W9-AIA-650

Professional JavaScript

**Nigel McFarlane, Andrea Chiarelli,
James De Carli, Sing Li, Stuart Updegrave,
Mark Wilcox, Cliff Wootton, Paul Wilton**

Wrox Press Ltd. ®

Professional JavaScript

© 1999 Wrox Press

All rights reserved. No part of this book may be reproduced, stored in a retrieval system or transmitted in any form or by any means, without the prior written permission of the publisher, except in the case of brief quotations embodied in critical articles or reviews.

The authors and publisher have made every effort in the preparation of this book to ensure the accuracy of the information. However, the information contained in this book is sold without warranty, either express or implied. Neither the authors, Wrox Press nor its dealers or distributors will be held liable for any damages caused or alleged to be caused either directly or indirectly by this book.

Published by Wrox Press Ltd
Arden House, 1102 Warwick Road, Acock's Green, Birmingham B27 6BH, UK
Printed in USA
ISBN 1-861002-70-X

Trademark Acknowledgements

Wrox has endeavored to provide trademark information about all the companies and products mentioned in this book by the appropriate use of capitals. However, Wrox cannot guarantee the accuracy of this information.

Credits

Authors
Nigel McFarlane
Andrea Chiarelli
James De Carli
Sing Li
Stuart Updegrave
Mark Wilcox
Paul Wilton
Cliff Wootton

Additional Material
Terry Constant
Jeff Hart

Editors
Daniel Maharry
Julian Skinner
Lums Thevathasan

Managing Editor
Victoria Hudgson

Development Editors
Greg Pearson
Jeremy Beacock

Project Manager
Sophie Edwards

Index
Andrew Criddle

Technical Reviewers
Damien Foggon
Rich Goldman
Jeff Hart
John Harris
Martin Honnen
Bob Lautenbach
Brent Noorda
Scott Roberts
Kris Rudin
Jon Stephens
Steve Williams

Design / Layout
Tom Bartlett
David Boyce
Mark Burdett
Will Fallon
Jonathan Jones
John McNulty

Illustrations
David Boyce
Will Fallon

Cover Design
Chris Morris

About the Authors

Nigel McFarlane

Nigel McFarlane lives the good life in Melbourne, Australia, where he works as a Senior Software Engineer for TUSC Computer Systems in the telecommunications industry. He's also worked a little for the big companies, and written the odd bit of submarine software. Because telecommunications started getting easy, predictable or manageable or something, so that life started settling down, he helped WROX with this and a previous book. That fixed that. He now also studies Physics and Mathematics at Latrobe University, where he hopes to learn something useful about satellites - originally he studied at The University of Melbourne, where he obtained a B.Sc. in Computer Science.

Within the computer industry he messes with C, C++, Perl, Browser and Web technology, communications, databases, PCs, Unix, whatever comes along really, not the least of which is JavaScript. He's written the odd bit of code he's proud of. He's had to touch FORTRAN a few times, but escaped COBOL entirely.

His standard line on writing books, or in fact doing anything, is give it a try and who knows what'll happen. Life's a bit like that. He doesn't own a TV, has a shamefully old computer, and only got an answering machine because his friends were ready to kill him.

When he's got a nanosecond of free time you might find him at the pub listening to Folk music, doing dinner-and-a-movie, sweating at Wu Gong (a martial art), or heading off to surf (very poorly) at Bell's Beach or thereabouts. Just lately you're more likely to find him collapsed in bed.

> *To Hilary, especially Hilary, but also Dave and Claudia, SteveO and O-pher-Christ Jones, for patience.*

Andrea Chiarelli

Andrea Chiarelli is an independent consultant with experience in software design and training. He holds a degree in Computer Science and a Master in Software Engineering, works for software companies and training centers in Tuscany (Italy) and is a contributing author to programming magazines such as ASPToday and Computer Programming (in Italian). His experience spans from database design to multimedia software developing. In recent years he's specialized in designing Internet and Intranet systems developing Web based applications and interfacing databases to the Web primarily using ASP.

When he isn't at work, he likes to read, paint and take long walks in the open air.

James De Carli

James R. De Carli is an Associate Director with Imperium Solutions, a Westport, Connecticut-based Microsoft Solution Provider Partner where he specializes in the design and development of custom internet and client/server database systems. Jim is also an Assistant Professor at Fairfield University where he teaches graduate Computer Science courses. He holds a Masters degree in Computer and Information Sciences and a Bachelors degree in Mathematics and Statistics. Having passed more than twenty Microsoft Certification exams, he has earned numerous technical certifications, including Microsoft Certified Systems Engineer (MCSE) and Microsoft Certified Solutions Developer (MCSD). Jim lives in Connecticut with his lifelong friend and wife, Cathy. and their two sons, Kenny and Robbie. Reach him on the Internet at jrdecarli@earthlink.net.

Sing Li

First bitten by the computer bug in 1978, Sing has grown up with the microprocessor revolution. His first 'PC' was a $99 do-it-yourself COSMIC ELF computer with 256 bytes of memory and a 1 bit LED display. For two decades, Sing has been an active author, consultant, speaker, instructor, and entrepreneur. His wide-ranging experience spans distributed architectures, multi-tiered Internet/Intranet systems, computer telephony, call center technology, and embedded systems. Sing has participated in several Wrox projects in the past, and has been working with (and writing about) Java and Jini since their very first alpha release. He is an active participant in the Jini community.

Stuart Updegrave

Stuart Updegrave has been a Web Developer since 1995, and is proficient in client and server JavaScript, HTML and CSS. Recent areas of interest include C programming and the incredible potential of XML to transform all facets of data exchange on the Internet. His current project aims to revolutionize the way in which developers access information. While waiting for snowboarding season to begin, he is on the hunt for his first home.

Mark Wilcox

Mark is the Web Administrator for the University of North Texas. He's also the author of *Implementing LDAP*, also published by Wrox Press, and is a regular columnist for Netscape's *ViewSource* magazine.

> *To my wife Jessica and to Dr. Kevin McKinney and Dr. Mitchel Kruger who made sure I was around to finish my chapter.*

Paul Wilton

After an initial start as a Visual Basic applications programmer, Paul found himself pulled into the net and has spent the last 18 months helping create internet and intranet solutions.

Currently he is developing web-based systems primarily using Visual Basic 6 and SQL Server 7 along with other numerous technologies.

> *Lots of love to my fiancée Catherine who ensures my sanity chip remains plugged in.*

Cliff Wootton

Cliff Wootton specializes in the development and integration of high performance media-based internet/intranet systems. His clients are companies needing solutions for publishing, graphics, multimedia and internet projects. Recent work includes architectural design and development of components for several award winning broadcast/entertainment websites. When he isn't developing software or content Cliff spends his time on music projects, playing bass and organizing seminars for musicians with his wife. Cliff also has three daughters who enjoy music and computing.

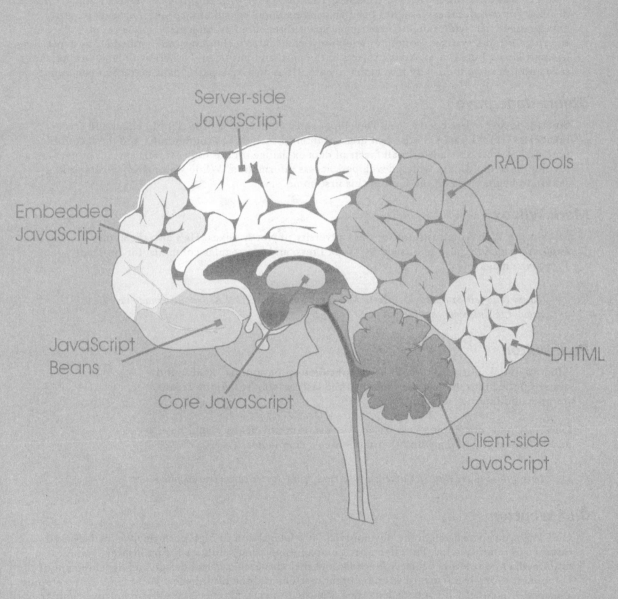

Table of Contents

Table of Contents

Chapter 2: Functions and Objects — 43

Chapter 3: Advanced Language Features — 63

Chapter 5: Windows and Frames 151

Chapter 7: Forms and Data 203

Chapter 8: Dynamic HTML   255

Chapter 11: Using Server-Side JavaScript With Netscape Enterprise Server 359

Chapter 13: ASP And JavaScript   419

Chapter 14: Building an E-Commerce Shop Front 457

Chapter 15: Applets and Java   523

Chapter 16: Java and JavaScript Beyond the Browser 555

Chapter 17: Debugging & Disappearing Data   581

Chapter 19: Rapid Application Development: Methodology, Tools & Components

Chapter 20: Windows and WSH 683

Chapter 21: High End Scripting With ScriptEase Desktop — 729

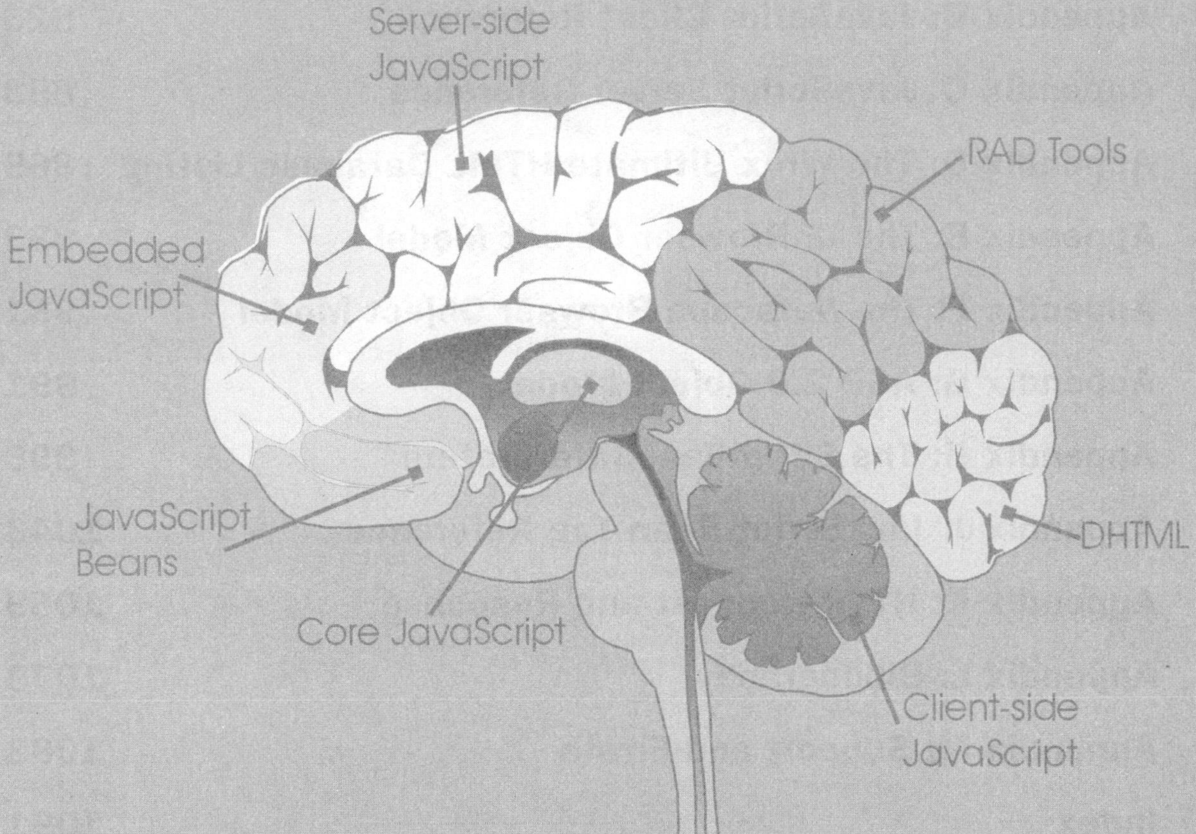

Server-side
JavaScript

RAD Tools

Embedded
JavaScript

JavaScript
Beans

Core JavaScript

DHTML

Client-side
JavaScript

Introduction

For a technology that didn't see the light of day until 1995, JavaScript has since swept the web development world to the point where it now has a near-universal presence on browsers and servers alike. When Netscape released version 2.0 of their Navigator web browser with an embedded scripting language – JavaScript 1.0 – the web became a much more interesting place to visit. A whole new world of dynamic interaction between users and browsers and between browsers and Web servers suddenly opened up and changed the use, purpose and scope of the web forever.

With the standardization of key Web technologies rapidly following, Netscape took their 1.1 release of JavaScript and submitted it to the European Computer Manufacturers Association (ECMA) for ratification as the standard for web scripting languages. The resultant specification, ECMAScript, defines the core JavaScript language. The implementers of JavaScript, Netscape included, then turned around and matched their languages to this specification.

JavaScript vs ECMAScript vs JScript

As this small history lesson may have hinted to you, JavaScript does not have a simple linear timeline to explain its formation over the last four years or so. The original JavaScript begat ECMAScript, which in turn begat later versions of JavaScript, JScript and other implementations. To clarify then, here's a rundown of what fits in where.

ECMAScript

ECMA (European Computer Manufacturers' Association) standard number 262 defines "the ECMAScript scripting language, a general purpose, cross-platform programming language" for public view at `http://www.ecma.ch/stand/ECMA-262.htm`. Originally submitted to ECMA in November 1996, ECMAScript specifies the core functionality of a cross-platform scripting language – JavaScript.

The ECMAScript standard is currently in its second edition. However, the changes made over the first edition are editorial only and specify nothing new to the implementation of the script at all. The first actual change to the language is due to take place around the turn of the year (1999/2000) with 'ECMAScript 2' set to specify a much fuller set of features including regular expression support and error handling.

The following table outlines which versions of JScript and JavaScript are compatible with ECMAScript:

JavaScript Version	ECMAScript Compliant?	JScript Version	ECMAScript Compliant?
1.0	No	1.0	No
1.1	Yes	2.0	No
1.2	No	3.0	Yes
1.3	Yes	4.0	Yes
1.4	Yes	5.0	Yes

It remains to be seen whether or not the features in JScript 5.0 and JavaScript 1.4 will comply with the guidelines in ECMAScript 2. Regardless of compliance, the JavaScript vendors have shown a free hand in innovating new features for their particular products.

JScript

JScript is Microsoft's own implementation of the ECMAScript standard. As you can see from the table above, it too has conformed to the standard since version 3.0, but apart from the original rough correspondence between JavaScript 1.1 and JScript 2.0, which were both put forward to help define the standard, there is no direct correlation between versions of JavaScript and JScript.

The following table demonstrates which product each version of JScript has appeared with so far. Note that these are all Microsoft products:

Application	Version Number				
	1.0	**2.0**	**3.0**	**4.0**	**5.0**
IE3.0	x				
IIS 3.0		x			
IE4.0			x		
IIS4.0			x		
WSH 1.0			x		
Visual Studio 6.0				x	
IE5.0					x
IIS5.0 (Windows 2000)					x

The JScript 5.0 scripting engine is also available for download from `http://msdn.microsoft.com/scripting` for use with IE3, IE4, IIS3, IIS4, Windows Script Host (WSH) and as a programming library for Visual Studio. Beware though that JScript does not run under Netscape browsers as **client-side** code. It also has some restrictions being run as **server-side** code in which capacity it can run only under IIS and as WSH scripts (which can in turn be run under CGI, so it's not all doom and gloom).

JavaScript

However, the standard implementation of JavaScript is that used by Netscape. This can be divided into three distinct parts: the core language, client-side and server-side extensions. **The core language** contains the fundamentals that mostly comply with the ECMAScript standard (but with a few extensions). Currently, it is at version 1.4 although there are only implementations up to version 1.3 in circulation at the moment.

The client-side set of extensions to JavaScript is currently based on the 1.3 core language and offers the ability to manipulate the web page's Document Object Model (DOM) and the various browsers' Object Models as we'll see in Chapters 4–10. The server-side set of extensions meanwhile are based on the 1.2 core and allows us to write standalone components, CGI programs, utilize key server-side objects (ASP and ADO, for example) and even to program our operating system's shell.

With Netscape having developed JavaScript, it is understandably their scripting language of choice, bundled it with their Navigator and Communicator browser packages and Enterprise Server. Microsoft too, through JScript, 'supports' JavaScript as shown.

Application	Version Number				
	1.0	1.1	1.2	1.3	1.4
Navigator 2.0x	x				
IE 3.0x	x	roughly			
Navigator 3.0x		x			
Enterprise Server 2.0		x			
Navigator 4.0 - 4.05			x		
Enterprise Server 3.0			x		
IE 4.0x			x		
Navigator 4.06 - 4.61				x	
IE 5.0x				x	roughly
Navigator 5.0 'Gecko'					x

This whole discussion would be redundant if client-side JavaScript could not be run on Internet Explorer, which it can, if a little inconsistently. Chapter 4 contains a much fuller discussion of the Microsoft / Netscape support story.

While Microsoft and Netscape browsers may both run compatible versions of ECMAScript implementations, the models with which one manipulates web pages and browser objects in Navigator and IE are completely at odds with each other, much like the Houses of Montague and Capulet. The WWW Consortium (W3C) has released one part of a complete specification for a standard Document Object Model that all browsers will eventually follow, (read it at `http://w3.org/TR/REC-DOM-Level-1.htm`) but for the time being, while it may or may not be possible for a Microsoft programmer to marry somebody from the house of Netscape and live happily ever after, to write a cross-browser program of any significant complexity is out of the question: you pretty much have to write two different versions.

Client-Side and Server-Side JavaScript

Some developers choose to use JavaScript solely on the client (in Navigator or another web browser). Larger-scale applications frequently have more complex needs, such as communicating with a relational database, providing continuity of information from one invocation to another of the application, or performing file manipulations on a server. For these more demanding situations, Netscape web servers contain server-side JavaScript, which has extra JavaScript objects to support server-side capabilities. ScriptEase too provides an extra set of objects for standalone **JavaScript applications** within its development environment. Note that when we talk of JavaScript applications, this implies that both server-side and client-side scripts have been incorporated into the code.

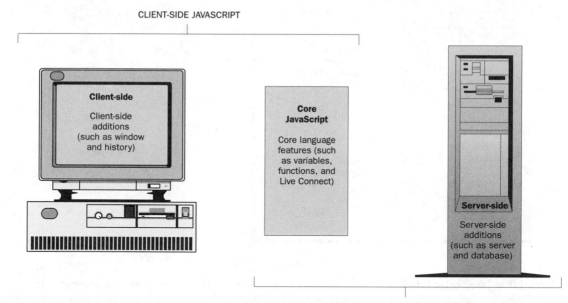

One key difference between client and server scripts, however, is how they are run. While client-side JavaScript is interpreted on the fly by the browser, server-side JavaScript is compiled first into byte codes, much like Java. JavaScript also has the ability, through Netscape's LiveConnect technology, to interact with actual Java code, even though the two sprang up from different areas.

ECMAScript Terminology

Since ECMAScript is the emerging standard for JavaScript, it's best to learn good habits at the start and to use its terminology. The ECMAScript standard only defines the most central features of JavaScript – its core language. This, it broadly categorizes into three parts and we can add a fourth here which connects those three together. This diagram illustrates how these parts fit together to form a JavaScript interpreter.

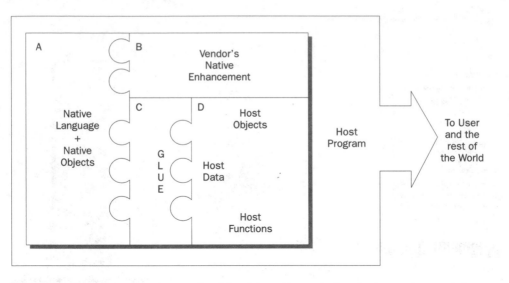

Recall that JavaScript loves to work with other software technologies such as web browsers. In ECMAScript/JavaScript, a **native** feature means a feature of the language that has solely to do with JavaScript. Such a feature might be the syntax for mathematical expressions, or variable names. Section A in the diagram above represents all the native features which go together to make ECMAScript. Section B shows that each JavaScript interpreter vendor might add **native enhancements** to the language to make their product more attractive, but these are still unique to JavaScript itself. Section D shows **host features**, which are features built into some other software that exist in their own right. In a web browser, these might be HTML documents, links, plug-ins, images or form elements. In a standalone interpreter they might be operating system calls or database functions. Finally, Section C shows these host features are connected to the native language by a little bit of software 'glue'. In summary, the main software (browser, server or operating system) is said to **host** the JavaScript interpreter, which consists of all four pieces combined. The ECMAScript standard doesn't find the glue section interesting enough to talk about. Browser vendors like to promote their own proprietary solutions for the glue section using technology brand names like ActiveX or COM, and LiveConnect.

A Word on Input and Output

JavaScript relies on host objects for all its input and output needs. It's a bit hard to experiment with the native language features without using host objects – you won't see anything. Therefore, here are some examples of how to perform basic output operations. These examples print "Hello, World!" on a single line on the screen, and nothing else.

An example using client-side JavaScript, in an HTML file to be loaded by a browser:

```
<HTML>
<BODY>
<SCRIPT LANGUAGE="JavaScript">
    document.write('Hello, World!<BR>');
</SCRIPT>
</BODY>
</HEAD>
```

An example using standalone JavaScript in a plain text file to be supplied to an interpreter (ScriptEase 4.10 in this case):

```
Clib.puts('Hello, World\n');
```

Server-side JavaScript and embedded JavaScript are a bit hard to set up for simple language tests so we'll skip them for now.

The functions document.write() and Clib.puts() are **host functions** (or host methods), not native features of the JavaScript language. All web browsers hosting JavaScript support document.write(), but since a standalone interpreter isn't a web browser, it has a different facility. The string 'Hello, World!\n' on the other hand, is a native JavaScript feature: a string constant. It's very common with JavaScript to see host and native features mixed up closely like this. In these examples, the single, 'Hello, World!\n' line can be replaced with any number of lines of JavaScript.

Some Key Features Of JavaScript

Predicting the Web's future in any detail is foolish to say the least, but there are trends to the whole system. One of them is that more and more people will write programs, without becoming programmers. So then, for those in this category, a word to the wise: learn the important principles we mention in Chapters 1-3 early and apply them in their programming practice. They will make your programming both more effective and more pleasurable, because most people derive pleasure from producing well-designed, well-crafted things. JavaScript is a great language to start programming in, and to start it well.

Why? Well, here are some reasons:

❑ Much of JavaScript's syntax and some of its semantics are adopted from C and C++. This will help any C or C++ programmers coming to JavaScript, and while it's still a big leap from C to JavaScript, at least some of the syntax will be familiar.

❑ **Regular expressions** are a prominent feature of JavaScript. These allow strings to be matched to certain patterns and empower JavaScript significantly as a tool for manipulating the text content of web pages.

❑ Functions are treated as first-class objects, which frequently makes code concise and elegant.

❑ JavaScript is well designed for object-oriented programming

❑ JavaScript objects are also associative arrays. You can refer to obj.propName as obj["propName"], and call obj.methodName() as obj["methodName"]. Since functions are treated as first-class objects, you can add methods by simple assignment. The strings that index the properties and methods of an object can be constructed at run time.

The Rest of the Book

So, what have you got to look forward to in the rest of this book? Well, we've divided the book into six parts:

❑ Chapters 1 - 3 lay out the core JavaScript language in its entirety, from variables and data types through to objects and functions.

❑ Chapters 4 - 10 drill down into client-side scripting and look at how we can use both the Document Object Model and the various browser object models to automate web pages.

❑ In Chapters 11 - 14 we move onto the server side and look at working with three main platforms: Internet Information Server and ASP, ScriptEase Web Server Edition and Netscape Enterprise Server.

❑ Chapters 15 - 18 then look at issues concerning any kind of JavaScript development: debugging, security, the RAD tools to use and the use of LiveConnect to make use of any Java applets or applications available.

❑ Finally, Chapters 19 - 21 look at the power of JavaScript outside of a web context, working with and manipulating the operating system itself. In particular, we'll look at working with the Windows Scripting Host, ScriptEase Desktop and Embedded JavaScript.

Who Should Read This Book?

This is a broad and at times in-depth book on JavaScript, which starts with the basics and works all the way up and all the way across to some quite advanced features. We've tried to include everything in this one book. If you have any of the following attributes, then this book should boost your skills, your knowledge and your output significantly:

❑ You can't get your application written with just a point-and-click tool or two, a bit of HTML and a bit of magic. It's gone past that and now you have to get something a bit deeper.

❑ You need to do it, but you don't have time to immerse yourself in low-level development tools like C compilers in which it takes ages to achieve the quick and dirty. You've got to get the job done faster with something that's more accessible.

❑ Half your job is battling with the web environment and web applications, a quarter is getting things done with PCs or servers and the last quarter is the hard stuff you're still looking for solutions to.

❑ You're a manager, educator or student and need to penetrate the capabilities that scripting, the World Wide Web and client-server applications provide to developers and users. You need a technical companion you can use to show you what the jungle is all about.

❑ You've got a fair knowledge of the subjects we cover, but you've got gaps that need filling, or you're looking to extend yourself.

If you're not in any of these categories, never fear: JavaScript is an interesting microcosm of the computing landscape and has enough turns and alleyways to be a curiosity in its own right. If you do choose this book that our many authors and editors have labored over, we wish you all the best with it and hope that you find it an eye-opening and enjoyable read.

What Do I Need to Use This Book?

To get to grips with the content of this book, you should have a knowledge of HTML and an up-to-date browser from either Microsoft (Internet Explorer 5.0) or Netscape (Navigator 4.61). You can also download evaluation copies of the ScriptEase products from http://www.nombas.com/ for use with Chapter 20.

Where You'll Find the Samples and Tools

If you want to try out the examples in this book, you can run them straight from our web site or you can download them as compressed files from the same site. The index page can be found at:

```
http://www.wrox.com/Store/Details.asp?Code=270X
```

If you're located in Europe or the United Kingdom, or you find that the site in the United States is down for maintenance, then you may want to try our UK site, which can be found at:

```
http://webdev.wrox.co.uk/books/270x/
```

Conventions

We have used a number of different styles of text and layout in the book to help differentiate between the different kinds of information. Here are examples of the styles we use and an explanation of what they mean:

> **Important pieces of information come in boxes like this**

- ❏ *Advice, hints, or background information comes in this type of font.*
- ❏ **Important Words** are in a bold type font
- ❏ Words that appear on the screen in menus like the <u>F</u>ile or <u>W</u>indow are in a similar font to the one that you see on screen
- ❏ Keys that you press on the keyboard, like *Ctrl* and *Enter*, are in italics
- ❏ Code has several fonts. If it's a word that we're talking about in the text, for example, when discussing the **For...Next** loop, it's in a bold font. If it's a block of code that you can type in as a program and run, then it's also in a gray box:

```
<STYLE TYPE = "text/javascript">
… Some Javascript …
</STYLE>
```

❏ Sometimes you'll see code in a mixture of styles, like this:

```
<HTML>
<HEAD>
<TITLE>Javascript Style Sheet Example</TITLE>
<STYLE  TYPE = "text/javascript">
tags.BODY.color = "black"
classes.base.DIV.color = "red"
</STYLE>
</HEAD>
```

❏ The code with a white background is code we've already looked at and that we don't wish to examine further.

These formats are designed to make sure that you know what it is you're looking at. I hope they make life easier.

We'll frequently use these abbreviations:

NC4	Netscape Communicator 4.x
IE5	Internet Explorer 5.x
ECMA	European Computer Manufacturers Association
W3C	World Wide Web Consortium
DOM	Document Object Model
OOP	Object-oriented programming

Tell Us What You Think

We've worked hard on this book to make it useful. We've tried to understand what you're willing to exchange your hard-earned money for, and we've tried to make the book live up to your expectations.

Please let us know what you think about this book. Tell us what we did wrong, and what we did right. This isn't just marketing flannel: we really do huddle around the e-mail to find out what you think. If you don't believe it, then send us a note. We'll answer, and we'll take whatever you say on board for future editions. The easiest way is to use e-mail:

feedback@wrox.com

You can also find more details about Wrox Press on our web site. There, you'll find the code from our latest books, sneak previews of forthcoming titles, and information about the authors and editors. You can order Wrox titles directly from the site, or find out where your nearest local bookstore with Wrox titles is located. The address of our site is:

http://www.wrox.com

Customer Support

If you find a mistake, please have a look at the errata page for this book on our web site first. The Support and Errata Appendix at the back of the book outlines how you can submit errata in much greater detail, if you are unsure. The full URL for the errata page is:

```
http://www.wrox.com/Consumer/Forums/AllErrata.asp?Forum=186100270x&Type=2
```

If you can't find an answer there, tell us about the problem and we'll do everything we can to answer promptly!

Just send us an e-mail to: `feedback@wrox.com`.

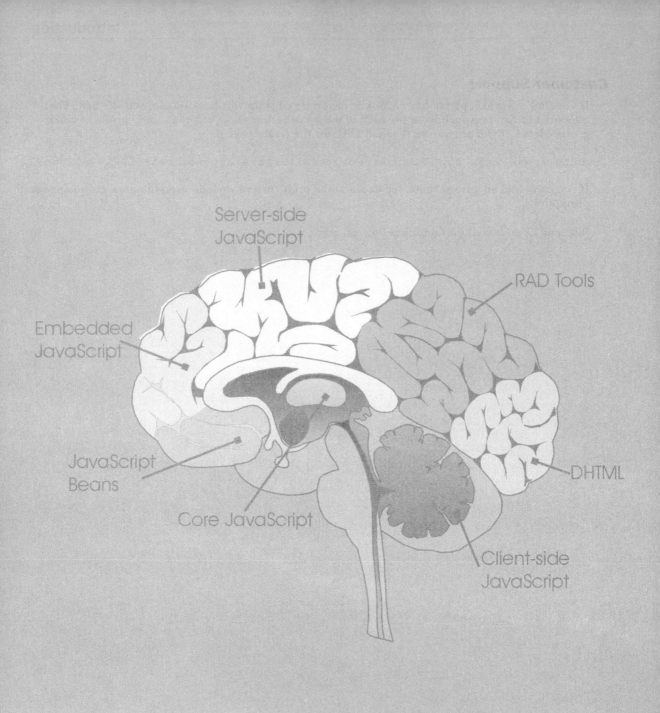

Core JavaScript Basics

As we've seen in the introduction, the core language describes the basic constructions and features that the client- and server-side extensions we use to write into the browser or on the server are built upon. Here in Chapter 1, we'll specifically take a look at the following:

- Writing scripts and Unicode
- Variables and Data Types
- Expressions
- Type Conversions
- Control Loops

This may seem a little basic, but there are a few pointers within even these rudimentary features that vary between versions and browser implementations. If you're new to JavaScript, then by the end of this chapter, you will be able to point to different parts of the language and construct basic programs, although they won't be very sophisticated or even that useful. The remaining core language features are covered in the next two chapters – here we're interested in the utter basics – so skip over this chapter and keep it as a reference if you know them already.

JavaScript 1.3 is the latest version of the core language to have been implemented in a browser and it is to this version that this first part of the book will attend. Netscape has indeed released version 1.4 of JavaScript, but this is currently implemented only in the pre-alpha release of Netscape 5.0, codenamed Gecko, which you can find at http://www.mozilla.org. This chapter is correct to version 1.3 and notes the changes made for 1.4 along the way.

Writing Scripts and the Unicode Standard

JavaScript scripts are designed to be readable by humans. To make this as easy as possible, they're generally stored in simple character-based files. This means that you don't need a special editor like Microsoft Word in order to view the file's contents – Edit, Vi, Notepad or any of many other text editors will do. So generally you can just open a new file and start typing. However, let us pause for a minute and look at how the JavaScript language supports the user 'just typing it in'.

The primary problem with 'just typing' is that everyone types in a different language, and every computer has different support for the characters typed. A set of characters supported by a given computer and the values the computer gives each one are collected together into a character set encoding. If everyone agrees on the encoding, then there is common ground for communication. This is not always the case. EBCDIC (IBM) and ASCII (Standards USA) are different encodings for the same English characters – 26 letters, 10 numbers and numerous punctuation marks and control characters. JIT is a very different character set that represents Japanese characters. JavaScript in particular needs a solution to this problem because it is commonly used in the World Wide Web, which is a highly international environment. English is still not the most common language in the world, even if it is nearly the common business language.

Enter the **Unicode 2.0 standard**, promoted and developed by the Unicode Consortium, `http://www.unicode.org`. Their achievement has been to squeeze all the characters in the world into a single set, the Unicode set, with some space left over for future additions. Each character in Unicode has a 16-bit (two byte) value that is unique. JavaScript programs are written in the Unicode character set. Since the first 128 characters match the ASCII character set – the one most English-speaking computer people have used for years – this is perfectly convenient for English speakers. A further plus for speakers of English, is that all the special JavaScript key words, or reserved words, happen to be English words. Yay.

However, there is one complexity. Unicode characters are 16 bits. Most Western computers are based on 8 bit characters that follow the ASCII standard or the PC standard (that's the one that looks like ASCII but has little happy faces, lines and corner symbols in it as well). So even if you have an editor that allows you to type in Unicode characters, you can't traditionally save the file as an ordinary text file. The solution to this is that the ECMAScript language allows *any* JavaScript program to be written using only the first 128 characters of Unicode, which is the same as ASCII. This means we only need 8 bits for a script, we can use all our familiar software tools, and the interpreter can convert what it reads to Unicode 16 bit when it interprets the script.

Of course, that would be great if both main browsers supported Unicode – IE has since version 4 but Navigator still supports only the ISO-Latin 1 character set. A word of warning also to European users whose keyboards support ISO Latin-1 – be aware that characters with diacritical marks like é *aren't* in the first 128 characters of Unicode.

What if we need a non-English character like Ψ or © ? There are two answers for 8 bit files. Outside of JavaScript strings and comments, the answer is: you can't do it. That's most of the script. Inside strings and comments you can, by using the special sequence of characters \uXXXX where XXXX are hexadecimal digits for the Unicode number for the character needed. So you won't actually *see* the character you want, but you'll be able to specify it.

To give a quick example, we mentioned earlier that ASCII corresponded to the first 128 characters in the Unicode set. The character 'A' for example can be referenced as \u0041 in Unicode or 0x41 in 8-bit character sets. Going back to our starter for ten, the Ψ symbol can be written as \u0470. There's more on strings, comments and hexadecimal numbers later in this chapter.

Finally let's not confuse character set encodings with fonts. A font like Helvetica determines what a particular character *looks* like. A character set encoding number for a particular character just tells you *which* character the character is. Lexicographers are probably grinding their teeth in frustration at this simplistic explanation but it's enough for our purposes. Fonts have nothing to do with it.

In summary, if you read and script in English – a fair assumption for this book – just type your script in like you would any text into a text file, and rely on the JavaScript interpreter to understand it all correctly. If you need special characters, move to a computer with good Unicode support, or just use the escape sequence technique on the rare occasion when it's unavoidable.

Variables and Data

It would be almost impossible to write a useful piece of JavaScript code without being able to store values and other data in memory within our program. There are two ways to represent data – stored inside a **variable** or directly typed in as a **literal**. A variable holds data provided by a literal like a shoebox holds a shoe. The example below illustrates both variables and literals. Variables are on the left of the equals signs and literal values are on the right. The first line is unique – in that line we have a variable that contains no data yet – an empty shoebox.

```
var new_value;
var cost = null;
var new_price = 10.95;
address = "23 Short St.";
var result = 'Result unknown';
result = true;
result = 1.08e+23;
result = 0x2Fe3;
result = 0377;
$name = "Jimmy Zed";
var first = 1, second = 2, last = 10;
```

One of things that make JavaScript easy to handle is that it is a weakly-typed language. This means that once declared, programmers still have the ability to change the type of value stored within the variable. Consider in the code above the variable `result`, which is first declared as a string type variable, and then a boolean, float, hexadecimal number and octal number. Compare this to a strongly-typed language like C++ in which once a variable is declared to be of a certain type, for example, an integer, it can no longer hold anything other than integer values.

However, data always has a **type**, so literals each have a type and variables take on the type of the data they contain. At this basic level, there are three primitive types – **boolean, number** and **string** – and two special values, **null** and **undefined**. We'll see these in the next section.

Variables should be declared using the keyword **var** whenever they are created. This makes sure that the interpreter creates a new variable in memory rather than assigning a new value to one declared earlier with a more global scope – a concept we'll deal with in Chapter 2.

Variables should also always be set to a value rather than created with an unspecified state, as new_value was in the example above. Variables that have unspecified contents, and variables used without having already been declared using var are sources of error and confusion, and should generally be avoided.

Don't forget either to give your variables meaningful names. It may seem easier to hand out a letter at a time, but you'll soon start wondering if it was e that contained the string, or if it was perhaps h and so on. There's no reasonable limit to the number of characters you can give to a variable name but there are a couple of rules that must be obeyed when creating and using valid variable names.

- ❑ JavaScript is case sensitive. Thus variable XYZ is different to variable xyz.
- ❑ Variable names must start with either a letter or an underscore (_). They may also start with a dollar sign ($) when using JavaScript 1.1 or later.
- ❑ Any subsequent characters in the name may include numbers (0-9) as well as those characters mentioned above.
- ❑ Variables cannot be given names that are already JavaScript reserved words. See the Inside Back Cover for this list.

Primitive Types and Core Properties

The three primitive types – **Boolean, Number** and **String** – are the simple building blocks of all data in JavaScript. Neither objects nor arrays, which are both important types in their own right, are primitive types.

Boolean

The Boolean type has only two values. The constants for these values are **true** and **false** and are only used for truth values. These constants are case-sensitive. Unlike some languages, false isn't exactly the same as 0 (zero), but it will convert to 0 when used where a number is expected, so it's much the same thing.

Number

The Number type deals with strings of digits containing an optional decimal point and an optional exponent. In effect, this means that it covers both floating point numbers and integers, unlike strongly – typed languages.

Floating point numbers store fractional numbers like 123.456, 2.0, .4763 and $5.3e^2$. Integers here are dealt with as floating point numbers with no decimal point. Number constants can be written plainly in decimal, or in computer exponential or hexadecimal or octal notation. For example, result is set to the equivalent of 255 in decimal in each line below.

```
result = 2.55e+2;    // Exponential
result = 0xFF;       // Hexadecimal
result = 0377;       // Octal
result = 255;        // Decimal
```

The Number type can cope with very large (or very small) values and negatives. Very large means up to about 10^{308}, very small means down to about 10^{-324}, if you're mathematically inclined.

Numbers are stored as "double precision floating point numbers" – a standard created by the IEEE organization (http://www.ieee.org) that mandates 64 bits (4 bytes) must be available for one value. The ECMAScript standard exactly follows this standard except in the treatment of NaN, which is discussed separately. There are, however, three awkward consequences of this approach:

❑ Numbers with lots of different digits will not be stored exactly, eg 123456789123456789 might be stored as 123456789123450000. This is because 64 bits can only hold so much, and will ignore the least important digits.

❑ Mathematical operations on 64-bit numbers are tricky to get right, and so two poorly written JavaScript interpreters might disagree very slightly on, for example, what 1 divided by 7 is.

❑ Finally, 64-bit numbers can be tricky to print out correctly. Sometimes two interpreters might print the same number out using slightly different digits. For example, is 2 divided by 3 printed out to 5 decimal places 0.66667 or 0.66666.

String

The String type deals with series of zero or more text characters. Checking against a strongly-typed language it too covers two normally separate variable types just as the Number type does – rows of zero or more characters as a unit and single characters.

A String is a row, not an array, of single characters. Of course, a String of exactly one character is as good as a single character, so that is the way a single character is represented.

There are a few special characters, known as **escape sequences**, which can be stored in a String, all of which begin with a '\'. The '\n' in 'Hello, World!\n' above is an example – it adds a new line character to the string. There are eight escape sequences specified in the ECMAScript besides \x and \u to indicate hex and unicode sequences as we have seen previously. They are:

Escape Sequence	Unicode Equivalent	Produces
\b	\u0008	backspace
\t	\u0009	horizontal tab
\n	\u000A	line feed (new line)
\f	\u000C	form feed
\r	\u000D	carriage return
\"	\u0022	double quote
\'	\u0027	single quote
\\	\u005C	backslash

Strings must start and end with either matching single or double quotes You should be careful when putting quotes intentionally inside Strings as the start and end quotes must match. For example:

```
var easy_string = "Hello Mum.";
var mixed_string = "Mum replied, 'Have a biscuit'";
var wrong_string = "'Thanks", I said.';   // Wrong. Quotes mismatched.
```

Browser versions of JavaScript are particularly bad at correctly handling the ASCII NUL character (also known as '\0')– so beware. NUL characters are often used with image data and digital signatures stored as strings. As this implies, strings are not under any onus to be legible to humans.

At this point, you should be aware that each of the primitive types has a corresponding object built into JavaScript which offers a number of properties and methods to make a coder's life easier. We'll meet these objects later in Chapter 2.

Null and Undefined

Besides the primitive types, JavaScript also defines two other core types, **Null** and **Undefined**.

```
var blank = null;
var new_value;
```

The Null type has only one value, **null**. The null value means 'no data' – it's used as a placeholder in a variable to let you know there's nothing useful in there.

The Undefined type is trickier. It also has one value, **undefined**, but this is often the same as null. If a variable's contents are unclear, because nothing (not even null) has ever been stored in it, then it's undefined, but for convenience, much of the time it acts as if it had a null value. Unless you are doing something advanced, undefined is usually bad news meaning your script isn't working properly.

In the example above, variable new_value is undefined because nothing is ever assigned to it. So is the variable old_value, because it doesn't appear in the example script at all.

Infinity and NaN

Two properties of the Number object, **NaN** and **Infinity**, have been 'promoted' to top-level properties in JavaScript 1.3.

NaN means 'Not a Number' and is the result of a mathematical operation that makes no sense. The classic example of this is trying to divide any number by zero. NaN is always unequal to any number, including itself.

As its name suggests, the property **Infinity** represents mathematical infinity, a number greater than any other number including itself.

The NaN and Infinity variables may be standard, but as part of JavaScript 1.3, they are too new for all but the most recently released browsers (IE5+, NC4.06+), but you can create them yourself if you want to stick close to the standard in your scripts. Here's how:

```
var NaN = 0/0;
var Infinity = 1e300 * 1e300;
```

The safest way to examine these special values is with some special utilities – isNaN(), isFinite() and typeof() – described later. These are just functions, a topic covered more generally in Chapter 2. There are also two constants for checking infinite values. They are Number.POSITIVE_INFINITY and Number.NEGATIVE_INFINITY. You can read more about them in Appendix A.

Don't rely on the special values printing out the same on all browsers, and don't do mathematics with these values if you're going to create them, as results can be unpredictable. Internet Explorer 3.02 with JScript 1.0 has no idea about NaN, it just silently converts it to 0 (zero). You can't tell the difference between undefined *and* null *using Netscape Navigator 2.02, and it doesn't understand* Number.POSITIVE_INFINITY *or* Number.NEGATIVE_INFINITY *either. It is not until both browsers reach version 4.0 that NaN will be highly bug-free.*

Arrays

Arrays let you store several pieces of data, usually with a common theme, under the same variable name in an ordered way. This can save you creating a heap of variables all with similar names. Let's work through some code:

```
var month_totals = new Array(12);
month_totals[3] = 1999.95;
month_totals[4] = 'No sales';

var a = 4;
document.write(month_totals[a]);
document.write(month_totals.length);
document.write(month_totals);

var days = new Array("Sun","Mon","Tue","Wed","Thu","Fri","Sat");
```

The variables `month_totals` and `days` are made into arrays by the as-yet cryptic code 'new `Array()`'. This call does two things.

❑ First, the initial number of items in the array is decided and stored in a hidden place called `length`. In line 1, it's set explicitly to 12.

❑ Second, some space in memory is set aside for the elements of the array (the variables we wish to group together), the number of which is kept in `length`.

The elements of an array are counted from 0 (zero), not one, so a three element array called `fred` has elements called `fred[0]`, `fred[1]` and `fred[2]`. The numbers 0, 1 or 2 are also known as the **index** of the element in the array. If you prefer to number from one rather than zero, just make the array one bigger in the first place and ignore the zero'th element. Arrays can be enlarged to contain more elements just by storing a value in an array element whose index is bigger than any that exists so far. Note also that array indices are not limited to numbers; assigning a value to `icecream[flavor]` is just as valid as assigning one to `icecream[1]`. There is an upper limit to all this however, but if you end up using a 4,294,967,295-element array, you really should consider dividing it into two.

As you can see from lines 2 and 3, array elements can contain different types of data. Line 2 assigns a Number value, `1999.95`, to the fourth element of the `month_totals` array, while line 3 assigns the String type value `'No sales'` to `month_totals[4]`.

Accessing array elements is easy. The first two `document.write()` lines display **No sales** and **12**. The third `document.write()` only needs to report that the variable printed is an object to match ECMAScript. However, Netscape Navigator will print out all the array elements, comma-separated, which is very handy.

Last but not least in our example code, the bottom line demonstrates a shorthand way of creating an Array and setting all its elements at the same time. In one fell swoop, we create a seven element array called days populated with seven String type values.

Navigator 2.02 doesn't know how to do 'new Array', and neither does Internet Explorer 3.02 with JScript 1.0 – the call wasn't implemented until JavaScript 1.1. Another problem arises when specifying LANGUAGE="JavaScript1.2" in the <SCRIPT> tag in your client-side code. Under these conditions, calling new Array(12) will create an array with one element, value 12, rather than an array of twelve undefined elements, as would be the case in any other circumstance.

We'll look more at arrays in Chapter 2.

Multi-Dimensional Arrays

Some collections of data aren't easily represented by a simple list of items. Grids, spreadsheets, matrices and so on are commonly stored not in simple arrays, but in multi-dimensional arrays where there is more than one index present. Multidimensional arrays also lend themselves to algorithms used for graphics. JavaScript doesn't directly support multi-dimensional arrays.

However, one of the things you can store in a JavaScript array element is another array. An array of arrays can be treated like a multidimensional array. This example creates a two-dimensional array of size two-by-two, and fills it with the values that make up the identity matrix – a mathematically useful thing.

```
var matrix = new Array(2);
matrix[0] = new Array(2);
matrix[1] = new Array(2);

matrix[0][0] = 1;
matrix[1][0] = 0;
matrix[0][1] = 0;
matrix[1][1] = 1;
```

Array Literals

The array example above creates a couple of arrays and stores them in a variable. But what if you want an array that's not necessarily stored in any variable, like a literal such as 'string value' or 99. If you just want to type the array straight into the script, you need an array literal:

```
var a = [];
var b = [1, 2, 3];
var c = ['a','b',,,'c'];
var d = ['a1','a2',['b1','b2'],'a3'];
```

In this example we are in fact assigning our literal arrays to variables – when we cover expressions later, you will be able to see that you can put a literal (array or otherwise) in an expression without any variables being needed. In this example, variables a and b are arrays with zero and 3 elements respectively. Variable c is a 5-element array but the indices of the supplied literals are 0, 1 and 4, not 0, 1 and 2. This is because elements 2 and 3 are present but undefined. Variable d is an array of 4 elements, but the third element (index value 2) is another array. That other array has 2 elements, 'b1' and 'b2'. You could access the 'b1' element using the d variable as follows:

```
    var e = d[2][0];
```

None of these arrays are limited to their initial size – you can change them afterwards.

> *The final trailing comma in the literal will be ignored by the interpreter. For example,* `['a',]`
> *is an array of length 1. Contrast with* `[,'a']` *which is treated as an array with two elements,*
> *the first of which is undefined.* `[,'a',,]` *meanwhile has three elements only the second of*
> *which has been defined.*

The last example shows that it's possible to create tree-like structures of data using arrays, but for such structures, you're really stretching arrays past the purpose they were intended for and you're better off using Objects, described in Chapter 2. Nevertheless, here is an example of a three level structure made from an array literal:

```
    var family =
    [ "gramps",
      "granny"
      [ "dad",
        "mum",
        [ "bub",
          "toddler",
        ],
        "uncle",
        "aunt",
        [ "terror",
          "teenager"
        ]
      ]
    ];
```

Array literals require at least JScript 3.0 or JavaScript 1.2

Statements, Blocks and Comments

It's all very well being able to store data, but most of the time you'd like to do something with it. This means writing a JavaScript program or script fragment. A **script fragment** is just a piece of JavaScript that is so small it doesn't deserve to be called a whole program. Most of the examples in this chapter are script fragments.

Regardless of what name it has, all JavaScript code consists of a sequence of **statements**. These statements are processed top-to-bottom, one at a time, unless you organize it otherwise. Statements can be grouped together into a **block** which can act as a single statement even though it contains many. Every statement also results in some action being made by the JavaScript engine unless it is either a do-nothing statement or a comment.

Comments are notes made by the coder that should help readers understand how the series statements fit together. They can either span over several lines, in which case they are enclosed by a `/* ... */` pair of delimiters, or they can be single-line comments, preceded by `//`. You can't embed comments inside a String constant. Single line comments will nest, meaning you can put a comment inside a comment, but multi-line ones won't. Additionally, single line comments can appear inside multi-line comments.

Here's an example program that prints out different text depending upon the value of the variable `result`. It also demonstrates the different types of comment:

```
var result;
result = 15                      // for this test, set it to 15
result = 5; result = 20;         // then set it again, just for fun

result
= 19;                            // final value is 19.

if ( result == 15 )
{
    /* this bit won't be printed
       because it's not 15
    */
    Clib.puts('The value is ')
    Clib.puts('still 15')
}
else
{
    /* this bit WILL be printed
       because it's not 15
    */
    Clib.puts('The value has been ');
    Clib.puts('changed to something else');
}
/* end of example */
;
```

Ignore the lines reading `if...` and `else ...` for the minute. Notice how some lines end with a semi-colon (`;`) and some don't. In JavaScript, semi-colons are the official way of saying a statement has ended. However, JavaScript lets the script writer be carefree – if a statement looks like it has finished even though there's no semi-colon, and then the line ends, JavaScript will assume you were lazy and act as though you did put one.

> It's good practice to *ALWAYS* put a semi-colon at the end of a statement as it makes tracking down problems easier, and some fancy editing tools can cope better if the semi-colons are there.

There are two blocks in the example above. Blocks are started by a left brace (`'{'`) and ended by a right brace(`}`) In this example, each block contains two statements (and a comment, but that's ignored). The line reading `if` only operates on a single statement, so a block is used to make two statements behave like one. Notice that blocks break the rules: there is no need for a trailing semi-colon. This is the only exception.

Note lines 3–6. Line 3 has two statements : `result = 5;` and `result = 20;`. Also, the single statement, `result = 19;` is split over lines 5 and 6. JavaScript is a **free-format language**. Provided you always use semi-colons, you can add as many spaces, tabs and blank lines as you like (**whitespace**), as long as you stick to the spots where spaces can normally appear. This is similar to HTML. Just like HTML, using a spacing and indentation standard will make the code easier to understand in six months time when it is revisited. This kind of thing for example won't work:

```
var my_string = "first line
                 second line"     // no returns allowed in strings - use \n
var copy = my_str ing;            // makes no sense. What does ing mean?
```

The orphaned semi-colon on the last line of our example is denoting neither the end of the previous block nor the end of the comment. Instead, it is simply a **'do-nothing'** statement. So, for example, should a script contain just `; ; ; ; ;` it would do nothing 5 times and then end.

One last point in passing. Our example uses `Clib.puts()` to output to the screen – a call that's only made only on the server-side or most likely for running in a standalone JavaScript interpreter. If our script fragment was intended for a browser, `document.write()` would have been used.

Statement Labels

This next script fragment uses statement labels – labels for short – to identify significant points in the statements making up the script:

```
start: var fruit = 0;
       var fruit_salad = 0;

       var apples = 3;
       var bananas = 2;
       var peaches = 4;

total: fruit=apples+bananas+peaches

serve: fruit_salad = fruit / 1000 * 1000
```

The labels `start`, `total` and `serve` are each associated with a single statement – the one on their immediate right. By themselves they have no effect at all (except possibly to make the script slightly easier to read), which makes them much like comments. However, coupled with some of the flow control commands described later on, labels provide signposts that allow the JavaScript interpreter to jump around within a script. Since blocks are statements, the following syntax is also correct:

```
var cup1 = 'empty'
var cup2 = 'empty'
var cup3 = 'ball here'

swap: {
    cup1 = cup3;
    cup3 = cup1;
    cup2 = cup1;
    cup3 = cup2;
    } // now where is it?
```

As long as you don't use one of the JavaScript reserved words for your label (see IBC for a complete list), it's up to you how you name your labels. Just be aware that labels were not supported until JavaScript1.2 so only the version 4 browsers can handle them. Labels are also not as flexible as the infamous 'goto' of the BASIC language, as you'll see later in the 'Flow Control' section.

Expressions and Conditions

With variables and statements, you can store as much data as you like, but eventually you'll want to manipulate it or check it. Expressions and Conditions are used for these two tasks. **Expressions** combine values into a new value whereas **conditions** compare values and return a Boolean truth value (`true` or `false`). Conditions are a kind of expression most often concerned with testing logical (truth or boolean) values.

Expressions and conditions combine variables and constant data (and other expressions and conditions) together via **operators**. Except for string manipulation, the operators are mostly identical to those of the "C" and Java languages. An important matter is **operator precedence**, which is a set of rules dictating how expressions are interpreted when more then one operator is present. Parentheses – '(' and ')' – can be used to force a different interpretation to that laid down by the precedence rules, which are detailed in Appendix A. Take, for example,

```
a = 5 + 6 * 7 + 8
a = (5 + 6) * (7 + 8)
```

In the operator precedence table, multiplication is done before addition, so the top line gives a the value 55. By adding parentheses, we force the additions to be evaluated first and a becomes equal to 165.

An operator has to work with something in order to operate. Operators are divided into **unary** operators that operate on one piece of data and **binary** operators that operate on two pieces of data, one on each side of the operator symbol. There is also a single **ternary** operator that uses three pieces of data.

Arithmetic Operators

Arithmetic operators are the familiar mathematical ones and are all binary operators: plus (+), minus (-), divide (/), multiply (*). There is also remainder (%) which gives the leftovers of a division. For example: 9 / 4 is 2.25, but 4 goes into 9 twice with one left over, so 9 % 4 is 1. This operator is also called 'modulo'. For division of real numbers, not integers, the leftover is a real number, so for example 5.5 % 2.2 = 1.1. Used carelessly, these operators can produce NaN or Infinity.

```
a = 2 + 3;   b = 2 * 3;   c = 2 / 3;   d = 2 - 3;   e = 2 % 3;
```

Microsoft products with JScript version 1.0 truncate floating point numbers to integers before applying %, so 5.5 % 2.2 = 1.

The obvious results of these expressions are a=5, b=6, c=0.6666667, d=1 and e=2 respectively.

Relational Operators

Relational operators are those used for comparisons and are all binary operators: less than (<), less than or equal to (<=), greater than (>), greater than or equal to (>=), equal (==), not equal (! =), strictly equal (===) and not strictly equal (! ==). Discussion of what exactly equals and strictly equals mean is deferred for the minute, but it's safe to say if the two things compared are of the same type, then equal means 'the same as' in the common sense way you'd expect.

```
a < b;   a >= b;   a == b;   (a + b) <= (c + d);   a === b;   c !== d;
```

The strictly equals operators === and !== were introduced in JavaScript 1.3 (IE5, NC4.06+) and are not part of the ECMAScript specification.

The results of these expressions, assuming the variables have values matching the previous arithmetic example, are: true, false, false, false, false, true.

Logical Operators

Logical operators go hand-in-hand with relational ones. They are **logical and** (&&), **logical or** (||), **logical not** (!). The first two are binary, and the last one unary. These operators let you combine the results of several variable tests into one result. 'Logical and' means both sides must be true, 'logical or' means at least one side must be true to yield a true result. 'Logical not' gives back the reverse of the true/false state of the value tested.

```
a && b;      a || b;      !a;      ( a<=b ) && ( c > d );      (!a && b) || c;
```

Sometimes logical expressions can get quite complicated. It is best to use parentheses wherever possible, both to aid the reader's understanding and to avoid obscure bugs. Note that as these operators are evaluated left to right, in the case of `false && aValue` and `true || aValue`, the expressions will return false and true respectively without evaluating `aValue`.

If a=true, b=false, c=true and d=false in the examples above, the results are: false, true, false, false, true.

Bit Operators

Bit operators treat Number types as a 32 bit value, change bits according to the operator and then convert the value back to the original Number type (decimal, hex, octal) when done. If you've never used a bit operator, then it's likely you never will – in which case ignore this stuff.

The operators are bitwise **NOT** (~), **AND** (&), **OR** (|), **XOR** (^), **left shift** (<<), **right shift** (>>), **unsigned right shift** (>>>). All are binary, except NOT which is unary. The dual right shift operators help keep JavaScript portable between different computers and are derived from Java. These operators aren't yet used much in Web-style applications.

```
a = ~a;      b = b & a;      c = c >> 2;      d = d >>> 2;
```

If a=1, b=2, c=-1 and d=-1 in this example, then the results are –2, 0, –1, 1073741823. Exciting (!).

Miscellaneous Unary Operators

Miscellaneous unary operators: these are **prefix** and **postfix increment** (++), **prefix** and **postfix decrement** (--), **unary plus** (+) and **unary minus** (-). Here are examples:

```
a++;    ++a;    a--;    --a;    +a;    b = -a;    b = 2 * a++;    b = 2 * ++a;
```

The unary minus is easiest to understand; it simply makes a negative number positive and vice versa. All the rest are really as valuable for their side effects as much as for their main effect. This is because they often provide a handy shorthand for longer expressions. The pre/post increment/decrement operators just give you a fast way of saying 'a = a + 1' or 'a = a-1' – they increase or decrease the variable they're applied to by one, which is a very common operation.

When ++ is placed before the variable it works on, that variable is incremented, and the new value is used in any expression it's part of. However, if ++ is placed after the variable it works on, the variable's old value (before increment) is used in the expression and then after that's over, the increment is applied as an afterthought. As the last statement in the example shows, it can get confusing if overused.

If a=1 at the start of the example above, then by the end a=3, and b has been set to –1, 2 and 6 respectively. The value for a as the example proceeds is:

- ❏ 2 – value of a incremented once and stored back in a
- ❏ 3 – value of a incremented once and stored back in a
- ❏ 2 – value of a decremented once and stored back in a
- ❏ 1 – value of a decremented once and stored back in a
- ❏ 1 – the value of a is converted to positive, but not stored back in a or anywhere else
- ❏ 1 – the value of a is converted to negative (-1) and stored in b, not a
- ❏ 2 – a is used in a multiplication (2 * 1) yielding 2, which is put in b, then a is incremented and stored back in a
- ❏ 3 – a is incremented to 3, stored back in a and then used in a multiplication (2 * 3) yielding 6 which is stored in b.

Care has to be taken if these operators are mixed with other operators in an expression, or used in an assignment, as this next example shows.

```
a = 5; c = a++ + 2;     // c = 7, not 8;

b = 10; c = ++b + 2;    // c = 13, not 12;

a = 6; b = 11; c = ( ++a == b++ );
                        // not obvious but c is false as 7 == 11 is false)
```

Unary plus won't change the sign of a Number (unary minus does that) or its value, so you might think it's useless. Nevertheless, it does force any variable it's used with to undergo type conversion (discussed later), and on rare (very rare) occasions that can be useful.

Assignment Operators

The **assignment operators** are the last general group of operators. Plain assignment (=) is the most obvious one. From one point of view it makes no sense to think of it as calculating any kind of expression, since usually it's just used to copy a value into a variable. But it may be looked at differently as follows: if the copy of the value is a result, and storing that value is seen as a side-effect, then it looks like an operator that does nothing to a value except pass it on untouched (and have a side-effect). If this doesn't sound plausible, consider this example:

```
a = 2; b = 2; c = 2;
d = ( a + ( b + ( c + 3 ) ) );          // d becomes 9
d = ( a = ( b = ( c = 3 ) ) );          // d ( and a, b, and c) becomes 3
d = a = b = c = 3;                      // d ( and a, b, and c) becomes 3
```

Line 2 is fairly straightforward, it's just 'd = a + b + c + 3' with more parentheses than are really needed. In Line 3 we can think like this: c is assigned 3, and passes 3 on, so (c = 3) is 3, then b is assigned that new 3, and so on. Finally, line 4 shows that the parentheses can be dropped, leaving us with a shorthand way of assigning the same value to numerous variables at once.

> **As for C and other C-like languages, mixing up = and == is a common source of bugs in JavaScript. See the chapter on debugging for some further discussion.**

There are other assignment operators: compound ones. All the bit and arithmetic operators can be combined with = in a way which allows simple expressions to be written in a shorthand way similar to ++ and --. Here is an example for plus. See Appendix A for the rest.

```
a += 3;                          // same as a = a + 3;
```

Other Operators

Three operators don't fit into any category. These are the ternary (meaning three-part) **conditional operator** ? :, the binary **comma operator** ',' and the binary **string concatenation operator** +. Finally, there are some operators that don't look much like operators. They are new, delete, void, typeof, in, instanceof, and this. Note that this last trio of operators work exclusively with objects and we look more closely at them in Chapter 2. They are mentioned here for completeness.

Ternary Conditions

The ternary conditional operator is a quick way of assigning one of two values to a variable, depending on some test. It's really just shorthand for a specific kind of if statement (ifs are described in the next section), and it is often used in place of simple ifs for brevity. It works like this:

```
a = 1; b = 2; c = 3; d = 4;
x = ( a > b ) ? c : d;           // x becomes 4
```

If the expression before the '?' (which should be a condition) is true, then the expression between the '?' and the ':' is assigned to x, otherwise the expression to the right of ':' is assigned to x. This can also get quite confusing if care isn't taken. Any of the expressions can contain further ternary operators so you can create a mess as well as a confusion if you don't show enough restraint.

Comma Operator

The comma operator's main use is for passing arguments to functions (described in Chapter 2), but technically it's a binary operator as well. What it does is evaluate its left value, throw the result away, evaluate its right value and pass that on. This might all seem useless until you realize that it allows you to put in your own side effects if you want them. Not generally advised, but here's an example:

```
a = 2; b = 3; c = 4; d = 5;
x = ( a++, c ) * ( b++, d );     // same as x=c*d; a++; b++; so why bother?
```

This example is pretty artificial really as the comma operator isn't used much at all, except in some declarations of a `for` loop, on which topic you can read later in this chapter.

String Concatenation

The string concatenation operator takes two String values and creates a new String which is the same as the two original strings run together. Some examples:

```
a = 'Red';
b = "Blue";
c = a + b + 'Yellow';                    // c becomes "RedBlueYellow".
d = a + 5;                               // d becomes 'Red5'.
```

This is really useful. Since + is already used with Numbers as the addition operator however, it can get a bit confusing. In the last line, one value is a String and one is a number, so how does + know whether to concatenate or to add them? The section on type conversion explains, but generally you are safe provided the one value that is a string doesn't contain numeric digits. No strings are damaged in the process of concatenation – in fact, a value which is a String type is always constant – unchangeable by any means. If you want to modify a String, you have to replace it wholly with another string. When the + operator is used for string concatenation, it tries hard to perceive its two supplied values as strings.

New and Delete

New and `delete` allow the creation and removal of objects, a topic covered in Chapter 2. We mention them briefly merely in order to be complete in listing all the operators.

> *delete is not available in Internet Explorer 3.02 or less, or Netscape 2.02 as it is officially a part only of JavaScript 1.2 and above. Netscape thus only officially supports* delete *in its 4.0 browser, but it won't generate an interpreter complaint if used in the 3.0 Netscape versions. In a language that is already garbage collected,* delete *is only useful if your JavaScript scripts start becoming sophisticated and have to manage lots of data.*

Void

Void is used for controlling expressions. All expressions calculate a value, normally the result of a comparison or a mathematical calculation. Sometimes it's preferable to just throw the result away, rather than storing it in a variable, particularly if the main aim of the expression is to achieve some side effect, such as changing a host object. Void causes the expression to report undefined, rather than what the expression's result would otherwise be.

```
a = 5;
document.write( void (++a) );            // displays 'undefined', not '6'.
```

> *void was introduced in JavaScript 1.1.*

Typeof

Typeof is used for identifying types. Given an expression or variable, it will return a string containing a word that describes the type of the expression's result or the variable's contents. Which word is returned is set down in full in Appendix A, but to demonstrate, here's a quick example.

```
var a = 'anything';
var b;
document.write(typeof(a));          // displays "string"
document.write(typeof(b));          // displays "undefined"
document.write(typeof(c));          // displays "undefined"
```

Typeof is one of the rare places where you can work with a variable that has never been declared with var. You can do this without generating an error. This is especially useful because you can check for the existence of variables with typeof.

Typeof () was introduced in JavaScript 1.1.

Type Conversion and Equality

JavaScript is called a loosely typed language because any variable or property can contain any type of data, but this flexibility doesn't come free. Every piece of data still has a type and there are several situations where decisions need to be made about how to handle those types. To save the script writer the overhead of making those decisions (typically required in a strongly typed language like Java), the JavaScript interpreter follows a set of built-in rules. Obscure and hard to find bugs can occur if these rules aren't appreciated by the script writer, but for normal cases it all works the way you'd expect it to. Generally speaking, the only time these rules apply is when **type conversion** happens – a piece of data of a given type needs to turn into another type. If you consider this example, you'll see there are a number of ambiguities that an efficient scripter should appreciate:

```
var u = String(5.35);               // 5.35 or "5.35" ?
var v = "10" + 23;                  // "1023" or 33 ?
var w = ( "10.5" == 10.5 );         // true or false ?

var x = new Object;
var y = x + 1;                      // what ?
```

In the following sections we'll develop enough rules for you to answer the questions posed in the comments of this example. First, the next bit cuts to the chase and shows you how to avoid problems. After that there's some minor agony covering the gritty details of the rules before you get to read something more palatable again.

Before we go into any of that however, we should return briefly to the question of the '**strictly equals**' operators, === and !==, that were introduced in JavaScript 1.3. These two operators compare not only the value of the variable but the type of the variable too. So, two variables are strictly equal to one another if both their value and type are the same. Compare this with the == and != operators in the rest of this section.

Quick and Safe Type Conversion

As you'll see below, comparisons are the main bugbear. The safest way to proceed with comparisons without wasting time on bugs, compatibility problems and obscure rules is to stick to three simple guidelines:

❑   Compare same types only – don't mix Numbers and Strings;

❑   If mixing is inevitable, force the conversion you want to happen.

❑   Avoid comparing things with `null`; just rely on the fact that conversion to the Boolean type is reliable.

This example illustrates these points:

```
var result = ( a+'' == b+'' );          // String comparison forced
    result = ( a-0 == b-0 );            // Number comparison forced
    result = ( !a == !b );              // Boolean comparison forced

if ( a != null ) { do_something(a); };   // possibly attracts bugs
if ( a ) { do_something(a); };           // more likely to avoid bugs

var message = "total errors: " + num_errors;   // always safe
```

Don't worry about concatenating Numbers and Strings together. It'll work. Note that Netscape's implementation of JavaScript1.2 disobeyed some of the type conversion rules, so you should avoid it if at all possible. The actual discrepancies are noted later.

Now for the type conversion details – one day you may need them. Skip to the Flow Control section if it starts to drive you crazy.

Primitive Type Conversion

In order to discuss type conversion, we'll first have to admit we haven't covered all of the data types yet. There is an Object type in JavaScript, described in detail in Chapter 2. Just think of it as another type for now, like String or Number.

ECMAScript says that any piece of data can be converted to each of the obvious primitive types: Boolean, Number and String. If the piece of data is an Object, then there is a mechanism in the object that can be used to convert it to a Number or a String. If the piece of data isn't an Object, then the JavaScript interpreter does the job itself, internally.

Conversion to Boolean

The conversion to Boolean is the easiest to grasp as this table shows

Original Type	Converted Boolean Value
Undefined	`false`
Null	`false`
Number	`false` if -0, +0, or NaN, else `true`
String	`false` if string length = 0, else `true`
Object	`true`

Conversion to Number

Again, the conversion to Number is not too tricky, with two exceptions.

Original Type	Converted Number Value
Undefined	NaN
Null	+0
Boolean	1 if true, 0 if false
String	See below
Object	Returns the value of the object as a Number if Boolean, Number or String object, else returns NaN

Converting a String to a Number is tricky if you rely on the interpreter converting. You can do it yourself with some object methods called parseInt() and parseFloat() but we haven't covered objects yet, and in any case the interpreter's own behavior needs to be stated.

To start with, either the String looks like a number or it doesn't. The latter case produces NaN, but the former case isn't simple. Because the Number type has a limit to the number of digits it can store, there is a special piece of agony the interpreter must go through to store the closest possible value to the number represented in the String. This is the business of **rounding**, and applies in the reverse situation as well – converting a Number to a String. This can be particularly irritating because the JavaScript implementations 1.1 and 1.0 (NC2, NC3, IE3, JScript3.0 or less) can cause 6 / 2 to equal 2.99999999 instead of 3 – although you usually have to pick more obscure number combinations to see this happening.

The URL http://developer.netscape.com/library/examples/JavaScript/rounding.html contains a JavaScript function that will round a variable that otherwise isn't rounding well. ECMAScript-compliant JavaScript will correctly round. This example reveals at least one problem in most Netscape browser versions; Microsoft browsers generally, but not always, round better.

```
var x = 0.03;
var y = 0.09+0.01;
var z = 1.23456789012345678;
document.write(x + ' ' + y + ' ' + z);
```

The moral of this example is: don't rely on the built-in support for number rounding if you want to display highly accurate numbers. If you have a JavaScript implementation that isn't rounding well, or if you are doing complex mathematics, then the ultra-safe way to compare Numbers is to use this old trick: instead of comparing two numbers against each other, calculate a difference and see if the difference is close enough to zero to satisfy you that they are the same.

```
var test_data = 1.23450000000001;
var tiny = 1e-10;
if ( Math.abs(test_data - 1.2345) < tiny)
{
                        // Math.abs() removes the sign of a Number
    document.write("so close it's the same as 1.2345.");
}
else
{
    document.write('some number other than 1.2345.');
}
```

Conversion to String

As we've seen already, the major sticking point when converting to Strings is when the original type is Number:

Original Type	Converted String Value
Undefined	"undefined"
Null	"null"
Boolean	"true" if true "false" if false
Number	"NaN" if NaN "0" if +0 or -0 "Infinity" if infinity else "xx" where xx is the number value. See above for discussion of rounding.
Object	Returns the value of the object as its built-in toString() method would, else "undefined". See Appendix A for more on toString().

The ability to convert to primitive types freely means that the following examples contain no ambiguities:

```
var u = String(23);          // "23"
var v = Number("44.55");       // 44.55
var w = +("0xFE99");         // 65177
var x = "23.45" - 10;        // 13.45 - minus only accepts Number types
var y = ( "fred" && 23 );    // true
var z = ( "0xFF" & 0xF0 );   // 0xF0 = 240
```

Easy Conversion of Mixed Types

Given the ability to convert between types at will, the following rules describe which conversions will occur when there is a mixture of types present. Step one is to identify what is a legal mixture and what isn't. Here it is according to the ECMAScript standard.

A mixture of types can only occur for binary operators. If a given binary operator only supports one type, then both pieces of data for that operator must either be of that type, or convertible to that type, otherwise an error results.

This takes care of most cases, such as all the bit operations, multiplication, subtraction and division. All those operators require two numeric (or convertible to numeric) types.

Remove these cases and the **polymorphic** binary operators are left. Polymorphic means "many shapes" and polymorphic operators are those that work with more than one type of data. The assignment operators and the comma operator are examples, but they are straightforward. The assignment operators always change the contents of their left-hand data item to match their right-hand item, and the comma operator doesn't combine its two data types in any meaningful way at all.

For all these cases, there's no confusion possible, and no need to do anything, except watch for complaints from the JavaScript interpreter.

Hard Conversion of Mixed Types

The problematic operators are the relational operators (==, <, >, <=, =>) and the string concatenation operator ('+') which is also used for addition. All these operators work with more than one type.

Since some types (such as some objects) can be converted to either Numbers or Strings, the conversion rules for these hard cases come down to describing which way the two arguments will be converted in which circumstances. All else being equal, arguments that are Objects have a preference as to which of String or Number they will convert to (usually Number, except for the Date type), and that preference can figure in the conversion decision as well.

The easiest case to understand is '+', the addition/concatenation operator. The rule is:

> **For + operators, if either argument is a String or converts preferentially to one, then do String concatenation, not addition. Otherwise, neither argument prefers to be a String so do Number addition.**

To apply this test to a specific example ask yourself: would either argument like to be a String? If so, concatenation is in order. The interpreter does the same thing.

For the relational operators, the situation is similar but the case for Strings is 'weaker'.

> **For >, >=, <, <= operators, if neither argument can be converted to a Number, then do string comparison, not numeric comparison. Otherwise, at least one argument can be converted to a Number, so do numeric comparison.**

To apply this test to a specific example, ask yourself: could either argument be a Number? If so, numeric comparison is in order. The interpreter does the same thing.

Remembering what happens in these two cases can be tricky because it can go either way (Number or String), and it's all a bit obscure. A memory trick that will act as a rough guide is to remember this:

"String plus: either String, String compare: neither Number"

The case of inequality and equality is different again:

> **For ==, != operators, first convert any Objects to their preferred primitive types. If the types are still different, convert any Boolean to a Number. If the types are still different, convert the non-Number argument to Number and compare as Numbers. Exception: null == undefined without any conversion required.**

To apply this test to a specific example, ask yourself: would both arguments prefer to be Strings? If so, a string equality test is in order, otherwise it's a numeric equality test.

These ECMAScript comparison rules all roughly agree with the pre-ECMAScript versions of JavaScript currently available. However, there is one particular trap to be wary of.

Netscape JavaScript 1.2 is Different

Netscape's JavaScript version 1.2 abandons most of the type conversion rules, incorrectly anticipating the standard. This means "3" != 3 (note the quotes), for example. Fortunately, if you don't explicitly ask for this version of JavaScript when you embed your script in a webpage, it works like the older versions of JavaScript that both the standard and Internet Explorer are closer to. Even more fortunately, in Netscape Navigator 4.0 if you don't explicitly request the 1.2 version, you still have access to all the 1.2 features, except for this specific change. Chapter 4 describes how to request different versions using the <SCRIPT> tag.

It's also true that bugs in the Microsoft and Netscape implementations make some of the more subtle comparisons unreliable. Early versions, before 4.0, get easily confused about comparisons with NaN, null and 0 when type conversions are involved.

Flow Control

All the examples to date show the simplest kind of statement: just assigning a value to a variable. The flow control syntax features of JavaScript give the script writer control over which JavaScript statements are executed and when. Without flow control, all scripts would start at the first statement, proceed rapidly to the last statement and then end immediately. Not very flexible if you want to do something over and over.

if..else

The if...else... statement causes the interpreter to choose between one or two alternative statements and execute at most one set. The syntax is:

```
if ( condition ) {
    statement or block
}
```

or

```
if ( condition ) {
    statement or block
}
else {
    statement or block
}
```

In the first form, if the condition is met, then the statement or block of statements is done, otherwise it is skipped. In the second form, if the condition is met, then the first statement or block is done, otherwise the second one is. Each possible block is called a **branch**. Since a block uses braces, but a statement doesn't, it follows that braces are optional (but advised for clarity's sake) if there is only one statement in a branch. Some examples:

```
if ( x == 5 ) {          // first example
    y = 6;
}

if ( name == "fred") {   // second example
    y = 6;
}
else {
    y = 7;
}

if ( x == y && a == b ) {    // third example
    x++;
    y++;
}
else {
    a++;
    b++;
}
```

The statements making up each branch are indented only for ease of reading. Like HTML, it makes no difference to the result if there's extra whitespace included. One standard mistake to make is to begin your statement with if (x = 5) rather than if (x == 5) as in the first example. See more on this in Chapter 17.

Finally, you can have a **cascading if**. This is an if statement that has multiple branches, as many as you like. The syntax is:

```
if ( condition ) {
    statement or block
}
else if ( another condition ) {     // repeat this middle part
    statement or block               // as many times as you like
}
else {
    statement or block
}
```

In this case, if the first condition is not met, then the second (and possibly, third, fourth, fifth, etc) conditions are tested. If any become true, the accompanying block will be executed, and no others. If none of the conditions are met, then the else block is executed as for the simple case. If any of the conditions are met, then subsequent else if sections will *not* be evaluated. This is similar to short circuit boolean evaluation, discussed above in the expressions section. In this case, conditions are only evaluated until one yields a true result. Even if there are two conditions exactly the same that evaluate to true (difficult to see why you would want to do this), only the first will actually be tested.

while

The while statement repeats a statement or block based on a condition. Its syntax is:

```
while ( condition ) {
    statement or block
}
```

If the condition is met, one repetition occurs. After that, the condition is checked again to see if there should be another repetition, and so on. If the condition is false initially, then no repetitions at all occur. Care has to be taken that the condition eventually stops the cycle or the loop will go on forever. Some examples:

```
var num = 134 - 1;                    // Example 1. Find the biggest factor of 134.
var finished = false;

while (finished == false) {
    if ( 134 % num == 0 ) {
        document.write('The biggest factor of 134 is ' + num);
        finished = true;
    }
    num--;
}

num = 1;                              // Example 2. Display all the numbers.
while (true) {                        // This loop never ends.
    document.write(++num + ' ');
}
```

do..while

The do...while statement is a variant on the while statement. Its syntax is:

```
do {
statement or block
} while ( condition )
```

In this variant, the statement or block is always executed at least once. After that, the condition is checked again to see if there should be another repetition, and so on. This is sometimes more convenient than while on its own because it matches better the logic of the problem you are trying to solve. If the condition is never true, then only one repetition will occur. Care must still be taken to see that the condition eventually stops the cycle or the loop will go on forever. Here is a previous example rewritten:

```
// example 1 again - biggest factor of 134.
var num = 134;
do {
    num--;
    if ( 134 % num == 0 ) {
        document.write('The biggest factor of 134 is ' + num);
    }
} while ( 134 % num != 0 )
```

This form of the `while` statement didn't make it into the original ECMAScript standard but is planned for version two. Netscape and Microsoft have both implemented it in the interim. You can find it in any version of JavaScript or JScript since 1.2 and 3.0 respectively.

for

The `for` loop statement is similar to the `while` loop but is a bit more complicated. Like `while`, it also allows the same statement or block to be repeated, but in this case a count is usually kept of the repetitions to make sure that the loop doesn't go on forever. The syntax is:

```
for ( setup; condition; change ) {
    statement or block
}
```

The statement or block is the repeated part. **setup** is a JavaScript statement that occurs before the first repetition occurs. **condition** is a JavaScript expression (usually a condition) that is evaluated before the repeated part is started. If it evaluates to false right at the start, no repetitions occur, and the statement or block is ignored. If it evaluates to true, then a repetition starts, or another repetition if one has already occurred. `change` is a JavaScript statement that occurs just before the condition is re-checked, and which usually affects whether the condition will pass or not. These examples show a very common idiom using the 3 parts within the brackets of the `for` statement to set, test and update a counter that controls the number of repetitions:

```
// first example
var fruit = Array(3);
fruit[0] = 'apple';
fruit[1] = 'pear';
fruit[2] = 'orange';

for (count=0; count <=2; count++) {               // display all fruit.
    document.write(fruit[count]+ ' ');
}

// second example
var new_line = '<BR>';
for (loop1=0; loop1 < 5; loop1++) {               // display a triangle of T's.
    for (loop2=0; loop2 < loop1; loop2++) {
        document.write('T');
    }
    document.write(new_line);
}

// third example
for (;;)                                          // do nothing forever.
    ;
```

The first loop produces this output:

```
apple pear orange
```

The second loop, which has a further loop inside it, produces this output:

```
T<BR>
TT<BR>
TTT<BR>
TTTT<BR>
TTTTT<BR>
```

The last loop produces nothing and never ends.

Zero or more of the three parts can be left out if they're not needed, but for this command, there must always be exactly two semi-colons between the `for` parentheses with no carefree semicolon omissions allowed. Going towards the other extreme, if you want to evaluate more than one expression in such a statement, use a bit of code like this:

```
for (x=0; !x; exp1, exp2, exp3)
```

`exp1`, `exp2` and `exp3` are whole expressions or statements, as many or few as you want. How does this work? We are using the comma operator. When the third part of the for statement is evaluated (the bit after the second semi-colon), each of `exp1`, `exp2` and `exp3` are evaluated in turn, and in each case the result is thrown away unless a deliberate attempt is made to save it (perhaps using =).

Finally, if you are not careful, you will end up with an infinite loop as in the case of the while statement. In the for case this is very bad practice because it can only really happen if the loop variable is messed around with a lot. The loop variable should just neatly count up or down to some limit and not be otherwise changed.

There is a second form of the `for` statement that is specifically for objects. See Chapter 2 for details.

break and continue

`break` and `continue` should only appear inside a block that is the repeated part of a `for`, `while`, `do..while` or `switch` statement (`switch` is discussed next). These statements give finer control over how a block of statements is repeated. **break** causes any repetition to stop immediately with no further repetitions. **continue** causes the current repetition to stop immediately, but the test for another repetition still goes ahead. Some examples:

```
var loop = 0;                         // Example 1. Display all multiples of
while ( ++loop < 200 ) {              // 7 less than 200.
    if ( loop % 7 != 0 ) {
        continue;
    }
    document.write(loop + ' ');
}

for (loop=1000; loop < 1099; loop++) {  // Example 2.
    if (loop % 99 == 0)                  // Find the first number bigger
        break;                           // than 1000 that is divisible by 99.
}
document.write(loop);
```

In the `while` loop, the loop variable will increment through all the values from 0 to 199. The first thing that happens in the loop is the `if` test, which will pass for all numbers not divisible by seven. Therefore, the branch or body of the `if` statement will execute. This is the `continue` statement, which sends control back to the `while` statement. Therefore, the number will only be written out if the `if` statement fails, which occurs when the number *is* divisible by seven.

In the `for` loop, the loop variable will increment through all the values from 1000 to 1098 in the ordinary case. However, if the `if` statement is ever satisfied, the `break` statement will execute. When or if that occurs, control will pass to the statement immediately following the `for` statement. So in this case, either 1099 or the last value of the loop variable is written out. Of course, the number written out will be **1089** ($1089 = 11$ times 99).

break and continue with labels

Recall that labels can be applied to any statement or block. `break` and `continue` can take an optional argument: a label name. When the `break` or `continue` occurs, the next statement to be executed will be the one that has the label attached. This sounds very flexible, but there are some restrictions – the label must be attached to a statement block that the `break` or `continue` is *inside*. This example illustrates:

```
label1: var x = 1;
label2: x = 2;
label3: {
label4:    x = 4;
label5:    {
label6:        x = 6;
               break label3;
label7:        x = 7;
           }
label8:    x = 8;
       }
// next statement will be this one
x = 99;
```

The variable x will be assigned values 1, 2, 4, 6 and 99 in turn. The `break` statement can only break to labels `label5` and `label3` because only those blocks enclose the break. Attempts to break to any of the other labels will cause a runtime error. When a break occurs, the first statement after the block broken out of will be the next to execute, so in the case of `label3`, this is the 'x = 99' variable assignment. The situation is similar for `continue`. In short, labels can be put anywhere, but only certain ones can be `break`'ed or `continue`'d to.

The above example isn't very useful, unless you have a particularly baroque scripting style. Where `break`s and `continue`s on block labels come in handy is this classic case:

```
// As I was going to St. Yves

var wife, sack, cat, kit;
var too_many = 100, so_far = 0;

giveup:
for (wife=1; wife<=7; wife++)
 for (sack=1; sack<=7; sack++)
  for (cat=1; cat<=7; cat++)
   for (kit=1; kit<=7; kit++)
   {
       if (++so_far > too_many)
         break giveup;  // stay home!
   }
// next statement here
```

In this example, the label `giveup` is attached to the outermost `for` loop. The outermost `for` loop is a block because it contains other statements – the second `for` loop in particular. If one gets overwhelmed by the number of kits, cats, sacks and wives, one doesn't want to break out of just the innermost loop (the kit loop), one wants to get all the way out. The break-to-a-label syntax allows this very neatly. Since the sole label is attached to the outermost for statement, the next statement executed will be beyond that loop, which is at the final line as the comment indicates. It's possible to manage without this break-label syntax support but you have to muck around with an extra boolean flag and do more checks in each loop.

As for the `do..while`, labelled `break` and `continue` didn't make it into version 1 of the ECMAScript standard but are planned for version 2.

> *Again, Netscape JavaScript 1.2 and JScript 3.0 (NC4+, IE4+) are the minimum versions required for labelled breaks and continues.*

switch

Sometimes you are faced with a lot of alternative paths through a script. The `switch` statement provides a neater mechanism for handling this problem than writing lots of `if` statements, provided the alternatives can be determined from the result of a single expression. An example:

```
switch (grade) {
case 'A':
  comment = 'Excellent';
  break;
case 'B':
case 'C':
case 'D':
  comment = 'OK';
  break;
default:
  comment = 'Not your day';
  break;
}
```

When the `switch` statement is executed, the expression in the brackets is evaluated and the interpreter starts searching for a `case` clause that has a matching value. When one is found, processing is resumed at that point. Notice that all the statements for a given `case` clause end with a break. This is to prevent the interpreter from blindly dropping through to the next `case` clause – `switch` is pretty dumb in that respect. Also notice that several `case` clauses can be 'stacked' so that if any of them match, the same group of statements will be executed. Finally if none of them match, then the `default` clause is picked for execution. If there is no `default` clause, then nothing is executed. It's good practice to always put a `default` clause in, even if all it does is `break` – that way you know that exactly one of the switch alternatives will always be executed.

The value that follows the `case` clause is a little tricky. It can be any Number or String literal, or any expression that involves constants only (such as `10*6+4` or `Math.PI`). ECMAScript 2 may allow the value to be any expression at all, but for now only constants are possible. It's possible to have different types of literals for different `case` values, although that has only obscure applications. The `switch` statement also missed out on version 1 of the ECMAScript standard.

Again, Netscape JavaScript 1.2 and JScript 3.0 are the minimum versions required for switch.

Summary

Data, types, variables, and the basic language constructs that handle them lie at the core of JavaScript and are the nuts and bolts you use to screw everything else together. Support for basic mathematics and logic and a step-by-step execution model are fundamental to JavaScript. Even within those simple features there are a few incompatibilities and subtleties to watch out for.

However, JavaScript's core language goes further than the discussion so far. Complex scripts using only the features of this chapter would be cumbersome and awash with trivial detail. In the next chapter it will be seen how simple data items can be conveniently aggregated together into objects, and how simple series of statements can be conveniently aggregated into functions.

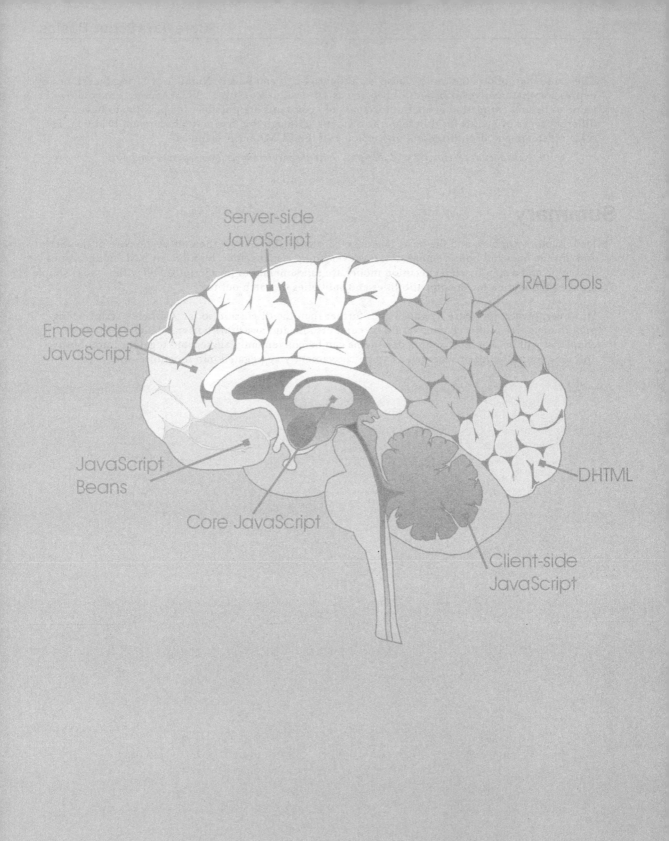

Functions and Objects

In this chapter you'll see how to go beyond simple variables and flow control in JavaScript as we look at how to create and work with functions and objects. If the script you are trying to write is complex, these aspects of the JavaScript language provide fundamental support for the design process that accompanies all well written programs – the grouping together (for easy re-use) of statements, data and other functions – albeit in different ways.

By learning to work with functions and objects, we can also start to work with the host objects we made reference to in the Introduction. Entities like windows in browsers, files in standalone scripts and database objects in web server scripts would be inaccessible to the JavaScripter otherwise. Recall from the Introduction that without host objects and functions, there's no way for a JavaScript script to communicate with the user or the outside world.

Besides looking at how to write your own functions and create your own objects, we'll also catch up with the rest of the top-level functions we haven't yet looked at. Remember that these functions are always accessible as they are part of the core language specification and not attached to any one particular object. We'll also run through JavaScript's native objects.

Functions

Functions group statements into a block and give that block a name so that it can be referred to by that name each time that group of statements needs to be run. In this way you don't have to retype the block each time you need it. When writing a function, you should use the following syntax:

```
function name(arguments)
{
    statements, possibly including 'return'
}
```

and, if we ever wished to run the statements in the above block, we would **call** or **invoke** the function with

```
name(Argument_Values);
```

Several points should be noted

- ❏ function is a JavaScript keyword like var or while.
- ❏ name is the unique name given to the function, which follows the rules for variable names.
- ❏ return is a keyword similar to break, which is optional and can only exist inside a function.
- ❏ arguments is an optional comma-separated list of variables which will be used inside a function, and is similar to the data that the expression operators work with.
- ❏ Argument_Values is a comma-separated list of data items to be used by a function when it has been called.

Functions are a departure from the rule 'execute a JavaScript statement as soon as you see it'. The **function definition** (where the function's statements and name are described) is merely noted by the interpreter for later use – it doesn't actually run until the function is called elsewhere.

Here are three example functions:

```
function say_hello()
{
    document.write('Hello. ');
    document.write('Welcome to the say_hello() function. ');
    return;
}

function add_together(first, second)
{
    var result = first + second;
    return result;
}

function add_all()
{
    var loop=0, sum=0;
    for ( loop = arguments.length-1; loop >=0; loop--)
        sum += arguments[loop];
    return sum;
}

// Now make them happen

say_hello();
var answer = add_together(5, 3);
document.write( answer + ' ' + add_together(10, 4) );
document.write( ' ' + add_all(1, 3, 5, 7, 9) );
```

As you can see, most of the effort is in defining the functions, that is, making the JavaScript interpreter aware they exist. This is equivalent to the `var` statement for variables. Only the last four lines make them "go". Should we actually run these, we would quickly see

Hello. Welcome to the say_hello() function. 8 14 25

A bit more terminology will go a long way towards the intelligent discussion of functions. When a function is called, the data specified between the parentheses are known as **arguments** or **parameters** and are said to be **passed** to the function. When a function has a value to hand back to the place it was called from, it is said to **return** that value.

There are several things going on in this example:

❑   `return` provides the simple and official way to finish a function or method, returning a value to the code that called it. We'll come back to `return` in a second.

❑   Functions are often declared to require some elements to be passed to them, just as `add_together()` does. Once the function is running, these act just like normal variables, except that they are unavailable outside the function, a bit like `break` is unusable outside a `for` or `while` loop. This availability or not of a variable depends on its **scope**.

❑   Even if no arguments are declared at the point where the `function` keyword appears, a function can still get at any that might be passed to it, as shown in `add_all()`. In this function, no arguments are declared but clearly five are sent to it (in the last line). Inside every function is a special Array called `arguments` (it's always present), that can be examined for the number and values of the arguments passed in. This allows a function to also handle the less common case where it is passed different numbers of arguments at different times. Should the function be passed more arguments than it has specified, those extra ones will be ignored but still available through the `arguments` array, as is the case with `add_all()`. On the other hand, should the function be passed fewer arguments, those not specified will be given the value `undefined`.

Back to the first of our three points. `return` can only be used within a function and can appear zero or more times there. If there is no value for the function to return, `return` can be omitted or written on its own, as it is in the `say_hello()` function above, and `undefined` is passed back to the calling code.

Usually, a function simply returns a value at its end, but you can use return more than once in a function. For example,

```
function die(how)
{
  if ( how != 'go quietly')
  {
    return "Yeeeaaarrrgghhh";
  }
  return;                        // the quiet way
}
```

It's not recommended to use `return` more than once in a function, for the practical reason that it makes the script harder to maintain.

In the following example, the way `return` is used isn't sensible since there are statements after it, and you will receive an error from the interpreter to boot if the browser is not a recent 4.0+ version:

```
function stage_death()
{
  var gasp = 'Ahhh ..';
  gasp += 'Ohhh ..';
  return gasp;
  gasp += '.. Alas!';
}
```

Function Scoping of Variables

The last two functions in the `add_all()` code example above have some variable declarations in them – `loop`, `sum` and `result`. These are not accessible outside the function they appear in, but they're not special like the `arguments` array. They do, however, illustrate the scope of a variable.

The **scope of a variable** is the part of the script over which the variable name can be referenced – that is, where you can use the variable in the program. Variables declared within a function are said to be **local** to that function as they are accessible only within the body of the function in which they are declared. Remember though that a variable does not exist before its declaration, so it is only available within a function from the point of its declaration until the end of the block in which it is defined.

On the flip-side of the coin, we have **global** variables, which are available for the entire duration of the script, but the word 'global' is a bit overloaded in JavaScript so we'll stick to local and non-local. This distinction is an attempt to reduce complexity by hiding variables from parts of the program where they'd be irrelevant. If that was all, then complexity would indeed be reduced, but the scoping rules also make it possible for us to work with two variables that have the same name provided they have different scopes. Should we choose to do so then on referencing the name, the variable with the 'innermost', or nearest, scope with that name will be used. For example:

```
var stuff = 'outside';

function do_it()
{
    var stuff = 'inside';
    document.write(stuff);
}

document.write(stuff);                    // display 'outside'
do_it();                                  // display 'inside'
```

New scopes aren't created inside `if` branches or in `while` or `for` statement blocks. Those kinds of blocks will obey whatever scopes were at work just before they began, however. Only functions (and methods) produce new scopes.

> *JavaScript is not like C in this respect. The reason is that there is no stack in JavaScript so a different mechanism is at work. See the section on scope chains in Chapter 3 for further information.*

Note that so far, we've only passed primitive values (numbers, in this case) to the functions in our examples. We said that the arguments passed to the function don't exist beyond the function. It's also true that the values used between the parentheses of the function call aren't affected by any goings-on within the function. After all those values are supplied from outside the function and have their own destiny.

We'll see under the discussion of objects shortly, that you can pass things to a function that exist both inside and outside the function and can be affected from both places.

Functions in Expressions

In Chapter 1, there was some discussion of operators that have side effects in expressions and conditions, such as the pre-increment operator (++). The main purpose of expressions and conditions is to return a value that is the result of a calculation. Not surprisingly then, you can nest function calls within function calls in much the same way as you can nest sums within sums. For example,

```
var sum = add( add(2,3) , add(4,5) );
```

will initialize sum with the value 14. Of course, this assumes the function add returns some value other than undefined, in which case it cannot be used as part of a larger expression.

Functions can do anything when called, including performing statements that are unrelated to the return value that they pass back. Since functions can participate in expressions and conditions, quite powerful side-effects can occur as this optimistic example shows:

```
var tasks_complete = solve_all_world_problems() + keep_everyone_happy();
```

The return values for the two functions are added together and stored in the tasks_complete variable. Whatever the statements in these functions are, it's likely they are large and complex ...

Native JavaScript Functions

JavaScript comes with a few generally useful ECMAScript native functions. These are parseInt(), parseFloat(),isNaN(), isFinite(), escape(), unescape(), and eval(). All of these are for String and Number manipulation, except eval() which is special.

Controlling Type Conversion – parseInt(), parseFloat()

parseInt() and parseFloat() are both used to extract Number type values from strings. As you can guess, the former will produce an integer and the latter a floating point number. For example:

```
var total   = '234.50 dollars';
var dollars = parseInt(total,10);   //Parse the number as a decimal
var dolhex = parseInt(total,16);    //Parse and convert hex number to decimal
var cents  = parseFloat(total);
document.write(dollars + ' ' + dolhex + ' ' + cents);
```

will produce the output 234 564 234.5.

`parseInt` works by taking the string passed to it, ignoring any initial whitespace and treating any integer that immediately follows as a number in the numerical base (decimal, octal, hex) specified in the second argument and returning a value in decimal. If it initially reads any non-whitespace character not considered to be a number in the specified base, it returns NaN. It also works with just the string argument by attempting to discern what base the number is in as it goes along according to the rules for writing alternative base numbers we met in Chapter 1. The strings '255', '0xFF' and '0377' would all return 255 through `parseInt()`.

`parseFloat()` works in much the same way as `parseInt()` but also treats decimal points and exponents as valid characters and works only in decimal. However, older versions of `parseFloat()` are not so liberal and will give an error if the string is not exactly a floating point number. This applies to JavaScript 1.2 or less (NC4.05-, IE4.0-).

> *Eagle-eyes may have spotted that NaN didn't exist in JavaScript 1.0 (NC2, IE3). In this case both parseFloat() and parseInt() returned 0.*

We'll use these functions again in Chapter 7 for processing forms and data.

Detecting Odd Values – isNaN(), isFinite()

`isNaN()` and `isFinite()` do just what you'd expect – return `true` if a supplied number is NaN in the former case and `false` if the number is +Infinity or -Infinity in the latter case. Without these functions it's tricky and ugly to detect these cases.

> *isNaN() was introduced in JavaScript1.1 (NC3+,IE4+) and isFinite() was introduced in JavaScript1.3 (NC4.06+, IE5+)*

Web Hacks – escape(), unescape()

The JavaScript language was born for use in web browsers. One consequence of this is that the `escape()` and `unescape()` functions crept into the core language even though they are mostly useful for constructing URLs. The standard for valid URLs – RFC 1738 – demands that if a URL contains non-alphanumeric characters with the exception of `*@-_+./` they should be encoded rather than used directly. A string passed to `escape()` returns a correctly encoded URL, and `unescape` reverses the process.

These functions are eventually going to change names in ECMAScript so that they will be called `URLencode()` and `URLdecode()`. It's almost guaranteed that the older names will survive in software for a long time, though. Here is an example of a URL before and after encoding by `escape()`. In case you're curious, file URLs just point to the local disk, in this case the C: drive.

```
file://C|/local/tmp/My Plan For World Domination!.doc
file://C|/local/tmp/My%20Plan%20For%20World%20Domination%21.doc
```

Note that the spaces are not returned as character codes in the Unicode set (\uXXXX), but rather as the hexcode for the ISO-Latin-1 character set. To this extent, `escape()` and `unescape()` do not follow the ECMAScript specification.

Evaluating Code – eval()

The function `eval()` takes a string, then examines and runs it as though it was a JavaScript script. We'll return to `eval` in Chapter 3.

Objects

Nothing makes some computer people more miserable than the word "object". Fortunately, JavaScript objects are extremely tame.

What is an object? In general terms, an object is one or more pieces of data and one or more useful functions all collected together into a neat item that can be easily carried around. Usually the data items and the functions are related and work together. Often an object has a particular identity, like 'person', so that it's possible to have many 'person' objects, each one for a different human being. The ability to carry all the stuff about a person or other kind of thing around in one neat item is a very handy and powerful feature of modern computer languages.

Advocates of other programming languages that support objects such as C++, Java, Ada and Eiffel are likely to become enraged by such a simple definition of objects. For these languages, defining and combining objects is a very exact science. However, JavaScript's loosely-typed and interpreted nature is perfectly suited to simple objects, so the definition is a good one in this case.

Here's an example of two JavaScript objects:

```
var thing = new Object;

thing.name  = 'Any old thing';
thing.age   = 59;
thing.hobby = 'moving as little as possible.';

thing.thing2 = new object;
thing.thing2.name = "thing's own thing";

delete thing;
```

In the object lifecycle, the `new` operator creates an object which is put into `thing`. `thing` is still an ordinary variable, it simply contains a new type of value – an object value. After that's complete, `thing` is neither `undefined` nor `null`. However, objects initially don't contain much of interest – **properties** and **methods** have to be added to them, like ingredients combined to make up a meal. Finally, objects can be got rid of, using `delete`. After `delete`, `thing` is `undefined`. (You can check this with `typeof()`.)

Properties

Lines 3 to 5 of the example above demonstrate the simple syntax used to add properties:

```
objectVariableName.propertyName = value
```

Objects can have as many properties as you can find different names for, and each property can contain a value of any type, including another object, as lines 7-8 demonstrate.

However, there is a catch – objects always have a parent object (just as `thing` is the parent of `thing2`) and it is they who have the final say whether or not we can delete their child object. This gets complex but the practical upshot is that only host objects, as opposed to any we have created using `new`, can deny the script permission to delete an object. This is like directory permissions under Unix or Windows NT, in that you need the right kind of directory permissions as well the right kind of file permissions for a delete.

But what's the parent object of `thing`? Well, as we'll see later, it commonly known as the **global object**, but for more information you'll have to read on. One point to note here is that only Internet Explorer 5.0 lets you explicitly delete new objects attached to the global object. However, an object will automatically disappear if the function in which it was created has ended *and* it is not passed onwards to the code that called the function. Chapter 17 , on disappearing data, has more to say about mechanisms that make objects go away.

Methods

If you have used another programming language, you might be familiar with concepts such as structures, records, tuples, or forms. An object that only has properties does for you about the same amount as these other common concepts. It's just data. However, objects can also contain **methods**, as this example shows:

```
function ordinary_say_hello()
{
    document.write("Hello.");
}

function special_print_name()
{
    document.write("My name is: " + this.name);
}

var thing = new Object;

thing.name = "Fred";
thing.say_hello = ordinary_say_hello;
thing.print_name = special_print_name;

thing.say_hello();
thing.print_name();
```

There are two apparently normal functions here, except that the second one has a mystery variable called `this`. Near the end of the script, two properties of the thing object apparently have function names put into them:

```
thing.say_hello = ordinary_say_hello;
thing.print_name = special_print_name;
```

Then right at the bottom, somehow the object properties began to look like functions:

```
thing.say_hello();
thing.print_name();
```

A method is just a function that likes to be inside, or be part of, an object. It does this by letting an object's property track it in the same way that properties and variables can track whole objects. When the method/function is called (as if it were a property of the object), the special `this` variable becomes available inside the method/function. `this` is a kind of placeholder for whichever object has called the function, and allows access to all the other properties of the object the function was called from. It's done like this (no pun intended) so that the function can always get at the properties of the object it was called from if it needs to, regardless of which object called it. Those properties are its siblings, in a way. However, when methods take advantage of the `this` variable, they can't usually be called as a plain function any more. Thus in the example above, `special_print_name()` must always be called as `thing.print_name`.

> *IE 5.0 will ignore the use of 'this' if a method is called as a plain function. All other browsers will give an error reporting 'this' is undefined.*

The secret mechanism here is that functions are also objects and so can be tracked like objects. But that's getting a bit ahead of ourselves.

Objects vs Primitive Types

There's a very important difference between an object and a variable holding an object. A JavaScript object is just like a bag of properties in no particular order, and that's a good way of viewing it. However, a JavaScript variable can't contain an arbitrary number of properties, it can hold only one piece of data. So the variable just contains one piece of data that tracks where the bag is (you can't get at this data) and since there may be more than one object around, it also tracks which object bag it is. The actual bag itself is separate from the variable's value. In programming parlance then, we say a variable like this contains a **reference** to an object. Just like a personal reference or a letter of introduction gives a potential employer personal details about yourself, so too the reference in a variable gives script statements access to (details about) the object being referred to.

This is important because up until now, dealing with primitive data has been easy; if a variable contains 2, and another variable gets assigned the value 2, that's fine because 2's are cheap – you can have as many as you like. This is also true for objects – you can have as many as you like – but it's often the case that one object will be shared between many variables, because it can be too much bother (or even impossible) to copy it. Here, three variables point at the one object:

```
var x = new Object;
var y = x;
var z = x;
delete x;          // y and z still point to the same Object.

new Useless();     // not wanted
```

In this example the object created is never deleted. This means `delete` is a bit tricky – it really means "make this variable stop tracking its object". If no variables are tracking an object, then the JavaScript interpreter will throw the object away (as happens automatically in line 5).

This distinction is particularly important when using functions. Variables can be passed to functions as arguments. They can contain either primitive types or objects. If you use a primitive type as a function argument, then the argument appearing inside the function is a copy of the one you passed it. This means your original copy can't be damaged from inside the function. However, if you pass an object to a function, a **copy isn't made**, so you are operating on the exact same object inside the function as outside, with consequences to the object that apply even after the function finishes. The former case is called **pass by value** (a copy of the value is passed), the latter case is called **pass by reference** (a reference to the same value is passed). To summarize, extra care is required in passing objects to functions as they are not proof against accidental damage inside the function. Here is an example of an object that is created outside a function, and yet is permanently modified when passed in to that function.

```
function fix_it(obj)
{
  obj.condition = 're-glazed';
}

var vase = new Object();
vase.condition = 'chipped';
fix_it(vase);
// vase.condition = 're-glazed' until further notice.
```

Prototypes and Constructors

So far we have seen that objects are just bags of properties and methods, which we defines as we see fit once we have created one with the new operator. Now suppose you wrote some JavaScript that stored employee's details in objects. You might have 20 items of data per employee and if you used one object for each employee, that's 20 property values per object, plus maybe 10 handy methods. So every time you add a new employee you have to set 20 properties and 10 methods on the new object you create. That's a lot of typing, especially when the methods are all the same for each employee (likely) and half the properties are the same for each employee. And all you'd have for your effort would be an object, which doesn't sound much like an employee record.

The `prototype` property fixes this, along with another special use of functions – **constructors**. Here's an example of a constructor and a prototype:

```
function display_it()
{
    document.write(this.name);
}

function Employee(name, age)
{
    this.name = name;
    this.age = age;
    this.status = 'Full time';
}

Employee.prototype.address = 'JS Industries, Station St.';
Employee.prototype.contact = '012 345 6789';
Employee.prototype.job = "Appear indispensable";
Employee.prototype.display = display_it;

var person1 = new Employee("Doe, John", 47);
var person2 = new Employee("Doe, Jane", 45);

person1.display() + document.write(" " + person2.contact);
```

The function named `Employee` isn't an ordinary function, because it uses the special `this` variable. It could be used as a method, but not in this example – there isn't any object property it's being assigned to. Instead it's being used with new to create an object. So this function is put to a third use: neither function nor method, instead it is an **object constructor**. The new operator assumes its argument is an object constructor and magically 'knows' the object's name, which is the constructor function's name.

The object created is a typical one except that the function `Employee` decorates it with extra properties automatically. If you create an object using 'new object', you don't get any new properties automatically. So constructor functions add value to the normal object construction process.

The extra properties created by a constructor function can be based on function arguments, since all the usual function rules apply. Therefore, this constructor achieves two ends: firstly it saves typing by letting the script writer reuse the statements in the constructor each time an object is created; secondly, it's a more meaningful word than just plain `object`.

Constructors are only a half solution to the problem of too many properties per object. If there were 20 properties and 10 methods per Employee object, that would be 30 arguments to the Employee constructor. That is hardly practical. Instead, there is a special property called `prototype`. Properties of the `prototype` property are copied magically into every object created by the matching constructor. So the two variables `person1` and `person2` both contain the same address, contact, job and display properties, even though the `Employee` constructor didn't explicitly set them. Notice that the word `prototype` is only required once where each `prototype` property is declared. This is a little bit like `var`.

There's one other reason why constructors are useful. In Netscape Navigator 2.02 and Internet Explorer 3.02, you can manipulate existing Arrays, but you can't make one via 'new Array' as the Array constructor function is not available. What you can do is make a special constructor that does an equivalent job. Here's how:

```
function MakeArray(size)
{
    var num = 0;
    this.length = size;
    for (var num = 1; num <= size; num++)
        this[num] = 0;
    return this;
}
```

In Navigator 2.02, setting the 'length' property as in this example is buggy and unreliable. In Netscape 3.0, the Array constructor numbers elements from 0, not from 1, and the elements are not initialized. However, the new versions 4.x of Navigator and Internet Explorer 4+ support using 'new Array..' Techniques to overcome this kind of incompatibility are discussed later.

Chapter 2

Object Literals

Just as it's possible to create an array from a literal value (recall the use of bracketed lists from Chapter 1), so too it's possible to create an object from a literal:

```
var obj1 = {};
var obj2 = { name:'Jo', age:25 };
var obj3 = { spreads:{
                        jam:10,
                        butter:3
                    }
            breads: {
                        white:true,
                        brown:false
                    }
            };
var obj4 = { twins: [ {name:'zig'},
                      {name:'zag'},
                    ]
            };
```

The strings before the colon symbols represent property names. What follows after the colon is the value that property can take on. The value part can be any JavaScript expression, but the name parts must appear plain and complete as they are here.

In this example, `obj1` tracks an object with no properties. `obj2` tracks an object with two properties `name` and `age`. `obj3` tracks an object with two properties `spreads` and `breads`, each of which also tracks an object with two properties.

In the above example, `obj4` is complex. `obj4` tracks an object with one property that is an array of two elements, and each of those elements is an object with one property – name. This last example has an array inside an object, but it could have easily been re-written so that the outermost item was an array literal and the inner one an object literal. There's no requirement that object literals enclose everything when object and array literals are mixed up. Of course, you have to get the order correct for the particular kind of data you want to store.

In order to use this feature, you'll need Netscape JavaScript 1.2 or JScript 3.0 (NC4+, IE4+)

The Secret Influence of Objects

Plain variables and primitive types like Number and String are straightforward. Why bother with objects? Well, for a start, at least, all the built-in objects have many useful properties and methods (listed in Appendix A) instantly available which you would otherwise have to write yourself. The real, compelling reason however is that if you scratch the surface, objects rule the world. Here's a many-faceted illustration, which is discussed at length in the following sections:

```
//Object equivalents of primitive types
var data0 = new Boolean("True");
var data1 = new Number("5");
var data2 = new String("Anything");
var data3 = data2.substring(1, 4) + data2.charAt(7);      // data3 = nythg (!)
```

```
//Function objects
var data4 = new Function("a, b", "return (a<b) ? a : b;");
                                              // return lesser value
data4(3, 5);

// Array objects
var data = new Array(2);
data.0 = "red";                  // same as data[0]
data.1 = "blue";                 // same as data[1]

var data5 = new object;
data5["shape"] = "square";       // same as data5.shape
data5["old cost"] = 10.95;       // same as data5.old cost (but that's an error)

// Native, host and global objects
var data6 = Math.round(3.45);    // equals 3
var data7 = new Date(1997, 7, 27);   // a day of the year
var data8 = new RegExp("ab+c");
```

Primitive Types Have Object Equivalents

The familiar primitive types can be treated like objects:

```
var data0 = new Boolean("True");
var data1 = new Number("5");
var data2 = new String("Anything");
var data3 = data2.substring(1, 4) + data2.charAt(7);     // data3 = nythg (!)
```

For both the Boolean and the Number type, having object equivalents is near useless and in the former case often confuses things. A couple of facts must be kept clear in your mind when using Boolean objects.

❑ The Boolean type truth values `true` and `false` are not the same as the Boolean object values `True` and `False`.

❑ As we saw the type conversion discussion in Chapter 1, any object that isn't `undefined` or `null` converts to the Boolean type value `true`. Even a Boolean object with the value `False`.

String values, on the other hand, have a bit of Jekyll and Hyde about them. On one hand, a String is just a humble piece of text surrounded by quotes – unchangeable. On the other hand, it's a complex object with a heap of methods that let you search, convert, split, concatenate and otherwise prod it in a number of useful ways as shown in line 4. JavaScript automatically converts primitive Strings to String objects when necessary, so it's all fairly invisible to the script writer. Appendix A has the full list and description of all these methods.

Functions Are Also Objects

Functions are objects and can be created like objects as this fragment from the main example shows:

```
var data4 = new Function("a, b", "return (a<b) ? a : b;");
                                              // return lesser value
data4(3, 5);
```

This is only useful for advanced stuff, but if you're desperate to create a function without a name, this is how.

It's also the case that ordinary functions (ones that start with the `function` keyword) are objects:

```
function im_an_object()
{
  var prop1;
  var prop2;
  if ( arguments.length > 2)
    return "At least 3 properties";
}

var obj = im_an_object;
obj(1,2,3);                 // do im_an_object
```

In this example, `prop1`, `prop2` and the `arguments` array are all properties of the Function object that corresponds to the function `im_an_object`. The syntax conveniently lets us overlook the fact that the function is an object but, as the penultimate line shows, we can assign and reference it from a variable just like other object types. We can even call the function using the assigned variable name as shown the last line of the example.

> *The ECMAScript standard process for version 2.0 is likely to mandate toSource() as a method name that always returns JavaScript code for the object that it's a part of. For a Function object, that would be the source code that the function was created with. At the time of writing, that is a little way off. Currently, the toString() method will return JavaScript source when applied to a function object for several vendor's implementations, particularly Netscape.*

Arrays Are Also Objects

Objects and arrays are interchangeable. You can add properties to arrays and array elements to objects, as well as the normal way around. So all the statements in the following examples are the same:

```
arr = new Array(3);         // make one of
obj = new Object;           // each type
arr['prop'] = 1;
obj.prop = 1;
arr.prop = 1;
obj['prop'] = 1;
```

As you can see, the familiar syntax for getting at array elements is interchangeable with the object property syntax. However, since property names aren't numbers, a string is used inside the square brackets. This is especially handy if the property name contains spaces, or you don't know what the property name is at the time. For example:

```
var data = new Array(2);
data.0 = "red";             // same as data[0]
data.1 = "blue";            // same as data[1]

var data5 = new object;
data5["shape"] = "square";  // same as data5.shape
data5["old cost"] = 10.95;  // same as data5.old cost (but that's an error)
```

You can always swap between styles, except for the case of the last line, which is an exception because the string between the brackets can't be turned into a legal variable or property name. IE users out there also lose out as it doesn't yet support the square-bracket-less way of accessing arrays as in lines 2-3.

Arrays are just objects but there is one special difference – you only get the automatically updated `length` property (and some handy array methods) with an official array, and it won't count properties of the array that are named by types other than numbers.

Native and Global Objects

If you look at it from the correct perspective, nearly everything is an object in JavaScript – there's no escape. There are four pre-defined objects in the core language we have yet to discuss. The first and easiest to deal with is **the `Object` object**. It sounds redundant until you realize that every other kind of object is based upon this one and it is from this they all 'inherit' the `prototype` property, and five other methods as follows:

Method	Description
toSource()	Returns the equivalent object literal for the object
toString()	Returns a string that represents the object
valueof()	Returns the primitive value of the object
watch()	Keeps an eye on a property and whe it is assigned a value, runs a specified function.
unwatch()	Unsets the `watch()` function

Let's look at some more code.

```
var data6 = Math.round(3.45);        // equals 3
var data7 = new Date(1997, 7, 27);   // a day of the year
var data8 = new RegExp("ab+c");
```

This example illustrates the remaining core objects we've yet to see: **Math**, **Date** and **RegExp**

Math is a rare example of a **built-in** JavaScript object – one which always exists for you to work with and so never needs to be created using the new operator. By using Math, you give yourself access to eight predefined mathematical values (pi, ln10, etc) and 18 standard mathematical operations like taking calculating the sine, cosine and tangent of a triangle. The full list can be found in Appendix A.

Date, as its name would suggest contains a host of methods (listed in Appendix A) for doing date-time calculations. Interestingly, the value of the date itself is stored as the number of milliseconds that have passed by since midnight, January 1, 1970. With 86,400,000 milliseconds in every day, you can imagine that the current date is actually stored in a Date object as a pretty large integer. Of course, a little logical thought will have you realize therefore that you cannot store a date before midnight January 1, 1970 as a result.

Finally, we come to regular expressions and the **RegExp** object. Or rather we don't, as we'll look at them in fine detail in Chapter 3. Suffice to say here that regular expressions are a convenient way to manipulate strings in a very precise, refined way. Both JScript (3.0+/ IE4+) and JavaScript (1.2+ /NC4+) support regular expression objects as new native objects.

The Global object

The biggest secret to working with objects is that there's always one around you. A given script might look like it just contains plain variables, but these variables are really properties of some object. In ECMAScript, this is the magic **global object** that you can't see or touch except by some other variable that was rigged to point at it before you arrived. In browser-hosted JavaScript, each window is an object that contains as properties any variables you care to make up. Every variable is a property of some object – it's just a matter of finding it.

Object Based Operators and Flow Control

To round off our discussion of objects before we get to the more intricate parts of JavaScript in Chapter 3, we're going to take a brief look at the object-based operators and flow control statements we've not yet looked at.

for..in

Sometimes an object's contents are unknown. If it were an array it would be easy to discover the contents by looking at the `length` property of the array and accessing all the elements starting at 0 (zero). It's not so easy for objects because the properties of the object aren't neatly ordered and their names can be arbitrary strings – millions to choose from. There has to be another mechanism.

The `for` statement discussed in Chapter 1 has a variant designed for this job. Its syntax is:

```
for ( variable in object-variable )
    statement or block
```

An example:

```
for ( prop in some_object )
{
    if ( typeof( some_object[prop] ) == "string" )
        document.write(" Property: " + prop + " has value: " + some_object[prop]);
}
```

This example steps through all the properties of the `some_object` variable (presumably containing an object) and displays only those properties containing strings.

Unfortunately, the `for..in` statement is a trap for beginners. "Ordinary" properties are reported as you would expect, but some special properties never appear. This can be a source of confusion. Typical examples are methods of objects that are supplied by the host, not by the script writer. The order in which properties are reported varies between JavaScript vendors, too.

with..

The point has been made that every variable is part of an object, which we might call the **current context,** the **current object**, or the **current scope**. Sometimes (usually for typing convenience) we might want to change the current scope. The `with` statement does this. Its syntax is:

```
with ( object )
    Statement or block
```

An example:

```
var unrealistically_long_name = new object;
unrealistically_long_name.sole_property = new object;
unrealistically_long_name.sole_property.first = "Ready";
unrealistically_long_name.sole_property.second = "Set";
unrealistically_long_name.sole_property.third = "Go";

with ( unrealistically_long_name.sole_property )
{
    document.write( first + ',' + second + ',' + third + '!');
    // Ready, Set, Go!
}
```

To display the three deepest level properties would take very long lines of code like lines 3, 4 and 5, were it not for the use of `with` surrounding the line producing the output. Further work could be saved by putting the last three assignments inside the `with` statement as well.

in and instanceof

Both `in` and `instanceof` were introduced in JavaScript 1.4, so no Netscape browser actually yet supports them, but for future implementations, we've added them in anyway.

```
var a = ("PI" in Math);         //a holds true
var b = new String;
var c = (b instanceof String);  //c holds true
```

As the discussion of the `for..in` loop may have suggested, the `in` operator returns `true` if a specified property does exist with the specified object. In the example, the `Math` object does have a property called `PI`, so `a` is `true`. Similarly, `instanceof` returns true if the left hand side variables is an object of the type specified on the right. `b` is a `String` object in the example, so `c` is also `true`.

Summary

Functions are a handy feature of JavaScript that let you re-use a piece of code without it having to appear more than once in your script. Objects allow the bundling of data and functions together into discrete lumps that are easy to manipulate and allow you to do cleaner and more organized design. The ease of use of JavaScript objects is one of the key appeals of the language – object features are powerful but have a reputation for being complex. No such reputation applies to ordinary JavaScript.

Objects in JavaScript go beyond mere utility, though. Objects are at the root of JavaScript's data manipulation model. It is important to develop an appreciation of how object-like most aspects of JavaScript are, because a) it helps when the problem gets tough, b) it leads to cleaner and more organised scripting, and c) that's how most features of the host that a JavaScript interpreter is embedded in make their appearance.

Having covered functions and objects, most of the features of the core JavaScript language have now been discussed. However, for very advanced scripting, there's a number of things hiding underneath the surface of the language worth knowing. Chapter 3 dwells on those subjects before the rest of the book dives off into looking at various host environments, such as web browsers.

Note that since this nearly brings the technical discussion of JavaScript native language features to a close, only the word Object appearing with its self-important initial capital letter will stand in future for the official ECMAScript definition of what a JavaScript object is. The more humble word 'object' (lowercase) will be used from now on to cover any bit of data that operates roughly like an object, having methods properties, and so on. We'll also use this distinction for Arrays and arrays.

For a much longer discussion of working with and building JavaScript Objects, you might like to peruse a copy of the Wrox Press book 'JavaScript Objects' by Tom Myers and Alexander Nakhimovsky (ISBN 1-861001-94-0)

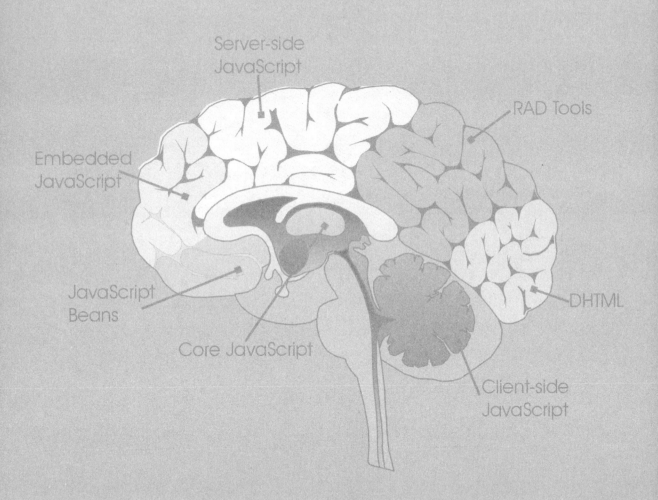

Advanced Language Features

It doesn't take much practice to be able to write some basic JavaScript. Chapters 1 and 2, combined with some information on a JavaScript-embedded host application such as a web browser, (like that in Chapter 4) are enough to get going. If you're impatient to get on with your web application, come back to this chapter later.

For those of you still reading, the JavaScript core language has some pretty fancy features we've not covered yet, and with the upcoming "ECMAScript 2" due for release in late 1999, more features of the language will be standardized. If you feel the need to tackle heavier-duty scripting tasks either inside web browsers or outside of them, then this chapter will give you the ammunition to do the job.

Just like many other modern languages, JavaScript scripts can be modeled in an "object-oriented" way. Recent innovations by Microsoft and Netscape introduce mechanisms to support generic "exception handling", "namespace management" and "regular expressions". In the following sections you'll see the language support available and some analysis of how well supported these grown-up features are.

Before jumping into these concepts, you first need to understand some JavaScript language plumbing. So here's that first.

Prototype and Scope Chains

JavaScript is an interpreted language. If it were a compiled language, every named object, property and method used in the source code could be nailed down during the compilation phase, removing all doubt as to what was what. Then, when the compiled program was run, the program or script could blindly charge ahead, confident that everything was organized perfectly in advance by the compiler. An interpreter requires a more sophisticated approach. At any time a newly named variable can spontaneously appear, and the interpreter has the job of managing and tracking it. The section on eval() at the end of this chapter shows how unpredictable this process can be.

In this next example, just accept for now that the strings in line 1, whose contents look suspiciously like a bit of JavaScript, do in fact get turned into runnable script somehow. The question is, how does JavaScript know to display the new_price variable in this (or in any other) script:

```
eval('var new_pr' + 'ice = 99.95; ');   // no variables - just a string
document.write(new_price);               // shows 99.95
```

Clearly, an interpreter can't look through the script and foresee every possible string that might contain valid JavaScript statements in advance. It must have some additional method of tracking what properties belong to what objects. This section explains the mechanisms at work.

Simplifications Revisited

JavaScript allows objects to be constructed as described in Chapter 2, using constructor functions and the prototype property. In that discussion, the implications of the prototype property were glossed over to a degree. In Chapter 17, when we tackle debugging, one of the common problems discussed is that of forgetting that the 'current object' within a web browser's form element's event handler is different to the usual object, which is the window object. In that discussion, just what a 'current object' might be is glossed over to a degree as well.

Recall that methods, variables and objects are all just properties of some other object, even if that other object is merely the global object. A property name is also called an **identifier**. When an identifier for a property (variables, objects, methods and functions are all properties too, recall) appears in a JavaScript program, two questions need answering in order to find out what it stands for:

❑   How is it decided whether an identifier matches a property of a given object?
❑   What objects should be examined to see if this identifier matches one of their properties?

The answers lie in the prototype mechanism in the first case, and in the scope chain mechanism in the second.

Prototype Chains

Prototype chains allow the JavaScript interpreter to determine whether a property exists for an object or not. Here is a typical object created via a JavaScript constructor:

```
function Thingy(name)
{
  this.name = name;
}

Thingy.prototype.color = 'blue';
Thingy.prototype.shape = 'round';

var thing = new Thingy('Jack');
```

Consider the composition of the `thing` object. JavaScript objects have properties, and each property can have only one value. If more than one value is required, the property must refer to another object. But hang on a minute. The `prototype` property for `Thingy` as declared above has two properties itself – `color` and `shape` – so it must refer to another object.

In fact, `typeof(Thingy.prototype)` reports "object". If the `prototype` property is an object, it must have its own prototype, assumedly called `Thingy.prototype.prototype`. What about that object's own prototype? Such behavior could go on forever.

Fortunately, in the normal case the ECMAScript standard says that a constructor function's `prototype` property is of type `Object`, and the actual prototype object's own `prototype` property is `null`, so there is only one step to the end of the chain. Normally, the only places to look for a property with a given name are directly in the object, and directly in the object's prototype object.

The example above could be re-written to explicitly define the object's prototype, rather than relying on the built-in `Object` prototype as above. For instance:

```
function Thingy_common_bits()
{
  this.prototype = null;
  this.colour = 'blue';
  this.shape = 'round';
}

function Thingy(name)
{
  this.name = name;
}

Thingy.prototype = new Thingy_common_bits();
var thing = new Thingy('Jack');
```

The behavior for the `thing` object is the same as before. The only difference is that now the `prototype` property is explicitly set to a new object using an object constructor `Thingy_common_bits()`. This example could be further changed to show a more general case:

```
function Thingy_bit1()                  // prototype constructor
{
  this.prototype = null;
  this.colour = 'blue';
}

function Thingy_bit2()                   // prototype's prototype constructor
{
  this.shape = 'round';
}

function Thingy(name)                     // object constructor
{
  this.name = name;
}

Thingy.prototype      = new Thingy_bit1();
Thingy_bit1.prototype = new Thingy_bit2();

var thing = new Thingy('Jack');    // object
```

The `thing` object still looks the same as the other examples, but this time it is contributed to by two prototype objects, one directly (its own prototype), and one indirectly (its prototype's prototype). This is a prototype chain. If the chain is exhausted without a given property name being found, the property is `undefined`.

Scope Chains

Prototype chains describe how to rummage around in an object looking for a property. How does JavaScript decide which object or objects to rummage around in?

A **scope chain** is used by the JavaScript interpreter in order to determine which objects to examine for a given property name. Each object so determined will then have its prototype chain examined. There must always be at least one candidate object, even if it is just the global object.

A scope chain's details are not accessible to the scriptwriter. It is part of the script's 'execution context', or 'thread of execution', or 'interpreter instance', or 'housekeeping data', whichever you prefer. All those terms mean it's something present you can rely on, provided you don't go outside the familiar embrace of the interpreter. There are some under-the-hood techniques involving special properties that start with double-underscore. However, they are mostly of use to programmers who embed JavaScript interpreters in other products and languages, and this book doesn't cover that topic extensively. See Chapter 22 for what we do cover on Embedded JavaScript.

According to ECMAScript, the scriptwriter can't directly interact with the scope chain. However, it is easy to change it, particularly using the `with` statement as this example shows:

```
var plant = 'Geranium';                 // == window.plant

var outside = new Object;               // == window.outside
outside.furniture = 'Banana Lounge';    // == window.outside.furniture
outside.plant = 'Willow';               // == window.outside.plant

outside.inside = new Object;            // == window.outside.inside
outside.inside.plant = 'Ficus';         // == window.outside.inside.plant
```

```
  alert(plant);
  with ( outside )
  {
    alert(plant);
    with ( inside )
    {
      alert(plant);
      alert(furniture);
    }
  }
```

Not surprisingly, the example displays alerts for Geranium, Willow and Ficus in that order. It may come as a surprise that Banana Lounge is then displayed as well, even though the inside object has no furniture property.

The reason Banana Lounge is displayed is that the with statement **does not replace** the object usually scrutinized when an identifier name is encountered. Instead, it **adds** an object to the scrutiny process.

The object added (the argument of the with statement) is the 'current object' or 'current scope', to use familiar terminology, but it is really just the first in a list of such objects. This list is called the scope chain. Objects in the scope chain are consulted in order until the identifier matches one of the object's properties.

In the above example, each with statement adds an object to the front of the scope chain when it starts, and removes that item when it ends. When the innermost statements are executed, the chain consists of three objects: inside, outside, and window. inside is consulted first.

The business of scope chains is a subtle source of bugs. Since it is possible to locate all the property names of all the objects in the scope chain, not just those of the object at the head of the chain, there are many more opportunities to accidentally clash with an existing name.

Finally, this extremely simple example leaps ahead a little, drawing elements from Chapter 4 on browsers and Chapter 7 on Forms and Data. It shows that the interpreter may organize the scope chain before a piece of script even starts running, based on the context in which it runs:

```
<HTML><HEAD>
<SCRIPT>
  function show_name(x)
  {
    alert(x);
  }
</SCRIPT>
</HEAD><BODY>
<FORM METHOD="POST" NAME="foofoo">
  <INPUT TYPE="button" NAME="Test Name" ONCLICK="show_name(name)">
</FORM>
</BODY></HTML>
```

In this example, both the show_name() function and the name property are correctly identified inside the event handler (the bit of code following ONCLICK in line 8). However, show_name() is only a property of the window object, while name is a property of the window, form and element (button) objects. Since the button's name is passed to the alert box, both window and button objects must be in the scope chain, and the button object must be before the window object. Very convenient, as it saves using 'window.show_name()' in the event handler code, but it does create extra opportunities for name mix-ups, as in the non-handler case.

Particularly confusing in web browsers can be the use of identifiers such as location which exist in both the window and document objects – that is why it is wise to prefix identifiers in browsers with 'window.' everywhere that is practical – see the debug chapter.

Is JavaScript Object-Oriented?

Programming languages that are **object-oriented** are considered to have powerful features above and beyond other, merely mortal languages. Moreover, the style in which developers must think when working with object-oriented languages differs from that of more traditional procedural languages like Pascal and C.

There's some debate about just exactly what features are required to make a language object-oriented. From a practical point of view though, these four features are probably enough to draw a Yes vote from most people:

❑ **Encapsulation** – data and operations on that data can be grouped together in a single entity: an object.

❑ **Aggregation** or **containment** – objects can have other objects inside them.

❑ **Inheritance** between object types – the nature of an object can depend on more than one definition.

❑ **Polymorphism** or **late binding** – the user doesn't always have to know the exact nature of an object in order to use one of its features. The system can figure out what is meant automatically.

> Just for completeness, we should really add a fifth item to our small list. However this one is more of a consequence of the other four rather than a fifth necessary feature of object-oriented programming.

❑ **Association**: objects can refer to other objects.

We'll look at each of these points in a minute, but to cut to the chase JavaScript scores highly on all fronts:

❑ **Encapsulation**: yes – but no information hiding.

❑ **Aggregation** or **containment**: yes – but no information hiding.

❑ **Inheritance**: yes – but inheritance concepts are different for a fully interpreted language.

❑ **Polymorphism** or **late binding**: yes – fundamental to the language.

❑ **Association**: yes – fundamental to the language.

Inheritance is a crucial concept for object-orientedness. Without inheritance, or so-called "robust support" for inheritance (meaning enough proper features built into the language), JavaScript could only be said to be **object-based**, not object-oriented. Object-based languages miss out on a convenient fit with some powerful software modeling techniques such as Unified Modeling Language (UML). Strongly typed languages such as C++, Java or ADA might take such a view of JavaScript. However, other interpreted languages such as Smalltalk and Perl would probably agree with JavaScript, so it comes down to picking sides. Pragmatically, you get some language assistance with JavaScript for inheritance, so that's probably enough to qualify.

But the key question is simple. Why would you want or need to start writing JavaScript scripts in an object-oriented fashion? JavaScript is probably at its best when it leaves the complex object handling stuff to the host software that the interpreter is embedded in. Your script can thus stay short and sweet and achieve powerful effects through the host objects exposed with no real need for an OO thought in your head.

Consider the point down the line however when your script starts to collect dozens of custom-made JavaScript objects. Relying on JavaScript's relaxed syntax at this stage to whip together a quick and dirty script is not going to work for you much longer and you will begin to need a more planned and designed approach. JavaScript centers around objects, therefore an object-oriented design is a natural and sane fit.

JavaScript Support for OO Concepts

As you walk down OO Programming Parkway, you'll realize a need to understand how to implement the tenets of this modus operandi in actual code, so in the next few pages we'll go through how each of the five important object-oriented concepts mentioned above fit into JavaScript.

Encapsulation

You'll remember from Chapter 2 that in JavaScript, pretty much everything is the property of an object (if it's not a method). Now take the following example.

```
function area()
{
  return this.dimension * this.dimension;
}

function Square(size)
{
  this.dimension = size;
  this.area = size * size;
}

var object1 = new Square(4);  // make one

var object2 = new Object;
    object2.dimension = 4;
    object2.area = 16;   // make another
```

It's pretty obvious that all the script does is to create two effectively identical objects. They both have the same properties and the same values associated with those properties. So what we can see from here is that ignoring how they got those properties, both objects group the two together under one umbrella which we can refer to – they **encapsulate** the properties.

In this example, `object1` is probably created in a more "object-like" manner since we bother to define all the features of the object in one place (in the constructor function `Square()`) before we make the object up. Functionally there is little difference.

In other object-oriented languages, **information hiding** goes hand-in-hand with encapsulation. This means that not only are the candidate data and functions collected together in one object, but also restrictions are placed on how the items can be extracted or accessed afterwards. Typically it is the candidate data items that are heavily restricted. In JavaScript, once the above objects are created there's nothing stopping you from getting at the dimension property thus:

```
var total = object1.dimension + object2.dimension;
object2.dimension = total;
```

If JavaScript had heavy restrictions you might have to create special methods to access the `dimension` property (after adding other special magic to hide it in the first place):

```
var total = object1.getSize() + object2.getSize();
object2.putSize(total);
```

You can still do this (except for the special magic required to do the hiding), but there's not much point. The solution for JavaScript is to relax – it's not that important. Access the property directly – the simple nature of JavaScript is designed to encourage a non-rigid approach.

Aggregation / Containment

Aggregation and **containment** in object-oriented terms mean the ability to store objects entirely inside other objects. As you've seen from Chapter 2, there is some simple syntax to do this. Here's an example:

```
var apple = new Object();
var pear  = new Object();
var peach = new Object();

var fruitbowl = new Object();
fruitbowl.item1 = apple;
fruitbowl.item2 = pear;
fruitbowl.item3 = peach;
```

The last object, `fruitbowl`, has several properties that are themselves objects. Aggregation/containment isn't much different to encapsulation in this respect; it's just that whole objects are collected together into another object rather than object parts collected together into a single object. As before with encapsulation, you could worry about hiding the contained objects, but it's much easier just to relax. However, in this case you can get *too* relaxed as this further example shows:

```
var pickle = new Object();
object3.flavor = "extra tart";
pickle_jar1.contents = pickle;
pickle_jar2.contents = pickle;
```

Lines 1 and 2 are fair enough encapsulation – an object with a single property is created. But in lines 3 and 4 both pickle jars (assumedly they're objects) are (also assumedly) trying to contain the pickle. This is not allowed as only one object can contain another. 100% of one pickle won't go into both of two pickle jars. Okay, you could put the pickle in one jar and that jar inside the other jar, but that's a different script. That script would actually be an example of association which we'll come to later.

The example illustrates that JavaScript *supports* aggregation/containment, but doesn't *enforce* it. Using a loosely-typed language lets you relax, but on the other hand it's up to you to make sure you don't confuse yourself. Lines 3 and 4 illustrate association, not encapsulation, aggregation or containment. When the conceptual idea separates from the things that the language lets you get away with, that's when C++ and Java programmers get excited and say that JavaScript only has "weak" (as opposed to "robust") support for OO. But as a relaxed scripter, who cares – as long as you accept the onus is on you to be clear about your design.

In an object oriented language: the peach is **part of** the fruitbowl, the fruitbowl **contains** a peach, or **has a** peach (sometimes officially written **HAS-A**).

Aggregation and containment are probably the most interesting object-like features to the scriptwriter. The reason is that Web browsers that host JavaScript have a large containment hierarchy (objects containing objects containing objects).

Inheritance

Inheritance in object-oriented terms means that an object's nature or essence or features come in part from itself, and in part from another object. It inherits the other object's features. That other object might be in the same position – in part described by itself and in part from a third object. In that case, the first object is also in part from the third. Objects can't be mutually derived from each other. Since there is a one-way order, the collection of interrelated object features is called an object hierarchy. Notice that the discussion focuses on object features not object **instances**. Features are descriptive of an object. An instance represents an actual object.

A classic example of inheritance comes from geometry:

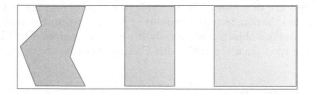

Here is a generic polygon, a polygon that is a rectangle, and a polygon that is a rectangle that is also a square. It's easy to see that rectangles inherit features from polygons. Polygons have a number of straight-edged sides that completely enclose a space and so do rectangles. However rectangles have some properties of their own as well: they must also have exactly 4 sides; opposite pairs of sides must be the same length; and all angles between adjacent sides must be 90 degrees. Further, it's true that squares fulfill all the rectangle criteria, so they can be said inherit the rectangle's features. Squares also have features uniquely their own. Not only must opposite sides of a square match in length and all angles be 90 degrees, but all sides must be equal in length as well.

The square depicted doesn't partially exist as part of the polygon depicted – clearly they are separate objects. It's just that the features of the more general polygon contribute to the features of the square. Sometimes you look or sound like one of your parents, but you're still yourself.

A bit of inheritance language: you can say squares **inherit** from rectangles. Squares are also the **derived** thing and rectangles are the **base** thing. Alternatively, squares are the **child** thing and rectangles the **parent** thing. It's also very common and expressively powerful to say "a square **is a** rectangle". This is sometime written `IS-A` to emphasize the specialized nature of the relationship. You can also say that a square **specializes** a rectangle, or that a rectangle **generalizes** a square.

For completeness, consider triangles. Triangles are polygons, but they're not rectangles. So it's possible for one base object type to have two different derived object types. The different derived object types are unrelated to each other. Such collections of inheritance relationships can be drawn like this:

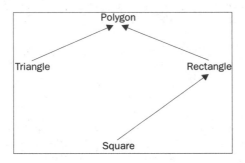

This is an inheritance hierarchy where the arrows point towards the parent. A popular notation for object modeling diagrams is **UML**, which you can read more about in *Instant UML by Pierre-Alain Muller (Wrox Press, 1997. ISBN 1-861000-87-1).*

JavaScript Prototype Chains

Inheritance can get pretty complex, so the way JavaScript handles it is deferred until all the other object oriented concepts are disposed of. Nevertheless, it should be easy to see that prototype chains are a good candidate for inheritance-type behavior in JavaScript, since an object appears to have all the properties of its prototype object. Alas, if only it were that simple. Organizing JavaScript inheritance is left to the next main section in this Chapter because there are a number of options to consider.

Polymorphism / Late-Binding

Polymorphism and **late-binding** are concepts designed to make computer objects a little like real-world objects, by ensuring that using common behavior doesn't require an in-depth knowledge of the object. An example from the real world is picking up and throwing things. Most small things, like pebbles, sticks, fruit, books, eggs and shoes can all be picked up and thrown, and you don't need to know too much about them in order to get them to sail through the air. You certainly don't need to know how many pips the fruit has, or whether the shoelaces on the shoes are nicely done up. You may have to modify your behavior a bit for some less common throwable objects, like houses, cats and loved ones but the principle is there – the details don't matter too much.

For strongly typed languages such as C++ and Java, acquiring this kind of "don't care" behavior is not trivial because the nature of all available objects is supposed to be strictly and completely known at all times. For those languages, the problem is solved with the technique of late-binding which, very roughly speaking, defers the "need to know everything" requirement until a given program is actually running. Such languages normally need to know everything at compile (preparation) time.

In the JavaScript case, the language is designed from scratch so that you don't have to care:

```
var thingo = new Object;
...      // do anything with thingo
thingo.gently_lob();
```

In JavaScript, everything is late-bound, because the language is interpreted – decisions about whether methods or properties exist are made at the last second. Secondly, JavaScript objects are loosely-typed, so the language never had a need to rigidly understand objects in the first place. In the example, it doesn't matter where thingo comes from, or what type it is, you can easily try to gently_lob() it, and the worst that will happen is that you'll get an error saying "no gently_lob() method". If a gently_lob() method exists, it'll be called without fuss, as you'd expect.

From this example you can see that JavaScript has very straightforward support from polymorphism.

Association

Association is not a core requirement for object-orientedness in a language, but it is used so much in object-oriented design that it's worth covering for completeness. Association is a powerful concept because it is the only way that objects can have access to each other without the "sole ownership" implications of containment as discussed above.

Because any JavaScript variable can track any object, association is implemented very naturally in the language. A simple example:

```
// Object separate to other concerns
var car = new Mini();
    car.capacity = 4;
    car.passengers = 0;

// Second as-yet unrelated object
var person = new Traveller();

if ( car.passengers < car.capacity )
{
  car.passengers++;
  person.transport = car; // associated here
}
```

In this example, many Traveller objects might use the same Mini object as their preferred transport. Hopefully checks will always be done so that sharing the object makes sense. In this case that means that no more than four Traveller objects should share the Mini object. When a Traveller object is finished with the Mini object, then this code might be used:

```
delete person.transport;
```

or alternatively

```
person.transport = null;
```

When this happens, the `Mini` object won't cease to exist, as the `car` variable will always point to it. But one less person will associate the `Mini` object with themselves.

For association, common language is to say: the `Traveller` object **uses a** `Mini` object. This is sometimes more formally written: **USES-A**. Because JavaScript provides no mechanism to distinguish between containment and association, it's up to the scriptwriter to put his design hat on and stay clear in his own mind which use is intended.

Implementing JavaScript Inheritance

JavaScript is weakest in its object-oriented support when it comes to inheritance. The features are there for you to do it, but unless you're organized, nothing will work as you expect. In order to see the issues, first a bit of theory about objects, classes, and instances.

Understanding Classes and Instances

If you have an object, then usually there are some properties containing data or methods in it. However it is also usually possible to write down some information *about* that object. At the simplest you can write down its name (from the constructor function perhaps) and the number and type of properties it has. In object-oriented lingo, that kind of information is called an **object class definition**. A class definition has the same role for an object that a type has for a primitive bit of data such as a number. "Class definition" and "object type" are interchangeable ideas. An actual object itself is called an **object instance**. Instance just means "one of" that type of object. Therefore it's common to see many object instances for a given object class. Recall Chapter 2 describes how to use a JavaScript object constructor to create as many objects as you like.

There is a general expectation in object-oriented languages that once the details of an object class are settled they won't change. Individual bits of data in an object instance might change, but not the class. This expectation comes from strongly typed languages like C++ and Java. In those languages, it's not a basic process to get at the information in an object class; you have to use an extra-special mechanism (like Run Time Type Information [RTTI] or Reflection) and you certainly can't change an object class once it exists. This is also consistent with the way primitive types work – you can easily change a variable holding a particular value of type Number (say 5) into a different value (say 6), but you can't change the Number type itself (say, by increasing the range of allowed numbers, or by banning negative numbers). If you did that, then maybe you would call the changed type BigPositiveNumber to distinguish it from the normal Number type.

This all helps to understand how objects that inherit information are managed. This diagram illustrates the pieces at work:

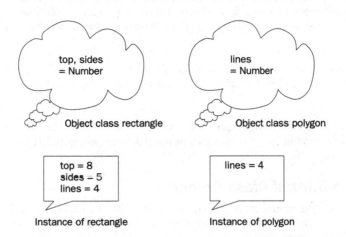

Notice how the classes and instances are nicely divided – instances exist (like speech) but classes are more abstract (like thought). In strongly typed languages like C++ and Java the two rarely meet, and classes are never modified.

In JavaScript, the picture is more like this:

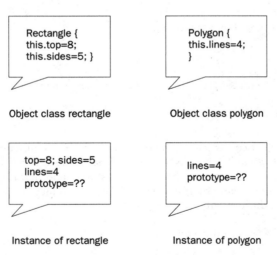

In JavaScript, classes are ordinary objects too – created when you make a constructor function. That means you can accidentally damage classes in your program. Or you can deliberately change classes. It also makes it easy to mix up class objects and "ordinary" instance objects. In fact the whole idea of separate, abstract classes breaks down a bit in JavaScript.

Because of this breakdown, it's better to focus on prototypes, which is the mechanism available. However, it pays to understand classes and instances. Both are implemented with the same mechanism (JavaScript Objects) and both are modifiable, so the objects available can become extremely fluid (and unpredictable). Sometimes it pays to be able to think in class/instance terms; but if you're a real computer guru then sometimes you'll want to throw out the class/instance split entirely.

There is one rock to cling to. A JavaScript object doesn't define host objects – they are defined elsewhere. Therefore you can nearly always be sure that host object definitions will never, ever, change.

In the above diagram there are some question marks. In particular, what does the prototype property get set to when you're trying to get rectangles to inherit from polygons? It turns out that there are two main possibilities.

Inheritance via a Shared Class Object

The simplest form of inheritance in JavaScript is for the object instance for the derived class to collect the information it inherits from the class definition object for its base class. Therefore this is a case of mixing up instance and class objects.

```
function Polygon()
{
  this.edges = 8;                    // octogons are the default
  this.regular = false;              // sides needn't be all the same
  this.area = new Function (...)     // some hard mathematics
}

function Rectangle(top_len, side_len)
{
  this.edges = 4;
  this.top = top_len;
  this.side = side_len;
  this.area = new Function("return this.top*this.sides");
}

Rectangle.prototype = new Polygon;
```

This example has two object constructors: the two functions. Since functions are objects in JavaScript, there are two new objects as well. There is also a third new object. It has been added to the `Rectangle` function object's prototype chain in the last line, and that is the only place it is accessible. That object can be thought of as a class definition object, because it is only really used at object creation time, and there is only ever one of it.

To create a new `Rectangle`, use this code:

```
var box = new Rectangle(8,3);
```

Afterwards the object's properties are:

```
box.edges = 4  // overrides Polygon
box.top = 8
box.side = 3
box.area = Function("return this.top*this.sides");
box.regular=false // from Polygon
```

The benefits of this approach are:

- ❑ Simplicity - inheritance is achieved with the single extra statement `Rectangle.prototype = ..`
- ❑ Properties in the derived objects correctly override base object properties.
- ❑ Information in the base object is not duplicated; it is looked up via the prototype chain.
- ❑ If you modify the base object, which is acting like a class definition, then *all* of the derived objects will see the change.
- ❑ Any amount of inheritance hierarchy is possible – `Square` objects could have `Rectangles` in their prototype chain and they would benefit from the `Polygon` class object instance as well.

However, this approach does have drawbacks. The problems mostly revolve around the fact that there is only *one* prototype chain for the `Rectangle` constructor, and it is shared between all `Rectangle` objects that are created. So any `Rectangle` object that modifies properties of the base class changes them for all `Rectangle` objects.

- ❑ Modifying the base class object's properties doesn't just affect the current object; it affects all objects of this type that are hanging around.
- ❑ The base class object's constructor (`Polygon()` in this case) can't have any arguments; or at least it must be able to survive without being passed any arguments.

You can work around the first problem by overriding all the base class objects properties in the derived instance object constructor (`Rectangle`). However, if you do that, overriding everything, one wonders why bother use inheritance at all – you might as well just have a separate object type.

Sometimes you *do* want properties in the base class to be updated by every derived instance ('static class variables'). Here's an example:

```
function Counter() { this.total=0; }
function StockItem() { this.total++; }
StockItem.prototype = new Counter;

var biscuits = new StockItem; // total = 1
var coffee = new StockItem; // total = 2
```

Every object contributes something to the shared property. In the example above, this property is a total of the objects currently existing (this simple example doesn't correctly decrease the total if objects go away).

Finally, if you can avoid changing any state in the base class object, then the approach we've outlined here can still be quite useful. You could put a store of constant data and methods in it that will be usable by all derived instance objects. The methods in the base class object can refer to properties in derived instances as well. Here's an example:

```
function Base(v)
{
  if (arguments.length != 0)
    this.value = v;
  this.double_up = new Function ("this.value*=2;")
}
```

```
function Derived(v) {this.value = v;}

Derived.prototype = new Base;

var obj = new Derived(5);
obj.double_up();    // this.value = 10
```

Notice how in this example the base class object uses, but may never define the `value` property. In that case, the derived instance object's `value` property will be doubled. The 'if' condition in the base class object is only true if the `Base()` function is used as a simple constructor, not when inheritance is at work. For C++ and Java experts: this mechanism works well for abstract base classes.

Inheritance via Object Masquerading

If you want to create a derived object instance, and you don't want the risk that it might be changed under you, then this is the approach to use. Here is the example from the last section slightly modified:

```
function Polygon()
{
  this.edges = 8;                 // octogons are the default
  this.regular = false;           // sides needn't be all the same
  this.area = new Function (...)  // some hard mathematics
}

function Rectangle(top_len,side_len)
{
  this.temp = Polygon;
  this.temp();
  delete this.temp; // or this.temp = null;
  this.edges = 4;
  this.top = top_len;
  this.side = side_len;
  this.area = new Function("return this.top*this.sides");
}
```

In addition to three new lines, the `prototype` assignment line at the end is missing as well. There are no prototype chains in this example at all. Instead, when the object is constructed, a temporary property is made for the base class' constructor, and that constructor is called as though it were a method of that object. All the properties set by the `Polygon` constructor are set directly in the `Rectangle` object. This has to be done first in the `Rectangle` constructor, because if it were last, some of the properties set by the derived object might be overridden by the base class constructor – back to front. In fact, when the base class constructor is called, it thinks that it is operating on an object whose destiny is to be of that base class type.

When the `temp()` method is called in the above example, you can supply arguments to it much like any method – of course those arguments should make sense when the `Polygon()` constructor gets them.

'ECMAScript 2' plans to replace this awkward three-statement approach with new, purpose-built functions requiring only a single statement:

```
this.call(Polygon, argument1, argument2, …)
```

or

```
this.apply(Polygon, array-of-arguments)
```

According to the draft of 'ECMAScript 2', the two functions differ only in how arguments are supplied to them. At the time of writing, these functions are too new to be relied upon much. Nevertheless, you can find them in Netscape browsers, versions 4.06 and greater and Internet Explorer 5.0, or where JScript 5.0 is installed.

The benefits of this second inheritance approach, regardless of what syntax you use are:

❑ The object shares no information with other objects after it is created and can be considered independent

❑ The "type" of the object is frozen at create time – no changes to the base class afterwards will affect it.

❑ Arguments can be passed to the base class constructor.

❑ Multiple inheritance is possible (see below).

The drawbacks of this approach are:

❑ If the base class inherits from an even-more-base class (e.g. Polygon might derive from Shape), then the derived class (Rectangle) won't benefit from that third class since it was never put in the prototype chain (for Rectangle objects).

If this line is added back at the very end, then the deeper-level inheritance problems go away.

```
Rectangle.prototype = new Polygon;
```

However, since all type properties of the base class were set directly into the derived class, all of the base class properties are now overridden – changes to the base class won't necessarily filter through to the derived class. So it is a mistake to think that doing this gives you all the benefits that were to be had in the first approach to inheritance.

Finally, this system supports multiple inheritance. The multiple inheritance it supports is only one level deep, however. All that is required is to repeat the trick at the core of this technique more than once:

```
...
function Rectangle(top_len,side_len)
{
  this.temp = Base1;       // first base class as before
  this.temp();
  delete this.temp;

  this.temp = Base2;       // second base class, similarly
  this.temp();
  delete this.temp;
  ...
}
```

Further Reading on Prototype Inheritance

These references are invaluable sources of information on prototype inheritance if you want to get your hands really dirty. The author acknowledges them as contributing to the information presented in this chapter.

At Sun Microsystems, `http://www.sunlabs.com/research/self/papers/papers.html` contains a number of articles about the Self language. Self may be considered the precursor to the JavaScript language in many respects.

At Netscape, `http://developer1.netscape.com:80/docs/manuals /communicator/jsobj/ contents.htm` has a comparison of the inheritance support available in JavaScript compared with Java.

Exception Handling

When a function or method is called, the only mechanism described to date for passing information back to the script fragment that called the function of method is the `return` statement. What if something goes wrong? This example illustrates:

```
function add_like_a_child(num1, num2)
{
  if ( num1 + num2 > 20 )
    return "finger & toe limit passed!"
  if ( num1 + num2 > 10 )
    return "finger limit passed!"
  return num1 + num2;
}
```

The problem with this function is that every time it gets used, additional code is required to check the return value. One never knows until after that check whether the function has failed to work usefully or not. In this case, you may have to do two checks, one for each unusual case. If the function was complex, you may have to do many checks. How tedious. Here's an example of using this function:

```
var result = add_like_a_child(3, 5)
if ( result == "finger & toe limit passed!")
{
  // do something to cope …
}
else if ( result == "finger limit passed!" )
{
  // do something else to cope …
}
// carry on normally if we reach this point.
```

In Java, this kind of difficult case is handled with `exceptions`. The general goal of exceptions is to provide a mechanism that reports when the extraordinary has happened. With such a mechanism in place, one can rely on return values reporting only the ordinary – normal, successful output from the function. With the extraordinary taken care of, there's no need for special, extra checks of the function's return value.

To a degree, JavaScript tries to mimic Java in its syntax. **Exceptions** are a proposed 'ECMAScript 2' enhancement to the language and appear in both Microsoft JScript 5.0 and JavaScript 1.4. They are likely to become a much-used feature of JavaScript in the future. The reason for this is based on the imperative that if an object is to be used in a script, the scriptwriter must have available access points where he can get at that object. These access points combined make up the object's **interface**, or **signature**. In computer language terms, the big three features of object interfaces are properties (also called attributes), methods and exceptions. Hence exceptions in JavaScript.

In Java you have to rigidly declare the type of thing that an exception is. True to form, in JavaScript your exception can be any old thing. Here's the official syntax for the JavaScript statements supporting exceptions. First, to create an exception:

```
throw expression;
```

Secondly, to handle an exception:

```
try
   statement-block
catch ( identifier )                    // variant1, can be repeated
   statement block
catch ( identifier if condition )       // variant2, can be repeated
   statement block
finally                                 // optional, at most one.
   statement block
```

Here is the example function above re-written:

```
function add_like_a_child(num1, num2)
{
  if ( num1 + num2 > 20 )
    throw "finger & toe limit passed!"
  if ( num1 + num2 > 10 )
    throw "finger limit passed!"
  return num1 + num2;
}
```

In this function, if a `throw` statement is ever executed, processing of the function stops, and the function returns immediately. No ordinary return value is returned. Instead, an exception is returned.

Here is the calling code rewritten:

```
var result;
try {
  result=add_like_a_child(3,5);
  if ( result == 8 )
  {
    // give chocolate
  }
  else
  {
    // give Brussels sprouts
  }
}
catch (error) {
  if ( error == "finger & toe limit passed!" )
  {
```

```
        // do something to cope
    }
    if ( error == "finger limit passed!" )
    {
        // do something else to cope
    }
}
```

In this script, the result variable might never be set in the third line. If the function returns an exception, processing immediately jumps straight to the `catch` statement, which has access to the exception in the error variable, and the statements in the block following the `catch` statement are executed instead. If there is no exception, and the function returns normally, then processing continues with the next statement in the `try` block, and when that block is finished, the `catch` block is stepped over entirely, similar to an unused branch of an `if` statement.

The whole explanation gets a lot easier once you know a little jargon, so here you go. If something goes wrong, you say the function **throws** an exception. The function is called in a **try block** and exceptions are **handled** in **catch blocks**. The **finally block** is executed if no exception is outstanding at the end.

The rules for how this complicated processing all works are as follows:

If a `throw` statement is reached in a function (or in any block-like piece of code), then that function will not continue. It will not return a value, and it will not return `void`. Instead, it will cease immediately and the exception will be created. In simplistic terms, the exception appears effectively by magic.

If the statement or function causing the exception *is not* inside a try block, then a runtime interpreter error will occur and the script will stop. If the statement or function is called inside another function, method or block, then that collection of statements will be aborted as well and the exception passed up to the next level of control until a try block is found, or an error results, as before.

If the statement or function causing an exception *is* inside a try block, then any further statements in the try block are ignored. The interpreter looks through any catch blocks that might be present. If one is found with satisfactory criteria, that single catch block is executed. If any exception remains, because no catch block has satisfactory criteria, or there are no catch blocks, or a catch block raised a new exception, then the finally clause is avoided. Otherwise, all is in order and the finally clause is executed.

What are catch block criteria? There are two cases, illustrated here:

```
catch (stuff) { ... }
```

and

```
catch (stuff if (stuff > "Error 1")) { ... }
```

In the first case, the catch block matches all exceptions. In the second case, the catch block only matches those exceptions that pass the if criteria. If there are multiple catch blocks, then the first case will catch everything, much like the default: clause of a switch statement, so it makes sense to put it last in the list of catch blocks. The stuff variable tracks the exception, and it acts within the catch block like a function parameter. The catch block treats the variable stuff in much the same way that this further script treats the variable stuff2:

```
function something(stuff2)
{
...
}
```

Exception Syntax vs 'if'

If you've never used exceptions before, you're likely to be very skeptical about the syntax arrangements required to get them working by now.

Common objections to the above example are:

❑ It's more verbose. There are actually more lines than the plain if case – too much effort!

❑ It looks pretty much like the first example structurally. Where's the improvement?

❑ The language is foreign. What's the matter with good old if?

For simple cases, it must be admitted that the argument for exceptions is weak; the exception-style code can definitely be bigger. More generally, the argument for using exception syntax goes like this:

❑ Exception syntax is clearer when lots of things go wrong.

❑ Once you're used to it, exception syntax is easier to read, because you learn to ignore catch blocks. Catch blocks cater for 1% of the code actually run (errors are rare) and contain 99% of the irrelevant detail (errors are messy to recover from).

❑ Exceptions are "better art" or "cleaner code" or "good programming style" (but try telling a C++ programmer that!).

❑ Exceptions are one of the big 3 features of objects – attributes, methods and exceptions. Get used to it.

It must be admitted that you don't always need exceptions. Simple scripts that just perform sequences of guaranteed operations have no need of exceptions at all, really.

Here is an example that shows exception syntax working for the scriptwriter rather than against:

```
// piece of code that could fail 20 different ways
try {
    // might cause 1 of 5 exceptions
    dodgy_task_1();
    // might cause 1 of 4 exceptions
    dodgy_task_2();
    // might cause 1 of 7 exceptions
    dodgy_task_3();
```

```
   // might cause 1 of 4 exceptions
   dodgy_task_4();
}
catch (everything)
{
   // scream blue murder
}
```

Because a `throw` statement immediately aborts the `try` block, each dodgy function can come straight after the other, confident that if something goes wrong, the latter ones will never be executed. We've saved a heap of `if` tests by using the `try` block in this case. Note that functions needn't have a return value (other than the default of `void`) in order to make use of exceptions.

Finally, you needn't restrict yourself to throwing primitive types. Here's some paired code that illustrates:

```
// throws an object
throw { err_string:"You're doomed", err_number: 23 };
```

This statement creates a two-property object and returns that as the thrown item.

```
// catches only error number 23
catch ( e if ( e.err_number == 23) ) { … }
```

This statement expects the exception to be an object with an `err_number` property, which clearly will be the case if the previous `throw` statement is responsible for the exception.

Exceptions vs Events vs Errors

If you've messed around with JavaScript in browsers a little before reading this book, then you might be aware that there exist triggers or events that can make JavaScript script fragments run, especially if a given web page contains forms. Are these exceptions or not?

These kinds of events are not generally considered exceptions. Events, generally occurring as a form of input from a user or a network, are expected, planned for, and normal occurrences. They are usually handled the same as normal data. Exceptions are not considered normal, and are usually used for error conditions – something went wrong that the script has been able to anticipate (with try/catch blocks), but can't really handle normally.

Sometimes it's easy to relate events and exceptions together. This is because the way a script gets ready for events is typically a little different to the way it receives plainer kinds of user input. This oddity of handling events can seem similar to the oddity of handling exceptions. Nevertheless, they are separate and different. Chapter 7 on Forms and Data gives a flavor of what ordinary events are like, and if you look there, you'll see there's not a mention of JavaScript exception syntax anywhere.

Exceptions Make Sense for Host Objects

A further reason for exception handling support in JavaScript is to be found in host objects. Without host objects JavaScript is nearly useless. What if those host objects generate exceptions as part of their attribute/method/exception interface? There must be a mechanism in place in JavaScript to support this kind of communication. This is especially the case if JavaScript is to work closely with Java, which has support for exceptions deeply ingrained in its language.

Exceptions Make Sense for Interpreter Errors

Some things that go wrong with JavaScript scripts can be pretty bad. If the scriptwriter has made a typographical error in some obscure part of a large script, it might never be detected until that script is installed in some critical place. That is the risk you take with an interpreted language.

If the interpreter comes to read the script and finds a typographical error, wouldn't it be nice if there was something that could be done about it rather than the whole script just stopping dead? This is a future direction for the ECMAScript standard – scripting errors might be reported as exceptions and handled by the system that starts the JavaScript interpreter in the first place.

eval() Concepts

Interpreted languages like JavaScript have a very useful peculiarity that compiled languages lack. Because the interpreter exists as part of the program that runs the script, the possibility exists that more interpretation of JavaScript statements can occur *after* the script has been read and started. We might call this **dynamic** or **run-time** evaluation to emphasize that it happens after the script gets going. Sometimes this might be called **piggyback embedding**.

Simple Dynamic Evaluation – Maps

Chapter 2 discussed how objects and arrays have interchangeable syntax. Recall that these two statements are equivalent:

```
object.property = "stuff"
array["property"] = "stuff"
```

Because the argument supplied to the array is an expression, it's possible to do handy things like this:

```
var all_cars = new CarCollection;
var car;
while ( (car=get_car_name()) != "" )
  all_cars[car.toLowerCase()] = get_registration(car);
```

In the last line, the variable car is used to create the property names of the `all_cars` object so that one property matches each car in the collection. Then each of those properties is set to a related value for that car – in this case the registration number. So if these collectable cars existed:

Model T Ford	A234
Goggomobile	MCI 223
Austin Lancer	JG 33

Then the properties of the `all_cars` object would be "`model t ford`", "`goggomobile`" and "`austin lancer`". Later we could refer to those properties as follows to dig out the related information:

```
var x = "model t ford";
all_cars[x];                    // "A234"
all_cars.goggomobile;           // "MCI 233"
all_cars["austin lancer"];      // "JG 33"
```

Effectively, the properties of the object depend on the data available, and that might not be known until runtime (if the user enters it, for example).

This ability to interchange between data and variable names is a powerful and common feature of scripting languages. In particular, this example shows a very commonly used structure dubbed alternatively a **map**, **mapping**, **associative array**, **hash**, or merely **dictionary**. The point is that it lets you get at a data value (a property's value) based on a unique key value (the property name), and it lets you keep a bunch of such pairs neatly together. It is a simple form of unordered index. Mathematicians say "There is a mapping from the set of collectable cars to the set of registration numbers for those cars". Whatever.

Note that in this example we'd be in trouble if a second Model T Ford turned up. That second car would have the same property name as the first and the system breaks down. That's why this approach is nearly always used for data that has a set of unique values only. Plenty of data is like that.

Turning Script Statements Into Data

Bits of JavaScript can be very simply turned back into data if you choose the right bits. Here are a couple of examples:

```
var greatgranddad = new Patriach;
greatgranddad.child1 = new Granddad;
// ...
// lots more family tree detail
// ...
var tree=greatgranddad.toString();   // If you specify JavaScript1.2
print_to_screen(tree);
```

In this example, a hierarchy of objects is created starting with Great-Granddad who clearly is the most senior. When the `toString()` method is called, the object is forced into a String type, and if you're lucky (because the different interpreter brands are a little varied in this functionality still) what will be printed to the screen will be a literal object matching the object's contents. In this case the literal would start:

```
{ child1:{ …
```

Note, however, that this functionality of `toString()` is only available if you specify LANGUAGE = "JavaScript1.2" when writing it. In JavaScript 1.3 and beyond (NC4.06+, IE5+), this functionality is taken on by `toSource()`.

A similar trick is possible with functions:

```
function first() { … }
function second() { … }
function third() { … }

function do_it()
{
  first()  || throw first.toString();
  second() || throw second.toString();
  third()  || throw third.toString();
}

try { do_it(); }
catch ( e ) { alert('failed: ' + e) }
```

In this example, you might be testing 3 functions for syntax problems. If any of them fail, returning `false`, their source code is returned as an exception, and the user (presumably) is shown the offending code via the `alert()` function in the catch block. Recall Microsoft's JScript 5.0 is the only implemented contender at this time of writing for `try` and `catch` statements.

In both these cases, the `toString()`/`toSource()` method is not always required – recall from Chapter 1 that there is automatic type conversion in JavaScript.

This process won't necessarily work everywhere. For example, JavaScript statements that aren't part of any function are harder to get back as data. The JavaScript interpreter in Internet Explorer 4.0 is a notable exception.

The Mighty eval()

The native function `eval()` is by far the most powerful native function in JavaScript, allowing a JavaScript string to be examined, interpreted and run as though it was a script.

```
var x=5, y=6, result=0;
var formula = "result = x*y;";
eval(formula);                    // result is now 30
```

The contents of the formula variable can be as complicated as you like – multiple statements, if-else logic, and so on. Provided the string contains valid JavaScript, everything works fine. However, if the string contains invalid JavaScript, the interpreter will give a runtime error and halt. Because the script fragment is hidden inside a string, the interpreter has no chance of detecting problems with it when it first reads the whole script. That means that syntax checks that would otherwise be performed at script startup time are delayed until the eval() statement is actually executed. That means you must take extreme care when using eval(), or else everything can come crashing down much later on, when you least expect it. Perhaps by the time this book is in your hands there will exist an interpreter that issues an exception instead.

Here's a more complicated example of eval(). This example runs a different function depending on whether the boss is around or not:

```
var type1 = "function work() { slog(); slog(); slog(); }";
var type2 = "function work() { rest(); rest(); rest(); }";

if ( boss )
   eval(type1);
else
   eval(type2);
eval("work()");
```

Notice how you can delay defining any kind of work at all until the boss is around. Handy.

eval() has the potential to be used pretty powerfully. Suppose you have an application that hosts a JavaScript interpreter. Suppose that application connects to another application, possibly on a remote computer that also hosts a JavaScript interpreter. A script in the local application could turn some script functions back into data using toSource(), and then send them to the remote application via a convenient host object. The remote application could then eval() the data, turning it back into scripts. This kind of architecture allows scripts to move around a computer network and execute in different places as "mobile agents", a very modern and fluid approach.

Basically this technique works anywhere you can store interpretable code in a string and execute it. Macintosh users may recognise that HyperCard does the same with the do command. In a Bourne shell window, you can write text out to a file with an echo statement, chmod it to make it executable and 'dot run' it into the current process space to achieve the same goal.

Piggyback embedding

Let's look at the way an eval() may help us out with some interesting problems.

Within the context of distributed JavaScript, you can put a function in a string, send the string to a script on another computer which then does an eval(), executes it, gets an answer, and passes the answer, the function, or a modified version of the function back to the sending computer, or possibly to another computer. So facilities that only really exist on one computer can be executed on request from a remote master machine.

The piggybacking comes from the way you carry one script around in another. Technically there is no limit to the number of enclosures within enclosures. The scripts can transcend languages and be embedded in completely foreign environments. For example, you could transfer a Bourne shell script inside a JavaScript script that was transferred across the network from a series of strings that were constructed in a source script written in Perl.

To construct these mechanisms you basically work backwards from the ultimate target environment, wrapping the scripts with increasing numbers of onion skin layers as you go.

Regular Expressions

Last, but definitely not least, we come to the topic of Regular Expressions (RE), a not-so-simple pattern of characters that can be used to match a sequence of characters in a string. Combined with the right method, regular expressions can perform some pretty heavyweight text search and replace duties. This is not limited to checking that someone has typed in the right kind of phone number in a form element or validating some other kind of data. We could, for instance, search through a bank's records and add new digits to everyone's bank account number or discover the number of times Homer says "Doh!" in the screenplay for an episode of The Simpsons.

JavaScript has had built-in support for Regular Expressions since version 1.2 in the shape of the `RegExp` object and a few certain methods attached to the `String` object, all of which we'll come to later, but before we have a look at these, we need to nail down how exactly you construct such an expression.

Rolling Your Own RE

When it comes to producing your own regular expressions, you have two options in JavaScript – you can write them either as literals or as objects. For example

```
var myRE = new RegExp("R2D2");
var myRE = /R2D2/;
```

Both these lines do the same thing – assign `myRE` with a reference to a newly created `RegExp` object whose expression will match an instance of the sequence "R2D2" in a string. The `RegExp` object contains the data for the RE you specify when that object is created. Easy. However, you can't really making use of the full power of regular expressions until you learn their alphabet and syntax.

The first point easily learned is that with the exception of two switches, every RE literal is contained within a pair of forward slashes.

```
var blankRE = /  /;
```

The two switches mentioned earlier are g and i, and affect directly how the search to match your regular expression is conducted. g, the global switch, tells the search to find every instance of your character sequence in the target string, rather than just to find the first and then stop looking. i, meanwhile, tells the search mechanism that the search is case insensitive. For instance:

```
var myRE = /R2D2/;      // finds first instance of R2D2
var myRE = /R2D2/i;     // finds first instance of r2d2, R2d2, r2D2 or R2D2
var myRE = /R2D2/g;     // finds all instances of R2D2
var myRE = /R2D2/gi;    // finds all instances of r2d2, R2d2, r2D2, or R2D2
```

With that out of the way, we'd better look and see what we can put inside the slashes.

The RE Alphabet

The alphabet for regular expressions incorporates all the alphanumeric characters, upper and lower case, and quite a few other special characters in the form of escape sequences, as shown below. Note that an escape sequence may match one or more ordinary characters or alternatively a special condition that isn't an ordinary character, like the start of a string, as we'll see in the pages to come.

Character to Match	Corresponding Escape Sequence
Any alphanumeric character (a-z, A-Z, 0-9)	Itself
Any of . ? / \ [ ] { } ( ) + * |	\ followed by the character. For example \{ matches {
Form feed	\f
New line	\n
Carriage return	\r
Horizontal tab	\t
Vertical tab	\v
ASCII with octal character number *Octal*	\o*Octal*
ASCII with hex character number *Hex*	\x*Hex*
Control-x where x is any control character	\cx
The beginning of a line or string	^
The end of a line or string	$
A word boundary	\b
Not a word boundary	\B
Single white space. (tab, space, etc)	\s
Single non white space	\S
Wildcard character. Anything but a new line	.

You should be familiar with what the first ten of these items will match up to – we've encountered them already at the very beginning of Chapter 1, so to demonstrate the rest, let's take an example text

Jimmy the Scot scooted his scooter through the park.

The Parky watched Jimmy do this

and we'll go through some easy examples:

```
var RE1 = /^Jimmy/;          //matches "Jimmy" on line 1 but not line 2
var RE2 = /his$/;            //matches "this" on line 2 but not "his" on line 1
var RE3 = /\bt/;             //matches " the" and " through" with front space
                             //but not "Scot" or "watched"
var RE4 = /\Bt/;             //matches "Scot" or "watched"
                             //but not " the" or " through"
var RE5 = /t\s./;            //matches "Scot scooted" but not "watched"
var RE6 = /t\S./;            //matches "watched" but not "Scot scoo"
```

From these examples, you can see that each character or escape character between the forward slashes of a regular expression stands for a single character only. Some escape characters will match more than one *kind* of normal character such as the whitespace escape sequence, but only match one character in *total*.

RE Syntax - Shortcuts and Options

If you've kept up with this discussion so far, you should have realized that this is not a very flexible system yet. Apart from the wildcard character – a period or full stop – we've yet to proffer any notation that specifies an option on single characters. For example, let's take a brand new string we want to match our regular expressions against.

```
dink fink link mink oink pink rink sink tink wink +ink _ink "ink
```

Now suppose we wished only to match link, mink, and wink from the string above. From what we know currently, the only option we have is to create three regular expressions – one for each word. Using the wildcard in /.ink/ will match every word in the string and that's not what we want.

There is, of course, a solution. By using square braces, [], we can specify which group of letters we want to match a certain character. So then we should use

```
var RE7 = /[lmw]ink/;        //matches "link", "mink" and "wink"
```

to get the desired matches. At the same time we can also use 'not-this-group' [^] to match every other word in the string.

```
var RE8 = /[^lmw]ink/;       //matches "dink", "fink", "oink", "pink", etc
                             //but not "link", "mink" and "wink"
```

This is all very well if you've got a few characters that you'd like to check in a single space, but when you've got ten or twelve, your RE is going to start looking quite unwieldy (or should that be unwieldier?). Fortunately, we can also specify ranges of characters using the hyphen, -, within the braces as a marker to indicate the range. For example, to match every word apart from tink and wink in the string, you could either of:

```
var RE9 = /[a-s]ink/;
var RE10 = /[^t-z]ink/;
```

By now you might have realized that in using a hyphen, [0-9] represents all the numerals, [a-z] the lower case letters and [A-Z] the uppercase. Again, we have some shortcuts for particular ranges of characters that make things more compact.

Shortcut	Represents the range..
\d	[0-9] Any number character
\D	[^0-9] Any non-number character
\w	[0-9a-zA-Z_] Any letter, numeral or underscore
\W	[^0-9a-zA-Z_] Any non-alphanumeric character except the underscore
\s	[\f\n\r\t\v] Any whitespace character
\S	[^ \f\n\r\t\v] Any non-whitespace character. NB Not the same as \w

There is one more thing to mention in this section - the alternation of the *or* symbol (I). Equivalent to the or operator in Chapter 1 (remember ||?), the alternation symbol matches any one group of symbols out of several groups specified. For example /(ab|cd)/ will match either two-character sequence. We use the parenthesis to remind ourselves how the two parts of the alternation are related – the use of parentheses here is used to add clarity in the same way that you can use parenthesis in common mathematical expressions. Let's look at some examples.

```
var RE11 = /^([1-9]|1[0-2]):[0-5]\d$/;      // Matches proper time values
var RE12 = /['"]/d/d/d['"]/;        // Matches a three digit number in quotes
var RE13 = /[123]|[^123]/;
```

Our last example, RE13, serves little purpose other than to illustrate the or symbol. In effect, it does the same job as the wildcard character..

RE Syntax - Repetition and References

There are still some limitations to what we can do with regular expressions, the most notable being that we have to write out explicitly how many characters we're searching for in our pattern. This is fine for small, well-defined patterns like example RE11 for matching time strings, but say we wanted to match any string in quotes and you are facing quite a challenge to match it with a group of expressions like RE12.

The solution comes from a number of special characters used to denote the repetition of a letter, number, etc as follows.

Characters	Meaning
?	Either zero or one match only
*	Zero or more matches
+	One or more matches
{n}	Exactly n matches
{n,m}	No less than n and no more than m matches
{n,}	At least n matches

Each of these characters should come directly after the character or group that you wish to denote is repeated as is demonstrated below.

```
var RE14 = /g?nash/;          //Matches gnash or nash
var RE15 = /g*nash/;          //Matches nash, gnash, ggnash, gggnash etc.
var RE16 = /g+nash/;          //Matches gansh, ggnash, etc but not nash
var RE17 = /go{2}p/;          //Matches goop, not gop or gooop
var RE18 = /go{3,}p/;         //Matches gooop, goooop, not gop or goop
var RE19 = /go{1,3}p/;        //Matches gop, goop and gooop only
var RE20 = /['"][^'"]*['"]/;  //Matches a quoted string of length 0-?
```

You can also specify a sequence of characters to be repeated by enclosing them in parentheses like so.

```
var RE21 = /\d{5}(-\d{4})?/;   //Matches zip codes
```

The use of parentheses brings us on neatly to our final piece of syntax – reference markers. Consider the strings 212-555-212, 628-932-628, "Quote 1" and 'Quote 2'. Each of them has a (series of) character(s) repeated after some others. Regular expressions allow us one more match test on strings – to match character strings against those stored elsewhere in the same string. In effect, we can search for a matching pair of quotes or brackets and subsequently do something with the contents. For example, we can ensure a user's name matches that written on his credit card or, in the case of calculating mathematical pi (π) that no single digit is repeated more than twice in a row. We do this with references.

Let's take the number example. The regular expression to match those numbers mentioned earlier would be /\d{3}-\d{3}-\d{3}/. In order to match the first group of three numbers with the last, we would alter that expression slightly to /(\d{3})-\d{3}-\1/. The new escape sequence here, \1, seeks out the first expression within a set of parentheses and finds out the match for that expression. Then it tries to match a later sequence of characters against that earlier qualifying match.

These reference escape sequences can refer to the nth set of parentheses in a regular expression, so it's not uncommon to see \2, \3, \4 etc in more complex expressions. In the case where the parentheses are nested \n refers to the pair of parentheses that begins with the nth left parentheses starting from the left. One final word of caution here. Should you use, for example \10, in your expression when there are not ten sets of parentheses present, JavaScript will take this as meaning the ASCII character with octal value 10 - in this case, a backspace. There are only 9 maximum matches allowed.

To conclude, regular expressions are built out of pattern matching elements that together form more sophisticated patterns. The pattern matching process takes a candidate string and matches it from left-to-right against the supplied regular expression pattern. If there is any possible match at all, the string matches. If there is no match, you can be sure there is no possible interpretation of the pattern that could work for the string. This is an impostant point you can rely on if the regular expression, or the string it works on starts becoming complex.

RE Methods and Properties

Now you know how to write your very own patterns, what do you do with them? Well, we've already discovered that there is a RegExp object that is automatically created when you assign a string pattern to a variable. Now it's time to meet the methods we use to do our dirty work with. There are two attached to the RegExp object and four to the String object that work with REs, as follows.

str.search()

The String object's search() method is the simplest of all the operations we cover here.

```
var str="96521234";
var reg= new RegExp("965");
var reg2= /123/;
var index=str.search(reg);              // index = 0
var index2=str.search (reg2);           // index2 = 4
```

As you can guess from our example, search simply looks through the String specified and returns to index the position of the first matching character sequence in the String. Note that String ignores the global switch 'g' in a RE literal and that this index value begins at 0 as line 4 demonstrates. If a match is not found, search returns -1.

str.split()

The split() method has been in the language since JavaScript 1.1, but with version 1.2 came support for it to take a regular expression argument.

```
var large_number = "212,0,456,0,67889";
var reg3 = /,\d,/;
var numberList = large_number.split(re);
                                  // numberList = ["212","456","67889"]
```

The purpose of split() is to take a string and return an array of string elements. Each element exists in the original string separated by characters matching the pattern sent to split() as its argument.

str.replace()

As you would imagine, the `replace()` method returns a brand new string that contains a copy of the original string with any matching part of it replaced accordingly. For example

```
reg4 = /happy/gi;
str4 = "I'm happy. You're Happy";
newstr4=str4.replace(reg4, "sad");    // newstr4 = "I'm sad. You're sad"
```

Notice the use of the global and case-insensitive switches. Without them `newstr4` would be assigned `"I'm sad. You're Happy"`.

`replace()` is actually a lot more useful than it would appear from this simple example. Recall from part two of our syntax discussion the use of `/1`, `/2`, etc to refer to the match for a parenthesized sub-expression. The `RegExp` object has similar properties called `$1`, `$2`. etc up to `$9`, equivalent to `/1` and so on which can be fed back into `replace()`. For example

```
reg5 = /(I am) (\s\w*.\s) (You are) (\s\w*)/;
str5 = "I am working. You are asleep";
newstr5 = str5.replace(reg5, "$3$2$1$4");
                              //newstr5 = "You are working. I am asleep"
```

As you can guess, $1 and $3 correspond to "I am" and "You are" respectively and are swapped accordingly by `replace()`.

str.match()

Our last string method, `match()`, is very similar to `replace()` except that instead of returning a new string, it returns an array of matches to the global regular expression as a result.

In the case that the regular expression does not contain the global switch, the first element of the array will always return the match for the complete expression while subsequent elements will hold $1, $2, etc.

```
reg6 = /(I am) (\s\w*.\s) (You are) (\s\w*)/;
str6 = "I am working. You are asleep";
var newarr6 = str6.match(reg6);
```

So in this example, `newarr[0]` holds "I am working. You are asleep", `newarr[1]` holds "I am", `newarr[2]` holds " working. " and so on.

re.test()

The first of the methods attached to the `RegExp` object is very similar to the `search()` method we looked at earlier. It simply returns a boolean value, true or false, depending on whether or not a pattern can be matched to a sequence of characters in the given string. For example:

```
var string="96521234";
var reg= /965/;
var isin = reg.test(string);            // isin = true
```

If the pattern has the global flag set, it will set the `lastIndex` property of the `RegExp` object (see below) and continue the search from that point in the string when called again. If it does not have the flag set, `lastIndex` will be reset to 0.

re.exec()

The last of our RE-utilizing methods is `exec()`, which acts in a similar fashion to `match()` when the global switch is not used. It also has useful side-effects. Let's start with an example.

```
var string="965212234";
var reg= /(\d{2}2)/g;                    //Look for two digits followed by a 2
var results = reg.exec(string);         // = ["652", "652"]   Call 1
var results = reg.exec(string);         // = ["122", "122"]   Call 2
```

exec does a little more than you may first have guessed. In fact it populates all the static properties of the `RegExp` object, the `reg` object and updates details of the array too. `exec()` also behaves the same as `test()` with respect to the global flag being set. Should it not find a match, `exec()` returns `null` for the array.

Given the code above, the following tables demonstrate what each call to `reg.exec(string)` populates various properties with.

Array Properties

Accessed as	After Call 1	After Call 2	Notes
results.index	1	4	Character position at which match occurred
results.input	965212234	965212234	The target string

Pattern Properties

Accessed as	After Call 1	After Call 2	Notes
reg.lastIndex	4	7	The index from which to begin the next search
reg.ignoreCase	false	false	Has the 'i' switch been used?
reg.global	true	true	Has the 'g' switch been used?
reg.source	(\d{2}2)	(\d{2}2)	The pattern being matched

Static Regular Expression Properties

Always referred to as properties of the generic `RegExp` object

Accessed as	After Call 1	After Call 2	Notes
RegExp. lastMatch	652	122	Last character sequence to match the pattern
RegExp. leftContext	9	9652	Characters to the left of the matching sequence
RegExp. rightContext	12234	34	Characters to the right of the matching sequence
RegExp.$1	652	122	See previous explanation
RcgExp. LastParen	652	122	The last substring match to a parenthesized subexpression.

As you can see, `exec()` does a lot of behind the scenes work, especially if you're running Navigator.

Limitations of exec() in Internet Explorer

The JScript version of `exec()` is quite limited in comparison to that in JavaScript in two ways:

- ❑ It does not support the 'run-on' style of operation when the global flag is set.
- ❑ JScript regular expressions only have five properties as follows

RegExp.index, RegExp.input : Equivalent to `results.index` and `results.input` as above.
RegExp.lastIndex, reg.source: Equivalent to `reg.lastIndex` and `reg.source` as above
RegExp.$1: Equivalent to `RegExp.$1` as above.

And so, with all that information behind us, we conclude our tour of regular expression support in JavaScript.

Summary

Beyond basic objects and syntax in JavaScript lurk some powerful and flexible features. Although the language easily and simply supports basic and trivial scripts, the scriptwriter can expand his horizons well past that if required. Support for Object-Oriented programming, including exceptions and inheritance lets the JavaScript language stand tall with the best. Self-evaluation of data as code and vice versa mean that JavaScript is even more amenable to advanced mobile code architectures than popular languages such as C++ and Java.

With the 'ECMAScript 2' standard still under development in late 1999 it is certain that these features will be standardized once the new version of the language is launched. Nevertheless, prototype and scope chains are fairly fundamental to JavaScript and can be relied upon almost everywhere.

Regardless of these advanced features, the basic language is still almost useless taken purely by itself. A host environment is needed in order for the interpreter to have an application domain to work with. Such a domain (e.g. web browsers) can be so interesting in its own right that high-end features of the language are entirely forgotten in the excitement. When that domain has been pushed beyond its obvious uses, advanced JavaScripters turn back to the more subtle language features for inspiration, innovation and solutions. In the meantime, the rest of this book considers those host applications – browsers, servers, shells, custom applications and others – and JavaScript's general role in extending their utility.

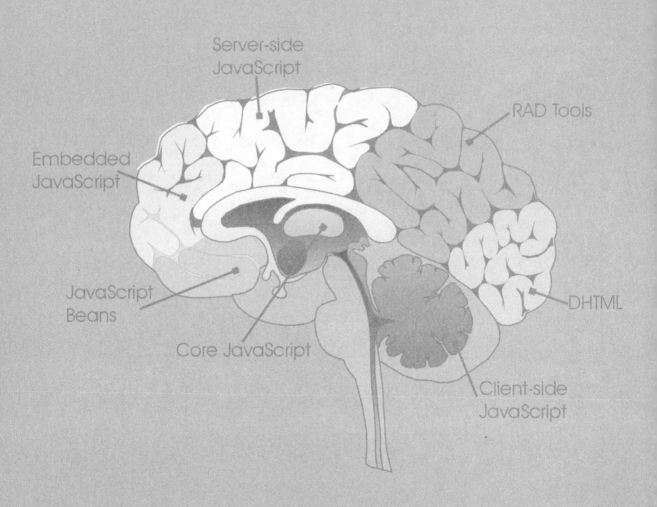

Basic Browser JavaScript

A JavaScript interpreter can't do much in a vacuum; it needs to work with a host program. The host program supplies all the interesting objects, functions and data that the interpreter operates on. Through these things, scripts can read input from a user, display output to a user, and perform computations in between.

Mainstream Browsers and JavaScript

JavaScript has its origins in the Internet and the World Wide Web, so it's no surprise that Web browsers are the places JavaScript is most frequently used. In most cases, this is achieved by adding JavaScript scripts to documents that normally only contain HTML tags and content.

Of the many, many web browsers available, Microsoft's Internet Explorer and Netscape's Navigator and Communicator have the lion's share of the market. JavaScript's impact on these mainstream browsers is considered the 'ordinary case' and we'll be looking at those browsers primarily. In this chapter we'll also briefly consider some of the less well known alternatives. Alas, unless their popularity improves, the lesser known browsers are likely to occupy only small niches in the browser marketplace.

Adding JavaScript to HTML

An HTML document that contains JavaScript can be looked at from two points of view. Looked at from the outside, as a mere textual document, there are only select places in an HTML document where JavaScript scripts can be added. Looked at from the inside as a collection of tags and content items, an HTML document consists of numerous interesting features that can be manipulated by any scripts that can get at those features. It is the former view that is described here.

Since JavaScript scripts can only be placed in HTML documents in certain spots, opportunities for acting upon the document or the browser displaying the document are limited. However, what JavaScript can do in an HTML document is:

❑ Affect document layout when HTML tags and content are still being loaded by the browser.

❑ Affect document layout after HTML tags and content have been loaded by the browser.

❑ Affect the number of browser windows and window-like objects currently displayed.

❑ Capture, mimic and modify actions the user of the browser might make.

❑ Perform basic automation and basic feedback tasks.

❑ Improve on the simple forms that HTML supports.

❑ Forward user actions onto applets, plug-ins and other foreign bodies embedded in the document.

Let's throw a little jargon in at this point. An HTML document may have JavaScript scripts **embedded** in it. The browser running these JavaScript/HTML pages **hosts** a JavaScript interpreter or has a JavaScript interpreter embedded in it.

<SCRIPT>

The <SCRIPT> HTML tag is the main way of connecting JavaScript to HTML. Any amount of JavaScript code can accompany the <SCRIPT> tag. It is a paired or block tag and has a number of attributes that can be set as this example shows:

```
<HTML>
<HEAD>

<SCRIPT>
  var step=1;                              // example 1.
</SCRIPT>

<SCRIPT LANGUAGE="JavaScript"> step=2;     // example 2.
</SCRIPT>

<SCRIPT LANGUAGE="JavaScript1.1"> step=3;  // example 3.
</SCRIPT>

<SCRIPT LANGUAGE="JavaScript1.3"> step=4;  // example 4.
</SCRIPT>

<SCRIPT SRC="myfunctions.js">              // example 5.
</SCRIPT>

<SCRIPT TYPE="text/JavaScript"> step=6;    // example 6. HTML 4.0
</SCRIPT>
</HEAD>
</HTML>
```

Examples from 1 to 4 inclusive show the most common use: **inline JavaScript**. This form is called inline JavaScript because the JavaScript code inside the document is *executed as soon as it is encountered* when the browser is reading the HTML file. The one exception is if JavaScript functions are defined – they are stored away for later. In these examples, the JavaScript scripts are very trivial – just assigning a value to a variable – but could easily be quite complex, which would halt reading of the HTML until the script finished.

Each of the first 4 examples illustrates a different point.

❑ Example 1 shows that just the plain tag is enough to identify its contents as a script.

❑ Example 2 shows that the <SCRIPT> tag is designed for all kinds of scripting languages, and that the LANGUAGE attribute identifies the particular language. JavaScript is the default language for most browsers, so leaving the LANGUAGE attribute off is harmless. If a browser does support scripting generally, but doesn't support the language specified, then the code between the tags is ignored.

❑ Examples 3 and 4 show that a particular language version can be specified. If the browser supports that language version, then the code is executed using that language version, otherwise it is ignored. Neither 'ECMAScript' nor 'JavaScript1.0' work as language names. 'JScript' only works in Internet Explorer 4+. If no language version or language is specified, the browser will choose the version and the language that it thinks is best.

Example 5 shows that a JavaScript script can be retrieved from another file. The value of the SRC attribute can be any valid URL that points to the file in question. This form is particularly handy if you have a large number of JavaScript functions that are used in several HTML documents. Rather than type the functions into every document, store them in a separate file containing pure JavaScript (no HTML) and use SRC in every HTML document that needs them. The content of the file will be executed immediately, in the same way as for the earlier cases, but it's not referred to as inline JavaScript because it isn't physically in the same file.

Example 5 should not use the LANGUAGE attribute either. This is because the source file is retrieved from somewhere external to the HTML document and, therefore, the web browser's normal mechanisms for detecting file type should be relied upon. Occasionally there is a problem getting this to work – if so, make sure any web server you use knows that a .js file is an 'application/x-JavaScript' MIME type with a .js filename extension. You can use URLs in the SRC attribute that accesses files on the local disk if you're not using a Web server. No special setup is required in that case.

The HTML 4.0 standard uses a different attribute, TYPE, specifying a MIME type of 'text/JavaScript' for JavaScript, but only Internet Explorer 4+ and Navigator 4+ support this attribute, so it's less portable. It is illustrated in example 6.

The two biggest benefits of inline JavaScript are that you can affect the HTML as it is being read and rendered in the browser, and you can declare functions for later use, possibly organized in a modular manner in separate files.

Inline Scripts

This example illustrates adding scripts to HTML, and using a function. All indenting is just for readability.

```
<HTML>
 <HEAD>
  <SCRIPT>
   function weather_comment()
   {
     if ( !Math.random )      // doesn't exist in Navigator 2.0
     {
      document.write('<PRE> -- weather called off due to rain --</PRE>');
     }
     else if ( Math.floor((Math.random()*2)) == 0 )
     {
      document.write("<STRONG>It's just awful.</STRONG>\n");
     }
     else
     {
      document.write("<EM>How wonderful it is!</EM>\n");
     }
   }
  </SCRIPT>
 </HEAD>
 <BODY>
  <P>Weather report for today:</P>
  <SCRIPT>
   weather_comment();         // add special stuff
  </SCRIPT>
  <P>End of report.</P>
 </BODY>
</HTML>
```

In the <HEAD> of the example, an inline script is used which does nothing except create a function. This is similar to the other activities that go on in the <HEAD> – no document content, but plenty of other setup information. Then, in the body, an inline script calls that new function which runs the infamous document.write(). The output of the document.write() is added to the plain HTML as it is displayed on the screen. This means the body part of the HTML will ultimately appear to be either this:

```
    <P> Weather report for today:</P>
 <STRONG> It's just awful.</STRONG>
    <P> End of report.</P>
```

or this:

```
    <P> Weather report for today:</P>
 <EM>How wonderful it is!</EM>
    <P> End of report.</P>
```

or for Netscape Navigator 2.02, which has no Math.random() method, this:

```
    <P> Weather report for today:</P>
 <PRE> -- weather called off due to rain -- </PRE>
    <P> End of report.</P>
```

and then will be rendered by the browser appropriately.

The important thing to note here is that while this example has managed to affect the HTML delivered to the user, once that HTML is delivered, it's impossible to change it again by this approach. We could use other fancy tricks such as Dynamic HTML to modify the HTML after it's rendered, but this technique only applies to the process of initial display.

Where to Put <SCRIPT>

An HTML document consists of a <HEAD> and <BODY> or a <HEAD> and a <FRAMESET>. There are three reasonable places to put <SCRIPT> tags:

- ❑ in the <HEAD> – recommended
- ❑ in the <BODY> – recommended
- ❑ after the <HEAD> but before the <BODY> or <FRAMESET> – not so good, but still possible.

In theory, the head contains no document content, only meta-information about the document. In theory, the head is completely read by the browser before any body elements are displayed. This makes the head a good place to put any JavaScript that does invisible setup. This means declaring all functions, native objects and variables in the head, and avoiding executing document.write() when the head is loaded, although both Internet Explorer and Navigator will handle output from the head if you use document.write() there anyway.

Another good reason for putting as much script as possible in the head is that the JavaScript interpreter only knows that functions, objects and variables exist after the browser has reached the point where they are created in the HTML document. If functions are declared at the bottom of the document and called from the top, you will get 'function undefined' errors all over the place. If data is declared at the bottom of the document and called from the top, you'll have the same problem.

The body is the obvious place to put inline code that can vary the HTML output. If the script in the body starts looking complex or repetitive, consider putting it in a function declared in the head, and just call it from the body. At the end of the body is a good place to put any JavaScript code that you want to happen when the tags and objects it works on are already displayed on the screen.

Documents containing a frameset instead of a body can't have any JavaScript inside the frameset (except JavaScript URLS, see below). This is a nuisance if you want to vary the frameset details using inline scripts. Instead, you can put a <SCRIPT> tag after the </HEAD> tag, and use it to write out the whole <FRAMESET> content (or the whole <BODY> content), avoiding the problem altogether. Since there aren't any ordinary tags in a frameset document, you're safe to do this, unless your script starts looking inside the contents of each frame. That's bad because each frame also has to load a document, and you can have the same unloaded object problem again.

Overall, browsers supporting JavaScript are quite liberal about where you can technically put <SCRIPT> tags. A script can be responsible for quite a lot of a given document's content as this rather suspect (but generally browser friendly) HTML example shows:

```
<!DOCTYPE HTML PUBLIC "-//W3C//DTD HTML 3.2//EN">
<SCRIPT>
  with ( document )
  {
    write('<HTML><HEAD>\n');
    write('<TITLE>Nearly all JavaScript!</TITLE>\n');
    write('</HEAD><BODY>\n');
    write('Who needs plain HTML?\n');
    write('<BR><HR></BODY></HTML>');
  }
</SCRIPT>
```

Further Variants

These first examples show all the common ways of embedding JavaScript into an HTML file. There are also some additional browser-specific methods. Netscape Navigator 4.0 (and the equivalent Communicator suite) has enhanced security options for JavaScript. The benefits of using these are twofold: your scripts can be protected from prying eyes, and your scripts can do more powerful things. This subject is explained in the security chapter, Chapter 18, including how the ARCHIVE and ID attributes can be used together. Common to both browsers at versions 4+ is support for JAR files, also explained under security.

Four Traps

JavaScript code stored in a document by itself is a straightforward matter. Embedding JavaScript into an HTML document, which has another kind of content and format altogether introduces some problems.

Firstly, you can't use </SCRIPT> inside inline JavaScript. When a browser picks through a file's text, it looks for tags indicating where various bits of information begin and end. Once it sees a <SCRIPT> tag it goes on the hunt for a matching </SCRIPT>, which eventually results in an error or a mess. So this example is problematic:

```
<HTML><BODY>                                    // Example 1
<SCRIPT>
var warning = 'do not ever put </SCRIPT> literally in a string';
</SCRIPT>
</BODY></HTML>
```

The whole output of this HTML example for old browsers is likely to be:

```
literally in a string';
```

when no output was probably intended. Newer browsers, Internet Explorer 4+ and Netscape 4.5+ produce no output (correct) but the variable warning is set to:

```
do not ever put literally in a string
```

So these browsers manage to ignore the tag altogether. A better approach is to chop up the tag like this:

```
var script_tag = '</SCR'+'IPT>';                // Example 2
var warning = 'do not ever put ' + script_tag + ' literally in a string';
```

Secondly, a similar problem occurs with printing any 'special' HTML characters. An example:

```
<HTML><BODY><SCRIPT>                              // Example 3
   // who's shorter?
   // (He is - she grew up, and he's earlier in the alphabet anyway).

   document.write(('Danny DeVito' < 'Shirley Temple') ?'Danny < Shirley'
                                            :'Shirley < Danny');
</SCRIPT></BODY></HTML>
```

The HTML produced looks like this, with the only output being Danny:

```
<HTML><BODY>
Danny<Shirley
</BODY></HTML>
```

<Shirley surely looks like a tag, but is unknown to the browser and therefore ignored. Do this instead:

```
// common knowledge anyway
document.write('Danny&lt;Shirley');    // also use this trick for &gt; and &amp;
```

Here, we're relying on the alternative entity syntax provided by HTML for characters such as <, > and &. There aren't any new JavaScript features here, just a better choice of HTML.

Thirdly, if the HTML file containing JavaScript script is publicly available on the Internet, there is another problem. There are many browsers that not only don't support a scripting language, but they haven't even heard of the <SCRIPT> tag also. When a browser discovers an unknown tag, it is discarded and ignored. In this case, example 2 is likely to produce this ugly output for the reader's consumption:

```
var script_tag = ''; var warning = 'do not ever put ' + script_tag + ' literally
in a string;
```

No modern browser has this problem, but it's impossible to tell what some people are using. You may be doing a blind person, or someone else who relies on a rare browser, a favor if you remember to solve this. There is a special feature of JavaScript that can help you out. If the first line of a JavaScript script is the HTML comment start symbol, then the JavaScript interpreter will ignore it, even though it is a JavaScript syntax error. This lets JavaScript code look like HTML comments for browsers with no clue about scripts. This is specific to browsers. An example:

```
<HTML><BODY><SCRIPT>
<!-- hide from old, stupid browsers

document.write('JavaScript rules, but not everywhere!');

// end comment -->
</SCRIPT></BODY></HTML>
```

The last problem has more to do with HTML rendering of tags than the tags themselves. Recall the weather example above. In that example, the `document.write()` calls contain strings that are terminated by the new line character '\n', meaning "start a new line at this point". In the generated HTML that results, you can see this has happened, because the 'End of report' line *in the generated HTML* starts on a line by itself. However, when the HTML is rendered for the user, new lines don't have any effect on the displayed output. This is because newlines are the same thing as whitespace in HTML. Therefore they are only useful when someone looks at the HTML source. Another example:

```
document.write('red\n');
document.write('blue\n');
document.write('yellow\n');
```

This does not visibly produce three lines of output. It appears to the user as:

```
red blue yellow
```

To insist on separate lines in the user output, use a `<BR>` HTML tag instead of a newline.

Taking all these traps into account, the 'Hello World!\n' example of Chapter 1 can be re-written and used as a template on which we can base all of our future JavaScripted HTML pages:

```
<HTML>
 <HEAD>
  <TITLE>First script ever</TITLE>

  <SCRIPT LANGUAGE="JavaScript">
  <!--hide it from old browsers
     var my_hello = 'Hello, World!';

    function say_it(stuff)
       {
           document.write(stuff)
       }
  // finish hiding -->
  </SCRIPT>

 </HEAD>
 <BODY>

  <SCRIPT LANGUAGE="JavaScript">
  <!--hide it from old browsers
     say_it(my_hello);
  // finish hiding -->
  </SCRIPT>

 </BODY>
</HTML>
```

This is a good general pattern to follow, even though it looks complicated for such a simple use.

JavaScript Entities

An HTML **entity reference** is a bit of HTML syntax that lets difficult-to-type characters be represented. Examples are   and Á. JavaScript entities are an extension to this syntax. This example draws two horizontal lines, but cleverly computes the lengths of the lines (which are normally specified as an HTML attribute) from some JavaScript variables and a bit of math. You couldn't do this without JavaScript, as either a <HR> tag has a fixed WIDTH attribute in plain HTML or none at all. The first line shows total units sold, the second the percent of a batch of 1000 units sold:

```
<HTML><HEAD>
  <SCRIPT>
    var pixels_per_unit = 25.4;
    var total_units = 8;
  </SCRIPT>
</HEAD>
<BODY>
  Bar graph showing number of units:<BR>
  <HR ALIGN=LEFT SIZE=10 WIDTH="&{pixels_per_unit * total_units};"><BR>

  Bar graph showing units as a percentage of 1000:<BR>
  <HR ALIGN=LEFT SIZE=10 WIDTH="&{ (pixels_per_unit*total_units/1000) * 100};%">

</BODY></HTML>
```

It's the values of the WIDTH attribute of the <HR> tags that contains the JavaScript entities. Everything between the curly braces is evaluated as a script and the result replaces the entity at the end, same as an HTML entity. Unlike HTML entity references, these can only be used in the value part of an HTML tag attribute, as shown, not in normal HTML content. Notice in the second <HR> that the result of the JavaScript entity is concatenated with '%'. Whatever other characters are in the value part of the tag attribute will concatenate with the JavaScript entity's value. Any JavaScript expression can be used between the braces. JavaScript entities are of limited use. They are supported only in Navigator 3.0+, and in fact the HTML 4.0 standard advises against persisting with the use of this feature. It's there if you want it.

JavaScript URLs

A JavaScript URL is a special kind of URL. Mostly, URLs contain some kind of address that leads to a file, an e-mail account, or a terminal session when that hypertext link is clicked on. JavaScript URLs are different in that they don't retrieve or send anything, except as a side effect. What they do instead is cause the immediate execution of a bit of script, without the overhead of any request to a web server.

JavaScript URLs only occupy a single line, so if they contain more than one JavaScript statement, semi-colons should be used. There are three places to put JavaScript URLs.

Interactive

All Netscape browsers, plus Internet Explorer 4+ support this functionality.

```
javascript:Math.PI * radius * radius
javascript:alert(top.name)
javascript:if ( top.page_number ) { alert(top.page_number.hits); }
```

The web browser user can type JavaScript URLs directly into the browser in the same way as for any URL. You can use the browser as a simple calculator, as in the first line above. A more common use is as a debugging aid, shown in the other two lines ('alert()' is a browser host function–more on that later). Typing JavaScript URLs interactively lets you examine any hidden (or not so hidden) contents of an HTML page, such as variables or properties. The URL has access to all the pages in the current window if frames are present. Here is a simple example based on this HTML source:

```
<HTML>
<HEAD><TITLE>Test Page</TITLE></HEAD>
<BODY>Test content</BODY>
</HTML>
```

From this next screen shot you can see the JavaScript URL typed, the content and title of the page, and the small alert box window that is the result of the JavaScript URL. Note that the title of the main window agrees with the data the URL dug out of the document and displayed in the small window:

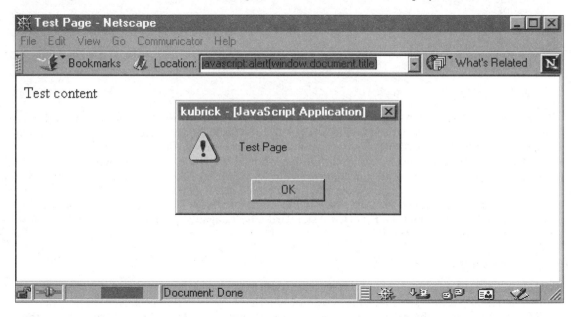

There's a lot happening in the above example. For now just accept that JavaScript URLs can get information out of HTML documents. The Windows and Frames chapter describes the rest of what's going on here.

If the URL is just typed as follows: 'javascript:' a special interpreter window appears that allows plain JavaScript to be typed in and executed straight away without the javascript: prefix. Here's a picture of the Netscape JavaScript interactive interpreter:

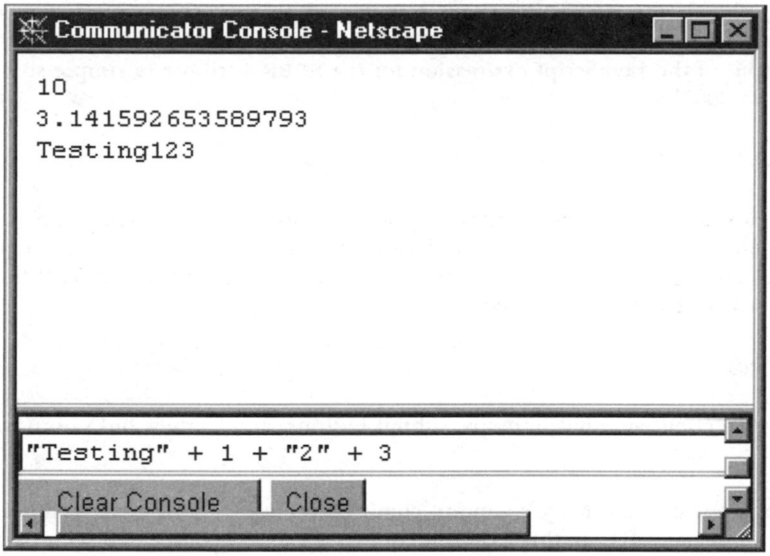

```
※ Communicator Console - Netscape                    _ □ ✕

10
3.141592 653589793
Testing123




"Testing" + 1 + "2" + 3                              ▲

   Clear Console  |  Close                           ▼
◄ ▢                                                  ► ◢
```

To get this display, first we typed `'javascript:'` where URLs are normally typed. Then, in order to get the output shown, we typed the following into the input box at the bottom:

```
3 + 4
Math.PI
"Testing" + 1 + "2" + 3
```

As Document Source

You can replace normal URLs in a document with `javascript:` ones. The result of the JavaScript expression will be that the contents are displayed if that URL is loaded. If the expression result is void, then no action will be taken, except for any side effects. This example shows three different uses, described below:

```
<HTML><BODY>
<SCRIPT>
  var quiz_results = "Your result for this test was: " + 23 + "%";

function update_results()
{
  quiz_results = "Perfect score!";
}

  var tiny = "#define x_width 1\n#define x_height 1\nstatic char x_bits[] =
            {0x00};";

</SCRIPT>

<A HREF="javascript:quiz_results">Click here to see your results</A><BR>
<A HREF="javascript:update_results()">Click here to improve your results</A>
<IMG SRC="javascript:tiny" NAME='Single pixel image'>

</BODY></HTML>
```

In the first <A> tag above, clicking on the link will result in a new page displaying a single line. Clicking on a plain link causes the current page to be replaced with a new page. In this case, the new page is the output of the JavaScript expression for the HREF attribute (a simple string in this case). The new page looks like:

```
    Your result for this test was: 23%
```

If the second <A> tag is clicked nothing will appear to happen since function update_results() returns void. So the current page is not replaced, and the update_score() function gets to do some invisible magic behind the scenes – in this case just changing a variable. If the first link is clicked afterwards this will be displayed:

```
    Perfect score!
```

This also works in client-side image maps, submit buttons, and frames, but not in Internet Explorer 3.0.

The third example shows an image's content coming from a JavaScript expression instead of from a file located at a normal URL. In this example, the image used is described by a string. This tactic is explained in more depth in Chapter 6 on Images and Multimedia. Internet Explorer 3.0 can not do this.

As Bookmarks

Netscape Navigator 4.0 will accept interactive JavaScript URLs as bookmarks. To create one, follow these steps. Click from the browser menu bar: Bookmarks, Edit Bookmarks. In the new window select an appropriate folder like Personal Toolbar Folder by clicking on the name, then click File, New Bookmark and enter the JavaScript URL along with the other details.

Care must be taken when creating these kinds of bookmarks. Any document from any source could be currently displayed when a user selects a bookmark. If the bookmark refers to any objects, variables or properties in the current page, extra checks should be included in the bookmark URL. This ensures the bookmark doesn't 'crash' if picked when the user is exploring some unexpected page.

<SERVER>, RUNAT and <% and %>

For completeness, we'll briefly mention some non-browser tags that can find their way into HTML pages. These tags are used just like the <SCRIPT> tag – JavaScript code is put between them. However, these tags are processed by the web server, not by the browser, so they should never appear when you do View Source from the browser menu.

<SERVER> is a Netscape-only tag, the RUNAT attribute is a Microsoft-only, one that applies to the <SCRIPT> tag, hence <SCRIPT RUNAT="server">. The funny looking pair of punctuation marks, <% and %>, are just Microsoft shorthanded for <SCRIPT RUNAT="server"> and </SCRIPT> respectively.

If these tags ever appear in your browser, you know your website is in trouble, because you are using the wrong specialist tags with the wrong web server. Other than that, they have no relevance to browsers.

<STYLE>

Styles allow formatting normally specified in HTML tags to be collected together and applied to tags repeatedly as a unit. JavaScript can be used with styles. A syntax is required to identify the contents of a style, with the most common syntax being that of the CSS-1 standard, which is what is currently implemented in most browsers.

From the JavaScript perspective, there are two issues with handling styles: creating them and working with them. When creating styles, there are variations in functionality provided by Internet Explorer 5.0 and Netscape 4.x.

Creating Netscape JavaScript StyleSheets (JSSS)

Stylesheets can be written in several different languages, one of which is JavaScript. JavaScript stylesheets conform to the CSS-1 stylesheet model, so they are equivalent to stylesheets written in CSS-1 syntax. JavaScript stylesheets are known by the acronym JSSS, and are only supported in the Netscape 4+ browsers. Internet Explorer 4+ has two alternative techniques toward the same end, demonstrated below:

```
<HTML><HEAD>
<STYLE TYPE="text/JavaScript">
 tags.P.borderWidth = 100;
 tags.P.borderStyle = 'none';              // or else a very thick border ensues
 tags.B.color = "red";
</STYLE>

<LINK REL=STYLESHEET TYPE="text/JavaScript" HREF="fancystyle" TITLE="Fancy">

</HEAD><BODY>
<P> Spacious paragraph ! </P>
<P><B>Angry spacious paragraph!</B></P>
</BODY></HTML>
```

The use of the `<STYLE>` tag shows that creation of stylesheets in JavaScript is just a matter of creating correctly named properties and assigning valid values. Capital 'P' and 'B' in the example stand for the `<P>`aragraph and `<B>`old tags respectively. The section describing the browser object model explains what properties exist. The CSS-1 concepts of **classes** and **ids** have a similar syntax.

The `<LINK>` tag in the head of an HTML document is supposed to identify dependencies between this document and other documents in a general manner. One such dependency is a JavaScript stylesheet, so this tag provides an alternative to embedding the stylesheet data directly in the document.

There are a few special JavaScript functions for JSSS:

```
<HTML><HEAD>
<STYLE TYPE="text/JavaScript">
 tags.H1.color = 'pink';
 tags.H1.margins(1,2,3,4);                  // set top, right, bottom, left margins.
                                            // paddings(), borderWidths() exist too.
 tags.H1.rgb(50,50,50);

 contextual(tags.H1, tags.B).fontStyle = "italic";

 function change_it()
 {
  if ( color == 'pink' ) fontStyle = "medium";
 }

 tags.I.apply = change_it();
</STYLE></HEAD></HTML>
```

This example doesn't do anything much; we're just illustrating a typical use of the various functions and their syntaxes.

The first few bits of the style details are simple. The `margins()` method is handy shorthand for setting the four margin properties all at once – it just saves typing. The `rgb()` method is similarly handy for specifying colors by value.

The next part of the style takes a bit of getting used to. `contextual()` is a method which lets one style depend on another, the equivalent of CSS-1 syntax like `'H1 B { font-style: italic}'`. As JavaScript it looks a bit unusual until you realize that `contextual()` is creating an object which has its `fontStyle` property set. `contextual()` can take any number of arguments, which means you can have any number of levels of tag nesting as a condition for the special style information.

The final part creates a JavaScript function and assigns it to the special property `apply` of the current style for the `<I>` tag. The `apply` property is an escape hatch for those special cases when it all becomes too hard. When the browser reads a tag and collects together the relevant style information, it first resolves how that tag's details will be displayed. Before displaying the tag details, it checks the `apply` property. If the `apply` property is set, then the assigned function is called which can then do any last-minute band-aid work required on the tag's ultimate style.

In this example, because `<B>` tags inside `<H1>` tags are shown as italic, some confusion might arise if `<I>` tags are also present inside the `<H1>` tag–they could look the same. The `apply` property is used to avoid this case. The `change_it()` function checks the color the tag details are going to be rendered in and, if the answer is `pink`, assumes that the `<I>` tag is inside a `<H1>` tag and so changes it to `medium` style.

Creating Internet Explorer Behaviors

Where Netscape innovates styles with JSSS, Microsoft innovates styles with **behaviors**. A behavior is a way of attaching some script to a style, and therefore to all the HTML tags of a given web page that adopt that style. This is done by storing the script in a specially formatted, separate file called a `.HTC` file (for HTml Component). In this respect, behaviors are an approach that is similar to using the `<SCRIPT SRC=>` tag and attribute, but there the similarity ends. Although events haven't been covered yet, it doesn't take too much imagination to see that there ought to be ways that JavaScript scripts can run when the user clicks on elements in a web page. Behaviors let styled-up tags run such scripts.

Here is a simple HTML document using an Internet Explorer 5.0 behavior:

```
<HTML><HEAD>
<STYLE>
  .help{behavior:url(help.htc)}
</STYLE>
</HEAD><BODY>
No response here
<DIV CLASS=help DELAY=2000> Click me for help </DIV>
No response here
</BODY></HTML>
```

The behavior is defined in line 3 in the STYLE block. It is activated if the user interacts with the <DIV> tag. Here is a very simple .HTC file:

```
<script language="JScript">
attachEvent("onclick", event_onclick);

function event_onclick()
{
  alert("Sorry, you're beyond help");
}
</script>
```

If the user clicks on the middle line, then the function in the .HTC file attached to the event runs, displaying a simple alert box (a window) with a message.

This behavior feature has advantages and drawbacks. Its advantage is that it stops the HTML web page from being littered with bits of JavaScript, which aids comprehension, and it saves you from having to duplicate JavaScript event handlers all over the place for like items in a web page, which saves effort. Its drawbacks are that if you use many behaviors, then you must draw many .HTC files over the Web into your browser, and that's slow. So slow, that you might have to wait some time before the behaviors are ready to be used. The magic DELAY attribute in the above example tells Internet Explorer "wait this long before displaying this tag, a behavior will probably be loaded by then". It could require some fairly complex code to be absolutely sure all the behaviors have loaded.

The .HTC file can be begun with some XML markup that associates events from the browser without having to use the attachEvent() function as shown here. This URL gives a fuller introduction: http://msdn.microsoft.com/workshop/essentials/versions/IE5behave.asp.

Manipulating Styles

In order for JavaScript to be able to do anything with stylesheets apart from specifying them, two things need to be possible: the style details need to be readable, and the style needs to be changeable by JavaScript.

In both 3.0 browsers, it is not possible to read or write style attributes outside the style definition. This means styles are both static (unchanging) and invisible to JavaScript.

In Netscape 4.0 browsers, styles can be changed. Additionally, if the style includes a position property of `absolute` or `relative`, then the style appears as a JavaScript Layer object. This has read/write properties matching all the CSS-1 positioning properties, which let scripts manipulate a style's location, size, visibility and stacking order in the document. The actual display of the HTML element or layer identified by the style is still static. This means that if a style is changed via JavaScript, any HTML elements already displayed won't automatically change to match the new values – the browser just doesn't give you that much control. The document that the element is a part of would have to be reloaded first (which might reset the changes anyway). The sole exception to this rule is the background color or image for an 'absolutely' or 'relatively' positioned style. In that case, you can change the background color at any time you like.

Internet Explorer 4.0 has an innovation called **dynamic styles**. Dynamic styles means that styles are fully exposed as host objects that JavaScript can manipulate after they are created and after the HTML document is displayed in the browser as well. Styles created with the <STYLE> tag and styles created with the HTML `STYLE=` attribute are accessible as JavaScript objects. This gives all the functionality of Navigator 4.0 layers, plus the ability to change all the other style properties. A change to one of these properties via JavaScript can result in parts of the document being re-examined and redrawn differently by the browser ('**reflowed**').

See Chapter 8 on Dynamic HTML for further discussion on manipulating styles from JavaScript.

<META>

This tag in HTML 4.0 provides a way of setting the default scripting language for an HTML document, and the default style definition language. The syntax is:

```
<META http-equiv="Content-Script-Type" content="text/JavaScript">
<META http-equiv="Content-Style-Type" content="text/JavaScript">
```

Since JavaScript is already the default, and Internet Explorer doesn't support JSSS, they're not of much use yet. Netscape 4.0 ignores the tag variants.

Events

HTML events are the main way JavaScript improves its interactivity with the user. An **event** is just a piece of input to the browser, usually from the user. **Event handlers** are bits of JavaScript code that execute in response to events.

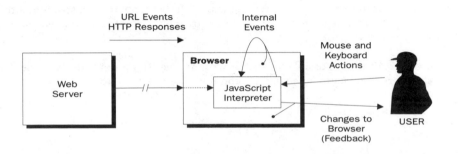

An **event model** describes how events are created and moved around by the software. The HTML 4.0 standard calls events relating to HTML **intrinsic events**. These are the browser events of most interest. The components of the HTML event model are:

- ❏ Special conditions causing events to occur.
- ❏ Special attributes in HTML tags for each event.
- ❏ Scripts to handle each event.
- ❏ A JavaScript host object that a given event acts on.
- ❏ Control passed temporarily to the JavaScript interpreter when an event occurs.
- ❏ Data accompanying the event.

From the scriptwriter's point of view, only components 3, 4, and 5 require any JavaScript code.

Creating Handlers

There are two ways to create JavaScript for HTML events: via HTML tags and via JavaScript host objects.

```
<HTML><HEAD><SCRIPT>
var shouts = 0;

function shout(obj)
{
  alert('What? Just: "' + this.value + '"\n\nLOUDER !!');
}
</SCRIPT></HEAD>
<BODY>
Shouting page. Type away, then hit the TAB key.<BR>

<FORM NAME="shouter"> First shout:
<INPUT TYPE="text" NAME="first" ONCHANGE="this.value='LOUDER !!!';return true;">
<BR> Second shout:
<INPUT TYPE="text">
<BR> Last shout:
<INPUT TYPE="text" NAME="last">
</FORM>

<SCRIPT>
document.shouter[1].onchange=shout;
document.shouter.last.onchange=shout;
</SCRIPT></BODY></HTML>
```

In this example there are three HTML text fields, all with onChange event handlers. Since HTML tag attributes are case insensitive, ONCHANGE could have been written onchange or onChange. In documentation, the convention is to use onChange, as will be done from here on. In JavaScript code, the equivalent property must be lowercase – onchange, except Netscape 4+ will allow onChange as well. Later in this section the implications of this handler are described. For now, run the example and see for yourself, or just note the syntax.

Analyzing the Example and Its Conventions

In the example above, the first text field has the event handler embedded in the HTML tag. Any amount of code can go here, but unless the handler is trivial as in the example, usually a function will be called.

117

Notice the this keyword is used. In Chapter 2, it was discussed how this gives access to the current object, or the object in whose scope the script is running. In the example above, the current object is the specific form element the user changed.

Also notice the return keyword is used. Unlike JavaScript URLs, JavaScript event handlers are supposed to always return true or false although this is: a) not enforced, b) not always necessary, and c) sometimes doesn't even do anything. Read about event processing further on in the book for the implications of true and false. For now, we just note that it is a good habit to always return true.

The last text field has an onChange event handler or **trigger**, but it's not specified in the <INPUT> tag. At the bottom of the example is a line with the word 'last' in it, which is the name for the third text element as specified in the tag. This line allocates the 'shout' function to the onChange event for that element. From JavaScript, if you want to be portable, you can only assign a whole function to an event, not a scrap of code as for the first function. For Internet Explorer 3.0+ you can use a different syntax: the FOR EVENT= HTML syntax to assign a scrap of code. This is not recommended unless you're sure that Internet Explorer is the only browser your users will use. Finally, you can portably assign an anonymous function if you don't want to declare one, but its harder to read what's going on.

Above the line assigning a handler to the last element is a similar line. This does the same thing, but for the middle HTML form element which has no name in the <INPUT> tag. This is an example of objects and arrays being (nearly) interchangeable in JavaScript.

Notice the shout() function declared in the head also uses the this keyword, so there is an expectation that it will be used as a method of an object, which is true. The shout() function also has one argument, obj. This argument is not used in early JavaScript browsers, and in those cases will always be null. In Navigator 4.0, an Event object associated with the event will be passed to the event handler function, containing interesting bits about the event. Internet Explorer 4+ looks at a global variable for event details, not a function argument.

Since the shout() function is declared in the <HEAD>, why put the JavaScript event handler assignment script elsewhere in the body? Because the browser works from the top of the HTML document down when displaying it to the user. This means some bits of the document, such as the text elements, appear before others. Before they appear, these elements don't exist, which would make it hard to assign event handlers to them. The assignment has to be done after the elements are created. Assigning handlers inside the element tag is the better method, because this problem is avoided and everything about the tag is in the one place. Here's an example of the page being tested. First, the page itself:

Secondly, the response from the event handler.

onError and Event Complications

Not all event handlers can be set in HTML tag attributes. The most notable exception is the onError event handler of Netscape 3.0 and 4.0. It can be set in the < IMG > tag using the ONERROR attribute. The event also occurs for windows and frames but there is no tag attribute to use. In those cases it must be set directly from a script. Again, the event model is described later in this chapter.

Secondly, Netscape 4.x supplies new event management routines in JavaScript: captureEvents(), releaseEvents(), routeEvent() and handleEvent(). In earlier versions, certain events fired certain event handlers, and that was it. With these new routines, those existing events can move to new places, firing handlers that previously wouldn't have taken part. This is a behavioral change, rather than a new place to put handlers.

Thirdly, Internet Explorer 4+ allows potential event handlers to be structured in a hierarchical manner, if the scriptwriter arranges it correctly. Events move up the hierarchy in a manner called **event bubbling**, starting with the most specific handler possible such as an individual HTML tag, and working up towards more general handlers such as window or document handlers. The event is disposed of when a potential event handler exists to receive the event. The handler is triggered, performs actions, and then may elect to stop the event from bubbling up any further.

Timer Events

There are ways of causing a JavaScript script to run other than with an HTML intrinsic event. The JavaScript function `setTimeout()` is an easy alternative:

```
<HTML><HEAD><SCRIPT>
function wake_up()
{
  alert('Fire, Flood, Famine!');            // Try to wake up the user.
  setTimeout('wake_up()', 2000);
}
setTimeout('wake_up()', 2000);              // 2000 milliseconds in the future
</SCRIPT></HEAD></HTML>
```

This page displays an alert box to the user every two seconds. The first time this occurred because the function wake_up() was scheduled in the second last line when the document was displayed. It reoccurred because the function reschedules itself just before it ends. The first argument to setTimeout() can be any valid JavaScript. If you run this example, you'll see that timers created with setTimeout() can be really irritating, but they're good at checking the state of a document or window, performing animation, or regularly reloading a document in case it has changed. This last case is a variant of '**client pull**' behavior where the browser regularly updates itself without the user doing anything. The setTimeout() function only acts once – if you want it to repeat you must reset it each time, as in this example, or change tactics and use a similar timer that does repeat, called setInterval().

Plug-in and ActiveX Events

Whenever plug-ins or ActiveX controls are engaged handling <EMBED> and <OBJECT> tags in HTML, JavaScript can also happen. This is because LiveConnect and ActiveX allow plugins and controls to run specific JavaScript functions or scripts. For Netscape, the <EMBED> tag must include the MAYSCRIPT attribute, or this kind of event won't be allowed. The special file type identified by these tags can actually contain bits of JavaScript script as part of its content. See Chapter 6 on Multimedia and Plugins for more details.

Java Exception Events

A mechanism similar to HTML events is to use Netscape's BeanConnect technology in Netscape 4.0 browsers. This allows JavaScript code to be invoked when a Java exception occurs in an applet, without a lot of extra effort required when the applet is written. Java exceptions are highly flexible things that can happen almost any time.

Microsoft Variations

Microsoft provides a bit of syntactic sugar to the JavaScript language that saves you from having to define and assign an event handler in two separate steps. This syntax allows you to prefix the function name with the name of the object it will be a method of (recall all functions are methods of some objects anyway). This works for Internet Explorer 4.0+

```
Function document.shouter.last.onchange()
{
. . . // same content
}
```

Of course this doesn't save you much if you need to assign the function to multiple handlers. There are other tactics you can use for that, but first you need to understand the way events are processed, see later in this chapter.

Other Oddities

`watch()` and `unwatch()` object methods are features aimed at easing JavaScript debugging, but they're only available in Netscape 4.0+ browsers. Apart from debugging, they do provide a general mechanism for calling an otherwise unconnected function when a plain object property has its value changed. This is not strictly an event-oriented mechanism. Chapter 17, Debugging illustrates the most common use of this feature.

Finally, Chapter 9 describes how dynamic updates to the browser's preferences can occur via JavaScript without any user interaction at all.

Adding JavaScript to News and E-mail Messages

Browsers at the 4.x+ level include the ability to send e-mail messages and news posts in HTML format. For Internet Explorer 4+, the e-mail client is Microsoft Outlook, or Outlook Express. Where HTML goes, JavaScript can go as well since the e-mail or newsreader that the message is read with contains a JavaScript interpreter and HTML renderer. Then the message in HTML format will run any JavaScript contained within it as would normally happen with an HTML-and-JavaScript web document. This raises a number of interesting possibilities which are reminiscent of Lotus Notes and other workflow style products:

- ❑ Including scripts that advise you when your e-mail has been read at the other end.
- ❑ Providing forms and surveys for readers to fill out.
- ❑ Demonstrating scripts to others.
- ❑ Producing multimedia messages, including 'spoken' audio messages.

The techniques to use here are the same as those for scripted HTML documents in general, which are covered in later chapters. If the reader of the message doesn't have a JavaScript/HTML enabled reader, all the JavaScript code and HTML tags will appear intermixed with the content intended for the reader – plain text is still the safest for e-mail and news conversations with the rest of the world.

Mixing JavaScript and VBScript

Microsoft's scripting architecture for Internet Explorer makes it possible to use a different language in each script block, simply by specifying the `language` attribute. It is then straightforward to call code in one language from another. At first glance these seems to be a great thing–and it used to be widely used–but today there are some alternatives you might want to consider before introducing the complexities of multiple languages. For example, you might want to mix languages to:

- ❑ Reuse code – If you have a library of code in one language, you can avoid having to rewrite it into another simply by calling across script blocks. Perhaps a better way to promote reuse, however, is to use DHTML or XML Scriptlets.

❑ Reuse skills – If different people on your team are trained in different languages, they can work together on the same page by mixing language calls. Of course, if you have enough code that this becomes an issue then the maintenance headaches from multiple languages might overshadow any savings.

❑ Leverage features not found in your "regular" language – Each interpreter has its own unique features and it can sometimes be worth the complexity of mixing languages to get at those features. Until fairly recently it was very worthwhile because, for example, VBScript didn't offer regular expressions and JScript didn't offer exception handling. In their latest releases both these shortcomings have been addressed and it's Microsoft's stated goal to make the languages functionally equivalent. But they still aren't quite equivalent so if you need these out-of-your-language features, you have a good reason to mix languages. We'll see two examples of this next.

It's important to keep in mind that mixing languages can extend to any interpreter on your machine that supports the IActiveScript interface. Depending on your situation, Perl or other languages that are available as ActiveX components can provide powerful facilities not directly available in JavaScript.

The example below calls VBScript from JScript to take advantage of its MsgBox function, which offers all the options available in a Win32 message box including changing the button names and displaying a message icon. These options go well beyond what a scriptwriter normally has available with the browser's built-in alert() and confirm() methods.

```
<HTML>
<HEAD>
<SCRIPT LANGUAGE="JScript">
<!--    //Define button values (same as VB/Win32 API MsgBox constants)

  var vbOK = 0;                        //Default is just an OK button
  var vbOKCancel = 1;                  //Display OK and Cancel buttons
  var vbAbortRetryIgnore = 2;          //Same for Abort, Retry, and Ignore
  var vbYesNoCancel = 3;               //...and so on
  var vbYesNo = 4;
  var vbRetryCancel = 5;

  //Define icons that show on message box
  var vbCritical = 16;                 //Display Critical Message (red X) icon
  var vbQuestion = 32;                 //Same for Warning Query icon.
  var vbExclamation = 48;              //...and so on
  var vbInformation = 64;
  var vbDefaultButton1 = 0;            //Make first button the default.
  var vbDefaultButton2 = 256;          //...and so on
  var vbDefaultButton3 = 512;
  var vbDefaultButton4 = 768;

  //Define "mode" of message box
  var vbApplicationModal = 0;      //Application modal; user must respond
                                   //before script continues. This is the default.
  var vbSystemModal = 4096;        //System modal--well not quite. Actually just
                                   //keeps message box "on top" of all other apps.

  function jsHandler() {
    //Call VB script to take advantage of better message box
    var iAns = vbsMessage(txtMessage.value,
                    vbYesNoCancel+vbQuestion, "Message from VBScript");
```

```
      //Example of how we might use returned value
      switch( iAns ) {
        case 1:          //OK
          alert("The user answered OK.");
          break;
        case 2:          //Cancel
          alert("The user wants to Cancel.");
          break;
        case 3:          //Abort
          alert("The user wants to Abort.");
          break;
        case 4:          //Retry
          alert("The user wants to Retry.");
          break;
        case 5:          //Ignore
          alert("The user wants to Ignore.");
          break;
        case 6:          //Yes
          alert("The user answered Yes.");
          break;
        case 7:          //no
          alert("The user answered No.");
          break;
        default:         //"Never" happens
          alert("We don't know what they want!");
          break;
      }
    }
//--></SCRIPT>

<SCRIPT LANGUAGE="VBScript"><!--

  Function vbsMessage( sMsg, iStyle, sTitle )
    vbsMessage = MsgBox( sMsg, iStyle, sTitle )
  End function
--></SCRIPT>

</HEAD>
<BODY>
<P>Enter your question here: <INPUT id=txtMessage></P>
<P><INPUT ID=cmdShowMe TYPE=button VALUE="Show Me" ONCLICK="jsHandler()"></P>

</BODY>
</HTML>
```

This example begins by defining some "constants" useful for the message box call. The mixed language call itself is very straightforward because all the primitive types map directly across. In fact the only common complexity in calling between these languages is VBScript's array type. JScript 3.0 introduced a special object (VBArray) to provide read-only access to VBScript arrays. For more on this special case, see the JScript documentation or http://msdn.microsoft.com/scripting/jscript/doc/jsobjVBArray.htm.

In addition to MsgBox, VBScript has a few other features that JScript writers will need to access in this way, at least until the next version of our beloved language. VBScript has better support for date and currency calculations, a handy RGB function, and really valuable formatting functions. Anyone who's ever fought with indexOf() and substring() to format a date or currency value will really appreciate these functions.

For an example of calling JScript from VBScript we need to stretch a little further, or simply go back a version of the language. If you are using a version of JScript prior to 3.0, then it's a good idea to wrap your JScript code in a VBScript procedure to take advantage of the latter's exception handling. For client-side code, if you have enough control over your users to know they are using IE, you might prefer to require IE4. This includes JScript 3.0 and hence lets you use its native `try..catch` mechanism. You might be stuck without version 3.0 however, if you are developing server side JScript for delivery on a server with IIS 3.0 or earlier.

Whatever the reason, if JScript 3.0 isn't available to you, something like the following could ensure you catch all errors:

```
<HTML>
<HEAD>
<SCRIPT LANGUAGE="JScript"><!--
  function jsHandler(){
    //The following statement won't work well!
    noSuchObj.missingProp = 2;
  }
//--></SCRIPT>

<SCRIPT LANGUAGE="VBScript"><!--
  ivbExclamation = 48

  'Wrap the JS handler in this nice safe VBS
  Function vbsHandler()
    On Error Resume Next

    jsHandler()
    If Err.number<> 0 Then
      msgbox "Sorry, we had an error", ivbExclamation
    End If
  End Function
'--></SCRIPT>

</HEAD>

<BODY>
<P>Click here to crash and burn:
<INPUT ID=cmdJS TYPE=button VALUE="Working Without a Net" ONCLICK="jsHandler()">
</P>
<P>Click here if you prefer to live safely:
<INPUT ID=cmdVBS TYPE=button VALUE="Nice and Safe" onclick="vbsHandler()">
</P>

</BODY>
</HTML>
```

In this example, we've purposely referenced a nonexistent object in the line

```
noSuchObj.missingProp = 2;
```

Depending on the user's setup of IE, they will get one of several error messages... possibly even offering to let them debug our code (never a good idea).

In contrast, the VBScript handler, which calls the same flawed JScript code, uses its 'On Error Resume Next' statement to catch the error and allow us to handle it slightly more elegantly.

For those familiar with Visual Basic for Applications or for Windows, please note VBScript doesn't support any of the other On Error variants so you can't say

```
On Error Goto X
```

You have to handle the error inline, as the example above shows. Unfortunately it's a little tough to write a general purpose VBScript error-handler because prior to version 5.0 as it didn't have the equivalent of an eval() function.

Mainstream Browser Event Models

Web browsers were originally designed to display plain HTML and that was all. Handling of user input via HTML intrinsic events is a more recent innovation. Client-side languages like JavaScript came after HTML, and for earlier browsers it shows. It is only with advent of the 4.0 browsers that event handling mechanisms are organized in a general and flexible way.

Microsoft and Netscape use different capitalization for event handler names. We're using the Netscape version here. Just convert to all-lowercase for the Microsoft equivalent.

The Good Old Days That Weren't So Good

In the simplest model for events, an event occurs, a handler fires and when it completes, then the event is over. Possibly the browser might do something afterwards. This is broadly how Netscape and Microsoft 3.0 browsers work. It's worth looking at these old browsers first, because the number of events in the version 4+ browsers are quite overwhelming. The events that appeared at the 3.0 level are the ones needed for the simplest and commonest scripting tasks, so they're a good place to start before diving in more deeply. Here is a list of those events:

Event Name	Action causing the event	After effect when event finishes
onAbort	User stops a page loading before an image in the page is complete.	Image cannot be fully displayed.
onBlur	Move the cursor from a text field or select list, click a different form element or raise a different browser window.	Input focus moves to the other window or form element.
onChange	Fill-in field or select menu item is changed and user then goes to another field.	Field or menu has a new value, field no longer has the input focus.
onClick	Click a hypertext link or any button-like object in a form, and this event fires.	Any action attached to the button occurs, e.g. form submission, form reset, or in the case of a link, navigation to a new URL.

Table Continued on Following Page

Event Name	Action causing the event	After effect when event finishes
onError	Bad JavaScript script or bad image in Netscape.	Interpreting of the script / loading of the image stops; error message.
onFocus	As for onBlur, except the event occurs on the thing moved to.	As for onBlur. In the case of a text field it is now ready for user input.
onLoad	HTML document or an image finishes loading.	All of the document/image is now readable. All JavaScript script has loaded.
onMouseOut	Mouse pointer moves over a link.	Status bar updates.
onMouseOver	Mouse pointer moves off a link.	Status bar resets.
onReset	Reset-style form button clicked.	Form's elements are unset.
onSubmit	Submit-style form button clicked.	Form is submitted; web page is replaced.
onUnload	Window closed or new URL navigated to by any means.	All HTML objects and JavaScript scripts in the page are wiped away.

These events, especially the ones that have to do with forms are very straightforward. If you have a modern browser, version 4.0+ then you can learn a great deal quite quickly just experimenting with these events. Try playing with this page:

```
<HTML><BODY><FORM>
<INPUT TYPE=text ONCHANGE="this.value=this.value.toUpperCase(); return true;">
<BR>
<INPUT TYPE=text ONCHANGE="this.value=this.value.toLowerCase(); return true;">
</FORM></BODY></HTML>
```

However, even for the older version 3.0 browsers, the simple table shown is not really sufficient. This second table shows that for some events, more than one handler of the same type might fire:

Event Name	3.0 handlers that might fire	User action that fires multiple handlers
onBlur	Frame, window, text and password fields.	Click on a different frame or window.
onError	Frame, window, image. (NC3 only)	Load a document containing a bad image.
onFocus	Frame, window, text and password fields.	Click on a field in a different frame. Click on a field or frame in a different window.

Table Continued on Following Page

Event Name	3.0 handlers that might fire	User action that fires multiple handlers
onLoad	Frame, window, image.	Load a document or frameset.
onReset	Reset button, form. (NC3 only)	Clear a form.
onSubmit	Submit button, form. (NC3 only)	Submit a form.

For these browsers there is little you can do to control this behavior, except avoid using specific combinations of handlers. Chapter 7 on Forms and Data and Chapter 17 on Debugging collect some wisdom on how to manage these events. The Appendices list every event by object.

If the situation is nontrivial for version 3.0 browsers, it follows that if more events or more features are added to the browser, something has to happen to give more control to the scriptwriter.

Event Innovations In 4.0 Browsers

The enhancements chosen by Microsoft and Netscape, the two main 4.0 browser vendors aren't that different in their overall functionality, but they do differ in the specific details.

When all the details (and learning) regarding event features for a given vendor are lumped into a pile, that pile is big enough that committing to a single browser suddenly seems very attractive. If you are concerned about portability, you need to make a deliberate decision at the start to keep it simple, or else you will be locked into a particular browser in no time.

Modern Events

The HTML 4.0 standard mandates a set of intrinsic events and these are supported to a lesser or greater degree by both 4.0 browsers. You can download the standard for HTML 4.0 by going to the www.w3c.org Website. In addition to the events already specified in the 3.0 browsers, there are ten general user input events that apply to every tag in the HTML document. These are: onKeyPress, onKeyup, onKeyDown, onClick, onDblClick, onMouseOver, onMouseOut, onMouseMove, onMouseDown and onMouseUp.

For Internet Explorer 4.0 and 5.0, these events are supported as described by the standard. Microsoft has gone to further lengths with their event processing model, describing the exact order in which events fire when multiple events occur.

For Netscape Navigator 4.0, only some objects support all these events. The ones that do are windows, frames, layers and link objects (the <A> tag with the HREF attribute set and the <AREA> tag are link objects). The onMouseMove handler is supported only via JavaScript, not via HTML tag attributes for that browser.

Both browsers support events beyond the HTML 4.0 standard. Netscape 4.0 supports only three: onResize, onDragDrop and onMove. Internet Explorer 4+ supports a multitude. Refer to the specific browser documentation – the detail is beyond this book's scope.

Netscape's lack of support for the ten user input events could be partially worked around by exploiting the support that is present for links. This example illustrates:

```
<HTML><HEAD>
  <STYLE TYPE="text/css">
     A:link { text-decoration: none; color: none }
  </STYLE>
</HEAD>
<BODY>
  Normal text
  <A HREF="http://localhost/" ONCLICK="return false;"
                              ONDBLCLICK="return false;">
     <STRONG>Interesting part <P> with tags<P></STRONG>
  </A>
  Normal text
</BODY></HTML>
```

If any mouse events are required for the <STRONG> tag, then use the event handlers of the surrounding <A> tag, as shown above. Key press and click events can be captured by the window and passed to <A> tag handlers as well – see the discussion further on event hierarchy. Generally speaking, Internet Explorer 4.0 and 5.0 have a much richer event model than Netscape 4.x.

Additional Structure

For Internet Explorer and Netscape 3.0 browsers, event handlers are organized in a common pool: when an event occurs, all the appropriate handlers in the pool are fired. In the 4.0 browsers, handlers are stored in a hierarchy that dictates which handler is the first candidate for a given event. An event may pass through several handlers, but if so, there is a definite order. Since event handlers are properties of JavaScript host objects, the hierarchy follows the browser's specific object model.

The crucial difference between Netscape and Microsoft implementations is that for Netscape, events travel down the hierarchy, for Microsoft they travel up. The Microsoft approach has been adopted by the DOM (Document Object Model) standard:

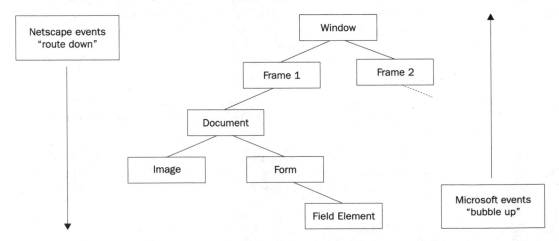

Not all events can flow through the hierarchy. Many of the Internet Explorer 4.0 event handlers, for example, are attached to specific objects. If the matching event occurs, either that object's handler or no handler at all will be called.

Not all objects in the hierarchy are exploited when an event flows through the structure. In the Navigator 4.0 case, only "large" objects like windows, layers and documents get a chance, plus any item at the bottom of the tree that the user interacted with to cause the event in the first place.

Additional Objects

As well as new event handlers and better organized event handlers, the 4.0 browsers also provide more event information. A new JavaScript object called the **Event object** (Netscape) or **event** (Microsoft) stores this data.

The event object is handled differently in the two browsers. In the Microsoft case, there is only one event object per browser window. All the event handlers must refer to this object. In the Netscape case, an event object is created for each event and is passed to the handler as an argument. This table gives an at-a-glance comparison of the two styles of event object:

IE 4.0 window.event properties	NC 4.0 Event object properties
User input:	
type	type
altKey, ctrlKey, shiftKey, keyCode, button	which, modifiers
Graphical position of event:	
screenX, screenY,	screenX, screenY,
clientX, clientY, offsetX, offsetY, x, y	layerX, layerY, pageX, pageY
Items marked out by mouse movements:	
fromElement, toElement	data
Progress and control information:	
reason, returnValue, cancelBubble	a separate routing mechanism is available that uses captureEvents(), releaseEvents(), routeEvent() and handleEvent()
Document element originating the event:	
srcElement, srcFilter	target
Special constants	
	MOUSEDOWN, MOUSEUP, CLICK, KEYDOWN, KEYUP, KEYPRESS, etc

You can make a JavaScript function that inspects such an object and acts as a general event handler. This is a good way to illustrate how the browsers differ. For Internet Explorer 4.0 such a handler looks like this:

```
function handy_event_handler()
{
  if ( window.event.type == "click" )
  {
    // do click stuff ...
    return true;
  }
  // and so on for other possibilities...
  return false
}
```

For Netscape Navigator 4.0, such a handler looks like this:

```
function handy_event_handler(new_event)
{
  if ( new_event.type == "click" )
  {
    // do click stuff ...
    return true;
  }
  // and so on for other possibilities...
  return false
}
```

For both browsers, a portable handler that works for simple handler tasks only:

```
function handy_event_handler(netscape_event)
{
  var real_event;
  real_event = (netscape_event) ? netscape_event : window.event;

  if ( real_event.type == "click" )
  {
    // do click stuff ...
    return true;
  }
  // and so on for other possibilities...
  return false
}
```

Managing Events in the Handler Hierarchy

If a given document has no event handlers, then all the event flow and structure provided by the browser has no effect. So, leaving event handlers out is a good way to avoid complexity. This isn't very practical if you are designing a highly interactive page.

If you restrict yourself to handlers that are attached to the most-specific HTML tags only, you avoid event flow effects up or down the hierarchy and still get to receive events. In this case you are operating in a similar manner to the 3.0 browser event model, except more events are possible.

If you need to use events at several levels of the object model, the real differences between Netscape and Microsoft show up. A different approach must be adopted for each brand if you want to fully exploit the object hierarchy. The general strategy for each browser type can be described this way:

❑ Microsoft events means mouse-catching: what mice you catch depends on where you put your traps, so lay traps and wait. What events you handle depends on where you put event handlers.

❑ Netscape events means traffic-policing: Where cars go depends on where you send them, so actively direct those you see. Which event handlers are invoked depends on where you direct events.

Microsoft

Managing events for Microsoft's 4.0 browser proceeds in the familiar pattern of previous browsers, so there's nothing radical to learn. When events proceed through handlers in the new event hierarchy, they do so one at a time – only one handler is active at any time. Two of the new properties of the `window.event` object need to be particularly borne in mind:

❑ `cancelBubble`. This property is a `true`/`false` value that controls what happens to the event after the current handler has finished. If you want the current handler to be the last one that services the event caught, set this property to `true`. Beware that Microsoft documentation says that a few events cannot be cancelled! This example illustrates canceling, it displays MIDDLE and INNER alert boxes only:

```
<HTML><BODY>
<DIV ONCLICK="alert('OUTER'); return true;">
  <DIV ONCLICK="alert('MIDDLE'); window.event.cancelBubble=true; return true;">
  <DIV ONCLICK="alert('INNER'); window.event.cancelBubble=false; return true;">
    Click Me
  </DIV>
  </DIV>
</DIV>
</BODY></HTML>
```

❑ `returnValue`. This property is a `true`/`false` value that controls whether the normal action of the event occurs (for example, submitting a form or navigating a link). Beware that actions of some events cannot be stopped, such as the unloading of a document associated with an `onUnLoad` event. The action for an event occurs after the last handler has finished. It is the `return` value of that last handler that normally dictates whether the action will happen, as for 3.0 browsers. This presents a problem if an earlier handler wants to have a say in the event's ultimate impact. The `returnValue` property provides an override mechanism for those earlier handlers. If it is ever set to `true` or `false`, so that it is no longer undefined, its value is used regardless of the `return` value of the last handler. This example will not follow the link even though all handlers return `true`, although it will pop up an alert box:

```
<HTML><BODY>
<A HREF="about:blank" ONCLICK="alert('A tag'); return true;">
 <DIV ONCLICK="alert('DIV tag'); window.event.returnValue=false; return true;">
Click Me
</DIV>
</A>
</BODY></HTML>
```

The bubbling and event action mechanisms are separate and don't affect each other.

Netscape

For Netscape, ordinary event handlers proceed in the same pattern as for 3.0 browsers, but the advanced features require a whole new concept. This concept is that window, document and layer objects can be interposed between the user and the object that an event is normally associated with, such as a button. The event may then be handled by this interposed object first. A general term for this kind of behavior is **filtering**, but it's just as easy to think of it as events arriving at the top of the document object model first, as described above. To do this requires three steps:

1. **Create handlers for the interposing object.** It is better to create and assign these directly in JavaScript, because their meaning in the web page is not as trivial as typical event handlers. When one of these handlers is called and then finishes, that is the end of all event processing for that event. Therefore, the return value of that handler dictates whether the event's action is canceled or not, as for earlier browser versions. If tag attributes are not used to define these handlers, the appropriate properties of the window, document or layer object must be assigned to.

2. **Start collecting events.** An interposed object does not automatically use these new handlers. The special function `captureEvents()` must be used to determine which events an interposed object will collect. The sole argument is a bitwise-OR'ed list of constants. These constants are similar to other JavaScript constants such as `Math.PI`. They represent the ten general user input events specified by HTML 4.0. `Event.MOUSEUP | Event.MOUSEDOWN | Event.KEYPRESS` is an example of three values bitwise-OR'ed together. Only the events specified in the bitmask are affected by the use of this function. The matching function `releaseEvents()` stops an interposed object from collecting events.

3. **Decide routing policy.** Once the interposed object is collecting events, those events will never be forwarded to their original destination (such as a form element) unless extra efforts are made. These efforts takes the form of two methods: `routeEvent()` and `handleEvent()`. A call to `routeEvent()` from within an event handler tells the browser to suspend the current handler, call other handlers that are involved and then return back to the point of suspension. So `routeEvent()` provides the mechanism for events to "route down" the object hierarchy. This behavior means handlers are **nested** – one handler is invoked from inside another. The other function `handleEvent()` is more radical. It is a method of the Window and Document (not Layer) objects. If such an object's method is called from within another handler then the event is passed to that object directly, ignoring any other objects expecting the event, and ignoring the normal hierarchy entirely.

Here is an example of two frames that illustrate a simple case of `handleEvent()`. To see it happen, click in either frame. All that this example does is to interpose a window between the two documents that each occupy on of the frames in the window. This is like putting two diamonds behind bulletproof glass – first you have to get through the glass. To illustrate `routeEvent()`, add a button to each frame with an `onClick` handler, and change `top.first.handleEvent(e)` to read `routeEvent(e)`.

```
<!-- frameset.htm -->
<HTML>
<FRAMESET ROWS="*,*">
<FRAME NAME="first" SRC="anyframe.htm">
<FRAME NAME="second" SRC="anyframe.htm">
</FRAMESET>
</HTML>
```

```
<!-- anyframe.htm -->
<HTML><BODY><SCRIPT>

document.write('This is the frame named "'+self.name+'"');  // visible content

function handle_it(e)                    // ordinary event handler, e is the event
{
  alert("Caught by frame: " + window.name);
  if ( window.name == "first" )
    alert("Preventing infinite loop");
  else
    return top.first.handleEvent(e);
  return true;
}

window.onMouseDown = handle_it;                              // assign handler
window.captureEvents(Event.MOUSEDOWN);  // in this case, filter just one event

</SCRIPT></BODY></HTML>
```

There is one complication that is due to frames. A frame might display a URL from a web site that is different to the website of the frameset document. A security hobble prevents parent documents from capturing that frame's events (more on this in Chapter 5). However, if the parent document and its scripts are signed or otherwise secure, the methods window.enableExternalCapture() and window.disableExternalCapture() can be used to free up or re-impose this restriction.

Other JavaScript-Enabled Browsers

In their most basic forms, HTML and JavaScript aren't complicated technologies to implement on software. There are dozens and dozens of web browsers now. Therefore it should be no surprise that the number of browsers supporting JavaScript is expanding ...although these other browsers don't have large market share. It's broadening to briefly consider the full landscape of possibilities before we return to the labor of learning the major browsers and their JavaScript inside and out. Who knows –particular features of these eclectic browsers might be especially suited to the task you have in mind.

Personal Computer Browsers

Before the World Wide Web and the browser sprang into existence as a source of digital entertainment, there was the personal computer. Personal computer these days generally means an Intel-based Microsoft Windows computer, but there are other personal, or home computers out there. Browsers and platforms vary, but JavaScript appears much the same across several of them.

Opera

Not many people achieve fame by being third, but Opera Software appears to have done it. Their JavaScript support is at the Netscape Navigator 3.0 level. The main version of their browser runs on Microsoft Windows and operates in MDF (multi-document format) as illustrated below, or it can run with free, floating windows like the other major browsers.

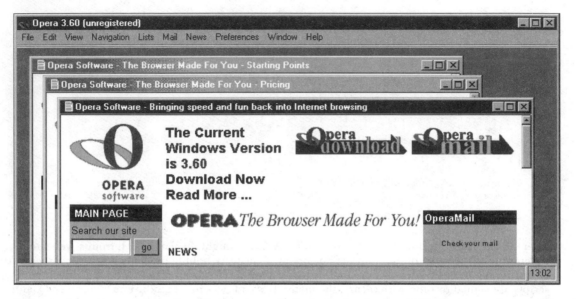

Why would you worry about JavaScript compatibility with this browser? There are a only a couple of niche reasons. Firstly, their browser still fits on a single floppy disk – the only browser that does and still supports JavaScript. So if you are supplying web files for someone to read on a disk, and if they display correctly with Opera, you can supply the whole browser on the disk as well – useful for mail-out programs. Secondly, Opera's so-called Project Magic shows the company's enthusiasm for porting the browser to every obscure computer under the sun. If you are a company of one serving a tiny market niche like the Amiga, then it probably pays to construct your scripts to support this browser, since that's what your customers will use. Finally, one possibly novel feature of Opera is its accessible keyboard support – every operation can be done from the keyboard. For automated testing of Web pages, this might make your life easier and provide you with a compatibility guarantee for pages developed mostly under IE.

Opera may need to weather some fierce competition from Netscape 5.0, which has stated design goals of 'fast and small like Opera, but better'. Only time will tell how well this company survives. Opera is downloadable from www.opera.com.

NeoPlanet

Another interesting PC browser is NeoPlanet, www.neoplanet.com. Instead of being written from nothing, this browser consists of the core of Netscape 5.0 *and* the core of Internet Explorer 4+. Using a simple button, you can view a given web page exactly as either major browser would display it. Because of this design, NeoPlanet doesn't give you much that is new, except possibly some amazingly subtle JavaScript compatibility bugs. However, they're working on giving you more features, and what they do give you is the chance to brighten the appearance of your browser up with some graphical magic, resulting in a look and feel (and sound) that seems more like a computer game than anything else. Here's an example of one of the many appearances of their browser – pretty slick, even before you start surfing, as is shown in this image.

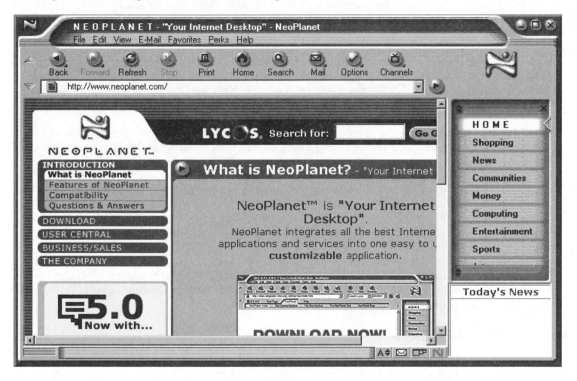

Not everything has to be concrete; if it's style over content for you, then NeoPlanet could be your thing.

Be

Be is a European hardware and software company that produces a personal computer called the BeBox aimed at the Multimedia market. Learning from experience gained at Apple, their computer has architecture optimized for fast multimedia formats like video, and attracts developers interested in those kinds of applications. To the ordinary user, it's still a point-and-click window-based (not Windows based) environment, so Be has a JavaScript capable browser. Unfortunately our research hasn't extended to any analysis of its worth, but if you are curious, have a look at www.be.com.

Ant

Similar to the BeBox, but older is the Acorn computer, now based on a RISCOS platform, popular as an educational computer in the UK. Tiny Ant Limited at www.ant.co.uk have produced a web browser for that computer with JavaScript support called Fresco. If you want to produce enhanced web pages for British school kids, perhaps you'd better have a look at what they've done.

Netscape Variants

It's worth briefly noting the group at www.mozilla.org who are developing Netscape 5.0. Their approach is sometimes confusing because they use a variety of nicknames for their browser, or the browser project, or the technologies in the browser. SeaMonkey, NGLayout, Mozilla, Gemini, Raptor and Navigator are roughly all the same thing – effort surrounding Netscape's flagship browser product.

The only thing that this group currently produces which could be considered a separate browser is the Gecko test software. Gecko is a facility for developers that let them test some of the new technologies in Netscape 5.0. By the time you read this, Netscape 5.0 will probably be available. You can download the current beta versions or just Gecko and have a fiddle if you are curious.

The Mozilla version-in-development of JavaScript is currently 1.5. This version introduces very few changes over 1.4 to date, the most obvious being tighter integration with the Java component of the browser.

Beyond the Mozilla organization are a couple of loosely related projects. The Cryptozilla project, being based outside the U.S.A. (in Australia) is not subject to the export restrictions that Netscape is. They've taken the Netscape browser source and put back strong (140-bit) encryption into it, so you can get the identical browser from their web site with better encryption if you want it. See www.cryptozilla.org.

Vastly more speculative are Internet discussions with regard to browsers named Jazilla and Jozilla respectively – noble plans to provide Netscape-like browsers written entirely in Java. Don't hold your breath waiting for these to deliver.

Apple, Unix and Others

The Apple and various Unix platforms are covered by the major browsers from Microsoft and Netscape. The major Unix platforms, Sun, HP, and Linux are supported by Netscape and Opera.

Set-Top Browsers

Not everyone in the industrialized world has a PC at home, but nearly everyone has a television and a telephone. If set-top boxes can give consumers access to cable TV or satellite TV, then why not to the Web and the Internet? Just plug the phone into the set-top box, add some software and away you go. There are several examples of browsers with JavaScript support that run on set-top boxes today, and they're worth a quick look. But before doing so, consider the implications of set-top technology.

The set-top and TV environment is a different one to that of the home computer. First, there is the technology – until we are shortly blessed with high definition digital television at a price mere humans can afford, all we have is an old TV set. That set has was designed for very low resolution compared with a computer monitor – just several hundred by several hundred pixels. Some fancy processing can smarten it up a bit, but there's still limits imposed by the surface of the picture tube. The bandwidth of an ordinary TV station's signal is low, and particularly bad in the U.S.A, which doesn't encourage picture tube makers to over-engineer much. Next, (especially) old TV screens are *designed* to be blurry – each pixel blends into the next one in order to create "natural" tones. Anyone who has used supertext subtitles for the hearing impaired or looked at the weather on the original TV hypertext systems know how big and chunky the text has to be in order to be both sharp and readable. Next, in a TV picture tube the intensity varies from color to color, whereas a computer monitor has a "flatter" response. This can result in bright colors "washing out" dimmer ones. All these effects impose severe constraints on what images, text, and layout you can get away with in a web page and still have it look good on a TV screen. Finally, instead of a keyboard and a mouse, there's just this remote control thingy – definitely no one wants to squat within arm's reach of the screen fiddling with the buttons in order to search the Web.

Beyond the limits of technology is the user. Your original TV couch potato has different expectations to a computer user when first hooking up to the Internet via a set-top browser. In particular, lots of typing is out, lots of passive entertainment is in – further constraints on the content provided. That remote control is fiddly to work with, and so the user doesn't want to be navigating and scrolling all over the place, which is more than likely given that you can't cram much HTML on his screen at a time.

All that aside, a set-top box is cheaper than a PC and there's enough demand for many companies to be working in the area. Set-top boxes have use outside the home too – in information kiosks and possibly in rugged environments where a PC made of delicate parts isn't welcome.

WebTV

WebTV is the best known and first visible set-top Web browser. Just like the major browsers, you get an email client as well as HTML. Supposedly with over a million users, WebTV is obviously quite popular. You can have a look at their site here: www.webtv.com.

The JavaScript support in WebTV is about at the Netscape 3.0 level. For HTML authors and script developers, the company provides set-top box emulation software that you can download and run for free on your web browser. This is just a browser that acts exactly like the set-top browser. The sole exception is that the emulator displays pages more clearly because the computer screen is better than the TV tube. Here is a picture of the main window:

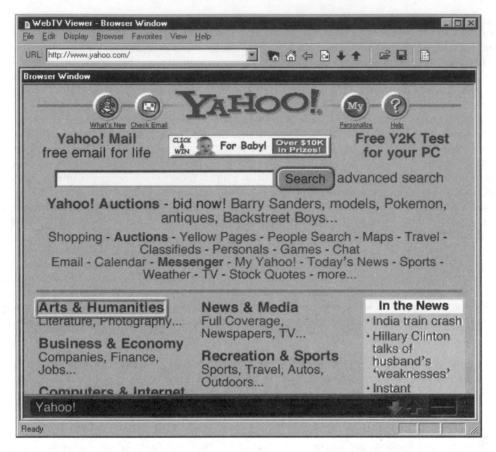

In the real set-top browser, there are no menus, window borders or toolbars – all you get to work with is the area inside the inner window named "Browser Window". This inner window can't be resized. The bright box around "Arts and Humanities" is what a hypertext link looks like – a single underline is too hard to see on a TV.

The second window of this browser looks like this:

This is the remote control that a real user has in their hand. By clicking the direction arrows, the user can move the bright box from link to link.

What does it all mean for JavaScript? Your JavaScript enhanced page may work on WebTV if you use only basic Netscape 3.0 features of the language and object model. The set-top box can't handle floating point numbers in JavaScript, and it can't open extra windows, so no `alert()` or `window.open()` – these are described in later chapters. The WebTV website has some documentation on what's in and what's out.

What the set-top box loses in compatibility it gains in its own fancy enhancements. Specifically, it has a markup language in addition to HTML called TVML. Between TVML, HTML and JavaScript, you can integrate live TV channels and static web pages together for some very fancy audio-visual results that are still difficult to achieve smoothly on a personal computer.

Finally, here's a screenshot of a great web site that looks lousy on WebTV:

This is a very crowded page for a low-resolution TV screen. The images down the left-hand and right-hand sides of the pages would be unreadable, because of their tiny text. Although they're advertising, a reader of this site would likely want to follow those images to explore their contents. Remember this is a picture of the emulator, not the real thing, and so is also artificially clear. At least the site designer hasn't elected to use fancy fonts, which would be completely lost in the set-top browser. Note the bright squares in the top right hand corner – the user would have to navigate with the remote control some distance before any of the news items' links could be reached. Great site, and it's fortunate that WebTV isn't hugely popular.

EnReach Technologies

EnReach Technologies at www.enreach.com aren't a consumer electronics company like WebTV. Instead, they are one step further down the development chain. Their set-top browser is a development kit that other companies can purchase and embed in a set-top device. Several companies have already done this. Here's a screen shot of their browser environment at work:

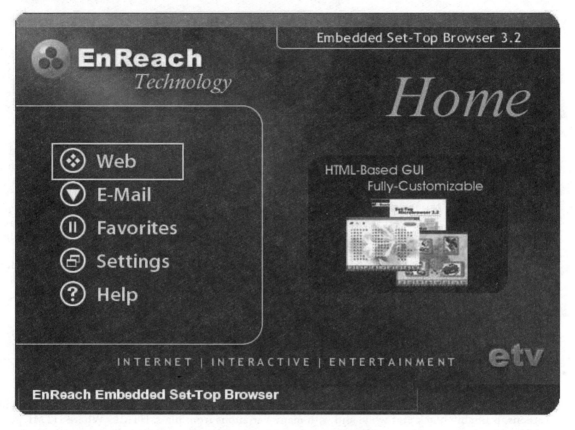

Unlike the WebTV pictures this is more like the actual TV image. Notice the lack of any form of navigation except icons and large text within the page – this really forces the Web page designer and client side scriptwriter to think about navigation.

Just like WebTV, the EnReach browser supports JavaScript to the Netscape 3.0 level. What's particularly interesting about this browser is that while some of its functionality is fixed, like the features that display HTML code and that do the Internet connection, others are not. In particular, the set-top browser is extendable – a developer embedding it in a set-top device can add other features like an e-mail client, a chat client or a news ticker for example. How are these features developed? In special JavaScript scripts which are put into the set-top box along with the browser. So not only can the browser act on JavaScript embedded in HTML pages, it is also partially made out of JavaScript scripts itself. Alas, this is far too narrow a field to get any further attention in this book.

Acorn

Finally in the set-top market, Acorn computers, developers of the Acorn PC also have a set-top browser with JavaScript support. See www.acorn.com for more details. Obviously, writing an HTML browser and adding JavaScript is not particularly difficult, and we can expect to see more variety still in JavaScript capable browsers in the future.

Really Different Browsers

A JavaScript enabled browser, whether in a PC or a set-top box, is nevertheless much the same thing. However, there are some even stranger places where JavaScript is found that we could still qualify as browsers, provided we broaden our minds a bit.

Adobe Acrobat

When people think of the PDF file format invented by Adobe, they usually think of a friendly, portable document format that can be used to display documents nicely and which provides good quality printouts. The Adobe Acrobat Reader is the free tool most people use for viewing PDF files.

However, the original design goals of the PDF format and the Acrobat Reader included some Web browser like features – hypertext links are the most obvious one, followed by incremental download from a remote site. However, the format also supports forms embedded in PDF documents. Where there's forms there's form data, and where there's form data there's user data entry mistakes and the need for validation. JavaScript code embedded in the document and an interpreter in the Reader software allows this validation to take place. You'll never see this JavaScript, unless you buy the full set of document preparation tools from Adobe – just Adobe Acrobat and Distiller isn't sufficient.

WAP

Our run down of JavaScript-enabled browsers wouldn't be complete without a nod of the head to WAP. What's a WAP? WAP stands for Wireless Application Protocol. The WAP consortium at www.wapforum.org is responsible for minting a collection of standards that will let users of handheld devices like PalmPilots and mobile phones access the Web.

At the end of these standards will be web browsers inside handheld devices with very small resolution screens, probably black and white and with many variations from plain HTML. Where HTML goes, so goes JavaScript, except the WAP consortium aren't happy with the ECMAScript standard (they thought it was too big for a handheld device). Instead, they went off and defined WAPScript – a new standard for a cut-down tiny version of JavaScript that will run in your new satellite pocket calculator and other grown-up toys. Never fear ... testing your ordinary Web-based JavaScript script's compatibility against a Nokia mobile phone is not something you'll need to do in any hurry.

Thus completes our roundup of browsers supporting JavaScript.

Browser Compatibility

If Internet Explorer and Netscape browsers were identical, scriptwriters would be saved a lot of worry. With increased support for standards, the differences when scripting basic tasks are becoming smaller and smaller, but still one has to be wary. Here we review versions and discuss strategies for handling differences.

Mainstream Browser Version Review

A mainstream browser is just one with a big share of the market. At August 1999, choosing a mainstream browser means choosing between Internet Explorer 4.0 or 5.0 and Netscape Navigator or Communicator 4.0 or 4.5 or 4.6. According to the Mozilla website, version 5.0 of the Mozilla browser, which is Communicator 5.0, will be released around the end of 1999.

Even within just one of the two major vendors, there are plenty of subtleties between versions, so let's briefly recap the versions and any broad JavaScript differences that might apply.

Navigator and Communicator Versions

The original Netscape 1.0 browser was based on the Mosaic browser developed by the academic and research community. It had no JavaScript support.

Netscape introduced JavaScript with version 2.0 of the Navigator product. There was no Communicator. With that release the core language and common host objects in the browser took on the basic form that they have kept ever since. However, many tiny features were changed in subsequent releases, and version 2.0 is just a memory now. This version of JavaScript was labeled 1.0.

Version 3.0 of Navigator cleaned up the language and slightly enhanced the browser object model from 2.0, establishing a de facto standard for the JavaScript language. This version was used as the basis of the ECMAScript standard, although this browser never complied with that standard. The version was labeled JavaScript 1.1.

The basic set of browser objects and events made available in 3.0 was significant because it is the minimal set that a browser can implement in order for its JavaScript support to be of basic use. This is still important because it is to this level that most of the more obscure browsers attempt to support JavaScript. It is also important because sticking to this limited set of features is a useful way of ensuring that Web pages stay simple enough that the blind and other disabled folk can still make use of the Web. Of course, the HTML as well as the JavaScript must be sympathetically designed for the pages to be sensible.

Netscape 4.0 introduced Communicator as the first non-free browser, and a free version of Navigator. The browser was becoming quite large. With the earliest versions of 4.0, such as 4.01, the free Navigator client did not have e-mail support, which was decried by the public, and soon changed with a new minor release. Communicator was subsequently declared free as well. Important JavaScript innovations for this version involved HTML+JavaScript support in mail and news items, and JavaScript support for stylesheet objects. This version of JavaScript was labeled 1.2.

With this release, Netscape started to slip behind Internet Explorer in functionality. The way the browser processed HTML made it hard for the Netscape programmers to provide full support for Dynamic HTML, and an unusual processing innovation in the event model failed to take off. Version 5.0 removes both these obstacles. The tiny increments in version, such as 4.01 and 4.02 mostly reflect security fixes that forced a new browser release.

Netscape 4.06 was an important minor version. There were new features released, such as ECMAScript standard compliance fixes in the JavaScript interpreter, and access to new objects such as `document.crypto`. This version was labeled JavaScript 1.3.

Simultaneously with 4.06, Netscape released version 4.5, again with JavaScript 1.3, but the primary difference between 4.5 and 4.0 was the bundling of MacroMedia Flash with the installation plus some support in e-mail for IMAP and LDAP protocols. These enhancements continued through 4.6 and onwards, but there was no change to the JavaScript language, and only a little to the objects it could access.

4.0 and 4.x versions continue to be released in minor versions that contain bug fixes only – at the time of writing 4.08 and 4.61 are the latest versions.

Internet Explorer Versions

If Internet Explorer 1.0 and 2.0 existed, they were lost in the hysteria surrounding Netscape. There was no JavaScript support in those versions.

Internet Explorer 3.0 was released in great haste, and it showed. Its JavaScript support, available for the first time, was labeled JScript 1.0 and was awful, especially for event handling. It was rapidly followed by 3.01 and 3.02, the latter of which contained JScript 3.0. By that stage, the JScript language was in good order, but the events and objects in the browser still weren't. Internet Explorer 3.0 tried to meet the Netscape 3.0 level of JavaScript functionality, very roughly. JScript could be upgraded separately via a web download, which created all kinds of configuration confusion for some. In typical Microsoft style, those early versions have disappeared without a trace from the Microsoft web sites.

With Internet Explorer 4.0, Microsoft exceeded Netscape's functionality (and browser size). The primary enhancement was good Dynamic HTML support – access to all the objects making up an HTML page from JavaScript. With JScript 5.0 and WSH released separately (JScript 4.0 only appeared in a particular commercial product bundle), Microsoft was first to claim ECMAScript functionality in a browser, and first to provide a browser that could also be used as a software object from a programming language. JScript 5.0 also was first to provide exception handling functionality.

The event model in IE 4.0 has been adopted by the Web standards body, W3C for the DOM – the Document Object Model Standard. Other features of IE4.0 also influenced standards such as HTML 4.0 and related stylesheet standards.

With the 4.0 browser, Microsoft caught up with Netscape in terms of browser market share. Around the time of this release, JavaScript in the form of JScript also achieved the status of a general scripting language on the Windows platform, although not as functional or as thoroughly supported as the mighty Visual Basic, or its cut-down version VBScript. Microsoft also released a service pack, IE4.0 SP1 for the browser, bringing the final 4.0 version to 4.01.

Microsoft continues to blur the line between a browser, an operating system with a graphical interface, and a set of development components with the release of Internet Explorer 5.0. In order to be sure of having an exact version of Internet Explorer, one must now have full configuration control over the MS-Windows installation, as the functionality between the browser and the operating system rely on many common elements. JavaScript's access to many Windows-related features new in IE5.0 is no more special than any programming language used on that platform.

Compatibility Techniques

Unfortunately, JavaScript browsers are not unequal but different as well. Netscape and Microsoft have been diverging in their advanced features as fast as possible in order to obtain a loyal customer base. Today's advanced features are tomorrow's backwards-compatibility nightmares.

Handling compatibility requires a two pronged attack: **readership strategies** and **technical tricks**.

Choose Readers

If you only intend to use JavaScript to set browser preferences, then readership isn't much of an issue. However, JavaScript is mostly embedded in HTML documents. Who is going to try and read these pages? Answer these questions and avoid masses of work being tripped up by compatibility issues.

❑ Are non-JavaScript browsers important? If so, don't bother with JavaScript at all. Once JavaScript 'infects' HTML, the HTML becomes very quickly reliant on it. Forms relying on JavaScript can still be submitted from plain browsers even though the JavaScript is ignored, which can have unexpected results.

❑ Are non-JavaScript browsers possible? If random web surfers can view your page, your page needs to 'gracefully downgrade' to readable plain HTML when viewed by them, with special care for forms.

❑ Do you control the browser version? In an Intranet application used only within one company, all users may have the same browser. It's then safe to use all features of that version, provided you are willing to upgrade your work if the browser version changes.

If none of the above are the case, then you are left with multiple JavaScript/browser versions to handle. You can still simplify matters, provided you don't mind losing some readership or having your content look bad in unexpected places:

❑ Ignore really old browsers. In late 1999, according to one poll, less than 1% of web surfers use Navigator 2.02.

❑ Support latest browsers only. This will cut down testing to one browser per vendor, but loses you a significant part of the readership, especially if latest versions are newly minted.

❑ Advocate one brand only. This cuts compatibility to one (or more) version. If your subject matter appeals mostly to users of one browser, for example Unix or Macintosh, don't bother with the others. Maybe you prefer a particular browser vendor.

❑ Support the most popular browsers. You can still reach about 90% of web surfers if you support only the version 4.0+ browsers. Adding version 3.0 support, which means no Dynamic HTML tricks, and you have 95% or more of the market. Web sites like www.yahoo.com have Browser Statistics sections you can be mystified by, although www.statmarket.com could be more useful.

A safe middle ground at this time of writing is to use the features in Netscape 3.0 JavaScript. Failing all that, you can spend a lot of time making your JavaScript work everywhere and gracefully downgrade everywhere else. Lots and lots of time.

Choose Tricks

Here are a variety of tricks for handling different browsers in JavaScript.

Supporting Ancient Browsers

```
<HTML><BODY><SCRIPT>
<!-- hide from old, stupid browsers
document.write('JavaScript rules, but only here!');
// end comment -->
</SCRIPT></BODY></HTML>
```

Shown earlier, comments hide script source from browsers that don't know <SCRIPT>.

Detecting Scripts are Ignored

```
<HTML><BODY><SCRIPT>
 alert("Off to the JavaScript page?");
 document.location.href = 'js_top.htm';
</SCRIPT>
<NOSCRIPT>Get a real browser, see it all!</NOSCRIPT>
</BODY></HTML>
```

The <NOSCRIPT> tag provides a method of dealing with browsers which refuse to interpret JavaScript, either because they can't or because the user has turned JavaScript off. The main use of this tag is to provide some feedback to the user asking them to go away or else enable JavaScript. It can be used, as in this example, to show a dummy page that is replaced if JavaScript is enabled. Although the alert in this case stops the 'real' page from loading automatically, it can easily be left out.

Detecting Versions

```
<HTML><HEAD>
<SCRIPT LANGUAGE="JavaScript">var v = 1.0</SCRIPT>
<SCRIPT LANGUAGE="JavaScript1.1">v = 1.1</SCRIPT>
<SCRIPT LANGUAGE="JavaScript1.2">v = 1.2</SCRIPT>
<SCRIPT LANGUAGE="JavaScript1.3">v = 1.3</SCRIPT>
<SCRIPT LANGUAGE="JavaScript1.4">v = 1.4</SCRIPT>
</HEAD><BODY><SCRIPT>
document.write(v);
</SCRIPT></BODY></HTML>
```

This script shows a simple way of detecting JavaScript versions– at the end, 'v' contains the highest version supported. If a rough guide is all you need it should suffice. Unfortunately, all it really tests is the tag attribute. JavaScript for Internet Explorer 3.0 on the PC and Macintosh are subtly different in features. JavaScript 1.1 is "supported" in Internet Explorer 3.0 with Jscript 2.0, but doesn't support all the features in Netscape's 1.1 implementation. Bugs and beta releases further cloud the water.

There are other ways of gathering information about the browser and JavaScript.

The `navigator.userAgent` property contains a unique string describing the browser version, brand and platform. Although it doesn't contain the JavaScript language version, it can sometimes be deduced. For example, Netscape 2.02 has the string `'Mozilla/2.02 (Win95;I)'` for the Windows-95 32-bit version and that version is known to support only JavaScript 1.0.

Via Netscape's LiveConnect and Java, the operating system and its version can be detected, provided Java support is enabled. This script will report `'Windows 95-4.0-Pentium'` for Netscape Navigator 3.03 32-bit for the PC we used to test with:

```
var str = '';
str += java.lang.System.getProperty('os.name');
str += java.lang.System.getProperty('os.version');
str += java.lang.System.getProperty('os.arch');
document.write(str);
```

This script works for Netscape 3.0 and 4.0 browsers.

A warning – watch out for the processor specific information in the above two example strings. 'I' and 'Pentium' may well vary if your computer doesn't have a genuine Pentium I processor, as most new computers don't now. It's safer to just test using the operating system version.

For Internet Explorer, the JavaScript version is accessible directly via special native functions. However, this requires at least JScript 2.0, or else the script will fail with no ability to trap errors. An example:

```
var str = '';
str += ' ' + ScriptEngineMajorVersion();
str += ' ' + ScriptEngineMinorVersion();
str += ' ' + ScriptEngineBuildVersion();
document.write(str);
```

Common output for this example would be `'2 0 1125'`.

As a last resort you can detect the JavaScript version by testing in the script for a specific feature or bug that you might know is unique to a given version.

Supporting Several Versions

Once the JavaScript version is known, there are three main strategies available: **separate pages**, **alternate script blocks**, and **object guarding**. Separate pages means creating separate HTML+JavaScript documents for each language version, and displaying the appropriate one. Alternative script blocks means providing <SCRIPT> blocks in the HTML for each version and using an `if` test at the start of each so that only the 'right' one does anything. Object guarding is perhaps the most flexible method. We guard the object we're not sure about with a test and only use it if the test passes. It is illustrated in this example:

```
<HTML><BODY>
… more HTML and JavaScript …
<SCRIPT>
if ( top.images ) { change_image(); }
</SCRIPT>
</BODY></HTML>
```

The `top.images` property is problematic in some browsers, so calling `change_image()` won't always work. In this example, by testing the property against `null`, nothing is done if it doesn't exist. This allows feature-by-feature compatibility without regard to versions, but it also means using a lot of extra `if`s if you use many non-portable features.

Which features should you watch out for? The Appendices extensively list the objects available, and specific well known problems are discussed in the subject areas throughout this book where they are most often used – for example, read about images in the Multimedia and Plugins chapter.

Alas, nothing will guard you against bugs. Netscape is good enough to publish theirs publicly on the www.`mozilla.org` web site (see bugzilla, the bug database), and there's Microsoft's knowledge base if you're patient with the response from www.`microsoft.com`, but even so, you're pretty much on your own if you find a bug in a browser. The public USENET JavaScript newsgroup comp.lang.javascript always contains a few battle-weary veterans of browser bugs and compatibility issues, and they might help you if your question hasn't been asked a million, million, million times before.

Summary

This chapter has described all the browser cracks and crevices into which JavaScript scripts can be stuffed.

With Internet Explorer and Netscape Navigator/Communicator having the lion's share of the web market, understanding where your client-side JavaScript can be put is a critical hurdle that needs jumping before you can do anything meaningful. The bottom line is, most JavaScript goes inside the HTML page.

However, we've also given a nod briefly to other browser possibilities where JavaScript applies. There are many other browsers, generally more humble and generally more obscure where you can expect your JavaScript to run correctly if it's simple. Beyond personal computers, set-top boxes and even mobile phones allow JavaScript or JavaScript-like scripting options in browsers.

For the rest of this book, we'll be concentrating on the JavaScript development environment for mainstream computing uses only. In particular, the next group of chapters will explore in detail the uses and abuses of JavaScript in the normal Web browser environment.

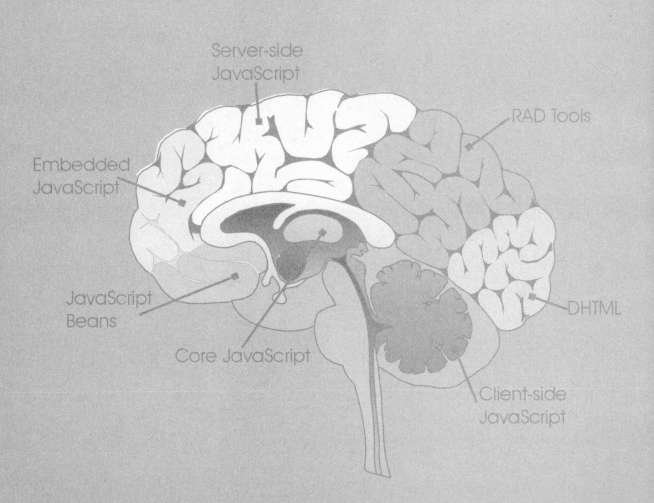

Server-side
JavaScript

RAD Tools

Embedded
JavaScript

JavaScript
Beans

Core JavaScript

DHTML

Client-side
JavaScript

Windows and Frames

Without a browser window to display it, there's not much point in creating HTML documents, much less adding JavaScript for special effects. This chapter explains how all the biggest parts of a browser hang together and what JavaScript techniques can be applied successfully to them. The biggest parts of a browser are the browser windows and any frames they might have.

Browser windows and frames live together with HTML documents in an edifice called the **Browser Object Model** or the **Document Object Model**. This edifice is a set of JavaScript host objects. This chapter is mainly concerned with the window object, which stands for a whole browser window or frame. Nearly as broad in scope is the Document object, which can stand for the whole content of a given browser window. A window object can often be handled from a JavaScript object called window. A document object can always be handled from a JavaScript object called document.

Messing with windows and frames using JavaScript is a game called "who controls the browser?" played between the scriptwriter and the user, with the browser's security features as umpire. The specifics of the security features are covered in Chapter 18.

The more specific objects in the Browser Object Model are described in later chapters, such as Chapter 6 "Multimedia and Plugins" and Chapter 7 "Forms and Data". See the Appendices for details on all the objects available.

Window Types

The more you think about it, the more windows there appear to be in a browser. They are controllable to different degrees from JavaScript.

Main Browser Windows

A browser can display more than one window at once. These windows hold the content the user normally views and each one is represented by a `window` object in JavaScript. They can be opened and closed and their history navigated via JavaScript, with some security limitations. All JavaScript variables and objects in an inline JavaScript script ultimately belong to one `window` object. Although windows are mostly used to display HTML documents, non-HTML windows exist as well, such as windows that display an `ftp://` URL.

Windows Displaying HTML

HTML documents are the most common contents of browser windows. It is with `window` objects that the scriptwriter most often tries to override the user's control of the browser. The `window` object's `open()` method or function is particularly important. This function should never be confused with the `open()` method of the Document object, discussed later. Suppose two HTML files exist as follows, plus a third that illustrates the `window.open()` method:

```
<!-- first.htm -->
<HTML><BODY>Boo!!</BODY></HTML>
```

```
<!-- second.htm -->
<HTML><BODY>I'm smaller</BODY></HTML>
```

Here is an example of the `open()` function:

```
<HTML><BODY><SCRIPT>
var win1 = open("first.htm","first",
                "resizable=no,height=200,width=200");

function show_it()
{
  var win2 = window.open("second.htm","second",
                "resizable=no,height=100,width=100");
}
</SCRIPT>
<A HREF="#" ONCLICK="show_it();"> Click me, Alice.</A>
</BODY></HTML>
```

Notice the use of the "#" URL. This is a plain HTML trick that prevents a page from being replaced when a link is followed. That won't work on Internet Explorer 3.0, but it will on 4.0 and 5.0. Here is the initial page, shown in Internet Explorer 4.0:

When this page is displayed, the inline script opens a second window:

If the link is clicked in the original window, then a further window is displayed:

This example shows several important points. The open() function provides the new window with a name (this is separate from its <TITLE>, which is set by the HTML document for the whole browser window) and a set of window property options. To avoid confusion between window properties and JavaScript properties, this chapter refers to traditional window properties such as menus and scrollbars as **decorations**. The options can stop toolbars from appearing, set the window size in pixels and so on. The open() function returns new window objects, which the variables win1 and win2 refer to. For win2, the open() function should be qualified with the object window because technically, the window isn't the current object for event handlers. For normal inline scripts, plain open() is enough.

The parts of the third argument to open() must be comma-separated, not space-separated, and not commas plus spaces. This picky syntax is a trap you can fall into with monotonous regularity. So a typical open() function call looks as follows:

```
variable-name = open("URL", "window-name", "option=value,option=value...");
```

One design issue in this example is that the win2 variable is only local to the show_it() function. This is usually a bad idea because when the function ends and the variable goes, you've lost track of the new window. It can be found again with open('','second'), but it's better to keep the variable somewhere more permanent, like win1, in case you want to use it.

Another design issue is that users often don't like unexpected windows popping up, especially without controls like menus on them, so you need a good reason to do it. Here are three fair reasons:

- ❑ Attempting to display something that requires precise pixel layout, such as layers animations.
- ❑ The window is a temporary popup-style window like help or a user warning.
- ❑ The features removed are compensated for with buttons, links and images in the new window.

open() is otherwise quite limited. Security issues prevent you from changing the decorations of an already open window (unless you use a secure script), or a window displaying pages from a different web site. There is no way to prevent the user from closing a window you've specially opened – to detect this you must keep track with a variable.

Finally, open() is not as general as you might like to think. A WebTV viewer has a small screen size if you count the number of pixels in each direction, and doesn't allow additional windows to open at all.

When It's Not HTML

Browser windows don't always display HTML documents. Sometimes they display directory information from FTP sites, gopher menus, or just a single image. windows only have a name if assigned one from JavaScript, otherwise they are anonymous and can't be found. So new windows displaying non-HTML information can't be touched or read by JavaScript. Existing windows that change their contents from HTML to something else will keep their name. If you have a variable referring to such a window, for Netscape all the existing properties of the object will be set to undefined (including the name property – somewhat bizarre). Internet Explorer 4.0 and 5.0 do a little better, properties that should be there are intact, like name and location, but the other properties are either undefined as in Netscape (usually the IE specific ones, like dialogTop), or give an error (like document). The name and the location property are intact in 3.02, but the other properties can't be examined at all.

The mail, news and bookmark organizer windows aren't accessible from HTML embedded JavaScript, but configuration preferences, scripted in JavaScript for Netscape 4.0 browsers (discussed in Chapter 9 – "Browser JavaScript from the Outside In") can affect their appearance and content. These preferences can also control the appearance of the first window that appears when the browser starts up.

Wysiwyg

In Netscape 3.0 only, resizing an HTML window can have an unusual side effect. If the HTML source comes in part from inline JavaScript, the URL displayed in the location bar can change. If the URL is `http://my.site.com/page.htm` it changes to `wysiwyg://56/http://my.site.com/page.htm`, where `56` is some random number.

Such a page is still a normal HTML page, accessible from JavaScript. The new-looking URL just reflects Netscape's attempts to cope with resizing, and the page's URL hasn't really changed. Ignore it. An example page that can be resized to show this behavior is:

```
<HTML><BODY><SCRIPT>
document.write('resize for Navigator 3.0 wysiwyg');
</SCRIPT></BODY></HTML>
```

You can't make up a `wysiwyg:` URL yourself.

View Source

The page that displays the HTML and JavaScript source for a given document isn't accessible from JavaScript.

In particular, there is no easy way to get the whole contents of the View Source page into JavaScript strings. Internet Explorer 4+ has a nearly equivalent, but separate mechanism for doing this, explained in the Dynamic HTML chapter.

Netscape browsers can be directed to display the View Source window from embedded JavaScript. Do this by opening a window with the URL `view-source:X` where X is the fully qualified URL of the document to view. This can be used as a debugging aid.

About, Help and Security Info

Online help is a necessity in today's computer applications. As Dynamic HTML (see Chapter 8) gives web authors the foundations they need to write full-featured applications with all the features and perks a native windows application can provide, it's not surprising to see efforts to make it possible to provide online help in a web environment also.

In the Netscape browsers, these windows are all just HTML pages, so in theory they are accessible directly from JavaScript. There isn't much reason to do so, but if you feel the urge to hack into the browser in order to find out how these windows are named, go ahead. The About page is easiest because it doesn't appear in a new window without a location bar.

Microsoft has created a standard called HTML Help that allows help information to be displayed in a browser window that looks similar to the Help Topics window that windows applications like Microsoft's Word and Excel display today. HTML Help is hosted in IE4+. To see it, click on the Content and Index menu item in the Help menu. The DHTML showHelp method is a useful tool. It takes the URL of an HTML Help page as well as a second optional parameter where arguments that control how the page is displayed can be specified. For example, if we have an HTML Help page called MyHelp.htm, then we'd show it with this simple line of code:

```
showHelp "MyHelp.htm"
```

Both Netscape and Microsoft have a software development kit (SDK) that assists in the creation of HTML help pages. Two good URLs for starting points are: Netscape's NetHelp at http://developer.netscape.com/products/index.html and Microsoft's HTML Help: http://msdn.microsoft.com/workshop/author/htmlhelp/default.asp.

Address Books and Bookmarks

Netscape Communicator 4.0+ can dynamically add entries to the Address book configuration popup. To see the style of these URLs, just view a piece of mail in Netscape Messenger, point the mouse at an e-mail address link, and read the status bar. You can put this URL in a link or use window.location.href, etc. Needs a little testing to work out if all the address book fields can be configured from this URL, and if the user still needs to dismiss the new window by hand.

IE 4.0+ has an AddFavorite() method which is a property of the window.external object. Favorites are equivalent to bookmarks in Microsoft language.

Neither Netscape nor Internet Explorer will let you add bookmarks without user interaction. You can overcome this restriction with security tricks – see Chapter 18.

Java

The Java interpreter controls two kinds of windows in addition to the space reserved for it with the <APPLET> or <OBJECT> tags. These kinds of windows are zero or more Java popup 'canvases' and the sole Java console. Both of these kinds of windows can be manipulated from JavaScript via ActiveX or LiveConnect. See Chapter 9, "Applets and Java". New canvases can be created this way, but the console cannot be displayed or hidden from JavaScript. You might want to create a canvas if you want to control a Java applet from JavaScript in an independent window. You might want to work with the console when debugging your scripts.

Warnings and Dialog Boxes

Depending on your preferences, especially security preferences, there are numerous warnings and dialog boxes that can appear during a web browsing session. Very few of these can be controlled directly from HTML embedded JavaScript. Some can be avoided by the use of secure scripts, or otherwise affected by configuration preferences.

However, three types of popups are custom-made for JavaScript use. They are created with methods of a window object and are called **alert**, **confirm** and **prompt** and are presented respectively below:

These examples are from Navigator 4.02 for windows 95. Where 'Text' appears, any JavaScript string can be substituted. Here is a script showing all three:

```
<HTML><BODY><SCRIPT>
var agree = false, notes = '';
agree = confirm('Love pumpkin?');
if ( agree )
    notes = prompt("Its good points?",'Type here');
else
    notes = prompt("Its bad points?",'Type here');
alert(notes + '\nYour mother would be proud.');
</SCRIPT></BODY></HTML>
```

confirm() returns a Boolean value. prompt() returns a string typed in by the user when the OK button is clicked, or null if the cancel button is clicked. alert() returns undefined which is much the same as not returning anything. The windows are always titled [JavaScript Application] or similar words for security reasons so the user can't be fooled into thinking they are something else.

These windows halt the script until the user responds. In Netscape this means halting all JavaScript in the browser. This behavior makes `alert()` and `confirm()` useful as simple debugging aids – use them to step through a script that isn't quite working yet. They are particularly useful for probing an existing page via JavaScript URLs:

```
javascript:alert(document.form1.field1.value)
```

Note the `document` object is used here – this alert displays an HTML field value that is part of an HTML document. These popups aren't HTML-style popups, they just display directly, and so end-of-line characters aren't lost. If you want fancy formatting, you have to do it yourself (or use a whole window that displays real HTML). To duplicate this code:

```
<HTML><BODY>
<STRONG>Snow White accomplices:</STRONG>
<UL><LI>Dopey<LI>Grumpy<LI>Doc</UL>
</BODY></HTML>
```

try this:

```
var message = 'SNOW WHITE ACCOMPLICES:\n'
              + ' o  Dopey\n o  Grumpy\n o  Doc';
alert(message);
```

If you really need fancy formatting, you can simulate these windows with HTML windows, using `window.open()` and display content formatted with HTML tags and form elements, but the window will not be **modal**. That is, the other windows will not be frozen when the new one appears. There are ways around this, however. The crudest way is to use the `setTimeout()` or `setInterval()` functions to call `window.focus()` in the new window every 10 milliseconds, so it stays on top. This technique must be used with Netscape 2.0-4.x. This technique also works with Internet Explorer 4+, but that browser also has special features if you don't care about portability. In this case, instead of opening a normal window, use the `ShowModalDialog()` method of the window object, which opens a window that always retains the input focus. Microsoft also have a `ShowModalessDialog()` variant for drop-down menu and help-like windows. Netscape 5.0 will have a `ShowDialog()` method.

JavaScript does not yet have a generalized message box function like Visual Basic's `MsgBox` function. If you are desperate for this and sure that only Internet Explorer browsers 4+ will be used, you can use the JScript-to-VBScript example in Chapter 4 to get access to these popups.

Layers, Frames and Scripts

Layers, frames and scripts are not windows in the user sense. Layers are `layer` objects, specific to Netscape 4+ only, which are either documents or pieces of documents. The closely related HTML concept of a piece of HTML that is a positional stylesheet isn't a window either. Scripts are whole documents taking up part of an existing window, but don't have a window object of their own. Frames appear as an array of window objects internally to scripts, but externally they are only a piece of a window. Both layers and frames act like containers for document information, just adding a few properties of their own, such as size and position. They don't have the status of a whole user-visible window – no toolbars or menus.

A frameset is not a window or an object at all, it is just a convenient tag for grouping and sizing a set of frames. It also provides a place for window event handlers to be specified.

Pop-up Menus

The user can make pop-up menus appear when right-clicking (Unix and windows 95/NT) on a document. You have to use advanced event handlers in the 4.0 level browsers in order to stop these from appearing.

On Unix only, Netscape 3.0 browsers have two variants of pop-up menus: one for frames and one for non-frames. You can alternate them by turning a non-frame document into a frame – just make a frameset document with a single frame that points to your original document. The reverse can also be done. Then you can disable the back option on these menus as described under history in the next section.

Window Organization

This section describes how windows work with each other. The discussion applies mostly to ordinary HTML document windows, not other windows such as mail readers.

Hierarchy

A browser can have more than one window open. No window is marked as special just because it was first, or because it opened the others – they are all equal. Each of those windows can either contain an HTML document with a <BODY>, or with a <FRAMESET>.

Each window has a window object, and each window object has two important properties: document and frames. The document property points to the document object matching the URL for the window. Frames is an array of (possibly zero) frame window objects. The frames array has a length property which reveals how many frames are *owned* by the main window object.

Consider these HTML documents:

```
<!-- rabbit.htm -->
<HTML><BODY>Rabbit.</BODY></HTML>
```

```
<!-- vsplit.htm -->
<HTML><FRAMESET COLS="*,*">
<FRAME SRC="rabbit.htm" NAME="bunny1">
<FRAME SRC="rabbit.htm" NAME="bunny2">
</FRAMESET></HTML>
```

```
<!-- three.htm -->
<HTML><FRAMESET ROWS="*,*">
<FRAME SRC="rabbit.htm" NAME="bunny3">
<FRAMESET COLS="*,*">
  <FRAME SRC="rabbit.htm" NAME="bunny4">
  <FRAME SRC="rabbit.htm" NAME="bunny5">
</FRAMESET></FRAMESET></HTML>
```

```
<!-- complex.htm -->
<HTML><FRAMESET ROWS="*,*">
  <FRAME SRC="rabbit.htm" NAME="bunny6">
  <FRAME SRC="vsplit.htm" NAME="bunny7">
</FRAMESET></HTML>
```

Displayed in small windows, the windows `rabbit.htm`, `vsplit.htm`, `three.htm`, and `complex.htm` (respectively):

The value of `frames.length` is 0, 2, 3, and 2 respectively. The third example shows that nested framesets don't do anything tricky – each frame is simple added to the frames array. The last example shows that if the URL for a frame turns out to be a frameset document, then it *is* tricky – the frames of the second frameset aren't counted in the first frameset individually, even though it looks the same visually. Instead they are counted once because the parent frame they are both part of is counted once. The structure of these four windows can be illustrated as follows:

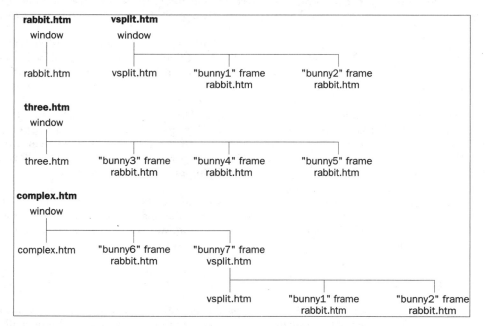

In the fourth example, to reach the lower left document (object) from the original, from the frameset document (called `top`) in JavaScript requires navigating the object hierarchy like this:

```
top.frames[1].frames[0].document;
```
or
```
top.bunny7.bunny1.document;
```

Frame names are object properties of the window object as well as frames array members – this is objects and arrays being almost the same again. If frames are deeply nested and documents are complex, referring to distant objects from the top down can be very cumbersome.

Finally, Internet Explorer 3.0, 4.0 and 5.0, Netscape 4.0 and 5.0, and HTML 4.0 allow floating frames: the <IFRAME> tag. Floating frames are specified in the document's <BODY> content. Nevertheless, they are added to the frames array of the window containing the document, just as <FRAMESET> frames are.

Window References

A well-defined hierarchy of windows, frames and documents brings order to complex HTML documents, but it doesn't make access to those objects particularly easy. Access between windows and within windows is made easier by special object properties.

In HTML, the special URLs _self, _parent, _top and _blank are often used to control which window or frame to load a URL into. Internet Explorer also has _search and _main. JavaScript has equivalent variables, called self, parent and top, which always point at window objects. These variables are properties of the window object. Blank does not exist because it is pointless to refer to a window which hasn't been created. There is also a window variable that is the same as self.

Like HTML, the top variable refers to the window object representing a whole visible window, regardless of its content. self refers to the window object that the script is most directly embedded in. parent is the same as self unless self is a frame, in which case parent is the window containing self's frameset document.

A script always executes inside the scope of some object. Usually this is the self window, which means window methods like open() and alert() don't require a prefix like self.open() or window.alert(). The longer form should be used if these methods are used inside an event handler, because for the current object there is usually not a window, and confusion will eventually occur if you don't develop the habit of properly qualifying properties and methods.

Some JavaScript host objects are **global** meaning they are available to use regardless of what object is current. Math is an example. top, self, and parent are like this, so top in particular is always available to use. They are also updated automatically if windows go away or framesets are replaced with other documents. If all else fails, start from top and work down.

Decorations

Other elements of a browser window exist as properties of the window object for that window. Security issues prevent some of these features being changed unless advanced techniques like signed scripts or configuration scripts are used.

❑   **Status bar**. The message in the status bar can be read and written to, but not the progress indicator. Chapter 6, "Multimedia and Plugins", has an example.

❑ **open()** can create a window without a status bar, by using the status=no option, but there is no way for a plain script or the user to put it back. This is very irritating in Netscape, because if a window with no status bar is the last one in the browser to shut down, the browser will start up without status bars from then on. The solution is to either edit the browser preferences file by hand, or have JavaScript open a window with a status bar, and shutdown the browser again using that window as the last window. In Navigator 4+, a signed script can expose or remove a status bar.

❑ **Scrollbars**. Scrollbars can be disabled in new windows via open() by using the scrollbars=no option. The user cannot put them back. Frames can also have scrollbars. These can't be exposed or removed once set.

❑ **Toolbars**. These cannot be read or changed by embedded JavaScript, except for open() which can create a window without them, by using the toolbar=no option. The user can put toolbars back at any time if the menubar is accessible.

❑ **Menubar.** As for toolbars, except once its gone, the user can't get it back.

❑ **Big N or E icon** (in the top right corner of the browser window). This can only be changed from a configuration script.

❑ **Window title bar**. The title string is a property of the top-level Document object in the window, not the window itself. The property is called **title**.

❑ The title bar and its close and resize icons are added by the computer's operating system, not the browser, and aren't visible inside JavaScript. You're stuck with them, unless you create an ActiveX control that specifically removes them.

Finally, Netscape 3+ has a **kiosk** mode that allows the browser to start up without most of the window decorations. IE 4+ has the equivalent functionality with **theater** mode. This is done in both browser cases with a command line option, -k. In Netscape 4+ the preferred way of doing this is to use open() and a mixture of its options that prevent the user from changing windows. This is called **canvas mode**. Internet Explorer 4 and 5 support this directly with a button on the browser toolbar called **Full screen mode**. An example of canvas mode which sets the correct options is:

```
<HTML><BODY><SCRIPT>
var details =   'alwaysRaised=yes,titlebar=no,left=0,top=0,width='
                + top.screen.width + ',height=' + top.screen.height;
</SCRIPT>

<A HREF="#" ONCLICK="window.open('about:blank','test',top.details);">
   Click Me
</A>
</BODY></HTML>
```

The only catch is that the JavaScript must be moved to a signed script or else the alwaysRaised option (illustrated above) is ignored. The alwaysRaised option prevents other windows and applications from appearing in front of the canvas mode window.

Finally, the actual window borders, buttons, menus and images can all be considered decorations of a given window. There is some discussion of the process in Chapter 9, "Browser JavaScript from the Outside In", which covers the subject of browser configuration more thoroughly.

163

Concurrency

If several windows and/or frames are downloading web documents at the same time, it's a race that anyone could win. If inline scripts that operate on other windows occur as part of the downloads, chaos can result. Without planning, it's impossible to know whether a variable or object exists yet in a given frame or window used by another window's script.

For Netscape browsers, the situation is not so bad. Using the footrace analogy, as the runners speed down the track next to each other, they juggle a ball between themselves. Only the runner with the ball can interpret a script. This means that for Netscape, you can always be confident that when you set or read a variable, it won't change at least until your script ends (when you pass the ball on). However, in Internet Explorer, every runner has a ball, so you can't even be sure about your variables from one statement to the next.

In technical speak, for both browsers version 4+, the browser is **multithreaded**. In the Netscape case, the interpreter occupies a single thread amongst those threads. In the Internet Explorer case, JScript can occupy more than one thread. In version 3.0 browsers, each window has a single thread with an interpreter.

Of course, a variable or object referred to only within its own window is straightforward.

The solutions for the general case are:

- ❑ Don't mess with other windows unless absolutely necessary.
- ❑ Only rely on windows that are known to be fully loaded.
- ❑ Use events to wait for windows to finish loading.
- ❑ If a critical window closes, close everything related.

Two key window events help achieve this: onLoad and onUnload. The onLoad event fires when a document is fully displayed. The onUnload event is a little less trustworthy due to bugs, but fires when a document is removed from visibility. Since these events are document-based, they apply to windows, frames and <LAYER> tags. These are the only two window events in HTML 4.0, but Netscape browsers 3.0 and 4+, and Internet Explorer 4+ have a heap of others. See the Appendices for a full list. An example of a multi-frame document that alerts the user when everything is loaded:

```
<!-- toplevel.htm -->
<HTML><HEAD>
<SCRIPT>
var total = 0;
var win = new Array();
function ready(w)        // report that this window is ready
{
    win[total++] = w;
    if ( total == 3 ) alert('All rabbits ready.');
}
</SCRIPT></HEAD>
<FRAMESET ROWS="*,*" ONLOAD="top.ready(this)">
<FRAME SRC="newbunny.htm">
<FRAME SRC="newbunny.htm">
</FRAMESET></HTML>
```

```
<!--newbunny.htm -->
<HTML><BODY ONLOAD="top.ready(this);">
Hop.
</BODY></HTML>
```

In this example, the alert only appears when the `ready()` function has been called enough times. That is enough by itself to detect everything's loaded. This example also stores the supplied `window` objects. In this case there's no real need to do so because the `frames` array already tracks each frame. However, this example can be adapted to the case where separate windows, not just frames, are loaded using `open()`. In that case the `win` array is needed to track those separate windows. Finally, you might be tempted to use `register` rather than `ready` for the function that reports the document is loaded. That is a bad idea, as `register` is a reserved word in JavaScript.

History

In the window hierarchy diagram above, each window or frame not only has a document object for its URL, it also has an object called `history`. This stores the URLs of all the past documents appearing in this window or frame. Methods of this object are used to navigate forwards and backwards through the list. The items in the list are just URL strings, not whole documents – you can't probe historical documents with scripts.

The most common uses of history are as follows:

```
<A HREF="#" ONCLICK="window.history.go(-1)">
   Boldly take a step backwards</A>
<A HREF="#" ONCLICK="window.location.reload()">
   Boldly go nowhere</A>
<A HREF="#" ONCLICK="window.location.reload(true)">
   Boldly go nowhere, but making a special effort</A>
<A HREF="#" ONCLICK="window.location.replace(url)">
   Boldly forget the past</A>
```

The first case returns to the previous document, which was probably stored in the browser's cache, just like the user's `Back` button. The second case refreshes the current page, again, probably from the browser's cache. The third does the same, but from its original source on a remote website somewhere (which may have changed). The last refreshes the current page, but also throws out all the history in the process, effectively disabling the user's `Back` button.

History features are bug-prone in Internet Explorer 3.0. Even in browsers where they work perfectly, your author isn't keen on them, apart from the occasional `go(-1)`. The official reason is that working out a clean and bullet-proof navigation model for users of a web-based application is hard enough without jumping back and forth between pages of unknown origin and content. That's the official reason. The real reason is that browser history mechanisms can drive you crazy.

Window Design

The appearance of your web page and the window(s) within which they are contained can vary drastically depending upon how you choose to present your information. A few design issues crop up when working with windows and are discussed below.

Multiple Windows

Simple document display doesn't often involve multiple windows. If you are trying to build an application that makes heavy use of forms, that is another matter. Multiple forms lead quickly to multiple windows.

Because the user can close a window at any time, maintaining a lot of random dependencies between windows just doesn't work well. Not only do you have to check window references before every use, you have to decide what to do when they've gone. Worse still, when a window closes all the objects and variables inside it vanish forever. Best to choose a simple architecture with fewer tricky possibilities. Two workable options are explored here.

Simple Approach

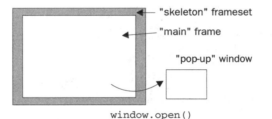

This example has a maximum of 2 windows. The 'skeleton' window contains one frame only, in which all the action such as form data entry happens. When user issues occur, the second window 'pop-up' appears, but only for temporary matters. While the pop-up window is open, the first window can't or shouldn't be modified. To stop the main window from doing anything, always use the same variable to track the pop-up window opened with open(). Then test that variable in all event handlers in the main window to make sure it's correct to go ahead with the event.

The frameset document in this example may appear useless, but it's critical. Control type data can be stored in the main window or its frameset document object. If the sole frame is used to change between pages of the web application, then the data in that frame is destroyed with each new page. But any data in the frameset window stays intact. If the main window is created without toolbars, the user can't damage the frameset window at all.

Enhancements: it may make sense to allow the user a second popup for Help text, or similar information, that doesn't lock the main window. The main menu can also benefit from a second frame in a strip containing buttons or links that allows the user to navigate pages in the other frame.

More Complex Approach

If you really do need multiple windows at a time, a more complex solution is as follows:

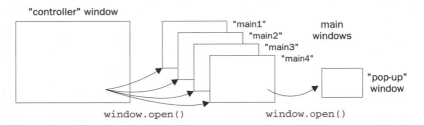

In this example, the controller window is dedicated to maintaining good order in the application. It does the entire opening and tracking of the main windows. If the controller window is shut down by the user, it shuts down all the main windows as well – they can't survive without it. If a main window wants to refer to another main window, it asks the controller window for a window reference via a function supplied in the controller window, like `top.opener.get_window('form3')`. Control information is stored in the controller window. Pop-ups and help are managed in each main window as for the simple case, or the controller window can be given responsibility.

A problem with this solution is that the controller window is always visible, and so must contain something sensible to look at, like a toolbar or a control pad. It's ineffective and confusing to users if you try and hide the controller window just by making it very small.

If one of the main windows is guaranteed to always exist, it can take on the role of the controller by being structured as for the simple approach – then no separate controller window is needed. However, there are always cases where the simple approach is limited. One such typical case is where a window displays constantly updating information – you can not afford to overwrite the window because the user goes elsewhere, so only the complex case will do.

Reopening Windows With Internet Explorer 4.0

Some Internet Explorer 4.0, but not 5.0, installations have a problem with re-opening existing windows. If a window is already open, then attempting to re-open it gives an error instead of the expected result. In the following example try clicking the first link, ignoring the new window, and clicking the second link in the original window:

```
<HTML><BODY>
<A HREF="page2.html" ONCLICK="window.open('page2.html', 'new_win'); return
false;">Page 2 </A>
<A HREF="page3.html" ONCLICK="window.open('page3.html', 'new_win'); return
false;">Page 3 </A>
</BODY></HTML>
```

The problem is that `window.open()` won't work properly if a window with the same name already exists. This is fixed in Internet Explorer 5.0. The work-around is to only open the new window if it doesn't already exist. You do this by checking a reference to the new window before you open it. You have to save that reference at some point too. Each of the `onClick` events above should have this bit of script instead:

```
if ( window.winref && !window.winref.closed)
   window.winref.replace('page2.html');
else
   window.winref = window.open('page2.html','new_win');
return false;
```

Of course, you may have to format it differently (or put it in a JavaScript function) in order to fit the code sensibly into the event handler. This code won't work on Internet Explorer 3.0, unfortunately, but it's good in all other 3+ versions.

Window Event Handling Tricks

A particularly tricky possibility involving window events has already been presented in Chapter 4. It explained how Netscape 4.0 browsers can send event information between windows.

Windows Without URLs

A window can avoid the overhead of downloading an HTML URL from some remote place by creating the HTML in the browser. Inline JavaScript can be used to generate the whole HTML document for a window, from another window. There are a few good reasons for doing this:

❑ The HTML is small and trivial, and Web connections can be slow.

❑ The HTML depends on some other data currently in the browser.

❑ The HTML page never ends, or continually refreshes, or other automation.

For greatest portability, the way to do this is to load an empty, dummy page as a place holder when the window is first created, and then re-write it straight away:

```
<!--blank.htm-->
<HTML></HTML>
```

```
<!--hello.htm-->
<HTML><HEAD><SCRIPT>
<!--
     var txt='<HTML><BODY>Hello, World! </BODY></HTML>';
     var win2 = open('blank.htm', 'win2');
     win2.document.open();
     win2.document.write(txt);
     win2.document.close();
// end comment -->
</SCRIPT></HEAD></HTML>
```

This example shows the use of the other common open() method - for the Document object. This kind of open() destroys the current document, leaving the window ready to receive new document information. document.close() shuts the door on any more data for this document.

Netscape has a few ease-of-use shortcuts. Its version of document.write() is smarter – it will automatically do a document.open() if one is required. Internet Explorer 5.0 will do this too. It is better to get into the habit of doing the open() yourself since earlier Microsoft browsers require it. The two files above can be shortened into one and made faster if Netscape-specific enhancements are used:

```
<!--hello.htm-->
<HTML><HEAD><SCRIPT>
<!-- avoid &lt; problems
    var new_page_content =
        '<HTML><BODY>Hello, World!<BR></BODY></HTML>'
    var page2 = open('about:blank', 'page2');
    page2.content = new_page_content;
    page2.location.href = 'javascript:new_page_content';
// end comment -->
</SCRIPT></HEAD></HTML>
```

In this example the entire HTML for a new page is loaded into a JavaScript variable. Then we open the new window with a dummy page. `about:blank` fills a Netscape window with nothing. This is a handy way of giving frames a temporary initial document when you know they are going to be reloaded shortly. This still works in Netscape 4+, but sometimes the window doesn't *look* empty, due to a bug (possibly this is a 'performance' change). `about:blank` is also available in Internet Explorer 4+. Next we copy the variable into the new page, which at least has a window object, even if it's otherwise empty. Then we tell the new page to go to a new URL - except the URL is a `javascript:` one, discussed in Chapter 4. The expression for this JavaScript URL is very simple - just a single variable. The result of that expression is the variable's content, which is a whole HTML page, so that's what is displayed in the new window.

Detecting Size

Early HTML tried to get away from any need-to-know sizes of screens or windows, but for more advanced applications the issue rears its ugly head again. There are two things worth knowing: the size of a given window in pixels, and the size of the whole computer screen.

Window Size

In Netscape browser versions 4.0, window, frame and layer sizes are directly accessible in `window` object properties like `innerWidth` and `innerHeight`. For Internet Explorer 4+, these aren't available, and it's better to use stylesheet properties like `pixelWidth` (described further in Chapter 8, "Dynamic HTML") to work out the size of the window from the top-level `<HTML>` object it displays. Prior to those versions, the only way to be sure of window and frame sizes is to set them explicitly using `window.open()` or tag attributes, and disable user resizing. For Internet Explorer 3+ you should be able to create a special ActiveX control to expose window sizes if you're desperate.

Screen Size

For the size of the user's screen in pixels, version 4+ browsers have a new `window` property called `screen` which is itself an object. It has various properties describing the screen size. Internet Explorer 4.0 is slightly different – it reports the actual number of colors, rather than the number of bits per color. To convert to bits for that browser, use this mathematics:

```
var colours = top.window.screen.colorDepth;
var bits = Math.log(colours)/Math.log(2);      // For IE 4.0 only.
```

In Navigator 3.0, you must resort to LiveConnect and get the data from Java as follows (this is still JavaScript):

```
if (navigator.javaEnabled())
{
  var obj = java.awt.Toolkit.getDefaultToolkit();
  obj = obj.getScreenSize();
  document.write(obj.width+'x'+obj.height);
}
```

If the user has Java turned off this won't work, in which case you'll have to resort to the last possibility: here, and for Internet Explorer 3.0 and Netscape 2.02, you must create a custom Java applet or ActiveX control. Either can detect the screen size and make it readable from JavaScript. Of course, ActiveX controls will only work on platforms that Microsoft supports.

Other People's Frames

Your carefully organized document can be loaded into a frame in someone else's document. This creates two problems: any visual effect you've planned can be spoiled by the content of unexpected sister frames, and the special variable top isn't the top you relied on any more. If the frame wrapping your document comes from a foreign web site, security limitations can trip you up as well.

The solution is to reload your document into top, but without touching any features that might fail due to security. Careful testing by Bob Stewart (mailto:webmaster@vmirror.com) yields logic which works with all relatively modern browsers. Thanks for permission to reproduce, Bob:

```
// First inline code of your document
if (parent.frames[1])
    parent.location.href = self.location.href;
```

The reverse can also be a problem: you are displaying a foreign document in a frame of your document. Either the foreigner overrides your frames, or their document isn't accessible any more and won't load. There's nothing you can do about the former case, except load their document in a separate window instead, perhaps one without user controls but on the other hand the latter case is worse. This results in a valid page being loaded, but not the one you expected. Better to be philosophic about this happening to start with.

Finally, you may want a page to appear only within a specific frameset document, probably a specific one. This simple test stops it from being loaded alone:

```
// first inline code in your document
if ( top == self )
    self.location.href = "frameset.htm";
```

Keeping Windows Intact

Some actions a script can take will spoil the appearance of a document. Submitting a form, requesting search results, sending email via HTML or even just clicking a link can stop a document that contains animations or interesting information from staying in good order. Chapter 7, Forms and Data, explains the mechanics for forms. Chapter 6, Multimedia and Plugins, explains the mechanics for images, animations and links.

Help Windows

You may want to supply help for a window's contents. There are a number of methods to try. Usually you want to help the user with either a small cue, or a more detailed discussion.

Small Cues

There isn't always the need to provide page after page of detailed explanations and reasons: a hint is often enough to help the user.

Alert, Confirm and Prompt Boxes

As discussed earlier, these simple little windows can provide basic feedback to the user when required. Being modal, they force the user to stop browsing and dispose of them before they continue. For some small cues, this is fine, but at times it can be intrusive, and so they shouldn't be overused for this purpose.

Status Message

The status message bar at the bottom of a main window is a handy place to cue the user. The biggest catch with it is that if the user can resize the window, you never know how much of your message is exposed to view. The easiest solution is to give up: write and hope. Keep the message short: imagine, for whatever reason, the user has set the system font size to 36 point! It's only a cue after all, not a warning.

There are two properties of the `window` object for the status bar: `status` and `defaultStatus`. The latter sets the status bar permanently, except for when the mouse pointer hovers over an interesting object like a link. Then the `status` property value is used instead. This means it only really makes sense to set the status property via an `onMouseOver` event. See the discussion in Chapter 6, Multimedia and Plugins.

You might give up on the status bar because there's not enough space, and create a one-line frame across the width of the window at the bottom. Then, at least, you'd have the full width of the window. You can use the 'windows without URLs' approach above to fill it whenever you need. Alternatively, you can put a single input text field into that thin frame and write messages into the field. None of these ideas are that much better than just using the status bar.

Chapter 5

Flyover Help

Typically called flyover help, bubble help or tool tips, browsers at the 4.0 level already do this for you, so upgrade if this is critical. Internet Explorer 4.0+ has the most support – the TITLE attribute of HTML 4.0 is used to show a tool tip over the tag it is part of. Netscape 4.0 will only produce these tiny windows for ALT attributes in <IMG> tags.

Extraordinarily desperate people will create a small window as a tooltip using window.open(), but why bother? It's slow, and it gets very tricky capturing the mouse movements and managing window focus so that the tiny window stays on top while the mouse hovers over the item of interest. Furthermore, browsers limit the minimum size of a window for paranoid security reasons (100x100 pixels in Netscape). To get around this limit you have to use a signed script, or write the tooltip window in ActiveX or Java.

For Netscape 3.0 and Microsoft 3.01 for the Macintosh, it's possible to mimic the Netscape 4.0 behavior. Use the technique described in the Multimedia and Plugins chapter for swapping images with an onMouseOver event. Make the second image the same as the first one, except that a tooltip appears to be embedded in it. When the images swap, the tooltip appears and disappears.

Finally, the resources of Dynamic HTML, described in Chapter 8, can be brought to bear on the problem of tooltips. This URL display tooltips using Dynamic HTML:
http://members.aol.com/MHall75819/JavaScript/tooltips.html

Detailed Information

When nothing but the facts will do, a window with hypertext information in it is just what HTML was designed for. Use window.open() and strip the new window of most of its controls, so the user can't surf the Web in the help window ... you never can tell how their minds work! There are a number of options for making the window appear on the screen.

Help Button

The most pain-free way to proceed is to just use a form button visible to the user. Most browsers don't even require that it be inside a <FORM> container, although Netscape 4.0 does. Very straightforward:

```
<INPUT TYPE="BUTTON" VALUE="Help" ONCLICK="show_help()">
```

show_help() is just your function containing all the window.open() plumbing.

Context Sensitive Help

A more aggressive approach is to open the help window with information specific to the bit of the window the user is interested in, not the whole window. There are two approaches: the form way, and the hard way.

The form way applies when the document in the window contains a form. Using onFocus triggers (described in detail in Chapter 7, Forms and Data), keep track of the current field the user is in by updating a separate variable. When a help button as described above is pressed, open the appropriate document for that field. A trivial example:

```
<HTML><HEAD><SCRIPT>
var field = "one";
function help()
{
    window.open("help_"+field+".htm", "help");
}
</SCRIPT></HEAD><BODY><FORM>
<INPUT TYPE="TEXT" NAME="one" ONFOCUS="top.field='one'">
<INPUT TYPE="TEXT" NAME="two" ONFOCUS="top.field='two'">
<INPUT TYPE="BUTTON" VALUE="Help" ONCLICK="window.help()">
</FORM></BODY></HTML>
```

In this example, `help_one.htm` and `help_two.htm` are help documents describing an individual field. The example could be varied so that different parts of a single document are displayed instead. This is done by using `<A NAME=''>` tags in the help file and modifying the function `help()` above as follows:

```
window.open("all_help.html#" + field, "help");
```

The hard way to do help is to organize matters so that when the user clicks anywhere in the screen, help appears for the item at that spot. In order to do this, you must use advanced event features of 4.0 version browsers, and lose some portability. The main problems to solve are:

❑ Convincing the user to click differently with the mouse for help.
❑ Partitioning the document logically into pieces;
❑ Identifying the item at the coordinates the user clicked.

For the end users, the normal left-click is fine for help if they understand some left-clicks do other things, like following links or setting checkboxes. Otherwise, pick any supported mouse button combination. It's possible to use the mouse to drop a 'help' icon onto the item required, if you want to use all the details of animation available in Dynamic HTML (Chapter 8).

Partitioning the document into pieces is a design approach that lends some structure to the document. Thinking of the document as a jigsaw puzzle of rectangular pieces is like making hot spots in an HTML image map. It makes it easier to define what help to show for each X,Y location in the document. Internet Explorer 4.0 does this for you, because all HTML elements are available to capture events. For Netscape Navigator 4.0, you have to use the whole window as one backdrop, and then make sure any areas which are to have help available are displayed via positionable styles, so the events can be captured in a `Layer` object. This means re-working a plain HTML document into one with positionable styles and layers located over (or containing) every interesting feature of the document.

To identify the item to give help on, use the Event object provided in different ways by the two 4.0 browsers. Then proceed as for the 'form way' above, opening the appropriate help page.

Chapter 8, Dynamic HTML, explains how to exploit these more advanced concepts. If all else fails, you can always turn to the HTML help software development kits (SDKs) mentioned earlier.

Built-in Help

In addition to the tactics described, configuration tools like Mission Control can be used to alter the basic menu items and toolbar icons of the browser. Bookmarks can form a simple help index and be locked so that the user can't remove them. Signed scripts in Navigator 4.0 can affect the 'Guide' menu, adding a help item for a specific application. See Chapter 18, Privacy, Security and Cookies.

Bad Documents and onError

Browsers can be quite tolerant of bad HTML, bad links and bad images. Often the document will finish displaying anyway. Netscape 3.0 and 4.x have a mechanism to allow it to be equally tolerant of bad JavaScript. This is the Netscape-specific onError event handler, present in Navigator 3.0 and 4.x.

Numerous errors can occur due to bad syntax, either when the document is loading, or later on in error handlers, and when eval() and setTimeout() occur. As a special 'other' case, errors can also occur when loading ('interpreting') an image – examining its URL or its content. When these errors appear the user gets an ugly error box. It is this kind of error that the onError handler is designed to manage. An example:

```
<HTML><HEAD><SCRIPT>
var ignore = true;
function catch_error()
{
   if ( ignore ) alert('Ignored ... sort of.');
   return ignore;
}
</SCRIPT></HEAD><BODY><SCRIPT>
onerror = null;
document.write('<BR><A HREF="x" ONCLICK="+++">No error</A>');
onerror = catch_error;
document.write('<BR><A HREF="x" ONCLICK="+++">Warning</A>');
ignore = false;
document.write('<BR><A HREF="x" ONCLICK="+++">Real error</A>');
document.write('<BR>Finished');
</SCRIPT></BODY></HTML>
```

The default behavior is that any error stops the document being read, and the error appears. In this example, the onerror handler is set three times, and there are three bad pieces of syntax – '+++' is not valid JavaScript:

❑ Firstly, the handler is set to null meaning ignore all errors, so No error appears, unmolested. Only <IMG> tags which have an OnError handler in that tag will be treated differently. In that sole case, responsibility for <IMG> errors devolves to the specific <IMG> tag's handler. That handler has the same choices as the document's onError handler.

❑ Secondly, the handler is set to the catch_error() function, which returns true due to the variable ignore, and pops up an alert (ignore has no special significance here, it's just a useful trick). When the alert is acknowledged, the Warning content appears unmolested.

❑ Finally, the handler is called again but returns false this time. An error results, and the browser gives up loading the document, so Finished never appears.

Netscape 4.06+ has a further trick up its sleeve here. Complaints from the browser can also be directed to the JavaScript console (discussed in Chapter 4 under 'JavaScript URLs') This is done via a preference sent in the Netscape `prefs.js` file:

```
user_pref("javascript.console.open_on_error", true);
```

If this line is in place when Netscape 4 starts up, any errors will cause the JavaScript console to appear.

As an alternative you might want the error to speak up for itself. To do that, just install an error handler at the start that does nothing but raise an alert. Here's an example of such a handler:

```
function error_alert(message)
{
  alert(message);
  return true;
}
onerror = error_alert;
```

Summary

Manipulating web browsers' windows and frames via JavaScript is mostly restricted to HTML document windows. Using scripts in this area creates tension between the control the scriptwriter and the browser user would like to have over the browser's features.

For basic document-style web pages, especially if they are publicly available on the Internet, keep it simple. Trying to limit the user's behavior is a valid goal, but takes work, and should be restricted to special purpose windows. Don't annoy users with extra windows, or useless windows just because you want more control as a scriptwriter – the user can always shut a window down.

For web-based applications, or whole systems delivered with a browser viewer, take a designed approach to limiting the user's behavior, so that a minimum of bad things can happen. Most toolbars give the users powers that can unexpectedly change your application setup. Configuration scripts, lockable preferences and signed scripts can enhance the script writers control over the browser beyond the basic features available in HTML-embedded JavaScript. Avoid old browsers for these applications where possible, and where impossible, stick to the simplest effects.

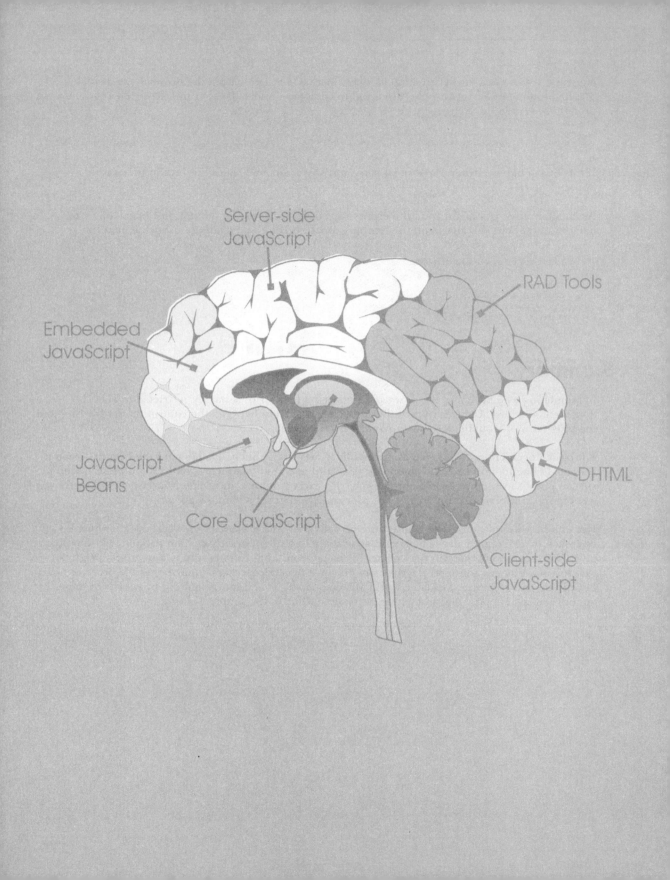

Multimedia and Plugins

Multimedia activity mostly occurs in a browser. Client-side JavaScript can be used as a control mechanism for exotic multimedia items embedded in an HTML document. Some features of the browser itself can be controlled in a dynamic way from scripts. Server-side or standalone JavaScript can play a part feeding the multimedia information to the browser.

This chapter discusses the multimedia possibilities created by combining JavaScript with plain HTML. Two technologies central to multimedia features used within plain HTML are ActiveX controls and Plugins. Plugins are a Netscape innovation, but work on virtually all browsers. ActiveX controls work primarily on Internet Explorer 3+ and allow installation and use of Windows-based components from the World Wide Web; because ActiveX controls are limited to use in Microsoft browsers, we will concentrate in this chapter on plugins. Further multimedia effects are made possible by combining JavaScript with Java or by using Dynamic HTML. These other possibilities are discussed in separate chapters.

A web browser has a pecking order that dictates how it handles a multimedia item. A file, message or URL which constitutes a multimedia item can be identified either with a DOS-style file extension or with a MIME message type. Usually the MIME type will only be available if the item has been retrieved from a web server, rather than from a local file system.

The browser uses these extensions and MIME types to identify how to display the item. There are two ways to call up such an item into the browser. The simpler way requires a URL pointing directly to the item to be typed in by the user or to be declared in a hypertext link (<A> tag) in an HTML page. The more complex way is to embed the object in the HTML document in an <OBJECT> or <EMBED> tag.

In either case, the browser first tries to handle (that is, to display or run) the item itself. If it can do this, as in the case of an HTML or plain text file, that is the end of the matter. If that is not possible, the item is handed to a plugin or to an ActiveX control that works with the browser to display or run the item. (This last step applies only to items specified in <OBJECT> or <EMBED> tags). If there is no suitable plugin or control available, or that option doesn't apply, a helper application (a separate program) is started to deal with it. If there's no suitable helper, the user gets the option of immediately installing a plugin or helper, saving the item to disk, or giving up.

Naturally, most of the following discussion will focus on visual effects, but remember that a multimedia item doesn't necessarily have to take up any space on the screen – sound clips, for example, are also multimedia items.

HTML Refresher

It pays to look before you leap. Basic multimedia is possible in a browser *without* using JavaScript. This section is a brief review of what you can get away with using plain HTML.

Color and Visibility

The numerous features of HTML allow colors to be chosen statically for many visible elements of a document, and also for the document's background. These features are now mostly deprecated in HTML 4.0 in favor of equivalent stylesheet properties, but are still widely available.

Stylesheets can further affect the appearance of HTML elements: they may become transparent, occlude other HTML elements, be occluded themselves, be clipped at the edges, or they may not be displayed at all.

Images

Many formats exist for storing and displaying single images (as opposed to animated images): GIF or PNG for graphics, JPEG for natural images, XBM, and others. GIF, JPEG and PNG have progressive formats so images are viewable as they are loaded. Use of a transparent color in a GIF image makes the image appear to be non-rectangular in shape. Making images look appealing is an art and a science all of its own.

The HTML <IMG> tag maps an image of any size into a rectangle in a browser window. The rectangle can be of a different size, scaling the image. The LOWSRC Netscape attribute allows a 'quick' image to display while the 'real' one is being retrieved.

Images in Other Elements

In addition, HTML allows images to appear in many other elements. <A> tags can have images in their content and client- or server-side image maps always have images in their content. In this way, the user can navigate by means of images to other URLs, possibly opening new windows in the process.

In HTML 4.0, an image can even appear as an `<INPUT>` element, due to the `<INPUT TYPE="image">` tag. This works in a similar way to a `SUBMIT` element, although in IE5, it also supports the `onClick` event.

```
<FORM ONSUBMIT=fnSubmit()>
    <INPUT TYPE=IMAGE SRC="wrox.gif" BORDER=0>
</FORM>

<SCRIPT>
    function fnSubmit()
    {
        // handle event here
    }
</SCRIPT>
```

We will see a development of this technique later on in this chapter.

The `BACKGROUND` attribute of the `<BODY>` tag tiles the document's background with the image. The following two very simple lines of HTML illustrate this:

```
<BODY BACKGROUND="wrox.gif">
</BODY>
```

The effect produced by this is to cover the browser window with a repeated image:

We can achieve the same effect with stylesheet properties such as background-image.

The 'single pixel image trick' is an old trick involving a tiny image one pixel wide and high. When the sole pixel is transparent, it is a crude way of aligning HTML elements when style sheets are not available. When not transparent, solid color rectangular blocks of any size are displayed. Both effects are achieved using the HEIGHT and WIDTH attributes of the <IMG> tag.

Animating Images

The 'animated GIF' mechanism inside GIF files allows simple animation by bundling a number of images into the one file. Pauses and endless loops are possible.

For fully animated images, the MPEG, QuickTime (usually MOV) and AVI standards are most common. These mostly require plugins. VRML is used to display three-dimensional images and animations, sometimes with user animation. The DYNSRC and START attributes of the <IMG> tag give crude control over animations in Microsoft browsers; greater control can be achieved using the DHTML behaviors introduced in IE5. DHTML behaviors are a means of attaching components to elements so that they behave in certain ways when specific events occur.

> *For more details on DHTML behaviors, see 'XML in IE5 Programmer's Reference', ISBN 1-861001-57-6, published by Wrox Press, or visit the Microsoft site at* http://msdn.microsoft.com/workshop/author/behaviors/overview.asp.

Images and plugins can be further clipped and overlaid using style sheets.

Sound

Sounds can be included in an HTML document using the <EMBED> or <OBJECT> tags. If the sound takes up no visible space in the browser, the proprietary <BGSOUND> tag of Microsoft, or Netscape's HIDDEN attribute for <EMBED> is used. Alternatively, display can be avoided by setting the display stylesheet property for the element to none.

Text

HTML text has a few simple effects available. Most of them are achieved with stylesheets, or pre-stylesheet tags, such as <FONT>. Moving the mouse over a hypertext link updates the status bar with the link's URL. Hyperlinks themselves are visibly different to other text. Microsoft's proprietary <MARQUEE> tag allows text to roll across the screen in several different ways. Netscape 4.0 allows a different font displayer to be installed into the browser or special additional fonts to be downloaded (if the user can be bothered). Flyover help appears for images (Navigator 4.0) or TITLE attributes (Internet Explorer 4.0).

JavaScript HTML Techniques

This section discusses what you can achieve with JavaScript and plain HTML, without stepping into the realm of Dynamic HTML.

Image Events

An image displayed in an HTML document can receive events, and therefore can have JavaScript event handlers. The reference section summarizes which events are available. There are two categories of events, which we may call **genuine events** and **derived events**.

Genuine Events

Only HTML 4.0 defines any standard events for images. In prior versions, there isn't even an `onClick` handler for image maps. Only Internet Explorer 4+ supports all these events. Netscape 4.x supports one or two. For portability, restrict yourself to `onMouseDown` and `onMouseUp`, and version 4+ browsers, or wait for further major upgrades from the vendors.

Netscape 3+ and Internet Explorer 5.0 support several events that apply chiefly to images. These are `onAbort`, `onError` and `onLoad`. These three events are designed to make loading of images a smooth and painless experience for the user, by handling problems as images load. The `onAbort` handler occurs when the user cancels the image download; `onError` occurs when there is a problem loading the image; and `onLoad` is raised when an image is fully displayed.

The `onError` event handler is useful if your document contains references to many images scattered over a number of web sites, such as a compilation page. It cannot be known how many of them will be available when the page loads. The `onError` event can be used to turn off complaints, as described in the 'Bad documents' section of the Windows and Frames chapter, Chapter 3.

An `onLoad` handler can prevent the user from proceeding before they have fully appreciated our pictures. Advertisements are a case in point; users may be inclined to ignore these if they can look at the web site's content straight away. This example shows how we might use `onLoad` to prevent the content being displayed before the advert has loaded:

```
<!-- frameset document -->
<HTML>
   <FRAMESET ROWS="*,*">
      <FRAME NAME="rubbish" SRC="advert.htm">
      <FRAME NAME="content" SRC="blank.htm">
   </FRAMESET>
</HTML>
```

```
<!-- frame advert.htm-->
<HTML>
   <HEAD>
      <SCRIPT>
         function more()
         {
            top.content.location.href = "content.htm";
         }
      </SCRIPT>
   </HEAD>
   <BODY>
      <IMG SRC="buy_it.gif" ONLOAD="more()">
   </BODY>
</HTML>
```

This displays a substitute page (blank.htm) until the onLoad event of the advert image is fired. Of course, if you want to use this technique, you'd better be sure that your content is worth waiting for, or users might decide to go somewhere else!

Just about the only reason for using onAbort is to help the user escape from a document that contains a huge, slow image. An example:

```
<HTML>
    <HEAD>
        <SCRIPT>
            function run_away()
            {
                window.location.href = window.history.go(-1);
            }
        </SCRIPT>
    </HEAD>
    <BODY>
        Another elephant crowd scene:<BR>
        <IMG SRC="peanut_hunt.jpg" ONABORT="run_away()">
    </BODY>
</HTML>
```

Big images should really be viewed in a window of their own (not in another HTML page) for the best possible appearance. One reason for this is that the browser will be better able to exploit the colors that the computer terminal has to offer, which can improve the image reproduction.

Derived Events

If an image is the sole content of another HTML tag, then user events for that tag are probably intended for the image. Several tricks can be achieved by this method.

The main approach with Netscape is to surround an image with an <A></A> hyperlink 'container', making onMouseOver, onMouseOut and onClick handlers available. This works in Navigator 3.0 and 4.x, and Internet Explorer 4.0 and 5.0. The alternative is to place the image within a <LAYER> tag (an element used to place content in overlapping layers), which can capture all the HTML 4.0 events. This alternative will only work in Navigator 4.x, as layers are proprietary to Netscape.

The event model exposed by Internet Explorer 4+ allows mouse actions and keypresses to bubble up through the HTML tag hierarchy regardless of tag. This means both Netscape's <A></A> alternative and numerous other tag combinations are possible. For Internet Explorer 3.0, the situation is very limited as neither Image objects nor onMouseOver triggers are fully functional.

The next section shows how to exploit these tactics.

Using the Image Object

JavaScript lets the scriptwriter create an Image object for an image located at a URL. This is quite special behavior because the Image object is directly exposed to JavaScript as a host object. So this browser script is completely correct:

```
var picture = new Image();
```

By comparison, you can't create a paragraph object to represent a <P> element, for example, in any browser by calling a JavaScript constructor, such as:

```
var para = new P();
```

It's true that there are other methods of creating a <P> tag from a script, for example using a `document.write('<P>')` statement or via DHTML, but no method is as direct as that available for the Image object. Alas, Internet Explorer 3.0 and Navigator 2.02 don't support this Image behavior.

The appendices list all the properties and methods of this object. The two essential properties are `src` and `complete`:

❑ `src` is a read/write property containing the URL of the actual image file represented by the object.

❑ `complete` is a read-only property indicating whether the browser has finished attempting to load the image file.

There are a couple of points to think about with these properties. Using `src`, one image file can be replaced with another, whether it is visible in the window display or not. With `complete`, we have to resort to event handlers or timers to find out whether the image is fully loaded or not. This is because there is no other easy way to 'wait' for the property to become `true`. It's easy to test with a simple `if` statement to see what the current value of the property is, but suppose that's not to our liking: what then? Consider this script:

```
var picture = new Image();
picture.src = 'CheshireCat.jpg';

// waste some time doing other tasks

if (picture.complete == true )
{
    // Great, on we go.
}
else
{
    // What now? Sit in a tight loop checking
    // forever until it is loaded? Very wasteful.
}
```

When a new URL is assigned to an `Image` object, it actually represents a scaled-to-fit version of the URL. `HEIGHT` and `WIDTH` attributes in <IMG> tags, or constructor function arguments in JavaScript, dictate the size the image file is scaled to fit. If neither are supplied, the image's natural size is used (no scaling). The upshot of this is that any image URL can be assigned to an `Image` object directly via a script statement and, if the width and height of the image are fixed it will always fit exactly the space that object takes up on the browser window.

This resizing-to-fit will always happen in the Netscape browsers, because the 4.x browsers can't reflow the document after it's loaded. However, in the case of Internet Explorer 4+, we have to remember to specify the `HEIGHT` and `WIDTH` tags or else when the second image loads, it could alter the page layout if its original size is different to that of the first image.

Replacing an Image

Here is the simplest example, replacing one image with another. It's easy to see how the `onClick` handler could be expanded to do more complex work such as retrieving the image URL from a text field the user filled in. Because the `Image` object underneath is a scaled image, this example will work with any replacement image, regardless of size—try changing the names in the script to any images you have lying around.

```
<HTML>
    <BODY>
        <FORM>
            <IMG HEIGHT=200 WIDTH=200 SRC="startup.gif">
            <INPUT TYPE="BUTTON" VALUE="Change Image"
                    ONCLICK="window.document.images[0].src = 'anything.jpg'">
        </FORM>
    </BODY>
</HTML>
```

Button Swaps

The button in the `<INPUT TYPE="button">` tag is rather boring. It's not hard to create two images that look like interesting buttons – one for when the button is selected, and one for when it isn't. This is so simple and useful that HTML 4.0 includes a general `<BUTTON>` tag, available only in Internet Explorer 4+. However, this tag merely highlights the edges of any enclosed image when the mouse is pressed. That leaves plenty of scope for very fancy buttons using images. This example makes the mock button change appearance when the mouse hovers over it.

```
<HTML>
    <BODY ALINK="black" VLINK="black" LINK="black">
        <FORM>
            <A HREF="javascript:void(0)"
                ONMOUSEOVER="window.document.images[0].src='down.gif'"
                ONMOUSEOUT="window.document.images[0].src='up.gif'"
                ONCLICK="alert('Click!');return false;">
            <IMG HEIGHT=100 WIDTH=100 BORDER=0 SRC="up.gif"></A>
        </FORM>
    </BODY>
</HTML>
```

If the second image looks the same as the first, except for an added small box of text, then we can use this technique to simulate flyover help (Microsoft tooltips). Since the `onClick` handler fires when the mouse is "over" the image, but not yet "out" of it, further changes to the image are possible when the click occurs. For example, an image of a button may generally appear ordinary, change to an image of a highlighted button when the mouse is over it, and change again to an image of a depressed button when the user clicks on it.

This example won't work for Internet Explorer 3.02, so see this page for a free Java applet that does the same thing, and works with both Microsoft and Netscape 3.0 browsers:
`http://www.omegagrafix.com/mouseover/mousover.html`.

Making Image Swaps Faster

Each time the `src` property changes for an image swap or for some other script manipulation of an image, the browser has to find the image. A lengthy delay can result if the image file isn't cached in the browser and needs to be retrieved over the network. If the image is already loaded and cached, this problem disappears. Here is a script that loads some images separate to any in the normal HTML of the page, and advises when they're completely loaded:

```
<HTML>
   <HEAD>
      <SCRIPT>
         var images_so_far = 0;
         var poster1 = new Image();
         var poster2 = new Image();
         var poster3 = new Image();

         function ImageCounter()
         {
            if (++images_so_far == 3)
            alert("All wise men present");
         }
      </SCRIPT>
   </HEAD>
   <BODY>
      <SCRIPT>
         poster1.src = 'elvis.gif';
         poster1.onLoad=ImageCounter();
         poster2.src = 'ghandi.gif';
         poster2.onLoad=ImageCounter();
         poster3.src = 'groucho.gif';
         poster3.onLoad=ImageCounter();
      </SCRIPT>
      Waiting ...
      <!-- the HTML document, incuding any IMG tags, go here -->
   </BODY>
</HTML>
```

`Image` objects loaded separately to those in the current document can be used to make image swaps look much faster to the user. This is because in the above example care was taken to load the other images right at the start of the main page load. It's a race to see who will finish loading first, but the other images have the best start they can get.

If you want to be sure that no image events are acted upon until all the images are loaded, then example needs to be modified as follows:

```
var all_ok = false;
function ImageCounter()
{
   if (++images_so_far == 3)
      window.all_ok = true;
}
```

And in addition all your image event handlers must be changed from perhaps:

```
<IMG SRC="whatever.gif"
   ONMOUSEOVER="doOver()"
   ONMOUSEOUT="doOut()">
```

to:

```
<IMG SRC="whatever.gif"
    ONMOUSEOVER="if(window.all_ok) doOver()"
    ONMOUSEOUT="if(window.all_ok) doOut()"
>
```

To keep the original simplicity of your event handlers, the check of the `all_ok` variable could alternatively be moved inside those handler functions.

Controlling Animation

Animated GIFs don't give you any control over their animation: they run, and you're stuck with them. Fancy plugins do give control, but often use file formats you can't create without tools. A middle ground using the `Image` object provides a crude form of fully controlled animation. Each of the frames in the animation is a distinct image with its own URL. When using this sort of animation, it's important to be certain that all the images have been cached using the technique above, or else the animation will start in a very jerky manner (it will improve with time). The following example shows a 'waiting' animation, controlled by the user. In this case, the animation images are named `wait-0.gif` through to `wait-7.gif` and appear as follows:

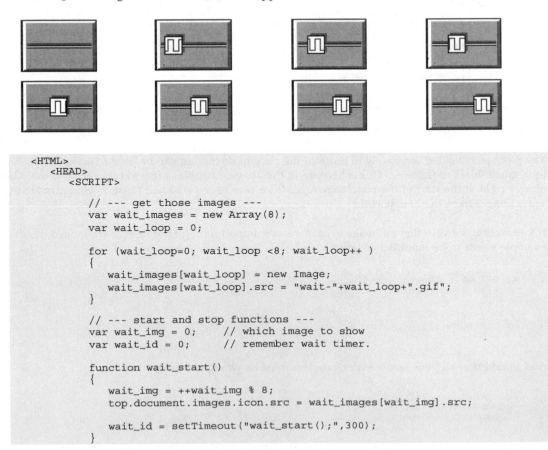

```
<HTML>
   <HEAD>
     <SCRIPT>

        // --- get those images ---
        var wait_images = new Array(8);
        var wait_loop = 0;

        for (wait_loop=0; wait_loop <8; wait_loop++ )
        {
           wait_images[wait_loop] = new Image;
           wait_images[wait_loop].src = "wait-"+wait_loop+".gif";
        }

        // --- start and stop functions ---
        var wait_img = 0;     // which image to show
        var wait_id = 0;      // remember wait timer.

        function wait_start()
        {
           wait_img = ++wait_img % 8;
           top.document.images.icon.src = wait_images[wait_img].src;

           wait_id = setTimeout("wait_start();",300);
        }
```

```
        function wait_stop()
        {
            clearTimeout(wait_id);
            top.document.images.icon.src = 'anything.gif';
        }
    </SCRIPT>
</HEAD>
<BODY>
    <IMG SRC="anything.gif" NAME="icon">
    <FORM>
        <INPUT TYPE="BUTTON" VALUE="Wait" ONCLICK="wait_start()">
        <INPUT TYPE="BUTTON" VALUE="Done" ONCLICK="wait_stop()">
    </FORM>
</BODY>
</HTML>
```

In this example, the timing and order of the images are all fully exposed in the wait_start()
routine, which could be arbitrarily complex. The small box moves from left to right, disappears, and
then repeats. However, it could just as easily move from right to left, or alternate directions, or jump
around randomly. It could start fast and then slow down. Only one function needs changing for each
of these effects.

Faking Menus and Popups

The 'button swap' section above shows how to mimic tooltips with images. If you have a large image,
then it is possible to mimic other graphical user interface (GUI) elements, like menus. GUI items that
require complex user input like dialog boxes are impractical, however.

The way to do this is to apply a general image replacement technique for this specific problem. The
general approach treats the space taken up by the initial image as a canvas (blank area) on which to
draw other images. If the 'background' color or texture of the images is the same as the document
background, this can appear quite effective, and is sometimes as convenient to do as Dynamic HTML
tricks. Consider the following images:

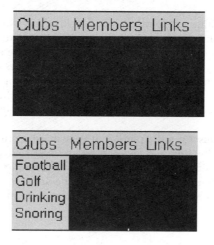

If there are no more than four menu items each in 'Members' and 'Links', the image space can be used to display all the different menus using 4 images. This setup relies on a client-side image map as follows (assume the images are 200x100 pixels with each word item being 60x20 pixels):

```
<HTML>
  <BODY>
    <SCRIPT>
    var dropped = false;
    var menu = 0;
    function update(item)
    {
      if ( !dropped )    // no submenu yet
      {
        if ( item != 1 && item !=6 && item != 11)
        {
          return;      // user clicked somewhere useless
        }
        if ( item == 1) {
          window.document.pic.src = 'fakemenu2.gif';
          dropped=true;
        }
        // two more if's for other menus ...
      }
      else
      {
        if ( menu == 1 && item == 1 )
          // do the football thing ...
          // 14 more if's for other menu items ...
      }
    }
    </SCRIPT>
    <MAP NAME="menu">
      <AREA COORDS="0,0,60,20" HREF="javascript:window.update(1)">
      <AREA COORDS="0,20,60,40" HREF="javascript:window.update(2)">
      <!— 5 x 3 = 15 AREA tags total ... -->
    </MAP>
    <IMG NAME="pic" SRC="fakemenu1.gif" USEMAP="#menu">
  </BODY>
</HTML>
```

The user is first presented with a single menu bar. Clicking anywhere in the image except the menu bar does nothing. Clicking on a menu bar item causes the image to change and a drop-down menu appears. Clicking on an item in the drop-down menu causes some arbitrary JavaScript to run. Clicking in empty space away from the drop down menu still does nothing. A more sophisticated example could clean up the menu bar afterwards or gray-out inappropriate options. The appearance of the drop-down menu could be animated via an animated GIF that ran through its images once and then stopped, with the drop-down menu fully exposed as the last image of the animation.

Obviously, the example menus are quite plain, but very artistic ones could just as easily be used. Provided that every pixel of the image is covered by an <AREA> tag, the user won't notice that some 'hot spots' apparently do nothing when clicked. This is because the mouse point will look the same everywhere on the image. There is no need to lay out the areas in a grid as has been done in this case; it's just convenient for menus. There is no need to stick to menus with this technique either.

Progress Meters

Progress meters are tricky to implement with image replacement techniques, because of the many stages progress can be at. It's quite possible to create them by designing 100 images (one for each percentage point of progress), but there's an easier way: use a single pixel image and a frame or layer. This is also easy with positioned elements and no images —extend the clipping region of a colored area as progress occurs, to expose more of the area. Here is an example of the image approach:

```
<HTML>
   <FRAMESET ROWS="40,*">
      <FRAME NAME="progress" SRC="blank.htm">
      <FRAME NAME="test" SRC="bar.htm">
   </FRAMESET>
</HTML>
```

```
<!-- blank.htm -->
<HTML></HTML>
```

```
<!-- bar.htm -->
<HTML>
   <HEAD>
      <SCRIPT>
         function draw(percent)
         {
            with (top.progress.document) {
               open();
               write('<HTML><BODY><IMG SRC="onepixel.gif" '+
                  'HEIGHT=10 WIDTH="' + percent*4 +
                  '"></BODY></HTML>');
               close();
            }
         }
         var percent = 10;
      </SCRIPT>
   </HEAD>
   <BODY>
      <FORM>
         <INPUT TYPE="BUTTON" VALUE="Progress"
               ONCLICK="window.draw(percent+=10)">
         <INPUT TYPE="BUTTON" VALUE="Backwards!"
               ONCLICK="window.draw(percent-=10)">
      </FORM>
   </BODY>
</HTML>
```

Although the updates are due to the user here, the draw() function could easily be called from anywhere within the code (possibly with better error checking on the passed-in value).
This example will run more slowly than a style sheet version, but it is extremely portable.

Local Processing

Retrieving URLs, for images, animations or otherwise, can be slow. There are a few small tricks that are more efficient than generating a possibly expensive URL request for the Web.

Multimedia Without URLs

It may not be necessary to reach across the Internet for animations and images. The simplest thing is to package your multimedia up and deliver it to the disk drive that holds the target web browser, making your pages work that way. If you are installing an information kiosk, or producing a game, that may be enough. A second possibility is to use Netscape's LiveCache feature – see http://www.home.it.netscape.com/navigator/v3.0/using/cachesetup.html. This allows web pages normally accessed by a web server to be bundled up into a local file (possibly on a CD) and still be accessible via their full URL. URLs are still used in these cases, but at least they are local to the browser's computer.

Finally, some trivial multimedia can be done directly in the browser.

Inline Images

Chapter 5 describes how JavaScript URLs can be used as document content. They can also be used as image content – specifically for an Image object's src property. If you can create the contents (not the URL) of an image directly in client-side JavaScript, you can display it without a web server. Note that this tactic only works with Netscape 3+ browsers.

Unfortunately, there are two catches. The first is that image content is hard to reproduce from any language. JPEG format is based on mathematical transforms, GIF is compressed (as well as being a proprietary format), and PNG is just as complex. The second is that Netscape browsers prior to 4.06 have this obscure bug in their JavaScript implementation:

```
'xxx\000yyy' == 'xxx';        // true !
'xxx\000yyy'.length == 3;     // true !
```

An ASCII NUL (zero value) character terminates a JavaScript string, and therefore can't be put inside one. This shuts out most image formats, since they contain binary data, and therefore randomly contain ASCII 0s.

Even with these issues, its still possible to create images from JavaScript. There are three suggested approaches:

❑ Steal the images from Java.

❑ Use Netscape 4.06+ browser only and use some free PNG format tools.

❑ Use the XBM format more generally with Netscape.

Stealing the images from Java means taking advantage of Netscape's LiveConnect features (see the chapters on JavaScript and Java). If it's too hard to create an image and get it into a string in JavaScript, then call a Java applet or library, get that applet or library to create the image, and then have that library return the image back as a string to JavaScript. This is fairly sophisticated stuff, and well beyond the scope of this book. However, if you are keen (or your Java programmer friend is keen) then read the chapters on Java and JavaScript (Chapters 15 and 16) and use the following URL as a jumping off point for the Java half of the problem: http://developer.java.sun.com/developer/onlineTraining/Programming/JDCBook/perf.html

For JavaScript formatting tools for the PNG image format, this gentleman has done an impressive job: http://www.elf.org/pnglets/. His files can easily be downloaded from: http://www.elf.org/js/. He's also had some limited success with the GIF format – alas, not as flexible as his PNG work.

Finally, the ancient and humble XBM format is still a possibility. This format allows us to create black and white bitmapped images. An XBM file contains plain text, not binary data, so there are no ASCII zeros to cause problems. We'll have a more in-depth look at this approach here. An XBM file looks like this (this is the file's source):

```
#define trash_width 16
#define trash_height 16
static char trash_bits[] = {
    0x00, 0x01, 0xe0, 0x0f, 0x10, 0x10, 0xf8, 0x3f, 0x10, 0x10, 0x50, 0x15,
    0x50, 0x15, 0x50, 0x15, 0x50, 0x15, 0x50, 0x15, 0x50, 0x15, 0x50, 0x15,
    0x50, 0x15, 0x10, 0x10, 0xe0, 0x0f, 0x00, 0x00};
```

Put into a JavaScript string it would look like this:

```
var trash_bmp = "#define trash_width 16\n" +
    "#define trash_height 16\n" +
    "static char trash_bits[] = {\n" +
    "    0x00, 0x01, 0xe0, 0x0f, 0x10, 0x10, 0xf8, 0x3f, \n" +
    "    0x10, 0x10, 0x50, 0x15, 0x50, 0x15, 0x50, 0x15, \n" +
    "    0x50, 0x15, 0x50, 0x15, 0x50, 0x15, 0x50, 0x15, \n" +
    "    0x50, 0x15, 0x10, 0x10, 0xe0, 0x0f, 0x00, 0x00};"
```

Somewhat ironically for XBM, this is a picture of a rubbish bin icon, height 16 pixels, width 16 pixels. Each hexadecimal value represents 8 pixels, each either on or off:

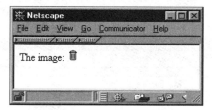

Once you have this text in a string, you can assign it to the `src` attribute of an `Image` object. Chapter 4's section on 'JavaScript URLs' shows an example of creating a one-pixel GIF this way.

What is this good for? If you refuse to access a Java applet, ActiveX control or plugin from JavaScript, then this or the PNG URLs above are your only way of doing graphics (black and white at that) in a browser with JavaScript. You can create an arbitrary image with patterns, or graphs, or pick up drawing movements made by the user, etc. That is left as an exercise to the reader...

For later sub-versions of Navigator 4.0, such as 4.04, the ASCII NUL bug is fixed, so the other image types are again a possibility—but beware! It is only fixed deep inside JavaScript where images are manipulated—if you try to display a string with an embedded NUL using `window.alert()` or `document.write()`, the bug is back. This problem doesn't occur in Internet Explorer.

Chapter 6

Status Bar Animations

Animating the status bar is a thrill nearly as cheap as XBM images. If you can write a string to it once, you can do so twice... and so on. This web site lists a number of different scrolling effects in JavaScript with the source code: `http://javascript.internet.com/scrolls/`

The debate is still open as to whether scrolling messages annoy the user, but the answer is probably yes. Here is the least annoying example your author could think of (watch the status bar carefully):

```
<HTML>
   <HEAD>
      <SCRIPT>
         var current = 0;
         var note = "The scrolling message from hell";
         function scroll_it()
         {
            current = (current == note.length) ? 0 : current+1;
            defaultStatus = note.substring (0, current)
                + note.charAt (current) .toUpperCase ()
                + note.substr(current+1, note.length);
            setTimeout("scroll_it()",100);
         }
         scroll_it();
      </SCRIPT>
   </HEAD>
</HTML>
```

Creating charts

On its web site, Netscape provides a handy script library for creating simple bar charts in a web page. Although it consists of no more than a set of plain JavaScript functions and a few `document.write()` statements, this script library shows how much you can achieve using only basic browser features. Here's a screen shot from Netscape's HOW-TO page at `http://developer.netscape.com:80/docs/technote/javascript/graph/`:

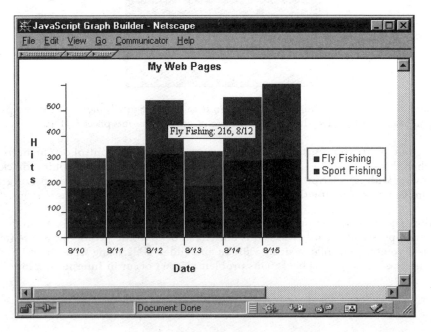

If you want more sophisticated charts, you really have to look outside JavaScript to embedding Microsoft Excel as an ActiveX object in your web page, or to a Java graphing applet. However, if you have Internet Explorer 4+ or Netscape 5.0, then this chart is just a glimpse of what's possible with Dynamic HTML - see Chapter 8.

Document Re-writing

The progress bar example illustrates how crude animation can be done by re-writing HTML documents. You can rewrite any HTML document, not just an `<IMG>` tag. To make this happen as smoothly as possible, follow that example, but avoid tables: always use `HEIGHT` and `WIDTH` attributes in `<IMG>` tags; minimize the number of URLs that have to be fetched in order to complete the page; and don't get your hopes up too high.

The URL Request Trap

In order to stop a browser from making requests from web servers, it's common to install JavaScript event handlers to capture events, or to install `javascript:` URLs to replace 'normal' URLs. However, there is a subtle difference between these two tactics.

When an `onClick` event handler for a link is invoked, it gives the script writer a chance to abort any URL request that would otherwise occur. That link might be in an `<A>` tag or a client-side image map's `<AREA>` tag. If the handler returns `false`, no URL request occurs (except for in Navigator 3.0, since `onClick` return values are ignored there). This approach is a straightforward way of intervening when a user tries to go to another URL by clicking a link.

However, a `javascript:` URL is still a URL, so substituting it for another URL in a tag doesn't technically stop the URL request. The request that is the `javascript:` URL is performed.

This subtle distinction is important, because if the browser detects that a URL is to be loaded, it gives up on the current document. When it gives up, any partially loaded components of the document, such as replacement images, streaming sound files, or animations stop as well. So avoid `javascript:` URLs in favor of event handlers in documents that contain many loading or reloading multimedia objects - they will stop other partially loaded items dead.

Microsoft 3.0 web browsers don't support `javascript:` URLs in client-side image maps anyway, so if you need to support 3.0 browsers, you're caught between the devil and the deep blue sea - non-portable `javascript:` URLs or (in 3.0 browsers) possibly buggy event handlers.

Creating Pauses and Delays

Controlling animation effects often means working with timing issues. Using animation may require us to create pauses in the processing of the page. Although JavaScript in browsers is good at scheduling events for the future via `setTimeout()` and `setInterval()`, it doesn't contain any `sleep()`, `wait()` or `pause()` style functions like this:

```
do_something();
wait(3);                    // three seconds pass impossible
do_something_else();
```

Implementing these pauses is therefore a bit tricky. There are two solutions:

- ❑ Apply brute force.
- ❑ Stop thinking about it.

The brute force solution looks like this:

```
function wait()
{
    var loop;
    for ( loop=0; loop < 10000; loop++)
        123.45 * loop * 67.890;
}
```

This function grabs the browser and doesn't let go until it has finished. The mathematics in the body of the `for` loop is just to give the computer something to do other than examining and incrementing the `loop` counter. This is heavy work for the browser's computer, but it works. The only problem is that it runs at different speeds for different browsers, and may not stop all browser windows if the browser is 'threaded', so that each window runs independently (e.g. Internet Explorer).

You can write a calibration function that detects the speed of the browser's computer and modifies the loop total accordingly, but it will only turn a guess into a rough estimate.

"Stop thinking about it" saves you from trying to breed a flying pig. Browsers think in terms of scheduling incoming events – items that need doing, either immediately, or at some time in the future. In order to do this they need to keep referring to their list of outstanding events to see what's due to be done. This approach doesn't fit well with the idea of "just stop for a second". You can usually re-express your goal as a series of events to be scheduled and use `setTimeout()` instead. Consider the following example.

You want to display some information (perhaps an image or some Dynamic HTML text) for a few seconds, and then change the information to something else. If the user is still viewing the page after two minutes, you want to change the information yet again, threatening to visit their mother if they don't hurry up and buy your product. Suppose you already have JavaScript functions created that do the actual displaying:

```
show_entry_advert();
show_main_advert();
show_warning();
```

What you'd like to do is something like this:

```
show_entry_advert();
// wait 5 seconds somehow
show_main_advert();
// wait 120 seconds somehow
show_warning();
```

As we've seen, this is problematic. A better solution is to plan all these things now, and leave it up to the browser to execute them:

```
show_entry_advert();                    // do this straight away.
setTimeout("show_main_advert()", 5000)  // 5000 milliseconds from now.
setTimeout("show_warning()", 125000)    // 5+120 seconds from now.
```

Your script finishes very quickly this way – only one function and two `setTimeout()` calls are made before the script ends. At two points in the future, somewhat magically (but really due to the browser remembering what you told it with `setTimeout()`) the other functions start up. This approach can be varied – you don't have to schedule everything at the start. Suppose `show_main_advert()` reads as follows:

```
function show_main_advert()
{
   // do some stuff;
   return true;
}
```

W can change it so that it is responsible for scheduling the next action:

```
function show_main_advert()
{
   // do some stuff;
   setTimeout("show_warning()", 120000);   // 120 seconds from now.
   return true;
}
```

In this case, our three-line scheduling process is reduced to two lines, because we are now scheduling one thing at a time, like making a daisy chain.

```
show_entry_advert();                    // do this straight away.
setTimeout("show_main_advert()", 5000)  // 5 seconds from now.
```

In 5 seconds time, a further activity will be scheduled 120 seconds further into the future by the `show_main_advert()` function.

Browser JavaScript and Plugins

Plugins allow clever multimedia effects such as coordinated sound and picture, and specialized graphics. Depending on the individual plugin, JavaScript can control these effects to varying degrees.

To refresh on terminology: when a browser retrieves a URL resource from the web, the resource arrives in a message with some identifying information. One part of this information is the MIME type, which uniquely describes the type of content the message contains. An ActiveX control is not a plugin – Microsoft Internet Explorer supports both ActiveX controls (general access to the browser computer) and Netscape-style plugins (intended to have little access to the browser computer).

As a script writer, before you can control a multimedia effect created by a plugin, you need to ensure that four things are present and correct: firstly, that the MIME type for the multimedia URL is known by the browser; secondly, that a plugin is installed for that MIME type; thirdly, that an <EMBED> or <OBJECT> tag exists for the multimedia data file, and fourthly, that the data file has loaded into the browser. Only when all those things have occurred does JavaScript have any chance of affecting the plugin.

Often it is sufficient to warn users of a web page that a particular plugin is required by putting a note in that page, or by letting the browser warn the user itself. You can usually be confident that common plugins are present, such as those supplied with the browser at installation. Alternatively, you can focus on the users interested in your page (who are likely to have the browsers correctly installed) and let the rest cope as they may. However, on the Internet there is no controlling users' browser installation, so technically, you should check (via a script) before making assumptions about how plugins can be controlled.

Plugin Object Model

The following diagram illustrates the essential parts of the browser object model for plugins. This is valid only for Netscape Browsers 3.x and 4.x. The embeds array also exists in Microsoft browsers, and no error is generated by calling navigator.plugins or navigator.mimeTypes; however, these return empty arrays.

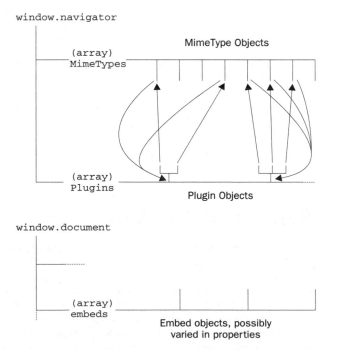

There are two parts to the model; the first relates to installation, and the second to specific HTML documents.

Installation Plugin Objects

Details of what plugins and MIME types have been installed in the browser are exposed to client-side JavaScript. There are two important object types: `MimeType` and `Plugin`. Appendix F documents their methods and properties. They are collected into arrays called `mimeTypes` and `plugins`. These arrays are accessible from the `window.navigator` object.

Every MIME type either has a plugin, or it doesn't. Each `MimeType` object in the `mimeTypes` array has a property `enabledPlugin` which is either `null` or refers to a `Plugin` object in the `plugins` array. If it is `null`, it means that MIME type must be handled by some other means. Only one plugin can handle a given MIME type.

One the other hand, every `Plugin` object in the `plugins` array looks like an array of MIME types. A `Plugin` object has a few descriptive properties but mostly its properties point to `MimeType` objects in the `mimeTypes` array. Each `plugin` can handle more than one MIME type, but no plugins can share MIME types.

If you type `about:plugins` in the location, you will see a report based on these browser objects for the currently installed plugins and their MIME types. You can see from the source of this page that it merely uses these objects.

There is no reason at all to modify these objects from JavaScript, and there is only one reason for examining them:

Detecting Correct Installation

It's no use trying to control a multimedia object in the browser if it's handled by an unexpected plugin. Fortunately, the MIME type of the multimedia URL and the plugin preferred is usually known in advance by the scriptwriter. This gives enough information to write a script that will detect the situation when it arrives at a user's browser. We need to check when the page loads that the correct plugin is enabled, and that it handles objects with our MIME type:

```
var known = true;

if ( ! navigator.plugins["QuickTime Plug-In"].enabledPlugin )
    known = false;        // the expected plugin is missing

else if ( ! navigator.plugins["QuickTime Plug-In"]["video/quicktime"])
    known = false;        // it's not configured for our type
```

Once a missing plugin is detected, there are two options: let the URL load, but script around it without touching it, or exclude the tags with the URL from the source HTML. Using the `known` flag from the above example:

```
function rewind_it()
{
    // ... rewind a quicktime movie back to frame 1.
}
if ( known )
{
    document.write('<EMBED SRC="film.mov" HEIGHT=260 WIDTH=320 '
                   + 'CONTROLLER=true LOOP=false AUTOPLAY=TRUE>');
    document.write('<INPUT TYPE="BUTTON" VALUE="Play" ONCLICK="rewind_it()">');
}
```

```
   else
   {
       // only use standard HTML parameters
       document.write('<EMBED SRC="film.mov" HEIGHT=260 WIDTH=320');
   }
```

Similarly for avoiding the whole problem:

```
if ( known )
{
    document.write('<EMBED SRC="film.mov" HEIGHT=260 WIDTH=320 '
                  + 'CONTROLLER=true LOOP=false AUTOPLAY=TRUE>');
    document.write('<INPUT TYPE="BUTTON" VALUE="Play" ONCLICK="rewind_it()">');
}
else
{
    document.write('<IMG SRC="get_quicktime.gif" HEIGHT=260 WIDTH=320>');
}
```

Document Plugin Objects

Detecting that a browser is configured with the plugin you want to use is only half the battle. To interact with the multimedia URL, it must be loaded into the browser. Just like the rest of an HTML document, this means a JavaScript host object will be created when that part of the document is reached. Just because the object is created doesn't mean that the whole related URL has been loaded – this is similar to the Image object. This object is called a plugin instance.

The embeds property is an array which contains one Embed object for each <EMBED> or <OBJECT> tag in the document. Internet Explorer 3.0 differs on this property – it is window.document.embeds in Netscape browsers and Internet Explorer 4+ and window.embeds in Explorer 3.0 only. A simple hack fixes this:

```
var myembeds = ( typeof(window.embeds) == "undefined" )
      ? window.document.embeds
      : window.embeds;          // use 'myembeds' from now on
```

The elements of the array appear in the order that they appear in the HTML source. The ugly part of the embeds array is that every Embed object has different properties and methods, depending on the plugin used to handle the URL. The plugin-specific parameters are only available from JavaScript if the plugin supplies them as Embed object properties (or by retrieving the whole tag as a string, as in Internet Explorer 4.0).

To find out the properties and methods a given plugin supplies, you have to look up information supplied by the plugin vendor (usually accessible on their web site). This is also the case for tag attributes specific to the plugin.

To find out if all the Embed objects have been created for a document, just use a synchronization tactic such as document onLoad handlers—see the section on 'Concurrency' in Chapter 5. Alternatively, you can repeatedly check the embeds.length property until it is as large as the number of embedded objects in the page.

Controlling Plugins Objects

There are two degrees of control over plugins supported from within JavaScript. Whether they are available depends on the individual plugin. They are:

❑ Embed object properties and methods

❑ Embed object properties and methods, plus callback functions

Apart from an Embed object, a plugin instance can cause a specially named JavaScript function to run. If the function exists, the plugin will run it at appropriate times. Since the function is written by the script writer, not the plugin vendor, this gives an escape hatch for the script writer to perform special actions on behalf of the plugin.

Simple Object Properties – LiveAudio

LiveAudio is a Netscape plugin installed by default with Navigator 4.0 designed for sound files. It supports several sound formats. When a LiveAudio plugin instance is created, perhaps in response to a tag like `<EMBED SRC="tidal.wav">`, an Embed object is created in the embeds array of the browser, which can then be accessed through script with the line:

```
document.embeds[0].method_name()
```

where *method_name* is one of the ones iterated below. The Netscape web page at `http://developer.netscape.com:80/docs/manuals/js/client/jsguide/liveaud.htm` describes the properties and methods of this object. Particularly noteworthy is the `IsReady()` method, which is just like the 'complete' property of the Image object. This mechanism can be used to tell if the sound file is fully downloaded yet. The LiveAudio plugin does not support any callback functions, so control of the plugin instance is one-way: from the scriptwriter to the plugin instance.

To illustrate a whole plugin, here are the properties and methods quoted from that document. These methods are very typical of plugins. In this list `int` (integer) is just a convention meaning a whole number is expected, rather than a string or fractional number:

Controlling functions (all Boolean):

❑ play(true/false or int,'URL of sound file')

❑ stop()

❑ pause()

❑ start_time(int seconds)

❑ end_time(int seconds)

❑ setvol(int percent)

❑ fade_to(int to_percent)

❑ fade_from_to(int from_percent,int to_percent)

❑ start_at_beginning(): Override a start_time()

❑ stop_at_end(): Override an end_time()

State indicators (all Boolean, except the last, which is an integer):

- ❑   `IsReady()`: Returns `true` if the plug-in instance has completed loading
- ❑   `IsPlaying()`: Returns `true` if the sound is currently playing
- ❑   `IsPaused()`: Returns `true` if the sound is currently paused
- ❑   `GetVolume()`: Returns the current volume as a percentage

Callback Functions – Shockwave Flash

ShockWave Flash is a plugin from Macromedia `http://www.macromedia.com`. The plugin displays sound and animation combined with a scripting language of its own, all bundled up into a multimedia file downloaded via a URL. When an `<EMBED>` tag specifies a ShockWave Flash file, the tag's NAME attribute must be set.

When the plugin instance is created, the Embed object contains specific methods and properties as for the LiveAudio plugin. However, the properties and methods are of course different. If the NAME attribute is set to `"demo"`, the plugin instance will look for the JavaScript function `demo_DoFSCommand()`. If the function exists, then it may be called from within the plugin instance at different times in the display of the loaded file.

This JavaScript function is invoked, runs and ends in response to a call made by the plugin, not by a web page loading or by a user generated event. In effect, the JavaScript function is part of the plugin's normal order of execution. The plugin subcontracts some work out to the JavaScript function, supplied by the web developer who is using the plugin.

Inside such a function might be a number of calls to methods of the Embed object that matches the plugin instance. This function could also draw new HTML buttons in a separate frame to be used to control the plugin, or display a prompt for the user in a `confirm()` dialog box. The plugin passes several arguments to the function that can be used to control what tasks the function performs each time it is called. These arguments come from information inside the downloaded file.

If another ShockWave Flash file is embedded in the HTML page, but with a different NAME attribute, it has a separate custom function, which would be called independent of the other embedded object.

This plugin does not create a special property to indicate when the file has completed its download. Instead, the callback function can be called when the file is fully loaded. If unique arguments are supplied to the function, the function can use them as a cue to detect that the download has finished.

See `http://www.macromedia.com/support/flash/ts/documents/tn4160.html`.

Summary

Where an HTML page contains images, but no animation, JavaScript can add simple animation. Where an HTML page contains fancy multimedia effects used by browser plugins or ActiveX controls, JavaScript can often manage these in ways beyond the power of the user. In either case, event handling for simple multimedia effects like images, sounds and movies are very limited in most browsers, unless another technical frontier is crossed and Dynamic HTML features are brought into bear on these issues. Although IE5 has a greatly extended event model, using these events is impossible if cross-browser support is at all an issue.

Performance is an issue with multimedia. Some simple animations are possible inside the browser without retrieving anything over a network. The `Image` object can be used to cache and preload images, so if it is necessary to load them from somewhere else they can still be presented speedily to the user. Simple support for timed script execution in client-side JavaScript helps enormously when attempting simple animations.

Using plugins carries its own risks. Unless the scriptwriter is in control of the user's browser, anything can be configured in the browser when a multimedia document is downloaded. To handle this situation robustly, the script writer must go to extra lengths to detect plugin support if the user is to be spared warning messages.

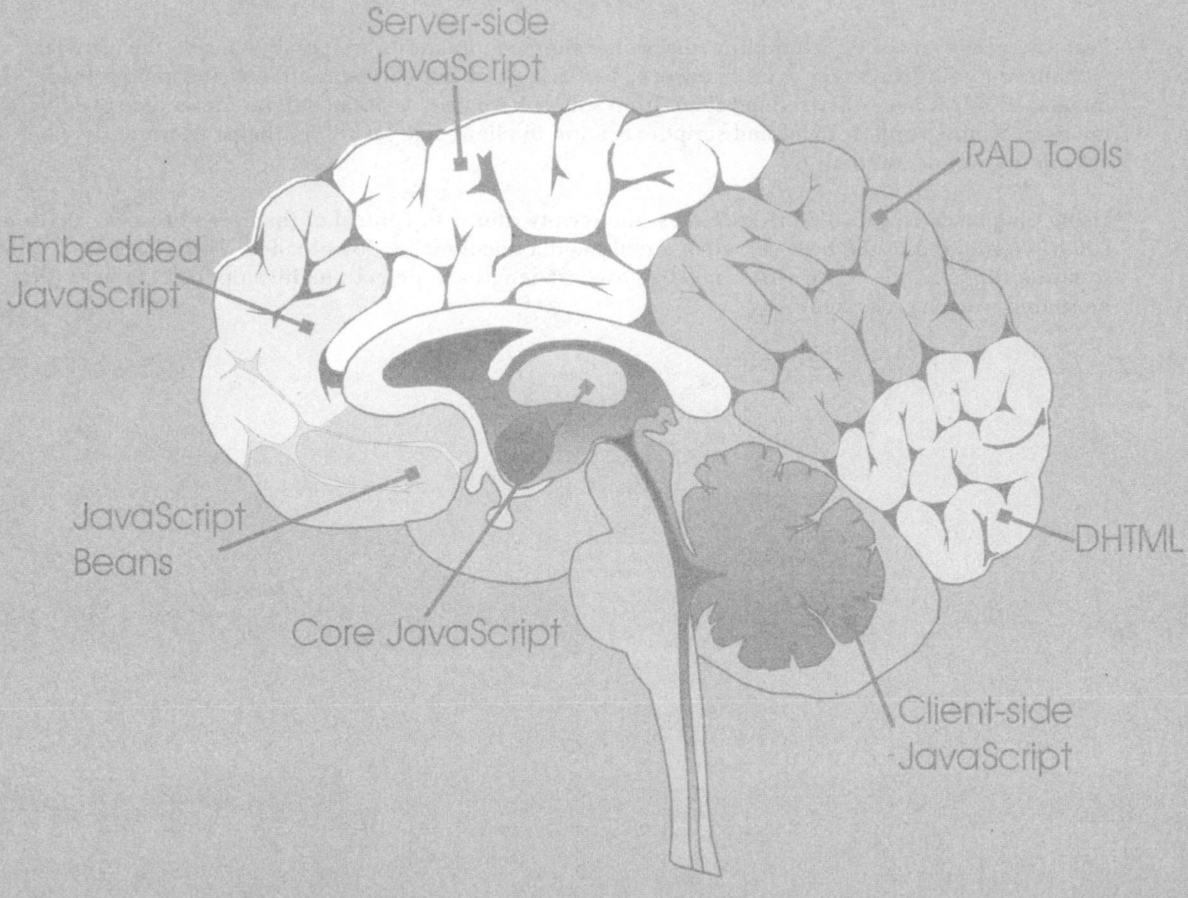

Server-side
JavaScript

RAD Tools

Embedded
JavaScript

JavaScript
Beans

Core JavaScript

Client-side
JavaScript

DHTML

Forms and Data

Without client-side scripting, a web browser can't do much except display information. HTML form elements by themselves aren't that flexible – all plain HTML form elements can do is send any user data directly to a web server. With the addition of JavaScript, a web browser's form elements take on some of the attributes of more data-oriented software tools such as 4GL form-building packages and spreadsheets. Without JavaScript or an alternate scripting language, some HTML tags like < INPUT TYPE="button" > are entirely useless.

Once data input is possible in a web browser, a browser page starts to look like the front end of a database client. However, the form support built into HTML doesn't supply many options for storing data. If web pages with forms are going to take on some of the attributes of database clients, then more flexible options are required. Once JavaScript enters the picture, there are several places in a browser where data can be stuffed apart from inside HTML fields.

The main problem with forms in an HTML document is that if the form is submitted, the data has to go somewhere to be processed. The chapters on server-side JavaScript describe how you can use JavaScript to handle that problem. This chapter describes only the management of forms and data on the client side.

Forms

JavaScript can interact with HTML forms directly in a number of ways. It can:

❑   Write out form element tags with inline JavaScript, as for other HTML tags.

❑   Act as event handlers for form elements, via HTML tag attributes or host object properties.

❑   Read and modify the values of form elements.

❑   Construct form elements in a limited way, or more flexibly if Dynamic HTML is used.

It is beyond these basic tasks that JavaScript adds real value to forms and HTML. The higher level tasks that JavaScript can achieve are:

❑   Validating and correcting user data.

❑   Performing calculations on user data.

❑   Storing and forwarding user data.

❑   Controlling user navigation through the data input process.

Because all these tasks can happen solely inside the browser, without any need for the World Wide Web, smoother form operation results. Without JavaScript, every form check or change requires that a form's details be passed to a web server for a response, which can slow processing considerably.

Form Objects

HTML forms are part of HTML documents, so it's no surprise that form-style tags are reflected in JavaScript as objects that are properties of the Document object.

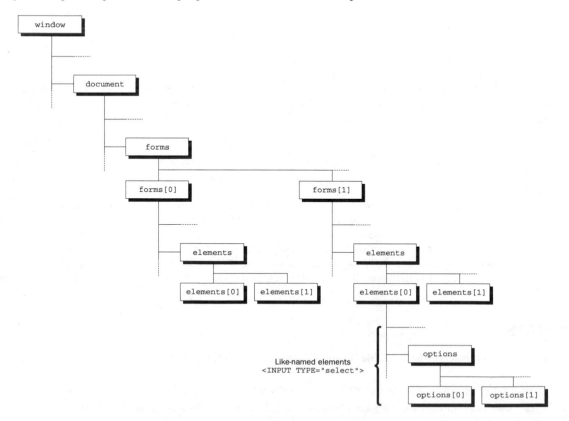

This diagram shows the basic structure of the forms part of the document object model. The specific methods and properties are listed in the Appendices. Key features are described in this chapter.

In addition to the objects in the above diagram, there are several miscellaneous features of web browsers that can assist with forms. These are also described in this chapter.

Form Objects Explained

An HTML document can contain more than one form, so the forms property near the top of the Document Object Model hierarchy is a JavaScript array with an array member for each <FORM> tag. These objects have as properties all the important attributes of the corresponding<FORM> tag.

Internet Explorer 3+ HTML documents can have text fields and buttons without any <FORM> tag, although this is not advised. If this is the case, then a single form object is created in forms[0]. An exception is if form controls exist both within and outside a <FORM> tag, then the ones outside the tag are ignored. For Netscape (all versions to 4.61) form elements must always be inside a <FORM> tag, or else they won't appear to the user or the scripter at all.

Each form object has an elements property that is an array. Each array element is one of the form controls in the HTML form. The form controls populate the array in the same order they appear in the HTML document's source, not as they appear on the screen. <INPUT>, <BUTTON>, <TEXTAREA>, and <SELECT> tags are all the form controls available and are represented as a 'forms' array element, one for each instance in the document. This includes <INPUT TYPE="HIDDEN">. Effectively, a 'form control' and a 'form element' are equivalent – the former emphasizes what the user visibly sees, the latter emphasizes an object the scriptwriter sees.

It's best to think of the individual element objects as being of a generic 'input' type of object, rather than being specifically a checkbox or textarea object. This is because these objects have in common several properties such as type, value, name, and form. The type property allows you to tell from within JavaScript what HTML tag was used to create the element you are examining. It reflects the TYPE attribute of the <INPUT> tag, as well as covering the <SELECT> tag and the <TEXTAREA> tag. The value property is the current data value held by the control. The name property reflects the NAME attribute of the corresponding tag. The form property refers back to the forms array element that this form control is a part of. In addition to these basic properties, there are properties which only apply to some types of control, and properties for event handlers (described further on). See the Appendices for complete lists of object properties.

Generally, none of the form or form element objects visible in JavaScript can be created or deleted. Some of their properties can be usefully set, like the element value property, but the structure of a given form can't be altered, except by re-writing the HTML using inline JavaScript or Internet Explorer 4+'s dynamic HTML access to the source.

For most form element types, this two-level hierarchy of forms and form elements covers it all. The <SELECT> form control is the exception. Within the element object for each <SELECT> tag is a property options. This is an array of further objects, one for each <OPTION> tag within the <SELECT> tag. The type of these <OPTION> tag objects, is Option. The Option object is a rare example of an HTML-related host object in the browser that can be created directly from JavaScript. This makes it similar to the Image object (see Chapter 6). Option objects can replace existing objects in the options array of a <SELECT> element, which means menu items can be changed. This is not possible with Internet Explorer 3.0, but is possible with 4.0 and 5.0.

Access to form elements and their properties is demonstrated with this form:

```
<HTML><BODY><FORM NAME="patient">
<BR> Insanity checklist. Enter number of weeks:
<INPUT NAME="weeks" TYPE="text">
<BR> Hearing voices? <INPUT NAME="symptom" TYPE="checkbox">
<BR> Seeing things?  <INPUT NAME="symptom" TYPE="checkbox">
<BR> Clothing preferences:
<SELECT NAME="attire">
   <OPTION VALUE="napolean"> Napolean Bonaparte
   <OPTION VALUE="strangelove"> Dr. Strangelove
</SELECT>
<INPUT TYPE="submit">
</FORM></BODY></HTML>
```

These properties are all valid for the example:

```
with ( top.document )
{
  forms[0].name;                        // = 'patient'
  forms[0].method;                      // = 'GET' (the default)
  forms[0].elements.length;             // = 5
  forms[0].elements[0].value;           // = '', the user can change it.
  forms[0].elements[0].onchange;        // null, no handler.
  forms[0].elements[1].name;            // = 'symptom'
  forms[0].elements[2].checked;         // = 'false', user clicked itable
  forms[0].elements[3].options.length;  // = 2
  forms[0].elements[3].options[1].value; // 'strangelove'
}
```

Note that the `value` property of the `text` element is always a string, even though the user is prompted for a number in this example.

The form element objects have a further useful feature that isn't covered by any property. In Chapter 1, there was some discussion on conversion of JavaScript types. To refresh, JavaScript objects are converted to strings where strings are expected, via the `toString()` method of the object. For form element objects, the conversion conveniently recreates the HTML that the object is based on. Therefore, this example produces a form with two identical input fields:

```
<HTML><BODY><FORM>
<INPUT TYPE="text" NAME="twin" VALUE="me too"><BR>
<SCRIPT>
document.write(document.forms[0].elements[0]+'<BR>');
</SCRIPT>
</FORM></BODY></HTML>
```

Alas this isn't required by the ECMAScript standard – the `toSource()` not `toString()` method is the only one that is required to give you back your source, and here the script is converting the element to a string. This trick works for all Netscape browsers, plus Internet Explorer 4.0, but not 5.0.

Naming Form Elements

With more than one form, or with many form elements, using array indices quickly becomes confusing, as the above example shows. Fortunately, form and element tags are accessible via their names as well, since objects and arrays are nearly the same thing in JavaScript. The NAME parameter of the appropriate tag is used as the property name. Here are the same properties using the property names instead of array indices:

```
with ( top.document )
{
patient.name;                    // pointless
patient.method;
patient.elements.length;         // pointless if all names are known
patient.weeks.value;
patient.weeks.onchange;
patient.symptom[0].name;         // this line and the next - special handling
patient.symptom[1].checked;
patient.diet.options.length;
patient.diet.options[1].value;
}
```

The 'named' notation is a lot clearer and almost identical structurally. There is one catch. In the source HTML document, the NAME attribute for both checkboxes is symptom. This might be by design, or possibly even required (mutually exclusive radio buttons have this constraint). If the checkboxes are referred to by array indices, there is no problem. Referring to the checkboxes via properties presents a difficulty, though: an object can't have two properties with the same name, whether it is a form element or not. If you wish to use property names, there must be some other solution.

The key to this problem is that, for like-named checkboxes, the property name no longer refers to just one of the elements. Instead, it refers to a new, intermediate object. In Navigator, this object's type is InputArray, and it is a JavaScript array. Each similarly named element is then a member of the InputArray array. This array can cryptically appear when buggy scripts are run with Netscape browsers. It helps to remember that each form element is just a type of input item, and therefore an InputArray is just an array of such items.

Using names can make life a lot easier, especially if they are short. For the unimaginative and the pathological haters of array syntax, use names such as form1. Recall JavaScript variables cannot start with a number so 1form is out. A big trap with naming elements is forgetting to avoid the numerous reserved words and other property names. Chapter 17, Debugging and Disappearing Data, covers this possibility in more detail. A simple example for now is:

```
<HTML><BODY><FORM>
Flagpole juggling survey. Enter pole length: <INPUT TYPE="text" NAME="length">
</FORM></BODY></HTML>
```

Clearly the document.forms[0] JavaScript object already has a length property, since it is an array. Don't do this.

Form Events

HTML intrinsic events are the main way the scriptwriter catches and processes form input. Such an event is defined as any event appearing in the HTML 4.0 standard.

If the user turns JavaScript support off in the browser, any form elements will have their default behavior. The reference section describes the full gory details of which events are supported where. Chapter 4 describes features common to all browser's events. Events commonly used in form processing are described here.

Here is an example that shows how event handling makes HTML documents more interactive and useful:

```
<HTML><HEAD><SCRIPT>
function applause()
{
  var answer = "Man is correct!\n" +
               "Man crawls when young, " +
               "walks when adult, " +
               "and uses a cane in old age\n" +
               "\nShould you meet a riddling Egyptian Sphinx," +
               "you'll be perfectly safe";
  alert(answer);
}
</SCRIPT></HEAD>
<BODY><FORM>
<H1>Riddle Page</H1>
What goes on four legs in the morning,
two during the day
and three in the evening?
<BR> <INPUT TYPE="radio"
            ONCLICK="alert('You seem confused too')">
     </INPUT>
A confused table
<BR> <INPUT TYPE="radio"
            ONCLICK="alert('Perhaps you have had too much Sun?')">
     </INPUT>
The Sun
<BR> <INPUT TYPE="radio" ONCLICK="applause()"> Man </INPUT>
</FORM></BODY></HTML>
```

In this simple example, the event handlers give the user additional information not otherwise displayed with the document.

The onClick event handler is probably the most common handler used. The main uses are for detecting checkbox and radio button changes and for carrying out arbitrary actions, such as opening new windows. The button type of the <INPUT> tag relies almost entirely on the onClick handler in order to do anything useful.

Alongside onClick is the onChange event. This event occurs when the user moves the cursor away from a form element whose value has been changed. Typically, this is a text, textarea, or select element.

The onBlur and onFocus event handlers occur when the user moves between fields in a form, and between frames or windows. Their main use is to control the way the user navigates between fields. In current browsers, they can be tricky to use portably and aren't advised for doing simple checks on fields.

The onReset and onSubmit events are the only ones that apply to a whole form. These events match the default actions of the <INPUT TYPE="submit"> and <INPUT TYPE="reset"> tags, and can only be applied to the <FORM> tag. This is both a good thing and a bad thing.

It is a good thing, because if you want to ensure that the user's data is submitted no matter what, you can confidently install scripts on these handlers. If the browser does not support JavaScript, then the form will still be submitted if the user clicks on a supplied submit button. If they do have JavaScript, your handlers run as a bonus.

It is a bad thing, because if you want to control exactly what the user submits, then using these handlers can see you come unstuck. While you rely on your handler to check that the data the user entered is valid, the user went and turned JavaScript off in the browser, or never had it anyway. In this case they can submit any data they want. In order to stop this happening, you should not use submit buttons, and instead use the <BUTTON> tag – put an onClick handler on that form element instead. There's no way the user can submit a form from a <BUTTON> tag with no JavaScript.

Apart from these events, many other events are defined in HTML 4.0 for form elements. These events such as onMouseMove and onKeyPress are rarely available in, or used for, HTML forms, although if you are creative, you'll probably find a use.

The main problem with events is trying to anticipate exactly how they will occur. Just knowing all the event handlers available is not enough information. A simple example is clicking on a text input field when another text input field currently holds the input cursor (the vertical bar). A number of events may result from this one action – onBlur and onChange in the original field, onClick and onFocus in the new field. The order in which these events occur is not standardized or consistent between browsers. If the handlers for these events further mimic user actions by calling form element object methods like click(), change(), blur() or focus(), then matters become quite complex. Too much reliance on the exact order of events will produce non-portable, fragile code that isn't even backwardly compatible. Two of the most common problems in this area are described here.

Microsoft 3.0 Handler Trap

Internet Explorer 3.0 provides us with a good example of the complexities of event handling. It has some unique features that fortunately, are superceded and improved on in versions 4.0 and 5.0. In that older browser, onChange, onBlur and onFocus handlers can behave very inconveniently. When one of these events fires, the browser reacts to the event with some internal actions, then calls an event handler, then does some further internal actions to finish up. Unfortunately, the further internal actions can undo just the thing you've been trying to achieve in the handler. An example:

```
<INPUT TYPE="radio" ONCLICK="this.checked=false">
```

This line attempts to keep the radio button unset, even if the user clicks it. However, the browser applies the results of the user's click after the event handler finishes, so it's set anyway.

To avoid these effects, defer processing until all the event handling rubbish is finished. This approach, which is compatible with other browsers, applies your handler as you expect. Try clicking the second radio button in this example:

```
<HTML><BODY><SCRIPT>
function real_handler()
{
  document.forms[0].r[0].checked=true;
}
</SCRIPT><FORM>
   <INPUT NAME="r" TYPE="radio">
   <INPUT NAME="r" TYPE="radio" ONCLICK="setTimeout('real_handler()',1)">
</FORM></BODY></HTML>
```

Internet Explorer 3.0 is bad enough in this area that it's worth avoiding altogether, if at all possible. The later versions are much more popular, in any event.

Current Field Problems

Another example of event handling differences stems from the concept of a **current field**. When an `onBlur` trigger fires, what should the current field be, where should the insertion point be, what field if any should gain focus? Microsoft and Netscape browsers answer differently at the 3.0 level. An example:

```
<INPUT TYPE="text" ONFOCUS="this.blur()">
```

This handler above attempts to make the field read-only, by automatically blurring it as soon as it gains focus. This won't work in Internet Explorer 3.0 for two reasons: firstly, because of the Microsoft trap described above; secondly because that browser requires that one field always be in focus. In that browser, you can only put focus somewhere else, not merely take it away from a field. This also won't work in Navigator 3.0. In that browser, you can have no fields focused, and a time-out delay isn't required to do it. However, there is a bug that leaves the insertion point in the current field if it is blurred from its own handler. The upshot is that this code will work for both browsers:

```
<HTML><BODY><SCRIPT>
function defocus()
{
  window.document.forms[0].two.focus();              // go to field 'two'.
}
</SCRIPT><FORM>
  <! this first field is the one that is set to be workably read-only >
  <INPUT NAME="one" TYPE="text" ONFOCUS="setTimeout('defocus()',1)">
  <! this field's only purpose is to have somewhere else to put the focus >
  <INPUT NAME="two" TYPE="text">
<SCRIPT>
// to start with, put the focus in element 'two':
document.forms[0].two.focus();</SCRIPT>
</FORM></BODY></HTML>
```

Other Form-like Features

It's possible to collect user-input without using `<FORM>`, `<INPUT>`, `<SELECT>` or `<TEXTAREA>` HTML tags. Usually forms are good enough, but a number of obscure possibilities present themselves that traditional HTML forms can't help with. For example:

- ❑ You need to prompt the user before the whole HTML page is loaded.
- ❑ You want to collect input from a narrow or hidden frame.
- ❑ The user has no keyboard, perhaps in an information kiosk or WebTV.

A further trap with traditional HTML forms applies to invisible forms. Forms can be created so that none of the form elements are ever visible to the user. Perhaps the form is in a hidden frame. From such a form it's not possible to submit its contents back to a web server. You can't cheat by using a mailto: URL instead, either. This is a browser security restriction designed to stop the scriptwriter from submitting data without the browser user being aware.

In summary, the other features you might want to bring to bear on data input problems are:

- ❑ Message boxes: `confirm()` and `prompt()`, described in Chapter 5, allow simple input.
- ❑ Dynamic HTML: you can mockup any kind of input you want with Dynamic HTML and receive input via events.

❑ Microsoft Data Binding: this technology allows data to be tied to various HTML tags.

❑ HTML Hyperlinks can be used to capture a single item of data if the user clicks on them. If the user has no keyboard then an image map of a keyboard can allow you to collect keyboard input anyway.

Each of these techniques is discussed later, but first let's take a look at data.

Data

The purpose of HTML form elements is to collect data, and if you're interested in JavaScript then you'll want to work on that data. Beyond accepting the user's input and fiddling with the data immediately afterwards, there are some larger issues. Some of these are:

❑ What format does input data have?

❑ Where is the data stored?

❑ How long does the data last?

What format does input data have? The major browsers, Navigator and Internet Explorer, come in many different localized versions. Each localized version has a different 8-bit character set. For a given version, forms will accept whatever data in that character set that the user's keyboard is configured to send. The upshot of this is that you can't guarantee that form data input will be in English for text and textarea fields. However, if your web page is written in English in the first place, then English input is obviously a highly likely event. For non-text field types, the data values are determined by the scriptwriter, or HTML author, so there's no issue there.

For the Where and How of data, read on.

The Storage Problem

The fundamental problem with HTML and browsers is that when the user surfs around the World Wide Web, documents viewed appear and disappear from the browser. What if you want some of the document information to hang around after a document's long gone? It's not so obvious how or where. Isn't there somewhere else within a browser to store information apart from HTML documents? Sometimes the answer is No. However there are several places within a browser that are good candidates for storing data and these are discussed below.

HTML Form Fields

The most obvious place to store data is in HTML form fields. The user can type information into the visible fields, and the scriptwriter can get and set the data via the appropriate `value` property of the form element. Form fields are just JavaScript host objects, so they act like JavaScript objects in most other respects.

Form fields have some other handy behaviors. If a form is submitted, there's no work required by the scriptwriter – the browser does all the conversion and submission for you. The `<INPUT TYPE=HIDDEN>` field is a godsend for scriptwriters who want to include extra, user-invisible information in a form.

Forms can have as many form elements as you like, and text fields can generally be as big as you like. There is a form-wide limit of 4096 bytes (4Kb) on form GET operations, but POST operations have no limit, however there are limits to how much data individual text elements will reliably hold. For example, there is an approximately 30000 character limit on reading the contents of a textarea. This is very similar to a defect in 3.0 versions of Netscape that couldn't manage scripts much bigger than 30000 characters. Somewhere in the browsers there is a 16-bit limit in this textarea respect. Recall that the METHOD attribute of the <FORM> tag defines which of GET and POST applies to a given form.

Forms have other limitations, too. The main one is that forms are part of an HTML document. If the document disappears, the form data generally disappears. If your browser is Netscape Navigator 3.0+ or Internet Explorer 4.0+, then you can rescue the data if you navigate back through history to the document in question (see Chapter 9 for an example). But if the browser shuts down, the data is gone.

Form data also suffers from performance problems. If a web page is slow to load, then the tags containing a form may take some time to appear and the scriptwriter has to coordinate this – see Chapter 5. Also data stored in a form can be slow to work with. If you have a complex script that manipulates form data in a repetitive way, your script can run inefficiently. Compare these two scripts:

```
<HTML><BODY><SCRIPT>
var i, j=0;
document.write((new Date)+'<BR>');
for (i=0; i < 10000; i++)
    j++;
document.write((new Date)+'<BR>');
</SCRIPT></BODY></HTML>
```

```
<HTML><BODY><FORM>
<INPUT TYPE=TEXT>
</FORM><SCRIPT>
var i, j=0;
var form_item = document.forms[0].elements[0];
document.write((new Date)+'<BR>');
for (i=0; i < 10000; i++)
{
   j++;
   form_item.value = j;
}
document.write((new Date)+'<BR>');
</SCRIPT></BODY></HTML>
```

In one test run, the first document took approximately 5 seconds to complete, but the second one took approximately 20 seconds, so text fields must be at least 3 times slower than JavaScript variables to set. This test was done on Windows 95.

JavaScript Variables and Objects

JavaScript variables are another obvious place to store data. Since each script fragment is part of a given document that is part of a browser window, JavaScript variables are by default properties of some window object. It's possible to store them as properties of most browser objects, though. JavaScript properties are a great place to store data, since you have the full flexibility of JavaScript at hand. All other data storage methods are restricted to strings, whereas JavaScript variables can be numbers or objects.

JavaScript variables have limitations. The user can't see the data unless you make an effort to display it somewhere. If you have several browser windows open at different URLs, security restrictions might make accessing variables in other windows problematic – see Chapter 11. JavaScript variables aren't automatically submitted anywhere, so you have to do that yourself. If browser windows or the browser entire closes down, then JavaScript variable data is lost. Unlike form element data, if you navigate back through history to old documents, you don't get any JavaScript variables back that that document might have contained. You may find some variables are reconstructed when the document is redisplayed, but strictly speaking they're new variables with the same name as old ones. JavaScript variables also have the same web page loading problems that form data has.

There is an exception to the rule that variable data is lost when a window closes down. The Netscape 4.0+ `window.navigator` object survives the closure of all browser windows except the last; so data stored there is slightly more robust.

For complex web applications it is common to see HTML pages that store handy information in JavaScript arrays. This data is then exploited once the document loads as though it were part of the document to start with:

```
<HTML><HEAD><SCRIPT>
var sleep_types = ['snooze', 'nap', '40 winks', 'cataleptic'];
</SCRIPT></HEAD>
<BODY><SCRIPT>
//… look up sleep type as required …
</SCRIPT></BODY></HTML>
```

There are two possibilities for storing data in JavaScript variables in a document. The difference depends on which object the variables are made properties of.

Separate To Document Object Model Objects

An ordinary script like this stores all its JavaScript variables as properties of the `window` object. When the document in the window is replaced, the variables are gone, even though the `window` object remains.

```
<HTML><HEAD><SCRIPT>
var head_stuff = "thinking"
</SCRIPT><BODY><SCRIPT>
var body_stuff = "feeling"
</SCRIPT></BODY></HTML>
```

Attached To Document Object Model Objects

Sometimes it's handy to decorate parts of a document with extra information. This example illustrates:

```
<HTML><BODY><FORM>
Mystery button page<BR>
<INPUT TYPE="button" VALUE="One">
<INPUT TYPE="button" VALUE="Two">
<INPUT TYPE="button" VALUE="Three">
</FORM><SCRIPT>
var messages = [ "10 seconds to detonation",
                 "Don't touch",
                 "Elevator ready" ];
var e;
for (e=0; e<3; e++)
{
```

```
    document.forms[0].elements[e].details = messages[e];
    document.forms[0].elements[e].onclick
      = function (e){alert(this.details);};
  }
</SCRIPT></BODY></HTML>
```

This example doesn't work on version 3.0 browsers, because we've used array literals (in line 7) and a nameless function in the 3rd last line. It's easy to work around those problems, but this kind of scripting is typically used only with browsers that support DHTML – versions 4.0 and higher.

None of the buttons in this example have explanatory labels. Instead, a property is added to each button object, with a description of that object. When the button event handler fires, that new property is handy and available. Clearly, any amount of data can be attached to existing objects in this way. The data will still disappear when the containing document disappears. The book, "JavaScript Objects" *(by Nakhimovsky and Myers, Wrox Press 1998)* illustrates this technique extensively.

A side-effect of this strategy might be obscurely useful at some point. If the property name you use clashes with an existing property of the object, then that existing property is replaced. This might be useful if for some reason you want to disable an object property, such as the window object's open property. It's very simple:

```
<HTML><BODY><SCRIPT>
window.open = null;
</SCRIPT></BODY></HTML>
```

Internet Explorer 4+ has easy HTML syntax for setting extra attributes.

```
<HTML><BODY><FORM>
<INPUT TYPE="text" NAME="myname" VALUE="myvalue" MYATTRIBUTE="myatt">
</FORM><SCRIPT>
alert(document.forms[0].myname.MYATTRIBUTE);
</SCRIPT></BODY></HTML>
```

As expected, this displays myatt inside the textbox popped up by alert(). Although Netscape will let you add new attributes to HTML tags, the information won't appear inside JavaScript when those tags are rendered.

Cookies

Chapter 18 on Privacy, Security and Cookies explains cookies, and is recommended for reading if you want to do anything at all with them. Within this chapter you only need to note that cookies are roughly like JavaScript variables except:

❑   They are more tedious to access from a script.

❑   They are automatically submitted to Web servers with all URL requests, which is very convenient.

❑   They can be shared between multiple windows in a browser.

❑   They can survive window, full browser shutdown, and computer shutdown.

Cookies are limited to storing strings of less than 4096 bytes each.

URLs

It might seem odd, but URLs are a potential place for storing data. If a web page is retrieved with a GET-style request, data is pinned to the end of the URL when the web server responds to an initial GET request from the browser. That URL then goes into the browser's history list. From JavaScript you can look through the history list and extract the data again. This is a read-only storage method – you can't change a historical URL. The size limit is as for URL size limits – 4096 bytes.

HTML/XML Tags and Content

Provided you have a browser that supports the DOM level 1 standard, it's possible to see the full text of an HTML document as data. Therefore it is also possible to store data inside the HTML document. Put another way, you can create extra HTML objects and insert them into the document for future access. Internet Explorer 4+ is the only browser to support this feature so far.

```
<HTML><BODY>
<DIV ID="astro" STYLE="visibility:hidden">
<SPAN ID="sun">Apollo, the sun king</SPAN>
<SPAN ID="moon">Luna, the mad woman</SPAN>
<SPAN ID="earth">Gaea, the provider</SPAN>
</DIV>
<SCRIPT>alert(document.all.astro.children[0].innerText)</SCRIPT>
</BODY><HTML>
```

In this example there are three astronomical entries: sun, moon and earth. None of the detail shows due to the style of the <DIV> tag. Using the Document Object Model of Internet Explorer 4.0+, you can treat these three items like an array of records. The alert box extracts the description for sun. Chapter 8 describes how to manipulate the window.document.all.astro.children collection so that data can be added or deleted.

Because Internet Explorer 4.0+ supports XML as well as HTML, this approach can be used in either markup language.

Data stored by this method won't be submitted with form submissions and disappears when the document is no longer viewed in the browser, since the data is effectively part of the document. There is another benefit to this approach. If there is a lot of data the HTML document will be quite large. In this approach, the data is stored directly in HTML so the document will be efficient to load.

Java, Plugins and Elsewhere

There are other places you can put your data using client-side JavaScript. When all else fails, you can escape out of the HTML environment entirely and store your variables somewhere else. The remaining candidates are the <OBJECT>, <APPLET> and <EMBED> tags. Only the first of these will be supported by HTML in the future.

Given sufficient security, <OBJECT> embedded objects, applets and plugins in a web page might store data anywhere: to local disk; across the network; within their own context inside the browser. Details really depend on the specific object, applet or plugin.

Java is an interesting case because a) the contents of Java applets are readily available from inline JavaScript within the same HTML document, and b) the lifetime of a Java applet can be longer than that of the parent HTML document. Chapter 9 describes the lifecycle of a Java applet within a browser and how to store data there.

Finally, you can always submit your data to a web server for storage via a GET or POST URL request, in true database style. In that case, you need to organize the server so that it doesn't wipe out the page your client-side script is in with its response

Storage Comparisons

This table contrasts the different storage techniques available. Because all are accessible from JavaScript within the browser, there's no obstacle to moving data around. Just use a bit of JavaScript to copy the data from one type of storage to another.

Storage type	Lifetime of storage type	Capacity of storage	Automatically sent to servers?
HTML <FORM> elements	HTML document + pages stored in history	Unlimited, but maximum of 4Kb when sent in a GET request	Yes
JavaScript variables	HTML document	unlimited	No
Cookies	Up to forever	at least 20 at 4Kb each	Yes
URLs	Browser session	up to 4Kb per URL	Yes
HTML/XML tags	HTML document	unlimited	No
Java	Browser session*	unlimited	No

* Can be extended with appropriate security in place.

For the remainder of this chapter we'll be considering mostly plain form elements, since they're where 90% of the action is.

Form Elements

Once you've got your web page set up to receive data, you may want to do something with that data. There are several common tasks.

Validation

Using JavaScript to check user-entered data in a browser gives the user better feedback. If the data is ever submitted, some program on the web server side will have to consume that data. If there are checks to be done on that data, and they can be done in the browser, then the user will get a fast response. If the server program knows that the browser has already done validation, life becomes a lot less complex at the server end, probably reducing the amount of information passed back and forth between the server and client. So validation benefits both the user and the web server, by reducing the number of packets that are sent/requested by the server/client, effectively freeing network bandwidth and allowing the server more time available to spend on other tasks.

However, the World Wide Web is a public place with folk of all kinds, and as we'll see shortly there's really no escape from validating at the server. Therefore, validation in the browser is of primary benefit to the user.

Validation Models

When to check the data the user enters is a design issue for validation. The options are form level validation, field level validation and key level validation.

Form level validation is the easiest. When the user attempts to submit the data, use an `onSubmit` or `onClick` event handler, check the user's work and reject the submission with an `alert()` pop-up if there are problems. If two fields depend on each other and the user picks a bad combination, a form level check can sometimes warn the user too late.

Field level validation isn't any harder, except more handlers are required. When the user leaves a field, or changes its state, a handler fires and a warning occurs if there is a problem. Unless the handlers are carefully organized to prevent the user from moving on when an error has occurred, a form-level recheck is required as well. This careful organization is very time consuming if portability and backwards compatibility are issues because of the complexities of event models, discussed earlier in this chapter.

Key level validation is an attempt to stop users from typing forbidden things at all. Trying to guarantee only uppercase alphabetic letters in a text field is an example. An event captures each keystroke the user types and allows it or ignores it. This degree of control has little to recommend it for forms, unless you are trying to implement your own keyboard shortcuts. It has its uses in Dynamic HTML, discussed in Chapter 8.

We advocate form-level validation, with additional field level checks whenever special cases arise. A simple example showing a mixture of the two is as follows:

```
<HTML><HEAD><SCRIPT>
function validate()
{
  with ( window.document.forms[0] )
  {
    if (    country.value.length != 2
         || !parseInt(postal.value,10)
         || parseInt(postal.value,10) < 0
       )
    {
      alert("Evidently you're lost.");
      return false;
    }
  }
  return true;
}
</SCRIPT></HEAD>
<BODY><FORM ACTION="POST" ONSUBMIT="return validate()">
<H3> Where are you? </H3>
<BR>Enter your two letter country code:
<INPUT TYPE="text" NAME="country" ONCHANGE="this.value=this.value.toLowerCase()">
<BR>Enter your postal code:
<INPUT TYPE="text" NAME="postal">
<BR><INPUT TYPE="submit">
</FORM></BODY></HTML>
```

This example does most validation in the <FORM>'s onSubmit event handler. A minor correction is applied in the first <INPUT> tag to provide the user with some quick and harmless feedback for that particular input item.

Regular Expressions

Netscape 4.0+ and Internet Explorer 4.0+ browsers support regular expressions. These make some validation tasks extremely simple, and are worth using if you can always rely on these browsers.

A regular expression is like a formula for a JavaScript string that must follow a specific format. Regular expressions use this format to describe another string format. When a normal string is examined with a regular expression, a conclusion is drawn about whether, or how, that normal string matches the format of the regular expression. So regular expressions are an analysis tool for strings – very handy for user input.

Regular expressions occupy two parts of the JavaScript language places: as methods of the String object, and in their own right in the form of the RegExp object. See the Reference Section for all the method names. The critical detail for validation is that the test(regexp) method of a String object returns true if the string is in the format dictated by the regexp regular expression, otherwise false.

These regular expressions are delimited by / characters instead of ' or " quotes in JavaScript source, so they're not strictly strings. The RegExp object is only used if a regular expression is stored in a string rather than embedded literally in the script source. In that case, the RegExp object acts like a little engine that converts and manages the string-embedded regular expression. This second case is an uncommon use of regular expressions.

Here's how to do it:

```
var str = "Eany Meany Miny Mo";
var bool = null;
bool = str.test(/Meany/);        // true - contains 'Meany'
bool = str.test(/^E/);           // true - starts with 'E'
bool = str.test(/[Nn][^yY]/);    // false - all n's and N's have a trailing y or Y
```

Regular expressions can be quite complex. Their syntax is copied exactly from the same feature in the Perl language. The Reference section describes the JavaScript functions that support regular expressions.

For the really gory details on regular expressions, visit this Perl URL: http://www.perl.com/CPAN/doc/manual/html/pod/perlre.html. Perl documentation on the web may automatically relocate you to an identical document at a closer web site, so don't be too surprised if you end up somewhere else.

Beware of very complex regular expressions! JavaScript Regular expressions are based on Perl regular expressions, but Perl regular expressions are subtly different between Perl 4.0 and Perl 5.0. If you have Netscape 3.0 or JScript 3.0 or less (found in Internet Explorer 3.0, old WSH 1.0 installations or rarely in Internet Explorer 4.0), then you have Perl version 4.0 regular expressions, not version 5.0. You can easily avoid compatibility problems if you use the basic and intermediate RE features but not the advanced features.

Numbers

`Text`, `textarea` and `password` form controls accept Strings, not Numbers. If the form demands a number from the user, it needs to be converted. Here is the worst thing to do:

```
Seats: <INPUT TYPE="text" ONCHANGE="if (!(this.value-0)) alert('Number
required');">
```

This example relies on automatic type conversion from a `String` to a `Number` to check the user's response. Apart from the fact that it will fail if the user types 0 (zero), the interpreter will fail entirely, stop all processing and give an error message, if the user types 'se#$a%jjz' or any other rubbish. This assumes that the browser has error detection pop-ups enabled, as described in the debugging chapter. Of course, users are all geniuses and never type things like that or disable their error messages ...

A better solution is to use two built-in JavaScript functions: `parseInt()` and `parseFloat()`. Both take `Strings` and attempt to read `Numbers` from them, either an integer, or a floating point number. This can be somewhat successful, especially `parseInt()` which can read Numbers in bases other than 10 if needed. These functions are unusual in that they are not part of any obvious JavaScript object. Examples:

```
var num1 = parseInt('23', 10);         // decimal
var num2 = parseInt('1AB2', 16);       // hexadecimal
var num3 = parseFloat('garbage');      // returns NaN
var num4 = parseFloat('123.45');
```

Unfortunately, these functions have two failings. First, they return NaN if the conversion fails, which is fine except that old browsers like Navigator 2.02 and Explorer 3.02 with JScript 1.0 can't cope with NaN or return 0 instead, leaving you to wonder what really happened. Secondly, both functions stop trying to read the string as soon as a number is successfully read. This example doesn't fail:

```
var num5 = parseFloat('3.1415926junk');      // num5 = Math.PI (roughly).
```

More irritatingly, neither does this:

```
var num6 = parseFloat('11.22.33');           // num6 = 11.22
```

There are three alternatives: accept the first thing typed and discard the rest, rely on having a 4.06+ Netscape or 4+ Internet Explorer browser and use the handy `isNaN()` function, or examine the user data thoroughly. The latter case means writing your own versions of `parseInt()` and `parseFloat()` that return NaN even if there is trailing garbage – for `parseFloat()` that is about 70 lines of JavaScript if thorough checking is done. Accepting the first thing typed works like this:

```
<SCRIPT>
function check_num(obj)
{
if (!parseInt(obj.value, 10))
    alert("Number required");
else
    obj.value = '' + parseInt(obj.value, 10);
}
</SCRIPT>
<INPUT TYPE="text" ONCHANGE="check_num(this)">
```

With `parseInt()`, the second argument is critical. It says what mathematical base to interpret the number in. Humans use base 10, the digits zero to nine. Without it, the interpreter will do its best with the first argument and might conclude it is any of octal, decimal or hexadecimal. If unwise users add leading zeros, '033' will be read as 27, because it looks like an octal number. Always specify the base.

These 4+ browser regular expressions will pass or fail a string as an integer and as a floating point number, including leading and trailing spaces, but won't tell you if they are effectively Infinity or not:

```
var int_format = /^[ ]*[+-]?\d+[ ]*$/;
var flt_format = /^[ ]*[+-]?\d*\.?\d*([eE][+-]?\d+)?[ ]*$/
vat data = '123';
int_format.test(data);          //integer
flt_format.test(data)           //floating point
```

Once you know the value supplied is a valid number, you can assign it directly to a variable with confidence like this:

```
var numeric_data = data - 0;
```

You could check it with `isFinite()` if you wanted to avoid NaNs.

Dates

Dates are an awful mess to validate in a web browser if you insist on the user typing the whole date in. Users of relational databases will know that there are a million ways to represent the same date. What to choose? The key to easy date validation is DON'T give the user choice in the first place.

The best solution for validating dates is to use **international date format**. This format spells the month out into three letters and keeps the rest of the date in digits so:

04-Jan-1998
29-Feb-1997

With this format, there's no confusion about what's a year or a month or which century applies. The examples show an English interpretation of the standard; for other languages it's different. However, since the language of your web page is likely to be English, it's no great crime to stick to English names for months.

Try to do dates this way:

```
<HTML><BODY><FORM>
<INPUT TYPE="text" MAXLENGTH=2 SIZE=2>-
<SELECT SIZE=12>
   <OPTION VALUE=1>Jan
   <OPTION VALUE=2>Feb
<!--… and so on … -->
</SELECT>-
<INPUT TYPE="text" MAXLENGTH=4 SIZE=4>
</FORM></BODY></HTML>
```

With this design, the user can't get the month wrong. You'll still need to check the year and day are sensible number values. The `selectedIndex` property of the form element will also give you the number of the month the user has chosen, but the months will be numbered from zero, not 1. Therefore its possibly more error free to include VALUE attributes as is done in the above example, and lookup those after you've worked out which element is selected. Lest we forget, the way to remember the number of days in a given month is:

30 days hath September,

April, June, and November,

All the rest have 31,

Excepting February alone,

Having 28 days, or 29 days in each leap year.

To tell if a year is a leap year, try this function (2000 AD is a leap year):

```
function isLeapYear(year)
{
    return (year % 4 == 0 && ( year % 100 !=0 || year % 400 ==0 ));
}
```

The Netscape validation library described a bit further on has some very useful date validation routines. Another wonderful resource for dates are the Date and Time Articles at www.irt.org. The most useful of which was last seen at: http://www.irt.org/articles/js043/index.htm.

Day / Month / Year Problems

If you live in the U.S. you'd be used to the Fourth of July being written so: 7/4/98. Unfortunately, much of the rest of the English speaking world doesn't see it that way; it can also be read 7th of April. This is bad for dates like 8/20/75, which are impossible where I live, but worse for those that can be read either way like 1/2/03. For this reason alone, avoid this format for date entry.

Year 2000 Problems

Even though the year 2000 may be passed when you read this, it can still cause you headaches for historical dates – perhaps your web pages reports on some old data. There are two things to do to make your life easy:

❑ If you can't use four digits for the year part of a date, make sure to set a **pivot year** (a 2 digit year) that lets you convert 2 digit years to 4 digit years reliably. For example, if 30 is the pivot year then the user entering 75 means 1975 because it's above the pivot, but 22 means 2022 because it's below.

❑ Avoid the `Date.getYear()` method. This method returns the number of year since 1900 in theory, so if the year is 2002, it should return 102. In practice it does, except Netscape 3.0 returns the actual year. This is very inconvenient because this function is usually used to extract the year of the current century. Instead, use the ECMAScript standard function `Date.getFullYear()`, which returns the four digit year. If the `getFullYear()` function doesn't exist, because you are using JScript 2.0 or 1.0, or Netscape browsers less than 4.06, you can add helpful functions yourself:

```
function getFullYear()
{
   var year = Date.getYear();
   return year < 1000 ? year + 1900 : year;
}

function getCenturyYear()
{
   return Date.getYear() % 100;
}
```

Year of Birth Problems

If you ask the user to type in the year they were born into an older browser, problems can occur.

Prior to the ECMAScript standard, there was no rule stating how JavaScript would store dates internally. The common method used in 3.0 browsers was to store the number of seconds since 1 January 1970 (this is a significant date for Unix computers). If you try and store an earlier date into a Date object in those browsers, results are unreliable. For those browsers, you'll have to come up with your own date system for earlier dates. With the ECMAScript standard, dates can now go way, way back. 1 January 1970 is still considered the "start" but dates before that are stored internally as negative numbers.

Thinking About Time Globally

If you expect your web page to be used all over the world, you can get confused very quickly if you keep all times in the local time of the user. Daylight saving, changing legislation and day-of-the-week issues can make it very difficult to know WHEN some form was submitted.

The key to making sense of times is to realize that when a particular moment occurs, it occurs all around the earth at the same time. So a moment is really independent of the local time. That means the number of seconds since 1 January 1970 in the U.K. (where Greenwich Mean Time, GMT = UTC [Universal Time Coordinated] was first set) to a given moment is the same for everyone. Number of seconds is therefore a universal time, provided we all agree to take England's 1 January 1970 as a starting point. When you convert that number of seconds to some local time, it might be this time or that, this day or that, but it will still be the same moment. The reverse is obviously not true – when it's midnight for me, it's probably morning for you.

So when you're deeply embedded in time and date calculations just close your eyes and think of England and everything will work out...

Validation Masks

Masks are similar to regular expressions, but less complex and easier to support across all browsers. The idea is that a format dictates allowable values for a field. Users of report creation tools and spreadsheets will be familiar with format masks – validation masks are a similar thing, but for input, not for output.

The simplest example is entering a monetary amount. This could be handled as a number, but inexperienced users might add '$', ',', '.' or even 'Y' symbols (damn, where's that pound sign on my keyboard). A mask can solve this by only accepting specific characters.

```
<SCRIPT>
// This function returns false if at any stage any part
// of the supplied mask does not match the supplied value
function check_mask(mask,value)
{
var i;
if ( value.length != mask.length )      // exact fit required
   return false;
for (i=0; i<mask.length; i++)           // look char. by char.
{
    if ( mask.charAt(i) == '#' )        // digit required
    {
        if ( !parseInt(value.charAt(i) && value.charAt(i) != '0')
            return false;
    }
    else                                // exact match required
    {
        if ( mask.charAt(i) != value.charAt(i) )
            return false;
    }
}
return true;
}
</SCRIPT>
<INPUT TYPE="text"
   ONCHANGE="if (!check_mask('$##.##',this.value)) alert('Bad value');">
<INPUT TYPE="text"
   ONCHANGE="if (!check_mask('$####.##',this.value)) alert('Bad value');">
```

In this example, the check_mask() function has a simple matching criteria: strings to check fail unless they exactly match the mask, except for certain character positions that may be any digit. The first input field can accept values from '$00.00' to '$99.99', the second from '$0000.00' to '$9999.99'.

Regular expressions to do the same job would be:

```
str.match(/^\$\d{2}\.\d{2}$/);      // $##.##
str.match(/^\$\d{4}\.\d{2}$/);      // $####.##
```

Domains, Lookups and Picklists

Another way to constrain a field's value is with a **domain**. A domain is just a set of allowable values for a variable or field. Some such sets can't be fully listed, such as every instant in the day. Others can, like the set of months of the year.

Where the set can be listed, a lookup is a function that checks a value against that set. A picklist displays the members of a domain as a guide for the user to choose from.

```
<HTML><BODY>
<SCRIPT LANGUAGE="JavaScript">

// an object with 12 properties
var months = { 'Jan':0,'Feb':0,'Mar':0,'Apr':0,'May':0,'Jun':0,
               'Jul':0,'Aug':0,'Sep':0,'Oct':0,'Nov':0,'Dec':0 };

//  check for times of the day
function is_time_domain(value)
{
    // the expected format is a simple Army time: 0 to 2359
    // with no colon (:), so 23:59 is not allowed.
    // Obviously it could be more complex.
```

223

```
        var num = parseInt(value,10);
        if (value.length != 4 )
           return false;
        if ( num <0 || num % 100 > 59 || num / 100 > 23)
           return false;
        return true;
}

// check for months of the year
function is_month_domain(value)
{
        // Could be more tolerant of capitalisation.
        return ( months[value] != null );     // true if it's there
}

// check for anything
function check_domain(domain, value)
{
        var result = false;
        if ( domain == 'TIME' )    result = is_time_domain(value);
        if ( domain == 'MONTH' )   result = is_month_domain(value);
        if (!result)
           alert('please enter data correctly');
        return result;
}
</SCRIPT>

<FORM>
<BR> Enter an Army time:
<INPUT TYPE="text" ONCHANGE="return check_domain('TIME',this.value)">
<BR> Enter a month in short format:
<INPUT TYPE="text" ONCHANGE="return check_domain('MONTH',this.value)">
</FORM>
</BODY></HTML>
```

In this example month entries could easily have been tested against the months object directly, but what we're emphasizing is that a single function passed a domain type and a value can be used everywhere for any domain evaluation you might have.

The most common form of a picklist is a simple menu using a <SELECT> tag. If the set of valid values in the domain are highly dynamic, e.g. available taxis in a taxi fleet, then the picklist is only as up-to-date as the time when the document was last loaded. If this isn't recent enough, a picklist can be created using window.open() to create a small scrollable window of values. This window is then the picklist. When a value is chosen, the window updates the field in the original document via a handler. Such a small window can load a fresh URL every time it is opened, and therefore is always up to date.

Netscape Validation Libraries

Before you get halfway through writing a whole heap of validation libraries, consider this URL from Netscape:
http://developer.netscape.com/docs/examples/javascript/formval/overview.html. There are a large number of pre-written validation routines here that you can steal for your own purposes. Beware that some functions depend on others, so you can't just rip out the one function that looks good for your purpose – either examine the function carefully, or just include the whole function library in your page.

These functions will work on most JavaScript enabled browsers, not just Netscape's.

Server Checks

If all else fails, the data in a form can be submitted to the web server for validation by server-side JavaScript or a CGI or ASP program. The only costs are in development time and performance, and of course, you must have development access to the web server environment.

Layout

There are several display techniques using JavaScript that build on the basic <FORM> tags of HTML.

Read-only Fields and Boilerplate

Sometimes form data in a document shouldn't be changeable by the user. Boilerplate text and read-only form fields can achieve this.

Boilerplate text is just all the content of a document that doesn't change. If a document is dynamically produced, like the results of a search query, then plain HTML text can be displayed. The catch with displaying form data this way is that JavaScript cannot change it, unless Dynamic HTML techniques are exploited. If form content displays a mixture of form controls and boilerplate text, and that form can be submitted, then there should be a hidden field duplicating each boilerplate data item, or else those items won't be submitted with the rest of the data.

To make existing form controls read-only, there are two alternatives: don't let the user get near the control or change the control's state back as soon as the user changes it. The first possibility is covered under 'Form events' and is perhaps a better approach for text, password and textarea fields. Alternatively, to change a field back to what it was before the user touched it, try these various tricks:

```
<HTML><BODY><FORM>

<!-- This case works for "text", "textarea" and "password" types -->
<INPUT TYPE="text" NAME="first" VALUE="Important" ONCHANGE="this.value=this.real">
<SCRIPT>
document.forms[0].first.real = document.forms[0].first.value;
</SCRIPT>

<!-- This case works for all checkboxes and for radio button groups of one -->
<INPUT TYPE="checkbox" NAME="second" ONCLICK="this.checked=!this.checked;">

<!-- This case works for radio button groups of more than one button -->
<INPUT TYPE="radio" NAME="third" CHECKED>
<INPUT TYPE="radio" NAME="third" ONCLICK="this.form.third[0].click()">
<INPUT TYPE="radio" NAME="third" ONCLICK="this.form.third[0].click()">

<!-- This case is solely for SELECT -->
<SELECT NAME="fourth" ONCHANGE="this.selectedIndex=this.realIndex">
<OPTION SELECTED VALUE="A"> Apples
<OPTION VALUE="B"> Banana
</SELECT>
<SCRIPT>
document.forms[0].fourth.realIndex = document.forms[0].fourth.selectedIndex;
</SCRIPT>

</FORM></BODY></HTML>
```

Submit, reset, button, hidden and image input types can't have their values set directly by the user at all, so they are ignored. Their normal action can be disabled with an onClick handler if desired.

Bugs: Internet Explorer 3.02 ignores the handler in the password case. Navigator 3.0 may crash if asked to display a radio button group of only one button. For radio buttons and select lists, Internet Explorer 3.02 has a trap in the use of its event handler – see the heading titled 'Internet Explorer 3.0 handler trap'. The file input type is problematic for event handlers – it appears to be buggy in all Netscape versions and you can't even be sure it is present at all with Explorer 3.0, since it's added to the browser's computer via a patch.

There are other solutions. HTML 4.0 has a READONLY attribute for form elements, which is the ultimate solution, but it is only supported in Internet Explorer 4+. A Java applet that displays a single piece of text can be exploited from JavaScript. A normal <INPUT> form control of type button, reset or submit can have its displayed value changed via JavaScript – although the user can still push the button, they can't change the displayed value. Finally, a Netscape <LAYER> can be used to write out a scrap of text in a specific position over a document. The Layer solution has the advantage that it can be made wider if the new text is longer than the old, but the disadvantage that the static page underneath must be carefully laid out so that the layer doesn't obscure anything important if it grows in size.

For the ultimate results in managing read-only screen data, one needs only to consider Dynamic HTML's ability to manage all the boilerplate text on a web page in intimate detail. See Chapter 8 for more details of Dynamic HTML.

Menus

The <SELECT> and <OPTION> tags with their single and multiple pick variants are the main mechanisms for displaying menus, but there are a few alternatives and subtleties.

The alternatives for drop-down menus are to use image map swaps as described in Multimedia and Plugins, Chapter 6, or to take advantage of positionable styles with Dynamic HTML. For plain, static menus that don't scroll or drop down, any set of clickable items such as a button bar can suffice.

However, the <SELECT> and <OPTION> tags have a trick or two of their own. As noted in 'Form objects' you can create your own Option objects, and change menus on the fly. There are some restrictions, however. It won't work in Internet Explorer 3.0, for one.

Replace a Menu Item

This is straightforward. The Option object's constructor function takes at least one argument: the displayed text in the <OPTION>tag content. There are further optional arguments. In order they are: the value from the VALUE attribute, the defaultSelected boolean state from the SELECTED attribute, and a final fourth argument, the selected boolean state, which says whether the option is currently selected or not.

```
<HTML><BODY><FORM NAME="cafe">
<SCRIPT>
function to_morning()
{
document.cafe.food.options[2] = new Option('Garlic Muesli', 'M1');
}
function to_evening()
{
```

```
document.cafe.food.options[2] = new Option('Garlic Quiche', 'M2');
}
</SCRIPT>
<INPUT TYPE="button" VALUE="Halitosis Cafe Morning Menu" ONCLICK="to_morning()">
<INPUT TYPE="button" VALUE="Halitosis Cafe Evening Menu" ONCLICK="to_evening()">
<SELECT NAME="food">
<OPTION VALUE="B1">Garlic Bread
<OPTION VALUE="S1">Garlic Soup
<OPTION VALUE="M1">Garlic Muesli
</SELECT>
</FORM></BODY><HTML>
```

When replacing an item as above, it's not strictly necessary to create a new `Option` object. Either of the functions shown could have been written using more conventional syntax as follows, but the `Option` object is there if you want it.

```
function to_lunchtime()
{
  document.cafe.food.options[2].value = "L2";
  document.cafe.food.options[2].text = "Garlic Coffee";
}
```

Remove or Gray Out a Menu Item

Removing items from a menu is easy. To remove the last item in the example above:

```
document.cafe.food.options.length--;
```

To remove an intermediate item, all the items can be moved up to fill the gap, or the item can be blanked out. From within JavaScript:

```
document.cafe.food.options[1] = new Option('','XX');
```

To initialize an item with blanks from HTML is trickier. The browser will collapse sequences of spaces into a single space. This is fine if other menu items have non-space strings. However, if all the menu items are formed from spaces, the menu will be only one character wide. The solution is to fill the menu item with non-breaking spaces, which aren't collapsed. An example in HTML:

```
<OPTION>     </OPTION>       <!-- 4 spaces -->
```

In JavaScript, four non-breaking spaces aren't the same as four ordinary spaces. Plain space has character code 32. Non-breaking space has character code 160, or in hexadecimal notation A0. Therefore, in JavaScript, four such characters are written as \xA0\xA0\xA0\xA0. If a menu control is part of a submitted form, and the item picked contains non-breaking spaces, then these different values will be sent with the submission as well. Any receiving CGI program or server-side JavaScript will then have to cope.

Because the text in the select menu items isn't HTML, only limited formatting options are available. This is much the same as `alert()` boxes. There is no way to fade a menu item, indicating it is unavailable. The best you can do is remove it entirely, or give the user some simple cue like surrounding the item's text in parentheses, and use an `onChange` event handler to complain if they pick it anyway.

Add Wide Menu Items

Netscape Navigator does not support reflowing an HTML document's contents if they change size. This goes for select menus as well. If you attempt to add menu items in that browser that have text wider than the widest existing item, the new item will appear truncated. There are two ways around this.

First alternative: plan ahead. Allocate enough space for all possible items. This option allocates 5 spaces:

```
<OPTION VALUE="X"> Hi    </OPTION>
```

or, if the menu is built from JavaScript originally:

```
var spaces5 = new Option('Hi\xA0\xA0\xA0', 'X'); // \xA0 is the   character
```

Second alternative: rewrite the whole <SELECT> contents, changing the HTML.

Internet Explorer 4+ doesn't have this 'wide item' problem at all; it will reflow the document, recreating the select list as required. For very wide items this could distort the normal layout of your page, as for all actions that cause a reflow.

Changing The Number of Items

You can add menu items quite simply, but not all Netscape browsers cope perfectly. An example:

```
with (document.cafe.food)
options[options.length] = new Option('Garlic Ice Cream','D1');
```

Under Windows 95, again for all Netscape versions, a drop down menu still appears, but that menu now has a scrollbar to accommodate extra items, rather than simply expanding in size. At least the non-dropdown version looks normal. To have the menu drop down to a new length, you have to re-write the whole <SELECT> tag or refresh the document's display entirely. The latter operation can be done by the statement `history.go(0)` which tells the browser to navigate (as if going backwards) to the current document.

Internet Explorer 4+ will correctly adjust the menu for you without any scrollbars appearing. A general solution for all browsers is to use in-place menus via the SIZE attribute of the <SELECT> tag rather than drop down menus.

Multi-Record Forms

There are several approaches to displaying more than one record at once in a document. The simplest is to have a <FORM> container for each record, which is straightforward. However, if all the records are to be part of a single form, some other approach is necessary.

Repeating Controls

A form can have multiple elements with the same name, so a simple solution is to use the same form elements repeatedly. Ten records with a street and suburb field each means ten text fields named `street` and ten named `suburb`. This may only require plain HTML. The main disadvantage is that many form elements lined up in a document can be hard on the eyes. This approach makes adding records difficult, unless extra spare fields are supplied. When the data is submitted, a large amount of data is sent, which can exceed the limits of some CGI systems and which can take some effort to extract in the receiving program.

List Viewers

A flexible approach is to store records in a set away from the user's view and only display the 'current' record. An example:

```
<HTML><HEAD><SCRIPT>
function Horse(kind)      // constructor - add other parameters as required
{
  this.kind = kind;
}

var list = new Array(); // the list of records, each an object.
var current = 0;
list[current++] = new Horse("Arab");
list[current++] = new Horse("Quarterhorse");
list[current++] = new Horse("Palamino");
list[current++] = new Horse("Gelding");
list[current++] = new Horse("Shetland Pony");
list[current++] = new Horse("Hack");
list[current++] = new Horse("Mule");

function next(form)
{
  if ( current + 1 < list.length )
    form.kind.value = list[++current].kind;
  else
    form.kind.value = list[list.length-1];
}
function previous(form)
{
  if ( current > 0 )
    form.kind.value = list[--current].kind;
}
</SCRIPT></HEAD><BODY><FORM>
<INPUT TYPE="text" NAME="kind">
<INPUT TYPE="button" VALUE="Next" ONCLICK="next(this.form);">
<INPUT TYPE="button" VALUE="Previous" ONCLICK="previous(this.form);">
</FORM>
<SCRIPT>
current=0; document.forms[0].kind.value=list[0].kind;
</SCRIPT></BODY></HTML>
```

It is easy to see how insert, delete, and update operations could work on the JavaScript `list` array via user buttons. The one visible record acts as like a "letterbox slot" into the list. More than one row at a time could be displayed using this approach. In order to submit anything, arrangements similar to the shopping cart example described later would have to be made.

Selectable HTML

HTML form controls don't provide very flexible layout options. If visual display is an issue, it may be better to render the records in boilerplate HTML, with only minimal form controls. This example reuses the data of the previous example:

```
// ... 'list' initialisation ..
</SCRIPT></HEAD><BODY><FORM><TABLE BORDER=1>
<SCRIPT>
var i;
for (i=0; i < list.length; i++)
{
document.write('<TR><TD><INPUT TYPE="radio" NAME="horse" VALUE="'+i+'">');
document.write('<TD>'+list[i].kind+'<TD>Other horsing around ...</TR>\n');
}
</SCRIPT></TABLE></FORM></BODY></HTML>
```

This example looks better but lacks any editable fields. Any record can be selected by checking its radio button. The value of the radio button contains enough information to identify the record – seed data again. In this case, the seed is the index of the `list` array. If that array didn't exist, perhaps because the page was the output of some search query, the seed data is sufficient to use as a query used to display the record in an editable form.

<Textarea>

`<Textarea>` tags provide a form control for multi-line input, which sounds perfect for multiple records. Their only obvious restriction is that their content must be plain text only, which is rather primitive.

For display only of multi-record data, you may find `textareas` of basic use. There are two traps. The first is that Windows and Unix differ over the end-of-line character, one requiring `\r\n`, the other just `\n`. As far as we're aware, this incompatibility is restricted to `textareas`. Fortunately the `\r\n` combination works in both places, so use that. A portable example displaying 3 lines:

```
<TEXTAREA ROWS=3 ONCHANGE="this.value='ten\r\ngreen\r\nbottles';">
No bottles yet
</TEXTAREA>
```

Unfortunately, the Macintosh requires just `\r`. If you want portability on all three platforms, you will have to avoid literal characters altogether. Instead, test the operating system using one of the compatibility techniques in Chapter 4, set a variable to the correct characters, and use that variable instead.

The second trap is the `autowrap` feature of the `textarea`. If a line extends past the physical width of the textarea, and the `COLS` attribute is set to a value, then the line will be broken unpredictably into two, spoiling the display. You can deal with this by setting the `WRAP` attribute to `off`, but then you must live with the possibility that all your text might not all appear – the user might need to scroll the textarea.

If the user can change the textarea's contents, the situation is much worse. `Textareas` were designed for plain text, not formatted information. Their word-wrapping behavior formats plain text nicely, but makes data entry of line-oriented information very difficult. You can't stop the user adding additional lines beyond the value of the `ROWS` attribute, and if the `COLS` attribute is set you can't stop the user from entering a long line that gets word wrapped, and that is then indistinguishable from two separate, smaller lines.

With careful processing of the textarea's value, you can reformat user input, but really this is so limited, it is not recommended. Desperate tactics: use a 4.0 browser and capture each keystroke the user makes over the textarea control and insert it into the textarea's value yourself from the scripting side.

Automatically Generated Records

For Internet Explorer 4.0+ it's possible to have the records of a multi-record form created when the form is sent from the web server. Use Microsoft's data binding features.

Custom Form Elements

Sometimes the various HTML tags that make up form elements seem a bit limited. If you really want to do something else, there's always a way.

Clickable Elements

Any HTML element that's clickable can be used to store simple form data. Usually that data just amounts to a flag that says 'I was picked'. The most traditional clickable elements are hypertext links (`<A HREF>` tags) and images. However, with the Dynamic HTML support in Internet Explorer 4+, any tag will do.

This example shows how to use links to simulate a simple radio button set arrangement. When a link is clicked, a URL request that is effectively a GET form request is sent with a single form element called `dress`. Although in this case each items full description is linked, there's nothing stopping you from making some other bit of HTML the link, leaving each item's description stated near it.

```
<HTML><BODY>
Dressing for Dinner? Choose your attire:<BR>
<A HREF="answer.html?dress=white_tie">Top Hat and Tails</A><BR>
<A HREF="answer.html?dress=black_tie">Tuxedo</A><BR>
<A HREF="answer.html?dress=casual">Slacks and Coat</A><BR>
<A HREF="answer.html?dress=punk">Safety Pins</A>
</BODY><HTML>
```

This Internet Explorer 4.0 example is a little more sophisticated; information is collected from the user's clicks until the submit link is clicked.

```
<HTML><BODY>
<SCRIPT>var palette='?palette=A';</SCRIPT>
Click on the colours of the rainbow that appeal, and then click on the pot of gold
to have your preference registered.<BR>
<DIV STYLE='background : red'
     ONCLICK='window.palette+="&col=red"'>
Colour 1</DIV>
<DIV STYLE='background : orange'
     ONCLICK='window.palette+="&col=orange"'>
Colour 2</DIV>
<!-- ... and so on ... -->
<DIV STYLE='background : violet'
     ONCLICK='window.palette+="&col=violet"'>
Colour 3</DIV>
<A HREF="#"
   ONCLICK="window.location.href+=palette; return false">
I'm the Pot!
</A>
</BODY></HTML>
```

In the second line, we're creating a dummy variable called `palette` that we're not really interested in. We do this because then we can add zero or more items to the string that it begins in a consistent way as shown in the `<DIV>` ONCLICK events. Otherwise we'd need tricky logic to test whether each item added was the first one or not - the first item must be preceded by ? and not by &.

Q&A Sessions

The prompt() and confirm() functions, described in Chapter 5, are the simplest way to get data from the user. You can even put these functions in the <HEAD> of a document so that you can gather data before any of the document is displayed:

```
<HTML><HEAD><SCRIPT>
var polite = confirm("Be nice?");
</SCRIPT></HEAD>
<BODY><SCRIPT>
if ( polite == true )
  document.write('Welcome to my home page')
else
  document.write('Waddaya want?')
</SCRIPT></BODY></HTML>
```

A second use of message boxes is when you want to implement a simple Question-and-Answer session, similar to a Microsoft Wizard dialog box. For such a system you can use a shopping cart arrangement with a separate HTML page for each stage of the Q&A, but for very simple uses a few simple dialog boxes might be enough:

```
<HTML><BODY>
Budget Examiner<BR>
<SCRIPT>
var income =    prompt("Enter your annual income",'');
var expenses = prompt("Enter your annual expenses",'');
var tax =       prompt("Enter your tax % as 2 digits",'');
if ( income * (1 - tax/100) > expenses)
  document.write("you still have spending money");
else
  document.write("you're broke!");
</SCRIPT></BODY></HTML>
```

In a real application (where you are doing more than just illustrating a point of design), when reading data from the user you should include all the proper input validation checking that has been discussed earlier in this chapter.

Dynamic HTML Replacements

The standard HTML form element controls are pretty inflexible in some ways. Some might even say dull. When form element controls are displayed on the screen, there isn't much chance to control the appearance of those elements. Using JavaScript and HTML, we can improve on nature.

The <INPUT TYPE="text"> tag is a good example — you have limited control over the font that the typed in text is displayed in; you can't resize the control once it's displayed; you can't do anything about the borders that surround the input box; you can't control the element's colors well; you can't do any of these things separately to other controls displayed on the page; you certainly can't control the space leading or trailing the control that separates it from surrounding text. This Internet Explorer 4+ Dynamic HTML example does give you those options though:

```
<HTML><BODY>
<!--  add styles as required  -->
Click on yellow and type away:
<SPAN ID="TextBox"
  STYLE="background: yellow; width: 2em; clip: rect(0 100 32 auto)"
  ONKEYPRESS="this.innerText+=String.fromCharCode(window.event.keyCode)"
>
</SPAN></BODY></HTML>
```

In this example, the <SPAN> tag acts as a textarea. Whenever a key is pressed while the mouse is over the <SPAN>, the key character is added to the <SPAN> contents, although you have to click once on the span to give it the input focus to start with. Because all of the style properties are exposed to JavaScript for this tag, we have fine control over the textarea's fonts, size and appearance. This rather crude and simple example can be enhanced quite a bit to support character deletion by backspacing or highlighting to show input focus and so on. It could also be constrained on the screen by clip regions and so on.

This example only works in Internet Explorer 4.0+.

Chapter 8, "Dynamic HTML", goes over dynamic HTML in more detail. That chapter also illustrates replacing the <SELECT> dropdown menu control with a dynamic HTML equivalent.

One of the commonest enhancements seen on the web doesn't have much Dynamic HTML at all. It is a set of fancy radio buttons with explanatory text. Each button lights up when the mouse hovers over it. This is a simple bit of JavaScript that merely uses the image swapping techniques described in Chapter 6, "Multimedia and Plugins", to provide a brighter alternative to normal radio buttons.

Tree Menus

A common control that isn't provided by the HTML form element tags is a tree menu or tree menu controller. This kind of control allows the user to navigate hierarchical data within a web document in a similar way to the Macintosh's Finder or Microsoft Window's Windows Explorer.

The book, "JavaScript Objects" *(by Nakhimovsky and Myers, Wrox Press 1998)* discusses tree-controllers at length, but in the meantime you might like to have a look at some tree controllers available on the World Wide Web. A fairly well documented Dynamic HTML controller is available at http://home.sol.no/~warnckew/tree_menu/. A controller that is less well documented but mimics Windows Explorer more closely is available at: http://www.geocities.com/Paris/LeftBank/2178/foldertree.html

Java and Bean Connect

If all else fails in JavaScript and HTML, you can always resort to Java. A Java applet can act as a single form input control. In Netscape 4.0+, Java-style controls can run in an HTML document even without an applet. Java applets can also manage their own form submission or have their data added to normal web form submission. Chapter 9 discusses how to do this.

Zones

Zones are a design technique for forms that don't require any JavaScript. Don't get confused with Internet Explorer security zones – we're talking about a design technique, not a browser feature here.

Zones are so useful that they're worth a mention anyway. A zone is just a rectangle of a web page used to collect similar information together. Zones are usually separated by blank space. This arrangement makes a page or a form easier for the eye to read and the brain to make sense of. There's no rocket science involved, usually just some appropriate HTML (such as <FIELDSET> and <LEGEND> tags of HTML 4.0) or simply some layout and design before you even touch the keyboard. Thinking in terms of zones is a good design strategy.

Both of these web pages contain the same content, but one is clearer and saner, just because like-minded information is collected together in separate areas. You needn't use table borders; any kind of layout that emphasizes collections of related items is good enough.

If you have a look around the web at some of the more expensive, corporate web sites, you'll see how zones are used to divide and draw the user's attention to different parts of the web page.

Form Design

Form elements can be collected together for a number of purposes. It pays to notice the general class of task the form is intended for, because once identified, techniques to follow become obvious. This section describes some general classes of forms, and the attendant issues.

Controls and Calculators

The simplest use of a form is a single button marked 'Just do it'. Such a form is typically used to control the browser or the user's navigation in the browser. The form elements used don't contain any data, or else the data they do contain is ignored. The point of the form is to make something else happen.

For such a form, there is usually little need to go beyond `onClick` event handlers. No data is required from the user; so many events are meaningless. No `submit` or `reset` form elements exist. Form elements may be unrelated. The form acts much like a collection of HTML hyperlinks. The appearance of buttons and checkboxes adds visual variety to a page whose only other features might be links, text and images. A simple example, that allows the user to navigate between several pages via buttons, is often called a **button bar**:

```
<!--frameset.htm-->
<HTML><FRAMESET ROWS="50,*">
<FRAME SRC="control.htm">
<FRAME NAME="main" SRC="home.htm">
</FRAMESET></HTML>
```

```
<!--control.htm-->
<HTML><BODY><FORM>
<TABLE BORDER=0><TR>
<TD><INPUT TYPE="button" VALUE="My Home"
ONCLICK="top.main.location.href='home.htm'">
<TD><INPUT TYPE="button" VALUE="Games"
ONCLICK="top.main.location.href='game.htm'">
<TD><INPUT TYPE="button" VALUE="Links"
ONCLICK="top.main.location.href='link.htm'">
<TD><INPUT TYPE="button" VALUE="Help" ONCLICK="top.main.location.href='link.htm'">
</TR></TABLE>
</FORM></BODY></HTML>
```

You can get the same result, but with a better looking button bar if you use image maps. Similarly, Dynamic HTML, described in chapter 8 can achieve the same effect, with full access to event handlers if you are using Internet Explorer 4.0+.

Beyond button bars, a similar but less simplistic use of forms puts the JavaScript interpreter under the user's control. The JavaScript interpreter supports basic mathematics and logic, so it can perform calculations on the user's behalf. The calculation is done in three stages: user input, processing & user feedback. The entire calculation occurs without accessing any other URL. Just like the button bar, no form data is forwarded anywhere. Unlike the button bar, the user might enter values into the form which are processed locally. There is still no need for a 'submit' button, or a button performing a submit action, but a 'reset' button might be used to clear the form. Because the user can enter data, the scriptwriter might need to validate that data in case rubbish has been entered, or control the user's navigation through the elements of the form. If the window containing the form closes, the form data is gone.

The classic example of this kind of processing is a hand calculator. A calculator just takes input from one place and produces output in another. A trivial example (which could do with some better error checking – more on that later):

```
<HTML><BODY><FORM>
<H4>Centimeters to Inches and back again converter</H4>
<INPUT TYPE="text" NAME="cm" ONCHANGE="this.form.inches.value = this.value *
2.54">
```

```
<INPUT TYPE="text" NAME="inches" ONCHANGE="this.form.cm.value = this.value /
2.54">
</FORM></BODY></HTML>
```

Type any number into either field, and see the other field update.

A very simple example of a desk-style calculator can be found at
`http://www.people.cornell.edu/pages/avr1/calculator.html`. This alternate page
points to a number of similar examples, some of them even useful, but not all of them are pure
JavaScript, so view the HTML source of each to confirm:
`http://www.yahoo.com/Computers_and_Internet/Hardware/Calculators/Online_Ca`
`lculators/JavaScript/`. A good example can be seen at this web address:
`http://sun1.bham.ac.uk/s.m.williams.bcm/apps/apps.html`.

The book, "JavaScript Objects" *(by Nakhimovsky and Myers, Wrox Press 1998)* has a lot more to say on
the design of JavaScript calculators.

Fire and Forget

The most common kind of form on the Internet is used to collect data from the browser user and is
then submitted once to a remote system. The user rarely, or never, sees the data again in the form
that it was entered. The two most common styles of these 'fire and forget' forms are **search requests**,
and **registration or feedback forms**. These forms are the kinds that HTML was designed to support
when <FORM> tags were first added to the HTML 2.0 standard. The form data is submitted to a web
server where it is processed by a specially developed system.

These kinds of forms have some features which combine to make them 'one use only' forms. The
form is contained in a single HTML document. The fields in the form are usually very simple: the
user starts at the first one, works down, and then submits. Once such a form is submitted there is
often no need to retain the form information in the browser – the document containing the form is
replaced with something else. The user rarely has a reason to return to the form document, unless it is
to start again. The data that the user enters is rarely rejected – at worst it might produce no useful
results. The information in the form doesn't have any complex relationships with other data, and
doesn't need to be maintained in the browser after the user has submitted it.

These forms are simple to construct because they rely heavily on the principle of **harmless data**. No
matter what the user enters, the system to which the data is submitted will cope. There is no need to
coordinate the form data with other information in the browser or maintain it in some special state.
JavaScript in the browser might do some validation on the data, but that's about all. Often these
forms can be constructed in plain HTML without any JavaScript at all.

An example of a simple 'fire and forget' style form is this page from Wrox web site:

Once you submit this form, the current page (with the form in it) disappears, to be replaced by another page. Very common practice. Other examples can be seen at http://www.yahoo.com, and http://www.hotbot.com

Shopping Carts

When forms need to span more than one HTML document, a **shopping cart** or **shopping trolley** is a design approach that overcomes some limiting factors of HTML.

A common use of forms is to allow users to place orders for goods. Shopping cart forms meet this need. The name derives from the user's typical behavior – they browse through the web site looking at goods, collecting desired items the same way that shoppers operate in a supermarket, and then buying them at the end. The equivalent of a physical shopping cart or trolley in a web form is a temporary storage place for form data.

Simple 'fire and forget' style forms would be enough for the job if it weren't for three issues.

The first issue is the matter of document size and presentation. web sites selling goods act as ordering systems, but they also have an advertising and sales function. If the site has many items for sale, a simple form solution would result in a huge HTML page that can be scrolled at length, takes a long time to load, and has possibly hundreds of form fields. web sites selling goods are better off mimicking the large printed catalogues that used to be delivered in the days before television (or now in the electronics industry). The user can turn to specific sections of interest, and choose items from each. This allows smaller HTML pages and better advertising focus on the user.

The second issue is that there is nowhere in plain HTML to temporarily store form data. For browsers without scripting support or Java, there is no choice but to maintain the shopping cart with the web server and ask the user to submit each item so it can be stored in the cart. Then a final extra submit tells the server the cart contents should be purchased.

The third issue is that HTML forms can't span several HTML documents. This makes the design goal of splitting any form into separate documents difficult.

With a modern browser, JavaScript comes to the rescue for all these issues. The tasks involved are as follows:

❑ Create a permanent place for the shopping cart.
❑ Create forms in each page of the catalogue.
❑ Organize for each form's data to be captured in the cart.
❑ Submit shopping cart data if the user decides to buy.

A full example follows. First, the creation of a shopping cart - the 'simple approach' to multiple windows described in Chapter 5 on Windows and Frames is used here. The shopping cart will be stored in a frameset document. One frame is used to control the catalogue paging and the other to display the actual pages.

```html
<!--catalog.htm -->
<HTML><HEAD><SCRIPT>
var cart = new Object;                    // The whole cart

function Item(name, price, quantity)      // cart item constructor
{
  this.name = name;
  this.price = price;
  this.quantity = quantity;
}
</SCRIPT></HEAD>
<FRAMESET ROWS="50,*">
<FRAME NAME="buttonbar" SRC="buttons.htm">
<FRAME NAME="page" SRC="welcome.htm">
</FRAMESET>
</HTML>
```

Each property of the `cart` object will be an ordered item. Each ordered item will have its own product code, making it unique. The control frame is ordinary; it doesn't even use a form:

```html
<!--buttons.htm -->
<HTML><BODY><TABLE BORDERS=0><TR>
<TD><A HREF="big.htm" TARGET="page">Big stuff</A>
<TD><A HREF="medium.htm" TARGET="page">Medium stuff</A>
```

```
<TD><A HREF="small.htm" TARGET="page">Small stuff</A>
<TD><A HREF="order.htm" TARGET="page">Place order</A>
</TR></TABLE></BODY></HTML>
```

The front page is just an introduction for the user:

```
<!--welcome.htm-->
<HTML><BODY>
Welcome to the Obscure Emporium! If no one wants it, we've got it!
</BODY></HTML>
```

Here is an image of the first page the user sees:

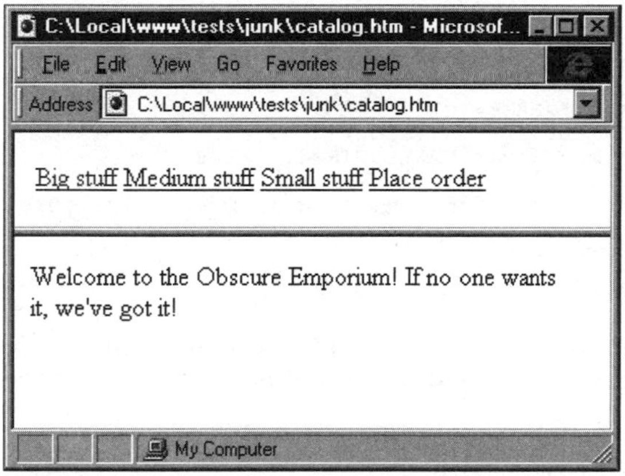

The catalogue pages all follow the same pattern. The first one is shown here:

```
<!--big.htm-->
<HTML><HEAD>
<SCRIPT>
function recall_selection()
{
  if ( top == self )            // make sure this is a frame.
    self.location.href = "catalog.htm";
  if (top.cart["CH"])
  {
    document.frm.c1.checked = true;
    document.frm.v1.value = top.cart["CH"].quantity;
  }
  if (top.cart["LV"])
  {
    document.frm.c2.checked = true;
    document.frm.v2.value = top.cart["LV"].quantity;
  }
  if (top.cart["AO"])
  {
    document.frm.c3.checked = true;
    document.frm.v3.value = top.cart["AO"].quantity;
  }
}
</SCRIPT>
<BODY ONLOAD="recall_selection()">
<SCRIPT>
if ( top == self )              // make sure this is a frame.
  self.location.href = catalog.htm";
</SCRIPT>
```

```
<FORM name="frm">
Big stuff for sale today.<BR>
Check the items required and enter a quantity for each
<BR><BR><BR><INPUT TYPE="checkbox" NAME='c1'
     ONCLICK="document.frm.v1.value='0'">
<INPUT TYPE="text" NAME='v1' MAXLENGTH=2 SIZE=2
     ONCHANGE=
     "top.cart['CH']=new top.Item('CombineHarvester',145000,this.value)"

>
Combine Harvester - $145,000.00
<BR>
<INPUT TYPE="checkbox" NAME='c2'
     ONCLICK="document.frm.v2.value='1'">
<INPUT TYPE="text" NAME='v2' MAXLENGTH=2 SIZE=2
     ONCHANGE=
     "top.cart['LV']=new top.Item('Lunar Vehicle',6000000,this.value)"
>
Lunar Re-entry Vehicle - $6,000,000.00
<BR>
<INPUT TYPE="checkbox" NAME='c3'
     ONCLICK="document.frm.v3.value='0'">
<INPUT TYPE="text" NAME='v3' MAXLENGTH=2 SIZE=2
     ONCHANGE=
     "top.cart['AO']=new top.Item('Arctic Ocean',123,this.value)"
>
Arctic Ocean - $123.00
</FORM></BODY></HTML>
```

Again, unless you are merely illustrating a point to someone, include proper validation everytime the user has latitude to enter something odd. If the user navigates to this page, it appears as follows:

In this example, two letter codes (CH, LV, AO) are used for each product line. Anything could be used. The example isn't formatted very well, nor does it do good validation – if the user ignores the instructions, problems can occur. It also needs work so that the user can back out of their choices. The main point of it is to show how items are put into the shopping cart using an onChange trigger. The recall_selection() function demonstrates how the form is loaded with any existing selections the user has made. This allows the page to be abandoned and revisited without any information being lost.

The last page is the ordering page that submits the data in the shopping cart to a web server. Here it is:

```
<!--order.htm-->
<HTML><BODY>
Your order currently consists of:<BR>
<SCRIPT>
var i;
var linetotal = 0, subtotal = 0;

for ( i in top.cart)
{
  document.write(' Item: '+top.cart[i].name);
  document.write(', '+top.cart[i].quantity+' at '+top.cart[i].price);
  linetotal = top.cart[i].quantity * top.cart[i].price;
  document.write(' each is: '+ linetotal + '<BR>');
  subtotal += linetotal;
}
document.write('<BR>Total due is: '+subtotal+'<BR>');
</SCRIPT>
<FORM METHOD="POST"> <! add an ACTION for your server-side program>
<SCRIPT>
var item;
for (i in top.cart)
{
  item = '<INPUT TYPE="hidden"' +
         ' NAME="' + i + '"' +
         ' VALUE="' + top.cart[i].quantity + '">';
  document.write(item);
}
</SCRIPT>
<BR>
Credit Card details (you won't feel a thing)
<INPUT TYPE="text" NAME="card_number">
<INPUT TYPE="submit" VALUE="Buy Now">
</FORM>
</BODY></HTML>
```

Typical output from this page might be:

The shopping cart details are extracted twice, once for the user to review, and once to create hidden fields (they could be visible if desired) in the form that is submitted. The data submitted consists of field name-value pairs; in this case, the name is the two-letter product code and the value is the number of items bought.

Notice that these forms (and all other submitted forms) make assumptions about the program at the web server site that will receive the submission. In this case, the scriptwriter assumes that such a program knows prices for all the items on sale, knows what the two-letter codes mean, and knows that the number supplied is a quantity, not a price. The form document and that program are a deliberate match.

This coordination between the server side and the browser side can require a lot of work if they are maintained separately. A more sophisticated strategy is to have the server-side create the HTML and JavaScript in the client side automatically, so that updates need only be done on the server side. This can be done with server-side JavaScript, CGI or ASP.

Forms for Data Management

Beyond forms that submit data only once are forms that are used to manage existing data. Typically, this data is in a database accessible via a web server. Databases tend to support four important operations: **insert**, **update**, **delete** and **fetch/select** - fetch or select is sometimes called **query**. Forms that are submitted only once are equivalent to just one database-style operation, typically insert (e.g. registration forms) or select requests (e.g. search engine queries). To fully support database-style operations requires a more sophisticated approach.

Browsers Versus 4GL Tools

Because browsers and web servers have a client-server relationship, and because JavaScript provides a generally flexible programming language for controlling the browser, it may seem that a web browser is a good tool to use as a database client development tool. However, it is only a primitive tool for such uses, compared with more specialized "4GL" database tools. On the other hand, 4GL database tools are primitive tools for developing Internet document retrieval systems, so that makes it even.

Traditional 4GL database clients provide a great deal of programmer support, being custom built for databases. Some of the features they support with little effort are:

❑ Automatic validation of simple types.

❑ 'Picklists' or 'select lists' recalled dynamically from the server.

❑ Logic for insert, delete, update and fetch operations.

❑ Automatic coordination of master-detail records.

❑ Support for multi-record forms.

❑ Fully synchronized operation.

❑ Log-in and security features.

❑ Systematic support for storing and saving variables.

❑ Systematic support for user navigation.

Few of these things are built into a web browser. To mimic a complex data management-style form in a web browser can be a lot of work and can generate a lot of JavaScript. Even then, it is possible the form document can't be crafted by hand, because it may require an up-to-the-second view of the database. In this case, the form document must be partially generated by an ASP or CGI program or by server-side JavaScript each time it is displayed.

If you don't feel like getting elbow deep in JavaScript code, then you might want to give up and go for one of the 4GL-like tools that can create web pages (with JavaScript) for you. Chapter 19, "Rapid Development", looks at these tools.

However, there are no total obstacles to achieving the features that 4GL tools offer you. If your goal is to explore the possibilities, feel free. If you have limited time, there are efficient ways to proceed, and they are the topics of this section.

Strategies That Ease Implementation

The simplest strategies are to avoid the technology or avoid the problems.

The technology can be avoided a number of ways. Custom tools instead of browsers or Java applets instead of JavaScript can be more productive for complicated forms, if the user base allows it. JDBC is a well defined Java standard for accessing databases, and the number of commercial Java applets supporting form-style interfaces to databases is increasing. Of course, Java applets are embeddable in HTML documents.

Avoiding the problems means keeping it simple. Two very time consuming processes when developing data management forms are supporting in-place editing and supporting master-detail record coordination. We look at how to make both easier. A third consumer of time is validation, so we look at that too. If the form is complex, adding validation script can take up considerable time. However, as described in Chapter 18, "Privacy, Security and Cookies", in a public arena like the Internet, validating the data in the browser is no guarantee of anything when the submitted data arrives at the server end. If that is your case, it might not be worth adding any user validation at all.

An easy trap to fall into when working with databases is to reflect the database structure directly in the fields of a document's forms. This means all fields in the database appear in the browser. This is not so bad for a simple document based on just one database record, but if there are 3 types of records in the database with 14, 15 and 16 fields each, a complex document might end up with all 45 fields displayed. Lots and lots of JavaScript can easily result trying to keep them all organized. A better approach is to focus on the task the user is trying to achieve with a given form, and supply only the fields necessary, regardless of the underlying database structure. When the data is submitted to the web server back-end, that back-end is responsible for sorting through the data, away from the user's view. This is **transaction processing**, a standard technique in the world of databases. In transaction processing, just the needed data is supplied by the client and then some dedicated program behind the web server grinds through the logic required to make it all happen.

In-place Editing

In-place editing occurs when the one form is used for both retrieving and modifying data. The advice of this section is **don't do it** - use the alternative we describe, which is to break up the functionality into many simple forms.

In-place editing looks good to the user. The user sees a single form, typically with a number of button options, one for each form function. Typical button options are add, display, delete and modify. When the user presses a button, the form is submitted as usual. When the submission returns with a new HTML document, it is exactly the same form. Usually only the data in the form has changed, so there is little that is new for the user to absorb. Here is a simple example – the source HTML is not important, it is the general look of the screen that is the point here:

The row of buttons performs different functions, but the user only ever sees this one screen. This kind of setup is hard work for the scriptwriter (especially a non-spunk scriptwriter!). Nearly all screens like this are going to have much bigger forms, too. A typical sequence of user actions in such a screen illustrates why it is difficult:

- ❑ The user partially fills in an empty form with search or fetch criteria, and submits.
- ❑ The form is replaced with an identical form containing the fetched data.
- ❑ The user modifies the fetched data and submits, causing an insert, update or further search.
- ❑ The form is replaced with an identical form containing the changed data.

There are many such sequences of steps. This requires a complex form that records many states because it is not always clear what action the user intends when changing the fields. Is it new search criteria for a fetch, or new data being inserted? What action did the user do last? Two deletes in a row may not make sense. These states are usually stored in JavaScript variables, and may include duplicating some or all of the form's data. These states have to be preserved somewhere in case the form document reloads or is submitted, and might have to contribute to the submission process as well. Argghhh!

A simpler approach is to separate out each operation into its own document. The key to this approach is to retain **seed data**, also called the **current key**. These values are enough information to identify the current data and to communicate between documents.

Here is an example based on scheduling waiter's shifts in a restaurant. If the waiters are all frustrated actors, chances are the staff will regularly need to be reorganized - fame and fortune only come at short notice. A 'duty' in this example is a match of a shift (a period of work) and a particular person. In this application, everything revolves around two seed values or keys: the shift_id and staff_id (id meaning identifier) variables. Each uniquely identifies a type of data (in true relational database style), and together they uniquely identify a duty (a composite key in relational language). To start with they're set to nothing.

In order to avoid dedicating the rest of this book to script extracts for this one example, only the essential features are included. Remember, this example is illustrative and doesn't include iron-clad anti-stupid-user logic; that would require much more script. Here's a screen shot of the menu and fetch/query option at work:

```
<!--main.htm - the top level document -->
<HTML><SCRIPT>
var shift_id = null;                // current key values
var staff_id = null;
</SCRIPT><FRAMESET ROWS="50,*">
<FRAME NAME="start" SRC="actions.htm">
<FRAME NAME="page" SRC="blank.htm">
</FRAMESET></HTML>
```

```
<!--actions.htm - controls for the user -->
<HTML><BODY>
<A HREF="fetch.htm" TARGET="page">Show duties</A> -
<A HREF="insert.htm" TARGET="page">Add duty</A> -
<A HREF="delete.htm" TARGET="page">Delete duty</A> -
<A HREF="update.htm" TARGET="page">Update duty</A>
</BODY></HTML>
```

These two documents above are similar to the shopping cart example.

```
<!--fetch.htm - search form to get current duties -->
<HTML><FORM>      <!-- add an ACTION for your ASP program -->
Enter shift name: <INPUT TYPE="text"><BR>
Enter staff name: <INPUT TYPE="text"><BR>
<INPUT TYPE="submit" VALUE="Get Duties">
</FORM></HTML>
```

This above form doesn't use the seed data, because the user is doing a new search. If the search succeeds, the page generated by the system behind the web server might look like this:

```
<!--results.htm - data resulting from the search -->
<HTML><BODY><FORM>      <!-- again, an action for the server -->
   Shift Name - Waiter Name - Rate - Tips <BR>
<INPUT TYPE="radio" ONCLICK="top.shift_id='3'; top.staff_id='13';">
Evening - Manuel - $10/hr - No Tips<BR>
<INPUT TYPE="radio" ONCLICK="top.shift_id='3'; top.staff_id='22';">
Evening - Elmer - $2/hr - Tips allowed<BR>
<INPUT TYPE="radio" ONCLICK="top.shift_id='3'; top.staff_id='9';">
Evening - Woody - $12/hr - Tips allowed<BR>
</FORM></BODY></HTML>
```

Output from this HTML looks like this:

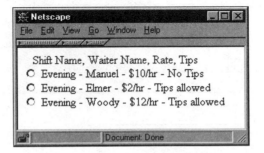

When the user selects one of the three displayed duties, the seed values for that duty is saved. The other three documents use these values. The update case, update.htm, might look like this:

```
<HTML><FORM>
<INPUT TYPE="hidden" NAME="shift_id" VALUE="&{top.shift_id}">
<INPUT TYPE="hidden" NAME="staff_id" VALUE="&{top.staff_id}">
<SCRIPT>
document.write('Current shift period: '+top.shift_id+'<BR>');
document.write('Current staff member: '+top.staff_id+'<BR>');
</SCRIPT>
<BR>Hourly Rate:
<INPUT TYPE="text" NAME="rate">
<BR>Tip policy:
<SELECT NAME="tips">
<OPTION VALUE="Y"> Tips allowed
<OPTION VALUE="N"> No tips allowed
<OPTION VALUE="R"> Customers tipped for staying
</SELECT>
<BR><INPUT TYPE="submit" VALUE="Update">
</FORM></HTML>
```

The only problem with this example is that the user is left wondering what a staff_id and a shift_id is. However, if this URL was returned by a CGI program rather than being hand-written, and the two ids were passed to that program, the real name for the shift and the staff member could be inserted into the document instead. The section on CGI discusses the mechanics of parameter passing. When this form is submitted, the replacement document might be merely:

```
<HTML><BODY>
Update succeeded.
</BODY></HTML>
```

The delete and insert cases follow in a similar manner. The insert case wouldn't need to use the seed values, as new user data would be the issue. It might check the new data doesn't clash with the current seed values.

Master-detail Coordination

Master-detail coordination means coordinating two forms so that they always match. Some 4GL products do this for you automatically, but that automatic process can create a dozen event handlers. In a web browser, you might have to script that many JavaScript event handlers manually in order to achieve the same effect.

The classic example of master detail coordination is an order-entry system. In such a system, one purchase order from a customer consists of a number of individual items required (entries) plus general information such as the customers name, order number and the date (the order). The details are entered into a computer to track the order. All kinds of rules apply: an order must have at least one entry; if an order is deleted, all the entries are deleted; when an order is added, entries must be added; when the user displays an order, all the matching entries should be displayed.

There are several problems here for the web developer:

❑　How to display and manage multiple records at once.

❑　How to coordinate two forms.

❑　How to ensure that when submitted, both forms succeed or fail together.

The section on display techniques describes methods of displaying multi-record sets. Coordinating forms is discussed here. Ensuring two submissions stand or fall together is discussed in the 'Complex Problems' section.

Finding an easy solution to coordination problems means using a similar pattern to that in the previous section. Functionality supplied to the user should be broken up into numerous, simple forms. In that previous section, the concept of seed or key data was used to target each simple form at specific data. A similar approach can be used here, but in a repeated way. Using the order-entry example, an important observation is that entries can't exist without an order. This means that the order details 'drive' the entry details – the order details must be specified before the entry details can be known. This allows the forms to drive the user's responses in a step by step manner. Here is a stripped down example showing insertion of an entry into an existing order:

```
<!--main.htm - the top level document -->
<HTML><SCRIPT>
var order_id = null;            // current order key
</SCRIPT><FRAMESET ROWS="50,*">
<FRAME NAME="start" SRC="order_actions.htm">
<FRAME NAME="order_page" SRC="blank.htm">
</FRAMESET></HTML>
```

```
<!-- order_actions.htm - controls for the user -->
<HTML><BODY>
<A HREF="fetch.htm" TARGET="order_page">Show order</A>
<A HREF="insert.htm" TARGET="order_page">Add order</A>
<A HREF="delete.htm" TARGET="order_page">Delete order</A>
<A HREF="update.htm" TARGET="order_page">Update order</A>
</BODY></HTML>
```

These two documents are almost identical to the last example. The fetch.htm document would be similar as well. Since this example is about inserting an entry into an order, not displaying an order, assume the user has displayed an order, which set the seed order_id value to 55, and then clicks the **Update order** button. In the previous example, this would be a single document. In this example, the document is a frameset with the same structure as the top level frameset, but focussed on an entry, not an order. When this new frameset is displayed, the user sees three frames: a top row, a left column, and the remainder.

```
<!--update.htm - let the user change an order or its details -->
<HTML><SCRIPT>
var entry_id = null;            // current entry key
</SCRIPT><FRAMESET COLS="100,*">
<FRAME SRC="entry_actions.htm">
<FRAME NAME="entry_page" SRC="order_update.htm">
</FRAMESET></HTML>
```

The order_update.htm document just contains a normal form, with a submit button and a hidden field containing the order_id stolen from top.order_id. When the user changes the form details (the order details) and presses submit, the order is changed, but no entries for the order are changed, so that document isn't illustrated. Here is the suspiciously familiar entry_actions.htm page:

```
<!-- entry_actions.htm - controls for the user -->
<HTML><BODY>
Choose entry action:<BR>
<A HREF="fetch.htm" TARGET="entry_page">Show entries</A><BR><BR>
<A HREF="insert.htm" TARGET="entry_page">Add entries</A><BR><BR>
<A HREF="delete.htm" TARGET="entry_page">Delete entries</A><BR><BR>
<A HREF="update.htm" TARGET="entry_page">Update entries</A><BR><BR>
```

```
<BR>
<A HREF="order_update.htm" TARGET="entry_page">Back to Order Update</A><BR>
</BODY></HTML>
```

Here is a screen shot of the application taken after the 'Update Order' (not 'Update Entry') link has been clicked:

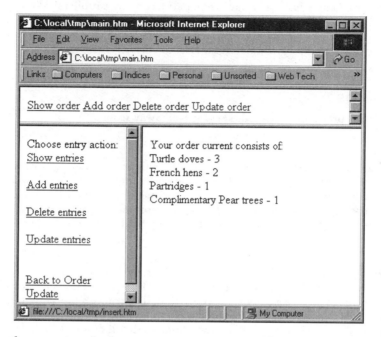

As you can see, the <BR> tags in the entry_actions.htm file are present only because this menu appears vertically on the left – a layout choice. The only frame remaining is the one in the bottom right-hand corner of the window that fills most of the space. The entry_actions.htm document gives the user the choice of four forms; just like the order_actions.htm document does, but focused on the particular entries, rather than on the more general orders.

The key difference is that for the 'order' screens (the master record), the seed value is just top.order_id, but for the 'entry' screens (each a detail record), the seed value is the combination of top.order_id and top.order_page.entry_id. This fully specifies which entry is being operated on. For displaying current data, displaying orders requires no order_id, unless the user searches for it specifically. Similarly, for displaying an order's entries, no entry_id is required, but the order_id is.

Using this approach, the user has to jump around a little more than for a single integrated screen, but the scriptwriter is spared a lot of coordination work, and the user can only make one simple and safe change at a time. If this seems a little confusing, try fully implementing the example in the previous section on 'in-place editing', then convert it to a fully working ordering system that has no entry records (and therefore no master-detail coordination), and finally add support for entries as described here.

Stripped of validation and other features that would make these forms robust, there is only a very small and manageable amount of client-side JavaScript required, as this example has shown. You are still required to create server-side JavaScript or CGI programs in order to service the submitted data.

Finally, master-detail coordination is an example of working with one-to-many relationships. One order has (possibly) many entries. These relationships can occur in "chains", for example: one order has many entries; one entry has many parts; one part has many suppliers. The approach described here can be applied to such chains which have more than one "**link**" (to burden an overused word with further meaning) – just keep nesting the framesets and adding seed values at each level. Only one record is ever operated on at a time, but the set of current seed values puts that record into a context.

Complex Problems

Some database style problems are worth keeping well away from.

Database Integrity

You can never be sure that data submitted by the user will be accepted by a database. Even if the user submits on good faith, the data may be conflict with other data and be rejected, or the database may become corrupt and fail entirely. This means you need to do error handling. That in itself is no great chore, but trying to anticipate or detect integrity problems *before* submitting is a great deal of effort for little benefit, or else is a hobby. Best to submit, wait and see what happens, and then act on the outcome.

Multiple Submits

Each submit in a web browser is a single action (an HTTP request) that is independent of all other requests. Submitting several times, say for several different forms on the same page, is several different actions. It is a great deal of effort to impose some kind of coordination system (usually called a transaction model) on such sets of submit operations so that they succeed or fail together. The difficulties of backing out from partially complete sets of submit operations are immense, not to mention the user's ability to interfere by shutting down the browser at no notice. Don't try to coordinate multiple submissions.

A better approach for the desperate is to use inline JavaScript to create an additional form. This form contains a duplicate of every field of every form to be submitted. Before submitting, copy all the values across to the additional form and submit that form only. This way the submit is done as a single item. A specially created server-side program then handles the complexity of the combined data.

Microsoft's Data Binding

Web browsers consist of many parts – HTML, JavaScript, plugins, ActiveX controls and Java. Just as LiveConnect and ActiveX are forms of glue that connects these parts together, so too is the Data-Binding feature of Internet Explorer 4.0+. Microsoft's data binding provides an alternate mechanism for managing server-based data in a web browser.

Data-binding has the goal of replacing a complex chunk of client-side JavaScript processing with some special built-in browser coordination of HTML tag attributes with ActiveX controls, plugins or Java. Using this system, single record and multi-record data displays can be had without any JavaScript logic being required – the browser handles it all.

Three steps are required to take advantage of data binding:

- ❑ Use of the special Microsoft proprietary DATASRC and DATAFLD tag attributes in HTML tags that will display the data to be bound. Not all Microsoft HTML tags support these attributes.

- ❑ Inclusion of a foreign item in the HTML page that can extract data from outside the browser. This foreign body can be a Java applet or an activex plugin.

- ❑ Maintenance of the data in some suitable form either behind the Web server that will serve up the data-bound pages, or on the user's local machine.

Because Data-Binding in its simplest form doesn't require much JavaScript, and is a fairly complex system in its own right, it's not pursued much here. However, it is an interesting alternative way of handling form-like data. Check out Wrox's Professional IE4 Programming for a complete discussion. Nevertheless, like everything else in a browser, if your work becomes sophisticated enough, you'll end up using buckets of JavaScript with Data Binding just like with the other technique mentioned here.

Avoiding Server Development

If you don't want to write CGI programs or server-side JavaScript, or you can't because you don't have access to the web server where your pages are stored, there are a few alternatives.

Using E-mail

A form can send its data to an e-mail address via a **mailto:** URL instead of an **http:** URL. To do this, just use <FORM ACTION=mailto:fred@obscure.com METHOD=POST ENCTYPE="text/plain">. This feature isn't supported in Internet Explorer 3.0 or in the early versions of Netscape Navigator 4.0 that are separate to the Communicator suite. There is no way to send e-mail without the user being warned, except for these two possibilities: use a signed script or ensure the user has turned off email warnings in the browser's preferences. Of course, if the email is to ultimately be successful, the web browser must have access to an e-mail service to start with, and their browser must be setup to use it. This means setting up Microsoft Outlook for Internet Explorer, or Netscape Messenger for Netscape Navigator.

This URL describes how to exploit the mailto: URL prefix to the maximum extent:
http://developer.netscape.com/viewsource/husted_mailto/mailto.html.

Using Cookies

A form's contents, or any data, can be packed into a cookie (see Chapter 18 for how) and stored with the user's browser. Each time the user visits the web page containing JavaScript, that JavaScript can examine the cookie and be reminded of what the user entered. This is limited in some respects - if the user uses a different browser, or removes the file containing their cookies, the data is lost. Cookies usually stay with the browser that received them, so they are not generally portable once saved.

Using Custom Packages

You might not be able to develop anything on the web server that stores your web pages, but you may be able to find or use helpful software installed by others there. See Chapter 13 onwards for details.

Avoiding HTTP Entirely

Form data and cookies are generally sent to servers from browsers via HTTP requests. However, it is possible to avoid working with HTTP entirely. There are other protocols that can be used. In particular, a browser that supports Java can send information back to the web server that it originates from via its general and flexible networking support. See the Applets and Java chapter. On top of this general networking support, protocols such as RPC, RMI, CORBA or DCOM can be exploited. Alternatively, a specialized plugin run from within a browser might send data by almost any method to other computers, provided that the user trusts the plugin.

Summary

Just like the other parts of an HTML document, HTML form elements make an appearance as host objects accessible from a browser-embedded JavaScript interpreter. From the JavaScript perspective there are some complexities with HTML forms that aren't obvious from the equivalent HTML tags, and the scriptwriter needs to beware of these. Furthermore, although HTML forms are an obvious and logical place to store user or developer data in a web document, they are not the only place by a long shot.

JavaScript allows the scriptwriter to add smarts to forms. The two main possibilities are smarter processing via scripting in validation, and better form element layout. When traditional HTML forms are too limited, JavaScript can exploit Dynamic HTML where its available to escape right out of the box and innovate more flexible form elements from scratch.

The flexibility provided by JavaScript makes a number of more complex form designs possible. Shopping carts, multi-record forms and master-detail forms are all examples. With client-side JavaScript, a web browser starts to look a bit like a traditional 4GL database client and some of the processing of those tools is possible, provided the scripter is wary of a number of design issues.

Finally, the main bugbear of forms is the question of where the data should be sent. There are a few browser escape hatches, but in general, scripting at the web server is required.

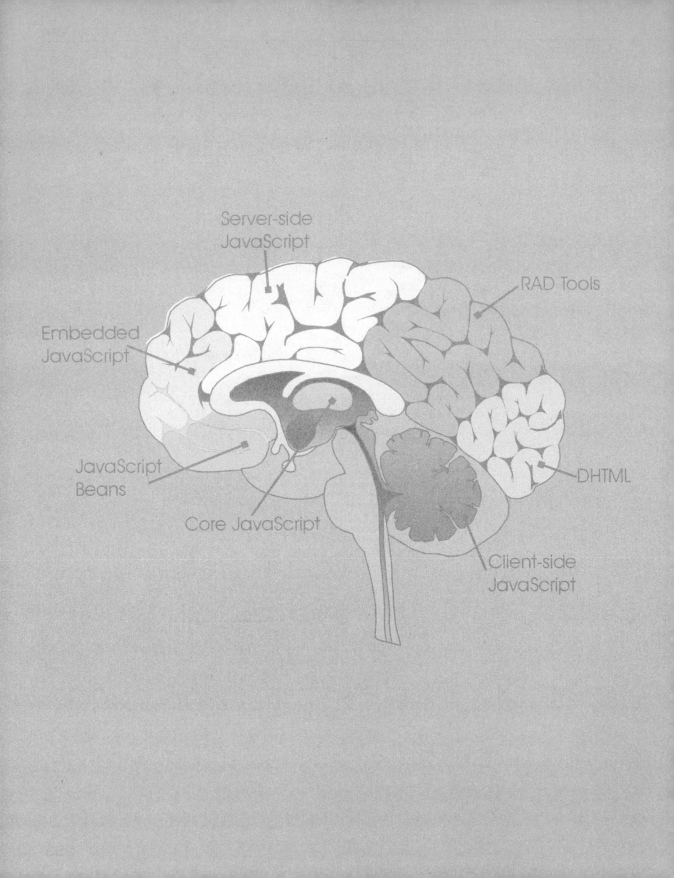

Dynamic HTML

Web pages vary greatly in their appearance. Some HTML web documents are merely informative, being no more than heading-laden text. Some web documents are both informative and interactive, such as HTML documents containing forms and a liberal dose of JavaScript. Magazine-style documents, strewn with images, applets and plugins, and sporting fancy styles, headings, colors and typefaces can be quite impressive visually, especially if backed-up by a good graphic artist. Via a few JavaScript multimedia tricks such as those outlined in Chapter 6, images can add a degree of animation. However, for truly impressive web pages, nothing beats the possibility of independently animating every single tag in a document and its contents, either in response to user actions, or without the user needing to do anything at all. This possibility is offered by a technology called **Dynamic HTML**.

Client-side JavaScript, with its timing mechanisms and access to host objects that reflect a document's content is absolutely crucial for Dynamic HTML. Viewed from the JavaScript perspective, it is the scriptwriter who creates dynamic behavior in a document that is otherwise just inactive HTML.

Dynamic HTML is a subject rich in information that really requires a book of its own, or better, several, since the implementations of DHTML in different browsers varies considerably. In this chapter we'll give you the foundations by discussing all the JavaScript and browser bricks and mortar that can be used to build Dynamic HTML pages. Accompanying these are examples of common tasks and the inevitable compatibility issues.

> *For a more in-depth view of DHTML as it is implemented in the latest versions of the main browsers, check out 'Instant Netscape Dynamic HTML', ISBN 1-861001-19-3 or 'IE5 Dynamic HTML Programmer's Reference', ISBN 1-861001-74-6, both from Wrox Press.*

What is Dynamic HTML?

The term Dynamic HTML is somewhat vague. In a general, hand-waving sense, it means any HTML document in a browser that exploits one or more specific technical features in order to create one or more specific visual effects. From a practical point of view, that is hardly a useful description. From the JavaScript perspective, we might define it this way:

Dynamic HTML, or DHTML, is essentially not a new variety of HTML, but rather an additional set of JavaScript functionality. These new JavaScript abililties allow access to more of the properties of the HTML elements within an HTML document, enabling the properties of those elements to be altered in a particular way, for example their visibility or position in the document. The <SPAN>, <DIV> and <STYLE> tags, and ID, CLASS and STYLE attributes of descriptive content tags are the ones most commonly used in concert with JavaScript to produce DHTML effects.

Before we delve into the mechanics of how to do this, let's step back a bit and see what Dynamic HTML means for a mere human being when we come to learning, programming and designing tasks.

DHTML as a Technology

Dynamic HTML can be viewed as an evolutionary step in browser technology, rather than an entirely new, alien technology.

JavaScript commands like window.alert('Frivolous Example') provide a very simple mechanism for changing what the browser displays. Such features are provided by a host object (the window object in this case) and have been available since the earliest days of JavaScript. As browsers developed, more host objects became available, and the extent of JavaScript's control over the browser environment grew. With the 4.x and 5.x browsers, the host objects available have reached a kind of critical mass, sufficient to allow very detailed control over the elements of a document, especially in the case of Internet Explorer 5.0. Taking advantage of this detailed control - ordinary JavaScript applied to newly exposed document features - is all Dynamic HTML really is. An important aspect of this control is that it happens *after* the document is fully loaded and rendered into the browser.

Put another way, there are five technologies which contribute to Dynamic HTML:

- ❏ An embedded scripting language (in our case, this of course means JavaScript).
- ❏ Styles and stylesheets.
- ❏ HTML.
- ❏ The Browser Object Model.
- ❏ The DOM - the Document Object Model (implemented only in IE5).

By the time all the latest enhancements for all these technologies are rolled together, compatibility levels between Netscape 4.x and Microsoft 4+ browsers are less than might be hoped. It is to be hoped that the level of compatibility between the 5.x browsers will be much greater (largely thanks to the DOM), but this will remain a pipedream until Communicator 5 is released.

JavaScript

JavaScript itself does not contribute much that is new to Dynamic HTML, other than providing access to the host objects innovated by the other technologies. However, it is the authority that orders those objects' behavior. One exception in the 4+ browsers is the method `setInterval()`, which is a very handy alternative to `setTimeout()`. Some Dynamic HTML techniques are repetitious - `setInterval()` allows a section of script code to run periodically, whereas `setTimeout()` schedules a action for only a single point in the future.

Styles

The properties that make up styles are the meat and drink of Dynamic HTML. By altering these style properties, the scriptwriter can change the appearance of an HTML document even after it is fully rendered on the screen. Styles may be expressed a number of ways, but the most common approaches, which are the ones that contribute to Dynamic HTML, are based on these standards:

- ❑ CSS1: Cascading Style Sheets Level 1. The text of the W3C recommendation can be viewed at `http://www.w3.org/TR/REC-CSS1-961217.html`.

- ❑ CSS2: Cascading Style Sheets Level 2. The specification is at `http://www.w3.org/TR/REC-CSS2/`.

- ❑ DOM2 Appendix E: ECMAScript language binding. This appendix specifies how elements are to be accessed through ECMAScript. The standard is at `http://www.w3.org/TR/WD-DOM-Level-2/ecma-script-language-binding.html`.

The CSS2 standard is yet to be implemented completely or correctly in any browser, although the Netscape 5.0 development program appears to be aggressively focused on standards compliance.

Internet Explorer 4.0 has enhancements to style sheets called **filters, transitions**. Filters may be used for a number of additional effects beyond style sheets' normal capabilities, and transitions allow simple animation effects. Internet Explorer 5.0 has further enhancements called **behaviors**. Behaviors allow you to attach scripts that are stored in a separate file to a specific style. When an event occurs on a HTML element that matches that style, the event is passed to a function in the behavior script, just as though it were a JavaScript event handler. This does not add much new functionality, but provides a cleaner and shorter way of attaching scripts to events, if you can rely on users having this browser. Netscape 4.x has ways of mimicking some of Internet Explorer's transitions using JavaScript – see `http://developer.netscape.com/viewsource/wyner_transition/wyner_transition.html`. However, Internet Explorer generally has greater functionality in terms of fancy style features.

HTML

With the advent of HTML 4.0, the `STYLE`, `CLASS` and `ID` attributes proliferate widely over most tags. These attributes allow style information to be attached to tags, and these are all accessible from JavaScript (albeit in different ways in Navigator and IE). The `<DIV>` and `<SPAN>` tags have new importance because of their ability to associate arbitrary chunks of HTML with a style.

Specific to Netscape 4.0 browsers are the `<LAYER>` and `<ILAYER>` tags. These tags allow overlapping layers to be placed in a document, with upper layers covering the content of those underneath. However, these elements have no future and are made redundant by the CSS2 standard. Only use `<LAYER>` and `<ILAYER>` if you are deeply committed to Navigator 4.x. The same effect can be achieved using the positioning attributes of normal stylesheets, so there's little value in using this alternative syntax.

The Browser Object Model

The Browser Object Model defines all of the JavaScript host objects in the browser. Although most of the objects which are not concerned with the structure of the HTML document are implemented in a similar way in different browsers, the way the HTML document is represented varies enormously. While all elements can be accessed through script in IE4 and IE5, not every element is available to JavaScript in Netscape 4.x browsers. Moreover, the way in which different elements are accessed can be different, so even where a JavaScript object representing an aspect of the HTML document has similar functionality in Netscape and Microsoft browsers, there is no guarantee that it can be accessed with the same code in both browsers. This variance in the Browser Object Models is perhaps the most serious problem for a DHTML programmer seeking to build web pages with cross-browser compatibility, but fortunately, there may be a solution in the not too distant future. The standard ratified by the W3C for a common Document Object Model will hopefully grant JavaScript programmers access to every element within an HTML document, in a way that will be identical in all browsers.

DOM - the Document Object Model

Unlike the Browser Object Model, the Document Object Model describes only those parts of the browser model that depend on the currently displayed HTML document. Because of the widespread adoption and therefore importance of HTML, the object model for HTML is undergoing standardization. DOM is that standard, with level 1 now released and implemented (with numerous additions) in Internet Explorer 5.0 only. Internet Explorer 4.0 has similar functionality, but varies on numerous points from the standard, which was still in development when that browser was released. Netscape 4.x and lower have only a fraction of the standard supported.

The exposure of the DOM to JavaScript provides access to all the elements of an HTML document. Style manipulation is the main benefit. In addition, IE4 and IE5 grant access to the original HTML source text from within JavaScript through the `innerHTML` and `outerHTML` properties. However, that is a Microsoft extension, rather than a standards-driven feature. Previously, we could only perform a View Source of the HTML source interactively.

Consequentially, the **DOM** allows the **content** of an HTML document to be changed after the document is loaded. This is the most dynamic aspect of Dynamic HTML.

The DOM and XML

This standard can be viewed at `http://www.w3c.org/DOM`. The specification is divided into two chapters. The first chapter describes the DOM with respect to Extensible Markup Language (XML). XML is a markup language similar in format to HTML, but with tags with no intrinsic "meaning": XML allows users to define their own tags and the structure of their documents. XML is a subset of another markup language, the Standard Generalized Markup Language (SGML), of which HTML is one specific application; hence the similarity in format. In fact, strictly-formed HTML is almost valid XML.

The exception is that XML does not allow empty elements (such as `<HR>`). To make such elements permissible in XML, we must supply a "dummy" closing tag (`<HR></HR>`), or a shortcut version of this (`<HR />`). These XML-style shortcuts are permitted in the XML-compatible IE5.

Because of this similarity, Chapter 1 of the specification for the DOM, which was written chiefly with XML in mind, can also be used with an HTML document. The DOM treats each element as a "node" in the document, and provides methods for script code to enumerate through these nodes, regardless of the type of the element in question (remember, that doesn't matter in XML, and the browser has no way of knowing what a specific tag "means"). This provides access to every element, and should in time allow DHTML programmers to bypass the vendor-specific Browser Object Models altogether. In the meantime, however, this dream is a reality only in IE5.

The DOM and HTML

The second chapter of the DOM is specific to HTML as an application of XML; it defines the methods and properties which HTML elements should expose, in addition to those which they should expose as XML `node` objects. This chapter too is only supported to any real extent by IE5, although some of the methods and properties defined by the W3C coincide with those already implemented by the major browsers. Chapters 1 and 2 of the DOM are sometimes referred to as the "XML DOM" and the "HTML DOM" respectively, although, as we have seen, this is not strictly accurate, since Chapter 1 relates also to HTML.

> *These two chapters of DOM Level 1 must be distinguished from the two levels. Level 1 describes the core features with which browsers should comply; Level 2, which is still a working draft, describes less fundamental aspects of the DOM.*

DHTML as an Art Form

Dynamic HTML can be viewed as a mode of expression for communicating with people, like other visual art forms such as painting, dance, or the iconized, mouse-driven graphics of a computer's desktop.

Like plain HTML, Dynamic HTML appears in a web browser window. Unlike plain HTML, the possibility of images, icons and text moving and reacting to each other creates a new mode of communication that the user must learn to interact with. This kind of interaction is particularly important when browsers are run in full screen mode, such as at information kiosks or via Netscape's Netcaster. In those cases, the user's normal mode of interaction for navigation tasks (via browser toolbars and menus) is not available, and Dynamic HTML features must substitute. The user must learn that interacting with particular elements of a Dynamic HTML page means that certain effects will follow.

The ability to position HTML elements at exact locations on a page allows elements to overlap. HTML is normally strictly two-dimensional. Overlapping elements in a browser page require some additional organization in the third dimension. However, browsers are not capable of full three-dimensional effects, and in any event all that is really required is a **stacking order** for overlapping elements. A stacking order merely dictates which item is on top of which other item. So a browser window that is 800 pixels by 600 pixels, with a stacking order for a particular page of perhaps 6 elements or fewer is called two-and-a-half dimensional, or 2.5D, since the third dimension is much smaller in 'size' than the other two.

Dynamic HTML draws inspiration from several other well-established media. It is strong on animated presentation graphics and slide shows. It is also similar to video-digital editing, in that it allows effects like panning, wipes, zooms and insets. Dynamic HTML also draws from the world of animation, as it allows crude but flexible animation features. Because HTML documents can be textual, Dynamic HTML also allows some unique tricks of its own - menu expansion is a simple example.

For good examples of the potential of Dynamic HTML, see the following web pages:

- ❑ Presentation. Use Navigator 4+ to view this hype from Netscape:
  `http://developer.netscape.com/devcon/jun97/key_1/directs.html`
- ❑ Video editing. Use Internet Explorer 4+ to view this simple page:
  `http://msdn.microsoft.com/workshop/author/dhtml/site/Scale1.htm`
- ❑ Animation. Use Navigator 4+ to interact with this winner of the Netscape 1997 Dynamic HTML contest:
  `http://developer.netscape.com/devcon/jun97/contest/freefall/index.html`
- ❑ Menu expansion. Use Internet Explorer 4+ to navigate through nearly any Microsoft website by moving the mouse over the menu strips that sit at the top of Microsoft's HTML pages, eg:
  `http://msdn.microsoft.com/`

Of course, Dynamic HTML has limitations as well. It may be a visual art form that can produce useful interrelationships between textual and iconic elements on a page, but because of these effects it is a poor vehicle for communication with visually impaired users. This is not because the browsers aren't sensitive to such people, its just because it's easy accidentally to build in problem features using Dynamic HTML once you start using it. It also isn't widely accessible outside the two major browsers, and even for those browsers, at least version 4.0 is required. Therefore it is a less conservative approach than plain HTML.

What's Possible Without JavaScript?

You should already be familiar with most of the features of HTML and CSS1 stylesheets. We will look briefly at some of the major features used to style HTML, as they are the building blocks for the more animated features of Dynamic HTML. This screenshot illustrates the effects that can be achieved with simple HTML STYLE attributes, without recourse to DHTML or JavaScript:

This is the HTML code for this page; as you can see, inline stylesheets can rapidly become quite unwieldy, even for such a simple page:

```
<HTML>
<HEAD>
<STYLE TYPE="text/css">
.style1 {font-size: 24pt;
         font-weight: bold;
         font-family: arial}

.style2 {position: absolute;
         top: 100;
         left: 100;
         border-width: thick;
         border-color: red;
         border-style: groove;
         font-family: Allegro BT;
         font-size: 16pt}

.style3 {position: absolute;
         top: 165;
         left: 260;
         border-width: thick;
         border-color: blue;
         border-style: ridge;
         font-family: Monotype Corsiva;
         font-size: 24pt}
</STYLE>
</HEAD>

<SPAN CLASS=style1>
Some Basic Styling Features
</SPAN>
<HR><BR><BR>

<DIV CLASS=style2>
A DIV element with<BR>a thick, red border<BR>with a groove.
</DIV>

<DIV CLASS=style3 Z-ORDER=1>
Another DIV with<BR>a blue border<BR>with a ridge.
</DIV>

</HTML>
```

Unfortunately, style properties are particularly browser-specific, and it can be quite difficult to achieve complex stylistic effects which will be reproduced in the same way in the different browsers. However, as the CSS standards mature, it is likely that browser support will increase, and this problem will diminish accordingly. In the meantime, it is still possible to design pages which will look (nearly) identical on the main browsers, even if it requires a little patient experimentation.

Font Control

The basic style features provide all the text control features normally found in word processors; font size, weight, family and decorative features such as underlining.

Text Spacing

Styles can also provide margin, padding and border spacing features which are **block formatting** information equivalent to 'paragraph formats' in word processors.

Positioning

Styles allow the element they apply to be located away from the normal position it would adopt when rendered in the normal layout flow by the browser. Absolute positioning allows the element to appear anywhere.

Superimposition

With absolute positioning a possibility, elements can overlap. The style mechanism defines a **z-order** which resolves which elements appear on top.

Visibility and Display

Elements can take up visual space in a document, but they can also not be allocated any space at all, much like hidden form fields. If they do take up space, then they can be visibly present (the normal case) or just withhold that space from other uses, as with the Netscape proprietory <SPACER> tag.

Clipping

The content of a styled element takes up a set area, known as a bounding box. If the element's content exceeds the capacity of the bounding box, it may be clipped. Clipping means the overflowing parts of the content do not appear.

Filters, Transitions and Behaviors

Internet Explorer 4+ supports filter and transition enhancements to styles that allow additional effects to be laid on top of other style information. In IE5, we can also associate stylistic features with particular events due to the introduction of DHTML behaviors. Microsoft also provides a number of default behaviors which can be attached to HTML elements and which, amongst other things, allow us to persist data between page visits, control animations and to find out about the capabilities of the client's browser.

<DIV> and <SPAN> Elements

Styles normally apply to a specific instance of an HTML tag. Sometimes the piece of content to be styled doesn't easily fit into one of the predefined tags. The <DIV> or <SPAN> tags can be used to mark out an arbitrary section of content. <DIV> provides a line break before and after the content.

<LAYER> and <ILAYER> Elements

The <LAYER> and <ILAYER> tags are an alternative syntax for absolutely positioned styles. They apply to Netscape 4.x browsers only, and are frequently considered a failed experiment, now that stylesheets are seen as the way forward. Everything we can do with layers and JavaScript in Netscape can be done with absolute positioning in stylesheets and JavaScript, even in Netscape. In fact, layers are just absolutely positioned styles, specified by an HTML tag rather than by a stylesheet element.

Embedded Animation

In Chapter 6, we looked briefly at the options for embedding already-animated objects into web pages, such as progressive GIFs. We also saw how we could provide a crude form of completely controlled animation using JavaScript.

Dynamic HTML Support in Browsers

Before diving in and examining each Dynamic HTML feature in detail, let's first survey the scene from on high. Dynamic HTML support in browsers is patchy, and even where an effort has been made to provide it, those provisions aren't necessarily complete.

The one line summary is that only Netscape 4+, Internet Explorer 4+ and browsers derived from Internet Explorer 4+ (like NeoPlanet) have any Dynamic HTML support. Fortunately, that's most of the web community, if you can believe the surveys.

Running through the versions, here's what you can work with, from least to most:

❑ Netscape 4.x: Positionable styles; improved event model; enhancement of Netscape layers.

❑ Internet Explorer 4.0: DOM Level 1 features (but without names matching the DOM standard); advanced event model; control over CSS1 style definitions; dynamic HTML tag rewriting; many Microsoft enhancements.

❑ Internet Explorer 5.0: As for 4.0, plus features nearly matching the DOM Level 1 standard; control over results of cascaded styles; many more Microsoft enhancements.

❑ Netscape 5.0 (still in development as this is being written): Advertised as religiously adhering to as many W3C standards (DOM Level 1, DOM Level 2, CSS1, CSS2) as can be squeezed in before release.

In order to get any serious level of Dynamic HTML support, Internet Explorer 4+ or Netscape 5+ is really the minimum requirement.

Since this is a chapter on DHTML and not a whole book, we'll refrain from going on and on about every one of the numerous properties and objects available in Internet Explorer 4+ and in the DOM at this time. Instead, we'll try to give you examples of each DHTML feature that is available to exploit. Once you've seen the various principles at work, you should have enough orientation to go out and conquer on your own, or at least have a structure to work with that you can add to as the need arises.

JavaScript DOM Host Objects

Provided that a HTML document is correctly composed so that the HTML markup in it is well-ordered, the HTML tags fit together in a tree hierarchy. Consider this example:

```
<HTML>
   <HEAD>
      <TITLE> Pink Page </TITLE>
   </HEAD>
   <BODY>
      <HI>Think Pink!</H1>
      <BLOCKQUOTE>
         All marshmellows, azaleas, but <STRONG> not </STRONG> panthers welcome.
      </BLOCKQUOTE>
   </BODY>
</HTML>
```

When displayed in the browser, this looks like this:

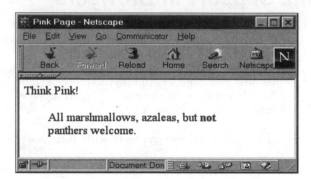

If we draw out this document in diagrammatic form, we can see the hierarchy more clearly:

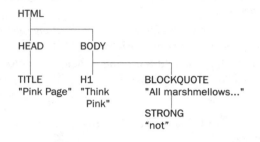

As we saw, the Document Object Model specifies that each tag in a given document should be represented by its own object. From this simple example it is easy to see how this could create quite large hierarchies. Imagine if these objects were named after their tags; to access a given tag's object from JavaScript would require quite long object references, possibly as follows:

```
top.document.html.body.blockquote.strong.contents; // doesn't quite work like this
```

This example is not too bad, but a complex document could be far worse, especially since most documents have more than one paragraph and you need to know which one you are talking about. An HTML table alone adds three levels of objects to the hierarchy. This example doesn't include any style information either. There has to be a better way, and there is.

Hierarchies versus Collections

Users of databases will be familiar with the idea of extracting important data out of a large database by use of a query. Users of event-driven systems would be familiar with extracting important data out of a large flood of events using a filter. In both cases, a reduction facility is available to expose only the interesting data – queries in one case, filters in the other. For HTML host objects in JavaScript, collections are the equivalent facility. A collection is just a group of related objects, which in JavaScript translates into an array of objects. In this section it will be seen that some collections are supplied ready to use, whereas you may have to do some work to get at other collections.

Therefore the DOM offers two ways of accessing host objects: by navigating the object hierarchy directly, which might be quite a lengthy process, and by extracting a collection of interesting items from the hierarchy and then looking at them directly.

Often the scriptwriter will know exactly which object is wanted, and will extract a collection from the hierarchy that reduces to the single object desired. At other times, a collection might be extracted that contains a group of matching items. Occasionally the scriptwriter might see fit to go poking through the hierarchy in detail if some complex analysis is required of the document. So both approaches have their place.

If a collection object is changed, the hierarchy is updated as well, and vice versa. The objects are the same in both cases, so the system is fully coordinated.

Object hierarchy

The DOM standard describes the important objects that are used to represent an HTML document inside a program such as a browser. The ECMAScript binding section of that standard describes the gory details of how this is to work in client-side JavaScript. The only browser attempting compliance at the time of writing is Internet Explorer 5.0, although the Netscape 5.0 development effort has laid out some goals for compliance. It's a great deal of effort to test a browser rigorously for compliance, so the truth of the matter for a given browser may never be fully known.

What is easy to say is that version 4, and to a much greater degree version 5, of Internet Explorer are the first available browsers to include support for the central, important features of the DOM. At the time of writing, they are the only such browsers. Since the DOM standard was completed after the release of Internet Explorer 4.0, it is hard to claim that that browser's implementation is compliant with the standard, but IE5 support for the DOM is much more complete.

The most important feature of any DOM-compliant browser is that all the tags in an HTML document must be accessible as objects. Internet Explorer sets a further benchmark: it should be possible to retrieve the HTML source that those tags objects originate from. Only Internet Explorer 4+ provides broadly useful functionality for both. The Netscape browsers released to date do not provide general support for either feature.

Meanwhile, the more obvious objects available to JavaScript in earlier versions of browsers still exist, such as forms and images. However, these are now considered separate to the 'main event' - the DOM. Of course, they still represent a convenient and compatible way of achieving a range of tasks within the browser.

You can read about the standard hierarchy provided by the DOM at `http://www.w3c.org/DOM`. The DOM Level 1 standard also contains an appendix on ECMAScript/JavaScript binding, which in plain English means that it describes the methods and properties that a DOM-compliant browser should expose. Unfortunately, only Internet Explorer 5.0 and the upcoming Netscape 5.0 support this release. In the meantime, the methods and properties supplied by Internet Exploter 4.0 (also existing in 5.0) are the most reliable for DHTML developed for that browser.

Navigating the hierarchy

For Internet Explorer 4+, locating an arbitrary HTML element's object revolves around the `document.all` property. This itself returns an `Array` object. Look at the following HTML code; after it we show the JavaScript statement needed to dig the actual HTML of the `<STRONG>` element out:

```
<HTML>
    <HEAD>
        <TITLE> My Title </TITLE>
    </HEAD>
    <BODY>
        <STRONG> strong text </STRONG>
    </BODY>
</HTML>
```

The HTML code behind the `<STRONG>` element may be accessed in this way:

```
alert(window.document.all[4].outerHTML);
```

This statement displays the following dialog box:

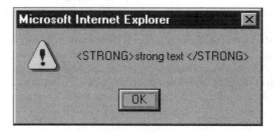

We'll see as we go on how this works, but for now it's enough to see that there's a JavaScript object we can rely on for this kind of information.

Since the `<BODY>` tag is the fifth array element, there must be four more before it, and there are: the `<HTML>`, `<HEAD>`, `<TITLE>` and `<BODY>` tags of our particular example page. The `all` property returns a reference to all the elements in the document, but there's a catch - a few tags are treated differently in IE4 compared to IE5. These are the `<HTML>` and `<HEAD>` tags, and all the tags within the head. In Internet Explorer 4.0 these are present, but not readable, whereas in 5.0, they can be read or changed. So `all` really means "all the parts of the body of the HTML document" if IE4 is involved. Any `<SCRIPT>` tags in the head can be retrieved another way via the `scripts` collection in 4.0.

> *Internet Explorer 5.0 also has a `window.all` property that also returns a collection; this contains all the items of the `document.all` collection plus more. If you are happy with only Internet Explorer 5.0, feel free to use this. However, if you have any desire to comply with the DOM standards, or want to plan for portability with other browsers, use `document.all`, not `window.all`.*

Let's return for a second to our "Think Pink!" example. We will rewrite this without a <HEAD> element, and with an ID attribute for each element within the body. In Internet Explorer 5.0, the <HTML> and any tags in the <HEAD> could have Id properties too, but this is sufficient for our purposes:

```
<HTML>
<BODY ID="page">
<H1 ID="intro">Think Pink!</H1>
<BLOCKQUOTE ID="quote">
All marshmallows, azaleas, but
<STRONG ID="extra"> not </STRONG> panthers welcome.
</BLOCKQUOTE>
</BODY>
</HTML>
```

These lines of JavaScript illustrate a number of points about accessing the objects which represent HTML tags:

```
var tag_object;

tag_object = document.all.page;            // The <BODY> tag
tag_object = document.all["page"];            // The <BODY> tag
tag_object = document.all[3];          // The <BODY> tag

tag_object = document.all.extra;              // The <STRONG> tag

tag_object = document.all.quote;                // The <BLOCKQUOTE> tag
tag_object = tag_object.children.extra;   // ... the ID="extra" sub-tag
tag_object = tag_object.parentElement;    // ... back to <BLOCKQUOTE>
```

The three lines at the top show that the all object is an array-style object, similar to the document.forms or window.frames objects in the browser. It has two crucial differences. Firstly, its properties are named after the ID attribute of their respective tags, not the NAME attribute. Secondly, all the document's tags appear in the array, not just the top-level tags, as the middle line of the example shows. This is because the all property is a **collection**.

What is a collection? In practical JavaScript terms, a collection is just an Array object. However, in Microsoft and general computer terms, a collection is much more flexible than an array. A collection is a set of items like an array, but doesn't necessarily have array indexes. Users of Visual Basic may recognize collections - in order to get items out of one, you often need a special object that you use to step through the collection. In client-side JavaScript it's not so hard - collections are always just arrays.

The last three lines of the above example illustrate how to move around the object hierarchy. Every tag object has these properties that hold the object hierarchy together and make navigation through it possible:

- ❑   children - an array of the tags immediately contained within this tag.
- ❑   parentElement - a simple property pointing back to this tag object's parent tag object.
- ❑   all - an array of all the tags contained directly or indirectly within this tag.

The first two properties, together with the `children.length` property (recall that a collection is an array), are enough to step through all the tag objects in the hierarchy. The hierarchy is a 'tree' structure, and since the tags are added to the hierarchy in the order in which they are discovered in the HTML source document, you can find all the tags by stepping through all the children arrays, and the children's children, and so on. In computer science terms this is a 'pre-order traversal' of the hierarchy.

If you want to experiment with the document tree in an interactive way, try this tool using Internet Explorer 5.0 from Microsoft: `http://www.microsoft.com/windows/ie/webaccess/webdevaccess.exe`. When it has been downloaded and installed, you'll find that if you right-click in the browser window, the context menu has an extra item 'Document Tree'. If you choose this item, you will be presented with a new window that lets you analyze the document tree of the first window. The tree is not so obvious because all properties or all objects, not just tree properties are shown. To make it work, click on `documentElement` at the top level. Another level under that element should appear. For each level from now on, the way to see all immediately contained tags of the current tag (shown at this level) is to click on the children sub-element which exposes the next level. Each contained tag that has an ID attribute will appear by ID attribute name. Each contained tag without an ID attribute will appear just as an array index.

Working with Tags via HTML Source

There's not much point navigating the object hierarchy if there is nothing worth having in there. Therefore, for Internet Explorer 4+, each tag object has four further properties: `innerText`, `outerText`, `innerHTML` and `outerHTML`. Each of these properties contains a different variant on the tag's contents. This table explains which to choose:

	Content only	Content and HTML tags
Include space used by tags	outerText	outerHTML
Exclude space used by tags	innerText	innerHTML

'Content only' means the scriptwriter only wants to see the content marked up by HTML tags, and not the tags as well. 'Include space used by tags' is used mostly for *replacing* the HTML source - it means that the piece of document to be replaced should include the tags that mark the beginning and the end of the element (such as `<DIV>` and `</DIV>`). You can replace HTML source by assigning a string to one of these properties.

The alert boxes for this example are shown below:

```
<HTML><BODY>
<H1 ID="testtag" STYLE="color:blue">My    <EM>Important</EM>    test</H1>
<SCRIPT>
alert(document.all.testtag.outerText);
alert(document.all.testtag.innerText);
alert(document.all.testtag.outerHTML);
alert(document.all.testtag.innerHTML);
</SCRIPT>
</BODY></HTML>
```

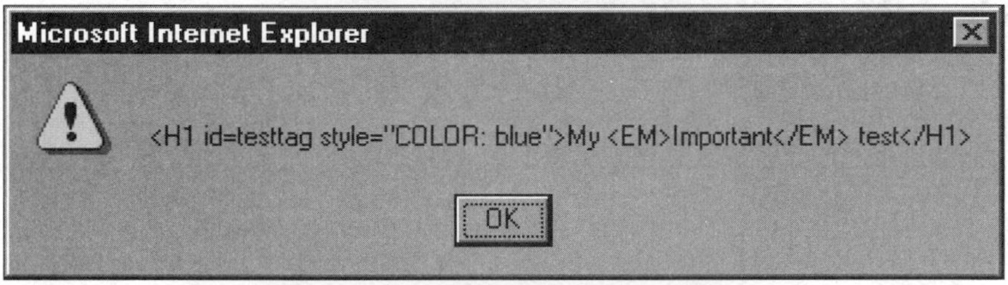

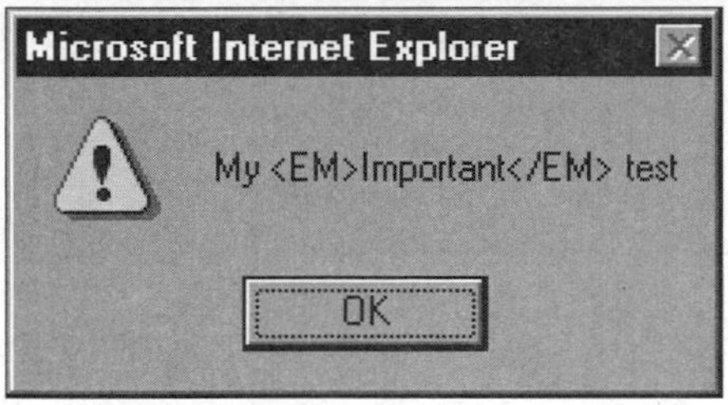

There is a further subtle effect at work in this example. Notice that the last two alerts do not retrieve the HTML source exactly as it appears above - there are spaces missing, and the quotes around testtag are gone. The HTML source is actually **reconstructed** from the browser's understanding of the document. This is slightly different to the View Source window that shows the original HTML document verbatim. Usually no meaningful information is lost. Note that retrieving the source of a JavaScript script or a JavaScript function does not suffer from this problem.

If you set the innerText or outerText properties, the text you supply will appear literally in the browser. If you set innerHTML or outerHTML, any tags in the new text will be interpreted before display. It is not until you try to change the document using the outerText/innerText properties that a difference appears between those two properties. The outerText case removes the delimiting tags as well as their content. Using the same HTML page, this code illustrates the four different effects that result from setting these four properties.

```
<HTML>
    <BODY>
        <H1 ID="testtag" STYLE="color:blue">My    <EM>Important</EM>    test</H1>
        <SCRIPT LANGUAGE="JavaScript">
            var prop;
            prop = prompt('Enter which field','');
            document.all.testtag[prop] = '<HR>new text<HR>';
        </SCRIPT>
    </BODY>
</HTML>
```

Type each property in response to the prompt window and click **OK**. Here are the results:

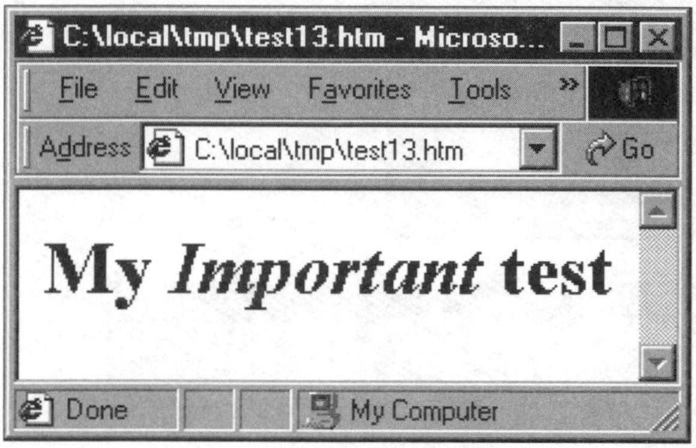

These first two images are the original and the result of `outerText`. The tags are not interpreted, but note that the `<H1>` tags have disappeared.

The HTML is still not interpreted in the next image, but the `<H1>` tags are intact because ths is the `innerText` case. The right image is the `outerHTML` case – the `<HR>` tags are interpreted and the `<H1>` tags are replaced.

Finally, using the `innerHTML` variant, the `<H1>` tags are intact and the tags within the supplied string are read and acted upon as well.

Working with Tags via Properties

Reading and setting the source for an HTML tag object is not very convenient if you are only interested in a single feature of that tag, such as an event handler or a tag attribute. There is a better way - each tag object has properties for all the valid tag attributes. This is consistent with the older-generation objects such as form text field objects, and works in exactly the same way.

A tag may have an attribute that isn't in any standard - recall that HTML is only an advisory markup language - or may have an attribute value that doesn't make sense. Such detail might be meaningful to some specific web server or HTML editor, even if browsers pass over it. It's hard to anticipate unknown attributes, so properties on the tag object aren't created for them. Tag objects support three special method properties that give access to these unknowns:

- ❑ getAttribute() - extract any attribute's literal value.
- ❑ setAttribute() - set any attribute to any value.
- ❑ removeAttribute() - throw an attribute for a given tag away.

Finally, the style property of a tag object is itself an object. Its own properties match any CSS1 or CSS2 attributes for that tag. Stylesheet names translate to JavaScript property names directly, except that hyphens are dropped in favor of a capital letter. So color becomes color, but background-color becomes backgroundColor. These properties of the style property aren't quite as flexible as normal JavaScript object properties, but the features of IE4+ are sufficient to make what's available very powerful when used. The features are:

- ❑ All style properties can be written, which is the most common case.
- ❑ Only style properties originating from a STYLE attribute in the tag, or from previous JavaScript statements can be read.
- ❑ Style information defined in <STYLE> tags is available elsewhere, not in the object for the element.

Object collections

Sometimes the scriptwriter isn't interested in the structure of a whole HTML document; just a slice of it. A typical example is user input via HTML forms. Usually we don't care how many nested <OL> tags surround the form - you just want to get at it. In JavaScript, a collection means an array object, and the like-minded objects are stored one per array element.

If it weren't for object collections, the Navigator 4.x browsers would have very little Dynamic HTML capability. Even Internet Explorer 4.0/5.0 would lose some important flexibility.

Using a collection is the easy part: access the correct array element, or a conveniently named property of the collection object, and you have the same object that you would have found if you had gone poking through the object hierarchy for it. For tag objects, this means access to the style, innerHTML, getAttribute() properties and so on, as described above, but beware! Most of these properties are specific to Internet Explorer 4.0.

The trick is to find or make the collection in the first place. There are several sources of collections.

Pre-created Collections

Some objects are so useful that they are always available from JavaScript. It's tempting to call them 'built-in' collections, but that term already means 'native JavaScript features' in ECMAScript language, so it is best not to overuse it. Pre-created is exactly what these collections are - they are right there in the browser without you having to do anything.

An obvious example of a readily available collection that's been met before is the document.forms object. Clearly this is a collection of <FORM> elements in the current document. Similarly, the document.images array is a collection of <IMG> elements, and the document.form[0].elements array is a collection of <INPUT>, <SELECT> and <TEXTAREA> tags (assuming there is at least one form present in the document). Viewed from the perspective of the DOM, we can say that all JavaScript-enabled browsers provide some DOM collections, but only one (Internet Explorer 4+) supports the *whole* DOM hierarchy directly. For the rest, the DOM hierarchy is 'invisible' except for popular bits of it such as the forms array.

For Internet Explorer 4+, a further example is the document.styleSheets object which is an array or collection of objects representing each <STYLE> or <LINK> tag in the document. Each of the collection elements has a property named rules, which is an array/collection of the individual CSS rules. Internet Explorer also has a scripts collection for all the <SCRIPT> sections in the document. Of course, document.all is the most useful pre-created collection for that browser. As we noted before, Internet Explorer 5.0 has a window.all collection as well.

For Netscape Navigator 4.x, there are three collections that contain style information: ids, tags, and layers. It is the third of these, layers which provides much of the Dynamic HTML functionality for that browser. The layers collection contains an object for every tag that has an *absolute* or *relatively*-positioned style. It also contains every instance of the <LAYER> and <ILAYER> tags. Each object in the layers collection contains properties matching all the CSS2 type attributes. The other two collections are mostly used for (statically) specifying JavaScript style sheets (JSSS).

With all these pre-created collections, you might wonder if there is a 'CSS Object Model', 'Script Object Model', or worse still a 'Collections Object Model' that describes a hierarchy of pre-created collections. There are some remarks in the DOM specification about support for the collections present in the 3.0 browsers, but beyond that we are mercifully spared another standard.

In-hierarchy Collections

A few collections are bundled up inside the DOM object hierarchy itself. Since only Internet Explorer 4+ has the DOM hierarchy, they are specific to that browser. Here are two examples:

- ❑ Children - for each tag object, all the tags directly contained in this one.
- ❑ filters - for each tag object, any style filters applying to this tag.

You might prefer to see the style property of each tag as a collection, but technically it's not an array object, since there's no length property.

User Extracted Collections

The most useful form of collection for complex HTML documents is the one you make yourself. Internet Explorer's features provide two ways of making a collection that consists of a subset of the document's tags or objects:

```
var id_collection  = document.all.item("id23");
var tag_collection = document.all.tags("P");
```

The first case draws out the tag objects for all of the tags in the document that have ID="id23" as an attribute. The second case draws out all the tag objects from the document that are <P> tags. In both cases, a whole collection (a JavaScript array) is created, not a single object.

Each tag object is referenced as an ordinary array member. There is also a shorthand notation for the item() method which allows a single tag object to be extracted. This script fragment illustrates both cases:

```
var all_headings = document.all.tags("H2");
all_headings[0].style.color = "blue";                    //  H2 now blue

var third_checkbox = document.all.item("boxlist1", 2);   // third checkbox
```

In the third line, a variation on the item() method is used. The new, second argument indicates which item of the collection is to be returned, rather than the whole collection. So for that third line, the user-extracted collection is only created temporarily - long enough for us to find the second collection member. Once the member element has been returned, the user-extracted collection disappears again, because no variable is used to record it.

Livening up HTML with JavaScript

The main thrust of Dynamic HTML is to make elements of a displayed HTML document change appearance and/or move around in the page. The elements of the HTML document can be woken up from their normally static and unchanging state in a number of increasingly dramatic ways:

- ❑ Change special embedded items only.
- ❑ Change appearance by modifying style sheets.
- ❑ Move existing elements within the page.
- ❑ Modify the document's fundamental content and structure.

The first possibility is covered elsewhere in this book where forms, multimedia, windows and Java are discussed. The remaining three possibilities are discussed here.

Before we jump in, a reminder about browser compatibility checks from Chapter 4. The two major browsers are different, and you'll need checks in virtually every DHTML page you write if you want it to be portable. The simplest way to test which browser you're in for DHTML work is to use the following tests:

```
if (document.layers) { ... }        // must be Netscape 4.x
if (document.all ) { ... }          // must be Internet Explorer 4+
```

Alternatively, we could check the `appName` property of the `navigator` object:

```
if (navigator.appName=="Netscape") {...}                    // using Navigator
if (navigator.appName=="Microsoft Internet Explorer") {...}  // using IE
```

We'll leave it to the case studies elsewhere in this book to show complete applications that are without portability problems. In this chapter we'll be illustrating technologies, and not always with the full cross-browser bells and whistles.

Simple Appearance Changes

You have built an HTML document, and you like it the way it is. You don't want to mess around with its layout or content, but somehow you would like it to be a bit more responsive to the user's input, or just a bit more flashy. Otherwise, you'd like the document to stay put. A classic example is highlighting a particular detail when an `onMouseOver` event occurs.

The way to achieve this kind of effect is to change style sheet properties. This is straightforward for Internet Explorer 4+. Netscape 4+ browsers require a more complicated approach.

The important style properties for this class of effects are:

- ❑ Color properties
- ❑ Clip properties
- ❑ Filter properties
- ❑ The visibility property
- ❑ Border properties
- ❑ Font properties

These style properties can be set as described earlier. The following common tasks illustrate some useful ends for this functionality.

onMouseOver Highlighting

Before Dynamic HTML, `onMouseOver` highlighting only meant swapping images, which wasn't always that fast. Not any more. This example takes advantage of Internet Explorer 4+'s font color changes, and general tag support for `onMouseOver` and `onMouseOut` to liven it up a bit:

```
<HTML>
   <BODY>
      Pick any item ... <BR>
      <OL>
         <LI ONMOUSEOVER="this.style.color='green'"
ONMOUSEOUT="this.style.color='black'">
            Pick me!
         <LI ONMOUSEOVER="this.style.color='green'"
ONMOUSEOUT="this.style.color='black'">
            No, pick me!
         <LI ONMOUSEOVER="this.style.color='green'"
ONMOUSEOUT="this.style.color='black'">
            Don't listen to them! Pick me!
         <LI ONMOUSEOVER="this.style.color='green'"
```

```
ONMOUSEOUT="this.style.color='black'">
            Pick me, or else I'll cry.
        </OL>
    </BODY>
</HTML>
```

The background color, or in fact any combination of style information, can also be set. However, the background color in particular is a little trickier. This is because the tag might not end on the screen where you think it ought to - try replacing color with backgroundColor in the above example. The solution is to use <SPAN> tags to give finer control to the script – as in the following example (again Internet Explorer 4+ specific):

```
<HTML>
    <BODY>
        Pick any item ... <BR>
        <OL>
            <LI>
                <SPAN ONMOUSEOVER="this.style.backgroundColor='yellow'"
                      ONMOUSEOUT="this.style.backgroundColor='white'">
                    Don't pick me!
                </SPAN>
            <LI>
                <SPAN ONMOUSEOVER="this.style.backgroundColor='yellow'"
                      ONMOUSEOUT="this.style.backgroundColor='white'">
                    Don't pick me either!
                </SPAN>
        </OL>
    </BODY>
</HTML>
```

There's always a catch. In this case, it's Netscape browsers. You can't set style properties in Navigator 4.x. However, there is an escape hatch: all Netscape Window objects can have their background color changed, and that includes layers. So this will work in a cross-browser way:

```
<HTML>
    <BODY>
        Before layer.
        <BR>
        <LAYER ONMOUSEOVER="this.bgColor='red'" ONMOUSEOUT="this.bgColor='white'">
            MouseOver me!
        </LAYER>
        <BR>
        After layer.
    </BODY>
</HTML>
```

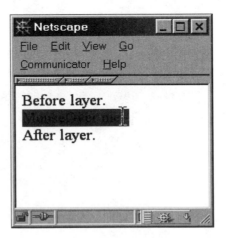

With Netscape, for changes more general than just the background color you must resort to more desperate tactics. See the section on 'Making a Dramatic Entrance' below for a solution.

Improved Menus

Again, prior to Dynamic HTML, your options for menus were restricted to the `<SELECT>` tag, and image swap tricks. The ability to clip HTML elements after the page is displayed opens up whole new possibilities if you use Internet Explorer 4+ features:

```
<HTML>
   <BODY>
      <STYLE TYPE="text/css">
         #menu1 { position: absolute; clip: rect(auto auto 16 auto) }
         #item  { background-color: red }
      </STYLE>

      <SCRIPT>
         function   pick(obj) { obj.style.backgroundColor="yellow"; return true; }
         function unpick(obj) { obj.style.backgroundColor="red"; return true;}
      </SCRIPT>

      <STRONG>
         <PRE>
            <DIV id="menu1"
                 ONMOUSEOVER="this.style.clip = 'rect(auto auto auto auto)'"
                 ONMOUSEOUT ="this.style.clip = 'rect(auto auto 16 auto)'">
            <SPAN ID="item">File  </SPAN>
            <SPAN ID="item">      </SPAN>
            <SPAN ID="item" ONMOUSEOVER="pick(this)" ONMOUSEOUT="unpick(this)">
                Open
            </SPAN>
            <SPAN ID="item" ONMOUSEOVER="pick(this)" ONMOUSEOUT="unpick(this)">
                Edit
            </SPAN>
            <SPAN ID="item" ONMOUSEOVER="pick(this)"
                ONMOUSEOUT="unpick(this)">Export</SPAN>
            <SPAN ID="item" ONMOUSEOVER="pick(this)"
                ONMOUSEOUT="unpick(this)">Import</SPAN>
            <SPAN ID="item" ONMOUSEOVER="pick(this)" ONMOUSEOUT="unpick(this)">
                Save
            </SPAN>
            <SPAN ID="item">      </SPAN>
            <SPAN ID="item" ONMOUSEOVER="pick(this)" ONMOUSEOUT="unpick(this)">
                Exit
            </SPAN>
            </DIV>
         </PRE>
      </STRONG>
   </BODY>
</HTML>
```

The keys to this example are the two handlers in the first `<DIV>` tag. They expose and hide most of the content of that element in response to the mouse, leaving only the word file.. permanently visible. Without clipping, the menu of seven items and two ruled lines would always appear. By altering the position of the bottom clip, the menu is exposed or removed as desired.

Note that this example is only an illustration. It needs quite a bit more handler work to be a fully working system: the onMouseOver/onMouseOut handlers for the ID="menu1" tag should be replaced with an onClick handler and the `<SPAN>` tags require onClick handlers too.

This kind of behavior is still possible in Netscape 4.x, but complicates the script once you put compatibility checks in to cater for the two different browsers. The main trap for the Netscape case is to realize that extra onMouseOver and onMouseOut events must be added to each `<SPAN>` block after the page has loaded, because the choice of absolute positioning technically makes that block a layer. The second compatibility trap is to note the different names in each browser for the style attributes and object properties that relate to background colors.

Making a Dramatic Entrance

Normally a document appears in the browser window as it downloads. The visibility style property can be used to alter this behavior. This Internet Explorer 4+ example mimics the kind of behavior you might typically see from a Java applet:

```
<HTML>
   <HEAD>
      <STYLE TYPE="text/css">
         #loading { position: absolute }
         #content { position: absolute; visibility: hidden }
      </STYLE>
      <SCRIPT>
         function display_it()
```

```
                    {
                        document.all.content.style.visibility='visible';
                        document.all.loading.style.visibility='hidden';
                    }
            </SCRIPT>
        </HEAD>
        <BODY ONLOAD="setTimeout('display_it()', 4000)">
            <DIV ID="loading" STYLE="color: orange">
                <H1>Loading, please wait ...</H1>
            </DIV>
            <DIV ID="content">
                Regrettably, anticipation exceeds the event in this case.
            </DIV>
        </BODY>
    </HTML>
```

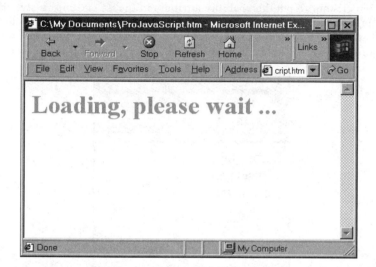

The `setTimeout()` call is only present to help simulate a slow-loading document - normally you would call `display_it()` immediately from the `onLoad` handler. To achieve the same effect in Netscape, just replace the `display_it()` function as follows:

```
function display_it()
{
    document.layers.content.visibility='visible';
    document.layers.loading.visibility='hidden';
}
```

Just replace `'layers'` with `'style'` for the same effect in Internet Explorer 4+.

This next example uses visibility to support fancy `onMouseOver` style changes for Netscape browsers:

```
<HTML>
    <BODY>
        <STYLE TYPE="text/css">
            .alternate {   color: red; background-color: yellow; }
        </STYLE>
        Before layer.
```

```
    <BR>
    <LAYER ONMOUSEOVER="window.document.layers[1].visibility='visible';
                       this.visibility='hidden'">
      MouseOver me!
    </LAYER>
    <LAYER CLASS="alternate" VISIBILITY=hide
           ONMOUSEOUT="window.document.layers[0].visibility='show';
                       this.visibility='hidden'">
      MouseOver me!
    </LAYER>
    <BR>
    After layer.
  </BODY>
</HTML>
```

It would have been cleaner to put the visibility attribute in the .alternate style class rather in the <LAYER> tag, but that's not possible because the layer doesn't inherit that attribute from the style definition - this is a quirk of Netscape layers that we also alluded to earlier when we had onMouseOver and onMouseOut events that needed to be reapplied if layers were to be used.

In this example, there are two layers, one exactly on top of the other, both with the same content. When the mouse moves over one, it disappears and the other appears. When the mouse moves out again, the reverse happens.

For Internet Explorer 4.0, filters are a further trick you can pull to control visibility of HTML elements. Filters are a Microsoft proprietary extension to stylesheets that provide a grab-bag of special effects. The effects can be applied to <DIV> tags and images. If used without thought, the effects produced can look very amateurish. The invert, chroma, and blendtrans options are the safest in terms of style. Refer to 'IE5 DHTML Programmers Reference' from Wrox Press for a detailed discussion of filters. There is a supporting web page that's relevant to this book too: http://webdev.wrox.co.uk/books/1746/Chapter04/FilterEx_JScript.htm.

Border Decorations and Other Nasties

Border style properties are yet another way of highlighting content in an HTML document. An extremely simple example for Internet Explorer 4.0 looks like this:

```
<HTML>
    <BODY>
        <CENTER>
            <H3 STYLE="color: green">Easy games of the Paeolithic Age #3: Trap the
Rock</H3>
            <DIV ID="prey"> One Rock </DIV>
            <FORM>
                <INPUT TYPE="button"
                       VALUE="Trap it now"
                       ONCLICK="document.all.prey.style.border='medium solid'">
            </FORM>
        </CENTER>
    </BODY>
</HTML>
```

Here are the before and after images:

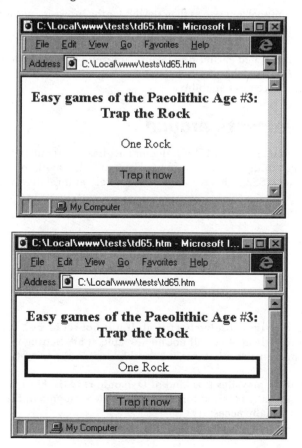

At first glance this example might not seem to reveal anything new, but look closely: when the button is pressed, the <DIV> tag is boxed, expanding slightly in the process, and the button moves slightly down the window to compensate (observe that the after case has acquired a scrollbar). Reload the document and press the button again to repeat the effect. The change in the <DIV> tag has resulted in the rest of the document being re-organized

This behavior is a powerful feature specific to Internet Explorer 4+ called **reflowing** the document. In simple examples as above it is very handy, taking care of the layout changes for you much like a modern word processor. In fact, most of the style properties not touched on yet in this chapter are likely to cause reflow to occur. All the margin, font, padding, border, spacing and text attributes are implicated.

It's worth being aware of this effect. There are several cases where you might not want reflow to occur:

- ❑ In very large documents, reflow can take some time if the changed point is near the top.
- ❑ In carefully laid out documents, you might not want your exact pixel settings to be moved around.
- ❑ If the user has an unusual font size as their default for the browser, reflow might ruin a document that otherwise appears well laid out.

All the style properties illustrated earlier don't cause any reflow. The section on 'Modifying Content and Structure' explains how to deliberately exploit the reflow feature of Internet Explorer 4+. Netscape browsers don't have this capability.

Moving HTML elements around

Beyond simple style enhancements to HTML documents lies re-organizing how the existing parts of the document are laid out in the browser window. Changing the layout of an HTML document comes down to manipulating the CSS2 style attributes of absolutely and relatively positioned elements.

The important style properties for this class of effect are:

- ❑ `position`
- ❑ `left`, `top`, `width` and `height`
- ❑ `clip` and `overflow`
- ❑ `z-index`

The `position` style property is absolutely critical. If it is not set to `relative` or `absolute`, then the element to which the style applies will not be movable at all. Setting the `position` property 'frees' the element for movement; otherwise it is 'embedded' in the rest of the document.

The idea of 2.5D animation pervades this kind of Dynamic HTML. For complex movement effects, the `z-order` must be carefully planned for all the movable elements in the page. However, for simple effects this is not usually necessary.

A further restriction on moving HTML around is that of coordinate systems: there must be some way to tell the difference between 'here' and 'there'. You need to decide at the start whether to fit in with the browser's layout of the document and use percentage measures, or whether to go straight to specific pixel-by-pixel measurements. If you want to do highly accurate movement, then you should create a non-resizable browser window using `window.open()` and perform all your movement within that window on a pixel-by-pixel basis.

Types of Movement

Movement of HTML elements can be expressed in several different ways. In the following examples, `balloon.gif` looks like this:

Of course, movement is not restricted to images - any kind of content can be used, from simple text to complex chunks of HTML markup.

Automated movement

User input isn't always required before HTML elements can move around. Via JavaScript, motion can be had automatically. This first example illustrates this:

```
<HTML>
    <HEAD>
        <STYLE>
            #zephyr { position: absolute; left: 0; top: 0; }
        </STYLE>
        <SCRIPT>
            function drift()
            {
                var z = document.all.zephyr.style;
                if ( z.pixelTop < 200 && z.pixelLeft == 0 ) z.pixelTop +=5;
                else if ( z.pixelLeft < 200 && z.pixelTop == 200 ) z.pixelLeft +=5;
                else if ( z.pixelTop <= 200 && z.pixelTop > 0 ) z.pixelTop -=5;
                else if ( z.pixelLeft <= 200 && z.pixelLeft > 0) z.pixelLeft -= 5;
            }
        </SCRIPT>
    </HEAD>
    <BODY ONLOAD="setInterval('drift()',1)">
        <DIV ID="zephyr">
            <IMG SRC="balloon.gif"><BR>
            Out, out and about!
        </DIV>
    </BODY>
</HTML>
```

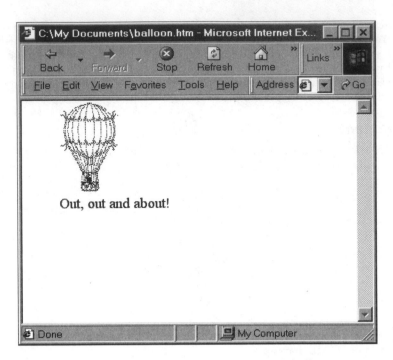

When viewed in Internet Explorer 4.0, this example displays the balloon moving in a square with diagonally opposite corners at pixel coordinates (0, 0) and (200, 200). There are several points to note here:

- ❑ Redrawing the absolutely positioned element takes time. The setInterval() delay is one millisecond; if the computer could perform at that pace, the balloon would travel around the square about 7 times a second, which it clearly does not.

- ❑ The script must finish ('let go') before the HTML element is redrawn - if you replace the setInterval() timing mechanism with a while() or for() loop inside the drift() function, it won't work, because JavaScript will always be in charge.

- ❑ Note the use of style properties that report pixel values as integers, not strings. Recall that 20px is a valid positional value, but that format is not as easy to work with as a plain number.

To make the example work in Netscape Navigator 4.0, replace the main function with this alternative:

```
function drift()
{
    var z = document.layers[0];
    if ( z.top < 200 && z.left == 0 ) z.top +=5;
    else if ( z.left < 200 && z.top == 200 ) z.left +=5;
    else if ( z.top <= 200 && z.top > 0 ) z.top -=5;
    else if ( z.left <= 200 && z.left > 0) z.left -= 5;
}
```

This example shows very typical differences between the two browsers. The detection technique described above could be used to make both browsers workable from the one HTML document.

This next very similar example shows how z-order can be used to plan overlapping animated areas. This example is specific to Internet Explorer 4+:

```html
<HTML>
   <HEAD>
      <STYLE>
         #zephyr { position: absolute; left: 0; top: 0; z-index: 1;
                   background-color: yellow;}
         #sirocco { position: absolute; left: 150; top: 150; z-index: 2; }
      </STYLE>
      <SCRIPT>
         function drift()
         {
            var z = document.all.zephyr.style;

            if ( z.pixelLeft == 0 && z.pixelTop == 0 )
               z.zIndex = ( z.zIndex == 1 ) ? 3 : 1;

            if ( z.pixelTop < 200 && z.pixelLeft == 0 ) z.pixelTop +=5;
            else if ( z.pixelLeft < 200 && z.pixelTop == 200 ) z.pixelLeft +=5;
            else if ( z.pixelTop <= 200 && z.pixelTop > 0 ) z.pixelTop -=5;
            else if ( z.pixelLeft <= 200 && z.pixelLeft > 0) z.pixelLeft -= 5;

            z = document.all.sirocco.style;
            if ( z.pixelTop < 250 && z.pixelLeft == 150 ) z.pixelTop +=5;
            else if ( z.pixelLeft < 250 && z.pixelTop == 250 ) z.pixelLeft +=5;
            else if ( z.pixelTop <= 250 && z.pixelTop > 150 ) z.pixelTop -=5;
            else if ( z.pixelLeft <= 250 && z.pixelLeft > 150) z.pixelLeft -= 5;
         }
      </SCRIPT>
   </HEAD>
   <BODY ONLOAD="setInterval('drift()',1)">
      <IMG ID="zephyr" SRC="balloon.gif">
      <DIV ID="sirocco"><IMG SRC="balloon.gif"><BR>In, in with a spin!</DIV>
   </BODY>
</HTML>
```

In the first balloon example the transparent nature of the balloon image was not obvious. 'Black' and 'transparent' are the only colors in that example, not 'black' and 'white'. In this second example, the original image now has a z-order that switches with each pass around the square, and a solid background color. The result is that on odd-numbered passes around the square, the first image can be seen 'through' the second image, but on even-numbered occasions, the first image blocks out the second image due to its solid background color.

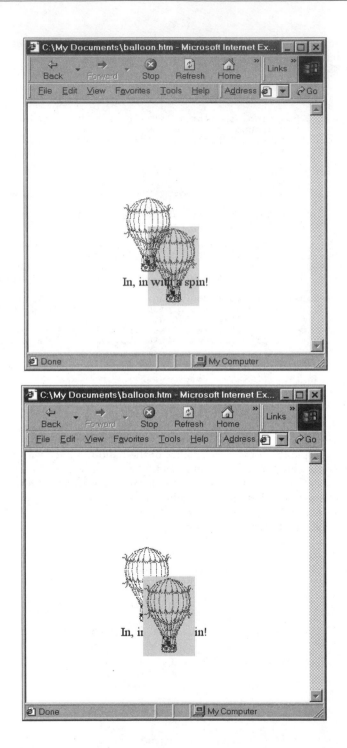

User Drag-Drop

Rather than rely on automation, sometimes the user wants to move an HTML element around on the page. This is more likely to be the case if the web page provides puzzles or games. There is an important distinction between dragging an item from *outside* of the browser onto a browser window (such as a file icon), and just moving an element around *inside* the window it belongs to. Only the latter case is discussed here, since the former leads into the complexities of operating systems.

For this latter case, the script author needs to provide the magic - there is no direct drag-and-drop support in the browser for moving positioned HTML elements. This can be a bit confusing to understand, so an analogy may help. Suppose the user is at a picnic, and sees a biscuit they want on the grass. Their hand reaches for the biscuit, but it moves. No matter how hard they try to grab the biscuit, it moves away. Eventually the picnickers organize themselves to box the biscuit in, revealing thousands of bored ants underneath engaged in psychological warfare against the human race. The ants are moving the biscuit in response to the user's hand movements.

Back in the browser it works almost the same, except the scriptwriter acts for the ants. When the user moves the mouse over the item to be dragged, the item moves in the mouse direction because JavaScript code underneath detected the mouse movement and moves the HTML item accordingly. The steps are:

❑ 'Prime' the item for dragging with an appropriate handler.

❑ Catch all onMouseMove events and update the item's position.

❑ 'Defuse' the item for dragging with an appropriate handler.

In other words, like this (for Internet Explorer 4+):

```
<HTML>
    <HEAD>
        <STYLE> #zephyr { position: absolute; left: 0; top: 0;} </STYLE>
        <SCRIPT>
            var primed = false;
            var new_x = 0;
            var new_y = 0;

            function set_drag() {
                if (!  window.primed && window.event.srcElement ==
document.all.zephyr)
                    window.primed = true;
                else
                    window.primed = false;
            }

            function handle_move()
            {
                if ( window.primed == true)
                {
                    window.new_x = window.event.x;
                    window.new_y = window.event.y;
                    setTimeout ("drag_it()",1);
                }
            }

            function drag_it()
            {
```

```
                with ( window.document.all.zephyr.style )
                {
                    pixelLeft = window.new_x - pixelWidth/2;
                    pixelTop  = window.new_y - pixelHeight/2;
                }
            }

        </SCRIPT>
    </HEAD>
    <BODY ONMOUSEMOVE="handle_move()" ONCLICK="set_drag();">
        <IMG ID="zephyr" SRC="balloon.gif"></IMG>
    </BODY>
</HTML>
```

This example lets you position the balloon anywhere you wish on the page, using the mouse.

There are three functions in this example: set_drag() is just a switch to turn dragging on and off; in this case the onClick handler is chosen, so the user must press and release the mouse button before dragging starts, and again on finishing; handle_move() picks up all move events from the window and updates the image. It uses a separate function drag_it() in a timer, not because of the limitation that JavaScript must 'let go' before the image's position changes, but because it gives the user time to move the mouse away from the dragged item. Try collapsing the statements from drag_it() into handle_move() and see how the dragged item 'sticks' to the mouse pointer in a frustrating way.

Modifying content and structure

As remarked earlier, even simple style changes in an HTML document can cause the current layout of a document to be disturbed. Thus most style changes aren't possible in Navigator 4.x, and in Internet Explorer 4+ cause the browser automatically to reflow as a result. For small changes, like expanding text by increasing its font size, this latter possibility is a useful but trivial feature. However, it can be exploited more thoroughly for good effect.

The most obvious example of this effect is collapsing menus, such as you might find in Apple Macintosh's Finder, or in the Windows Explorer utility of Microsoft Windows. Using the `innerHTML` and `outerHTML` properties discussed earlier, this is fairly straightforward to achieve:

```
<HTML>
    <HEAD>
        <SCRIPT>
            var hairy_exposed = false;
            var scaly_exposed = false;
            var bugs_exposed = false;

            function show_details(obj)
            {
                if ( eval(obj.id+"_exposed" ) == false )    // show the exploded list
                {
                    obj.innerHTML = document.all[obj.id+"_list"].innerHTML;
                    eval(obj.id+"_exposed=true");
                }
                else                                        // collapse the list
                {
                    obj.children[0].outerHTML='';
                    eval(obj.id+"_exposed=false");
                }
            }
        </SCRIPT>
    </HEAD>
    <BODY>
        <DIV ID="hairy_list" STYLE="display: none">
            <UL> <LI> Mammals <LI> Marsupials <LI> Monotremes </UL>
        </DIV>
        <DIV ID="scaly_list" STYLE="display: none">
            <UL> <LI> Fish <LI> Reptiles <LI> Birds .. sort of </UL>
        </DIV>
        <DIV ID="bugs_list" STYLE="display: none">
            <UL> <LI> Creepy crawlies <LI> Stinging things
                <LI> Slugs and stuff <LI> Ugh - Germs </UL>
        </DIV>
        <H2> Amateur's guide to the animal kingdom</H2>
        <UL>
            <LI ID="hairy" ONCLICK="show_details(this)">Hairy things</LI>
            <LI ID="scaly" ONCLICK="show_details(this)">Scaly things</LI>
            <LI ID="bugs" ONCLICK="show_details(this)">Bugs</LI>
        </UL>
    </BODY>
</HTML>
```

In this example, the three <DIV> elements are just invisible storage areas for HTML used as replacement text later, hence the `display: none` style information. You could just as easily store the HTML in plain JavaScript strings, but that's very cumbersome to type in. Since the <DIV> tags appear as objects in the DOM hierarchy, access to their original HTML is as easy (or easier in this case) as literal strings. When the user clicks on the line items, an expanded, two level view for that item appears. Note the careful use of `innerHTML` and `outerHTML` to make this happen.

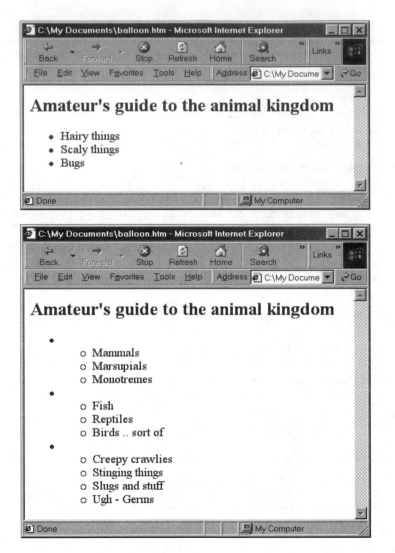

However, this example has a problem. When you replace one tag's contents with another, you lose the original contents. In this example, the main headings disappear forever, even though their bullet-points remain. The script could save the old values somewhere and replace them later, but there is a better way.

Each tag object supports an `insertAdjacentHTML()` method. This method allows new content to be slipped into the document before or after the tag of the current tag object. It takes two arguments: a special keyword indicating exactly where to insert (`BeforeBegin`, `AfterBegin`, `BeforeEnd`, `AfterEnd`), and the HTML content to insert. As with the `innerHTML`/`innerText` pair of properties, there is also an `insertAdjacentText()` method. To fix the behavior of the above example, replace the first branch of the `if` statement with these statements:

```
obj.insertAdjacentHTML("BeforeEnd", document.all[obj.id+"_list"].innerHTML);
eval(obj.id+"_exposed=true");
```

The result is much more satisfactory:

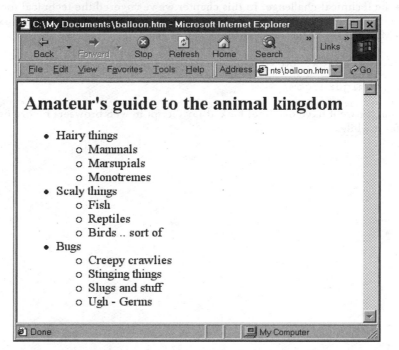

These features provide a flexible way of manipulating the document's source. They rely on some knowledge of the document's current structure in order to identify the bits that are of interest. Browser users, on the other hand, aren't encumbered with structured views of HTML. When a browser user selects part of a document in a browser window by dragging and highlighting with the mouse, any amount of content might be selected. The user doesn't care where tag boundaries might lie. To handle that behavior, Internet Explorer 4.0 supports a special TextRange object. TextRange objects require a bit of study before you can exploit them usefully, so their features are left to books more closely focussed on Dynamic HTML.

Summary

Netscape and Microsoft 4.0 browsers expose a lot of new host objects to JavaScript's control. The ability to manipulate fragments of a single HTML document, known as Dynamic HTML, puts a number of new techniques at the scriptwriter's (and HTML author's) disposal. Using these techniques, a browser window graduates from a mostly static information display device, to a (possibly highly) animated and interactive communication media. This evolution allows browsers to take up some of the space normally reserved by other tools, such as in the area of presentation graphics.

Regrettably, both vendors continue to add incompatible features as they anticipate or innovate ahead of the standardization process. Fortunately, the Document Object Model is both standard-driven and central to these new features. Because of their more recent release, Internet Explorer 4.0 and 5.0 have far greater support for this standard than Netscape's 4.x browser offerings.

Leaving aside incompatibilities, Dynamic HTML is a big subject, and one where the design challenge is as great as the technical challenge. In this chapter we've covered the technical toolset required and some of the basic techniques. For more information and inspiration, check out Wrox's various Dynamic HTML titles, or have a look at these web pages:

```
http://www.webreview.com/wr/pub/guides/style/style.html
http://www.dynamicdrive.com/
http://www.htmlguru.com/
```

In the next chapter we'll have one final look at JavaScript in web browsers before heading off into other lands for a while.

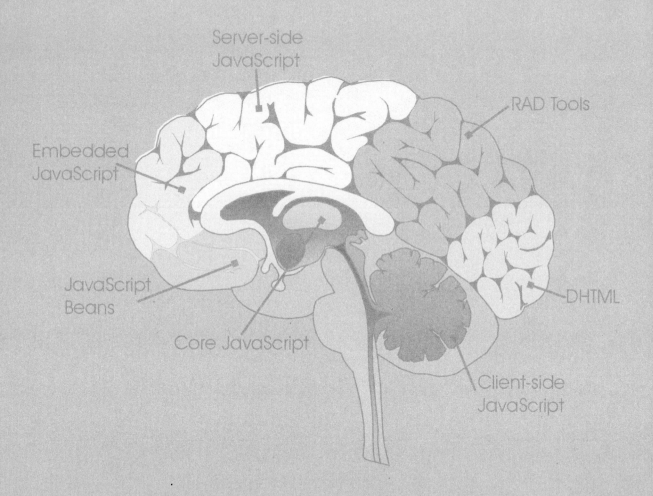

Browser JavaScript From The Outside In

In the previous chapters we've seen how JavaScript can be embedded in an HTML page. A user loads HTML pages into a browser when surfing the Web, and when the browser displays the pages, the JavaScript contained within does its thing. In this common scenario, the browser application itself doesn't get much attention. At most we might compare its display and processing idiosyncrasies with other browsers. When doing so, the browser is generally seen merely as a viewing tool for web pages, rather than as an interesting object in its own right.

In this chapter we'll see that matters are not quite that simple. There are a number of ways to interact with a web browser that have little to do with HTML. JavaScript rises to the fore again as a useful – in some cases, the only useful – way to set up these interactions.

What can we do with JavaScript and browsers other than enhance the display of HTML? We can set browser preferences, organise for e-mail to be automatically processed, run the browser without any human user at all and even escape out of the normal confines of the browser to display web pages in a number of alternative and innovative ways.

There is a common theme to this potpourri of techniques. All these things are configuration style activities that act *on* the browser and not necessarily *in* it. This means that the scriptwriter must generally have access to the browser from the outside: from the computer that the browser is running on. This is the reverse of the normal web development approach where we care little about the user's computer and are generally prevented by a number of security measures from doing much with it anyway. This time we don't care much about the HTML – the browser and its computer are the interesting target. Therefore the techniques in this chapter are only of use to the browser user or those who have access to the browser user's computer.

Configuring Browsers With JavaScript

Look under the menus named Edit and then Preferences when running Netscape 4.0 browsers, and you'll see a large number of configuration options. Look under Tools...Options in Internet Explorer and you'll see an equally large number of preferences. Normally these are set by hand when a person controls the browser, but they can also be set via JavaScript scripts without any user interaction.

The logistics for Internet Explorer and Netscape Navigator are completely different, so we consider each one in turn. In each case, only version 4.0 and greater browsers are recent enough to cover all these features.

Netscape 4.0+ Browsers

In the Netscape case, not only can the browser's preferences be changed via a JavaScript script; they are in fact stored as a JavaScript script. However, before plunging in, there are many items it doesn't cover, mostly because they are large or repetitive – the script only contains small configuration items. The preferences script does not cover these items:

- ❏ Lists of news servers and newsgroups subscribed to
- ❏ Records of what e-mail, news items and Web pages have been visited (except for the URLs that appear as history in the browser – those *are* in the script)
- ❏ Bookmarks, digital certificates, cookies and applets
- ❏ The browser Web page cache
- ❏ Items listed in the drop-down menus.

Other than that, everything you can setup in the browser can be set in the configuration

Preferences and Prefs.js

In Netscape Navigator 4.0, there is a new method of storing all the preferences that can be set for the browser, such as colors of links, locations of toolbars and sizes of windows. In Netscape 3.0, the browser is restricted to the user preferences accessible from the Options menu. Further changes are made possible via the version 3.0 Admin Kit product, known under version 4.0 as Mission Control.

Three Scripts

In 4.0, three scripts, which are all JavaScript scripts, can be used to control the browser. The three scripts are prefs.js, netscape.cfg, and config.jsc. .jsc stands for 'JavaScript configuration'. These scripts are consulted by the browser, in the order listed, when it starts up with later files overriding earlier ones. The first two are stored on the same computer as the browser, and the third one at any valid URL.

The script prefs.js (or preferences.js on Unix) stores all the user preference information. It is read when the browser starts up, and written by the browser when the browser shuts down, so it can't be changed by hand when the browser is running. If the browser is not running, it can be changed like any text file. If the user manipulates preferences via the Edit menu Preferences... popup, this will change the script when the browser shuts down. The only reason to edit by hand is to add one of a few special preferences that make developing in JavaScript easier – these can't be added from the browser. There can be a different prefs.js for each user profile created in Netscape 4.0.

The script `netscape.cfg` replaces the `netscape.lck` file of Netscape 3.0. This script stores user preferences that override the `prefs.js` script. It also stores other preferences inaccessible to the user, such as menu options and the 'big-N' animated icon. Lastly, it stores reference information about the `config.jsc` script. The `netscape.cfg` script is encrypted so that the browser user can't touch it or read it, giving system administrators a way to permanently set browser features. It can be created by hand, but an easier approach is to use Netscape's Mission Control product. This product contains a Configuration Editor tool that provides a GUI for the `netscape.cfg` script just like the **Edit, Preferences...** browser window does for the `prefs.js` file. Mission Control also contains an InstallBuilder tool that can deliver the encrypted `netscape.cfg` script to the computer which will run the browser.

The script `config.jsc`, if it exists, in turn overrides the `netscape.cfg` script. It can have the same range of content as the `netscape.cfg` script, but is stored as a plain readable file, not an encrypted one. It can be written by the Configuration Editor, or by hand, as for `netscape.cfg`. It is usually stored apart from the browser user's computer. The script's URL can be used to update a browser's configuration regularly, not merely once at startup time, by including re-read instructions in the local `netscape.cfg`. This is especially powerful if `config.jsc` changes between reads – features can be regularly turned off and on like TV channels going off-air. This script's main use is for administrators who need to manage many browser installations at once – all browsers can be configured from one `config.jsc` URL.

Here is an example fragment from the `prefs.js` script:

```
// Netscape User Preferences
// This is a generated file!  Do not edit.

user_pref("autoupdate.enabled", false);
user_pref("browser.bookmark_columns_win", "v1 2 1:5000 2:5000 4:2500 3:1999");
user_pref("browser.bookmark_window_rect", "225,10,561,403");
user_pref("browser.cache.check_doc_frequency", 1);
user_pref("browser.cache.disk_cache_size", 10240);
user_pref("browser.cache.memory_cache_size", 4096);
user_pref("browser.download_directory", "C:\\local\\users\\nigel\\js\\");
user_pref("browser.startup.homepage",
"http://antwrp.gsfc.nasa.gov/apod/astropix.html");
user_pref("browser.startup.homepage_override", false);
user_pref("browser.url_history.URL_1", "www.tusc.com.au");
user_pref("browser.url_history.URL_2", "www.latrobe.edu.au");
... and so on ...
```

The first two lines are just a JavaScript comment generated by the browser when the file is generated at browser shutdown time. Despite this warning, it's OK to modify this file, provided that you do it carefully, and when the browser isn't running. All the usual JavaScript language features are available, like flow control statements and mathematical expressions, but since the sole purpose of this file is to supply configuration data to the browser, there's usually no need for anything fancy. Thus the use of JavaScript in this file is very limited. From inside the browser, provided you have the right security set, using the `window.navigator.preferences()` method you can do other magic with the preferences. Read Chapter 18 for the security constraints.

The first argument to the `user_pref()` function is a string, but its contents in the above examples look suspiciously like a JavaScript property reference. You might be tempted to try:

```
browser.download_directory = "C:\\TEMP\\";
```

or something similar. This won't work – see the discussion below under 'Help! What Are These Objects, Anyway?'. The short answer is that although there is a host object browser with a property `download_directory`, it's not exposed directly to the JavaScript interpreter.

This URL describes all the preferences available up to and including Netscape 4.5: `http://developer.netscape.com/docs/manuals/deploymt/jsprefs.htm`. Note that there are a number of backwards compatibility and debugging options that can be set in these scripts that can't be turned on from the GUI dialog boxes that the browser supplies. Have a poke around `http://home.netscape.com/browsers/index.html` for some technical notes on these special preferences. If you do set one of these preferences by hand in the preferences script, then it will be read at browser startup time, and Netscape will remember to write it out again at browser shutdown time, so it won't be lost.

Proxies and Proxy.pac

Netscape browsers require access to the Internet or some other network to be useful. One way of managing this access for Netscape 4.0 only is via JavaScript. Separate to the general `prefs.js` file is a file that routes information requests from the browser out to the world at large. One preference in the `prefs.js` file records the name of this file if it is used. First, some background on how information requests from browsers to the Internet and Web work.

A browser on the Internet uses a number of services on the user's behalf. These are the common functions of the browser like web pages, news, file transfer (ftp) and electronic mail. Each of these services demands that the browser connect to a server (such as web servers or news servers) in order to do any useful work.

In the simplest case, the browser connects to servers directly using widely known public address information, but this creates security problems for the computer the browser runs on. Usually there is one or more 'proxy', 'firewall' or 'gateway' computer interposed between the browser and the actual Internet. Private address information points the browser to the proxy instead of to the world at large, reducing security problems.

For performance or organizational reasons, the browser user might want to pick and choose between proxies (if more than one is available) for each and every URL request made. The proxy configuration file, written in JavaScript, allows the user to set policy stating what kind of URLs go to which servers. Each time a URL request is made, the URL is processed by a JavaScript function in the configuration file that decides how to proceed.

In order to make this easy, the browser supplies some native JavaScript functions for picking apart URLs. These are only available when used in the proxy configuration file. The job of the proxy file is to define the function `FindProxyForURL` and nothing else. Two arguments are always passed: the full URL to be fetched, and the piece of the URL containing the host name only, for convenience of use in the function.

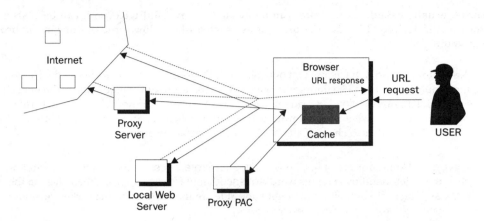

In the following example, imagine a browser is used on a PC in a small corporate Intranet with Internet access via 3 hosts: one for SOCKS (a "secure sockets" protocol) connections, and two for all other 'normal' Internet URLs. There might be two either for redundancy or for performance reasons.

```
// proxy.pac file

function FindProxyForURL(url, host)
{
  if (isPlainHostName(host) || isInNet(host, "192.123.234.0") )
    return "DIRECT";

  else if ( url.substring(0, 6) == "https:" || url.substring(0, 6) == "snews:")
    return "SOCKS sockshost:1081";

  else
  {
    if ( Math.random() < 0.5 )
        return "PROXY proxy1:1080 ; proxy2:1080";
    else
        return "PROXY proxy2:1080 ; proxy1:1080";
  }
}
```

First, note that `String` and `Math` functions are available – this is JavaScript. Second, there are some 'helper' functions used, such as `isPlainHostName()`. These save a lot of complex string operations, and allow conversion between hostnames and IP addresses (the underlying technical name for a computer). Avoid doing conversions, because there is a performance penalty. Finally, the function has to return a string in a specific format; most of the interesting formats are illustrated here. This string advises the browser how to get the URL.

In this example, there are three `if` branches. The first branch is taken if the user types a URL with a simple hostname (like `http://localserver/top/index.html`) or a hostname that is in the company network, which is called `192.123.234.0` in this example. A direct connection results, using the widely known public addresses for the Web. This is internal to the company, so all the fuss about proxies and security is ignored. The second branch identifies `https` and `snews` style URLs (which use the magic SOCKS protocol) and reports back to use the special SOCKS proxy. The third branch returns both of the ordinary proxies for everything else. When more than one proxy is returned, the browser tries them in order until it succeeds. To prevent the first one in the list always being used and the other standing idle (even though both work), the `Math.random()` function ensures they are returned in a random order.

This script, usually called `proxy.pac`, can be located at any valid URL, so it can be shared by many browser users if desired. To make the browser use such a file, follow these options in the browser menu system:

❑ Navigator 2.0 and 3.0: Choose **Options, Network Preferences** ..., then choose the **Proxies** tab in the resulting window. The third radio button **Automatic Proxy Configuration** is the one; click and enter a URL, press **Reload** to read the new script. Your browser now obeys the new rules. Test by navigating to somewhere well known, such as `http://www.yahoo.com`. On Unix versions of Netscape remember to choose **Options, Save Options** afterwards.

❑ Navigator/Communicator 4.0: Choose **Edit,** then **Preferences** ... In the resulting window, double-click in the left-hand pane on the word **Advanced** until **Proxies** appears, then click on the word **Proxies**. The radio buttons on the right hand side are the same as for the earlier versions of Navigator, so proceed as described above.

If the proxy file's URL is provided by a web server, then that server is contacted 'directly' in order to get the file, so you don't need a proxy file in order to get the proxy file. You can tell that files with a `.pac` extension are special to the browser – just try to load the `proxy.pac` directly into the browser window via its URL and you'll get an unusual error from the browser.

E-mail and News Filters

Netscape 4.0 has a little-known filtering feature that can make reading e-mail and news a less onerous and more pleasant activity. This is really worthwhile if you're used to working through dozens or hundreds of news and e-mail messages every day and would like some kind of automatic sorting to occur. When the user calls up the Message Center, Messenger Mailbox or Collabra Discussion Groups window of Netscape Communicator, the first thing that happens is that the browser starts downloading unread news and e-mail items. JavaScript can be used to customize the processing that occurs when Netscape sorts through these new items prior to displaying them for the user.

A warning for the unwary – this feature of Netscape can be tricky to use and there's little documentation. It certainly doesn't yet have the powerful filtering functionality that some mail and newsreaders have.

Processing Model

The JavaScript filter mechanism is similar to the event handler mechanism used within an HTML page. In the HTML case, the scriptwriter has to identify which event the handler needs to be set against. Next, some JavaScript for the handler is written. Finally, the script is installed in the right spot in the HTML. In the case of e-mail and news filters, there are two events, which we'll informally call the "onNewEmail event" and the "OnNewNews event". These aren't really official names - there aren't any – we're just using them to ease the explanation. The handler for these events must be a whole JavaScript function, not just a script fragment like `this.value = this.value.toUpperCase()`. The handlers are installed into special configuration files where they do nothing until one of the events occurs, sparking the browser to read and possibly execute them.

An important difference with the HTML event system is that each event in this case can have more than one handler. If there are several handlers turned 'on' for the OnNewEmail event, then the event will fire and run every such handler in turn. The result is that the information attached to the event can be passed to and through a number of handlers, possibly being modified in the process, so the handlers are more commonly called filters. The information that's passed to the handler is an object that represents one e-mail or news item.

Therefore, each mail or news item that comes in may cause many filters (handlers) to fire, and a given filter may fire many times if there are a lot of new mail or news items.

Finally, a warning – what constitutes a new message is a little fuzzy. If your mail is stored on an IMAP server, then no messages are stored with the local browser. When the browser requests e-mail items from the IMAP server, all items are downloaded, so all items are filtered, even if they've been seen and read before.

Setting Up Filters

Filters can be set up directly within Netscape by the user using point and click, or by hand creation of JavaScript. Only simple filters can be set up from within the browser. Be sure to have an up to date copy of the browser before experimenting with this – version 4.08 or 4.6 at least. Earlier versions do not work well. The hand-creation way is described here, but for completeness, to create filters via dialog boxes, look in the menu system of the Message Center window of Netscape Communicator under Edit, Message Filters... Look under Mail Filters in the Communicator MailBox window.

Two files are required to make filters. One does not require any JavaScript – it is used to register the filters in a similar way to onClick handlers in HTML. The other contains the JavaScript code. Both must be created on a per-user basis, as they are part of the user preferences for the browser. Both files are plain text files, editable with any text editor. Where these files go depends on whether you have a simple setup, with plain downloaded mail and news, or a more complex setup where you have one or more IMAP sources of e-mail and/or more than one news server.

Let's consider the simple case first: plain downloaded and locally stored e-mail and a single default news server.

The first file is called mailrule on UNIX and is stored under the .netscape directory. On MS Windows the file is called rules.dat and is stored under the Mail subdirectory of the specific user whose preferences are being changed. The second file is called filters.js and goes in the same directory as the first file.

In the complicated case, if you use IMAP as the source of your e-mail, then you will need to put these files instead under the ImapMail/<IMAP servername> subdirectory instead. If you have more than one IMAP server, you will need to put the files under every server directory that you want the filters to be used on. Although the mail filtering works with this setup, your humble author sweated a fair bit and still couldn't get the news filtering functionality to work when there are multiple IMAP e-mail servers and multiple news servers. Not recommended in this case.

The following discussions relate to the simple case of plain downloaded e-mail and a single news server.

The `mailrule` file is used to match handlers against events. Its format matches the simple `.ini` format used extensively in MS Windows 3.1. Here is a sample:

```
name="Test"
enabled="yes"
type="2"
scriptName="NoSpamFilter"
```

The `name` property is the name of the filter. The `scriptName` property is the name of the JavaScript function in the `filters.js` file. The `type` property identifies whether the event is OnNewEmail (use the number 2) or OnNewNews (use the number 8). These numbers are just magic numbers that mean something deep in the guts of the browser. The `enabled` flag allows you to create extra filters without them doing anything. Set it to `no` if they are to be disabled. This lets you create a library of filters and activate only the ones you're currently interested in. To add a second filter, just add four more lines the same, with a blank line after the first filter. The `name` and `scriptName` properties must be unique.

You might be tempted to think this file is a JavaScript file, but it's not – so adding semicolons and such won't work. If you create a filter using the dialog box of the browser, you'll see some extra lines in the file afterwards; you don't need these for your JavaScript filters.

The `filters.js` file is just a normal JavaScript file. Here's a simple example:

```
// My message filters

function NoSpamFilter(message)
{
  var sub = message.subject;
  if (sub.toUpperCase.indexOf("MAKE MONEY FAST") != -1)
  {
    message.trash();
  }
}
```

Every time a new message arrives at the browser, this function is run. A message object is passed to the function and its properties can be examined using normal JavaScript logic. If you elect to do something different with the message then you can call one of its methods to change its fate. Otherwise, if you leave the message object alone, the message will appear as though nothing happened. In this example, the message is put in the trash folder if the subject line contains MAKE MONEY FAST. If there was another filter after this one, something else might happen to the message as well.

There are only a limited number of things you can do with filtering, and they all depend on exploiting the properties and methods of the message object that's passed to your filter function. None of the methods need be supplied any values as arguments.

❑ `killThread()` and `watchThread()` ignore and mark the thread that the message is part of, respectively. This lets you ignore rubbish discussions and remember to note interesting ones.

❑ `trash()` effectively deletes the message, putting it in the trash folder before you see it.

❑ If you set the folder property of the message, the message will go into that folder instead of the inbox. Folder names should read `mailbox:folder-name`; the folder must exist before the filter is applied; and the folder must be on the local computer – IMAP folders not supported.

❑ You can set the `priority` property to a priority like the ones in Messenger (High for example).

❑ You can set whether the message has been read with the `read` property – use `true` or `false`.

❑ Apart from that, the message object has a property for each header line in the message (but all in lowercase) so you can examine the `subject`, `from` or `sender` properties. For header lines that are more than one word, you can use the alternate array syntax of JavaScript – this time use correct capitalization, e.g. `message["Reply-To"]`.

Help! What Are These Objects, Anyway?

JavaScript scripts generally act on objects and their properties. After fiddling with the Netscape configuration scripts for a while, it's easy to see that there are at least a couple of objects involved that are part of the browser, but don't appear to be part of the Document Object Model, or even the Browser Object Model. Just what are they?

The Netscape browser is built out of many, many different types of objects. Some of these are a consequence of HTML pages the browser has loaded, some are part of the browser's very nature. Not all of the objects that are part of the browser's very nature are exposed to JavaScript – that is, there are host objects in the browser that JavaScript can't get access to. The ones used by the scripts in this section are exposed to JavaScript, *but only when the script comes from the particular source described above.* So the Netscape browser has a mechanism where it can selectively expose host objects to JavaScript, depending on where the JavaScript comes from. Beyond that, there's not much value in dwelling on what the objects are, since their use is so highly restricted.

If we briefly look forward a few chapters to the discussion on cookies (Chapter 18), it can be seen that cookies are accessed in a similar "arm's length" way to the way preferences are set – the objects acted on aren't directly available to the scriptwriter in either case.

Internet Explorer 4.0+

If you're an old hand at throwing together quick scripts for Microsoft Windows, perhaps in Visual Basic, then the scripting options for Internet Explorer are easy to understand because they follow the same general pattern as other scriptable Windows applications such as Microsoft Excel. All the configuration information in the IE case is stored either in the Windows registry or is not stored at all.

Directly Scriptable Preferences

Later on in this chapter we'll see how the Internet Explorer browser can be treated as an ActiveX object, with all that implies. For the purposes of configuration that means that we can work on the browser from any language that has a COM interface to ActiveX components. The Windows Script Host (WSH), discussed elsewhere, is one such tool, and JScript is a language that can be used with WSH. Therefore, we can do some configuration work with the Internet Explorer objects using JScript under WSH.

Here's an example:

```
var ie = WScript.CreateObject("InternetExplorer.Application");

ie.Height = 640;
ie.Width = 480;
ie.ToolBar = false;
ie.Resizable = false;
ie.Navigate("http://www.wrox.com", 8);
ie.Visible = true;
```

This example script opens Internet Explorer with the size of the viewing area fixed, and all the menu and toolbar controls removed from the user's access. This allows you to control exactly the screen size used by the browser – useful if you have a web application which could be messed up if the user opened other windows or navigated forwards and back through pages.

Unfortunately, this kind of thing only allows us to modify a few of the simple display characteristics of the browser at startup time. If we want to configure the browser more deeply from JavaScript, we have to look elsewhere

Scriptable Registry Preferences

Most of the Browser configuration in Internet Explorer is stored with the configuration information for other Microsoft applications – in the Windows registry. Again WSH and JScript provide a method for changing the browser configuration, this time in a manner that's much more like the preferences file of Netscape. The WSHShell object of WSH provides for reading and writing of registry items. Don't forget to use double-backslash or else the strings meant to be key names will be mistranslated:

```
var WSHShell = WScript.CreateObject("WScript.Shell");
WSHShell.RegWrite("HKCU\\MyRegKeyName\\", "My Register Key Value");
```

For Internet Explorer the main obstacle is that the various preferences are located in several different areas of the registry, so lets go through them.

Remember: if you want to modify the registry, tread lightly, and back it up beforehand!

For preferences specific to one user, this section of the registry is the one to attack:

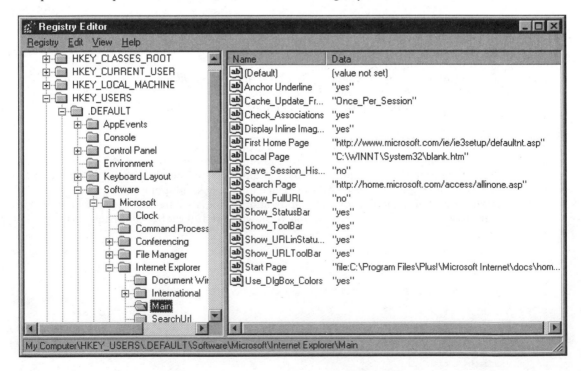

This screenshot is from a Windows NT 4.0 SP3 computer. We're showing the default user here because it's easy to see the whole hierarchy and some of the properties, but typically you will want to modify the properties for one of the non-default users – they are identified by a long string of numbers under HKEY_USERS that in part represents the Microsoft license for that user. Most users will have far more properties under Main than the default user has here. The folders that are siblings of the Main folder contain interesting configuration items as well.

For configuration information about basic Internet and Web connectivity, such as proxies and servers, it's appropriate to look elsewhere. This is because those basic connectivity items are really part of Windows itself and not part of the browser, even though they're accessible from within the browser via the Tools then Internet Options ... menu items (in IE5). You should plan and research carefully before fiddling with these items from scripts as they are part of the lower level Windows configuration and Microsoft advises against changing them this way. Microsoft recommends using the tools provided in the Control Panel to do these tasks. Here is a snapshot of the most obvious configuration items in the registry. You might find the format varies a bit for Internet Explorer 5.0 – these are IE4.0 screen shots.

Note the fully qualified registry path at the bottom of the screen, as it wasn't practical this time to include a snapshot from the very top down. Again, these items are found under the HKEY_USERS branch of the registry, repeated for each separate user. Again, we are showing the default user only, because an ordinary user is packed with more information than can easily be put here. It's obvious what some items are - for example the User Agent string is the browser type and version that Internet Explorer (3.02 in this case) reports with every web server query. Changing the items that are timing settings may have profound and unwanted effects on your computer – **you've been warned**. If you examine the settings for your particular user, you'll see many more of the kind of options that are easy to understand.

The third configuration area of Internet Explorer relates to extending the browser's functionality. It's possible to create client or helper applications and also browser extensions. These features of Internet Explorer 4.0 and higher allow powerful customizations of the browser, some involving scripts or other programs. Alas, delving into extensions is beyond the scope of this book, so you're referred to these Microsoft URLs if you want to explore those technologies. For configuring client programs, possibly JavaScript ones, that act as helpers:
`http://msdn.microsoft.com/workshop/browser/configuration/clientreg/clientr egistrylayout.asp`. For configuring browser extensions that enhance toolbars and other user-action features of Internet Explorer, possibly with scripts again, look at:
`http://msdn.microsoft.com/workshop/browser/ext/overview/overview.asp`
These extensions also have their entries in the registry.

Any deeper exploration of configuration options than this, and one is no longer merely configuring, one is just about developing one's own browser, albeit with a fair wad of help from Microsoft. So we'll leave it at that.

Running Browsers from JavaScript

From the previous section it's easy to see the use of JavaScript-based browser configuration files. However, it's possible to go further – we can actively control browsers from scripts. In order to do this we rely on the browsers being good citizens of the operating system under which they run. By being good citizens, the browsers provide a standard interface to the outside world we can exploit with a script.

In this section it will be seen that the amount of control you have over the browser depends on how deeply it integrates with the system it runs on. In summary, Internet Explorer provides varied and useful interfaces, whereas Netscape provides almost none, so most of the discussion relates to Internet Explorer alone.

Browsers As Runnable Programs

The simplest thing you can do from JavaScript is to run a program. That program could be a browser. You can do this using Nombas' ScriptEase or Microsoft's WSH and JScript. Here's a WSH example:

```
var shell;
shell = WScript.CreateObject("WScript.Shell");
shell.run("C:\\Program Files\\Netscape\\Communicator\\Program\\netscape.exe",
          0,
          true);
```

For Netscape, that is all the choice you have from a script, apart from including a few command line options. That is pretty uninspiring. If you need them, the options are described here:
`http://developer.netscape.com:80/docs/manuals/deploymt/options.htm`.

You can do this kind of thing with Internet Explorer as well, but there are vastly more flexible alternatives with that browser. Consider the following possibilities.

Browsers as JavaScript Objects

We touched briefly on a technique for running Internet Explorer from JavaScript rather than from the user's command in the last section. Let's revisit that example briefly:

```
var ie = WScript.CreateObject("InternetExplorer.Application");

ie.Height = 640;
ie.Width = 480;
ie.ToolBar = false;
ie.resizable = false;
ie.Navigate("http://www.wrox.com", 8);
ie.Visible = true;
```

This is very different to just running some program without knowing much about it. Here we're doing something to the browser's insides as well.

To gain some perspective on this sample script, have a look at the Internet Explorer program, which is named `iexplore.exe`. This program is less than 100 Kilobytes in size. That is hardly enough for an application with the many features of Internet Explorer. The Internet Explorer browser is actually this one file plus a collection of other, separate pieces. The `iexplore.exe` program is small because "all" it does is tie those other pieces together into a whole browser. Most of the functionality is in the pieces. If we know enough about the pieces, we discover new and flexible scripting options, rather than just having to start the whole browser, as in the Netscape case.

Internet Explorer-like Objects

There are two main objects useful from scripts are the `WebBrowser` object and the `InternetExplorer` object. Both of these are ActiveX objects, and so they can be exploited from any ActiveX aware language, including Microsoft's WSH + JScript. These aren't really intended to be used from inside normal client-side JavaScript in a web browser.

The `WebBrowser` object is the simpler object of the two. It displays a single HTML window in which any URL can be displayed. If one of the links in the window is clicked, then the next URL will be displayed in that same window. History and bookmarks are maintained by the object, so it is much like a small browser. Unfortunately, to exploit the `WebBrowser` control, you really need a full development environment such as the Visual Basic Applications suite before you can get at it.

The `InternetExplorer` object is the one that is visible and easily accessible on any PC that the browser is installed on. This is the one you are most likely to use because no special products or licenses are required. It provides the full multi-window and toolbar-decorated environment of Internet Explorer; in effect it *is* the object that stands for all of Internet Explorer. This is the object used in the script example above. This URL describes all the properties and methods that are available on the `InternetExplorer` object:
http://msdn.microsoft.com/workshop/browser/webbrowser/reference/objects/InternetExplorer.asp.

As we said earlier, most of these options only have cosmetic effects when the ActiveX object starts up. However, the object also supports a number of events and access to the Browser and Document Object Models inside the running browser. That access allows a number of very sophisticated uses. We can dig down into the HTML page being displayed by the browser as far as we want. For example, we can change <DIV> and <SPAN> sections, fill in <FORM> <INPUT> elements or do other processing as though we were running ordinary JavaScript script statements embedded in the HTML. Here is a simple fragment of script following on from the last that illustrates the principle:

```
var win = ie.window;
if ( win.document) WScript.echo(win.document.form[0].element[0].value);
```

This works (provided the document gets a chance to load first) because, unlike Netscape, Internet Explorer exposes the Document Object Model to programmatic control from outside the browser. In order to do this, merely use the techniques described in Chapter 20 (on WSH), plus the Browser Object Model as a guide to the object hierarchy. You can use the WSH 'event sink' techniques described at `http://msdn.microsoft.com/scripting` with Internet Explorer just as you can with Microsoft Excel or Word, so that you can capture in your script browser events. This means that if the browser is displaying an HTML page, and the page has buttons or other items that support HTML events, then when the user fires those events by interacting with the page your script can capture them.

Disguised Browser-like Objects

For completeness we briefly mention two other browser-like objects, tucked deep in the Internet Explorer software.

The magic file `MSHTML.dll` contains the simplest and least functional browser of all. It is a COM/OLE object that just presents a single undecorated window containing a single HTML page. If the user clicks a link, a new instance of the object and a new window is always created. This object is so low level that it is really meant for use from languages such as C and C++, but for the desperate, you could expose this object to WSH and JScript and exploit it from there.

Finally, the Microsoft Windows Help system has changed from the help available with Windows 95 and its predecessors. The new help system is called HTML Help and uses a HTML browser-like interface to display help documents. The window that the help system displays has different toolbars and menus to the other browser windows, reflecting its specific focus. This HTML Help window is also an ActiveX object, one that you can download from Microsoft's Web Workshop web pages (formerly SiteBuilder) if you haven't already got it as part of another upgrade (such as IE5.0 or Windows 98 or Windows 2000). However, you will need to buy the Visual Basic for Applications development tool before you have the correct software to exploit the object properly, even if you want to use it from JScript, not VBScript or Visual Basic.

Browsers As Operating Systems

The final level of integration with the Windows operating system that Internet Explorer 4.0+ can perform is via Active Desktop. In this case, the browser and operating system Graphical User Interface virtually merge together into one system so that the two become difficult to distinguish. In this case the browser becomes just one facility of the operating system and if we are to discuss controlling it from JavaScript/JScript scripts, then we might as well discuss scripting activities under Windows in general. To cover general scripting facilities under Windows requires not only this book but a number of others as well.

From this chapter's perspective, which is to introduce in some depth all the different ways of using JavaScript to interact with the outside parts of browsers, Active Desktop doesn't really provide us with any new options. We can resort to general WSH scripting, but that's covered in Chapter 20.

Browsers and Push Content

The implications of **push technology** on the Internet was a topic of much discussion in 1997. Push technology derives from comparisons between the Web and other media such as television, radio and print. In those other media, the user/consumer/audience is almost entirely passive, whereas the Web generally requires the user to direct matters with the mouse and keyboard. Push technology opens the opportunity for web pages to "push" information (whether documents, applets or otherwise) into the user's browser (or wherever) without much user interaction, rather than the user actively "pulling" (downloading). Hysteria surrounding the advent of push technology stems from the possibility that a web content provider can take a much larger role in the user's viewing choices: the user subscribes/tunes in/buys a content agreement, and the provider varies the content over time. This is the type of opportunity that television stations, newspaper publishers, stock exchanges and CNN represent – potentially big business. Furthermore, if the content is software rather than just data, it also represents a chance for software vendors to update user's computers remotely – more power to the vendors.

Unfortunately, it is not so easy. For TV, radio and print, it doesn't matter if a user switches off – TV and radio signals are broadcast without regard for individual users, and newspapers are disposed of if they are not sold. For the Internet and the Web, there needs to be an understanding that the user's computer is switched on before anything can be pushed to it. So Web content can't just be blindly pushed into the arms of a browser from the content provider end. Also, since security is an issue, the user's computer can't be rummaged through by the content provider to see what to update. Finally, with Internet bandwidth increasing oh-so-slowly, the content provider can't saturate the Internet with content updates on the assumption that someone might want them.

Enter Netscape and Microsoft's browsers and Marimba's Castanet technology. Despite the fact that Internet newsgroup feeds and media news feeds have been operating effectively in a "push" manner for years, these tools are seen as central to the possibility of push. Netcaster is Netscape's offering aimed at this market. While these tools may look like push technology on the surface, underneath it is a different story; no content server takes the initiative, although one might respond to a "push" tool's request.

These tools also promote the idea of **channels** – a stream of content from one source – paralleling radio and TV. Netscape and Microsoft have gone to great lengths to sign up channel providers that will add value to the technology that they sell to users.

In these enlightened, post-1997 times, push content for the masses tends to be focussed around Java applets that act like news or stock tickers, or around that old standby, e-mail. Nevertheless, the infrastructure for push content is there in the browsers, and will be exploited in some niche of the ever-expanding Internet. For some really well designed push content, alas, beyond this book's scope, you might like to have a look at how WebTV integrates HTML and television channels into the one screen. Check out `http://www.webtv.com`.

Netscape Netcaster

Netscape's Communicator 4.0 product has a `window.components` property that is an array. Obviously the plan must be to populate this array with a suite of add-on components in the same way that the `window.plugins` array can be populated with a suite of third-party plugins. Netcaster is the first and only such component offering to date. For Netscape 4.0 it is downloaded and installed separate to the main Communicator installation process.

This is what Netcaster means to the scriptwriter:

❑ Yet another place to configure Netscape's browsers via JavaScript.

❑ Two further host objects to interact with in the browser.

❑ Special constraints to take into account when developing client-side JavaScript.

❑ Functionality to do graphics and text *outside* of any browser window.

What Netcaster Really Is

At the core of Netcaster is the same old stuff as the rest of the Netscape browser: web pages, URLs, HTML, Java, JavaScript and HTTP. The fancy "push" content is typically just web pages. Separate to these familiar, core technologies are four innovations:

❑ Fancy browser graphics. There is a new user control called the Channel Finder which looks like a toolbar crossed with a bookmark list - that is roughly all it is.

❑ A new **webtop** window. This is a variant on the possibilities of the window.open() method. It allows the whole computer screen to be used as a single browser window, and can be located behind other screen elements such as icons, menus and applications. It wastes no space with window decorations.

❑ A configurable **web crawler**. A web crawler is just a piece of software that browses the Web automatically as though it were a highly methodical user.

❑ Marimba software included. The Netscape browser can use this software to download content instead of the normal, direct approach via HTTP if the Netcaster user so chooses. Castanet is beyond the scope of this book.

Without the distractions of the graphical enhancements, what you have is a web browser that can browse on its own.

How It Works

When the Netcaster component is installed and activated, the Channel Finder contains a little database of channels, just as the bookmark list is a database of bookmarks. When the browser is running, there are two people steering in parallel: the user who controls the normal Web, e-mail and news windows, and the Netcaster web crawler functionality that controls any "active" channels.

Each channel is defined by a URL, some timing information, some window positioning information, and some trivia. The timing information controls how often the web crawler will examine the URL of the channel. The web crawler retrieves the URL's document, and recursively follows all the HTML-embedded links, retrieving subsidiary documents as well, up to a configured limit. These are stored in a document cache similar to the normal browser cache. If the channel is visible, the content is displayed as well. Once the web crawler has finished, it stops activity until the timing information tells it to try again. At that point it crawls again, fetching any updates that might have occurred in the meantime.

The Netcaster component is designed to be useable when the browser is offline – not connected to the Internet. In that case, attempts to view a channel just result in the channel's cached documents being displayed.

What It Is Good For

Netcaster gives the user several new ways to interact with the Web:

- ❑ A lazy way to find out what's new. By subscribing to a channel, the user makes the content provider do the work of searching out and assembling content.

- ❑ Acheaper way to surf the Web. By efficiently crawling the Web, the user can download heaps of information at the fastest rate possible, then disconnect and view the information offline at a more relaxed pace.

- ❑ An easy way to focus on special interests. By subscribing to a channel, the user elects a topic of interest, and waits for the news. Of course, the user becomes a target market in the process.

- ❑ A non-intrusive way to stay up-to-date. Since the Netcaster channels can appear on the screen's backdrop ('webtop'), the user can do other tasks without interruption, while the backdrop updates according to channel content changes.

Because Netcaster is partially an automated web browsing system, it obeys the etiquette rules for **web robots**. Web robots are automated web browsers ('web crawlers'), and etiquette rules are a system of checks that stop automated web browsers from dominating the Internet with their activities. Each web site has a `robots.txt` file which defines how much (if any) web crawling is allowed at that site. The Netcaster component of Communicator follows the etiquette rules by identifying itself as a robot. This has a downside: some sites might refuse to respond to Netcaster URL requests. Obviously, channel sites are unlikely to refuse.

Working With Channels

Development of web pages viewed via a channel is much the same as any web page. It is the creation of new channels that involves a unique interaction with JavaScript.

New Host Objects

There are two JavaScript host objects worth considering.

The `window.components["netcaster"]` is one of these objects. This is the 'top level' object for the Netcaster subsystem of Communicator. It is undefined if Netcaster hasn't been installed. Its most interesting features are as follows:

- ❑ `active` property. Contains a Boolean value indicating whether Netcaster is running or not.
- ❑ `activate()` method. Start Netcaster.
- ❑ `getChannelObject()` method. Ask for a new `channel` object.
- ❑ `addChannel()` method. Submit a `channel` object to Netcaster, creating a new channel.

The last two functions represent a change of tack for JavaScript objects. Up until now, it has usually been sufficient to use the JavaScript `new` operator to create new objects. The approach used by Netcaster is more formal – the scriptwriter must request a new object from the Netcaster subsystem and submit it back after it has been worked on. Here is a simple example, assuming Netcaster is installed:

```
var nc_top = components["netcaster"];
nc_top.activate();                // make sure Netcaster is turned on
if (nc_top.active == true)
{
```

```
    import nc_top.getChannelObject; // Extract usable functions from
    import nc_top.addChannel;       // Netcaster, which is otherwise secure.

    var channel = nc_top.getChannelObject(); // new Channel object.

// work on the 'channel' object
    addChannel(channel);            // modified and 'submitted' to Netcaster.
}
```

The `Channel` object itself is a configuration object. It contains no methods, only properties. The scriptwriter's job is to assign values to the properties until the new channel is fully defined. To read about all the channel object properties, consult the Netscape Netcaster manual: `http://developer.netscape.com/library/documentation/netcast/devguide/index.html`.

Here is an example that shows the critical properties required to get going quickly:

```
// add to the above example:

channel.url = ("http://www.wrox.com");   // channel URL
channel.name = ("WROX Books");  // name appears in Channel Finder

channel.depth = 2;              // links deep the webcrawler will go

channel.intervalTime = 3600;    // optional update frequency in minutes
                                // No updates occur if not specified

channel.maxCacheSize = 1000000; // optional limit on disk space (bytes)

channel.mode = "webtop";        // appearance (others: "full", "window")
channel.type = 1;               // retrieval mechanism (2 = Castanet)
```

Remember that all this scripting is just put inside a normal HTML document.

JavaScript Inside Channels

Web pages designed for channel viewing force two constraints onto the scriptwriter.

Firstly, channels can be viewed offline. The web crawler inside Netcaster attempts to ensure that all files required for the channel are sniffed out when the channel is downloaded. However it only looks at URLs embedded in tags in HTML documents. This means that any URLs referred to from inside JavaScript, such as Image pre-loading or random links will not work unless the URLs are also visible from HTML. The scriptwriter should therefore avoid these features.

Secondly, if the channel is displayed to the user in "webtop" or "full" mode, the scriptwriter can't really use `window.open()` to open new windows or use multi-window tricks such as help, because that will spoil the background effect of the channel. Scrollbars, toolbars and menus aren't available either. This puts all the responsibility on the scriptwriter to provide navigation mechanisms for the user. Apart from ordinary `<A HREF>` links, this means extensive use of Dynamic HTML.

Microsoft Channels

Channels plus the Active Desktop is the Microsoft equivalent of Netscape's Netcaster. Setting up channels doesn't particularly require any JavaScript, though, so it's not of much interest here. For more on Microsoft's Channels, try WROX's "Professional IE4 Programming". Of course, the pages that are displayed using Microsoft Channels are HTML pages similar to the ones that Netscape Netcaster uses, and being ordinary HTML they can contain client-side JavaScript in all the forms described elsewhere in this book.

JavaScript Inside Browser Objects

There is one further approach that allows JavaScript scripts to contribute something to a web Browser's behavior. Elsewhere we've described how basic client-side JavaScript is carried along with a HTML document and executed within the web browser's display. In this chapter we've seen how JavaScript scripts can affect a browser's state if applied in a select number of ways from the outside of the browser. The final option is to disguise JavaScript scripts as something else and get at the web browser as if by stealth, from the inside.

In order to do this we must hide the script inside some other thing that will be loaded into the browser, and then give it a chance to run. Technically this is not really different to normal client side JavaScript, since you are still loading content over the Web from elsewhere, but in practice it's more subtle, because none of the objects in the HTML page look like they have any JavaScript in them.

Most of these approaches are covered in other chapters in this book, so they're just listed for completeness here:

- ❑ Microsoft DHTML Scriptlets 1.0/HTML components. DHTML scriptlets/HTML components act like anonymous objects when loaded into Internet Explorer, and it's not obvious that there is any JavaScript inside them. Chapter 22 discusses scriptlets in more detail.
- ❑ Microsoft Scriptlets 2.0 looks just like any other ActiveX/OLE/COM object and if there's any JavaScript at work, it's non-obvious.
- ❑ We can always can fall back on the mighty eval() feature of the core JavaScript language. If our browser page has access to a cookie, or some form data, or some user input, or a GET-style URL with a query string, and in any of those cases the data happens to be JavaScript statements stored in a string, then they can be promptly executed by the use of eval(). This function is discussed in some detail in Chapter 3.

One final, rather brain-bending possibility involves this bit of HTML, which contains primarily a Java (not JavaScript) applet:

```
<HTML><BODY>

<APPLET CODEBASE="local" CODE="start.class" HEIGHT=10 WIDTH=10 MAYSCRIPT>

</BODY></HTML>
```

The <APPLET> tag, innovated by Netscape is the main way of embedding Java applets in an HTML document. Although JavaScript scripts have access to Java applet internals, in the same way that JavaScript scripts have access to plugins, Java applets don't always have access to JavaScript objects. The MAYSCRIPT attribute supplied by the HTML author grants permission for that to happen.

With the MAYSCRIPT attribute turned on, code in the Java applet (written in Java, of course) can reach out of the applet page into the rest of the HTML page and mess around with it a bit – poking into form elements, doing Dynamic HTML or calling existing JavaScript functions that were embedded in the HTML. Of course, you need to learn Java to understand what the applet's intentions are. That's all well and good, but there's no hidden JavaScript so far.

We've seen briefly that there are versions of the JavaScript interpreter written in Java, such as FESI and Rhino. What if part of the applet loaded by this page contains a JavaScript interpreter written in Java? What if another part of the applet contains a JavaScript script, or a Rhino-compiled JavaScript script? The script saved in the applet is then run by the interpreter in the applet. The script's goal is to reach out into the HTML in the browser to run scripts embedded in the HTML that run on the interpreter that normally accompanies the browser and...aargh, it's all too much! The point is that there are numerous and sophisticated combinations of Java and JavaScript interpreters when they act together. We'd need to describe the Java Language and some complex interactions between the two languages to properly understand what's going on. Suffice to say scripts can lurk inside applets (perhaps more simply than this scenario, too) and they can be executed in the normal browser environment. Moral to the story: Don't use MAYSCRIPT unless you trust the applets you are using.

Documentation on LiveConnect, which is the Netscape interface between Java and JavaScript in the browser, at http://developer.netscape.com will point you into the right direction if you want to explore this further.

Summary

This chapter has described all the cracks and crevices outside an HTML document into which JavaScript scripts can be stuffed which still having some relevance to the browser environment.

Although HTML pages are the most common place to find JavaScript, there are diverse options. Netscape is increasingly dependent on the language for a variety of configuration tasks, and in fact some features of the browser can only be activated by explicit use of specially named and placed scripts. Although this isn't the case for Internet Explorer, that browser is instead well exposed to the Microsoft Windows environment – WSH and JScript scripts can be brought to bear in a number of administrative ways.

Browsers are also sufficiently complex now that it's possible to break JavaScript away from the traditional embedded-in-HTML role in a number of ways. Component objects of Internet Explorer can be exploited to drive mini-browsers with varying features. Channels and desktop modes of normal browsers can be activated with JavaScript and allow display of web content in non-traditional formats outside an ordinary browser window.

Finally, because JavaScript is interpreted, anywhere that an interpreter and some script source can be hidden away and then loaded into a browser, becomes a possible vehicle for attacking the browser-scripting problem from an innovative angle. Components of JavaScript and integrated interactions with Java allow for complex scripting possibilities – a subject only touched on here.

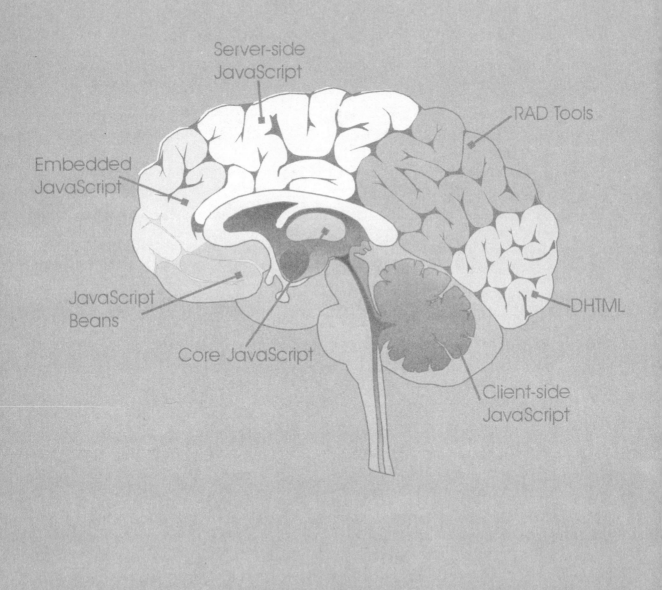

Server-side
JavaScript

RAD Tools

Embedded
JavaScript

JavaScript
Beans

Core JavaScript

Client-side
JavaScript

DHTML

Creating a JavaScript Family Tree Photo Album

Now that we've had a look at much of the potential of JavaScript, now seems like an appropriate time to see how this all works in practice and to apply our knowledge to a substantial project. In this chapter, we will look at a case study which uses JavaScript to create a Family Tree Photo Album. The album will allow us to manage and display photographs of our current family, as well as ancestors, in a very-easy-to-find manner over the Internet.

We will start (as all projects should!) by considering the specific requirements of the application. Then we will discuss alternative design approaches and tradeoffs. Finally, we will examine in detail the code of the implementation. In fact, we will look at two different implementations of the project within this chapter.

One feature of this case study is that all the programming logic will be coded in JavaScript, with a little help from the browser's object model, DHTML, and Java. By the end of this project, we will have hands-on experience of:

- ❑ Working with JavaScript and DHTML to create dynamic attributes and dynamic content.
- ❑ Creating a re-usable tree controller using only JavaScript and DHTML.
- ❑ Using JavaScript to assist in submitting a form through e-mail, without server-based CGI.
- ❑ Simulating the operation of a cross-browser compatible modal dialog box using JavaScript.
- ❑ Embedding a Java applet into a web page, and interfacing it to work with JavaScript.
- ❑ Writing JavaScript code that will work on the latest versions of both Netscape and Microsoft browsers (Netscape 4.61 and IE 5.0).

❑ Implementing a tree controller that works with version 4.x and later browsers.

❑ Creating a tree controller solution that works with Netscape 3+ browsers.

Before we can proceed further, let us take a quick look at how the application that we're building will actually work.

The Photo Album Application

This is how we want our Family Tree Photo Album to look when it's completed:

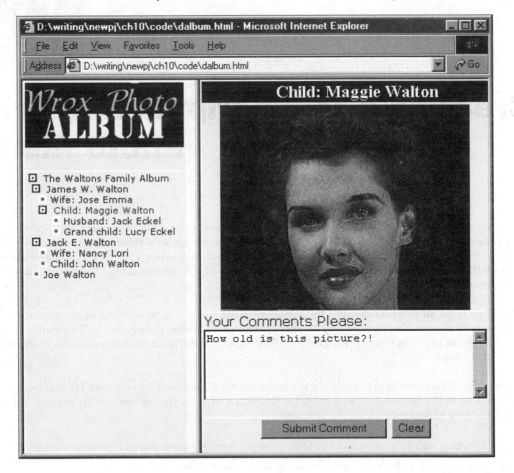

The user will typically:

❑ Navigate through the family tree by clicking on the left pane, collapsing or expanding subtrees.

❑ View the photograph of a family member by clicking on his or her name in the tree.

❑ Submit a comment to the webmaster on any family member picture.

The page will consist of two frames:

- A Tree Controller Page (the left-hand frame), which will allow the user to navigate through the family tree.
- A Photo Display Page (on the right), where the picture of the family member will appear, and where the user will be given the chance to send a comment to the webmaster.

When a user submits a comment, he or she should get a chance to confirm the message before it is sent.

Requirements of the Project

Other requirements for the project are that:

- The application should work with the latest versions of the two major browsers (Internet Explorer 5.0 and Netscape Communicator 4.61).
- No CGI (server-side processing) support will be available; comments will have to be submitted via e-mail.

Implementation Strategy

We will actually be working through three different versions of the project. In the first version, we will work with Internet Explorer 4/5 and the DHTML that it supports. This will illustrate some of the power of the Microsoft object model and its implementation of DHTML. We will be building a reusable tree controller completely in raw JavaScript. It will also give us a chance to see how JavaScript can be put to good use building a relatively complex application.

When we've got the application running smoothly in Internet Explorer, we will look at the problems that must be overcome to build a cross-browser version of the page. The second version of our project will have cross-browser compatibility for Netscape 4.x and Internet Explorer 4+ versions. Since these browser versions support DHTML (although with substantially different browser object models), we can accomplish a reasonable compromise.

In the third and final version, we examine the work required to make our application compatible with Netscape 3.0 browsers. Version 3.x browsers do not support DHTML, so we will need another solution. Much of the complexity goes away in this version because we take the "easy way out" and use a pre-fabricated component to implement the tree controller.

Designing the Application

All of our application versions will share the same basic design; only the implementation (and coding) differs. The basic problems that we must solve in the application are to:

- Implement a tree controller which graphically displays hierarchical data.
- Dynamically change the picture and title displayed in the Photo Display Page when the user clicks on a tree controller link.
- Display a pop-up modal dialog box.
- Submit comments via e-mail from a form on the page.

A Tree Controller Displaying Hierarchical Data

Our approach here is to introduce a simple text-based description language to describe the family tree data. Next, we create a mini-parser which scans this description and builds the actual graphic tree for the controller. We will call our description language the mini-Hierarchical Data Markup Language (mHDML). The figure below illustrates this process:

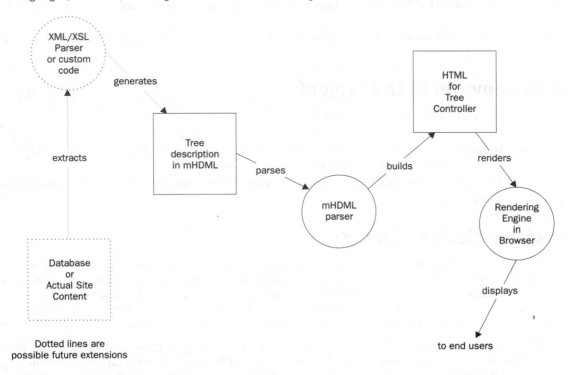

The additional flexibility, as illustrated in this figure, is the possibility of generating the actual mHDML automatically using a server-based custom process or XML/XSL (Chapters 11 to 14 will show you how to use JavaScript on the server). It is still a good idea to maintain mHDML as an intermediate stage because it avoids the necessity of a client which supports an XML parser. This allows the tree display to vary as the actual server content changes – for example, if new family members are added. Another possibility might be a tree view which navigates to an Internet site and which is automatically updated.

Changing Pictures and Titles Dynamically

To change the picture and title displayed on the Photo Display frame, there are two possible approaches:

❑   Directly modify the attributes of the associated <DIV> and <IMG> tags, causing the browser's rendering engine to display the new data.

❑   Send data for a new title and a new image to JavaScript code within the Photo Display frame, and get the JavaScript code to generate the actual HTML to display that new data.

It turns out that we will be using both methods, the first one in our first, IE-specific implementation, and the second in the last two versions.

Displaying a Modal Dialog Box

If the browser supports display of a modal dialog, it will obviously be a trivial matter to achieve this. In our Microsoft-specific solution, we will use IE5 support for modal dialogs. However, Netscape browsers unfortunately do not support modal dialog boxes directly in any reliable cross-platform manner (although Netsacpe 4.x on Windows does support a modal dialog option). To ensure backwards compatibility with version 3.x browsers, we have to emulate the behavior of a modal dialog box by repeatedly setting the focus. We will design a solution in this way which will work with both Netscape and IE.

Submitting a Form Using E-mail

Fortunately, this is a standard feature of both leading browsers. The general approach is to use a specific ACTION attribute in the <FORM> tag:

```
<FORM NAME="myform" ACTION="mailto:lsing@working.com"
      ENCTYPE="text/plain" METHOD="post">
```

The form data will be submitted as an e-mail to the recipient (in this case, lsing@working.com), in "text/plain" or unencoded format. You will have to change the e-mail address in the source code during testing, so that you will receive the test e-mail yourself, instead of the webmaster or systems administrator.

Obviously, the browser must be configured to send e-mail for this to work properly. In Internet Explorer 5, you must ensure that Outlook Express is the default application for sending and receiving e-mail. In Netscape 4.61, configure the Mail & Newsgroups setting under Edit | Preferences. In earlier versions of the browsers, the actual method of configuration may vary.

The Family Tree

This screenshot shows the family tree that we will be working with. It belongs to a fictitious family called the Waltons.

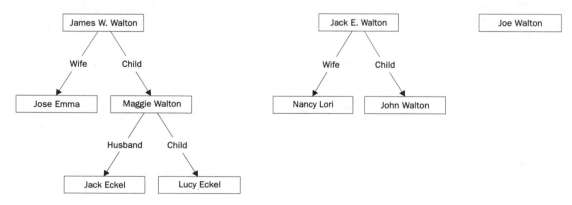

The associated picture files of each family member are:

Name	JPG file
James W. Walton	WALT1.JPG
Jose Emma	WALT2.JPG
Maggie Walton	WALT3.JPG
Jack Eckel	WALT4.JPG
Lucy Eckel	WALT5.JPG
Jack E. Walton	WALT6.JPG
Nancy Lori	WALT7.JPG
John Walton	WALT8.JPG
Joe Walton	WALT9.JPG

These picture files can be found in the source code distribution.

An IE-Specific DHTML Application

As we stated earlier, our first solution will be created using Internet Explorer 5, but will also be tested to ensure compatibility with Internet Explorer 4.01. It makes extensive use of JavaScript and DHTML.

The Main Application Frame

The main application page is called dalbum.html and can be found with the source code on the Wrox web site. It contains just a frameset, which links to two other HTML pages: ietree.html for the tree control page, and iepage.html for the Photo Display frame. A third page, called iedlg.html is used for a modal dialog when the user submits a comment from the Photo Display Page. Splitting up the page into frames in this way enables us to take a "divide and conquer" approach to development.

```
<HTML>
   <HEAD>
   </HEAD>
   <FRAMESET COLS="210,*">
      <FRAME SRC="ietree.html" NAME="treectrl" ALIGN="left" MARGINWIDTH=0
             NORESIZE SCROLLING="no">
      <FRAME SRC="iepage.html" NAME="albpage" MARGINWIDTH=0
             NORESIZE SCROLLING="no">
   </FRAMESET>
</HTML>
```

Implementing the Photo Display Page

The Photo Display Page consists of three general areas:

- ❑ Title area
- ❑ Picture area
- ❑ Comments form

We will build a table to manage the layout of the three areas; each area will occupy one cell in the table. We will use a `<DIV>` tag to mark out the title area, giving it a custom white-on-black format, and providing us with the ability to change its content dynamically later on. The picture area consists simply of a straightforward `<IMG>` element, whose `SRC` attribute we will modify when we want to display different photos. The comment form is a standard `<FORM>` element. We will create a custom `SUBMIT` button handler for this form. Clicking the submit button will launch a modal dialog box confirming the message.

Creating a Modal Dialog Box

Creating a modal dialog box is simple using DHTML in IE5 (this also works in IE4). It can be accomplished through the `showModalDialog()` method of the `window` object. The syntax for this method is:

```
var returnValue = window.showModalDialog(URL, Args, Options);
```

where:

Element Name	Description
`returnValue`	A value returned by the dialog box. It is returned by setting the `returnValue` property of the `window` object which represents the dialog box.
`URL`	The URL for the page to be displayed within the dialog box.
`Args`	A variable containing the arguments to be passed into the dialog box. The dialog box page can access this via the `window.dialogArguments` property.
`Options`	A string, in stylesheet format, controlling the width, height, placement, and appearance of the window. It can contain: `dialogWidth`, `dialogHeight`, `dialogTop`, `dialogLeft`, `center`, `help`, `resizable` and `status` attributes.

The modal dialog displayed by this command is a Win32 application modal dialog box. This ensures that the parent browser window cannot get focus back unless the dialog is closed.

Passing Data into Modal Dialog Boxes

The source code for the Photo Display Page is in the `iepage.html` file. Let us examine it in details. The first island of script code contains the `showform()` function. This function prepares the arguments for passing into the modal dialog box, and then it displays the dialog via the `showModalDialog()` method.

```
<HTML>
    <HEAD>
        <SCRIPT LANGUAGE="JScript">
            function showform()
            {
                var myArgs=new Array(2);
                myArgs[0]=document.all.cmttxt.value;
                myArgs[1]=document.all.showpic.src;

                var result=showModalDialog("iedlg.html", myArgs,
                    "dialogHeight:250px;dialogWidth:300px;status:no;help:no;");
            }
        </SCRIPT>
    </HEAD>
```

The variable `myArgs` is the array containing the arguments which are to be passed into the dialog box. The first item contains the comment entered by the user. This is taken from the `<TEXTAREA>` element called `cmttxt`, where the user will enter any comments. The second item is the name of the image file for the photo being displayed when the comment was entered. This name is available from the `SRC` attribute of our `<IMG>` tag. Note that the URL of the page displayed inside the dialog, the first parameter in the `showModalDialog()` call, is that for the `iedlg.html` page. We will examine the code for this page shortly.

Designing the Page Layout

In the next part of the Photo Display Page, we design the customized heading for the page. This part of the code places the actual text for the title, initially set to `"The Waltons Family Album"`, within a `<DIV>` tag called `picTitle`. When a user clicks on a selection from the tree controller, the controller will use DHTML to modify this title directly.

```
<BODY STYLE="font-size:8pt;font-family:Verdana,Arial,Helvetica;">
    <TABLE WIDTH=300 BORDER=0 ALIGN=left>
        <TR><TD bgcolor="black">
            <CENTER>
                <DIV ID="picTitle" STYLE="color:white; font-size:16pt;
                                          font-weight:bold;
                                          font-family:Times,Times Roman;">
                    The Waltons Family Album
                </DIV>
            </CENTER>
        </TD></TR>
```

Similar to the way in which the title was changed, the tree controller will also be able to modify the SRC attribute of the `<IMG>` tag directly when the user clicks on a selection.

```
<TR><TD BGCOLOR="lightyellow">
    <CENTER>
        <IMG NAME="showpic" SRC="album.gif" width=300 height=250>
    </CENTER>
</TD></TR>
```

Adding a Message Confirmation Dialog

The comment form is designed to be processed entirely in JavaScript. It does not submit the form to the server with the GET or POST method, as traditional forms do. Instead, when the Submit Comment button is pressed, the showform() function is called to display the modal dialog. We will design the dialog box to look like this:

This dialog is used to confirm the message, and allow the user to enter his or her name before actually sending the message.

```
    <TR><TD BGCOLOR="lightyellow">
       <FORM NAME="comment">
          Your Comments Please:<BR>
          <TEXTAREA NAME="cmttxt" COLS=40 ROWS=5></TEXTAREA><BR>
    </TD></TR>
    <TR><TD BGCOLOR="lightyellow">
       <CENTER>
          <INPUT TYPE="button" ONCLICK="showform()"
                 VALUE="Submit Comment">
          <INPUT TYPE="reset" VALUE="Clear">
       </CENTER>
    </FORM>
    </TD></TR>
    </TABLE>

    </BODY>
    </HTML>
```

That wraps it up for the Photo Display Page. There is very little JavaScript code, apart from the showform() function for displaying the modal dialog box. Let us turn our attention now to the design of the page which will represent this dialog box.

Implementing the Modal Dialog Box

The code for the Modal Dialog page is in the iedlg.html file in the source code. This is an important technique, so let's examine this code line by line. In the <HEAD> section, we first define a function called delayClose(), called when the dialog box is closed. There is a good reason why we need this function.

Recall that the message entered by the user will be submitted via e-mail. When a form is not submitted to the server via a GET or POST transaction, Internet Explorer will not close the form or transfer to another page. This means that we must explicitly implement the behavior that we want. In this case, we want to give the application some time to send the e-mail, and then close the window (our modal dialog box):

```
<HTML>
    <HEAD>
        <TITLE>Confirm Message</TITLE>
        <SCRIPT>
        <!--
            function delayClose() {
                setTimeout('top.close()',8000);
            }
```

Escaping Quotes in JavaScript Generated Forms

The next function we'll define in the <HEAD> section is the escQuote() function to escape quotation marks in the comment text. To understand why this function is necessary, we need to understand better how the message entered on the Photo Display Page ends up in the e-mail message sent from the Confirm Message modal dialog box. This diagram shows the process our code will follow, from the user entering a comment to an e-mail being sent to the webmaster:

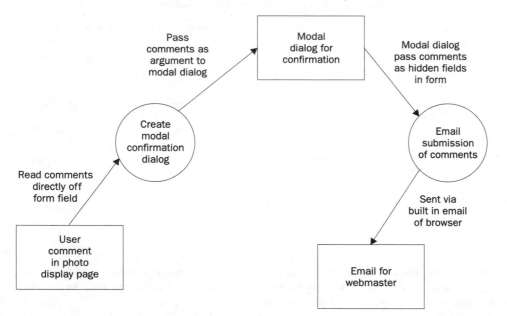

We can see that the argument passed into the modal dialog box is used to create part of the HTML confirmation page where the message is re-displayed. In fact, it is also used to create HTML for two hidden fields within the modal dialog box form. Conceptually, the code that will generate these two hidden fields will look something like this:

```
<SCRIPT>
    document.write("<INPUT NAME='pic' TYPE='hidden' VALUE='" +
                    window.dialogArguments[1] + "'>");
    document.write("<INPUT NAME='mesg' TYPE='hidden' VALUE='" +
                    window.dialogArguments[0] + "'>");
</SCRIPT>
```

Note how the hidden <INPUT> tags are made part of the HTML document. In particular, notice that the mesg field value – window.dialogArguments[0] – is written inside a pair of single quotes ('). This field value must not include an embedded single quote, otherwise the generated HTML code will not be syntactically correct. For this reason, we have written a JavaScript function called escQuote() to replace any embedded single quotes with an asterisk (*). We cannot use the standard JavaScript escape()/unescape() functions because the resulting message text will be emailed using the "text/plain" unencoded data type. Here's our implementation of the escQuote() function:

```
function escQuote(inStr)
{
    var tpArray = inStr.split("'");
    var escMsg;
    if (tpArray.length > 1)
        escMsg = tpArray.join("*");
    else
        escMsg = inStr;
    return escMsg;
}
//-->
</SCRIPT>
</HEAD>
```

The escQuote() function demonstrates the powerful methods provided by the JavaScript String object. We can replace all the single quotes within a string with asterisks by simply calling the split() method, removing the quotes and separating the string into an array of tokens; and followed by a join() method, gluing the array of tokens back using the new asterisk separator. Note that we assume that there is no regular expression support (i.e. cannot use the replace() method) to avoid having to change this function for our 3.x-compatible version later.

Argument Data inside a Modal Dialog Box

The next part of the modal dialog page redisplays the message entered so that users can confirm that this is really the message they want to send. This is done by accessing the dialogArguments array which we passed in as a parameter. The argument array is the second parameter of the original showModalDialog() call:

```
<BODY BGCOLOR="lightyellow" STYLE="font-size:12;
    font-family:Verdana,Arial,Helvetica;" SCROLL=no>
<TABLE WIDTH=100%>
    <TR>
        <TD>
            Your Message:<BR>
        </TD>
    </TR>
    <TR>
        <TD bgcolor="white" valign="top" height=120
            style="font-size:10;font-family:courier;">
            <SCRIPT>
                document.write(window.dialogArguments[0]);
            </SCRIPT>
        </TD>
    </TR>
```

Submitting Form Information via E-mail

Next comes the actual form that we will submit via e-mail. In the `<FORM>` tag, notice the
`ACTION="mailto…"` attribute used to specify e-mail processing. The `ENCTYPE` attribute is included
to ensure that the transmitted message is not escaped for special characters, but transmitted as
unfiltered text instead. The `METHOD="post"` attribute must be included to ensure the form is
submitted properly:

```
        <TR>
          <TD>
            <BR>
            <FORM NAME="myform"  ACTION="mailto:lsing@working.com"
                    ENCTYPE="text/plain" METHOD="post" ONSUBMIT="delayClose()">
              Name:  
              <INPUT NAME='myname' TYPE="text"><BR>
              <SCRIPT>
                document.write("<INPUT NAME='pic' TYPE='hidden' VALUE='" +
                                window.dialogArguments[1] + "'>");
                document.write("<INPUT NAME='mesg' TYPE='hidden' VALUE='" +
                                escQuote(window.dialogArguments[0]) + "'>");
              </SCRIPT>
              <INPUT TYPE="SUBMIT" VALUE="Send Comment Now">
              <INPUT TYPE="button" VALUE="Cancel" ONCLICK="top.close()">
            </FORM>
          </TD>
        </TR>
      </TABLE>
    </BODY>
  </HTML>
```

We have already seen why we have to include the `delayClose()` function. Here it is hooked in so
that the modal dialog box will close a few seconds after the user has submitted the message. We see
here the generation of the two hidden fields required for form submission. Note the use of the
`escQuote()` function on the actual message within the `mesg` hidden field.

This completes our coverage of the modal dialog box page. We will now look at the most complex
page in the entire project: the page that implements the tree controller, `ietree.html`.

A Tree Controller in Pure JavaScript

A tree controller displays hierarchical data in a graphical tree form, in a similar way to Windows
Explorer. The user can expand and collapse the various levels of the tree to increase or reduce the
level of detail respectively. For our sample family tree, a completely collapsed tree will look like this:

⊞ The Waltons Family Album

Clicking on the + sign at the left of the item will expand the tree, so that the tree controller shows all the first level nodes. This will appear thus:

⊡ The Waltons Family Album
⊞ James W. Walton
⊞ Jack E. Walton
• Joe Walton

Finally, if we expand the tree controller to its full level of details by clicking all the remaining + icons, we will see this:

⊡ The Waltons Family Album
⊡ James W. Walton
  • Wife: Jose Emma
  ⊡ Child: Maggie Walton
    • Husband: Jack Eckel
    • Grand child: Lucy Eckel
⊡ Jack E. Walton
  • Wife: Nancy Lori
  • Child: John Walton
• Joe Walton

By clicking on any link displayed, the tree controller will change the picture displayed on the Photo Display Page.

Rendering Collapsing Tree Elements

To render the collapsing tree elements, we need the following:

❑ Small icons which will indicate the state/type of the tree element (whether it is expanded or collapsed, whether it has children or not).

❑ A way to show and hide the tree elements dynamically.

We will use these three small graphic icon GIF files to display the state of the tree elements:

+   EXPAND. GIF

●   FIXED.GIF

   LEAF.GIF

A single tree element will always consists of one of these graphics, followed by a string to be displayed.

In HTML, we will mark off the icons and the text inside a <SPAN> tag. Using this approach will allow us to work on the combined graphics and text as a single unit. In particular, it allows us to control the visibility of the entire element. Here is an example of how it appears conceptually in HTML:

```
<SPAN><IMG SRC='expand.gif'>  Waltons Family</SPAN>
```

To show the actual level of the tree, we can use a varying number of spaces before the display of the image within the span. We will be constructing these indentations programmatically later on. For example, the HTML content of a second level element may be:

```
<SPAN>    <IMG SRC='fixed.gif'>  Sam Walton</SPAN>
```

Dynamic Attributes and Fly-by Animation

We use Internet Explorer's ability to accept dynamically defined attributes to help us implement fly-by animation. As the user moves the cursor over the selectable elements that are displayed in the tree control, each element will change color. This creates a "flashing effect" when the mouse is moved over the selection. In our case, the item will either be displayed in "dark" black or "bright" red. In order to implement this effect, we need to persist information on each element that supports it. The information we want to keep is:

❑ Whether an element should be fly-by animated.
❑ The current state of an element: dark or bright.

We will keep this information so that we can use one single set of event handlers for the entire document. Within the event handler, we will be checking these attribute values to determine what action to perform if any. Using dynamically defined attributes, we can add a marker attribute to the <SPAN> tag to mark a specific element as eligible for fly-by animation. We will use a new FLASHER attribute. Using such a dynamic attribute will enable us to stop certain elements flashing if the need arises (by leaving out the attribute). Now, a typical second level element may have the following HTML:

```
<SPAN FLASHER>    
   <IMG SRC='fixed.gif'>  Sam Walton
</SPAN>
```

One unique benefit of DHTML is the ability to define our very own custom attributes (like FLASHER). We can use the element.getAttribute() method to check the value of these custom attributes.

In implementing the actual fly-by animation, we use a CSS class to format the small-font red (or black) characters. By switching the class associated with an element in JavaScript, we can cause the tree element to flash. This doubles as a way to keep track of the current brightness of a flashing element. We can use the CSS class to mark a flashing element as either "dark" or "bright". The second level element with this improvement will end up with:

```
<SPAN CLASS="dark" FLASHER>    
   <IMG SRC='fixed.gif'>  Sam Walton
</SPAN>
```

Last but not least, if we need to be able to react to mouse clicks on these elements, we can simply make the inner content a hyperlink. For example:

```
<SPAN CLASS="dark" FLASHER>    
   <IMG SRC='fixed.gif'>  
   <A href="http://www.mynode.com/~samw/">Sam Walton</A>
</SPAN>
```

Or, if we need more flexible event handling than simply transferring to a URL, we can use an ONCLICK handler:

```
<SPAN CLASS="dark" FLASHER>    
   <IMG SRC='fixed.gif' ONCLICK="handleClk()">   Sam Walton
</SPAN>
```

Note that we restrict the onClick event handler here within the <IMG> tag because it is clicking the icons that will cause the tree to expand or collapse. Clicking on the text itself will instead cause the picture in the Photo Display Page.

Use of Cascading DIV and SPANS

The actual expanding and collapsing tree elements are implemented using cascading (or nested) <DIV> tag. We are going to take advantage of the ability of Microsoft's rendering engine to perform repeated layout immediately after the visibility of an element has been modified via the display:none style attribute.

Conceptually, a collapsed tree element looks like:

```
<SPAN CLASS="dark" FLASHER>... visible top level element ...</SPAN>
<DIV ID="out1d" STYLE="display:none">
   <SPAN CLASS="dark" FLASHER>...hidden sub level element...</SPAN>
   <SPAN CLASS="dark" FLASHER>...hidden sub level element...</SPAN>
   ...more hidden sub level elements...</DIV>
```

An expanded tree element can be expressed as:

```
<SPAN CLASS="dark" FLASHER>... visible top level element ...</SPAN>
<DIV ID="out1d">
   <SPAN CLASS="dark" FLASHER>...visible sub level elements...</SPAN>
   <SPAN CLASS="dark" FLASHER>... visible sub level elements...</SPAN>
   ...more visible sub level elements...</DIV>
```

Notice how we can expand or collapse an element simply by changing the display:none STYLE attribute. This can easily be done through the JavaScript code. To collapse an element:

```
document.all.out1d.style.display = "none";
```

Or to expand an element:

```
document.all.out1d.style.display = "";
```

While the technique detailed above can be used to expand and collapse one single tree element, it can also be used to expand and collapse multiple tree elements. These other elements can include other collapsible tree elements as well. Therefore, in the general case, this is how a final collapsible tree may look like in DHTML:

```
<SPAN CLASS="dark" FLASHER>  
   <IMG SRC='expand.gif'>  Collapsable Main
</SPAN>
<DIV ID="firslev" STYLE="display:none">
   <SPAN CLASS="dark" FLASHER>    
      <IMG SRC='expand.gif'>  Another Level
   </SPAN>
   <DIV ID="seclev" STYLE="display:none">
      <SPAN CLASS="dark" FLASHER>      
         <IMG SRC='leaf.gif'>  Inner Level
      </SPAN>

      <!-- ... more nested levels ... -->

   </DIV>
   <DIV>
      <SPAN CLASS="dark" FLASHER>  
         <IMG SRC='leaf.gif'>  A Standalone Level
      </SPAN>

      <!-- ... more collapsing elements ... -->

   </DIV>
</DIV>
```

If we orchestrate carefully the collapsing and expanding of these elements with changing the GIF icons and the end user's mouse clicks (via onClick event handlers), we can directly provide the tree controller functionality in JavaScript. We will see how this is done in code very shortly.

Tree Controller Algorithm

However, before we move on to some actual code, we have one last problem that needs some consideration: how will we structure the data for our family tree? Of course, one way would be to hard-code the tree according as above, with collapsing <DIV> elements. There are two disadvantages to this approach:

❑ Any change in the data can be difficult and error prone, because structured data is mixed hopelessly within HTML.

❑ The resulting tree controller is good only for this application, and we will have to hard-code all over again should we need to use the controller for another application.

Now, if we only have a language that can simply describe the tree data that we need to display to the tree controller, that would solve the problem. As well as describing the tree structure of the data, this language must also allow us to associate the appropriate behavior with "what to do" when the user selects the specific tree element. Those familiar with XML (Extensible Markup Language) will see that this is very close to the motivation for XML. However, for our purposes we do not need a formal schema nor the bulky complexity associated with typical XML parsers. Lacking a pre-fabricated solution, we strike out and invent our own simple description language.

A Simple Description Language

Keeping things as straightforward as possible, we want out mini-markup language to look like this:

```
<LVL0 ITEXT="desc text" IURL="action" ITARGET=""></LVL0>
   <LVL1 ITEXT= "desc text" IURL="action" ITARGET=""></LVL1>
   ...
     <LVLn ...></LVLn>
   ...
   <LVL1 ITEXT="desc text" IURL="action" ITARGET=""></LVL1>
```

We can see above how each successive level of the tree is marked out by a `<LVLn>` tag. `<LVL0>` is the outer-most level. Each higher level is collapsible within its parent. For example, all the `<LVL2>` elements immediately following a `<LVL1>` element are collapsible within the `<LVL1>` element, etc.

This allows us to describe the exact hierarchical relationship between the elements. The data itself is embedded in the tags as the custom dynamic attribute `ITEXT`. We have done this in order to facilitate parsing using JavaScript. The associated behavior is specified via the `IURL` and `ITARGET` dynamic attributes. During parsing, these attributes can be easily accessed by the parser using the `element.getAttribute()` method.

Since the specification for HTML 3+ requires that unknown tags be left alone by the browser, we can embed the entire tree description into the body of the document. Should we ever want to reuse the tree controller, all we will need to do will be to replace this description.

Parser Pseudo-code

A new data description language would be pretty useless without a way to parse and use the data. Thanks to IE's ability to access every element of an HTML page through its object model and its ability to define and access dynamic attributes, writing the required parser is actually quite a simple exercise.

Examining the mini-language that we have just defined, and matching it with the cascading `<DIV>` and `<SPAN>` HTML code that we must generate, we see the following patterns:

- ❑ For every transition from a lower `<LVL>` to the next higher `<LVL>` tag, we must generate an open `<DIV>` immediately after the `<SPAN>` for the element.

- ❑ For every transition from a higher `<LVL>` to a lower `<LVL>`, we must generate one or more `</DIV>` closing tags after generating the `<SPAN>` for the higher level element.

- ❑ For every element with the same `<LVL>` as the previous one, we simply generate the corresponding `<SPAN>`.

The first and second of these patterns will require us to be able to "look ahead" at least one `<LVL>` tag, or always remember the last `<LVL>` tag. This is necessary in order positively to identify a "transition" between levels. For the sake of simplicity, we will choose always to remember the last `<LVL>` tag.

Here is the final pseudo-code for our parser:

```
prevLevel = null;
current level = 0;
loop through all the <LVL> tags in the description;
   if (prevLevel = null)
   {
```

```
        // store the initial element information
        set prevLevel = <LVL> tag;
        set current level to <LVL> tag's level;
        skip to loop condition check;
    }

    if (<LVL> tag  > current level)
    {
        generate the previous level <SPAN>
        generate an open <DIV>
        set current level to <LVL> tag
    }
    else
    {
        generate the previous level <SPAN>
        if (<LVL> tag < current level)
            {
            generate as many </DIV> as necessary
            set current level to <LVL> tag
            }
    }
end loop;
// process the last element
repeat loop operation one more time by using a <LVL0> tag
```

We will see the actual JavaScript implementation of this pseudo-code shortly.

Implementing the Tree Controller

You will find the implementation of the entire tree controller in the `ietree.html` file in the source code. Let us take a detailed line-by-line look at how the above algorithm is implemented.

Stylesheet-Based Fly-by Animation

First, we must define the CSS attributes for the brightness of the display elements used during fly-by animation. We can see the `bright` class has red lettering, while the `dark` class has black lettering. We set a small font size and a hand-shaped cursor for `<SPAN>` elements. This will ensure that all our displayed text will be in a small font, since all our displayed text inside an element is inside `<SPAN>` tags, as we explained earlier:

```
<HTML>
    <HEAD>
        <STYLE>
            SPAN {cursor: hand ; font-size: 8pt; font-
family:Verdana,Arial,Helvetica;}
            .bright {color: red ; font-size: 8pt; font-
family:Verdana,Arial,Helvetica;}
            .dark {color: black ; font-size: 8pt; font-
family:Verdana,Arial,Helvetica;}
        </STYLE>
```

Defining State Variables for Tree Controller

Next, we will implement the parser. The parser will use a number of variables. Of specific importance here is the `builtHTML` string variable, which will hold the entire HTML page that we will generate during the parsing process. The approach we take in creating the tree controller is:

❑   To build the HTML code describing the entire controller by parsing the data and generating the `builtHTML` string.

❑ To create dynamic content consisting of the entire `builtHTML` string by replacing the `innerHTML` property of a `<DIV>` within an `ONLOAD` event handler for the document.

This approach, rather than adding elements as we parse, has two advantages:

❑ We avoid the unpleasant flickering of the tree controller display which occurs when elements are added one at a time.

❑ We speed up the generation process for the tree controller by rendering the HTML only once.

```
<SCRIPT LANGUAGE="JScript">
    var curLevel = 0;
    var prevElement = null;
    var prevLevel;
    var prevID;
    var builtHTML = "";
```

A Minimal Hierachical Markup Language Parser

The core code for the parser is contained in a function called `MakeTree()`. You can compare it to the pseudo-code covered earlier understand to how it works. By iterating through the `document.all` collection from the browser's object model, we have access to every tagged element inside the HTML document. Rememeber that this collection includes the non-HTML tags that we have defined for our mini-language. We speed up the tag scanning process somewhat by starting at the `<BODY>` tag, at `document.body.soureIndex+1`:

```
function MakeTree() {
    var coll = document.all;
    var level;
    var id;
    var tagBegin;
    for (i=document.body.sourceIndex+1; i<coll.length; i++) {
        switch (coll[i].tagName.substring(0,3)) {
            case "LVL":
                level = parseInt(coll[i].tagName.charAt(3));
                break;
            default:
                level = -1;
        }
        if (level!=-1) {
            id = i;
            addElem(coll[i], level, id);
        }
    }
    addElem(prevElement,0, prevID);
    divWrap();
    //    document.all.Debug.outerText = MyTree.innerHTML;
}
```

Notice that the core operation of the loop is factored out into the `addElem()` function. This is necessary to facilitate the same operation for the final element (see the pseudo-code).

The commented out code is for debugging. We will have more to say about this shortly.

Generating Cascading <DIV> and <SPAN> HTML Code

The addElem() function contains the guts of the parser operation. It performs the one-behind processing as we defined in our earlier pseudo-code. Notice how all the HTML code for the cascading <DIV> and <SPAN> elements are concatenated together in the builtHTML string variable.

```
function addElem(el, level, id) {
    if (prevElement == null)
    {
        prevElement = el;
        prevLevel = level;
        prevID = id;
        return;
    }
    var s = " ";
    for (var j=0; j<prevLevel; j++)
        s = s + s;

    if (level > curLevel)
    {
        builtHTML += "<SPAN STYLE='cursor:hand' CLASS='dark'  IURL='"
                  + prevElement.getAttribute('IURL')
                  + "' FLASHER>"
                  + s
                  + "<IMG SRC='expand.gif' ID='OUT"
                  + prevID.toString()
                  + "' CLASS='collapsible' >   "
                  + prevElement.getAttribute('ITEXT')
                  + "<BR></SPAN>"
                  + "<DIV ID='OUT"
                  + prevID.toString()
                  + "D' STYLE='display:none'  >";
        curLevel = level;
    }
    else
    {
        builtHTML += "<SPAN STYLE='cursor:hand'  CLASS='dark' IURL='"
                  + prevElement.getAttribute('IURL')
                  + "' FLASHER>"
                  + s
                  + "<IMG SRC='leaf.gif'> "
                  + prevElement.getAttribute('ITEXT')
                  + "<BR></SPAN>";
        if (level < curLevel)
        {
            for (var tplev = level; tplev < curLevel; tplev++)
                builtHTML += "</DIV>";
            curLevel = level;
        }
    }

    prevElement = el;
    prevLevel = level;
    prevID = id;
}
```

Adding Dynamic Contents using DHTML

To close off any pending open <DIV> tags, we will write a function named divWrap(). Another very important purpose of this function is actually to render our builtHTML string. We have a <DIV> placeholder in the document body, called MyTree, that is initially blank. By inserting the builtHTML string into this <DIV>, the tree control is immediately rendered. We perform this task by setting the innerHTML property of the MyTree element:

```
function divWrap() {
   while (curLevel > 0)
   {
      builtHTML +=        "</DIV>";
      curLevel--;
   }
   document.all.MyTree.innerHTML=builtHTML;
}
```

The next few functions in the source code are event handlers; we will cover them later since they do not relate directly to the rendering of the tree controller.

Data in Our Mini Hierachical Data Markup Language

The next portion of the file contains the <BODY> of the document. Note the hooking of the ONLOAD event handler to MakeTree(). This will ensure that the controller will be constructed properly once the page has finished loading.

The description of the family tree data is inserted right here. Using the custom <LVL> tags, we define the structure of the data for the tree. Notice how we have also embedded the behavioral information of which GIF file to display, for each element, via the IURL dynamic attribute. These tags are all ignored by the IE rendering engine since they are not recognized HTML tags.

```
<BODY  ONLOAD="MakeTree()">

<LVL0  ITEXT="The Waltons Family Album" IURL="album.gif" ITARGET=""></LVL0>
   <LVL1  ITEXT= "James W. Walton" IURL="walt1.jpg" ITARGET=""></LVL1>
      <LVL2  ITEXT="Wife: Jose Emma" IURL="walt2.jpg" ITARGET=""></LVL2>
      <LVL2  ITEXT="Child: Maggie Walton" IURL="walt3.jpg" ITARGET=""></LVL2>
         <LVL3  ITEXT="Husband: Jack Eckel" IURL="walt4.jpg" ITARGET=""></LVL3>
         <LVL3  ITEXT="Grand child: Lucy Eckel" IURL="walt5.jpg"
             ITARGET=""></LVL3>
   <LVL1  ITEXT="Jack E. Walton"  IURL="walt6.jpg" ITARGET=""></LVL1>
      <LVL2  ITEXT="Wife: Nancy Lori" IURL="walt7.jpg" ITARGET=""></LVL2>
      <LVL2  ITEXT="Child: John Walton" IURL="walt8.jpg" ITARGET=""></LVL2>
   <LVL1  ITEXT="Joe Walton"  IURL="walt9.jpg" ITARGET=""></LVL1>
```

Creating Placeholders for Dynamic Contents

Now we get on to the real start of the displayed HTML page. At the top, we have a logo, and the tree controller will be inside the <DIV> at the bottom. Initially, it is completely blank. Once we have executed our parser on the data description, the <DIV ID=MyTree> element will be filled up with the HTML code representing the tree controller.

```
<TABLE WIDTH=95% BORDER=0 ALIGN=left>
   <TR><TD>
      <IMG SRC="Logo.gif">
   </TD></TR>
   <TR><TD BGCOLOR="lightyellow"> </TD></TR>
   <TR><TD WIDTH=200 HEIGHT=340 VALIGN="top" BGCOLOR="lightyellow">
   <DIV ID=MyTree>
   </DIV>
```

Debugging Dynamic Content Pages

When creating dynamic contents, it is sometimes difficult to determine what went wrong if things do not display as expected. It is useful if we can see what our code actually generates. A useful debug technique is to define a placeholder for displaying the raw HTML text that is generated – in text form! We have included a `<DIV ID=Debug>` element for exactly this purpose. If you uncomment the debug line in the `MakeTree()` function, this area will be filled with the actual generated HTML from the parser. When enabling debugging, it is useful to load the `ietree.html` file directly into the browser instead of going through `dalbum.html`. Examining this generated HTML text will enable you to locate problems quickly.

```
    <DIV ID=Debug>
    </DIV>
    </TD></TR>
</TABLE>
```

Handling Mouse Clicks for Collapsing Elements

The next portion of the code sets the event handlers for the page. We are going to hook this handler for the entire document. This means the tree controller since the page contains nothing else.

```
<SCRIPT LANUGAGE="JScript">
   document.onclick = clickHandler;
   document.onmouseover = MakeBright;
   document.onmouseout = MakeDark;
</SCRIPT>

</BODY>
</HTML>
```

Now, we will examine the event handlers themselves. These functions are the ones we omitted earlier when we were examining the `<HEAD>` section of the page. In `clickHandler()`, we determine if the GIF icon of one of the tree elements has been clicked on. These icons are all assigned the attribute `CLASS="collapsible"` upon generation for easy identification. If such an icon is clicked on, we toggle the display attribute of its style to show or hide its associated `<DIV>` tree. We also swap the GIF file accordingly (between the square with a + inside and the square with a dot inside).

```
function clickHandler() {
   var colId, colElem ;
   var tpURL;
   gifElem = window.event.srcElement;

   if (gifElem.className -- "collapsible") {

      colId = gifElem.id + "D";
      colElem = document.all(colId);

      if (colElem.style.display == "none") {
         colElem.style.display = "" ;
         gifElem.src = "fixed.gif" ;
      } else {
         colElem.style.display = "none" ;
         gifElem.src = "expand.gif" ;
      }
   }
}
```

Handling Mouse Clicks for Photo Display and Title Changes

If the user has clicked on the text of one of the FLASHER elements, the mouse click will be associated with the <SPAN> element. Since the element should have been highlighted during the fly-by animation, we can check simply whether the element belongs to the bright class. Processing the click involves changing the photo and title on the Photo Display Page. This is done by extracting the file name to display from the dynamic attribute IURL, and setting the SRC attribute of the <IMG> tag, and the innerText property of the title <DIV> tag in the iepage.html frame.

```
if (gifElem.className == "bright")
{
    with (parent.frames[1].document.all)
    {
        showpic.src = gifElem.getAttribute("IURL");
        picTitle.innerText = gifElem.innerText;
    }
}
```

Helper Routines for Dynamic Fly-by Animation

MakeBright() and MakeDark() are two helper routines used to assist in highlighting and darkening the selectable element creating fly-by animation. They are hooked up to the MOUSEOVER event for the document. Inside the function, a check is made to ensure the element involved has the FLASHER attribute. If so, we will change the CSS class associated with the element, causing its appearance to change:

```
function MakeBright() {
    el = event.srcElement ;
    if (el.getAttribute("FLASHER") != null) {
        el.className = "bright" ;
    }
}

function MakeDark() {
    el = event.srcElement ;
    if (el.getAttribute("FLASHER") != null) {
        el.className = "dark";
    }
}
</SCRIPT>
</HEAD>
```

This concludes our coverage of the code for the version 1 solution. We are now ready to test the application.

Testing the Family Tree Photo Album

You can test the photo album application by opening the dalbum.html file inside your IE5 (or IE 4.X) browser. Here are some suggestions for testing/exploration:

❑ Expand and collapse the elements in the tree controller.

❑ Move the mouse around the elements in the tree controller, and see the fly-by animation.

❑ Click on a family member and see the title and photo displayed change.

❑ Fill in a comment and submit it to see the argument passing and modal dialog handling.

❑ Confirm and submit the comment from the modal dialog to see the delayed close routine, and e-mail based submission of the form.

❑ Enter a comment that contains a single quote, and read the confirmation of the message to see what happened.

❑ Modify or create your own tree control by changing the data description.

Once you're satisfied that everything is working as specified, you will be ready for some bad news. The bad news is that many things will simply not work in Netscape.

Things that Don't Work in Netscape

There are more than enough differences between Netscape's and Microsoft's versions of Dynamic HTML to ensure that our Photo Album application will not work on Netscape browsers. The list of differences is quite long, but we will look at some of the more important ones here:

❑ While supporting the <DIV> and <LAYER> tag, visibility toggle, and fine positioning, Netscape's page rendering engine does not reexecute when element attributes are changed; this alone makes the collapsing and expanding action of the tree controller extremely difficult to implement.

❑ Netscape's browser object model does not uniformly expose every non-HTML, user-defined tag as an object accessible from JavaScript.

❑ Netscape's Browser Object Model does not support dynamic content creation in the same way as Microsoft.

❑ Netscape has no built-in support for creating modal dialog boxes from JavaScript that is reliable across multiple versions or platforms

Because of these differences, getting the Photo Album to work by tweaking the same set of code is almost possible. Instead, we must reconsider our implementation strategy with a goal towards creating a cross-browser solution.

A Version 4.x Cross-Browser Application

We will overcome the differences between the browsers one at a time. The two most prominent problems that we must solve are:

❑ Creating a cross-browser tree controller.

❑ Creating cross-browser modal dialogs.

To create a cross-browser tree controller, we will need to either write new code or find some existing library code to use. Fortunately, such a library does exist.

Using the Netscape Collapsible List Library

Netscape provides a library of JavaScript code that does essentially what we have done in our tree controller, except that it works with Netscape's DHTML based on <LAYER> tags. As a bonus, this library also work reasonably within Internet Explorer 5/4.x using <DIV> tags. You can find the library code at this URL:

http://developer.netscape.com/docs/technote/dynhtml/collapse/list.js

The information on how to use this library is located at:

http://developer.netscape.com/docs/technote/dynhtml/collapse/index.html

Using this library greatly simplifies our coding for the tree controller. Essentially, we only need to create the list structures required and the library code takes care of the positioning, rendering, and event handling for us. Compared to our custom code, the library has the following minor disadvantages:

❑ The library does not handle fly-by animation, and it cannot be added easily.
❑ The list management and rendering routine is quite slow, especially if the list is large.
❑ The library does not support parsing of a generic list description language; hard-coding is required.

Despite these disadvantages, the library has one very important advantage: it works with 4.x versions of both Internet Explorer and Netscape browsers when used properly.

So let's take a look the code of our solution created using this library.

The Main Frame Document

The main HTML document is called nsalbum.html and again contains just a frameset with two frames:

```
<HTML>
    <HEAD>
    </HEAD>
    <FRAMESET COLS="325,*">
        <FRAME SRC="nstree.html" NAME="treectrl" ALIGN="left" MARGINWIDTH=0
            NORESIZE SCROLLING="no">
        <FRAME SRC="dpage.html" NAME="albpage" MARGINWIDTH=0
            NORESIZE SCROLLING="no">
    </FRAMESET>
</HTML>
```

Note that we are now using nstree.html for the tree control, and dpage.html for the photo display page. While nstree.hml hosts the tree control based on the collapsible list library, we will be creating dpage.html in such a way that it is fully reusable for our last version of the project.

Creating the Tree Controller

The tree controller code, as in all our versions, is confined to one HTML file, in this case nstree.html.

Here, `resize.js` is a JavaScript fix for Dynamic HTML rendering problems with Netscape 4.0x browsers during resizing. It ignores browser versions that do not exhibit the resize bug. The code can be downloaded from:

`http://developer.netscape.com/docs/technote/dynhtml/collapse/resize.js`.

The `list.js` file contains the actual library.

```
<HTML>
    <HEAD>
        <SCRIPT LANGUAGE="JavaScript1.2" SRC="resize.js"></SCRIPT>
        <SCRIPT LANGUAGE="JavaScript1.2" SRC="list.js"></SCRIPT>
```

Our main logic for creating the list to be displayed is contained within a function called `init()`. This is the `ONLOAD` handler for our tree controller, similar to our `MakeTree()` function in the first version. The function first tests for the browser version, and gives a warning if the browser version is not at least 4.0:

```
<SCRIPT LANGUAGE="JavaScript">

function init() {
    if(parseInt(navigator.appVersion) < 4) {
        alert("You need a 4.0+ browser to run this.");
        return;
    }
```

Next, we need to set the variables containing the height and width of each row within our tree. Here, we are using a height of 23 pixels, and a width depending on the size of the window. Note that `document.layers` will exist only for Netscape browsers. We also set the color of the list elements to white (`#ffffff`), and only the top-level element to visible.

```
    var height = 23;
    if(document.layers) width = window.innerWidth  -5 ;
    else width = document.body.clientWidth - 5;

    var backColor = "#ffffff";
    var visible = true;
    var leafVisible = false;
```

In the next large section of the code we will create the sublists for our family tree data, and attach them one at a time to the list or sublist with which they are associated. Each sublist is exactly equivalent to a collapsible `<DIV>` section in our first version. The `addList()` method is used to attach a sublist to an existing list or sublist. A higher level element can be associated with each sublist during the `addList()` call; this is identical to the `<SPAN>` associated with each collapsible `<DIV>`. The following section of code sets up the complete tree:

```
nsTree = new List(visible, width, height, backColor);

mySub = new List(leafVisible, width, height, backColor);
nsTree.addList(mySub, "The Waltons Family Album");

mySub2 = new List(leafVisible, width, height, backColor);
mySub2.addItem("<A HREF='dpage.html?walt2.jpg&Wife%3a%20Jose%20Emma' "+
            "TARGET='albpage'>Wife: Jose Emma</A>");
mySub.addList(mySub2,  "<A HREF='dpage.html?walt1.jpg&James%20W.%20Walton' "+
                    "TARGET='albpage'>James W. Walton<A>");
```

```
mySub3 = new List(leafVisible, width, height, backColor);
mySub3.addItem("<A HREF='dpage.html?walt4.jpg&Husband%3a%20Jack%20Eckel' "+
        "TARGET='albpage'>Husband: Jack Eckel</A>");
mySub3.addItem("<A HREF='dpage.html?walt5.jpg&Grand%20child%3a%20Lucy%20Eckel'"+
        " TARGET='albpage'>Grand child: Lucy Eckel</A>");
mySub2.addList(mySub3, "<A HREF='dpage.html?walt3.jpg&Child%3a%20Maggie%20"+
                "Walton' TARGET='albpage'>Child: Maggie Walton</A>");

mySub4 = new List(leafVisible, width, height, backColor);
mySub4.addItem("<A HREF='dpage.html?walt7.jpg&Wife%3a%20Nancy%20Lori' "+
        "TARGET='albpage'>Wife: Nancy Lori</a>");
mySub4.addItem("<A HREF='dpage.html?walt8.jpg&Child%3a%20John%20Walton' "+
        "TARGET='albpage'>Child: John Walton</A>");
mySub.addList(mySub4, "<A HREF='dpage.html?walt6.jpg&Jack%20E.%20Walton' "+
                "TARGET='albpage'>Jack E. Walton</A>");

mySub.addItem("<A HREF='dpage.html?walt9.jpg&Joe%20Walton' "+
        "TARGET='albpage'>Joe Walton</A>");
```

Since there is no parser available, we have encoded the IURL information directly into the item as a hyperlink with an extended URL. This will enable the user to click directly on the link to the change the picture being displayed.

A Word on Extended URL Hyperlinks

The extended URL we create simulates a CGI GET query by adding a question mark (?) at the end of the URL, and a set of name/value pairs afterwards. One valid URL may be:

```
http://www.walt.com/dpage.html?walt1.jpg&Title
```

The page being loaded, dpage.html in the Photo Display Page frame, can then examine its own URL and pull the name/value pairs in the query. It can then use this information to generate HTML code that will display the corresponding picture and title.

One thing to be careful of here is that the parameters after the question mark must not contain blanks or other special characters. Instead, it should be an escaped URL. This means that blanks and certain special characters must be replaced by their Unicode equivalent and as %xx where xx is the hexidecimal Unicode value for the character.

Escaping Special Characters for the Extended URLs

We can see the escaping of special characters for the form GET URLs. Here is the decoding for the special characters that we have used in the code:

Character	Code
space	%20
:	%3a

Compared to the previous Tree Controller page, this one is barren! The JavaScript library has truly taken much of the complexity out of the equation.

Setting Fonts Used in Lists/Sublists

To change the default font (`<BASEFONT>`), the `setFont()` method must be called for each list or sublist that is created. The next section of code changes the font for the entire list to small blue type:

```
nsTree.setFont("<FONT FACE='Verdana,Arial,Helvetica' COLOR='blue' "+
               "SIZE=-1><BOLD>","</BOLD></FONT>");
mySub.setFont("<FONT FACE='Verdana,Arial,Helvetica' COLOR='blue' "+
               "SIZE=-1><BOLD>","</BOLD></FONT>");
mySub2.setFont("<FONT FACE='Verdana,Arial,Helvetica' COLOR='blue' "+
               "SIZE=-1><BOLD>","</BOLD></FONT>");
mySub3.setFont("<FONT FACE='Verdana,Arial,Helvetica' COLOR='blue' "+
               "SIZE=-1><BOLD>","</BOLD></FONT>");
mySub4.setFont("<FONT FACE='Verdana,Arial,Helvetica' COLOR='blue' "+
               "SIZE=-1><BOLD>","</BOLD></FONT>");
```

The very last part of the `init()` function simply creates the tree by calling the `build()` method. The two parameters specify the x and y co-ordinates in pixels relative to the top-left corner of the current window. In this case, we use `y=95` to position the control below the logo:

```
    nsTree.build(8,95);
}
</SCRIPT>
```

Apart from specifying the `ONLOAD` event handler, the rest of the `nstree.html` file contains style information and the fixed `<DIV>` elements that are necessary for Internet Explorer compatibility. The library requires that one of these `lItemx` elements be created for each level of the list. In our case, we have nine levels, so we have created items `0` to `8`:

```
    <STYLE TYPE="text/css">
        #lItem0 { position:absolute; }
        #lItem1 { position:absolute; }
        #lItem2 { position:absolute; }
        #lItem3 { position:absolute; }
        #lItem4 { position:absolute; }
        #lItem5 { position:absolute; }
        #lItem6 { position:absolute; }
        #lItem7 { position:absolute; }
        #lItem8 { position:absolute; }
    </STYLE>
</HEAD>

<BODY ONLOAD="init();">
    <IMG WIDTH="191" HEIGHT="79" SRC="Logo.gif">
    <DIV ID="lItem0" NAME="lItem0"></DIV>
    <DIV ID="lItem1" NAME="lItem1"></DIV>
    <DIV ID="lItem2" NAME="lItem2"></DIV>
    <DIV ID="lItem3" NAME="lItem3"></DIV>
    <DIV ID="lItem4" NAME="lItem4"></DIV>
    <DIV ID="lItem5" NAME="lItem5"></DIV>
    <DIV ID="lItem6" NAME="lItem6"></DIV>
    <DIV ID="lItem7" NAME="lItem7"></DIV>
    <DIV ID="lItem8" NAME="lItem8"></DIV>
</BODY>

</HTML>
```

Simulating A Modal Dialog Box

The lack of native modal dialog support means that we must simulate modal dialog behavior using standard HTML windows. The `window.open()` method can be used for creating such a dialog. In order to simulate modal behavior, we must ensure that the parent browser window will not steal the focus away from the dialog. One naive way to attempt to accomplish this is to use `setTimeout()` to create a timer that will regularly set focus back to the dialog window.

This actually will not work as intended. The main reason is that there are form elements within the modal dialog that can receive focus. When the timer sets the focus to the dialog window, the form element that the user is interacting with will lose focus. While this will maintain the dialog in focus all the time, it will also create an endless lockup loop.

To get around this problem, we can add a variable to the dialog. This variable will be set in the `ONFOCUS` handler of each active form element. Since the variable tracks which HTML control has the focus at any given time, the timer can then set the focus back to the element that was in focus.

This cross-browser technique works relatively well in simulating the behavior of modal dialog boxes.

The New Photo Display Page

You can find the new Photo Display Page as `dpage.html` in the source code. Let us take a look at how this page will decode the extended URL and generate the appropriate title and picture links

Extracting Values from the Extended URL

The script code right at the beginning of the page will decode the extended URL. First and foremost, the entire URL (including all the information in the query) will be available through the browser's object model via the `document.location` property.

We assign the full URL to a string array called `tpstr`, and then call the `String` object's `split` method with `"?"` as the argument. This places the query string (if there is one) in the second element of the resulting array, or `paramList[1]`.

Note that we also include the Netscape 4.0 resize rendering fix, the `resize.js` script:

```
<HTML>
   <HEAD>
      <SCRIPT LANGUAGE="JavaScript1.2" SRC="resize.js"></SCRIPT>
      <SCRIPT>
         var urlList;
         var tpstr = new String(document.location);
         var paramList = tpstr.split("?");
         var mytitle; var mygif;
```

The next part of the code will set a variable called `mytitle` to the title we want to display and a variable called `mygif` to the name of the GIF file to display. We will use default of `"Walton Family Album"` and `"album.gif"` if no parameters are found. Note how we need to split up the title and GIF parameters, and unescape the title (which might contain hex code representing blanks and special characters):

```
if (paramList.length > 1)
{
  urlList = paramList[1].split("&");
  mytitle = unescape(urlList[1]);
  mygif = urlList[0];
}
else
{
  mytitle = "Walton Family Album";
  mygif = "album.gif";
}
```

Escaping Quotes in Generated HTML Code

Next comes a function that we are already familiar with. This one swaps any single quotes (') with an asterisk (*). It is needed here for the same reason as in the previous version: when we generate the hidden fields in the modal dialog box form, we need to make sure it does not contain any single quotes.

One interesting thing to note is that we will not have a separate HTML file for the modal dialog form. Instead, we will have the code to generate the form right inside dpage.html.

```
function escQuote(inStr)
{
    var tpArray = inStr.split("'");
    var escMsg;
    if (tpArray.length > 1)
        escMsg = tpArray.join("*");
    else
        escMsg = inStr;
    return escMsg;
}
```

Using window.open() to Simulate Modal Dialog

The showform() function in this version uses the window.open() method instead of the showModalDialog() method, since this method works on both browsers. It is important to note that this function actually returns a reference to the newly created window, which we will assign to a variable called mywin. The fact that we can maintain a reference (in the parent window) to the newly created child window allows us to do something not possible with the showModalDialog() method. We will see what this is in the next section.

```
function showform()
{
    var mywin= window.open("", "newwin", "resizable=no,width=300,height=250");
```

Generating Dialog Content Dynamically With document.write()

That's right: we will actually generate the entire content of what goes into the modal dialog right here within dpage.html. There is no need to figure out how to pass parameters into the modal dialog, since we write() the data right into the HTML. Note how we break up the <SCRIPT> tag using string concatenation (see Chapter 3) within document.write().

```
with (mywin.document)
{
    open();
    write("<HTML><HEAD><SCRI" + "PT>var myElem = self; "+
        "setTimeout('setmyfocus()',500);");
    write("function setmyfocus() { ");
    write("myElem.focus(); setTimeout('setmyfocus()',500);}");
    write("</SCRI" + "PT><TITLE>Verify Comment</TITLE></HEAD>");
    write("<BODY BGCOLOR='lightyellow' STYLE='font-size:12;"+
        "font-family:Verdana,Arial,Helvetica;' SCROLL=no>");
    write("<TABLE WIDTH=100%><TR><TD>Your Message:<BR>");
    write("</TD></TR><TR><TD bgcolor='white' valign='top' height=120 "+
        "style='font-size:10;font-family:courier;'>");
    write(document.forms[0].elements[0].value);
    write("</TD></TR><TR><TD><BR><FORM NAME='myform' "+
        "ACTION='mailto:lsing@interlog.com' ENCTYPE='text/plain' "+
        "METHOD='post' >");
    write("Name:  <BR><INPUT NAME='myname' TYPE='text' "+
        "ONFOCUS='myElem=this'><BR>");
    write("<INPUT TYPE='hidden' NAME='pic' VALUE='" + mygif +"'>");
    write("<INPUT TYPE='hidden' NAME='mesg' VALUE='" +
        escQuote(document.forms[0].elements[0].value) + "'>");
    // onsubmit does not work reliably with e-mail on NS4.61
    write("<INPUT TYPE='submit' VALUE='Send Comment Now' ONFOCUS='myElem=this' "+
        "ONCLICK='setTimeout(\"self.close()\",10000)'>");
    write("<INPUT TYPE='button' VALUE='Cancel' ONFOCUS='myElem=this' "+
        "ONCLICK='self.close()'></FORM>");
    write("</TD></TR></TABLE>");
    write("</BODY></HTML>");
    close();
    }
}
</SCRIPT>
</HEAD>
```

Maintaining Focus on A Modeless Window

It's now time to take a detour and examine the HTML code for rendering the dialog box; this is the very same HTML that we `document.write()` into the dialog. The first part sets up the timer that will repeatedly set focus to the window, simulating modal behaviour. Notice that the focus is set to a variable called `myElem`:

```
<HTML>
    <HEAD>
        <SCRIPT>
            var myElem = self;
            setTimeout('setmyfocus()',500);");
            function setmyfocus() {
                myElem.focus();
                setTimeout('setmyfocus()',500);
            }
        </SCRIPT>
```

The next part repeats the message entered, so that the user can confirm it:

```
        <TITLE>Verify Comment</TITLE>
    </HEAD>
    <BODY BGCOLOR='lightyellow' STYLE='font-size:12;
                 font-family:Verdana,Arial,Helvetica;'
        SCROLL=no>
    <TABLE WIDTH=100%>
        <TR><TD>Your Message:<BR>
        </TD></TR>
        <TR><TD bgcolor='white' valign='top' height=120 style='font-size:10;
                font-family:courier;'>
            ...message entered by user...
        </TD></TR>
```

Next comes our form. Notice how every element in the form has an ONFOCUS handler that updates the myElem variable. This is necessary to ensure that focus is set to the correct element by the timer.

From a purist's point of view, the dialog is not actually modal. It is still possible for the user to type quickly into the main browser window or to click one of its elements. Assuming that your user is vicious, and attempts to beat your 0.5 second timer, you may have some problems with this implementation. In practice, the implementation is more than adequate to simulate modal behavior.

```
      <TR><TD><BR>
        <FORM NAME='myform' ACTION='mailto:lsing@interlog.com'
              ENCTYPE='text/plain' METHOD='post'>
        Name:  <BR>
        <INPUT NAME='myname' TYPE='text' ONFOCUS='myElem=this'><BR>
        <INPUT TYPE='hidden' NAME='pic' VALUE='...GIF Name...'>
        <INPUT TYPE='hidden' NAME='mesg'
              VALUE='...Quote Escaped Message...'>
        <INPUT TYPE='submit' VALUE='Send Comment Now'
              ONFOCUS='myElem=this'
              ONCLICK='setTimeout("self.close()",10000)'>
        <INPUT TYPE='button' VALUE='Cancel' ONFOCUS='myElem=this'
              ONCLICK='self.close()'>
        </FORM>
      </TD></TR>
    </TABLE>
  </BODY>
</HTML>
```

The values of the two hidden fields pic and mesg are readily available within this frame, so we simply use document.write() to write the values in. Note that we do not use ONSUBMIT, but instead ONCLICK to start a timer before the dialog window is closed. It turns out that using ONSUBMIT to submit an e-mail is less than reliable for Netscape 4.61. Hooking the event handler for the ONCLICK event will work for both Navigator and Internet Explorer.

Generating Title and Picture Display

Since we have already set the mytitle and mygif variables earlier, it is a trivial matter to generate the HTML code with document.write() to display the correct title and image.

```
<BODY  STYLE="font-size:8pt;font-family:Verdana,Arial,Helvetica;">

  <TABLE WIDTH=300 BORDER=0 ALIGN=left>
```

Handling 3.x Level Browsers

For 3.x level browsers, we cannot use the CSS formatting and <DIV> tags to render the nice white-on-black title. Instead, we simply use a larger font to display the title:

```
      <SCRIPT LANGUAGE="JavaScript">
        document.write("<TR><TD");
        if (navigator.appVersion.substring(0,1) == "3")
        {
          mytitle = "<CENTER><FONT SIZE=+2>" + mytitle + "</FONT></CENTER>";
          document.write(">");
        }
        else
          document.write(" BGCOLOR='black'>");
      </SCRIPT>
```

The rest of the code can remain since even 3.x browsers support changing the SRC of an < IMG > tag:

```
<CENTER>
    <DIV ID="picTitle" STYLE="color:white;font-size:16pt;"+
            "font-weight:bold; font-family:Times,Times Roman;">
        <SCRIPT>
            document.write(mytitle);
        </SCRIPT>
    </DIV>
</CENTER></TD></TR>
<TR><TD BGCOLOR="lightyellow">
    <CENTER>
        <SCRIPT>
            document.write("<IMG ID='showpic' SRC='" + mygif +
                    "' WIDTH=300 HEIGHT=250>");
        </SCRIPT>
    </CENTER>
</TD></TR>
```

Comments Form with Confirmation Dialog

The final section of this page contains a form where users can add comments. This is exactly the same as in the first version. When the user clicks the **Send Comment** button, the showform() function is called to display the confirmation modal dialog box:

```
<TR><TD BGCOLOR="lightyellow">
    <FORM NAME="comment">
        Your Comments Please :<BR>
        <TEXTAREA ID="cmttxt" COLS=40 ROWS=5></TEXTAREA><BR>
</TD></TR>
<TR><TD BGCOLOR="lightyellow">
    <CENTER>
        <INPUT TYPE="button" VALUE="Send Comment" ONCLICK="showform()">
        <INPUT TYPE="reset" VALUE="Clear">
    </CENTER></FORM>
</TD></TR>
</TABLE>
</BODY>

</HTML>
```

That's all the coding we need for our second version, so it's time to test the application with 4.x and 5.x browsers.

Testing the Cross-Browser Solution

To test the cross-browser compatibility of this version of the Photo Album Application, you could try some or all of the following browsers:

❑ Netscape 4.61 or later

❑ Internet Explorer 5.0 or later

❑ Netscape 4.06

❑ Internet Explorer 4.01

Test the collapsible lists, check that the photos change when you select different members of the family tree, try out the modal dialog box, and so on.

Here's what our test with Internet Explorer 4.01 SP1 looks like:

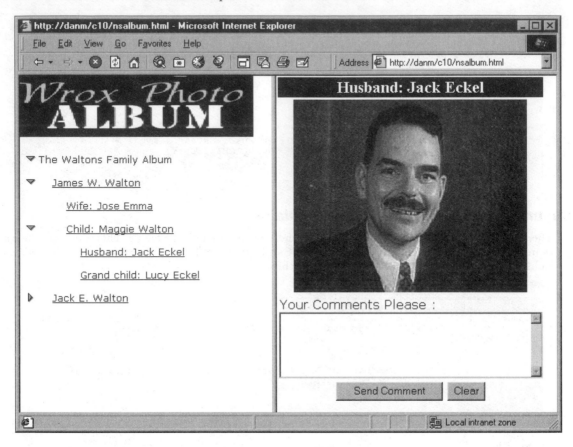

Caveat: File URL Differences Between IE Versions

When testing the application, you should be hosting the pages off a local server. While it is possible to test with IE 5 by directly opening the file, some versions of IE 4.x may not handle the `location.href` and `location.href.search` properties properly with file-based URLs. In fact, you will not get any parameters after the question mark in an extended URL. This will result in no change on the Picture Display Page when a link is clicked on the Tree Controller Page. If you test pages from a web server, even if the server is local, this will not be a problem.

A Backwards Compatible Solution

Now, for our finale, we will write a version of our Family Tree Photo Album that will work even in Netscape 3.x browsers (specifically Netscape Navigator Gold 3.04 or later). Let's look now at what we have to do to achieve this.

Eliminating Dynamic Content Dependency

The limitations of the Netscape 3.x rendering engine don't give us much choice. We *must* eliminate our dependency on any DHTML-dependent code. This means that the `list.js` library that we were using in Solution 2 is out of the question. While it is still possible to keep state on the page (via a cookie) and to rewrite the entire document every time the user selects a different family member, this is at best extremely awkward.

Instead, we have selected a solution that dodges the problem, and pushes all the "hard work" onto a Java applet. All the dynamic changes that are necessary to manage a tree controller are now performed within the applet. A Java applet is a small Java program that can be embedded into a web page. Like ActiveX controls and certain visual plug-ins, it manages its own area of screen real estate within a web page. We will cover Java applets at length in Chapter 15. The only important (and highly desirable) feature of a Java applet over JavaScript coding is that the code will work across browsers and platforms and does not depend on any browser-specific features.

A Versatile Tree Controller Applet from the Web

The tree controller applet that we have selected is one available freely over the Internet. It is written by davidg@spigots.com in the UK. The latest version can be downloaded from:

`http://www.demon.co.uk/davidg/outline.htm`.

Of all the available tree controllers available in applet form, we have selected this applet because:

- ❏ It is available as freeware.
- ❏ It is very small and lightweight.
- ❏ Several sophisticated web sites have used this applet as the main user interface, testifying to its robustness for production use.
- ❏ It works perfectly in the latest browsers (IE5 and NC4.61).

The Main Album Page

The main frameset page for the 3.x compatible browser album application is almost identical to that for the Internet Explorer version. You can find it as the `album.html` page in the distributed source code:

```
<HTML>
  <HEAD>
  </HEAD>
  <FRAMESET COLS="200,*">
    <FRAME SRC="treectrl.html" NAME="treectrl" ALIGN="left"
           MARGINWIDTH=0 NORESIZE
           SCROLLING="no">
    <FRAME SRC="dpage.html" NAME="albpage" MARGINWIDTH=0
           NORESIZE SCROLLING="no">
  </FRAMESET>
</HTML>
```

A Quick Word on Java Applets

Since the tree controller that we will use is a Java applet, we should take a sneak preview to the content of Chapter 15. Here is all that we will need to know for now:

❑ A Java applet is a program written in the Java programming language.

❑ The Java programming language is designed for the Internet and can run across a variety of operating systems, machines and browsers.

❑ A Java applet is downloaded over the Internet and executed by the browser; a "sandbox" security model ensures that the Java applet cannot do anything malicious to our system.

❑ Both Internet Explorer and Netscape support Java applets since their 3.x versions.

❑ When a Java applet executes, a Java interpreter (called the Java Virtual Machine or JVM) is started; this interpreter is independent of the JavaScript interpreter for script code.

❑ Java applets reside in .class files (binary files compiled by a Java compiler); the JVM interprets these binary files during runtime.

Embedding a Java Applet in an HTML Page

A Java applet is embedded into a web page with an HTML <APPLET> element. The syntax for this is:

```
<APPLET NAME="anApplet" CODE="..class file.." WIDTH=200 HEIGHT=340></APPLET>
```

The CODE="" attribute specifies the name of the program (.class) file to load for the Java applet. In our case, the Java applet is contained in a file called Outline.class.

The WIDTH and HEIGHT attributes specify the size of the area on the screen where the Java applet will be displayed. Once specified, only the code within the Java applet can write within this area.

Working with the Outline Applet

The Outline tree controller applet looks as follows when embedded into a web page:

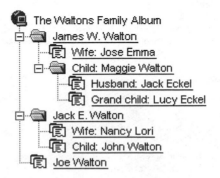

It bears a strong resemblance to our two JavaScript versions, and functions identically. In fact, the only very obvious difference is the icons used for expanding and collapsing the tree. Even the way that the data for describing the tree is specified is very similar. The applet uses its own variety of mini-data description language.

The Outline Applet Markup Language

The applet's data description language is as straightforward as our mHDML language, although it uses recognized HTML tags. The typical syntax is as follows:

```
<LI>top level information</LI>
<UL>
    <LI>second level information</LI>
    <UL>
        <LI>third level information</LI>
        ..more nested levels..
    </UL>
    <LI>second level informaiton</LI>
    ..more information..
</UL>
```

We can summarize the syntax very simply:

❑   Each tree element must be in <LI></LI> tags.

❑   Each collapsible level must be enclosed in <UL></UL> tags.

To make any of the elements act as a hyperlink, we just add the appropriate HTML <A> tags. A target attribute is also used since the new URL may be in another frame. An example element with a hyperlink might look like this:

```
<LI><A HREF="http://www.walts.com/walton" TARGET="albpage">Sam Walton<A></LI>
```

In fact, the markup style for this description language is very similar to our JavaScript version. If you can imagine a tool that could transform <LI> tags to <SPAN> tags, and <UL> tags to <DIV> tags, one can see how one format can automatically translate to the other.

It might be a good exercise to convert the existing JavaScript tree controller to use this style of markup for the data description language.

Limitations of the Outline Applet

Using the applet on our web page is extremely simple. We just embed the applet in the page and supply the tree description. That's all. The applet takes care of the rest of the operation.

Unfortunately, because of the way the applet functions – and to a large degree the way that Java applets can interact with the browser (as we shall see in Chapter 15) – there are some limitations as to what we can do with it:

❑   The effect of clicking on a link is restricted to changing a URL in another frame; unlike our JavaScript tree controller, we cannot cause a JavaScript function to be called.

❑   The graphics used in the tree controller are built into the applet and cannot be changed.

The second limitation is trivial. However, it turns out that the first limitation is quite severe. In the JavaScript version of the tree controller, we modified the SRC attribute of an <IMG> tag and the innerText property of a <DIV> tag to change the title and photo in the Photo Display frame. Since we cannot call a JavaScript function when the user clicks on a tree element, this is not possible. The only obvious solution is to create one web page per picture to be displayed. While this would work, it is definitely not a desirable solution.

Another apparent solution that comes to mind is to use a JavaScript URL (see Chapter 4) such as:

```
"javascript:doclick(this.pic);"
```

Unfortunately, this does not work with this applet. The applet will recognize the URL as invalid.

To overcome this limitation, we will use the same technique as we did in Solution 2: we will use extended URLs which carry the picture and title information in a query after the question mark.

Laying Out the Tree Controller Page

Since the tree controller page in this project is by far the simplest, we will examine it first. You can find this page in the `treectrl.html` file. This page is laid out identically to the JavaScript version. At the top, we have our logo displayed:

```
<HTML>
    <HEAD></HEAD>
    <BODY>
        <TABLE WIDTH=95% BORDER=0 ALIGN=left>
            <TR><TD>
                <IMG SRC="Logo.gif">
            </TD></TR>
            <TR><TD> </TD></TR>
            <TR><TD WIDTH=200 HEIGHT=340 VALIGN="top">
```

Adding the Hierachical Markup Description

Next, we have the embedded applet, and the description of the tree in the applet's data definition language. Notice how the description is sandwiched between the opening and closing `<APPLET>` and `</APPLET>` tags:

```
<APPLET CODE="Outline" WIDTH=200 HEIGHT=340>
    <LI>The Waltons Family Album</LI>
    <UL>
        <LI><A HREF="dpage.html?walt1.jpg&James%20W.%20Walton"
               TARGET="albpage">James W. Walton</A></LI>
        <UL>
            <LI><A HREF="dpage.html?walt2.jpg&Wife%3a%20Jose%20Emma"
                   TARGET="albpage">Wife: Jose Emma</A></LI>
            <LI><A HREF="dpage.html?walt3.jpg&Child%3a%20Maggie%20Walton"
                   TARGET="albpage">Child: Maggie Walton</A></LI>
            <UL>
                <LI><A HREF="dpage.html?walt4.jpg&Husband%3a%20Jack%20Eckel"
                       TARGET="albpage">Husband: Jack Eckel</A></LI>
                <LI><A HREF="dpage.html?walt5.jpg&Grand%20child%3a%20Lucy%20Eckel"
                       TARGET="albpage">Grand child: Lucy Eckel</A></LI>
            </UL>
        </UL>
        <LI><A HREF="dpage.html?walt6.jpg&Jack%20E.%20Walton"
               TARGET="albpage">Jack E. Walton</A></LI>
        <UL>
            <LI><A HREF="dpage.html?walt7.jpg&Wife%3a%20Nancy%20Lori"
                   TARGET="albpage">Wife: Nancy Lori</A></LI>
            <LI><A HREF="dpage.html?walt8.jpg&Child%3a%20John%20Walton"
                   TARGET="albpage">Child: John Walton</A></LI>
        </UL>
        <LI><A HREF="dpage.html?walt9.jpg&Joe%20Walton"
               TARGET="albpage">Joe Walton</A></LI>
    </UL>
</APPLET>
</TD></TR>
</TABLE>

</BODY>
</HTML>
```

Creating The Photo Display Page

Amazingly enough, we do not have to create a new Photo Display Page. In fact, our `dpage.html` page from the last version is precisely what we need for this solution as well. This saves us a significant amount of work.

That is all the code for the 3.x browser compatible version of our photo album. As you can see, this version is considerably less complicated than the first two, since we pass most of the work onto the Java applet.

Testing the 3.x Browser Compatible Photo Album

To test this cross-browser photo album, try loading the `album.html` page from these browsers:

- ❑ Internet Explorer 5 or later
- ❑ Netscape Navigator 4.61 or later
- ❑ Internet Explorer 4.01
- ❑ Netscape Navigator 4.06
- ❑ Netscape Navigator 3.04

There are a few configuration details to bear in mind when you test and experiment with this version:

- ❑ Make sure Java is enabled for your browser (it is typically enabled by default).
- ❑ Make sure your browser is configured to send e-mails, or the e-mail submission will not work. You may also experience problems when you try to submit e-mails if you use an external program (such as Eudora) for your e-mail.
- ❑ Remember to change the `mailto:` address in the code to your own e-mail address.
- ❑ Make sure that all the required files come from the same web server, or at least a local server; the Java sandbox security model is especially sensitive to this.

When you finally submit the comment form, please note that the browser will display a warning similar to this:

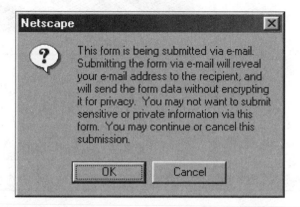

Or, for Internet Explorer:

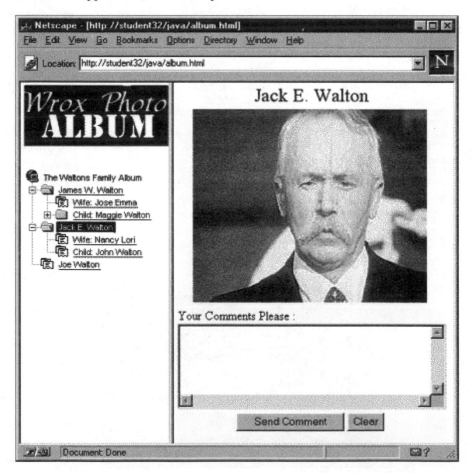

This is a routine security message to notify users that their e-mail address will be revealed through submitting a form. Click on OK and the message will be on its way.

This is how our test appeared on the Netscape 3.04 browser:

Summary

We have discovered the hard way that in real life cross-browser JavaScript programming is much more difficult than we would like it to be. In fact, it is more of a black art than a science. With every new version of browser and scripting technology release, a new Pandora's Box of incompatibilities and problems is opened. The good news is that this evolution will ensure proficient JavaScript developers a long and prosperous career ahead of them; the bad news that a project sometimes never seems to finish.

While programming using Microsoft Dynamic HTML in their Internet Explorer version 4 and 5 browsers can be both fun and efficient, it also immediately locks out any compatibility with Netscape-based browsers. In fact, creating our tree controller entirely in JavaScript within Internet Explorer browser was quite straightforward once we had worked out the design.

We discovered that JavaScript libraries are available and that several from Netscape are actually cross-browser compatible, albeit requiring a 4.x level browser.

On solution to deal with 3.x browser compatibility is to use Java applets (if we can find one that fits our requirements). Java applets provide a way of achieving cross-browser compatibility with complex functionality that is beyond anything possible with JavaScript and the Browser Object Model. In many real-life scenarios, deploying a Java applet can save considerable coding and design time while adding cross-browser compatibility to a web-based application. With the typical large memory that modern web browsing machines have, the performance penalty traditionally associated with Java applets are quickly disappearing.

The very bottom line is that JavaScript is not just a simple "glue" or "play" programming language, but one that can be used to create sophisticated and complex applications – with a little help. If this is the only message that you remember after reading this book, you can consider the journey worthwhile.

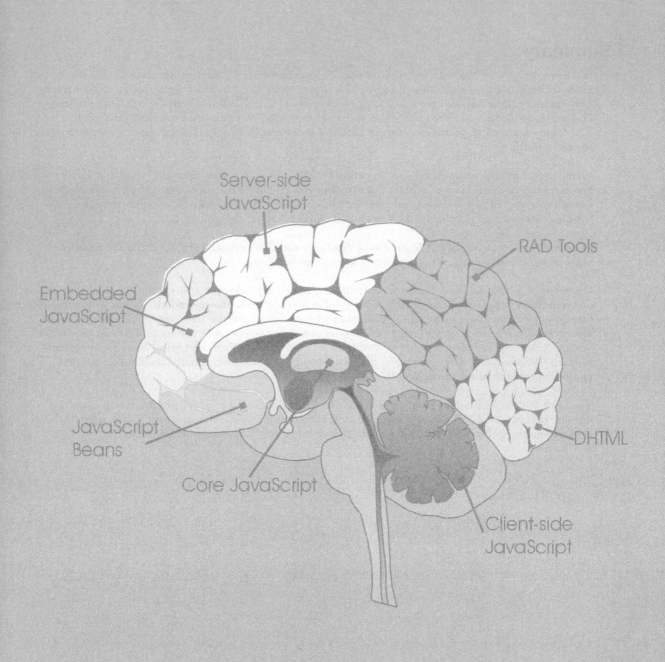

Using Server-Side JavaScript With Netscape Enterprise Server

In this chapter we are going to discuss how Netscape's **Server-Side JavaScript (SSJS)** application service on the **Netscape Enterprise Server (NES)** lets you extend your client-side JavaScript knowledge for server-side web development.

Starting in NES version 2, Netscape made available SSJS as one of its options for server-side development, along with CGI, Java servlets (which were not compliant with the Sun Java servlet specification) and the **Netscape Server Application Programming Interface (NSAPI)**. More functionality was added to SSJS in version 3 to make it a much more capable development language, in particular for web-enabling database applications. NES 4, which should be shipping by the time you read this, comes with a Sun Java servlet compliant engine.

SSJS is designed to fill in a particular programming niche, in fact the same niche ASP and CGI are designed to fill. This niche is primarily made up of people who need to create server-side web applications, in particular database applications, who have little or no "real" programming experience, but have at least a minimum knowledge of client-side JavaScript. Because it's easier to protect a server from malicious code (e.g. we only have to worry about the settings on a few machines as opposed to millions of clients), the JavaScript environment in SSJS has a lot more functions. These functions include the ability to send e-mail, access files residing on the server, built-in persistence mechanisms, the ability to connect to Java classes (well you can also do that with client-side Java) and C plugins that can extend JavaScript, as well as access remote databases.

We will cover the following topics:

- Why SSJS?
- What the SSJS development environment has to offer
- Developing a SSJS database application
- SSJS vs CGI, SSJS vs ASP, SSJS vs JSP

Why SSJS?

So why you would want to use SSJS for your web development? Remember that unfortunately SSJS is only available at the moment with the Netscape Enterprise Server. But since the JavaScript engine is now an open-source project as part of the ongoing Mozilla project (see `http://www.mozilla.org/rhino` for more information), there is nothing to prevent it from really being ported to, say, Apache. Someone would have to write the necessary code to hook it into Apache and then write all of the code to develop the same SSJS objects.

Ease of Development

Probably the most common reason someone chooses to use SSJS is that they already know JavaScript from developing web pages and they want to apply the basic knowledge they have to server-side programming.

Writing your own server-side code under NES is pretty straightforward too, accomplished in three easy steps.

- SSJS code can be inserted into any page containing HTML and client-side code by delimiting it with a pair of `<SERVER>..</SERVER>` tags.
- Once the collection of pages that forms your web application has been completed, you need to compile them into a SSJS application using the `jsac` compiler.
- With your compiled application, it's then a simple matter to tell NES where your application is and what constraints to put upon it.

We'll cover each of these steps in more detail later on in the chapter, as we work through an example SSJS application, but as a brief example, here is the ubiquitous "Hello World" page in the form of a SSJS application:

```
<HTML>
<HEAD>
   <TITLE>
       SSJS Example 1
   </TITLE>
</HEAD>

<BODY BGCOLOR="#0000FF" TEXT="#FFFFFF">
<SERVER>
   var msg = "Hello World!";
   write(msg+"<br>");
</SERVER>
<TABLE BORDER=1>
<TR>
```

```
      <TD BGCOLOR=`(request.ip == "127.0.0.1" ? "#FF0000" : "#00FF00")`>
         This color is backtick generated
      </TD>
      <TD>
         This color is standard
      </TD>
   </TR>
   </TABLE>
   </BODY>
   </HTML>
```

As you can see in our first example, the backtick (`) can also be used to enable SSJS code in an HTML page. The backtick is useful to include SSJS code inside HTML tags, where it would be otherwise impossible to add the <SERVER> tag.

If you are wondering why we use the backtick, well for one, both the single and double quote are already reserved for other uses. The other reason is that the backtick is a standard symbol for calling external operations in many other programming languages like Perl.

Once compiled, our Hello World app looks like this:

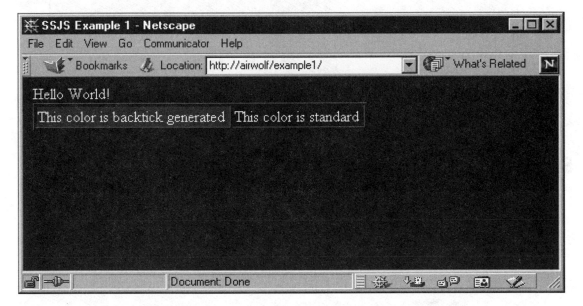

Now of course if you've spent hours, days or even months on developing an SSJS application, you don't want your competitors or lazy programmers out there stealing your code. When the SSJS application is run, only the client presentation code is passed to the browser, as you can see by looking at the View Source screen from Communicator.

```
Source of: http://airwolf/example1/ - Netscape
<html>
<head>
<title>
SSJS Example 1
</title>
</head>
<body bgcolor="#0000FF" text="#FFFFFF">
Hello World!<br>
<table border=1>
<tr>
<td bgcolor="#FF0000">This color is backtick generated
</td>
<td>This color is standard
</td>
</tr>
</table>
</body>
</html>
```

Look at the HTML here and then go back to the earlier code example and you will see that there is not a single server specific tag in there.

Setting Up SSJS

Obviously before you can use SSJS, you'll need a copy of the Netscape Enterprise Server – I used version 3.62 for the examples in this chapter – and for our main application, you'll also need a copy of the Netscape Directory Server (or any other LDAP server, but I used Netscape DS), both of which are available for a free 60 day evaluation at http://www.iplanet.com/downloads/testdrive/index.html. NES 3 has been out for at least two years and is the most popular version of NES. As I was writing this chapter the beta for NES 4 was out, but it had a lot of bugs in its SSJS engine, so I chose not to cover it.

Installing Netscape Enterprise Server

If you have ever installed a web server before, installing NES is a piece of cake. You simply start the installation wizard and answer the questions it presents to you. If you're not working with LDAP, you don't need to set up the LDAP authentication mentioned in the first dialog screen of the installation wizard, but do remember to make a note of the Administrator ID and password you choose to use as well as the port number the wizard assigns to your web-based admin pages. Note that this port number is randomly selected, so forge it at your peril.

Once NES has installed, go to your admin URL and check that a web server has been set up.

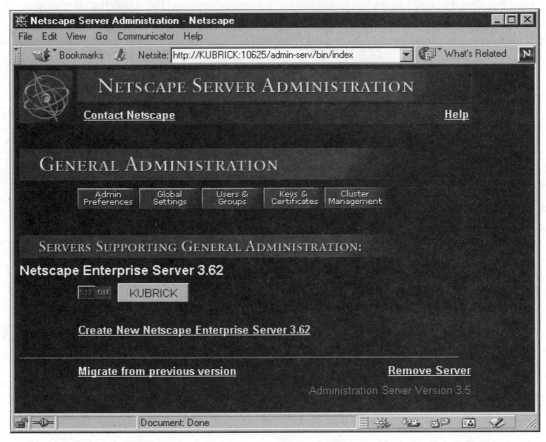

All being well, you should see a screen very much like this one. The key thing to look for is the 'ON webServerName' button under the heading 'Servers Supporting General Administration'. If this hasn't appeared, then choose 'Create New Netscape Enterprise Server' and fill in the details accordingly. If it has appeared, then click the button with the web server's name and then choose Network Settings from the subsequent left hand side navigation bar. In the screen that appears, check that the ServerName entry in the form is the name of your server. If it isn't fill it in correctly and hit OK.

These simple steps will actually set up a NES server instance for serving web pages and other web applications such as SSJS. Complete installation instructions can be found online at http://home.netscape.com/eng/server/webserver/3.0/

Installing Netscape Directory Server

Installing the Netscape Directory server is a bit trickier. However, we're not looking for a full directory service implementation here, just a simple LDAP datastore. The installation wizard takes care of all the hard work. Use your common sense to fill in the relevant dialogs and do make sure you write down all the passwords and ports you set yourself up to use.

For our example application, we chose the "custom" installation option at the beginning of the installation wizard and accepted all the default settings, except for the following screen.

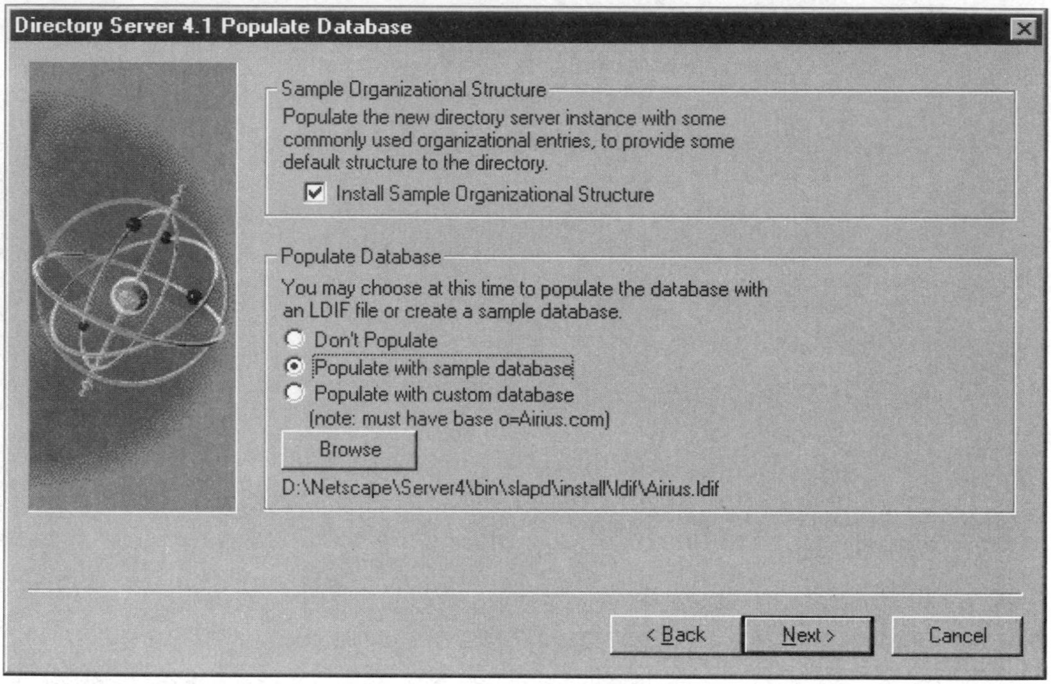

On this screen, we've overturned the default and said 'yes' to both importing the suggested schema and the example LDIF data. Full installation instructions for Directory Server can be found online at http://home.netscape.com/eng/server/directory/.

Turning SSJS "on"

To setup the Netscape Enterprise Server for using SSJS is actually pretty simple. All you must do is to tell the NES that you would like to enable the SSJS interpreter. From the admin home page in NES then:

- ❑ Hit the button labelled with your web server's name.
- ❑ In the resulting screen, select Programs from the top navigation bar.
- ❑ Now you'll be able to select Server Side Javascript from the left hand side and get to the following screen below.
- ❑ Select Yes to the question, 'Activate the Server Side Javascript application environment?' and press OK.

On most operating systems you can run multiple web servers and NES has been developed so that you can choose to enable SSJS on only the particular web servers you wish to run it. Following the steps shown here, you have now told a specific server to enable the SSJS interpreter and also told it to require the NES administrator password before allowing anyone to enter the SSJS Application Manager screen:

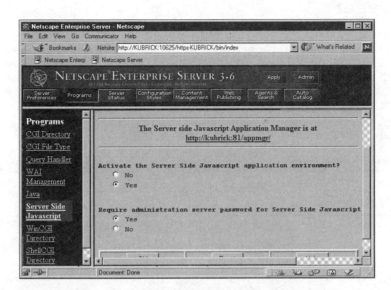

If you click on the URL in this screen you will be taken to the SSJS Application Manager which is shown in our next screenshot:

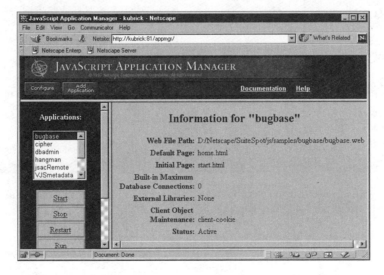

From the SSJS Application Manager screen you can add, remove and configure all of your SSJS applications. You can also start, stop, restart, debug and run your applications from this screen as well. If you click on the Run link you will be taken directly to your application as it appears to the end-user. If you click on the Debug link, you will be taken to the SSJS Debugger.

SSJS Debugger

One of the best things about the SSJS Application manager is its debugger. The debugger enables you to run the application in a live environment, while simultaneously being able to view what's going on "behind the scenes". While you don't have the ability to "step-through" line by line or set breaks (places you tell the server where you want to stop the application) like you do with a programming environment like Visual C++, it's a lot better than the way we typically program and debug blindly when doing CGI development.

Here is an example screenshot of the SSJS Debugger window:

The left frame will show you what's going on in the server. This includes the values of the four server objects: **request**, **client**, **project** and **server**.

It will also show the results of any server generated error messages (e.g. messages that would be logged to the server's error logs) that occurred because of something that happened in your application.

Debug()

You will often find yourself in the situation where you need to see the state of a given variable, or to find out where you are in an application (e.g. usually this is done as a print statement that says something like "I've just connected to the database", etc.). In most programming environments we print these various results straight to the screen and then are forced to go back and clean up our code at the end before we put the application in production. In SSJS you can do this, but you don't have to worry about removing the statements at the end. This is because SSJS includes a function called `debug()`.

The `debug()` function will write its output to the left frame in the SSJS debugger, but when run as a production code (e.g. outside of the SSJS debugger), the end-user will not see anything that the `debug()` statement prints.

It's extremely easy to use. Just think of it as a `write()` function that only displays debug statements.

Here's an example of how to use this function:

```
<SERVER>
...
debug ("started applications");
...
var v = 3;

debug ("The value of v is " + v);
...
</SERVER>
```

See isn't that simple? And I can personally attest to its functionality and that the SSJS debugger has made SSJS development much easier than otherwise possible. Sometimes I really wish I had a debugger like SSJS when doing traditional CGI programming, in particular when my application dies and all I get back is the dreaded "500 Server Error" message without any output.

Working with SSJS

Without any further ado let's get straight into some code. Over the next twenty or so pages we're going to develop an SSJS application that interacts with a relational database, uses LDAP for authentication and uses an external Java library to provide functionality that JavaScript doesn't yet include.

Web-Based Voting with SSJS and LDAP

Our example application is a web-based voting system. One use for this system could be to enable users of your portal (doesn't everyone have one of those now?) to vote on a particular question. Or perhaps in an environment where you have a more secure means of determining identity (e.g. through the use of smart-cards or biometrics) you could actually use the system for a local election of leaders (e.g. vote in the city council race on-line).

The application will use Microsoft Access for its relational database. Access is not the best choice for a production use system, but it is a database that most of you will have and is easily set up for use with SSJS, which are two primary criteria for selecting anything when you write a book on a general subject. Please feel free to use an alternative DB in place of Access.

In our DB, we'll create two tables, one to store the results of the votes so far and one to say whether or not a user has voted. In any voting system you want to eliminate or at least minimize ballot-stuffing, so we will have a table that will simply say whether a user has voted or not. There will not be anything that says how a user voted on a particular question.

We will also be using an LDAP server and my SSJS LDAP library for the actual user authentication. While I've used Netscape Directory Server as my LDAP server, you should be able to use any LDAP server that contains userids and passwords. Bottom line, you'll need an LDAP server to use this application as it relies on the server to authenticate a user who wants to vote.

Why do we use LDAP for authentication? Well for two reasons. One reason is simply so that I can show you how to extend SSJS with Java. The other reason is that your organization will most likely have an LDAP server either available to you now or soon in the future. Probably the primary reason for using LDAP right now is to centralize the user authentication database. By doing this and making that database openly available within your organization, you can improve your overall organizational security while minimizing the need to develop your own authentication systems for each database application you build.

To illustrate, if we didn't use LDAP for our authentication system in our example, we would have to write an authentication system into our database, which means a user would have to register with the system and remember yet another password. Hopefully by using LDAP, this id and password will be the same id and password they use to login to the majority of systems they come into contact with. This means the user is happier (and hopefully in turn more productive) because they have to remember fewer ids and passwords, while your security is improved because when a user leaves, you can easily remove all of their access by deleting the account in a single source.

We're not going into a full-blown discussion of an LDAP-based system here, but if you'd like to read more about it, you can pick up a copy of 'Implementing LDAP' by Mark Wilcox (ISBN 1861002211, Wrox Press).

An Ingredient List for our Example

Here are the components (or ingredients) for our example SSJS application:

- ❑ Netscape Enterprise Server
- ❑ Netscape Directory Server or another available LDAP server
- ❑ Microsoft Access
- ❑ SSJSLDAP library
- ❑ SSJS code

You should be familiar with all but the fourth item on the list, a library of routines that enhance the LDAP functionality within SSJS that are freely downloadable on the web. We'll come to these in a moment.

How it all Fits Together

Before we start looking at the code in depth, I thought it would be helpful to understand how each page fits together. The first page the user sees is the initial log-in page called `login.htm`. Technically however, this is actually the second page run as `init.htm` is loaded when either the Enterprise Server is first set up or when the log-in page calls it. As its name would suggest, `init.htm` takes care of initializing the database and the various LDAP objects used in the app. It will be called automatically if the application detects either a null database or LDAP object.

Once the user has logged in (as either a user in the example LDAP database or as an entry you have added to the LDAP server), the application checks that you are both a registered voter (if you have added the user's information to the database before) and that you have not voted previously. If the user passes all of these conditions then they are allowed to vote. This is accomplished within two files – `authenticate.htm` and `vote.htm`.

Voting takes place on our fifth page – `ballot.htm` – though it appears as only the second to the client. Here we define a simple voting form, the contents of which are sent to `process.htm` for it to update both database tables accordingly to take account of the choice made and that the user is no longer eligible to vote. After the user has voted, they are simply taken back to the login screen.

From the login screen, you also have the option of seeing the current vote standings via `results.htm`.

I wanted to keep the code examples for this application simple so it's very plain, but since each page uses simple HTML for output, you could do anything you want to improve the display. A neat addition would be to render the results as a graphic, though I'll leave that up to you.

A few things to note before we go any further. First of all, if you don't want to have to copy out all the code in the next few pages, you can download all the necessary code and database from Wrox's support website at `http://www.wrox.com/books/270x`. If however you decide you'd like nothing better than to copy the code straight out from the book, please be aware that in order to keep the code easy to read, I've sometimes split one line into two or three. When this has been done I've ended the line with an underscore (_) to denote that the line is continued on the next one down.

Setting Up the Database

Now we've had a runthrough how all the pieces will fit together, it's time to get started on building our app. The first thing on our list is to build the underlying database. Remember that we're using an Access database in the example here although you have the option to use another, more robust database.

We'll need two tables. The `voter` table simply keeps track of who has voted and who has not. It has three fields as shown.

Field Name	Data Type	Description
uidcounter	AutoNumber	
uid	Text	UID of person voting
hasvoted	Yes/No	Whether has voted or not

Meanwhile, the `votes` table keeps track of the votes for and against. It too has three fields.

Field Name	Data Type	Description
voteskey	Number	
yesvote	Number	number of yes votes
novote	Number	number of no votes

Open up a new database project in Access, then create the two tables as shown above and save the database as `vote.mdb`. In order for our application to see it, we'll have to create an open connection to it in the form of a System DSN.

From your Windows Start menu, find the ODBC32 Control Panel and select the **System DSN** tab. As we are creating a new connection, click **Add** and then the **Microsoft Access Drivers** from the next dialog. The next screen you'll see should be filled out like so:

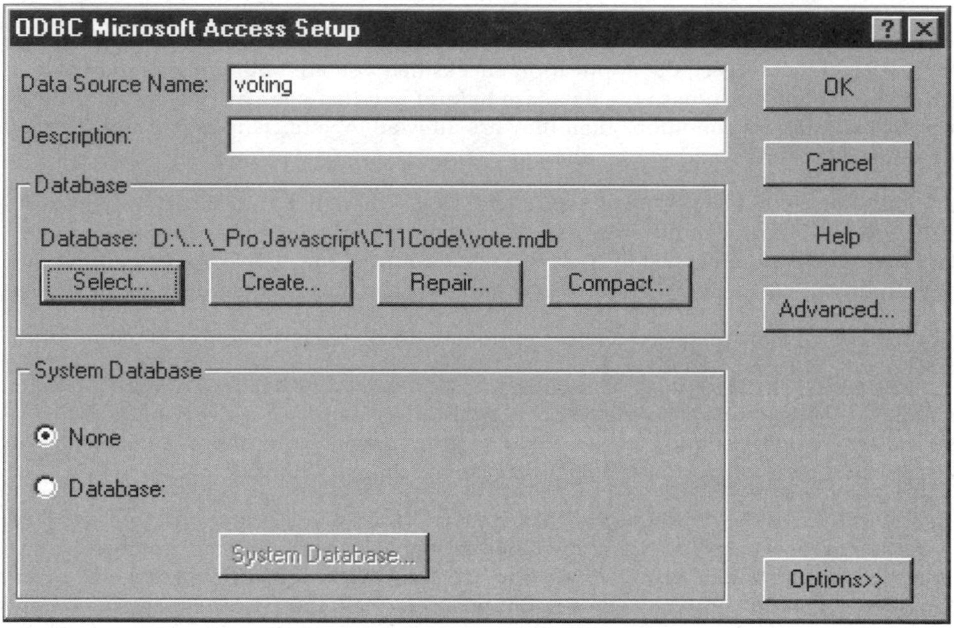

Hit the **Select** button to locate your copy of `vote.mdb` and name the DSN `voting`. Finally, press OK and your DSN is created.

It would be a good idea at this stage to add a few voters (matching the data found in the example `Airius.ldif` file that comes with Netscape Directory server) to `vote.mdb`.

Installing SSJS LDAP

Our next step is to install the Java library that improve the LDAP functionality in SSJS, which is available for download at `http://courses.unt.edu/mewilcox/ldap/`.

The process to get these working is a little bit more involved than we've had so far, so pay close attention.

❏ Navigate your way back to the Server-Side JavaScript admin screen as shown earlier. Hit the Java link in the left hand side navigation bar and switch the Java interpreter on. Make a note of where Java servlets are to be stored.

❏ Download the Netscape LDAP Java SDK from `http://devedge.netscape.com/directory` and install it on your system.

❑ Go to the directory `<server root>\plugins\java` and make a directory there called `local-classes`, if it doesn't already exist.

❑ Find the files `ldapfilt.jar` and `ldapjdk.jar` in the packages directory of the LDAP Java SDK, copy them into the `local-classes` directory and then unzip them. This will create a `netscape` and a `com` directory. (In a future version of the Enterprise server, you won't have to unzip the jar files.)

❑ CD into the `local-classes` directory and make a directory called `mark`.

❑ CD into the `mark` directory and make a directory called `ldap`.

❑ Place the `SSJSLDAP.class` file in the `<server root>\plugins\java\local-classes\mark\ldap\` directory.

❑ Restart the Enterprise Server.

❑ When you compile your web file for your SSJS applications, just make sure that you include the `LDAP.js` file when you run the JavaScript Compiler.

And So To The Code

With all our setup done, we finally come to the writing of the code. Because SSJS works from inside HTML files, the application is usually broken up into several different HTML files which can become hard to manage. You can store often-used functions in JS files (e.g. stored with `.js` extensions) and include those files when you compile your application, but, like other include files, JS files can't be called on their own – you must call the functions inside `<SERVER>` tags.

Init.htm

Our first page, `init.htm`, is run in the background either when NES first starts up or by a hidden call in our log-in page, which we'll come to next. However, it's run, `init.htm` is the page that initializes all of our database and LDAP connection objects.

```
<HTML>
<HEAD>
    <TITLE>
        Voting Initialization
    </TITLE>
</HEAD>

<BODY>
    You shouldn't see this page.
</BODY>
```

Remember SSJS code is delimited by `<SERVER>` tags.

```
<SERVER>
    // create a pool of 5 connections
    // anonymous database access with write rights, probably not
    // a good idea in practice ;)
```

First thing to do is create a `DbPool` object, which will manage our pool of database connections. We simply tell it what protocol to use, the name of the database, any authentication information, and whether or not we want transactions to commit or not.

```
project.appPool = new DbPool("ODBC","voting","","","",5,true);
```

Next we specify some variables for our LDAP object. Remember how during the section on installing Directory Server we told you to write down all those names and passwords? Here's where you use them.

```
//LDAP setup - note the settings below reflect the default NDS installation

//set to your LDAP host
project.host = "airwolf";

//set to your LDAP port
project.port = 389;

//set to your Directory Base
//change to match your server's
project.searchBase = "o=airius.com"

//the Distinguished Name you are going to use
//project.mgr_dn = "";
//Password for the Distinguished Name
//maybe blank for mgr_dn & mgr_pw if directory allows anonymous searches
//project.mgr_pw = "";

// Grab an LDAP object
var ldap = new LDAP(project.host, parseInt(project.port), project.searchBase,
                    parseInt(0), project.mgr_dn,project.mgr_pw);
```

Here is an example of the debug() statement for use to make sure we got an LDAP object successfully.

```
debug("set ldap"+ldap);

//authenticate if necessary
//ldap.authenticate(project.mgr_dn,project.mgr_pw);
//set your scope
ldap.setSearchScope(parseInt(ldap.SCOPE_SUB));
```

The redirect in the following code is irrelevant when init.htm is called during application or server startup. However, in order to make better use of the code, I've included it so that I can reuse the code should project.ldap need to be reinitialized. Thus, in the start page (login.htm) I've included the following lines:

```
if (project.ldap == void(0)) {
  redirect('init.htm');
}
```

This checks for the existance of project.ldap and redirects back to this page if needed.

```
if (ldap == null)
{               // connection could not be made
   write("Failed to connect to LDAP server. _
         See error log or Java Console<br>");
}
else
{               // store the connection in the project object.
   project.ldap = ldap;
   redirect("login.htm");
}
</SERVER>
</HTML>>
```

Login.htm

With our initial setup code out of the way, it's time to create the first screen that the user will see - login.htm. It's not a particularly interesting page however, consisting of just a standard HTML form and a small piece of SSJS code to make sure the database and LDAP connections have been initialized.

```
<HTML>
<HEAD>
    <TITLE>
        Voting Login Page
    </TITLE>
</HEAD>
<BODY BGCOLOR = "#ffffff">

<SERVER>
    //make sure LDAP object initialized
    if (project.ldap == void(0))
    {
        redirect('init.htm');
    }
</SERVER>

<FONT SIZE = +2>SSJS Voting Example</FONT>
<BR><BR>
<B>Please login</B>
<BR>

<FORM METHOD="POST" ACTION="authenticate.htm">
    <TABLE BORDER=0>
    <TR>
        <TD ALIGN="right"> <B>uid:</B> </TD>
        <TD> <INPUT NAME="uid"> </TD>
    </TR>
    <TR>
        <TD ALIGN="right"> <B>password:</B> </TD>
        <TD> <INPUT TYPE="password" NAME="password"> </TD>
    </TR>
    <TR>
        <TD> <INPUT TYPE="submit"> </TD>
    </TR>
    </TABLE>
</FORM>
<HR>
<A HREF="results.htm">See the results</A>
</BODY>
</HTML>
```

Authenticate.htm

Once a user has entered his or her details and pressed Submit, the details are passed to authenticate.htm to make sure they're valid. First thing to do is make sure we have some live connection to our LDAP directory to validate details against.

```
<HTML>
<HEAD>
    <TITLE>
        Authenticate Voting
    </TITLE>
</HEAD>
<BODY BGCOLOR="#ffffff">
<SERVER>
```

```
    var ldap = project.ldap;

    if (ldap.connection == null)
    {
        write("project.ldap.connection has no properties. Please make sure the _
                Directory server and the Enterprise server are functioning _
                correctly.<br>");
        write("<A HREF=\"init.htm\">Click here to try and reconnect</A><br>");
    }
    else
    {
```

Assuming all is well, we pull the entered `userid` and `password` from the `request` object. We'll come back to exactly what the `request` object is later in the chapter.

```
    var user = request.uid;
    var passwd= request.password;

    var searchFilter = "(uid=" + user + ")";
    var entryDN = ldap.getDN(searchFilter);
```

LDAP requires the Distinguished Name (DN) of the entry to check for successful authentication, so we retrieve the DN of the user.

```
    //prevent anonymous logins
    if ((user == "") || (passwd == ""))
    {
        redirect("login.htm");
    }

    //store userid in client variable so we can get it later for voting
    client.user = user;

    loggedin = ldap.authenticate(entryDN,passwd);
```

If authentication is successful, then we take the user to the second vetting page, otherwise we send them to the login page. We can accomplish either with the `redirect()` function, which redirects the browser to the URL specified in the function.

```
    //success go to voting page
    if (loggedin == true)
    {
        redirect("vote.htm");
    }
    else
    {
        redirect("login.htm");
    }
    }
</SERVER>
</BODY>
</HTML>
```

Vote.htm

There are still two cases in which an authenticated user is not allowed to vote. They might not be registered to vote or, alternatively, they might have already voted. `Vote.htm` checks for both cases and only if neither of the above cases apply do we finally pass them onto the ballot page.

```
<HTML>
<HEAD>
   <TITLE>
      Voting Page
   </TITLE>
</HEAD>

<BODY BGCOLOR="#ffffff">
<SERVER>
```

First we get the `userid` from the `client` object.

```
//get the voter uid
var user = client.user;
```

Next we grab one of the available connections to the database from the connection pool we created in `init.htm`. We give it a name – `checkVoters` – for debugging purposes, and tell it to set the database connection timeout to 10 seconds. We then test for failure to connect by checking to see if the variable is `null` or not.

```
// initialize our connection to voting database
var voteConn = null;

// get the connection
// name connection for debugging purposes
// set server timeout to 10 seconds

voteConn = project.appPool.connection("checkVoters",10);

if (voteConn == null)
{
   write('<FONT COLOR="#ff0000">Error: Unable to connect to database  _
         </FONT>');
}
```

Here we build our SQL statement and then pass it to the database, which returns a `cursor` object. A database cursor is an object that represents the results of a database query. If the user is not found, we let the user know and then log them out. If you remember, we preloaded the database with all of the user-ids from the `Airius.ldif` file that comes with the Netscape Directory server.

```
sql = "SELECT voter.uid, voter.hasvoted FROM voter _
      WHERE (voter.uid = '"+ user + "')";
var voterCursor = voteConn.cursor(sql);

if (!voterCursor.next())
{
   write('<h2> No voter found matching: ' + user + '</h2>');
   client.user = "";

   //here we allow the user to try again
   //In a real application, something should at least be logged in
   write('<A HREF="login.htm">Try again</A>');
}
```

If we get this far, then we know that the user is a registered voter. The next step we do is check and see if the voter has already voted or not. This is relatively easy because SSJS automatically sets the object variables of the `cursor` object to the field names of the database results.

```
    else      // we got a "real" voter
    {
        // check to see if they have voted yet
        // we don't want any ballot stuffing ;)
        if ( voterCursor.hasvoted == 1)
        {
            write('<h2> voter: '+ user + ' has voted</h2>');

            //again we should do better error handling
            write('<A HREF="login.htm">Try again</A>');
        }
```

The user hasn't voted yet, so we close the cursor, release the connection and then we take the user to the actual ballot.

```
    else
    {
        //okay you can vote!
        //first close the cursor
        voterCursor.close();

        //next release current connection
        voteConn.release();

        // now the user can go to the voting booth
        redirect("ballot.htm");
    }
}
</SERVER>
</BODY>
</HTML>
```

Ballot.htm

Finally we get to the page where we can vote. As you may already have guessed, this another simple form with two radio buttons for yes and no and a submit button.

```
<HTML>
<HEAD>
    <TITLE>
        Voting Ballot
    </TITLE>
</HEAD>

<BODY BGCOLOR="#ffffff">
```

Covering the case where someone may try and come directly to this page, we have another redirect to login.htm in case we haven't got an authenticated user.

```
<SERVER>
    var user = client.user;
    if (user == "")
    {
        redirect("login.htm");
    }
</SERVER>
```

Now here's the ballot form itself. The form contents are POSTed to process.htm so that they are hidden in the HTML header rather than in full view appended to the header as they would be if the form was GETed.

```
<FORM METHOD="POST" action="process.htm">
   <TABLE BORDER=0>
   <TR>
      <TD><B>Voting Question: Is SSJS a viable alternative to CGI?</B></TD>
   </TR>
   <TR>
      <TD>yes</TD>
      <TD></INPUT TYPE="radio" name="q1" value="yes" checked></TD>
   </TR>
   <TR>
      <TD>no</TD>
      <TD></INPUT TYPE="radio" name="q1" value="no"></TD>
   </TR>
   <TR>
      <TD></INPUT TYPE="submit"></TD>
   </TR>
   </TABLE>
   <A HREF="exit.htm">Logout</A>
</FORM>
</BODY>
</HTML>
```

Process.htm

Now that the user has expressed his right to vote, we need to register their opinion in our database and note that they have voted. This we do inside process.htm. First, we need a connection the database, which we make in the same way as before.

```
<HTML>
<HEAD>
   <TITLE>
      Process Votes
   </TITLE>
</HEAD>

<BODY BGCOLOR="#ffffff">
<H2> Voting Results</H2>

<SERVER>
   //get the voter uid
   var user = client.user;

   // voting db connection
   var voteConn = null;

   // get the connection
   // name connection for debugging purposes
   // set server timeout to 10 seconds
   voteConn = project.appPool.connection("checkVoters",10);

   if (voteConn == null)
   {
      write('<FONT COLOR="#ff0000">Error: Unable to connect to database _
         </FONT>');
   }
```

In order to update the vote count, we must get the choice from the ballot and then the current vote results from the database. If we were using a more traditional database engine such as Oracle or Microsoft SQL Server, we could tell the server we would like an updatable cursor, but Access doesn't support such an option.

```
//update vote
var ballot = request.q1;

//get current results
sql = "SELECT votes.yesvote, votes.novote FROM votes _
        WHERE ((votes.voteskey) = 1)";

//make it an updateable cursor
//voteConn.beginTransaction();
//for db's that support updateable cursors like Oracle
//var counterCursor = voteConn.cursor(sql,true); // ditto

var counterCursor = voteConn.cursor(sql);
if (!counterCursor.next())
{
    write('<h2> No voting results found matching key 1</h2>');
    var err = voteConn.majorErrorCode() + ": " + _
            voteConn.majorErrorMessage();
    write('<h2><font color="#ff0000">' + err + '</FONT></h2>');
}
else
{
```

In the next few lines of code we update both tables in the database using standard SQL statements and the execute() function of the connection object. Remember that we are updating both the vote count and that the user has now registered his vote and cannot do so again.

```
if (ballot == "yes")
{
    counterCursor.yesvote = counterCursor.yesvote + 1 ;
    sql = "UPDATE votes SET votes.yesvote = "+ counterCursor.yesvote + _
        " WHERE ((votes.voteskey) = 1)";
}

if (ballot == "no")
{
    counterCursor.novote = counterCursor.novote + 1;
    sql = "UPDATE votes SET votes.novote = "+ counterCursor.novote + _
        " WHERE ((votes.voteskey) = 1)";
}

// var results =   counterCursor.updateRow("votes");
//updateable if db supports updatable cursors
// must use pass-through SQL for Access

var results = voteConn.execute(sql);

if (results > 0)
{
    write('<h2> Error occurred: ');
    var err = voteConn.majorErrorCode() + ": " + _
            voteConn.majorErrorMessage();
    write(err + '</h2>');
}
else
{
    write('<font color = "#ff0000">updated successfully!</FONT><br>');
    // voteConn.commitTransaction();
    //if db supports transactions
}
```

```
        //now update voter so that it shows they have voted
        sql = "UPDATE voter SET voter.hasvoted = 1 _
            WHERE ((voter.uid='" + user +"'))";
        var results = voteConn.execute(sql);

        if (results > 0)
        {
            write('<h2> Error occurred during voter update: ');
            var err = voteConn.majorErrorCode() + ": " + _
                voteConn.majorErrorMessage();
            write(err + '</h2>');
        }
    }
}
</SERVER>

<HR>
<A HREF="exit.htm">Exit the System</A>;
</BODY>
</HTML>
```

Results.htm

So now we've authenticated our users, registered their votes, updated our counts accordingly and flagged that the users no longer eligible to vote. How do we see the current state of the vote? Easy – we hit the link to results.htm. If you've actually been typing this out rather than running it from the code download, you may notice that there's not much code here we haven't already come across.

```
<HTML>
<HEAD>
    <TITLE>
        Voting Results
    </TITLE>
</HEAD>

<BODY BGCOLOR="#ffffff">
<H2> Voting Results</H2>

<SERVER>
    //get the voter uid
    var user = client.user;

    // voting db connection
    var voteConn = null;

    // get the connection
    // name connection for debugging purposes
    // set server timeout to 10 seconds
    voteConn = project.appPool.connection("checkVoters",10);

    if (voteConn == null)
    {
        write('<FONT COLOR="#ff0000">Error: Unable to connect to database _
            </FONT>');
    }

    // build the cursor to handle results
    var sql = "SELECT votes.voteskey, votes.yesvote,votes.novote FROM votes";
    var voterCursor = voteConn.cursor(sql);
```

```
       if (!voterCursor.next())
       {
           write('<h2> No voters found </h2>');
       }
       else
       {
           write('<TABLE BORDER=0>');
           write('<TR><TD>question</TD><TD>yes</TD><TD>no</TD></TR>');
           do
           {
               write('<TR><TD>' + voterCursor.voteskey + '</TD>');
               write('<TD>' + voterCursor.yesvote + '</TD>');
               write('<TD>' + voterCursor.novote + '</TD></TR>');
           } while (voterCursor.next());

           write('</TABLE>');
       }
       voterCursor.close();
       voteConn.release();
</SERVER>
<HR>
<A HREF="login.htm">Vote!</A>
</BODY>
</HTML>
```

Exit.htm

Last but not least, you've probably noticed that on a few of the screens we've given the user the ability to log out. This is handled by the exit.htm file which simply sets the client.user variable to nothing.

```
<HTML>
<HEAD>
    <TITLE>
        Exit Voting Booth
    </TITLE>
</HEAD>
<BODY BGCOLOR="#ffffff">
<SERVER>
    client.user="";
    redirect("login.htm");
</SERVER>
</BODY>
</HTML>
```

Using The jsac Compiler

After you have typed up all of your code, the next step is to compile your application using the jsac compiler. Note, of course, this applies to every SSJS application you write, not just the one we've made here.

Much to many people's taste, jsac is a command line based compiler which can be found in the <server-root>\bin\https\ directory. In order to run it, you need open up a DOS window and then navigate to that directory. You then have four different possible ways in which to call the compiler – please excuse the syntax.

```
jsac [-cdv] [-l charSet] -o binaryFile [-i] inputFile1 [-i] inputFile2
jsac [-cdv] -o binaryFile -f includeFile
jsac [-cdv] -o binaryFile -p directory -f includeFile -r errorFile
jsac -h
```

Real helpful, isn't it.

Fortunately, everything becomes quite a bit clearer once you've cast your eyes down a list of the flags and what they mean.

Flag	Meaning
-c	This switch checks the syntax of your SSJS application but doesn't compile it.
-d	This will print out all of the SSJS code in your application on the screen.
-v	This will run the compiler in verbose mode, which is useful when trying to solve a particularly hard to kill bug.
-l	Specifies the character set being used in the pages to be compiled. e.g. iso-8859, euc-kr, etc.
-h/-?	Either one of these switches will display the jsac command line help.
-o	Use this switch to specify the name of the compiled SSJS application file. It must end in a .web file extension.
-p	This switch tells the compiler to append the directory name after -p (e.g. -p /usr/local/include/ssjs) in front of the file names.
-f	This switch enables you to create a SSJS "makefile". You list each of your files in a text file, one file per line.
-i	Allows you to specify an HTML or JS file for inclusion in your application. If you simply just pass the name of a file (e.g. login.htm or library.js) this switch is implied.
-r	Allows you to redirect messages on the console to the file name you specify with this switch.

To make it easier on yourself, I recommend adding the jsac directory to your path. Many SSJS developers also place their SSJS compilation statements into batch files to make it easier to compile because you must specify each HTML and JS source file into your compilation statement.

Here's how I compiled the application we've just completed, which I called vote.web. Note that you should copy the LDAP.js file containing the LDAP routines for SSJS LDAP into your application folder before making this call:

```
jsac -o vote.web init.htm authenticate.htm login.htm vote.htm ballot.htm
exit.htm process.htm results.htm LDAP.js
```

This will compile your application into SSJS bytecode which can then be used by the SSJS interpreter in your Netscape Enterprise server.

Telling NES About Your Application

The next step is to tell the Enterprise server about your application, via the SSJS Application Manager, which you'll recall can be found at `http://server-root/appmgr`:

Click Add Application in the top navigation bar and then fill in the values accordingly. From top to bottom they are:

- ❑ The name you want to refer to your application by
- ❑ The location of the compiled WEB file
- ❑ The page you wish to have loaded when the user types in the default URL
- ❑ The page that contains any initialization code
- ❑ The maximum number of database connections the application can have open
- ❑ Any external C libraries the application uses
- ❑ The format you want the client object stored as (I usually leave it as the default which is client cookies)

Once you've added them in, click OK and your application is now installed. The settings for our voting application are in the screenshot above. Note that if you recompile the application, you must restart it for the changes to take effect.

To see the application we've built in action simply type the URL: `http://server-root/vote/`. The URL is always the name of the WEB file, minus the `.web` extension.

Building and Using SSJS Libraries

Besides storing your SSJS code in HTML, you can also store your functions inside separate .js files. These files are like their client-side JavaScript brethren; they allow you to share commonly used JavaScript functions in your JavaScript applications.

Unlike client-side JavaScript however, you don't have to specify which .js file contains the function you need. Instead you just call the routine and when you compile your SSJS application, you include the .js file with the rest of your files, just as we did with LDAP.js in our example. By doing this the SSJS JavaScript interpreter already "knows" the routine the code refers to and calls it for you.

The SSJS Environment

So now we've got SSJS installed, the server set up and switched on, created our first SSJS applications and even got it running. What else can we do with it? In this section we'll look at the rest of the SSJS environment and what other server-side functionality NES offers to rival the competition.

LiveWire (Database Access)

One of the most popular uses of the web right now is to provide an easy to use and consistent interface to applications. One of the most popular reasons to build web applications is to simplify access to databases. Because the web interface is so prevalent and easy to use/administer it's hard to find a new database application that at least doesn't take a web interface into account during its initial design.

One of the problems that developers have is how to hook a database up to the web. When SSJS was first developed there weren't any easy solutions. This problem space was one SSJS was designed specifically to fill – to make it easy to hook databases into the web. It's all done with Netscape's SSJS database interface known as **LiveWire**.

LiveWire contains the DbPool object we used in our example application and several functions to connect and operate on a variety of databases. This NES3 object succeeds the database object in NES2 which should no longer be used.

The variety of databases you can interact with is large. SSJS is capable of talking to Oracle, Informix and Sybase natively (e.g. using these databases' native drivers) and also to any other database that supports the popular ODBC protocol. Even if you're running a UNIX version of NES and the database is on a Windows-based platform, as long as the database is ODBC-compliant, one can talk to the other.

Because the database access is through standard JavaScript objects and functions, you don't have to worry about learning a new or difficult syntax for communicating with databases either. SSJS supports many of the popular RDBMS operations using pass-through SQL. What this means is that the SQL commands are sent as plain text to the database, which then interprets them, as opposed to having the SQL commands precompiled and then sent to the database. Pass-through SQL is slower than "straight-through" SQL (though it does allow you to switch database vendors without having to change your entire program), but you can improve performance by using stored procedures as we'll demonstrate in Chapter 14.

Persistence – Maintaining State

SSJS makes it easier on the developer for persisting information and maintaining state – the global properties and information that need to be available to the application at all times rather than just for a single page. In fact, SSJS provides us with three persistence-related objects to make use of:

❑ **server** : Data stored in the `server` object is available to all applications and is stored there until the server process is restarted. You can also use this object to get information about the particular server your application is running on.

❑ **project** : Data stored in the `project` object is available to all instances of a particular application and is stored there until the application is restarted. Each project has its own `project` object.

❑ **client** : Data stored in the `client` object is available to the application and is a viable way of storing information for each client that accesses the application. The data in the client application is only available to the application that was accessed; it cannot be shared between different SSJS applications. SSJS allows the developer to choose between several different mechanisms as to how the client information is physically stored. This type of object can be used to track user sessions because the client object only lasts as long as the user's (e.g. client) session with the application.

This graph shows you comparisons of the lifetimes of the various SSJS persistence objects.

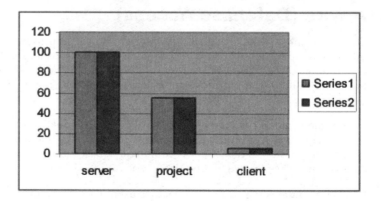

To store data in any of these objects, you simply add a new property to them. For example, to store a person's name in the client object, you would type:

```
<SERVER>
...
client.name = request.full_name;
...
</SERVER>
```

and to get it back later, it's a simple matter of calling the variable, like so:

```
<SERVER>
...
var name = client.name;
...
</SERVER>
```

The data in the `server` and `project` objects are kept in memory. While doing this speeds up data access, it also eats up resources that can either slow down the responsiveness of your web server or crash it.

It is a good idea then to store persistent information in the `client` object as opposed to the `server` or `project` objects unless you have data that needs to be shared between applications. This is because data stored in the `client` object is stored in files either on the client (e.g. client-cookies) or on the server.

Now if you think it's kind of strange to store client information on the server instead of on the client, you have to understand your users and your environment. As a veteran web application developer I can tell you that I consider client-cookies the best alternative. They are easy, simple and standardized, exactly what the developers of the cookie specification were looking for. Unfortunately cookies have gotten a bad reputation thanks to a few unscrupulous advertisers and lots of misinformation. It's very possible your users simply won't accept cookies because they fear you'll sell their cookie data to someone else. See Chapter 18 for a frank rebuttal of the panic-mongering that has been aimed at cookies in recent times.

Choosing the client Object Maintainence Mechanism

As we've already seen, when creating a new SSJS application, we must tell NES which particular mechanism we want to use to store the data that the `client` object contains. Look once again at the new application dialog and you'll find that there are actually five different methods, all transparent to the user, but with differing consequences for the server. They are:

- ❑ **Client cookie** : Stores the data in a cookie in the web browser. You are limited to 20 variables because the cookie specification only allows you store 20 cookies per application and you are limited to data under 4K in size. This is the default method. Note that client cookies are not easily shared outside of SSJS applications.

- ❑ **Client URL** : The data is stored as URL encoded data in the query string of all of the links used in the application. You must also use the `addClient` function to get the values of this method if your application generates an URL.

- ❑ **Server IP** : The data is stored on the server in an indexed database that uses the client's IP address as the index to the database. You should only use this if your clients have fixed assigned IP addresses.

- ❑ **Server cookie** : The data is stored on the server in an indexed database that is indexed by a unique value. This value is stored in a single client cookie.

- ❑ **Server URL** : The data is stored on the server in an indexed database that is indexed by a unique value. The value is stored in the query string of all of the links of the application. You must also use the `addClient` function to get the values that are stored with this method.

Performance

Obviously if you are developing web applications you are concerned with performance and SSJS addresses this issue in three key ways.

First of all, SSJS executes in the same process space as the NES server in the same way that Java Server Pages execute in the same process as their web server. This means there is not the extra overhead of starting a new process like there is in CGI or ASP. One downside to this however is that should SSJS applications crash, so will the web server, unlike CGI or ASP apps.

Second, as we've seen already, every SSJS application must be precompiled into intermediate bytecode and stored as .web files (simply called web files). Like Java bytecode, **SSJS bytecode is OS-independent** and can be used to deliver the logic of your program (you still have to provide any graphics, multimedia or Java class files) without having to give out the source. Instead, when NES is told of an application's existence, it compiles the bytecode into native code for use on that particular OS.

Finally, SSJS improves database performance with the use of the `DbPool` and `StoredProc` objects. The `DbPool` object maintains a "pool" of connections to a database so that your application doesn't have to wait for a database connection to be established (which is often the highest overhead of any database operation). The `StoredProc` object allows you to call a stored procedure on the database, which can improve SQL queries several magnitudes over pass-through SQL because the actual SQL code is already compiled into the database's native code and only needs to know to be executed with the correct parameters.

LiveConnect (Java)

While SSJS has many built in functions, it obviously can't do everything. One of the most popular options to extend SSJS is to use Java classes via the **LiveConnect** interface. If, for example, you wish to use one of the standard Java classes in your application, you can access it via the fully-qualified class name like this:

```
<SERVER>
...
var javastring = java.lang.String;
...
</SERVER>
```

Otherwise you have to use the `Packages` object like this:

```
<SERVER>
...
var  myobj = Packages.com.something.Myobj;
...
</SERVER>
```

To use a Java class, you must do two things.

❑ Activate the server-side Java service in NES (which is the same screen you use to activate Java Servlets).

❑ If you wish to use any non-standard Java classes, you must store the class files in the `<NES server root>/plugins/java/local-classes` directory.

Note that you can only use JAR (Java ARchive) files if you are using NES version 3.6 or later. The only exceptions to this rule are certain packages on NT (like the Netscape Directory SDK for Java) which cause NES's Java Virtual Machine resident JIT (Just In Time) interpreter to crash, meaning they cannot be used with any version of NES as a JAR file. This is a known bug with the Symantec JIT on Windows NT in its JVM before JDK 1.1.7.

Extending SSJS with Server Plug-ins

Of course sometimes Java is not going to fit the bill. Either there's not a Java class available to do what you want or you need the extra speed a native library gives you. Luckily, SSJS enables you to do that – the LiveWire and LiveConnect interfaces being excellent examples of exactly this technique. You can compile a function that can be called from SSJS that then executes the native code you need access to (the function is compiled as a DLL on Windows and a Shared Object on UNIX).

This way you can get the benefits of native code, but you can call the code from SSJS using the familiar JavaScript language.

To use a native library from SSJS, first you must register the function with the SSJS engine.

```
<SERVER>
...
 var isRegistered = registerCFunction("myCLib", _
                                "c:/code/myclib.dll",/ "myCLibArguments");
 if (isRegistered == true)
 {
```

Then we can call the function with any arguments we need to provide.

```
    var returnValue = callC("myClib", "first arg", 99, "my last argument");
    write(returnValue);
 }
 else
 {
   write("registerCFunction() returned false, " + _
         "check server error log for details")
 }
...
</SERVER>
```

Standard SSJS Objects

SSJS is standard JavaScript 1.2 and has all of the standard JavaScript objects and functions including regular expressions. Of course it doesn't have any of the browser-related objects like the `document` object. We'll briefly look at the SSJS specific objects here, but for a complete reference containing the objects and all of their methods as well as the SSJS specific functions, you should look at Appendix C.

- ❑ **client**: Contains data that is stored via the client (e.g. web browser) and contains methods to specify how long to store that data.
- ❑ **Connection**: Used to actually interact with a database.
- ❑ **Cursor**: Provides a handle to retrieve data from database.
- ❑ **database**: This object was the original mechanism use to connect to a database, and has been deprecated in NES 3 in favor of DbPool.
- ❑ **DbPool**: This object is now the preferred mechanism used to connect to the database.

- ❏ **File**: Allows you to read and write files that are stored on the server.
- ❏ **Lock**: Allows you to lock and unlock variables. Locked variables cannot be accessed by any other application.
- ❏ **project**: Allows you to store and access variables that need to be shared between instances of a particular SSJS application.
- ❏ **request**: Allows you to access variables that are a part of an individual HTTP request including client username, IP address, browser and, of course, submitted form data.
- ❏ **ResultSet**: Allows you to manipulate the results of a SQL operation.
- ❏ **SendMail**: Allows you to send mail from a SSJS application.
- ❏ **server**: Allows you get information about the server and also to store information that needs to be shared across all SSJS applications.
- ❏ **StoredProc**: Allows you to access stored procedures in databases.

CGI

As you'll read in the next chapter, the most common way for web clients to send data back to the server is through the **Common Gateway Interface (CGI)**. CGI programs are passed data from the client via the web server. These programs run separately from the web server and thus can be developed in any language of the programmer's choice – UNIX shell, Visual Basic, C/C++, Python, Java, ADA, Perl and, of course, JavaScript to name but some. I've heard a rumor that someone has even written some using the old QBasic language from DOS 5. The Perl programming language is by far the most popular of the languages used for CGI development. This is primarily because Perl excels in handling and parsing text, which of course is what 99% of the Web is.

CGI Problems

Unfortunately, CGI suffers from two major problems:

One is that it doesn't scale well. This is because each time the server must handle a CGI request, it must start up a separate CGI process. Each process takes up its own memory, CPU time and other overheads. If enough requests come in, the server either will be slow to respond, or fail to respond because it won't have enough resources. There is also the possibility the entire machine may crash if your CGI programs take up too many resources, which is not a good way to build friends on the web.

Secondly, CGI is not the most friendly of programming environments. Now, while I'm a decent Perl hacker and can even get by with C if I need to, most of the web developers that I have met are not typical programmers. For them, hacking out their JavaScript code for browser detection is the closest they have ever gotten to developing a "real" application and they have never seen the inside of a Programming 101 Computer Science course. Typically what happens is that they need to hook a database up to the Web, perhaps even with some simple authentication including a mechanism to keep people "logged in" over several pages. Now as a super-programmer I'm sure I could build a Perl CGI program in a short amount of time using cookies and the Perl DBI interface to hook to a database, but that's not your typical web developer. This is a major reason why application environments such as SSJS, ASP, Allaire ColdFusion and even Java Server Pages have been developed.

CGI Solutions

The original and still the best solution to solving CGI's scalability problems has been the development of server APIs. These server APIs give programmers the ability to write CGI-like programs that are able to run in the same "process space" as the web server. That is, the web server no longer has to start up a separate process for each CGI request.

Unfortunately server API programming is even harder than CGI. You are forced to use C or C++ instead of your favorite development language. If you screw up your server plug-in, it will crash the entire web server. If you screw up your CGI program, it will usually only crash itself and not the entire web server. You also lose the cross-platform functionality you have with SSJS. While all popular web servers support a server API, each one is different. Even if the web server is cross platform, you must recompile your server API for each platform before you can use it. And even fewer number of web developers have the skill or the access to develop server API applications.

Luckily there are several middle grounds such as SSJS, ASP and **Java Server Pages (JSP)**.

SSJS is actually implemented as a NSAPI plug-in. This means that when your SSJS application runs, it runs in the same "process space" as the web server, which gives it an immediate performance gain over CGI. And since the SSJS plug-in is already compiled and installed with the Netscape Enterprise Server, you don't have to worry about compiling for your particular platform. Because you are using JavaScript as your development language, you don't have to worry about memory management or platform management because JavaScript manages the memory for you and SSJS is cross-platform like Java.

SSJS gives you many of the speed advantages of a server API plug-in, but also has the advantage of being JavaScript; a language you already know. The analogy I like to use is that SSJS is like a Porsche car. A Porsche allows you to go real fast if you want to, but still with most of the comforts you are used to in a luxury car. A server API plug-in is like an Indy race car. It goes real fast (much faster than the Porsche) but only in the hands of a very skilled driver, backed by a very skilled pit crew and without ANY of the comforts of a luxury car.

While SSJS is more scalable than traditional CGI, it is certainly not the most scalable solution. If your site is taking on millions of hits a day, you probably want something better such as the Netscape Application Server or to develop your application using one of the server-side APIs like NSAPI.

On the bright side though is the fact that most web applications don't ever see this type of traffic (though they often wish they did) and SSJS will most likely fit the bill quite nicely.

ASP

Chapters 13 and 14 demonstrate the use of Active Server Pages (ASP), a Microsoft development environment designed to make it easier and more efficient to develop web-based applications.

The nice thing about ASP is that if you know Visual Basic, it's very easy to come up to speed with ASP. While it is indeed possible to use other languages such as JavaScript and Perl as ASP development languages, VBScript remains the most popular ASP language. If you know HTML and a bit of scripting language like VBScript or JavaScript you can quickly create web applications in ASP; particularly ones that interact with databases.

On the flip-side of ASP are the issues of performance and platform dependence. ASP pages are always interpreted which really adds a great deal of overhead to your web applications. Even if you just hit reload on a page, the ASP script must be re-run through the ASP engine. This adds an extra second or two to the execution of the script, which can be the difference between a visitor staying or leaving your site. ASP is also primarily a Windows-only server product. However if you're happy with using Microsoft's Internet Information Server as your web server, then go for it. For those of you with non-Windows machines, there are several third party ASP engines on the market if you want to have a look at ASP. Check out www.halcyonsoft.com and www.chilisoft.com for more details.

JSP

Java Server Pages (JSP) are the Java community's answer to both SSJS and ASP – a part of the Java Servlet standard which is quickly gaining in popularity.

JSP, like ASP and SSJS, enable you to add application logic into HTML pages. JSP pages are compiled by the JSP engine into Java servlets, "on the fly". This means that the first visitor to your site will pay a slight performance penalty as the application is compiled, but the rest of your visitors get a performance boost.

Java servlets (remember these are what JSP pages become) are like server API functions because they don't add extra CPU processes, running instead in the same process as the servlet engine. The servlet engine may be a stand-alone application (like Apache JServ) or in the same process. This gives you an added performance boost because it doesn't have to be reinterpreted or compiled, it's just run.

And finally Java servlets are a standard. They can be run on any platform that supports Java (without having to be rewritten or recompiled) including all of the popular web servers on the market. Sun and the Apache group are also working on an open-source Java servlet server called Jakarta (which will replace both the Sun Java web server and the Apache JServ engine).

You can find out more about JSP at http://java.sun.com.

Conclusion

In this chapter we discussed the use of server-side JavaScript in the Netscape Enterprise web server and created a small SSJS voting booth application.

We learned why it can be an effective option to traditional CGI, in particular when you need to connect to a database over the Web and looked at several of the key features to making SSJS an appealing option for server-side web development.

Finally, we also gave a brief introduction to ASP and JSP, two other similarly featured server-side technologies which you can use as an alternative to sever-side JavaScript.

If you would like to learn more about SSJS check out the Netscape Developer's JavaScript Central site at http://developer.netscape.com/js/.

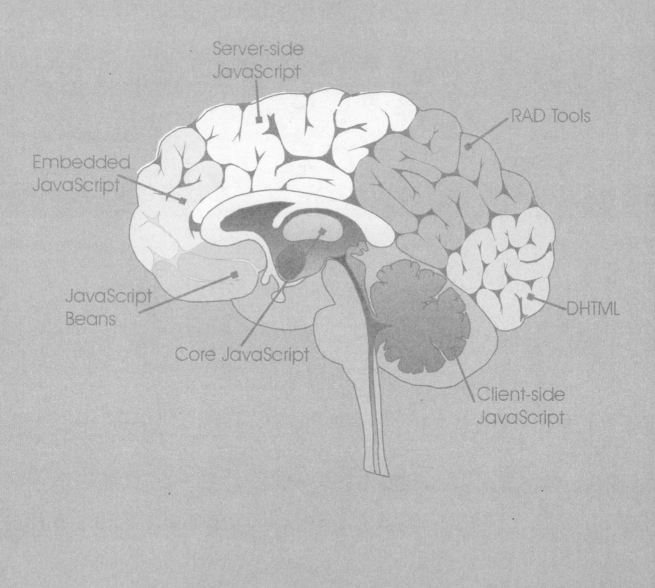

CGI and ScriptEase:WSE

In the previous chapter, we saw how using server-side code in our web pages allowed us to do things not possible when writing on the client side only. One possible way in which create such code is to create compiled server-side JavaScript files that run under Netscape Enterprise Server. Another far less limiting way is to script all your server-side operations as CGI programs. CGI (Common Gateway Interface) is the grand-daddy of server-side technologies and has the major plus point that because it has been around for so long, and has its specification as a standard, that once you write a CGI program for use on one platform it's more than likely to work on all the others as well.

To explore CGI, we're going to make specific use of the ScriptEase:Web Server Edition (SE:WSE) JavaScript-based CGI handler that offers some useful facilities that other solutions may lack. Specifically in this chapter, we'll look at:

- ❑ Why we'd want to use CGI in the first place
- ❑ How CGI works
- ❑ SE:WSE, it's functionality and many cool features

To finish, we'll also run through some sample CGI scripts, so you can get the idea of how JavaScript CGI is written.

Why CGI?

CGI programs have all the functionality of both Server-Side JavaScript and Active Server Pages but also the added advantages of cross-platform compatibility and multi-lingual support. Because CGI has been around for so long and been accepted as a web standard, practically every platform can run some CGI adapter that conforms to the specification. There is no requirement that a web server implements the CGI specification, but it is so useful that most web servers do.

CGI programs are also distinct from the web server and the pages they create, meaning that:

❑ If the CGI program crashes, it won't automatically kill the web server too

❑ They can be written in any language

The proviso then, is to make sure that each server contains an implementation of the language the script has been written in. The content that makes up such a program is never revealed to the browser user. It is only the output of such a program that ultimately reaches the user.

CGI also has a few tricks up its output sleeve too. Normally its dynamic page generation would be set up to create some HTML to be sent back to the client. However, it is becoming more commonplace to generate image data on the fly. That may be simply to replay some image data from a cache or database or even to generate and render a pixel map directly.

Theoretically, it is possible to generate dynamically any kind of data that a web browser can use. In practice, however, it's still quite a complex operation to generate image data and so far the dynamic generation of streamed video tends to be done with specialized hardware and software systems.

All the useful things we can do on the server-side however do not come without some effort. In order for anything to happen, someone has to write a CGI script and then install it on the web server. Then when a page is called, the CGI back-end will run the script. The great benefit of a scripted back-end is that the scripts can be adjusted and used right away without the need for recompilation, unlike SSJS, as we saw last chapter. More sophisticated script-based systems like WebObjects, StoryServer and Cold Fusion may do some partial just-in-time compilation and may in fact cache the compiled scripts and output data to improve performance.

How Does It All Work?

A web server responds to a request from a browser by following the supplied URL to locate some data, which it then sends back to the browser. In any ordinary case – for example, retrieving some HTML – this is done by finding and opening a file, reading its contents and forwarding that content onwards. Incorporating CGI on your server however, provides us with an alternative plan of action. Instead of finding and opening a file, the web server finds and runs a program. The output of the program is the content that is send back to the user. The program that was executed then ends.

That's the short version anyway. It is, of course, a bit more complicated than that.

The HTTP/CGI Connection

When you type a URL into the location box of a web server and press the return key, or when you click on an active link in a web page, your browser sends a message to the web server. Actually, it's a little smarter than that because it can do all kinds of things if you use different URL methods, but only a couple will end up running a CGI program so the rest can be ignored for now.

The web server handles the request, either by locating a static resource to return, building a response itself or delegating the response construction to another service and waiting for its output. Whichever it chooses to do, the response is then constructed and sent back to the browser. This is called the **request-response chain** and looks like this:

The browser to server connection may pass through some intermediate caching proxy servers which is why here we refer to the request-response chain when we are looking at the end to end behavior from the point of view of a web browser. We might call it a request-response loop when we consider just what happens at the target web server.

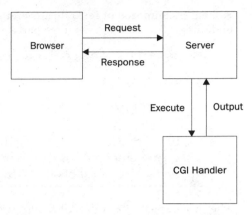

We can now walk through that request-response chain from beginning to end to see how our CGI handler gets executed and how it interacts with the web server. To keep things from getting too complex, we'll ignore the effects of having proxy servers between the browser and server.

It all starts with the URL you enter in your browser. The eventual path it takes to get to the server is more involved than you would have imagined.

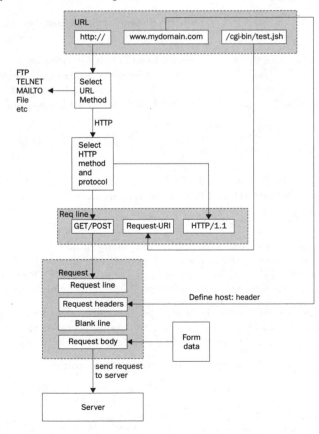

A URL is composed of several parts and although relative URLs may appear as if they do not, in the end, they all share the same three-part composition:

```
<URL method>://<host>/<absolute path>
```

For example:

```
http://www.mydomain.com/admin/readme.txt
```

> The browser will send a request to a web server if the URL method is `http` or `https`. It will go to other kinds of servers or trigger client-side actions for other values. See Appendix K for a list of other URL methods and what they do.

The browser will break this URL into its component parts so it can select a protocol handler and build an **HTTP request** targeted at the host. It will also add other information to the request. If a relative URL is used, then the missing information will be filled in based upon the fully qualified URL of the current document.

The HTTP Request

The HTTP request to be constructed is made up of several parts, some of which are derived from the original fully qualified URL.

At the top of a request comes the actual **request line**. This is followed by a sequence of header lines which are added by the browser. Some are **request headers**, some are general headers and a few are entity headers. The distinctions are subtle and really aimed at helping server engineers understand and implement them. Finally, an optional **entity body** may be added by the browser.

Let's have a look at each of these in detail.

The Request Line

Like a URL, the request line is composed of three distinct parts – the HTTP request method, the absolute document path and an HTTP protocol version number:

```
<HTTP request method> <Request-URI> <HTTP version>
```

The HTTP protocol specifies several possible request methods as you can see in Appendix K, although for CGI we would normally expect to use either GET or POST. Remember not to mix up the URL method with the HTTP request method; one selects the HTTP protocol to send the request by, while the other tells the server how to read with the request when it arrives.

On the Internet, technology is constantly being updated and so the browser needs to tell the web server what version of the HTTP protocol it can understand. As far as the request is concerned, the browser will add a version number for the HTTP protocol it is able to cope with.

Here is an example request line taking all these factors into consideration:

```
GET /admin/readme.txt HTTP/1.1
```

Note that the request line has trimmed the URL to remove the URL method and the target host. All that is left is the full path to the target document. This is called the Request-URI. It might sometimes also be called an entity although that relates more to the construction of a request or response.

The request line can also include parameter values. For GET requests, these parameters will be appended to a question mark as name\value pairs forming a 'query string' and then to the end of the URI. For example

```
GET /admin/readme.txt?a=1&b=3 HTTP/1.1
```

For POST requests, these same name\value pairs are placed in the request entity body, further down the request. Wherever they're placed however, your CGI adapter will unwrap these and present them to you for easy access.

If your request-URI does not contain a file and simply ends with a directory name, the web server will use an internal mechanism to supply a default index file name. It is up to your webmaster to define this but it is good practice to not rely on it being defined. It is far better to explicitly and fully describe the URI. If you are rigorous in this, traffic analyzer software will stand a better chance of detecting site entry points where users begin to access your site.

The Request Headers

A set of request header lines follows the request line. Each line is composed of a keyword followed by a colon and a value. They look a lot like mail headers and it's quite common to find headers constructed like this in all kinds of Internet protocols.

There are about twenty of these headers commonly used but you may encounter other ones that are implementation dependent. There are many dozens actually and new ones can be created as needed. A limited set of them is defined as part of the HTTP specification.

Some headers will get eaten by the web server before your CGI program ever sees them. Others are not really very useful but a few can give you a great deal of help when creating dynamic content.

You may find that you have to change your web server's configuration to allow certain headers through to the CGI back-end. It's not always necessary and depends on the CGI adapter in your web server. It is likely though that you will find the common headers already configured by default. It depends greatly on the browser and sometimes even how the user has set it up as to whether you will ever see some of these headers.

Bearing this in mind, the table below lists the set of the most useful headers you'll come across. We will see how to get at them shortly when we are inside the CGI handler environment.

Header	Description
Content-Length	Used in conjunction with Content-Type to extract data from a POSTed request entity body.
Content-Type	Used by the CGI adapter to convert the POSTed request entity body into accessible parameters. Used in conjunction with Content-Length.

Table continued on following page...

Header	Description
Cookie	Not actually specified as part of the HTTP protocol but will be used by the browser to append any cookies to the request that the server receiving the request may have previously sent it. For more on cookies see Chapter 18.
From	The user-provided e-mail address might be presented in this header. The client browser may not be configured to supply this value so it may not always be available.
Host	Selects one of the virtual hosts on the server. It contains the value of the <host> portion of the original URL.
Referer	Indicates the page that the browser was displaying when the user clicked on a link. You will often get a blank value for this if a location was typed in, or if the link was in a local file-based bookmark page. Framesets can also yield an empty referer value on some browsers but not others.
User-Agent	Contains what sort of browser was being used. Note that this may not always contain a human-readable string however. Custom-made browsers and spiders often choose not to identify themselves in this fashion.

Many more request and response headers are listed in Appendix K.

The Request Entity Body

The request entity body is optional and is used by some of the HTTP request methods to supplement the information provided on the URL request line. It is separated from the headers by a blank line. If there is an entity body, then the Content-Type: and Content-Length: header lines should also be supplied.

You will most often find this used in a POST request to convey the contents of a form back to the CGI handler – a distinct advantage over appending it to a URL, especially when the contents of the form are large and bulky. You can also transfer binary data in the entity body which you cannot do in the URL without encoding it and even then there are limits on the size of URL before it becomes unreasonably large.

Putting The Whole Request Together

Now that we have covered the basic structure of a Request Message, let's put all the pieces together to illustrate an example message from the client to the web server. First, we will start with a URL embedded in a link on a page:

```
<A href="http://www.mydomain.com/cgi-bin/test.jse">ClickMe</A>
```

Inside the browser, this is unwrapped and a request message is constructed like this:

```
GET /cgi-bin/test.jse HTTP/1.1
Host: www.mydomain.com
From: me@myaddress.com
User-Agent: Mozilla/4.0 (......)
Accept: text/*
Accept-Encoding: gzip
Cookie: USERID=1994545
```

The browser uses the hostname and does a lookup via DNS to locate the IP address for the host. Then it opens a connection on port 80 at that IP address. The server acknowledges the connection and the browser sends the request message. Then it waits on the server for a response.

The Server Response

Now it gets interesting. The server receives the request and looks at the content of it to determine what to do next. It notes that the browser can cope with HTTP/1.1 protocol which means it could maintain the connection and send back several responses without a new connection needing to be made.

Then it looks at the header values. If there is a `Cookie` header and it can deal with cookies, it digests those attached into a form that can be read by the CGI handler. Other headers may trigger certain 'browser match' handlers to set up the request-response loop at the server end in a particular way. The `Accept` header's encoding value is also noted because the response may be transferred in a compressed form for performance if the server knows the browser can cope with it.

If there is an entity body, the `Content-Type` and `Content-Length` headers determine how that is unpacked. The URI is stripped down to its component parts and the path is checked against a map. Finally, if the server is configured correctly, in this example it will know that it has a CGI program to call.

Having packaged up the headers and any parameter values from the request URI, the web server now tries to execute the CGI handler. How it does this exactly depends on the web server and the platform it is running on. The net result is that we find ourselves inside a program or script, with an environment built around us that reflects the current state of the world as the web server sees it and any request parameters and form values readily to hand if we want to use them.

Of course if the web server cannot find or execute the CGI program, it simply sends back an error page.

Inside the CGI Handler

Inside the CGI handler, we can unpack the parameters the web server has given us, make some observations about the state of the world and manufacture a suitable response. By the time we're ready to create a response, we will have clear access to:

- ❑ The HTTP Headers that haven't been 'cleared' from the server
- ❑ Any parameters or form contents that were appended to the request message
- ❑ The values stored in any cookies that we have previously sent the browser

This last item in particular will help us maintain state between requests and track users. We should also be able to determine the kind of browser the user sent the request from and with that knowledge we can work round some of the variations in functionality that different browsers support as we've seen earlier in the book.

Constructing a Response

There are two parts to a server response: a **header block** and a **body**. The header block is composed of header lines, some of which might well include the same HTTP headers we've already seen in the client request. This is then followed by a blank line and the body of the response – the HTML\JavaScript etc.

Inside our CGI handler, we can construct any kind of response we like – it's simply a matter of populating the CGI buffer with lines like:

```
cgi.out("Print Me");
```

and then ending the program. We could also add any number of headers to set cookies, last-modified times, cache control and expiry times on the response or possibly even our own custom headers if we so desired. Note that cookie data only needs to be sent back if it has to change the current value in the cookie or reset its expiry date.

From CGI to the Browser

The web server waits on the CGI handler for its output. It knows when the CGI handler is finished and the output is complete. At that point it can add any headers it wants to and send it back to the browser.

Note that we do not put in a `Content-length` header at this stage – the web server will do that for us automatically. It needs to measure the content length anyway so that it can record the value in the access log. This it can do as it makes each CGI call as a separate transaction and the connection to the browser requires the content length to be specified so it can receive multiple responses on a single connection.

Eventually, the response arrives back in the web browser where it is stored in the local cache in case it is required again and displayed on the screen. Any response headers that the browser can use are unpacked along the way. Cookies are stored if necessary, expiry times are registered in the cache log and the connection to the web server closed unless there is more incoming traffic.

If you want to read more about the CGI standard, these two sites are rather good,

```
http://hoohoo.ncsa.uiuc.edu/cgi/
http://www.w3.org/hypertext/WWW/CGI
```

as are these two on the subject of URLs:

```
http://www.ncsa.uiuc.edu/demoweb/url-primer.html
http://www.w3.org/hypertext/WWW/Addressing/Addressing.html
```

Note that as we've described how the HTTP protocol and CGI interface work together, we've done it in a server-independent way. That is, we have not described any particular server but a very idealized model that all servers are built around. Each server must comply with the various protocols but how they implement them internally may differ from one product to another. They are all configurable but some have a GUI and others have an editable text file. They are certainly not all configurable to the same extent but for the purposes of CGI handling and our discussion here, they are all remarkably similar.

CGI is tightly interwoven with the actual HTTP protocol itself, and the particular CGI handler we're going to use, ScriptEase:Web Server Edition, does an excellent job of making sure all the HTTP request and response is at your fingertips.

The 'Susie' Solution

ScriptEase:Web Server Edition, or SE:WSE (pronounced 'Susie') as it's more easily called is an excellent JavaScript-based CGI handler with a number of handy features built-in:

❑ Portability across many platforms and web servers by using a common interpreter core

❑ Support for ISAPI, WinCGI, ACGI and LCGI

❑ Access to strongly typed data (ScriptEase interpreters have additional types), allowing more precise calculations, e.g. integer calculations

❑ Powerful C language standard function library and OS calls – see Appendix H for more details

❑ Pre-formatted function libraries to support HTML generation

❑ Portability. Web sites with a non-trivial server-side back-end can move from web provider to web provider and still be sure their scripts will perform as expected. Only CGI is required and that is a standard feature available from almost any ISP

❑ Multi-tiered distributed scripting

❑ IDE debugger tool

❑ Support for secure access

❑ Ability to web-enable legacy applications

The main differentiator of ScriptEase interpreters is their ease of access to low level nitty-gritty C and Unix functions. It's generally available in a wider variety of configurations than other products. This makes it a powerful programming tool that is suitable for a wide range of jobs.

JavaScript and ScriptEase

Developing JavaScript-based CGI scripts to work with SE:WSE really is very simple. Just to whet your appetite, here is an example SE:WSE script which generates a very simple dynamic page:

```
cgi.out("Content-Type: text/html \r \n");
cgi.out("\r \n");

cgi.out("<HTML>");
cgi.out("<BODY>");
cgi.out("A CGI test page");
cgi.out("</BODY>");
cgi.out("</HTML>");
```

ScriptEase interpreters have a lot of extensions to the basic JavaScript functionality. Many of these extensions are provided in the pre-processor and the object containing the C language standard library handlers. These give you access to files on the server that client-side scripts would not have. You are also able to control other asset and resource privileges far more effectively in the server.

Installing SE:WSE

Installing and setting up SE:WSE on your server is quite simple. Because it is available for such a wide variety of platforms and servers you should check the instructions supplied with the install kit for any special considerations for your system. The installation is remarkably similar across all platforms.

Installing and configuring SE:WSE on your server is a matter of following these simple steps.

- ❑ Download the correct version for your operating system from
  `http://www.nombas.com/us/download/index.htm#sewse`
- ❑ Run the install script. The installer will unpack and customize the files it installs according to the options you specify. The HTML files that it writes contain helpful online documentation and they will be edited as they are installed so that they work correctly in your server environment. It asks you questions about where the CGI directory is and where the HTML documents are kept so it can install the online manuals. If you have purchased a license, you will need your license key at this point
- ❑ When the installer finishes, it will automatically run the configuration tool – SEWSECFG – which allows you to setup the security features built into SE:WSE. It is important that you configure these correctly. When you define password values, anticipate the way people may try to generate passwords and make up values that are unlikely to be cracked easily

The Windows NT 4.0 version of ScriptEase will run on Windows 2000 with IIS5.0, but requires a lot more coercion to run properly than it does on Windows NT 4 and IIS 4.0. Uninstalling is simply a case of deleting the files that the installer created.

Testing the Installation

Once you have installed and configured the SE:WSE software, you can test that it works by requesting a page with a browser. Make sure the web server is running first and then request a URL according to the details you specified during installation. For example:

```
http://www.mysite.com/scriptease/index.html
```

This might be different according to the values you specified during the installation. It may also be somewhat platform specific. If you are in doubt, check your document tree for the folders that the installation placed there and try accessing the files at that location. You may need to adjust the URL to cope with case sensitivity and whether you are using the `.htm` or `.html` extension.

If this works you should see a page with some links on it and a big ScriptEase logo center top. To make sure the CGI handler is working, hit the Arcade link on the page and then look for the 'Verify installation' link in the top right of the arcade page. The Verify link will display a message from SE:WSE telling you it is working. A second link to try is the CGI Fields URL at the bottom of the arcade page. This will tell you what server values are presented to the CGI interface. You can change these by re-configuring the server setup. If you use Apache, this is the `httpd.conf` file but your server may have a GUI admin tool as an alternative. If necessary, you may need to rebuild the server after modifying the sources for the CGI adapter if you need some esoteric header to be passed through.

If it does not work properly, and really there is not much to go wrong, there is some debugging advice in the read-me document that came with your installation kit.

At this point you should have a working web server that is able to create dynamic pages. OK, we have not hooked it up to a database yet but we can do a lot with flat files without needing a database at all. There are large set of example scripts provided with your installation so you can begin experimenting right away.

UNIX Installation Problems

Be aware that on some platforms (in particular UNIX) the installer and config tools may convert your answers to all lower case. This can be a problem if you have your web site installed in directories whose names have an upper case letter in them. You can work round this but you may find that all the sample code is written with hard coded URLs embedded inside it and they point at an HTDOCs and CGI-BIN that are rooted in a lower case version of your base path.

Setting up the secure paths will require colon characters instead of semi-colon characters as the documentation suggests.

Other Possible Installation Problems

Checking through the read-me document that was supplied with your installation kit is worthwhile. It might tell you about some known problems with your server platform. That will save some valuable debugging time when you encounter them later.

Known issues include the possibility that binary image data may not make it back through your web server from the CGI interface resulting in broken or corrupted GIF image data apparently coming out of the `cgi.out()` function. The likelihood is that `cgi.out()` is operating perfectly fine but that there's a problem in your web server. It is impossible to cover all the likely causes but here are some suggestions:

❑ The CGI interface may not be 8-bit binary transparent. That means that 7-bit characters make it through fine and HTML is delivered in a useable form. Binary image data loses one bit of information and gets corrupted accordingly.

❑ The web server may not be configured to support all the MIME types you need.

❑ There may be a buffering problem in the CGI interface.

❑ You could have a memory or CPU resource limit set for sub-processes that prevent the image data from being processed correctly.

The CGI interface in your web server simply may not allow binary data to be delivered. Bugs in code like this sometimes only show up when you 'push the envelope' of performance. Dynamically generating GIF data is still a rare enough requirement that many people will not have tried it. Some web servers may not have been tested thoroughly for this capability.

Activating a Script

As far as the user browser is concerned, there is very little difference between receiving the contents of a static file or the dynamically generated output of a script. At the server, however, the two are quite distinct. A request for a static resource simply requires the relevant file to be located in a document collection and sent off. For a script-generated response however, the server needs to be able to locate the script processor, call it and then pass on the name of the script to be executed.

With the basic SE:WSE setup, on a Windows server you might receive a URL like this:

```
http://www.oursite.com/cgi-bin/sewse.exe?C:/example.jse
```

This refers to a script called `example.jse` that lives in the root directory of the C:\ drive in the server. It gets loaded into the SE:WSE interpreter that lives in the `CGI-BIN` directory that the web server controls.

On a UNIX machine, that URL might become something like this:

```
http://www.oursite.com/cgi-bin/sewse?/scripts/example.jse
```

The script is still called `example.jse` but it lives in a `scripts` directory on the server. The SE:WSE interpreter also no longer has the `.exe` file extension – it's simply not necessary in UNIX. Although this works, it gives away the name of the script interpreter and how to call it directly. Potentially, this is a security risk. Having published this interface, a nefarious hacker may choose to exploit your SE:WSE interpreter by passing arbitrary parameters to it.

Hiding the Interpreter Details

On some platforms, and on UNIX in particular, you can move the interpreter to a separate location and call the script directly. An associative mechanism then runs the script in the interpreter without giving away the location of the interpreter. In the UNIX environment, we move the `sewse` interpreter executable to `/usr/local/bin` and make sure that the environment the web server runs in will look in there for an executable. We do that by modifying UNIX's `PATH` environment variable to include `/usr/local/bin` if it does not already. Then we modify the scripts, placing this text in the first line of each one that is called directly by the CGI mechanism:

```
#!/usr/local/bin/sewse
```

Now we store the script in the `CGI-BIN` directory of the server and we can then call them directly with a URL like this:

```
http://www.oursite.com/cgi-bin/example.jse
```

Now, for this to work slightly more elegantly, we could configure Apache with a `Rewrite` directive to associate the `jse` file type to the `cgi-bin` directory. In doing so successfully, we can shorten the URL even more to something like this

```
http://www.oursite.com/example.jse
```

for inclusion in an anchor tag or form action attribute. This is good because the more we hide server-side configuration details on the server-side, the less likely we are to hard code it into the web pages themselves and that is a significant benefit.

ScriptEase CGI Extensions

ScriptEase interpreters support some feature extensions that after a while you will really enjoy having available. These include the ability to:

- ❑ Use conditional statements at the pre-processor stage
- ❑ Define manifest constants and macros
- ❑ Include external source code into your programs
- ❑ Link in compiled library code
- ❑ Use C-library function calls
- ❑ Use other libraries for OS support
- ❑ Easily access HTTP Header Values

The first four of these options are implemented by additions to the CGI pre-processor as we'll see in a minute and the last of these as you may realize is very important given how tightly CGI is tied into the HTTP request-response loop. For more information on the C library function calls and other libraries available for inclusion in your CGI programs, see Appendix H.

Additions to the Pre-Processor

The ScriptEase CGI pre-processor operates in a similar way to that of a C language compiler, processing the source code before starting to interpret and execute it. By correctly making use of the pre-processor then, you can create code that configures itself at run-time according to certain definitions that you have previously set up within the source code. For example, you could define a constant that switches code functionality on or off in 30 different places in the script. You would never want to do 30 edits to the code before running it but a manifest constant in a #define statement can be modified once in a single line to the same effect. For instance

```
#define USER_SUPPORT 3

if (USER_SUPPORT == 3)
{
 cgi.out("The user name is ");
 cgi.out(USER_NAME);
}
```

At the next level up, you could use this idea in conjunction with #ifdef (if defined) statements to determine whether actual blocks of code are included or not in the execution of the program.

```
#ifdef DEBUG_LEVEL
 Clib.printf("Debugging level %d\ n", DEBUG_LEVEL);
#endif
```

#include and #link also give the program access to extra code, with the former inserting some or all the contents of a specified file into the program and the latter providing your program with access to (but not including in your source) runtime-loadable compiled code libraries. Typically, these libraries can give your programs high performance functionality that accesses the deepest core capabilities of your platform. For example:

```
#include <string.jsh>
```

You can place an explicit path in the include or you can leave the path off. If you do, then ScriptEase searches some locations that were configured when the interpreter was installed. These were specified under the JSEPath value.

ScriptEase is smart enough to only include a file once, but you should be careful with nested includes as it's not always obvious in what order the includes will be used. Other platforms that support an #include capability may not allow nested includes to operate. Be wary if portability is an issue and it's probably sensible to include only a single level of external files and not have them including any others internally.

SE:WSE ships with a large number of libraries of pre-written functions you can use. Library files are plain text files having the extension .jsh. See Appendix H for more details on this collection of resource libraries.

Note that you do not have to compile your code to make use of the pre-processor. It is invoked automatically by the interpreter as it loads the script ready for execution.

Getting HTTP Header Values

One great advantage to using ScriptEase as opposed to other CGI interpreters is that a great many of the server environment variables you'll use in your scripts are converted automatically into native JavaScript variables. For example, the HTTP header called `Request-Method:` becomes the environment variable `REQUEST_METHOD` and so on. It does this through its CGI adapter module (although it may be called something else on your server).

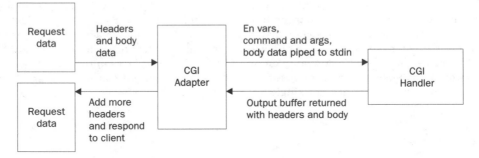

To find out what environment variables you have available you could run the following script.

Note that the first line is a UNIX directive pointing to where the script interpreter is. By including it, you can then call the script directly from the web server rather than calling it indirectly as a parameter to the SE:WSE handler. On non-UNIX-like systems, such as Windows, that do not support this feature you can omit the first line.

```
#!/usr/local/bin/sewse

function main(argc, argv)
{
  var envList = Clib.getenv();
  var itemName;

  cgi.out("Content-Type: text/html \r \n");
  cgi.out("\r \n");

  cgi.out("<HTML>");
  cgi.out("<HEAD>");
  cgi.out("<TITLE>");
  cgi.out("Display All Environment Variables");
  cgi.out("</TITLE>");
  cgi.out("</HEAD>");
  cgi.out("<BODY>");

  for (var ii=0; (itemName = envList[ii]); ii++)
  {
    if (itemName != null)
    {
      cgi.out(itemName);
      cgi.out(" = ");
      cgi.out(Clib.getenv(itemName));
      cgi.out("<BR>");
    }
    else
    {
      break;
    }
  }
  cgi.out("</BODY>");
  cgi.out("</HTML>");
}
```

ScriptEase Parameter Handling

Regardless of whether a form's content has been POSTed or GETed, SE:WSE users have easy access to it. Given the name of the variable you want to access, the function cgi.getVar() retrieves the form values for the script and any character encoding that was necessary to transfer them within the request is handled automatically for you too. For example:

```
cgi.getVar("NAME");
```

If the cgi.getVar() is unable to get the value of the variable, it returns NULL, otherwise cgi.var() works as follows (depending on the type of form element in question):

- ❑ If you are retrieving data from a text field, the text will be returned.
- ❑ If you are retrieving the value of a check box, ON will be returned if the box was checked, and NULL will be returned if it was not.
- ❑ If you are retrieving the value of a set of radio buttons, the VALUE attribute of the checked button will be returned, or NULL if none of the buttons is checked.
- ❑ cgi.getVar() may also be called with no parameters, in which case it returns an array of all valid variable names.

Any parameters sent to your CGI programs as a query string attached to a URL or within the request entity body are also converted into a readily useable format and SE:WSE provides an additional parameter passing mechanism besides the query parameters that normally follow the question mark.

Data may be passed as a command line parameter to a CGI script by appending it to the end of the URL for the script preceded by a '+' sign. This can only be used if the value is a constant since a name\value pair will not work in this situation. It is good for selecting alternative page processing methods within the same script. You might pass a parameter to the script telling it which page made the CGI call although this is not to be confused with the value in the Referer header. You might do it like this:

```
<A HREF=http://www.oursite.com/cgi-bin/example.jse+homepage>
<A HREF=http://www.oursite.com/cgi-bin/example.jse+newspage>
```

In this case, either homepage, or newspage will be passed to example.jse as the first command line argument, depending on which link was selected. The value will be passed to the script as a string and stored both as argv[1] which is local to the main function, and as _argv[1] which is available globally. For example, this line would make sense anywhere in your script:

```
referingPage = _argv[1];
```

Alternatively, to access the command line argument from within the main function, use this fragment of code:

```
function main(argc,argv)
{
 referingPage = argv[1];
}
```

In both cases, you will get the page name (homepage or newspage, depending on which link accesses the script) and store it in the variable referingPage.

The ScriptEase Environment

Up to now, we've looked solely at the features in ScriptEase that give us easy access to the information we can glean from the request-response loop and how to send a very simple response back. Before we go into some more involved examples of CGI scripts, let's look at what other server-side functionality ScriptEase can give us.

Database Access

SE:WSE scripts can access any database with a live ODBC (Open DataBase Connectivity) connection pointing to it. If you don't already have ODBC functionality, Nombas supply a set of ODBC setup files for this reason from their download page at
`http://www.nombas.com/us/download/index.htm`. They also distribute a demonstration database for you to experiment with as part of SE:WSE itself. Unhappily though, it is not immediately available.

In order to connect to a database, you must create a Data Source to it named 'Nombas' registered in the ODBC configuration. You must also run the database setup script as demonstrated in the online manual you installed with SE:WSE to populate the tables within. There are obviously problems inherent in the fact that the Data Source must be named 'Nombas'; you have to make sure that all the tables you'll need are available under this name and it's nigh on impossible to partition up the database and access different parts under different Data Source names.

With the set-up done, you'll need a section of code that includes the ODBC wrapper functions that access the ODBC binary library. This would be placed somewhere near the top of your script:

```
#if defined(_WINDOWS_) || defined(_WIN32_) || defined(_UNIX_)
#include "odbc.jsh"
#else
#include "idspodbc.jsh"
#endif
```

You can then create a database object to hold the database name and access details. Like this:

```
#ifdef _UNIX_
  nombasDatabase.databasename = "www.dbservers.com:MYDB";
  nombasDatabase.username = "user12";
  nombasDatabase.password = "accessAAA";
#else
  nombasDatabase.databasename = "Nombas";
#endif
```

Now you can start the database, read some data and close it again. There are several examples shipped with the installation kit and more still online at Nombas and in the other ScriptEase interpreter kits. Of course, this does not preclude you from experimenting with your own ideas.

Maintaining State

As with all server-side technologies, it's not within the power of CGI to simply query a client's browser about its current state. So you have to make assumptions in the server and depend on values the browser has returned in the request. You may need to use cookies or encoded URL values and preserve some session state in your server-side back-end.

Preserving session state can be very useful but it has some technical issues that make it tricky. Each session has a previously defined time-out value after which state variables expire. Thus if a session times out, any subsequent requests that originated in that session can arrive without any context in which to exist. If a user goes to lunch and continues when they return, their session cache may have expired in the meantime. Maintaining session integrity through static sections of the site (for example, a number of pages not containing any CGI script) is also tricky so a combination of cookies, hidden form fields and encoded URLs could be used very effectively.

The present version of SE:WSE is executed once for each request and does not remain persistent between calls. It parses and interprets the script and then exits. Because it does not run in a persistent condition, if you want to maintain some state information during a session so that activities on one page can influence another, you will need to implement that in your scripts. With the capabilities that ScriptEase interpreters have for file I/O, you can preserve session state in a flat-file cache in the server. So long as you can convey some session identifying value between requests this is not too hard to manage.

With respect to this issue, you may want to incorporate some or all of the following ideas for a session manager into your CGI handler:

- ❏ A way to create, update and destroy session keys
- ❏ A session cache manager, possibly using cookies for state storage
- ❏ Using the additional ScriptEase parameter handler, +, to pass back in any state variables from a cookie to the handler

The ScriptEase Debugger

One thing that does come with SE:WSE but is not automatically installed is ScriptEase's remote IDE Debugger tool. This will prove extremely useful when you are developing your server-side scripts. Often the only access you would have to a server back-end is via the web server itself or through a telnet connection to the server machines where you can watch debugging logs. The IDE allows you to work through the web server interface and debug your scripts line by line and variable by variable. This is really great because you are debugging through the same interface that it delivers the client code.

In this example, you can see the script source window with the currently executing line indicated. There is a window showing the values of local variables for that function and another showing the global variables. Having a tool like this to diagnose errors in JavaScript that is running in a server can help solve the most difficult problems. We can also augment our debugging capabilities with custom scripts as we'll see in a while.

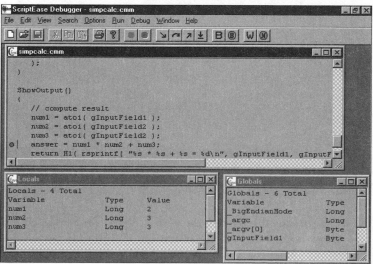

Some Example Scripts

It would be rude to talk about setting up the interpreter and all the features of ScriptEase on offer without at least demonstrating a few scripts. But before we do, let's return to the first principle of server-side programming – generating output for the client to read.

Sending Output with cgi.out()

Having received a client request, you need to return something to the client when the CGI program is run: a server response. This is done with a series of calls to the cgi.out() function.

> **The cgi.out() mechanism is built around a buffer that can be cleared and rewritten possibly several times during the execution of the script. It is quite useful to be able to detect an error and completely purge and rewrite the buffer. The downside of this is that streaming techniques are not possible because the buffer is not returned until the script exits. Mechanisms for streaming responses may be added to a later version of ScriptEase.**

The first call to cgi.out() creates this buffer to contain the HTML page that your program will generate and writes whatever you give it to the buffer. Each subsequent call then appends the next line of the HTML string to the buffer, unless, that is, we call cgi.out(null) which will erase the entire contents of the buffer. When the script terminates, whatever's left in the buffer is sent back to the client.

The first portion of the CGI output buffer must contain the content type of the document being returned. For HTML documents, this looks like:

```
cgi.out("Content-Type: text/html \r \n");
cgi.out("\r \n");
```

This example, which we saw earlier, generates a simple HTML document:

```
cgi.out("Content-Type: text/html \r \n");
cgi.out("\r \n");

cgi.out("<HTML>");
cgi.out("<HEAD>");
cgi.out("<TITLE>");
cgi.out("ScriptEase HTML Example");
cgi.out("</TITLE>");
cgi.out("</HEAD>");

cgi.out("<BODY>");
cgi.out("<H2>");
cgi.out("Simple Messages are best!");
cgi.out("</H2>");
cgi.out("</BODY>");
cgi.out("</HTML>");
```

As we've already discovered, the server response is composed of the response headers, a blank line and a response entity body.

The minimum header you should return would be the Content-Type value. You should be careful to collect all the headers together before outputting the blank line. A short cut would be to code the Content-Type line like this:

```
cgi.out("Content-Type: text/html\ r\ n\ r\ n");
```

The danger here is that you will place subsequent headers after this line and the will actually end up being outside the header block. In the examples in this chapter, the content type is shown as follows, even when it is the only header line being returned in the response:

```
cgi.out("Content-Type: text/html\ r\ n");
cgi.out("\ r\ n");
```

This is less ambiguous and you are more likely to place additional headers in the right location.

Redirect Responses

When a client requests a page that has moved elsewhere, a simple set of three headers should be returned from the server, indicating that the page has moved and the new location it can be found at. It is then up to the client to either request the new location or go someplace else.

Here is a short CGI handler script that returns a permanent redirect:

```
#!/usr/local/bin/sewse

cgi.out("Content-Type: text/plain \r \n");
cgi.out("Status: 301 Moved Permanently \r \n");
cgi.out("Location: http://www.elsewhere.com/ \r \n");
cgi.out("\r \n");

cgi.out("If you see this, your browser");
cgi.out("does not handle 301 status codes correctly");
```

Note that both ASP and SSJS have much simpler ways of dealing with this situation.

Custom CGI Error Handling

It's in the nature of a piece of code not to work, at least the first time anyway. When a CGI program fails for some reason (data corruption, lack of resources or a bug, typically), the browser will report a fatal error to the user. In this case all you can do is fix the originating problem. A less serious case is where the CGI program detects something has gone wrong, and cannot complete normal processing – for example when submitted data cannot be stored in a database due to clashing data.

When the error is not a fatal one, you can either display a special error page, or redisplay the current page with an error message. The next two examples show both methods. Both check the name entered in a form to see if it is boring, and if so, they report an error.

The first script – `error1.cgi` – generates a separate page for the error:

```
#!/usr/local/bin/sewse          //Unix-alike OS users only

function show_html()
{
  cgi.out("Content-Type: text/html \r \n");
  cgi.out("\r \n");

  cgi.out("<HTML>");
  cgi.out("<BODY>");

  // Uncomment one of the following two lines. Which depends on your OS
  // Top line for UNIX, bottom line for Windows
  // cgi.out("<FORM METHOD=\"POST\">");
  // cgi.out("<FORM ACTION=\"http://myserver/cgi-bin/sewse.exe?error1.cgi\"
           METHOD=\"POST\">");

  cgi.out("Enter surname ...");
  cgi.out("<INPUT TYPE=\"text\" NAME=\"surname\">");
  cgi.out("<INPUT TYPE=\"submit\">");
  cgi.out("</FORM>");
  cgi.out("</BODY>");
  cgi.out("</HTML>");
}

// Create global variable
var surname;

// called without submit
function main ()
{
  if ( (surname = cgi.getVar("SURNAME"))== NULL || surname=="")
  {
    show_html();
  }
  else
  {
    if ( surname.toUpperCase() == "SMITH"
        || surname.toUpperCase() == "WONG"
        || surname.toUpperCase() == "SINGH"
        || surname.toUpperCase() == "BROWN" )
    {
      cgi.out("Content-Type: text/html \r \n");
      cgi.out("\r \n");

      cgi.out("<HTML>");
      cgi.out("<BODY>");
      cgi.out("Warning! Boring name alert!");
      cgi.out("</BODY>");
      cgi.out("</HTML>");
    }
    else
    {
      show_html();
    }
  }
}
```

And, as promised, while functionally the same, this version of the script – `error2.cgi` – will always display the same page but include an error message on screen as well should an error occur.

```
#!/usr/local/bin/sewse          //Unix-alike OS users only

function show_html(err_text)
{
  cgi.out("Content-Type: text/html \r \n");
  cgi.out("\r \n");

  cgi.out("<HTML>");
  cgi.out("<HEAD>");
  cgi.out("<SCRIPT>");

  if ( err_text )
  {
    cgi.out("var error_string = \""+err_text+"\";\n");
  }
  else
  {
    cgi.out("var error_string = null;\n");
  }

  cgi.out("if (error_string) alert(error_string);\n");
  cgi.out("</SCRIPT>");
  cgi.out("</HEAD>");
  cgi.out("<BODY>");


  // Uncomment one of the following two lines. Which depends on your OS
  // Top line for UNIX, bottom line for Windows
  // cgi.out("<FORM METHOD=\"POST\">");
  // cgi.out("<FORM ACTION=\"http://myserver/cgi-bin/sewse.exe?error2.cgi\"
            METHOD=\"POST\">");

  cgi.out("Enter surname ...");
  cgi.out("<INPUT TYPE=\"text\" NAME=\"surname\">");
  cgi.out("<INPUT TYPE=\"submit\">");
  cgi.out("</FORM>");
  cgi.out("</BODY>");
  cgi.out("</HTML>");
}

// Create global variable
var surname;

function main(argc, argv)
{
  if ( (surname= cgi.getVar("SURNAME"))== NULL || surname=="")
  {
    show_html("Hello"); // called separate to submit
  }
  else
  {
    if ( surname.toUpperCase() == "SMITH"
        || surname.toUpperCase() == "WONG"
        || surname.toUpperCase() == "SINGH"
        || surname.toUpperCase() == "TRAN" )
    {
      show_html("Warning! Boring Name.");
    }
    else
    {
      show_html("Hello");
    }
  }
}
```

The variable `error_string` only appears in the browser. The variable `err_text` only appears in the CGI program. The browser always checks the variable `error_string` via inline JavaScript when loading the HTML, to see if anything went wrong.

CGI Form Handlers

Last but not least we come to the main reason why the majority of people use Perl and its excellent regular expression support – dealing with forms.

There's no right or wrong way to write a CGI form handler, but one of the more elegant solutions is to write one that generates the initial form as well as dealing with a user's submitted data. In effect, such a handler would have three tasks:

❑   **Document generator**. On start-up the handler need be called with no parameters triggering it to generate the form.

❑   **Form submission handler**. As a user submits data, the handler is called again but this time with the user's submission as parameters to the call.

❑   **Form validator**. If the contents of the form have been entered incorrectly, the handler returns the form again for resubmission, else it returns a simple acknowledgement.

Even from this bold statement of intent, you may already have realized that there is more subtlety to even the simple task of forms handling than you may have first thought. In the next few sections, we'll look at some of these subtleties in more detail.

GET Versus POST for Form Data

As we've already noted, there are two ways to submit form data to a web server: GET and POST.

❑   The GET method attaches the form data to the end of the URL in the submit request as a 'query string' separated by a question mark (?) character from the rest of the URL.

❑   The POST request sends the form data as a separate, but attached message in the submit request.

Although the methods of transmission are different, both do use a special code for the form data so that it is not confused with any other parts of the submit request. They also both have their pros and cons.

To its advantage, a GET request can be 'remembered' as a bookmark as it attaches form data to a URL. Likewise, this also means that the user can read the data being submitted by looking down the URL's query string. However, URLs have a maximum length, so GET is no good for forms with lots of data or indeed with any data that needs to be secure. GET is intended to be used where the form submission does not change the web site it is sent to at all. Search engine requests are a classic example.

POST form data is attached as a separate body section to the URL and can be any size, so it is reliable for all forms. The user cannot see the POSTed data either, which means that it's a little more secure as well. However, POST requests do not have unique URLs like GET and very, very, big POST requests can create problems for little web servers with only simple CGI support. POST requests are meant to be used where the form submission changes or stores something on the web site. Registration forms are a classic example. There are also issues regarding log analysis that may require the form data to be available for processing so that you can determine what dynamic content was served. You might have had that data present with GET requests but it's not there with POST and so reporting can become a significant technical challenge.

Accessing Form Values as Parameters

Regardless of whether a form's content has been POSTed or GETed, SE:WSE users have easy access to it. Given the name of the variable you want to access, the function cgi.getVar() retrieves the form values for the script and any character encoding that was necessary to transfer them in the request is handled automatically for you too. For example:

```
cgi.getVar("NAME");
```

If the cgi.getVar() is unable to get the value of the variable, it returns NULL, otherwise it works as follows, depending on the type of form element in question:

- ❑ If you are retrieving data from a text field, the text will be returned.
- ❑ If you are retrieving the value of a check box, ON will be returned if the box was checked, and NULL will be returned if it was not.
- ❑ If you are retrieving the value of a set of radio buttons, the VALUE attribute of the checked button will be returned, or NULL if none of the buttons is checked.
- ❑ cgi.getVar() may also be called with no parameters, in which case it returns an array of all valid variable names.

Here is an example that displays the values of all valid variables supplied by a submit:

```
#!/usr/local/bin/sewse

function main(argc, argv)
{
 var variableList = cgi.getVar();
 var itemName;

 cgi.out("Content-Type: text/html\ r\ n");
 cgi.out("\ r\ n");

 cgi.out("<HTML>");
 cgi.out("<HEAD>");
 cgi.out("<TITLE>");
 cgi.out("Display All Form Variables");
 cgi.out("</TITLE>");
 cgi.out("</HEAD>");
 cgi.out("<BODY>");

 for (var ii=0; ((itemName = variableList[ii]) != null); ii++)
 {
 if (itemName != null)
 {
 cgi.out(itemName);
 cgi.out(" = ");
 cgi.out(cgi.getVar(itemName));
 cgi.out("<BR>");
 }
 else
 {
 break;
 }
 }

 cgi.out("</BODY>");
 cgi.out("</HTML>");
}
```

Preserving Form Variables Between Pages

One thing to remember in general, and not just with respect to the CGI handler we hypothesized earlier, is what happens to the contents of a form and particularly any inline JavaScript variables when the form is submitted. Netscape browsers preserve the data in an HTML form after a submit occurs, in case the replacement form is the same one. If so, the data is put back again. IE4 and above also store the data internally in case you wish to resubmit it. However, neither browser persists the value of a form's contents or any JavaScript variables across pages. To do that, we must write a little script.

For example, suppose the following document is generated from a CGI program:

```
<HTML>
<BODY>
<FORM>
<INPUT NAME="lonely" TYPE="text" VALUE="I'm here!">
</FORM>
</BODY>
</HTML>
```

The lonely field will always be filled. A CGI program could read the old value of the field on submit, and put it back in the generated document. Here is such a CGI program, written in SE:WSE JavaScript:

```
#!/usr/local/bin/sewse      //UNIX Only

function main(argc, argv)
{
 var lonely_field = cgi.getVar("lonely");

 // Check for call with no submit data
 if ( !lonely_field )
 {
 lonely_field = "";
 }

 cgi.out("Content-Type: text/html \r \n");
 cgi.out("\r \n");

 cgi.out("<HTML>");
 cgi.out("<BODY>");
\\ Uncomment one of the following two lines. Which depends on your OS
  \\ Top line for UNIX, bottom line for Windows
  \\ cgi.out("<FORM>");
  \\ cgi.out("<FORM ACTION=\"http://myserver/cgi-bin/sewse.exe?persist.cgi\"
          METHOD=\"POST\">");

 cgi.out("<INPUT NAME=\"lonely\" TYPE=\"text\" VALUE=\"");
 cgi.out(lonely_field);
 cgi.out("\ >");
 cgi.out("</FORM>");
 cgi.out("</BODY>");
 cgi.out("</HTML>");
}
```

Each time the CGI program is run, the VALUE attribute of the text field changes to any value submitted.

Otherwise, the simplest way to avoid wiping out data is to choose a target window away from the submission window, if the user requires no feedback. The next simplest is to avoid submitting from the form in question entirely, as described next.

Handmade Submits

Both `GET` and `POST` style requests can be made from an HTML document that has no form, using JavaScript.

For `POST` requests, the only way to achieve this is to create or use an HTML form in another document. Whatever data is required can be copied into that form. Typically, that form is in a frame of zero height or width so that it is invisible on the screen of the client browser. This also allows the user to continue interacting with the main document while the form submit is in progress.

For `GET` requests, the URL containing the form data can be constructed by hand without any HTML, but it still requires a (possibly hidden) window to be loaded into. Use `window.location.href` or `document.replace()` to apply the new URL. The format of the URL is:

```
http://host/path?name1=value1&name2=value2&name3=value3...
```

Where `name1`, `name2`, `name3` are HTML `NAME` attribute values for fields, and `value1`, `value2`, `value3` are the field values. If two form elements have the same name, there should be two `name=value` pairs, one for each element.

That alone, however, is not enough. URL syntax demands that the URL follow encoding rules so that no special or dangerous characters appear. JavaScript provides the life-saving `escape()` function to do just this, and `unescape()` to change back, if necessary. Be careful to only escape the portions you need to. You will have to escape the URL as individual components. This is the WRONG way to do it:

```
var my_url;
my_url = "http://search.yahoo.com/bin/search?p=help me!";
var fixed_url=escape(my_url);
```

Here we do it correctly, only escaping the parts that need to be escaped:

```
var my_parm = "p";
var my_valu = "help me!";

var my_url = "http://search.yahoo.com/bin/search";

var fixed_url = my_url + "?" + escape(my_parm) + "=" + escape(my_valu);
```

The 'fixed' version looks like this:

```
http://search.yahoo.com/bin/search?p=help+me%21
```

You can now insert the fixed up URL into the document or use it in a button handler as you like.

Summary

We have covered a lot of territory since starting this chapter. CGI is a powerful means of hooking into dynamic page generators. As you have seen from this chapter, just being able to write a reasonably neat JavaScript is not enough. To exploit the benefits of CGI, you need to understand the request-response loop and a little bit of server functionality.

The SE:WSE interpreter is a better than average tool for developing CGI back-ends. It is simple to deploy, easy to learn and inexpensive to buy. It is certainly good for some quite powerful implementations.

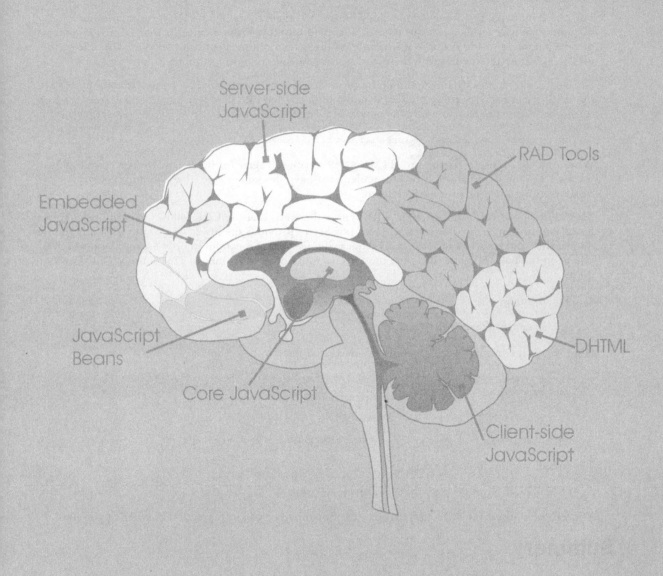

ASP And JavaScript

ASP – Active Server Pages – has grown very quickly since its inception in late '96 and is now one of the most popular server-side frameworks for developing web applications available, offering developers a powerful server-side object model to work with, the ability to integrate server-side components into their applications and the freedom to work in the scripting language of their choice. VBScript may be the default language, but by adding:

```
<%@ LANGUAGE="JavaScript" %>
```

to the head of each page, you can use JavaScript to develop ASP applications. In fact, you can set and use any scripting language, as long as the ActiveX scripting engine for it is provided (JavaScript is provided as part of the ASP engine). This chapter will focus on how to use JavaScript within the ASP framework. In particular it will cover:

- ❏ How an ASP page is rendered when requested
- ❏ ASP syntax and JavaScript features
- ❏ The ASP object model
- ❏ Integrating server-side components into your pages
- ❏ Configuring your ASP applications
- ❏ A loan planning example

With ASP, web developers can implement scripts with the same power as CGI, but with an easier syntax. These scripts can govern many advanced server-side tasks, such as HTTP request and session management, distributing and updating cookies and certificates, page redirection, and transfer to name but three.

Some ASP Fundamentals

The first release of ASP arrived as part of Microsoft's Internet Information Server (IIS) 3.0 for Windows NT Server in December 1996 and was subsequently updated to version 2.0 with the release of IIS 4.0 as part of the freely available (from their web site) NT Option Pack in December 1997.

For those of you with Windows NT Workstation or Windows 9x, Microsoft also included ASP in their Personal Web Server software which is available for these platforms. The latest versions of PWS can be found in:

❑ The NT Option Pack (for NT Workstation/Windows 95)

❑ Windows 98 Install disk (for Windows 98)

❑ Visual Studio 6.0 Disk 2

On Windows 2000, both Server and Workstation (now known as Professional) run IIS5.0 and ASP 3.0.

In whichever case, the ASP framework is fully integrated with the Windows web server architecture and is able to exploit its features. Unlike CGI, ASP doesn't start up a new process for each script it executes. It loads only when the first script is executed and shares the same memory space with the web server. In fact, the ASP engine is an Internet Server Application Programming Interface (ISAPI) extension (ASP.DLL), so it inherits all the performance benefits that this technology provides.

Beyond the world of PCs and Microsoft Windows, both Chili!soft and Halcyon Software have developed implementations of the ASP framework for Netscape servers on both PC and various Unix platforms.

ASP Applications

In recent years, the concept of the web site has gradually converged upon the notion of the software application. What yesterday was just a web site now has some aspect of a software application, while what was an application now typically features some characteristics of a web site.

ASP has aided this blurring of ideas by introducing the concept of an **ASP application** – a collection of HTML pages, ASP pages, COM components and other resources considered as one functional entity – that draws many parallels with the more typical applications we see today built with C++ or Visual Basic. Such applications are built upon a heterogeneous set of elements – a browser, a web server, the ASP engine, the software components installed on the server, etc. – glued together by a scripting language and the ASP object model. As we shall see, it is with the object model that ASP application developers may overcome some of the key differences between their applications and those not based around the web or the HTTP protocol: the lack of state (or continuity of information between pages) and both application-level and session-level variables.

How ASP works

An ASP page is a text-based file comprised of any combination of HTML and scripting code. Any scripting code delimited by `<% ... %>` (a shorthand for `<SCRIPT RUNAT=SERVER> ... </SCRIPT>`) tags is deemed to be server-side code and is interpreted by the ASP engine to generate either further HTML for rendering on the client or more client-side code. All HTML code and any other content outside the delimiters is just ignored by the ASP engine. The following is a simple example of an ASP page that states whether a random number minus 0.5 is positive or negative:

```
<%@ Language=JavaScript%>
<HTML>
<BODY>
<%
   var x = Math.random() - 0.5;
   if (x >= 0) {
      Response.Write(x + " is <B>non-negative</B>")
   } else {
      Response.Write(x + " is <B>negative</B>")
   }
%>
</BODY>
</HTML>
```

By saving this with the file extension .asp, for example as sum.asp, the server recognizes it as an ASP page and activates the ASP engine to process the page before sending it to the browser whenever it is requested by a user. On viewing the source code of an ASP page, all you'll ever see will be HTML and client-side code. Once run, any server-side code in the page will disappear. For example, the code could be reduced to:

```
<HTML>
<BODY>
   0.11032074897909305 is <B>non-negative</B>
</BODY>
</HTML>
```

or possibly:

```
<HTML>
<BODY>
   -0.18027657376016154 is <B>negative</B>
</BODY>
</HTML>
```

before it is sent to the browser. Diagrammatically, the whole ASP process looks like this:

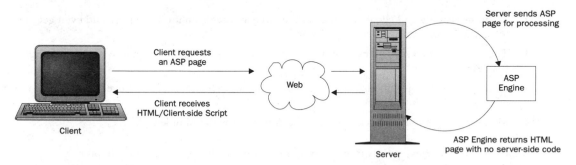

From this picture we can see that:

- ❑ The user requests an ASP page by sending an HTTP request to the web server.
- ❑ The web server gets the .asp file and sends it to the ASP engine for processing.
- ❑ The ASP engine processes any server-side script in the page obtaining an HTML page as a result.
- ❑ The web server sends the resulting HTML page to the client via HTTP.

Even if the above steps look simple at a first glance, ASP beginners sometimes get them confused. Understanding this process helps in fixing errors and in building advanced ASP applications that exploit both server-side and client-side scripting. It also gives you the ability to determine where a problem occurs (i.e. on the client side or on the server side) and when it occurs (i.e. at which step it occurs).

ASP scripts are interpreted and compiled on the fly the first time a user accesses a page. This has two benefits:

❑ The developer doesn't need to compile the scripts before running them because the ASP engine does this automatically.

❑ The script execution is a bit slower only the first time the page containing it is requested by the user; subsequent executions will not require the compilation step.

Of course, as for any scripting environment, the performance is not comparable to compiled and optimized programming languages, but the ASP architecture is independent of the language used with it.

The ASP Arsenal

Well "Hooray", you cry. "So far you've shown us yet another way to do exactly what server-side JavaScript and ScriptEase\CGI can do. Why should I use ASP and not the other two?" A good question that we'll devote pretty much the rest of the chapter to. The simple answer is that you can do pretty much everything the other two techniques can do and a lot more besides. The only restriction – being remedied by Chili!soft et al. – is that ASP is only available as part of Microsoft's web server family: Personal Web Server and Internet Information Server (IIS).

That aside, by using JavaScript and ASP as your server-side technology, you can instantly:

❑ Write server-side and client-side code in the same language, on the same page and even get the former to dynamically generate the latter.

❑ Take advantage of ASP's language-neutral status to make use of VBScript as well as JavaScript in your ASP page.

❑ Access the ASP object model with its concise but comprehensive access to every server-side aspect of client browser interaction.

❑ Make use of both your own and supplied components with a simple call.

We'll look at each of these points in more detail throughout the course of this chapter.

Interleaving Client-Side and Server-Side Script

Server-side scripting has many advantages for the developer. It hides script from the user and enables the dynamic creation of HTML pages with no need to download any additional plug-ins or COM controls.

On the other hand, the client remains the best place to execute certain types of script. Consider what would happen if you tried to validate data from a form on the server. If some value was in error, the server would have to send back an error message and the client would have to fill out the form again and resubmit it. This implies a considerable delay for the user, extra work for the server and increased traffic on the network. Not, you'll agree, very efficient.

The solution then is simple – we incorporate our client-side code into ASP pages. Remember that all server-side script is delimited by `<% ... %>` or `<SCRIPT RUNAT=SERVER>...</SCRIPT>` tags, so the server won't touch any script that isn't in these tags, leaving the browser to interpret and execute it, as it does plain HTML.

Working this way, you can have pages which access both the server's object model with server-side code and the browser's object model and user interface with client-side code. Remember that server-side code cannot access browser elements, nor client-side code server-side objects. It is important understanding this distinction in order to localize where and determine why problems occur.

Our first example simply shows both types of script co-existing together in an ASP page to generate a form dynamically and then validate the user's entries:

```
<%@ Language="JavaScript" %>
<HTML>
<HEAD>

<SCRIPT>
function Validate()
{
   if (document.myForm.username.value == "")
   {
      alert("Enter your name, please!");
      return false
   }
   document.myForm.submit();
   return true
}
</SCRIPT>

<%
   var Choices = new Array("Music","Visual_Arts","Sport","Hobby","Travelling");
   var i;
%>
</HEAD>

<BODY>
<FORM NAME="myForm" METHOD="post" ACTION="process.asp">
   Enter your name:
   <INPUT TYPE="text" NAME="username" SIZE="30">
   <BR>
   Enter your choice:
   <SELECT NAME="choice">
<%
   for (i = 0; i<5; i++)
   {
%>
      <OPTION VALUE=<%= Choices[i] %> > <%= Choices[i] %>
<%
   }
%>
   </SELECT>
   <P>
   <INPUT TYPE="button" VALUE="Submit" onClick="Validate()">
   <INPUT TYPE="reset">
</FORM>
</BODY>
</HTML>
```

This ASP page dynamically builds the OPTION values of a SELECT control from values stored in an array. It also provides the browser with a client-side script checking whether the user entered his name.

The symbols < % = ... % > are a shorthand form of < % Response.Write ... % >, which is used to write text and/or HTML directly to the browser. We will discuss this method in more detail later in the chapter.

The form's action page, process.asp, neatly demonstrates a simple instance of server-side script dynamically generating client-side code. It doesn't manage the Sport, Hobby and Travelling choices in the form, but you can easily add them.

```
<%@ Language="JavaScript" %>
<%
var ImagesToShow = new Array(3);
var i;

if (Request.Form("choice") == "Music")
{
    ImagesToShow[0] = "mozart.gif";
    ImagesToShow[1] = "beethoven.gif";
    ImagesToShow[2] = "chopin.gif"
}

if (Request.Form("choice") == "Visual_Arts")
{
    ImagesToShow[0] = "vangogh.gif";
    ImagesToShow[1] = "michelangelo.gif";
    ImagesToShow[2] = "picasso.gif"
}
%>

<HTML>
<HEAD>
<SCRIPT>
var AllImages = new Array()
var CurrentImage = 0

<%
    for (i = 0; i < 3; i++)
    {
        Response.Write("AllImages[" + i + "] = '" + ImagesToShow[i] + "';")
    }
%>

function NextImage()
{
    if (CurrentImage == <%= i-1 %>)
    {
        CurrentImage = 0
    }
    else
    {
        CurrentImage = CurrentImage + 1
    }
    document.images["slide"].src = AllImages[CurrentImage]
}
</SCRIPT>
</HEAD>

<BODY>
    <IMG SRC=<%= ImagesToShow[0] %> NAME="slide">
    <P>
    <INPUT TYPE="button" VALUE="Next Image" onClick="NextImage()">
</BODY>
</HTML>
```

This page works by creating a server-side array of image filenames dependant upon the choice sent by the user. Then it dynamically creates the client-side code to populate a client-side array in order to manage a slide show, similar to that one shown in Chapter 10. Should the reader choose the `Visual_Arts` option in the form then, the following HTML would be generated:

```
<HTML>
<HEAD>
<SCRIPT>
var AllImages = new Array()
var CurrentImage = 0

AllImages[0] = 'vangogh.gif';
AllImages[1] = 'michelangelo.gif';
AllImages[2] = 'picasso.gif';

function NextImage()
{
    if (CurrentImage == 2)
    {
        CurrentImage = 0
    }
    else
    {
        CurrentImage = CurrentImage + 1
    }
    document.images["slide"].src = AllImages[CurrentImage]
}
</SCRIPT>
</HEAD>
<BODY>

<IMG SRC=vangogh.gif NAME="slide">
<P>
<INPUT TYPE="button" VALUE="Next Image" onClick="NextImage()">
</BODY>
</HTML>
```

Most client-side scriptwriters already use JavaScript, so the jump to use it on the server side as well is a small one.

Mixing JavaScript and VBScript

As we've seen in Chapter 4, it's quite possible to have client-side code that takes advantage of both VBScript's and JavaScript's strengths. While we may choose to use JavaScript's superior array management and mathematical functions, we can still make use of, for example, VBScript's `FormatCurrency()` function, which is unique to that particular script.

And, just as the distinction is made in client-side code, telling the ASP interpreter which script you're using is simply a matter of defining a new script block. Consider that we've already used the line

```
<%@ LANGUAGE = "JavaScript" %>
```

at the head of the page, indicating that JavaScript (or JScript - the words are interchangeable in ASP) should be the default server-side language for this page. All script within `<%  ...  %>` tags will then be taken as JavaScript and any server-side VBScript to be run should be enclosed in a `<SCRIPT RUNAT="server" LANGUAGE="VBScript">  ...  </SCRIPT>` tag pair.

You could write a JavaScript function with the same functionality of a VBScript built-in function such as `FormatCurrency()`, but it would be much easier to reference it like this:

```
<SCRIPT LANGUAGE="VBScript" RUNAT="Server">
Function FormatValue(Value)
    FormatValue = FormatCurrency(Value)
End Function
</SCRIPT>
```

Now you can use `FormatValue()` inside your JavaScript script as a normal JavaScript function. Of course, the same approach applies to VBScript scripts using JavaScript functions.

You can also share data between JavaScript and VBScript script blocks by declaring variables at page level scope. That is, outside of any function and therefore accessible by any script in the page. To demonstrate, the following code shows a variable declared as a VBScript variable and used in a JavaScript script:

```
<SCRIPT LANGUAGE="VBScript" RUNAT="Server">
Dim X
X = 10
</SCRIPT>

<SCRIPT LANGUAGE="JavaScript" RUNAT="Server">
X = X + 1;
</SCRIPT>
```

Note that a little more care needs to be taken when sharing arrays between script types. A VBScript array can be used in the JavaScript environment but uses the index notation of VBScript – that is, we must write `myArray(2)` rather than `myArray[2]`.

VBScript and JavaScript interactions in an ASP page increase the power of this server-side development platform, allowing you to exploit existing functionality without rewriting scripting code. For more information, take a look at the section on mixing JavaScript and VBScript in Chapter 4. All the tenets there apply equally to server-side scripting as well.

The ASP Object Model

Every server-side scripting platform provides the developer with access to server functionality. We've seen how CGI uses compiled programs on the server to work with disparate pages while Enterprise Server users compile SSJS files into a single Java-like application that covers both sides of the client-server divide.

ASP, in its turn, lets scriptwriters gain access to server functionality through a very neat set of built-in ActiveX/COM objects. Each object – `Response`, `Request`, `Session`, `Application`, `Server` and `ObjectContext` – represents distinct functions provided by the server seen as a whole: the operating system server, the web server and other applications installed on the server.

The Request Object

The `Request` object enables us to access information contained in an HTTP request – essentially what it was the client wanted of the server and the HTTP information the browser used to send that request to the browser. To do this, the ASP engine analyzes the HTTP request message and places information into specially designed data containers, called **collections**, of which the Request object has five – `Form`, `QueryString`, `Cookies`, `ServerVariables` and `ClientCertificate`.

We can access elements in a collection by specifying the name or the index. We can use the following general syntax to access the information in the `Request` object:

```
Request.CollectionName(VariableName)
```

where `CollectionName` is the name of one of the following collections and `VariableName` is the name of the variable in the collection that you want to access.

The Request.Form Collection

When you design an HTML page containing a form, one thing you have to specify is how the information contained in that form is sent to the server. There are two methods (with corresponding HTTP options): `POST` and `GET`.

When the contents of a form are `POST`ed, they are sent as part of the HTTP header message that clients do not see and can be retrieved as items in the `Request.Form` collection. Consider the following:

```
<FORM METHOD="post" ACTION="submit.asp">
<P>
Insert your first name: <INPUT TYPE="text" NAME="firstname" SIZE="30">
<P>
Insert your e-mail address: <INPUT TYPE="text" NAME="email" SIZE="30">
<P>
<INPUT TYPE="submit">
</FORM>
```

In our example, the form `POST`s the data to `submit.asp` to echo it back to the screen. In `submit.asp` then, we could use the following two lines of ASP code to do just that:

```
Your name is <%= Request.Form("firstname") %> and
your e-mail address is <%= Request.Form("email") %>
```

Note how each item in the form has a corresponding item in the `Request.Form` collection whose name is the same as the form elements `NAME` property.

The Request.QueryString Collection

The `QueryString` collection allows our ASP script to retrieve the values from query strings: the parameters tacked onto the end of a URL after a question mark. For example:

```
http://www.server.com/submit.asp?firstname=John&email=john@wrox.com
```

It also clears up the question of what happens to the contents of a form that is submitted with a `GET` rather than a `POST` directive. In this case, the contents are appended to the URL as a query string, and are hence retrievable through the `Request.QueryString` collection. For instance, should the form in the previous example have been declared as:

```
<FORM METHOD="get" ACTION="submit.asp">
```

we would need to retrieve the parameters through the `QueryString` collection, for example with the lines:

```
Your name is <%= Request.Querystring("firstname") %> and
your e-mail address is <%= Request.Querystring("email") %>
```

The Request.Cookies Collection

The `Request` object also allows you to read cookies stored on the client machine. Cookies are small files saved on the client by the web server; they generally contain information identifying the client or record information about the client's preferences.

> *Note that the `Request` object cannot write to the client, so in order to send a cookie to the client, we must use the `Cookies` collection of the `Response` object (which we will meet shortly).*

Cookies are appended to any HTTP request for a URL with which they are associated. They can then be accessed through the `Request` object's `Cookies` collection, by specifying its name as in the following example:

```
<%= Request.Cookies("myCookie") %>
```

This example shows how to access information stored in a cookie called `myCookie`, so long as it isn't a dictionary cookie. A dictionary cookie is a cookie that has more than one value stored in it. We can access a given item in a dictionary cookie in the following way:

```
<%= Request.Cookies("myCookie")("myKey") %>
```

To determine whether a cookie is a dictionary cookie (that is, whether it has keys or subitems), we can use the `HasKeys` property, as in the following script:

```
<%= Request.Cookies("myCookie").HasKeys %>
```

This property will be `True` if `myCookie` is a dictionary cookie, and `False` otherwise.

The Request.ServerVariables Collection

When as ASP application is executed, there's a plethora of information that's passed across. This isn't just data about the application – it also includes information such as the name of the user who ran the application, where the application is located, the server name, what port the request was sent to – in fact, the whole environment in which the application was executed. These important bits of information are all stored in individual variables known as **environment variables**. This list of variables is predefined by the server and a list is provided in Appendix K.

These environment variables can be set by the server or by the client. For example, the `SERVER_SOFTWARE` variable returns the name and version of the HTTP server, while the `REMOTE_ADDR` displays the IP address of the requesting machine.

We can access environment variables in ASP Script through the `ServerVariables` collection of the `Request` object, adding the name of the specific variable we want to access:

```
This server uses <%= Request.ServerVariables("SERVER_SOFTWARE") %><BR>
Your IP address is <%= Request.ServerVariables("REMOTE_ADDR") %>
```

The following screenshot illustrates the result of executing this script:

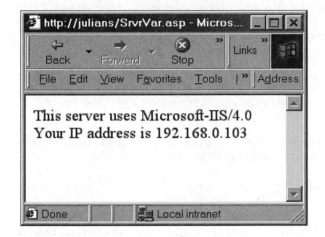

The Request.ClientCertificate Collection

When a client makes a secure connection to a server, it may be necessary for each end to be certain of the identity of the other. This can be achieved by means of a **digital certificate**, which contains information about the organization or individual. These certificates are issued by a trusted third party known as a **Certificate Authority**.

The information within the digital certificate can be accessed from ASP script through the ClientCertificate collection of the Request object. This helps to verify that information is coming from a trusted client. In particular, it allows us to retrieve certification fields (that is, items of information in the digital certificate) from a web browser which is using the Secure Sockets Layer (SSL) protocol to create a secure connection to the web server. We can retrieve each certification field by referencing the appropriate key of the collection. For example, the following code displays the expiration date of the client's digital certificate:

```
This certification will expire on <%= Request.ClientCertificate("ValidUntil") %>
```

Other information that we can retrieve from ClientCertificate collection includes the company name, the certificate's serial number, the binary stream of the entire certificate content, etc.

Request Object Properties

The Request object also provides one property and one method. The sole property is TotalBytes, which returns the total number of bytes in the body of the HTTP request. For example, the following code displays the number of bytes sent by the browser:

```
The server received <%= Request.TotalBytes %> bytes
```

Request Object Methods

The only method that the Request object provides is BinaryRead. This is used to read raw data sent to the server from a POST request. It requires a parameter which stipulates the number of bytes to be read; the following example uses this method in conjunction with the TotalBytes property to read the entire binary content of the body of the HTTP request:

```
<%
var BinaryInformation
BinaryInformation = Request.BinaryRead(Request.TotalBytes)
%>
```

The Request object provides a short version of the general syntax to access information stored in the collections. This short syntax is as follows:

```
Request(VariableName)
```

Using this shorthand syntax, we can omit the name of the collection. ASP will search for the variable in the collections in the order: QueryString, Form, Cookies, ClientCertificate, ServerVariables. The first variable that matches VariableName will be returned. Although this mechanism is available, for readability and performance reasons, we recommend explicit collection access. This will also avoid any risk of retrieving the wrong variable should two or more variables in different collections share the same name.

The Response Object

ASP also provides a built-in Response object which we can use to control and manage the data sent to the browser. We can use this object to send text to the browser, store values in cookies, control server-side and client-side caching of data, send HTTP header information, or to redirect the browser to another web page. All of these actions can be performed through the Response object's collections, properties and methods, as we shall see in the following section.

The Response.Cookies Collection

The Response object provides just one collection, the Cookies collection. As we mentioned earlier, the Request.Cookies collection cannot be used to write a cookie to the client; however, the Response.Cookies collection allows us to do just that. Through this collection, we can set the values of cookies which already exist, and create new cookies.

Both tasks are achieved in the same way: by setting the value of the cookie. If the cookie doesn't already exist, it will be created; if it does, it will take the new value we give it. For example, the following code will keep tabs on the number of times a particular user has visited a page:

```
<%@ LANGUAGE="JavaScript" %>
<%
if (Request.Cookies("myCookie")=="") {
    Response.Cookies("myCookie")=1;
}
else {
    Response.Cookies("myCookie")=Number(Request.Cookies("myCookie"))+1;
}
%>
```

Notice how we always set the value of the cookie in the Response.Cookies collection, but read the value from the Request.Cookies collection.

If we wish to make our cookie a dictionary cookie, we simply specify value for the individual keys. For example, suppose we wanted to keep track of the last time the user visited our page, as well as the total number of visits:

```
<%@ LANGUAGE="JavaScript" %>
<%
if (Request.Cookies("myCookie")=="") {
    Response.Cookies("myCookie")("noOfVisits")=1;
}
else {
    Response.Cookies("myCookie")("noOfVisits")=
        Number(Request.Cookies("myCookie")("noOfVisits"))+1;
}
Response.Cookies("myCookie")("lastVisit")=Date();
%>
```

Each cookie has a set of attributes that specify information about the cookie itself. The attributes can be one of the following:

Name	Description
Expires	The date on which the cookie will expire.
Domain	The domain to which cookies will be issued.
Path	The path of the folder in the domain to which cookies will be sent.
Secure	Specifies whether the cookie is to be delivered over a secure channel. Its value can be True or False.
HasKeys	Indicates whether the cookie is a dictionary cookie; that is, whether multiple values are stored within the cookie. This attribute is read-only and its value can be True or False.

The following example stores the user name in a cookie and sets the cookie's expiry date, domain and path:

```
<%
Response.Cookies("UserName") = "Mickey Mouse"
Response.Cookies("UserName").Expires = "December 31, 2000"
Response.Cookies("UserName").Domain = "cartoons.com"
Response.Cookies("UserName").Path = "/users"
%>
```

Note that we cannot write information to a cookie after any HTTP header information has been sent to the requesting browser. In other words, we cannot send cookie information to the browser after any HTML tags have been already sent; this will cause an error. We should therefore set cookie information within the first lines of our ASP code. Alternatively, we should enable output buffering, as seen below.

The Response.Write Method

The Write method is the most commonly used method of the Response object. This method allows us to send information in the output stream to the browser from within the ASP delimiters. Its syntax is:

```
Response.Write(text)
```

For example, the following code sends an HTML formatted text to the user:

```
<% Response.Write("<H1>Welcome to my web site</H1>") %>
```

The `Write` method is especially useful if you want to send content back to the user within a procedure:

```
<%
if (HasAccess) {
    Response.Write("<H1>Welcome to my web site</H1>")
} else {
    Response.Write("<H1>Sorry, you cannot access this web site!</H1> ")
}
%>
```

Notice that the following script produces exactly the same output as the previous one:

```
<% if (HasAccess) { %>
    <H1>Welcome to my web site</H1>
<% } else { %>
    <H1>Sorry, you cannot access this web site!</H1>
<% } %>
```

In addition, the `<%=` syntax we met earlier can be considered a shorthand form of `Response.Write`.

The Response.Redirect Method

Another common use of the `Response` object is to redirect the browser to another web site. The `Redirect` method allows you to redirect the browser to another URL. The syntax is as follows:

```
Response.Redirect(URL)
```

For instance, the previous example could be modified in the following way to redirect the user to the appropriate page after authentication:

```
<%
if (HasAccess) {
    Response.Redirect("welcome.asp")
} else {
    Response.Redirect("noaccess.asp")
}
%>
```

An error will be generated if the `Redirect` method is used when content has already been sent back to the browser, unless the `Response.Buffer` property is set to `True`.

The Response.Buffer Property

The `Buffer` property controls when information is sent to the client. If its value is set to `True`, the ASP page output is buffered – that is, the server does not send output to the browser until all of the server scripts on the current page have been processed. If its value is set to `False` (the default), the page output is sent to the browser while it is still being processed by the server. If buffering is disabled, we cannot send an HTTP response after any HTML output has been sent. This means, for example, that we cannot send any cookies to the client unless no output has been sent to the browser.

To enable or disable output buffering, the `Buffer` property should be set to the appropriate value as the first line of ASP script in the page. We cannot change the `Buffer` property after output has been sent to the browser; this will generate a runtime error.

Managing the Server Buffer

Page buffering is useful when, at some point in the processing of a page, we don't want to send previous content to the browser. We can manage the server buffer with a number of methods: the `Clear` method will empty the buffer of any content, `Flush` to send the buffered output to the browser immediately, and `End` to stop processing the ASP page and send the buffered output to the browser. It can be a good idea to call this at the end of every page which has used the `Response` object. The following example illustrates the use server buffering in an ASP page:

```
<% Response.Buffer = True %>
<HTML>
<BODY>
...
<%
if (Request.Form("Name") == "") {
    Response.Clear()
    Response.Redirect("getname.asp")
}
else {
    Response.Write(Request.Form("Name"))
}
%>
</BODY>
</HTML>
```

This example page starts by setting the `Response.Buffer` property to `True` to prevent output being sent straight to the browser. We then check the value of a form element; if this is empty, we discard all buffered data (using the `Response.Clear` method) and redirect the browser to another ASP page. Otherwise, we display the value of the form element.

Notice that redirection is possible in this example because no output has yet been sent to the browser due to our `Response.Buffer=True` statement. Although buffering the output improves server performance, it has a potential drawback if the ASP page has long scripts: the user might be forced to wait a considerable time before the script is processed.

Expiring Cached Pages

Through the `Response` object we can also control the browser's mechanism for caching pages. This can be accomplished with the `Expires` property; this property sets the number of minutes the page will remain active in the browser's cache. For example, to avoid a page caching at all, so that the browser is forced to reload the page every time it is viewed, we should set `Response.Expires = -780`. This is thirteen hours behind the current time; this value is used to ensure that the page won't be cached due to any difference in the time zones of the server and browser.

If we wish to specify the exact time and date a page will expire in the browser's cache, the `ExpiresAbsolute` property allows us to do this. The following example forces the current page to expire on December 31, 2000 at 12:00 AM:

```
<% Response.ExpiresAbsolute = "Dec 31, 2000 12:00:00" %>
```

Adding Information to the HTTP Header

However, not all browsers interpret this information correctly; some simply ignore it. In this case we can send customized information in the HTTP header. To add information to the HTTP header, we can use the `AddHeader` method of the `Response` object. This has the following syntax:

```
Response.AddHeader(name, value)
```

where `name` is the name of the variable to be added to the header and `value` is the value assigned to this variable. For instance, we could add a variable `pragma` with the value `no-cache` to the HTTP header in order to instruct the browser not to cache the current page:

```
<% Response.AddHeader "pragma", "no-cache" %>
```

The Session Object

The `Session` object, together with the `Application` object, contributes to the transformation of a collection of Active Server Pages into a true application. This object enables us to overcome the intrinsic stateless nature of the HTTP protocol: HTTP manages each browser request independently from previous requests, and without any memory of them. In many web applications this can be a big problem. The `Session` object helps us to manage information about multiple requests by the same user.

A session is the period of time during which a user is interacting with an ASP application. The session starts when a user requests a URL of an `.asp` file in an application. Sessions automatically end if the user has not requested or refreshed a page in an application for a specified period of time. This value is 20 minutes by default. However, as we will see, it is possible to end a session explicitly, or to set a different timeout interval.

The `Session` object represents a session in the ASP object model. It enables us to store variables that have **session scope** – that is, which are accessible from any page within the same session. We can declare a `Session` variable following this syntax:

```
Session("VariableName")
```

Suppose a user has submitted his or her name through a form. When the first page in an ASP application is accessed, the session starts, and we can store the user name in a session variable:

```
<% Session("UserName") = Request.Form("UserName") %>
```

Now we can use the value stored in `Session("UserName")` in every ASP page accessed during the current session. For instance, if the user accesses a special offer page during the session, we can display a customized message, greeting the user with the name retrieved from the session variable:

```
<H1>Welcome <%= Session("UserName") %>, this special offer is for you!</H1>
```

We can store any data in session variables, including objects. However, we cannot store built-in objects in it (such as the `Request` and `Response` objects and so on). The following code tries to store the `Request` object in a session variable:

```
<% Session("myvar") = Request %>
```

This will cause a runtime error.

The persistence of variables within a session is based on the cookie mechanism. The first time a user requests an .asp file within a given application, ASP generates a **SessionID**, and then sends a response to the user's browser to create a cookie for the SessionID. The SessionID is a GUID (Globally Unique Identifier) – a number produced by a complex algorithm that identifies the user's session. The user's SessionID cookie, which the browser sends in the HTTP request header, enables ASP to access the information associated with it and is stored on the server, rather than on the client. Each time the web server receives a request for a page, it checks the HTTP request header for a SessionID cookie, and then looks for corresponding information, such as session variables.

While most browsers support cookies, some do not. If a user's browser does not support cookies, ASP will still generate a SessionID for that client, but a new SessionID will be generated each time a page is visited.

Ending Sessions

If, for a specific session, we want to set a timeout interval that is longer than the 20-minute default, we can set the Timeout property of the Session object. For example, the following script sets a timeout interval of 30 minutes:

```
<% Session.Timeout = 30 %>
```

However, we cannot set the timeout interval to be less than the default value.

We can also explicitly end a session with the Abandon method of the Session object. For example, we can provide a Quit button on a form with the ACTION attribute set to the URL of an .asp file that contains the following command:

```
<% Session.Abandon() %>
```

The Application Object

Together with the Session object, the Application object helps the developer to maintain state, that is the ability to retain information. While the Session object enables us to persist information for a specific user for the duration of an ASP session, the Application object is used to store information which is shared among all users of a single ASP-based application. An ASP application starts when the first page of an ASP application is requested by any user. It ends when the web server is shut down.

In a similar way as for the Session object, the Application object allows us to store information at the application level. These application variables can be accessed by any user. We can use the following syntax to declare application level variables:

```
Application(VariableName)
```

Although the value of an application variable can be read by any user, we have to perform some extra operations in order to modify its value, because of the possibility of a conflict if more than one user attempts to modify the value at the same time. Before we can change the value of an application variable, we have to lock the Application object. After we have changed its value, we must unlock the object again to free it for other users. The following script shows how to implement a simple page counter using an application variable:

```
<%
Application.Lock()
Application("Counter") = Application("Counter") + 1
Application.Unlock()
%>
This page has been visited by <%= Application("Counter") %> visitors.
```

The Server Object

The Server object is used to control the administrative functions of the web server and to perform any operations related to the HTTP service. It also allows us to create instances of server components, as we shall see in the next section.

The Server.ScriptTimeout Property

The Server object has only one property, ScriptTimeout. This property specifies the maximum length of time a script can run before it will be terminated. This prevents a process from running endlessly. The default value is 90 seconds. If the script in a page takes longer than the time specified by this property, the script will be stopped and a script timeout error displayed. If we have complex scripts in a page, we can set the timeout interval to a different value. The following example sets the timeout value for scripts to two minutes:

```
<% Server.ScriptTimeout = 120 %>
```

The Server.CreateObject Method

The most commonly used method of the Server object is the CreateObject method. This allows us to create an instance of an external object and is used to instantiate ASP components. The syntax is:

```
Server.CreateObject(ObjectClass)
```

where ObjectClass is the class or type of object to be instantiated. We will see how to use this method in more detail in next section.

The Server.MapPath Method

The MapPath method maps the specified relative or virtual path to the corresponding physical directory on the server. The following example uses this method to map the physical path of the example.asp file:

```
<%= Server.MapPath("/example.asp")%>
```

This produces the following output:

c:\inetpub\wwwroot\example.asp

Using Server-Side Components

As well as these 'built-in' objects, a number of components are provided by applications such as Microsoft Exchange, Transaction Server, etc., and, indeed, by IIS itself. These components contain yet more objects – **server components** – to extend the functionality of the web server beyond the traditional HTTP response/request arena. These objects give us the ability to access databases, create, manage and send e-mails, manage the local file system, and so on. Unlike the built-in objects, however, these objects are external to the ASP environment, so they need to be instantiated ('switched on' if you will) before they can be used.

Furthermore, we can build your own components in any programming language supporting the **Component Object Model** (COM) standard. This topic is treated in much more detail in 'Beginning Components for ASP' (ISBN 1-861002-88-2, Wrox Press).

Remember that we can use all these objects only in server-side scripts. Client-side scripts cannot access these objects, just as our server-side scripts have no access to the Browser Object Model.

In some cases, external components are needed to perform specific operations. There are three typical reasons for using external components:

❑ To gain access to functions that are not supported by JavaScript or by other scripting languages.

❑ To speed up an ASP application which contains complex logic.

❑ To re-use components by sharing them with other applications.

Built-in objects are directly available in the ASP environment and do not need to be instantiated. When we wish to use external objects, we must first instantiate them using the `CreateObject` method of the `Server` object.

As we shall see, ASP provides some external objects to help us accomplish common tasks. However, we can use any COM-compliant component within our ASP pages.

Using Generic COM Objects

As we already know, to gain access to an external object we first have to instantiate it with the `CreateObject` method of the `Server` object. The syntax for this is:

```
Server.CreateObject(ObjectClass)
```

where `ObjectClass` is the Programmatic Identifier, or ProgID, for the object. This identifier uniquely identifies the class of the object which we want to instantiate, and takes the following format:

```
AppName.ObjectType
```

where `AppName` is the name of the application hosting the object and `ObjectType` is the class or type of the object to create. For example, the following script instantiates an object from a class `Account` provided by the COM component `Bank`:

```
<% myAccount = Server.CreateObject("Bank.Account") %>
```

The `CreateObject` method returns a reference to the newly created object. The previous example assigns this reference to the `myAccount` variable. We can then use this variable as an object of the class `Account`; that is, we can use its properties and its methods.

When we assign an object created by the `CreateObject` method to a page-level variable, as in the example above, the object is destroyed when the page has finished processing. If we need to access the same component a number of times, in most situations we will benefit from using an application- or session-level object; we will see how to do this in the section on "The Global.asa file" below. Creating an object only once (rather than repeatedly re-instantiating as it is needed again) reduces the overhead required to constantly create and destroy the object. And, more importantly, it allows the object to preserve state.

Using System Objects

As we have already implied, the ASP scripting engine provides several object additions to the built-in objects of the ASP Object Model. These objects provide us with a means of accessing file and system management functions. They can be accessed by instantiating classes of the ActiveX `Scripting` component. The `Scripting` component provides access to six objects and three collections:

Object	Description
FileSystemObject object	Provides access to the file system on the server and the objects (files, folders and drives) within it.
Drive object	Represents a physical disk drive which is available to the server.
Drives collection	A collection containing all the available Drive objects.
Folder object	Represents a folder or directory within the file system.
Folders collection	A collection of all the Folder objects in the system.
File object	Represents a file within one of the Folder objects.
Files collection	A collection of all the File objects in the system.
TextStream object	Provides access to contents of a file in the file system as a stream of text; any file with contents in a text-readable form can be opened as a TextStream object.
Dictionary object	Used to store and access data in name/value pairs. Each item in the dictionary has a name (also called a key), which uniquely identifies that item, and a value.

The most important of these objects is probably the `FileSystemObject`, so we shall look at this in a bit more detail.

The FileSystemObject Object

The `FileSystemObject` object enables us to control file system elements such as files, directories and drives. The code below illustrates the use of this object by creating a function which calculates the available space on a given drive:

```
<%@ LANGUAGE="JavaScript" %>

<%
function ShowAvailableSpace(drive) {
    var fs, d, s;

    fs = Server.CreateObject("Scripting.FileSystemObject");
    d = fs.GetDrive(drive);
    s = "Drive " + drive.toUpperCase( ) + " [";
    s = s + d.VolumeName + "] ";
    s = s + "Available Space: " + d.AvailableSpace/1024 + " Kbytes";
    return(s);
}

%>

...

<% Response.write(ShowAvailableSpace("C")) %>
```

The function first creates an instance of the `FileSystemObject` object; we then call the `GetDrive` method of the `FileSystemObject` to access the `Drive` object specified by the `drive` parameter. The function then uses this `Drive` object to build the output string; we get the volume name of the drive from its `VolumeName` property and the available space in bytes from the `AvailableSpace` property.

Executing this function will cause a message similar to this to be written to the browser:

C: WINNT Available Space: 129664 Kbytes

In its turn, the `FileSystemObject` object provides access to three more objects:

- ❑ `Drive`. A `Drive` object can be accessed through the `GetDrive(DriveName)` method of the `FileSystemObject`, which we saw in the function above.
- ❑ `File`. A specific `File` object will be returned by the `GetFile(FileName)` method of the `FileSystemObject`.
- ❑ `Folder`. A specific `Folder` object can be referenced through the `GetFolder(FolderName)` method of the `FileSystemObject`.

The `FileSystemObject` object also provides collections to manage and to access each of these objects:

- ❑ `Drives`
- ❑ `Files`
- ❑ `Folders`

These collections can be referenced through the `Drives`, `Files` and `Folders` properties respectively of the `FileSystemObject`. For example, to reference the `Drives` collection:

```
objFSO=Server.CreateObject("Scripting.FileSystemObject");
colDrives=objFSO.Drives;
```

We can then access a specific `Drive` object through this collection:

```
objCDrive=colDrives("C");
```

This is identical to the syntax we met above:

```
objCDrive=objFSO.GetDrive("C");
```

The TextStream Object

Although we can manage files using the `File` object, the `FileSystemObject` object also provides the `TextStream` object to facilitate sequential access to files. The following example uses the `TextStream` object to write a line of text into a file:

```
<%
var fs = Server.CreateObject("Scripting.FileSystemObject");
var a = fs.CreateTextFile("c:\testfile.txt", true);
a.WriteLine("This is a test.");
a.Close;
%>
```

As well as creating objects through the `Server` object's `CreateObject` method, JavaScript allows us to instantiate ActiveX objects (which includes the `Scripting` objects) by defining them as new `ActiveXObject` objects. In fact, we can use the syntax:

```
ObjectVariable = new ActiveXObject(ClassName)
```

whenever we might use:

```
ObjectVariable = Server.CreateObject(ClassName)
```

Incidentally, the `ActiveXObject` constructor is also available in client-side JScript.

External Components Provided by ASP

Several external components are shipped and installed with ASP. These components provide us with common functions for developing an ASP application.

For example, the **Browser Capabilities** component allows us to determine the capabilities of the requesting browser. This feature can be used to tailor the content we send to a browser, based on the features supported by that browser. Because new versions of browsers are constantly being released, it is imperative to have the latest version of this component. It can be downloaded from `http://www.asptracker.com`.

The following example uses the Browser Capabilities component to display a table showing some of the features supported by the current browser:

```
<%@ LANGUAGE="JavaScript" %>
<% bc = Server.CreateObject("MSWC.BrowserType") %>

<TABLE BORDER=1>
<TR>
   <TD>Browser Type</TD>
   <TD><%= bc.browser %></TD>
</TR>
<TR>
   <TD>Browser Version</TD>
   <TD><%= bc.version %></TD>
</TR>
<TR>
   <TD>Support Frames?</td>
   <TD><% if (bc.frames) { %> Yes <% } else { %> No <% } %></TD>
</TR>
<TR>
   <TD>Support ActiveX controls?</TD>
   <TD><% if (bc.activexcontrols) { %> Yes <% } else { %> No <% } %></TD>
</TR>
<TR>
   <TD>Support JavaScript?</TD>
   <TD><% if (bc.javascript) { %> Yes <% } else { %> No <% } %></TD>
</TR>
<TR>
   <TD>Support VBScript?</TD>
   <TD><% if (bc.vbscript) { %> Yes <% } else { %> No <% } %></TD>
</TR>
</TABLE>
```

The result of executing this code with the IE4 browser is:

Browser Type	IE
Browser Version	4.0
Support Frames?	Yes
Support ActiveX controls?	Yes
Support JavaScript?	Yes
Support VBScript?	Yes

Other external server-side components provided by ASP include:

Name	Description	Class
Ad Rotator	Automates the rotation of advertisement images on a web page.	`MSWC.AdRotator`
Permission Checker	Verifies whether the requesting user has permission to access a file.	`MSWC.PermissionChecker`
Content Linking	Manages a list of URLs so that we can link the pages in a web site like the pages in a book.	`MSWC.NextLink`
Page Counter	Keeps track of how many times a specific page has been accessed	`MSWC.PageCounter`

ADO	Allows database access via ActiveX Data Objects. It allows us to create ADO `Connection`, `Recordset` and `Command` objects.	`ADODB.Connection`
		`ADODB.Recordset`
		`ADODB.Command`

Configuring ASP applications

The ASP engine has a default behavior based on certain configuration settings. We have already met some of these settings which control the page caching and the timeout value for scripts, as well as the directive to set the default scripting language. We can specify these settings and others at three different levels: at the page level, at the session level, or at the application level.

This section will deal with configuring various aspects of an ASP application.

ASP directives

ASP directives enable us to specify configuration settings at the page level, overriding global settings. The directives only apply inside the ASP page that contains them. The ASP directives must be located on the first line of the ASP page. The general syntax is:

```
<%@ DirectiveName=Value %>
```

where *Value* is the value assigned to the directive and *DirectiveName* is one of the following:

Name	Description
CodePage	Sets the code page for an ASP page; this is a character set which can include letters, numbers, punctuation marks and other symbols, and which can differ for various languages.
EnableSessionState	Controls whether session tracking is applied to the ASP page.
Language	Sets the primary scripting language for the ASP page.
LCID	Sets the locale identifier for the current ASP page so that various local formats can be supported.
Transaction	Indicates that the ASP script is to be treated as a transaction monitored by MTS.

Although in most situations we can use spaces around the equal sign in a directive, this is not permitted by the technical specification. In addition, no space should be between the opening <% and the @ symbol. Both these issues are important considerations for compatibility with future releases of ASP. If we need to specify more than one directive, they are included in a single line (always the first line of the page):

```
<%@ Language="JavaScript" EnableSessionState=False %>
```

This sets JavaScript as the default scripting language for the current page and disables session management.

These directives are very important. As pointed out at the beginning of this chapter, the default scripting language for an ASP page is VBScript rather than JavaScript if we don't include the Language directive, so the ASP engine will try to interpret our JavaScript as VBScript. We can set JavaScript as the default language for the current page by inserting the following directive as the first line of the page:

```
<%@ LANGUAGE="JavaScript" %>
```

The strings JScript and JavaScript can be used indifferently. Notice the presence of the @ symbol to the right of the <% delimiter. This indicates that what follows is information for the ASP engine and doesn't have to be processed as scripting code. This feature allows the developer to use different scripting languages in the same application, providing information about the language used for each page. In a following section we will see how to set JavaScript as the default scripting language for an ASP application and/or for the whole ASP environment.

The Global.asa file

The Global.asa file is an optional file in which we can specify event scripts and declare objects that have session or application scope. It is not a content file displayed to the users; instead it stores event information and objects which are used globally by the application. This file must be named Global.asa and must be stored in the root directory of the application. An application can only have one Global.asa file.

Global.asa files can contain only the following:

- ❑ Application-level event handlers
- ❑ Handlers for events triggered when the ASP application starts (Application_OnStart) and ends (Application_OnEnd)
- ❑ Session-level event handlers
- ❑ Handlers for events triggered when one session starts (Session_OnStart) or ends (Session_OnEnd)
- ❑ <OBJECT> declarations
- ❑ Object declarations with application or session scope

When the ASP application or session starts or ends, the ASP engine looks in the Global.asa file for a handler for the event and processes it. The Global.asa file can only include tags of the form <SCRIPT RUNAT=SERVER>; we cannot use the shorthand <% ... %> tags.

The following is an example of Global.asa file:

```
<SCRIPT LANGUAGE="JavaScript" RUNAT="server">
function Application_OnStart() {
    var StartDay = new Date()
    Application("StartTime") = StartDay.getTime()
}

function Session_OnStart() {
    var StartDay = new Date()
    Session("StartTime") = StartDay.getTime()
}
</SCRIPT>
```

When the ASP application starts, the start time is assigned to the StartTime application variable. Similarly, when a new session starts, the start time is assigned to the StartTime session variable. We can use these variables to display information about the running time of application or session:

```
<% var Now = new Date() %>
This application has been running for <%= (Now.getTime() -
Application("StartTime"))/1000 %> seconds.<BR>
You have been connected to this application for <%= (Now.getTime() -
Session("StartTime"))/1000 %> seconds.<BR>
```

We can also exploit the `Global.asa` file to declare objects with session or application scope. We can accomplish this by using the extended `<OBJECT>` tag:

```
<OBJECT RUNAT = "server" SCOPE ="session" ID="ThisBrowser"
PROGID="MSWC.BrowserType">
</OBJECT>
```

The objects declared in the `Global.asa` file can be used by any script in the ASP application. For example, we could reference the object `ThisBrowser` from any page in the application:

```
<%= ThisBrowser.Browser %>
```

The Metabase and Registry Settings

Many global settings for the ASP scripting engine are stored in two special data structures: the **Metabase** and the **Registry**. The Metabase is a hierarchical database used to store configuration information about the IIS 4.0 server. It contains configuration settings that can affect the behavior of ASP applications. We can edit most of the Metabase settings through the Internet Service Manager. Here we can set the default scripting language for all applications, determine whether the web server has to send error messages to the browser, enable ASP debugging and so on. This screenshot shows the panel of the Internet Service Manager where we can set most of the application-level properties.

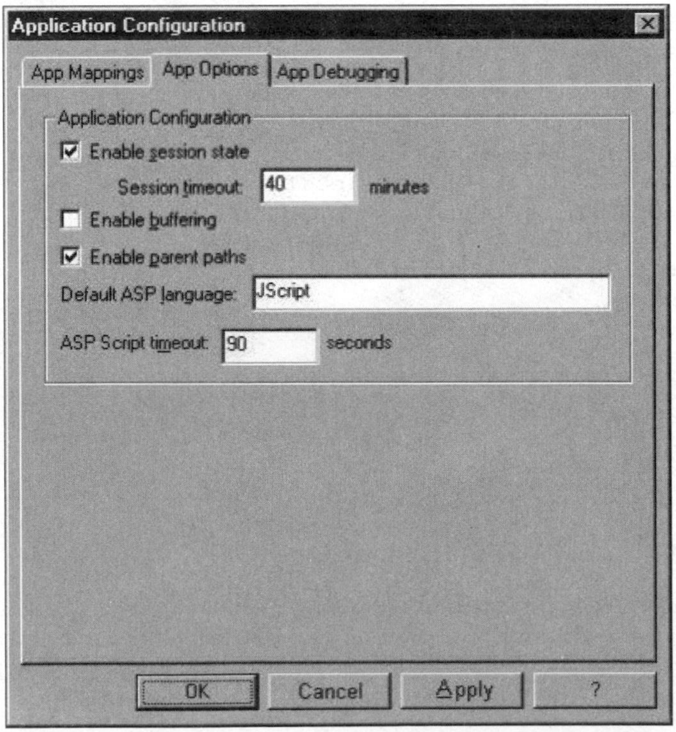

Some of these Metabase settings can also be found in the system **Registry**, although this is due to change in ASP 3.0, when all settings for ASP will be moved to the Metabase. The ASP settings in the Registry can be found in the path:

```
HKEY_LOCAL_MACHINE\System\CurrentControlSet\Services\W3SVC\ASP\Parameters
```

Component Interaction

One of the main benefits of ASP is its ability to make use of COM components. This allows us to extend the web server processing power and to re-use existing software components.

Most components used in ASP applications are dynamic link libraries (DLLs). Components of this type are called **in-process** components because they execute in the same process as the application which calls them. An out-of-process component is a component that executes in a separate process on the same machine. Typically **out-of-process** components are executable components (EXE files). If you try to instantiate an executable component using the CreateObject method, an error similar to the following may occur:

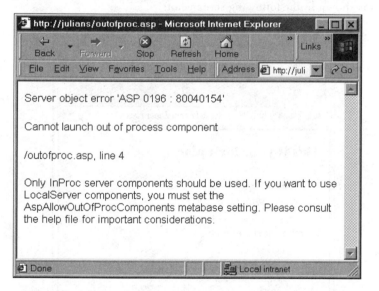

In general, only in-process server components should be used. If we want to use local server components, we must set AspAllowOutOfProcComponents in the Metabase. The help files should be consulted if you wish to do this. Note that in ASP 3.0 this Metabase setting now defaults to true, so out-of-process components may be instantiated at any time.

This error is the result of a safety mechanism in ASP that prevents the launch of out-of-process components. This is in place because there are security concerns that should be considered when launching out-of-process components. In addition to these security concerns, DLLs are also generally preferred because they bring performance benefits over EXEs and can hosted by Microsoft Transaction Server (MTS).

Sometimes, however, we want our ASP application to interact with full applications, such as Microsoft Excel or Microsoft Word. This allows us to exploit advanced functionality such as complex calculations or spell checking which we don't want to code in JavaScript. This actually requires us to interact with out-of-process components. In order to enable this kind of interaction, we have to enable the `AspAllowOutOfProcessComponents` setting in the Metabase. Managing the Metabase is a complex subject which is beyond the scope of this chapter. You can find more information and examples at `http://msdn.microsoft.com/workshop/server/components/outproc.asp`.

A Practical Example

Before we move away from JavaScript in ASP, we will have a look at a practical example and develop an application that will use most of the ASP features seen in this chapter. This application will enable the user to plan a loan on the basis of the total amount loaned and the monthly payments he or she wants to make. Users will be able to build their plan interactively according to their needs. The resulting plan displays the number of payments required to pay back the loan and gives details about the distribution of interest and capital for each payment. An example of what the user will see as result of his plan is shown in the following screenshot:

When the user is satisfied with the plan, the data can be saved on the server. At any point, it will be possible to query the server about the status of the plan by providing the loan number and the number of last payment. Thus, the user will be able to see how much interest has been paid and how much capital still has to be paid back. This is what the user will see when the loan status is queried:

The ASP application we are going to build will interact with a server-side component which provides the functions for making the complex interest calculations. This component, named `Financial`, provides an object, `Loan`, with a number of properties and methods that we will need to make these calculations. The table below summarizes the items we will use in this example:

Name	Type	Description
Rate	Property	The interest rate for each payment.
PV	Property	The amount of the loan (present value).
PaymentAmount	Property	The amount of each payment.
NumberOfPayments()	Method	Calculates the number of payments required for the loan on the basis of the current data.
LoanPlan()	Method	Calculates the loan plan using the current data. Detailed results are stored in the Interests and Capitals collections.

Table Continued on Following Page

Name	Type	Description
Interests	Collection	A collection containing the interest amount for each payment.
Capitals	Collection	A collection containing the amount of capital returned for each payment.
NPayments	Property	The number of payments in which the loan will be paid back.
SaveLoanData()	Method	Saves the current loan data on the server. This method returns the reference number associated with the loan.
GetLoanData(LN)	Method	Loads the data for the loan identified by the LN parameter. Data is stored in the Rate, PV, PaymentAmount and NPayments properties.
LoanStatus(PN)	Method	Calculates the current status of the loan given the last payment number (PN). Results are stored in the PaidInterest, ReturnedCapital and RemainingCapital properties.
PaidInterest	Property	The interest already paid.
ReturnedCapital	Property	The capital already paid back.
RemainingCapital	Property	The capital still to be paid back.

The ASP application consists of the following files:

- default.htm. This is the main page that links to the LoanPlan() and LoanStatus() functions.
- planning.asp. This page allows the user to enter data in order to create a loan plan.
- loanplan.asp. This page builds a loan plan according to the data submitted by the user.
- saveloan.asp. Here the user can save the loan data on the server; this causes an identification number associated with the loan to be displayed.
- status.htm. Here the user can query the server about the status of a loan.
- loanstatus.asp. This page retrieves loan data from the server and displays its current status.
- error.asp. This page manages any errors which occur when the loan data is accessed.

The application has also a Global.asa file containing some global variables. It contains two functions which manage the Application_OnStart event and the Session_OnStart event. When the ASP application starts, the Application_OnStart() function initializes three global variables defining the annual interest rate, the maximum amount of a loan and the minimum payment for each month. These values will be used by the application for validating the user's input.

When a new session starts, the Session_OnStart() function instantiates the Loan object using the Server.CreateObject method. The resulting object instance is stored in a session variable so that it can be accessed at any time during the current user session.

The `Global.asa` file looks like this:

```
<SCRIPT LANGUAGE="JavaScript" RUNAT="server">
function Application_OnStart() {
    Application("Rate") = 0.08
    Application("MaxLoan") = 50000
    Application("MinPayment") = 100
}

function Session_OnStart() {
Session("Loan") = Server.CreateObject("Financial.Loan")
}
</SCRIPT>
```

When the user chooses to build a loan plan, the `planning.asp` page is requested from the web server. This page includes a simple form to allow the user to input details for the loan and to submit the loan amount and the monthly payment amount to the ASP application. Its code is as follows:

```
<%@ LANGUAGE="JavaScript" %>

<HTML>
<HEAD>

<SCRIPT>
function CheckData() {
    if (!(parseInt(document.frmLoan.LoanValue.value) > 0)) {
        alert("You must enter a valid value for the loan")
        document.frmLoan.LoanValue.focus()
        return false
    }

    if (parseInt(document.frmLoan.LoanValue.value) > <%= Application("MaxLoan") %>)
    {
        alert("The loan cannot exceed $ " + <%= Application("MaxLoan") %>)
        document.frmLoan.LoanValue.focus()
        return false
    }

    if (!(parseInt(document.frmLoan.PaymentValue.value) > 0)) {
        alert("You must enter a valid value for the monthly payment")
        document.frmLoan.PaymentValue.focus()
        return false
    }

    if (parseInt(document.frmLoan.PaymentValue.value) <
        <%= Application("MinPayment") %>) {
        alert("The monthly payment cannot be less than $ " +
            <%= Application("MinPayment") %>)
        document.frmLoan.PaymentValue.focus()
        return false
    }

    if (parseInt(document.frmLoan.PaymentValue.value) >
        parseInt(document.frmLoan.LoanValue.value)) {
        alert("The monthly payment cannot be greater than the loan")
        document.frmLoan.LoanValue.focus()
        return false
    }
    document.frmLoan.submit()
    return true
}
</SCRIPT>

</HEAD>
<BODY>
```

```
<H1>Loan Plan</H1>
<HR WIDTH="70%">

Insert the amount of the loan you need and the amount of each periodical payment.
<BR>
You will get the number of monthly payments and a detailed plan of your payments
at the interest rate of <%= Application("Rate") * 100 %>% per year.
<P>

<FORM NAME="frmLoan" METHOD="post" ACTION="loanplan.asp">

    The Loan Value: <INPUT TYPE="text" NAME="LoanValue" SIZE="10">
    <BR>
    The Amount of each monthly Payment: <INPUT TYPE="text" NAME="PaymentValue"
SIZE="10">
    <P>

    <INPUT TYPE="button" VALUE="Submit" onClick="CheckData()">
    <INPUT TYPE="reset">

</FORM>

</BODY>
</HTML>
```

As you can see, the ASP page provides a client-side JavaScript function to validate the data entered by the user. This script is first pre-processed by the ASP engine to set the maximum amount for a loan and the minimum for a monthly payment. These are taken from the application variables set in the `Global.asa` file. This approach provides a flexible way of updating the ASP application with new values without updating every script (whether server-side or client-side) which uses them.

The data submitted through the form is sent to the `loanplan.asp` page. Here, the `Loan` object is called to calculate the monthly payments. The results are then returned to the user:

```
<%@ LANGUAGE="JavaScript" %>

<HTML>
<BODY>

<%
var Payments

Session("Loan").Rate = Application("Rate")/12
Session("Loan").PV = Request.Form("LoanValue")
Session("Loan").PaymentAmount = Request.Form("PaymentValue")

Payments = Session("Loan").NumberOfPayments()

Session("Loan").LoanPlan()
%>

<H3> This is your loan plan</H3>

Loan value: $ <%=Request.Form("LoanValue") %><BR>
Monthly Payment: $ <%= Request.Form("PaymentValue") %>
<P>

Number of payments: <%= Payments %>
<P>

<TABLE BORDER="1">

<TR>
<TD> <B>Payment N.</B> </TD>
<TD> <B>Interest</B> </TD>
<TD> <B>Capital</B> </TD>
</TR>
```

```
<%
var i
var TotalInterests = 0
var TotalCapitals = 0

for (i=0;i<Payments;i++) {
   TotalInterests = TotalInterests + Session("Loan").Interests(i)
   TotalCapitals = TotalCapitals + Session("Loan").Capitals(i)
%>

<TR>
<TD> <%= i + 1 %> </TD>
<TD> $ <%= Session("Loan").Interests(i) %> </TD>
<TD> $ <%= Session("Loan").Capitals(i) %> </TD>
</TR>

<%}%>

<TR>
<TD><B>Totals</B></TD>
<TD> $ <%= TotalInterests %></TD>
<TD> $ <%= TotalCapitals %></TD>
</TR>

</TABLE>
<P>

<FORM METHOD="post" ACTION="saveloan.asp">
   <INPUT TYPE="submit" VALUE="Save Loan Plan">
   <INPUT TYPE="button" VALUE="Back" onClick="javascript:history.back()">
</FORM>

</BODY>
</HTML>
```

Let's have a look at this code to see what it does. First it sets the values for the current loan plan request, then executes the NumberOfPayments() and the LoanPlan() methods to calculate the data the user is waiting for. It can then display the results using the properties of the Loan object. Specifically, the Payments variable is set to the total number or payments required to pay back the loan (returned by the NumberOfPayments() method) and the details about the interest and capital paid are returned from the Interests and Capitals collections. The script also calculates the total amount for interests and capitals.

At the bottom of the resulting page, two buttons are displayed: the first allows the user to save the current plan; the second goes back to the previous page in order to refine the current loan plan and submit it again to the server.

If the user clicks on the **Save Loan Plan** button, the saveloan.asp page is executed by the ASP engine:

```
<%@ LANGUAGE="JavaScript"%>

<%
var LoanNumber = Session("Loan").SaveLoanData()
%>

<HTML>
<HEAD>
</HEAD>
<BODY>

You Loan Number is <%= LoanNumber %>. <BR>
Use it for future reference to your loan.
<P>
```

```
       Back to <A HREF="default.htm">Loan Manager</A>

       </BODY>
       </HTML>
```

This page simply executes the SaveLoanData() method of the Loan object, which saves the loan data on the server and displays the loan number generated by the method itself. Notice how the Loan object is referenced using the session variable Session("Loan").

The user might want to know the status of his loan plan in order to decide whether to continue with the plan or to pay off the remaining capital. This can be done through the status.htm page:

```
<HTML>
<HEAD>

<SCRIPT>
function CheckData() {
    if (!(parseInt(document.frmStatus.LoanNumber.value) > 0)) {
        alert("You must enter a valid Loan number")
        document.frmStatus.LoanNumber.focus()
        return false
    }

    if (!(parseInt(document.frmStatus.PaymentNumber.value) > 0)) {
        alert("You must enter a valid value for the payment number")
        document.frmStatus.PaymentNumber.focus()
        return false
    }

    document.frmStatus.submit()
    return true
}
</SCRIPT>

</HEAD>
<BODY>

<H1>Loan Status</H1>
<HR WIDTH="70%">

Insert your Loan number and the number of the last payment.
<BR>
You will get the current status of your loan.
<P>

<FORM NAME="frmStatus" METHOD="post" ACTION="loanstatus.asp">

The Loan Number: <INPUT TYPE="text" NAME="LoanNumber" SIZE="6">
<BR>
The number of your last Payment:
<INPUT TYPE="text" NAME="PaymentNumber" SIZE="3">
<P>

<INPUT TYPE="button" VALUE="Submit" onClick="CheckData()">
<INPUT TYPE="reset">

</FORM>

</BODY>
</HTML>
```

As you can see, this is a standard HTML file, with no ASP. The user is prompted to enter the loan number of the loan plan to be checked and the number of the last payment that was made. This data is sent to the loanstatus.asp page, where it is processed.

The loanstatus.asp page creates an instance of the Loan object, calls the GetLoanData()
method to retrieve the details for the loan with the specified loan number and executes the
LoanStatus method in order to calculate the current status of the loan. This is the code for the
loanstatus.asp page:

```
<%@ LANGUAGE="JavaScript" %>

<%
var Payments

if (Session("Loan").GetLoanData(Request.Form("LoanNumber")) == 0) {
    Response.Redirect("error.asp?code=LoanNumber")
}

if (parseInt(Request.Form("PaymentNumber")) >
        parseInt(Session("Loan").NPayments)) {
    Response.Redirect("error.asp?code=PaymentNumber")
}

Session("Loan").LoanStatus(Request.Form("PaymentNumber"))

%>

<HTML>
<BODY>


<H3> This is your loan status</H3>

Loan value: <%= Session("Loan").PV %><BR>
Interest rate per year: <%= Math.round(Session("Loan").Rate * 12 * 100) %>%<BR>
Monthly Payment: <%= Session("Loan").PaymentAmount %><BR>
Number of payments: <%= Session("Loan").NPayments %>
<P>

Last payment number: <%= Request.Form("PaymentNumber") %> <BR>
Paid Interest: <%= Session("Loan").PaidInterest %> <BR>
Returned Capital: <%= Session("Loan").ReturnedCapital %> <BR>
Remaining Capital: <%= Session("Loan").RemainingCapital %> <BR>
<P>

<FORM>
<INPUT TYPE="button" VALUE="Back" onClick="javascript:history.back()">
<INPUT TYPE="button" VALUE="Loan Manager"
onClick="document.location='default.htm'">
</FORM>

</BODY>
</HTML>
```

Notice that the script controls whether data entered by the user is correct. In particular, if the Loan
object cannot retrieve a loan plan with the number provided by the user, the GetLoanData method
returns 0. In this case, the JavaScript code redirects the browser to the error.asp page passing the
query string code=LoanNumber in order to manage this situation. Also, if the user entered a
payment number which was greater then the total number of payments for the loan plan, the script
redirects the browser to the error.asp page with the query string code=PaymentNumber. This
sort of data validation must be performed on the server side because it has to compare data stored on
the server. This complements the data validation which was performed on the client, where we
ensured that valid numerical values were entered. The rest of the ASP page simply displays data
retrieved from the properties of the Loan object.

The `error.asp` page simply displays appropriate error messages when the user submits invalid data for the loan status request:

```
<%@ LANGUAGE="JavaScript"%>

<HTML>

<HEAD>
</HEAD>

<BODY>

<%
if (Request.QueryString("code") == "LoanNumber") {
   Response.Write("The loan number you provided does not exist! Try again.<P>")
   Response.Write("<A HREF='status.htm'>Loan Status</A>")
}

if (Request.QueryString("code") == "PaymentNumber") {
   Response.Write("The payment number you provided is greater "+
                  "than the total number of payments!<BR>")
   Response.Write("Maybe you have paid back the entire loan.<P>")
   Response.Write("<A HREF='status.htm'>Loan Status</A>")
}

%>

</BODY>
</HTML>
```

When the browser was redirected to this page, we appended an error code to the URL as a query string; the script analyzes this string and displays the message for the specific error which occurred.

Summary

This chapter showed how to use JavaScript within the Active Server Pages framework. It explained how we can use ASP to generate content dynamically and introduced the syntactical features that allow us to embed JavaScript code into HTML tags. We also considered the interaction between client-side and server-side scripting, and illustrated a mixed use of JavaScript together with VBScript. We then took a whirlwind tour of the ASP object model, looking at each of the individual built-in objects: the `Request`, `Response`, `Application`, `Session` and `Server` objects. In addition, we looked at the system objects available in ASP through the `Scripting` object and considered other external components. We also took a very quick look at configuring the settings for ASP. Finally, the chapter concluded with an example application which implemented most of the ASP features introduced throughout the chapter.

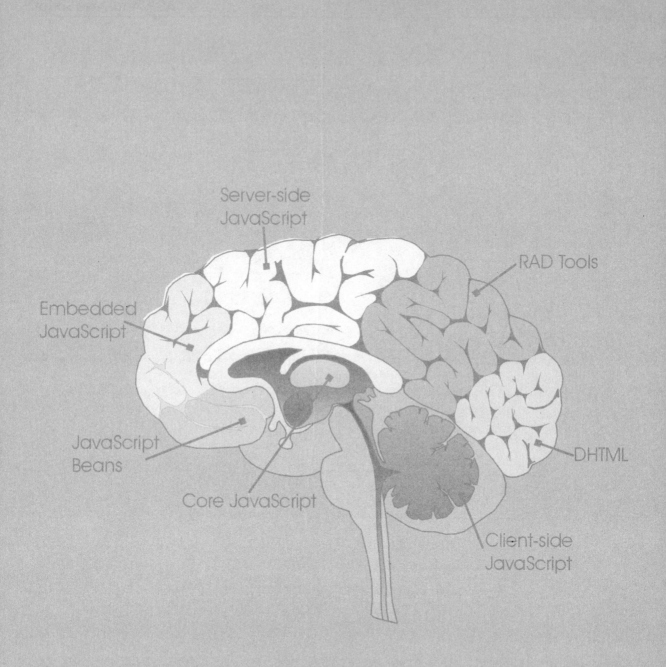

Building an E-Commerce Shop Front

In this chapter we will be building an electronic store front and online ordering system for an imaginary company called MusicMadOnline.com. It will include many of the essential elements required for an online store such as the ability to browse stock, a shopping basket and an online ordering system.

In this chapter you will learn how to:

❑ Build dynamic pages using server-side JScript v5 and ADO 2.1 to pull information from a SQL Server 7 database

❑ Validate form based user input using client-side JavaScript

❑ Persist state from page to page using cookies

❑ Harness Active Server Page's transaction support via MTS (Microsoft Transaction Server) to process orders and store user orders in a database

❑ Send e-mails using Microsoft's CDONTS (Collaboration Data Objects for Windows NT Server)

To work through this example, you will need access to Windows NT Server 4 or Windows 2000 with SQL7.0, JScript v5.0, IIS4 or 5, MTS, a simple mail server and a text editor installed upon it. Note also that where we have split lines of code onto two or more lines for clarity's sake, this has been marked with an underscore.

MusicMadOnline.com

Our imaginary client MusicMadOnline.com sells music compact discs and wants an online store to sell their products. They want customers to be able to browse their electronic shelves based on music genre. However they don't want their product lists or the categories to be hardwired in to the HTML pages although they do require the addition of new products and categories to be reflected automatically in the HTML pages.

Once the customer has selected their goods they must then be able to place an order online using a credit card for payment. Once an order has been accepted, the shipping department must be notified by e-mail of the customer's delivery address and items to be sent. The customer must also be notified by e-mail that their order has been accepted and will be delivered shortly.

Design aims

Businesses want to make money and can't afford to turn away customers. It's for this reason that the client-side part of MusicMadOnline.com has been designed to work on Internet Explorer and Netscape Navigator browsers version 3 and above. If we want to include Dynamic HTML effects particular to say IE4 or 5 then separate pages would most likely have to be written. Although it is possible to include support for different browsers in the same page, things can quickly get confusing.

On the server-side we have control of what version of JavaScript we use. Here I have used features available in JavaScript 1.2 and in particular those available in Microsoft's JScript Version 5.0 which comes with Internet Explorer 5.0 (IE5). If you don't want to install IE5 on your server than you can download the version 5.0 scripting engine from the Microsoft site (http://msdn.microsoft.com/scripting/jscript/default.htm) and install it on your server. Perhaps the best reason for upgrading to JScript v5 is its support of exception handling using the try...catch statement, but more on this later.

In anticipation of our online store being hugely popular we need to ensure it can cope with large numbers concurrent users and database transactions. It may be tempting to use something like Microsoft Access as our back end database, but as even Microsoft admit, Access won't cut it for high numbers of concurrent users. Instead I have used SQL Server 7 as the back-end database, though there are plenty of other high-end databases available which can provide the power we need.

SQL Server 7 also provides a greater level of sophistication, such as compiled stored procedures, which by modularizing our database code will make it more maintainable and as a bonus achieve greater scalability through being pre-compiled.

When dealing with large databases ensuring they don't become corrupted is always important. By this I mean that we don't want the situation where halfway through processing a customer's order we hit an unexpected error causing our application to drop out leaving the database in an inconsistent state. Either a transaction completes fully and the customer gets their goods or it fails and is rolled back completely and the customer is informed of this fact and where possible given information on why it happened and how they can proceed to complete their order. To help us with this objective we will make use of support for Microsoft Transaction Server transactions in ASP.

Setting Up The Database

Our first task is to create a new database. Use SQL Server's Enterprise Manager to create a new database and name it `MusicMad`. To do this open up the console root until the name of your server is displayed. Then open it up to display the current databases.

Right click on **Databases** in the left panel and select **New Database**. Enter the name `MusicMad` into the name box and click **OK**. The default settings for the database are fine for our purposes.

Next we need to create a new user called `MMCustomer` with the password `Madforit` and give them access to the MusicMad database. In the Enterprise Manager main console area open up the **Security** root so you can see **Logins** and right click it. Select **New Login**. Enter `MMCustomer` for the name, check the **SQL Server authentication** radio button and enter `Madforit` in the password box. Use the drop down combo box to change the default database to **MusicMad**.

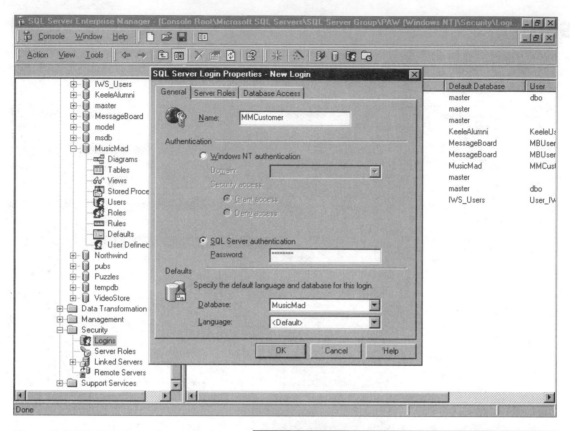

Then click the **Database Access** tab at the top of the dialog and check the **MusicMad** box to give the user access to our database. Click **OK** and you'll be asked to confirm the password. Re-enter it and click **OK** to close the dialog box.

Creating the Tables

The database consists of six tables as shown in the diagram below:

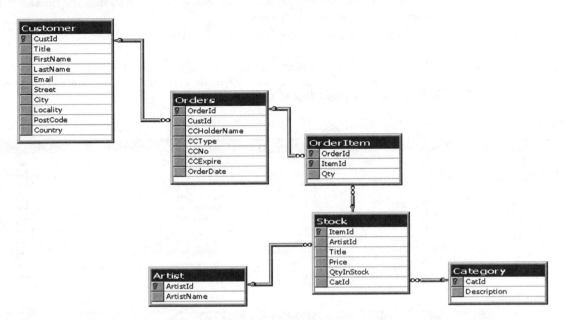

When a customer places a new order its details go into the Orders table and the customer details such as name and address in the Customer table. The Customer table's primary key field CustId is also in Orders as a foreign key and links the two together.Meanwhile OrderItems stores the items making up an order and is linked to the Orders table using the OrderId.

Normalizing the data by splitting into separate tables helps keep the database size to a minimum by avoiding data duplication. For a real world system you might want to take it further and have customers create a login before they can order goods and store the customer details just once in the Customer table. If they shop again they can log in and won't have to re-enter their details.

Information about individual goods is stored in the Stock table, which also has links to Artist and Category. Again this helps reduce data duplication, especially as we start inputting many albums in stock by the same artist. With this arrangement only the integer ArtistId is duplicated in the Stock table. It also allows extra details about an artist to be included easily and efficiently. The Category table stores all the different music genres of modern music, for example rock, pop, dance, acid house, etc. Again we could add extra information about the genre if we want.

The steps to follow to create each of the six tables are identical:

- ❑ Open up the Console Root tree in Enterprise Manager so that you can see the MusicMad database.
- ❑ Open up MusicMad so that Tables is visible.
- ❑ Right click on Tables, select New Table, and a dialog box will appear for you to enter the name you want to give the new table.

- ❑ Having done that click **OK** then create the fields for each table as shown below.
- ❑ A key icon next to a field name indicates a **primary key field**. To set a field as a primary key, right click anywhere on it and select **Set Primary Key**. In the case of setting more than one field as primary key, select both first and then right click.
- ❑ After each table has been created close the design screen, making sure you have saved first.

Note: CustId in the Customer table, OrderId in the Orders table and ItemId in the Stock table are Identity fields. This means that they are automatically allocated a new value when a new row is inserted. Check the Identity check box to make them identity fields.

Customer Table

Column Name	Datatype	Length	Precision	Scale	Allow Nulls	Default Value	Identity	Identity Seed	Identity Increment	Is RowGuid
CustId	int	4	10	0			✓	1	1	
Title	varchar	4	0	0						
FirstName	varchar	50	0	0						
LastName	varchar	50	0	0						
Email	varchar	75	0	0						
Street	varchar	75	0	0						
City	varchar	50	0	0						
Locality	varchar	50	0	0						
PostCode	varchar	15	0	0						
Country	varchar	50	0	0						

Orders Table

Column Name	Datatype	Length	Precision	Scale	Allow Nulls	Default Value	Identity	Identity Seed	Identity Increment	Is RowGuid
OrderId	int	4	10	0			✓	1	1	
CustId	int	4	10	0						
CCHolderName	varchar	50	0	0						
CCType	varchar	25	0	0						
CCNo	varchar	50	0	0						
CCExpire	varchar	7	0	0						
OrderDate	datetime	8	0	0						

OrderItem Table

Column Name	Datatype	Length	Precision	Scale	Allow Nulls	Default Value	Identity	Identity Seed	Identity Increment	Is RowGuid
OrderId	int	4	10	0						
ItemId	int	4	10	0						
Qty	int	4	10	0						

Stock Table

Column Name	Datatype	Length	Precision	Scale	Allow Nulls	Default Value	Identity	Identity Seed	Identity Increment	Is RowGuid
ItemId	int	4	10	0						
ArtistId	int	4	10	0						
Title	varchar	50	0	0						
Price	money	8	19	4	✓					
QtyInStock	int	4	10	0						
CatId	int	4	10	0	✓					

Category Table

	Column Name	Datatype	Length	Precision	Scale	Allow Nulls	Default Value	Identity	Identity Seed	Identity Increment	Is RowGuid
▽	CatId	int	4	10	0	☐		☐			☐
	Description	varchar	50	0	0	☐		☐			☐
▶						☐		☐			☐

Artist table

	Column Name	Datatype	Length	Precision	Scale	Allow Nulls	Default Value	Identity	Identity Seed	Identity Increment	Is RowGuid
▽▶	ArtistId	int	4	10	0	☐		☐			☐
	ArtistName	varchar	50	0	0	☐		☐			☐
							☐		☐		☐

Referential Integrity

To ensure data integrity we need to put constraints on what can be added to and deleted from the table. For example it would not make sense to have an `ArtistId` in the `Stock` table that does not exist in the `Artist` table.

The easiest and quickest way to add these constraints is from the database diagram view. The first step is to create a new database diagram:

- ❑ From Enterprise Manager open up the MusicMad database so that you can see the Diagrams branch.

- ❑ Right click Diagrams and select New Database Diagram.

- ❑ If you're using the full version of SQL Server then the database diagram wizard dialog will pop-up. Use it to add all the tables to the diagram. (*Editor's Note: If the wizard doesn't work when you use it, close and restart Enterprise Manager and then repeat the steps above. That seems to fix it*).

- ❑ If you're using a developer version of SQL Server then you need to drag the tables from the Add Table dialog.

With the tables on the diagram, you can arrange them neatly by drag-and-dropping them to the required position. For example:

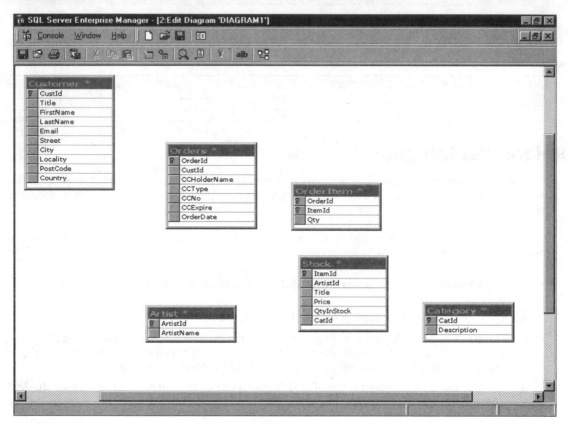

Now we can add the relationships between tables. The rules to enforce are:

1. For each order there must be a corresponding customer.

2. For each order item there must be a corresponding order.

3. For each order item there must be a corresponding stock item.

4. For each stock item there must be an artist and a category.

For the first constraint you need to left click and hold down the mouse on the gray box next to CustId in the Orders table then, keeping the mouse button held down, drag over to CustId in the Customer table then let go. You should see a **Create Relationship** dialog box (like the one below) pop-up with details of the fields and tables involved in the relationship. Just click **OK** and the relationship will be created. Note that the 'bars' between tables will not necessarily point to the two fields but you can move them so they do.

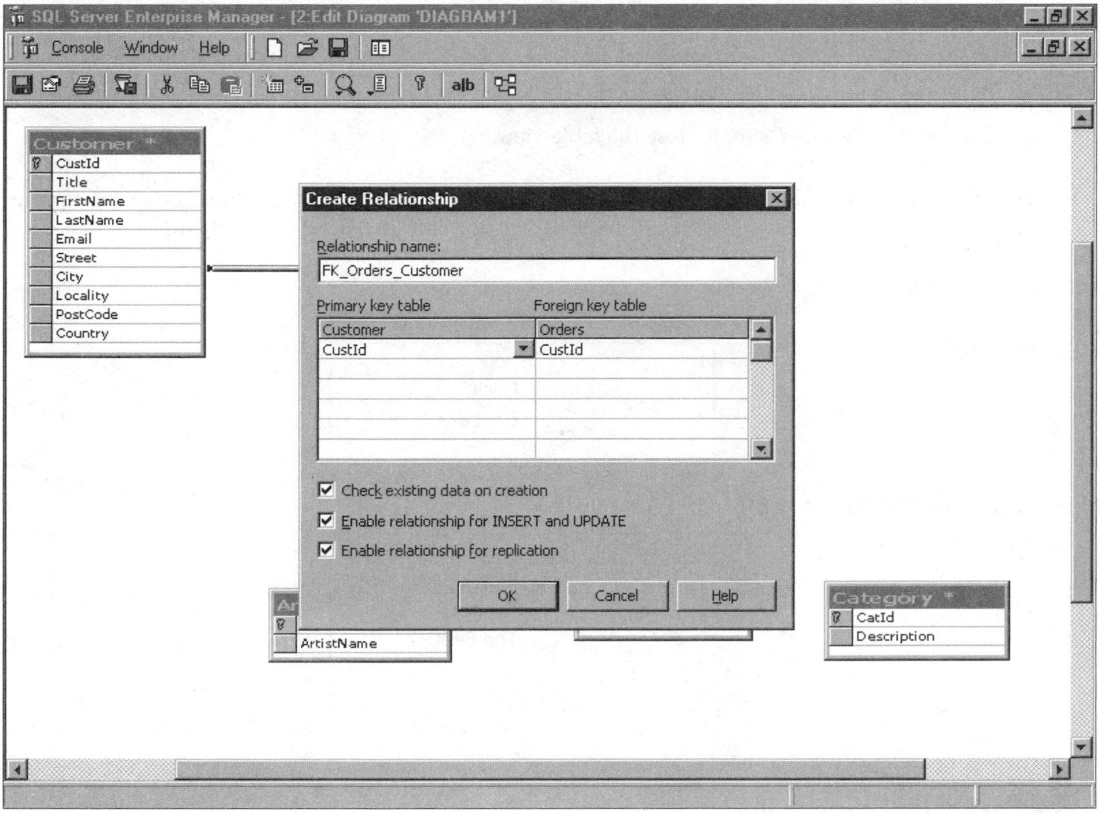

Follow the steps above and do the same for the following tables:

- ❑ Click and drag from `OrderItem`, `OrderId` field to `Orders`, `OrderId` field.
- ❑ Click and drag from `OrderItem`, `ItemId` field to `Stock`, `ItemId` field.
- ❑ Click and drag from `Stock`, `ArtistId` field to `Artist`, `ArtistId` field.
- ❑ Click and drag from `Stock`, `CatId` field to `Category`, `CatId` field.

Make sure you save the diagram then close the diagram view.

Sample Data

Now would be a good time to add sample data to the database. You'll need to add data to the `Category`, `Artist` and `Stock` tables. The constraints we added above should prevent you adding an item to the `Stock` table and giving it an `ArtistId` which does not exist in the `Artist` table and similarly for the `CatId` and the `Category` table.

Shown below is some sample data to get you started. With SQL Server 7.0 comes the ability to type your data directly into the table. For example, to type data into the `Category` table:

- ❑ From Enterprise Manager open up the MusicMad database so that you can see the Tables branch.
- ❑ Right click on the Category table and select Open Table and then Return all Rows.
- ❑ Click into a box and start typing.
- ❑ To save your entries, simply close the table view.

We've included some example data here to get you started, but please do add some more of your own favorite records. A music shop with only five records for sale is a poor one indeed.

Sample Data for the Category Table

CatId	Description
1	Pop
2	Rock
3	Dance

Sample Data for the Artist Table

ArtistId	ArtistName
1	REM
2	Orbital
3	The Beatles
4	U2
5	Orb
6	saint etienne

Sample Data for the Stock Table

ItemId	ArtistId	Title	Price	QtyInStock	CatId
1	1	Up	9.99	5	2
2	1	Automatic for the P	9.99	10	2
3	1	Monster	11.99	5	2
4	2	In Sides	9.99	5	3
5	3	Abbey Road	9.99	10	1

There's no need to add sample data to the Customer, Orders or OrderItems tables as we'll do that using the web site.

Building the Basic Website

We have completed the foundations of our database. We will create the stored procedures as we need them. Our next task is to create the HTML and scripting for the MusicMad web site.

Creating the Initial Frameset

The site consists of two basic frames. The top frame contains a menu bar with links for browsing the site and remains in view at all times. The bottom frame is where the action is at and will be used for displaying all the other pages on the site.

There are two client-side JavaScript functions inside the page. The first returns the value of the cookie whose name is passed as the function's parameter. As discussed in further detail in Chapter 18, `document.cookie` returns all the cookies for that web site but does not provide a way of retrieving just one particular cookie. The string returned by `document.cookie` takes the format `cookiename=cookievalue; cookiename=cookievalue;` and so on...

The second function handles the `frasetMain_onload()` event. As the web site relies heavily on cookies, particularly for the shopping basket we need to check the user has cookie's enabled. Though this site is designed only for cookie supporting browsers, they can be disabled under a browser's security options. We need to check for this and if the user accesses a part of the site which requires cookies then we will inform them they need to be enabled to use the web site.

Methods for checking if cookies are enabled vary from browser to browser, but I have used one which works for version 3 browsers and above. We set a global variable in the `window_onload` event of the top frame that we can access later from child windows.

```
<HTML>
<HEAD>
<SCRIPT language="JavaScript">
var cookiesEnabled = false;

// Retrieves particular cookie
function getCookie(cookieName)
{
    var cookieFoundAt;
    var cookieValue;

    // find start position in cookie string
    cookieFoundAt = document.cookie.indexOf(cookieName + "=");

    if (cookieFoundAt < 0)
        {
        cookieValue = "";
        }
    else
        {
        // move to actual start of cookie's data
        cookieFoundAt = document.cookie.indexOf("=",cookieFoundAt);
        cookieFoundAt++;

        // find end position of cookie's data
        cookieEnd = document.cookie.indexOf(";", cookieFoundAt);
        if (cookieEnd == -1)
            {
            cookieEnd = document.cookie.length - 1;
            }
        cookieValue =document.cookie.substring(cookieFoundAt,cookieEnd);
        }
    return cookieValue;
}
```

```
// Check whether cookies enabled
function frasetMain_onload()
{
   document.cookie = "Enabled=true";
   var cookieValid = document.cookie;

   // if retrieving the VALUE we just set actually works
   // then we know cookies enabled
   if (cookieValid.indexOf("Enabled=true") != -1)
   {
      cookiesEnabled = true;
   }
   else
   {
      cookiesEnabled = false;
      alert("You need to enable cookies on your browser to take advantage of our
            online ordering");
   }
}
</SCRIPT>
<TITLE>Welcome to MusicMadness.Com</TITLE>
</HEAD>
<FRAMESET  BORDER=5 ROWS="62,*" NAME="frasetMain" onLoad="frasetMain_onload()">
   <!-- MenuBar Top Frame -->
   <FRAME SCROLLING="NO" SRC="top_menu.asp" NAME="fraTop" NORESIZE>
      <!-- Main area - where most of the displaying of information occurs -->
   <FRAME SCROLLING="AUTO" SRC="home.asp" NAME="fraMain" NORESIZE>
</FRAMESET>
</HTML>
```

With this page completed you need to save it as `MusicMad.htm`. To make life easy for yourself create a new directory called `MusicMad` and put it in there. This is where we will put all the files for this project. You may also wish to make this a virtual directory on your development machine and share it as `MusicMad` for easy access during development and testing. Note that all of these files are available as part of the source code download for this book from `http://www.wrox.com` and that the entire of this will be running as a demo from `http://rapid.wrox.com/books/270x`.

Displaying A List Of Categories

To allow the user to browse the available music categories we need to dynamically produce a list of categories contained in the database table `Category`.

To retrieve the data from the database we must create a new stored procedure and name it `ListCategories`:

❑   In Enterprise Manager under the MusicMad database root, right click **Stored Procedures** and select **New Stored Procedure**.

❑   Add the following SQL and then click **OK** to return to the main view:

```
CREATE PROCEDURE [ListCategories] AS
SELECT CatId, Description FROM Category
ORDER BY Description
```

You'll need to give `MMCustomer` execute permissions for the stored procedure.

Right-click the newly created stored procedure and select **Manage Permissions** from under the **All Tasks** menu. Tick the **EXEC** check box for `MMCustomer` as shown below and then click **OK** to close the dialog box.

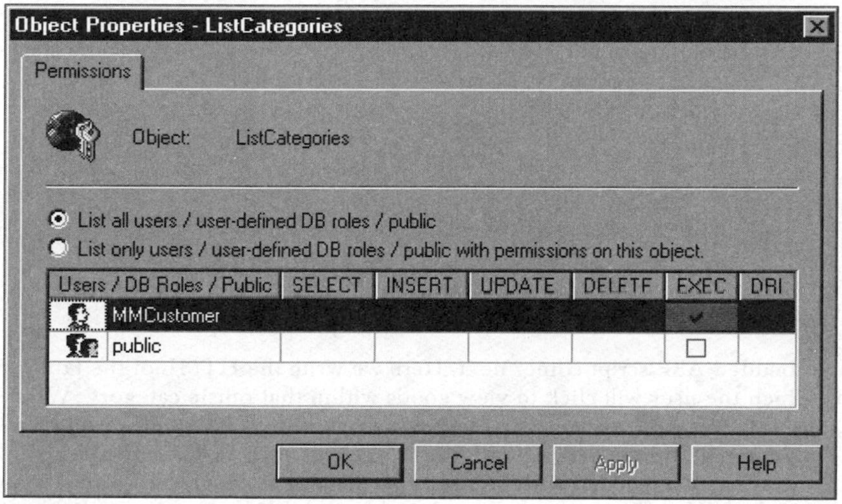

The stored procedure is now complete and you need to return to your HTML editor to create the page that uses it.

Some Standard Include Files

Web page and scripting creation do not easily lend themselves to code reuse. However, one way of accomplishing code reuse is server-side include files whereby a file is included within a page by use of the `<!--#include file="">` directive available with NT Server via ASP.

The next piece of scripting we will write is an include file to create a dynamic list of music categories available for browsing. Taking the information from the `Category` table in the database, this include file creates a table of links which when clicked takes the user to a list of goods available within that category.

Using the server-side include directive we will incorporate this file in a number of pages in the web site demonstrating code reuse.

The CategoryList Include File

The first thing our ASP code does is create an ADODB Recordset to obtain a list of categories from the database. We use the ASP Server object's `CreateObject` method to create a new `ADODB.Recordset` object. The Recordset's `Open` method fetches the data we need by executing the `ListCategories` stored procedure we created earlier. `sdbConnString` is a global variable defined outside of the include file, in another server-side include file that is inserted into every ASP page in the web site, but we will come to this in good time.

```
<%
    // Number of table cells per row
    var iNoPerRow = 4;
    var loRS;
    var scategoryDesc;
```

```
    // Create ADODB.Recordset object then execute of ListCatgeories
    // stored procedure
    loRS = Server.CreateObject("ADODB.Recordset");
    loRS.Open("Exec ListCategories", sdbConnString);
%>
```

Next we have the starting tags of our HTML table. The ASP code following is the start of our while loop which loops though the recordset rows and creates our table's rows and cells:

```
<TABLE>
<TR>
<%
    // Loop though the returned recordset
    // populating table cells/links
    while (!(loRS.Eof))
    {
        scategoryDesc = loRS("Description");
%>
```

HTML with embedded ASP script comes next. Here we write the HTML of the table cell, inserting the hyperlink which the user will click to view goods within that music category. We append the CatId and Category Description to the end of the hyperlink's URL. The ASP page which this link navigates to can pick up the data from the ASP Request object's QueryString collection. Note that Description has been coded with the escape method to ensure no confusion occurs when it is passed as part of a URL. Characters such as the ampersand (&) are converted into their ASCII value so they are not confused with an ampersand which indicates another item of data in the URL.

```
<TD WIDTH="150" height="50">
    <FONT SIZE=5 COLOR=#FF8040 FACE="Comic Sans MS">
    <STRONG>
        <A HREF="Browse.asp?CatId=<%=loRS("CatId")%>
                &Description=<%=escape(scategoryDesc)%>
                &StartItemId=-1">
            <%=loRS("Description")%>
        </A>
    </STRONG></FONT>
</TD>
```

Finally we come to the end of the while loop and table:

```
<%
        // Decrement row counter - if hit our limit for the row
        // start a new row
        iNoPerRow--;
        if (iNoPerRow == 0)
        {
            Response.Write("</TR><TR>");
            iNoPerRow = 4;
        }
        loRS.MoveNext();
    }   // end of while loop
    loRS.Close();
    loRS = null;
%>
</TABLE>
```

Save the include file as `CategoryList.inc` into the MusicMad directory you created earlier. The `.inc` extension is not compulsory for include files but it is the one recommended by Microsoft.

The Global Include File

Our next task is to create another include file which will be added at the start of all our ASP pages using the include directive. It contains a number of global constants and general functions.

At the very top of the file on a separate line by itself is an ASP preprocessing directive. This must be the first line and it must be separate from other ASP code or the page will fail. There are a number of ASP preprocessing directives, some of which we will come to later, but this particular one sets the default language for all ASP on this page to JScript:

```
<%@ Language="JScript"%>
```

Next a couple of global constants used in the web site are declared. The `sdbConnString` is our connection string we use in our ADO statements to connect to the database. I have used a DSN-less connection for ease of set up (there is no set up needed!). If you prefer, you can set up an ODBC data source which does make it easier to change data sources without changing any code. Even if you never change your database you may change its location to another server, something you can easily do with an ODBC data source.

Most of the database connection string is self-explanatory. However some needs further explanation. The `Provider` is our database, here SQL Server 7. `Initial Catalog` is our database. In `Data Source` we have used a period (full stop). This is an alias for the local server, similar to using `localhost` for the local web server. If you find this does not work, for example if your SQL Server database is not installed or you are using a Win95/98 machine, then replace the period with the name of the SQL Server your database is installed on.

`Response.Buffer = true` buffers the sending of page content and has been used to allow us to change cookie values once the HTTP header has been written. When the response is buffered, the result of the ASP code (HTML and client-side script) is stored in the server's memory until either the end of the page is reached or a `Response.Flush` or `Response.End` methods are called. Buffering also means that we can change a cookie in server-side ASP code even after the `<HTML>` tag, something otherwise disallowed.

```
<%
 // Global Constants

Response.Buffer = true;

// DSN-less Connection String to database
var sdbConnString =  "Provider=SQLOLEDB.1;Password=madforit;Persist Security
Info=True;User ID=MMCustomer;Initial Catalog=MusicMad;Data Source=.";

// Number of goods per page to display
var lMaxPerPage = 15;
```

Next we come to the code for the first of the two functions included with the include file. This is part of our web site's shopping basket functionality. It extracts cookie data for a particular stock item contained within the basket – the `ItemId`, which is the same as that defined in the database, is used for identifying items. Data held within the cookie for a particular item includes `ItemId`, `Qty`, `ArtistName`, `Item Description` and the `Price` of an individual item. It is contained in a single string which uses & to delimit data within an item and the £ to indicate the end of the item's data.

```
function getItemFromCookie(lItemId, sCookie)
{
    // Find Item start and end
    var lStart = sCookie.indexOf(lItemId + "&");
    var lEnd = sCookie.indexOf("£",lStart + 1);

    // put that into a new string - excluding £ at end
    var sItem = sCookie.slice(lStart,--lEnd);
    var ItemData = sItem.split("&");
    return ItemData
}
```

The getItemFromCookie functions counterpart is the setItemToCookie function. Its parameters are ItemData, an array containing ItemId, ArtistName, item Description and Price, and the current value of the basket cookie.

There are three situations the routine deals with:

❑   The item already exists in the basket in which case we need to update its quantity.

❑   If the updated quantity is zero then the item needs to be deleted from the basket, otherwise we override the existing value.

❑   If the item is not already in the basket then we need to concatenate it to the end of the basket cookie string.

Regular Expressions, a powerful feature of JavaScript versions 1.2 and above, and the string object's replace method are used to update an existing quantity. For example, if we had an ItemId of 12, with a current Qty of 2, ArtistName "REM", Description "Monster" and Price of 9.99 then the cookie for that item will look like:

```
ID12&2&REM&Monster&9.99£&
```

Our regular expression created by the line new RegExp(lItemId + "&[0-9]+"), will be:

```
ID12&[0-9]+
```

This will match any occurrences of ID12& and any number of digits (which make up the quantity). [0-9] indicates any character in the range 0 – 9 (i.e. any digit). The + indicates that one or more of the previous character, i.e. a digit, must follow.

```
function setItemToCookie(ItemData, sCookie)
{
    // ItemData is array with elements
    // ItemId,Qty,ArtistName,Title,Price
    var sBasketCookie = new String(sCookie);
    var lItemId = new String(ItemData[0]);

    // Is that item already in the basket
    var lItemStart = sBasketCookie.indexOf(lItemId + "&")

    // update qty of existing Item
    if (lItemStart >= 0)
    {
        // If new VALUE is not 0 then update Qty
        if (ItemData[1] > 0)
        {
```

```
               var SearchPattern = new RegExp(lItemId + "&[0-9]+");
               sBasketCookie = sBasketCookie.replace(SearchPattern,lItemId + _
                                            "&" + ItemData[1]);
         }
         else
         {
            // new Item Qty is 0 so remove it from basket
            var lItemEnd = sBasketCookie.indexOf("£&",lItemStart + 1) + 2;
            sBasketCookie = sBasketCookie.replace _
                         (sBasketCookie.slice(lItemStart,lItemEnd),"");
         }
      }
      else
      {
         // Item not in basket already - so add it
         sBasketCookie = sBasketCookie.concat(lItemId + "&",ItemData[1] + _
                      "&",ItemData[2] + "&",ItemData[3] + _
                      "&",ItemData[4] + "&");
      }

      return sBasketCookie;

}

%>
```

Save this page as `ServerSideGlobalDef.inc`.

The Homepage

The homepage is the first page displayed in the main frame when the user browses to the web site. It displays the site name and lists the music categories available for browsing using `CategoryList.inc` we created above.

```
<!--#include file="ServerSideGlobalDef.inc"-->
<HTML>
<HEAD></HEAD>

<BODY>
<BASEFONT SIZE=3 COLOR=#004080 FACE="Comic Sans MS,MS Sans Serif,Arial">
    <H1 ALIGN="CENTER">
        <FONT COLOR=#004080 FACE="Comic Sans MS">MusicMadOnline.com</FONT>
    </H1>
    <H3 ALIGN="CENTER">
        <FONT COLOR=#004080 FACE="Comic Sans MS">
            Prices so low we must be insane!!!
        </FONT>
    </H3>
    <DIV align="center">
    <FONT FACE="Comic Sans MS" color="#FF8040">
        Browse our categories below for great bargins, <BR>
        all available to purchase online with our secure online ordering
        system.
    </FONT>
    <P>
        <!--#include file="CategoryList.inc"-->
    </P>
    </DIV>
</BODY>
</HTML>
```

Save the file as `Home.asp`

The Menu Bar

The menu bar will contain three links, a link to the home page, a link to the shopping basket and a link to the checkout. Also in the menu bar is a form with an HTML select tag with a list of categories and a button which when clicked will navigate the user to the category selected in the select tag.

First we add our server-side global include file. Next we add the client-side scripting for the Checkout link. Script has been used here rather than an `<A>` tag with an `href` property because we need to check a few things before deciding where to navigate to. If cookies are disabled then we need to inform the user that they won't be able to proceed and cancel the event by returning false.

If the basket is empty then there is no point going to the checkout so we navigate to a page informing them their basket is empty. If cookies are enabled and the basket contains goods then we navigate to the checkout.

```
<!--#include file="ServerSideGlobalDef.inc"-->
<HTML>
<HEAD>
<SCRIPT language='javascript'>

function linkCheckout_onClick()
{

    if (parent.cookiesEnabled == false)
    {
```

```
        // cookies disabled - so checkout will not function
        // inform user then cancel event
        alert("You require cookies to be enabled to order online");
        return false;
    }
    else if (parent.getCookie("Basket") == "")
    {
        // Empty basket - go to empty basket page
        parent.fraMain.location.href = "emptybasket.asp";
    }
    else
    {
        // something in basket to buy - so go to checkout.
        parent.fraMain.location.href = "Checkout_frame.htm";
    }
    return true;
}
```

The next event we will code is that for the view basket link. The same principles apply for this link as the checkout.

```
function linkViewBasket_onClick()
{

    if (parent.cookiesEnabled == false)
    {
        // cookies disabled - so basket will not function
        // inform user then cancel event
        alert("You require cookies to be enabled to order online");
        return false;
    }
    else if (parent.getCookie("Basket") == "")
    {
        // Empty basket - go to empty basket page
        parent.fraMain.location.href = "emptybasket.asp";
    }
    else
    {
        // basket has contents - display basket page in main frame
        parent.fraMain.location.href = "viewbasket.asp"
    }
    return true;
}
```

Finally we add the event handler for the go button which when clicked navigates the main window to view goods in the category selected in the select control.

```
function cmdGoBrowse_onclick()
{
    var sURL = document.frmMenu.cboBrowse.options _
                    [document.frmMenu.cboBrowse.selectedIndex].VALUE;
    parent.fraMain.location.href = sURL;
}

</SCRIPT>
```

Now we need to add the links we have just coded for. They are contained within a table for formatting, this way we can space them evenly and horizontally across the frame.

```
</HEAD>
<BODY BACKGROUND="musicbk2.jpg">
<BASE TARGET="fraMain">
<TABLE>
```

```
<TR ALIGN="CENTER">
  <TD VALIGN="TOP" WIDTH="150">
    <A HREF="home.asp">
      <STRONG>
        <FONT FACE="comic sans ms" COLOR=#FF8040>Home</FONT>
      </STRONG>
    </A>
  </TD>
  <TD VALIGN="TOP" WIDTH="150">
    <A HREF="#" TARGET="_self" NAME="linkViewBasket"
              onClick="return linkViewBasket_onClick();">
      <STRONG>
        <FONT FACE="comic sans ms" COLOR=#FF8040>
          Shopping Basket
        </FONT>
      </STRONG>
    </A>
  </TD>
  <TD VALIGN="TOP" WIDTH="150">
    <A HREF="#" TARGET="_self" NAME="linkCheckout"
              onClick="return linkCheckout_onClick()">
      <STRONG>
        <FONT FACE="comic sans ms" COLOR=#FF8040>Checkout</FONT>
      </STRONG>
    </A>
  </TD>
```

Our next task is to create the form containing the drop down select box which contains a list of music categories the user can browse and a button which when clicked navigates the main frame to view the available items in the selected category.

The option tags for the select control need to be created dynamically on the fly using ASP to create the HTML based on data pulled from the Category table. We use the same stored procedure we used for the CategoryList.inc include file.

In fact the code is very similar to that in CategoryList.inc except here we are creating option tags rather than table cell tags. The value for the option tags is the URL for the browse.asp page with the CatId and Description added to the end (which is then retrieved by ASP script in browse.asp).

```
<TD VALIGN="top" WIDTH="200">
<FORM METHOD=POST NAME="frmMenu">

<%
var loRS;
loRS = Server.CreateObject("ADODB.Recordset");
loRS.Open("Exec ListCategories", sdbConnString);
%>

    <STRONG>
        <FONT FACE="comic sans ms" COLOR=#FF8040>Browse</FONT>
    </STRONG>
    <SELECT NAME="cboBrowse" SIZE="1" onChange="cmdGoBrowse_onclick()">
<%
while (!(loRS.Eof))
{
%>
        <OPTION VALUE="Browse.asp?CatId=<%=loRS("CatId")%>& _
                    Description=<%=escape(loRS("Description"))%>& _
                    StartItemId=-1">
          <%=loRS("Description")%>
        </OPTION>
<%
```

```
        loRS.MoveNext();
    }
    loRS = null;
%>

    </SELECT>
    <INPUT TYPE="Button" NAME="cmdGoBrowse" _
            onClick="cmdGoBrowse_onclick()" VALUE="Go">
    </FORM>
```

Finally we finish off the page by adding the close tags for the table and the page itself.

```
    </TD>
 </TR>
 </TABLE>
 </BODY>
 </HTML>
```

Save the page as `top_menu.asp`.

A First Look

We have done enough to be able to browse to the web site. Currently that's as far as we can go, but you can confirm that the dynamic creation of the list of categories in the home page and in the select tag are working.

Producing a Dynamic Product List

Our next task is to dynamically create a page displaying goods contained within a particular category of music as shown above. We also need to limit how many items are displayed per page; if our stock contains more than can be displayed, then we need a facility to go to the next page and back to the previous one. What we don't want is the customer being presented with a page containing a hundred plus long list. They'll get fed up of scrolling down long before they actually get to the end. Also a long page will be slow in downloading.

First, let's create the `ListStockByCategory` stored procedure following the same steps as we did for `ListCategories`. It takes two input parameters, `CatId` and `StartItemId`. To prevent the length of a page becoming unmanageable for the user we only return the first 16 rows with the first item having an `ItemId` greater then `@StartItemId`. We match item details and artist details using an inner join of the `Stock` table and the `Artist` table.

```
CREATE PROCEDURE [ListStockByCategory]
(@CatId int, @StartItemId int = -1)
AS

SELECT TOP 16  S.ItemId, ArtistName, Title, Price, QtyInStock
FROM (Stock S JOIN Artist A ON S.ArtistId = A.ArtistId)
WHERE S.CatId = @CatId AND S.ItemId >= @StartItemId
ORDER BY ItemId
```

After you have completed the code click **OK** and close the dialog box. As before you'll need to give `MMCustomer` Execute permissions for this stored procedure.

Next we create the page itself.

The number of items per page is determined by the `lMaxPerPage` variable we define in the server-side global include file. Its value has been set to 15 but you may wish to vary this, though if you do so you'll also need to alter the `ListStockByCategory` stored procedure which returns 16 records.

The `ListStockByCategory` stored procedure returns the next 16 records starting with the `StartItemId` we pass it. We display the first 15 of them and use the `ItemId` of the 16th as the `StartItemId` for our next 15. If we have a full page then next and previous links are included which reload this page, but with the `StartItemId` passed in the link's URL determining whether it's the next or previous 15 items that are displayed. A `StartItemId` of −1 retrieves the very first page of stock.

Its time to take a look at the code. Having included our `ServerSideGlobalDef.inc` file, we set the page to expire as soon as it has been written to the client's browser. The list of items we produce also includes whether they are in stock. By stopping the page from being cached we can ensure the user sees up-to-date stock availability information every time they browse the stock.

Next we retrieve the data passed in the URL by using the `Request.QueryString` collection. We can then use this information to create a new recordset and populate it using our `ListStockByCategory` stored procedure.

```
<!--#include file="ServerSideGlobalDef.inc"-->
<% Response.Expires = -1; %>
<HTML>
<%
    // Retrieve the data we included in the link
    var scatTitle = unescape(Request.QueryString("Description"));
    var lCatId = Request.QueryString("CatId");
    var lstartItemId = Request.QueryString("StartItemId");
```

```
            var sRowBGColor = "oldlace";
            var savailable;
            var lRecordCount = 0;
            var loRS;
            loRS = Server.CreateObject("ADODB.Recordset");

            loRS.Open("Exec ListStockByCategory " + lCatId + _
                    "," + lstartItemId, sdbConnString);
    %>
```

Next we create our table tag and start looping through the rows in the recordset. The background color for each row is alternated so it's obvious where a product's row starts and ends, even if it has wrapped on to a second line. A variable contains the color value and is simply alternated between ivory and oldlace HTML colors.

Having dealt with the row color we need to deal with the stock availability by creating a string containing either "In Stock" or "Unavailable" which we will display in a table cell and the surlData variable to give the href value of the **Add to Basket** hyperlink. If stock is available then its value will point to the additem page with the item details added to the end of the URL. If no stock is available, or cookies are not enabled, then the value will be a JavaScript line which alerts the user that they can't proceed because either no stock exists or cookies are disabled.

```
<BODY>
<H1 ALIGN="CENTER">
    <FONT FACE="Comic Sans MS" color="Navy"><%=scatTitle%></FONT>
</H1>
<DIV align="center">
<TABLE>

<%
    while (!(loRS.Eof))
    {
        // Alternate the row's background colour
        sRowBGColor = (sRowBGColor == "ivory"? "oldlace" : "ivory");
        lRecordCount++;

        // Create the Item availability string
        if (loRS("QtyInStock") > 0)
        {
            savailable = "In Stock";
        }
        else
        {
            savailable = "<FONT color='#808080'>Unavailable</FONT>";
        }

        // Determine what ACTION clicking a product's add item link
        // does. If stock we want to add the item, if no stock or if
        // cookies disabled then inform user
        if (savailable == "In Stock")
        {
            surlData = "AddToBasket.asp?ID" + escape(loRS("ItemId") + _
                        "&1&" + loRS("ArtistName") + "&" + loRS("Title") + _
                        "&" + loRS("Price") + "£&");
        }
        else
        {
            surlData = "javascript:{alert('Sorry this item is currently _
                                        out of stock')}";
        }

%>
```

The creation of the individual item row occurs next with cells populated with our recordset row's values. Note the **Add to Basket** hyperlink has an `onClick` event handler defined which returns the value of the `cookiesEnabled` variable in the parent window `MusicMad.htm` page. If it's false, indicating that cookies are disabled, any attempts to add to the basket will be cancelled.

```
<TR bgcolor="<%= sRowBGColor %>">
   <TD WIDTH="125">
      <FONT FACE="Comic Sans MS" SIZE="-1"><%=loRS("ArtistName")%></FONT>
   </TD>
   <TD WIDTH="250">
      <FONT FACE="Comic Sans MS" SIZE="-1"><%=loRS("Title")%></FONT>
   </TD>
   <TD WIDTH="45">
      <FONT FACE="Comic Sans MS" SIZE="-1">£<%=loRS("Price")%></FONT>
   </TD>
   <TD WIDTH="85">
      <FONT FACE="Comic Sans MS" SIZE="-1"><%=savailable%></FONT>
   </TD>
   <TD WIDTH="90">
      <FONT FACE="Comic Sans MS" SIZE="-1">
      <A HREF="<%=surlData%>" onClick="return parent.cookiesEnabled" >
         Add to Basket
      </A>
      </FONT>
   </TD>
</TR>
```

Having moved to the next record, we check to see if we have come to the last record. If so, we can add a previous and next page hyperlink if appropriate. If the `lstartItemId` was -1 then this was the first page requested so there is no need to put a previous page link.

If we have gone past the maximum per page allowed then we don't display the next record, but, instead, display a next page link with a `startItemId` of that last record (so we know that if the user clicks the link the page will contain at least one record), then we break out of the `while` loop.

```
<%
      loRS.MoveNext();

      // Has the end of the page been reached
      if (lRecordCount == lMaxPerPage || loRS.Eof)
      {
%>
<TR>
<%
         // If this is not the first page then add previous link
         if (lstartItemId != -1)
         {
%>
            <TD COLSPAN=4 ALIGN="RIGHT">
               <A HREF="javascript:history.back();">Previous Page</A>
            </TD>
<%
         }
         // If last item then add link to next page
         if (!loRS.Eof)
         {
%>
            <TD COLSPAN=5 ALIGN="RIGHT">
               <A HREF="Browse.asp?CatId=<%=lCatId %>& _
                                 Description=<%=escape(scatTitle)%>& _
                                 StartItemId=<%=loRS("ItemId")%>">
                  Next Page
```

```
                    </A>
                </TD>
    <%
            }
    %>
    </TR>
    <%
            break;
        }
    }
    loRS = null;
    %>
    </TABLE>
    </DIV>
    </BODY>
    </HTML>
```

Save this page with your other files as browse.asp.

Testing times

You should now be able to browse to the home page and view a list of the products available.

The MusicMad Shopping basket

The MusicMad shopping basket relies exclusively on cookies, in particular the basket cookie which we set. Given we have server-side programming available to us you may wonder why we still use cookies stored on the client machine for storing our basket's contents instead of say, session variables or the database.

The main reason is scalability. Storing any data on the server consumes the finite server resources available. On a popular web site at peak times user sessions could run into hundreds of thousands, maybe more. Session variables consume resources until the user's session times out, which is 20 minutes by default. Using a database to store basket contents is a possibility but again your database could grow very large, even if just temporarily. It also requires database connection each time a user accesses their basket which, again, is costly in terms of server memory and processing time. It's likely the user's machine has more than sufficient resources to cope with our shopping basket's storage and processing, so it makes sense to distribute responsibility here.

Adding Items to the Basket

When we wrote the code which dynamically creates a page with a list of products, we also put an <A> tag for each item with **Add to Basket** as the link's text and AddToBasket.asp as its href property. We also appended ItemId, the number of CDs wanted (by default 1), ArtistName, record Title and Price per item to the end of the <A> tag's href. We can now retrieve those values in our server-side ASP script.

The values passed in the URL were also escaped into a URL-encoded form. Effectively, this means that non-alphabetic characters were converted to a hexadecimal format. For example, a space would become %20 if there were any in the link. So, the first thing we must do is unescape those values and split them up into the individual data values for ItemId, ArtistName etc. We use the ItemId to check there is not already one of those items already in the basket. If there is then we get the current quantity in the basket and add one to it. Finally, we use the setItemCookie function that's been made available by including our server-side global module at the top of the page. It's perhaps worth mentioning here that server-side include directives cannot have include directives in them to other files, precluding the errors inherent in an 'include chain'. This is managed as ASP has a one-step preprocessing stage by any server-side code is executed and the include statement is dealt with in this stage.

```
<!--#include file="ServerSideGlobalDef.inc"-->
<%
   // decode query string from HTTP form
   var sQueryString = unescape(Request.QueryString);
   var sBasketCookie = new String(Request.Cookies("Basket"));

   // String is in form
   // IDItemId&Qty&ArtistName&Description&Price
   var NewItemData = sQueryString.split("&");

   if (sBasketCookie.indexOf(NewItemData[0] + "&") >= 0 )
   {
     var ExistItemData = getItemFromCookie(NewItemData[0],sBasketCookie);
     NewItemData[1] =parseInt(NewItemData[1])+parseInt(ExistItemData[1]);
   }

   Response.Cookies("Basket")=setItemToCookie(NewItemData,sBasketCookie);
%>
```

We complete the page by adding a message informing the user what has just been successfully added to their basket.

It's also nice, from a user interface point of view, to give them the option to view their basket or proceed to the checkout by putting a form with two buttons on the page. The onClick event handler code has been added to the HTML tags and simply replaces the current page of the main frame with the relevant pages for viewing the basket, which we create next, and the checkout page which will be created later.

```
<HTML>
<BODY>
<BR><BR><BR>
<P align="center">
   <FONT FACE="Comic Sans MS" SIZE="3">
      1 copy of <STRONG><%= NewItemData[3] %></STRONG><BR>
      by <STRONG><%= NewItemData[2] %></STRONG>
      has been added to your shopping basket
   </FONT>
</P>

<DIV align="center">
<FORM ACTION="" method="POST">
   <INPUT TYPE="Button" NAME="cmdCheckout" VALUE="Proceed to Checkout" _
         onClick="window.location.replace('checkout_frame.htm')">
   <INPUT TYPE="Button" NAME="cmdBasket" VALUE="View Basket"  _
         onClick="window.location.replace('viewbasket.asp')">
</FORM>
</DIV>
</BODY>
</HTML>
```

Save the page as `AddToBasket.asp`

Viewing the Basket's Contents

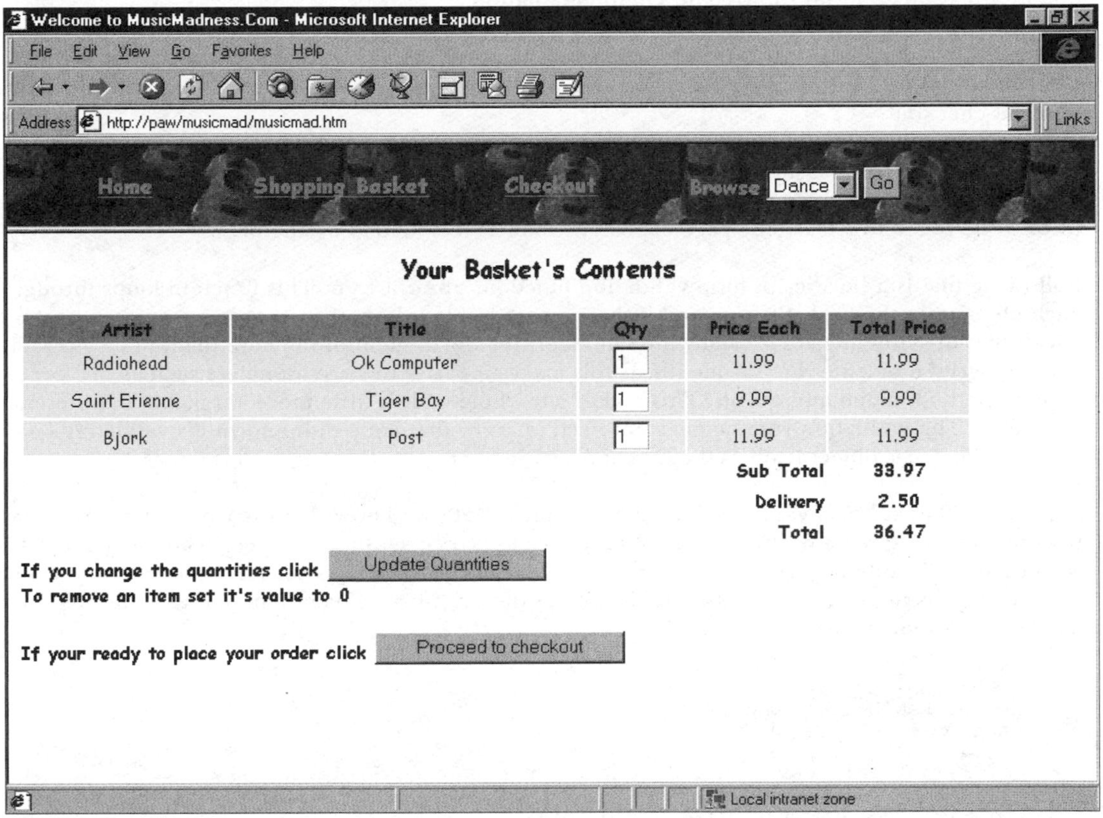

The screenshot above shows what we are aiming for as regards the contents and layout of the basket. As well as showing each item, the quantity, price and total price we also have a summary of the order cost at the end.

Before we create the page that views the basket, we are going to create another server-side include file: `Basket.inc`. As you will see later, viewing the contents of the basket is something we need to do in a number of different places on the site, so by creating an include file we keep the code in one place making debugging and maintenance easier.

The basket include file retrieves each item from the basket cookie used to store the goods and produces a table listing the item's artist, description, quantity selected, price per item and cost of the total quantity of that item in the basket. Finally at the end of the table it produces a sub total of the cost of all the items, cost of delivery and final cost.

The include file uses a variable bReadOnly which we define and set outside the include file. If bReadOnly is false then in each item row in the table, the quantity of each item is displayed inside a text box. Below the table is a button which when clicked updates the quantities based on the values in the quantity boxes. If the user wishes to remove an item from the basket they enter 0 in its quantity text box and hit the Update Quantities button.

If bReadOnly has been set to true then quantities are displayed as plain text and there is no Update Quantities button. This gives us a method of displaying a non-updateable summary of basket items at checkout.

Our first task is to make sure the user is viewing the very latest details and not a stale cached version of the basket. We can accomplish this by setting the Response.Expires property to -1, as we did in browse.asp, to ensure the page expires as soon as it is loaded by the browser.

Following that is a JavaScript form validation function, checkQtys. This function loops through each element in the basket's form and if the element is a text box, (i.e. its type property is text) we check that the contents are a valid whole number. It's worth mentioning here that the <FORM> tag is actually written outside the include file as this makes it easier to set parameters such as the form's action, method, name and events. This makes our whole code a little more adaptable to different situations. The validation routine does not need to know the name of the form it's validating because we pass the form object itself as the function's parameter.

If parsing the text box's value to an integer produces NaN, we know that the user has entered some invalid value. We react to this with a warning message, then set focus to the offending element and select the text inside it (just to make things really clear to the user). Also, false is returned from the function and is important if this routine is used as the onSubmit event handler, as returning false cancels the submit event.

```
<% Response.Expires = -1; %>
<SCRIPT LANGUAGE="JavaScript">
function checkQtys(theForm)
{
   for (var iElement = 0; iElement < theForm.length;iElement++)
   {
      if (theForm[iElement].TYPE == "text")
      {
         if (isNaN(parseInt(theForm[iElement].VALUE)) || _
             (parseInt(theForm[iElement].VALUE) < 0))
         {
            alert("The quantity you have entered is invalid\n _
                   Only whole numbers are valid in this box");
            theForm[iElement].focus();
            theForm[iElement].select();
            return false;
         }
      }
   }
   return true;
}
</SCRIPT>
```

Following the validation script we define the table and its headers and then start looping through the basket's contents. As we saw above, each item in the basket cookie is in the format:

```
ItemId&Qty&ArtistName&Title&Price£&
```

We split the basket cookie into an array with the ampersand delimiting each piece of data. We know each item has 5 pieces of data associated with it so our loop increments in steps of 5. The item price is delimited by a £ sign which we need to remove using JavaScript's `replace` method. We also keep a running total of the cost of each row (`item cost * quantity`) which we display at the bottom of the table.

As we loop through the data for each item we add table cells displaying the item's `ArtistName`, `Title` and we add a hidden input box with the `ItemId` which forms part of any form post action taken in updating quantities.

```
<TABLE BORDER=0>
<TR  BGCOLOR="#9F9F9F">
   <TH><FONT FACE="Comic Sans MS" SIZE="2">Artist</FONT></TH>
   <TH><FONT FACE="Comic Sans MS" SIZE="2">Title</FONT></TH>
   <TH><FONT FACE="Comic Sans MS" SIZE="2">Qty</FONT></TH>
   <TH><FONT FACE="Comic Sans MS" SIZE="2">Price Each</FONT></TH>
   <TH><FONT FACE="Comic Sans MS" SIZE="2">Total Price</FONT></TH>
</TR>
<%
   var sbasketItems = new String(Request.Cookies("Basket"));
   var lTotal = 0;
   var lItemTotal = 0;

   // Each item's data in form
   // ItemId&Qty&ArtistName&Title&Price£
   sbasketItems = sbasketItems.split("&");

   // loop through each item in basket
   for (var lcounter=0; lcounter<sbasketItems.length-1; _
           lcounter=lcounter+5)
   {
      // the price delimited by a £ sign - need to remove that
      // using string.replace method
      sbasketItems[lcounter+4] = sbasketItems[lcounter+4].replace(/£/,"");

      // calculate item total
      lItemTotal = (sbasketItems[lcounter+1] * sbasketItems[lcounter+4]);

      // add item total to grand total to be displayed as
      // summary at end of table
      lTotal = lItemTotal + lTotal;
%>

<TR>
   <TD ALIGN="CENTER" WIDTH="150" BGCOLOR="#EFEFEF">
      <FONT FACE="Comic Sans MS" SIZE="2">
         <!-- ArtistName -->
         <%=sbasketItems[lcounter + 2]%>
      </FONT>
   </TD>
   <TD ALIGN="CENTER" WIDTH="250" BGCOLOR="#EFEFEF">
      <FONT FACE="Comic Sans MS" SIZE="2">
         <!-- Title -->
         <%=sbasketItems[lcounter + 3]%>
      </FONT>
   </TD>
   <TD ALIGN="CENTER" WIDTH="75" BGCOLOR="#EFEFEF">
      <!-- ItemId in hidden INPUT box-->
      <INPUT NAME="txt<%=sbasketItems[lcounter]%>" TYPE="hidden"
             VALUE="<%=sbasketItems[lcounter]%>">
```

Next the bReadOnly variable determining whether this basket summary is updateable comes in to play. If the basket's item quantities can't be updated then the quantity is displayed as plain text and a hidden input box is placed on the form and is used after a form post action to determine item quantity.

If this is to be an updateable summary then a visible text input box is put in a cell and is given the same name as a hidden one would. This means any code using the basket's form does not need to know if this was an updateable or otherwise view of the basket.

```
<%
    if (bReadOnly == true)
    {
        Response.Write('<FONT FACE="Comic Sans MS" SIZE="2">' + _
                        sbasketItems[lcounter + 1] + '</FONT>');
%>

    <!-- hidden Quantity INPUT box -->
    <INPUT NAME="txtQty<%=sbasketItems[lcounter]%>" TYPE="hidden"
            VALUE="<%=sbasketItems[lcounter + 1]%>" SIZE="3">
<%
    }
    else
    {
%>
    <!-- visible Quantity INPUT box -->
    <INPUT NAME="txtQty<%=sbasketItems[lcounter]%>" TYPE="text"
            VALUE="<%=sbasketItems[lcounter + 1]%>" SIZE="2"
            MAXLENGTH="2">
<%
    }
%>
    </TD>
```

Finally, we reach the end of the for loop creating the table's rows but keep looping until we have displayed all of the basket's contents. At the end of each row we add the item's cost and the sub total for that row based on item cost multiplied by quantity wanted.

```
<TD ALIGN="CENTER" WIDTH="100" BGCOLOR="#EFEFEF">
    <FONT FACE="Comic Sans MS" SIZE="2">
        <!-- Cost per item -->
        <%=sbasketItems[lcounter + 4]%>
    </FONT>
</TD>
<TD ALIGN="CENTER" WIDTH="100" BGCOLOR="#EFEFEF">
    <FONT FACE="Comic Sans MS" SIZE="2">
        <!-- total cost for quantity ordered -->
        <%=lItemTotal%>
    </FONT>
</TD>
</TR>

<%
    }
%>
```

However, we have not yet finished creating the table. The table is completed by producing a summary of the total cost of items, delivery charges, and finally, the total cost of the order as it currently stands.

```
<!-- Cost Summary -->
<TR>
   <TD COLSPAN=4 ALIGN="RIGHT">
      <FONT FACE="Comic Sans MS" SIZE="2">
      <STRONG>
         Sub Total
      </STRONG>
      </FONT>
   </TD>
   <TD ALIGN="CENTER">
      <FONT FACE="Comic Sans MS" SIZE="2">
      <STRONG>
         <!-- Cost sub total for basket -->
         <%=lTotal%>
      </STRONG>
      </FONT>
   </TD>
</TR>

<TR>
   <TD COLSPAN=4 ALIGN="RIGHT">
      <FONT FACE="Comic Sans MS" SIZE="2">
      <STRONG>
         Delivery
      </STRONG>
      </FONT>
   </TD>
   <TD ALIGN="CENTER">
      <FONT FACE="Comic Sans MS" SIZE="2">
      <STRONG>
      2.50
      </STRONG>
      </FONT>
   </TD>
</TR>

<TR>
   <TD COLSPAN=4 ALIGN="RIGHT">
      <FONT FACE="Comic Sans MS" SIZE="2">
      <STRONG>
         Total
      </STRONG>
      </FONT>
   </TD>
   <TD ALIGN="CENTER">
      <FONT FACE="Comic Sans MS" SIZE="2">
      <STRONG>
         <!-- total including delivery -->
         <%=lTotal + 2.5%>
      </STRONG>
      </FONT>
   </TD>
</TR>
</TABLE>
```

With the table's creation finished our final task is again linked with the bReadOnly. If this is an updateable summary then we add a submit button to submit item quantity changes.

```
<%
   if (bReadOnly == false)
   {
%>

<FONT FACE="Comic Sans MS" SIZE="2">
   <STRONG>
      If you change the quantities click
      <INPUT NAME="Submit" TYPE="submit"
```

```
                    VALUE="Update Quantities" ALIGN=top>
        <BR>
        To remove an item set it's VALUE to 0
      </STRONG>
   </FONT>

<%
     }
%>
```

Save the file as `Basket.inc`.

Our final task in enabling the user to view the basket is the `viewbasket.asp` page itself. As most of the work is done by the `Basket.inc` include file, this page is fairly simple. We define the form that will contain the basket contents, include `Basket.inc` and add a button the user can press to go directly to the checkout. The form's action property has been set as `UpdateQty.asp` and it's this page, which we come to next, that actually handles the alteration of item quantities when the user hits the update quantity submit button.

```
<!--#include file="ServerSideGlobalDef.inc"-->
<%
    // Used by basket.inc - determines whether amounts updateable
    var bReadOnly = false;
%>

<HTML>
<BODY>
<DIV align="center">
    <H3>
    <FONT FACE="comic sans ms" color="Navy">
        Your Basket's Contents
    </FONT>
    </H3>
</DIV>

<FORM METHOD=POST ACTION="UpdateQty.asp"
      NAME="frmItems" onSubmit="return checkQtys(this)">

    <!--#include file="basket.inc"-->
    <P align="left">
        <FONT FACE="Comic Sans MS" SIZE="2">
        <STRONG>
            If you're ready to place your order click
        </STRONG>
        </FONT>
        <INPUT TYPE="Button" NAME="cmdCheckout" VALUE="Proceed to checkout"
                onClick="window.location.href = 'checkout_frame.htm'">
    </P>
</FORM>
</BODY>
</HTML>
```

Save the page as `viewbasket.asp`

Updating the Basket's Quantities

The penultimate page of our shopping basket is the `UpdateQty.asp` page. When the user clicks the update button on the shopping basket page, it can either

- ❑ Bring them to this page which does the work of updating the shopping basket and redisplaying it, or

- ❑ Redirect them to the emptybasket.asp page if they have deleted all its contents by setting the quantities to zero.

As displaying the basket is done by Basket.inc and the ServerSideGlobalDef.inc include file handles the storing and retrieval of data from the basket cookie, there is actually little to do here.

The ASP retrieves the current basket cookie's value then loops through the form elements that have been submitted, which contain two elements per item: the ItemId and the new quantity to be set. The new quantity value is set using the setItemToCookie function in ServerSideGlobalDef.inc. Finally, the basket cookie is updated and we display the basket with its updated quantities using the Basket.inc include file.

```
<!--#include file="ServerSideGlobalDef.inc"-->
<%

   var sBasketCookie = new String(Request.Cookies("Basket"));
   var sItemID;
   var ExistItemData;
   var NewItemData;
   var lQty;

   // loop through form elements submitted
   for (var lCounter=1; lCounter<Request.Form.Count; lCounter=lCounter+2)
   {
      // Get ItemId
      sItemId = new String(Request.Form(lCounter));

      // Get Quantity
      lQty = new String(Request.Form(lCounter + 1));
      lQty = parseInt(lQty);

      // Get items existing details
      NewItemData = getItemFromCookie(sItemId, sBasketCookie);

      // set new quantity
      NewItemData[1] = lQty;

      // update basket cookie
      sBasketCookie = setItemToCookie(NewItemData, sBasketCookie);
   }

   // Set new VALUE for basket cookie
   Response.Cookies("Basket") = sBasketCookie;
   if (Request.Cookies("Basket") == "")
   {
      Response.Redirect("emptybasket.asp");
   }
   var bReadOnly = false;
%>

<HTML>
<HEAD></HEAD>

<BODY>
<FORM METHOD=POST ACTION="UpdateQty.asp"
      NAME="frmItems" onSubmit="return checkQtys(this)">
   <!--#include file="basket.inc"-->
</FORM>
</BODY>
</HTML>
```

Save the file as `UpdateQty.asp`

Viewing an Empty Basket

Our final basket page is the one displayed when the shopping basket is empty. The page contains a message informing them of the basket's empty state and a list of categories to browse so the customer can fill the basket up again. The customer will arrive at this page if they try to view the basket and it's empty or if they update the basket quantities to remove all items.

```
<!--#include file="ServerSideGlobalDef.inc"-->
<HTML>
<HEAD></HEAD>

<BODY>
<P align="CENTER">
    <FONT FACE="Comic Sans MS" SIZE="3" color="Navy">
        Your basket is currently empty<BR>
        Fill it with items from our wide selection of music.
    </FONT>
</P>
<P>
    <DIV align="center"><!--#include file="categorylist.inc"--></DIV>
</P>

</BODY>
</HTML>
```

Save the page as `EmptyBasket.asp`

Testing the Basket

Check that the basket is working by adding a few items from the product list pages, viewing the basket and updating quantities it contains.

Check 'em Out – The Online Ordering System

The online ordering system's information gathering takes place over three pages with a fourth page at the end displaying a final summary of the order which the user can accept or go back and alter if they are not happy. At some point in the checkout process, prior to any credit card details being transmitted to the server, we would normally switch to a secure connection using Secure Sockets Layer (SSL) which encrypts all data before it's sent to the web server.

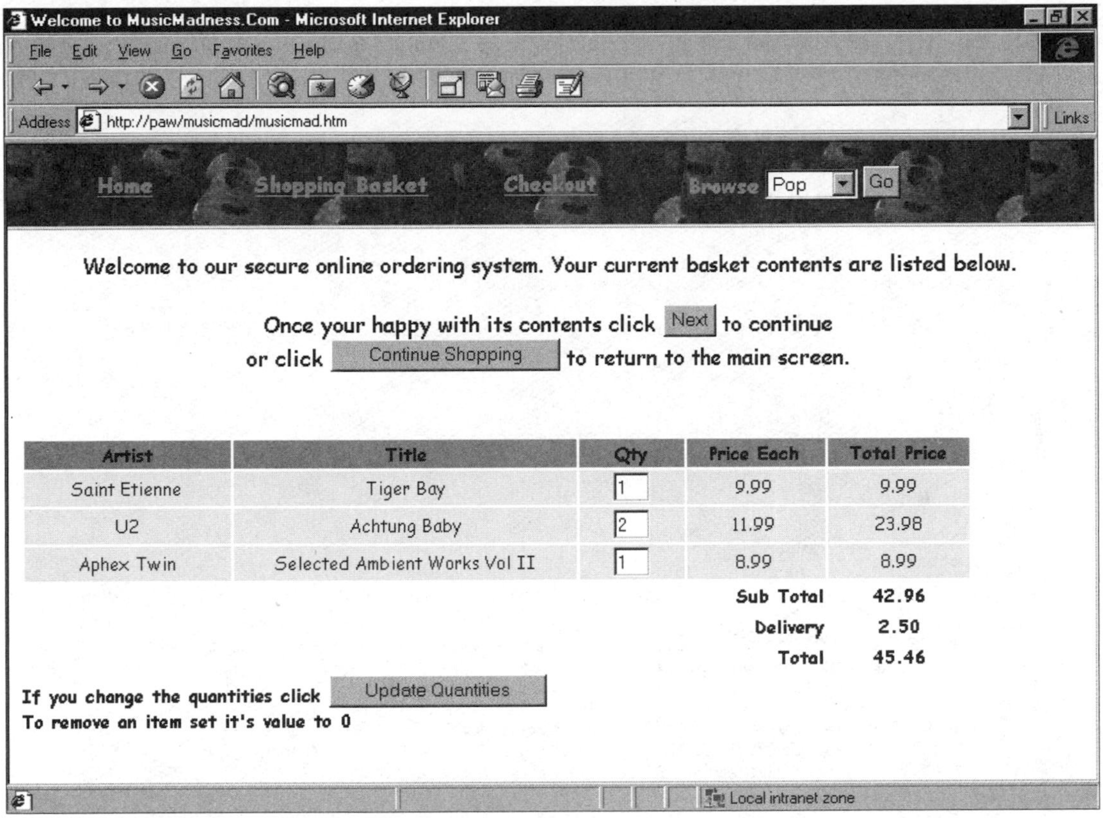

The first of the four screens splits the main frame into two more frames

❑   The top frame contains the 'welcome to the online ordering system' blurb and buttons to go to the next screen.

❑ · The bottom frame contains our shopping basket and serves the dual purpose of confirming what the user is about to buy and giving them an opportunity to change their mind about the quantities.

First we need to create the frameset page and save it as `checkout_frame.htm`

```
<HTML>
<FRAMESET FRAMEBORDER=0 BORDER=0 ROWS="140,*">
    <FRAME SCROLLING="NO" SRC="checkout.asp" FRAMEBORDER="NO"
        NAME="fraCheckoutTop" NORESIZE>
    <FRAME SCROLLING="AUTO" SRC="checkoutbasket.asp" FRAMEBORDER="NO"
        NAME="fraCheckoutBottom" NORESIZE>
</FRAMESET>
</HTML>
```

Now lets create `Checkout.asp`, which is displayed in the top part of the frameset. For the `cmdNext` button a function has been created for the `onClick` event. Here we check that there is still something left in the basket to buy (after user changes to the basket's contents) using the shopping basket in the lower frame. If there is still something in the basket then we continue to the next page.

The `cmdBrowse` button gives the shopper another opportunity to shop themselves penniless by going back to the category list page. The JavaScript has been included in the event definition itself as it's just one line so there's little point creating a separate function.

```
<!--#include file="ServerSideGlobalDef.inc"-->
<HTML>
<HEAD>
<SCRIPT language='javascript'>
function cmdNext_onClick()
{
    // if as a result of changes to the basket it's empty, inform user
    if (parent.parent.getCookie("Basket") == "")
    {
        alert("Your basket is empty - click Continue Shopping to fill it _
                up with our excellent bargains");
    }
    else
    {
        // go to page 2 of checkout process
        this.parent.location.href="personaldetails.asp";
    }
    return true;
}
</SCRIPT>
</HEAD>

<BODY>
<CENTER>
<FONT FACE="Comic Sans MS" SIZE="3" color="Navy">
    Welcome to our secure online ordering system.
    Your current basket contents are listed below.
<FORM>
    Once you're happy with its contents click
    <INPUT NAME="cmdNext" TYPE="button" VALUE="Next" ALIGN=top
            onClick="cmdNext_onClick()">
    to continue <BR>
    or click
    <INPUT NAME="cmdBrowse" TYPE="button" VALUE="Continue Shopping"
            ALIGN=top onClick="parent.location.href='home.asp'">
    to return to the main screen.
</FORM>
</FONT>
</CENTER>
</BODY>
</HTML>
```

Save the page as `Checkout.asp`

The final page in the checkout frameset is the shopping basket. It's very similar to the main shopping basket and uses the same code by incorporating the `Basket.inc` file, which does most of the work of displaying the basket. `bReadOnly` has been set to false so that the user can update the contents of the basket.

```
<!--#include file="ServerSideGlobalDef.inc"-->
<%
    bReadOnly = false;
%>
<HTML>
<HEAD>
</HEAD>
<BODY>
<FORM METHOD=POST ACTION="UpdateQty.asp" NAME="frmItems" onSubmit="return
checkQtys(this)">
<!--#include file="basket.inc"-->
```

```
</FORM>
</BODY>
</HTML>
```

Save the page as `CheckoutBasket.asp`

Obtaining the User's Details

The next two pages obtain the necessary information about the customer to process their order.

The first page obtains information regarding name and delivery address. We also obtain their e-mail address as we use that later to send them conformation of their order.

In between the <HEAD> tags we include a new include file – `checkout_validate.inc` – into this page which we'll create shortly. As its name suggests, this file contains a number of client-side JavaScript functions which will be used to validate the form's content when the user clicks the submit button. We have added an event handler for the form's `onSubmit` event which calls one of the validate functions inside `checkout_validate.inc`. The value returned by this function will prove important: if `false` is returned then the form's submit action will be cancelled. Also note that in the `onSubmit` event handler we call `checkCompleted` and pass it one argument – `this`, which in this context refers to the element that is the cause of the event firing. Here, it is the form itself.

```
<% @LANGUAGE="JScript" %>
<HTML>
<HEAD>
   <!--#include file="checkout_validate.inc"-->
</HEAD>

<BODY>
<CENTER>
<FORM METHOD=POST ACTION="checkoutcredit.asp"
      onSubmit="return checkCompleted(this)">
```

The remainder of the page consists of the form elements contained within a table for formatting. At the top is a group of radio buttons for selecting the customer's title. When the form is submitted only the value of the radio button that has been selected by the user will be sent.

The remainder of the form consists of input boxes, each of which has its maxlength property set to match the maximum size of the relevant database field which acts as a basic form of validation. At least we know the user has not entered a string value length greater than we can store. The problem comes if we change the size of the database fields, as we must remember to update the page. This problem could be overcome by building the page dynamically using ASP script. Using ADO we could obtain the correct sizes of each field and populate the maxlengths on the basis of this information. This would increase maintainability but at the expense of scalability as server processing load would be increased significantly. Here I have gone for scalability by having static values.

The last input element in the form is a text box for the customer's country. It would help ensure valid data if we changed this to a select element with a drop down list of countries rather than a text box. For this example I kept it as a text box to save typing a long list of countries!

```
<FONT FACE="Comic Sans MS" SIZE="3" color="Navy">
   Please enter your NAME, address and e-mail address below.<BR>
</FONT>
<TABLE>
<TR>
   <TD><FONT FACE="Comic Sans MS" SIZE="2">Title</FONT></TD>
   <TD>
      <FONT FACE="Comic Sans MS" SIZE="2">
      Mr<INPUT NAME="radTitle" TYPE="radio" VALUE="Mr">
      Mrs<INPUT NAME="radTitle" TYPE="radio" VALUE="Mrs">
      Miss<INPUT NAME="radTitle" TYPE="radio" VALUE="Miss">
      Ms.<INPUT NAME="radTitle" TYPE="radio" VALUE="Ms.">
      Dr.<INPUT NAME="radTitle" TYPE="radio" VALUE="Dr.">
      </FONT>
   </TD>
</TR>
<TR>
   <TD><FONT FACE="Comic Sans MS" SIZE="2">First Name</FONT>
   <TD><INPUT TYPE="Text" NAME="txtFirstName" maxlength="50">
</TR>
<TR>
   <TD><FONT FACE="Comic Sans MS" SIZE="2">Last Name</FONT>
   <TD><INPUT TYPE="Text" NAME="txtLastName" maxlength="50">
</TR>
<TR>
   <TD><FONT FACE="Comic Sans MS" SIZE="2">E-mail Address</FONT>
   <TD><INPUT TYPE="Text" NAME="txtEmail" maxlength="75">
</TR>
<TR>
   <TD><FONT FACE="Comic Sans MS" SIZE="2">Street</FONT>
   <TD><INPUT TYPE="Text" NAME="txtStreet" maxlength="75">
</TR>
<TR>
```

```
                <TD><FONT FACE="Comic Sans MS" SIZE="2">City</FONT>
                <TD><INPUT TYPE="Text" NAME="txtCity" maxlength="50">
            </TR>
            <TR>
                <TD><FONT FACE="Comic Sans MS" SIZE="2">County/State</FONT>
                <TD><INPUT TYPE="Text" NAME="txtLocality" maxlength="50">
            </TR>
            <TR>
                <TD><FONT FACE="Comic Sans MS" SIZE="2">Post/Zip Code</FONT>
                <TD><INPUT TYPE="Text" NAME="txtPostCode" maxlength="15">
            </TR>
            <TR>
                <TD><FONT FACE="Comic Sans MS" SIZE="2">Country</FONT>
                <TD><INPUT TYPE="Text" NAME="txtCountry" maxlength="50">
            </TR>
            <TR>
                <TD COLSPAN=2>
                    <INPUT TYPE="reset" NAME="cmdReset" VALUE="Clear form">
                    <INPUT TYPE="button" NAME="cmdPrevious"  VALUE=" Back "
                        onClick="window.location.href='checkout_frame.htm'">
                    <INPUT TYPE="submit" NAME="cmdSubmit" VALUE="Continue">
                </TD>
            </TR>
            </TABLE>
    </FORM>
    </CENTER>
    </BODY>
    </HTML>
```

Save the page as `PersonalDetails.asp`

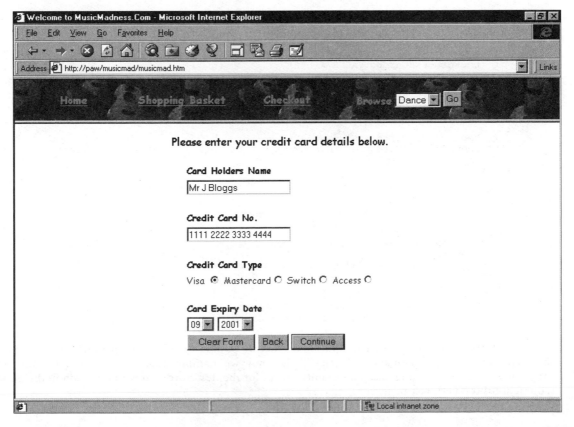

The final page, as far as inputting user details is concerned, is `CheckoutCredit.asp` which gets that all important information we need to get our hands on the user's money!

It's smaller in terms of number of visible page elements, but more complex in terms of validation as we have a radio group, a couple of select elements with dates that need validating and a text box which must contain a valid number only. Again, all of the validation functions are in the `checkout_validate.inc` file we include inside the head of this page. Because there is more to check in this form than on the personal details page form, a separate function has been created to handle the `onSubmit` event. Using functions defined in `checkout_validate.inc`, it checks that the form is fully completed, the credit card number actually contains numbers and that the card expiry date is valid. If any of these checks fails then the form submit event is cancelled by returning `false`. As in the previous page's `onSubmit`, we are passing a reference to the form as a parameter of the function handling the `onSubmit`.

```
<% @LANGUAGE="JScript" %>
<HTML>
<HEAD>
<!--#include file="checkout_validate.inc"-->
<SCRIPT LANGUAGE="JavaScript">

function frmCredit_onsubmit(theForm)
{
    // Check form fully filled in
    if (checkCompleted(theForm) == false)
    {
        return false;
    }

    // Remove everything except numbers from CardNo
    theForm.txtCardNo.VALUE = numericOnly(theForm.txtCardNo.VALUE);

    // If removing all but numbers results in nothing then alert user
    if (theForm.txtCardNo.VALUE == "")
    {
        alert("Your have entered your credit card number incorrectly");
        theForm.txtCardNo.focus();
        return false;
    }

    // check credit card expiry date is valid
    if (checkCardExpDate(theForm.cboExpMonth,theForm.cboExpYear) == false)
    {
        return false;
    }
}
</SCRIPT>

</HEAD>
<BODY>
<FONT FACE="Comic Sans MS" SIZE="3" color="Navy">
    <P align="center">
        Please enter your credit card details below.
    </P>
</FONT>

<FORM METHOD=POST NAME="frmCredit" ACTION="checkoutconfirm.asp"
        onSubmit="return frmCredit_onsubmit(this)">
```

The next form elements are hidden input boxes that we populate using ASP script with the values the user submitted in the personal details page. This is how we maintain state over the course of the four pages involved in obtaining customer details except for the items ordered which remain in the basket cookie until the very last page.

```
<INPUT TYPE="HIDDEN" NAME="txtTitle"
       VALUE="<%=Request.Form("radTitle")%>">
<INPUT TYPE="HIDDEN" NAME="txtFirstName"
       VALUE="<%=Request.Form("txtFirstName")%>">
<INPUT TYPE="HIDDEN" NAME="txtLastName"
       VALUE="<%=Request.Form("txtLastName")%>">
<INPUT TYPE="HIDDEN" NAME="txtEmail"
       VALUE="<%=Request.Form("txtEmail")%>">
<INPUT TYPE="HIDDEN" NAME="txtStreet"
       VALUE="<%=Request.Form("txtStreet")%>">
<INPUT TYPE="HIDDEN" NAME="txtCity"
       VALUE="<%=Request.Form("txtCity")%>">
<INPUT TYPE="HIDDEN" NAME="txtLocality"
       VALUE="<%=Request.Form("txtLocality")%>">
<INPUT TYPE="HIDDEN" NAME="txtPostCode"
       VALUE="<%=Request.Form("txtPostCode")%>">
<INPUT TYPE="HIDDEN" NAME="txtCountry"
       VALUE="<%=Request.Form("txtCountry")%>">
```

The remainder of the page consists of the form elements into which the customers enter their credit card details. Card expiry date has been based upon two drop down select elements: one for the month and one for the year. This ensures that the user can enter only valid values, which is particularly important for dates as there are so many variations possible. For example, if we just used a text box, 11/1999, 11-99,11 01 are all valid but would cause us headaches if we had to deal with each possibility.

The cmdPrevious button at the end of the form contains history.back() in its onClick event rather than specifying the page with window.location.href='personaldetails.asp'. If the history object's back() method is used then the personal details page is displayed with all the information that the user filled in. Using location.href however returns you to a blank form to fill out once again.

```
<DIV align="center">
<TABLE>
<TR>
   <TD COLSPAN=4>
      <STRONG>
         <FONT FACE="Comic Sans MS" SIZE="2">Card Holders Name</FONT>
      </STRONG>
   </TD>
</TR>
<TR>
   <TD COLSPAN="4">
      <INPUT TYPE="TEXT" NAME="txtCardHolderName" maxlength="50">
   </TD>
</TR>
<TR>
   <TD COLSPAN=4>
      <BR>
      <STRONG>
         <FONT FACE="Comic Sans MS" SIZE="2">Credit Card No.</FONT>
      </STRONG>
   </TD>
</TR>
<TR>
   <TD COLSPAN="4">
      <INPUT TYPE="TEXT" NAME="txtCardNo" maxlength=20>
   </TD>
</TR>
<TR>
   <TD COLSPAN=4>
   <BR>
```

```
            <STRONG>
                <FONT FACE="Comic Sans MS" SIZE="2">Credit Card Type</FONT>
            </STRONG>
        </TD>
    </TR>
    <TR>
        <TD>
            <FONT FACE="Comic Sans MS" SIZE="2">Visa</FONT>
            <INPUT NAME="radCardType" TYPE="radio" VALUE="Visa">
        </TD>
        <TD>
            <FONT FACE="Comic Sans MS" SIZE="2">Mastercard</FONT>
            <INPUT NAME="radCardType" TYPE="radio" VALUE="Mastercard">
        </TD>
        <TD>
            <FONT FACE="Comic Sans MS" SIZE="2">Switch</FONT>
            <INPUT NAME="radCardType" TYPE="radio" VALUE="Switch">
        </TD>
        <TD>
            <FONT FACE="Comic Sans MS" SIZE="2">Access</FONT>
            <INPUT NAME="radCardType" TYPE="radio" VALUE="Access">
        </TD>
    </TR>
    <TR>
        <TD COLSPAN="4">
        <BR>
            <STRONG>
                <FONT FACE="Comic Sans MS" SIZE="2">Card Expiry Date</FONT>
            </STRONG>
        </TD>
    </TR>
    <TR>
        <TD COLSPAN="4">
            <FONT FACE="Comic Sans MS" SIZE="2">
            <SELECT NAME="cboExpMonth" SIZE="1">
                <OPTION VALUE="01">01</OPTION>
                <OPTION VALUE="02">02</OPTION>
                <OPTION VALUE="03">03</OPTION>
                <OPTION VALUE="04">04</OPTION>
                <OPTION VALUE="05">05</OPTION>
                <OPTION VALUE="06">06</OPTION>
                <OPTION VALUE="07">07</OPTION>
                <OPTION VALUE="08">08</OPTION>
                <OPTION VALUE="09">09</OPTION>
                <OPTION VALUE="10">10</OPTION>
                <OPTION VALUE="11">11</OPTION>
                <OPTION VALUE="12">12</OPTION>
            </SELECT>
            <SELECT NAME="cboExpYear" SIZE="1">
                <OPTION VALUE="1999">1999</OPTION>
                <OPTION VALUE="2000">2000</OPTION>
                <OPTION VALUE="2001">2001</OPTION>
                <OPTION VALUE="2002">2002</OPTION>
                <OPTION VALUE="2003">2003</OPTION>
                <OPTION VALUE="2004">2003</OPTION>
                <OPTION VALUE="2005">2003</OPTION>
            </SELECT>
            </FONT>
        </TD>
    </TR>
    <TR>
        <TD COLSPAN="4">
            <INPUT NAME="reset" TYPE="reset" VALUE="Clear Form">
            <INPUT NAME="cmdPrevious" TYPE="button" VALUE="Back"
                    onClick="history.back()">
            <INPUT NAME="Submit" TYPE="submit" VALUE="Continue">
        </TD>
    </TR>
```

```
      </TABLE>
      </DIV>
   </FORM>
   </BODY>
   </HTML>
```

Save the page as `CheckoutCredit.asp`

Validating the User's Details

Our next task is to create the `checkout_validate.inc` file we have included in both the personal details page and the credit card info page.

It contains four client-side functions, the first of which is `numericOnly`. This function goes through each character in a string and checks to see if it's a valid character or not – as specified by `sValidChars`. If it's not valid (i.e. not a number), the character is removed and when all characters have been checked, the function returns what's left.

```javascript
<script language="JavaScript">

// Removes all characters which are not digits
// from a string
function numericOnly(sString)
{
   var sNumericOnly = "";
   var sValidChars = "1234567890";
   for (var iCharPos = 0; iCharPos < sString.length; iCharPos++)
   {
      if (sValidChars.indexOf(sString.charAt(iCharPos)) != -1)
      {
         sNumericOnly = sNumericOnly + sString.charAt(iCharPos);
      }
   }
   return sNumericOnly;
}
```

Note that if we didn't have to worry about version 3 browsers, we could make good use of the version 4 browsers' support for JavaScript 1.2 and replace the function with the line:

```javascript
sString = sString.replace(/(\D)+/g,"")
```

Visual Basic developers will recognize the next function we create which trims all white space – tab, space, and line feed – characters from the beginning and end of a string. In effect this is the JavaScript equivalent of the VB `trim` statement.

Our `trim` function works by looping through from the start of the string checking each character to see if it's white space or not. If it hits a non-whitespace character it breaks out of the loop and we have found the start of the valid string. The same algorithm, but starting from the end of the string, finds the last valid character at the end of the string.

```javascript
// Removes all whitespace characters
// from start and end of a string
function trim(sString)
{
   sTrimmedString = "";
   if (sString != "")
   {
```

```
        var iStart = 0;
        var iEnd = sString.length - 1;
        var sWhitespace = " \t\f\n\r\v";

        while (sWhitespace.indexOf(sString.charAt(iStart)) != -1)
        {
            iStart++;
            if (iStart > iEnd)
                break;
        }

        // If the string not just whitespace
        if (iStart <= iEnd)
        {
            while (sWhitespace.indexOf(sString.charAt(iEnd)) != -1)
                iEnd--;
            sTrimmedString = sString.substring(iStart,++iEnd);
        }
    }
    return sTrimmedString;
}
```

Again, using regular expressions and the string object's `replace` method, the whole function could be achieved in two lines.

```
sString = sString.replace(/^[\s]+/g,"");
sString = sString.replace(/[\s]+$/g,"");
```

Our third function ensures that the user has completed all the form elements. It loops through each element in the `Form.Elements[]` collection, which can be abbreviated to `Form[]`, and if it's an `text` or `radio` element, it checks it has a value. For radio button groups we need to loop though each radio button in the group and check to see if one has been selected. The naming convention I have used for radio buttons is to prefix the name with `rad`. To let the user know which element has failed validation the name of the radio button can be used with the `rad` prefix removed to make it more readable.

```
// Checks all text boxes and radio button groups
// have a VALUE entered
function checkCompleted(theForm)
{
    var bRadioChecked;
    var sElementGroupName;
    var theElement;

    // loop through all elements on form
    for (var iElement = 0; iElement < theForm.length;iElement++)
    {
        theElement = theForm[iElement];

        // <INPUT TYPE="TEXT">
        if (theElement.TYPE == "text")
        {
            if (trim(theElement.VALUE) == "")
            {
                alert("You must complete all the form details");
                theElement.focus();
                theElement.select();
                return false;
            }
        }
```

```
            // <INPUT TYPE="RADIO">
            else if (theElement.TYPE == "radio")
            {
                bRadioChecked = false;
                sElementGroupName = theElement.NAME;

                // all radio buttons in a group have the same NAME
                // so loop through all radio elements with same NAME
                // until one true or last one reached
                while (theElement.NAME == sElementGroupName)
                {
                    if (theElement.checked == true)
                    {
                        bRadioChecked = true;
                    }
                    iElement++;
                    theElement = theForm[iElement];
                }

                if (bRadioChecked == false)
                {
                    // radio button names in form radCreditCard
                    // so just cut off first 3 characters
                    alert("Please select your " + _
                        sElementGroupName.substring(3,sElementGroupName.length));
                    return false;
                }
                iElement--;
            }
        }
        return true;
    }
```

The final validation routine checks our `cboExpMonth` and `cboExpYear` select elements that make up the card expiry date to see that the card date has not already expired. However, we encounter a problem here in that the values returned by the `Date` object in JavaScript are particularly platform and browser dependent – some browsers return `99` as the year, others the full 4 digits `1999`. Here we get round the problem by assuming the year 2000 if the value returned by the `getYear()` method is 0 or by simply adding 1900 if it's another value below 1900. Note that if we were using JavaScript 1.3 (IE5, NC4.06+) or JScript5, the `getFullYear()` method of the Date object would solve this problem.

If the current year is the same as the year the user selected and the month is before the current month then we know the card has expired and we inform the user.

```
// Checks card not expired already
function checkCardExpDate(cboExpMonth,cboExpYear)
{
    var nowDate = new Date();
    var nowYear = nowDate.getYear();
    var nowMonth = nowDate.getMonth() + 1;
    var expYear = cboExpYear.options[cboExpYear.selectedIndex].VALUE;
    var expMonth = cboExpMonth.options[cboExpMonth.selectedIndex].VALUE;

    // some browsers return only 99 for the year so we need
    // to compensate for that
    if (nowYear == 0)
    {
        nowYear = 2000;
    }
    if (nowYear < 1900)
```

```
    {
        nowYear = nowYear + 1900;
    }
    if (expYear <= nowYear)
    {
        if (expMonth < nowMonth)
        {
            alert("According to the date you have entered, _
                  your credit card has expired")
            cboExpMonth.focus();
            return false;
        }
    }
}
</SCRIPT>
```

Save this file as `checkout_validate.inc`.

The End – A Final Summary of the Order Details

The final page, before the user commits to purchasing, is the summary page. We have all the details we need to complete the order and we are giving the customer one last chance to check the details before sending their order.

The form contains all the information the user has entered and will be passed in the final form submit. The information obtained from the previous forms is placed at the top of the page in hidden text boxes whose values we populate using server-side JScript.

```
<!--#include file="ServerSideGlobalDef.inc"-->
<HTML>
<HEAD>
    <TITLE>Confirm Details</TITLE>
</HEAD>

<BODY>
<FORM ACTION="ProcessOrder.asp" method="POST">

    <!-- Name/Address Details -->
    <INPUT TYPE="HIDDEN" NAME="txtTitle"
           VALUE="<%=Request.Form("txtTitle")%>">
    <INPUT TYPE="HIDDEN" NAME="txtFirstName"
           VALUE="<%=Request.Form("txtFirstName")%>">
    <INPUT TYPE="HIDDEN" NAME="txtLastName"
           VALUE="<%=Request.Form("txtLastName")%>">
    <INPUT TYPE="HIDDEN" NAME="txtEmail"
           VALUE="<%=Request.Form("txtEmail")%>">
    <INPUT TYPE="HIDDEN" NAME="txtStreet"
           VALUE="<%=Request.Form("txtStreet")%>">
    <INPUT TYPE="HIDDEN" NAME="txtCity"
           VALUE="<%=Request.Form("txtCity")%>">
    <INPUT TYPE="HIDDEN" NAME="txtLocality"
           VALUE="<%=Request.Form("txtLocality")%>">
    <INPUT TYPE="HIDDEN" NAME="txtPostCode"
           VALUE="<%=Request.Form("txtPostCode")%>">
    <INPUT TYPE="HIDDEN" NAME="txtCountry"
           VALUE="<%=Request.Form("txtCountry")%>">
```

```
<!-- Credit Card Details -->
<INPUT TYPE="HIDDEN" NAME="txtCCHolderName"
       VALUE="<%=Request.Form("txtCardHolderName") %>">
<INPUT TYPE="HIDDEN" NAME="txtCCNo"
       VALUE="<%=Request.Form("txtCardNo") %>">
<INPUT TYPE="HIDDEN" NAME="txtCCType"
       VALUE="<%=Request.Form("radCardType") %>">
<INPUT TYPE="HIDDEN" NAME="txtCCExpire"
       VALUE="<%=Request.Form("cboExpMonth") + "/" + _
              Request.Form("cboExpYear") %>">
```

Our next task is to display a summary of the information the user entered starting with the actual items in the order. We use the `Basket.inc` file we created earlier (and used for the shopping basket) to actually display the summary, this time we want it to be read only so `bReadOnly` is set to `true`. The `Basket.inc` file has hidden input elements with the `ItemId`'s and quantities of the order and these will be sent when the form is submitted.

```
<!-- Summarize Order details -->
<FONT FACE="Comic Sans MS" SIZE="+1" color="Navy">
   <P>Your order details are listed below.</P>
   <P>
      Once you have confirmed the details click
      <INPUT TYPE="Submit" NAME="cmdSubmit" VALUE="Submit Order">
      to send your order
   </P>
</FONT>
<STRONG><FONT FACE="Comic Sans MS" SIZE="3" color="#FF8040">
   <br>The following items<br><br>
</FONT></STRONG>

<!-- Summary of items in order -->
<%
   bReadOnly = true;
%>
<!--#include file="Basket.inc"-->
<STRONG><FONT FACE="Comic Sans MS" SIZE="3" color="#FF8040">
   Will be delivered to<br>
</FONT></STRONG>
```

The next summary we display is that of the customer's name and address details which we format by placing inside a table. The values are populated by ASP script which retrieves them from those posted in the form submit that brought us to this page.

```
<!-- Summary of NAME and address for delivery -->
<TABLE cellspacing="2" cellpadding="2" border="0">
<TR>
   <TD>
      <STRONG><FONT FACE="Comic Sans MS" SIZE="2">
         <%=Request.Form("txtTitle")%> 
         <%=Request.Form("txtFirstName")%> 
         <%=Request.Form("txtLastName")%>
      </FONT></STRONG>
   </TD>
</TR>
<TR>
   <TD>
      <STRONG><FONT FACE="Comic Sans MS" SIZE="2">
         <%=Request.Form("txtStreet")%>
      </FONT></STRONG>
   </TD>
</TR>
<TR>
   <TD>
```

```
        <STRONG><FONT FACE="Comic Sans MS" SIZE="2">
            <%=Request.Form("txtCity")%>
        </FONT></STRONG>
        </TD>
    </TR>
    <TR>
        <TD>
        <STRONG><FONT FACE="Comic Sans MS" SIZE="2">
            <%=Request.Form("txtLocality")%>
        </FONT></STRONG>
        </TD>
    </TR>
    <TR>
        <TD>
        <STRONG><FONT FACE="Comic Sans MS" SIZE="2">
            <%=Request.Form("txtPostCode")%>
        </FONT></STRONG>
        </TD>
    </TR>
    <TR>
        <TD>
        <STRONG><FONT FACE="Comic Sans MS" SIZE="2">
            <%=Request.Form("txtCountry")%>
        </FONT></STRONG>
        </TD>
    </TR>
</TABLE>
```

The summary is completed with a summary of the credit card details and a restating of exactly how much will be debited from the card.

```
<!-- Summary of amount to be charged to credit card -->
<br>
<STRONG><FONT FACE="Comic Sans MS" SIZE="3" color="#FF8040">
    A total of <FONT color="Black">&pound;<%=lTotal + 2.5 %></FONT>
    will be debited from your <%=Request.Form("radCardType")%> card
    (Card details below)
</FONT></STRONG>

<!-- Show summary of card details -->
<TABLE>
<TR>
    <TD>
        <STRONG><FONT FACE="Comic Sans MS" SIZE="2">
            Name of credit card holder :
        </FONT></STRONG>
    </TD>
    <TD>
        <STRONG><FONT FACE="Comic Sans MS" SIZE="2">
            <%=Request.Form("txtCardHolderName")%>
        </FONT></STRONG>
    </TD>
</TR>
<TR>
    <TD>
        <STRONG><FONT FACE="Comic Sans MS" SIZE="2">
            Card Number
        </FONT></STRONG>
    </TD>
    <TD>
        <STRONG><FONT FACE="Comic Sans MS" SIZE="2">
            <%= Request.Form("txtCardNo") %>
        </FONT></STRONG>
    </TD>
</TR>
<TR>
```

```
        <TD>
            <STRONG><FONT FACE="Comic Sans MS" SIZE="2">
                Expiry Date
            </FONT></STRONG>
        </TD>
        <TD>
            <STRONG><FONT FACE="Comic Sans MS" SIZE="2">
                <%=Request.Form("cboExpMonth")%> / _
                <%=Request.Form("cboExpYear") %>
            </FONT></STRONG>
        </TD>
    </TR>
    </TABLE>

    <STRONG><FONT FACE="Comic Sans MS" SIZE="2">
        Click
        <INPUT TYPE="Submit" NAME="cmdSubmitBottom" VALUE="Purchase items">
        to send your order
    </FONT></STRONG>
</FORM>
</BODY>
</HTML>
```

Save the page as `CheckoutConfirm.asp`

Check out the Checkout

Before continuing it's worth testing the checkout code so far before we move on to the order processing.

Processing the Order

The user has hit submit in the order summary page (`CheckoutConfirm.asp`) and its action has brought us here, to `ProcessOrder.asp`, where we will extract the information and process the order. The order items, customer name and address and credit card information will be written to the database using the stored procedures we are about to create.

Transaction Integrity

It's very important that the order transaction should succeed completely and the customer gets the goods they requested, or the transaction must fail unequivocally and we must handle this failure and deal with it as we are best able. For example we don't want to add their name and address to the database then find we are unable to complete the order leaving a name and delivery address in the database but an order with no items.

The most likely failure is that we have insufficient stock to complete the customer's order. Although we checked that the stock was available when the customer first added items to their basket, time has passed since then during which someone else may have bought the remaining stock. If we are unable to fully complete the customer's order, because we are short of one or more items, then we need to inform the customer and give them the option of either proceeding with the amounts available or canceling completely.

We face certain difficulties. We need to check that sufficient quantities of each item are in stock. But if we do that first, then try and update the database we may find in that fraction of a second another concurrent user has got in first and bought our items.

I have dealt with this by checking the items exist and removing them from the database in the same stored procedure. But what if the customer has ordered 10 different items and item 9 of the list is out of stock and the customer wants to completely cancel the order? Do we keep a list of items that have been removed from the stock table and use that information to put the items back on the shelf as it were?

It all seems to be getting a little complex and too much like hard work so lets make it easier for ourselves and enlist the help of Microsoft Transaction Server and the transaction functionality it makes available to ASP.

The central focus for transactions in ASP is the ObjectContext object. This has two methods, SetComplete and SetAbort and two events, OnTransactionCommit and OnTransactionAbort.

If we wish to rollback all the database writes made in a transaction, we call the SetAbort method. If our transaction processing has completed successfully then we make a call to SetComplete and all the database changes will become permanent. Calling SetAbort results in the OnTransactionAbort event firing and SetComplete in OnTransactionCommit being fired. Note that even if SetComplete is called in one part of the code, any other part of the code calling SetAbort will cause the transaction to abort.

Although MTS will rollback all database changes, it does not currently rollback any other changes that might have occurred, for example a change to a file on disk. Also, the database must support the XA protocol – a two phase protocol that allows applications and resource managers to communicate with a transaction manager – which currently limits it to SQL Server. A further limitation is that transaction support is only valid for one page, essentially the page becomes a transaction and this must be committed or aborted before any more pages are loaded otherwise the transaction will abort.

More Stored Procedures

Before we create the ProcessOrder.asp page we need to create the 3 stored procedures it requires.

First, we need a stored procedure to add the customer's and the new order's details to the database. The stored procedure consists of 2 insert statements which add the data from the forms filled in by the customer. Because we want to make sure any error is handled and the ASP page's transaction aborted we have added error checks after each insert. If an error occurs global variable @@Error will contain its value, otherwise it contains zero. Therefore if @@Error is not zero we end the stored procedure and return @@Error which our ASP code can pick up as a return parameter of an ADO Command object.

You'll remember that our Customer and Orders table both have a primary key field which is an identity field, inserting a row automatically puts the next number in sequence in those fields. We need to know this number for later when we add order items or want to get back the customer details. To do this we use the @@Identity variable which SQL Server populates with the last identity number inserted. Thus, the @@Identity values for CustId and OrderId are put in the output variables @CustId and @OrderId which we can access later in the ASP page.

```
CREATE PROCEDURE [NewOrder]
(  @Title varchar(4), @FirstName varchar(50), @LastName varchar(50),
   @Email varchar(75), @Street varchar(75), @City varchar(50),
   @Locality varchar(50),   @PostCode varchar(15), @Country varchar(50),
   @CCHolderName varchar(50), @CCType varchar(25), @CCNo varchar(20),
   @CCExpire varchar(7), @CustId int OUTPUT, @OrderId int OUTPUT)
AS

-- Insert Customer details
INSERT INTO Customer ( Title, FirstName, LastName, Email, Street, City, _
                    Locality, PostCode, Country)
       VALUES ( @Title, @FirstName, @LastName, @Email, @Street, @City, _
               @Locality, @PostCode, @Country)

IF (@@ERROR <> 0) GOTO on_error

-- Retrieve the automatically generated CustId VALUE
SET @CustId = @@IDENTITY

-- Insert order details
INSERT INTO Orders (CustId,CCHolderName,CCType,CCNo,CCExpire,OrderDate)
       VALUES (@CustId,@CCHolderName,@CCType,@CCNo,@CCExpire,GetDate())

IF (@@ERROR <> 0) GOTO on_error

-- Retrieve VALUE automatically put into OrderId field
SET @OrderId = @@IDENTITY

RETURN(0)

on_error:

RETURN(@@ERROR)
```

Our second stored procedure is the one that adds each item of the order to the database. First we check stock levels are sufficient to fulfill the order. We raise an error if the levels are too low to let the calling ASP program know. We return zero if everything was successful or the error number otherwise.

```
CREATE PROCEDURE [AddOrderItem]
( @OrderId int, @ItemId int, @Qty int)
AS

DECLARE @Return int

-- check suffcent stock available
IF (SELECT QtyInStock FROM Stock WHERE ItemId = @ItemId) < @Qty
BEGIN
    SET @Return = 547
    GOTO on_error
END
```

Next we reduce the stock levels by the order quantity.

```
-- deduct stock levels
UPDATE Stock
SET QtyInStock = QtyInStock - @Qty
WHERE ItemId = @ItemId

IF (@@ERROR <> 0)
BEGIN
    SET @Return = @@ERROR
    GOTO on_error
END
```

Finally, we add the order item information to the `OrderItem` table.

```
-- add item to orderitem table
INSERT INTO OrderItem(OrderId,ItemId,Qty)
       VALUES (@OrderId, @ItemId, @Qty)

IF (@@ERROR <> 0)
BEGIN
   SET @Return = @@ERROR
   GOTO on_error
END

RETURN 0

on_error:

RETURN @Return
```

Our final stored procedure for this page is `ItemAvailability` which is used to return stock item information and quantity.

```
CREATE PROCEDURE [ItemAvailability]
( @ItemId int )
AS
SELECT ArtistName, Title, QtyInStock
FROM Stock JOIN Artist ON Artist.ArtistId = Stock.ArtistId
WHERE ItemId = @ItemId
```

Before we continue we need to give the database user `MMCustomer` Execute permissions to the three stored procedures.

Building our Order Processing Page

OK, now let's make a start on creating `ProcessOrder.asp`

At the very top of the page are two pre-processor directives, the first stating that this page requires a new transaction, the second making the default language JScript. We need to explicitly state we want this to be a transaction-based page by using the `TRANSACTION` pre-processor directive.

```
<%@ TRANSACTION=Requires_New Language="JScript" %>
```

Next we define some page level variables and set the page to buffer which means no response will be sent to the client browser until we reach the end of the page or we explicitly say so. This allows us to redirect the response in mid flow.

Event code has been written for `OnTransactionAbort` and `OnTransactionCommit`. `OnTransactionAbort` checks the error number and if it's not 547 – indicating an error of insufficient stock – then the response is redirected to the `transerror.asp` page which lists the error cause. `OnTransactionCommit` clears the basket cookie, then redirects to the `acceptOrder.asp` page which displays a success message and e-mails the customer and the shipping department who actually sends the goods.

```
<%
    Response.Buffer = true;
    // Database connection string
    var sdbConnString =   "Provider=SQLOLEDB.1;Password=madforit; _
                           Persist Security Info=True;User ID=MMCustomer; _
                           Initial Catalog=MusicMad;Data Source=.";
    var iErrorNo = 0;
    var sErrorDescription;

    // Index of first Item element in form
    var iItemElementStart = 1;

    // ADO constants make code more readable
    var adCmdStoredProc = 4;
    var adParamReturnValue = 4;
    var adParamInput = 1;
    var adParamOutput = 2;
    var adVarChar = 200;
    var adInteger = 3;

function OnTransactionAbort()
{
    // If error is not insufficient stock
    if (iErrorNo != 547)
    {
        Response.Redirect("transerror.asp?" + escape(sErrorDescription));
    }
}

function OnTransactionCommit()
{
    // Everything went ok - re-direct to confirmation page
    Response.Cookies("Basket")= "";
    Response.Redirect("acceptorder.asp?" + iOrderId);
}
```

Now we open up a connection to the database and create a command object which we will use to execute our stored procedure `NewOrder`. `NewOrder` will add the customer and credit card details to the database.

Note the whole of the transaction code is inside a JScript 5.0 `try…catch` clause. If any other non-database errors occur we can catch them and ensure the transaction is aborted.

```
// Process order form
try
{
    var loConn = Server.CreateObject("ADODB.Connection");
    var loCommand = Server.CreateObject("ADODB.Command");
    var loParam;
    var iCustId = -1;
    var iOrderId = -1;
    loConn.Open(sdbConnString);

    // Create ADO command object which will execute our stored procedure
    loCommand.CommandText = "NewOrder";
    loCommand.CommandType = adCmdStoredProc;
    loCommand.Name = "NewOrder";
```

Before we can execute the ADO Command we need to append the parameters the stored procedure expects and this is the task of the next piece of code.

There are a lot of parameters to append but the method is the same for each.

❑ First a new parameter object is created using the ADO command object's `CreateParameter` method whose arguments are parameter name, parameter type, direction, size and default value.

❑ Then the new parameter is appended to the `Command` object using the `Append` method.

The first parameter we define is the return value which is an integer. If a return value is expected then it must always be the first parameter appended. Here the return value is used to notify us of any errors that occurred inside the stored procedure. The remaining parameters except for the last two are input parameters used to pass values to the stored procedure. The final two parameters are output parameters which the stored procedure populates with the `CustId` of the customer row added to the database and `OrderId` of the order.

```
// @Title, @FirstName varchar(50), @LastName varchar(50),
// @Email varchar(75), @Street varchar(75)

loParam = loCommand.CreateParameter("RV",adInteger, _
                                    adParamReturnValue);
loCommand.Parameters.Append(loParam);

loParam = loCommand.CreateParameter("Title",adVarChar,adParamInput, _
                                    4, Request.Form("txtTitle"));
loCommand.Parameters.Append(loParam);

loParam = loCommand.CreateParameter("FirstName", adVarChar, _
                                    adParamInput, 50, _
                                    Request.Form("txtFirstName"));
loCommand.Parameters.Append(loParam);

loParam = loCommand.CreateParameter("LastName", adVarChar, _
                                    adParamInput, 50, _
                                    Request.Form("txtLastName"));
loCommand.Parameters.Append(loParam);

loParam = loCommand.CreateParameter("Email", adVarChar, adParamInput,_
                                    75, Request.Form("txtEmail"));
loCommand.Parameters.Append(loParam);

loParam = loCommand.CreateParameter("Street", adVarChar, adParamInput,
                                    75, Request.Form("txtStreet"));
loCommand.Parameters.Append(loParam);

//@City varchar(50), @Locality varchar(50), @Country varchar(50)
loParam = loCommand.CreateParameter("City", adVarChar, adParamInput, _
                                    50, Request.Form("txtCity"));
loCommand.Parameters.Append(loParam);

loParam = loCommand.CreateParameter("Locality", adVarChar, _
                                    adParamInput, 50, _
                                    Request.Form("txtLocality"));
loCommand.Parameters.Append(loParam);

loParam = loCommand.CreateParameter("PostCode", adVarChar, _
                                    adParamInput, 15, _
                                    Request.Form("txtPostCode"));
loCommand.Parameters.Append(loParam);

loParam = loCommand.CreateParameter("Country", adVarChar, _
                                    adParamInput, 50, _
                                    Request.Form("txtCountry"));
loCommand.Parameters.Append(loParam);
```

```
    // @CCHolderName varchar(50), @CCType varchar(25),
    // @CCNo varchar(20), @CCExpire varchar(7)
    loParam = loCommand.CreateParameter("CCHolderName", adVarChar, _
                                        adParamInput, 50, _
                                        Request.Form("txtCCHolderName"));
    loCommand.Parameters.Append(loParam);

    loParam = loCommand.CreateParameter("CCType", adVarChar, adParamInput,
                                        25, Request.Form("txtCCType"));
    loCommand.Parameters.Append(loParam);

    loParam = loCommand.CreateParameter("CCNo", adVarChar, adParamInput, _
                                        20, Request.Form("txtCCNo"));
    loCommand.Parameters.Append(loParam);

    loParam = loCommand.CreateParameter("CCExpire", adVarChar, _
                                        adParamInput, 7, _
                                        Request.Form("txtCCExpire"));
    loCommand.Parameters.Append(loParam);

    // @CustId int, @OrderId int
    loParam = loCommand.CreateParameter("CustId", adInteger, _
                                        adParamOutput);
    loCommand.Parameters.Append(loParam);

    loParam = loCommand.CreateParameter("OrderId", adInteger, _
                                        adParamOutput);
    loCommand.Parameters.Append(loParam);
```

The `Command`'s connection is set to the ADO Connection we opened and the `Command` is executed.

```
    loCommand.ActiveConnection = loConn;

    loCommand.Execute();
```

If there were any problems with the stored procedure's execution, its return value will not be zero and we need to abort this transaction. Calling `ObjectContext.SetAbort` will abort the transaction and cause `OnTransactionAbort` to fire and run any 'clean-up code' we put there. In our case this is where we redirect the user to the `transerror.asp` page.

If all has gone without error then we can start processing the order items. We create the command object we will use to execute the `AddOrderItem` stored procedure then we append the parameters.

```
    // check if stored procedure executed ok
    // abort transaction if failed
    if (loCommand.Parameters("RV") != 0)
    {
        // get Stored Procs return VALUE
        iErrorNo = loCommand.Parameters("RV");
        ObjectContext.SetAbort;
    }
    else
    {
        // Retrieve CustId and OrderId from
        // stored procs output variables
        iCustId = loCommand.Parameters("CustId");
        iOrderId = loCommand.Parameters("OrderId");

        // Create new command object
        // to add each order item detail to database
        loCommand = null;
        loCommand = Server.CreateObject("ADODB.Command");
```

```
loCommand.CommandText = "AddOrderItem";
loCommand.CommandType = adCmdStoredProc;
loCommand.Name = "AddOrderItem";

//Append Parameters @OrderId int, @ItemId int, @Qty int
loParam = loCommand.CreateParameter("RV", adInteger, _
                                    adParamReturnValue);
loCommand.Parameters.Append(loParam);

loParam = loCommand.CreateParameter("OrderId", adInteger, _
                                    adParamInput,0,iOrderId);
loCommand.Parameters.Append(loParam);

loParam = loCommand.CreateParameter("ItemId", adInteger, _
                                    adParamInput);
loCommand.Parameters.Append(loParam);

loParam = loCommand.CreateParameter("Qty", adInteger, _
                                    adParamInput);
loCommand.Parameters.Append(loParam);
loCommand.ActiveConnection = loConn;
```

Having created our `Command` object we can reuse it as we loop through the form elements containing the `ItemIds` and quantities making up the order. After each item has been added using the stored procedure we check that the return value is zero indicating no errors. If there were errors then we call `ObjectContext.SetAbort` and break out of the loop. Calling `SetAbort` will roll back all the order items already added to the database as well as the customer and order details added to the database. We are therefore assured that the database will not become corrupted by half completed transactions.

Remember that a return value of `547` indicates an error due to insufficient stock and we will write the code to handle that soon. If it's any other error then the `OnTransactionAbort` event, which fires as a result of calling `SetAbort`, will redirect the response to `transerror.asp` – a page we have yet to create.

Assuming that all has gone well, we call `SetComplete` to indicate the transaction's success and to ensure the data gets committed to the database. The `OnTransactionCommit` event fires and the customer is directed to a page confirming the transactions success and e-mails both them and the order shipping department.

```
var sElementKey;
var iItemId;
var iQty;

// Loop through the item form elements
for (var iElementCounter = iItemElementStart; _
     iElementCounter <= Request.Form.Count; iElementCounter++)
{
   sElementKey = new String(Request.Form.Key(iElementCounter));

   // if element NAME starts with ID its an item form element
   if (sElementKey.substr(3,2) == "ID")
   {
      // Get ItemId from form VALUE passed
      iItemId = parseInt _
                   (sElementKey.substring(5,sElementKey.length));

      // move to next element which is quantity VALUE for that item
      iElementCounter++;

      // get quantity
      iQty = parseInt(Request.Form(iElementCounter));
```

```
            // set command's parameters
            loCommand.Parameters("ItemId") = iItemId;
            loCommand.Parameters("Qty") = iQty;

            // execute stored procedure
            loCommand.Execute();

            // Any errors?
            if (loCommand.Parameters("RV") != 0)
            {
                // set iErrorNo, abort transaction and break out of loop
                iErrorNo = loCommand.Parameters("RV");
                ObjectContext.SetAbort;
                break;
            }
        }
    }
}
    // only set complete if transaction complete with no errors
    if (iErrorNo == 0)
        ObjectContext.SetComplete;
}
```

Finally we come to the end of our order processing script and the `catch` part of the `try` statement we set at the beginning of the code. If an error occurs in our code, the statements here execute and we are able to store the description in `sErrorDescription` and abort the transaction which will lead to the page being redirected to `transerror.asp` by `OnTransactionAbort`.

```
catch(e)
{
    sErrorDescription = e;
    ObjectContext.SetAbort;
}

%>
```

Save the page as `ProcessOrder.asp`.

Roll with it – Degrading Gracefully When It All Goes Wrong

We have not finished with the `ProcessOrder.asp` page yet: we need to add some code to handle the out of stock error (547) in a more user friendly way then just redirecting to an error page.

The out of stock problem is dealt with by displaying a list of the order items not available in sufficient quantity to fulfill the order and letting the user choose to either cancel the order completely or proceed with the amounts available. If the order was successful, or any error other than out of stock occurred, then the user will be redirected to another page elsewhere and will never see the HTML we are about to create.

The ASP page will be processed in totality even if re-direction occurs, so, to avoid the overhead of the order failed code, we nest it inside an if statement. Place the code at the bottom of the page immediately following the code we just created.

```
<HTML>
<BODY>
<%

    // If error is Out Of Stock then create HTML
    if (iErrorNo == 547)
    {

%>
```

The next task is to create a form replicating the form elements originally passed when the customer submitted their order – the last thing they want to do is be retyping the information. The form action returns to this page for reprocessing, this time hopefully with sufficient stock (though it is possible others may place orders whilst this customer is thinking about what to do).

```
<H2>Sorry we are unable to fully satisfy your order</H2>
<P>
<FORM ACTION="ProcessOrder.asp" method="POST">
    We do not currently have suffient stock for some items in your order,
    details listed below<BR>

    <!-- Name/Address Details -->
    <INPUT TYPE="HIDDEN" NAME="txtTitle"
        VALUE="<%=Request.Form("txtTitle")%>">
    <INPUT TYPE="HIDDEN" NAME="txtFirstName"
        VALUE="<%=Request.Form("txtFirstName")%>">
    <INPUT TYPE="HIDDEN" NAME="txtLastName"
        VALUE="<%=Request.Form("txtLastName")%>">
    <INPUT TYPE="HIDDEN" NAME="txtEmail"
        VALUE="<%=Request.Form("txtEmail")%>">
    <INPUT TYPE="HIDDEN" NAME="txtStreet"
        VALUE="<%=Request.Form("txtStreet")%>">
    <INPUT TYPE="HIDDEN" NAME="txtCity"
        VALUE="<%=Request.Form("txtCity")%>">
    <INPUT TYPE="HIDDEN" NAME="txtLocality"
        VALUE="<%=Request.Form("txtLocality")%>">
    <INPUT TYPE="HIDDEN" NAME="txtPostCode"
        VALUE="<%=Request.Form("txtPostCode")%>">
    <INPUT TYPE="HIDDEN" NAME="txtCountry"
        VALUE="<%=Request.Form("txtCountry")%>">


    <!-- Credit Card Details -->
    <INPUT TYPE="HIDDEN" NAME="txtCCHolderName"
        VALUE="<%= Request.Form("txtCCHolderName") %>">
    <INPUT TYPE="HIDDEN" NAME="txtCCNo"
        VALUE="<%= Request.Form("txtCCNo") %>">
    <INPUT TYPE="HIDDEN" NAME="txtCCType"
        VALUE="<%= Request.Form("txtCCType") %>">
    <INPUT TYPE="HIDDEN" NAME="txtCCExpire"
        VALUE="<%= Request.Form("txtCCExpire") %>">
```

We need to create a list of the items the customer ordered and check the availability of each item. In order to do so, we use the ItemAvailability stored procedure to retrieve the quantities available. Then we create a new command object which will be reused to execute the stored procedure as we loop though the shopping basket's items.

```
<%
   var loRS;

   // Create new command object
   loCommand = null;
   loCommand = Server.CreateObject("ADODB.Command");
   loCommand.CommandText = "ItemAvailability";
   loCommand.CommandType = adCmdStoredProc;
   loCommand.Name = "ItemAvailability";

   //@ItemId int
   loParam =loCommand.CreateParameter("ItemId", adInteger, adParamInput);
   loCommand.Parameters.Append(loParam);

   loCommand.ActiveConnection = loConn;
```

Next we start looping though the item elements in the form, retrieving the ItemId and quantity and using this information to access the database with the Command object and find out how many we actually have in stock.

```
   var sElementKey;
   var iItemId;
   var iQty;
   var iQtyInStock;
   for (var iElementCounter = iItemElementStart; _
        iElementCounter <= Request.Form.Count; iElementCounter++)
   {
      sElementKey = new String(Request.Form.Key(iElementCounter));

      // If this is an item element
      if (sElementKey.substr(3,2) == "ID")
      {
         // get ItemId
         iItemId = parseInt(sElementKey.substring(5,sElementKey.length));
         iElementCounter++;

         // Get desired quantity
         iQty = parseInt(Request.Form(iElementCounter));

         // access database to see how many are actually available
         loCommand.Parameters("ItemId") = iItemId;
         loRS = loCommand.Execute();
         iQtyInStock = loRS("QtyInStock");
```

If we find that there is insufficient stock available for the item we need to let the customer know. If there is no stock at all then we tell the user, otherwise we tell them how many are actually available. We also create hidden form elements to store the ItemId and quantities actually available. If the user goes ahead with the quantities available then this information can be retrieved after the form post.

We are only informing the user of problem items so if there are sufficient available we just create the hidden form elements for ItemId and quantity. The loop continues though each item.

```
         // If insufficient stock
         if (iQtyInStock < iQty)
         {
            // no stock at all - so no able to provide any of this item
            if (iQtyInStock == 0)
            {
%>
```

515

```
    <P><STRONG>
        <%= loRS("Title") %>  by <%= loRS("ArtistName") %> is currently
        unavailable, we hope to have new stock in shortly
    </STRONG></P>
<%
            }
            else
            // some stock available but not enough
            {
%>
    <P>
        <STRONG>
            You requested <%= iQty %> copies of <%= loRS("Title") %> by
            <%= loRS("ArtistName") %>, but unfortunately we only have
            <%= iQtyInStock %> in stock
        </STRONG>
        <INPUT TYPE="Hidden" NAME="<%= "txtID" + iItemId %>"
            VALUE="<%= "ID" + iItemId %>">
        <INPUT TYPE="Hidden" NAME="<%= "txtQtyID" + iItemId %>"
            VALUE="<%= iQtyInStock %>">
    </P>
<%
            }
        }
        else
        // suffcient stock - add hidden elements to form
        {
%>
    <INPUT TYPE="Hidden" NAME="<%= "txtID" + iItemId %>"
        VALUE="<%= "ID" + iItemId %>">
    <INPUT TYPE="Hidden" NAME="<%= "txtQtyID" + iItemId %>"
        VALUE="<%= iQtyInStock %>">
<%
        }
    }
}
%>
```

Finally we add two buttons giving the customer the choice of continuing with the available amounts or canceling altogether.

```
    <P>
        Click <INPUT TYPE="Submit" NAME="cmdSubmit" VALUE="Process Order">
        to submit your order with the maximum amount amounts available.
    </P>
    <P>
        Click <INPUT TYPE="button" NAME="cmdCancel" VALUE="Cancel Order"
                onClick="window.location.replace('ordercancel.htm');">
        to end this transaction, no monies have been debited from your
        credit card.
    </P>
</FORM>
<%
    }
    // close database connection
    loConn.Close();
    loConn = null;
%>

</BODY>
</HTML>
```

We have completed this page so re-save the file before closing it and continuing.

The OrderCancel and TransactionError Pages

Let's take the `ordercancel.htm` page first. Here we inform the user that no money has been debited from their card and give them the option to continue shopping.

```html
<HTML>
<BODY>
<DIV ALIGN="center">
   <FONT FACE="Comic Sans MS" SIZE="4">
      Your order has been cancelled successfully.<br>
      No monies will be deducted from your credit card
   </FONT>

   <FORM ACTION="" method="POST">
      <INPUT TYPE="button" NAME="cmdMainPage" VALUE="Continue shopping"
             onClick="top.location.replace('musicmad.htm')">
   </FORM>
</DIV>
</BODY>
</HTML>
```

Save the page as `ordercancel.htm` before continuing.

For the `transerror.asp` page we reassure them that no money has been debited and will also display the error message, more for our benefit when trying to debug. The actual error description was passed in the URL by the `OnTransactionAbort` method of the `processorder.asp` page which redirected us here.

```asp
<!--#include file="ServerSideGlobalDef.inc"-->
<%
   var sErrorDescription  = unescape(Request.QueryString);
%>
<HTML>
<HEAD></HEAD>
<BODY>
<FONT FACE="Comic Sans MS" SIZE="3">
   Due to a technical fault we have been unable to complete your
   order.<BR>
   Your order has been cancelled and no monies will be deducted from your
   credit card.<BR>
   The problem is listed below
</FONT>
<BR>
<P><%= sErrorDescription %></P>
</BODY>
</HTML>
```

This page needs to be saved as `transerror.asp`.

Sweetness Follows – Order Transaction Completed Successfully

The transaction has completed successfully, the sun is shining and MusicMadOnline.com are a few dollars richer. All that needs doing now is to e-mail the order shipping department telling them what to send and to whom. We'll also e-mail the customer just to confirm the order is being sent. The page itself also displays confirmation and a thank you message.

To send an e-mail we will use Collaboration Data Objects for Windows NT Server, which are installed on NT Server when you install Option Pack 4. You'll need to either have a mail server, such as Microsoft Exchange, located on your server machine or use SMTP (Simple Mail Transfer Protocol) to divert messages to a machine with a mail server. If you don't have a mail server on your machine, using SMTP's smart host facility enables you to point to your mail server. Open up the IIS console and check that SMTP is loaded and running on your server machine. Right click the SMTP service and choose **Properties**. Select the **Delivery** tab and in the **S**mart host property enter either your mail server's IP address or friendly name. Now messages should be routed for delivery to your mail server.

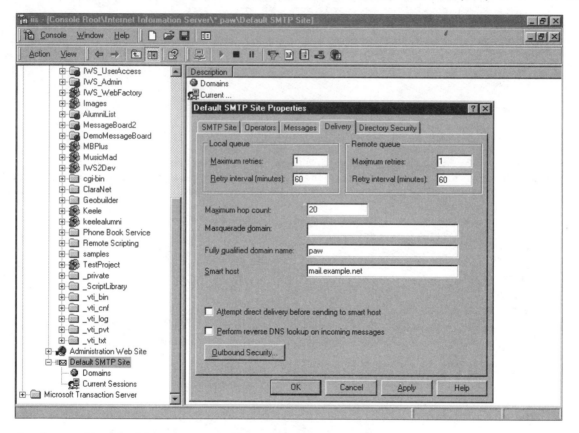

Our first goal is to build up the text for the e-mails, retrieving the information from the database. To do this we need to create two more stored procedures.

First, to retrieve the customer details, we need to create a `CustomerDetails` stored procedure. We know the `OrderId` as it's passed from the proceeding page so we can use that to do a join between the `Orders` table and `Customer` table.

```
CREATE PROCEDURE [CustomerDetails]
( @OrderId int )
AS
SELECT Title, FirstName, LastName, Email, Street,
       City,Locality,PostCode,Country
FROM Orders JOIN Customer ON Customer.CustId = Orders.CustId
WHERE Orders.OrderId = @OrderId
```

Our second stored procedure is `OrderDetails`, which returns details of each item the customer ordered.

```
CREATE PROCEDURE [OrderDetails]
( @OrderId int )
AS
SELECT OrderItem.ItemId, Qty, ArtistName, Title, Price
FROM (OrderItem JOIN Stock ON Stock.ItemId = OrderItem.ItemId) JOIN _
      Artist ON Artist.ArtistId = Stock.ArtistId
WHERE OrderItem.OrderId = @OrderId
```

Before leaving Enterprise Manager remember to give `MMCustomer` Exec permissions for both the stored procedures.

Now to create the `AcceptOrder.asp` page. We appended the `OrderId` to the end of the URL in `ProcessOrder.asp` when we redirected to this page. We can now retrieve it using `Response.QueryString`. This information is all we need to start pulling back customer and order information from the database.

Having created a new `ADO.Connection` object and opened a connection to the database we then populate a Recordset using the `CustomerDetails` query.

```
<!--#include file="ServerSideGlobalDef.inc"-->
<%

    // Get Order info
    var sCustEmail = "Thank you for shopping with MusicMadOnline.com\n\n _
                    The following items\n\n";
    var sOrderDeptEmail = "Send the following items - \n\n";
    var sAddress = "";
    var iTotal = 0;
    var iOrderId = Request.QueryString;
    var loConn = Server.CreateObject("ADODB.Connection");
    var loRS;

    // Retrieve customer details from database
    loConn.Open(sdbConnString);
    loRS = loConn.Execute("CustomerDetails " + iOrderId);
```

Now we can retrieve the customer's address and e-mail address from the database before closing the recordset.

```
    // create customer address part of e-mail
    sAddress = sAddress.concat(loRS("Title"), " ", loRS("FirstName"), _
                    " ", loRS("LastName"),"\n");
    sAddress = sAddress.concat(loRS("Street"), "\n", loRS("City"), "\n", _
                    loRS("Locality"), "\n");
    sAddress = sAddress.concat(loRS("PostCode"), "\n", loRS("Country"), _
                    "\n");

    sEmail = new String(loRS("Email"));

    loRS.Close();
```

Now we need to build up a list of the items the customer has ordered. Another recordset is created using the `OrderDetails` stored procedure and we then loop though it row by row building up the e-mail's text: one e-mail for the shipping department and one as confirmation for the customer.

```
    // Retrive order details - list of all items to be sent
    loRS = loConn.Execute("OrderDetails " + iOrderId);

    // create the order detail par of the e-mail
    while (!loRS.Eof)
    {
        sCustEmail = sCustEmail.concat(loRS("Title"), " by ", _
                    loRS("ArtistName"), " Qty ", loRS("Qty"), " @ £", _
                    loRS("Price"), "\n");
        iTotal = iTotal + loRS("Qty") * loRS("Price");
        sOrderDeptEmail = sOrderDeptEmail.concat("ItemId : ", _
                    loRS("ItemId"), "\nArtist Name : ", _
                    loRS("ArtistName"), "\nTitle : ", loRS("Title"), _
                    "\nQty : ", loRS("Qty"), "\n\n");
        loRS.MoveNext();
    }

    loRS.Close();
    loConn.Close();
    loRS = null;
    loConn = null;

    // complete e-mail message
    sOrderDeptEmail = sOrderDeptEmail.concat _
                            ("\n\nto the address below\n\n",sAddress);
    sCustEmail = sCustEmail.concat("\n\nHave been shipped to\n\n",
                            sAddress, "\n\n£", iTotal + 2.5, _
                        " will be debited from your credit card\n");
    sCustEmail = sCustEmail.concat("\nIf you have any queries please _
                            email us at orders@MusicMadOnline.com");
```

With the e-mail message created we can now send it using CDONTS's `NewMail` object.

First we create a new `NewMail` object, simply use `NewMail`'s `Send` method to send the e-mail. The `Send` method has 5 parameters: From E-mail Address, Send to E-mail Address, Subject, Message Body and importance. I have left the importance parameter at its default value of normal.

The `NewMail` object is a use once and throw away object. If we want to send another e-mail we must create a new `NewMail` object.

```
    loEMailer = Server.CreateObject("CDONTS.Newmail");

    // Email order person
    loEMailer.Send("NewOrder@MusicmMad.com",
                "shipping@MusicMadOnline.com", "New Order",
                sOrderDeptEmail);

    // Email Customer
    var loEMailer = Server.CreateObject("CDONTS.Newmail");
    loEMailer.Send("Orders@MusicMadOnline.com", sEmail, _
                "Your order with MusicMadOnline.com", sCustEmail);

%>
<HTML>
```

Finally, lets create the page text itself confirming the order transaction's success.

```
<HEAD>
    <TITLE>Order Successful</TITLE>
</HEAD>
<BODY>
```

```
<DIV ALIGN="center">
   <FONT FACE="Comic Sans MS" SIZE="5" color="Navy">
      Your order was successful
   </FONT>
   <FONT FACE="Comic Sans MS" SIZE="3" color="BLACK">
      <P>
         Your goods will be sent to you shortly.
         Confirmation of your order items have been e-mailed to you
      </P>
   </FONT>
   <FONT FACE="Comic Sans MS" SIZE="4" color="#FF8040">
      <P>
         Thank you for shopping with MusicMadOnline.com
      </P>
   </FONT>

   <FORM ACTION="" METHOD="POST">
      <INPUT TYPE="Button" NAME="cmdGoShop" VALUE="Contine Shopping"
             onClick="window.location.replace('home.asp');">
   </FORM>
</DIV>
</BODY>
</HTML>
```

Save the page as `AcceptOrder.asp`.

Online Store Complete

Congratulations you've made it to the end! Hopefully along the way you have learned the basic techniques for an online store. Now you can take it further and improve on the foundations laid.

One of the most useful additions would be a customer log-in facility, which would save database space for you and the hassle of retyping their details for the customer. It also provides the opportunity to find out more about your customers and perhaps keep them informed of updates to the web site or new product lines.

You may also decide that with 70% of people browsing with a version 4+ browser that you can afford to rewrite this in JavaScript 1.2 and make use of some of the advanced features that offers, particularly in string manipulation.

Taking things further with a component written in Java, C++ or Visual Basic you could implement full credit card checking, such as verifying account details and obtaining authorization.

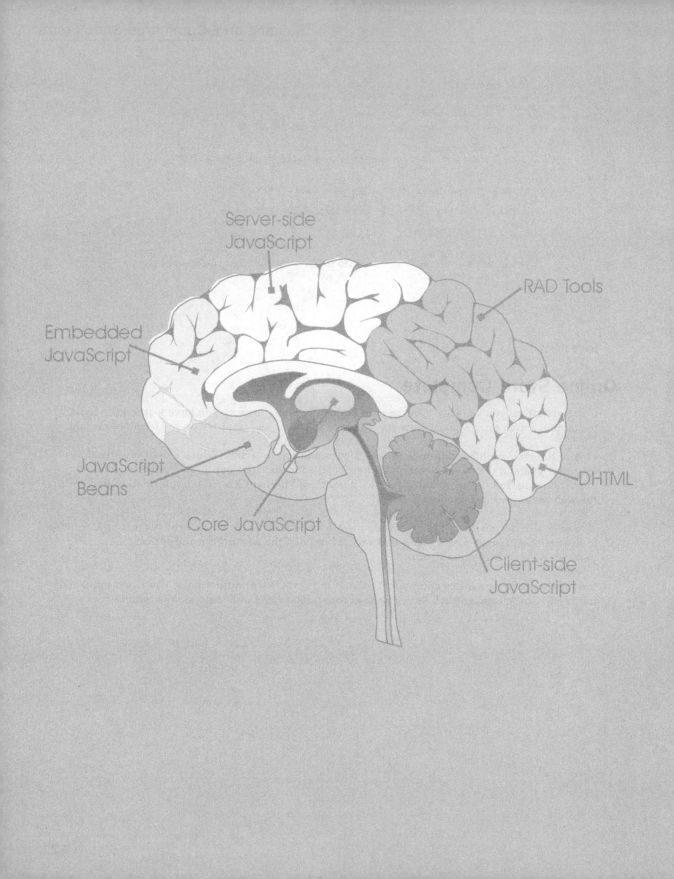

Applets and Java

We have seen how plug-ins and images can be controlled by client-side JavaScript when embedded in an HTML document. In the case study in Chapter 10, we embedded a tree controller Java applet to do the essentially the same thing. However, the interaction between JavaScript and Java can be substantially more complicated and flexible than the one between JavaScript and plug-ins. This is due to the fact that Java is a general-purpose programming language. In fact, as Sun Microsystems never tire of saying, Java is an entire computing platform in its own right.

Because of the legal rift between Sun and Microsoft, and especially because of Microsoft's insistence on using its own system object model (called COM) in Internet Explorer, the evolution of Java support on Netscape browsers has been consistently more faithful to the original specifications. As a result, supporting Java applets on Microsoft browsers can become a love/hate affair. In this chapter, we will focus on what can be done with Java on Netscape browsers, and will make special note of cross browser compatible features.

Neither browser, however, can be guaranteed to support the latest Java release. Even if the browsers released a new version with each release date, installed browsers wouldn't be up-to-date. Sun have therefore released a Java runtime environment (JRE) with each recent version of Java. This includes a plug-in that can be downloaded to provide the correct Java class versions. This makes the APPLET tag redundant, as the plug-in uses the Netscape and IE specific tags EMBED and OBJECT. For more information, see the documentation at http://java.sun.com/products/plugin/index.html.

Using JavaScript, you can knit together Java applets embedded in a Web page with other elements of the page and each other. As we have seen with our Photo Album case study, Java plus HTML plus JavaScript lets you create applications, not just applets.

Furthermore, using Java from JavaScript greatly expands the functionality available in JavaScript. Graphics, file operation and networking functionality are all missing from client-side JavaScript. With easy access to Java, JavaScript programs suddenly have vast new realms to play with. The 'platform', as provided by the Java libraries and runtime environment, immediately becomes available for use via JavaScript.

This book assumes you have no prior knowledge of Java. But there are some things you might want to achieve with JavaScript that just can't be done without a little Java. This chapter explains how to do those tasks, the technical basis behind them, and the noteworthy Java concepts needed to make sense of it all. We will be coding four complete Java applets from scratch in this chapter:

- ❑ A simple `HelloWorld` applet for the warm-up act

- ❑ An applet that allows you to 'break out' of JavaScript, and draw graphic lines directly on a drawing surface displayed on a web page

- ❑ A cross browser compatible Java applet that will 'reach back' and interface with JavaScript code. It will work with 4.x level browsers

- ❑ A cross-browser and 3.x version compatible applet. This will explain how to code applets that will work harmoniously with JavaScript even on the oldest Java supporting browsers

If you have not programmed in Java before, this chapter will let you get your hands wet working with some code. If you have started Java programming or are already a competent Java programmer, this chapter should shed some light on how to leverage the flexibility and dynamism inherent in JavaScript to create great web-based applications quickly and effectively.

Note that it is also possible for JavaScript to interact with Java in a standalone program. This opens up dramatic possibilities not available in an Internet scenario. This exciting functionality will be discussed in Chapter 16. Only JavaScript and Java interactions that occur within the web browser context are discussed in this chapter.

Java Basics for JavaScript Scriptwriters

For a detailed tutorial on Java, try *Beginning Java 2* by Ivor Horton (Wrox Press, ISBN 1-861002-23-8), or check out the online trails at http://java.sun.com/docs/books/tutorial/. There is only a superficial treatment here.

A Sanity Check

There are more than a few reasons to delve into Java from the JavaScript scriptwriter's perspective. They include, but are not limited to:

❑ JavaScript and HTML are just too crude for the fancy display you are trying to create

❑ You want to use signed JavaScript scripts

❑ You want to communicate with a program on a web server from the browser

❑ You want to tie applets and HTML together into a cohesive application

❑ There are features missing in JavaScript, available only in Java

❑ You want to create a compelling cross-browser compatible user experience, but JavaScript alone falls short of delivering it

❑ You want to use it "because it's there"

Java and JavaScript Compared

As for JavaScript scripts, Java programs come in standalone and host-embedded varieties. In Java terminology, these are 'applications' and 'applets' respectively. On the client-side, applets run within the context of a browser and are subject to security constraints. Their server-side equivalents, servlets, run within the context of a web server and enhance its processing ability through customized behavior. Only client-side applets are discussed in this chapter. For more details on servlets, take a look at *Professional Java Server Programming* (Wrox Press, ISBN 1-861002-77-7).

From the point of view of a person using someone else's Java applets in a browser, applets look much like plug-in data or ActiveX controls. A Java applet is loaded over the Web from a file of binary data using a special HTML tag - <APPLET>. Applet activity is often restricted to a specific rectangle on the screen, allocated to it by the tag, or to special windows that the applet opens itself.

> *It is also possible to embed applets using an <OBJECT> or <EMBED> tag on some browsers; this essentially treats the applet as part of a plug-in written in Java. As we saw earlier, this gives the applet developer more flexibility in which version of Java they can use.*

Internally JavaScript and Java aren't that far apart. Both have syntaxes that borrow common elements from the C language. Both have object concepts. Programs written in both languages can be loaded into browsers via URLs. JavaScript scripts rely on an interpreter in the browser; Java applets also rely on a browser-side interpreter or runtime library except that that second interpreter has a fancy name: the Java Virtual Machine (JVM). In both cases, the interpreter allows the program or script to be portable across different types of computer.

In a typical browser, the JavaScript interpreter and the JVM are two very separate beasts running in a completely independent fashion. The figure below gives an idea of the isolation between the two subsystems. This separation gives rise to many co-ordination and interoperability problems.

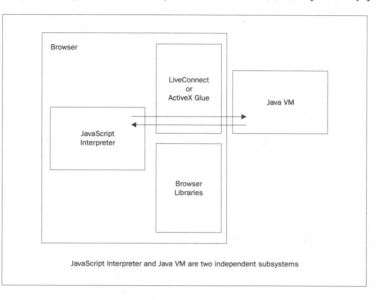

Browser

LiveConnect
or
ActiveX Glue

Java VM

JavaScript
Interpreter

Browser
Libraries

JavaScript Interpreter and Java VM are two independent subsystems

From the point of view of development there are three crucial differences between the two languages:

Firstly, Java source code requires an extra preparation step before it is useable. This step, called **compilation**, takes the readable Java source, typically in a `.java` file, and outputs a stream of binary **bytecode** data into a `.class` file. This serves to check that the developer's readable code is syntactically correct and secure. It is also this bytecode format that is loaded across the Web and interpreted by the JVM. Because the format is not character-based, it can't easily be embedded in HTML files as JavaScript can. Since the applet source never appears in the browser, there is no 'View Source' option for Java applets.

Part of Java's philosophy is that the same code, once compiled, should run on any JVM, and one way to ensure this is to have strong support for a core set of functionality available on every platform. The runtime Java support typically found in modern browsers (including libraries of code to create user-interfaces, graphics, multi-media, databases and handle data structures, etc.) allows bytecode `.class` files to have typically very small footprint, enabling them to be downloaded quickly.

Secondly, types and objects have a much larger hand in Java than JavaScript. Java is **strongly typed**, not loosely typed, so the developer must use `String` variables for `String`-typed values and `Integer` variables for `Integer`-typed values, etc. The Java language syntax doesn't hide the developer from objects, as is sometimes the case in JavaScript. Java requires object concepts from the very beginning. Quick program or script fragments like JavaScript event handlers aren't possible - only whole objects can be created in Java. The developer spends a lot of time getting classes right - classes define the type of an object in a way that is much more specific than the simple constructor functions of JavaScript. In general, Java programs are more formal, methodical, and disciplined. However, as JavaScript is used more in more complex and larger web applications, this distinction may not remain as clear-cut. JavaScript programmers will also have to be more formal, methodical and disciplined in order to write high quality, robust and maintainable code.

Thirdly, Java does not come with ready and immediate access to the browser's features. It does have its own useful libraries of objects, but these are aimed more at creating entire applications – such as a browser – within Java, rather than accessing the parts of the browser in which the Java interpreter is embedded. In fact, Sun has a commercial product called HotJava that is a complete web browser written completely in Java; and it supports embedded JavaScript on web pages. From a Java applet, it is extra effort to get at browser features such as HTML form elements in documents. This difficulty stems from the Java language designers' initial desire to keep Java separate and isolated from other software systems - both for reasons of security and platform independence. As the earlier discussion on separate subsystems has illustrated, this can add significant complexity.

Because of these three things, the development model for Java is a little different to JavaScript. With JavaScript, you create your HTML page, decorate it with script bits that act on that page's objects, and load it into a browser to see if it works. With Java, you first create your objects (or tie together the ones provided by the Java runtime library) and compile them to see if they have problems. If not, the resulting bytecode files are loaded via a special tag in an HTML document, and you see if they work within the restricted area of the screen allocated to them.

Last but not least, the terminology used in each of the two languages can vary considerably. This is perhaps the main obstacle for the scriptwriter.

Java's Special Browser Status

From the outside, Java applets can appear like any form of multimedia, such as images or plug-in data. Assuming there is no difference at all between these technologies is a trap for the scriptwriter. There are a number of special behaviours that set applets apart from other complex tags.

An Applet of Objects

Images, sounds, animation and other items embedded in an HTML document are loaded across the web from one file each (JavaScript image animation, described in Chapter 6 is an exception). An AVI movie, for example, isn't usually split across a number of files.

Java is not like that. A single applet can consist of many objects stemming from a variety of classes. In the simplest case, each class has a separate file. In the typical and crudest case, each class needs to be fetched separately across the network (and it's not hard to be more efficient than this). The JVM part of the browser consolidates them together as they arrive, and runs the complete applet.

The implications for the scriptwriter are:

- ❏ Just because the main or initial class of an applet is loaded, that doesn't mean the whole applet is in memory. Web page loading problems extend to applets in new ways.
- ❏ Some or all of the core Java classes can be (and are) permanently stored on the browser's local disk, because they are commonly used and there are big performance gains. These classes are defined and created either by Sun or by the browser vendor. A browser should have compatible versions of these classes, ready to use by your Web application's applets without downloading them all over the network.
- ❏ Because classes can be stored on the local computer, Netscape browsers allow their use by the scriptwriter *without* any applet being present in the browser (this is accomplished through their LiveConnect technology). Because these local classes exist, JavaScript can rely on them for some operations like file writing. This is convenient and also saves duplicating functionality across two languages.

In a more complex (but still typical) case, these separate files are often grouped together for performance reasons into single `.zip` or `.jar` (Java Archive) files, both at Web sites and in the browser's local folders. However, the idea of separate files for separate classes is still a cornerstone of Java's architecture.

Applet Lifecycle Surprises

Suppose an HTML document containing an image and some JavaScript is loaded into a browser window. If the user then browses to a different URL, you would expect that the first document, its image and its script variables would be gone, whatever 'gone' means. This example illustrates that:

```
<HTML><BODY>
<SCRIPT>

if ( typeof(saved) == "undefined" )
    var saved = 10;
else
    saved *= 2;

alert(saved);
</SCRIPT>
<IMG SRC="anyimage.gif">
<FORM><INPUT TYPE="text"></FORM>
</BODY></HTML>
```

To run this example, view it and then go backwards one and forward one, via the browser buttons. This test shows that the alert always shows 10 so the variable `saved` is not saved. You would expect browser caching of the two files (the document and `anyimage.gif`) to work for you, but the document's state from the last time the document was viewed is gone. Otherwise the alert would show 20 on the second viewing, and double each time you repeated the test.

However, life is not always that simple. If you use a Netscape browser, or Internet Explorer 4 or later, and type something into the lone field before the above test - the lone field's value *is* remembered. So, there are exceptions to the rule that nothing is remembered.

Java is a big exception. When you leave a URL that contains an applet, that applet is not necessarily wiped away. When you return to the URL, not only does the applet remain loaded, but also the applet's state (all of its variables and objects) is fully preserved as well. This is not an absolute - there are a number of reasons why you can't rely entirely on it - but it is the common case and a fair guide. It's even possible that the applet continued to work after the URL was left. It is easy to understand why this may be the case if we recall our discussion on the separate and independent system that the browser and the Java VM runs within.

The implication for the scriptwriter is that knowing when applets are loaded or 'fresh' (i.e. have yet to run for the first time) is a non-trivial affair.

JavaScript as an Applet Communication Conduit

Because Java applets have the power of a programming language behind them, they have the potential to communicate with each other. Images don't normally do this - otherwise there might be some unusually entertaining Web sites to visit! The mechanism for such communication may reside purely within Java; be assisted by HTML-supplied tag information; be enabled by glue technologies like ActiveX or LiveConnect; or occur via intermediate JavaScript scripts.

The implications for the scriptwriter are:

❑   JavaScript can interact with a single applet

❑   JavaScript is a useful intermediary for tying together applets

For this latter scenario, one can imagine a web page featuring a complex user interface created using a combination of Java-based UI widgets and standard HTML elements, and all co-ordinated via JavaScript.

The Authoritative Role of Java: Security Master

Because Java is held in high regard on the Internet, some of the responsibilities otherwise held by the non-Java parts of Web browsers have been given to it. In particular, Java has taken on the role of security manager for many aspects of the 4.x browsers. This is especially the case for Netscape. Plug-ins and ActiveX controls rarely provide fundamental services to the browser in a like manner.

JavaScript scripts must therefore appeal to the Java security manager if they want to perform insecure operations. We'll see more of that in the section *The Java Security Model* later.

Creating Java Applets

To get a feel for how creating a Java applet differs from writing JavaScript programs, let's create everybody's favourite `HelloWorld` applet in Java. Despite sophisticated Interactive Development Environments for Java development, many hardcore Java programmers still use a trusty text editor, such as vi or notepad for their daily development activities.

Other than the editor, you will need the following to start Java development.

❑   Acquire a copy of the Java development system. The simplest one is the JDK (Java Development Kit) from Sun, available for many platforms and for free. Look on http://java.sun.com.

❑   Understand the tools. The JDK comes with a `javac` program that is the compiler, and an `appletviewer` program that lets you test your applets without a browser. `appletviewer` is in effect a mini-browser that supports only one HTML tag, `<APPLET>`. The `javac` compiler doesn't combine your various Java classes together into a `.jar` file. You need the `jar` packager program to do that, which also forms part of the JDK.

❑   Set up your environment. The JDK tools need to be on your `PATH` variable. Next, the magic `CLASSPATH` environment variable must be set to the appropriate directories and JAR files. Usually just the present directory, `.`, is sufficient. `CLASSPATH` is less finicky in JDK 1.2.x because the path for system library classes is now kept in the system registry. Read your JDK documentation carefully. Lastly, the class to be compiled must have a filename that **matches** the class name, excepting the file extension.

Assuming that you have already installed the latest version of JDK and have set up your environment, use your favorite editor and enter the following code:

```
import java.applet.Applet;
import java.awt.*;

public class HelloWorld extends Applet {

    String myGreeting;

    public void paint(Graphics g) {
        myGreeting = "Hello World!";
        g.drawString(myGreeting, 30, 30);
    }
}
```

Save this file as `HelloWorld.java`.

Examining this simple code, we can see some glaring differences between JavaScript and Java:

❑ Every variable must be declared and have a fixed type (the `myGreeting` variable is of type `String`)

❑ Every programming element in Java is a class or belongs inside a class (even our `HelloWorld` applet)

❑ Java has rich library support that simplifies programming (the `import` statement brings in the required library)

❑ Object inheritance is supported and used heavily throughout (`extends Applet` means to inherit from the `Applet` class, and greatly simplifies the code needed to create an applet)

To compile the `.java` file into the binary `.class` file, type in from the command line:

`javac HelloWorld.java`

This should produce the `HelloWorld.class` applet file. Now create a simple `app.html` file containing:

```
<HTML>
<HEAD><TITLE>Hello World Applet</TITLE>
</HEAD>
<BODY>
    <APPLET CODE="HelloWorld" WIDTH=300  HEIGHT=250>
    </APPLET>
</BODY>
</HTML>
```

530

Load this file up in Netscape, and appreciate how easy it is to create a Java applet. Your very first Java applet should look like this:

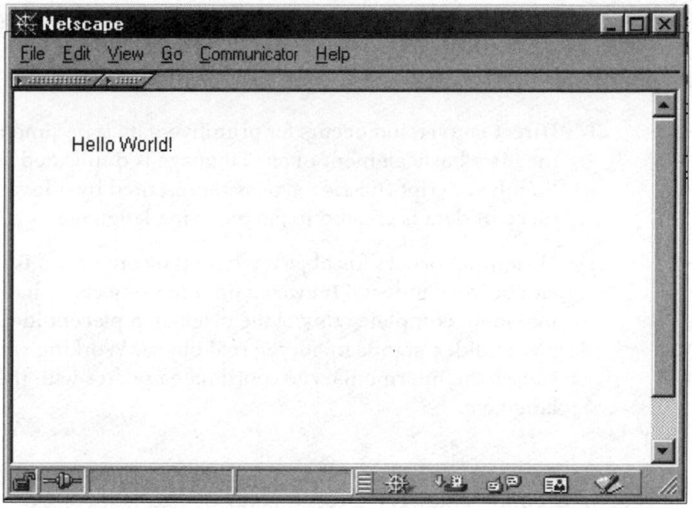

Crossing the Subsystems Boundary

The actual lines of code required to go from one language to the other (from the JavaScript subsystem to the Java VM) are very simple. The concepts behind the code need a little more work.

> Needless to say, in order to communicate between the two languages, both must be turned on in the preferences or options windows of the browser.

How Java and JavaScript Interact

In JavaScript, only JavaScript types, objects and syntax are allowed. In Java, only Java types, objects and syntax are allowed. These rules can never be broken.

If two human beings speak different languages, then an intermediary who knows both is required. So it is with Java and JavaScript, and the intermediary is LiveConnect for Netscape or ActiveX for Microsoft browsers. The intermediary's job is to *convert* from one language to the other. There are four things to convert:

❑ Primitive data types

❑ Objects

❑ Method and function calls

❑ Events

These things have roughly the same meaning in both Java and JavaScript languages, which makes the intermediary's conversion job relatively easy and efficient. There are two kinds of conversion.

- ❏ **Direct conversion** occurs for primitive data types, method calls, and events. Direct conversion means a basic element of one language is duplicated as a similar basic feature of the other language. So a JavaScript `Number` type is represented by a Java `Float` type when it is passed to Java. A new piece of data is created in the receiving language.

- ❏ **Wrapping** occurs for objects where the conversion is otherwise not so easy. Representing objects can be very messy if they contain other objects or have inheritance/prototype features. Instead of making a complete copy of the original, a placeholder is supplied in the second language. This placeholder 'stands in' for the real object. Working with the placeholder in the second language causes the intermediary to coordinate updates with the original object still stored in the first language.

In order to understand wrapping, think of a pottery kiln. The pots in the kiln are like Java objects inside the Java language environment. If you were to extract a pot to some other environment, you'd have to use asbestos gloves or an insulated tool to handle it. This at-a-distance approach is how JavaScript handles Java objects.

This table describes the conversions that occur. Java is unlike JavaScript in that there are both primitive types (numbers and characters and the like), and classes representing the primitive types. Literal values always have a primitive type (e.g. `float`) but variable's objects may be of the equivalent class type (e.g. `Float`).

Starting from JavaScript	Result in Java	Starting from Java	Result in JavaScript
Primitive Types			
Undefined	Cannot be converted	null	Null
`Boolean`	`Boolean`	`Boolean`	`Boolean`
`Number`	`Float`	`Float`	`Number`
`String`	`String`	`String`	`String`
Objects			
Host object	`JSObject` wrapper	`JSObject` wrapper	Real JavaScript object
Real JavaScript object	`JSObject` wrapper	Any real Java object	Wrapped Java object
Wrapped Java object	Real Java object	Array of objects	Wrapped Java object that allows array indices.

Starting from JavaScript	Result in Java	Starting from Java	Result in JavaScript
Method calls			
Wrapped Java object method call	Method call on real Java object	`JSObject.call()`	Named method of real JavaScript object called
Wrapped Java object's property is used	Property of real Java object is used	`JSObject.getMember()` `JSObject.setMember()`	Property of real JavaScript object is used
		`JSObject.getSlot()` `JSObject.setSlot()`	Array element of real JavaScript object is used
Events and Exceptions			
		Java exception thrown	JavaScript `onError` event

Calling Java from JavaScript

Recall that JavaScript is a loosely-typed language. Within JavaScript, values are converted between types automatically as appropriate. This policy applies to interacting with Java as well - all the conversion is done for you automatically, making the process particularly easy.

Java Connection Points

Java objects appear in the JavaScript browser object model as though they were host objects. Access to Java is achieved through the properties and methods of these objects. There are two kinds: applet objects and local class library objects.

window.document.applets

Just as `window.document.embeds` is an array of Plug-in objects embedded in an HTML document, `window.document.applets` is an array of the applets in that document. For example, to access the very first applet embedded in an HTML page:

```
window.document.applets[0];
```

If the HTML tag describing the applet has a NAME attribute (NAME=myapplet, for example), this can be used to identify the particular applet:

```
window.document.myapplet;
```

Each of the JavaScript array members is an object. Every Java applet has a main object that is the centre point of the applet. The objects that are JavaScript array elements are placeholders for the main objects of applets.

How do you know what properties apply to what applet? There are three options:

❏ Make the applet yourself

❏ Look at the applet source code

❏ Find documentation on the applet

JavaScript Graphics and Drawing with Java

We will see how argument conversion works, and how to make calls from JavaScript into Java applet methods by working through an example. The example examines how we can harness the power of Java's graphic libraries to create graphics drawing on a web page. In fact, without Java, your alternative to providing graphics drawing on web page is quite limited. A Java applet enables JavaScript to control powerful graphic libraries such as AWT, Swing and the Java2D APIs.

Our example here will use the AWT library and allow JavaScript code to control line drawing on the display area of a web browser. This is what the application looks like:

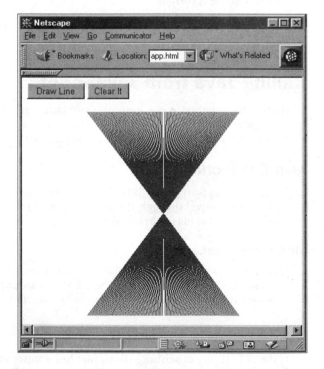

When you press the Draw Line button, the JavaScript script will repeatedly draw symmetry lines on the display area. The JavaScript program actually does this by repeatedly calling the drawLine() method provided by the applet. Clicking on the Clear button will clear the drawing screen. This is also done via a cross-subsystem call to the clearAll() method of the applet.

Here is the code for the HTML page, you can find it in the `LineApp.html` file:

```
<HTML>
<HEAD>
<SCRIPT>
var pressCount = 0;
var initX = 199;
var maxY = 299;

function drawIt()
{
    pressCount++;
    var sX = initX - (pressCount * 2);
    var eX = initX + (pressCount * 2);

    document.myApp.drawLine(sX, 0, eX, maxY);
    document.myApp.drawLine(sX, maxY, eX, 0);
}
</SCRIPT>
</HEAD>
<BODY>
<FORM NAME="myForm">
<INPUT TYPE="button" VALUE="Draw Line" onclick="drawIt()">
<INPUT TYPE="button" VALUE="Clear It" ONCLICK="pressCount=0;
document.myApp.clearAll()">
</FORM><APPLET NAME="myApp" CODE="LineApp.class" HEIGHT=300 WIDTH=400></APPLET>
</BODY>
</HTML>
```

In the `drawIt()` function, notice how the applet's `drawLine()` method is called:

```
document.myApp.drawLine(sX, 0, eX, maxY);
```

This is much the same as a host object, or a DHTML element. In the Java applet code we will examine later, the `drawLine()` method (the Java term for a function within an class) has the following calling signature:

```
public void drawLine(int sx, int sy, int ex, int ey);
```

Note how we rely on the type conversion service for the parameters provided by the LiveConnect or ActiveX interface layer between the two subsystems. The number variables and constants we passed from JavaScript just get converted to the required `int` type for the Java method call.

Now for the Java code. You can compile it yourself with `javac`, or use the class file that we have provided. The source is found in the `LineApp.java` file.

The first part of the Java program simply defines a new class, called ALine, that will be used in the actual applet. The ALine class bundles the properties of a line (like the start and end position, as well as its color) with the behavior of a line (how to draw itself). This design is typical of object-oriented programming languages such as Java.

```java
import java.awt.*;

class ALine {
    int startX;
    int startY;
    int endX;
    int endY;
    Color lineColor;

    public ALine(int sx, int sy, int ex, int ey, Color clr) {
        startX = sx;
        startY = sy;
        endX = ex;
        endY = ey;
        lineColor = clr;
    }

    public void draw(Graphics g) {
        g.setColor(lineColor);
        g.drawLine(startX, startY, endX, endY);
    }
}
```

The next portion of the code is the actual applet. The applet maintain a list of lines that it is supposed to draw. Screen updates occurs only at certain time, or when the repaint() method is called. These screen updates occurs automatically on an as-needed basis. The repaint() default implementation will call the user-defined paint() method to refresh the screen. When these updates occur, the paint() method will iterate through the list of lines and ask each one to draw itself onto the graphics context.

The public methods, which are exposed to JavaScript, are drawLine() and clearAll().They simply add an ALine object instance to the list and release all the lines on the list respectively. The paint() method is also public, but we have inherited and overridden this method to do our own painting; it is not called directly from JavaScript.

```java
import java.applet.Applet;
import java.awt.*;

public class LineApp extends Applet {
    int initCount = 0;
    int startCount = 0;
    int stopCount = 0;
    int destroyCount = 0;
    int drawIndex = 0;
    ALine drawList[] = new ALine[500];

    public void paint(Graphics g) {
        g.setColor(Color.white);
        g.fillRect(0, 0, size().width, size().height);

        for (int i = 0; i < drawIndex; i++)
            drawList[i].draw(g);
    }
```

```
        public void drawLine(int sx, int sy, int ex, int ey) {
            drawList[drawIndex] = new ALine(sx, sy, ex, ey, Color.red);
            drawIndex++;
            repaint();
        }

        public void clearAll() {
            drawIndex = 0;
            repaint();
        }
    }
```

Try out the application by loading the `LineApp.html` page in a browser. You will see how easy it is to get JavaScript code talking to Java applets on a per-method granularity.

This example have shown us that:

❑ Calling the method of a Java applet from JavaScript is as easy as calling the methods of a host object

❑ Parameter data type conversion between JavaScript and Java is automatic, and it is designed to usually 'do the right thing'

❑ Making a Java applet work for you on a scripted web page is easy, and often offers a less complex solution to an otherwise complex problem

Common JavaScript to Java Calling Problems

What if the number or type of the arguments varies between a call from JavaScript and its Java definition?

The inter-subsystem glue layer, LiveConnect or ActiveX, will try very hard to do a proper conversion for you. If conversion is not possible, you may see a message similar to this:

```
Alert - Netscape                                          _ □ X
JavaScript Error: no Java method Hello2.greet matching JavaScript
arguments (string, string)




                              OK
```

Java methods are not generally as flexible as JavaScript methods. Each method usually has an exact number of arguments with exact types. The moral to the story is not to rely on type conversion - be organized enough to always supply the right number of values of the right types.

JavaScript Direct System Access via window.Packages

Applets are formed from class files. Some of these class files are standard classes. Just as the browser object model is the meat and drink of JavaScript, so are the standard classes for Java. One can think of them as the Java equivalents to the native and built-in JavaScript objects provided by the ECMAScript specification. These classes are stored locally with the browser, and for Navigator 3.x and Navigator 4.x can be accessed directly from JavaScript.

The window.Packages property gives access to these classes. Inconveniently, packages is a reserved word in JavaScript, so the uppercase 'P' is required. These Java classes are formed into a hierarchy, but it's not an object hierarchy (a hierarchy of object instances) - rather it's a class hierarchy (a hierarchy of object types), with each class appearing at most once. A class hierarchy is the static specification of classes and their inheritance relationship whereas an object hierarchy is a runtime grouping of object instances. The class hierarchy is multilevel, so these are all valid classes:

```
window.Packages.java.lang.System;
window.Packages.netscape.security.PrivilegeManager;
window.Packages.sun.tools.debug.StackFrame;
window.Packages.com.somethingsoft.stuff.Special;
```

Apart from the Packages.java case, the first word after Packages is by convention the name of a company that invented that part of the class hierarchy, hence sun, netscape and the new hopeful somethingsoft. Technically, such a name should be preceded by org or com, in a similar way to domain names, but in reverse. Because the java, netscape and sun cases are so commonly used, these three cases *only* are also accessible *without* the Packages keyword:

```
window.java.lang.System;
window.netscape.security.PrivilegeManager;
window.sun.tools.debug.StackFrame;
```

The online documentation for developers at http://java.sun.com describes the whole hierarchy of classes.

Several example of using these classes have been illustrated already. In Chapter 17, on Debugging, we'll make good use of this simple example:

```
java.lang.System.out.println("Window name is: " + top.name);
```

This example writes the supplied data out to the Java console, and looks straightforward. However, there is a twist in the tail: the hierarchy referred to is a hierarchy of classes, not objects. So when the println() method is called, what object does it belong to? We'll also use this next line in Chapter 17 to show where is the return data extracted from:

```
str = java.lang.System.getProperty('os.name');
```

The answer is that the properties and methods of a Java object can optionally be static. Normally a method is associated with an object, so there is one per object of a given class. Static methods are associated with the class, not a particular object (class instance), so there is one *total*, independent of, and shared by, all objects of the class. This imaginary applet illustrates the following:

```
import java.applet.Applet;
import java.awt.Graphics;

public class Example extends Applet {
    static public String data = 'test';  // Always available, shared by objects

    public void first() {                 // Available when an Example object is
                                          // present
    }

    static public void second() {         // Available without an Example object
    }
}
```

The `second()` method is `static` and therefore can be used like the `println()` method we saw earlier, without any object instance being needed. The `first()` method is not static and can only be called as part of an object. The `data` variable (a class **attribute**) is also `static`, so it is accessible - there will always be exactly one copy of the variable. For JavaScript scriptwriters, `static` Java methods and attributes are the easiest to use.

For non-static members, a different approach is required. This Netscape-only JavaScript function exploits local classes:

```
function save_it(filename, filedata)
{
    netscape.security.PrivilegeManager.enablePrivilege("UniversalFileAccess");
    var jo_writer = new java.io.FileWriter(jo_file);
    jo_writer.write(filedata,0,filedata.length);
    jo_writer.close();
    netscape.security.PrivilegeManager.disablePrivilege("UniversalFileAccess");
}
```

The lines starting `netscape...` exploit static methods as above. To use other Java methods, first a Java object must be created, and then the method can be invoked from this object. In this example, two JavaScript objects that wrap one Java object each are created - `jo_file` and `jo_stream`. The calls to the security manager request permission to write to the local file system via these objects, which would otherwise not be allowed.

This example is effectively 'arms-length' Java programming - the whole example is written in JavaScript. No Java object or method is ever directly touched - only Java object wrappers and Java method wrappers. Each time a Java method wrapper is called, processing 'descends' into the Java language, does the work and then returns to JavaScript. The second new operation shows how a wrapped Java object can be handed to a wrapped Java method as an argument. When it is passed to Java it all unwraps properly and the real Java method is called with the real Java object.

In order to fully exploit this feature you need to be conversant with the Java standard class hierarchies. If you are, you can achieve quite a lot using JavaScript that would otherwise require an applet. The only catch is that this approach is slower than directly using an applet, because of all the wrapping and unwrapping that goes on.

Understanding the Applet Lifecycle

As remarked earlier, applets can exhibit some odd behavior when loading or running. If the applet you are trying to manage from JavaScript disappears, spits errors, won't start, or is generally difficult, review these details.

When Applets are Loaded

Inside Java there is a bit of functionality called a **class loader** that is responsible for retrieving applet class files from across the Internet. It is a lazy soul. It only retrieves applet files when they are absolutely needed. This means an applet can spend a long time in a partially loaded state if it has sufficient classes at hand to do useful work.

For a currently running applet, you can be confident that the main class of the applet has loaded - otherwise the applet couldn't have started. If you call a method of an applet from JavaScript, and that method requires additional classes to be loaded, then execution will halt while the class loader fetches whatever is needed. This can result in very jerky behaviour if the applet irregularly stalls to augment itself with further classes. Also, browsers have a security hobble that prevents JavaScript from making network connections. For Netscape browsers less than version 4.0, this hobble extends to the network connections used to retrieve applet class files. In those cases, if JavaScript calls an applet method that requires classes to be loaded, an error will occur.

To avoid both of these problems, the applet creator should enhance the applet so that when it starts, all the classes are retrieved straightaway. We'll see how in a moment. Interested readers are also referred to the Netscape developer support site for more information, `http://developer.netscape.com`.

What Applets Do

Applets lead complicated lives. An image is either loading or loaded, but applets can be in any one of six states. Three of these start the applet up and three shut it down.

The official names for the three startup states are **Loaded**, **Initialized** and **Started**. When a new document with an applet is displayed in the browser, the applet quickly passes through each of these states, ending with Started:

❑ **Loaded** means the main class of the applet has been retrieved by the class loader.

❑ **Initialized** means the special `init()` method of the applet has been called. This gives the applet designer a chance to do some preparation work before the applet is officially started. You can use the `init()` class to load all the classes you need to make the applet work without pause or in conjunction with JavaScript in older Netscape browsers.

❑ **Started** means the applet is running, or expecting user input.

The official names for the three shutdown states are **Stopped**, **Destroyed** and **Disposed**. When an applet is due to be removed, or the browser is shutdown, the applet quickly passes through each of these states, ending with Disposed:

❑ **Stopped**. The applet is not running but all its state (data and objects) is intact.

❑ **Destroyed**. The special destroy() method of the applet has been called. This gives the applet designer a change to do any special cleanup required before the applet finally goes away.

❑ **Disposed**. All the applet's content is discarded - it is gone.

For Microsoft browsers, the use of these states is straightforward. When a URL with an applet is displayed in a window, the three startup states are run through. If the URL is replaced with another one, the shutdown states are run through. Netscape browsers are not so easy.

Netscape browsers attempt to give applets more flexibility. They do this by allowing applets to survive as long as the document they are a part of is retained somewhere in the browser's history. If a URL containing an applet is moved to the history list because the user displays a different URL, the applet is merely stopped, not destroyed. If the original URL is returned to, the applet is started again.

The consequences are that without planning ahead, the scriptwriter can't tell if the applet is running for the first time, or continuing from where it last left off. The way to overcome this is to get the Java applet to set a JavaScript variable in its init() method. When the document loads, if the JavaScript variable exists, the applet is running for the first time. If it doesn't, the Java applet is picking up where it left off. See the *Handling JavaScript from Java* section for how to do this.

There is a further complication with this system. If the user creates a very long history of pages, all with applets, a great deal of the computer's resources will be spent holding on to Stopped applets that aren't visible. Netscape browsers handle this by setting an arbitrary maximum of 10 applets held in this way. If more than 10 occur, some will be moved to Destroyed and then Disposed. If the page is returned to, those applets will be restarted from the beginning. This is not easy for the scriptwriter to handle - better to accept that the applet was aborted in an untimely way and start again. However, the limit of 10 can be lifted higher for Netscape 4.0 with this JavaScript statement:

```
netscape.applet.Control.setAppletPruningThreshold(99);   // 99 applets? - plenty.
```

Finally, there is a second complication. Java is a general programming language and there are ways of avoiding the strict interpretation of these six states. The best the browser can do is *label* the applet as being in one of the states, and hope that its functionality follows suit in the expected way. An applet need only re-write the stop() method of the Applet class to achieve this. In a perfect world this would be documented with the applet...

How to Start Again

If you are confused about the state of a given applet you can force a complete reload from the remote location the applet came from as follows:

❑ Simultaneously, *Shift* and the Reload button on Netscape browsers

❑ Simultaneously, *Ctrl* and the Refresh button on Microsoft browsers

How to Detect the Version of Java in Use

This code snippet will report the version of the JVM running inside your browser. Applets can be developed to support a specific version of JVM or use the lowest common denominator approach, depending on application requirements.

```
javascript:alert(java.lang.System.getProperty('java.version'));
```

Handling JavaScript from Java

The Java language doesn't automatically provide easy access to the browser's HTML features, such as form elements. By communicating from Java to JavaScript, JavaScript's access to those features can be exploited by Java.

The MAYSCRIPT attribute of the <APPLET> tag, and the Java JSObject and JSException classes provide the mechanism for communicating with JavaScript. These features are Netscape innovations applying to Navigator 3.x and 4. x. Thanks to LiveConnect compatibility, applets and HTML pages developed using these features will also run on the latest Internet Explorer 4.x and 5.x browsers. However, the only officially supported way to call from within Microsoft's Java VM into the JavaScript subsystem when dealing with Microsoft Internet Explorer product is through their COM technology. Our focus in the rest of this chapter will be on Netscape's implementation since it is – to all intents and purposes – currently the cross-browser solution for the problem.

In practice, the need to call JavaScript from Java seldom occurs. Because of this low demand, there is no true cross browser way of accessing the JavaScript subsystem from Java. Although we will cover a technique for doing so, it's usually a special case. That may well change in the near future with current developments in the Web and XML world.

MAYSCRIPT

If the MAYSCRIPT attribute is not present, no communication from Java to JavaScript is possible. You can always go from JavaScript to Java, however. The reason behind this is that an HTML document author or a JavaScript scriptwriter might want to use a third party applet, but might not trust the applet enough to be willing to expose their own work to that applet. Without MAYSCRIPT, the applet is trapped in Java-land. Chapter 4 has an example of MAYSCRIPT.

If there is more than one applet embedded in a given page, some may have the MAYSCRIPT attribute and others not. This is a more flexible arrangement than page signing, discussed in Chapter 18, where all the JavaScript is signed, or none of it is. However, flexibility creates a complication. Because Java applets can interact with each other directly, a non-MAYSCRIPTed applet might try to get access to JavaScript by communicating with a MAYSCRIPTed applet that does have access. That could be bad.

Such a security hole is prevented by the class loader that applets rely on to get into the browser in the first place. Two applets share a class loader only if the CODEBASE, ARCHIVE and MAYSCRIPT attributes for both applets' tag match *and* if the applets are embedded in the same document. Otherwise, they have a separate class loader. So, on a typical single page of applets, there might be two class loaders used: one for MAYSCRIPTed applets, and one for the rest. This has the additional limitation of preventing applets in different frames (for example) talking directly to each other under all circumstances. For those applets, MAYSCRIPT and JavaScript must be used, or else Netscape 4.0's BeanConnect enhancements to LiveConnect investigated.

The *Errors and Events* section below illustrates what happens when there are mix-ups with
MAYSCRIPT.

JSObject

Just as JavaScript relies on the document.applets and Packages JavaScript objects to get access
to Java, Java relies on objects of the netscape.javascript.JSObject Java class. This class is
used for all possible types of JavaScript objects, no matter what typeof() might report for the
object.

JSObject.getWindow()

It's fine to use JSObject to represent all JavaScript objects within Java, but how do you get the first
such object? JSObject has a static method called getWindow() which returns a Java object that
wraps the JavaScript object that window tracks. This example applet illustrates that call:

```
import java.applet.Applet;
import netscape.javascript.*;        // Required for JavaScript access

public class Test extends Applet {
    JSObject window;                  // To match the JavaScript one of the same name

    public void init() {
        window = JSObject.getWindow(this);
        // .. more stuff ..
    }

    // .. more stuff ..
}
```

Compile it with the following command, to use the Java runtime JAR file provided with Netscape 4.x
communicator. This JAR file contains the netscape.javascript package:

```
C:\>javac -classpath C:\Netscape\communicator\program\java\classes\java40.jar
Test.java
```

Since the init() method is responsible for organising the applet before it really gets going, it's a
logical place to grab the JavaScript window object. Stored in a property of the instance, it's available
from then on. See the *Errors and Events* section later for why you might grab the window object
outside init() instead.

Finding a JavaScript Object

Once you have the window object, it's just a matter of stepping through the JavaScript object
hierarchy until you reach the bit you want. This Java code snippet locates the
window.document.location object using the getMember() method of the JSObject wrapper
object to return a second wrapper object for the specified sub-object. The casting to JSObject is
necessary since all return objects have JSObject as their base class (i.e. they inherit from
JSObject):

```
// ... more ...
JSObject win = JSObject.getWindow(this);
JSObject doc = (JSObject)win.getMember("document");
JSObject loc = (JSObject)doc.getMember("location");    // Found it
// ... more ...
```

Chapter 15

Executing any JavaScript Code

It's also possible to run an arbitrary piece of JavaScript from within Java. This includes declaring new JavaScript functions, or attaching new properties to existing JavaScript objects. If you specifically prefer the floating point math in JavaScript (there's no real reason to) you can do this:

```
// Find the area of a circle, radius 2, using JavaScript
JSObject window = JSObject.getWindow(this);
Number area = (Number)window.eval("Math.PI * " + 2 + " * " + 2);
```

Notice how the addition sign can be used for string concatenation in Java just as it is in JavaScript. This functionality is the easiest way to interact with JavaScript browser objects as these examples show.

❑   Populate an HTML text field with a Java value:

```
JSObject.getWindow(this).eval("window.document.form1.field1.value = " +
java_string);
```

❑   Make an alert appear with a Java string as the message:

```
JSObject.getWindow(this).eval("window.alert('message from Java')");
```

In both these cases, the wrapped copy of the JavaScript window object is only temporarily created - long enough for the eval() method to pass the statements to JavaScript and return.

Since the class file is compiled into a binary format, the bits of JavaScript in the class file are very difficult for the browser user to look at. This may be the best way for scriptwriters to protect their code from being stolen, but it is a great deal of effort to go to, and is *still* not as secure as digital signing, because of the possibility of a hacker decompiling the applet. If the JavaScript is stored as Java strings, possibly with a simple encryption like the 'rot13' encryption used on the Internet in the days before encrypted e-mail, then it is a great deal of effort for even a hacker to get the script. But it's still possible: all a suitable maniac requires is a reverse Java-compiler (a decompiler) and time better spent on something else.

Calling from Java to JavaScript - A Banner Rotator Applet

Another way to execute JavaScript code is using the window.call() method. Let us illustrate how this is done through a practical example. It is an ad banner rotator applet that you may have seen on some websites. Our version rotates through three advertisements with a 5 seconds interval. If the user clicks on any of the ads, the rotator applet will call back into a JavaScript function to carry out some custom operation. The following figure shows the applet in action:

Here is the code of the hosting HTML page. You can find it in the `banner.html` file.

```
<HTML>
<HEAD>
<SCRIPT>
function adClicked(inURL)
{
    document.location = inURL;
}
</SCRIPT>
</HEAD>
<BODY>

<APPLET NAME="myApp" CODE="SimpleBanner.class" HEIGHT=60 WIDTH=468 MAYSCRIPT>
<PARAM NAME="ad0" VALUE="ad1.gif">
<PARAM NAME="url0" VALUE="ndest1.html">
<PARAM NAME="ad1" VALUE="ad2.gif">
<PARAM NAME="url1" VALUE="ndest2.html">
<PARAM NAME="ad2" VALUE="ad3.gif">
<PARAM NAME="url2" VALUE="ndest3.html">
</APPLET>
</BODY>
</HTML>
```

The `adClicked()` function is the callback that the applet will make if the user clicks on one of the displayed banner. The parameter, `inURL`, will reflect the URL corresponding to the banner clicked. This is a very simple action that can accomplished by other means, but it suffices here. Of course, one can easily rewrite the `adClicked()` function to perform other more complex duties. The point we are trying to illustrate is the flexibility offered by being able to make callbacks from Java into the JavaScript subsystem.

Note the `<PARAM>` tags used to pass the ads and destination URL information into the applet. This is the only official way of passing initialization data from an HTML page into an applet upon loading. We obviously need the `MAYSCRIPT` attribute since the Java applet will be making a callback.

Below is the Java applet code, you can find the source in the `SimpleBanner.java` file. A synopsis of what is happening with this code is:

❑ All the banner ads and associated destination URLs are read into two arrays, an image array called `adImages`, and a `String` array called `adURLs`

❑ A thread (a very lightweight process) is spawned to run in the background, see the `run()` method. This thread, called `rotator`, will wake up every `DELAY_TIME` (5 seconds) and change a variable called `currentAd` – it is this action that causes the ad to rotate

❑ The `paint()` method always displays the banner associated with the `currentAd` variable on the screen

❑ A mouse click handler is written to invoke a method called `performJSAction()` whenever the banner is clicked on

❑ The `performJSAction()` methods grabs the URL associated with the `currentAd` variable, and calls back into the JavaScript function called `adClicked()`. The URL is passed as an argument during this call. This call is made through `window.call()`, after obtaining the window reference through the `JSObject`

You can track this action through the following code.

```
import netscape.javascript.JSObject;
import java.applet.*;
import java.awt.*;
import java.awt.event.*;
import java.net.*;

public class SimpleBanner extends Applet implements Runnable {
    Thread rotator;
    Image banners;

    JSObject window = null;

    String tpGif;
    String tpURL;
    int currentAd = 0;
    int adCount = 0;
    static final int MAX_ADS = 20;
    static final int DELAY_TIME = 5000; // ms
    Image adImages[] = new Image[MAX_ADS];
    String adURLs[] = new String[MAX_ADS];

    public void init() {
        for (int i = 0; i < MAX_ADS; i++) {
            if ((tpGif = getParameter("ad" + i)) == null) {
                adCount = i;
                break;
            }

            adURLs[i] = getParameter("url" + i);
            adImages[i] = getImage(getDocumentBase(), tpGif);
        }

        addMouseListener(new MouseAdapter() {
                        public void mouseClicked(MouseEvent e) {
                            System.out.println("in here ... clicked");
                            performJSAction();
                        }
                    });

        rotator = new Thread(this);
        rotator.start();
    }

    public void paint(Graphics g) {
        g.drawImage(adImages[currentAd], 0, 0, this);
    }

    public void update(Graphics g) {
        paint(g);
    }

    public void start() {
        rotator.resume();
    }

    public void stop() {
        rotator.suspend();
    }

    public void destroy() {
        rotator.stop();
        rotator.destroy();
    }
```

```
    public void run() {
        while (true) {
            try {
                Thread.currentThread().sleep(DELAY_TIME);
                currentAd = (currentAd + 1) % adCount;
            } catch (InterruptedException e) {
            }

            repaint();
        }
    }

    public void ChangeAd() {
        currentAd = (currentAd + 1) % adCount;
        repaint();
    }

    public void performJSAction() {
        if (window == null)
            window = JSObject.getWindow(this);

        Object testArray[] = new Object[1];
        testArray[0] = new String(adURLs[currentAd]);
        window.call("adClicked", testArray);
    }
}
```

The above code will run with the latest version of the Netscape browser, 4.x. In fact, thanks to compatibility with Netscape's LiveConnect, you can also run it as-is using Internet Explorer 4.x or 5. Unless you have a server supporting SSL to serve your web pages via the secure https: protocol or you sign your applets, you must tell Netscape explicitly to trust your code as a security principal (see *The Java Security Model* later in this chapter). You must override the security manager by providing CODEBASE PRINCIPAL. Currently, this can only be done via editing of the prefs.js (or preferences.js on UNIX) file in your user directory:

```
user_pref("signed.applets.codebase_principal_support", true);
```

Enabling CODEBASE PRINCIPAL essentially asks Netscape to temporary trust all code coming from the non-secure codebase server or directory. This should only be enabled for development purposes. This line should be added only while the Netscape browser is not running.

Not all problems requires an explicit callback across the two subsystems. In fact, we could have done our URL switching in the previous example without such a call. Doing so will enable our solution to work even with 3.x level browsers. The next section will illustrate how the problem can be solved without the callback.

Banner Rotator: A 3.x Compatible and Cross Browser Solution

A Java applet can live happily and the programmer can avoid headaches by staying within the Java subsystem (without calling across to JavaScript). This is especially true if the application is to be deployed on the Internet rather than an intranet, where 3.x level browsers are still prevalent. For our example, we can solve the problem by using a method from the standard Java applet library class that supports the applet context.

The applet context can be obtained from the applet.getAppletContext() method. The method on the applet context that we are interested in is called showDocument(). This method allows us to cause the browser to change its displayed page, without ever exiting the Java security sandbox to do so.

You can find the source code to this in the `DualBanner.java` file. The changes are minimal - in the `init()` method, we now have the mouse click handler calling `moveURL()`:

```
public void init() {
    addMouseListener(new MouseAdapter() {
                    public void mouseClicked(MouseEvent e) {
                        System.out.println("in here ... clicked");
                        moveURL();
                    }
                });

    for (int i = 0; i < MAX_ADS; i++) {
        if ((tpGif = getParameter("ad" + i)) == null) {
            adCount = i;
            break;
        }

        adURLs[i] = getParameter("url" + i);
        adImages[i] = getImage(getDocumentBase(), tpGif);
    }

    rotator = new Thread(this);
    rotator.start();
}
```

And the `moveURL()` function is defined as:

```
public void moveURL() {
    try {
        getAppletContext().showDocument(new URL(getDocumentBase(),
                                        adURLs[currentAd]));
    } catch (Exception ex) {
    }
}
```

You can find the revised cross browser host file in `dbanner.html` (it just points to the `DualBanner` class and removes the scripting), and the Java source file for the updated applet in the `DualBanner.java` file. In hindsight, we now realize why the versatile tree controller applet used in the Chapter 10 case study does not provide a way to call back into a JavaScript function. It did so to maintain cross-browser compatibility and is thus applicable to the largest possible user base. We see in this example that compatibility is less of an issue if we eliminate the cross sub-system calls. The reader is encouraged to try writing a pure JavaScript based banner program as an exercise.

Lessons Well Learnt - Keep it Simple

Some observations that we can make from our code examination for Java to JavaScript calling are:

❑ Examine design alternatives if you feel that Java to JavaScript calling is necessary; it is seldom the only solution

❑ If you know you will be using secured servers and fixed level of browsers throughout the lifetime of your Intranet project, then maybe you have a case for doing Java to JavaScript calling

Errors and Exceptions

The Java compiler and interpreter are very fussy about data types and so on, so numerous errors that are hard to track down in JavaScript yield a message almost immediately in Java. However, problems can still happen. In Java, bad things usually result in an exception being thrown. An **exception** is just a particular type of Java object. The fact that it is **thrown** means that some piece of code that could have been well-behaved encountered an unusual condition and issued a complaint instead. The complaint takes the form of an exception object which is catered for by special Java syntax distantly related to `if` statements - the `try-catch` blocks you saw in the code of the previous two examples.

There are different classes of Java exceptions. The `netscape.javascript.JSException` class is just for JavaScript-related exceptions. Java code that calls JavaScript can be written to either specially handle this exception type, or leave it up to someone else. Unlike the `JSObject` class, the `JSException` class doesn't reflect any object in the browser hierarchy.

Because this class is really for Java programmers, its details aren't of much interest to a scriptwriter. However, scriptwriters need to understand that `JSException` exceptions (and Java exceptions generally) can cause JavaScript `onError` event handlers to execute. This only occurs if an exception is thrown and it is not **caught** (captured and handled) inside the Java applet. This applet shows the case where a `JSException` is handled without using the JavaScript `onError` handler:

```
import java.applet.Applet;
import netscape.javascript.*;

public class Test extends Applet {
    public void test_it() {
        JSObject win = JSObject.getWindow(this);
        try {
            throw new JSException();            // Force a JSException to be created
        } catch (JSException e) {
            JSObject.getWindow(this).eval("alert('Exception detected')"); //Caught it
        }
    }
}
```

In this applet, the `catch` statement ensures that the `Exception` never reaches JavaScript. The content of the catch block does choose to show a JavaScript alert, but it could just as easily be silent.

There is a possibility that can occur if a Java applet attempts to exploit JavaScript features when the `MAYSCRIPT` attribute is missing. An exception will result as for the other cases but not if the attempt in made inside the applet's `init()` method. The applet has yet to start when the `init()` method is called, so the normal exception system isn't supported. Instead, the user will be warned on the status line of the browser window that a `MAYSCRIPT` attribute is missing.

With the latest version of Netscape browser, JavaScript exception messages no longer pops up annoying alert boxes. However, you can still obtain the same exception information by calling up the JavaScript console (i.e. typing `javascript:` as a URL entry).

The Java Security Model

Apart from the general security provided by a browser, Java has its own security system. Both Netscape and Microsoft browsers take advantage of that security system in order to control access to dangerous features such as the writing of files on the browser's local computer. Each vendor does it differently. The model is used for the whole browser, not just for the JVM part of it.

For Microsoft Internet Explorer 4.x, the Authenticode code signing system allows the Java security information to be included as data with the code being signed, whether Java or JavaScript. Apart from organising the signing process, described in Chapter 18, there are no implications for JavaScript scripts. A correctly signed script will be able to exploit secure Java features via ActiveX the same as non-secured features.

For Netscape Communicator 4.x, the security information must be included as part of the content of JavaScript scripts and Java applets. The script can be signed or not signed. If not signed, the user will not be able to exploit secure Java features because of the untrusted principal (only digital certificates are by default trusted). As explained earlier in the banner example, one can make a setting change in the prefs.js file to ask the browser to trust the codebase as the principal. It is a scriptwriting task to setup the security access properly, and the details contributed by Java are discussed here.

Java Security Theory

Security normally applies to people - login accounts, locks on doors or identity checks. Those people who are considered 'safe' have passwords, keys, and ID which give them access to computers, rooms and expensive nightclubs. People aren't the issue for the Java security model. Foreign code loaded into a browser is - whether it is Java or JavaScript code.

Java 1.1 Security

The security model adopted for the 4.0 browsers is based on the security model innovated for the 1.1 release of Java.

For this model, the precious resources that need to be kept safe are called **targets**. A target is a general name - it could be anything deemed important. For Java, it means classes that do possibly insecure things, like network connections or file writing. For JavaScript it means all those Java classes plus various features of the browser only available to signed scripts, like the alwaysRaised option of the window.open() method in JavaScript 1.2.

The access mechanism for these targets is called a **privilege**. Once a suitable privilege is **granted**, the target's precious features may be exploited. Before they actually are exploited, a switch must be thrown to put the target in unsafe mode - this is called **enabling** the privilege. The privilege ought to be **disabled** when it is finished with.

The protagonist that requests privileges be granted is called a **principal**. Conceptually, anything can be a principal. Under this security model, however, only digital certificates are trusted as principals. In our case, if we made the appropriate change in the prefs.js file, our Java codebase can also be made the principal (only advised during testing). A codebase means a place that program code originates from. A place that program code originates from means a URL, and a URL means a file like a Java .class file, a JavaScript .js file, a Java-embedded HTML file or any other suitable format for code or scripts such as .jar files.

So a principal requests privileges be granted for particular targets such as Java classes or browser features, and once they are, enables those privileges, performs the functionality of interest, and disables them until that functionality is needed again. The questions remaining are: who grants the privileges, and what privileges do they grant? The browser grants them, either automatically by verifying an attached digital certificate, or by prompting the user for permission. The Java standard plus the browser maker define the privileges, so you have to refer to documentation. See the Reference section for Netscape's list. This diagram summarises the interactions:

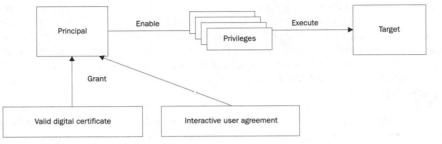

Manageable Privileges

The security system is supposed to be 'fine grained'. This means that the features that are targets are primitive and numerous in nature, and can be granted individually. This is beneficial for programmers who want close-up control of the system, but can be an administration headache. Simple operations like creating and copying a file might require privileges for several targets to be granted. More complex scripts might ask for dozens of privileges. Whether it's the user that has to grant the privileges interactively, or the developer who has to organise the signed scripts, this is not so practical.

A macro target is a target which is a collection of other targets. By requesting privileges on a macro target, all the privilege requests for the collection are made. Macro targets usually group a small number of like-minded targets, like all file targets, or all networking targets. This serves to reduce the administration problem somewhat. Macro targets are used in exactly the same way as other targets.

Microsoft's Internet Explorer 4.x goes one step further, introducing security zones. A security zone is a just a collection of targets, macro or otherwise that specifies a whole security profile for a given principal (script or file). This way, all the required targets are bundled into a single named item. The browser can then be loaded with a number of security zones, and scripts and applets indicate which zone they require privileges for. The zone description can be 'dumbed down' sufficiently that the user can make an informed decision about whether to grant access or not.

Netscape Use of Features

You may well be sick of the sight of this JavaScript function, since this is its third appearance:

```
function save_it(filename, filedata);
{
    netscape.security.PrivilegeManager.enablePrivilege("UniversalFileWrite");
    var jo_file   = new java.io.FileOutputStream(filename);
    var jo_stream = new java.io.DataOutputStream(jo_file);
    jo_stream.writeChars(filedata);
    jo_stream.close();
    netscape.security.PrivilegeManager.disablePrivilege("UniversalFileWrite");
}
```

The **privilege manager** is the part of Java and of the browser that allows privileges to be enabled and disabled. It is stored in local class files with the browser so it is directly accessible from JavaScript whether an applet exists in the HTML document or not.

Summary

The features that Java and Java applets make available in browsers create new horizons for JavaScript scriptwriters. Via glue technologies like ActiveX and LiveConnect nearly all the features of Java can be exploited from JavaScript. The only drawback to a scriptwriter may be that the necessity of learning many Java concepts can be burdensome. To be a well-rounded web application designer, the need to learn Java as an application design tool cannot be underestimated. Fortunately, every sign points to great rewards ahead for scriptwriters who take the extra time to master the Java programming language.

While technology and methods do exist for Java applet code to call back into the JavaScript subsystem, there is seldom any absolute need for this. In fact, doing so require venturing outside the basic Java sandbox (and browser basic) security model; and you must be prepared for dealing with highly browser specific and/or even version specific support issues.

Two important issues when dealing with Java are applet lifetimes and security. The former can easily confuse the situation when the scriptwriter is testing JavaScript web applications. The latter is indispensable if the scriptwriter wishes to exceed the ordinary bounds of the browser's functionality.

Through an exploration of four complete applets, we have observed first hand how to code both JavaScript programs and Java applets that can inter-work with each other within a web application.

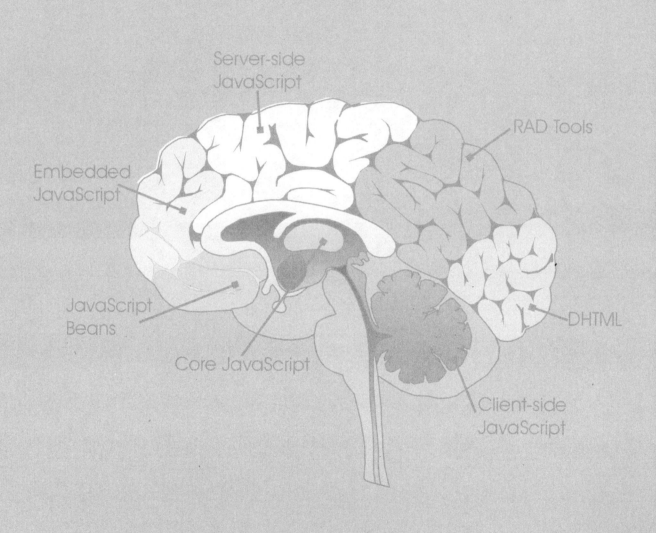

Server-side
JavaScript

RAD Tools

Embedded
JavaScript

JavaScript
Beans

Core JavaScript

DHTML

Client-side
JavaScript

Java and JavaScript Beyond the Browser

We've seen in the previous chapter that Java and JavaScript together can form a dynamic combination in creating potent web based applications. Unfortunately, we seem to be restricted at every turn because of the stringent security requirement of the browser, and of the Java applet sandbox security model. It's the equivalent of owning a private jet plane, but use it only to taxi along the ground all the time – a highly frustrating situation. If only we could break out of these security shackles....

Examined on its own merit, Java as a platform is evolving very quickly, with a new API or library being announced almost every other week. Developer support for the technology is phenomenal. There now exists more than a critical mass of Java code and code libraries available that most application problems can be solved efficiently using a combination of pre-existing components and some custom coding.

On the Internet, JavaScript acts as the glue of choice for webmasters the world over. It is also one of the easiest programming languages to learn and master. Its easy-to-program nature, combined with wide availability on almost all current browsers, makes it one of the most frequently used programming language in the computing world.

What if we can harness the best of all worlds, and:

❑ Inherit the ease of learning, simple programming model, quick prototyping, and no compilation required characteristics of JavaScript

❑ Inherit the robust libraries, huge base of existing applications and APIs in all problem domains, provided by Java

- Have the ability to code robust, custom reusable modules using a proven language like Java
- Have the ability to break out of all security restrictions, and develop full blown stand-alone applications
- Have all these benefits all rolled into one development technology, with no independently running isolated subsystem to navigate

What if we can have all of the above? Well, we would have invented FESI!

Introducing FESI

FESI (pronounced like fuzzy) is an unassuming acronym for **FREE EcmaScript Interpreter**, an ECMAScript interpreter written in Java. The ECMAScript supported by FESI conforms to ECMA 262, June 1997 specifications and was written by Jean-Marc Lugrin. Furthermore, release 1.1.2 (dated May 8, 1999) has built-in support for Java 1.2, Swing 1.1 and CORBA Accessors. The Swing 1.1 support provides a large library of user interface widgets, while CORBA Accessors provides FESI with access to the world of distributed CORBA objects. We will code some of the Swing widgets later on in this chapter but CORBA is out of the scope of this chapter. Interested readers should have a look at http://www.omg.org/ for more information.

Here is the schematic diagram for what FESI really is:

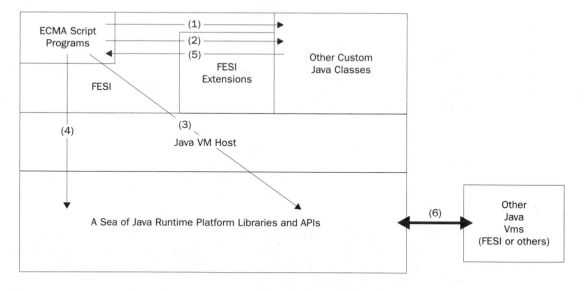

FESI combines JavaScript and Java into one single subsystem

FESI effectively combines the flexibility and impromptu nature of JavaScript with the powerful and robust quality of Java into one single seamless subsystem. Here are just some of the possibilities this architecture provide:

❑ **Direct Java Access** (1) – JavaScript calling to Custom Java Code that we write

❑ **Assisted Java Access** (2) – JavaScript calling into Custom Java Code through FESI extensions (for example, File I/O capabilities)

❑ **Assisted Java Library Access** (3) – JavaScript calling into Java Libraries through FESI extensions (for example, relational database access via JDBC through database extension)

❑ **Direct Java Library Access** (4) – JavaScript calling into Java Libraries directly (for example, Swing and AWT GUI access)

❑ **Embedded JavaScript functionality in Java Programs** (5) – Java programs using embedded JavaScript as dynamic, flexible, easily transmittable and portable behavior sharing mechanism

❑ **JavaScript-based cross-network distributed programming** (6) – JavaScript calling through network to distributed components, network services, or other JavaScript based agents

JavaScript writers of the world, rejoice! The countless hours that you have spent on mastering the syntax and idiosyncrasies of ECMAScript are about to pay off. Without going back to programming school, you now have the ability to program powerful, fully-fledged standalone applications.

Locating and Installing FESI

Before you can successfully install FESI, you must download and have installed the latest version of the JDK from Sun. If you have compiled the samples in the last chapter, you've already got the JDK installed properly. Otherwise, you can download them from `http://java.sun.com/products/OV_jdkProduct.html`

At the time of writing, the most current edition is version 1.2.2 which works great with FESI. You must also have **jar** installed to expand the FESI kit. Fortunately, this is part of the JDK and is installed with it.

The latest version of FESI can be found at `http://home.worldcom.ch/jmlugrin/fesi/`. All the binaries that you will need to run FESI are included in `fesikit.zip` which you should download. If you're a Java fanatic and would like to see how FESI is put together, you can also get the source code as `fesisrc.zip`.

❑ To get FESI up and running, just follow these simple steps.

❑ Unzip `fesikit.zip` to a suitable directory

❑ Add the `fesi\bin` directory to your PATH

❑ Create a new environment variable called `FESI_HOME` and set it to the root of the FESI directories

❑ Unpack the fesikit archive with the command **jar -xf fesikit.jar**. The files will be unpacked and placed into a fesi sub-directory within the current directory.

❑ Go into the `fesi\bin` directory and run `setup.bat`. This will start the FESI based installation script.

First, it will detect the version of JDK:

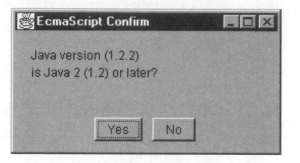

In our case, we have 1.2.2 so you can answer YES to the prompt.
Next, it will choose a directory into which the installation will create several command files later.

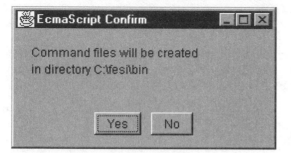

Click **Yes** to select the default directory. Next, it will detect the Swing GUI library path.

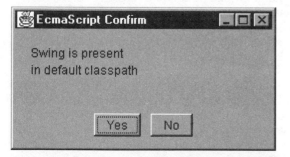

Since all of the JDK 1.2.x versions have Swing built-in, answer **Yes** to this prompt as well.
Finally, it will start writing out the command files.

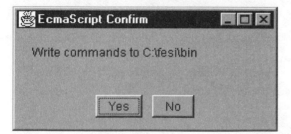

And the last dialog box gives you some hints on how to use the command files to start FESI.

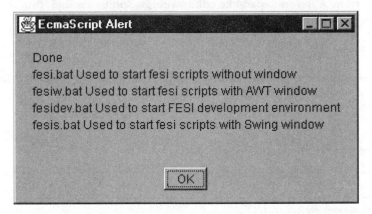

This concludes the installation of FESI. We're now ready to rock' n' roll. Let's write our very first FESI program.

First FESI Program - Hello World

We are really eager to start programming with FESI, so let's jump right into the development tool that is included with the distribution: the FESI IDE.

The Amazing Interactive Development Environment

To start this super powerful IDE, run `fesidev.bat` from the `fesi\bin` directory and you'll quickly see the following screen.

```
FESI - EcmaScript interpreter                                    _ □ X
File   Edit   Help
FESI (pronounced like 'fuzzy'): an EcmaScript Interpreter
Copyright (c) Jean-Marc Lugrin, 1998 - Version: 1.1.2 (8-May-1999)
Interactive read eval print loop - type @help for a list of commands
>
```

If it reminds you of Notepad, welcome to hard-core coder's paradise. In fact, the FESI IDE could well be characterized as 'Notepad with a RUN Button'.

There are many ways you can interact with this IDE. First off, let us write our first program by selecting the File menu and select New. A new notepad-like editor window will be created. Into this window, type our very first Hello World program:

```
alert("Hello world");
```

Okay, we challenge all language enthusiasts to beat the conciseness and brevity of this Hello World program. Makes one proud to be a JavaScript scriptwriter! While `alert()` is not part of the ECMAScript specification, it is provided as a part of the built-in I/O library extension for FESI. Save this file as `myHello1.es`.

For your reference, there are three standard file extensions used in conjunction with FESI:

Extension	Purpose
`.es`	FESI program that uses standard I/O
`.esw`	FESI program that uses the GUI based on Java AWT or Swing (Java Foundation Classes)
`.js`	JavaScript program executable in FESI. Typically, a pure FESI program should use the other two extension while `.JS` should be reserved for programs that may also be executed from a browser or server-side JavaScript system

This standard is a suggested convention and is not currently enforced by any tools.

To run our exciting FESI program, select Execute from the Run menu, or press F4 on your keyboard. Voila!

We have just learnt how to use the FESI IDE and written our very first FESI program. If you're anxious to try out all the rest of FESI's ability, go ahead and experiment with your own programs. Realize that FESI implements a pretty full set of ECMAScript objects and commands, so you can try out quite a few things immediately without reading any further. For the more patient reader, we will continue to cover more FESI basics.

FESI Fundamentals

We will warm up to FESI application coding by first covering the fundamentals. We need to become comfortable with the basic IDE operation, execution procedure, and several input/output techniques.

Interactive Evaluation

If you return to the original FESI window, you will notice that it has a prompt ">" displayed. This is the interactive evelution console. The output from programs executed within the IDE and directed to standard output will show up here. Anything you type into the console will be immediately evaluated by the ECMAScript interpreter. Try entering the one line Hello World program again by typing the single line on the console.

```
alert("Hello World!");
```

Notice that we didn't even have to create a text file to run the program! Now, if you are curious about what the current time is:

```
Date();
```

You could also try out some code that previously required a browser to test:

```
parseInt("12234THIS");
```

You are not limited to a single line program on the interactive console. If you want to see the value of the current time in milliseconds format, try these two consecutive lines:

```
var vdate = new Date();
vdate.valueOf();
```

Due to its high interactivity and friendliness with Java, FESI is a powerful interactive test tool for Java classes. Its ability to run scripts from a file adds to the flexibility by offering automated testing.

From the console, there is also a set of special OS-like commands that you can use to affect your development and debugging environment. For example, you may have noticed the nice message in your FESI console saying 'type @help for a list of commands'? Well, @help is one of them and this is the full list.

Command	Description
@about	Prints copyright and contact information for the author.
@clear	Clears the interactive console. Do this frequently between runs to make output easier to read.
@debugEvent @debugLoader @debugJavaAccess @debugParse	These commands toggle flags that are checked by the FESI interpreter when executing your code. Setting them to true can produce a large amount of debug information on the console and significantly slow down execution. They are useful for detailed debugging should the need arise.
@describe	Gives a detailed description of any variables/objects. For example, if you have a Java object as a variable, it will print its class, all its constructors, methods and properties.

Table Continued on Following Page

Command	Description
@detail	Provides the execution time taken, and the returned value from the previous evaluation.
@exit	Closes the console.
@expand	Extract all the JavaScript code from an HTML file between <SCRIPT></SCRIPT> tags and execute them. This treats each line of JavaScript as if they are keyed into the console. After execution, the variable values are available for examination.
@extensions	Shows all the extensions that are loaded. Extensions are Java classes that provide additional functionality (other than the ECMA specs) to FESI programs. In many cases, these extensions are substantially more scripter-friendly than libraries designed specifically for Java – which FESI can also access directly.
@help	Prints a list of available @commands from the console.
@list	Examines and displays the properties of an object.
@listAll	
@load	Load and run a script file with .es, .js, or .esw extension
@memory	Gives you an idea of how much memory is free out of total available.
@path	Display what the file/class loading path is set to currently.
@pwd	Displays the current working directory.
@reset	Reset the state of the interpreter. You will lose any variables or objects currently defined. With version 1.1.2, this may crash occasionally.
@test	Reads a "test" file. These files are created specifically to run automated testing scripts. We will have more to say about them in the FESI Techniques section later in this chapter.
@version	Prints out the version number of the interpreter.

FESI from the Command Line

If you want to execute FESI programs from the command line as batch files, there are three command line run commands created during the FESI install process that you should use.

Command File	Comment
fesi.bat	Runs the program with output and error going to the command line console.
fesis.bat	Runs the interpreter with Java Swing GUI support.
fesiw.bat	Runs the interpreter with Java AWT GUI support.

So, for example, if you want to run a FESI program called showdays.es that prints output to the command line, you would type:

```
fesi showdays.es
```

at the command prompt. In all three cases, the execution of the program will terminate with the very first error encountered.

Basic User Input and Output with FESI

As exciting as our Hello World program was, you will not be surprised to learn that FESI supports all the basic input and output functions. To demonstrate, we'll use one of the files that come as part of the source code download for this book – `simpleio.es`. This and the rest of the code for the book is available from `http://www.wrox.com/Consumer/Store/Download.asp?Category =Consumer`.

To load `simpleio.es` into the IDE,

❑ Select New from the File menu to create a new editor window.

❑ Select File|Open, navigate to the file and hit Open

You will see:

```
// Simple input and output demo

alert("This is an alert box!");

var tp = confirm("Do you know this is a confirm Box?");
writeln("You indicated " + tp);

var tpStr = prompt("What do you think about FESI?");
writeln("You just told me " + tpStr);

load("lonealrt.es");
```

We have already worked with `alert()`. It allows us to output a current status or warning to the user without any fuss. The next useful function is `confirm()` which displays a verification box containing a Yes and a No button. The return value is a boolean variable of either `true` or `false`.

The `prompt()` function displays a prompt, and collects an input string that is returned to the script. In our case, the dialog box looks like:

The `writeln()` function displays to the standard output, in this case we will find the output in the IDE console. All of these functions are provided courtesy of the I\O support library provided as a standard part of FESI.

Finally, the `load()` function will load and execute a FESI program. The load path is determined by an environment variable called `FESI.path`. This can be set when FESI is started. All the command files set this to the `fesi\bin` (current) directory. Therefore, we should copy the `lonealrt.es` file to `fesi\bin` to get this working. The `lonealrt.es` file contains the trivial line:

```
alert("I have been loaded!");
```

File I\O with FESI

If you open the `testfile.es` script file and examine it, you will see some of the file input and output functions supported by FESI.

This program:

❑ Removes the file named `testfile.txt` if it exists

❑ Writes 100 lines into a new `testfile.txt`

❑ Prints the file absolute path

❑ Loads the entire file back into memory

❑ Separates the lines

❑ Prints the third line of the file

The FESI source to perform this is:

```
// simple FESI code showing file I\O support

var fileToWorkWith = File("testfile.txt");
fileToWorkWith.remove();

fileToWorkWith.open();
for (i=1; i<=100; i++)
{
   fileToWorkWith.writeln("Number is "+i);
}
fileToWorkWith.close();

alert ("File is at " + fileToWorkWith.getAbsolutePath());

var allString=fileToWorkWith.readAll();

var strSplit = allString.split("\n");

alert ("The third line says " + strSplit[2]);
```

Examining the code, we can see here that files are represented by a `File` variable created via:

```
var fileToWorkWith = File("testfile.txt");
```

Everything else in the code is straightforward.

- ❑ `remove()` deletes a file
- ❑ `open()`, `writeln()`, and `close()` all work as you would expect.
- ❑ `getAbsolutePath()` returns the full path to the file in your machine's directory structure.
- ❑ `readAll()` reads every line of the file into a single string.

Directory Manipulations with FESI

The objects and methods that are used in manipulating directory entries and contents are identical to those for files. To demonstrate this, you can load another of the download files for the book, `testdir.es`, which contains a directory testing program.

This program finds all the files and directories within the current directory (probably `fesi\bin`) and for each item in the directory, it will

- ❑ Print whether it is a file or a directory
- ❑ Print the item's name
- ❑ Print the size of the file/directory
- ❑ Print its last modification date

The whole thing is pretty similar to the command line `dir` command.

```
// demonstrates directory manipulations
// using FESI

var dirToWorkWith = File(".");
var myDir = dirToWorkWith.list();

var myCount = 0;

while (myCount < myDir.length )
{
  write(" "+(myCount + 1) + ": ");
  tpFile = File(myDir[myCount]);
  if(tpFile.isFile())
   write(" File: " + myDir[myCount]);
  else
   write(" Dir: " + myDir[myCount]);

  writeln("\t" + tpFile.getLength() + "\t" + tpFile.lastModified());
  myCount++;
}
```

From the code, we can see that the `File` variable type also has some methods for working with directories.

- ❑ `list()` provides a `String` array of the names of all the items in the directory
- ❑ `isFile()` and `isDirectory()` determine if a `File` type variable is a directory or a file
- ❑ `getLength()` method returns the length of a file
- ❑ `lastModified()` method returns a `Date` variable representing the last modification date.

FESI and the GUI

Other than the alert(), confirm(), and prompt() global functions, the basic FESI system does not provide any additional graphical user interface support. Thankfully, FESI's famous partner, Java, has more than its share of great GUI libraries. You will find that there are more than enough graphical user interface element choices to jazz up any application.

As a FESI developer using the Java Development Kit (JDK) support, you have a choice of two families of GUI builder components:

❑ The Java AWT Library, or
❑ The Java Foundation Classes (Swing Library)

The AWT library has been around with Java since 1.0.x versions. It is a "just enough" library of GUI components. Swing on the other hand, is only available with JDK 1.2 and beyond. It is a very large collection of very sophisticated user interface elements that can be completely customized.

Exploiting The Classic Java AWT Library

To familiarize yourself with the available AWT library, run the awttest.esw program from your FESI IDE. Here is what you will see:

The source code to create the above UI is:

```
Frame = java.awt.Frame;
Label = java.awt.Label;
Button = java.awt.Button;
Checkbox = java.awt.Checkbox;
CheckboxGroup = java.awt.CheckboxGroup;
Choice = java.awt.Choice;
List = java.awt.List;
TextField = java.awt.TextField;
TextArea = java.awt.TextArea;
Panel = java.awt.Panel;
FlowLayout = java.awt.FlowLayout;
```

```
var myFrame = new Frame("AWT Components");
myFrame.setLayout(new FlowLayout());

var myPanel1 = new Panel();
myPanel1.add(new Label("Hello World!"));
myPanel1.add(new Button("Hello World!"));
myPanel1.add(new Checkbox("Bold"));
myPanel1.add(new Checkbox("Italics"));

var myPanel2 = new Panel();
var myCheckGroup = new CheckboxGroup();
myPanel2.add(new Checkbox("1st",myCheckGroup, true));
myPanel2.add(new Checkbox("2nd",myCheckGroup, false));
myPanel2.add(new Checkbox("3rd",myCheckGroup, false));

var myChoice = new Choice();
myChoice.add("Times Roman");
myChoice.add("Helvetica");
myChoice.add("Bookman");
myPanel2.add(myChoice);

var myPanel3 = new Panel();
var myList = new List(5, false);
myList.add("Monday");
myList.add("Tuesday");
myList.add("Wednesday");
myList.add("Thursday");
myList.add("Friday");
myPanel3.add(myList);
myPanel3.add(new TextField("",15));

var myPanel4 = new Panel();
myPanel4.add(new TextArea(5,20));
myFrame.add(myPanel1);
myFrame.add(myPanel2);
myFrame.add(myPanel3);
myFrame.add(myPanel4);
// Show the result
myFrame.pack();
myFrame.show();

// Dispose the frame when the window closes
myFrame.onWindowClosing="this.dispose();";
```

Note how easy it is to access Java classes from FESI. We used `Panels` to lay out the four individual sections, and then we add them to the `Frame`. This is very standard Java UI construction technique. To recap, these are the UI components available through AWT:

Component	Description
Label	A piece of text in component form.
Button	Graphical button that can be clicked.
Checkbox	A single square that can be checked or unchecked; when added to a CheckboxGroup, however, they become toggling radio buttons with only one checked within the group at anytime
Choice	A drop down combo box for selecting value.
List	Multiple values visible version of a selector.
TextField	For entering a single line of text.
TextArea	For entering multiple lines of text.

You should be able to spot the direct correspondence between these elements and those in an HTML form. This limits the type of user interfaces that can be created with AWT components.

Great Widgets from the Java Swing Library

The JFC (Swing) library is way too large for a FESI sample program. There are so many user interface widgets and variations that you've got to have the on-line help right by your side to assist when you're working with them. To get an idea of what I mean, have a look at
http://java.sun.com/products/jdk/1.2/docs/api/index.html

The best way to learn about what is available with the JFC library is to run a Java applet called SwingSet that is supplied with the JDK. You can find it in the jdk\demo\jfc\SwingSet directory.

Open a command prompt window, navigate to the SwingSet directory and type appletviewer SwingSetApplet.html. All being well, you should see something like the screenshot below in front of you. Note that should AppletViewer fail to load our applet with the message you may need to unpack the class files from the swingset.jar file. You can do this with the command jar -xf swingset.jar.

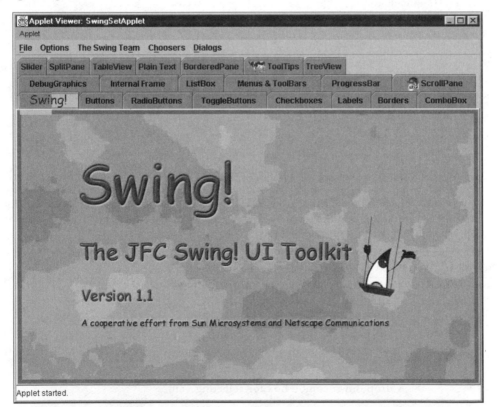

By clicking on the various tabs, you will see all the components available from the JFC, and the type of customization and control over their appearance possible. You can spend hours discovering all its variations. Most of these components and customizability are also available to FESI script writers.

To understand how we work with Swing components in FESI, here is some simple code to start up a JFC frame. You can find it as jfctest.esw in the code download for this book.

```
Swing = Packages.javax.swing;
JFrame = Swing.JFrame;
JButton = Swing.JButton;
JPanel = Swing.JPanel;
JTextField = Swing.JTextField;
JLabel = Swing.JLabel;

var myPanel = new JPanel();
var myLabel = new JLabel("Name:");
var myTxt = new JTextField(10);

myPanel.add(myLabel);
myPanel.add(myTxt);

var myPanel2 = new JPanel();
myPanel2.add(new JButton("Submit"));

// Now create the frame
var myFrame = new JFrame("Wrox JFC FESI Demo");
myFrame.getContentPane().add("North", myPanel);
myFrame.getContentPane().add("South", myPanel2);
myFrame.pack();
myFrame.setVisible(true);
myFrame.onWindowClosing = "this.dispose();";
```

Most of the code is very similar to the AWT version. The only important thing to watch out for is the additional frame.getContentPane() step required when adding components to a frame. If you do not call getContentPane(), the component may not display correctly.

This is what the program will display:

Note that all the remaining sample programs we'll use in this chapter will use JFC to generate their GUIs.

Hooking Event Handlers in FESI

Note that in both the AWT and the JFC examples, we have the line:

```
myFrame.onWindowClosing = "this.dispose();";
```

This statement associates (hooks) an event handler action with a specific event that an object may fire. In this case, the Frame object may fire a WindowClosing event. Many Java components and objects will fire events. This built-in FESI event handling mechanism allow us to react to Java component and object events.

The technique used above is to set an 'on<EventName>' property for the object, and set it to a string that contains the action to evaluate when the event fires. This gives us a great flexibility in how we choose to handle the event. Another accepted way of hooking an event handler is to assign to the 'on<EventName>' property an actual ECMAScript function that takes the event as a parameter. For example:

```
function myHandler(myEvent)
{
 ...
 use info from myEvent here
 ...
}

frame.onWindowClosing = myHandler;
```

You will find this second form useful if you need to access event specific information within the handler function. This is very similar to the way document object model events are handled within browsers by JavaScript.

FESI and the Database

Most commercial software developed today uses a Relational Database Management System (RDBMS) for the storage and retrieval of persistent data of any volume. In fact, RDBMS products host the vital business data of most enterprises in corporate America. It is no wonder that database administration, design, and programming remains one of the hottest fields in I.T. this decade. For the most part, due to the weak support for RDBMS in browser products, JavaScript writers were counted out of this lucrative picture... until now.

FESI Access to SQL Server, ORACLE, DB2, etc. via JDBC

FESI provides a standard extension that interfaces directly to JDBC (Java Database Connectivity), allowing ECMAScript programs to directly access and manipulate data stored in RDBMSes.

The idea behind JDBC is to provide a uniform, somewhat object-based API for accessing any RDBMS data source. JDBC itself is a mature technology that had been working since JDK 1.1. Most major RDBMS vendors have created and provide JDBC drivers with the latest versions of their products – ORACLE, DB2, Sybase, Informix, SQL Server, etc.. The figure below illustrates how JDBC can provide a single API that works with a variety of RDBMS products.

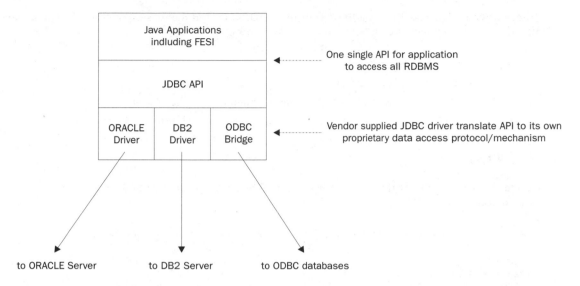

While most JDBC API calls are directly accessible via the Java class access capability of FESI, the database extension provided by FESI makes this task substantially easier, providing several classes (for example, one called Database) that can be easily configured and called using standard types within JavaScript. Using this extension, we will now write a JFC based application that will display the data from an RDBMS table in a grid format.

A Simple Database Table Viewer

To get this sample running, you must have access to a database and its JDBC driver. If you're using the download code the book, you will find an Access database called Members.mdb that you should use for this example and we'll be using the Sun-supplied JDBC-to-ODBC bridge driver included with JDK 1.2.x. This is a JDBC driver that can make calls through ODBC to use ODBC data sources.

If you've not got access to Access (no pun intended), the database you should create must have a table called MAIN with the following fields.

	Field Name	Data Type
	NAME	Text
🔑	ID	Number
	PHONE	Text

ID should be the primary key for the table. After creating the table, you should populate the table with some data. If you're using the download version of Members.mdb, these records are already in the table.

	NAME	ID	PHONE
▶	JOHN	2213	327-0012
	JOE	2312	232-2929
	MARY	3321	982-2911

571

For those of you using `Members.mdb` or your own ODBC-rooted database, you'll need to create an ODBC data source called `PEOPLE`. To do this in Windows:

❑ Open the ODBC Control Panel

❑ Select the System DSN tab and click Add

❑ Make sure Microsoft Access Driver (*.mdb) is highlighted and click Finish

❑ Give 'PEOPLE' as the Data Source Name and using the Select button, locate `Members.mdb` or your own database.

❑ Click OK

The code to create this GUI table viewer is contained in `testdb.es`, available as part of the book download code. This is what it contains:

```
Swing = Packages.javax.swing; // Just change this line if it moves

JFrame = Swing.JFrame;
JPanel = Swing.JPanel;
JTable = Swing.JTable;
JScrollPane = Swing.JScrollPane;
```

After defining the shortcut to the JFC classes we need, we load the required JDBC driver. In our case, it is the JDBC-to-ODBC bridge delivered with JDK 1.2.x. If you are using another JDBC driver, you will need to change the code here. The string used in the `db.connect()` method call will also vary with different JDBC drivers. Consult your JDBC driver documentation for details.

```
db= new Database("sun.jdbc.odbc.JdbcOdbcDriver");
writeln(db.getLastError());
db.connect("jdbc:odbc:PEOPLE");
```

`db` is of type `Database`, a class provided by the DB-support extension in FESI. The statement that actually does the query is executed via the `db.executeRetrieval()` method.

```
result = db.executeRetrieval("select * from MAIN");

// Create the panel and its content
panel = new JPanel();
dbTable = new JTable(8, result.length);
scrltable = new JScrollPane(dbTable);
dbTable.setToolTipText("Database Table content");
panel.add(scrltable);
```

Now, we create the JFC table. Notice that we are allowing up to 8 rows initially, and the column width corresponding to the number of fields from the resultset. With most JDBC drivers, it is not possible to know how many rows there are in the complete resultset after a query without fetching all the rows. Next, we will go through each row, and set the corresponding cell in the JTable to the corresponding field value.

```
var rowCount = 0;
var colCount = 0;

while (result.next())
{
  colCount = 0;
  for (c in result)
  {
   tpItem = result.getColumnItem(c);
   writeln("Column: " + c + ": " + tpItem);
   dbTable.setValueAt(tpItem, rowCount, colCount);
   colCount++;
  }
  rowCount++;
}
```

It's good programming practice to disconnect from the database as soon as possible. In our example then, we disconnect once we have completed the resultset row transversal – before completing our GUI setup.

```
db.disconnect();

// Now create the frame
frame = new JFrame("Wrox FESI Database Viewer");
frame.getContentPane().add("Center", panel);

frame.pack();
frame.setVisible(true);
frame.onWindowClosing = "frame.dispose();exit();";
```

If you have the JDBC driver connected properly, you should see all the rows of the table display in a spreadsheet like grid within a JFC frame.

FESI allows you to quickly glue various technologies together to create practical applications. This example illustrates how easy it is to use ECMAScript for gluing JDBC and JFC together to create a graphical database table viewer. We will now get more practice writing FESI applications by attacking an even more complex problem.

Building a Reminder System

Time to put FESI to work on a moderately complex project, so we're going to build a message reminder system. Why? Well, we haven't done it yet, so it'll make a change. This system will allow us to add reminder messages, and the time for the reminder. The application stores this information and alerts the user with the appropriate message when the time comes due.

To get this system working at a very minimal level, we will need to implement the following components for this application:

❑ A friendly Graphical User Interface for reminder messages input

❑ A list structure to store the list of reminder messages

❑ A timer mechanism to regularly check the list for expiry

So the first thing to try is the following command at the FESI IDE console:

```
setTimeout("alert('it works',3000);");
```

Unfortunately, the response is:

```
[[Error: Runtime error no global function named 'setTimeout'
detected at line 1 in string: 'setTimeout("alert('it works',3000);");']]
```

A good try – if the FESI support had a setTimeout() function, one of our three problems would have been solved immediately. Lacking support from the FESI implementation and extensions, our next stop will be the Java libraries. Looking through the API reference (http://java.sun.com/products/jdk/1.2/docs/api/index.html), we found a Swing Timer class that will do the job. We can set the notification interval and the class will fire an event when the interval expires.

Next, we need to create a data structure that will allow us to hold the list of reminders. Again we'll use a Swing component called a JList to keep track of this for us. As a bonus, it will also enable the user to see all the pending reminders visually.

The JFC-based user interface of the reminder system will look like this:

Quite nice really. It works in a quite straightforward way as well:

- ❑ Users can enter alert messages and how long (in minutes) before they appear.
- ❑ Once they've pressed Add, each separate reminder will be displayed in the console.
- ❑ When the relevant time comes, an alert will pop up with the reminder message.
- ❑ When the user dismisses the alert, the corresponding reminder will be removed from the list.

Alarm.esw contains the source code to implement the alarm system, so let's step through that. The first section establish shortcuts to the JFC classes, and the Timer class that we will need.

```
Swing = Packages.javax.swing;
JFrame = Swing.JFrame;
JButton = Swing.JButton;
JPanel = Swing.JPanel;
JList = Swing.JList;
JScrollPane = Swing.JScrollPane;
JTextField = Swing.JTextField;
JLabel = Swing.JLabel;
Vector = java.util.Vector;
myModel = Swing.DefaultListModel;
JTimer = Swing.Timer;
JComboBox = Swing.JComboBox;
```

Next, we create the list where the reminders will be kept, as well as the time and message text field that make up the user interface.

```
// Create the panel and its content
var panel = new JPanel();
var alrmlist = new JList(new myModel());
var scrllist = new JScrollPane(alrmlist);

alrmlist.setToolTipText("List of alarm items");

var lbl1 = new JLabel("Time");
var txt1 = new JTextField(5);
var lbl2 = new JLabel("Msg");
var txt2 = new JTextField(20);
var but1 = new JButton("Add");

var panel2 = new JPanel();
panel2.add(lbl1);
panel2.add(txt1);
panel2.add(lbl2);
panel2.add(txt2);
panel2.add(but1);

panel.add(scrllist);
```

Lastly, we create the application frame and add the UI elements to it.

```
// Now create the frame
var frame = new JFrame("Wrox FESI Reminders");
frame.getContentPane().add("Center", panel);
frame.getContentPane().add("South",panel2);
frame.pack();
frame.setVisible(true);
frame.onWindowClosing = "this.dispose();";
```

Now if the user hits the **Add** button, we'll want to add an entry for the reminder into our list, so we need to associate an 'Add button click' to a function we'll call `addEntry()`. This is done by hooking to the `Action` event fired by the `JButton`. Remember that the general format for hooking an event to an object is:

```
<object>.on<EventName> = <string with ECMAScript to evaluate>;
```

so we're going to need the line

```
but1.onAction = "addEntry();";
```

Setting Up the Timer

Now, we initialize the `Timer` class to fire every 15 seconds (15,000 milliseconds). Notice that `JTimer` has no constructor that takes an empty argument list. Instead, we must call it with some initial value and then reset them immediately using its methods. We've used a dummy `JComboBox` object here because it implements the `ActionListener` interface that the `JTimer` constructor requires.

The `ActionListener` interface is a Java interface specified for listening to events that an object may fire. In this case, we are specifically interested in the `Action` event from the `JTimer` object.

```
var myTimer = new JTimer(10000,new JComboBox());
myTimer.setDelay(15000);
myTimer.setRepeats(true);
```

We hook the `Action` event with a `CheckSchedule()` function. This function will be executed every 15 seconds unless the timer is disabled.

```
myTimer.onAction = "CheckSchedule();";
myTimer.start();
```

Here is the `addEntry()` function. Notice that we convert the alarm date/time into its millisecond format and store that number directly in the `JList` on the user interface! Or at least, that's what we would do. It turns out that FESI has a minor bug in dealing with very large numbers typically associated with dates. Therefore, we must divide the number of milliseconds by 1000, making it the number of seconds that we will be storing in the `JList`.

```
function addEntry()
{
  var curTime = 0;
  curTime = new Date();
  var diffMs = parseInt(txt1.getText()) * 60000;
  curTime = new Date(curTime.valueOf() + diffMs);

  var textToAdd = curTime.toString() + "-" + txt2.getText() + "-" +
                  Math.round(curTime.valueOf()/1000);
  alrmlist.getModel().addElement(textToAdd);
  txt1.setText("");
  txt2.setText("");
}
```

CheckSchedule() is called every 15 seconds. It will traverse the entire JList and check each reminder against the current time. For every expired reminder, it will alert the user with the reminder message. Once the user acknowledges the alert, it will remove the reminder from the JList. Just in case the user does not see the alert, we disable the timer during the notification to avoid deadlock.

```
function CheckSchedule()
{
  myTimer.stop();
  var cursize = alrmlist.getModel().getSize();
  var dateonly;

  for (var i=0; i< cursize; i++)
  {
    tpString = alrmlist.getModel().getElementAt(i);
    var ctime = 0;
    ctime = new Date();
    dateSegs = tpString.split("-");
    var tp2 = parseInt(dateSegs[2]);
    var  mntime = new Date(tp2 * 1000);

    if ( ctime.valueOf() >= mntime.valueOf() )
    {
      alert(dateSegs[1]);
      alrmlist.getModel().removeElementAt(i);
      break;
    }
  } // end of for loop
  myTimer.restart();
}
```

Where Do We Go From Here?

We hope you are as impressed with FESI (and JavaScript) as we are. Not only do we have the most used web programming language on our hand, but we have also mastered a first class application programming language. Interested readers should spend some good time experimenting with FESI and study its documentation. Meanwhile, we will blue-sky a little and consider what else FESI may enable us to do.

Rapid Prototyping

The code we have written so far has been very lightweight by any standard. Even the entire final reminder system sample fits under a couple pages of scripting code. This lends itself well to the rapid prototyping of applications. The text-based source code, and the no-compilation required interpreter both make design iterations or testing variations a very easy task to accomplish.

Test Harnesses

You can use the special @test directive in your FESI files to perform automated tests. Any file referred by the @test directive will be executed using a special test mode. Ordinarily, FESI will stop execution upon the first error encountered. In the test mode, FESI will execute each test preceded by the name of the test, and it will skip to the next @test if an error is encountered during a test execution.

This simple modification in behavior makes automated regression testing possible with FESI. One can develop a suite of tests to run against new code, ensuring that no old features are broken because of recent updates and/or enhancements.

Agents and Mobile Code

Imagine FESI code that can be manufactured by an AI engine, and then sent to a remote destination for execution. This may sound a little far-fetched, but the flexibility of FESI makes this a distinct possibility in the near future. In fact, you can find a link to an XML-RPC project right off the FESI web site. This project enables the remote execution of code based on a lightweight protocol that can be tunneled through any communication conduit that supports ASCII text. The code is already working. In many ways, the future is here today.

The World is Your Oyster

FESI allows every JavaScript script writer to adopt the most brilliant kid in town: Java and its vast code base and resources. The exciting coverage in this chapter has barely scratched the universe of possibilities.

Experiment and have fun. The only missing ingredient in the equation is your imagination. The only story not yet told is how you will be able to leverage your expertise of JavaScript, through the power of FESI, to solve the problems of the world.

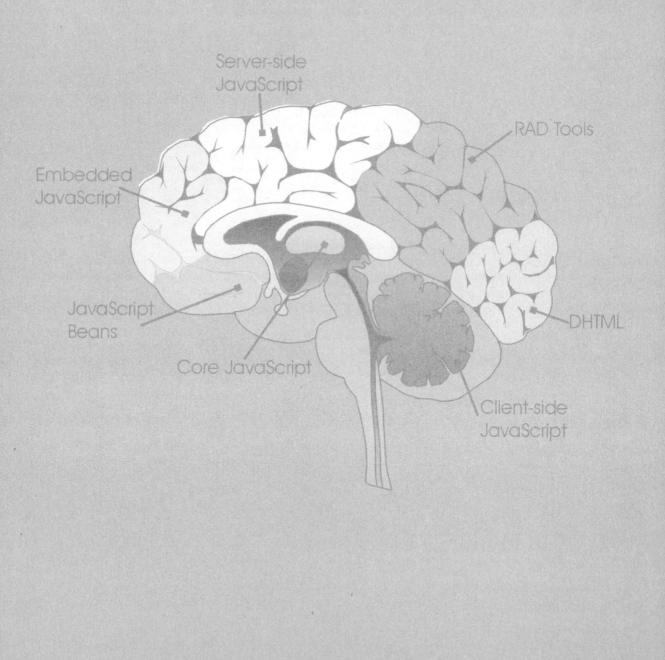

Debugging & Disappearing Data

Reading a JavaScript book is one thing; debugging an uncooperative script is another. Because JavaScript is interpreted, the feedback you receive about your script's health is mostly limited to warnings about syntax problems. Once syntax problems are overcome, the few runtime diagnostics available generally translate into "I tried to do it, but something didn't exist".

JavaScript is intended to be a quick-and-easy interpreted and interactive language, often requiring only a few statements. There is no compiler rigorously checking your scripts before allowing them to be used. Consequently, it is very easy to become sloppy in your programming habits. Many problems are due merely to this.

Apart from the poor human creating the scripts, there are some genuine traps. This chapter outlines these traps and serves as a memory jogger for problematic issues highlighted elsewhere in the book. Know Thy Enemy...or Enemies, as the case may be.

A look is also taken at manual debugging techniques.

Problems With Language Basics

If you are new to programming or to JavaScript, you are going to make all these mistakes. Old hands will nod sagely and say "Oh yes, the single-equals problem". Don't be fooled, they do it too. Even now. Think of these mistakes as a rite of passage and a fact of life.

Dangling Else Leaves You Dangling

Sometimes it is not clear which `if` a given `else` belongs to. The indenting designed to make it clear can just make it worse. This case has both bad formatting and a logic error:

```
if ( result != "win" )
   if ( result == "lose" )
     do_lose();
else
   do_win();
```

In this example, you never win. The `else` branch belongs to the inner, second `if`. No amount of formatting will make the interpreter think otherwise. The way to avoid this is: **always use curly brackets** (braces) – then the trap cannot be fallen into. You can win in this re-cast example:

```
if ( result != "win" )
{
   if ( result == "lose" )
   {
     do_lose();
   }
}
else
{
   do_win();
}
```

This book is itself guilty of avoiding the braces at times – probably there's no defense, but it's unlikely you'd enjoy seeing pages of extra braces either.

= Isn't Always Equal To The Task

This is a very common typo:

```
var x = 1; if ( x = 0 ) alert ("made it");
```

Probably what was meant:

```
var x = 1; if ( x == 0 ) alert ("made it");
```

Chapter 1 describes how the equality operator can be viewed as an expression. Expressions can appear in `if` statements. The mistaken example above is therefore not a syntax error: in the `if` part the variable `x` quietly gets reassigned the value 0, is then evaluated for truth or falsehood, passes, and the alert incorrectly appears.

Early Netscape 4.0 browsers, such as 4.05 are helpful enough to produce this error message if such a situation is detected. JavaScript processing is not suspended just because the window appears. This is different to the behavior of the `window.alert()` method, and to that of normal syntax error messages.

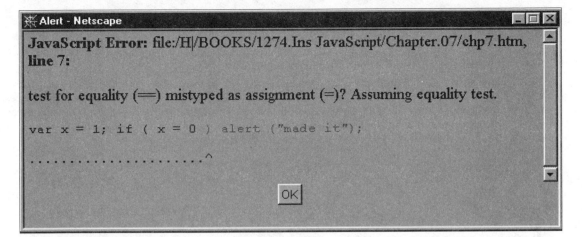

Unfortunately, this message can be quite irritating, and can interfere with perfectly legal JavaScript scripts. If you're stuck with a particular browser version, then there is a way around idiomatic use that causes this error. An **idiom** is a form of expression. This is a common idiom used in JavaScript and other C-like languages:

```
var result = null;
if ( (result=calculate_it()) > 0 )
  use_it(result);
```

In this example you keep calculating and using the result until the result's not greater than zero any more. The above script is exactly the same as the following one:

```
var result = null
result=calculate_it();
if ( result > 0 )
{
  use_it(result);
  result = calculate_it();
}
```

The first example is often preferred, because there are fewer lines to comprehend and only one place where the variable `result` is updated. Scripters are a lazy and terse bunch, sometimes. Unfortunately, for the browsers noted, the first example causes the pop-up to appear. You might want to use this idiom without the interference of the Netscape pop-up. If desperate, avoid the pop-up as follows, using the rarely used comma operator or use the alternate, more verbose statement layout:

```
var result = null;
if ( result=calculate_it(), result > 0)
  use_it(result);
```

for..in.. Has It In For You

As briefly described in Chapter 2, the `for..in..` syntax is used to find the names of all the properties of a JavaScript object. The problem is that it does not always work as you expect – some properties don't appear and some objects don't seem to have any properties at all. You can do little about this because it is a product decision made by the developers of the JavaScript interpreter. Usually this problem only occurs when you are hacking into the browser "off the beaten track" for your own devious ends.

Your only strategies are:

❑ know the property names in advance

❑ appreciate why they are hidden from inspection and accept it

To know an object's properties in advance, resort to documentation such as this book's Appendices. The only other tactic possible is to probe the object in question, one property at a time, using array syntax. This takes a very long time, and is only for the desperate. An example for 4.0 browsers which finds all the lower-case single-character properties of the document object:

```
function probe(obj)
{
  var i;
  var code = 'a'.charCodeAt(0);

  for (i=0; i < 26; i++)
  {
    if ( obj[(code+i).toString()] )
      alert ('found property: '+ (code+i).toString());
  }
}

probe(top.document);
```

A larger and more complex version could find all the properties of an object, but just finding all properties with six letters or less is 300 million tests – hardly worth it unless you enjoy running scripts overnight.

According to the ECMAScript standard, a given property of an object has a few **attributes** describing that property, such as property name and property value. One such attribute is the DontEnum attribute. If this attribute is present, then the property won't be revealed by a for...in... loop. This is how object properties are excluded in such loops.

There are several reasons why some host object properties have this DontEnum attribute. The simplest one is that some properties aren't interesting. Every method of an object is also a property of that object. It is pointless trying to interact with a method property if the object is a host object. An example for Navigator 4.0:

```
<HTML><BODY><SCRIPT>
alert(document.open);
document.open = "Fruit Salad";
alert(document.open);
</SCRIPT></BODY></HTML>
```

This script displays the following alerts, and messes up the document object in the process. The open() method is not accessible afterwards for creating new browser windows.

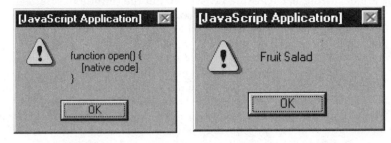

A second reason for non-enumerable properties is that some host objects don't follow the same rules as JavaScript. Java classes exposed as JavaScript host objects in a browser are an example. The JavaScript property java.lang isn't really an object, but a package of object types (also called a class library) – java.lang.io is a subpackage of that package, but isn't an object either. A **package** is merely a group of related objects collected together. These classes are stored on disk and it isn't easy, efficient or even that useful to sift through them looking for java.lang members that might be objects. In any event, the browsers won't let you do it. Therefore, this item and the others relating to Java classes can't be enumerated at all from JavaScript.

Note that the above discussion relates to Java *classes* accessed from JavaScript only, not Java *objects* accessed from JavaScript. You can enumerate through a Java object from JavaScript as normal.

Falling Foul of Types

It is so easy to do quick-and-dirty client-side JavaScript. A loosely typed language really saves a lot of messing around otherwise spent organizing the right kind of data for the right kind of variables. Once finished, specially gifted people called users come along and expose gaping holes in your scripts. JavaScript may well have untyped variables, but all the data itself is fully typed, and users will find a way to make your script trip over this distinction, trust me.

Chapter 1 describes how type conversion works in JavaScript. The most common trap is to develop all your scripts with Netscape 4.0 browsers and then discover that it doesn't work on any other browsers because you rely on the special behavior of Netscape's JavaScript 1.2 != and == operators. Don't use <SCRIPT LANGUAGE="JavaScript1.2"> when developing, unless portability is not required. It's probably safest to leave the LANGUAGE attribute out altogether, since JavaScript is the default browser scripting language anyway. If you must specify it, use LANGUAGE="JavaScript". If you are sure your users will only use a really recent browser, then LANGUAGE="JavaScript 1.3" or LANGUAGE="JavaScript 1.4" is also a good option, as you then have available the error handling events of those versions.

Chapter 7 described validation and the numerous evils of converting user input into numbers. If your CGI program is crashing, your e-mail is not arriving properly, or JavaScript is popping up errors on some obscure browser, first go back and check that all numeric values entered by the user are carefully validated.

Finally, older browsers have limited JavaScript support for types (also described in Chapter 1). If you want to support those browsers, don't be fancy with null, NaN, typeof() or Array objects.

Missing <SCRIPT> Portions

If syntax errors are occurring in client-side JavaScript, but the script looks perfect, review the discussion in Chapter 4 on embedding JavaScript in HTML. Certain combinations of characters confuse the browser and it can give up believing that a script is present.

A related problem is restricted to 16-bit versions of the Netscape browsers developed for Microsoft's Windows 3.1 platform. If a single piece of HTML-embedded JavaScript exceeds about 32 Kilobytes, the remainder will be silently discarded due to memory limitations. Syntax errors or 'XX Not Found' errors will result. There is a simple workaround – break up <SCRIPT>..</SCRIPT> tag pairs that contain a lot of JavaScript into several smaller ones. Here's a trivial example of breaking up a script – it's not 32K in size (that would be really boring), but it illustrates the principle. First before:

```
<HTML><BODY><SCRIPT>
// big script section!
var x =0;
x =1;
x=2;
x=3;
// lots more
x=99999;
</SCRIPT></BODY></HTML>
```

then after:

```
<HTML><BODY><SCRIPT>
// big script section!
var x =0;
x =1;
x=2;
</SCRIPT><SCRIPT>
x=3;
// lots more
x=99999;
</SCRIPT></BODY></HTML>
```

Problems With Variables

Variables are ultimately properties of objects and object models, but their use is so common that a few specific remarks are warranted.

Variables Belong To Somebody

In client-side JavaScript – in fact in *all* JavaScript – there is a notion of the current object that stems from complicated discussions of scope chains covered in Chapter 3. The simple outcome for browsers is that the current object is usually the window object. This is easy to forget by the time you write var x=0; for the 100th time, as the window object doesn't seem to play any part in that statement. If you want to access a variable from an HTML event handler or another window, you should identify it by its owning object, because the window object is *not* the current object in those cases. It's easy to say "but I can use window object methods and properties like open() and document from a form element event handler!". That's true - you can access those things from a form element event handler (due to scope chains, and provided the current object doesn't have its own property of the same name), but the window object still isn't the current object for setting properties. Here are some correct examples:

```
<INPUT TYPE="text" ONCHANGE="window.user_input = this.value; return true;">
```

```
top.opener.frames[0].my_time = "11:53";
```

If you don't, you may just set a property on the current object, rather than on the current window (usually a form input control like a text field) where it will usually remain, ignored. Here's a non-working example:

```
<INPUT TYPE="text" ONCHANGE=" user_input = this.value">
```

This example set the `user_input` property of some text element of some form. It also fails to return true or false. This is bad practice – always return true or false.

String Truncation

Beware of string constants that are over 80 characters. Some earlier browsers can't handle them. Just break them up into smaller chunks – it is easier to read anyway. This example has only short strings but it illustrates the principle:

```
var big_string  = "first chunk "
                + "second chunk "
                + "third chunk ";
```

Beware of the null character problem in Netscape browsers: `"xxx\000yyy".length` is only 3 except for recent Netscape 4.0 releases; the y characters are lost to view. For all browsers, attempting to display such a string with `alert()` or `document.write()` is generally problematic as all will understand the string to be xxx only and not xxx\000yyy.

String Shortening

Finally, `document.write()` can be used to output a string as a piece of HTML. However, when the HTML is displayed, any repeated spaces in the string will be collapsed together into one, and end of line characters are ignored. This is just a product of the way HTML's freely formatted language is processed – not a JavaScript feature – but it can get in the way of what you're trying to achieve. If you intended multiple spaces, then instead use the HTML non-breaking-space character like this:

```
var try1 = "Left      Right\n\n\nBelow";
var try2 = "Left     Right<BR><BR><BR>Below";

document.write(try1);          // wrong
document.write(try2);          // right
```

Frustratingly, this solution can cause problems if you overuse it. It definitely applies when you are constructing HTML *pages* from JavaScript, but not when you are altering HTML *values*. Here's a classic mistake that's easy to fall into – in this example we're trying to put the string L   R (which has two spaces) into the sole form element:

```
<HTML><BODY><FORM>
<INPUT TYPE="text" NAME="tryit">
<SCRIPT>
var try3 = 'L  R';            // HTML codes for spaces
var try4 = 'L\xA0\xA0R';                // Unicode codes for spaces
```

```
document.forms[0].tryit.value = try3;    // wrong
document.forms[0].tryit.value = try4;    // right

</SCRIPT></FORM></BODY></HTML>
```

Comment one line out, and done the wrong way, the window looks like this:

Done the right way, it looks like this:

This confusion arises because when set the initial value of a text field directly in HTML, like this from JavaScript:

```
document.write('<INPUT TYPE="text" VALUE="L  R">');
```

or like this directly in your HTML document:

```
<INPUT TYPE="text" VALUE="L  R">
```

then the HTML version of the non-breaking spaces is used. Summary: only use the Unicode version in the common case where you are setting an object's value from JavaScript, not when you are setting an HTML tag's value by any method.

Naming Problems

Choosing a name for a variable is more error-prone in JavaScript than in other computer languages.

There are a few specific traps:

❑ Variables are case sensitive, but not strictly everywhere – JScript 1.0 event handlers are the exceptions.

❑ Cookie variable names are not JavaScript variables, so different rules apply there – see the cookie section.

❑ Limitations on variable name size aren't well advertised and vary between interpreters, so use shorter names.

The more general problem, which applies mostly to client-side JavaScript and complex standalone scripts, is that numerous names are off-limits. A very harmless looking example:

```
var int = 23;          // reserved word
var name = "Fred";     // changes an existing property
var open = true;       // dumps an existing method
```

The variable `int` is a problem because `int` is a reserved word. This is easily detected by the interpreter. The `name` variable is more obscure. In client-side JavaScript the current object is usually the `window` object. That window object already has a property called `name`. After this script fragment is run, the window's name has changed – mostly harmless, unless another window relies on the old name, in which case there will be problems. The open variable has problems as discussed earlier – the `window` object has now had a method replaced with a simple data value, and it can't be reversed. Further discussion on these problems can be found elsewhere in this book:

❑ The 'Events and Forms' section illustrates further examples of these problems.

❑ Chapter 3 describes how scope chain concepts also contribute to this problem.

❑ The Appendices and the JavaScript Reserved Words list (inside back cover) list all the reserved words and other names that are already taken. The best advice is to avoid the lot.

A further naming issue derives from the advent of stylesheets and Dynamic HTML. Because of these innovations, HTML tag names now appear as objects and properties within client-side JavaScript. Although they are always capitalized and generally contained within the style parts of the document object model, these names should be avoided as well, or else confusion can ensue. Some HTML tags match common variable names like `I`, `SUB`, `MAP`, `HEAD`, `CODE`, `A`, `DIR` and `BASE`. Avoid. Particularly avoid using all-uppercase variable names for constants: a practice common in many programming languages. Remember that if even if you set such a property in the window object (which is well away from the objects making up the document), it could still be a source of subtle clashes from event handlers because it is in the scope chain of other like-named properties.

Just around the corner is the XML standard. This is a complementary markup language to HTML that allows a document to define its own, unique tag names. This makes it even more important to stay out of the habit of using uppercase names, although this standard is case-sensitive, as these arbitrary names will in future also be reflected as JavaScript objects.

Problems With Events and Forms

Beyond trivial uses, events and forms are the most difficult aspects of client-side JavaScript to script in a robust and portable manner. Variations between browsers make designing complex forms to suit everyone akin to tightrope walking. The best single piece of advice is don't bother trying to get your script to work on Internet Explorer 3.0 or Netscape Navigator 3.0 for Unix. The event handling is very poorly implemented in the Internet Explorer 3.0 case, with some events making no sense at all. In the Netscape 3.0 for Unix case, some event handlers are missing entirely. Abandon these browsers.

Events

Numerous event issues are covered in Chapter 7. The appendices also list the events attached to each object, and Chapter 4 has a gentle introduction to the browser event models and some of their quirks. If your event handlers aren't doing anything, the most common reasons are listed here:

- You are forgetting to return `true` or `false`, and you need to.
- You are incorrectly using the `this` property.
- You are testing with a Unix version of Netscape Navigator 3.0.
- You are using a Netscape `onUnload` event handler, version 4.0 or earlier.
- You are using Internet Explorer 3.0 form events.
- You forgot that event models differ between browser brands.

Let's look at these one at a time.

You are forgetting to return true or false, and you need to.

All event handlers should in theory return true or false. A common problem occurs when a handy function normally meant for non-event scripts is used in an event handler. It is easy to forget that `return` has to be explicitly stated in the event handler. In this example, the hyperlink is always followed, no matter what conclusion the `isValid()` function reaches:

```
<HTML><BODY><SCRIPT>
function isValid(str)                    // test if strings start with 'A'.
{
  return (str.charAt(0,1) == 'A');
}
</SCRIPT>

<FORM NAME="test">
<INPUT TYPE="text" NAME="stuff">
<BR>
<A HREF="javascript:alert('Valid')"
   ONCLICK="isValid(top.document.test.stuff.value)">
test it
</A>
</FORM></BODY></HTML>
```

The `onClick` handler should read:

```
ONCLICK="return isValid(top.document.test.stuff.value)"
```

In this particular case, a Netscape 3.0 browser design flaw that causes a return value of `false` to be ignored specifically for the `<A>` `onClick` handler further complicates the matter.

You are incorrectly using the this property.

This script runs fine, but (probably unintentionally) creates a property on the Text input type object called `total_clicks`. It is this property that is incremented, not the property of the same name that belongs to the `window` object – mostly useless behavior:

```
<HTML><BODY><SCRIPT>
var total_clicks = 0;
</SCRIPT>
<FORM>
<INPUT TYPE="button" VALUE="Click Me" ONCLICK="this.total_clicks++">
<INPUT TYPE="button" VALUE="Show Total" ONCLICK="alert(window.total_clicks)">
</FORM></BODY></HTML>
```

You are testing with a Unix version of Netscape Navigator 3.0.

`onBlur` and `onFocus` event handlers don't work at all with this browser.

You are using a Netscape onUnload event handler.

This handler is buggy for all Netscape browsers up to and including 4.61 and can be very unreliable. The problem is that the browser sometimes becomes confused by the twin tasks of having to destroy all the objects of the page that's being unloaded, and having to do something with them via the event handler at the same time. Avoid.

You are using Internet Explorer 3.0 form events

Form events are frustrating in this old browser because sometimes an action will fire two events, and the later one will partially cancel out the former one. Chapter 7, on Forms and Data describes a workaround. Only this old version is affected.

You forgot that event models differ between browser brands

Chapter 4 describes how subtle differences in event handling behavior make controlling the input cursor and navigation in a form problematic.

Errors and Undefined Data

If your event handler is causing JavaScript complaints, first check if the tag for the event handler is `<INPUT TYPE="text">`. If so, you should check that validation is not causing type conversion problems.

If not, then you may be falling prey to these problems:

```
<HTML><BODY><FORM NAME="location">        // problem line
Address:
<INPUT TYPE="text" NAME="address">
Delivery Method:
<INPUT TYPE="text NAME="method"          // problem line
ONCHANGE="alert(top.document.location.method.value)">
</FORM></BODY></HTML>
```

There are two problems with this document. The first is that the onChange handler always reports "undefined". This is because the form control's name ("method") clashes with the property of the Form object also called method. Don't use Form object property or method names as <INPUT> item names. The second problem is similar. The form's name is 'location', but forms are properties of the document object and there is already a location property of the document object. Therefore, while this by chance works for Netscape, it may confuse Microsoft browsers.

Scope chains, described in Chapter 3 describe more fully the underlying complexities here.

Finally, there is a further forms scenario that causes confusion in all browsers released to date. The scriptwriter starts with a document, usually much more complex than this:

```
<HTML><BODY><FORM>
Want one? <INPUT TYPE="checkbox" NAME="box1" VALUE="yes" ONCLICK="alert('Why
not!')">
</FORM></BODY></HTML>
```

and decides to enhance it. Rather than wreck the existing tags, text is copied and experimented with:

```
<HTML><BODY><FORM>
```

```
<SCRIPT>var state = false;</SCRIPT>
Want one? <INPUT TYPE="checkbox" NAME="box1" VALUE="yes"          <!copy>
        ONCLICK="alert(top.document.forms[0].box1.checked)">      <!copy>
```

```
Want one? <INPUT TYPE="checkbox" NAME="box1" VALUE="yes" ONCLICK="alert('Why
not!')">
</FORM></BODY></HTML>
```

In this case, the first checkbox always reports undefined even though a checkbox object has a checked property that reflects the state of the box. The problem is that there are now *two* input elements named box1, so the JavaScript object top.document.forms[0].box1 is an InputArray object (so-named by Netscape), not a checkbox object and has no checked method. The onClick handler should read:

```
ONCLICK="alert(top.document.forms[0].box1[0].checked)">
```

Chapter 7, on Forms and Data discusses this feature further.

Problems At Load Time

When an HTML document is loaded into a browser, the HTML elements are exposed to JavaScript sequentially and any embedded objects such as images, applets and plugins load at their own pace. It is no use trying to access a JavaScript object that doesn't exist yet, whether it is HTML or something foreign.

Store as much JavaScript as possible in the <HEAD> section of the document as described in Chapter 4. Avoid other problems by following the advice of Chapter 5 and use the onLoad event handler. Chapter 6 describes how to ensure that images and plugins have fully loaded.

Obscure Netscape Problems

Firstly, avoid the `onUnload` handlers as noted earlier.

Secondly, there is a complication with `<A>` hypertext links. The browser assumes that if a link is clicked and any `onClick` handler returns `true`, then the current document is to be replaced. Normally this is a fair assumption, but not when the `HREF` attribute's URL is a `javascript:` URL. This URL might return void, meaning no action is to be taken. Nevertheless, the browser ceases to load any embedded items that are still loading, assuming they are to be overwritten anyway. To avoid this problem, use a URL of `javascript://` (i.e. nothing but a JavaScript comment) and perform other actions required in the `onClick` handler. This will only work for Netscape 3.0 and higher.

Finally, there is a plain bug with Netscape 4.0 browsers that are version 4.03 or less: an `onLoad` handler for an image loaded via an Image object does not do anything. An `onLoad` handler for an image loaded via an `<IMG>` tag does work.

Problems With The Browser Object Model

In addition to variable, event and form reasons, there are other traps within the JavaScript browser objects that can make data appear to vanish.

Omitting the document Property

One of the most common problems is to forget the `document` property. A script writer might make all the right moves: name every tag, window and frame with the `NAME` attribute, avoid reserved words and use window references to ensure the correct object is being referred to – but still can't get it right. This is a long, but typical example that refers to a form value in a form in a frame in a window pointed to by the current window:

```
var temp = top.user_window.body_frame.user_form.comment_field.value;
```

This is the fixed version:

```
var temp = top.user_window.body_frame.document.user_form.comment_field.value;
```

Leaving out the `document` property is the commonest error. In Internet Explorer 4+, this is not an issue in the simple case, because there is some special processing. It works like this: if a property accidentally looked for in the `window` object doesn't exist, then look in any `document` property of that `window` object and return any property of that `document` object that matches the property initially sought. In the simple case, this is exactly what you wanted. However, if you are doing more complex processing, where you want to be explicit about which objects you check for properties, then you have to remember this feature is at work. This is similar to the scope traps you can become tangled in when using event handlers.

A less common issue that can cause confusion is this script:

```
alert(top.document);
```

This will cause an error with Internet Explorer 3.0, 4.0 and 4.01. IE5.0 will do better and report `[object]`, . But for Netscape, the alert box which does appear contains nothing. When a JavaScript expression type-converts a `document` object to a string, the result is just a zero-length string. This is probably for security reasons.

It's Not The Expected Browser

For Netscape and Microsoft products, the browser models are not the same. Your non-trivial JavaScript-enabled HTML document is almost certain to fail if you test it on only one browser and then expect it to run on another. You have to use the compatibility tricks described in Chapter 4 to work around areas where they differ.

Image and Option objects are a common example. Internet Explorer 3.0 does not generally support them. No Microsoft browser supports the Plugin, MimeType or Layer object, although 5.0 has `navigator.mimeType` and `navigator.plugin` properties. No Netscape browser supports the `scripts` array property or the `event` Window property of Microsoft browsers.

The 4.0 level browsers and higher differ considerably in the objects that reflect style sheet properties in an HTML document. Chapter 8, Dynamic HTML, has some discussion of compatibility issues.

Worst of all, advanced features of the event handling models in the 4.0 browser brands are sufficiently different to almost guarantee non-compatibility. If you aren't willing to do some serious thinking to ensure that your event handling logic works in both places, then don't expect it to be portable. Stick to basic event handling.

General Naming Problems

The 'Problems with variables' section describes the pitfalls of poorly named variables. This is really the case for objects of all descriptions. The general rules are:

❑ If an object reflects an HTML tag, don't let the NAME attribute's value clash with any property or method of its parent object.

❑ Don't use reserved words from any of the reserved words lists.

❑ Don't use all-uppercase letters lest they be confused with HTML tag names.

Problems With Cookies

Cookies are already designed to appear and disappear according to the path and domain of the currently viewed HTML document, and due to their own expiry time, so creating a flock (a jar?) of them is asking for trouble. Cookies can make life extremely complex and are slow to debug and fix if problems occur.

For trouble-free client-side cookies: keep the number used to one, set the path to ` ` (the most general path), and either set no expiry time or an expiry time that is way, way in the future.

For trouble-free server-side cookies: ensure cookies arrive separately to form parameters; you can have both a parameter and a cookie with the same name, so keep them separate. When writing `Set-cookie` headers to send to the client, make sure they are written *before* the `Content-Type:` header, and don't forget a `Date:` header if the connection is likely to be slow.

Most cookie problems occur in the browser.

Disappearing Cookies

There are many valid reasons why a cookie might not appear:

❑   The expiry time for the cookie has been reached, and it has disappeared normally.

❑   Your document stored at some URL like `http://www.test.com/public/file.htm` is trying to use a cookie with a path like `/public/part1/section1`. The URL is too general for the highly specific cookie.

❑   The user reloaded a window or frame's URL and the newly loaded document contained instructions to re-set the cookie with an expiry time in the past, so it goes away immediately.

❑   The user reloaded a window or frame with a different URL, and since the domain or path of the new URL no longer matches, the cookie isn't visible.

❑   You are using too many cookies – you've hit the Netscape 20 cookie limit and a cookie has been discarded (usually the oldest, least used cookie).

❑   You created the cookie without an expiry date, and then shut down the browser. The cookie is not written to the cookie file, and is gone.

A cookie might disappear if there are two windows running that have similar URLs. The first window may rely on a given cookie, but the second window may just as easily delete that same one.

Finally, cookies aren't very permanent. The user can always delete the cookie file when the browser is shut down, or use `javascript:` URLs to delete a cookie directly in the browser.

Cookie Value Won't Change

You set and set and set a particular cookie, but no matter what you do, you just can't get that new value back from the `document.cookie` property. One of several things is happening:

❑   Your cookie handling routines aren't quite right. Try the standard ones advocated in Chapter 18.

❑   You are trying to set a cookie that isn't accessible from the current document's URL. Check the path and domain attributes you are supplying.

❑   You have two cookies with the same name, because the path attribute isn't correct somewhere. When you read the cookie, you get the other one that you didn't touch. Test this with the debug URL in Chapter 18.

❑   Your expectations of the `document.cookie` property are too high. Read Chapter 18 on this property – not all the cookie information is available.

Cookie Values Change For No Reason

One of the most attractive reasons for using cookies is as a repository for global data – data that is not attached to any window or document, and is accessible everywhere. However, this comes with a catch.

The catch is coordination. Unless specific security measures are taken, the user can open as many browser windows as desired, and interact with them in any order. This makes it easy for one window or frame to interfere with a cookie set by another window. If the two windows view the same URL, interference is more likely than not. It is nearly impossible to guarantee that a window can update a cookie to a specific value and be confident at a later point that the cookie is unchanged.

To see this, just imagine a form that sets a cookie when a button is pressed. Later, when the user submits the form, the expectation is that the cookie will be sent with the submission. However, if two windows called A and B both show the form, the user can do this: click the button in A; click the button in B; submit in A. The cookie is sent with the B value from the A form – a mess.

Don't do this, or keep your cookie use very, very, simple. If you need to store some data globally, reconsider your design. Use a `<FRAMESET>` document instead of separate windows and store the data in JavaScript variables in the frameset document. At worst, store the data in a Java applet, and ensure the applet continues to run after its host document is closed.

Debugging Techniques

There are a number of effective debugging techniques available for JavaScript programs, ranging from the trivial to the complete.

Client-side JavaScript

For HTML-embedded JavaScript, the crudest debugging tool is `document.write()`. Even if it messes up your HTML document, at least you get some feedback while you are testing. Coupled with a `window.open()` command, you can send the output to another window if you desire.

JavaScript used for Internet connection proxy configuration files, or for browser preference files in Netscape browsers are not amenable to debugging – you have to try it, and if it doesn't work, try it differently. At least the preferences are also exposed to HTML-embedded JavaScript if secure scripts are used.

Alerts

Using `window.alert()` functions embedded in inline JavaScript scripts is the simplest way of stopping the JavaScript interpreter at a given point or points when a document is loading. The message in the alert box can reveal the value of any interesting data as well. This is the simplest way to debug complex logic that involves lots of `if` statements and function calls – just add an alert to the suspect branch or function and you'll know whether it's being executed or not. Alerts are particularly effective with `javascript` URLs as well.

javascript: URLs

Once an HTML document is fully loaded, `document.write()` isn't of much use. Inline alerts won't help if the script has finished running. `javascript:` URLs, which you can type in at any time in the browser window's address or location field allow you to probe the browser and document and see what the current state is. This example shows a window's URL:

```
javascript:alert(top.location.href);
```

However, `javascript:` URLs can be used more generally. Provided you are patient and careful, any amount of JavaScript can be included. This example displays all the element numbers of the first form that have value properties:

```
javascript:var i; for (i=0;i< document.forms[0].elements.length;i){ alert(i); }
```

Finally, any function or method in the browser that is otherwise available to JavaScript can be called. This means you can force a form `submit()` directly, perform a `click()` on a button, or call any of your own functions. This example deletes a cookie using the popular routines, which are assumed to be included in the document somewhere:

```
javascript:DeleteCookie("biscuit3");
```

Java Console Logging

If you don't want to disturb a document when it is loading, but you want a record of what happened, you can log information to the Java console. You can watch the console as the document loads or examine it after the fact. The approach is very similar to `document.write()`, just embed statements as follows at strategic points in your script:

```
java.lang.System.out.println("Window name is: "+top.name);
```

This version does not write an end-of-line character to the console:

```
java.lang.System.out.print('more..');
```

This works for Netscape 3.0 and 4.0.

File Logging

If logging output to the console is not permanent or spacious enough, the client-side JavaScript can write to files on the test computer's local disk (assuming it has one). All that is required is that security hobbles in the browser that prevent this type of behavior are turned off.

JavaScript Console Diagnostics and Unexpected Silences

For Netscape only browsers, version 4.06 or higher, sometimes diagnostic information is logged rather than an error thrown if a client-side script has a problem. Consider this simple script:

```
<HTML><BODY><FORM NAME="fomr1">          <! typo: 'form1' intended>
<INPUT TYPE="text" NAME="field1" VALUE="Test Data">
</FORM>
<SCRIPT>
alert(document.form1.field1.value);      // intended meaning
</SCRIPT></BODY></HTML>
```

For recent Netscape browsers, you might not get an error message popup warning you something is wrong; instead the `alert()` statement will appear to be ignored. This is because in those more recent browsers, errors can be re-directed to the JavaScript console. You need to type `javascript:` in the location box at the top of the browser window before you can see this information:

```
Communicator Console - Netscape                    _ □ X

JavaScript Error: file:C|/local/tmp/test2.htm,
line 5:

document.form1 has no properties.



javascript typein


┌──────────────────────────────────────────────────┐
└──────────────────────────────────────────────────┘
  Clear Console      Close
```

These two Netscape user preferences control the browser's console behavior:

```
user_pref("javascript.console.open_on_error", true);     // or false
user_pref("javascript.classic.error_alerts", true );     // or false
```

If the first of these is set to `true`, the above window automatically appears, otherwise you have to call it up yourself. If the second preference is set to `true`, then the user will be confronted with error messages each time there is a problem. Therefore, for debugging your Web pages, choose `true` and `false` respectively. For relieving the user of irritating message boxes, set their browser to `false` and `false` (the default).

Watch Points

Netscape 4.0 introduces watch points. Watch points allow code to execute when a property is changed. Only debugging tools normally take advantage of these, but they are equally useable directly by scriptwriters. Here is an example derived from remarks by Netscape's Brendan Eich, the JavaScript inventor.

```
<HTML><BODY><SCRIPT>
function display_it(id,oldval,newval)
{
  document.write('test.' + id + ' was: ' + oldval +
                        ' - now is: ' + newval +'<BR>');
  return newval;
}

var test = new Object;

test.watch("prop", display_it);      // start watching property "prop"
test.prop = "first";
delete test.prop;                    // still watch even with the property gone
test.prop = "second";
test.unwatch('prop');                // stop watching property "prop"
test.prop = "third";

</SCRIPT></BODY></HTML>
```

The key is the special `watch()` and `unwatch()` methods which exist for every object, like `valueOf()` and `toString()`. You register interest in a specific property and nominate a function to call when it changes. The function can do anything, including making the change different by not returning the new value passed to it as an argument. The output of this example is:

```
test.prop was: undefined - now is: first
test.prop was: first - now is: second
```

Debuggers

Both Microsoft and Netscape have free JavaScript-in-the-browser debuggers. If you prefer an Integrated Development Environment (IDE) style of development, where the one tool is used for development, testing and debugging, these tools may appeal. For the Microsoft debugger, you can make it start from a script with a simple `debugger` statement (assuming you've installed the tool in the first place):

```
<HTML><BODY><SCRIPT>
debugger;                            // starts the debugger
var x =1;                            // runs under the debugger's control
</SCRIPT></BODY></HTML>
```

Server-side JavaScript

Server-side JavaScript also supports techniques for debugging.

Firstly, all the techniques for client-side JavaScript are relevant to a degree as the server-side scripts ultimately produce client-side HTML and possibly client-side JavaScript as well. However, these cannot be used to halt server-side JavaScript as it runs, or confirm that a piece of JavaScript is executing on the server.

Secondly, since server-side JavaScript is securely 'behind' or 'within' a web server, the web server's file system can be used to create log files. The `File` object of Netscape's Enterprise Server is an example of a mechanism that allows this. Since a web server is involved, the server's own logs can be exploited to see URL requests, form parameters and cookie data travelling to the server and back. Server-side code often interacts with relational databases, and such products have logging system of their own.

For ASP scripts on a Microsoft platform, the Microsoft script debugger can be used to debug script fragments as for the browser environment.

Finally, Chapter 11 displays integrated features in the Netscape Enterprise Server server-side system, which allows the scriptwriter to see an execution trace of the server side code as it occurs.

Standalone JavaScript

Since standalone JavaScript has much the same flexibility as any third-generation programming language, the options for debugging are numerous.

As for client-side JavaScript, the quickest and dirtiest method of debugging is to write out debug information, for example:

```
Clib.puts("Current PATH is: " + Clib.getenv("PATH") + "\n");
```

The example of a client-side `alert()` in standalone JavaScript is a little harder to duplicate. Standalone JavaScript is not embedded in a complex browser-like application that supplies lots of support for graphical objects like alert boxes.

Nevertheless, it is not many lines of script to produce an alert box. Standalone JavaScript versions like ScriptEase 4.1 for Windows 95 have a library of functions that give access to the Windows 95 graphical user interface. If you are new to programming, that is a large and time-consuming can of worms to open. However, if you have a desire to program graphical user interfaces, feel free.

File Logging

The `Clib.puts()` example above just writes data to the display window that the script was run from. It is just as easy to log to a file. Only a few lines are required:

```
var fp = Clib.fopen("logfile","w");              // open log file for writing

Clib.fprintf(fp,"%s", "My logged message\n");    // write out a formatted line
Clib.fputs(fp, "My other logged message\n");     // write out just a string

Clib.fclose(fp);                                 // close the log file neatly
```

The `fputs()` and `fprintf()` lines appear as often as logged messages are necessary.

CGI Emulation

When a CGI program goes wrong, it's often not easy to see why, since a web server – not a human – controls it. However, a CGI program can be run without a Web server, provided it receives input matching the input a Web server would supply. If the program is written in a flexible scripting language like JavaScript, this is not hard to setup, but it is beyond the scope of this book.

Debuggers

As for the browsers, a debugging tool for ScriptEase 4.0 standalone JavaScript is available, and the Microsoft Script Debugger will work for standalone scripts as for in a Web browser.

Summary

The interpreted and loosely typed nature of JavaScript means that errors are often reported without detailed explanations of what went wrong. The ability to add names to the object hierarchy of a browser can result in obscure errors when new names clash with existing ones.

Elements of a browser that can appear and disappear cause the same thing to happen to the data they make available to JavaScript. Windows, cookies and separately loaded items such as images are all examples.

However, there are plenty of ways to probe a given script's behavior, ranging from simple interactive inquiries to full-blown visual debugging environments. Simple techniques are often sufficient to pick up the commonest problem cases. For the rest, you must accept that convenience of an interpreted language gives flexibility with one hand, but with the other puts the onus on the scriptwriter to use a degree of care.

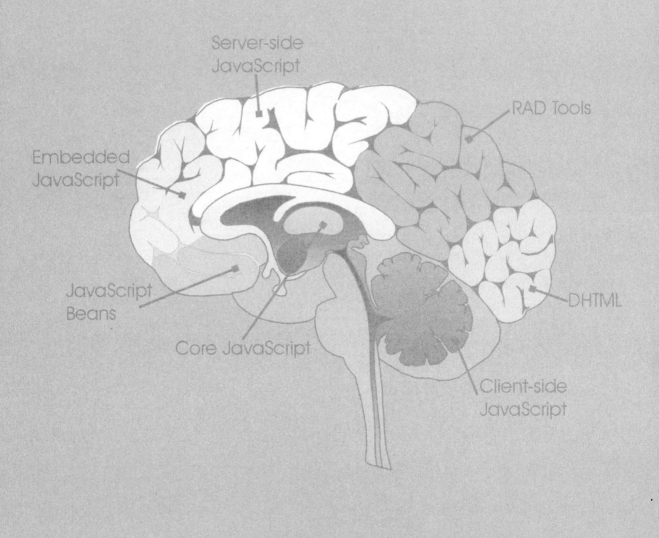

Server-side
JavaScript

RAD Tools

Embedded
JavaScript

JavaScript
Beans

Core JavaScript

DHTML

Client-side
JavaScript

Privacy, Security and Cookies

JavaScript scripts used on the Internet come with a number of risks. Allowing any old script, written by a possibly anonymous script writer, to do something unknown to a trusting person's computer is a risk for that trusting person. On the other hand, to allow an anonymous person to obtain a script that is someone else's property presents a risk to the owner of the script. There are numerous mechanisms available that help address these safety issues.

What your script does to your own property is your own concern. It's when your property and scripts are mingled with other people's property and scripts that risks arise, and people are likely to become annoyed, upset or even litigious. **Privacy** matters set the boundaries of what shouldn't or can't be shared. **Security** matters set the boundaries of good behavior when there is a need to share. **Security hobbles** prevent scripts from crossing either kind of boundary without appropriate permission.

In this chapter, you'll see what you can and can't get away with, and how to forge trust with other parties such as web browser users. Once that trust is forged you'll see how to get away with scripts that otherwise wouldn't be possible.

Privacy

One person's treasured privacy is another person's jail cell. Security hobbles that grant privacy to one participant in a shared system take functionality away from someone else. The three main players in such shared systems are browser users, scriptwriters and webmasters.

If a security system is in place, then browser security hobbles are not generally enforced. So privacy issues only really apply in an unsecured environment, such as ordinary use of the World Wide web.

Privacy for Browser Users

For users of JavaScript enabled browsers, requesting a URL represents a risk if it contains JavaScript. Without security hobbles, a JavaScript script could seize control of the browser, or possibly the browser's computer. The simplest form of privacy for the user is to turn JavaScript support off in the browser via the browser preferences. This can't be done from within an HTML embedded JavaScript script, except by specially arranging use of the `navigator.preference` property in Netscape Navigator 4.0+. Even then the browser must be shut down and restarted for it to take effect. It can be set in the `prefs.js` preference file for Netscape 3+, or via any of the configuration techniques described in the 'Browser JavaScript From The Outside In' chapter.

A number of JavaScript bugs that create security risks have been identified in version 3.0 and 4.0 browsers. To avoid as many of these as possible, make sure you have the absolutely latest version of the browser available. For example, at this time of writing Netscape 4.61 is the latest 4.x Netscape browser. This web page: `http://www-genome.wi.mit.edu/WWW/faqs/wwwsf?/html` is a good starting point for JavaScript security bug information.

There are several kinds of security hobbles that protect the browser user's privacy.

I/O Restrictions

The main input mechanism for a browser is via user interaction with the browser's graphical interface. The main output mechanism is the display of HTML to that graphical interface, or the requesting of documents over the web via URLs. All of these can be done to a degree from JavaScript, as we've seen in earlier chapters. However, it is nearly always true that client-side JavaScript is restrained from doing any other input or output, like writing to the user's computer's disk or network without the user's permission. Generally, the user can be confident that no changes are occurring to the local computer outside of the browser. There is the odd exception, however. Writing to files, to network connections, and to the display are the main sources of risk. Display-related restrictions are discussed later. Writing to files and to network connections are generally impossible without special arrangements and are described next.

Local Scripts

If a browser loads a script directly from the local computer without using a web server, then that script can do anything the language and host objects allow. The user may get a warning and an option to back out, depending on how the browser's security preferences are set up.

JScript 3.0 and later can take advantage of a pack of filesystem access objects. These objects are stored in a system file called `scrrun.dll`, supplied as part of the WSH, JScript or VBScript installation. You can get this file, available as part of the scripting engine downloads, at `http://msdn.microsoft.com/scripting`. It adds `FileSystemObject`, `TextStream`, `File` and `Folder` objects which allow local files to be removed or renamed as well as created or changed, but this is only possible for Internet Explorer 3+, and browser security options must be lowered by the user for this to happen. The main purpose of this JavaScript add-on is to make server-side JavaScript programs more useful.

Netscape JavaScript can also write to local files, but there is no direct support in the language. Instead, Java objects supply this functionality – those objects must be accessed from JavaScript via LiveConnect. Here is an example of writing a user-supplied string to a user-supplied filename. The 'Capability-based Security' section below explains the mechanics of obtaining these permissions.

```
<HTML><BODY><SCRIPT>
function save_it(jo_file, filedata)
{
    netscape.security.PrivilegeManager.enablePrivilege("UniversalFileAccess");
    var jo_writer = new java.io.FileWriter(jo_file);
    jo_writer.write(filedata,0,filedata.length);
    jo_writer.close();
    netscape.security.PrivilegeManager.disablePrivilege("UniversalFileAccess");
}
</SCRIPT>
<FORM>
File Name: <INPUT TYPE="text" NAME="file"><BR>
File Data: <INPUT TYPE="text" NAME="data"
                  ONCHANGE="save_it(this.form.file.value, this.value)">
</FORM></BODY></HTML>
```

This example also requires some agreement from the user before it can go ahead – see the Security section. Microsoft browsers can also take advantage of Java to write to local files, but the security mechanisms are different. In particular, the `netscape.security...` permission request lines aren't required for Microsoft browsers.

Java Connections

A browser that supports Java applets can make network connections. With ActiveX or LiveConnect, JavaScript scripts can control these applet connections. Chapter 15 describes how.

However, without a security agreement, the connections are of limited use. Java applets are downloaded via a URL in an `<APPLET>` or `<OBJECT>` HTML tag. Only the computer supplying the page for that URL can be connected to. If the tag includes a `CODEBASE` URL, then the computer at that `CODEBASE` URL is the only possibility for connections. In either case, the applet can only contact the host that it came from.

A more subtle possibility stems from the fact that one Java applet may converse directly with another. However, the part of the Java system that loads applets also ensures that applets from different sites can't communicate with each other. This prevents one applet from exploiting the network connections available to another.

Cookies

Cookies are described in a later section of this chapter. The cookie data available to web servers doesn't include any very private information such as the user's name, so risk from cookies is minimal. Long-lived cookies are stored in a file on the browser's computer. However, this file is a plain data file with a maximum size of approximately 1200 Kilobytes for Netscape. Other than taking up space, this file doesn't do anything outside the browser environment. A cookie file will normally be only one or two Kilobytes. The Microsoft Internet Explorer cookie file can grow indefinitely, so in theory a malicious web site could load your Internet Explorer computer up with cookies until it chokes. In practice, no one appears to have bothered yet.

Netscape Mission Control

The `netscape.cfg` file of Netscape 4+ browsers can be configured to give away control of the user's preferences. A JavaScript script stored on a webserver as described in Chapter 4 takes over the role of security for the browser. In a company environment, this usually poses no privacy risks. Similarly, for Microsoft, the AutoAdmin tools, or other tools that can set registry entries remotely may be used to configure the Internet Explorer browser's security restrictions. However, for the Microsoft case, this security management activity doesn't use much JavaScript, being implemented in other ways, and if no JavaScript is involved, it's not really worth exploring the attendant issues here. Use of Netscape's Mission Control is briefly described in Chapter 4.

Window Limitations

The main form of output from client-side JavaScript is not to files and network connections, but to the browser itself. JavaScript can affect windows in a browser in three ways:

❑ Write new content to browser windows.

❑ Change window decorations such as toolbars and menus.

❑ Modify JavaScript host objects and variables within windows.

The user can have more than one browser window open at a time. The user can also have more than one URL per window if frames are present, and those URLs can come from different web sites. If it were not for a number of security hobbles, JavaScript could use its control over windows to:

❑ Forge or manipulate content displayed from other web sites, misrepresenting those sites.

❑ Make the browser uncontrollable by the user.

❑ Wreck the JavaScript data and objects stored in windows displaying other web sites.

Two concepts are central to the window security features that prevent these things from happening.

Every Window Is An Island

To understand JavaScript window security restrictions, first take a step back and reflect on the ECMAScript standard. If you skipped Chapter 3, it'll help to go back and look at it before reading on here.

In ECMAScript terminology, an **execution environment** is a stage on which scripts can perform (execute), whether those scripts are standalone or in web client or server applications. When an execution environment is created, such as in a browser, a good question is "What is the current object?" The standard states that all built-in objects and built-in functions in a script are part of a special 'global' object, which is the current scope when that script starts executing. Even functions like parseInt() can therefore be viewed as a method of an object.

However, there is not just one global object in a JavaScript-capable web browser. Instead, the browser has a global object for each browser window currently open. These global objects each have a property window that refers back to that global object. These window properties provide a named hook so that the scriptwriter can get access to that global object.

Each global object is like a bucket in which all the data specific to the window can be stored, making it easy to access. Therefore, the window property sits at the top of a hierarchy (or a pool) of data that includes all the JavaScript variables, objects and host objects in that window. If the window is closed, everything owned directly or indirectly by the global object is tracked down and cleaned up. If a window is open, then all items within that one bucket are on the same footing – they can all access each other.

This makes each window fully self-contained and independent. It also makes it easy to keep scripts from interfering with other windows, since they can only ultimately belong to one global object. Viewed from the JavaScript perspective, the browser is not a single hierarchy or pool of objects and properties, it is a number of hierarchies or pools.

Unfortunately, life is rarely that simple. In reality, one window will often contain JavaScript variables that refer to objects or properties in other windows. A simple example is the `window.open()` method – the return value can be stored in a variable in the containing window but refers to the global object in the newly created window. Similarly, the newly created window's global object has an `opener` property referring back to the old window.

At the time of writing this, the ECMAScript standard doesn't specify how the communicating-between-globals system works. The answer for browsers is glue software: LiveConnect for Netscape and features of ActiveX/OLE/COM for Internet Explorer. This glue is effectively invisible except when window ownership issues are important. The owner of a window is the host address of the window's main URL, for example `www.something.com:80`. Attempts to work with properties or methods in a different window first have to pass checks based on the owners of the two windows. This script can be used to show the dynamic behavior involved:

```
<HTML><BODY><SCRIPT>
var win2 = null;

function open_local() { top.win2=window.open(window.location.href,'test'); }

function open_remote() { top.win2=window.open('http://www.wrox.com','test'); }

function show_it()
{
  window.document.forms[0].one.value = top.win2;
  window.document.forms[0].two.value = top.win2.name;
  window.document.forms[0].three.value = top.win2.location.href;
}
</SCRIPT><FORM>
<INPUT TYPE="button" VALUE="Open local window" ONCLICK="open_local()">
<INPUT TYPE="button" VALUE="Open remote window" ONCLICK="open_remote()">
<INPUT TYPE="button" VALUE="Show window details" ONCLICK="show_it()">
<INPUT TYPE="button" VALUE="Go backwards" ONCLICK="window.history.go(-1)">
<BR>
Type of win2: <INPUT NAME="one" TYPE="text"><BR>
Name of win2: <INPUT NAME="two" TYPE="text"><BR>
URL  of win2: <INPUT NAME="three" TYPE="text"><BR>
</FORM></BODY></HTML>
```

When displayed, the document looks like this:

This HTML page has four purposes:

❑ Create a second window with a URL that is at the same Web site as the main window.

❑ Create a second window with a URL that is at a different Web site as the main window.

❑ Display some state information about the second window.

❑ Provide content for the second window when the URL for that window is at the same Web site.

The Show window details button is used to report the current state of the auto-created window.

The following discussion pertains to Netscape behavior. Before pressing either of the open buttons, reporting the current state produces an error because the second window is not open and therefore win2 is not yet an object. If a local window is opened, the name and URL will display correctly. If a remote window is opened, then an error results trying to get its URL (assuming you don't own the WROX web site). If you navigate with that new window back to a local web page, either via the Open local window button or directly using the window toolbars, the URL is accessible again.

When the window is off-limits, Netscape's error is:

Access disallowed from scripts at http://mysite.com/tests/remote_test.htm to documents in another domain.

This message assumes that the mysite.com site is where you are doing the testing.

If the second window is closed, a number of obscure errors can occur, depending on the version and whether Java is enabled or not. It is better not to examine a closed window object, except to test if the window *is* closed by looking at the Boolean value window.closed.

If this script is run with Internet Explorer 3.0 and JScript 1.0, none of the second window's properties are accessible, including window.closed. This shows that JavaScript inter-window access is not a requirement of JavaScript, but a feature implemented and supported by the browser itself. For the 4.0 and 5.0 Internet Explorer browsers, the cross domain-access is also prevented, so the situation is similar. However, which objects and properties *are* available differs slightly – see the discussion in Chapter 5 on Windows and Frames under the heading 'When It's Not HTML'.

Every Window Is Free

Without security arrangements granting the scriptwriter special privileges, some browser features can't be removed from the user's control. In this section, these features are merely characterized. Later on, when security is discussed, under 'Capability-based Security' there is a more in-depth look. For now, these features typically are:

❑ Existing windows can't have toolbars or other window decorations removed or added.

❑ Documents from other sites loaded into frames can't have their events stolen by the frameset.

❑ Windows can't be created so small that the user can't read the contents.

❑ Windows can't permanently obscure other windows, or grab the user's input focus and keep it.

Canvas and kiosk mode, in particular, in which a single window takes over the whole screen, requires special privileges for Netscape 4+ browsers. For these browsers, the user can drop the above restrictions on scripts by changing their browser preferences as described in the 'Privacy For Scriptwriters' section. For full documentation on which methods require special privileges before they can be used refer to:
`http://developer.netscape.com:80/docs/manuals/index.html?content=security.html` and in particular the download links titled 'Introduction to the Capabilities classes' and 'Netscape System Targets'. As usual, full URLs are in Appendix L.

Resource Limiting Features

Browsers are designed to limit the user to a fraction of the resources of the browser's computer:

❑ **Disk space.** Pages loaded from a given Web server can't consume more than 80 Kilobytes of space in a Netscape browser's cookie file – more than that can be consumed with Internet Explorer. Creating new JavaScript Image objects, or writing new HTML pages is still subject to the caching restrictions that the browser user puts in place when setting the browser's preferences. If the user has all caching turned off, Images or pages won't be cached if they aren't part of a currently displayed window.

❑ **Memory.** Internet Explorer 4.0+ allows the user to place an upper limit on the amount of memory that a newly downloaded ActiveX control can consume. Otherwise, browsers can still consume large amounts of memory. The video memory used for graphics and windows is easy for most browsers to consume, especially if there are many windows, frames and images displayed.

Such memory protection systems aren't foolproof. Even for normal memory and non-ActiveX controls, this script fragment will bring most browsers quickly to their knees. **Don't try this script** unless you're willing to lose any unsaved information and re-boot your PC:

```
<HTML><BODY><SCRIPT>
var big_string = "double me up!";

while (true)
{
    big_string = big_string + big_string;       // 20 iterations equals all
your memory...
}
</SCRIPT></BODY></HTML>
```

Memory limitations also apply to Java applets in Netscape Navigator. Sometimes these applets are 'cleaned up' to save memory, which can also impact JavaScript.

❑ **Network Connections.** JavaScript scripts may open many windows, but the maximum number of connections set by the user via preferences will still be observed. Any additional windows will have to wait for a free connection.

❑ **CPU.** Netscape browsers and Internet Explorer 4.0+ will abort any JavaScript script that executes more than one million "instructions" (a vague term used by the vendors, probably meaning one JavaScript statement) before finishing. This is designed to prevent scripts from locking the user out of the browser permanently, not to prevent the browser from consuming large amounts of CPU time. This feature can be annoying if you are trying to do long, complex calculations with the interpreter. The user still has access to window menus and toolbars. There is also a workaround: break the task into steps and only run one step at a time. Here is a before-and-after example:

```
<HTML><BODY><SCRIPT>
var total = 234;
var new_items = 2555666;
function dumb_add()       // addition for people with only one finger
{
  while (new_items)       // won't complete: 2,555,666 iterations > 1,000,000
  {
    new_items--;
    total++;
  }
}
dumb_add();
alert('New total is: '+total);
</SCRIPT></BODY></HTML>
```

In the workaround case below, the browser will still be busy 99% of the time, but because the executing script breaks off regularly for a millisecond, the browser is satisfied that the user still has a chance to do things, and doesn't ever report an error. The browser will therefore be able to respond to user input, but only slowly, especially if that input means other scripts need to run. At the same time, the long-running script will be able to eventually complete all its processing.

```
<HTML><BODY><SCRIPT>
var total = 234;
var new_items = 2555666;

function dumb_add()                  // Do addition for people with only one finger
{
    var steps = 10000;               // don't run for too long
    while (new_items && steps)
    {
      steps--;
      new_items--;
      total++;
    }
    if ( new_items )
      setTimeout('dumb_add()',1);
    else
      alert('New total is: '+total);
}
dumb_add();
</SCRIPT></BODY></HTML>
```

Other Risks

There are other risks for the user when using a browser on the Internet, but not many of them involve JavaScript. A few do:

❑   Submitting HTML forms. The user's name or e-mail address cannot be obtained by a web site due to a form being submitted, unless the user has made special security arrangements. So submitting forms is generally safe for the user.

❑   Client-side JavaScript cannot silently e-mail a user when the user browses to a Web page. The user always gets the opportunity to confirm or cancel the submission.

❑   The user can configure a helper application to run when a particular file type (MIME type) is fetched across the network. Configuring a standalone JavaScript interpreter to run when JavaScript files are received is a risky choice, unless the interpreter has a security system of its own. This is because a downloaded standalone script will then automatically run, doing who-knows-what.

- ❑ In modern browsers the user can release all of the restrictions in the browser that require a security agreement. To do this in Internet Explorer 4.0, in the **Options** dialog box, under **Security**, set the **Minimum Security** level to **None**. In Netscape 4.0 browsers, shut down all of the Netscape windows and modify by hand the `prefs.js` file. That file is stored in the Netscape installation area: there is one for each browser user and one for the default user. Add this line and restart the browser:

```
user_pref("signed.applets.codebase_principal_support", true);
```

This line means that every computer that supplies a script to the browser can be trusted to supply safe scripts. Obviously this is not realistic and so this option is usually only needed in test environments. Even after supplying this line, the user is still prompted a grand total of once in order to confirm it's ok to trust the script.

Privacy for Browser Scripters

For scriptwriters, the two main privacy issues are preventing scripts from being stolen, and preventing scripts from being wrecked. The task is harder for JavaScript than it is for Java or other kinds of program because the script source and the executable program are one and the same.

For standalone scripts, neither issue is a problem, unless someone else has access to your computer or your account. If those scripts are used as CGI or ASP programs behind a web server, then there is also no problem, unless the web server itself has a security problem.

For server-side JavaScript, the scripts are stored and executed with the web server, so provided that server is secure, no web user can access them. HTML files sent to the user are usually stripped of any server-side JavaScript in the web server before delivery.

For client-side JavaScript, the situation is much worse. There is no way to systematically protect JavaScript code except by entering into a security arrangement with the user. There are a few partial solutions.

Hiding Source Code

Client-side JavaScript has virtually no protection on the web. If you need your web pages and its JavaScript to be publicly available, you might as well give up, and accept that the work you do is there to be stolen and modified as any web user sees fit. It is non-trivial (except for experts) to break-in to a web site and damage your original HTML and .js files, so at least the pages delivered by the web server are sent in good order, even if the user does something with it afterwards. If server break-ins concern you, use a tried and tested Unix variant such as Linux for your web site and test its security with the SATAN tool: `http://www.fish.com/satan/`. If you don't like the name, try SAINT instead, at `http://wwdsilx.wwdsi.com/saint/`.

Once the JavaScript is in the web browser, there are only a few things that can be done to protect it. In particular, this code does not protect anything:

```
<HTML><HEAD>
<SCRIPT SRC="secret.js"></SCRIPT>
</HEAD></HTML>
```

The JavaScript in the file secret.js may not appear when the user chooses to View Source for this document, but its URL is obvious. The user only needs to type the full URL for the file into the browser, retrieve the file, and then do View Source again. Browsers can display plain text files as well as HTML files, and a .js file is typically a plain text file.

For a user on the web who views publicly available HTML, there are few foolproof tactics for protecting or hiding client-side JavaScript. The nearest thing is to embed your JavaScript in a Java applet, using the Netscape LiveConnect features of Java. That is a lot of work for non-trivial JavaScript. Further information on embedding and LiveConnect can be found in Chapter 22.

An easier but less effective tactic is to protect your scripts by making the job of copying them less palatable, rather than impossible.

Relying On Microsoft

Microsoft provides a tool called the Microsoft Script Encoder that turns readable JavaScript into unreadable gobbledygook. This tool can be downloaded for free from http://msdn.microsoft.com/scripting/ as a component of the Microsoft Scripting Engine. It does a good job of hiding your precious scripts from lazy thieves, but isn't robust enough to entirely guarantee anything. In particular, a genius thief can unencode the scripts encoded by this tool, so don't bet the family jewels on it. Fortunately, most thieves aren't geniuses.

To get encoding working you need the Microsoft Script Encoder tool and at least version 5.0 of JScript. Use of the encoder is restricted to Microsoft environments – no Netscape.

The encoder tool is a simple command line driven one – run it from an MS-DOS window. The current version is version 1.0.

Here is a simple example of using the encoder. First, a plain HTML file called before.htm:

```
<HTML><BODY>
<SCRIPT>
  alert('Page has started loading');
</SCRIPT>
<FORM>
Your information goes here:
<INPUT TYPE="text"
   ONCHANGE="this.value=this.value.toUpperCase()"
   WIDTH=10>
</FORM></BODY></HTML>
```

Here is the command that encodes the file:

```
C:\Program Files\Microsoft Script Encoder > screnc before.htm after.htm
```

Here is the encoded file, created in after.htm:

```
<HTML><BODY>
<SCRIPT language =
JScript.Encode>#@~^LAAAAA==@#@&P~mV•DYvBhCo•P4lkPdOmDY• [P^Wl9rUoE#p@#@&^#~@</SCRIP
T>
<FORM>
Your information goes here:
<INPUT TYPE="text"
   ONCHANGE="this.value=this.value.toUpperCase()"
   WIDTH=10>
</FORM></BODY></HTML>
```

The encoder has translated the contents of the <SCRIPT> block from one language – JScript – to another – JScript.Encode. Jscript.Encode is a special Microsoft variant of JavaScript that is designed to be readable by computers, not humans (it is a tokenized stream of JavaScript statements, if you like). As you can see, the first script block re-written in JScript.Encode is now very hard to identify as an alert() statement. The encoder doesn't hide JavaScript event handlers at all so that code is still exposed. We can fix that by varying the original content to look like this:

```
<HTML><BODY>
<SCRIPT>alert('Page has started loading');</SCRIPT>
<FORM>
  Your information goes here: <INPUT TYPE="text" WIDTH=10>
</FORM>
<SCRIPT>
  function do_change() { this.value=this.value.toUpperCase();}
  document.forms[0].elements[0].onchange = do_change;
</SCRIPT>
</BODY></HTML>
```

The encoded copy now looks like:

```
<HTML><BODY>
<SCRIPT language =
JScript.Encode>#@~^IgAAAA==C^+.D`EnlT+,4lkPdYmDOn9PVKCNbxoEbI^#~@</SCRIPT>
<FORM>
  Your information goes here: <INPUT TYPE="text" WIDTH=10>
</FORM>
<SCRIPT language = JScript.Encode>#@~^fwAAAA==@#@&P~6E      mYbW
~NK{^tmxLnv#PP~Y4k/c-CV!+{Y4kd 7lsE• YKj22•DZCd•`bi}@#@&P~9W1E:•xD 0KDh/]!D
•V+snxD/$ZD W     m41Uon~{P[W|^tmxLnp@#@&^#~@</SCRIPT>
</BODY></HTML>
```

Now the event handler is hidden as well. This is the same tactic that you can use if you don't want to do Page Signing of an HTML page but you can do Object Signing (see later for more on this stuff).

Such an encoded page is loaded into a browser via a normal URL, and the JavaScript's effect is identical to the unencoded version, but there are a few restrictions:

❑ Using a source-level debugger on an encoded script is not practical.

❑ Only Internet Explorer 4.0+ can handle an encoded script.

❑ Even if the right browser is present, only computers with the encoding tools installed as well can handle an encoded script.

Therefore, unless Microsoft ends up entirely dominating the browser market, encoding is only useful where you control the browser user's computer. Encoding applies to other uses of Microsoft JScript too, such as JScript in ASP. However, its benefit is easiest to see in the browser. Be mindful that various claims have already been made in Usenet newsgroups that the encoding scheme has been 'cracked' – the system is not intended to be robust security.

Making It Too Much Effort

If you need your web pages to be viewable in all browsers then Microsoft encoding isn't currently an option, and therefore your scripts must be *au naturel*. However, there are some simple barriers that will make the job harder, and encourage any thieving culprits to give up. The most common tricks that make scripts difficult to read are:

❑ Put the whole HTML or JavaScript file contents on one line. Many CGI programs that produce HTML don't put line breaks into the generated HTML file. This helps keep the file as small as possible, improving download performance. You can do the same with your JavaScript `<SCRIPT>` sections. The script stealer has to create a formatting program to fix this, or do it by hand. If your JavaScript code is CGI generated, it is easy to apply a filter to the output that turns all return characters into spaces.

❑ Use obfuscation (confusion) techniques. It's possible, or even common, to write really unclear code that no one can understand. Since JavaScript has syntax related to C, some research of the obfuscation techniques in C may help you create unreadable code.

❑ Use a code-shrouding program. Such a program takes your readable JavaScript source, and translates it to equivalent source, but with formatting removed and all symbolic names replaced with randomly generated names. You keep the original source, in case you need to make further changes, which are re-shrouded as needed. An example showing a function before and after shrouding:

```
// before
function calculate_interest(principal, percent_rate, yearly_calculations, term)
{
    var factor = 1 + percent_rate/yearly_calculations/100;      // one lot of
interest
    return principal * Math.pow(factor, yearly_calculations * term);
}
```

```
// after
function a01(a02,a03,a04,a05){var a06=1+a03/a04;return a02*Math.pow(a06,a04*a05);}
```

The new function works the same as the original but its meaning is a near mystery. JMyth is one such tool for JavaScript: `http://www.geocities.com/SiliconValley/Vista/5233/jmyth.htm`.

Unfortunately, such tools have severe limitations. Firstly, as the example shows, built-in objects, methods and properties can't be renamed. These are often a large part of the code, and can give away the code's intent. Secondly, the translation is almost guaranteed to produce non-working code if `eval()`, `setTimeout()` or `setInterval()` are used, since their string arguments are actually code in disguise. Translators are usually too dumb to detect these more complex cases, so the arguments refer to original names, not translated ones. There are other similar problems which translators can't easily detect as well. Finally, if the document is a frame, referring to functions or variables in another frame, the translator has the further job of coordinating all the changes across documents.

Leaving aside these limitations, you may still find such a tool useful.

Making It Impolite

If you put a copyright statement in comments at the top of your code and ask that others should not use it, or at least, if they do, then the code is attributed back to you, people might just do it. If the information is "published" (exposed on the web) then you automatically have some copyright rights in countries that respect the Berne convention (most countries), provided you identify yourself as the author.

Making It Password Protected

The section on privacy for web servers describes several ways you can control user access to your browser JavaScript in the first place. However, once the user has access, they can do with the scripts as they please again.

The Most Practical Approach

In the end, worrying about theft is probably not productive. The main problem is identifying when your script has been taken and used elsewhere, and by whom – almost impossible to enforce or police on the Web. Most client-side JavaScript code is small and uninspired, and uses well-known techniques that aren't new in any case.

Discouraging Onlookers

As a scriptwriter interested in privacy, your main enemy might be evil websurfers, but they're not the only enemy. Your JavaScript-enabled web pages and any responses from the browser user may pass through any number of intermediate computers as part of their delivery, and those computers could be run by evil server administrators. What to do about these people?

Hiding Downloaded Scripts

When a user requests a URL from a web server, everyone between the user and the web server has a chance to look at it. Most browsers now include support for a network protocol called the Secure Sockets Layer (SSL). If support for this is turned on, then all data sent between the browser and any web servers with the same support will be hidden from intermediate systems. It can also deny all but your friends access to the web server that provides your scripts.

However, once the user has the data, such as a .js file, they may do anything with it without using secure means, such as forwarding it via e-mail. Therefore, even with SSL, files are only as safe as the recipient is. The main purpose of SSL is to extend the safety of web page delivery from the web server out beyond the browser to the browser user. Therefore the gory details are discussed under web server security further on.

Privacy For Web Servers

There are a few JavaScript security issues for webmasters. However, most of the security issues aren't JavaScript related. Since this is a JavaScript book they're only touched on briefly.

Web Server Certificates

Web **server certificates** let you control user access to web servers via the **Secure Sockets Layer – SSL**. SSL just uses some low-level magic on top of the Internet's basic TCP/IP network to hide information like web page request and responses from onlookers and the uninvited. This includes hiding JavaScript. Briefly, in order to use SSL you need a number of items:

- ❑ A server certificate
- ❑ A CA (Certificate Authority) certificate matching the server certificate
- ❑ An SSL capable Web browser
- ❑ A download point for the certificates, or the certificates installed in all user's browsers
- ❑ An SSL capable Web server to securely hold your Web pages

The CA certificate is a second certificate that is used to check the validity of the real server certificate. It represents the authority that issues and checks the server certificate, and is supposed to be a very well known and credible certificate. When an SSL connection is attempted, certificates are exchanged between the ends of the connection and the big tick is given only if the certificate authority in the server certificate is present and correct as well. The mechanics of organizing and validating certificates are described in more detail under 'Object Signing'.

Once you have these items, web development is pretty much as normal. The only change is that you should replace any references to `http:` with `https:` in any URLs you might have.

Here's how to get these items.

❑ Server Certificates can be had from most certificate vendors. VeriSign (`www.verisign.com`), Thawte (`www.thawte.com`) and Belsign (`www.belsign.com`) are the big three. VeriSign provides free test certificates with a 14-day expiry period. Otherwise, the server certificate will cost you, and they generally expire after a time.

❑ CA Certificates come from the Web pages of individual certificate authorities. Netscape and Microsoft browsers come pre-loaded with most CA certificates, so those are no effort to get. If you choose some other authority for your server certificate, then you approach the authority for the CA certificate via their Web site. Finally, you could pay up for a self-managed solution like Netscape's Certificate Server, which allows you to be your own CA. You ask yourself for the CA certificate, and if you think you're OK, then you hand it over to yourself …

❑ SSL support exists in both the major browsers. Make sure your browser choice has SSL 3.0 support – the latest version – and turn on SSL in the preferences of the browser.

❑ You need a download point or a distribution strategy for your certificates because you won't be the only person who tries to connect to your secure Web site. Provided your Web server is set up correctly, you can just supply the certificate via an `<A>` tag. Of course, if you make the certificate entirely accessible to the public, it'll be accessible to criminals as well, so you can't do that. You have to do something complex, non-technical and bureaucratic in the Web site to ensure only credible people can have access. Forcing people to telephone you for the certificate URL, or a password to access it, is a start.

❑ For a secure Web server, you may have to pay up for Netscape or Microsoft Web servers. However, there is an alternative. The Apache Web server is top quality and is free, but doesn't normally support SSL; yet there is a special free-outside-of-the-USA version that does. See `www.cryptsoft.com` – they have added a free version of SSL called SSLEAY to Apache.

All this SSL has very little to do with JavaScript, except that it hides script content as effectively as it hides all other kinds of content – HTML, Java and the rest.

Security Problems

For webmasters, there are a few JavaScript issues that create problems on the web site's computer.

CGI-BIN Trap On Windows NT

Standalone JavaScript scripts require an interpreter. If that standalone script is used as a CGI program, the interpreter is typically stored with the web server. By convention, a directory called `cgi-bin` is used. However, on Windows NT, this exposes the interpreter to the web user's control – they can submit URLs that have attached script commands, which are then executed by the interpreter. Such commands could read or delete files, or cause other similar problems. Put the interpreter elsewhere for Windows NT web sites.

Chapter 12 has many examples of how a ScriptEase 4.0 JavaScript interpreter can be controlled via command line arguments sent via CGI.

HTML Form Submissions

An issue affecting both server-side JavaScript and standalone JavaScript in CGI programs relates to form submissions. Forms are submitted from web browsers, and without security agreements, the data in a web browser is insecure. An HTML form which submits to a web server can be pulled apart by a hostile user (maybe it's a tax form), mimicked or rewritten in another page and submitted from that page. If the form is normally subject to complex JavaScript validation, all that validation can be ripped out by the hostile user and data submitted that would otherwise be stopped by validation. Alternatively, the user could write a different form that submits to the same CGI program.

Therefore, the receiving program can't assume the form data is in good order, just because some users have proper client-side JavaScript validation in place. Making this assumption when it's not true can result in the CGI program failing which might even crash the web server's computer if it fails spectacularly.

If the submitting user is not trustworthy, as on the public Internet, then all the submitted form data should be thoroughly checked in the server-side JavaScript or CGI program to avoid surprises. Relying on client-side JavaScript only works in a secure environment such as a corporate Intranet.

This trivial example illustrates why any kind of assumption about public form data is bad. This is the original:

```
<HTML><BODY><FORM ACTION="update.cgi">
Enter account balance:
<INPUT TYPE="text" ONCHANGE="if (!parseInt(this.value))  this.value='NO-
BALANCE';">
<INPUT TYPE="submit">
</FORM></BODY></HTML>
```

This is a copy created by a hostile user:

```
<HTML><BODY><FORM ACTION="update.cgi">
Enter account balance:
<INPUT TYPE="text">
<INPUT TYPE="submit">
</FORM></BODY></HTML>
```

In the first case, the form will always submit a valid, numeric balance, or else the special string NO-BALANCE. It might therefore seem reasonable for the update.cgi program to expect only these particular values. However, the hacked copy submits to exactly the same CGI program, and can accept any string, including negative numbers and random garbage. Therefore the CGI program cannot afford to trust client-side JavaScript to do its job in an insecure public arena.

The hostile user can become even more hostile:

```
<HTML><BODY><FORM ACTION="update.cgi">
Enter any garbage:
<INPUT NAME="blah" TYPE="checkbox">
<TEXTAREA NAME="blah"></TEXTAREA>
<INPUT TYPE="submit">
</FORM></BODY></HTML>
```

In this case, the number, names and types of form elements are all different to the intended page. The information is still submitted to the same CGI program, so a complete mess will likely result unless that CGI program checks what it gets carefully.

eval()

Because of the trap with form submissions, data supplied by the user is highly suspect and should be checked thoroughly. Use of eval() in web server JavaScript should be examined very, very carefully if the argument passed to this method comes from the user, or else unexpected statements might be run. Standalone JavaScript that supports functions like system(), open() or GetObject() calls are equally cause for concern, because any user-supplied data used as arguments to these functions might cause unexpected programs to run.

JavaScript Tactics For Website Access

The best tactic for secure web site access is to use SSL. That's a lot of bother and often expensive, so surely there's an easier way. Perhaps it's good enough to fool most of the people all of the time. Perhaps you'd like to merely direct people to particular parts of your web site, rather than insist and police. JavaScript can help you achieve these softer solutions.

One simple solution relies on the popular Apache web Server. Using Apache, you can dictate who has access to what URLs on a per-file or per-directory basis. This approach relies on a part of the HTTP protocol that's used to service URL requests. The part is called HTTP Authentication, and it's not very secure. Since this isn't a book on configuring web servers, perhaps have a look at WROX's "Professional Web Site Optimization" by Ware et al (ISBN: 1-861000-74-X).

Simple JavaScript Password Checking

Using JavaScript, this HTML document performs the most rudimentary password checking imaginable:

```
<HTML><BODY><SCRIPT>
var passwd = prompt("Enter password:", "")
this.location.href = passwd+".htm";
</SCRIPT></BODY></HTML>
```

If the user doesn't know the name of the entry page, then access fails. Even if the user looks at the JavaScript code, nothing secret is revealed. This simple kind of thing is more than enough to keep out ignorant passers-by. On another page you'd supply a form where the user would submit a request for access and perhaps then you'd then e-mail them the password. It's like trying to get into a nightclub without being a member. However, this kind of system is not very secure, because an evil user can attempt as many times as they like to guess the file name, or even set up an automatic system to check all possibilities.

This URL provides a tutorial on how to set this system up in a slightly more complex manner: http://junior.apk.net/~jbarta/tutor/keeper/index.html. This second URL sells products based on the same principles, one written in Java and one in JavaScript: http://www.ebutterfly.com/eb/ebgate.html.

Security

JavaScript security issues are mostly confined to the World Wide Web. Security issues for non-CGI standalone JavaScript scripts are the same as for standalone scripts in any language.

For the web, the basic security model supplied by web browsers keeps JavaScript scripts harmless and restricted, and browser users anonymous. As a scriptwriter, you may want to overcome one or both of these restrictions. In order to do so, you must come to a security arrangement with the user.

In the Privacy section, digital certificates were briefly touched on. Here they're explained in more detail.

Script-based Security

Privacy restrictions in a browser are at the user's discretion. If you want the restrictions lowered for your script, you have to convince the user, and provide systematic support so that it happens smoothly. Using SSL and server certificates does not achieve anything in this regard. A different kind of certificate is required to overcome browser restrictions.

The alternative to a web server certificate is a **code-signing** or **object signing certificate**. Instead of securing the connection between the browser and the server with a web server certificate, an object signing certificate is used to secure a particular piece or pieces of a program.

Technically this is achieved by **signing** the script, and by embedding the script in a compatible web page to be viewed by a compatible browser. Netscape and Microsoft browsers have different systems for handling signed programs, but both are based on the same concepts. Netscape call it **object signing**, Microsoft **Authenticode**. These systems are more commonly used for signing other downloadable and executable items such as plugins, ActiveX controls, and Java applets, but it is client-side JavaScript that is of interest here.

Microsoft's signing system cannot be used to directly sign browser JavaScript scripts – only Netscape 4+ supports a full script signing system. Internet Explorer 4+ using Microsoft's DHTML Scriptlet 1.0, also called DHTML component 1.0, functionality can control how scripts are used to a degree, but it is not a complete or robust security solution. In Internet Explorer 4.0+, you need to put your special script into an ActiveX control or Java applet and sign that object instead. ActiveX controls aren't strictly JavaScript so they're not discussed here. ActiveX controls may be created from JavaScript – using Microsoft Scriptlets 2.0 features. See Chapters 15 and 22 for more on ActiveX and Microsoft Scriptlets.

Signing of scripts has to be done in a manner that prevents tampering, or else there is no value in it. This means using some kind of secret code that can be checked after it is used. Computer encryption and cryptography provide such codes. Cryptography is a very complex matter, so for a thorough discussion, see this URL `http://www.rsa.com/rsalabs/newfaq/home.html`.

In summary, the steps for creating signed JavaScript are:

❑ Prepare the HTML page correctly.

❑ Create any special functionality needed in the in-line JavaScript.

❑ Sign the script, and install it in a Web site.

❑ Get the browser user to trust the script when it is loaded.

How HTML Is Used To Support Signed Scripts

Chapter 4 covers basic use of the <SCRIPT> tag with LANGUAGE and SRC attributes and the <OBJECT> tag. That is enough for plain inline JavaScript, but not for signed scripts. There are three problems from the HTML perspective:

- ❑ How to tell the difference between signed scripts and plain scripts?
- ❑ How to prevent unsafe plain scripts and signed scripts from interacting?
- ❑ How to stop users and hackers altering inline JavaScript to exploit signed features?

The Netscape approach is to provide a general mechanism that works with all client-side JavaScript. Solutions for the three problems above are explained in turn.

Telling Signed and Unsigned Scripts Apart

Netscape signed and unsigned scripts are distinguished with a new type of file. This type could be specific to JavaScript files, but instead a general format that works with all kinds of files is used. This is called a **JAR file**, or **Java AR**chive file, invented by Sun Microsystems. Such a file needn't contain Java stuff – the name just reflects the file's first use. One such file can contain many other files. The <SCRIPT> tag has an ARCHIVE attribute that specifies the file name. The SRC attribute is still required to identify the specific JavaScript file. An example:

```
<SCRIPT ARCHIVE="stock_updates.jar" SRC="ticker.js"></SCRIPT>
```

This way, the signing information is attached to the file and the actual JavaScript source is the same as always. Assembling a JAR file is part of the signing process and is discussed shortly.

For inline JavaScript that is embedded in an HTML file, signed <SCRIPT> tags can be identified by the use of an ID attribute, plus an ARCHIVE attribute either in that tag or in an earlier tag:

```
<SCRIPT ARCHIVE="misc.jar" ID=1> var first = 1; </SCRIPT>
<SCRIPT ID=2> var second = 2; </SCRIPT>
```

Keeping Signed and Unsigned Scripts From Interacting

Keeping signed and unsigned scripts separate is simple. Normally inline JavaScript and event handlers share all the JavaScript data in the page. Nothing stops one piece of script from using any of the data, such as form elements or other JavaScript functions, even if it comes from a signed script. So the rule is *all signed or none signed*. This way the page is entirely secure or entirely insecure. If you miss adding one ID to any piece of script in a page, then the security is blown for all the pieces of script in that page.

You can make it more complex than this simple rule if you wish. See http://developer.netscape.com/library/documentation/communicator/jssec/index.htm.

Preventing Signed Scripts From Being Changed

The problem of preventing changes to scripts is complex. Suppose an HTML page has three secure inline blocks of JavaScript specified via three <SCRIPT> tags. What stops someone saving the document to disk, modifying it and then presenting it to others as a 'safe' script? What stops that same person from loading their modified version up into their browser and submitting forms from it instead of from the official version? Inline scripts are open to abuse since they are delivered exposed to the user with the rest of the HTML contents. The solution is extra, separate checking, managed outside the page in question.

This extra checking uses the HTML ID attribute. This attribute is a way of identifying a particular occurrence of an HTML tag. So an ID can be used to identify every inline script and every tag with event handlers in a page. There is a Netscape rule that says: every signed HTML page containing inline scripts must have at least one JAR file, even if there is no SRC attribute. This creates a place to put data for the extra, separate checks. Every script piece, including handlers, must have a separate ID value, except for <SCRIPT> tags with SRC, since that SRC file is in the JAR file anyway.

The extra checks take the form of a checksum or hash value for each piece of script. These are just unique series of numbers that act like fingerprints for a given script piece. When the HTML page loads, the script pieces are picked out and hashed, and the new hash value compared with the one in the JAR file matching the ID of that script piece. A match means all is well. A non-match means the page has been interfered with – a security breach. This arrangement means the HTML document can be loaded via a normal URL whether it's signed or not. If a security breach is detected, the document will be treated as an unsigned script.

The upshot of all this is that the HTML document must be separately processed once by its author so the JAR file can be filled with the hash values. This is called **page signing**. Inline JavaScript, JavaScript event handlers and JavaScript entities can all be signed. JavaScript URLs can't be signed, and therefore can't be used in the normal way in HTML. If you want them to be checked as well, write them out via a document.write() inside a <SCRIPT> tag. Since the script tag is signed, and it contains the javascript: URL, that URL will be signed as well.

```
<HTML><BODY>
<SCRIPT ARCHIVE="special.jar" ID="1">
    document.write('first script piece');
</SCRIPT>
<SCRIPT ID="2">
    document.write('second script piece');
    document.write('<A HREF="javascript:alert(\'still piece two\')">Click me</A>');
</SCRIPT>
<FORM>
<INPUT TYPE="button" VALUE="Click me" ID="3" ONCLICK="alert('piece three');">
</FORM></BODY></HTML>
```

Why would Netscape encourage an approach that requires extra administrative tag attributes when writing HTML pages? One reason might be that this system allows several different web sites to contribute to the one HTML page in a mutually trustworthy way. That means several different companies can have their web services connected together into one integrated page. That in turn might be the beginning of integrated and public inter-company software applications. Imagine buying a car from a web site where the credit company, car detailer, car sales yard and registration service had all their features collected together into a single page you could access once. It doesn't look like this kind of integration is taking off as a popular solution yet. It seems more likely that user-less interchange of XML pages will allow this kind of thing to happen in the future, and a web presence provider will just give the user something simple and HTML to deal with.

Using Secure Script Features

Marking inline JavaScript with special HTML attributes is only half the content of signed scripts. The script logic itself must be created as well. Special features beyond plain client-side JavaScript's capabilities must be required in the script or else there's no point signing anything, just like in the real world – there's no point signing a check for $0.00. These special features come from two sources: new items in the browser object model, and the Java language.

Some example special features from the browser object model are:

❑ Simple parameters such as the `alwaysRaised` option of the `window.open()` function which allows you to thrust a browser window into the user's face and keep it there, no matter what.

❑ Whole functions such as `enableExternalCapture()` which allow you to put another Web site's page inside one of your document's frames and steal all its events so that your code processes them instead.

❑ Access to otherwise private data such as writing into browser windows that display pages from other Web sites, or messing with those other Web page's form data.

❑ Submitting forms and e-mail without the browser user knowing.

Within JavaScript, all the special features are just more host objects, methods and properties. Outside of signed scripts, these features do nothing or cause errors when you try and use them. Example special features provided by Java (but still inside the browser) are:

❑ Reading and writing files on the user's local disk using the Java I/O libraries.

❑ Managing digital certificates and encryption using Java's Security services.

❑ Connecting to arbitrary computers and servers elsewhere on the Internet, not just the one that the Web page came from, using Java's networking library.

Via ActiveX or LiveConnect, Java is the main mechanism that signed JavaScript uses for special features. Plain Java is restricted to a harmless subset of the Java functionality, just as plain JavaScript is restricted to harmless control of the browser. Signed scripts (or signed applets) can gain access to the rest of the Java functionality. Writing to local files and connecting to an arbitrary computer over the Internet are two possibilities.

Later on, under 'Security' there is some discussion of the Java security model that gives access to these features and to which signed JavaScript scripts must comply. From a practical perspective, the key points for 4.0 browsers are:

❑ The Java Security Manager, which is a part of Java, controls all the signed (secure) access in the browser. This means that JavaScript scripts have to appeal to that manager before any special abilities are granted.

❑ Appeals by JavaScript may require user confirmation, even though the script is signed, because that is what the Java security model demands. A signed script might be denied permission by the user, and never gain those permissions, so some error checking is required.

❑ By convention, a signed script only requests specific special abilities for short sections of script, and then lets go of them. This is to minimize the time that permissions for special abilities hang around. It's not strictly required that this convention be followed, and it's not followed at all for Internet Explorer 4+.

Here is a simple example of a signed script, for Netscape 4.0+ browsers. This example turns the user's toolbars on and off every second. That'll teach them to think twice before accepting signed scripts from malicious authors...

```
<HTML><BODY>
<SCRIPT ARCHIVE="sample.jar" ID="1">
function handler()
{
  alert('Very cautious of you - commendable');
  return true;
}

window.onerror = handler;                         // called if user denies access

function flash_toolbars()
{
  netscape.security.PrivilegeManager.enablePrivilege("UniversalBrowserWrite");
  window.personalbar.visible = ! window.personalbar.visible;
  window.toolbar.visible     = ! window.toolbar.visible;
  netscape.security.PrivilegeManager.disablePrivilege("UniversalBrowserWrite");
  setTimeout('flash_toolbars()',500);
}
flash_toolbars();
</SCRIPT></BODY></HTML>
```

Signing The Scripts

Once the client-side JavaScript content is created, that content must be signed. Signing the content lets the user confirm the origin of the script. They can then make a decision about whether to accept it or not. Signing scripts is different for Netscape and Microsoft 4.0 browsers.

Signing In Theory

Unlike web server certificates, the scriptwriter has to take a bit more of an active hand when code signing is concerned, and it can be very confusing. The big three sources of confusion with signing are human roles, terminology, and how it all hangs together.

'Human roles' refers to who is providing the secure information, and what the intended audience is. For signed scripts, the scriptwriter is providing the information, and the intended audience is any web user who will accept the script. This might seem obvious, but there are other kinds of signing that can happen on the Internet. Apart from similarly signed objects like plugins and applets, whole web sites can be signed, or a single e-mail note can be signed. For those other applications, the roles can be different. Here scripts are the focus.

Some terminology. The central concept is a **digital certificate**, or **digital ID**. This is the thing that is exposed to users, and is just a piece of data like everything else in computing. **Certificate authorities** (or CAs) are organizations that issue certificates. Certificates contain **digital signatures** that identify specific individuals. Developers have to manage digital signatures. Digital signatures are formed using techniques called **message digests** and **hashes**. Tools used by developers and users that aid the signing process implement these techniques. At the bottom of the pile is a theory called **public key encryption**, which makes the whole system go. If the developer loses his personal keys that are part of the public key encryption method, it's all over – start again at the top with a new certificate.

Why all these concepts? Because it matches the way people work. Suppose you were a bank, and a customer asked you for a line of credit, like a credit card or a home loan. You wouldn't just supply the money without checking the person out – you would ask for proof of identity. If the person just pointed to themselves and said "This is me", you wouldn't be satisfied. You would require them to do two things: provide proof, and provide a signature. Proof just means getting other people you trust to point to that person and say "Yes, he is who he says he is". Those other trustworthy bodies tend to be large, conservative organizations, like other banks, social security, medical benefits or driving registration authorities. Once proof is produced, each time the customer asks to withdraw money, their signature is provided, and you contact your trusted friends to see if there have been any problems with that signature since its last use. In the real world this last check might be relaxed, but not on the Internet.

In the case of the web, the user and their browser are the bank; the scriptwriter is the customer seeking access to the browser's features. The web browser holds certificates for a number of trustworthy bodies – certificate authorities. The scriptwriter has a code-signing certificate issued by a certificate authority, who has scrutinized the scriptwriter first. The scriptwriter signs scripts with a pen (a signing tool) and ink (the keys supplied with the certificate), and includes a photocopy (certificate) of the signature of the trustworthy body (the certificate authority) to confirm his identity. When the user loads the signed script, the scriptwriter's signature is examined. If it is unknown, the certificate authority's signature is examined. If it is a known certificate authority the scriptwriter's signature passes, the script is accepted, and the scriptwriter can get at the browser's secure features. The user can be warned via special browser dialog popups when this is happening. These dialogs serve to explain to the user who wants to do what to their browser.

So much for theory.

Signing In Practice

In practice, there are three different approaches:

❑   Doing without the hassle

❑   Netscape 4.0 object signing

❑   Netscape 4.0 page signing

For these processes, the scriptwriter needs to be properly set-up. If you are going to do it for real, the requirements are a computer that has installed the browser that is the target browser for your end-user of the web page containing the signed script. Ideally this should be your development computer as well. If not, you will need FTP access to that development computer. Your browser computer needs web access. You need an e-mail account that you can read, but it doesn't have to be on your computer (for example, RocketMail, HotMail, or Yahoo Mail remote e-mail accounts are sufficient).

If you just want to test out the signing system, you can get by without the e-mail, and you'll only need web access to download some tools at the start.

You must also have a certificate in order to do the signing – we'll explain how to get one shortly.

Doing Without The Hassle

As a developer, the signing process can get in the way of your development, slowing you down. To get going quickly you have several choices: use a test-only signing system, disable security or develop using local files only.

If you use a test-only signing system, you can test all the security aspects of the signing system, but you don't get the genuine security of proper signing. See 'Object Signing' below for the steps you need.

If you disable security, then it has to stay disabled for all users' browsers. To disable security, read the section above entitled 'Other Risks'. If you do this, the browsers are exposed to everyone's scripts, not just yours. For Netscape, put this line in the `prefs.js` configuration file and restart. For Internet Explorer, drop security restrictions to None in the browser's properties dialog.

```
user_pref("signed.applets.codebase_principal_support", true);
```

If you're developing locally, all security restrictions are eased, but you're committed to using a `file:` URL for the top-most document and keeping all references relative so that the files can be easily moved later if required. If you use any secure features of JavaScript, then the scripts won't work without signing if you move them to a web server later. Otherwise, you'll have to copy them to every computer that a user's browser is installed on.

A further alternative that saves hassle is to organize a certificate for a whole web server, rather than individual web pages. Server certificates are different to code-signing certificates, but they still require some configuration in the browser (and installation in the web server). However, this approach does not open up the browser's security; it just keeps information between the browser and the server secure. The process for acquiring the web server certificates is similar to the process for acquiring a code signing certificate, outlined in the next section.

Obtaining a Certificate

All of the signing methods require that you obtain a personal certificate. There are four classes of certificate, ranging from 1 to 4. Class 1 one means minimal identity checks on you. Class 4 means even your hair follicles have been inspected. For testing, Class 1 is sufficient, but only Class 2 and onwards carry sufficient credibility to count for anything in the real world. Class 2 and onwards are not free. Most of the popular CA organizations don't bother supplying Class 1 certificates. Simple tools supplied by Microsoft and Netscape will generate a Class 1 certificate for nothing. These are the so-called **test certificates**.

If you choose to go with a real certificate, prepare for bureaucracy. Certificates require numerous personal details, and a method of payment. You'll also have to wait several days. There are different kinds of certificates, so get the right one: a developer, code or object signing certificate (all the same thing). The certificates used for testing in this book came from Thawte Certification, `http://www.thawte.com`. Their service is international and doesn't currently suffer from U.S.-specific restrictions. It also allows you to deal with a more local representative who can comply with your country's specific privacy laws. Very handy if you don't like accumulating charges for international phone calls.

Actually acquiring the certificate starts with applying via the Certificate Authority's web site, using your browser to fill in a form. Next you do the paperwork and payment. Finally, when the certificate is ready you retrieve it from the CA's web site, again using your browser (it's only a file, after all). This last step appears to happen by magic, but just follow the instructions and use a simple nickname for the certificate, avoiding a password if possible. As for the discussion on cookies further on in this chapter, your browser is responsible for maintaining the certificate. Your browser is actually a certificate database, storing all the certificates you ever acquire in browser configuration files. Once the certificate is stored, you can view its details via the browser's security options.

There is one other piece of data that is stored. This is your encryption key for the certificate. It is stored in a separate file, often with a `.p12` extension. Lose this file, and you've lost control of your certificate. If you accidentally delete the certificate, you can get it back if you have this file. Otherwise, this file doesn't come into play.

Object Signing

Object signing signs things that are stored *outside* an HTML document. Applets, plugins and `.js` files are examples. This signing method doesn't sign anything between `<SCRIPT>` and `</SCRIPT>` tags. This is also the simplest way to sign Netscape scripts. If you can limit your client-side JavaScript to external `.js` files only, do it this way. This means event handlers must be assigned from scripts, not specified in HTML tags, which is a lot of bother from the scriptwriter's perspective, but actual signing is easier. A simple example that illustrates signing and use of signed features by toggling the location bar:

```
// greeting.js

netscape.security.PrivilegeManager.enablePrivilege("UniversalBrowserWrite");
top.locationbar.visible = ! top.locationbar.visible;
netscape.security.PrivilegeManager.disablePrivilege("UniversalBrowserWrite");

if ( Math.random() > 0.5 )
  document.write('Happy Birthday!<BR>');
else
  document.write('Merry Christmas!<BR>');
```

```
<!-- object.htm -->
<HTML><BODY>
Welcome to the random acts of kindness page. Just for you:<BR>
<SCRIPT ARCHIVE="greet.jar" SRC="greeting.js"></SCRIPT>
</BODY></HTML>
```

The file `greeting.js` is what you want to sign, but you can't sign a plain `.js` file. The file must be put inside a JAR archive. A JAR archive has two parts: a JAR format, and a JAR file. The JAR format is a group of files set up in a particular arrangement. A JAR file is a single file that collects together all the files in the group. The JAR format is quite detailed and tricky. You can read about it here if you wish:
`http://developer.netscape.com/library/documentation/signedobj/jarfile/index.html`.

It's hard work and error prone assembling a JAR file by hand, so it's better to use a tool. Netscape provided the JAR Packager, an applet that provides a simple, handy GUI that does the job. Because the applet was stored on your local computer, rather than downloaded from a remote URL, it could create the JAR file locally as well. This tool was replaced by version 0.60 of the **Netscape Signing Tool**, known as "Zigbert".

Zigbert has itself been superseded by versions of the signing tool: 1.1, 1.0, and beta versions. The Netscape Signing Tool does everything that the JAR Packager does, and more, all from the command line. Look here for documentation and a download location:
`http://developer.netscape.com/software/signedobj/jarpack.html`. Unless you have some backward compatibility problem, get the latest, 1.1 which operates on Netscape 4.0+ browsers. The Signing Tool is easy to run manually – from the MS-DOS prompt in the Microsoft Windows case. The tool is also available on Unix.

What you can do with the Netscape Signing Tool 1.1:

❑ Create test certificates

❑ Create the JAR format around your `.js` files.

❑ Inspect your browser's certificates from the command line.

❑ Sign your `.js` files stored in the JAR format with a certificate.

❑ Confirm all is well with the signing and the certificates.

What you have to do yourself:

❑ Organize and locate your certificates, test or otherwise

❑ Drive the tool so it does what you want

Here are the steps for signing an object that is a JavaScript source file.

❑ Download the tool and install it in a new, empty directory.

❑ Copy the `key3.db` and `cert7.db` Netscape certificate files to the same directory. These files are ordinarily stored under the Netscape install area of your computer, on a per-user basis. Each user can have a different certificate database.

❑ If you need to create a test certificate, do so with the command `signtool -G "my test cert" -d "."`. The first quoted argument will be the nickname for the new certificate. Save away any other files that are new after this step – they are the certificate's keys.

❑ Make a sub-directory, e.g. `test`, in the current directory. Put your `.js` files in there, e.g. `greeting.js` from the example above.

❑ You can review your existing certificates with `signtool -L -d "."`. You should also check that you have the CA certificate for the issuer of your certificate if you're not using a test certificate. If you are using a test certificate, the test certificate is it's own CA certificate – no separate CA certificate is required.

❑ Sign using the certificate nickname: `signtool -d"." -k"my thawte cert" -z greet.jar test`. This step also creates the JAR file in the current directory.

❑ Verify that the signing process has worked: `signtool -v greet.jar`

❑ You can now move the `greet.jar` file to the same directory as the `object.html` file that refers to it.

Your signed JavaScript should now run in the browser without any user warnings and without any security hobbles.

Page Signing

The Netscape object signing case (above) is all very well, but it doesn't allow signing of event handlers and inline JavaScript code, only `.js` files. An extra level of complexity is required to cover this more extensive requirement. Consider this example, similar to the last:

```
<!-- page.htm -->
<HTML><BODY>
<SCRIPT ARCHIVE="greet2.jar" SRC="greeting2.js"></SCRIPT>
<FORM>
<SCRIPT ID=1>
```

```
netscape.security.PrivilegeManager.enablePrivilege("UniversalBrowserWrite");
top.locationbar.visible = ! top.locationbar.visible;
netscape.security.PrivilegeManager.disablePrivilege("UniversalBrowserWrite");

document.write('Random act of kindness button: ');
</SCRIPT>
<INPUT TYPE="button" VALUE="Go Ahead" ONCLICK="greet()" ID=2>
</FORM></BODY></HTML>
```

and the `greeting2.js` file:

```
// greeting2.js
function greet()
{
  if ( Math.random() > 0.5 )
    alert('Happy Birthday!');
  else
    alert('Merry Christmas!');
}
```

As for the last section, the Netscape Signing Tool is required. The signing steps are identical, except for the step that creates the actual JAR file. This time, add the magic -J option: `signtool -J -d"." -k"my thawte cert" -z greet2.jar test`. The -J option tells the tool to hunt for JavaScript script fragments inside all HTML files in the target directory.

The tool will warn you if any <SCRIPT> blocks are missing ID attributes, so you can't get a bad JAR file using this process. It will sign event handlers, inline JavaScript, and JavaScript entities, but not `javascript:` URLs.

You now have a JAR file ready to use without any security warnings or hobbles in place. If you want to check that the page signing process does secure the HTML file against tampering, try removing one of the ID attributes and reload the page. The browser will now report that the page is unsigned when the page is reloaded.

Finally, if you include any external style sheet information in a signed page via the <LINK> tag, then that stylesheet page must be a signed object as for the `.js` example above, or else the page signing won't stick, and the page will act as though it is unsigned still.

Capability-based Security

Up until now, we've considered security in the browser to be an either-or matter; either you can't access any security features, or you have a signed script and the world is your oyster. In this section it will be seen that there is a middle ground. This middle ground revolves around the interaction of JavaScript scripts, the browser and the Java facilities that are also embedded in the browser. Once these facilities are understood, it will be clear exactly how this example, from earlier, achieves its goals:

```
netscape.security.PrivilegeManager.enablePrivilege("UniversalFileAccess");
var jo_writer = new java.io.FileWriter(jo_file);
    jo_writer.write(filedata,0,filedata.length);
    jo_writer.close();
netscape.security.PrivilegeManager.disablePrivilege("UniversalFileAccess");
```

The key thing to note in this example is that it only requests the secure privileges that it needs – access to files in this case. This is a lot more delicate than just dropping all the security in the browser.

This discussion pertains only to Netscape 4.x+ browsers. As we'll see in the next section, there are other security models that apply to these and other browsers, but it is the Netscape one that holds most of the interest from the JavaScripting perspective.

The Java Security Model

Apart from the general security provided by a browser, Java has its own security system. Both Netscape and Microsoft browsers take advantage of that security system in order to control access to dangerous features such as the writing of files on the browser's local computer. Each vendor does it differently. The model is used for the whole browser, not just for the JVM part of it.

First, let's admit that there are multiple Java security models, depending on versions. We're only interested in the Java 1.1 model because:

❑ The Java 1.0 security model doesn't allow any flexibility at all – you can't choose security based on capabilities, so it gives the scripter nothing.

❑ The Java 1.1 security model runs in Netscape 4.x browsers and has the good stuff – flexible control of capabilities.

❑ The Java 1.2 = 2.0 security model isn't currently compatible with available Web browsers (unless you obtain the Java plugin) and in any event, has a more sophisticated security structure again. That security structure allows you to sign a Java JAR file that has only partial security privileges, but no JavaScript is involved at all. In order to do that, two new concepts not covered here – policies and domains – are required.

For Microsoft Internet Explorer 4+, the Authenticode code signing system allows the Java 1.1 security information to be included as data with the code being signed, whether Java or JavaScript. Apart from organizing the signing process, described earlier, there are no implications for JavaScript scripts at all. A correctly signed script will be able to exploit secure Java features via ActiveX the same as non-secured features.

For Netscape Communicator 4.x, the security information must be included as part of the content of JavaScript scripts and Java applets. The script can be signed or not signed. If not signed, the user will be warned when particular secure features are requested. It is a scriptwriting task to setup the security access properly, and the required Java specifics are discussed here.

Java Security Theory

Security normally applies to people – login accounts, locks on doors or identity checks. Those people who are considered 'safe' have passwords, keys, and ID which give them access to computers, rooms and expensive nightclubs. People aren't the issue for the Java security model. Foreign code loaded into a browser is – whether it is Java or JavaScript code. A fuller understanding of Java security theory needs the discussion of:

❑ **Java 1.1 security**.
The security model adopted for the 4.0 browsers is based on the security model innovated in the 1.1 release of Java.

For this model, the precious resources that need to be kept safe are called **targets**. A target is a general name – it could be anything deemed important. For Java, it means Java classes that do possibly insecure things, like network connections or file writing. For JavaScript it means all those Java classes plus various features of the browser only available to signed scripts, like the alwaysRaised option of the window.open() method in JavaScript 1.2+.

The access mechanism for these targets is called a **privilege**. Once a suitable privilege is **granted**, the target's precious features may be exploited. Before they actually are exploited, a switch must be thrown to put the target in unsafe mode – this is called **enabling** the privilege. The privilege ought to be **disabled** when it is finished with.

The protagonist that requests privileges be granted is called a **principal**. That is also a general name – anything could be a principal. In the case of Java, the principals are **codebases**. A codebase means a place that program code originates from. A place that program code originates from means a URL, and a URL means a file like a Java .class file, a JavaScript .js file, a Java-embedded HTML file or any other suitable format for code or scripts such as .jar files.

So a principal (a script or program) requests privileges be granted for particular targets such as Java classes or browser features, and once they are, enables those privileges, performs the functionality of interest, and disables them until that functionality is needed again. The questions remaining are: who grants the privileges, and what privileges? The browser grants privileges, either automatically by verifying an attached digital certificate, or by prompting the user for permission. The Java standard plus the browser maker defines the privileges, so you have to refer to documentation. See the Appendices for URLs of Netscape's list. This diagram summarizes the interactions:

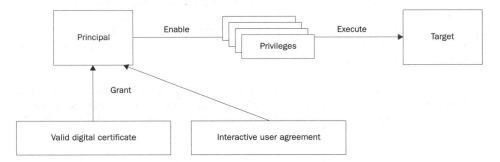

Said again in words, when a signed object comes into the browser (possibly with a valid certificate), and the user accepts it as secure, then the script acts to enable the privileges it needs. Having acquired those privileges the bits of special functionality required are then executed.

❑ **Manageable Privileges**
The security system is supposed to be 'fine grained'. This means that the features that are targets are primitive and numerous in nature, and can be granted individually. This is beneficial for programmers who want close-up control of the system, but can be an administration headache. Simple operations like creating and copying a file might require privileges for several targets to be granted. More complex scripts might ask for dozens of privileges. Whether it's the user that has to grant the privileges interactively, or the developer who has to organize the signed scripts, this is not so practical.

A macro target is a target that is a collection of other targets. By requesting privileges on a macro target, all the privilege requests for the collection are made. Macro targets usually group a small number of like-minded targets, like all file targets, or all networking targets. This serves to reduce the administration problem somewhat. Macro targets are used in exactly the same way as other targets.

Microsoft's Internet Explorer 4.0 goes one step further, introducing security zones. A security zone is a just a collection of targets, macro or otherwise that specifies a whole security profile for a given principal (script or file). This way, all the required targets are bundled into a single named item. The browser can then be loaded with a number of security zones, and scripts and applets indicate which zone they require privileges for. The zone description can be "dumbed down" sufficiently that the user can make an informed decision about whether to grant access or not. But in that browser, all this is configured without JavaScript.

❑ **Netscape use of features**
You may well be sick of the sight of this JavaScript function, since this is its third appearance:

```
function save_it(filename, filedata);
{

netscape.security.PrivilegeManager.enablePrivilege("UniversalFileWrite");
    var jo_file   = new java.io.FileOutputStream(filename);
    var jo_stream = new java.io.DataOutputStream(jo_file);
    jo_stream.writeChars(filedata);
    jo_stream.close();

netscape.security.PrivilegeManager.disablePrivilege("UniversalFileWrite");
}
```

All the pieces should fall together for this example now. The **privilege manager** is the part of Java and of the browser that allows privileges to be enabled and disabled. It is stored in local class files with the browser so it is directly accessible from JavaScript whether an applet exists in the HTML document or not.

To review: this chapter discusses calling Java methods from JavaScript and the Java security model and the general mechanics of signed scripts.

The only thing not shown is the granting of privileges. There is no JavaScript required for this – the browser takes care of it when the URL containing the script is loaded.

For Netscape 4.x, note that the privilege manager, targets and privileges are all defined by Netscape. Collectively they are called the Capability Classes. Although created by Netscape, it is Java standards that dictate that they work together as described.

User-based Security

User-based security means forcing the user to login to a web server before any of its documents, scripts or server-side programs can be used. Once the user supplies the correct information, they are trusted to download the web pages. The computer protocol underneath the web (HTTP) doesn't provide comprehensive support for user logins, so you have to make do with the basics available.

There are three main approaches, none of which require much JavaScript. They are:

❑ use the HTTP authentication system, which requires special web server configuration;

❑ use an HTML form that supplies a username and password to a CGI program (or server-side JavaScript) when submitted, and which returns a cookie that can be used to track the user afterwards. If your server-side JavaScript connects to a database, this is the preferred method. Any passwords sent to the server in this manner are exposed to the view of anyone intercepting the message on the way, so it is not a perfect solution;

❑ Server certificates.

The first two options are described in: `http://www.webthing.com/tutorials/login.html`. If you decide to use the second technique, you will need a method of encrypting the supplied password in your CGI program and possibly in the browser as well.

The third approach uses the same technology as signed scripts, but otherwise isn't covered here. You require a server certificate instead of an object signing certificate to proceed.

Cookies

Cookies are a form of data passed both ways between web browsers and servers. Cookies sent to a user's browser have some very light implications for privacy. Cookies can be managed from JavaScript.

Cookie Theory

It might sound like an obscure branch of theoretical physics, and possibly have some similar-looking enthusiasts, but the mysteries of cookies are quick to penetrate.

Cookies Enhance Web Requests

The communication between web browser and web server is defined by the HTTP network protocol. That protocol says that each URL request and the consequent response form a pair of messages independent of the past and the future. Without something fancy like JavaScript and frames, there is no method for maintaining information between requests, and no mechanism to let the web server receive or send any such information. Cookies are an enhancement to HTTP that let this happen. Originally proposed for standards consideration by Netscape Communications (their proposal is at `http://www.netscape.com/newsref/std/cookie_spec.html`), the most official specification is easily readable here: `http://www.cis.ohio-state.edu/htbin/rfc/rfc2109.html`. Most of the basic points of the specification are covered in the following sections.

Each URL or HTTP request made by a browser user is turned into lines of text called headers for sending to the web server. When the web server issues a response, the same happens. Cookies are just extra header lines containing cookie-style information. This is all invisible to the user, unless the user chooses the 'Warn me when cookies are sent' browser preference. So user requests and web server responses may occur with or without invisible cookies riding piggyback.

A key point is that the piggybacked cookies in the web server response get stored in the browser once received. Although a browser also reports its current cookies to the server when it makes requests, the server generally doesn't save them. This is almost the reverse of HTML form submissions: the browser has the long-term responsibility for the data not the server; the server says what to change, not the browser. However, the browser can use JavaScript to set its own cookies as well.

Anatomy of a Cookie

A cookie is much like a JavaScript variable, with a name and a value. However, unlike a variable, the existence of a cookie depends on several other attributes as well. This is because cookies can arrive at a browser from any web site in the world and need to be kept separate.

A cookie has the following attributes:

name

A cookie name is a string of characters. The rules are different to JavaScript variable names, but commonsense applies: use alphanumerics and underscores. Avoid using '$'. Cookie names are NOT case-sensitive. Watch out that browsers will let you set separate cookies differing only in case. This can create a real mess if those cookies are passed to web-servers that treat them caselessly and are then returned. Just stick to lowercase, always. To really understand the naming rules, read the HTTP 1.1 standard. 'fred', 'my_big_cookie' and 'user66' are all valid cookie names. There are no reserved words or variable name limits.

value

The value part of a cookie is a string of any characters. That string must follow the rules for URLs which means the `escape()` and `unescape()` functions should be applied if one is set by JavaScript. The name and string together should be less than 4095 bytes. There are no `undefined` or `null` values for cookies, but zero length strings are possible.

domain

If two different web sites are viewed in a browser, they shouldn't be able to affect each other's cookies. Cookies have a domain property that restricts their visibility to one or more web sites.

Consider an example URL `http://www.altavista.yellowpages.com.au/index.html`. Any cookies with domain `www.altavista.yellowpages.com.au` are readable from this page. Domains are also hierarchical – cookies with these domains: `.altavista.yellowpages.com.au`, `.yellowpages.com.au` and `.com.au` could all be picked up by that URL in the browser. The leading full stop is required for partial addresses. To prevent bored university students making a cookie visible to every web page in the world, at least two domain portions must be specified.

In practice, the domain attribute isn't used much, because it defaults to the domain of the document it piggybacked into the browser on (very sensible), and because it's unlikely that you would want to share a cookie with another web site anyway.

Chapter 18

path

In a similar manner to domains, the path attribute of a cookie restricts a cookie's visibility to a particular part of a web-server's directory tree. A web page such as `http://www.microsoft.com/jscript` might have a cookie with path `/jscript`, which is only relevant to the JScript pages of that site. If a second cookie with the same name and domain also exists, but with the path `''` (equivalent to `'/'`), then the web page would only see the first cookie, because its path is a closer match to the URL's path.

Paths represent directories, not individual files, so `/usr/local/tmp` is correct, but `/usr/local/tmp/myfile.htm` isn't. Forward slashes (`'/'` not `'\'`) should be used. Trailing slashes as in `/usr/local/tmp/` should be avoided. That is why the top-level path is `''` (a zero-length string), not `'/'`.

The name, domain and path combine to fully identify an individual cookie.

expiry time

The expiry time provides one of two cleanup mechanisms for cookies (see the next section for the other). Without such mechanisms, cookies might just build up in the browser forever, until the user's computer fills up.

The expiry time is optional. It is a moment in time. Without one, a cookie will survive only while the browser is running. With one, a cookie will survive even if the browser shuts down, but it will be discarded at the time dictated. If the time passes when the browser is down, the cookie is discarded when it next starts up. If the time dictated is zero or in the past, the cookie will be discarded immediately.

secure flag

This is a true/false attribute, which hints whether the cookie is too private for plain URL requests. The browser should only make secure (SSL) URL requests when sending this cookie. This attribute is less commonly used.

Browser Cookie Restrictions

Browsers place restrictions on the number of cookies that can be held at any one time. The restrictions are:

- ❏ 20 cookies maximum per domain.
- ❏ 4096 bytes per cookie description.
- ❏ 300 cookies overall maximum.

The standard, RFC 2109 (http://www.w3.org/Protocols/rfc2109/rfc2109) sets these maximums. Netscape's specification and browsers say these maximums, in an attempt to guarantee that all your disk space won't be consumed.

If you rely heavily on cookies, you will soon exceed the Netscape limit of 20. In that case, that browser will throw out one of the 20 when the 21st arrives. This is a source of obscure bugs. It is better to use only one cookie, and pack multi-variable data into it via JavaScript utility routines – 4096 bytes is quite a lot of space. Internet Explorer doesn't have the 20 cookies per domain limit.

The Netscape file that the cookie data resides in when the browser is shut down is called `cookies.txt` on Windows and Unix, and resides in the Netscape installation area (under each user for Netscape Communicator). It is a plain text file, automatically generated by the browser on shutdown, similar to the `prefs.js` file. The user can always delete this file if the browser is shutdown, which removes all cookies from their system. An example file:

```
# Netscape HTTP Cookie File
# http://www.netscape.com/newsref/std/cookiespec.html
# This is a generated file!  Do not edit.
www.geocities.comFALSE / FALSE        937972424    GeoId 2035695874900187870
.linkexchange.comTRUE  / FALSE        942191819    SAFE_COOKIE
       3425efc81808cebe
www.macromedia.com     FALSE  FALSE       877627211     plugs      yes
```

The large number in the middle is expiry time in seconds from 1 January 1970. From this example, you can see that most web sites set one cookie only, and then it only contains a unique ID. web sites often use this ID to look up their own records on the visitor holding the ID.

The equivalent files for Internet Explorer 4+ are stored by default in the `C:\WINDOWS\COOKIES` directory in `.TXT` files with the user's name. These are *almost* readable. Ironically, if you copy the files to a Unix computer, they are easily readable.

JavaScript and Cookies

Using JavaScript, cookies can be accessed from the browser, from a CGI program, and from server side JavaScript. The first two methods are examined here.

In The Browser

Cookies in the browser revolve around the JavaScript `window.document.cookie` property that first appeared in Netscape Navigator 2.0. This property is unlike other JavaScript object properties for a number of reasons:

❑ It isn't really related to its parent object, in this case the document object.

❑ Although it's singular in name, it holds all the visible cookies – but it's not an array.

❑ If you set the cookie property, its new value won't always match what you set it to.

The property's contents (it's a string) doesn't even look complete – what's going on? An example value:

```
bookmark1=face.htm; my_id=541263; quote=Et%20tu,%20Brutus
```

The `cookie` property is really just a service point for managing the browser's cookies. It doesn't directly represent the current cookie data. This is different to the other properties in JavaScript, such as the forms array which exactly matches each `<FORM>` tag. When you set the `cookie` property, your data is handed to the browser's cookie management software. When you read the `cookie` property, you get a report in a single string of the cookies that are currently visible and unexpired for the current window's domain and path. Only name and value attributes are supplied in this report.

This means that when looking for a specific cookie, you must pick the cookie property's string apart. You can't know when a cookie expires or will be visible without explicitly re-setting it. When setting a cookie, you must use a string in a specific format. That format is:

```
[name]=[value]; expires=[date]; path=[directory]; domain=[domain-name]; secure
```

You supply the items in brackets – leave the brackets themselves out. Each semi-colon separated item is optional, except the first. The [value] part must be run through the escape() function first. The date for expires requires the exact format that the toGMTString() method of the Date object produces:

```
// example date: 'Mon, 13 Oct 1997 12:40:34 GMT'
```

Managing cookie strings can be maddening because of the way they work with document.cookie. Fortunately Bill Dortch solved much of the problem for everyone. This URL http://www.hidaho.com/cookies/cookie.txt contains SetCookie(), DeleteCookie() and GetCookie() routines that do most of the hard work. The URL can easily be converted into a .js file. Here's the SetCookie() function from that file.

```
function SetCookie (name,value,expires,path,domain,secure) {
   document.cookie = name + "=" + escape (value) +
      ((expires) ? "; expires=" + expires.toGMTString() : "") +
      ((path) ? "; path=" + path : "") +
      ((domain) ? "; domain=" + domain : "") +
      ((secure) ? "; secure" : "");
}
```

And here's the example of its use – note all trailing arguments are optional:

```
SetCookie ("ccname", "hIdaho Design ColorCenter", expdate);
SetCookie ("tempvar", "This is a temporary cookie.");
SetCookie ("ubiquitous", "This cookie will work anywhere in this
domain",null,"/");
```

There are extensive comments in the URL supplied above.

In CGI Programs

Sometimes CGI programs are responsible for a URL's content. A CGI program is called at the end of a URL request, so it can read the cookies that the browser reports. A CGI program also produces the URL response, so it can set cookies that the browser will remember.

This example is standalone JavaScript written in ScriptEase 4.1. It is launched from a .BAT DOS file, is intended as a CGI program, and shows cookie reading and writing:

```
@echo OFF
C:\local\install\ScriptEase\win32\secon32 %0.bat > %OUTPUT_FILE%
GOTO SE_EXIT

// JavaScript script starts here

var this_moment = new Date;

var all_cookies = Clib.getenv('HTTP_COOKIE');          // Received from browser
```

```
// Output HTTP/URL Response Headers
// puts() is like document.write()

Clib.puts("Set-cookie: test_name=test_data;\n");      // Sent to browser in header
Clib.puts("Date: " + this_moment.toGMTString() + "\n");
Clib.puts("Content-type: text/html\n\n");

// Output HTML

Clib.puts("<HTML><BODY>\n");
Clib.puts("Cookie report from browser:<BR>");
Clib.puts(all_cookies);
Clib.puts("</BODY></HTML>\n");

// JavaScript script ends here

:SE_EXIT
```

This example does not use the customized-for-CGI ScriptEase JavaScript interpreter, because it is easier here to see the 'raw' response headers that include the cookie data. The line containing Set-cookie shows a new cookie being sent to the browser, called test_name. The format for this line is usually the same as that written to the document.cookie property (see above). The line containing getenv shows the CGI program reading the cookie information sent by the browser. The web server puts it in an environment variable, usually in the same format as is read from the document.cookie JavaScript property.

Notice the Date: header line. If cookie headers are added with an expiry date, the Date: header tells the browser what the time was in the CGI program when the expiry was set. This helps the browser avoid becoming confused about when the cookie should expire.

Because of differences between web servers, the CGI headers in this example may need subtle changes for a specific server even though the style shown here is quite standard.

Using Cookies

Cookies can be put to a number of simple uses. When cookie problems occur, this JavaScript URL is very useful for debugging. It produces a readable report if many cookies are present:

```
JavaScript:alert(document.cookie.split(';').join('\n'))
```

Logging In Users

Cookies can be used to force browser users to supply usernames and passwords before viewing web pages. web servers already have a mechanism for doing this called 'HTTP Authentication', but if you don't like that system, you can use cookies instead. The steps are:

❑   Create an ordinary HTML form to accept username and password.

❑   Submit that form to a 'login' CGI program that validates the form details. The user name and password might be validated against entries in a private file on the web server, like /etc/passwd on Unix.

❑   Have the login CGI program return a failure page if the details are wrong.

❑   Have the login CGI program return the first real page if the details are right.

637

❑   Return a special cookie to the browser if the details are right. This cookie is used to track the user when browsing through pages of the web site.

❑   Each page on the site should be accessible through a second CGI program. This second program checks the cookie before delivering the requested page. This is because a user might try and get around the login screen by going directly to the URL of another page. The cookie created cannot be as simple as `login=true;`, because an expert user might see this cookie and just create it with a JavaScript: URL next time he enters the web site, avoiding the login again. The cookie value should be different each time the user logs in (perhaps containing an encrypted time) so that subsequent checks can confirm that the value supplied is recent.

In general, this is not a highly secure login mechanism, but it does prevent unknown users from easily entering your web site. It is less efficient than 'HTTP Authentication'.

If you don't have the opportunity to use CGI programs, you might think that the password can be checked in client-side JavaScript, and then proceed directly to the next page. Yes it can, but it's not secure, because the browser user can always view the JavaScript source and therefore workaround the password-checking code.

Cookies As Bookmarks

There is no way to automate the creation of bookmarks from JavaScript. There is no way to automatically navigate to a specific bookmark. Cookies can be used to workaround these restrictions.

A cookie with an expiry date set way into the future will exist effectively forever. A cookie whose value is a URL can always be used as a bookmark. A simple example:

```
<!-- redirect.htm -->
<HTML><HEAD>
<SCRIPT SRC="cookie_functions.js"></SCRIPT>
</HEAD><BODY>
<SCRIPT>
function go_there()
{
  if ( GetCookie('favorite') )
  {
    window.location.href = GetCookie('favorite');
  }
}

setTimeout("go_there()",10000);                    // 10 seconds delay
</SCRIPT>
Returning you to your favorite location on our website ...
</BODY></HTML>
```

Provided the `favorite` cookie has been set at some time in the past, the user can be returned there automatically. This cookie could be set by client-side JavaScript, either automatically or in response to some user input, or it could be set in the browser in the response from a CGI program.

More than one bookmark is possible – use more than one cookie, or if the Netscape 20 cookie limit is close, concatenate all the bookmarks together into one cookie's value and unpack them when needed.

User Preferences

Along with bookmarks, cookies can be used to store a limited range of user preferences. The range is limited because of security hobbles. As for the last section these can be set in a number of ways.

Common preference choices might be:

- ❑ background color
- ❑ choice of frames or no-frames display
- ❑ choice of in-line images or text only display
- ❑ choice of navigation menu style
- ❑ font size

As the page is downloaded, inline JavaScript can check for special preference cookies and switch to the appropriate page, or adapt the page layout as required.

User Profiling

A web site can use a cookie to track a user's movements around the site. Web servers already have facilities for tracking the number of times each web page gets loaded, but cookies allow extra information to be supplied. Without the user's agreement, nothing can be stored in the cookie that exposes the real identity of the user, but the cookie can be used to show that the anonymous user is the same anonymous user as last time. Also see 'Cookie Traps' below.

Visit Counter

Possibly the simplest use of a cookie is to store a number in it and increment it each time the user loads a page that lies in the cookies domain and path. This gives the HTML author a simple way of establishing familiarity with the user. An example:

```
<HTML><BODY><SCRIPT SRC="cookie_functions.js"></SCRIPT>
<SCRIPT>
var visits = GetCookie("counter");
if ( visits && parseInt(visits) )
{
    SetCookie("counter", ++parseInt(visits) + "");
    document.write("Hello old friend on your "+visits+" visit<BR>");
    self.location.href = "top.html";
}
else
{
    var expires = new Date();
    expires.setTime(expires.getTime() + 3E11);        // about 10 years = "forever"
    SetCookie("counter", "1", expires, "");
    document.write("Welcome, Stranger.<BR>");
}

</SCRIPT>
<A HREF="top.html">Enter here</A>
</BODY></HTML>
```

Shopping Carts

Recall from Chapter 7 that shopping carts work around the limitation that HTML forms are restricted to one document. If you don't want to use a hidden frame and JavaScript variables to store the cart's contents, you can use cookies. There isn't much difference. The main benefit is that cookies are easier to submit to a web server – you don't have to recreate an HTML form, they are submitted directly with every URL request. The main disadvantage is that you have to pack your cart items into and out of the cookie, which can be annoying.

Cookie Traps

From the point of view of security, the web site `http://www.doubleclick.com` is worth considering. As briefly discussed in 'Privacy', cookies can't expose a user's true identity. However, they can be used to identify that an anonymous user is the same anonymous user as last time. This site has an advertising network that collects profiles of browser users by using cookies. The first time the user views an advertisement from this network, the cookie is set. Subsequently, when the user views a page anywhere in the network, the cookie is discovered, and the user's presence is reported back to the network's data-collection service. Like tracking a wild animal, cookie footprints reveal the users habits, which advertisers can then take advantage of. The next time the user views a page in the network, an advertisement appears tailored to the user's current habits. If you like tea, everywhere you go will eventually advertise tea leaves.

Chapter 17, covering debugging, points out some common traps with cookies.

Summary

Privacy and security concerns serve to make client-side JavaScript a complex matter.

By default, the browser user is safe, and the client-side JavaScript scriptwriter is not. The scriptwriter's activity is restricted by security hobbles, and the scripts are exposed to the user's whim. For JavaScript outside the browser such as server-side JavaScript and standalone JavaScript in CGI programs, the scriptwriter has the same protections as any general programming language.

Half-hearted attempts at security such as code shrouding may keep the ignorant and lazy at bay, but ultimately provide no security at all. In order to be properly secure, a complete solution involving digital certificates is required. This is not usually free and requires extra organization and tools. Users may need to be educated as well, since they should just accept every security alert the browser presents them with.

Cookies are a mechanism that resides in the gray area between secure and insecure. Useful for maintaining data in the browser client and for tracking browser users, they have some light implications on security. Their behavior in browsers is unusual compared with other browser features, and can only be controlled from the browser via JavaScript.

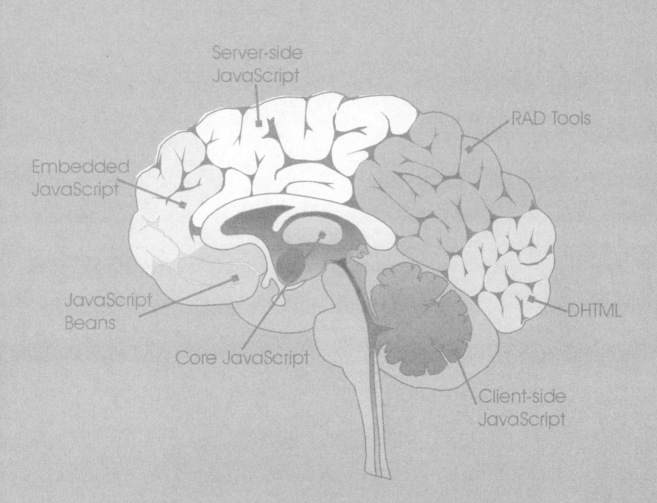

Rapid Application Development: Methodology, Tools & Components

When discussing resources that can be used for Rapid Application Development (**RAD**), it is worth considering just what RAD actually is. With a good understanding of what RAD is all about, you can better appreciate what the available resources have to offer. In this chapter we will discuss the methodology behind RAD. Then we will take a brief look at some of the many tools available to the RAD developer. Since code reuse is important to RAD, we'll also discuss the use of components and then show how JavaScript components can be created and used in web applications.

Like so many terms in our technical vocabulary, if you ask ten software developers what RAD is, you will probably get more than ten completely different answers. Most likely, if there actually is a true definition to the term, it is meaningful only in an academic sense. Ever since the term RAD was coined by James Martin, in his definitive 1991 book, *Rapid Application Development*, it has evolved into a variety of similar meanings for the typical developer. In almost all of these meanings, RAD is described as an approach to building software that deals with balancing time scales and functionality with planning, design, development, and testing in order to quickly create a product with the highest value.

RAD was developed because there is a need to be more responsive to today's fast-paced development environment. Everyone wants their software to do more, do things better, cost less, and they want it yesterday. Often software development projects have fixed time frames, fixed budgets and use a limited number of resources, i.e. people and money. The longer the development cycles lasts, the more likely there will be pressure to add or change things – but you are still expected to maintain the timelines and the budget! In these situations something must be sacrificed. The only choices available to you are:

- ❑ Extend the deadline
- ❑ Add more developers (and therefore, more money)
- ❑ Lower the quality
- ❑ Drop features and/or reduce functionality
- ❑ Use some combination of the above

The real solution to the above-mentioned problem is not to get stuck in the undesirable situation to begin with. The primary purpose of Rapid Application Development is precisely that – to avoid these problems. RAD combats scope creep by limiting the project's exposure to change. This statement may seem counter-intuitive. RAD doesn't eliminate change, but allows it to be better managed. How does RAD better manage change? The answer has much to do with how it breaks a project into a series of smaller projects, each with a shortened development life cycle. Within a shorter project duration, scope creep is reduced and better managed. Also, RAD encourages that when changes are made, they are incorporated early on or when changes can be properly evaluated, and before large investments are made in development and testing. The net result is that, in theory, budgets are suitably constrained and schedules are kept. I say "in theory" because there is no single methodology that is guaranteed to work. What works in one environment can fall short in another. But with that said, RAD still offers many benefits and can usually be an aid with development.

RAD and Development Cycles

In RAD, a project is broken down into a series of iterative development cycles. Rather than having a single end product, a series of releases is produced. The initial release is not the same as a prototype, although prototypes may play a role. Each release delivers 100% usability of the features it contains. Prototypes typically illustrate all the features of the final product, although each feature does not work 100%. Prototypes can be used in the RAD environment in a number of ways to:

- ❑ Explore early design alternatives
- ❑ Test critical technologies and components
- ❑ Increase team understanding
- ❑ Help gather feedback from end-users
- ❑ Illustrate the final product in order to manage expectations and increase enthusiasm and customer buy-in

However, it must be stressed that the fundamental principle of iterative development is that each iteration of the development cycle delivers a functional version of the final system. Each release has a very limited scope but extends the quality and/or functionality of the prior release.

Historically, another major risk to a project's success is lack of end-user involvement. With RAD, when an iteration is completed, the new release can be evaluated by all interested parties. After the end-users see each release you might find that what was thought to be a useful and productive feature may fail to meet expectations. Alternatively, some minor feature may prove to be exceptionally useful and you may wish to expand its capabilities. This periodic evaluation helps manage user expectations and can be used to prioritize the feature set of the next release. The tremendous advantage of this reprioritizing is that we can quickly and efficiently adapt to the rapid changes in business.

The iterative approach has many direct benefits to the developer as well. Even the best developer rarely performs complex, monolithic tasks with the first attempt. However, most developers are very good at making many small refinements and improvements. With each release, the development team learns more about the application as a solution to a business problem. The team also becomes more familiar with the technologies used. Armed with more knowledge, clearer understanding, and a better skill set, the team can make even better decisions and work more effectively with each new release.

Iterations also help to keep the project within its budget. If the budget is about to be exceeded, development can halt and a functioning product still exists. Even if all of the functionality is not included in the last release, having an application with 85% of the features that works 100% of the time is usually better that a product with 100% of the features but works only 85% of the time.

Tools for the RAD Developer

Although an iterative approach to development has many benefits, the developer still needs help to accomplish his or her work. It is virtually impossible to produce applications sufficiently fast without having a good set of development tools and a set of reusable components. Occasionally you might see a website with a note that claims that it was produced using nothing more than Notepad or some other simple text editor, but those sites are typically small and unsophisticated. RAD developers need efficient, time-saving tools if they are to meet tight deadlines.

As always, use the right tool for the right job. If you are building a prototype, why not let wizards and code generators do some of the work for you? Haven't yet memorized all of the tags required in JavaScript? Using a product like Macromedia's Dreamweaver, which allows you to drag and drop objects and commands, will save you hours of sifting through reference materials. Having a hard time tracking down that nagging problem with your component sitting on the web server? How about letting Microsoft Script Debugger save you from a weekend of debugging? Since RAD takes an iterative approach producing many releases, you should consider using a version management system. There are many useful products available to help today's web developer, and more are coming out each month. The following sections provide brief introductions to a few of the many tools useful to the RAD developer using JavaScript.

Borland IntraBuilder

Borland IntraBuilder is a bundle of tools that offer numerous features especially useful to the RAD developer. IntraBuilder includes an application development IDE called Designer, and a scalable, high-performance application server for creating multi-tier web applications. It supports several Web servers, most major databases, all HTML standards, and server-side JavaScript capabilities.

645

Borland offers IntraBuilder in three versions. The basic developer edition, simply called IntraBuilder, includes:

- ❑ IntraBuilder Designer
- ❑ IntraBuilder Server
- ❑ IntraBuilder Agent
- ❑ Borland Web Server

IntraBuilder Professional includes everything found in the basic developer edition but adds the following:

- ❑ Netscape FastTrack Web Server
- ❑ Borland Database Engine
- ❑ SQL Links for Borland InterBase and Microsoft SQL Server
- ❑ Support for CGI, NSAPI (Netscape FastTrack Enterprise Server), and ISAPI (Microsoft Internet Information Server)

The high-end edition of IntraBuilder is called IntraBuilder Client/Server. This edition expands upon IntraBuilder Professional with:

- ❑ A multiple-instances version of their IntraBuilder Designer
- ❑ Multiple IntraBuilder Server service agents on multiple machines
- ❑ Remote IntraBuilder service agents

For today's RAD developer, only the Professional or Client/Server editions are serious choices.

In an effort to help make thin clients, IntraBuilder Client/Server allows the developer to control how much JavaScript is to be sent to the client. By allowing remote IntraBuilder Agents to be installed on multiple servers to spread the workload, IntraBuilder Client/Server also encourages more scalable applications. The IntraBuilder Broker, included in all three editions, routes requests from browsers to an available IntraBuilder Agent. IntraBuilder Professional and IntraBuilder Client/Server can use multiple local agents, while the basic edition can use only a single local agent.

IntraBuilder makes JavaScript programming easier in a number of ways. IntraBuilder's wizards, called Experts, may be used to generate data forms, home pages, and reports quickly. These automated Experts take you step-by-step through common tasks such as creating new tables, interactive forms, and customized reports. A web page Expert generates web pages based upon selections that you make for layout style, text, colors, fonts and images. The Visual Form and Report designers allow you to work with a graphical UI, having the designers generate most of the JavaScript code for you. You can easily create a data form with support for queries and filters by checking two boxes during the forms Expert process. After the designers generate the code, you will still probably need to make some manual updates, but most of the tedious work is done for you quickly and easily.

Borland includes with IntraBuilder custom extensions for JavaScript to add new classes, exception handlers, and methods. By using these extensions, you can create robust and reusable components. Once your components have been created, you can easily add them to the numerous pre-built components found in the Component Palette. Once on the palette, you add the components to a page simply by dragging them from the Component Palette to the page. Because IntraBuilder applications generate pure HTML code, they can run in any browser on any platform.

Macromedia DreamWeaver

Although some may look at Macromedia's Dreamweaver as just a tool to make HTML a little easier, it is really for heavy-duty professional Web page creation, design and management. Although useful to developers at any level, Dreamweaver is geared more for advanced authoring and not for the less experienced developer. Although it is not dedicated strictly to JavaScript development, it is still a useful tool for the JavaScript developer. It provides a wide-range of templates and automated tools that provide complete control over the way pages look and act within a Web browser. Dreamweaver provides a wide-range of features such as absolute positioning, timeline animation, and Dynamic HTML. It sports easy drag-and-drop tables and frames, browser targeting/error reporting, extensible behaviors, and server file-locking.

Its use of templates makes life more convenient for the web developer. Templates can be created with editable and non-editable regions, which you can then use to base other pages on. By having pages based upon these templates, updates to pages are easily managed since changes made to a template are automatically applied to the pages that were created from the template. This saves valuable time for the RAD developer. Another time-saving feature is Dreamweaver's ability to leverage existing files. It can easily import existing documents such as HTML files and Microsoft Word documents so you can leverage existing work.

The DreamWeaver site, at http://www.macromedia.com/software/dreamweaver/, allows you to download a free evaluation version of the product. The site also provides many free enhancements to the product via plug-in modules called extensions. Some of the extensions available included enhanced support for Oracle8i, music and multimedia, e-commerce, and cookie management.

Microsoft Visual Studio, Enterprise Edition

Microsoft Visual Studio is a bundle of integrated development tools that offer many conveniences that you would expect a good RAD tool to provide. Visual Studio includes Microsoft Visual InterDev (VI), Microsoft Visual Basic, Microsoft Visual C++, Microsoft Visual SourceSafe, and numerous other tools and utilities. Considering that more and more web applications use a mixture of technologies with N-tiers, having all of the tools needed in an integrated IDE is quite compelling. With such a wide range of products offered in VS, you have what you need to produce solutions for many situations. Also, the products in the VS package have very robust IDEs and numerous code generating features so a RAD developer should seriously consider using them.

Although this suite is it is not specifically designed around JavaScript, Visual InterDev has a very strong focus on JScript, Microsoft's take on JavaScript. VI includes a number of wizards that generate server side JavaScript code to handle HTML interfacing. VI supports DHTML and Active Server Pages (ASPs) using COM objects for delivering content on the fly, has end-to-end debugging capacity for both the client and the server side, and makes a good solution for web-based applications connecting to databases. Its Visual Design-Time Controls allow developers to visually construct complex data-bound forms and reports. The point-and-click script building supports both client and server side components in both VBScript and JScript.

One very successful approach to building large volume, database web sites is to use middle tier components. Visual Basic allows the programmer to develop COM components easily without having to bother about the thread management, memory management, COM GUID generation and COM Interface details that a C++ programmer has to deal with. If you need the extra performance in your COM objects, you have Visual C++ in the bundle to use. Regardless of which product you use to create the COM component, they integrate easily with Visual InterDev created ASP pages.

The many conveniences offered with VS help make development fast and accurate. With its auto-complete, IntelliSense technology, properties and methods of objects are selected on the fly rather than having to type a lot of code. Its numerous wizards help with many common tasks such as creating database forms and default pages. Rather than writing a lot of custom scripting code from scratch, you can easily drag and drop components onto a design and then attach scripting code to those components. Visual Studio also offers a highly rated debugging environment allowing you to debug the entire web site – scripts, ASPs, VB middle-tier objects, and even stored procedures on back-end databases.

On the whole, Visual Studio provides a rich web development environment for creating scalable applications. But with this said, VS isn't for everyone. It does require some developer expertise to be able to push it to its full potential and it virtually requires Windows NT on the back end. VS relies heavily upon using COM/DCOM and (arguably) does not readily support CORBA objects. To get those most out of the product, you should consider using Microsoft Internet Information Server with related Back Office tools, such as Microsoft Transaction Server. But even this is not much of a big deal since Microsoft provides many of these products for free. The decision to use Visual Studio will probably be influenced greatly by the existing architecture you are working with. If you are already on NT and using SQL Server or Oracle, then VS is a sensible choice.

Microsoft Visual SourceSafe

With one of the critical features of RAD being the production of many releases of an application, it becomes a chore (or a nightmare) keeping the many files of the various releases organized. Issues also arise when two or more developers need to work on the same file at the same time. This is where a good version management tool becomes a lifesaver.

Microsoft Visual SourceSafe (VSS) is used to keep track of your files during the many development iterations in RAD development. VSS is bundled with many of Microsoft's products, including Microsoft Visual Studio and Microsoft Visual Basic, but it is also available as a stand-alone product.

VSS works by taking historical 'snapshots' and saving those snapshots in a database. Once stored in the database, any prior version of your code can easily be accessed. VSS provides a "differences" feature, which shows you what and where the changes are between two or more versions of a file. This is helpful when two or more developers need to make updates to a file at the same time and then later these two "editions" need to be merged into a single module.

VSS can be used to prevent developers from overwriting each other's changes by providing a "check out" feature. When a file is checked out by a developer, that developer takes "ownership" and is allowed read-write access to the file. Other developers can still read the file or make copies, but they cannot save their changes to the original source.

Although VSS comes standard with a number of Microsoft development tools like Visual Basic, it is geared for use with any type of file, and not just files from Microsoft products. Files from a variety of technologies may be managed by VSS at the same time, such as an HTML web page, Java component, sound file, graphics, or specification document.

Take a look at Microsoft's site under `http://msdn.microsoft.com/ssafe/` for more information concerning VSS.

NetObjects ScriptBuilder

ScriptBuilder from NetObjects provides a dedicated script development environment that complements your existing HTML authoring products. By using ScriptBuilder, Web developers can write scripts to add sophisticated animation effects, advanced transaction capabilities, and other advanced application functionality to their web sites.

ScriptBuilder is what NetObjects Inc. calls a "script development environment" (SDE) rather than an Integrated Design Environment (IDE). This difference in naming is due, in large part, to ScriptBuilder's focus on creating and editing scripts. ScriptBuilder combines a powerful script editor with a visual point-and-click interface that speeds development by enabling developers to re-use scripts or parts of scripts. The product is not limited to JavaScript, as it supports all the major scripting languages such as Microsoft JScript, Microsoft VBScript, Perl and LotusScript. ScriptBuilder even supports the use of JavaScript components called JavaScript Beans. The technologies used by ScriptBuilder go beyond scripting with its support of HTML, DHTML, IBM Java Server Pages (JSP), and ColdFusion Markup Language. ScriptBuilder provides a good way to bridge the gap between Netscape, Microsoft, IBM, and Sun Microsystems Web scripting environments.

NetObjects ScriptBuilder supplies a special help system, called Dr. Scripto, which provides information on work-arounds to common browser incompatibilities. The help system is context sensitive and can bring you to the appropriate help page when ScriptBuilder's script inspector detects potential version and browser incompatibilities.

Its autoscripting feature is similar to Word's Autotext feature or Visual InterDev's Intellisense by expanding keywords automatically as you type the word. Such minor features like this make a major impact on the time required to type code correctly. The Syntax Checker works remarkably well with JavaScript and VBScript to allow you concentrate more on what the code is meant to do rather than caring about typos.

One of the many features that set this tool apart from many others is its ability to allow you to save, organize, and reuse code libraries, components, and portions of scripts. The Toolbox in ScriptBuilder is actually a repository for code snippets, which you can drag and drop into the editor window. Scripts may be sorted by name, category, description, and browser version support, and can be previewed, edited, and easily inserted into active documents. Although this script library includes a number of items, you can easily add your own code for use on JavaScripts, VBScripts, ASP pages, and HTML pages. The ScriptBuilder site provides additional code snippets that you can download for free.

ScriptBuilder offers a range of other features to make your development efforts easier. The Script Inspector evaluates which browser versions are needed to run scripts and makes it easy to find flagged language elements. An Internal Preview feature speeds the testing and debugging of your page and the Info Tree feature provides a single, integrated reference point for language elements. Document Map finds embedded functions and scriptable objects visually, allowing you to navigate long and complex Web pages quickly.

ScriptBuilder also includes Script Component Pad, a utility for creating and editing JavaScript components. The interface is exceptionally easy to use. You add properties, methods, events, and parameters to the object with a click of a button and then fill in a form to specify such attributes as the name or data type. You may also view the source code for the component to construct the coding for the methods or to manually construct the component interface. The components that are created are stored in an external file that defines the component using XML. Once this file is created, it may be added to ScriptBuilder's Component Library.

To download a free trial copy of NetObjects ScriptBuilder, visit:
http://www.netobjects.com/products/

Netscape JavaScript Debugger

As the name implies, Netscape JavaScript Debugger from Netscape is a debugging tool for client-side JavaScript code. The tool is offered as a stand-alone product as well as part of Netscape Visual JavaScript. It runs on multiple platforms (Windows 9x/NT, Mac PPC, Solaris, and Irix) and runs well with almost any type of HTML authoring tools.

You can use the debugger while you develop your JavaScript applications to determine what is happening in your applications as they run. Using such features as conditional breakpoints, a call stack, watch mechanisms, and single-step execution, you can find issues quickly. JavaScript Debugger also provides signed script support, an Automatic Error Reporter Window, and a Page List feature that displays a sorted list of loaded pages.

Although JavaScript Debugger doesn't do everything a RAD developer may need, it is a good bare-bones debugger and is worth considering – especially since it is free of charge. You may download Netscape JavaScript debugger from:

```
http://developer.netscape.com/software/jsdebug.html#download
```

Netscape Visual JavaScript

Netscape has a tool for the developer of JavaScript code called Visual JavaScript (VJS). The good people at Netscape have put a great deal of effort into this product to make it practical and convenient to develop JavaScript applications. It allows developers to use drag and drop for components and visual programming. JVS has native hooks for Oracle, Sybase, and DB2, and supports ODBC for most others. Visual JavaScript provides Database Application Page Wizards, client-side JavaScript and Page Builder features. Such features allow you to incorporate sophisticated functionality into your applications with little or no coding.

As expected, it works exceptionally well with other Netscape products. It has an extensible palette of components, which makes it easy to tap into the functionality of Netscape Enterprise Server, Netscape Messaging Server, and Netscape Directory Server. The palette supports the import of CORBA services, JavaBeans, and JavaScript components (more JavaScript components later).

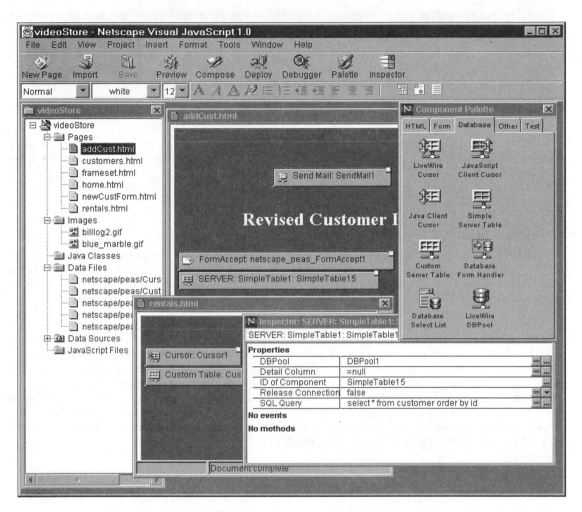

The product comes in two flavors, Visual JavaScript and Visual JavaScript Pro. The Pro edition is a superset of Visual JavaScript and includes Netscape Enterprise Server, Netscape Communicator and Personal Oracle Lite.

You can download an evaluation copy of Netscape Visual JavaScript from `http://www-hk1.netscape.com/download/archive/tools_index.html#vjs` or `http://www.cnet.com/Resources/Swcentral/PC/Result/TitleDetail/0,160,0-23962-g,00.html`. There also an update to Visual JavaScript found at `http://developer.netscape.com/software/vjspatch.html`.

Netscape Visual JavaScript Component Developer's Kit

As the name implies, the Netscape Visual JavaScript Component Developer's Kit (CDK) is targeted at the component developer. Its focus is on developing components to be used in conjunction with Visual JavaScript. With such components, you can more easily build complete cross platform applications. The CDK is actually a series of HTML-based pages with links to reference material, sample applications and other resources.

The CDK is available at http://developer.netscape.com/tech/components/. From this page, you can either use the CDK online or download it. Having the downloaded version is somewhat easier to use since all of the samples and help files are more easily accessible.

The CDK focuses on developing and deploying components for applications developed with Visual JavaScript and platform discussions are based on Netscape Communicator 4.xx. For JavaScript components, the CDK describes how to create and import components into the VJS palette. The CDK also contains sample code that implement Java and CORBA objects as VJS components.

The CDK contains a collection of examples to introduce the basic concepts of component creation. These examples are categorized from simple, intermediate, and advanced. Included in the samples are topics such as how to create basic client-side and server-side JavaScript Bean (JSB) components, how to package a JavaBean in a JAR, how to use events with your JSB, and how to work with Dynamic HTML and JSBs.

Enterprise Application Studio

Enterprise Application Studio (EAStudio) is a comprehensive toolset that provides everything you need to develop applications in any combination of three key architectures: client/server, Web, and distributed. This suite of tools and its excellent support materials helps you get your head around the complexities of using multiple technologies and simplifies the overall development process.

EAStudio includes Enterprise Application Server 3.0, PowerBuilder 7.0, and PowerJ 3.0. Most of the EAStudio modules have been available as separate products for a few years, but EAStudio has not just bundled these together, but refined them into a trim, well-integrated package. For example, EAServer 3.0 is actually Jaguar Component Transaction Server (Jaguar CTS) and PowerDynamo (a web application server). PowerBuilder, Sybase's flagship development environment, is the long-standing language-independent visual tool that has gained a legacy following from its pioneering days as a RAD tool. Other major modules included Adaptive Server Anywhere (a database server that evolved from SQL Anywhere), PowerSite (for website creation and management), InfoMaker (a report generator) and PowerDesigner AppModeler.

PowerJ, the Java development tool, is a noteworthy product. It provides with full support for all Java 1.x AWT objects, Java Foundation Classes (JFC), data-centric visual containers and the excellent JClass components. Source-code is easily accessible for each class developed, and a contextual pop-up menu is available to search for available methods or component interfaces. It has a very good interface with its tabbed palettes and customizable toolbars. PowerJ provides a built-in converter for migrating from the various versions of Java (1.02, 1.1, Java 2) which have various incompatibilities. You just save the 1.02 project as 1.1+.

Data management is one of the most important parts of designing and developing an application. EAStudio supports almost any kind of database through ODBC and JDBC. One of the bundled tools that can help make working with your data much easier is DataWindow. This tool comes close to being a universal data formatter – a report writer, form creator, and grid maker all in one. DataWindow has been available in earlier versions of PowerBuilder, but with EAStudio, it is available as an independent file. A DataWindow is a component that typically takes the result set of a SQL query and can mold it into various presentations including tabular, composite, crosstab, freeform, grid, and group layouts. The layout may then be incorporated into an HTML page that you design in PowerSite or in a deployable PowerJ Java application.

The Jaguar CTS is one of the showpieces of the Sybase Enterprise Application Server. As its name implies, Jaguar works with components – JavaBeans, CORBA, ActiveX, and COM. You can construct an application that uses Jaguar CTS from any or all of these components. Jaguar itself manages them all according to CORBA specifications. Jaguar CTS does much more than managing components, such as database connection and caching, session and component lifecycle management, transaction processing, and debugging. Jaguar allows you to debug your applications in three ways: component only, client only, or by both client and component. The debugging tools provided are sophisticated and take some learning, but easy enough to isolate the location of bugs and step though the relevant code.

Using PowerSite and PowerDynamo, EAStudio provides a complete system for developing, maintaining and deploying web sites. Web sites can be created and maintained by PowerSite. PowerDynamo, a web application server, sits between the web server and database server to help manage the creation of HTML pages containing dynamic data. PowerDynamo is programmable through DynaScript (an ECMA version of JavaScript) and it supports XML through queries that can produce either HTML or XML. PowerDynamo can also handle XML-specific tags to manipulate XML documents.

EAStudio can be easily installed in Unix or Windows environments and the supporting documentation is highly rated. In fact, all of the documentation, tutorials, and wizards are very well constructed. Having these available will make performing complex tasks fairly easy. Features such as Sybase's Reference Card system and Parameter Wizard, which helps you fill in the arguments of complicated methods, lets you concentrate on your coding while providing all the support you need when you can't remember details. Given the support from excellent documentation and training tools, it's a system that most developers will understand and probably master. Enterprise Application Studio should earn a place on the shortlist of application development products.

RAD and Components

Tools and methodology are not the only items the RAD developer needs to consider. Reusing existing code can save a great deal of time and effort. But the existing code needs to be easy to understand and to incorporate into the next application. If the code is poorly designed it may be error prone and time consuming to reuse. One way RAD encourages us to use existing code is through the use of components.

Characteristics of Components

There are a number of characteristics that comprise a well-constructed component. The ideal component should be usable in almost any application. It should be easy to use and be able to interact with other code as needed. It shouldn't try to do too many things, but rather provide a particular service. Using code, the developer can then stitch together different combinations of these components to construct the features that the application must offer.

In order for a component to be usable in a variety of applications without great effort, it should be modular, that is, self-contained. When you place the component into your application, it should contain everything it needs to function. The component should minimize its reliance upon other entities and perform all of the activities it needs to execute its task. This independence from outside objects is referred to as having *loose coupling*. It is true that a component can never be 100% independent and some outside assistance will be needed, but the more self-sufficient a component is the better.

Self-sufficiency does not imply that the component should try to do everything. A well constructed component performs one task, performs only that task, and performs that task well. By having a collection of limited-use components to work with, you can pick and choose which capabilities you want to offer in your application and avoid bloated code and unused features. Having a single dedicated purpose is referred to as having *high cohesion*.

As an example, consider a calendar widget that allows a user to select a date. It should be able to display itself and handle the user interactions to select some date, including error trapping. It should be able to keep track of its own internal settings, and provide a return value of the date selected. The widget should not have to depend upon some helper component. It does only one thing – allow the user to select a date. It does not transport data. It does not establish connections. It does only one thing and minimizes its dependencies upon other objects to work. Its single purpose – to provide a way to select a date – implies that it is highly cohesive. Its ability to perform its function without depending upon other components implies that it is loosely coupled.

Well-constructed components are reusable also because they are understandable to the application. This is achieved by having a clearly defined **interface**. This interface is a contract between the component and the application that uses it. This contract clearly outlines how the component gets information and what information that component will return. As a contract, this interface should not change. We should be able to use the same component in different applications and it should always behave the same in each application as long as we manipulate it the same way. With some languages used to develop components, if new versions of the component are needed, additional interfaces may be added to provide access to the new features of the component. By adding additional interfaces the existing interfaces remain static. If the interface must change, then there is a risk that the outside code that uses the component will need to be changed and often this means loss of 100% backward compatibility. Having this contract allows for *introspection*. Introspection allows a tool, such as Visual JavaScript, to examine the object and "read" its features, thus allowing it to be incorporated as part of the development environment.

The interface also helps isolate the developer from the internal workings of component itself. Being a contract, the interface should remain consistent but *how* the component processes information sent to it or *how* it generates return values can change. This allows for upgrades and bug fixes to components without having to change the applications that use the components.

The Component Interface

When we create components we must develop an understandable interface by defining three types of elements: properties, methods, and events. Properties will store data. Methods contain code that is executed to provide behavior. Events will provide a triggering mechanism to indicate that something has happened. Together, these three elements define how the developer can use the component.

Properties, methods, and events of components operate just as they would with other objects you have used in JavaScript, but as a component developer, you decide exactly how these interface members behave. When building properties for components, you can create functions that process the data that is stored within the component. For example, an American telephone number can be assigned to a property as "(203) 555-1929". When the object receives this data, it strips off the non-numeric characters to reduce storage requirements. Later, when the property value is requested, the object re-inserts these characters as needed. Components also may be designed to generate events as well as respond to events. The events generated by the component may be broadcast to the rest of the application or may be responded to internally by the component.

Object Models

From an abstract standpoint, all components should look similar – black boxes with easy to use interfaces. In reality, there are several competing approaches. These approaches, called **component models**, include, among others, CORBA, JavaBeans, JavaScript Beans, and Component Object Model (COM)/Distributed Component Object Model (DCOM). Although the implementations may differ, the approach taken by each component model is essentially the same. Each approach allows a component developer to construct objects with properties, methods, and events handlers. Once these objects have been created, they are added to a **container**, which may be a browser, an application being developed (like a Visual Basic application or web page) or even an application such as a word processor, database, or web server. Once the component is inserted into the container, their interfaces are accessible by scripts.

Not only can components be accessed by their containers, the components may also access their containers. For example, we might want to instruct the browser to navigate to a different page or display a dialog. Just as the component has an interface, the container may possess its own interface. If the container is a browser, this access is through the browser's **object model**. An object model is a collection of objects, each with its own interface, and a defined relationship between these objects, usually in some hierarchy. The relationships may be organized as a hierarchy because one object often contains one or more of another object.

We use a scripting language, such as JavaScript, to access the objects within the object model just as if they were other components. If fact, you have already been accessing much of the browser's object model in previous chapters of this book. Each time you use `document.write`, you are accessing the document object from the browser's object model!

The most popular browsers on the market use variations of a document object model (DOM) specification that has been developed by the W3C. (The DOM Level 1 specification can found at `http://www.w3.org/TR/REC-DOM-Level-1/`.) Although each browser manufacturer may use a slightly different version of the DOM in their products, the similarities are very strong. Unfortunately, these differences are significant enough that care must be given to detect which object model is in use when the code runs and that the code behaves appropriately. The object models found on web servers can vary greatly as well and it is commonplace for server-side components to be written specifically for individual servers.

Scripting Language Components

Components created using CORBA, JavaBeans or COM traditionally have been developed with some third generation language such as C++, Java, or Visual Basic. With the generation of "version 4 browsers", such as those from Netscape and Microsoft, developers of web applications are able to utilize components written in scripting languages, such as JavaScript. While Netscape calls their components "JavaScript Beans" (or JSBs for short), Microsoft refers to their components as "Windows Script Components" (WSCs).

Even though the two companies developed different approaches to constructing their scripting language components, these approaches have a great deal in common. As new versions of the scripting languages are released, the similarities grow stronger. The reason for this is that many of the scripting languages are based upon the ECMAScript Specification. In June 1999, the ECMA released a standard for developing components for languages that follow the ECMAScript specification (`http://www.ecma.ch/stand/ECMA-290.htm`). With this new specification available, it is reasonable to expect that scripting components will become wore widely used and more interchangeable.

The European Computer Manufacturer's Association (ECMA) is an international, Europe-based industry association founded in 1961 and dedicated to the standardization of information and communication systems. ECMA Standards are developed by highly qualified experts from the information technology and telecommunication industry with the commitment to provide in a consensus mode technical solutions ready for implementation in product development and conformity testing. You can find out more about ECMA by visiting their web site at `http://www.ecma.ch.`

Scripting language components are more than just code snippits that are cut and pasted into code. These components simplify Web application development by providing an object-oriented programming model to HTML and script programming. You can process forms by writing standard event handlers and by calling methods. Because the components are reusable, you don't have to write as much script code and that code tends to be simpler. The end result is that you can create applications more quickly and with fewer errors.

To convert standard script into a component, the code must be "wrapped" so that it is self-contained and provides an interface. When Netscape developed JavaScript Beans, they used what they learned from packaging Java into JavaBeans and were clever enough to come up with a way to wrap not just JavaScript, but also JavaBeans, CORBA objects and DHMTL. Microsoft was clever too. Their Windows Script Components provide an easy way to create reusable COM objects using script languages such as VBScript, PERLScript, PScript, and Python. NetObjects also came up with an approach that uses XML which can wrap all of the major scripting languages and provide support for many other component technologies.

One interesting difference between the approaches of Microsoft and Netscape is that WSC uses a runtime DLL for processing the interface whereas JSBs relies upon the browser's own scripting engine. Each has its strengths and weaknesses. By depending upon a runtime DLL, WSCs can't operate on platforms that don't support the DLL. So far, that excludes everything but Windows. Not having this requirement, JSBs may be more easily deployable across multiple platforms, but they are susceptible to quirks of the scripting engine used in whatever browser the component is running on.

JavaScript Beans

Simply stated, beans are custom-built components. Like any component in object-based programming, they are intended to be reusable. As RAD developers, we wish to reuse prior code as often as possible and if the components are well engineered, the time-saving from using components can be tremendous. JavaScript Beans (JSBs) are similar to JavaBeans in that they are both components, but Javascript Beans have the potential of being much more universally usable. This claim is due, in part, to the way they are constructed, and in part to the way they are deployed.

Note: Since coffee (also known as Java) is made from coffee beans, Sun Microsystems used the same term to refer to components of its Java language. Since JavaScript was named partially because of its relationship to the Java language (and partially as a marketing move), it inherited the term 'bean' when referring to its own components.

The specifications for JSBs are intended to define every last detail and type a JavaScript object may contain, so they are easily imported into a visual web application builder such as Visual JavaScript. JavaScript Beans work by creating a definition of the component in a text file, with the functions of the component written in JavaScript. This text file is then "imported" into the development tool as an object. Once the component has been imported, the developer uses it within an HTML page just as they would a button or other object. No actual HTML content exists in the component, but the code with the component may use `document.write()` to generate HTML.

Since the tags used for the JSB itself are based upon SGML (the markup language that HTML is based upon) and the code is in JavaScript, your development tool is able to produce a web page that runs on any browser that supports JavaScript. This means that JSBs are capable of being cross-platform. Of course, there may be some differences in behavior from browser to browser, since JavaScript in an interpreted language and therefore is at the mercy of the script engine executing the code. One of the most significant incompatibility issues involves Microsoft Internet Explorer 5, which, arguably, does not fully support JSBs as implemented with VJS and ScriptBuilder.

Even though JSBs are designed to work seamlessly with Java, JSBs are not Java applets. Both are considered components and therefore offer similar capabilities. JSBs come into play at design-time whilst applets are more run-time oriented. One way of looking at the difference is that JSBs are used by the developer to build additional logic and HTML code at design time. Java applets are "black boxes" that only influence what happens at run-time. It is the processing of the JSB at design-time that produces simple JavaScript and HTML that makes JSBs usable on virtually any web browser.

Another difference between JSBs and Java applets is that JSBs are designed to be **Universal Containers**. That is, containers which may encapsulate HTML, Dynamic HTML, and even Java. Of course, adding such advanced technologies as DHTML may make the JSB less cross-platform.

In order for JSBs to work as well as they do, a detailed specification was designed for producing and implementing JSBs. Some of the things that the JSB specifications tried to achieve include:

- Mimic the JavaBean `BeanInfo` class used to describe Java components for greater familiarity to Java developers
- Mimic the format of HTML for greater familiarity to script writers
- Easy integration with existing technologies, such as Java, HTML, and DHTML
- Make for easy inclusion into web development tools

Under the hood, a JSB is essentially your JavaScript code stored in a datafile that also contains technical information about the JSB. This file describes the structure of the JSB and how it may be included within an HTML document. Like an HTML file, this text file uses an extensive set of HTML-like tags. (In fact these tags are an extension of the same SGML markup definition language used to define HTML). Apart from tags, the content of the JSB file is pure JavaScript. The tags used allow us to define the parts of the JSB such as a constructor method, method definition, property definition, event definition, and definitions for the object's interface.

Typically, the skeleton of a JSB file looks like the following:

```
<JSB>
    <JSB_DESCRIPTOR ...>
    <JSB_ICON...>
    <JSB_PROPERTY ...>

    <JSB_EVENT ...>

    <JSB_METHOD ...>
        <JSB_PARAMETER ...>
    </JSB_METHOD>

    <JSB_CONSTRUCTOR ...>
    </JSB_CONSTRUCTOR>
</JSB>
```

The JSB file structure is modeled on the JavaBeans `BeanInfo` class, so if you are already familiar with Java, you already know about JSB files.

Building and Implementing a Simple JavaScript Bean

Before a developer can use a JavaScript Bean, the component itself must be created. This is done with a text editor such as Notepad or JavaScript Editor from E-Port Software (download a free copy from `http://e-port.yeah.net`). After the component has been coded and saved in a text file, that component must be added to a development tool that supports JavaScript Beans, such as Visual JavaScript or ScriptBuilder. It is this text file that informs the development tool how to interact with the object. Once the component is included as part of the development tool, the developer may then use that component in a web application. To test the component in a page, you must have browser that supports JavaScript.

When the developer creates a JSB file, they use HTML-like tags to specify the various parts within the component. Most JSB tags have attributes that provide unique tag information. For example, all tags have a `NAME` attribute that provides a unique identifier for the tag. The names you assign to attributes must be unique throughout a JSB file. Furthermore, the names should not duplicate JavaScript or JSB reserved words. Reserved words are those keywords that provide JS or JSB syntax, such as `SRC` or `SCRIPT`.

The following is the ubiquitous "Hello World" example:

```
<JSB>
    <JSB_DESCRIPTOR NAME="HelloWorld">
    <JSB_CONSTRUCTOR>
        function HelloWorld (params)
        {
            alert("Hello World!");
        }
    </JSB_CONSTRUCTOR>
</JSB>
```

The `<JSB>` and `</JSB>` tags identify the beginning and ending of the component. The `<JSB_DESCRIPTOR>` tag is used for the descriptor section. This section is used to identify the JSB, which in our example we named "HelloWorld".

When the JSB is first referenced, it is instantiated. When a JSB is instantiated, the function defined as its **constructor** is executed. So in our "Hello World" demo, as soon as our object is first used, the function `HelloWorld()` is executed which causes the `alert()` box to be shown. Constructor functions must always be present in your JSB file, even if the constructor doesn't do anything. Constructor functions hold a similar role to DOS's `AUTOEXEC.BAT` file, typically they are used to initialize variables and generally setup the component.

> **Note: The name used in the constructor must match the name in the descriptor section exactly.**

The constructor function contains a reference to "`params`". Although this reference is not used in our simple demo, it is used when the component is placed upon the web page to assign an ID to instances of the component. Later on we will discuss how `params` is used in some detail.

If we place our component on a page and then load that page in our browser, the component gets created and the JavaScript alert "Hello World!" appears. To demonstrate this, we will use Netscape Visual JavaScript to produce the page and then we will load that page into a browser.

Open Netscape Visual JavaScript and when prompted, create a new project called "JSB".

Using your favorite text editor (like Notepad or Netscape's JavaScript Editor), type in the following code exactly as it appears. Make sure that you pay close attention to upper and lower case. JavaScript, and therefore JavaScript Beans, is sensitive to case.

```
<JSB>
<JSB_DESCRIPTOR NAME="HelloWorld">
   <JSB_CONSTRUCTOR>
      function HelloWorld (params)
      {
         alert("Hello World!");
      }
   </JSB_CONSTRUCTOR>
</JSB>
```

Save the file as "`helloworld.jsb`" in the project folder for JSB. This folder is typically found at `C:\Program Files\Netscape Visual JavaScript\Projects\JSB`. Please note the lowercase `.jsb` file extension. If you are using Notepad, make sure that the "Save as type" dropdown is set to "All Files" or Notepad will add a `.txt` extension automatically.

Click on the "Palette" icon in the toolbar to display a tabbed window that contains several collections of components.

Let's add a new tab to the palette to place our JavaScript bean. To do this, right-click on the Palette window and select New Tab. A new tab named "Unnamed" will appear. Next, right-click on this new tab and select Rename Tab. The cursor will move to the title of the tab. Use the delete key to delete the existing name and then type "Wrox". Press the *Enter* key to finish.

Now to import the JavaScript Bean file. Right-click on the Palette window and select "From JSB file..." from the "Install Component(s)" menu. A dialog window titled "Load Java Script File" will appear.

Use the browse button to select the `helloworld.jsb` file that you just saved. Then click the **OK** button to confirm your selection. An icon representing the component will appear in the current tab of the Palette window. You may need to use the scrollbars to scroll down to the bottom of the tab to see the newly installed component.

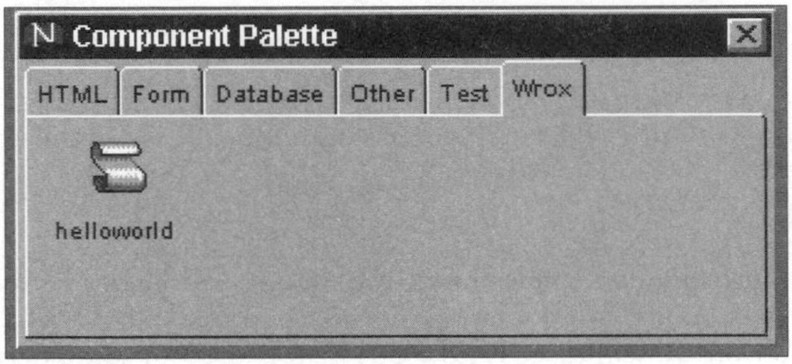

Click on the "New Page" icon found in the toolbar. A dialog window will appear prompting you for the new page type. Select "Blank Page Template" and then click on OK. A new window will appear in the Visual JavaScript editor.

From the Palette window, drag our new component onto the page. Visual JavaScript should appear similar to the following illustration:

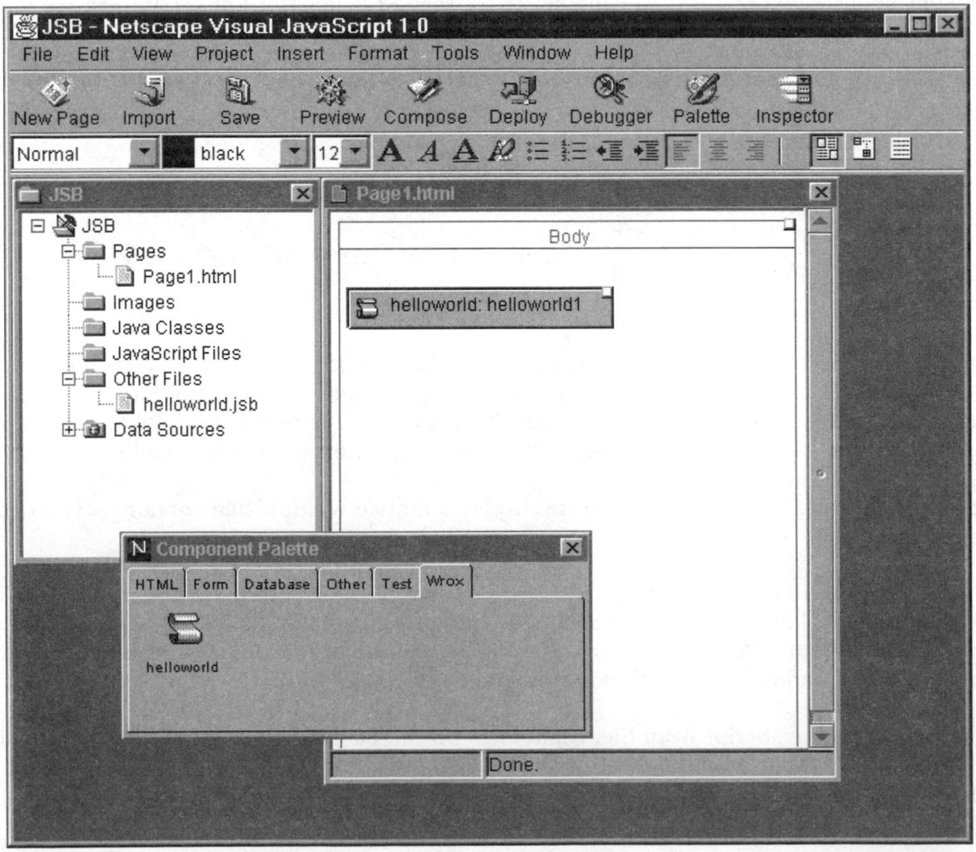

Click on the **Save** icon in the toolbar and then click on the **Deploy** button in the toolbar and deploy this page to a local folder.

Open up your browser and using the **File | Open...** menu item, open the page you just saved. When the page opens, the alert box will be displayed.

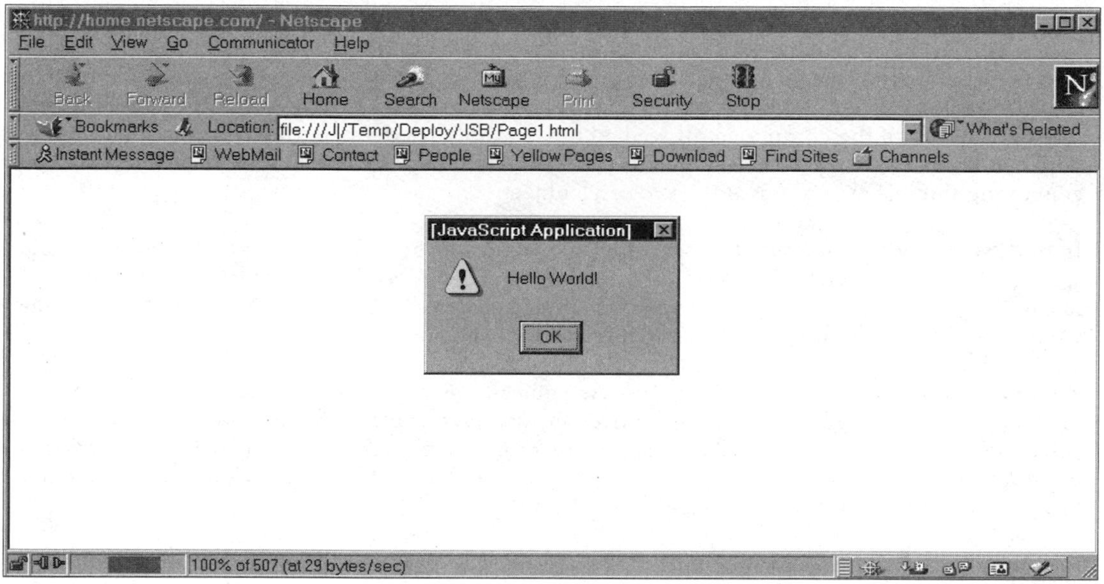

It is worth investigating just how the page was constructed with the JSB. From within the browser, right-click on the page and select the View Source. The code generated should appear similar to the following:

```
<HTML><HEAD><SCRIPT PURPOSE="JSConstructor" CLASS="HelloWorld">

        function HelloWorld (params)
        {
                alert("Hello World!");
        }


</SCRIPT></HEAD><BODY><P><SCRIPT LANGUAGE="JavaScript" PURPOSE="ObjectInst"
ID="HelloWorld1" CLASS="HelloWorld" DISPLAYNAME="HelloWorld"
SHORTDESCRIPTION="HelloWorld" ICONNAME="TagScript">

//automatically generated script
params = new Object();
params.id = "HelloWorld1";
HelloWorld1 = new HelloWorld(params);

</SCRIPT></P><SCRIPT PURPOSE=ConnectorInfo>

</SCRIPT></BODY></HTML>
```

Visual JavaScript generated a series of <SCRIPT> tags. The first of these <SCRIPT> tags defines the bean itself and the second tag declares an instance of the bean. The name of the component is used to generate the ID of each instance of the component, therefore the ID of this instance is "HelloWorld1". If an additional instance of the component were added to the code, a new <SCRIPT> tag would be generated that would be identical to the second <SCRIPT> tag, but declaring an instance with an ID of "HelloWorld2".

With the source for the page exposed, we can now see how params is being used. The params reference acts as a gateway to assign properties to our component. First params is declared to be a new object of some yet-unknown type. Next, values are assigned to properties of this new object, in this case the ID of the component. If we had other properties defined, they would use the params object as well. After the params object is assigned its property, it is then used as a template for generating the instance of our HelloWorld1 object.

In our JSB file, we didn't directly use params at all so we could have left out all references to it. In spite of this fact, the params object will always be needed to assign the ID to the component instance, so the params = new Object(); and params.id = "HelloWorld1"; statements would have been automatically generated for us.

There is another observation of note here. As you can see, all of the internal code of the bean is visible. This is one significant difference from using a Java applet. The JSB code needs to be exposed since JavaScript is an interpreted language. Thinking this through, we find that JavaScript Beans are no more (or less) secure than HTML code. Anyone who knows how to view the source code in a browser will see just what you did and how you did it.

More About Describing the Component

There are a number of additional attributes that may be included to better describe your JSB components. For a given component you can specify descriptions for your component, add icons, and even include a hyperlink to a URL for online help.

As discussed above, the NAME attribute of the <JSB_DESCRIPTOR> tag is used to generate the default ID of each instance of the component. Unfortunately, there are some technical and practical restrictions placed on what you can name a component. You should not use most non-alphabetical characters, nor should the name be very long or duplicate reserved words in JavaScript. Often these names are somewhat cryptic and may not be as descriptive as you might like. The good news is that the JSB file structure gives you some other ways to better present your components.

The SHORTDESCRIPTION attribute of the <JSB_DESCRIPTOR> tag allows you to provide a meaningful description for the user of the component. If you do not specify this attribute in the JSB file, it is automatically generated for you using the value of the NAME attribute. The value of this attribute is displayed as the tooltip when you hover your mouse over the component on either the Component Palette or on an instance of the component on a page.

To provide a help system for using your component, you may add the HELP_URL attribute within the <JSB_DESCRIPTOR> tag. This attribute may be assigned a string that contains a valid URL. Application developers can view the URL's page in their browser when they choose **More Info** from the VJS menu. The value of the HELP_URL attribute may be prefaced with the literal string "$INSTALLDIR" to force VJS to load the help page from a local folder relative to the VJS installation folder.

The following are a few examples of how this attribute may be assigned:

```
HELP_URL=http://www.wrox.com/componenthelp.html#widget
HELP_URL=file:///doc/help.htm#widget"
HELP_URL="$INSTALLDIR/doc/help.htm#widget"
```

The first example identifies some Internet web page, which resides as part of a web site on a remote web server. (This is a fictitious example, so don't actually try the link). The second example specifies some file on the user's local machine on the current drive. The third example also specifies a file on the user's local machine, but the file must reside in a folder inside the directory Visual JavaScript was installed to. This third form is often considered the most preferable since it helps assure that a help file moves with a component and its given VJS palette.

A component definition can include an optional `<JSB_ICON>` tag that provides information for a 16x16 pixel color GIF for the component's icon. This section follows the `<JSB_DESCRIPTOR>` tag and contains only a single attribute, `ICONNAME`, which specifies a 'base' file. Some development tools require a 16 x 16 pixel image while other, such as Visual JavaScript, requires both a 16 x 16 and a 32 x 32 pixel image. The file specified by this attribute is always the 16 x 16 pixel file. If a 32 x 32 pixel file is needed, its name is assumed to be the same as the filename provided, except it will have '32' appended. For example, if `ICONNAME` is assigned the string value `"jsbicon.gif"`, then the 32 x 32 pixel file will be assumed to have the name `"jsbicon32.gif"`.

Adding Properties to a JSB

For many components to be useful to a developer, there must be some mechanism to assign customizable settings to the component. Such information is assigned through the use of properties and may be done at design time, run time, or both. As with most object-oriented development, the assignment of properties uses the `object.property = value` format. To use the value of a property, simply reference the property using the `object.property` format. Consider the following JavaScript statements:

```
dog.breed = "German Shepherd";
dog.name = "Victoria";
dog.age = 12;
alert("My "+dog.breed+" dog, named "+dog.name+" is now "+dog.age+" years old")
```

The first statement would assign a value of "German Shepherd" for a property named "breed" for an object named "dog". The second would assign the value "Victoria" to the name property, and the third statement would assign the number twelve to the age property. The last statement displays these property values in an alert window.

When constructing our JavaScript Bean, we use a property descriptor tag, `<JSB_PROPERTY>` to identify the property's name, data type, and default value. Like the descriptor tag, the `<JSB_PROPERTY>` tag does not have an ending tag. To define the properties in the above example, we could use the following:

```
<JSB_DESCRIPTOR NAME="dog">
<JSB_PROPERTY NAME="breed" TYPE="string" DEFAULT_VALUE="mut">
<JSB_PROPERTY NAME="name" TYPE="string">
<JSB_PROPERTY NAME="age" TYPE="int">
    :
    :
</JSB>
```

665

It is considered good practice to always specify the data type for each property. This is done to help ensure that the developers who use your component will use the component correctly. The data type may be cast as any valid JavaScript data type. It may also be cast as a fully qualified Java class.

In our "Hello World" example, we shall add a property that specifies what message is to be displayed. If no message is assigned, the component will display the default of "Hello World!". As you saw in the earlier example, this code uses an object called params.

Using your text editor make the following changes to the code. Save this updated version of the new file as "HelloWorldA.jsb" in the Projects/JSB folder.

```
<JSB>
<JSB_DESCRIPTOR NAME="HelloWorldA">
<JSB_PROPERTY NAME="AlertMessage" TYPE="string" DEFAULT_VALUE="Hello World!">
    <JSB_CONSTRUCTOR>
    function HelloWorldA (params)
    {
        this.AlertMessage = params.AlertMessage;
        alert(this.AlertMessage);
    }
    </JSB_CONSTRUCTOR>
</JSB>
```

Right-click on the Palette window and select "Install Component(s)" then "From JSB file...". Use the browse button to select the HelloWorldA.jsb file that you just saved. Now two different HelloWorld component icons will be displayed in the current tab of the Palette window.

So we don't get confused between the first and second versions of our component, let's delete the instance of our first component before we add our new component. To delete the instance, click on the instance on the page, then right-click your mouse and choose Delete.

Now add our new component to the page.... From the Palette window, drag our new component onto the page. Now let's check to verify that our property is usable. To do so, double-click on the component on the page. The Inspector window will appear describing our component. Two properties will be listed, "ID of Component" and "Alert Message." If the inspector window did not display any properties then an error was probably made in typing out the code for the component. If the two properties are displayed, then we can start to use them.

Design Time Changes to Properties

As developers, we want to assign our own value to the AlertMessage property when we are designing our pages. When we first added this component to the page, the value we specified under the property descriptor's DEFAULT_VALUE attribute was automatically assigned. To change this, we can use this Inspector window. Click on the ellipsis button (the three dots) found on the far right of the line in the Inspector window that describes the AlertMessage property. A data entry dialog window will appear. Change the text to say "Wow! This is Easy!" and then click on the OK button. The Inspector window should then reflect this change. This change only affects this instance of the component. If we were to add another instance of our HelloWorldA component, its AlertMessage property would again be "Hello World! "

While we are discussing changing the values of properties, we can also change the ID of this component. Typically, having components named Widget1, Widget2, and so on is hard to keep track of. To avoid this we use a standard naming convention that can identify both the class of the component as well as its use. For example, we might have two components used to connect to two different databases, one database from the Sales department and the second from the Accounting department. Both components are the "JavaScript Client Cursor" found in the Database tab of the Component Palette. The IDs that we might use could be "ccurSales" and "ccurAcct". By using the same prefix in each name, we can easily see that these components are of the same class. In our simple example changing the name doesn't buy us much, but let's go ahead anyway, just for the experience. Change the ID of our HelloWorldA1 component to "hwDemo".

Now, let's take a look at the source code. You'll need to first click on the page window before selecting Source from the View menu.

```
<HTML><HEAD><SCRIPT PURPOSE="JSConstructor" CLASS="HelloWorldA">

</SCRIPT></HEAD><BODY><P><SCRIPT LANGUAGE="JavaScript" PURPOSE="ObjectInst"
ID="hwDemo" CLASS="HelloWorldA" DISPLAYNAME="HelloWorldA"
SHORTDESCRIPTION="HelloWorldA" ICONNAME="TagScript">

//automatically generated script
params = new Object();
params.AlertMessage = "Wow! This is easy!";
params.id = "hwDemo";
hwDemo = new HelloWorldA(params);

</SCRIPT></P><SCRIPT PURPOSE=ConnectorInfo>

</SCRIPT></BODY></HTML>
```

As you can see, the code is still structured much as is was in our previous example, with `<HTML>`, `<HEAD>`, and `<SCRIPT>` tag pairs. As expected, the ID of our component has been changed to `hwDemo` and the `AlertMessage` now contains the new text value.

The big difference in this new source code is the use of the `params` object. We use `params` as a gateway to assign properties to our component. First we declare `params` to be a new object of some yet-unknown type. Next, we assign values to properties to this new object (in our prior example, we didn't directly use this at all and we could have left out all references to it). In our second component, we again use `params` to assign the value of another property, namely `AlertMessage`. Once all of our properties have been assigned to the `params` object, we use it to instantiate our component with the line `hwDemo = new HelloWorldA(params);`.

More About Properties

There are a few more comments concerning properties worth mentioning here.

It is very common for an object or component to have a default property. By declaring a default property you can make coding simpler and faster as it helps increase execution speed. Coding is simpler because, when a default property is assigned, the property doesn't have to be explicitly specified in the code. For example, if the `"InvoiceNumber"` property of the `"Invoice"` component was the default, then the following two statements would be equivalent:

```
Invoice.InvoiceNumber = 4026;
Invoice = 4026;
```

The speed of execution is also increased, although this increase may not always be noticeable. The reason for the increase in performance has to do with how the interpreter accesses the various members of the component's interface. When any given property is referenced, the interpreter must find the property in the collection of available properties. When a property is identified as the default, that property is placed first in the internal workings of the component. By being at the top of the list of properties, the interpreter always finds it first.

The ISDEFAULT attribute is used to declare the default property. Unlike most attributes, ISDEFAULT is not assigned a value. It is the existence of this attribute that causes it to be in effect. This attribute is optional and if it is not used with any of the properties declared, then the first property listed in the JSB file automatically becomes the default property. If more than one property is assigned the ISDEFAULT attribute, the first property with this attribute becomes the default, and all other ISDEFAULT attributes for properties are ignored.

Being able to set certain properties at design time may not make sense. For example, a property that reports the currently displayed field in a database table is meaningless until run time, when the application accesses the database. Similarly, there may be properties that should be set only at design time. As a component developer, we have a great deal of control over when a property can be set. Using attributes of the Property Descriptor such as DESIGNTIMEREADONLY and RUNTIMEACCESS, we can specify that a property will be allowed to be set only at design time, only at run time, or at both design and run time.

When a property value is set, we can perform validation to ensure that the right data is being applied. The VALUESET attribute allows us to specify a range of allowed values for the property. For example, if we wished to limit a property "Gender" to receive only the values "M" or "F", we could use:

```
VALUESET="M","F"
```

For another illustration on the use of this attribute, consider the following example of a property from the DBSource component found in Visual JavaScript. This property tag defines a property named dbType, which limits the acceptable values to a list of supported databases.

```
<JSB_PROPERTY NAME="dbType" DISPLAYNAME="Database Type"
    VALUESET="ORACLE,INFORMIX,SYBASE,ODBC-SQL Anywhere,ODBC-SQL Server,ODBC-Access"
    SHORTDESCRIPTION="Database type"
    :
>
```

For string values, the VALUESET attribute requires commas to separate each value. For numeric properties, VALUESET can be a comma-delimited list of values or ranges. The ranges use a min:max pattern, such as "0:10", which would limit the acceptable values to zero through ten, inclusively. Ranges may also be mixed with individual values, such as "0:10,20,30", which would limit value to 0 through ten as well as twenty and thirty.

Adding Methods to a JSB

When we wish to add behavior to a component, the behavior is typically coded as a method. Unlike properties, which can be set at either design time or at run time, a method can only be executed at run time.

Any data that a method acts upon is supplied by either the calling routine as a parameter or from a property previously set in the object. To create a method, use the <JSB_METHOD> and </JSB_METHOD> descriptor tags. This tag pair will define what function will execute when that method is called, the type of data it will return, if any, and any arguments it might take. The method should have some function defined with the same name, typically contained within the JSB constructor. When the method is called, it is this function which is executed.

You might ask yourself why go through the effort of declaring a method rather than calling the function directly. The reason is, in object-based programming, it is considered safer to require that the calling routine communicate only through the object's interface. By associating the method with a function, you are providing a mechanism for which the outside world can invoke an internal function. It is by declaring a function for a method that a developer may access the functions within the component. This mechanism is also used by the authoring tool to inform the developer what the method is and what arguments it takes.

Another reason for encapsulating properties and methods within an object and forcing the developer to access the object via its interface is for maintenance. If, for any reason, you need to change the inner workings of the function, the routines that use the component would not need to change since they act upon the method and not the function the method uses.

Some methods will return values while others may not. If a method does return a value, the method definition must use the TYPE attribute to specify the data type of the return value. It is always good practice to specify a return value data type whenever possible. Like properties, this attribute may cast the return data type as any valid JavaScript data type or a fully qualified Java class. For example, the following defines a method that returns a string value:

```
<JSB_METHOD NAME="getURL"
    TYPE="string"
    >
</JSB_METHOD>
```

If the method does not return a value, set the TYPE attribute to "void", as in the following example:

```
<JSB_METHOD NAME="addRow"
    TYPE="void"
    >
</JSB_METHOD>
```

If a method accepts parameters, these parameters must also be specified using embedded tags. For example, the following code defines a method that has three parameters and returns a value. This method's return value as well as each parameter is cast as a Java String data type.

```
<JSB_METHOD NAME="directionChange" TYPE="java.lang.String">
    <JSB_PARAMETER NAME="propertyName" TYPE="java.lang.String">
    <JSB_PARAMETER NAME="oldValue" TYPE="java.lang.String">
    <JSB_PARAMETER NAME="newValue" TYPE="java.lang.String">
</JSB_METHOD>
```

In our HelloWorld example, we will create a method that actually displays the message. To demonstrate that the function is actually doing something, we will have it perform a trivial operation on the text of the message.

```
<JSB>
    <JSB_DESCRIPTOR NAME="HelloWorldB"
        DISPLAYNAME="Hello World demonstration with functions."
        EVENTMODEL="JS"
        >
    <JSB_PROPERTY NAME="AlertMessage"
        PROPTYPE="JS"
        TYPE="string"
```

```
            DEFAULT_VALUE="Hello World"
            SHORTDESCRIPTION="Content of message to be displayed"
            >
    <JSB_METHOD NAME="ShowMessage" TYPE="void" >
        <JSB_PARAMETER NAME="strContent"
        TYPE="string"
        >
    </JSB_METHOD>

    <JSB_CONSTRUCTOR>

        function ShowMessage(strMessage)
        {
            // Process the argument passed and display it.
            var strText;
            strText = strMessage + "!!!";
            alert(strText);
        }

        function HelloWorldB (params)
        {
            this.AlertMessage=params.AlertMessage;
            ShowMessage(this.AlertMessage);
        }

    </JSB_CONSTRUCTOR>
</JSB>
```

Now let's test the component to see the interface in action at run time. We'll place a button on the page and use its events to invoke the ShowMessage() method in our component. From within Visual JavaScript, drag the **Button** component from the **Form** tab of the Component Palette onto the page. Now we need to associate the button with our component. To do this, we first double-click on the button to display the Inspector Window. Under the section that lists events, click on the ellipsis for the onClick event. This will display the Connection Builder window.

Click on the "Script Builder" button at the bottom of the window to display the Script Builder window. From the Script Builder window, select HelloWorldB1 from the Component dropdown list. A list of methods from the component will be displayed under the "Call Method" tab. Select the ShowMessage() method and then click the "Add Action" button. This copies the code to call the method into the "onClick script handler" text box. Edit this code so that the argument passed is "Hello Again".

```
HelloWorldB1.ShowMessage('Hello Again');
```

Now select the OK button to close the Script Builder window and then select Apply. Close the window by selecting Done.

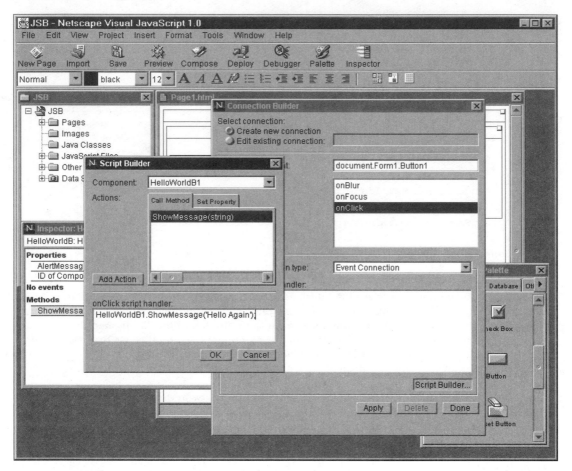

Now save the page, deploy the project and open the page in your browser. The AlertMessage again will be displayed when the page is opened, and an additional message will appear with each click on the button.

Processing Properties Using Methods

We have seen how each property of a component is identified with its own <JSB_PROPERTY> tag. So far, we have used properties as if they were variables by directly assigning values to them and retrieving values directly from them. Although this approach may be convenient, it doesn't provide data validation. It is true that we can add the VALUESET attribute to add a certain level of protection, but often this attribute alone is not sufficient. Take the situation where the value assigned is required to be one that exists in a database table. Since the developer usually does not know beforehand the values that will be stored in the table, the VALUESET attribute doesn't meet our needs. In order for the data to be properly validated, a connection to the database needs to be made and then the value looked for in the appropriate table. This process requires coding that a simple property can't provide. To get around this limitation, we may assign methods to do the processing for us whenever the value of the property changes.

Like properties in C++ and Visual Basic, properties in JavaScript components may be set and retrieved through Get and Set methods defined by the READMETHOD and WRITEMETHOD attributes within the <JSB_PROPERTY> tag:

```
READMETHOD="methodname"
WRITEMETHOD="methodname"
```

Where *methodname* corresponds to the name of a <JSB_METHOD> tag defined elsewhere in the JSB file.

The Get method uses an expression of the type *object.property* to retrieve a value. The Set method is created using an assignment expression to set the property. You can have a READMETHOD attribute without a WRITEMETHOD attribute, and vice-versa.

There are a few important notes about using Get and Set methods. The return value of the Get (READMETHOD) method is the same as the property's TYPE attribute since this method will supply the value of the property. Also, the Set method may only possess a single parameter and that parameter must match the property's TYPE attribute.

It is interesting to note that regardless of whether or not you specify a READMETHOD and/or WRITEMETHOD attribute, methods will be used to process the property values. If the Get and Set methods are not specified, or if they are null, they are created automatically at design time. These generated methods do very little besides directly referencing the property, but they are there nevertheless.

One final item to consider when using Get and Set methods with properties is developer access to these functions. Since the purpose of these methods is to process the value of the property when that property changes, there is little reason for the developer to have direct access to these methods. To make a method "invisible" to the developer, use the ISEXPERT attribute. This attribute takes no arguments. As long as the method tag contains this attribute, the method will not be displayed in the Inspector window of the development tool.

If we wanted to have our component use Get and Set routines for processing the AlertMessage property, we could use the following code. The behavior is exactly as it was before, but with this implementation, we have the option of adding additional processing code for data validation.

```
<JSB>
    <JSB_DESCRIPTOR NAME="HelloWorldC"
        DISPLAYNAME="Hello World demonstration."
        >

    <JSB_PROPERTY NAME="AlertMessage"
        PROPTYPE="JS"
        TYPE="string"
        DEFAULT_VALUE="Hello World"
        READMETHOD="GetAlertMessage"
        WRITEMETHOD="SetAlertMessage"
        ISDEFAULT
        SHORTDESCRIPTION="Content of message to be displayed"
        >

    <JSB_METHOD NAME="GetAlertMessage"
        TYPE="string"
        ISEXPERT
        >
    </JSB_METHOD>
```

673

```
        <JSB_METHOD NAME="SetAlertMessage"
            TYPE="void"
            ISEXPERT
            >
                <JSB_PARAMETER NAME="NewValue"
                    TYPE="string"
                    >
        </JSB_METHOD>

        <JSB_METHOD NAME="ShowMessage" TYPE="void" >
            <JSB_PARAMETER NAME="strContent"
                TYPE="string"
                >
        </JSB_METHOD>

        <JSB_CONSTRUCTOR>

            function GetAlertMessage()
            {
                return this.AlertMessage;
            }

            function SetAlertMessage(strNewValue)
            {
                this.AlertMessage = strNewValue;
            }

            function ShowMessage(strMessage)
            {
                // Process the argument passed and display it.
                var strText;
                strText = strMessage + "!!!";
                alert(strText);
            }

            //***
            // The constructor
            //
            function HelloWorldC (params)
            {
                this.AlertMessage=params.AlertMessage;
                this.SetAlertMessage=params.SetAlertMessage;
                this.GetAlertMessage=params.GetAlertMessage;
                ShowMessage(this.AlertMessage);
            }

        </JSB_CONSTRUCTOR>

    </JSB>
```

Having Property Changes Throw Events

Once a property is defined, it may be configured so that an onChange event is triggered when the property value changes. This association of a property and an event is called **binding** the property. The code that is executed when an event occurs (also called **thrown**) is called the **event handler**.

To have the property change cause an event to fire and then have an event handler respond to the event, three things need to be done. First, you need to specify that the property will cause an onChange event. Next, you need to define a function that will provide the behavior of the component when the event is thrown. Finally, you need to associate that function with the onChange event.

To throw an onChange event when a change is made to a property, add the ISBOUND attribute to the property's property tag. This attribute is not assigned any value. It is the presence of this attribute in the property tag which enables the property to throw the onChange event. For example:

```
<JSB_PROPERTY NAME="value"
    TYPE="string"
    ISBOUND
    SHORTDESCRIPTION="item to process."
    >
```

If we wanted to make the AlertMessage property of our HelloWorld JSB cause an onChange event when its value is altered, all we need to do is add the ISBOUND attribute to the AlertMessage property definition.

Now that we can cause an onChange event, we need to create an event handler. The event handler is simply a function that you define. This function is constructed no differently than the SetAlertMessage() or ShowMessage() functions that were created earlier.

The final step is to define the onChange event itself, which is done using the <JSB_EVENT> tag. To understand the attributes used in tag, let's briefly discuss some of the mechanics of events. Recall that events are based upon the concept of **event producers** that trigger events, and **event listeners**, that respond to triggered events. When a bound property of a component changes, the component is said to be the event producer. If the component responds to its own events, then it is also the event listener. The routine that is executed when the event listener responds is often called the **listener method**. Since many web applications use a mixture of technologies that may use events, we need to identify which **event model** will be used for each event in the component. The event model governs the internal mechanisms of how the event is structured and processed.

In the <JSB_EVENT> tag, use the NAME attribute to specify the name of the event being defined. In this case, the name of the event is "onChange". The LISTENERMETHODS attribute is used to specify the method (or methods) that will execute when the event is thrown. Also, there are several settings that you may use with the EVENTMODEL attribute to specify the event model: "JS", "AWT11", and "HTML". "JS" specifies the standard JavaScript event model. This is often a good setting to try if you have doubts about which event model setting to use. "AWT11" refers to the Abstract Windowing Toolkit used for Java 1.1 components, so this setting is often used when your component needs to interact with Java components or for events that use listener methods to connect components. The "HTML" setting is used when interacting with standard HTML components (e.g. form elements) such as the onClick event.

> *An event model must be specified for every event definition. There are two ways to define an event model. The first is when you declare a default event model for the entire component in the <JSB_DESCRIPTOR> tag using the EVENTMODEL attribute. The second way is when you declare a specific event model type for each event by using the EVENTMODEL attribute with the <JSB_EVENT> tag. If EVENTMODEL is found in both the Component Descriptor and in an event tag, the event tag's EVENTMODEL attribute will be used. If EVENTMODEL is omitted in <JSB_DESCRIPTOR>, you must supply a separate EVENTMODEL attribute for each event and property that uses an event.*

When objects are notified of event triggers, it is through their interfaces, therefore we must specify an interface for our event to communicate with. This is done with the <JSB_INTERFACE> tag. (Since JSBs were modeled after JavaBeans, the <JSB_INTERFACE> tag often identifies the Java package and class that defines the event handler.) Also, a JSB file may have more than one <JSB_INTERFACE> tag, so we need to specify for each <JSB_EVENT> tag the name of the interface that will be listened to. This is done by the LISTENERTYPE attribute of the <JSB_EVENT> tag.

The following is an example of an event declaration and its associated interface:

```
<JSB>
    <JSB_EVENT NAME="onClick"
        EVENTMODEL="JS"
        LISTENERTYPE="onClickListener"
        LISTENERMETHODS="onClick"
        >
    <JSB_METHOD NAME="onClick">
    </JSB_METHOD>

    <JSB_INTERFACE NAME="onClickListener">
</JSB>
```

Where Component Execution Occurs

When a component runs, it may execute on either the client machine (for instance in a browser) or on a server machine. Unless you specify the environment where your component is to execute, it may be executed in any location. If you specify where execution occurs, you can use the ENV attribute within the Component's Descriptor (<JSB_DESCRIPTOR>) tag.

The ENV attribute has the value 'either' as its default, which indicates that the application developer will decide where execution should occur. If you set the ENV to 'client' then the component will execute on the client. When the JSB file is processed, its code is automatically placed within <SCRIPT> tags in the HTML document. A value of 'server' forces execution on the server. When the JSB file is processed, its code is automatically placed within <SERVER> tags in the HTML document.

The following is the JSB descriptor tag used to identify a mail component that will execute on the server.

```
<JSB_DESCRIPTOR NAME="netscape.peas.Sendmail"
    DISPLAYNAME="SendMail"
    ISHIDDEN
    ENV="server"
    SHORTDESCRIPTION="Server SendMail Object"
    >
```

There is also a fourth setting for the ENV attribute with the <JSB_CONSTRUCTOR> tag: the value of both. This setting is used when you want some portions to be executed on each machine. When using the value both, an instance is created on both the client and the server and you choose where each property and method reside. The way you do this is to use the ENV attribute again within the <JSB_PROPERTY> and <JSB_METHOD> tags. As with the Component Descriptor tag, the value of ENV may be client, server, or both, but the either value is not permitted. If you don't specify an ENV attribute within a property or method declaration, the value both is assumed.

Here is an example of a method defined to execute on the client:

```
<JSB_METHOD NAME="setValue"
   TYPE="void"
   ENV="client"
   >
      <JSB_PARAMETER NAME="newValue"
         TYPE="string"
         >
</JSB_METHOD>
```

When using the `either` or `both` options with either the `<JSB_CONSTRUCTOR>` or individual properties or methods, make sure that you test the component on both machines. When possible, you should force execution to the client machine by temporarily setting the option to `client` and then testing it. Next, test the component when it is forced to run on the server. Only after testing the component on each machine should you then test using the `either` or `both` settings.

For any component that can run on the server, you must create a separate JS file on the server that defines the component's constructor function, and point to that file in the SRC attribute of the `<JSB_CONSTRUCTOR>` tag. For example:

```
<JSB_CONSTRUCTOR SRC="SampleScrollingBanner.js">
</JSB_CONSTRUCTOR>
```

Packaging Components for Import

Most simple JSBs may be imported directly into the component palette of your development tool. In general, components that consist of more than one file, such as a component that uses JS files to provide additional support routines or for components with icon files, must be packaged into a Java Archive Resource (JAR) file. The JAR file is then used to import the component into the development tool. JAR files may be created by using the Java Developer Kit (JDK) JAR packager utility, which is available from Sun Microsystems (`http://java.sun.com`).

To create the JAR file using the JAR packager in the JDK, use the follow steps as a guideline:

Create a temporary folder and copy the files used by the component to this folder. This should include all subfolders.

Create a "manifest file" named "`MANIFEST.MF`" in the temporary folder. Manifest files are ASCII text files that list all the files to be included in the JAR file.

The first line in this file should contain this:

```
Manifest-Version: 1.0
```

For each file to be included in the JAR file there should be an entry in the manifest file. Each entry will contain at least one line that gives the case-sensitive name of the file. If the file is in a subfolder, use '/' (forward-slash) as the separator. If the line specifies a JSB, a second line must be present with the text `Java-Bean: True`.

677

```
Manifest-Version: 1.0

Name: common/helloworld.jsb
Java-Bean: True

Name: common/class2.class
Java-Bean: True
```

Use the JAR compiler to create a JAR file, using at the DOS prompt:

```
jar cfm jar-name manifest-name beanfile1, beanfile2, …
```

Here is an example of using this command, which assumes that all of the required files are located in a subfolder named helloworld that is inside the temporary working directory:

```
jar cfm HelloWorld.jar HELLOWORLD.MF helloworld/*
```

You now have a JAR file containing your components which can be used to import your component! To verify that the JAR file has all of the intended files contained in it, use the command:

```
jar tf  jar-name
```

There is another way to examine and extract the contents of a JAR file. Since the JAR file specification saves the file in the same format used by WinZip (go to http://www.winzip.com for a free copy), you may use the WinZip utility to open the JAR file.

For more details concerning using the JAR utility, take a look at the Netscape's web site: http://developer.netscape.com/docs/manuals/components/cdk/ref/8_jar.htm#10 08099.

See also: http://java.sun.com/products/jdk/1.2/docs/tooldocs/win32/jar.html

Evaluating Component Models

As was mentioned earlier in this chapter, there are many different component models available to developers today. Even Visual JavaScript currently supports three different component models: JavaScript Beans, Java Beans, and CORBA objects. Each model has its weaknesses and strength, so how does a developer decide which to use? The answer, in large part, depends upon your needs, your background, and your current situation. If you have never worked with Java before, then the benefits of using JavaBeans are lessened. If your development team has a big investment in DCOM components, is it worth using lots of CORBA components? Similar arguments can be made for each component model and the decision to use one component model over another can only be made on a case-by-case basis. Assuming that you are not predisposed to one model over another, the apparent strengths and weakness of each model can be considered when making your decisions.

JavaScript Beans, although potentially cross platform, are currently supported by only a handful of application development tools and therefore not widely used (yet). With the recent battles between Microsoft and Netscape, it does not seem likely that Microsoft products will support the importing of JSBs in their products – especially since Microsoft is advocating their own scripting language VBScript and their own scripting components, WSCs. Each year Microsoft is gaining more and more market share with each of their product lines, so without Microsoft support, the pressure on third-party tool developers to make JSB capable products will be limited. But now that the ECMA has released their standards for developing scripting components (http://www.ecma.ch/stand/ECMA-290.htm) there is hope of Microsoft and Netscape finding some middle ground in future releases of their components.

JSBs have a few other disadvantages worth noting. By their very nature as scripting components, JSBs are at the mercy of the scripting engine, so execution speed may vary greatly from environment to environment. Beyond the Netscape Visual JavaScript Component Developer's Kit (CDK) and this book, there are currently few resources to tap into for help and code. But this is changing, albeit slowly. You are still much more likely to find free JavaBeans, JavaBean code, and web sites dedicated to Java Beans than JavaScript Beans.

On the up side, JavaScript Beans offer several advantages that may make its disadvantages seem trivial. They are fairly easy to use and are based upon HTML-like tags and JavaScript. Anyone with even a small amount of JavaScript and HTML experience can quickly get up to speed with developing the components. And as we have seen, the construction of the components doesn't require any special tools. A simple text editor such as Notepad will suffice, although a tool like VJS or ScriptBuilder will be required to implement the component. Since the end-result of a JSB is JavaScript, they may be executed virtually anywhere. JSBs are designed to be universal containers and may be used to encapsulate a variety of technologies, such as Java Beans, CORBA objects, and DHTML. JSBs run on either the client, the server, or both and have access to native JavaScript database objects on the server-side.

If you are not yet confident about using JavaScript Beans, you may be after considering the alternatives. Whether you are a fan or not of Microsoft, one obvious answer is Microsoft DCOM components. One downside of Microsoft's approach is the seeming requirement of using their server and middle-tier products, which not everyone is using. But each year, Microsoft is making better and better products and they are capturing more and more market share, so the availability of such back-end products may not be a big issue in the future. Another Microsoft solution is Windows Script Components, but these components are not supported by Netscape.

What about JavaBeans? Java takes a very interesting and powerful approach to its component architecture and has the potential to become the standard model in the future. But again, Microsoft enters the equation. With the recent "disagreements" between Sun and Microsoft, widespread use of Java may be impacted. Java also has the disadvantage of having a fairly steep learning curve for the novice developer. There are also performance and incompatibility issues that have surfaced.

CORBA provides another potentially great solution. It has been the approach of choice for many development shops that need cross-platform, multi-language support. Although still an immature technology, there are accepted specification standards for CORBA and a significant number of vendors supporting the technology. Although the future of CORBA looks bright for the many heterogeneous corporate environments, CORBA does have its share of disadvantages. These include greater overhead, scaling issues, and incompatibilities from proprietary extensions.

To be fair, each approach is well thought out and each works well. Although people tend to want to rally behind a single solution, I feel that having more than one component model available is actually a good thing. As each model matures, they tend to borrow the best features of their competitors. In the long run, the beneficiaries will be the developers and the clients that they build products for. But today, with these many competing models, it may be difficult to decide which is best for your particular situation. This indecision is yet another reason to consider using JavaScript Beans. With their ability to encapsulate various technologies and other component models, JSBs provide an elegant solution to meet today's needs until the other component models mature and gain more wide spread acceptance.

Summary

Today's fast-paced business places demands upon the developer that requires him (or her) to produce products faster and with higher value. To meet these challenges Rapid Application Development can help. The RAD developer uses a combination of iterative project management, tools, and reusable code. JavaScript Beans are one such way to develop truly cross-platform universal components.

In this chapter, we have covered:

- What Rapid Application development is and the approach RAD takes to balancing time scales and functionality with planning, design, development, and testing using the principle of iterative project cycles

- RAD Tools - a brief introduction to some of the many useful products available to help today's web developer

- What makes a useful component: that a well-engineered component will be self-contained, with high cohesion, loose coupling, and a well-defined interface of properties, methods, and events

- What components are and what characteristics make up a well-constructed component

- How to construct a JavaScript Bean - using a text editor to code the .jsb file; adding the component file to a development tool; using that component in a web application; and testing the application in a browser

- Implementing a JavaScript Bean - The various tags embedded in a component definition to describe the component itself, its properties, methods, and events.

- Distributing JavaScript Beans - Considerations for packaging and deploying components using JAR files

- Advantages and Disadvantages of JSBs - JSBs are just one of several component models available, each with their own strengths and weaknesses

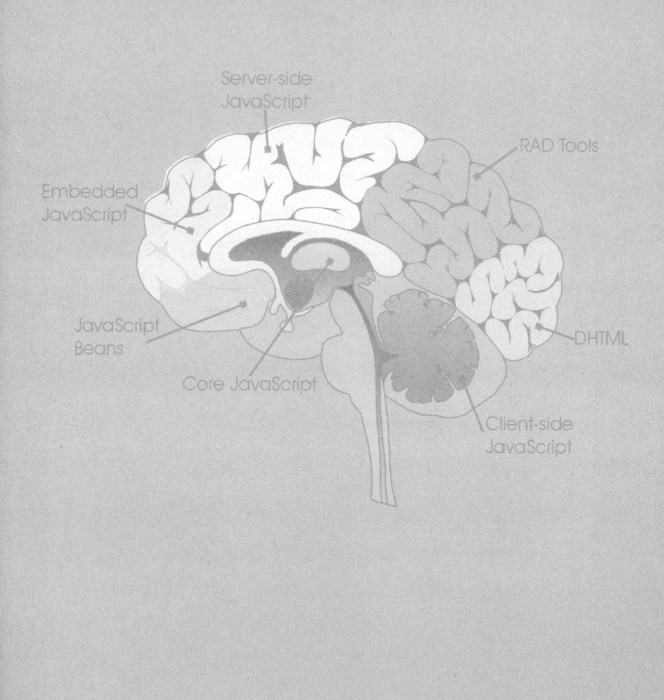

Server-side
JavaScript

RAD Tools

Embedded
JavaScript

JavaScript
Beans

Core JavaScript

Client-side
JavaScript

DHTML

Windows and WSH

As we have seen, JavaScript can be an extremely powerful language when used for web applications, both on the client and on the server. However, JavaScript is not restricted to these environments – there are numerous ways in which it can be applied to common tasks and to provide solutions for everyday problems such as controlling logons, administering machines and automating applications. The concept of JavaScript as a stand-alone scripting language is firmly established in the third paragraph of the ECMAScript standard:

"ECMAScript was originally designed to be a **web scripting language**, providing a mechanism to enliven web pages in browsers and to perform server computation as part of a Web-based client-server architecture. ECMAScript can provide core scripting capabilities for a variety of host environments, and therefore the core scripting language is specified in this document apart from any particular host environment."

One product that is available to help in solving these tasks is Microsoft's **Windows Script Host** (or WSH for short), which is a language-neutral environment available for Windows 9x, Windows NT 4.0 (Option Pack 4 or later) and Windows 2000.

WSH is a technology that exposes some of the internals of the Microsoft Windows family of operating systems to script developers. By itself, it provides very little except potential; when coupled with Microsoft's JScript, however, WSH provides JavaScript access to the Component Object Model of Windows and many of its applications. This includes applications like Internet Explorer, Microsoft Excel and NotePad – in fact, any application which exposes an automation interface can be scripted through WSH. Since it is language-independent, WSH also provides the facility to write scripts in VBScript.

Microsoft WSH and JScript

Prior to the release of Windows Script Host (WSH), the primary way to programmatically control the Windows environment was through command-line batch files, which date back to the days of MS-DOS. As anyone who has tried to automate tasks through the use of batch files is well aware, the amount of control provided is relatively limited. WSH solves this problem by providing a host that provides direct access to the computer at the file system level. Just as Unix computers have shell scripts and Macintoshes have AppleScript, now Microsoft Windows has WSH.

As mentioned above, WSH is a language-neutral environment. Because it works with any ActiveX scripting engine, developers can now write code to automate tasks using VBScript, JScript, or any other language that third parties have made available in the form of an ActiveX scripting engine. At the time of writing, an ActiveX scripting engine was also available for Perl.

WSH provides two interfaces, which allow us to execute scripts either from the command line, or from within the Windows environment:

Cscript.exe, the command-line interface for executing script files, can be run as follows:

❑ Open the Run dialog (Start | Run) or a command window (in Windows 9x, this is done via Start | Programs | MS-DOS Prompt – or Start | Programs | Command Prompt in Windows NT).

❑ Execute the script by typing into the command line cscript, followed by the path and filename of the script file to execute:

```
cscript c:\folderName\scriptName.js
```

Wscript.exe allows us to execute files in several ways:

❑ If the file type is registered to execute within WSH, we can run a script by simply double-clicking on its icon in any folder-view window.

❑ Using the Run command dialog, you can simply type in the full path and name of the script.

❑ Also from the Run dialog, we can invoke Wscript.exe, in exactly the same way that we can call Cscript.exe from the command line:

```
wscript c:\folderName\scriptName.js
```

WSH 2.0 New Features

Windows Script Host 2.0 is currently in beta release; the final release is scheduled to ship with Windows 2000. WSH 2.0 offers many new features and is a considerable improvement over WSH 1.0. A few of the new features (many of which were added as a result of user requests) are:

❑ Support for file inclusion

❑ The ability to use multiple languages within the same script job (pay attention to that word **job** – you will see it again)

- ❑ Support for drag-and-drop functionality
- ❑ Access to external objects and type libraries
- ❑ Stronger debugging capability
- ❑ A way of pausing scripts
- ❑ Standard input/output and standard error support
- ❑ Enhanced logon script capabilities

A new type of script file has been created, which utilizes an XML syntax that provides much of the new functionality listed above. This schema includes the tags `<script>`, `<object>` and `<job>`, among others. We'll look at the way this all works shortly.

The `WshShell` object has been enhanced to support the activation of arbitrary programs currently running on a computer, as well as being able to emulate data being sent to the application from the keyboard, using the methods `AppActivate()` and `SendKeys()`. Using these methods, we can send a sequence of keystrokes to an application running on our machine where they'll be executed as if they had been typed locally. This provides access to legacy applications and allows us to automate them in many cases where this would not otherwise have been possible.

There are enhancements to a number of area that will help system administrators. In WSH 1.0, there was a facility for adding printers. This was done through the `AddPrinterConnection()` method, which suffered from some design limitations – the most significant being that network printers added in this fashion were only accessible from DOS. This has been augmented in WSH 2.0 by the `AddWindowsPrinterConnection()` method, which creates connections which are visible from Windows.

There is also a set of methods for accessing the Windows Registry which have been added to the `WshShell` object. These allow developers to write to and read from the Windows registry.

Finally, WSH 2.0 provides access to Active Directory Service Interfaces (ADSI) and Windows Management Instrumentation (WMI) technology. These services provide access to a wide range of information regarding both the local machine and the network in which it resides.

Starting Up With WSH

Before we look in detail at Windows Script Host, let's first see how we get started, and where we can get WSH.

First Get the Software

If your operating system is Windows 98, Windows NT 4.0 with Option Pack 4 installed, or Windows 2000, this is easy – you already have Windows Script Host! However, you may want to ensure that you have the latest version in order to run the scripts included in this chapter. You can download it from the Microsoft Scripting Technologies Web site at `http://msdn.microsoft.com/scripting/windowshost/`. Version 5 of the Windows Script engines for JScript and VBScript are included with WSH 2.0.

It's also a good idea to install the WSH references locally; the site provides all of the documentation in a single HTML Help file.

If you want to do more than just the basics, you'll need documentation on the objects in the Scripting Runtime Library which is available at
`http://msdn.microsoft.com/scripting/JScript/download/jsdoc.exe`.

Orienting Yourself

When you load WSH onto your system, it acquires the ability to recognize new file types and display appropriate icons for them. Here are the whiz-bang new icons you get with WSH:

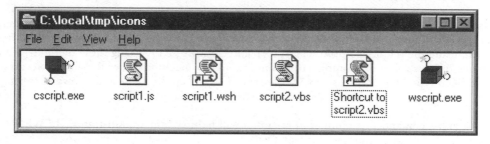

Cscript.exe and `wscript.exe` are host programs for JavaScript interpreters. There are two because `cscript.exe` is designed to be used from the Microsoft Windows console (basically a MS-DOS box within Windows) while `wscript.exe` is intended to interface directly with the GUI desktop. There's not actually much difference between them. The icons for these things must be amongst the most mysterious Microsoft have invented!

The files `script1.js` and `script2.vbs` are user-created scripts. Although you can't see it on the printed page, the little scroll image used for `.js` files is yellow, and the scroll for `.vbs` files is blue. The `.js` extension means JavaScript, while `.vbs` means Visual Basic Script. A discussion on the use of VBScript with WSH would be out of place in a book on JavaScript, but WSH support for VBScript is tremendously useful all the same. WSH also has the potential to support many other scripting languages, so long as an ActiveX scripting engine exists.

As with most Windows icons you can create shortcuts – as the VBScript shortcut illustrates. There is another option too. A `.wsh` file is a small configuration file roughly following the `.ini` file format of previous Windows versions. These `.wsh` files are good for customizing the way a script is started up – we can have several different `.wsh` files for a single script. The `.wsh` icon is blue text on a white scroll. We will look at these in a bit more detail later on in the chapter.

If you run `cscript.exe` with no arguments directly from a MS-DOS window, this is what you'll see:

```
MS-DOS Prompt                                              _ □ ×

Microsoft(R) Windows NT(TM)
(C) Copyright 1985-1996 Microsoft Corp.

C:\>cscript
Microsoft (R) Windows Scripting Host Version 5.0 for Windows
Copyright (C) Microsoft Corporation 1996-1997. All rights reserved.

Usage: CScript scriptname.extension [option...] [arguments...]

Options:
//B            Batch mode: Suppresses script errors and prompts from displaying
//H:CScript    Changes the default scripting host to CScript.exe
//H:WScript    Changes the default scripting host to WScript.exe (default)
//I            Interactive mode (default, opposite of //B)
//Logo         Display logo (default)
//Nologo       Prevent logo display: No banner will be shown at execution time
//S            Save current command line options for this user
//T:nn         Time out in seconds:  Maximum time a script is permitted to run

C:\>
```

If you run `wscript.exe` from an MS-DOS window, you'll get no output in the MS-DOS window, instead you'll see this dialog box:

When you click OK, nothing happens. Notice that `cscript` provides command-line options to let you control which of the two execution environments is run when a script icon is clicked – one has to be the default or else Windows wouldn't know what to do. Not much can happen if you don't supply a script. The timeout features are a security feature designed to stop a script from accidentally running out of control.

The difference between `cscript` and `wscript` becomes important when you are debugging a faulty script. Once you get going, error output to the script console can be a lot easier to deal with than the error pop-ups produced by `wscript`. `Cscript` is recommended for debugging scripts.

On the surface, that's all there is to WSH and JavaScript.

Time to move on to the fun stuff – writing some actual code! It's a good idea to create a new working directory so that you can have all of your test files in a single location. The rest of the chapter will assume that the folder in question is `"c:\wsh"`.

Hello World

To get started, let's something simple. Here are several variations on that old warhorse, "Hello, World!", one of the simplest programs imaginable. Try not to fall asleep! First:

In your working folder, create a new text file named `hello.js`. Open this file, and enter the following line of code:

```
WScript.Echo("Hello, World!");
```

As mentioned previously, there are several ways to execute this application. The output is different depending on whether you run `cscript` or `wscript`. Let's see what happens when we execute it on the command line:

❑   Open a command window.

❑   Execute the following command:

```
cscript c:\wsh\hello.js
```

You should see a few lines of copyright information, and then your expected output:

```
C:\>cscript c:\wsh\hello.js
Microsoft (R) Windows Script Host Version 5.1 for Windows
Copyright (C) Microsoft Corporation 1996-1999. All rights reserved.

Hello, World!

C:\>_
```

Note that you can permanently stop this copyright info from displaying by executing the following statement:

```
cscript //nologo //s
```

We will see more about this later, when we look at setting personal options for WSH. For now, let's see if it behaves any differently when run from within Windows:

❏ Open an Explorer window and navigate to your test directory.

❏ Execute your file by double-clicking on it.

As is to be expected, the result is a little different: You should receive a standard Windows popup dialog:

This is to be expected – echoing a response to the user is very different in a command prompt environment to working within the Windows GUI. With cscript, there's no simple way to avoid the black MS-DOS window, so wscript is the logical (and the default) choice behind desktop icons.

The Echo() function is pretty limited. WSH can use the Popup() method (exposed via the WshShell object), which allows slightly more versatile output. It can also be used for simple messages.

```
var shell = WScript.CreateObject("WScript.Shell");
shell.Popup("Hello, World!\n",0,"Hello World Script");
```

The two interpreters are pretty similar, really. There's no difference in output at all, except you'll get the familiar black DOS box as well when you execute scripts using cscript:

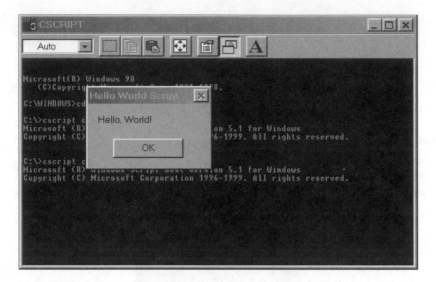

But "Hello, World!" can get a lot fancier than this. Try this example (you'll need Microsoft Office 97 installed for it to work):

```
var doc = WScript.CreateObject("Word.Application");
doc.Visible = true;
doc.Documents.Add();
with(doc.ActiveDocument.Shapes)
{
    AddTextEffect(21, "Hello, World!", "Arial Black",
                36, false,  false, 200, 150);
}
```

The result looks something like this:

WSH Unique Features

Windows Script Host provides an object model that allows developers to connect to other computers on a network, access the Windows Registry and file system, and to work with the Windows 2000 Active Directory Service Interfaces (ADSI) and Windows Management Instrumentation (WMI) object models. Additionally, WSH allows you to use ActiveX controls and applications that provide an automation interface, such as Microsoft Word and Excel.

WSH Elements

With WSH 1.0, developers were limited to using a single scripting language to access the system – the host determined the appropriate action based on the extension of the file being executed. Thus, in the case of a JScript file, Windows mapped its `.js` extension to WSH, which controlled its execution, passing the contents of the file to the JScript engine.

The features available in WSH 2.0 are quite an improvement over version 1.0, primarily due to the fact that, in addition to JScript and VBScript files, the host now recognizes a new file type: Windows Script file `.wsf` (note that the first two betas of WSH 2.0 use the extension `.ws` for Windows Script files. According to a post in Microsoft's WSH newsgroup, this extension will no longer be supported in the final release because this extension is already in use by a product with a large installed base, though it is apparently not registered as such in common file-extension databases). The Windows Script file provides increased functionality and flexibility over that available from `.js` and `.vbs` files, through the use of a simple XML syntax. The following description of the XML elements available in the WSH schema assumes some familiarity with tag-based markup and container models such as that used in HTML.

Unless stated otherwise, all of these tags are container tags, meaning that each requires matching opening and closing tags, as follows:

```
<tag>
    content goes here
</tag>
```

If you are new to XML, please note one crucial difference from HTML syntax. All empty elements in XML require a terminating slash in order to be recognized as valid elements by the XML parsing engine:

```
<element attrib="value"/>
```

Empty elements exist in HTML as well – such as `<IMG>` and `<BR>`. Since HTML does not have such a rigid syntax as XML, empty HTML elements do not need the terminating slash. The reason for the difference is that XML requires every opening tag to have a corresponding closing tag. In the case of empty elements, the open and close are the same.

<?xml?>

This is the standard XML declaration and, if included, forces WSH to parse the file rigidly as XML, enforcing case-sensitivity. This is not a container tag; although we have just said that XML does not allow elements without closing tags, there are one or two exceptions to this. These include processing instructions, which are enclosed in special `<? ... ?>` delimiters, and comments, which take the normal HTML form `<!-- ... -->`. Processing instructions contain instructions for the application which parses the XML. The XML declaration is a special processing instruction which informs the application processing the XML of the version of XML in use (at the moment, `"1.0"` is the only available version). This element is optional, and must be the first tag to appear when used.

The syntax for this element is:

```
<?xml version="1.0" [standalone="yes"]?>
```

<?job?>

This element is a processing instruction (and hence not a container tag) that specifies error-handling attributes. This is an empty element, and should appear prior to the first `<job>` tag:

```
<?job error="true|false|1|0" debug="true|false|1|0"?>
```

<package>

This optional element provides a way for developers to include the code for more than one job within a single file:

```
<package>
    <job id="job1">
       <!-- do something -->
    </job>
    <job id="job2">
        <!-- do something else -->
    </job>
</package>
```

<job>

This element provides a method for defining multiple jobs within a single file, used in conjunction with the `<package>` tag:

```
<job [id="jobID"]>
    <!-- do something -->
</job>
```

<object>

This optional element is used to define scriptable external objects without using methods such as `CreateObject()` or `GetObject()`. Objects defined using the `<object>` tag are available globally. This is an empty element. This element must be placed within a `<job>` element:

```
<object id="objID" [classid="clsid:GUID" | progid="programID"]/>
```

<reference>

This element is optional and provides an inclusion mechanism to be used as a way to access type library information without actually instantiating an object. This is an empty element which must come within a `<job>` element:

```
<reference [object="progID"|guid="typelibGUID"] [version="version"]/>
```

<resource>

This element is optional and allows developers to declare string or numeric data to be used within a WSH application, while keeping this data separate from the actual script code. Commonly used for strings that require localization. Like the `<object>` and `<reference>` elements, this element must belong to a `<job>` element. Note that support for `<resource>` was evidently added in Beta 2 of WSH 2.0, and documentation of this tag was not included in the HTML Help file available for the beta release. Hopefully this situation will be remedied for the final release:

```
<job>
    <resource id="resErr">
        An error has occurred in this script.
    </resource>
    <script language="JScript">
        // catch an error
        Wscript.Echo(getResource("resErr"));
    </script>
</job>
```

<script>

This tag uses the familiar HTML syntax. It can be used for external script inclusion by setting the `src` attribute to a valid file or UNC path, or for embedding script code directly into your WSH application. Again, the `<script>` element is a child element of `<job>`:

```
<script [language="jscript|vbscript"] [src="sFilePath"]>
    // script code here ...
</script>
```

When WSH scripts are being developed with strict adherence to XML conventions enabled (due to the inclusion of the `<?xml?>` tag), inline script should be wrapped in a special text section called a CDATA section. This prevents certain characters within the script code (such as the symbols for less than (<), greater than (>) or bitwise or Boolean "and" operations (& or &&)) being interpreted as XML delimiters or as special XML characters. In order to avoid this problem, use the following syntax when following XML-based lexical rules:

```
<?xml version="1.0"?>
<script language="JScript">
    <![CDATA[
        // script code here ...
    ]]>
</script>
```

Including the text in a CDATA section informs the XML parser that all information included within the CDATA block should be treated as literal character data, not as XML which needs to be parsed. For more information on CDATA sections, see the World Wide Web Consortium's XML 1.0 Recommendation at `http://www.w3.org/TR/1998/REC-xml-19980210`.

For additional documentation on the optional attributes of these elements, see the online documentation available on the Microsoft Scripting Technologies Web site `http://msdn.microsoft.com/scripting/windowshost/`. Full documentation is also available from this site for download as an HTML help file.

WSH Objects

Every object-oriented programming environment provides a hierarchy of objects which developers can use to implement solutions, and Windows Script Host is no different. WSH contains a core set of objects, with properties and methods, which can be used to access other computers on a network, import external scriptable objects for use within an application, or connect with Windows or the Windows shell.

When we use JScript as your interpreter, we of course have the usual JavaScript host objects – `Array`, `String`, `Function`, and so on. WSH only really contains a single host object of its own, `WScript`, which it makes available to the interpreter. However, there are numerous other objects which are children of `WScript`, and which we can access through WSH.

The WScript Object

The root of the WSH object model is the `WScript` object. This object provides the properties and methods that allow developers to access name and path information for the script file being executed, to determine which version of the Microsoft scripting engine is currently installed, work with external objects, provide user interaction (as we have already seen) and delay or terminate script execution.

WScript Properties

Property	Description
Application	Exposes the `WScript` object's `IDispatch` interface. Translated, that means, "this is how you gain programmatic access to an external application's objects, properties and methods".
Arguments	Returns a collection of all arguments passed to the current script either on the command line or in the shortcut used to access the file.
FullName	Returns a string containing the complete path to the file being executed.
Name	Returns a string containing the user-friendly name of the `WScript` object.
Network	Provides access to Windows-based networking, such as mapping or removing network drives, adding network printer connections, etc.
Path	Returns a string containing the parent directory of the active WSH environment (`cscript.exe` or `wscript.exe`).
ScriptFullName	Returns a string containing the complete path to the script currently executing.
ScriptName	Returns a string containing the filename of the script currently executing.

Property	Description
StdErr	Provides access to the script's error output stream. This stream is write-only. This property is only available to scripts being executed from within the command-line host environment cscript.exe.
StdIn	Provides access to the script's input stream. This stream is read-only. This property is only available to scripts being executed from within the command-line host environment cscript.exe.
StdOut	Provides access to script's output stream. This stream is write-only. Only available to scripts being executed from within the command-line host environment cscript.exe.
Version	Returns a string containing the version number of Windows Script Host.

All of the above properties are accessed using the following syntax:

```
WScript.PropertyName
```

Here is an example of what you can do, given these property values. This is your first port of call in any WSH script. The example script supplied with WSH 1.0 called excel.js illustrates some of the properties of this object. Assuming this script has been downloaded to the test directory C:\WSH\, you can access the example this way:

```
wscript excel.js foo bar fred nerk
```

When it runs, the script will open Excel and enter into a worksheet the name and current value and a description of a number of the properties of the WScript object. Notice that the Count of the Arguments collection is set to four, the number of parameters we passed into excel.js, and that Arguments has one item for each of those parameters:

```
Microsoft Excel - Book1
File  Edit  View  Insert  Format  Tools  Data  Window  Help
C15        =
```

	A	B	C
1	Property Name	Value	Description
2	Name	Windows Scripting Host	Application Friendly Name
3	Version	5	Application Version
4	FullName	C:\WINNT\system32\wscript.exe	Application Context: Fully Qualified Name
5	Path	C:\WINNT\system32	Application Context: Path Only
6	Interactive	TRUE	State of Interactive Mode
7	Arguments.Count	4	Number of command line arguments
8	Arguments(0)	foo	
9	Arguments(1)	bar	
10	Arguments(2)	fred	
11	Arguments(3)	nerk	
12			

```
Sheet1 / Sheet2 / Sheet3 /
Ready
```

This kind of information is nice to have. But this is not the end of the story: the `WScript` object also has some useful methods. Let's look at those next.

WScript Methods

What makes the `WScript` object really useful is its two methods, `CreateObject()` and `GetObject()`. These methods allow the script developer to get access many other objects, and it's these objects that are interesting to play with and which we use to get much of the job done.

CreateObject()

Creates an instance of an automation object from the `ProgID` passed in and provides the script with a hook which allows us to access properties and call methods of the created object:

```
var objFoo = WScript.CreateObject(sProgID[,sPrefix]);
```

For example, the following script creates an instance of the Microsoft Word application and makes it visible; we used this in the last of our "Hello, World!" examples (requires Word 97 or greater):

```
var objWord = WScript.CreateObject("Word.Application");
objWord.Visible = true;
```

The argument `sPrefix` provides script developers a hook into the event model of the controlled object. The sample code included in the section on "Controlling Browsers" below, includes an example which shows how to use this argument to allow a script to handle events fired by the created application.

DisconnectObject()

Removes an active instance of an object created by `CreateObject()` or `GetObject()` calls:

```
WScript.DisconnectObject(objID);
```

Echo()

Displays the argument(s) passed in on the screen. As we have already seen, the way in which the arguments are displayed depends on the host. If `cscript.exe` is the host, arguments to `Echo()` are displayed on the command line. If `wscript.exe` is the host, arguments will be displayed in a Windows popup dialog. The syntax is:

```
WScript.Echo(sArg|nArg[, ...]);
// where sArg = string
// and nArg = numeric
```

GetObject()

This method is similar to `CreateObject()`. It creates an instance of an automation object from a file or `ProgID`. This gives us access to an object that already exists somewhere on our computer – such as a version of a program which is already running, or an application with an unknown automation interface:

```
WScript.GetObject(sPath[, sProgID][,sPrefix]);
```

The following example (which requires Word 97 or greater) gets a reference to a Word document called test.doc in the C:/WSH/ directory (an error will be generated if this file does not exist):

```
var objDoc = WScript.GetObject( "c:\\wsh\\test.doc" );
var objApp = objDoc.Application;
objApp.Visible = true;
```

Quit()

Terminates host execution and returns the argument as an error code. In other words, it kills the current instance of cscript or wscript:

```
WScript.Quit([nErrCode]);
```

Sleep()

Temporarily suspends execution of the active script for the time specified (in milliseconds). After this period has passed, control is returned to the script:

```
WScript.Sleep(nDelay);
```

Some functions take a unique identifier for the object in question as an input argument and return an object reference that you can store it in a variable. Finding that list of unique identifiers and their uses is a bit of a voyage of discovery. We're not going to go into in the details of the Microsoft Windows Component Object Model management facilities as this subject can fill an entire book in itself. Suffice to say that two quickie methods of looking for unique ID's are:

❑   Run regedit and look at the second half of the long list under the top-level item HKEY_CLASSES_ROOT.

❑   Get the OLEView tool from Microsoft and become familiar with that. You can obtain it via the web from http://www.microsoft.com/com/resource/oleview.asp.

You'll also need proper documentation on the objects you intend to use. A painless start is to try 'Professional IE4 Programming', from Wrox Press, which explains how to add a few objects to Internet Explorer 4.0. For additional documentation resources, see the references for this chapter in Appendix L.

Additional Built-in Objects

Microsoft's documentation for WSH 2.0 lists several other objects that are available for building WSH applications. The majority of these are documented via a "friendly name", but are actually exposed as child properties or collections of the WScript object itself. The following list contains the object names as documented:

❑   WshArguments
❑   WshEnvironment
❑   WshNetwork
❑   WshShell
❑   WshShortcut
❑   WshSpecialFolders
❑   WshUrlShortcut

The following sections contain the friendly names as a point of reference, while the samples included within each section demonstrate the proper access methods.

Accessing Command-Line Arguments (WshArguments Object)

You might not be the argumentative type, but arguments in the programming sense are very useful for passing information into a script for it to work on. Creating scripts which work with arguments is a good step towards writing reusable code.

Consider for a moment what it's like to work in the DOS prompt. Most command-line executables use arguments in order to determine the right thing to do. For example, to navigate within a directory structure:

```
cd wsh
```

In this instance, `cd` is the name of the executable file (for 'change directory'), while `wsh` is the name of the directory to make active – it is an argument passed to `cd`.

The `WshArguments` object is a collection of the arguments passed into a script. Developers creating scripts designed to execute on the command-line may immediately see the benefits of working with the `Arguments` property. However, within WSH, there is another good reason to use this property – it is used to implement drag-and-drop functionality.

A final argument (pun intended) is that using this property allows developers to reuse script code within other scripts, by running the script in question as if it were executing on the command-line, passing whatever arguments may be necessary at run-time.

The `WshArguments` object is accessed through the `WScript.Arguments` property.

Properties

Property	Description
`Item`	Returns the specified argument from the collection.
`Length`	Returns the number of items in the collection (also implemented as `length`).

Methods

Method	Description
`Count()`	Returns the number of items in the collection (`Count` is implemented as a method for use within JScript, whereas it is implemented as a property for use with VBScript).

Note that the `Length` property is functionally equivalent to the `Count()` method. Microsoft's scripting documentation states that the `Length` property is included for compatibility with JScript. The following example uses `length` since this will be more familiar to JavaScript developers. In addition, the example uses the familiar syntax `collectionName(index)`, instead of the more rigorous `collectionName.Item(index)`. Since `Item` is the default property of `WshArguments`, the object can be indexed directly without specifying this property explicitly.

This example echoes all arguments passed to the script (either via drag-drop or the command line) back to the user:

```
var cArgs = WScript.Arguments;
var sArgs = "Passed arguments:\n";
for (var i = 0; i < cArgs.length; i++) {
    // cArgs.length == cArgs.Count()
    sArgs += "\n arg" + i + ": " + cArgs(i);
}
WScript.Echo(sArgs);
```

Network Communications (WshNetwork Object)

Windows Script Host is commonly used for creating login scripts for computers which are part of a corporate network. These scripts can make it easier for users to do their work by mapping to commonly-used network file servers and connecting to one or more network printers. This is where WshNetwork comes in handy. This object provides important functionality to be used for all network connectivity needs.

WshNetwork is accessed by creating an instance of WScript.Network.

Properties

Property	Description
ComputerName	Returns the computer's name.
UserDomain	Returns the domain name of the current user.
UserName	Returns the user name for the current user.

Methods

Method	Description
AddPrinterConnection()	Adds a printer connection to the network (but, as we mentioned above, this connection won't be visible from Windows – only from DOS).
AddWindowsPrinterConnection()	Adds a printer connection to the network which will be visible from Windows.
EnumNetworkDrives()	Allows us to enumerate through the drives available to the network.
EnumPrinterConnections()	Allows us to enumerate through the printer connections available to the network.
MapNetworkDrive()	Establishes a connection and maps a network drive.
RemoveNetworkDrive()	Removes a connection to a network drive.
RemovePrinterConnection()	Removes a printer connection.
SetDefaultPrinter()	Sets the default printer.

Note that the two methods `EnumNetworkDrives()` and `EnumPrinterConnections()` have somewhat unusual return values, in that there are two values returned in the collection. The first is the local resource (drive letter or port) while the second is the mapped network share. Thus, in the following example, `collNetDrive(0)` will contain `"Z"`, and `collNetDrive(1)` will contain `\\server\share`.

The following sample makes use of all the properties and methods of the `WshNetwork` object. (Please note that this example requires an active network connection to work correctly. In addition, running this script on your computer may end up modifying your network setup).

```
var objNet, collNetDrive, collNetPrint;
objNet = WScript.CreateObject("WScript.Network");

WScript.Echo
(
    "Computer Name:\t" + objNet.ComputerName + "\n" +
    "Current User:\t" + objNet.UserName + "\n" +
    "User Domain:\t" + objNet.UserDomain
);

objNet.MapNetworkDrive("Z:", "\\\\server\\share");
collNetDrive = objNet.EnumNetworkDrives();
// echo all networked drives
for (var i = 0; i < collNetDrive.Count(); i++)
{
    WScript.Echo("\n" + collNetDrive.Item(i));
}
objNet.RemoveNetworkDrive("Z:");

objNet.AddWindowsPrinterConnection("\\\\printserver\\share");
objNet.SetDefaultPrinter("\\\\printserver\\share");
collNetPrint = objNet.EnumPrinterConnections();
// echo all networked printers
for (var j = 0; j < collNetPrint.Count(); j++)
{
    WScript.Echo("\n" + collNetPrint.Item(j));
}
objNet.RemovePrinterConnection("LPT1:");
```

Interacting with the Windows Shell (WshShell Object)

In the `WshShell` object, Windows Script Host provides a convenient way to gain access to system environment variables, create shortcuts, access Windows special folders such as the desktop, and add or remove entries from the Registry. In addition, it is possible to create more customized dialogs for user interaction through the use of the `WshShell` object.

Developers should create an instance of the object `WScript.Shell` in order to work with the properties listed below. Further references to the `WshShell` object will refer to this created instance:

```
var objShell = WScript.CreateObject("WScript.Shell");
```

The `WshShell` object is also useful because it is the only object discussed so far capable of recording feedback from the user – through its `Popup()` method. We'll discuss this in more detail later on, in the section on 'Communicating with the User'.

System Environment Variables (WshEnvironment Object)

When a developer needs to access information about the system such as the operating system version or the processor type, the place to look is within the system's environment variables. WSH provides a way of accessing this information through the `Environment` property of the `WshShell` object. This returns a `WshEnvironment` object, which in turn provides access to the environment variables.

There are four sets of environment variables available: system, user, volatile, and process. Accessing a variable set other than the default is shown in the example below. Please note that if you wish to access the default set of environment variables, do not use an empty set of parentheses after the `Environment` keyword; doing so will generate a script error.

```
var objShell = WScript.CreateObject("WScript.Shell");
var objSysEnv = objShell.Environment("process");
WScript.Echo(objSysEnv("WINDIR"));
WScript.Echo(objSysEnv("PATH"));
```

Due to the internal structure of Windows NT 4 and Windows 2000, much more information is available when accessing system environment information under these systems than when using Windows 95/98:

- ❑ Windows NT/Windows 2000: all environment variable types are available: `System`, `User`, `Volatile`, and `Process`. If no type is passed, the default is `System`.

- ❑ Windows 95/Windows 98: only environment variables of type `"Process"` are available. This will be the default if no value is specified.

Working with Windows Special Folders (WshSpecialFolders Object)

Whether you are aware of it or not, you're probably quite familiar with most of the special folders available within the Windows environment. For example, the Start Menu and Desktop are simply folders – just ones that have special display characteristics within Windows.

Imagine that you're setting up ten machines for a group of new employees in your company. While doing this, you want to create a set of common sub-menus off the Start menu. Perhaps you also want to provide links to some common setup servers on the user's desktop. This should be an easy task, but there's a trick to it: it's up to you to figure out where these folders are. The actual file location of Windows special folders is dependent on the default Windows installation directory, so they may not be in the same place on one computer as they are on another. The `WSHSpecialFolders` collection helps developers get around this, making it very easy to access these folders; this example code displays the locations of the Desktop and Startup folders:

```
var objShell = WScript.CreateObject("WScript.Shell");
var objSpecFldrs = objShell.SpecialFolders;
WScript.Echo(objSpecFldrs("Desktop"));
WScript.Echo(objSpecFldrs("Startup"));
```

The following list includes the names of some of the more frequently used special folders. See the WSH documentation for a complete list:

- ❑ Desktop
- ❑ Favorites
- ❑ MyDocuments
- ❑ Programs
- ❑ Recent
- ❑ SendTo
- ❑ StartMenu
- ❑ Startup

Remember that the file locations to which these shortcuts resolve is dependent upon the actual user profile in use when the shortcut is created. This is always a consideration when using Windows NT 4.0 or Windows 2000, and will also be an issue if user profiles are active on an installation of Windows 9x.

Shortcuts and URLs (WshShortcut, WshURLShortcut Objects)

Now that you know how to get a handle to Windows special folders, it's easy to complete the scenario envisioned above, and add items to the Start menu or place a shortcut on the desktop. WSH has two objects to represent shortcuts – the WshShortcut object for a normal file shortcut, and WshURLShortcut for a URL shortcut. The same method of the WshShell object is used for creating both WshShortcut and WshURLShorcut objects – the primary difference is in the file extension given to the actual shortcut file: If the extension is .lnk, a standard WshShortcut object is created, whereas a WshURLShortcut object is created when the file extension is .url.

Properties

The WshShortcut object has all of these properties; WshURLShortcut has only FullName and TargetPath.

Property	Description
Arguments	Returns a collection of the arguments passed into the file opened by the shortcut.
Description	A description for the shortcut.
FullName	The full path and filename for the shortcut.
Hotkey	A string representing the combination of keys which launches the shortcut (e.g. "Ctrl+Alt+h").
IconLocation	The path, filename and index of the icon for the shortcut.
TargetPath	The full path and filename or URL for the target of the shortcut.
WindowStyle	A constant specifying the style for the application window.
WorkingDirectory	The directory from which to start the executable.

Methods

Both `WshShortcut` and `WshURLShortcut` have only one method, `Save()`:

Method	Description
Save()	Saves the shortcut to the location specified in the `FullName` property.

This example creates a shortcut to the Start Menu on the desktop called `WSHtest.lnk`:

```
var objShell = WScript.CreateObject("WScript.Shell");
var sPath = objShell.SpecialFolders("Desktop") + "\\WSHtest.lnk";
var objShortcut = objShell.CreateShortcut(sPath);
objShortcut.Description = "Test shortcut created from WSH.";
objShortcut.TargetPath = objShell.SpecialFolders("StartMenu");
objShortcut.Save();
```

Modifying the Windows Registry

The Windows Registry is a shared database of key/value pairs that is used to store configuration information regarding system hardware, installed applications and user profiles, among other information. An example use of the Registry might be an application that needs to persist information about the preferences of the current user. Within Windows, the easiest way to do this is by setting one or more keys in the Registry. WSH makes creating, reading and removing Registry keys quite painless.

> **It is very important to be very careful when modifying Registry settings. Making incorrect changes to the Registry can cause your system to become unstable or unusable. If you are not familiar with the inner workings of the Registry you are strongly advised to do some reading on the subject before beginning to experiment on your own.**

For example, to set, read and then delete a test value in the Registry:

```
WScript.Echo("Setting Registry value");
var objShell = WScript.CreateObject("WScript.Shell");
objShell.RegWrite("HKCU\\WSHTestKey", "WSH test value");
WScript.Echo(
   "Reading Registry key\n\n" +
   "value:\t" + objShell.RegRead("HKCU\\WSHTestKey")
);
WScript.Echo("Deleting Registry key");
objShell.RegDelete("HKCU\\WSHTestKey");
```

If we had wanted to set an actual Registry key, as opposed to a single value, we could have done this quite easily as well, by ending the string argument passed to `RegWrite()` with a backslash (of course, in JScript that needs to be two backslashes):

```
objShell.RegWrite("HKCU\\WSHTestKey\\", "WSH test key");
```

Using External Objects with WSH

Up to this point we've been examining objects that are part of WSH. However, there is much more to the world of Windows Scripting than the objects that are made available from within WSH. Through the `GetObject()` and `CreateObject()` methods of the `WScript` object, developers are able to access any object which provides a COM interface, including ActiveX controls and OLE Automation servers such as Word, Excel and Internet Explorer.

The following section will explore some of the more common external objects which may be used within a WSH solution.

Scripting Runtime Library Objects

Microsoft's Scripting RunTime library (SRT), which ships with the JScript and VBScript engines, provides ways to access the Windows file system and create, read and write files. It also contains a `Dictionary` object which most closely resembles an associative array (for all you Perl fans out there).

Managing the File System

Perhaps the most useful feature of the SRT is the file system access it provides. The core object for this is called the `FileSystemObject` (FSO). This provides interfaces to files, folders and drives, either individually or as collections.

Since a complete analysis of the FSO could easily make up a chapter in itself, we will have to content ourselves with saying that the FSO provides access to three objects – the `File`, `Folder` and `Drive` objects, which respectively represent a physical file, folder and disk drive in the file system – and three corresponding collections: `Files`, `Folders` and `Drives`. It also provides methods for creating, accessing, copying and deleting files and folders, and for navigating through the file system. We will show an example that makes use of a variety of FSO functionality. The names of the FSO interfaces are all fairly self-explanatory, so little additional explanation will be provided – see the references for this chapter in Appendix L for links to extensive reference material on all features of the SRT.

The following sample only utilizes a small amount of the functionality provided by the `FileSystemObject` – gaining access to the `C:` drive and printing out the free space and the type of file system on the drive, and a list of all the top-level subfolders (not recursive) within the root folder.

```
var objFSO       = WScript.CreateObject("Scripting.FileSystemObject");
var objDrive     = objFSO.GetDrive("c");
var iFree        = objDrive.FreeSpace;
var objFolder    = objFSO.GetFolder("c:\\");
var objEnum      = new Enumerator(objFolder.SubFolders);
var iCount       = 0;
var s            = Line(Line("System Information:"));
var sSubFolders  = Line("Subfolders:");

for ( ; !objEnum.atEnd(); objEnum.moveNext())
{
    sSubFolders += Line("\t" + objEnum.item().Name);
}

s += Line("Free space on drive C: " + iFree + " bytes");
s += Line("File system on drive C: " + objDrive.FileSystem);
s += Line("Drive C: contains " + objFolder.SubFolders.Count +
          "subfolders");
s += Line(sSubFolders);
```

```
    WScript.Echo(s);

    function Line(str)
    {
        return str + "\n";
    }
```

There is one interesting thing to note here – look at the following line of code:

```
    var objEnum = new Enumerator(objFolder.SubFolders);
```

The `Enumerator` object may be unfamiliar if your experience is mostly with client-side scripting. This object provides a way to iterate through collections of objects. This is similar to looping through an array – more on the distinction when we look at array traps later on.

Many more examples are available in the Scripting Runtime Library Reference available on the Windows Script Technologies web site – included in the references in Appendix L.

File I/O

If you've been following closely, you might have noticed that there are a few methods in the list above which refer to text files: `CreateTextFile()` and `OpenTextFile()`. These two methods of the FSO object return a `TextStream` object, which is the key to file input and output in Microsoft's Wide World of Scripting.

For developers who have a modicum of experience with file I/O, the names of the `TextStream` methods and properties should look familiar. The example below shows how to work with the `TextStream` object; again, detailed reference and explanation should be sought elsewhere.

Working with a `TextStream` object is very easy: create an instance of the `FileSystemObject`, use it to reference a file, and call the `File` object's method `OpenAsTextStream()`.

```
    var objFSO  = WScript.CreateObject("Scripting.FileSystemObject");
    var objFile = objFSO.GetFile("test.txt");
    var objTS   = objFile.OpenAsTextStream();
    var iCount  = 0;

    while (!objTS.AtEndOfStream)
    {
        objTS.ReadLine();
        iCount++;
    }

    WScript.Echo(objFile.Name + " contains " + iCount + " line(s).");
```

Reading the Dictionary

The Scripting Runtime also contains a `Dictionary` object, which allows for the storage of key/value pairs of data in an associative fashion. Each individual item stored in the dictionary is associated with a unique key, allowing for easy indexing to a specific item. This removes the overhead required (in terms of additional code and processing) when working with traditional one-dimensional JScript arrays – for example, there is no need to loop through the elements of an array to find a specific item when you can simply query for the existence of a given key.

Items can be of any JScript data type, while the keys are most commonly either numeric or string values – imagine trying to create a `Dictionary` using Boolean values as keys! However, any data type other than an array is allowed as the key value.

This example creates an instance of the `Dictionary` object and adds a key named `"myKey1"` with a value `"myValue1"`:

```
// create an instance of the Dictionary, and add an item
var objDict = WScript.CreateObject("Scripting.Dictionary");
objDict.add ("myKey1", "myValue1");
// echo property if item exists
if (objDict.Exists("myKey1"))
{
    WScript.Echo(objDict.Item("myKey1"));
}
```

Automating Windows Applications

As we've seen above, accessing and manipulating objects using WSH is pretty simple, assuming you know the ProgID of the object in question. This idea is easily extensible to OLE Automation servers such as Internet Explorer or the applications included in Microsoft Office. Using the `GetObject()` method, it is even possible to create an instance of an application without knowing the ProgID, simply by retrieving a file accessed by the application in question. For example, we can create an instance of Microsoft Word (using Word 97 or later) by passing the path to a `.doc` file as the first argument in a `GetObject()` call. We can then get a reference to the application using the document's `Application` property.

After launching an application in this manner, we can access and modify its properties and call internal methods, as exhibited previously with the Scripting Runtime Library. By using optional arguments for the object creation methods, we can even write functions that respond to internal events fired by an application instantiated in this fashion.

The following examples show how to create an instance of Microsoft Word both by using its ProgID and by retrieving the application through an associated file type.

In this first example, an instance of Word is created and a new document added. Then a text string is added to the new document using the `WshShell` methods `AppActivate()` and `SendKeys()` – only available in WSH 2.0. Finally, the `Save()` method of the document is called, which displays the default **Save As** dialog since this is a new file. You should save the created document as `test.doc` in your WSH test folder and close Word before running the next script.

```
var objShell = WScript.CreateObject("WScript.Shell");
var objWord = WScript.CreateObject("Word.Application");
var objDoc = objWord.Documents.Add();
objWord.Visible = true;
objShell.AppActivate("Document1");
objShell.SendKeys(
  "This Word document was created using " +
  "Windows Script Host automation."
);
WScript.Sleep(500);
objDoc.Save();
```

The second example retrieves an instance of Word from the document handle, then adds another line of text as proof of its presence:

```
var objDoc = WScript.GetObject("c:\\wsh\\test.doc");
objDoc.Application.Visible = true;
var objRange = objDoc.Range();
objRange.InsertAfter("\n\nThis text added in second example.");
objDoc.Save();
```

These are obviously very simple examples of automating Windows applications, and as such are meant to serve mostly informative purposes. When working with external applications, you will be well served by familiarizing yourself with the object model inherent to the application itself. For Microsoft Office applications, the Object Browser installed along with the VBA editor is a great tool for finding out more about exposed interfaces.

ActiveX Objects

Working with ActiveX controls is little different to creating instances of Word and other automation servers – particularly if the control exposes a ProgID which can be used to get a handle to the object in question. However, even when no ProgID is available, a crafty scripter can still gain access to the inner mysteries if he or she knows the object's Class ID. Remember the <object> element which was covered earlier? That's the way to gain access to controls which only expose a CLSID value.

Once you have a handle on the control, all you need is a good reference to its internals. Sometimes this can be attained through the use of the Visual Basic Object Browser, which is also included in Microsoft Office applications because of the integration of VBA (Visual Basic for Applications) into the Office suite. Another useful tool for gleaning controls is Microsoft's OLE/COM Object Viewer – the URL for downloading this is included in Appendix L.

JavaScript Language Traps

For web developers, moving to WSH may be a little tricky. There are some tricks and traps involved in using JScript outside of the familiar model of programming web pages. Additionally, developers coming to WSH from other directions – such as traditional client applications written in Visual Basic – will encounter some new quirks inherent to development using JScript as the programming language. This next section will cover some common pitfalls and provide ways to get around these problems.

If you are not using the latest revision, you'll find that WSH version 1.0 isn't quite perfect. Until you upgrade to version 2.0, you should beware of these few oddities that vary from standard JavaScript behavior. It appears that in the rush to release WSH 1.0, a few VBScript features have leaked through WSH into JScript.

Various aspects of these traps will get you quite early on as you get to know WSH. For example, if you are already having problems with the WScript.Arguments object, read on.

Array Traps

As most web developers are aware, one of the core JavaScript data types is represented by the Array object. Arrays are probably familiar to anyone with a modicum of programming experience – they can be used as a storage mechanism for groups of data, regardless of the type of information being stored. Thus, a single JavaScript array may contain strings, numbers, objects and even other arrays as child elements. The method in which this disparate information is handled rests in the hands of the individual scripter. The following is a simple example of an array:

```
var myArray = ["foo", "bar", "baz"];
for (var i = 0; i < myArray.length; i++)
{
    window.alert(myArray[i]);
}
```

As shown in this example, all members of an array are directly accessible using the syntax `arrayName[index]`. However, many object models contain objects which appear to behave like arrays, but are more properly thought of as enumerated collections, which cannot be accessed through indexes in the same way that arrays can. JScript provides an extension to the core ECMAScript specification to address the problem – the `Enumerator` object.

This object can be used to iterate through the members of a collection in a linear fashion; that is, using an `Enumerator`, it is possible to move from one item to the next through the collection. In addition, it is possible to move to the first item in a collection, and to query whether you have reached its end.

The collections available as children of the `FileSystemObject` are examples of this type of construct – namely the `Files`, `Folders` and `Drives` collections.

Imagine that you are required to ensure that each computer on your network has a few common folders available from the Windows Desktop. The following example shows how you could iterate through all of the subfolders on the Desktop in order to make sure that all the proper folders are in place:

```
var objShell = WScript.CreateObject("WScript.Shell");
var sDesktopPath = objShell.SpecialFolders("Desktop");
var objFSO = WScript.CreateObject("Scripting.FileSystemObject");
var objDesktop = objFSO.GetFolder(sDesktopPath);
var enumFolders = new Enumerator(objDesktop.SubFolders);

while (!enumFolders.atEnd())
{
    var objFolder = enumFolders.item();
    // your logic here to verify existence of required folders
    enumFolders.moveNext();
}
```

Case Sensitivity and Naming Collisions

Time to face facts – there are rules that have to be followed sometimes. One of those rules is that when developing using JScript, we have to pay particular attention to proper casing of object, property and method names.

The issue of case sensitivity in JScript is something of a double-edged sword. If you start coding in JScript after working with a language such as Visual Basic (which has much looser rules regarding case), you can spend many frustrated hours wondering why your code isn't working. On the other hand, if you're a web developer moving into the world of stand-alone scripting, you run into a whole mess of problems inherent to that particular background.

First off, let's address Joe VeeBee. Bad news, Joe. JScript knows the difference between an `item` and an `Item`. VB thinks they are the same thing, whereas JScript treats the two as unique creations. Counting on the documentation to point you in the right direction might not always be the right idea – even Microsoft's Scripting Runtime Reference documentation contains sample code (written in VBScript) that has examples of incorrect naming – such as `Wscript` instead of `WScript` – which will cause your scripts to break if you attempt to port the code to JScript. The references themselves are correct, but the samples can be frustrating (this refers to docs live with the WSH 2.0 Beta 2 release – hopefully these problems will be corrected by the time you read this).

All this talk of sensitivity is making me feel very PC – let's see if we can get into a bit of trouble here. As you know, rules are made to be broken. There are some quirks in the design of WSH – which result in case **insensitivity**! We've already seen one instance of this previously in our look at WshArguments – its Length property works as length as well. Here's another case where sensitivity rules are broken:

```
WScript.echo("This works");
WScript.Echo("This also works");
```

Not a big deal, but if you're used to JavaScript case-sensitivity or rely on the interpreter correcting you when you get the case wrong, then watch out. You have to be careful here, because most objects' property names *are* case-sensitive. Better to stick to the official case as documented (not as used in sample code) so you don't get confused.

And how about poor Jane JScripter? She's got troubles too – but they stem more from inconsistencies in Application Programming Interfaces, or APIs. Let's use the same example from above: the Enumerator object has an item() method, while the child collections of the FileSystemObject each contain an Item property. And how about our poor Count(), from WshArguments? In VBScript, it's a property. In JScript, it's a method. What a mess.

The best way to handle these problems is to learn the syntax of the particular API you happen to be working with at the time, and keep the reference materials handy.

Hierarchy Traps

For the web developer who uses JavaScript exclusively for client-side scripting, switching to a new development arena can be a frightening prospect for many reasons. Certainly one of the more challenging of these is the requirement to learn the intricacies of a new object model. As if ironing out the details of the previous traps weren't enough, there is also the need to learn new object hierarchies in order to be successful.

As an example, let's take another look at the FileSystemObject. Hanging off the root object are an interrelated set of methods and properties which often must be combined in order to achieve the desired end result. Suppose we want to get a reference to a file, and we know the path to it:

```
var objFile = objFSO.GetFile(path);
```

We might expect that a similar method GetFiles() might exist, which would return all files from a given folder path. Unfortunately, it's not that easy. We have to reference the folder in question and then access its Files property, which returns a collection (remember, collections are different to arrays!). If we then want to do something with each file in turn, we have to use an Enumerator to iterate through the members of the collection:

```
var objFolder = objFSO.GetFolder(path);
var collFiles = new Enumerator(objFolder.Files);
// code to iterate files
```

The best advice possible is this: before working with an unfamiliar object model, get the reference for it. Keep it close by – maybe under your pillow – for easy access when you just can't figure it out on your own. You'll be glad you did.

Of course, this only covers some of the pitfalls inherent in JavaScript development – there are many more that are simply features of the language itself. For example, when working with the `Date` object, it's vital to remember that the designers who initially built JavaScript decided that months should index from 0 instead of 1 – so December is the eleventh month when we write JavaScript code.

Also, remember that the backslash character `"\"` is used as an escape in strings, so it has a special meaning. This can cause trouble when working with file paths. The folder `c:\foo\bar\` is now `c:\\foo\\bar\\` when accessed from script.

Still others traps stem from the blurring in the minds of some web developers between the core JavaScript language and the prevalent scripting object model – that of the web browser. Try to use `alert()` in a WSH script, and you'll only get an error.

General ECMAScript Traps

Beware of some of the ECMAScript tricks you may be used to: `typeof()`, `toString()` and `toSource()` don't yet work on all objects. This example illustrates a shortcoming in WSH 1.0 and 2.0:

```
var dict = ActiveXObject("Scripting.Dictionary");
WScript.echo(dict);
```

This might only produce an error like this:

```
Cscript string.js
C:\TMP\STRING.JS: Microsoft JScript runtime error: type mismatch
```

Those kinds of common ECMAScript operations are all fine on the built in JavaScript objects such as `Date`; just not on host objects.

Working with More Than One Script

Thus far we've mostly examined simple individual scripts – stand-alone code snippets which contain all the functionality needed in a single package. This model works well for one-off projects or for building initial prototypes. However, there are many good reasons why we should consider working with multiple scripts when building a project. For example, designing a set of base code modules which can be reused in larger projects allows a developer to spend less time rewriting code as well as requiring less debugging and testing once it is known that the modules behave as expected. Another good reason to work with multiple scripts is that this allows a project to contain several different scripting languages where appropriate – perhaps a desired feature is easier to implement in one language than another. The use of multiple scripts in a single project facilitates such inter-mixing of components.

Even if you don't design a module library, after you've written a few scripts, you're sure to collect a general-purpose function or two. Before long you'll be cutting and pasting common functions every time you start a new script. Surely there's a way you can store stuff in one script and include it in another as you need to.

If you are using WSH version 1.0, you'll have to look forward to the XML support and other enhancements that Microsoft has planned for WSH 2.0 and then upgrade. Neither WSH 1.0 nor JScript 5.0 has direct support for including files like the #include statement or <SCRIPT SRC= ...> tag of other languages.

That doesn't mean you're sunk. There's more than one way to skin a cat, as they say where I come from. Read on for a version 1 workaround.

Direct Inclusion of Scripts

When it is determined that a project calls for a multi-script approach, an easy way to achieve this is through simple inclusion of one or more distinct script files into a single master application. Implementing this is quite simple in WSH, by using a .ws file which uses the <SCRIPT SRC=""> syntax to import the script directly. Suppose we have a file hello.ws as follows:

```
<job>
   <script script language="VBScript" src="hello.vbs"></script>
   <script script language="JScript" src="hello.js"></script>
</job>
```

And two files, hello.vbs and hello.js, which echo to the user greetings from both VBScript and JScript:

```
' hello.vbs:
WScript.Echo "Hello from VBScript"
```

```
// hello.js:
WScript.Echo("Hello from JScript");
```

Running hello.ws (e.g. by just double-clicking on its icon) will cause the two files to be run consecutively (in the order they occur in the hello.ws file).

If we are using the older version, the simplest way to access modular code functionality from a script is to use the Scripting Runtime Library:

```
var objFSO = WScript.CreateObject("Scripting.FileSystemObject");
var objInc = objFSO.OpenTextFile("c:\\wsh\\module.js", 1);
eval(objInc.ReadAll());
objInc.Close();  // tidy up
delete objInc;   // tidy up
delete objFSO;   // tidy up
```

The magic digit 1 means "Open this file for reading".

By giving a little bit of thought to modularity of design in your actual module implementation (recursive modularity?), you can make it a little cleaner to include multiple files, by adding the following function into your source:

```
function include(sFile)
{
   var objFSO = WScript.CreateObject("Scripting.FileSystemObject");
   var objInc = objFSO.OpenTextFile(sFile, 1);
   return objInc.ReadAll();
}
```

Which can then be used as follows:

```
eval(include("c:\\wsh\\incFile1.js"));
eval(include("c:\\wsh\\incFile2.js"));
```

Tricky stuff! You might ask: Why not call `eval()` inside the `include()` function? Ahhh... because you want the global version of `eval()` to run, not the local `Function` object's `eval()`. Otherwise the file's code is only included inside the `include()` function. If we had access to the global object's `eval()`, that would be another matter.

A final note – the import/export keywords of JavaScript don't help you out here – these keywords make existing JavaScript code available from a new parent object, they don't add any new stuff to the script from outside.

Running Other Scripts Separately

By using the `WScript.Run()` method, it is possible to execute scripts within a new process. This is equivalent to executing the script from the Run dialog or from a DOS prompt. One benefit provided by this facility is that it allows us to call an external script, passing objects from the first script as arguments. We can customize whether your script suspends execution until the new process has returned, or whether it should continue on its merry way. If we leave out the last two arguments on the second line, the result will always be zero, even if there's a problem running the other script. If we change `true` to `false`, the program won't wait for the other script to finish before continuing.

The following script will execute our old "Hello, World!" example in a new process:

```
var objShell = WScript.CreateObject("WScript.Shell");
objShell.Run("hello.ws", 0, true);
```

Delegation to Other Objects

If you want the benefit of some other bit of JavaScript code, but you don't want it cluttering up your nice script, you can include it at arm's length. The way to do this is to treat the included script as an object. There are at least two ways of doing this:

Use the **Microsoft Scripting Control**. This allows us to start pieces of script code from the control itself. The object we see is a controller that runs the second script.

Use **Windows Script Components**. These components, previously referred to as scriptlets, allow developers to create fully-fledged COM components using script alone – no more compiling. Provided that the object is registered correctly, we can use `GetObject()` to locate and use it just as we can with other objects such as traditional automation servers or compiled COM objects.

Information about both of these technologies can be found at `http://msdn.microsoft.com/scripting/`.

WSH Techniques

So far we've covered the core of the Windows Script Host object model, working with external objects, and some possible problems developers may face when working with WSH. Now let's move on to some ways in which we can actually get things done using WSH.

Customizing WSH Behavior

Firstly, make sure that WSH is working the way that you want it to. We can override default settings for any script executing within either environment, as well as being able to set options for a particular script individually.

Adjusting Options on the Command Line

`Cscript.exe` accepts a set of command-line parameters – you've already seen `//nologo` – which toggle various sets of behavior including the default execution environment, the length of time a script can execute before a timeout occurs, and whether debugging is enabled. The following table shows available switches, with descriptions for each.

Switch	Description
`//I`	Interactive: allows script errors and prompts to appear. (This is a default setting.)
`//B`	Batch: quiet mode – overrides error/prompt display. Opposite of `//I`.
`//T:XX`	Sets the length of time (in seconds) before a script timeout occurs.
`//logo`	Shows copyright information (only if the script is executed on the command line). (This is a default setting.)
`//nologo`	Prevents copyright information from being displayed. Opposite of `//logo`.
`//H:CScript` or `//H:WScript`	Registers the default script host. (The default is `WScript.exe`.)
`//S`	Saves current command-line settings.
`//?`	Displays all command-line parameters.
`//E:engine`	Executes the script with the specified scripting engine.
`//D`	Enables debugging.
`//X`	Executes the script within the debugger.
`//Job:<JobID>`	Executes a selected `job` from a `.ws` file containing multiple jobs.

For example, if you always want to execute scripts in a command-line setting, without the logo and with debugging enabled, you could execute the following line to save your preferred options:

```
cscript //nologo //H:CScript //D //S
```

Creating .WSH Files

Perhaps you don't need or want to modify the settings for every script you execute – but do need to be able to control individual files. You're in luck – this too is possible. You can create control files, which have the extension .wsh, which allow us to control settings for individual scripts.

In order to create a .wsh file, right-click on a file associated with WSH (thus, a file with the extension .js, .vbs, or .ws). Select Pr**o**perties, and then the Script tab from the context menu which is displayed. From here we can change the timeout default and whether logo information should be displayed on the command-line:

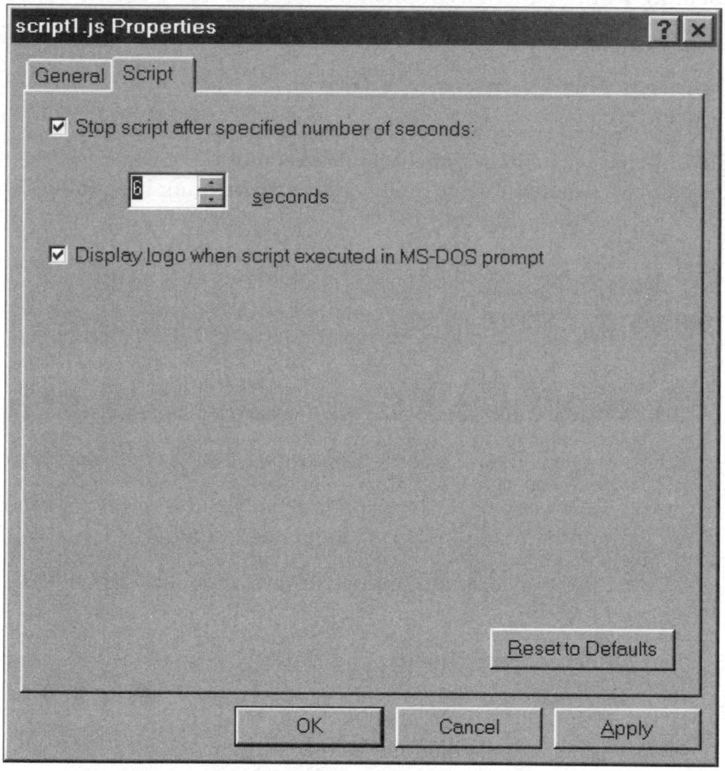

When we apply or accept any changes we have made, a new file will be created, with the same name as the script in question, but with the extension .wsh, which records these custom settings. Script1.wsh illustrated above has the following contents:

```
[ScriptFile]
Path=C:\WSH\script1.js

[Options]
Timeout=6
DisplayLogo=1
```

Controlling Browsers

We've seen in previous examples that Windows applications can be easily automated through WSH scripts. One such application that provides an automation interface is Microsoft Internet Explorer. Imagine for a moment that you are developing a logon script for machine setup – it may ensure that all of the proper network drives are mapped, that a shared printer is installed on your machine – all routine logon tasks. You may have also been given an additional requirement: at the start of each session, an instance of Internet Explorer should be opened, loading the company's intranet site.

Creating an instance of IE is simple – no more complex than the example used to create Word a few pages back:

```
var sIE_App = "InternetExplorer.Application";
var objIE = WScript.CreateObject(sIE_App, "IE_");
objIE.Navigate("http://www.example.com/");

function IE_DocumentComplete()
{
    objIE.Visible = true;
}
```

In this example, we simply create a browser instance and navigate to a predefined URL. Once the requested page has finished loading, the browser instance fires a `DocumentComplete` event, which we take as our cue to make the browser window visible. Note the syntax used in the second line:

```
var objIE = WScript.CreateObject(sAutoApp, "IE_" );
```

The second argument in the `CreateObject()` method call is the optional argument which allows developers to get access to the event model of the child application. This argument prefaces the name of the event as the name of event-handler function, as used in the sample code:

```
function IE_DocumentComplete()
```

This function is called when the `DocumentComplete()` event is fired when the page has finished loading.

Thus far we've created a browser instance, but we don't do much with it at this point – it is created with the same appearance as the last window the user closed. However, we've already covered all the basic functionality we need: setting properties, calling methods and handling events. Controlling browsers (or any other created applications) is nothing more than this. The next several examples will build a small script module which will be useful as a foundation for building user interfaces later on.

First off, it's important to remember that we're dealing with a web browser interface now. We have already established a hook into the application's event model – why not give ourselves access to the familiar IE object model. We can do this by caching a reference to `objIE.Document` property, which is equivalent to the `document` object in client-side scripting. Any document properties available in client script written for the web are now available to WSH. The highlighted lines of code below add the document reference:

```
var sProgID = "InternetExplorer.Application";
var objIE = WScript.CreateObject(sProgID, "IE_");
var objDoc;    // used to get hook into IE DOM
objIE.Navigate("about:blank");
```

```
function IE_DocumentComplete()
{
    objDoc = objIE.Document;
    objDoc.title = "Example.com: Intranet Site";
}
```

Now we start to take control! The company's name should be reflected in the title bar of our intranet browser – we've set this in the DocumentComplete handler.

Let's assume that we want the browser window to have a certain configuration at each user login – perhaps it should always show the Address, Menu, Status and toolbars, as well as a standard size:

```
with (objIE)
{
    AddressBar = true;
    ToolBar = true;
    MenuBar = true;
    StatusBar = true;
    Width = 400;
    Height = 450;
}
```

Finally, we make the window visible:

```
objIE.Visible = true;
```

There you have it – a customized browser window! Of course, there's much more we can do with this window by using the two object models available to us at this point: the one provided by InternetExplorer.Application, and the client-side Document Object Model accessed through objIE.Document. For more information on both object models, see the references in Appendix L.

Communicating With the User

As we have seen in some of the examples, user interaction can be a very important part of a WSH application. Up to this point, we've only seen dialog examples using the Echo() method. This method, however, is limited in its usefulness since it only offers the ability to send information to the user. It does not return a value, nor offer the user the possibility to cancel an action. These are certainly important features for an application that requires user input or decision-making capability.

Luckily, there's more than one way to provide user interaction. Here are a few possibilities:

❑   Using the extended pop-up functionality natively available within WSH

❑   Creating custom HTML forms to provide a mechanism for user input

❑   Working with Windows common dialogs or external user interface applications or controls

The following section will examine each of these options.

WshShell.Popup()

Let's start off with a simple Popup exercise:

```
var objShell = WScript.CreateObject("WScript.Shell");
objShell.Popup("Hello, World (take two)");
```

This example uses the `WshShell` object's `Popup()` method to display a dialog box rather than our old friend the `Echo()` method. The resulting dialog looks very similar to the results from a simple `Echo()` call executed through `wscript.exe`, but that's only a hint of what's possible using the `Popup()` method. We've already seen one difference between `Popup()` and `Echo()`. Whereas `Echo()` only takes a single type of argument (namely, one or more items of textual or numeric data to display), `Popup()` allows developers to create full-featured dialogs.

In fact, `Popup()` can take up to four arguments:

```
nReturn = WshShell.Popup(sText, nDelay, sTitle, nWindowType);
```

Argument	Description
sText	Text to be displayed in the dialog.
nDelay	Number of seconds to wait before automatically closing the dialog. Use 0 if dialog must be dismissed by user.
sTitle	Text to be displayed in title bar of dialog.
nWindowType	Integer representing information regarding button configuration, icon to be displayed, and more (for a complete reference, see the documentation for "MsgBox constants" available either online at `http://msdn.microsoft.com/library/` or on the MSDN Library CD).

The following example creates a new dialog utilizing all of the features available in the `WshShell.Popup()` method:

```javascript
var sText = "Isn't this dialog better?";
var sTitle = "Advanced \"Hello World\" Example";
var iType = 3;    // use yes, no, cancel buttons
iType += 48;      // add exclamation icon
var objShell = WScript.CreateObject("WScript.Shell");
var intReturn = objShell.Popup(sText, 0, sTitle, iType);
objShell.Popup("Popup() return value: " + intReturn);
```

This example captures the return value from the fancy pop-up and echoes it back to the user. Capturing the return value allows developers to create conditional code to execute based on the user's response (building on the previous example):

```javascript
var sBtnClicked;
switch (intReturn)
{
   case 2: // cancel
      sBtnClicked = "Cancel";
      break;
   case 6: // yes
      sBtnClicked = "Yes";
      break;
   case 7: // no
      sBtnClicked = "No";
      break;
}
objShell.Popup("You clicked " + sBtnClicked);
```

Combining VBScript with JScript

Unfortunately, JScript does not supply any method for user interaction as a part of the core language (the methods `alert()`, `prompt()` and `confirm()` are part of the Browser Object Model exposed by Internet Explorer, and not included in core JScript). However, VBScript does have some capacity for interactivity in its `MsgBox()` and `InputBox()` methods. Of the two, `InputBox()` is of greater interest, as `MsgBox()` provides functionality equivalent to `WshShell.Popup()`. As seen previously, `Popup()` simply echoes a message to the user and returns an integer value based on the key pressed in the dialog. `InputBox()` provides a slightly greater level of interactivity by prompting users for a response.

The following example uses VBScript to create an input box with text passed by the caller. It returns a string containing the user's input (which we show with an `Echo()`) (save the following code as `inputbox.ws` in order to execute it – this will only work if you have WSH 2.0; you will need to change the extension to `.wsf` if you are using the final release of WSH 2.0):

```
<?xml version="1.0" standalone="yes"?>
<job>
    <script language="VBScript">
        <![CDATA[
            Function ShowInputBox(str)
                ShowInputBox = InputBox(str)
            End Function
        ]]>
    </script>
    <script language="JScript">
        <![CDATA[
            var sMsg = "hello from a VBS InputBox";
            var sInput = ShowInputBox(sMsg);
            WScript.Echo(sInput);
        ]]>
    </script>
</job>
```

You might want to take a moment to review the XML tags (introduced at the start of the chapter) used in constructing `.ws`/`.wsf` files at this point. We'll be seeing more of them from here on.

We're definitely moving in the direction of more interactivity at this point, but have reached the limits of WSH's capacity for user interaction. In order to process input beyond which button was clicked and simple text input, we have to use external objects. Since most developers with an interest in WSH will probably already be familiar with client-side scripting in a Web browser, let's start there.

Browser Dialog Boxes

Right off the bat you should be aware that controlling a web browser interface and setting up clean communications between a WSH script and its hosted browser instance is not the easiest way to go about creating a user interface for input. There are quite a few ActiveX controls which are designed specifically for this purpose, and it seems that more appear each week.

However, in order to provide a complete range of input options, we'll start off by using a hosted instance of Internet Explorer. We already have some of the code we'll need, from the previous section on "Controlling Browsers".

This example makes use of the `include` capability provided in WSH 2.0, by breaking the code into reusable chunks. There are four parts to the script:

- ❑ `objIE.js`: Creates the browser instance and sets up access to IE's Browser Object Model.
- ❑ `dialog.js`: Customizes settings for the specific browser instance.
- ❑ `html_dialog.htm`: File to be loaded into the browser window.
- ❑ `ie_inst.ws`: The master file used to pull all the pieces together.

Let's look at each piece of code individually. First, we create the browser instance – this should be familiar from our earlier example:

```javascript
var sIE_progID = "InternetExplorer.Application";
var objIE      = WScript.CreateObject(sIE_progID, "IE_");
var objDoc     = null;      // used to get hook into IE DOM

function IE_DocumentComplete(pDisp, URL)
{
    objDoc = objIE.Document;
}
```

Next, we need to set custom values for this instance. Since it will be used as a dialog, we can dispense with the address bar, status bar, etc. In addition, there should be no need to resize or to allow files to be dropped onto the window. The last task is to set the window's width and height. Once again, this code will look familiar, but the settings are customized for the needs of the current application:

```javascript
with (objIE)
{
    RegisterAsDropTarget = false;
    AddressBar           = false;
    ToolBar              = false;
    MenuBar              = false;
    StatusBar            = false;
    Resizable            = false;
    Width                = 400;
    Height               = 300;
}
```

Next comes our HTML file. There are several interesting things going on here, which will be described individually after we've seen all the code:

```html
<HTML>
<HEAD>
<TITLE>HTML Dialog from WSH</TITLE>
<SCRIPT TYPE="text/javascript">
    window.onload = win_load;

    function win_load()
    {
        var iX = screen.width / 2 - document.body.offsetWidth / 2;
        var iY = screen.height / 2 - document.body.offsetHeight / 2;
        window.moveTo( iX, iY );
        btnUpdate.onclick = btn_click;
    }

    function btn_click()
    {
        document.body.setAttribute("UPDATE", "true");
    }
```

```
</SCRIPT>
</HEAD>

<BODY SCROLL="no" UPDATE="false">
<!--
    UPDATE is an expando property used to notify
    the host script when it can grab information
-->
<P>This is a non-modal dialog window built for user interaction.</P>
<TABLE CELLSPACING="2">
<TR>
<TD ALIGN="right">What is your name?</TD>
<TD ROWSPAN="3"> </TD>
<TD><INPUT TYPE="text" ID="txtName"></TD>
<TD ROWSPAN="3" WIDTH="20"> </TD>
</TR>
<TR>
<TD ALIGN="right">What is your quest?</TD>
<TD><INPUT TYPE="text" ID="txtQuest"></TD>
</TR>
<TR>
<TD ALIGN="right">What is your favorite color?</TD>
<TD><INPUT TYPE="text" ID="txtColor"></TD>
</TR>
<TR>
<TD COLSPAN="2"> </TD>
<TD COLSPAN="2"><BR><INPUT TYPE="button" VALUE="Update Values"
ID="btnUpdate"></TD>
</TR>
</TABLE>
</BODY>
</HTML>
```

The first thing to look at here is the client-side script in the page, which serves two purposes: centering the window in the screen, and handling the button click.

Since WSH doesn't have a built-in method to access screen resolution, the first function (which is called when the onload event fires) takes advantage of IE's screen object to calculate the proper placement for the window based on screen resolution and window size. This function also assigns the event handler for when the update button is clicked.

The second function changes the value of the UPDATE expando or dynamic property of the <BODY> element. This is the mechanism used to inform the controlling script that it can continue execution – it has been waiting patiently for this change to take place up to this point.

The only other interesting bit of code here is the assignment <BODY ... UPDATE="false">. This is the expando property mentioned previously. For those unfamiliar with expando properties, they essentially allow developers to assign custom properties to any element in the HTML document. Used here in conjunction with the second function, UPDATE provides a method for the WSH script to determine that the browser window is set to relinquish control back to its host.

The final piece to this puzzle is the driver file, which includes the first two external scripts and steps through the actual execution of events.

```
<?xml version="1.0" standalone="yes"?>
<job id="jobIE_Inst">
    <script language="jscript" src="objIE.js"></script>
    <script language="jscript" src="dialog.js"></script>
    <script language="jscript">
        <![CDATA[
```

```
          objIE.Navigate("c:\\wsh\\html_dialog.htm");

          // wait a bit - time to hook the document
          while (!objDoc)
          {
              WScript.Sleep(100);
          }

          var cAll  = objDoc.all;
          var oBody = objDoc.body;

          objIE.Visible = true;

          // wait until button is clicked
          while ("false" == oBody.getAttribute("UPDATE"))
              ; // do nothing

          var sName  = cAll("txtName").value + "\n";
          var sQuest = cAll("txtQuest").value + "\n";
          var sColor = cAll("txtColor").value + "\n";

          objIE.Quit();
          objIE = null;
          WScript.Echo( "Your input:\n\n" + sName + sQuest + sColor );
          WScript.Quit();

      ]]>
    </script>
  </job>
```

This script is responsible for most of the functionality of the application. It navigates to the proper document, hooks into the necessary parts of the Browser Object Model, stores the user's input in local variables when it becomes available, then echoes that input back to the user and performs application cleanup.

As exhibited here, it is possible to use Internet Explorer as a front end for your scripts when you need to accept user input, but it should be easier.

External Programs

Good news – it is! Perhaps the simplest way to provide user interaction within a WSH application is to use a helper application, such as an ActiveX control designed specifically for this purpose. An excellent example of such a control is WshKit, created by Dino Esposito for his book 'Windows Script Host Programmer's Reference', ISBN 1-861002-65-3, from Wrox Press. WshKit contains a DialogBox property which makes it easy to populate and query forms contained in HTML pages loaded into the DialogBox containers.

The following code is a simple example for working with WshKit.DialogBox. It first instantiates the object, then attempts to load an HTML page containing form objects (in this instance, text boxes) which have an ID attribute assigned; this ID is the hook which is used by WshKit to access the objects.

```
<HTML>
<HEAD>
<TITLE>WshKit.DialogBox Sample</TITLE>
</HEAD>

<BODY SCROLL="no" TIP="Hi, Monty! How's your Python?">
<!--
    TIP is used for "status bar" information
    any element can have a TIP applied
-->
```

```
<P>Please fill out the following information:</P>

<TABLE CELLSPACING="2" ALIGN="center">
<TR>
    <TD ALIGN="right">What is your name?</TD>
    <TD> </TD>
    <TD><INPUT TYPE="text" ID="txtName"/></TD>
</TR>
<TR>
    <TD ALIGN="right">What is your quest?</TD>
    <TD> </TD>
    <TD><INPUT TYPE="text" ID="txtQuest"/></TD>
</TR>
<TR>
    <TD ALIGN="right">What is your favorite color?</TD>
    <TD> </TD>
    <TD><INPUT TYPE="text" ID="txtColor"/></TD>
</TR>
</TABLE>

<P>Clicking "OK" will store the current values in local variables, and echo the
values back to you.</P>
<P>Clicking "Cancel" will discard form information.</P>
</BODY>
</HTML>
```

If the loading is successful, the script initializes the form fields as well as resizing and displaying the dialog window, by calling the handler object's Show() method. This method also serves as the return mechanism for the object: when its OK or Cancel buttons are clicked, the object returns a Boolean value. When the window is dismissed, the script handles the return value – if the OK button is pressed, the current form values are stored into local variables within the script, and are then echoed back to the user.

```
var objDialog = WScript.CreateObject("WshKit.DialogBox");
var boolRet = objDialog.Create("path://wshkit_dialog.htm");
// path:// is an internal protocol used by WshKit
// check for successful creation
if (boolRet)
{
    objDialog.SetItemValue("txtName", "");
    objDialog.SetItemValue("txtQuest", "");
    objDialog.SetItemValue("txtColor", "");
    objDialog.Move(0, 0, 450, 350);
    // get return value from dialog
    if (objDialog.Show("center"))
    {
        var sVal1 = objDialog.GetItemValue("txtName");
        var sVal2 = objDialog.GetItemValue("txtQuest");
        var sVal3 = objDialog.GetItemValue("txtColor");
        WScript.Echo(sVal1 + "\n" + sVal2 + "\n" + sVal3);
    }
}
```

Note the difference in size between this script and the previous one. The fact that we're using an external object results in a dramatic reduction of the amount of code required – much of the functionality is wrapped up into the WshKit helper object.

Of course, this is only one small example of how Windows Script Host can be used with external objects in order to provide user interaction. WshKit also provides classes for browsing the local computer or network, data input, and mail-sending capability.

There are many other objects available for use with WSH. The web sites listed in Appendix L contain information about some of these objects, as well as making them available for download.

Controlling PC Setup at Windows Startup

Enough small samples – we've finally reached the point where we are ready to put all of the pieces of the jigsaw together.

This last section will present a basic logon script which:

❑   Maps several network drives

❑   Connects a network printer (only under Windows NT)

❑   Determines whether the latest anti-virus software is installed

❑   Synchronizes the computer's clock with a central time source

❑   Opens a browser window onto the company intranet

Let's take a look at the code first – the actual logon script as well as external scripts used by the logon, and then we'll describe a few pieces as necessary. You may want to take another quick look at the XML information at the start of this chapter before digging into the code; it's used more extensively here than in any of the previous examples.

Our main `.ws` file, which links the other files together, is called `logon.ws`:

```
<?xml version="1.0" standalone="yes"?>

<!--

   logon.ws

   This file is the monster logon script which establishes
   connection of set file and printer shares, checks for current
   version of antivirus SW install, synchs local system time
   with a network resource, and opens browser window to
   company intranet

-->

<job id="jobLogon">

   <object id="objIE" progid="InternetExplorer.Application" />

   <resource id="resUpgrade">
      You have an old version of AntiVirusVendor Software installed.
      Please install the latest version from the following Web site:

         http://intranetsite/virus/

      Upgrade now?
   </resource>

   <script language="jscript" src="\\\\someserver\\shared\\commonObj.js">
   </script>
   <script language="jscript"
         src="\\\\someserver\\shared\\mapDriveOrPrinter.js">
   </script>
   <script language="jscript" src="http://intranetsite/virus/latest.js">
   </script>
   <script language="jscript" src="http://intranetsite/virus/antivirus.js">
   </script>
   <script language="jscript">
      <![CDATA[
```

```
        // map three network drives
        // syntax: MapDrive(sharename, driveletter)
        MapDrive("\\\\appserver\\apps", "Z");
        MapDrive("\\\\fileserver\\files", "Y");
        MapDrive("\\\\toolserver\\tools", "X");

        // connect a network printer (only if OS is Windows NT)
        // syntax: AddPrinter(printerpath)
        AddPrinter("\\\\printserver\\share");

        // synchronize computer's clock with a central time source
        objShell.Run("net time \\\\timeserver /set /yes");

        // is latest anti-virus software installed?
        // functionality pulled in from 'latest.js' & 'antivirus.js'
        CheckAntiVirusStatus();

        // open a browser window onto the company intranet
        // unless user chose to upgrade anti-virus SW
        // then go to anti-virus site
        if (6 == iVirusRet)     // "yes" chosen in upgrade dialog
        {
            objIE.Navigate("http://supde/virus/");
        }
        else
        {
            objIE.Navigate("http://supde/");
        }
        objIE.Visible = true;
    ]]>
  </script>
</job>
```

This file pulls together many of the different pieces of functionality made available by WSH:

❑ Since it is an actual Windows Script file (as opposed to a more basic .js file), it can create the browser without the use of an additional CreateObject() call.

❑ It utilizes the <resource> element to store a notification message.

❑ It imports several external scripts – using both web and file connections to do so.

❑ It executes a command-line application.

Since most of the actual functionality is hidden in the external script files, this file can be more compact and readable. So, on to the include files...

The first file, commonObj.js, simply creates global instances of a few native WSH objects for later processing assistance:

```
/*
    commonObj.js
    - creates instances of required objects
*/

var objNet    = WScript.CreateObject("WScript.Network");
var objShell  = WScript.CreateObject("WScript.Shell");
var objFSO    = WScript.CreateObject("Scripting.FileSystemObject");
var objSystem = objShell.Environment("System");
```

The `mapDriveOrPrinter.js` script provides two abstraction functions, which encapsulate a predefined set of functionality into a single concise wrapper. The first function provides error handling when mapping a network drive, while the second sets a default printer connection:

```javascript
/*
   mapDriveOrPrinter.js
   - provides wrapper functions to map network drives
     and printer shares
*/

var enmDrives = new Enumerator(objFSO.Drives);
var arrDrives = new Array;
var i = 0;

for (enmDrives.moveFirst();
     !enmDrives.atEnd();
     enmDrives.moveNext())
{
    arrDrives[i++] = enmDrives.item().DriveLetter.toLowerCase();
}


function MapDrive(sSharePath, sLetter)
{
    var bDriveInUse = false;
    sLetter = sLetter.toLowerCase();

    for (var i = 0; i < arrDrives.length; i++)
    {
        if (sLetter == arrDrives[i])
        {
            bDriveInUse = true;
            break;
        }
    }

    if (!bDriveInUse)
    {
        if (objFSO.FolderExists(sSharePath))
        {
            objNet.MapNetworkDrive(sLetter + ":", sSharePath);
        }
        else
        {
            WScript.Echo("unable to locate server share " + sSharePath);
        }
    }
}

function AddPrinter( sPrinterPath )
{
    // if printer share exists and OS == Windows NT
    // add printer and set as default
    // (Win 9x requires second arg: driver name [as string])

    if ("Windows_NT" == objSystem("OS"))
    {
        objNet.AddWindowsPrinterConnection(sPrinterPath);
    }

    objNet.SetDefaultPrinter( sPrinterPath );
}
```

The next script, `latest.js`, is very simple – a single line of code which declares a variable to be used when checking for the most recent anti-virus update. This file should be automatically updated whenever a version update is made available on the network.

```
/*
   latest.js
   - network file called for version comparison between
     local antivirus install and latest available version

   !! this file can be manually updated to reflect new versions !!
   !! but should be auto generated with each new release        !!
*/

var iCurrVer = 090199;    // date representation of latest update
```

The final script, `antivirus.js` compares the latest available version of the anti-virus software with the locally-installed version. This function returns a Boolean value to be used later inline.

```
/*
   antivirus.js
   - determine whether the latest antivirus software is installed
   - assumes existence of following regkey:
     HKCU\Software\AntiVirusVendor\LatestUpdate
*/

var iVirusRet;

function CheckAntiVirusStatus()
{
   var iInstVer = objShell.RegRead
                  ("HKCU\\Software\\AntiVirusVendor\\LatestUpdate");

   if (iCurrVer > iInstVer)
   {
      iVirusRet = objShell.Popup (getResource("resUpgrade"), // window msg
                  0,                                         // no auto-hide
                  "Antivirus upgrade required",              // window title
                  48 + 4);                                   // window styles
                                                    // exclamation + yes/no
   }
}
```

Summary

Hopefully this chapter has provided you with an incentive to start using Windows Script Host to automate tasks within Windows. As you have probably gathered by now, WSH is an extremely powerful addition to any developer's toolbox. Amongst the topics we looked at in this quick introduction to WSH were:

❑   The new features introduced in WSII 2.0

❑   The XML elements used in `.ws` (`.wsf`) files

❑   The WSH object model

❑   Traps and pitfalls involved in using JavaScript with WSH

❑   Using `.ws` files to combine a number of scripts

❑   Some techniques to use when programming with WSH

❑   A practical example demonstrating some of the power of WSH

One common usage of WSH which we have not covered here is in the area of network administration. WSH is rapidly becoming a favorite tool of network administrators who use it in conjunction with ADSI (Active Directory Service Interfaces) and WMI (Windows Management Instrumentation) for managing directory resources and sharing information in an enterprise setting.

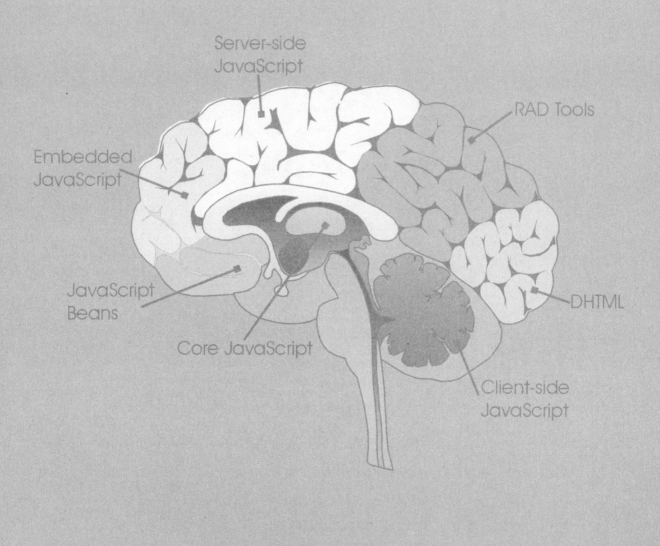

High End Scripting With ScriptEase Desktop

What Does It Do?

JavaScript interpreters need a host program in order to do anything useful. You've seen in previous chapters how Web browsers and Web servers are ideal systems for JavaScript to work on. However, it cuts both ways. Once the interpreter is embedded in a host program, it is also constrained by that program. For example, you can't do pop-up windows from server-side JavaScript, because there are no pop-up windows in the Web server host. What if you need more flexibility? What if you want to let your scripting instincts go crazy?

In this chapter you'll see how JavaScript, using ScriptEase Desktop, can lead you far beyond the Web environment into places foreign and mind expanding. Outside the Web, JavaScript choices are numerous and varied.

ScriptEase is rather different to most of the other JavaScript interpreters. It supports the ECMA compliant standard functionality you would expect it to. However, in addition, it provides a lot of extended capabilities by way of additional libraries of C language functions and special purpose objects. Its socket interface provides a way of building servers and clients that would be very difficult in other interpreters. On top of all that its platform coverage is as wide as any of the competing products. Because it supports a pre-processor as well, you can build scripts that are portable across every system you are likely to need to support in an enterprise wide environment.

In Appendix H, the extended capabilities are covered in detail and at the end of this chapter is an extensive demonstration of the Distributed Scripting capabilities of ScriptEase.

Standalone JavaScript On The Desktop

All you need is the ScriptEase Desktop JavaScript interpreter that uses the whole computer as its host program. That way every feature of the computer is at the command of the scriptwriter – printers, graphics, networking, files, applications, viewers, databases, running programs, everything. Before we delve into the intricacies of desktop automation with ScriptEase, we will take a short look at some of the other alternatives.

Standalone JavaScript scripts provide you with capabilities similar to Visual Basic. After you've had your fill of JavaScript in HTML pages, and you've experienced the costs associated with maintaining a web server with server-side scripting, this is the way to get some simple jobs done and at the same time expand your skills and your horizons.

As you'll see, choosing which standalone JavaScript interpreter to play with has a big impact on what you can do. The W3C consortium (`www.w3c.org`) may be a force for standardization in browsers, but there's no such umpire for standalone interpreters. Beyond the basic language features, each interpreter goes its own way.

Here, we are only considering one of the JavaScript host scripting interpreters and not looking at other scripting languages. Yes there are other scripting languages (and we haven't forgotten AppleScript or UNIX shell scripting). But this is a JavaScript book. At the time of writing, there are four major variants of standalone JavaScript (and more are likely to follow). These are:

- ❏ ScriptEase DeskTop from Nombas, Inc
- ❏ Windows Script Host (WSH) with JScript from Microsoft
- ❏ FESI by Jean-Marc Lugrin.
- ❏ Rhino from Netscape.

Aside from these, NGS and JSRef are two more JavaScript interpreters currently available. However, they don't take advantage of any host objects much. This makes them of limited use unless your mission is to add host objects yourself. Chapter 22, Embedded JavaScript, describes how you might make use of interpreters with no pre-existing host objects. To use them though, you will have build a framework within which they can exist. That's not impossible and these days with the support they provide its not actually very difficult either but it is easier to stand on someone else's shoulders and benefit from what they've achieved already if all you are interested in doing is a little automation with JavaScript. Chapter 16 discusses FESI in detail while Chapter 20 covers WSH and JScript. Now we can devote our attention to ScriptEase.

ScriptEase Desktop 4.10

ScriptEase is a suite of scripting tools from Nombas, Inc. Nombas are at `www.nombas.com`. Version 4.10 is the latest version and the scripting language is ECMAScript compliant, with some Nombas extensions. ScriptEase:Desktop is the standalone interpreter amongst the suite of tools. This tool runs portably across a variety of platforms, including Windows, Macintosh and Unix, although you can easily lock yourself in to one platform if you exploit that platform's functionality. It can be evaluated for free, but otherwise is a commercial product. It isn't very expensive to buy so there isn't really any reason not to pay the modest fees to continue using it.

All By Itself

Here are two examples, of standalone JavaScript scripts written in ScriptEase. The first is not very complicated:

```
Screen.writeln("A simple one line script");
```

The statement above could be replaced with:

```
Clib.puts("A simple one line script");
```

This example illustrates that ScriptEase has JavaScript at its core with the support of the standard C library available. It is a little more sophisticated. We load a variable with a text string and then delete a sub-string from it. If the sub-string does not exist then nothing happens. After that we test the result of performing the delete. That result will be false if the delete didn't actually happen. So changing the assignment so that the string in the id variables does not contain JavaScript would cause the else code block to be executed:

```
#include "string.jsh"

var id = "Nombas ScriptEase 4.10 JavaScript";
var brand = id.delStr("JavaScript");

if ( brand )
{
  Screen.write("JavaScript type is: %50.50s\n", brand);
}
else
{
  Screen.write("Not JavaScript? Identity crisis!");
}
```

Each of these examples would be in a separate file. The ScriptEase interpreter can read a script stored in a file with any extension, so .js is fine, although .jse is the preferred extension. .jsh is the preferred extension for #include'd files.

> Be aware that there is a possible conflict of file types here because the Microsoft scripting team are now proposing use of the .jse file extension within the JScript/WSH world. This is only an issue if you plan to use both scripting systems in close proximity.

The first example shows the Screen.writeln function and the 'put string' function Clib.puts() which are the equivalent of document.write(). The second example uses the 'print formatted' function Clib.printf(), which does the same thing, but gives fine control over the format of the output. This isn't HTML, so output to the screen or elsewhere appears exactly as you specify it. The %50.50s characters are an example of a specific format.

The second example also shows a 'hash include' in the first line. This allows another script to be include in the main script, replacing the #include which is called a directive. The HTML equivalent is <SCRIPT SRC="string.js">. Any code in the script included is interpreted straight away – in this case it is included so further on the handy method string.delStr() can be used to return a string minus a specified piece, or null. If you want to be a purist, you could use plain, old JavaScript and do an id.replace("JavaScript", "") but we wanted to show you #includes and other stuff.

Command Line Variations

These examples show JavaScript being run from the command line on a Windows system:

```
C:\SE> secon32 example1.jse ready set go

C:\SE> sewin32 "Clib.printf('A piece of pie: %d', Math.PI * 0.2);"
```

And this on a UNIX platform:

```
$ se < example3 > output
```

There are different interpreter programs to suit different compatibility issues and different computers. This explains why there are several different executables shown.

The first example shows how to specify a .jse file and supply starting information to it (ready, set and go). The second example shows directly executing JavaScript without any file, similar to a JavaScript URL in HTML. The last example shows that the interpreter can handle having the source of its script and of its output redirected from/to another file. Whether your Windows platform can support this UNIX-like command line depends on the command line interpreter you are running. You could add a Bourne shell CLI to Windows NT for example.

Batch Files

In addition to the above mechanisms, JavaScript standalone scripts can be embedded in batch files. On the PC, batch files are .BAT files and are handled as follows:

```
@echo off
SEcon32 %0.bat %1 %2 %3 % 4 %5 %6 %7 %8 %9
GOTO SE_EXIT

// All the script including #include's goes here
Clib.puts("Boo! JavaScript strikes.");

:SE_EXIT
```

When DOS runs this script, because of the GOTO, DOS only sees the first three lines and the last. In the second line, the ScriptEase interpreter is fed the *same* file, and is smart enough to know that a .BAT file means ignore all lines except those between GOTO SE_EXIT and :SE_EXIT, which must be the script.

On UNIX, batch files have a special start line instead:

```
#!/usr/local/bin/se
// script and #includes from here on
Clib.puts('JavaScript back at work\n');
```

This example assumes ScriptEase was installed in the /usr/local/bin directory.

It's a neat trick available to scripts that you execute from the shell. The shell (usually Bourne, Korn, or C Shell) will look in the first line of the script being run. If it sees a comment symbol (hash) followed by an exclamation mark, it looks at the rest of the line to see if it is an executable program. If it is, then it executes that program and then tells it to run the script on its behalf. It's called shell switching and allows you to write shell scripts in any language and execute them from any shell, regardless of whether they were written for that shell or not.

Getting ready for ScriptEase Desktop 4.10

ScriptEase Desktop, as you would expect, is very easy to install. You will find that the installation procedure is different for each platform. For example, the Windows install is a self-extracting executable file. It has an un-installer as well, which will remove ScriptEase from your system. The installation of ScriptEase on Windows does not affect any other parts of the Windows environment although bear in mind that the .jse file type may already be associated with parts of WSH.

Installing on UNIX is accomplished by the make utility. However, it executes a ScriptEase script to do the installation. This is an interesting example of how you can do some quite complex systems administration tasks with a JavaScript engine.

As is the case with all Nombas products, the manual is extensive and complete. At some 300 pages it covers a lot of territory.

ScriptEase Desktop Unique Features

Like all the ScriptEase interpreters, the desktop variety supports all the usual language extensions:

- ❑ Pre-processor support
- ❑ Built-in C language library
- ❑ Built-in System extension library
- ❑ #include libraries of script functions
- ❑ #link includable libraries supplied with the install kit
- ❑ #if/#ifdef conditional code blocks
- ❑ A specialized programmer's editor
- ❑ An IDE debugger
- ❑ cFunction support
- ❑ Most ECMAScript compliant standard JavaScript objects are extended with additional methods
- ❑ Dynamic object support
- ❑ The Buffer object class

When the ScriptEase shell environment is started, it can be configured to auto-load some initial files. They provided a way to enhance the basic capabilities of ScriptEase in an easily configured way. You can also filter shells on an individual command basis or at the character level. ScriptEase also supports GUI interface for running script as well.

Script Inclusions and Pre-Processing

All versions of the ScriptEase interpreter come packaged with a set of scripts that can be included to provide extra functions. There are also a set of compiled libraries that can be loaded at run-time to extend ScriptEase's capabilities.

Script source is loaded with the #include pre-processor directive while compiled libraries are loaded with the #link directive.

The pre-processor also supports #if, #else, #elseif, #endif conditional execution, just like the C language pre-processor.

The pre-processor also includes support for defining macros or manifest constants. If you are already used to using the C language and have begun using JavaScript you should find this useful. These provide a way to conditionally switch sections of code in and out of your project.

The pre-processor also defines some fixed constant values that you can take advantage of to build conditional versions of your scripts for different computing platforms.

The following values are set up for you to determine which platform you are running in. Several may be set at once:

Constant	Environment
DOS	MS-DOS
DOS32	MS-DOS with extended memory
MAC	Macintosh
NWLNM	Netware Network LAN Manager
_OS2_	OS/2
UNIX	UNIX (all variants)
WINDOWS	Windows 16 bit
WIN32	Windows 32 bit
95CON	Windows 95/98 in console mode
95WIN	Windows 95/98 in GUI mode
NTCON	Windows NT in Console mode
NTWIN	Windows NT in GUI mode
SHELL	Defined if you are running in a shell

Note that LAN Manager is a legacy system and this constant is likely to only be set when running on a server system of some sort.

Host Objects

There are a variety of objects that allow you to interact with the host computer. Here are some brief details of them:

❑ **Screen**
This object is used to display content on the console display. It supports a variety of methods such as `write()`, `writeln()`, `clear()`, `cursor()`, `handle()`, `setBackground()`, `setForeground()`, and `size()`. With these calls you should be able to do pretty much all you want with the text based console screen.

❑ **SElib**
This provides access to the host environment. It is through this object representation of a library that you can interact with file systems, memory, windows, messages and script execution mechanisms.

Library, Utility, and Sample Scripts

ScriptEase Desktop comes with a rich set of scripts that may be used by registered users when developing scripts of their own. These scripts come in three varieties.

Library Scripts

These are source text libraries of objects, methods, properties, functions, and values that you can include in your own projects. They are designed in a way that they extend the ScriptEase language even though they are written in ScriptEase itself.

Utility Scripts

These are routines that perform useful and real world tasks. They are already written to save effort for programmers. You would not normally include these into your own projects although they may contain useful fragments of code. They are run from the command line.

Sample Scripts

These are examples of scripting for various purposes. They are useful as starting points for your own scripting exploits.

All scripts share one thing in common. Users may use these scripts, or portions of them, in their own scripts. Users might want to use some scripts as starting points in more comprehensive projects.

Library scripts are found in the `include` folder, utility scripts in the `utility` folder, and sample scripts in the `sample` folder. This breakdown applies to scripts that work on all platforms. A similar breakdown applies to scripts for particular platforms. For example, ScriptEase for Win32 has library scripts in an `include` folder and `sample` scripts in a sample folder. Both of these folders are inside the `Win32` folder, where the utility scripts reside.

The file names for scripts adhere to the 8.3 naming convention since ScriptEase allows multiple platforms to share scripts. The file names are as descriptive as possible under the restrictions of this naming convention. But the descriptions that follow should be helpful in providing an overview. The routines chosen are those for general use, that is, for all platforms, and those for the most popular platform, Win32.

The scripts you can readily include into your projects are listed in Appendix H, where the ScriptEase language is covered in general for all the different ScriptEase variants.

ScriptEase Desktop Techniques

If you are developing code for a variety of projects and you find yourself implementing the same or a similar solution several times over, you could build a library of functions and include the library into each of the target projects. That way you would only need to maintain one copy of the functionality. Be careful that you understand the consequences of modifying one of the routines in the library though because if you change something in the library, you could possibly break every single project that includes it.

Formatted Reports

Formatted reports are quite tricky to do in JavaScript. However, because we have the `Clib` extensions, which provide lots of extra functionality, we can do formatted reports really easily. In the C language, this is done with `printf()` and a group of related functions that let us output formatted text to files, strings or as the result returned by a function call.

Here is another way to do "Hello World":

```
Clib.printf("Hello World!");
```

With `Clib.printf()` support any of the complex formatting we might do in the C language becomes available to us in JavaScript. For example:

```
Clib.printf("Count %d, %d, %d\n", 1, 2, 3);
```

This will output:

```
Count 1, 2, 3
```

Now if we wanted to make sure these would be nicely justified when numbers larger than 10 were listed, we might do this:

```
Clib.printf("Count %4.4d, %4.4d, %4.4d\n", 1, 2, 3);
```

Now the output is justified into zero leading 4 digit values:

```
Count 0001, 0002, 0003
```

This is a lot easier than building strings, adding leading zeros and trimming the front of the string off until they are the right length.

Keyboard Capture and Macros

All of the usual support for keyboard capture that you expect to have available in the C language is available within ScriptEase. These function calls will be useful for this sort of thing:

Code example	Description
`var passwordCharacter = Clib.getch();`	Get a character without echo.
`var readInputStreamChar = Clib.getchar();`	Get next character from standard input.
`var menuSelection = Clib.getche();`	Get a character with echo.
`var userName = Clib.gets();`	Get a string terminated by a return key.

`if (Clib.kbhit())`
`{`
`  // Read the keyboard as above`
`}`
	Check to see if there are any keystrokes to fetch. This is useful to prevent a blocking action.

Remote JavaScript

ScriptEase comes with built in socket handlers. OK, maybe if you haven't done hardcore socket listeners and talkers in C language, you might not appreciate just what a miracle this neat socket support is.

Now if I hadn't seen it with my own eyes, I would not have believed it was possible to implement a web server inside a JavaScript interpreter. However, the `httpd.jse` sample code does just that.

It uses socket listeners to implement the server side and even forks child processes to handle multiple requests. Now that is very impressive. It's this hard:

```
var new_sock = sockaccept(sock,loc);

if( Unix.fork() )
{
  // Parent side of fork handler
  closesocket(new_sock);
  continue;
}
else
{
  // Child side of fork handler
  handle_request(new_sock,loc);
  closesocket(new_sock);
  Clib.exit(0);
}
```

That's it. Well there are a few bells-and-whistles but you can build servers and clients to talk to one another remotely, very easily.

To gain access to this functionality requires that you link in the compiled socket library like this somewhere near the top of your script:

```
#link "sesock"
```

Thereafter you can do similar things in your own projects.

An Example Using Distributed Scripting Protocol

ScriptEase Desktop has a Distributed Scripting Protocol (DSP) that allows one computer to run scripts on, not from, another computer. The core of DSP is implemented in a library file, sedsp.dll, with enhanced routines that are defined in idsp.jsh and dspfile.jsh. The Internet DSP (iDSP) will be discussed first. Then DSP using files will be discussed in comparison to iDSP. One nice feature about iDSP and DSP is that they use the same routines and syntax, the only difference is in initial code, which establishes communication between a server and a client.

In general, Distributed Scripting Protocol – iDSP or DSP with files – allows a computer to run scripts on another computer. Communication between a DSP server and a DSP client is bi-directional and scripts can be executed on both computers. As an example of how DSP could be used in a network, suppose that you wanted to run scripts and programs on multiple computers, all under the control of one computer that would schedule and coordinate the activities of all computers. The controlling computer could send ScriptEase commands, even complete scripts, to other computers. Responses could be received, even ScriptEase commands to run on the controlling computer. Such control is not limited to a local area network (LAN), but can be done across the Internet. Of course, DSP with files is limited to a network in which files can be accessed in shared directories.

The iDSP Interface

Internet Distributed Scripting Protocol is more robust than Distributed Scripting Protocol, which relies on files, and is recommended for more serious work. iDSP uses sockets which means that a server can respond to multiple clients connecting to it. DSP uses files and can only work with one client at a time.

An iDSP Server

The following script, idspsrvr.jse, is a simple script that begins a server for distributed scripting. The entire server is implemented in less than twenty JavaScript statements, and these statements include informational and error messages. The comments in the script explain the details of running the script. After running the script, the computer waits for connections and JavaScript statements from client scripts. Remember, the port assignments for servers and clients must match. The easiest strategy is to use the default value, that is, do not specify a port for the server or client.

To execute this script on a Windows system, tell the interpreter its name and also the port number it needs to listen on for internet connections. Like this:

```
sewin32.exe idspsrvr.jse [port]
```

If you omit the port number, the script will use a default value (Port 1066) which is defined in the idsp.jsh file. This script will start up an iDSP server on the specified port and service any incoming connections until they are closed. The script will allow any commands to be executed, so it should not be used in security-sensitive situations. The script will run until the user cancels the script with a *Ctrl-C*. Here are some examples. Start iDSP server on default port 1066:

```
sewin32.exe idspsrvr.jse
```

Start iDSP server, specifying the default port:

```
secon32.exe idspsrvr.jse 1066
```

Start iDSP server, specifying another port. If the default is not used, then the client script must specify the same port as the server is listening on:

```
secon32.exe idspsrvr.jse 1011
```

Here is the script:

```
#include "idsp.jsh"

function main(argc, argv)
{
  // Get port to which to listen or use default port
  var port = (argv[1]) ? Number(argv[1]) : DEFAULT_IDSP_PORT;

  // Establish connection and get new DSP object
  var serverConnection = new iDSPServer(port);

  if(serverConnection == null)
  {
   // Error message if problem connecting to port
   Screen.writeln("Unable to bind to port " + port);
  }
  else
  {
   Screen.writeln("iDSP server running at " + Socket.hostName() + ":" + port);
   while(true)
   {
     // idsp.jsh: Like Socket.ready() in the Socket library.
     // Like iDSPServer.accept() except that a timeout is allowed.
     // Allows user interaction. But basically checks connection.
     while(!serverConnection.ready(250)) ;

     // idsp.jsh: Like Socket.accept() in the Socket library.
     // After the connection is verified, create an iDSP
     // object for the verified connection. This object is used
     // for now.
     var curConnection = serverConnection.accept();

     if(curConnection != null)
     {
      Screen.writeln("Incoming DSP request from " +
            curConnection.dspConnection.remoteHost());

      try
      {
        while( curConnection.dspService() ) ;
        Screen.writeln("Connection closed");
      }
      catch(error)
      {
        Screen.writeln("Connection lost: " + error);
      }
     }
   }

   // Technically, it can never get here, so this line is redundant
   serverConnection.close();
  }
}
```

When the iDSP server script first runs, it displays the following message (assuming that the computer name is main):

```
iDSP server running at main:1066
```

Now that the iDSP server script is running, you may run a client script to communicate with the server. The following client script is simple, illustrating several ways to send JavaScript statements to the server. When you run the script, you must specify the host machine using an IP or URL address.

You have another option if you are working with a network. You may assign IP addresses to machines in your network that are not visible to the Internet as a whole, that is, they are internal addresses. The IP addresses that you may use are:

```
10.0.0.0   -- 10.255.255.255
90.0.0.0   -- 90.255.255.255
172.16.0.0 -- 172.31.255.255
192.168.0.0 -- 192.168.255.255
```

You may then map computer names to these IP addresses. In Windows you may edit the hosts file in the Windows directory. For example, if you have a computer named main and if you assign it the IP address of 90.0.0.10, then you may add the following line to the hosts file:

```
90.0.0.10  main
```

After such mapping, you may use main for name of the host machine with a client script. Of course, you could skip these steps and simply use the IP address of the computer or the URL address of a computer on the Internet.

The iDSP Client

Now you can run the client script. It is called idspcli.jse and you execute it much like the server script. It has an additional parameter to indicate the host where the server script is running. Run it like this:

```
sewin32.exe idspcli.jse [host] [port]
```

The host value is the Internet address (IP/URL/Computer name) of the computer running an iDSP server script. Default is localhost. The port value is the port to which the server listens for Internet connection. Default is DEFAULT_IDSP_PORT (defined as 1066 in idsp.jsh). This must be the same as the port the server is listening on. If the server was started with a different port number, then you must use that same value here or the connection will not be made.

This script starts a connection with a computer that is running an iDSP server script. The connection is accomplished using Internet protocol. The purpose of the connection is to run ScriptEase commands on the host/server computer by means of distributed scripting. This script is quite simple and sends several simple statements to be executed on the server computer. Here are some examples of how to run it. Start iDSP client on default port 1066:

```
sewin32.exe idspcli.jse
```

Start iDSP client, specifying the default port:

```
secon32.exe idspcli.jse 1066
```

Start iDSP client, specifying another port. If the default is not used, then the server script must specify the same port:

```
secon32.exe idspcli.jse 1011
```

And here is the client script:

```
#include "idsp.jsh"

function main(argc, argv)
{
  // Get host IP/URL/Computer name and port, or defaults
  // Use the conditional operators to set host and port values
  var host = (argv[1]) ? argv[1] : "localhost";
  var port = (argv[2]) ? Number(argv[2]) : DEFAULT_IDSP_PORT;

  var connection = new iDSP(host, port);
  if(connection != null)
  {
   // If a connection is made, send the following commands

   // Display a hello message on the host/server computer
   connection.Screen.writeln("Hello from idspcli!");
   // Include write.jsh, which has enhanced write methods, and display
   // a message, using one of the methods, on the host computer.
   connection.eval(`#include "write.jsh"; Writeln("write.jsh was included");`);
   // Run multiple statments as if they were script on the host
   // computer. ScriptEase will concatenate without needing the plus signs.
   var ScriptLines =
     `Screen.writeln("This is line one");`
     `Screen.writeln("This is line two");`
     `Screen.writeln("This is line three");`;
   connection.eval(ScriptLines);
   // Execute an external program on the host computer, assuming that
   // the host computer has the program "notepad.exe".
   connection.SElib.spawn(P_NOWAIT, "notepad.exe");

   // Close this current connection. The host will continue to listen
   // to port for other connections/scripts.
   connection.dspClose();
  }
  else
  {
   // Show error message
   throw "Unable to connect to " + host + ":" + port;
  }
}
```

When this script is run, it connects and displays the following lines of text on the host computer (assuming that the client script is run on a computer with an IP address of 90.0.0.11):

```
Incoming DSP request from 90.0.0.11
Hello from idspcli!
write.jsh was included
This is line one
This is line two
This is line three
Connection closed
```

741

Before the connection is actually closed, the application `notepad.exe` is run on the host computer. Before looking at some of the details, remember that the host is not simply carrying out some DSP commands. ScriptEase statements are actually being run on the host computer, statements from a client computer.

In this illustration, simple statements are used that are executed on the host computer. It is possible to send entire script files from a client to a server to run as if they were files on the host. It is also possible for the server to send statements and data back to the client. But this illustration is simple by design. The first line is produced by the server with information about which client has connected. The second line of display is done by the DSP statement:

```
connection.Screen.writeln("Hello from idspcli!");
```

The identifier connection is a DSP object. Normal ScriptEase methods become methods of the DSP object. Any method in ScriptEase may be passed to the host computer by attaching it to the DSP object as a method. Objects and methods that are part of the global space of the remote machine are available locally as methods of the DSP object. The third line of display is produced by the following statement:

```
connection.eval(`#include "write.jsh"; Writeln("write.jsh was included");`);
```

We use the `eval()` statement to go beyond sending methods only. In this line, we use the enhanced function `Writeln()` to display the line of text. So we have to include `write.jsh` to use the function. The problem is that `#include` is a preprocessor directive. By using `eval()`, we are able to use such pre-processor directives. Another approach would be to have the server script itself include all library files that might be used. If the server script were to include `write.jsh` when it is first run, then the following line would be appropriate:

```
connection.Writeln("write.jsh was included");
```

The fourth, fifth, and sixth lines are displayed by assigning multiple statements to one variable and then using `eval()` which runs each of the statements. A similar technique could be used with an entire standalone script file. Further, ScriptEase has a function, `SElib.interpret()`, which is more robust than `eval()`. You might find yourself using the `interpret()` method instead of `eval()`.

The last line of the display indicates that the current connection on the port is closed. But the last statement passed from the client to the host, before closing the connection, is:

```
connection.SElib.spawn(P_NOWAIT, "notepad.exe");
```

Before the connection is closed, the `notepad.exe` application is started. You may start any application on a host, as shown here, and pass parameters to the application being run. Parameters would simply follow the application name.

DSP, as implemented in ScriptEase, is powerful and simple with capabilities far beyond these illustrations. But, these scripts illustrate some basic essentials.

The DSP Interface

As stated above, DSP with files and iDSP use the same statements and syntax. The only difference is in making the initial connection by use of files or Internet protocol. When a connection is made, by either method, a DSP object is defined. All subsequent operations are done with this object.

DSP with files has two significant limitations. First, the performance is a bit slower. Second, a server can connect and work properly only with one client at a time. But, for simple use, DSP with files might be a better choice.

For comparison purposes, a DSP server and a DSP client script are shown below. These scripts accomplish the same things as the scripts shown for iDSP. The only differences are in how the server and client connect and in the loop used to keep the DSP server alive after a connection is closed. The comments following the code explain the details of using the scripts.

A DSP Server

This script is called dspsrvr.jse and contains the server end code. This script is very simple, largely for illustrative purposes. You run it like this:

```
sewin32.exe dspsrvr.jse [infile] [outfile]
```

There are two parameters:

❑ The infile value is a file specification, complete path specification, or UNC specification. That is, infile may be a filespec, pathspec, or network file. The parameter infile specifies the file from which the server receives statements to execute. These statements are sent to the server script from client scripts. The infile for the server script corresponds to the outfile for the client.

❑ The outfile value is also a file specification, complete path specification, or UNC specification. That is, outfile may be a filespec, pathspec, or network file. The parameter outfile specifies the file to which the server writes statements to be received by a client script. The outfile for the server corresponds to the infile for the client.

Description: a generic server script run on a host computer using files to communicate with client computers; file DSP is simple and useful on a local area network, but is not as robust as Internet DSP; the server remains running until *Ctrl-C* is pressed.

Note the infile and outfile parameters for both the dspsrvr.jse and dspcli.jse scripts. These files need to correspond. The server infile corresponds to the client outfile, and the server outfile corresponds to the client infile. That is, output from one script is input for the other. Though both the server and the client specify two files, they are the same two files, that is, only two files are created. These files must be accessible by both the server and the client. Although they appear to be files, they are connected across the network so there is no contention over multiple processes having the same files open.

This script differs from its iDSP counterparts in that this script uses files to pass information and the iDSP scripts use Internet protocol to pass information.

Here are some examples of how to run the script. In our examples we assume that the host computer is main. The interpreter executable is omitted at the beginnings of the command line examples (see syntax above).

Firstly start the file DSP server using files in the root directory of drive c: of the host computer:

```
dspsrvr.jse c:\dspsrvr.in c:\dspsrvr.out
```

The following command line arguments would use a common directory on a computer named main in a network.

```
dspsrvr.jse \\main\common\dspsrvr.in \\main\common\dspsrvr.out
```

When we get to the client script, the examples in dspcli.jse correspond with these. The DSP server script follows:

```
#include "dspfile.jsh"

function main(argc, argv)
{
  // Get the in and out filespecs passed on the command line
  var filFromClient = (argv[2]) ? argv[2] : "dspsrvr.in";
  var filToClient  = (argv[1]) ? argv[1] : "dspsrvr.out";

  while (true)
  {
   // Establish connection and get new DSP object
   var serverConnection = new fileDSP(filFromClient, filToClient);

   if(serverConnection != null)
   {
     while(serverConnection.dspService());
   }
  }
}
```

A DSP Client

Now let's examine the client end script to use with this server. It is called dspcli.jse and runs with this syntax:

```
sewin32.exe dspcli.jse [infile] [outfile]
```

It has similar input/output files to the server. The infile value is a file specification, complete path specification, or UNC specification. That is, infile may be a filespec, pathspec, or network file. The parameter infile specifies the file from which the client receives statements. These statements are sent to the client script from server scripts. The infile for the client script corresponds to the outfile for the server.

The outfile value is another file specification, similar to the infile. The parameter outfile specifies the file to which the client writes statements to be received by a server script. The outfile for the client corresponds to the infile for a server.

Description: a client script run on a computer using files to communicate with a host.

Here are some example startup commands that correspond with the examples used to start the server. In our examples we, again, assume that the host computer is main. The interpreter executable is omitted at the beginnings of the command line examples (see syntax above).

First start a file DSP client using files in the root directory of drive c: of the host computer:

```
dspcli.jse \\main\c\dspsrvr.out \\main\c\dspsrvr.in
```

The following command line arguments would use a common directory on a computer named main in a network:

```
dspcli.jse \\main\common\dspsrvr.out \\main\common\dspsrvr.in
```

The DSP client script follows:

```
#include "dspfile.jsh"

function main(argc, argv)
{
   // Get the in and out filespecs passed on the command line
   var filFromServer = (argv[1]) ? argv[1] : "dspsrvr.out";
   var filToServer   = (argv[2]) ? argv[2] : "dspsrvr.in";

   // Establish connection and get new DSP object
   var connection = new fileDSP(filFromServer, filToServer);
   if(connection != null)
   {
    // If a connection is made, send the following commands

    // Display a hello message on the host/server computer
    connection.Screen.writeln("Hello from dspcli!");
    // Include write.jsh, which has enhanced write methods, and display
    // a message, using one of the methods, on the host computer.
    connection.eval(`#include "write.jsh"; Writeln("write.jsh was included");`);
    // Run multiple statments as if they were script on the host
    // computer. ScripEase concatenates the strings withbout the plus sign.
    var ScriptLines =
       `Screen.writeln("This is line one");`
       `Screen.writeln("This is line two");`
       `Screen.writeln("This is line three");`;
    connection.eval(ScriptLines);
    // Execute an external program on the host computer, assuming that
    // the host computer has the program "notepad.exe".
    connection.SElib.spawn(P_NOWAIT, "notepad.exe");

    // Close this file connection
    connection.dspClose();
   }
}
```

All of the descriptions about the statements in iDSP scripts also apply here, to the DSP scripts.

Observations on DSP and iDSP

This section about Distributed Scripting Protocol, as implemented in ScriptEase, demonstrates several things. First, distributed scripting is a simple, powerful, and useful tool to use with computers on a network or the Internet. Second, the DSP object for connections shows how simple, powerful, and useful objects are as implemented in JavaScript. Third, ScriptEase has very useful extensions implemented in objects, such as, Screen and SElib, as shown in these scripts.

One last observation. In a multitasking operating system, such as, Win32, you may run these scripts without command line arguments or with them, if you provide the correct information. You must run the server and client scripts from separate DOS sessions or as separate command lines to Windows. You may develop and tests DSP scripts on one machine. If you are working with DSP with files and are using the defaults, then the server and client scripts must be in the same directory.

Summary

In this chapter we've very briefly explored the capabilities of ScriptEase Desktop Edition and looked at an example piece of code developed in it.

ScriptEase is a profoundly useful tool and because it is available in so many different contexts (Embeddable, CGI, Desktop, Shell scripting) you can achieve great reusability with the scripts you develop for it.

ScriptEase Desktop is just one of a number of tools and technologies available to ease the pains of script building and ensuring that the resultant script is portable. What you use will probably be determined by the availability, ease of use, price, results achievable, and progression that the product allows. ScriptEase Desktop scores well on all these counts, but it may or may not be your cup of tea. We would advise that you try as many of the tools available before deciding which, if any, suits you.

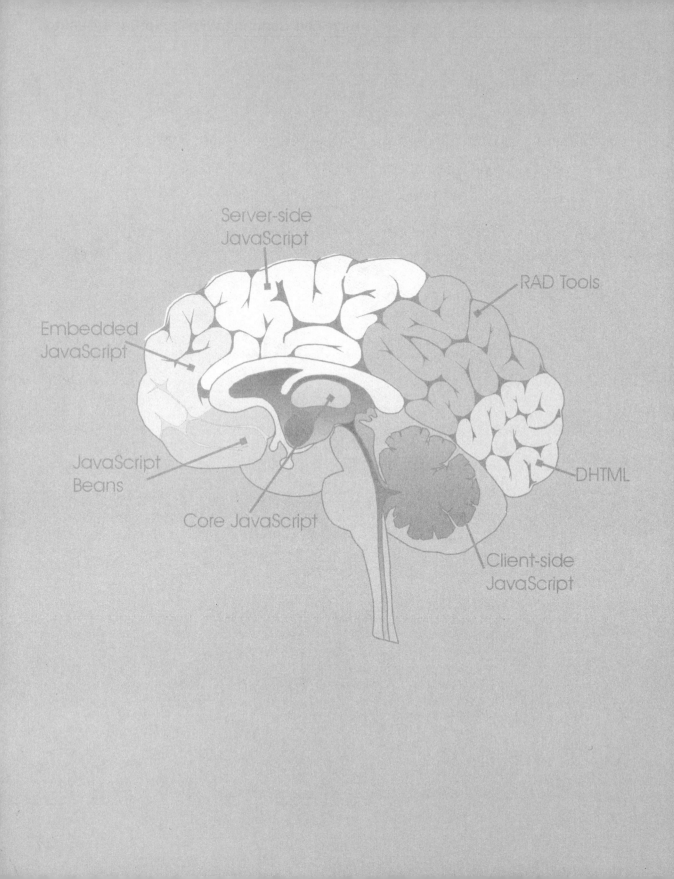

Embedded JavaScript

Who, Why and What For?

This chapter is aimed at developers who would like to deploy JavaScript as part of their existing applications. You may have a legacy product that requires some automation and JavaScript can be an effective way to add capabilities that your end users will find accessible due to the language already being familiar.

Why would you want to embed a JavaScript interpreter in an application? Well clearly, embedding one into a browser allows you to execute client-side JavaScript that is delivered inside the received HTML or is referred to and included. Either way, the server supplies some JavaScript that gets executed inside the browser.

Certainly there are limitations to what you are able to do in the context of a web browser. These limitations, however, are not technical. The client side JavaScript interpreter is purposely inhibited to prevent an attack on your computer by a malicious intruder. Imagine if it were possible to download a page of JavaScript that could overwrite any file on your system. The same limitations are imposed on Java applets too.

This means that, in some contexts, it may be quite appropriate to allow JavaScript scripts to have access to the rest of the machine's resources. You may still want to impose some access controls so that the scripts are executed under the normal security regime you impose.

On a server, you might allow certain users to access particular directories but not others. Server-side JavaScript interpreters need to operate within this security model.

It may be very useful to provide script execution facilities inside your own applications. This can be useful regardless of whether you are deploying networked applications or web servers.

Scripting is a helpful way of automating all kinds of activities. It may also be a way to develop bespoke application software within a basic framework. You could build a toolkit of useful components and call them under control of a script to realize a finished one-off custom application for example.

This chapter will look at some of the various implementations you can download and try for yourself. Where possible, some examples of how they are installed and used are also presented.

Embed What Inside What?

When we talk about embedding JavaScript, what exactly do we mean? What gets embedded in what? Just installing a JavaScript interpreter on a server may be sufficient. For other solutions, binding the interpreter tightly into your application's infrastructure may be appropriate or even necessary. In that situation, you might hold the JavaScript to be executed in a buffer somewhere in memory. It is run by telling the interpreter where it is so it can parse and execute the script content.

Some JavaScript interpreters are written in other languages, so your choice of interpreter may require that you build other software into your application as well to support the JavaScript interpreter.

You may find that a ready to run solution is easiest to implement and that to use it you need to be able to spawn sub-processes or connect to a persistent process via a socket.

The particular architecture you choose will be dictated by the facilities you need. Perhaps only one of the embeddable interpreters provides a critical feature that you simply have to have. That interpreter may need to run in a particular way and, therefore, the technology choices are made for you. On the other hand licensing issues may determine what you are able to ship as part of your product. All of these factors will affect the way you embed a JavaScript interpreter into your product.

Some interpreters let you embed JavaScript inside Perl while you could also embed Perl calls inside JavaScript. On the basis that scripts in one language could potentially request execution of scripts in any other, this could get very confusing.

JavaScript Interpreters

There are a variety of JavaScript interpreters available. Because this is a popular development area at present, there may be new product offerings appearing more frequently. Of course, in this book we are focussing on JavaScript and some of the recent innovations are deploying JavaScript where previously you might have used other technologies. This doesn't render them obsolete but provides you with an alternative. There are also add-on technologies that allow you to integrate JavaScript with other languages and tools.

What's Out There?

Here are a few examples (including additional integration technologies as well). We will give each one just a brief introduction before we start to explore them in detail:

JSRef Library

This is the Netscape reference implementation of JavaScript. Subject to licensing under the Netscape Public License, there is a great deal you can do with this interpreter. It is the basic engine that is used inside the Mozilla browser, which you will know already as Netscape Navigator. If you also embed it into a server side application the same JavaScript interpreter can be deployed server side and client side if this is important to your application.

You can integrate this interpreter with Perl through the PerlConnect interface and Java through the LiveConnect interface.

More resources for this interpreter are available at this URL:
`http://lxr.mozilla.org/mozilla/source/js/src/`.

LiveConnect

Server-side JavaScript applications can be connected to Java components or classes on the server using LiveConnect. And, using Java, connection to CORBA-compliant distributed objects is possible, giving further extensibility. More information about LiveConnect can be found at:
`http://developer.netscape.com/tech/javascript/index.html`.
More detail on LiveConnect can be found under 'Integrating JSRef With Java'.

PerlConnect

Mozilla's site says, "PerlConnect provides glue for the developer between JavaScript and Perl. It currently consists of two parts, PerlConnect implemented in C and JS.pm, a Perl module written using XSUBs. PerlConnect and JS.pm allow calling Perl from JS and JS from Perl, respectively. Whenever possible, it is attempted to achieve the maximum level of transparency for calling one language from the other. This is done by converting values between the two languages, creating wrappers around objects, and emulating the standard language syntax." This and more can be found at: `http://lxr.mozilla.org/mozilla/source/js/src/perlconnect/README.html#66` 'Integrating JSRef With Perl' has more on PerlConnect.

ScriptEase

ScriptEase is a versatile JavaScript interpreter core that is available in a variety of different configurations. It is available for embedding into your own applications in the form of an Integration Software Developer Kit (ISDK). It is also available as a desktop automation tool for both Macintosh, and Windows. Actually, it is available to automate other desktops too but these are likely the most popular. Finally, it is available as a CGI based web server back end for dynamically generating pages. Chapter 12 discusses this Web Server Edition (WSE) in great detail and the Desktop version is covered in Chapter 21.

Chapter 22

FESI

FESI (Free ECMAScript interpreter) is a JavaScript interpreter written in Java, not in the native format of your computer. Applications written in Java are easily accessible using FESI. While its use is restricted to those tasks that are purely Java, it benefits from the portability of the Java language. FESI is a free tool, provided you give the author credit. Its source is also freely available to inspect. FESI can be downloaded from: `http://home.worldcom.ch/~jmlugrin/fesi/index.html`. FESI implementation is covered in Chapter 16.

Rhino

This takes a script and compiles it into Java byte codes and executes the script as Java. Like FESI, this means that the potential range of platforms you can reach is generally quite wide. Since this interpreter is derived in part from the release of the Netscape source code under an open source agreement, you should check the Netscape Public License if you plan to ship a product that includes Rhino. You will need to comply with the licensing terms therein, although they aren't that difficult to cope with under most circumstances. There may be licensing stipulations that limit the use of Rhino in certain applications. For example, it may be harder to obtain permission to build a standalone interpreter than to use Rhino in an embedded product and there may also be limitations on redistributing the source code. Rhino is available at this URL: `http://www.mozilla.org/rhino/`.

NGS

This is a JavaScript interpreter available under the GNU Public License arrangements. That means you get the full source and can modify it, as you need. At present this implementation is not 100% compatible with the JavaScript language standard. It is still a work in progress development project but nevertheless may provide the functionality you need.

The home page for the NGS JavaScript interpreter where you'll find the install kit and documentation is at this location: `http://www.ngs.fi/js/`. NGS is also available at this URL: `http://www.debian.org/Packages/stable/interpreters/ngs-js.html`.

Microsoft WSH

Microsoft calls this a universal scripting host for scripting languages. In that sense, it's perhaps similar to the Open Scripting Architecture on the Macintosh platform. Both provide a framework within which script interpreters can run. Neither do anything on their own.

The Microsoft Windows Script Host (WSH) is a tool that will allow you to run JScript natively within the base operating system. It will also support Visual Basic Scripting Edition code. It is aimed at users of Windows 95 or Windows NT primarily. Using scripting languages you are already familiar with, from other environments and contexts, you can now automate common tasks to create more powerful macros and logon scripts for your systems. WSH has been available at version 1.0 for some time. As new versions of Windows are shipped, WSH is becoming more widely available without you needing to install it yourself. Version 2.0 is becoming available in beta form at the time of writing. The new version will add more features and deal with some of the difficulties that users have encountered with the earlier version. Resources for WSH are at this URL: `http://msdn.microsoft.com/scripting`. Read Chapter 20 for in-depth WSH coverage.

JScript Library

JScript is a script interpreter based on JavaScript. It's available from Microsoft and is shipped as an integral part of the Windows Script Host and Internet Explorer. However, it is also available as a separate item that can be embedded within your own applications. Both JScript and VBScript are available either as a ready to run binary or as source code. The conditions for using them in a ready to run binary form are that you include a mention of Microsoft in your application's copyrights message. A license agreement with Microsoft is necessary to obtain the source code for JScript or VBScript. One alternative to shipping the interpreter yourself is to build in the necessary hooks to the interpreter and encourage your end users to download the binaries from the Microsoft web site. JScript resources are at: `http://msdn.microsoft.com/scripting`.

Microsoft Scriptlets

It is understandable that people sometimes get confused between WSH and Microsoft Scriptlets and think they are the same thing – Scriptlets are not WSH scripts. Scriptlets are used for making HTML from XML and JavaScript. The more recent version can also make ActiveX components. In IE5, Scriptlets are called HTML Components (or HTCs for short). They aren't used for desktop automation, which is one of the primary goals for WSH. WSH scripts are genuinely standalone scripts, perhaps very like shell scripts in a lot of ways.

A very informative discussion on what Scriptlets are and how they work can be found at: `http://msdn.microsoft.com/workshop/languages/clinic/xmlscript.asp`.

JSRef Library

This is the reference implementation available from Netscape. You will most likely encounter this when it is already embedded into a web server.

The sources are available to build the interpreter as a library. All sources from Netscape are likely to fall under the general terms of the Netscape Public License. You should consult this first of all to see whether the embedding you plan complies with the terms of that license. The license can be viewed online at: `http://www.mozilla.org/NPL/`.

JSRef Server Side Context

The server side implementation of JSRef JavaScript is accomplished by compiling the JavaScript into byte codes that are then executed through a run-time engine in the web server.

The starting point is the static HTML that would arrive in the client browser. Then, those parts that need to be dynamically generated are replaced with server side JavaScript code enclosed in `<SERVER></SERVER>` tags. These would be scattered throughout the HTML file wherever you wanted to generate HTML at run-time.

The file is then compiled into the byte code format and executed in the run-time system when the user calls it. The result is some dynamically generated HTML with the `<SERVER></SERVER>` tags replaced by content generated by the JavaScript code.

Obtaining The Sources

You can download the source for this from Netscape at this URL:
http://lxr.mozilla.org/mozilla/source/js/src/.

This source will build a library or DLL containing the JavaScript run-time support. This includes the following:

- ❏ Compiler
- ❏ Interpreter
- ❏ Decompiler
- ❏ Garbage collector
- ❏ Atom manager
- ❏ Standard classes

When you build the kit, the resulting binaries include a small JavaScript shell environment that you can use to test your scripts.

Building JSRef

The build kit provides support for building JSRef on the following platforms:

Windows

The build kit is compatible with Microsoft Visual C version 4.2 or 5.0 and comes with the necessary .mdp files to build the projects. If you are using Visual C version 6.0, the Integrated Development Environment (IDE) will convert the project from the older versions. An additional makefile.win provides a means to build the JS-engine for use in the Mozilla browser but it should not be used to build the standalone JS-engine. Command line building is also supported. The resulting binaries are an executable shell called js.exe and a run-time library called js32.dll. Both of these may be created as debug or released code versions.

Macintosh

The build kit for the Apple Macintosh platform requires Code Warrior 3.x although later versions of Code Warrior should convert the project files as needed when you try and load them. The building instructions are quite straightforward. Simply load the project file and select Make from the menu.

UNIX

Building JSRef on UNIX is accomplished with gmake. As is the case with Windows, there are make files to build the embedded JS-engine for the Mozilla browser as well as the standalone. Makefile.ref is the correct one to use for the standalone. On UNIX, you need to install a configuration file with a .mk extension into the js/src/config directory. This specifies the compiler and linker to be used during the make. It also allows the command line options to be customized. The following UNIX variants are supported:

- Solaris

- AIX

- HP-UX

- OSF

- IRIX

- x86 Linux

For most platforms, you can either use the vendor-supplied compiler or the publicly available gcc compiler. This is not an alternative on HP-UX however because gcc won't link correctly with shared libraries on that platform. This may change in a later revision of gcc.

It is possible to configure the make process to automatically build a LiveConnect installation at the same time.

Windows NT

According to the JSRef documentation, the Windows NT build kit operates in the same way as the UNIX kit.

For further information, consult the documentation supplied with the JSRef sources for other build options and the latest details of platform availability.

Accessing The JSRef API

Because JSRef is implemented in the C language, embedding it into a C based application is probably the easiest of all the target embeds. However, as long as the compiler and linker you use are compatible at the object code level and provided you make sure that you pass arguments correctly, you can bind this to code written in any language. Arguments are passed by value or by reference. Passing by reference means a pointer to the value or a variable that contains it, or even a function that would return the passed in value. Results being returned to the caller need to have a receiving variable passed by reference or pointer to an expression evaluation where the value can be written.

Access to API calls is via public function names. There is a convention that these are all prefaced with upper case JS_ and the remainder of the name has capitalized **intercaps**. For example:

- `JS_Init()`

- `JS_NewObject()`

- `JS_NewContext()`

Macros are in ALL_CAPS, which is a commonplace convention that you will already be familiar with.

DLL entry points have supporting macro calls to set the Windows secret type qualifiers up correctly. Similarly, callbacks from DLLs are also wrapped in macros. Windows programmers used to working with DLL based implementations should find all the information they need in the documentation.

The JSRef source documentation also describes other naming conventions that you may need to be aware of.

In the source kit, an example framework that initializes the API and shows some example functions is a good starting point for embedding the interpreter in your own application. Bear in mind that because this is a starting point, you may need to do more or less than this depending on the complexity of your embedding requirements. Here is an outline of the basic requirements:

Starting Up

You need to consider tuning the parameters in the startup code to avoid memory wastage. The exact details depend on what you plan to do with the scripts that are run through the interpreter. The factor that most affects this is the depth of nested code you plan to support or whether the stack is extremely fluid and changing a great deal.

At startup, you need to initialize the engine, create a context, make a global object and add the standard classes to it. There is API support to do all this with simple calls from your application.

Defining Objects and Properties

There are facilities to create one-off objects, enumerators and switch case support. After constructing them, accessor methods for generic properties need to be set-up. Again the API provides helpful support for this.

Defining Functions

Next, if you need them, you will create native functions, build an array of them and set them up on your global object.

Defining Classes

Using the global object, the initialization so far is connected up with a constructor function, a prototype object, properties of that object and of the construction. This is done with a single call to a class initializer provided by the API.

Running Scripts

At this point we are ready to execute a script. The script should be contained in a C string. That is an array of bytes with a terminating NULL character. You can use larger non-null terminated buffers if you pass the length in. The hard work is done in the JS_EvaluateScript() function via the API.

Calling Functions Directly

Function calls are supported via the JS_CallFunctionName() API routine. This uses the look up information you provided during the setup to dispatch the call to the right method and of course you indicate the object to which you want the message directed as an argument to this call.

Shutting Down

When you have finished, you should shut the JS engine down in an orderly manner. This is quite simple and requires that you destroy each context you created during startup and then call a finish mechanism in the API to clean up at the end.

Debugging Support

There is a debugging API but it may be subject to revision. You should consult the documentation for up to date information on the debugging support. At this stage, debugging provides traps, watch points and line number to program counter mappings which can all help you to locate spurious lines of JavaScript as it is executed.

Integrating JSRef With Perl

If your project requires it, you can integrate JSRef with Perl using the PerlConnect and JS.pm modules. This is what we might call 'glueware'. PerlConnect is implemented in C language and JS.pm is a Perl module written using XSUBs. Using these two components, you can call Perl code from JavaScript or JavaScript from Perl. Both of these modules achieve a high degree of transparency by converting values between the two languages, constructing object wrappers and emulating the standard language syntax.

The Perl interpreter is created inside the JavaScript environment and then passing it Perl code to be executed via an eval() method. This is a neat 'Piggyback Embedding' trick. Although you can apparently instantiate more than one Perl interpreter, the PerlConnect implementation actually only runs a single instance internally. So you could do something like this:

```
perl_interp_1 = new Perl;
perl_interp_2 = new Perl;
perl_interp_1.eval("$a=20")
```

This created two Perl interpreters but executed an eval() on only one of them. Because there is only one instance, both perl_interp_1["$a"] and perl_interp_2["$a"] will yield the same result.

The PerlConnect documentation describes more examples of how you can build complex Perl scripts and execute them through the eval() interface.

Using JS.pm from Perl is just as straightforward and uses a very similar eval() syntax in the Perl context. For more details, refer to the documentation at: http://lxr.mozilla.org/mozilla/source/js/src/perlconnect/

Integrating JSRef With Java

LiveConnect is a library that allows JavaScript and Java virtual machines to interact with one another. It allows JavaScript to access Java fields and invoke Java methods. From the other direction, it allows Java code to access JavaScript object properties and evaluate arbitrary JavaScript code.

This was originally an integrated part of the Netscape Navigator browser and JavaScript support but now it is available as a standalone library. That means it can be embedded into other projects more easily.

Live connect is available for the same range of platforms as the JSRef libraries.

To use LiveConnect with your existing Java installation you need to update the CLASSPATH variable to point to the js/src/liveconnect/classes sub-directory. This is necessary to ensure objects can be exchanged between the two environments. If the CLASSPATH variable is not set correctly you can test for it by running a debug build version of LiveConnect and watching for an initialization error. If there is a problem you should see this message:

Initialization error: Can't load class netscape/JavaScript/JSObject

There are some things that remain an area of weakness in this integration. They are gradually being addressed as LiveConnect is revised. You should still be aware of the limitations though because they may affect the sort of things you allow your embedded scripts to do. There are also some useful enhancements that are available only in the latest version of LiveConnect. If you are using older versions you may want to upgrade to revision 3 or later of LiveConnect. Here are some areas you should consider carefully:

Windows Builds

When building LiveConnect on Windows, there are several alternate build systems. The Integrated Development Environment (IDE) build system is less complete but provides more facilities for debugging. The gmake build system is more complete because it builds the necessary Java classes as well as the LiveConnect binaries.

Thread Safe Builds

By default when you build LiveConnect on any platform it is not thread safe. If you need a thread safe build, there are a special set of headers and libraries that you must use. These can be downloaded from the Mozilla web site and are discussed in the LiveConnect documentation. There are also configuration parameters that you need to define to complete the build.

Ambiguity When Invoking Java Methods From JavaScript

Versions of LiveConnect prior to revision 3 had some difficulty in consistently connecting to the required overloaded method. It depended on locating the first available matching method in the Java reflection API's. There is no specification for the ordering of methods when they are enumerated in this way and it meant that different JVM implementations might yield a different method. The rules have been enhanced and no longer depend on the position a method takes up in an enumerated set. There is still some potential ambiguity but it is much more reliable and not affected by differences in the underlying JVM implementations.

Ambiguity Between Data Types

Even with the improved overloaded method resolution techniques, the JavaScript number data type can map to Java methods containing floating-point or integral types. JavaScript will see Java byte, char, short, int, long, float, and double as the all-inclusive number type. To work round this, it may be necessary to bypass the method overload resolution process altogether and explicitly specify the method to be invoked.

Static Method Linking

Older versions of LiveConnect could only be invoked using the class name. Now, you can invoke them as class or instance methods.

String Data Type Conversion

It used to be necessary to convert Java strings to JS strings before using them as receivers of JavaScript string methods. This was normally accomplished by appending an empty string. The interface handles this more effectively now and this coercion is not required any more. Now `java.langString` objects and their sub-classes inherit all the methods of JavaScript strings. You are now able to use them like this:

```
str = new java.lang.StringBuffer("Drink Java!");
str.insert(6, "Hot ");
```

The string buffer variable `str` now contains the text `Drink Hot Java!`

Array Conversion

`JavaArray` objects inherit the methods of the JavaScript `Array.prototype` in the same way. This allows you to apply many (but not all) of the JavaScript utility methods to `JavaArray` objects.

Performance Issues

There is still some ongoing work required to improve performance. There are issues with calling Java methods with respect to the handling of private data in `JSFunction` objects. Future versions of LiveConnect will be more efficient.

Another issue is to do with hash table access to Java objects from within JavaScript. This is related to the intricacies of thread handling.

Some reference counting mechanisms can lead to garbage collection being unable to remove `JavaSclassDescriptors` when they are no longer needed. This happens relatively rarely, but for they may not be freed until `JSJ_Shutdown()` is called.

There are some shortcomings in the handling of global variables when used with multiple JVMs.

Garbage collection can have problems when a JavaScript object refers to a Java object that refers back to a JavaScript object. Because the two environments manage garbage collection independently, there can be issues that prevent objects being collected.

ScriptEase ISDK

The ScriptEase Integration SDK is a means of embedding an ECMA-compliant JavaScript interpreter into your application for whatever scripting purposes you desire.

ScriptEase is also available as a desktop automation system and a back end web server CGI driven dynamic page generator. It's effective and useful in both of those roles. The SDK gives you a third way to deploy the interpreter.

The documentation for this product is impressive. The manual for the SDK alone is some 350 pages long with other similar sized manuals for the web server edition and the desktop version.

Platforms Supported

SE:ISDK is available on a range of platforms and the manufacturers (Nombas Inc.) are keen to support other platforms on an as requested basis.

Currently, it is available on:

- ❑ DOS
- ❑ OS/2
- ❑ Windows 16 bit
- ❑ Windows 32 bit
- ❑ Macintosh
- ❑ A variety of UNIX environments

Ease Of Integration

Each set of library file sources includes a set of sample applications demonstrating how to integrate the SDK. In addition, since you get the sources, you can make modifications yourself and, even without writing custom additions, there are a range of compiler-time pre-processor options that you can use to turn various functionality on and off when you build the ISDK libraries.

Integrating With Other Languages

The ScriptEase Integration SDK is intended for use with C or C++ based systems. However, if your build system is object code compatible, then you can integrate this with other language developments as long as you have a reliable calling and argument passing mechanism. This usually means that you need to be able to call functions by addresses and pass arguments by reference. In some languages, this might require that you wrap the calls and arguments in conversion functions.

New Features In The Latest Release

The latest release is version 4.10 and supports these new features:

Implicit Parents

By setting a flag using an attributes function, the `this` variable will inherit from parents which are searched recursively as the scope chain is created from the current object up to the global object at the head of the chain.

Operator Overloading

This is enhanced to support new types. For example, you can now add two complex numbers together as if they were simple scalar variables. Likewise, you can now perform matrix operations and complex algebraic computations.

Updates To The Libraries

The ISDK (and in fact all the other ScriptEase products) contain a large and rich set of libraries to provide additional functionality. These have been enhanced.

Uppercase Keywords Are Now Abolished

Previous versions allowed some uppercase variants of keywords to be parsed. This is no longer permitted and in compliance with the ECMAScript directives.

Additional Flags

Several new flags have been added to the environment to allow the environment and behaviors to be modified. These mostly affect calling conventions internally and externally.

Additional Functions In The API

Variable searches, Boolean handling, string table management and callback mechanisms all benefit from new functionality.

Deprecated Functions and Structures

Some older functionality has been superceded by new API facilities. The old function calls are preserved for backward compatibility but should no longer be used.

Building The ISDK

When you build the ISDK, the pre-processor options provide a way to configure the build. Generally, you would define the same pre-processor options when you build your application.

Many of these options are to do with memory management and for most of them, the ISDK will define sensible defaults. This area is often encountered in portability modules and because ScriptEase is available on such a wide variety of platforms, it has a larger than normal suite of options to set up for proper configuration.

There are also a great many options that can tailor the script execution environment to allow or disallow certain functionality. Basically, if you have deactivated features at compile time, its difficult for people to penetrate the core interpreter to 'patch in' functionality that you would prefer they didn't have. A system of run-time flags is less efficient and easier to subvert. Since you may want to use the script interpreter within a somewhat secure situation, this could be important.

Here is an outline of what you have available:

You need to define the platform the build is being targeted at. These options are built into the ISDK to control conditional compilation based on the platform type. One of these must be set to define the target. The default depends on the settings in your compiler:

- ❑ _JSE_DOS16_

- ❑ _JSE_DOS32_

- ❑ _JSE_OS2TEXT_

- ❑ _JSE_OS2PM_

- ❑ _JSE_WIN16_

- ❑ _JSE_WIN32_

- ❑ _JSE_WINCE_

- ❑ _JSE_CON32_

- ❑ _JSE_NWNLM_

- ❑ _JSE_UNIX_

- ❑ _JSE_390_

- ❑ _JSE_MAC_

- ❑ _JSE_PALMOS_

- ❑ _JSE_PSX_

The linking method is controlled by these options: one of these, if other than the default _JSE_LIB_ is required, must be set before compiling:

- ❑ _JSE_DLLLOAD_

- ❑ _JSE_DLLRUN_

- ❑ _JSE_LIB_

You need to define whether you are building the core interpreter or an application that is going to call it. The default is JSETOOLKIT_APP and the others are:

- ❑ JSETOOLKIT_APP

- ❑ JSETOOLKIT_CORE

You need to define the native number format. The value you assign to JSE_FLOATING_POINT indicates whether jsenumber supports floating point values or not. The default is floating point numbers to be supported.

You should define whether UNICODE is supported or not. By default, the UNICODE switch is on for the Windows CE platform and off for all others. This is controlled by the JSE_UNICODE value.

An area that always plagues portable software is the byte ordering within words and longer data types. This should be handled automatically by the compiler but you may need to adjust the values in JSETYPES.H to define one of the following:

- ❑ BYTE_ORDER

- ❑ _BYTE_ORDER

- ❑ BIG_ENDIAN

Another portability issue is the size of pointer values. Some systems have a 16-bit pointer size that limits the memory architecture that can be reached. Others have 32 bits. By default the pointer size is assumed to be 32 bits long. This is controlled with:

- ❑   JSE_POINTER_SIZE

- ❑   JSE_POINTER_SINT

- ❑   JSE_POINTER_UINT

Array indexing is controlled with:

- ❑   JSE_POINTER_SINDEX

- ❑   JSE_POINTER_UINDEX

There are performance gains to be had by limiting the array index value size according to the limits imposed by the memory pointer architecture.

Memory access requires that you define _NEAR_, _FAR_, NEAR_CALL and FAR_CALL appropriately.

Inter segment memory management may require that you define JSE_NO_HUGE.

A switch allows you to export/import pre-compiled scripts. This is controlled with JSE_TOKENSRC and JSE_TOKJENDST.

Security guard mechanisms are activated with JSE_SECUREJSE if needed.

If you want to enable the C-like extensions that Nombas have added to the ECMAScript language, then set JSE_C_EXTENSIONS. By default this is active anyway.

Run-time linking of external libraries is controlled by JSE_LINK and includes are controlled by JSE_INCLUDE.

Conditional execution of script lines inside pre-processor constructs can be enabled or not. This applies to the pre-processor that is invoked on the scripts as they are parsed. Whether this is available at the scripting level is controlled by the JSE_CONDITIONAL_COMPILE option.

You can choose to read script files and interpret them or to only interpret script that is in memory and loaded already. This is controlled by JSE_TOOLKIT_APPSOURCE.

ECMAScript inheritance is enabled through the JSE_PROTOTYPES option and dynamic object creation is controlled with JSE_DYNAMIC_OBS.

Parameter checking at the API level can be simple or can be more exacting. This is controlled by setting the JSE_API_ASSERTLEVEL value appropriately. The function names are included in assertion error reports depending on the setting of JSE_API_ASSERTNAMES.

The switching on of the compiler portion of the interpreter is controlled by the `JSE_COMPILER` value. This can reduce the code size and can allow you to ship an application that contains only pre-compiled scripts. The compiler simply will not interpret plain text source. This renders your application more secure and less prone to interference by end users.

If you are prepared to trade off memory, you can use inline functions (which are like C language macros). You gain performance but use more memory. Control whether this is available with `JSE_INLINES`.

You can compile to favor low memory usage at the expense of performance. The core interpreter has some sections of code that will run slower but in a smaller memory architecture. To favor memory use over speed, set the `JSE_MIN_MEMORY` option.

Since ECMAScript does not define a buffer data type, you can control the native data type of the buffer object inside ScriptEase. Set the `JSE_TYPE_BUFFER` value accordingly.

De-compiling interpreted script may be something you want to have available during development but not build into a shipping product. Its a long pre-processor option name but `JSE_CREATEFUNCTIONTEXTVARIABLE` allows you to turn de-compilation help on and off.

File name lists can be cached by setting `JSE_GETFILENAMELIST` as necessary. Discarding the list can save a small amount of memory.

Debugging can make use of breakpoint tests. This can be enabled with `JSE_BREAKPOINT_TEST` if you need it.

Memory usage can be debugged when the `JSE_MEM_DEBUG` option is set. This will considerably slow down the execution but will allow the interpreter to monitor memory usage to help you diagnose problems.

When a system is running, it allocates and frees memory areas as needed. If your interpreter needs to allocate and free many small items very quickly, the memory can become fragmented and performance will suffer as a result. You can reduce this problem by allocating larger chunks of memory and setting them up as pools within which an alternative allocate/free mechanism can operate. The pool can then be freed as a whole when all the objects within it are released. Switch this on with `JSE_FAST_MEMPOOL` if you think you need it.

Variables can be reference counted as they are retained and released. It is possible that you can encounter leak situations where objects are not being retained by anything but are not freed and never get de-allocated. The `JSE_CYCLIC_CHECK` and `JSE_FULL_CYCLIC_CHECK` options control some garbage collection that might help in low memory situations.

String tables can be managed in a variety of ways. The `JSE_HASH_STRINGS` option can affect table management to improve performance or conserve memory. You can switch to a shared single string table for all interprets and threads with the `JSE_ONE_STRING_TABLE` option.

The `NDEBUG` option determines whether extra debugging code is included. Most C compilers use this convention to control debugging code.

Integrating Your Application

The process of integrating the ScriptEase ISDK with your application is fairly straightforward and well conceived.

The interpreter engine can be built in the following ways:

- ❑ As a static library and then hard linked directly into your code.
- ❑ A shareable library that is loaded with your code and the links resolved at run-time.
- ❑ A DLL for use in Windows or OS/2.
- ❑ A code fragment library for use in the Macintosh environment.
- ❑ A shared object for UNIX ELF systems.

Initializing the interpreter engine requires a few simple steps in your code. Conceptually the process is very similar to that used in JSRef, but with ScriptEase it's a lot less complex.

There are basically three steps:

- ❑ Initialize the engine and create a context in which it can run.
- ❑ Register any functions and objects you want to make available within the scripting environment.
- ❑ Provide a wrapper to translate variables between the JavaScript and C language environments.

Below are some example fragments of code that illustrate how this is done with ScriptEase ISDK. The initialization call must be made at least once before any other ISDK calls are made. This must be called only once per application instance. Your application would include a line something like this:

```
int ver = jseInitializeEngine();
```

After this line is executed, the `int` variable `ver` contains the version number of the interpreter you have just initialized.

Now you need to get a context within which the scripting session can operate. This can be done several times, if necessary, so that you can have multiple contexts active at the same time. Here is how you initialize the interpreter context:

```
jseExternalLinkParameters linkparams;
memset(linkparams, 0, sizeof(linkparams));
jseContext jsecontext = jseInitializeExternalLink(appdata, linkparams);
```

The jseContext identifier returned at this point will be required for almost every call to the ISDK. That is how you make sure that a call is routed to the right context and how you manage multiple scripting environments simultaneously. The linkparams structure is used to control how the session is run. The appdata parameter contains a 'cookie' that is available inside the interpreter so it can find any data you want to have available to the session. For example, use it to define the session's global variables by means of a pointer value. Refer to the ISDK manuals for more details and an example.

Last of all, you need to create a function library table. This is simply an array of structures that describe the functions and objects to register with the jseContext. There are a set of macros that assist with the building of these function tables so its not very hard to do. The example code fragment below creates a Rectangle object and assigns it to the context as a global object. It also defines a method at the same time. The method will return the area of the rectangle object.

```
functionTable =
{
    JSE_LIBOBJECT("Rectangle", "_rectangle", 2, 2, jseDefaultAttr, jseFunc_Secure);
    JSE_LIBMETHOD("area", "_rectarea", 0, 0, jseDefaultAttr, jseFunc_secure);
    JSE_FUNC_END();
}
```

The wrapper functions are provided so that JavaScript can call them and they can then convert incoming values to C language compatible forms. Then when your function call is complete, your return values are then converted back to object property formats so that they are accessible from within the JavaScript environment

On the whole, the ScriptEase mechanisms are well thought out and implemented in a convenient way.

Areas Of Difficulty

There are, at the time of writing (with reference to version 4.10 of ScriptEase), some minor outstanding problems that you should take into consideration. These will likely be addressed in future releases in any case. The following issues are relevant to the core interpreter:

When a script error is encountered, the error reporting mechanism presents details of the line number where the error occurred. The line counting can get out of synchronization with the source script if literal strings are concatenated with a line break somewhere in the expression. The release notes describe a solution and work around to deal with this.

Assignments on a line that lacks a trailing semicolon may not be interpreted correctly. There is a fix for this in the release notes.

There are some arithmetic errors if you are using buffers or are using cfunctions. This is fixed in the next release and may not affect all scripts anyway.

ToString() and ToBuffer() functions may crash on systems that are unable to allocate zero length buffers. A simple work around is to modify the internal malloc() support to add 1 to the requested size. This is fixed in the next release and the documentation describes how to correct it.

If you are using earlier versions, prior to release 4.10b, then there are other issues detailed in the Core Interpreter errata. This is available online at:
http://www.nombas.com/us/devspace/errata/core/index.htm

Apart from the core interpreter problems, there are some issues with the standard objects and function libraries. The problems are generally all fixed in version 4.10c but are outstanding in earlier versions. There are issues regarding dates, bsearch, qsort and other areas. You will find these detailed in the errata at:

http://www.nombas.com/us/devspace/errata/objfunc/index.htm.

There are no recent problems with the #link libraries. Some functional improvements were made at revision 4.03c though. Their errata details are at:

http://www.nombas.com/us/devspace/errata/link/index.htm.

With the ISDK at version 4.10c, there are still some outstanding problems. The errata details some work arounds that will help. These require your consideration as you build the integration kit:

- ❑ An important fix needs to be applied to DEFINE.C before you build.

- ❑ Memory access needs to be fixed for callDelete() functions to work properly.

- ❑ The eval() function requires a small patch so that it operates correctly with the JSE_MULTIPLE_GLOBAL option.

- ❑ Microsoft Visual C compiler version 6 requires a date object fix. The corrective action is to turn off some compile time options in the Integrated Development Environment (IDE).

- ❑ Implicit parenting requires a fix that you need add. Details are in the documentation.

- ❑ Versions prior to version 4.10c exhibit other problems, details of them can be found at:
  http://www.nombas.com/us/devspace/errata/isdk/index.htm.

FESI

FESI comprises a set of Java packages that allow you to add the ECMA Scripting language as a macro mechanism on top of Java. The integration with Java is very strong, which makes it a very useful tool for testing Java library implementations.

Applications written in Java are easily accessible using FESI. While its use is restricted to those tasks that are purely Java, it benefits from the portability of the Java language. FESI is a free tool, provided you give the author credit. Its source is also freely available to inspect. FESI can be obtained from:

http://home.worldcom.ch/~jmlugrin/fesi/index.html.

Like all the other interpreters, FESI is constantly being updated and released. At the time of writing, it is at revision 1.1.2 and is compatible with Java 1.2, Swing 1.1 and the CORBA accessors.

Chapter 16 describes how to use FESI in great detail. Here we only need to consider briefly what is necessary to embed FESI in your applications.

Getting FESI Ready For Embedding

Installing FESI is quite straightforward and because it is based on Java you can experiment with it on a variety of platforms. Also because it is based on Java, you could embed it within your own applications as long they are written in Java as well or have access to a Java VM and can run Java code internally.

If you are installing on platforms other than Windows, you may need to edit some files to place the correct configuration details in them. This might only require that you add the Java or jre command and set the classpath properly.

Once the configuration is done, you can run the interpreter. The FESIIW will run the AWT version and FESIIS will run the Swing version. On the Windows platform, you can make associations to ensure that FESI is run when JavaScripts are executed from the desktop.

An Embedding Example

Here is an example of a simple embedding of the interpreter into a Java environment. You can create an interpreter simply by following this pattern:

```java
import java.io.*;
import FESI.jslib.*;
public class SimpleIntrp {
    public static void main(String args[]) {
        // Create the interpreter
        JSGlobalObject global = null;
        try {
            global = JSUtil.makeEvaluator();
        } catch (JSException e) {
            System.err.println(e);
            System.exit(1);
        }
        DataInputStream ins = new DataInputStream(System.in);
        String input = null;
        // read eval print loop
        while (true) {
            System.out.print("> "); System.out.flush();
            try {
                input = ins.readLine();
            } catch (IOException e) {
                System.exit(0);
            }
            if (input == null) break;
            try {
                Object result = global.eval(input);
                if (result!=null) System.out.println(result.toString());
            } catch (JSException e) {
                System.out.println(e.getMessage());
                if (DEBUG)
                    e.printStackTrace();
                    Exception oe = e.getOriginalException();
                    if (oe!=null) {
                        oe.printStackTrace();
                    } ;
                    System.out.println(e.getMessage());
                System.out.println(e.getMessage());
            }
        } // while
    }
}
```

There is a more extensive example shipped with the FESI installation kit.

Rhino Overview

The Rhino interpreter runs in a Java environment. Because of this, you will need to install and build a working Java VM before you can install Rhino and use it. This gives you other issues to consider, such as which VM to build and which version to use. You may want to share a VM between several applications or use a different Java VM for each one. To build Rhino, you will need a Java VM that is compliant with JDK version 1.1. This will enable you to build a Rhino interpreter that implements the core JavaScript language although this won't contain any objects or methods for manipulating HTML documents.

Here are the main features of Rhino:

❑   Supports all the capabilities of JavaScript version 1.4.

❑   Extensions to the ECMA standard in accordance with the working group expectations.

❑   Compatible with LiveConnect which allows scripting access to Java.

❑   Your JavaScript scripts can be executed in a command line shell.

❑   A built in compiler that translates JavaScript source files into Java class files

❑   Deprecated language features from JavaScript 1.2 are no longer supported.

❑   Textual messages are retrieved from external property files allowing different national language variants to be supported easily.

You should note however that the JavaScript compiler is not available in the free source version of Rhino and is subject to a separate commercial licensing arrangement. The free source version runs as an interpreter rather than compiling the JavaScript into Java bytecodes. If performance is an issue for your embedding project, you should consider the commercial license to gain access to the compiler.

As Rhino is a Netscape product, it may fall under the general terms of the Netscape Public license. You should consult this first of all to see whether the embedding you plan complies with the terms of that license. The license can be viewed online at: `http://www.mozilla.org/NPL/`.

The Latest Version

Rhino is being updated all the time with new features and additions. Rhino was first released under the open source arrangement and has been revised somewhat since then. Because a lot of this information is subject to change and is being revised frequently, the most up to date details are best sourced from the web references.

Rhino has been updated to support the LiveConnect version 3 specification. This provided overloaded method resolution, which enhances the integration between JavaScript and Java. Basically the object methods are called more consistently and are resolved more reliably. You can see more information about this at the location:
`http://www.mozilla.org/js/liveconnect/lc3_proposal.html`.

There have been some semantic changes to the `defineClass` method supported by the `scriptableObject`. You will find more details here:
`http://www.mozilla.org/js/rhino/org/mozilla/JavaScript/ScriptableObject.html`.

When you have built Rhino, you can start the command line shell using the -jar option in Java 2 and there are two new variables added to hold details of the environment and history. There was an issue raised at the JavaOne conference that suggested it might be unhelpful to allow access to the whole suite of Java classes from within a JavaScript. The outcome has been the addition of some security support that allows the embedding engineers to choose which classes are accessible to the scriptwriter. There are more details here:
http://www.mozilla.org/js/rhino/org/mozilla/JavaScript/SecuritySupport.html.

There are other security related changes with regard to allowing the JavaScript interpreter to create new classes in the Java environment from within an executing JavaScript. The security facilities in Rhino provide the ability to track the origin of a code fragment (and any code fragments that it may generate itself). This allows for the implementation of a URL-based security policy for your embedded JavaScript interpreter that is similar to the one embodied in Netscape Navigator.

The support for security related options is probably more sophisticated in Rhino than in any of the other alternative embeddable script interpreters.

Getting The Source

There are two principal ways of getting the code, via FTP here:
http://www.mozilla.org/download.html. Or using the CVS source code management tools from here: http://www.mozilla.org/cvs.html. If you need the most recent version of the sources, then the CVS mechanism will keep you right up to date. It is slower than FTP and also it is possible that you may synchronize to a part-working release. The FTP accessible copy is updated on a daily basis and is checked to ensure that the sources that are published can be built into a working system. The CVS sources *may* give you this guarantee. You need to choose carefully whether you need the very latest version or a reliable build. For a production system, it is likely you would use FTP and freeze a particular version of Rhino simply to give you the stability to build on that for embedding.

Building a Rhino

Details of embedding requirements, pre-requisites, installing, and building Rhino on a variety of operating systems can be found at http://www.mozilla.org/build/. The various pages that this index site leads to will also provide details of environment variables that need to be set prior to building and links can be found to references for limitations and performance issues.

NGS

The NGS JavaScript interpreter is available as a General Purpose Language (GPL) licensed source kit implemented in C language. Since you get the full source you can modify or enhance it as you need to. At present this implementation is not 100% compatible with the JavaScript language standard. It is still a work in progress development project but nevertheless may provide the functionality you need.

This particular implementation is designed to be re-entrant and therefore thread safe. That means you can be running multiple interpretation threads at the same time. It is intended to be extensible by means of user-defined commands and classes. Internally, the JavaScript code is compiled to byte-code that is executed by a virtual machine.

Because the project is at an early stage in its development you may encounter some limitations. However, since the source is freely available, contributions from other developers may accelerate the implementation of new features. For now, you'll have the least trouble compiling NGS if you build it on a Linux based system, although it would be possible to build it on other platforms.

The home page for the NGS JavaScript interpreter where you'll find the install kit and documentation is at: `http://www.ngs.fi/js/`. On the home page you will find up-to-date information about the interpreter, its development, releases, and current status.

At the time of writing, the current version, was js-0.2.0. The author welcomes ideas and contributions towards the ongoing development.

NGS is also available at this URL:
`http://www.debian.org/Packages/stable/interpreters/ngs-js.html`.

Note: NGS requires several other libraries to be available before you can use it. These should all be available from the download site or it will have links that point at where you can get them.

Microsoft WSH

The Microsoft Windows Script Host is a language-independent scripting host for 32-bit Windows operating system platforms. It is being integrated in current versions of Windows and can be added to older versions with an install kit that you can download from the Microsoft web site at:

`http://msdn.microsoft.com/scripting`

There is also a new version of WSH on the horizon (version 2.0) which is currently available as a beta release or is integral in the latest versions of Windows (as of the time of writing). Chapter 20 deals with WSH.

The JScript interpreter

JScript was originally designed to be a general purpose scripting language. It was intended to appeal to the many existing programmers who were used to working with C, C++ and Java already. Because of that, it 'borrows' many features from those languages where it is appropriate. However it is a language in its own right and has many features and attributes not available in C or Java. It was also designed to be capable of being used not just in the browser, but also for server side scripting and desktop automation.

The language has many features that provide flexible and sophisticated support for your implementation needs. It has a very broad reach and is designed so that it will operate in any browser on any platform.

JScript is a completely dynamic language. That means that you can effectively redefine your program as it executes. While there are certainly risks to supporting self-modifying code, it does provide the absolute ultimate in flexibility when you are designing a solution to a problem. This can be really useful when developing DHTML based pages because DHTML allows you to dynamically manipulate the object model.

A popular feature enjoyed by Perl programmers is its implementation of Regular Expressions. The JScript implementation is a close relative of Perl, Perl programmers needing to use JScript for the first time will be relieved to know. Because regular expressions are a very useful way to search text strings, this is especially useful when JScript is being deployed on the server side.

The eval() feature provides a way to execute code directly from a buffer. You can manufacture the code at run-time and execute there and then. This is hard to do in compiled languages but is a useful feature of interpreted environments. This can be very useful when used to send scripts to a remote machine. The text of the script can be transferred and evaluated on the target machine. This is very similar in concept to the Remote Shell (rsh) facilities in UNIX and the Remote Procedure Call (rpc) implementations in compiled languages most often used in C and sometimes in Java where it goes under the name of Remote Method Invocation (RMI).

Embedding Microsoft JScript

The Microsoft JScript is a JavaScript interpreter is available already embedded as an integral part of the Windows Script Host. You can also obtain it as a separate item to be embedded within your own applications. Depending on your needs and very likely the size of your development or licensing budget it is available either as a ready to run binary or source code.

It is unusual for something as valuable to be made available as source code like this but there are already a large number of script interpreters available for free on the internet so its likely that Microsoft felt more comfortable with that model than you would normally expect. However, that is subject to a licensing agreement where the binary distribution is virtually free of any licensing conditions.

Features and Benefits Of Embedded JScript

The JScript interpreter can be integrated according to the definitions covered by the Microsoft Active Scripting standard. This gives you some useful advantages:

❑ If your application is available over the Internet, you don't have to maintain your own copies of JScript. Your users could just as easily download the runtime binaries from: http://msdn.microsoft.com/scripting.

❑ Because the interface between your application and the JScript interpreter is standardized and should remain stable from one release to another, your users can upgrade the JScript core and gain access to new features without you needing to supply updates for your application.

❑ You can add your own objects and functionality to JScript without having to modify the core binary.

❑ All the applications in a machine that use JScript can all share a single DLL in memory. This means that the working set of your application is smaller since it is sharing JScript with other applications such as IE 4.0 for example.

❑ You can integrate JScript into your application by means of Active-X scripting. This is an open standard that can be used by any scripting language.

❑ By doing the necessary work to embed JScript into your application, the ActiveX scripting approach actually means you have done all that is necessary to embed any language into your application. The result is that you are not tied to any particular scripting language and your users can choose alternatives later on.

The licensing is very simple and straightforward for the binary version. It is a little more involved for the source license and requires that you sign an agreement with Microsoft.

Platform Availability

JScript interpreters are available or being developed for the following platforms:

- ❏ Microsoft Windows 3.1
- ❏ Microsoft Windows 95
- ❏ Microsoft Windows 98
- ❏ Microsoft Windows 2000
- ❏ Microsoft Windows NT for Intel
- ❏ Microsoft Windows NT for DEC Alpha
- ❏ Apple Macintosh
- ❏ HP-UX
- ❏ Sun Microsystems Solaris

The New Version 5.0 Support

JScript was revised to version 5.0 and shares a lot of common features with Visual Basic version 5.0. Because they are administered together (with all the other scripting related technology at Microsoft), their release schedules now track in parallel. They are also somewhat geared to the release schedule of the WSH framework in which they are likely to be used increasingly in the future.

One of the most popular changes from JScript 3.1 to JScript 5.0 is the addition of the exception handling support. This is especially useful on a server where it's very useful to be able to catch exceptions. Now, exception handling is provided in a way that is expected to be ECMAScript compliant with the try...catch notation.

JScript now implements DCOM support but uses the ActiveXObject rather than CreateObject. Here is an example:

```
var myObj = new ActiveXObject("RemoteObj", "\\server");
```

This creates an object called myObj that has been registered on \\server. After the object is created, it behaves as if it were a local object.

The new version 5.0 scripting support adds a script encoding facility to obfuscate the code you build into web pages. This is of little benefit in the server other than to lock up the code in a way that makes it difficult for end users to 'tinker' with it. In the client, it prevents people from recycling your script code without your knowledge. However there are limits to its availability on all browsers and at present, it is only supported on IE5.

A Really Small Example

A great benefit of scripting is that if you get it right, you can build custom versions of your applications even after the engineering design is pretty much frozen. The important thing is to 'Factor' your application. What that means is for example in a GUI based application, you would detach the menu and UI handling code from the functional code. The UI stuff can then be built into a framework and the function code can be provided as a collection of objects or event handling fragments. You then connect the two together through a scripting layer. This means you can add a menu item really quickly with the minimum amount of software development.

First off, your design should have an object model. It depends on the tools you have used and the development regimes in force as to whether this is visible or not. If you have developed in Visual Basic, then you should have everything you need. Otherwise, your application should support the IDispatch facility.

You need to tell the script engine about your object model. For more details on that check at: http://msdn.microsoft.com/scripting/hosting.htm.

In a Visual Basic application, add a script control to the project and put an instance of it into your form. Then you need to call the addObject method, passing it Name, Object and addMembers values. Assume you have a text box in your form called MyTextBox, you could add it like this:

```
ScriptControl.AddObject "MyTextBox", txtEditor
```

Scripts being run in the WSH environment could store a text value in there with a line of JavaScript code like this:

```
MyTextBox.text = "Script defined text";
```

To provide the script text in a way it can be executed, the script·control object supports an addcode method. Lets assume you have an extra text box called CodeText where the script source lives. The script source needs to be properly structured with function names in JScript or Procedure blocks in VBScript. You could pass this to the script control like this:

```
ScriptControl.AddCode txtCodeText.Text
```

Now the script controller knows about your code but won't do anything with it. To run it, do this:

```
ScriptControl.Run testFunction
```

This assumes there is a function called testFunction() in the source code you have loaded.

OK, its very simple. But, here we can only scratch the surface, so you'll need to read the WSH documentation for details of how to deploy an embedded JScript or VBScript interpreter into your own projects.

MS Scriptlets vs. WSH Scripts

Microsoft Scriptlets *are not* WSH scripts. They come in two kinds. An older version scriptlet and a newer version 2 scriptlet. They serve different uses. In IE5, scriptlets are now called HTML Components or HTCs. See the MSDN web site for more details at: `http://msdn.microsoft.com/workshop`.

The version 1 scriptlet variety is now referred to generically as a DHTML scriptlet. It is a way of making an HTML object specifically for use in a Web browser out of XML and JavaScript sources.

A version 2 scriptlet, arguably a 'real' scriptlet, is made from XML and JavaScript too. However, the difference is that it creates an object in the true Microsoft COM or ActiveX style. This is more generally useful and certainly more powerful than a DHTML scriptlet.

WSH scripts *are* standalone JavaScript code and are not scriptlets at all.

For all your Microsoft scripting needs, go to: `http://msdn.microsoft.com/scripting`. There are some sample programs there that will get you oriented into the right frame of mind quite quickly. However, they don't show any really heavy duty programming features. You will find other useful resources here: `http://wsh.glazier.co.nz/`. An extensive article on Scriptlets can be found at this location: `http://msdn.microsoft.com/workshop/languages/clinic/xmlscript.asp`. You can also join the newsgroup to discuss Scriptlets at: `news://msnews.microsoft.com/public.scripting.scriptlets`.

Scriptlet Varieties

Scriptlets were originally introduced with Internet Explorer version 4.0 and were intended for creating user interface components to be used in HTML pages. Now the concept has been expanded to provide a more general purpose component that can be used server side as well as client side.

Previously, Scriptlets were written with HTML and Script code. DHTML extensions to HTML provide additional functionality. As of IE version 5, scriptlets can be written around XML and Script code and are useful wherever you might use COM.

You can now build Scriptlets with VBScript, JScript and Perl, all constructed within an XML framework.

What's In a Scriptlet?

Scriptlets are built with XML from the following primitive elements:

Element name	Description
<SCRIPTLET>	This encloses the entire scriptlet definition.
<REGISTRATION>	The information necessary to register your scriptlet as a COM component. However this may not be required if your host application does not use the Windows registry when it creates an instance of the applet. You need to understand ActiveX registry mechanisms and ClassID values to fully utilitize this tag.
<IMPLEMENTS>	This describes the COM interface handler. That determines what sort of COM component the scriptlet will be. This might indicate that the component is an Automation Handler for example.
<PROPERTY>	This is a mechanism for mapping the internal script accessible properties and making them available as COM properties. Property blocks can own <GET> and <PUT> elements to dictate whether they are read-only, write-only or read-write.
<GET>	This is enclosed inside a <PROPERTY> elements and indicates that it can only return its value, you cannot change it from outside.
<PUT>	This is enclosed inside a <PROPERTY> elements and renders a <PROPERTY> value mutable. This allows you to define a new value for it externally.
<METHOD>	In the same way that <PROPERTY> values are exposed as COM properties, this makes the internal script methods/functions accessible as COM methods.
<EVENT>	Used to attach internal scriptlet code to events that happen in a browser. These are used when developing DHTML behavior scriptlets. You don't have to register these scriptlets before using them and so you can skip the <REGISTRATION> element.
<SCRIPT>	This is the script container where the logic of your scriptlet lives. An automation component might have several <SCRIPT> blocks. These blocks can be written in JScript, VBScript or Perl and as third parties develop scriptlet compatible interpreters, other languages will be supported in the future.

Summary

This chapter has described many alternative embeddable interpreters and ways in which you might add them to your own applications. The alternatives can be bewildering given that you need to consider functionality, portability, cost and licensing deals even before dealing with the technicalities.

Although HTML pages are still the most common place to find JavaScript, there are alternatives and it is catching on in other contexts very rapidly. Netscape is increasingly dependent on the language for a variety of tasks. Web servers use JavaScript to turn read-only HTML documents into usefully interactive applications. Fancy web servers do this via server-side JavaScript, simpler ones rely on standalone interpreters and CGI. Standalone JavaScript is a general programming language adaptable to any task. The desperate can put JavaScript inside Java or Perl and even turn things inside out and call Java or Perl from JavaScript instead.

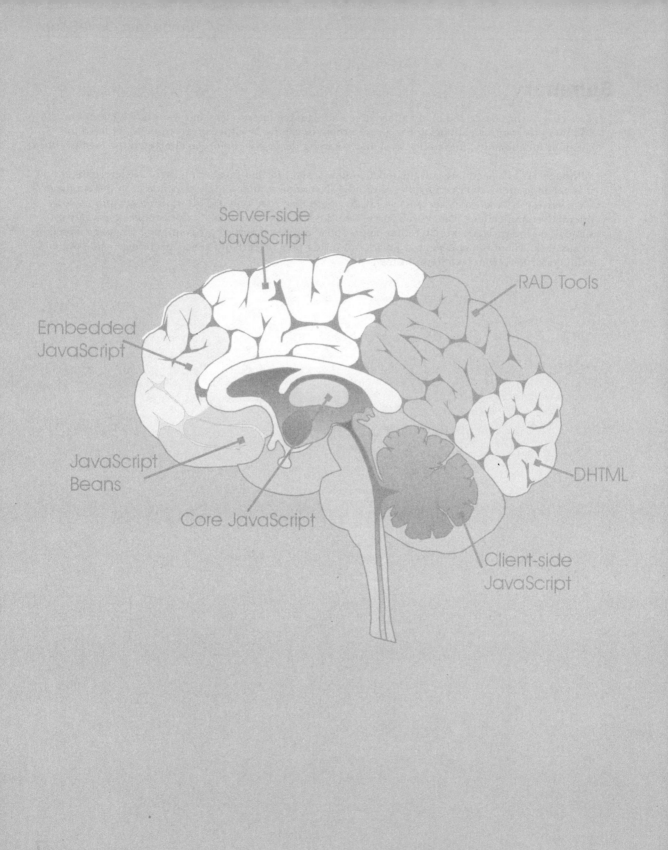

JavaScript Core Reference

This appendix outlines the syntax of all the JavaScript core language functions and object methods. If changes have occurred over versions, they have been noted.

Browser Reference

The Internet Explorer support for JavaScript (not JScript) is flaky but works in most cases.

Language Version	Navigator Version	IE Version
JavaScript 1.0, JScript 1.0	2.0x	3.0x
JavaScript 1.1	3.0x	–
JavaScript 1.2, JScript 3.0	4.0 - 4.05	4.0x
JavaScript 1.3	4.06 - 4.61	–
JavaScript 1.4, JScript 5.0	5.0	5.0x

JavaScript Operators

Assignment operators were introduced in JavaScript 1.0, JScript 1.0.

Name	Introduced	Example	Meaning
Assignment	JavaScript **1.0** JScript **1.0**	v1 = v2	
Shorthand Addition *or* Shorthand Concatenation	JavaScript **1.0** JScript **1.0**	v1 += v2	v1 = v1 + v2
Shorthand Subtraction	JavaScript **1.0** JScript **1.0**	v1 -= v2	v1 = v1 - v2
Shorthand Multiplication	JavaScript **1.0** JScript **1.0**	v1 *= v2	v1 = v1 * v2
Shorthand Division	JavaScript **1.0** JScript **1.0**	v1 /= v2	v1 = v1 / v2
Shorthand Modulus	JavaScript **1.0** JScript **1.0**	v1 %= v2	v1 = v1 % v2
Shorthand left shift	JavaScript **1.0** JScript **1.0**	v1 <<= v2	v1 = v1 << v2
Shorthand right shift	JavaScript **1.0** JScript **1.0**	v1 >>= v2	v1 = v1 >> v2
Shorthand zero fill right shift	JavaScript **1.0** JScript **1.0**	v1 >>>= v2	v1 = v1 >>> v2
Shorthand AND	JavaScript **1.0** JScript **1.0**	v1 &= v2	v1 = v1 & v2
Shorthand XOR	JavaScript **1.0** JScript **1.0**	v1 ^= v2	v1 = v1 ^ v2
Shorthand OR	JavaScript **1.0** JScript **1.0**	v1 |= v2	v1 = v1 | v2

Comparison operators were first introduced in JavaScript 1.0 though a few changes have been made as noted. If v1=1 and v2=2, the following statements are all true. Boolean literal values `true` and `false` are returned by the comparisons.

In JavaScript 1.4, `==` has been deprecated with respect to Objects in favor of `JSObject.equals`. In JavaScript 1.2 only, neither `==` or `!==` attempted type conversion before returning a value.

Name	Introduced	Example	Meaning
Equal	JavaScript **1.0** JScript **1.0**	`v1 == 1`	True if two operands are strictly equal or equal once cast to the same type.
Not Equal	JavaScript **1.0** JScript **1.0**	`v1 != v2`	True if two operands are not strictly equal or not equal once cast to the same type.
Greater Than	JavaScript **1.0** JScript **1.0**	`v2 > v1`	True if LHS operand is greater than RHS operand
Greater Than Or Equal	JavaScript **1.0** JScript **1.0**	`v2 >= v2`	True if LHS operand is greater than or equal to RHS operand
Less Than	JavaScript **1.0** JScript **1.0**	`v1 < v2`	True if LHS operand is less than RHS operand
Less Than Or Equal	JavaScript **1.0** JScript **1.0**	`v1 <= v1`	True if LHS operand is less than or equal to RHS operand
Strictly Equal	JavaScript **1.3** JScript **1.0**	`v2 === v2`	Not in ECMA-262. True if operands are equal and of same type.
Not Strictly Equal	JavaScript **1.3** JScript **1.0**	`v1 !== v2`	Not in ECMA-262. True if operands are not strictly equal

Arithmetic operators were first introduced in JavaScript 1.0 and JScript 1.0.

Name	Introduced	Example	Result
Addition	JavaScript **1.0** JScript **1.0**	`v1 + v2`	Sum of v1 and v2 Concatenation of v1 and v2, if they are strings
Subtraction	JavaScript **1.0** JScript **1.0**	`v1 - v2`	Difference of v1 and v2
Multiplication	JavaScript **1.0** JScript **1.0**	`v1 * v2`	Product of v1 and v2
Division	JavaScript **1.0** JScript **1.0**	`v1 / v2`	Quotient of v2 into v1
Modulus	JavaScript **1.0** JScript **1.0**	`v1 % v2`	Integer remainder of dividing v1 by v2
Prefix Increment	JavaScript **1.0** JScript **1.0**	`++v1 * v2`	(v1 + 1) * v2
Postfix Increment	JavaScript **1.0** JScript **1.0**	`v1++ * v2`	(v1 * v2). v1 is then incremented by 1
Prefix Decrement	JavaScript **1.0** JScript **1.0**	`--v1 * v2`	(v1 – 1) * v2
Postfix Decrement	JavaScript **1.0** JScript **1.0**	`v1-- * v2`	(v1 * v2). v1 is then decremented by 1

Bitwise logical operators were first introduced in JavaScript 1.0 and JScript 1.0. They work by converting values in v1 and v2 to 32-bit binary numbers and then comparing the individual bits of these two binary numbers. The result is returned as a normal decimal number.

Name	Introduced	Example	Result
Bitwise AND	JavaScript **1.0** JScript **1.0**	`v1 & v2`	ANDs each pair of corresponding bits
Bitwise OR	JavaScript **1.0** JScript **1.0**	`v1	v2`	ORs each pair of corresponding bits
Bitwise XOR	JavaScript **1.0** JScript **1.0**	`v1 ^ v2`	XORs each pair of corresponding bits
Bitwise NOT	JavaScript **1.0** JScript **1.0**	`~v1`	Inverts all the bits in the number

Bitwise shift operators were first introduced in JavaScript 1.0 and JScript 1.0. They work by converting values in v1 to 32-bit binary numbers and then moving the bits in the number to the left or the right by the specified number of places.

Name	Introduced	Example	Result
Left Shift	JavaScript **1.0** JScript **1.0**	`v1 << v2`	Shifts v1 to the left by v2 places, filling the new gaps in with zeros
Right Shift	JavaScript **1.0** JScript **1.0**	`v1 >> v2`	Shifts v1 to the right by v2 places, ignoring the bits shifted off the number
Zero-fill Right Shift	JavaScript **1.0** JScript **1.0**	`v1 >>> v2`	Shifts v1 to the right by v2 places, ignoring the bits shifted off the number and adding v2 zeros to the left of the number

Logical operators were first introduced in JavaScript 1.0, JScript 1.0. Should return one of the Boolean literals, `true` or `false`. However, this may not happen if either v1 or v2 is neither a Boolean value nor a value that easily converts to a Boolean value, such as 0, 1, `null`, the empty string or `undefined`.

Name	Introduced	Example	Result
Logical AND	JavaScript **1.0** JScript **1.0**	`v1 && v2`	Returns `true` if both v1 and v2 are true, `false` otherwise. Will not evaluate v2 if v1 is false.
Logical OR	JavaScript **1.0** JScript **1.0**	`v1 || v2`	Returns `false` if both v1 and v2 are false, `true` otherwise. Will not evaluate v2 if v1 is true.
Logical NOT	JavaScript **1.0** JScript **1.0**	`!v1`	Returns `false` if v1 is true, `true` otherwise.

Several operators have been introduced to JavaScript to deal with **objects**:

Name	Introduced	Example	Description

`delete`	JavaScript **1.2**
	 JScript **3.0**
		`delete someObject`
		 `delete someObject.property`
		 `delete someArray[index]`
			Deletes an object, one of its properties or the element of an array at the specified index.

`in`	JavaScript **1.4**	`property in someObject`	Not in ECMA-262. Returns `true` if `someObject` has the named property. Not supported by Internet Explorer.
`instanceof`	JavaScript **1.4** JScript **5.0**	`someObject instanceof objectType`	Not in ECMA-262. Returns `true` if `someObject` is of type `objectType`.
`new`	JavaScript **1.0** JScript **1.0**	`someObject = new objectType (parameterList)`	Creates a new instance of an object with type `objectType`. The `parameterList` obeys a constructor function specified elsewhere.
`this`	JavaScript **1.0** JScript **1.0**	`this` `this.property`	Refers to the current object.

There are several other miscellaneous operators in JavaScript:

Name	Introduced	Example	Description
Conditional Operator	JavaScript **1.0** JScript **1.0**	`evalquery ?` `v1 : v2`	If `evalquery` is true, the operator returns v1, else it returns v2.
Comma Operator	JavaScript **1.0** JScript **1.0**	`eval1, eval2`	Evaluates both `eval1` and `eval2` while treating the two as one expression.
`typeof`	JavaScript **1.1** JScript **1.0**	`typeof v1` `typeof (v1)`	Returns a string holding the type of v1, which is not evaluated.
`void`	JavaScript **1.1** JScript **2.0**	`void eval1` `void (eval1)`	Evaluates `eval1` but does not return a value.

Operator Precedence

Does `1 + 2 * 3 = 1 + (2 * 3) = 7` or does it equal `(1 + 2) * 3 = 6`?

The ECMAScript standard doesn't yet clearly document operator precedence. However, JavaScript closely follows Java, and Java closely follows C. The table shows precedence with highest at the top, and like operators grouped together. The third column explains whether to read `1+2+3+4` as `((1+2)+3)+4` or `1+(2+(3+(4)))`.

Operator type	Operators	Evaluation order for like elements
postfix operators	`[] () . expr++` `expr--`	left to right
unary operators	`++expr --expr` `+expr -expr ~ !`	right to left
object management or cast	`delete new typeof` `void`	right to left
multiplicative	`* / %`	left to right
additive	`+ -`	left to right
shift	`<< >> >>>`	left to right
relational	`< > <= >= in` `instanceof`	left to right
equality	`== != === !==`	left to right
bitwise AND	`&`	left to right

Table Continued on Following Page

Operator type	Operators	Evaluation order for like elements
bitwise exclusive OR	^	left to right
bitwise inclusive OR	|	left to right
logical AND	&&	left to right
logical OR	||	left to right
conditional	? :	right to left
assignment	= += -= *= /= %= &= ^= |= <<= >>= >>>=	right to left
multiple evaluation	,	left to right

JavaScript Statements

The following tables describe core JavaScript statements.

Declarations

Statement	Introduced	Example	Description

var	JavaScript **1.0**
	 JScript **1.0**
		`var Number;`
		 `var Number = 6;`
		 `var N1, N2, N3 = 6;`
			Used to declare a variable. Initializing it to a value is optional at the time of declaration.

function	JavaScript **1.0**
	 JScript **1.0**
		`function doItNow()`
		 `{`
		    `statements`
		 `}`
		
		 `function doThis(p1,`
		 `p2, p3) {`
		    `statements`
		 `}`
			Used to declare a function with the specified parameters, which can be strings, numbers or objects.
			
			 To return a value the function must use the return statement.

Loops

Statement	Introduced	Example	Description
do...while	JavaScript **1.2** JScript **3.0**	```do statements --test; while (0 <= test);```	Not in ECMA-262. Executes the statements specified until the test condition after the while evaluates to false. The statements are executed at least once because the test condition is evaluated last.
for	JavaScript **1.0** JScript **1.0**	```for (var i=0; i<15; i++) { var x += i; doSomething(x); }```	Creates a loop controlled according to the three optional expressions enclosed in the parentheses after the for and separated by semicolons. The first of these three expressions is the initial-expression, the second is the test condition, and the third is the increment-expression.
for...in	JavaScript **1.0** JScript **1.0**	```for (var i in obj) { return obj[i]; }```	Used to iterate over all the properties of an object using a variable. For each property the specified statements within the loop are executed.
if...else	JavaScript **1.0** JScript **1.0**	```if (x <= y) { thing += x; x++; } else thing += y;```	Executes a block of statements if the condition evaluates to true. If the condition evaluates to false, another block of statements can be executed.
while	JavaScript **1.0** JScript **1.0**	```while(y < 3) { doSomething() ; }```	Executes a block of statements if a test condition evaluates to true. The loop then repeats, testing the condition with each repeat, ceasing if the condition evaluates to false.

Execution Control Statements

Statement	Introduced	Example	Description

break	JavaScript **1.0**
	
	JScript **1.0**
		<pre>function
		loopWithBreak(b)
		
		{
		    var x = 0;
		    while (x < 20)
		
		    {
		      if (10 == x)
		        break;
		      x++;
		
		    }
		    return x*b;
		}</pre>
			Used within a while or for loop to terminate the loop and transfer program control to the statement following the loop.
			
			Can also be used with a label to break to a particular program position outside of the loop.

continue	JavaScript **1.0**
	
	JScript **1.0**
		<pre>function
		loopWithContinue(c)
		
		{
		
		    var count = 0;
		
		    while (count < 16)
		
		    {
		
		      if (0 == (++count
		% 2))
		
		        continue;
		
		      return count*c;
		
		    }
		
		}</pre>
			Used to stop execution of the block of statements in the current iteration of a while or for loop, and execution of the loop continues with the next iteration.

Statement	Introduced	Example	Description
`label`	JavaScript **1.2** JScript **3.0**	```function breakWithLabel(b) { var outer, inr = 0; myFirstLabel: while (++outer < 12) { for(inr=0;inr<12;inr++) { if(6 == outer) break myFirstLabel; return inr*outer; } } }```	An identifier that can be used with `break` or `continue` statements to indicate where the program should continue execution after the loop execution is stopped.
`return`	JavaScript **1.0** JScript **1.0**	```function returnSthg(x, y) { return x/y; }```	Used to specify the value to be returned by a function.
`switch`	JavaScript **1.2** JScript **3.0**	```switch(x) { case 0 : doSomething(); break; case 1 : doSomethingElse(); break; default : doThisInstead(); }```	Not in ECMA-262. Specifies various blocks of statements to be executed depending on the value of the expression passed in as the argument. Similar to a Visual Basic `Select Case` statement.

Table Continued on Following Page

Statement	Introduced	Example	Description

with	JavaScript **1.0**
	
	 JScript **1.0**
		```with(myObject)```
		```{```
		``` myProperty="New Value";```
		```}```
			Specifies the default object for a set of statements.

Exception Statements

These were introduced in JavaScript 1.4, and are consequently not supported in Netscape implementations of JavaScript; however, they are supported by Internet Explorer 5.

Statement	Introduced	Example	Description

throw	JavaScript **1.4**
	
	 JScript **5.0**
		```function ValidateDay(DayOfWk)```
		```{```
		``` if (DayOfWk < 1 | DayOfWk > 7)```
		``` {```
		``` throw "Invalid day of week";```
		``` }```
		```}```
			Not in ECMA-262.
			
			 Throws a custom exception defined by the user.

Statement	Introduced	Example	Description
try...catch	JavaScript **1.4** JScript **5.0**	```function catchException() { try { throw "Errors occurred"; } catch(excptn) { alert(excptn); } finally { doSomething(); } }```	Not in ECMA-262. Executes the statements in the try block; if any exceptions occur, these are handled in the catch block. The finally block allows us to stipulate statements that will be executed after both the try and catch statements.

Conditional Compile Statements

These are specific to JScript and are not supported by Netscape Navigator or Enterprise Server. Introduced in JScript 3.0, these statements allow JScript code to be compiled only if certain conditions are met. Conditional compilation also provides access to the conditional compilation variables, which provide information about the platform and version of JavaScript in use. Conditional compilation statements should be placed inside comments, where they will be ignored by browsers which do not support conditional compilation.

Statement	Introduced	Example	Description
`@cc_on`	JScript **3.0**	`/*@cc_on @*/`	Turns conditional compilation on.

`@if...`
`@elif...`
`@else...`
`@end`
	JScript **3.0**	`/*@if`
		`(@_jscript_version==5)`
		
		`    alert("Glad you've`
		`got the latest version`
		`of JScript!");`
		
		`@elif`
		`(@_jscript_version>2)`
		
		`    alert("It's not the`
		`latest version, but`
		`it'll do!");`
		
		`@else @*/`
		
		`    alert("You're not`
		`using IE, or your`
		`browser's too old!");`
		
		`/*@end @*/`
			Compiles the following code only if the given condition equates to true. The `@elif` statement allows for another condition to be tested, and `@else` supplies a default if no conditions are met.

`@set`	JScript **3.0**	`/*@set @v1=23 @*/`	Allows variables to be created for use in conditionally compiled code. The variable must start with the character `@`.

Predefined Conditional Compilation Variables

These predefined variables return information about the system and platform on which the browser is running and can be accessed when conditional compilation is enabled.

Variable	Description
`@_alpha`	Returns `true` if the browser is running on a DEC Alpha machine, otherwise `NaN`.
`@_jscript`	Returns `true` if the browser supports JScript. This always returns `true`.
`@_jscript_build`	Returns the build number for the version of JScript in use.
`@_jscript_version`	Returns the version number for the version of JScript in use.
`@_mac`	Returns `true` if the browser is running on an Apple Macintosh machine, otherwise `NaN`.

Variable	Description
@_mc680x0	Returns true if the browser is running on a Motorola 680x0 machine, otherwise NaN.
@_PowerPC	Returns true if the browser is running on a Motorola Power PC machine, otherwise NaN.
@_win16	Returns true if the browser is running on a Windows 16-bit platform, otherwise NaN.
@_win32	Returns true if the browser is running on a Windows 32-bit platform, otherwise NaN.
@_x86	Returns true if the browser is running on an IBM PC or compatible, otherwise NaN.

Other Statements

Statement	Introduced	Example	Description
comment	JavaScript 1.0 JScript 1.0	`// one-line comment` `/* multiple-line comment, of any length */`	Notes which are ignored by the script engine, and which can be used to explain the code.
import	JavaScript 1.2	`import myObject.myProperty, myObject.myFunction`	Allows a script to import objects and their properties and methods which have been exported from another script. Not supported by Internet Explorer.
export	JavaScript 1.2	`export myProperty, myFunction`	Allows a signed script to export objects and their properties and methods, so that they can be imported by other scripts. Not supported by Internet Explorer.

Top-Level Properties and Functions

These are core properties and functions which are not associated with any lower-level object, although in the terminology used by ECMAScript and by JScript they are described as properties and methods of the global object.

Top-Level Properties

These were introduced in JavaScript 1.3 and JScript 3.0, but in previous versions Infinity and Nan existed as properties of the Number object.

Property	Introduced	Example	Description
Infinity	JavaScript **1.3** JScript **3.0**	```function getNumber(x)\n{\n if (isFinite(x))\n {\n return x;\n }\n else\n {\n return Infinity;\n }\n}```	Returns infinity.
NaN	JavaScript **1.3** JScript **3.0**	```function getNumber(x)\n{\n if (isNaN(x))\n {\n return NaN;\n }\n else\n {\n return x;\n }\n}```	Returns a value which is not a number.

Property	Introduced	Example	Description

undefined	JavaScript 1.3	`if (v1 == undefined)`
		`{`
		`    alert("Variable not defined");`
		`}`
		`else`
		`{`
		`    alert("Value is " + v1);`
		`}`
			Indicates that a value has not been assigned to a variable. Not supported by Internet Explorer.

Top-Level Functions

Function	Introduced	Example	Description
escape	JavaScript 1.0 JScript 1.0	`str1 = escape("&");` `// str1 == "%26"`	Used to encode a string in the ISO Latin-1 character set, for example to add to a URL.

eval	JavaScript 1.0
	JScript 1.0
		`strOp = "*";`
		`v1 = 10;`
		`strCode = "v1 = v1" + strOp + "2";`
		`eval (strCode);`
		`alert(v1);`
			Returns the result of the JavaScript code, which is passed in as a parameter.

Table Continued on Following Page

Function	Introduced	Example	Description
isFinite	JavaScript **1.3** JScript **3.0**	```function getNumber(x)

{

    if (isFinite(x))

    {

        return x;

    }

    else

    {

        return Infinity;

    }

}``` | Indicates whether the argument is a finite number. |
| isNaN | JavaScript **1.0** (Unix only), **1.1**

JScript **1.0** | ```function getNumber(x)

{

    if (isNaN(x))

    {

        return NaN;

    }

    else

    {

        return x;

    }

}``` | Indicates if the argument is not a number. |
| Number | JavaScript **1.2**

JScript **2.0** | ```function getNumber(strNum)

{

    return Number(strNum);

}``` | Converts an object to a number. |

Function	Introduced	Example	Description

parseFloat	JavaScript **1.0**
	
	JScript **1.0**
		``x =
		parseFloat("21.99
		");```
		
		`// x == 21.99`
			Parses a string and returns it as a floating-point number.

parseInt	JavaScript **1.0**
	
	JScript **1.0**
		``x =
		parseInt("21.99")
		;```
		
		`//x == 21`
		
		``x =
		parseInt("FF",
		16);```
		
		`//x == 255`
			Parses a string and returns it as an integer. An optional second parameter specifies the base of the number to be converted.

String	JavaScript **1.2**
	
	JScript **1.0**
		``objDate = new
		Date(940000000000
		);```
		
		``strDate=String(ob
		jDate);```
		
		``/*strDate == "Fri
		Oct 15 16:06:40
		UTC+0100 1999" */```
			Converts an object to a string.

unescape	JavaScript **1.0**
	
	JScript **1.0**
		``str1 =
		unescape("%28");```
		
		`//str1 == "("`
			Returns the ASCII string for the specified hexadecimal encoding value.

JavaScript Core Objects

The following tables describe the objects available in the JavaScript core language and their methods and properties.

ActiveXObject

The ActiveXObject object represents an ActiveX object when accessed from within JScript code. Introduced in JScript 3.0; not ECMAScript or Netscape JavaScript. Created with the ActiveXObject constructor; for example, to create a Microsoft Word document, we would write:

```
var objActiveX = new ActiveXObject("Word.Document");
```

The properties and methods of this object will be those of the ActiveX object thus created. For example, the following code opens a Word document and writes some text to it and to the HTML page:

```
var objActiveX = new ActiveXObject("Word.Document");
strText="This is being written both to the HTML page and to the Word document.";
objActiveX.application.selection.typeText(strText);
document.write(strText);
```

Array

The `Array` object represents an array of variables. It was introduced in JavaScript 1.1 and JScript 2.0. An `Array` object is created with the `Array` constructor:

```
var objArray = new Array(10) // an array of 11 elements
var objArray = new Array("1", "2", "4") // an array of 3 elements
```

Properties

Property	Introduced	Description
constructor	JavaScript **1.1** JScript **2.0**	Used to reference the constructor function for the object.
index	JavaScript **1.2**	Not in ECMA-262. The zero-based index indicating the position in the string which matches a regular expression. Not supported by Internet Explorer.
input	JavaScript **1.2**	Not in ECMA-262. Returns the string against which a regular expression was matched. Not supported by Internet Explorer.
length	JavaScript **1.1** JScript **2.0**	Returns the number of elements in the array.
prototype	JavaScript **1.1** JScript **2.0**	Returns the prototype for the object, which can be used to extend the object's interface.

Methods

Method	Introduced	Description
concat	JavaScript **1.2** JScript **3.0**	Not in ECMA-262. Concatenates two arrays and returns the new array thus formed.
join	JavaScript **1.1** JScript **2.0**	Joins all the elements of an array into a single string.
pop	JavaScript **1.2**	Not in ECMA-262. Pops the last element from the end of the array and returns that element. Not supported by Internet Explorer.

Method	Introduced	Description
push	JavaScript **1.2**	Not in ECMA-262. Pushes one or more elements onto the end of the array and returns the new length of the array. (In JavaScript 1.2, the last element rather than the new length is returned.) Not supported by Internet Explorer.
reverse	JavaScript **1.1** JScript **2.0**	Reverses the order of the elements in the array, so that the first element becomes the last and the last becomes the first.
shift	JavaScript **1.2**	Not in ECMA-262. Removes the first element from the beginning of the array and returns that element. Not supported by Internet Explorer.
slice	JavaScript **1.2** JScript **3.0**	Not in ECMA-262. Returns a subarray from the array.
sort	JavaScript **1.1** JScript **2.0**	Sorts the elements of the array.
splice	JavaScript **1.2**	Not in ECMA-262. Adds, removes or replaces elements in the array. Not supported by Internet Explorer.
toSource	JavaScript **1.3**	Not in ECMA-262. Returns a string containing the source code for the Array object. Not supported by Internet Explorer.
toString	JavaScript **1.1** JScript **2.0**	Converts the Array object into a string.
unshift	JavaScript **1.2**	Not in ECMA-262. Adds elements to the beginning of the array and returns the new length. Not supported by Internet Explorer.
valueOf	JavaScript **1.1** JScript **2.0**	Returns the primitive value of the array.

In Netscape JavaScript, this object also inherits the methods watch and unwatch from the Object object (not ECMAScript or IE).

Boolean

The `Boolean` object is used as a wrapper for a Boolean value. It was introduced in JavaScript 1.1 and JScript 2.0. It is created with the `Boolean` constructor, which takes as a parameter the initial value for the object (if this is not a Boolean value, it will be converted into one):

```
var objBoolean = new Boolean("true");
```

Properties

Property	Introduced	Description
constructor	JavaScript **1.1** JScript **2.0**	Specifies the function that creates an object's prototype.
prototype	JavaScript **1.1** JScript **2.0**	Returns the prototype for the object, which can be used to extend the object's interface.

Methods

Method	Introduced	Description
toSource	JavaScript **1.3**	Not in ECMA-262. Returns a string containing the source code for the `Boolean` object. Not supported by Internet Explorer.
toString	JavaScript **1.1** JScript **2.0**	Converts the `Boolean` object into a string.
valueOf	JavaScript **1.1** JScript **2.0**	Returns the primitive value of the `Boolean` object.

In Netscape JavaScript, this object also inherits the methods `watch` and `unwatch` from the `Object` object (not ECMAScript or IE).

Date

The `Date` object is used to represent a given date-time. It was introduced in JavaScript 1.0 and JScript 1.0. Created with the `Date` constructor:

```
objDate = new Date() // Current date-time
objDate = new Date(940000000000) //milliseconds since Jan 1 1970 00:00:00
objDate = new Date("Jan 1, 1999");
objDate = new Date(1999,11,31,8,0) //31 Dec 1999 08:00:00
```

Properties

Property	Introduced	Description
constructor	JavaScript **1.1** JScript **2.0**	Used to reference the constructor function for the object.
prototype	JavaScript **1.1** JScript **2.0**	Returns the prototype for the object, which can be used to extend the object's interface.

Methods

Method	Introduced	Description
getDate	JavaScript **1.0** JScript **1.0**	Retrieves the date in the month from the Date object.
getDay	JavaScript **1.0** JScript **1.0**	Retrieves the day of the week from the Date object .
getFullYear	JavaScript **1.3** JScript **3.0**	Retrieves the full year from the Date object.
getHours	JavaScript **1.0** JScript **1.0**	Retrieves the hour of the day from the Date object.
getMilliseconds	JavaScript **1.3** JScript **3.0**	Retrieves the number of milliseconds from the Date object.
getMinutes	JavaScript **1.0** JScript **1.0**	Retrieves the number of minutes from the Date object.
getMonth	JavaScript **1.0** JScript **1.0**	Retrieves the month from the Date object.
getSeconds	JavaScript **1.0** JScript **1.0**	Retrieves the number of seconds from the Date object.
getTime	JavaScript **1.0** JScript **1.0**	Retrieves the number of milliseconds since January 1 1970 00:00:00 from the Date object.

Table Continued on Following Page

Method	Introduced	Description
getTimezoneOffset	JavaScript **1.0** JScript **1.0**	Retrieves the difference in minutes between the local time zone and UTC.
getUTCDate	JavaScript **1.3** JScript **3.0**	Retrieves the date in the month from the Date object adjusted to universal time.
getUTCDay	JavaScript **1.3** JScript **3.0**	Retrieves the day of the week from the Date object adjusted to universal time.
getUTCFullYear	JavaScript **1.3** JScript **3.0**	Retrieves the year from the Date object adjusted to universal time.
getUTCHours	JavaScript **1.3** JScript **3.0**	Retrieves the hour of the day from the Date object adjusted to universal time.
getUTCMilliseconds	JavaScript **1.3** JScript **3.0**	Retrieves the number of milliseconds from the Date object adjusted to universal time.
getUTCMinutes	JavaScript **1.3** JScript **3.0**	Retrieves the number of minutes from the Date object adjusted to universal time.
getUTCMonth	JavaScript **1.3** JScript **3.0**	Retrieves the month from the Date object adjusted to universal time.
getUTCSeconds	JavaScript **1.3** JScript **3.0**	Retrieves the number of seconds from the Date object adjusted to universal time.
getVarDate	JScript **3.0**	Not in ECMA-262 or Netscape JavaScript. Returns the date in VT_DATE format (used for communicating with ActiveX objects).
getYear	JavaScript **1.0** JScript **1.0**	Retrieves the year from the Date object.
parse	JavaScript **1.0** JScript **1.0**	Retrieves the number of milliseconds in a date since January 1 1970 00:00:00, local time.
setDate	JavaScript **1.0** JScript **1.0**	Sets the date in the month for the Date object.

Method	Introduced	Description
setFullYear	JavaScript **1.3** JScript **3.0**	Sets the full year for the Date object.
setHours	JavaScript **1.0** JScript **1.0**	Sets the hour of the day for the Date object.
setMilliseconds	JavaScript **1.3** JScript **3.0**	Sets the number of milliseconds for the Date object.
setMinutes	JavaScript **1.0** JScript **1.0**	Sets the number of minutes for the Date object.
setMonth	JavaScript **1.0** JScript **1.0**	Sets the month for the Date object.
setSeconds	JavaScript **1.0** JScript **1.0**	Sets the number of seconds for the Date object.
setTime	JavaScript **1.0** JScript **1.0**	Sets the time for the Date object according to the number of milliseconds since January 1 1970 00:00:00.
setUTCDate	JavaScript **1.3** JScript **3.0**	Sets the date in the month for the Date object according to universal time.
setUTCFullYear	JavaScript **1.3** JScript **3.0**	Sets the full year for the Date object according to universal time.
setUTCHours	JavaScript **1.3** JScript **3.0**	Sets the hour of the day for the Date object according to universal time.
setUTCMilliseconds	JavaScript **1.3** JScript **3.0**	Sets the number of milliseconds for the Date object according to universal time.
setUTCMinutes	JavaScript **1.3** JScript **3.0**	Sets the number of minutes for the Date object according to universal time.
setUTCMonth	JavaScript **1.3** JScript **3.0**	Sets the month for the Date object according to universal time.

Table Continued on Following Page

Method	Introduced	Description
setUTCSeconds	JavaScript **1.3** JScript **3.0**	Sets the number of seconds for the Date object according to universal time.
setYear	JavaScript **1.0** JScript **1.0**	Sets the year for the Date object.
toGMTString	JavaScript **1.0** JScript **1.0**	Converts the Date object to a string according to Greenwich Mean Time. Replaced by toUTCString.
toLocaleString	JavaScript **1.0** JScript **1.0**	Converts the Date object to a string according to the local time zone.
toSource	JavaScript **1.3**	Returns a string containing the source code for the Date object.
toString	JavaScript **1.1**	Converts the Date object into a string.
toUTCString	JavaScript **1.3**	Not in ECMA-262. Converts the Date object to a string according to universal time. Not supported by Internet Explorer.
UTC	JavaScript **1.0** JScript **1.0**	Retrieves the number of milliseconds in a date since January 1 1970 00:00:00, universal time.
valueOf	JavaScript **1.1** JScript **2.0**	Returns the primitive value of the Date object.

In Netscape JavaScript, this object also inherits the methods watch and unwatch from the Object object (not ECMAScript or IE).

Enumerator

The Enumerator object allows us to iterate through the items in a collection. Introduced in JScript 3.0; not ECMAScript or Netscape JavaScript. It is created through the Enumerator constructor; the collection to be enumerated is passed in as a parameter. For example, this code creates an Enumerator object for the forms collection in an HTML page:

```
<FORM NAME="form1">
<INPUT TYPE=BUTTON VALUE="Click me!">
</FORM>

<FORM NAME="form1">
<INPUT TYPE=BUTTON VALUE="No, click me instead!">
</FORM>
```

```
<SCRIPT>
var colForms = document.forms;
var objEnum = new Enumerator(colForms);
</SCRIPT>
```

Methods

Method	Introduced	Description
AtEnd	JScript **3.0**	Returns true if the Enumerator is at the end of the collection.
Item	JScript **3.0**	Returns the item at the current position in the collection.
MoveFirst	JScript **3.0**	Moves to the first item in the collection.
MoveNext	JScript **3.0**	Moves to the next item in the collection.

Function

Represents a block of JavaScript code which is to be compiled as a function. Introduced in JavaScript 1.1, JScript 2.0. A Function object is created with the Function constructor. For example, to create an object which represents the following function, which adds two values passed in as parameters:

```
function fnAddition(v1,v2) {
    return v1+v2
}
```

We could create a Function object as follows; the names of the parameters for the function are passed in to the Function constructor, followed by the body of the function:

```
var fnAddition = new Function ("v1", "v2", "return v1+v2");
```

We can then call this as though it were a normal function:

```
var total = fnAddition(4,3);
```

Properties

Property	Introduced	Description
arguments	JavaScript **1.1** JScript **2.0**	An array containing the parameters passed into the function (replaced in Netscape JavaScript by arguments as a local variable within the Function object).
arguments.callee	JavaScript **1.2**	Returns the body of the current Function object (replaced by the callee property of the arguments local variable). Not supported by Internet Explorer.

Table Continued on Following Page

Property	Introduced	Description
`arguments.caller`	JavaScript **1.1**	Not in ECMA-262. Returns the name of the function which called the current `Function` object (replaced by the `caller` property of the `arguments` local variable). Not supported by Internet Explorer.
`arguments.length`	JavaScript **1.1** JScript **2.0**	Returns the number of parameters passed into the function (replaced in Netscape JavaScript by the `length` property of the `arguments` local variable).
`arity`	JavaScript **1.2**	Not in ECMA-262. Returns the number of parameters expected by the function. Replaced by the `length` property. Not supported by Internet Explorer.
`caller`	JScript **2.0**	Not in ECMA-262 or Netscape JavaScript. Returns a reference to the function which called the current `Function` object.
`constructor`	JavaScript **1.1** JScript **2.0**	Used to reference the constructor function for the object.
`length`	JavaScript **1.1**	Returns the number of parameters expected by the function. This differs from `arguments.length`, which returns the number of parameters actually passed into the function. Not supported by Internet Explorer.
`prototype`	JavaScript **1.1** JScript **2.0**	Returns the prototype for the object, which can be used to extend the object's interface.

Methods

Method	Introduced	Description
`apply`	JavaScript **1.3**	Not in ECMA-262. Applies a method of one object in the context of the object which calls the method. Not supported by Internet Explorer.
`call`	JavaScript **1.3**	Not in ECMA-262. Executes a method of one object in the context of the object which calls the method. Not supported by Internet Explorer.
`toSource`	JavaScript **1.3**	Not in ECMA-262. Returns a string containing the source code for the `Function` object. Not supported by Internet Explorer.
`toString`	JavaScript **1.1** JScript **2.0**	Converts the `Function` object into a string.
`valueOf`	JavaScript **1.1** JScript **2.0**	Returns the primitive value of the `Function` object.

java

This is merely a synonym for `Packages.java`. Introduced in JavaScript 1.1, but not supported by ECMAScript or Internet Explorer.

JavaArray

Represents a Java array accessed from within JavaScript. Introduced in JavaScript 1.1; not supported by ECMAScript or Internet Explorer. Created by Java methods that return an array.

Properties

Property	Introduced	Description
`length`	JavaScript **1.1**	Not in ECMA-262. The number of elements in the Java array.

Methods

Method	Introduced	Description
toString	JavaScript **1.1**	Not in ECMA-262. In JavaScript 1.4, this method is overridden by the toString method of the java.lang.Object superclass. In earlier versions, this method returns a string which identifies the object as a JavaArray.

In JavaScript 1.4, the JavaArray object also inherits methods from the Java array superclass java.lang.Object.

JavaClass

Used to reference a Java class from within JavaScript. Introduced in JavaScript 1.1; not supported by ECMAScript or Internet Explorer. Created through the Packages object; for example, the following code gets a reference to the Java Date class provided by the java.util package:

```
var javaDate = Packages.java.util.Date;
```

Properties

The properties of a JavaClass object are the static fields of the Java class.

Methods

The methods of a JavaClass object are the static methods of the Java class.

JavaObject

Represents a Java object accessed from within JavaScript code. Introduced in JavaScript 1.1; not supported by ECMAScript or Internet Explorer. Created by any Java method which returns an object, or using the new keyword with the Packages object:

```
var javaDate = new Packages.java.util.Date;
```

Properties

Inherits the public properties of the Java class of which it is an instance. It also inherits the properties of any superclass of which the Java class is a member.

Methods

Inherits the public methods of the Java class of which it is an instance. It also inherits methods from java.lang.Object and from any other superclass of which the Java class is a member.

JavaPackage

Represents a Java package when accessed from within JavaScript code. Introduced in JavaScript 1.1; not ECMAScript. Created through the `Packages` object:

```
var javaUtilPackage = Packages.java.util;
```

Properties

The properties of a `JavaPackage` are the `JavaClass` and `JavaPackage` objects which it contains.

Math

The `Math` object provides methods and properties used for mathematical calculations. Introduced in JavaScript 1.0, JScript 1.0. The `Math` object is a top-level object, which can be accessed without a constructor.

Properties

Property	Introduced	Description
E	JavaScript **1.0** JScript **1.0**	Returns Euler's constant (the base of natural logarithms) (approximately 2.718).
LN10	JavaScript **1.0** JScript **1.0**	Returns the natural logarithm of 10 (approximately 2.302).
LN2	JavaScript **1.0** JScript **1.0**	Returns the natural logarithm of 2 (approximately 0.693).
LOG10E	JavaScript **1.0** JScript **1.0**	Returns the base 10 logarithm of E (approximately 0.434).
LOG2E	JavaScript **1.0** JScript **1.0**	Returns the base 2 logarithm of E (approximately 1.442).
PI	JavaScript **1.0** JScript **1.0**	Returns PI, the ratio of the circumference of a circle to its diameter (approximately 3.142).
SQRT1_2	JavaScript **1.0** JScript **1.0**	Returns the square root of 1/2 (approximately 0.707).
SQRT2	JavaScript **1.0** JScript **1.0**	Returns the square root of 2 (approximately 1.414).

Methods

Method	Introduced	Description
abs	JavaScript **1.0** JScript **1.0**	Returns the absolute (positive) value of a number.
acos	JavaScript **1.0** JScript **1.0**	Returns the arccosine of a number (in radians).
asin	JavaScript **1.0** JScript **1.0**	Returns the arcsine of a number (in radians).
atan	JavaScript **1.0** JScript **1.0**	Returns the arctangent of a number (in radians).
atan2	JavaScript **1.0** JScript **2.0**	Returns the angle (in radians) between the x-axis and the position represented by the y and x coordinates passed in as parameters.
ceil	JavaScript **1.0** JScript **1.0**	Returns the value of a number rounded up to the nearest integer.
cos	JavaScript **1.0** JScript **1.0**	Returns the cosine of a number.
exp	JavaScript **1.0** JScript **1.0**	Returns E to the power of the argument passed in.
floor	JavaScript **1.0** JScript **1.0**	Returns the value of a number rounded down to the nearest integer.
log	JavaScript **1.0** JScript **1.0**	Returns the natural logarithm (base E) of a number.
max	JavaScript **1.0** JScript **1.0**	Returns the greater of two numbers passed in as parameters.
min	JavaScript **1.0** JScript **1.0**	Returns the lesser of two numbers passed in as parameters.

Method	Introduced	Description
Pow	JavaScript **1.0** JScript **1.0**	Returns the first parameter raised to the power of the second.
random	JavaScript **1.0** (Unix only), **1.1** JScript **1.0**	Returns a pseudo-random number between 0 and 1.
round	JavaScript **1.0** JScript **1.0**	Returns the value of a number rounded up or down to the nearest integer.
sin	JavaScript **1.0** JScript **1.0**	Returns the sine of a number.
sqrt	JavaScript **1.0** JScript **1.0**	Returns the square root of a number.
tan	JavaScript **1.0** JScript **1.0**	Returns the tangent of a number.

In Netscape JavaScript, this object also inherits the methods watch and unwatch from the Object object (not ECMAScript or IE).

netscape

This is merely a synonym for Packages.netscape. Introduced in JavaScript 1.1; not ECMAScript or Internet Explorer.

Number

The Number object acts as a wrapper for primitive numeric values. Introduced in JavaScript 1.1, JScript 2.0. A Number object is created using the Number constructor with the initial value for the number passed in as a parameter:

```
var myNum = new Number(27);
```

Properties

Property	Introduced	Description
constructor	JavaScript **1.1** JScript **2.0**	Used to reference the constructor function for the object.
MAX_VALUE	JavaScript **1.1** JScript **2.0**	Returns the largest number which can be represented in JavaScript (approximately 1.79E+308).
MIN_VALUE	JavaScript **1.1** JScript **2.0**	Returns the smallest number which can be represented in JavaScript (5E-324).
NaN	JavaScript **1.1** JScript **2.0**	Returns a value which is "not a number".
NEGATIVE_INFINITY	JavaScript **1.1** JScript **2.0**	Returns a value representing negative infinity.
POSITIVE_INFINITY	JavaScript **1.1** JScript **2.0**	Returns a value representing (positive) infinity.
prototype	JavaScript **1.1** JScript **2.0**	Returns the prototype for the object, which can be used to extend the object's interface.

Methods

Method	Introduced	Description
toSource	JavaScript **1.3**	Not in ECMA-262. Returns a string containing the source code for the Number object. Not supported by Internet Explorer.
toString	JavaScript **1.1** JScript **2.0**	Converts the Number object into a string.
valueOf	JavaScript **1.1** JScript **2.0**	Returns the primitive value of the Number object.

In Netscape JavaScript, this object also inherits the methods watch and unwatch from the Object object (not ECMAScript or IE).

Object

`Object` is the primitive type for JavaScript objects, from which all other objects are descended (that is, all other objects inherit the methods and properties of the `Object` object). Introduced in JavaScript 1.0, JScript 3.0. An `Object` object is created using the `Object` constructor:

```
var myObj = new Object();
```

Properties

Property	Introduced	Description
constructor	JavaScript **1.1** JScript **3.0**	Used to reference the constructor function for the object.
prototype	JavaScript **1.1** JScript **3.0**	Returns the prototype for the object, which can be used to extend the object's interface.

Methods

Method	Introduced	Description
eval	JavaScript **1.0**	Not in ECMA-262. Evaluates a string of JavaScript code in the context of the specified object. Not supported in Internet Explorer and no longer available in Netscape JavaScript: replaced by the top-level `eval` function.
toSource	JavaScript **1.3**	Returns a string containing the source code for the `Object` object. Not supported by Internet Explorer.
toString	JavaScript **1.0** JScript **3.0**	Converts the `Object` object into a string.
unwatch	JavaScript **1.2**	Not in ECMA-262. Removes from the object's property a watchpoint that was added with the `watch` method. Not supported by Internet Explorer.
valueOf	JavaScript **1.1** JScript **3.0**	Returns the primitive value of the `Object` object.
watch	JavaScript **1.2**	Not in ECMA-262. Allows us to specify a function which will be called when a value is assigned to the specified property of the object. Not supported by Internet Explorer.

Packages

Allows access to Java packages from within JavaScript code. Introduced in JavaScript 1.1; not supported by ECMAScript or Internet Explorer. This is a top-level object which does not need to be created with a constructor. The `Packages` object takes as its properties the Java package which is to be accessed; for example, to get a reference to the Java package `java.util`, we would write:

```
var javaUtilPackage = Packages.java.util;
```

RegExp

The `RegExp` object is used to contain the pattern for a regular expression. Introduced in JavaScript 1.2 and JScript 3.0; not supported by ECMAScript. `RegExp` objects can be created in two ways: with the `RegExp` constructor, or using a text literal. For example, the following code creates a regular expression which performs a global match for `"Smith"` or `"Smyth"`:

```
var objRegExp = new RegExp("Sm[iy]th", "g");
```

Or:

```
var objRegExp = /Sm[iy]th/g;
```

The second argument may be omitted, or may be one or both of the following flags:

- ❑ g: global match
- ❑ i: ignore case

Properties

Some of these properties have both long and short names. The short names are derived from the Perl programming language.

Property	Introduced	Description
`$1`, `$2`, ... `$9`	JavaScript **1.2** JScript **3.0**	Not in ECMA-262. Matches placed in parentheses and remembered. Not supported by Internet Explorer.
`$_`	JavaScript **1.2** JScript **3.0**	See `input`.
`$*`	JavaScript **1.2**	See `multiline`.
`$&`	JavaScript **1.2**	See `lastMatch`.
`$+`	JavaScript **1.2**	See `lastParen`.

Property	Introduced	Description
$`	JavaScript **1.2**	See `leftContext`.
$'	JavaScript **1.2**	See `rightContext`.
constructor	JavaScript **1.2** JScript **3.0**	Used to reference the constructor function for the object.
global	JavaScript **1.2**	Not in ECMA-262. Indicates whether all possible matches in the string are to be made, or only the first. Corresponds to the `g` flag. Not supported by Internet Explorer.
ignoreCase	JavaScript **1.2**	Not in ECMA-262. Indicates whether the match is to be case-insensitive. Corresponds to the `i` flag. Not supported by Internet Explorer.
index	JScript **3.0**	Not in ECMA-262 or Netscape JavaScript. The position of the first match in the string.
input	JavaScript **1.2** JScript **3.0**	Not in ECMA-262. The string against which the regular expression is matched.
lastIndex	JavaScript **1.2** JScript **3.0**	Not in ECMA-262. The position in the string from which the next match is to be started.
lastMatch	JavaScript **1.2**	Not in ECMA-262. The last characters to be matched. Not supported by Internet Explorer.
lastParen	JavaScript **1.2**	Not in ECMA-262. The last match placed in parentheses and remembered (if any occurred). Not supported by Internet Explorer.
leftContext	JavaScript **1.2**	Not in ECMA-262. The substring preceding the most recent match. Not supported by Internet Explorer.

Table Continued on Following Page

Property	Introduced	Description
multiline	JavaScript **1.2**	Not in ECMA-262. Indicates whether strings are to be searched across multiple lines. Not supported by Internet Explorer.
prototype	JavaScript **1.2** JScript **3.0**	Returns the prototype for the object, which can be used to extend the object's interface.
rightContext	JavaScript **1.2**	Not in ECMA-262. The substring following the most recent match. Not supported by Internet Explorer.
source	JavaScript **1.2** JScript **3.0**	Not in ECMA-262. The text of the pattern for the regular expression.

Methods

Method	Introduced	Description
compile	JavaScript **1.2** JScript **3.0**	Not in ECMA-262. Compiles the RegExp object.
exec	JavaScript **1.2** JScript **3.0**	Not in ECMA-262. Executes a search for a match in the string parameter passed in.
test	JavaScript **1.2** JScript **3.0**	Not in ECMA-262. Tests for a match in the string parameter passed in.
toSource	JavaScript **1.3**	Not in ECMA-262. Returns a string containing the source code for the RegExp object. Not supported by Internet Explorer.
toString	JavaScript **1.2** JScript **3.0**	Converts the RegExp object into a string.
valueOf	JavaScript **1.2** JScript **3.0**	Returns the primitive value of the RegExp object.

In Netscape JavaScript, this object also inherits the methods watch and unwatch from the Object object (not ECMAScript or IE).

The following table lists the special characters which may be used in regular expressions:

Character	Examples	Function
\	/n/ matches n /\n/ matches a linefeed character /^/ matches the start of a line /\^/ matches ^	For characters that are by default treated as normal characters, the backslash indicates that the next character is to be interpreted with a special value. For characters that are usually treated as special characters, the backslash indicates that the next character is to be interpreted as a normal character.
^	/^A/ matches the first but not the second A in "A man called Adam"	Matches the start of a line or of the input.
$	/r$/ matches only the last r in "horror"	Matches the end of a line or of the input.
*	/ro*/ matches r in "right", ro in "wrong" and "roo" in "room"	Matches the preceding character zero or more times.
+	/l+/ matches l in "life", ll in "still" and lll in "stilllife"	Matches the preceding character once or more. For example, /a+/ matches the 'a' in "candy" and all the a's in "caaaaaaandy."
?	/Smythe?/ matches "Smyth" and "Smythe"	Matches the preceding character once or zero times.
.	/.b/ matches the second but not the first b in "blob"	Matches any character apart from the newline character.
(x)	/(Smythe?)/ matches "Smyth" and "Smythe" in "John Smyth and Rob Smythe" and allows the substrings to be retrieved as RegExp.$1 and RegExp.$2 respectively.	Matches x and remembers the match. The matched substring can be retrieved from the elements of the array which results from the match, or from the RegExp object's properties $1, $2 ... $9 or lastParen.
x|y	/Smith|Smythe/ matches "Smith" and "Smythe"	Matches either x or y (where x and y are blocks of characters).
{n}	/l{2}/ matches ll in "still" and the first two ls in "stilllife"	Matches exactly n instances of the preceding character (where n is a positive integer).

Table Continued on Following Page

Character	Examples	Function
{n, }	/l{2,}/ matches ll in "still" and lll in "stilllife"	Matches n or more instances of the preceding character (where n is a positive integer).
{n, m}	/l{1,2}/ matches l in "life", ll in "still" and the first two ls in "stilllife"	Matches between n and m instances of the preceding character (where n and m are positive integers).
[xyz]	[ab] matches a and b [a-c] matches a, b and c	Matches any one of the characters in the square brackets. A range of characters in the alphabet can be matched using a hyphen.
[^xyz]	[^aeiouy] matches s in "easy" [^a-y] matches z in "lazy"	Matches any character except for those not enclosed in the square brackets. A range of characters in the alphabet can be specified using a hyphen.
[\b]		Matches a backspace.
\b	/t\b/ matches the first t in "about time"	Matches a word boundary (for example, a space or the end of a line).
\B	/t\Bi/ matches ti in "it is time"	Matches when there is no word boundary in this position.
\cX	/\cA/ matches *ctrl-A*	Matches a control character.
\d	/IE\d/ matches IE4, IE5, etc.	Matches a digit character. This is identical to [0-9].
\D	/\D/ matches the decimal point in "3.142"	Matches any character which is not a digit. This is identical to [^0-9].
\f		Matches a form-feed character.
\n		Matches a line-feed character.
\r		Matches a carriage return character.
\s	/\s/ matches the space in "not now"	Matches any whitespace character, including space, tab, line-feed, etc. This is identical to [\f\n\r\t\v].
\S	/\S/ matches a in " a "	Matches any character other than a whitespace character. This is identical to [^ \f\n\r\t\v].
\t		Matches a tab character.

Character	Examples	Function
\v		Matches a vertical tab character.
\w	/\w/ matches O in "O?!" and 1 in "$1"	Matches any alphanumeric character or the underscore. This is identical to [A-Za-z0-9_].
\W	/\W/ matches $ in "$10million" and @ in "j_smith@wrox"	Matches any non-alphanumeric character (excluding the underscore). This is identical to [^A-Za-z0-9_].
\n	/(Joh?n) and \1/ matches John and John in "John and John's friend" but does not match "John and Jon"	Matches the last substring which matched the nth match placed in parentheses and remembered (where n is a positive integer).
\ooctal \xhex	/\x25/ matches %	Matches the character corresponding to the specified octal or hexadecimal escape value.

String

The String object is used to contain a string of characters. Introduced in JavaScript 1.0 and JScript 1.0. This must be distinguished from a string literal, but the methods and properties of the String object can also be accessed by a string literal, since a temporary object will be created when they are called. Created with the String constructor:

```
var objString = new String("This is a string object.");
```

Properties

Property	Introduced	Description
constructor	JavaScript 1.1 JScript 2.0	Used to reference the constructor function for the object.
length	JavaScript 1.0 JScript 1.0	Returns the number of characters in the string.
prototype	JavaScript 1.1 JScript 2.0	Returns the prototype for the object, which can be used to extend the object's interface.

Methods

Method	Introduced	Description
anchor	JavaScript **1.0** JScript **1.0**	Not in ECMA-262. Returns an HTML anchor element. This can be used as a target for another link but cannot be used to link to another document or part of a document.
big	JavaScript **1.0** JScript **1.0**	Not in ECMA-262. Encloses the string in <BIG>...</BIG> tags.
blink	JavaScript **1.0** JScript **1.0**	Not in ECMA-262. Encloses the string in <BLINK>...</BLINK> tags.
bold	JavaScript **1.0** JScript **1.0**	Not in ECMA-262. Encloses the string in <B>...</B> tags.
charAt	JavaScript **1.0** JScript **1.0**	Returns the character at the specified position in the string.
charCodeAt	JavaScript **1.2** JScript **3.0**	Returns the Unicode value of the character at the specified position in the string.
concat	JavaScript **1.2** JScript **3.0**	Not in ECMA-262. Concatenates the strings supplied as arguments and returns the string thus formed.
fixed	JavaScript **1.0** JScript **1.0**	Not in ECMA-262. Encloses the string in <TT>...</TT> tags.
fontcolor	JavaScript **1.0** JScript **1.0**	Not in ECMA-262. Encloses the string in <FONT COLOR=*string*>...</FONT> tags.
fontsize	JavaScript **1.0** JScript **1.0**	Not in ECMA-262. Encloses the string in <FONT SIZE=*string*>...</FONT> tags.
fromCharCode	JavaScript **1.2** JScript **3.0**	Returns the string formed from the concatenation of the characters represented by the supplied Unicode values.

Method	Introduced	Description
indexOf	JavaScript **1.0** JScript **1.0**	Returns the position within the String object of the first match for the supplied substring. Returns -1 if the substring is not found.
italics	JavaScript **1.0** JScript **1.0**	Not in ECMA-262. Encloses the string in `<I>...</I>` tags.
lastIndexOf	JavaScript **1.0** JScript **1.0**	Returns the position within the String object of the last match for the supplied substring. Returns -1 if the substring is not found.
link	JavaScript **1.0** JScript **1.0**	Not in ECMA-262. Creates an HTML link element that can be used to link to another web page.
match	JavaScript **1.2** JScript **3.0**	Not in ECMA-262. Used to match a regular expression against a string.
replace	JavaScript **1.2** JScript **3.0**	Not in ECMA-262. Used to replace a substring which matches a regular expression with a new value.
search	JavaScript **1.2** JScript **3.0**	Not in ECMA-262. Searches for a match between a regular expression and the string.
slice	JavaScript **1.0** JScript **3.0**	Not in ECMA-262. Returns a substring of the String object.
small	JavaScript **1.0** JScript **1.0**	Not in ECMA-262. Encloses the string in `<SMALL>...</SMALL>` tags.
split	JavaScript **1.1** JScript **3.0**	Splits a String object into an array of strings by separating the string into substrings.
strike	JavaScript **1.0** JScript **1.0**	Not in ECMA-262. Encloses the string in `<STRIKE>...</STRIKE>` tags.

Table Continued on Following Page

Method	Introduced	Description
sub	JavaScript **1.0** JScript **1.0**	Not in ECMA-262. Encloses the string in `<SUB>...</SUB>` tags.
substr	JavaScript **1.0** JScript **3.0**	Not in ECMA-262. Returns a substring of the characters from the given starting position and containing the specified number of characters.
substring	JavaScript **1.0** JScript **1.0**	Returns a substring of the characters between two positions in the string.
sup	JavaScript **1.0** JScript **1.0**	Not in ECMA-262. Encloses the string in `<SUP>...</SUP>` tags.
toLowerCase	JavaScript **1.0** JScript **1.0**	Returns the string converted to lower case.
toSource	JavaScript **1.3**	Not in ECMA-262. Returns a string containing the source code for the `String` object. Not supported by Internet Explorer.
toString	JavaScript **1.1** JScript **2.0**	Converts the `String` object into a string.
toUpperCase	JavaScript **1.0** JScript **1.0**	Returns the string converted to upper case.
valueOf	JavaScript **1.1** JScript **2.0**	Returns the primitive value of the `String` object.

In Netscape JavaScript, this object also inherits the methods `watch` and `unwatch` from the `Object` object (not ECMAScript or IE).

sun

A synonym for `Packages.sun`. Introduced in JavaScript 1.1; not supported by ECMAScript.

VBArray

The `VBArray` object represents in JScript an array created in Visual Basic or VBScript. Introduced in JScript 3.0; not supported by ECMAScript or Netscape JavaScript. A JScript `VBArray` object is created with the `VBArray` constructor, which takes a Visual Basic array as a parameter. The following code builds an array in VBScript and creates from that a JScript `VBArray` object:

```
<SCRIPT LANGUAGE=VBScript>
function getArray()
dim arrVB(1)
arrVB(0)=100
arrVB(1)=250
getArray=arrVB
End Function
</SCRIPT>

<SCRIPT LANGUAGE=JavaScript>
var vbArr = new VBArray(getArray());
</SCRIPT>
```

Methods

Method	Introduced	Description
dimensions	JScript 3.0	Returns the number of dimensions in the VBArray.
getItem	JScript 3.0	Retrieves the specified element from the VBArray.
lbound	JScript 3.0	Retrieves the index position of the first element in the VBArray.
toArray	JScript 3.0	Converts the VBArray into a normal JScript array.
ubound	JScript 3.0	Retrieves the index position of the last element in the VBArray.

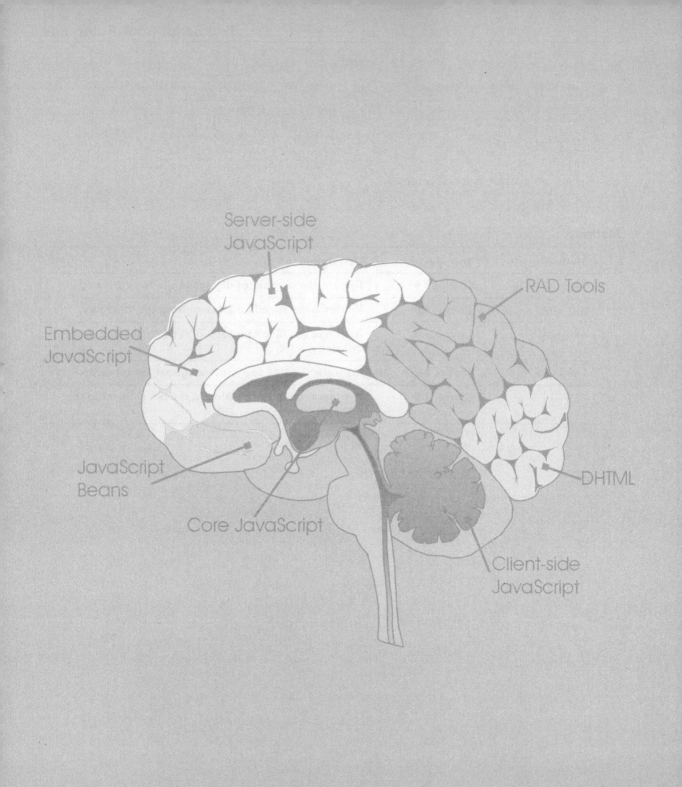

JavaScript Client Reference

The tables on the following tables represent the additional features of the JavaScript language which are available on the client. Netscape Navigator 4 supports JavaScript only up to version 1.3, so features added to the core language in version 1.4 are not supported. However, they may be supported in Internet Explorer 5.0, which broadly supports JavaScript 1.4. Since ECMAScript supports only the core language, none of the features described in this appendix are compatible with ECMAScript. The additions to the core language available in client-side JavaScript are concerned almost with the browser object model. Since the browser object models for Internet Explorer and Navigator are given in detail in Appendices D and E, this appendix will confine itself to objects, methods and properties which are common to both models, and which can therefore be used for cross-browser scripting.

Operators

These are identical to those of the JavaScript core language, except that the object operators `in` and `instanceof`, which were not introduced until JavaScript 1.4, are not supported in Netscape client-side JavaScript. However, `instanceof` is supported by IE5.

Statements

These are identical to those of the JavaScript core language, except that the exception functions `throw` and `try...catch`, which were introduced in JavaScript 1.4, are not supported by Netscape Navigator, although they are supported by IE5.

Events

The following tables describe the events available in client-side JavaScript. Note that the elements supporting these events differ considerably in Netscape Navigator and Internet Explorer.

To handle an event, the event and the function to handle it must be specified in the HTML element for which the event applies:

```
<FORM>
<INPUT TYPE="BUTTON" VALUE="Click here!" ONCLICK=fnEventHandler()>
</FORM>

<SCRIPT>
function fnEventHandler() {
// handle the event here
}
</SCRIPT>
```

Mouse Events

Event	Introduced	Description
onClick	JavaScript **1.0**	Raised when the user clicks on an HTML control.
onDblClick	JavaScript **1.2**	Raised when the user double-clicks on an HTML control.
onMouseDown	JavaScript **1.2**	Raised when the user presses a mouse button.
onMouseMove	JavaScript **1.2**	Raised when the user moves the mouse pointer.
onMouseOut	JavaScript **1.1**	Raised when the user moves the mouse pointer out from within an HTML control.
onMouseOver	JavaScript **1.0**	Raised when the user moves the mouse pointer over an HTML control.
onMouseUp	JavaScript **1.2**	Raised when the user releases the mouse button.

Keyboard Events

Event	Introduced	Description
onKeyDown	JavaScript **1.2**	Raised when the user presses a key on the keyboard.
onKeyPress	JavaScript **1.2**	Raised when the user presses a key on the keyboard. This event will be raised continually until the user releases the key.
onKeyUp	JavaScript **1.2**	Raised when the user releases a key which had been pressed.

HTML Control Events

Event	Introduced	Description
onBlur	JavaScript **1.0**	Raised when an HTML control loses focus.
onChange	JavaScript **1.0**	Raised when an HTML control loses focus and its value has changed.
onFocus	JavaScript **1.0**	Raised when focus is set to the HTML control.
onReset	JavaScript **1.1**	Raised when the user resets a form.
onSelect	JavaScript **1.0**	Raised when the user selects text in an HTML control.
onSubmit	JavaScript **1.0**	Raised when the user submits a form.

Window Events

Event	Introduced	Description
onLoad	JavaScript **1.0**	Raised when the window has completed loading.
onResize	JavaScript **1.2**	Raised when the user resizes the window.
onUnload	JavaScript **1.0**	Executes JavaScript code when the user exits a document.

Other Events

Event	Introduced	Description
onAbort	JavaScript **1.1**	Raised when the user aborts loading an image.
onError	JavaScript **1.1**	Raised when an error occurs loading the page.

Top-Level Functions

In addition to the core top-level functions, two extra functions are available in client-side JavaScript. These are not supported in Internet Explorer.

Function	Introduced	Example	Description
taint	JavaScript **1.1** (removed **1.2**)	v1=taint(v2)	Secures data and prevents it being passed to the server without the user's permission.
untaint	JavaScript **1.1** (removed **1.2**)	v1=untaint(v2)	Removes tainting from data and allows it to be passed to the server.

Objects

The following objects are supported in client-side JavaScript, in addition to the core objects.

Anchor

An `Anchor` object represents an HTML `<ANCHOR>` element. Introduced in JavaScript 1.0. `Anchor` objects can be created either through HTML `<A>` tags or through the `anchor` method of the `String` object. The following example shows how to create an `Anchor` object in HTML code and reference it in JavaScript:

```
<A NAME="myAnchor" href="http://www.wrox.com">Wrox Press</A>

<SCRIPT LANGUAGE="JavaScript">
var objAnchor=document.anchors[0];
</SCRIPT>
```

In Navigator, the anchor can be referred to by its `NAME`:

```
var objAnchor=document.anchors['myAnchor'];
```

However, this will not work in Internet Explorer; instead, we must use `document.all` if we wish to use the anchor's name:

```
var objAnchor=document.all['myAnchor'];
```

However, this will generate a message in Navigator, so the first method is to be recommended.

Properties

The only property shared by the `Anchor` object in NC and IE is name:

Property	Introduced	Description
name	JavaScript **1.2**	Indicates the name of the anchor. Corresponds to the NAME attribute.

Methods

No methods are shared by the NC and IE `Anchor` objects.

Applet

Represents a Java applet. Introduced in JavaScript 1.1, JScript 3.0. `Applet` objects are created with an HTML `<APPLET>` element and referenced through the `applets` collection of the `document` object:

```
<APPLET CODEBASE="http://mysite.com/applets/samples/" CODE="myapp.class"
        WIDTH=250 HEIGHT=150 NAME="myApp">
   <PARAM NAME="Quantity" VALUE="34372">
   <PARAM NAME="Color" VALUE="BrightPink">
</APPLET>

<SCRIPT>
var objApplet=document.applets['myApp'];
</SCRIPT>
```

Properties

The `Applet` object inherits the public properties of the Java applet.

Methods

The `Applet` object inherits the public methods of the Java applet.

Area

`Area` objects define an area of an image as an image map; they are a type of `Link` object. Introduced in JavaScript 1.1, JScript 3.0.

Button

Represents an HTML button element. Introduced in JavaScript 1.0, JScript 1.0. To create a `Button` object, use the HTML `<INPUT>` tag with a `TYPE` attribute equal to `"BUTTON"`:

```
<FORM NAME="myForm">
<INPUT TYPE=BUTTON VALUE="Click me!" NAME="myButton">
</FORM>

<SCRIPT LANGUAGE="JavaScript">
var objButton=document.forms['myForm'].elements['myButton'];
</SCRIPT>
```

The following events are supported by the `Button` object in both NC and IE:

- ❑ onBlur
- ❑ onClick
- ❑ onFocus
- ❑ onMouseDown
- ❑ onMouseUp

Properties

Property	Introduced	Description
form	JavaScript **1.0**	References the form to which the `Button` object belongs.
name	JavaScript **1.0**	Indicates the name of the button. Corresponds to the `NAME` attribute.
type	JavaScript **1.1**	Indicates the type of element, corresponding to the `TYPE` attribute. This will return `"button"`.
value	JavaScript **1.0**	Indicates the value of the element, corresponding to the `VALUE` attribute.

Methods

Method	Introduced	Description
blur	JavaScript **1.0**	Causes the element to lose focus.
click	JavaScript **1.0**	Simulates a mouse-click on the element and fires the onClick event.
focus	JavaScript **1.0**	Causes the element to receive focus.

This object also inherits the methods watch and unwatch from the Object object.

Checkbox

The Checkbox object represents an HTML checkbox. Introduced in JavaScript 1.0, JScript 1.0. To create a Checkbox object, use the HTML <INPUT> element with the TYPE attribute set to "CHECKBOX":

```
<FORM NAME="myForm">
<INPUT NAME="Check1" TYPE=CHECKBOX>Check me!
</FORM>

<SCRIPT LANGUAGE="JavaScript">
var objCheck=document.forms['myForm'].elements['Check1'];
</SCRIPT>
```

The following events are supported by the Checkbox object:

- ❑ onBlur
- ❑ onClick
- ❑ onFocus

Properties

Property	Introduced	Description
checked	JavaScript **1.0**	Indicates whether the checkbox is currently checked.
defaultChecked	JavaScript **1.0**	Indicates whether the checkbox is checked by default.
form	JavaScript **1.0**	References the form to which the Checkbox object belongs.
name	JavaScript **1.0**	Indicates the name of the checkbox. Corresponds to the NAME attribute.
type	JavaScript **1.1**	Indicates the type of element, corresponding to the TYPE attribute. This will return "checkbox".
value	JavaScript **1.0**	Indicates the value of the element, corresponding to the VALUE attribute.

Methods

Method	Introduced	Description
blur	JavaScript **1.0**	Causes the element to lose focus.
click	JavaScript **1.0**	Simulates a mouse-click on the element and fires the onClick event.
focus	JavaScript **1.0**	Causes the element to receive focus.

document

Represents the current document. Introduced in JavaScript 1.0, JScript 1.0. Created with the HTML <BODY> tag and referenced with the document keyword:

```
<BODY>
The body of the page goes here.
</BODY>
<SCRIPT LANGUAGE="JavaScript">
var objDoc=document;
</SCRIPT>
```

The following events are supported by the document object. However, note that events placed in the <BODY> tag apply to the window rather than the document object:

❑ onClick
❑ onDblClick
❑ onKeyDown
❑ onKeyPress
❑ onKeyUp
❑ onMouseDown
❑ onMouseUp

Properties

Property	Introduced	Description
alinkColor	JavaScript **1.0**	Indicates the color of active links in the document, corresponding to the ALINK attribute.
anchors	JavaScript **1.0**	Returns an array of the anchor elements in the document.
applets	JavaScript **1.1**	Returns an array of the applet elements in the document.
bgColor	JavaScript **1.0**	Indicates the background color for the document, corresponding to the BGCOLOR attribute.
cookie	JavaScript **1.0**	Indicates the value of a cookie.

Table Continued on Following Page

Property	Introduced	Description
domain	JavaScript **1.1**	Indicates the domain name of the server.
embeds	JavaScript **1.1**	Returns an array of embedded objects in the document.
fgColor	JavaScript **1.0**	Indicates the foreground color for text in the document, corresponding to the TEXT attribute.
form_name	JavaScript **1.1**	References the named form.
forms	JavaScript **1.1**	Returns an array of the forms in the document.
images	JavaScript **1.1**	Returns an array of the images in the document.
lastModified	JavaScript **1.0**	Indicates when the document was last modified.
linkColor	JavaScript **1.0**	Indicates the default color for links in the document, corresponding to the LINK attribute.
links	JavaScript **1.0**	Returns an array of the links in the document.
referrer	JavaScript **1.0**	Returns the URL of the document which called the current document.
title	JavaScript **1.0**	Indicates the title of the document, corresponding to the contents of the <TITLE> tag.
URL	JavaScript **1.0**	Returns the URL of the document.
vlinkColor	JavaScript **1.0**	Indicates the color of links which have been visited, corresponding to the VLINK attribute.

Methods

Method	Introduced	Description
close	JavaScript **1.0**	Closes an output stream and forces data to display.
open	JavaScript **1.0**	Opens a stream to collect the output of write or writeln methods.
write	JavaScript **1.0**	Writes a string of HTML to the document.
writeln	JavaScript **1.0**	Writes a line of HTML to the document.

event

The event object represents a JavaScript event. Introduced in JavaScript 1.2, JScript 3.0. These objects are created automatically when an event occurs, and cannot be created programmatically. We can retrieve a reference to the event by passing event in as a parameter to the event handler:

```
<FORM NAME="myForm" ONSUBMIT=catchEvent(event)>
<INPUT TYPE=SUBMIT VALUE="Click me!">
</FORM>
<SCRIPT LANGUAGE="JavaScript">
function catchEvent(objEvent)
{
alert(objEvent.type);
}
</SCRIPT>
```

Properties

Not all of these properties are relevant to each event type.

Property	Introduced	Description
screenX	JavaScript 1.2	Indicates the horizontal position of the mouse pointer, relative to the user's screen.
screenY	JavaScript 1.2	Indicates the vertical position of the mouse pointer, relative to the user's screen.
type	JavaScript 1.2	Indicates the type of the current event.
x	JavaScript 1.2	In Navigator, this indicates the width of the object when passed with the resize event, or the horizontal position of the mouse pointer, relative to the layer in which the event occurred. In IE, it indicates the horizontal position of the mouse pointer relative to the parent element.
y	JavaScript 1.2	In Navigator, this indicates the height of the object when passed with the resize event, or the vertical position of the mouse pointer, relative to the layer in which the event occurred. In IE, it indicates the vertical position of the mouse pointer relative to the parent element.

FileUpload

Represents a file <INPUT> element. Introduced in JavaScript 1.0, JScript 3.0. Created with an HTML <INPUT> element with the TYPE attribute set to "FILE":

```
<FORM NAME="myForm" ONSUBMIT=fnSubmit()>
<INPUT NAME="myFile" TYPE=FILE>
</FORM>
<SCRIPT LANGUAGE="JavaScript">
function fnSubmit() {
var objFile = document.forms['myForm'].elements['myFile'];
}
</SCRIPT>
```

The following event handlers are supported by the `FileUpload` object:

- ❑ onBlur
- ❑ onFocus

Properties

Property	Introduced	Description
form	JavaScript **1.0**	References the form to which the `FileUpload` object belongs.
name	JavaScript **1.0**	Indicates the name of the `FileUpload` object. Corresponds to the `NAME` attribute.
type	JavaScript **1.1**	Indicates the type of element, corresponding to the `TYPE` attribute. This will return `"file"`.
value	JavaScript **1.0**	Indicates the value of the element, corresponding to the `VALUE` attribute.

Methods

Method	Introduced	Description
blur	JavaScript **1.0**	Causes the element to lose focus.
focus	JavaScript **1.0**	Causes the element to receive focus.
select	JavaScript **1.0**	Selects the input area of the `FileUpload` object.

Form

Represents an HTML form. Introduced in JavaScript 1.0, JScript 1.0. `Form` objects are created with the HTML `<FORM>` tag and referenced through the `forms` property of the `document` object:

```
<FORM NAME="myForm" ONSUBMIT=fnSubmit()>
<INPUT TYPE=SUBMIT VALUE="Click me!">
</FORM>

<SCRIPT LANGUAGE="JavaScript">
function fnSubmit()
{
var objForm = document.forms['myForm'];
}
</SCRIPT>
```

Two event handlers are supported by the `Form` object:

- ❑ onReset
- ❑ onSubmit

Properties

Property	Introduced	Description
action	JavaScript **1.0**	Contains the URL to which the form will be submitted and corresponds the ACTION attribute.
elements	JavaScript **1.0**	Returns an array of the elements in the form.
encoding	JavaScript **1.0**	Indicates the encoding type for the form and corresponds to the ENCTYPE attribute.
method	JavaScript **1.0**	Indicates the HTTP method to be used to submit the form ("post" or "get") and corresponds to the METHOD attribute.
name	JavaScript **1.0**	Indicates the name of the form. Corresponds to the NAME attribute.
target	JavaScript **1.0**	Indicates the window at which the contents will be targeted and corresponds to the TARGET attribute.

Methods

Method	Introduced	Description
reset	JavaScript **1.1**	Resets the form to its default state.
submit	JavaScript **1.0**	Submits the form.

Frame

JavaScript actually represents a frame using a window object. Every Frame object is a window object, and has all the methods and properties of a window object. However, a window that is a frame differs slightly from a top-level window. To create and reference a frame, we use the HTML <FRAMESET> and <FRAME> elements and the frames property of the window object.

Hidden

The Hidden object represents a hidden HTML input element, used to send information to the server which you don't want to appear on the page (but note that this information is appended to the URL when submitted). Introduced in JavaScript 1.0, JScript 1.0. The Hidden object is created with an HTML <INPUT> tag with the TYPE attribute set to "HIDDEN" and referenced through the forms property of the document object:

```
<FORM NAME="myForm">
<INPUT NAME="hidden" TYPE=HIDDEN VALUE="You can't see this!">
</FORM>

<SCRIPT LANGUAGE="JavaScript">
var objHidden=document.forms['myForm'].elements['hidden'];
</SCRIPT>
```

Properties

Property	Introduced	Description
form	JavaScript **1.0**	References the form to which the Hidden object belongs.
name	JavaScript **1.0**	Indicates the name of the Hidden object. Corresponds to the NAME attribute.
type	JavaScript **1.1**	Indicates the type of element, corresponding to the TYPE attribute. This will return "hidden".
value	JavaScript **1.0**	Indicates the value of the element, corresponding to the VALUE attribute.

History

The History object is used to contain information about the URLs the user has previously visited. Introduced in JavaScript 1.0, JScript 1.0. The History object cannot be created programmatically but can be referenced through the history property of the window object:

```
var objHistory=window.history;
```

Properties

Property	Introduced	Description
length	JavaScript **1.0**	Indicates the number of entries in the history list.

Methods

Method	Introduced	Description
back	JavaScript **1.0**	Loads the previous URL in the history list.
forward	JavaScript **1.0**	Loads the next URL in the history list.
go	JavaScript **1.0**	Loads the specified URL from the history list.

Image

Represents an image in the HTML page. Introduced in JavaScript 1.1, JScript 3.0. The Image object can be created with the Image constructor:

```
var objImage=new Image();
```

Alternatively, it can be created with an HTML <IMG> tag and referenced with the images property of the document object:

```
<IMG SRC="myPicture.gif" NAME="myPicture">
<SCRIPT LANGUAGE="JavaScript">
var objImage=document.images['myPicture'];
</SCRIPT>
```

The following event handlers are supported by the `Image` object:

- ❑ `onAbort`
- ❑ `onError`
- ❑ `onLoad`

Properties

Property	Introduced	Description
`border`	JavaScript **1.1**	Indicates the width of the border around the image and corresponds to the `BORDER` attribute.
`complete`	JavaScript **1.1**	Indicates whether the browser has completed loading the image.
`height`	JavaScript **1.1**	Indicates the height of the image and corresponds to the `HEIGHT` attribute.
`hspace`	JavaScript **1.1**	Indicates the size of the horizontal margin and corresponds to the `HSPACE` attribute.
`lowsrc`	JavaScript **1.1**	Indicates the URL for a lower resolution image to load before the 'real' image is displayed, and corresponds to the `LOWSRC` attribute.
`name`	JavaScript **1.1**	Indicates the name of the image. Corresponds to the `NAME` attribute.
`src`	JavaScript **1.1**	Indicates the URL for the image and corresponds to the `SRC` attribute.
`vspace`	JavaScript **1.1**	Indicates the size of the vertical margin and corresponds to the `VSPACE` attribute.
`width`	JavaScript **1.1**	Indicates the width of the image and corresponds to the `WIDTH` attribute.

Link

Represents a link to another page or to another part of the same page. Introduced in JavaScript 1.0, JScript 1.0. Created through the `link` method of the `String` object or through HTML `<A>` or `<AREA>` tags; in the latter case, it will referenced through the `links` property of the `document` object:

```
<A HREF="http://www.wrox.com">Wrox Press</A>

<SCRIPT LANGUAGE="JavaScript">
objLink = document.links[0];
</SCRIPT>
```

Note that the `Link` object cannot be referenced through its `NAME` attribute, either in Navigator or in Internet Explorer.

The following events are supported by the Link object:

- ❑ onClick
- ❑ onDblClick
- ❑ onKeyDown
- ❑ onKeyPress
- ❑ onKeyUp
- ❑ onMouseDown
- ❑ onMouseOut
- ❑ onMouseUp
- ❑ onMouseOver

Properties

Property	Introduced	Description
hash	JavaScript 1.0	Indicates the anchor part of the URL.
host	JavaScript 1.0	Indicates the hostname and IP address of the URL.
hostname	JavaScript 1.0	Indicates the hostname from the URL.
href	JavaScript 1.0	Indicates the entire URL.
pathname	JavaScript 1.0	Indicates the path and filename of an object.
port	JavaScript 1.0	Indicates the port number in the URL.
protocol	JavaScript 1.0	Indicates the transport protocol to use (e.g. "http:" or "https:"), including the colon.
search	JavaScript 1.0	Indicates the query string appended to the URL.
target	JavaScript 1.0	Indicates the window at which the contents will be targeted and corresponds to the TARGET attribute.

Location

The Location object represents the web page currently being displayed in the browser. Introduced in JavaScript 1.0, JScript 1.0. The Location object cannot be created programmatically, but can be referenced through the location property of the window object:

```
var objLoc = window.location;
```

Properties

Property	Introduced	Description
hash	JavaScript 1.0	Indicates the anchor part of the URL.
host	JavaScript 1.0	Indicates the hostname and IP address of the URL.

Property	Introduced	Description
hostname	JavaScript **1.0**	Indicates the hostname from the URL.
href	JavaScript **1.0**	Indicates the entire URL.
pathname	JavaScript **1.0**	Indicates the path and filename of an object.
port	JavaScript **1.0**	Indicates the port number in the URL.
protocol	JavaScript **1.0**	Indicates the transport protocol to use (e.g. `"http:"` or `"https:"`), including the colon.
search	JavaScript **1.0**	Indicates the query string appended to the URL.

Methods

Method	Introduced	Description
reload	JavaScript **1.1**	Reloads the current document.
replace	JavaScript **1.1**	Loads the specified URL over the current history entry.

navigator

This object represents the browser and contains information about the type and version of browser in use. Introduced in JavaScript 1.0, JScript 1.0. This object cannot be created programmatically, but can be referenced through the `navigator` keyword:

```
var objNav = navigator;
```

Properties

Property	Introduced	Description
appCodeName	JavaScript **1.0**	Returns the code name of the browser. This is `"Mozilla"` for both Navigator and Internet Explorer.
appName	JavaScript **1.0**	Returns the name of the browser. This is `"Netscape"` for Navigator and `"Microsoft Internet Explorer"` for IE.
appVersion	JavaScript **1.0**	Returns information about the browser, including the version number and the platform on which it is running.
mimeTypes	JavaScript **1.1**	Returns an array of the MIME types supported by the client. Included for compatibility only in IE, and returns an empty array.
platform	JavaScript **1.2**	Returns a string indicating the operating system on which the browser is running (for example, `"Win32"`).
plugins	JavaScript **1.1**	Returns an array of the plug-ins installed. Included for compatibility only in IE, and returns an empty array.

Methods

Method	Introduced	Description
javaEnabled	JavaScript **1.1**	Indicates whether Java is enabled.
taintEnabled	JavaScript **1.1** (removed **1.2**)	Specifies whether data tainting is enabled. Data tainting is not supported by IE, so this always returns false.

Option

Represents an option in an HTML <SELECT> element. Introduced in JavaScript 1.0, JScript 1.0. An Option object can be created in two ways; it can be created on the fly with the Option constructor. The following code demonstrates both methods, creating a <SELECT> element with options for "Yes" and "No", and adding a third "Don't know" option on the fly:

```
<FORM NAME="myForm">
<SELECT NAME="mySelect">
<OPTION>Yes
<OPTION>No
</SELECT>
</FORM>

<SCRIPT LANGUAGE="JavaScript">
var objSelect=document.forms['myForm'].elements['mySelect'];
var objOption=new Option("Don't know");
objSelect.options[2]=objOption;
</SCRIPT>
```

Properties

Property	Introduced	Description
defaultSelected	JavaScript **1.1**	Indicates whether the option is selected by default when the page is loaded.
index	JavaScript **1.0**	The zero-based index position of an option in the array of options for the selection list.
selected	JavaScript **1.0**	Indicates whether the option is currently selected.
text	JavaScript **1.0**	Indicates the text for the option.
value	JavaScript **1.0**	Indicates the value of the element, corresponding to the VALUE attribute.

Password

Represents a password input element. Introduced in JavaScript 1.0, JScript 1.0. Created through an HTML <INPUT> element with the TYPE attribute set to "PASSWORD" and referenced through the elements array of a Form object:

```
<FORM ONSUBMIT=fnSubmit()>
<INPUT NAME=myPWD TYPE=PASSWORD>
<INPUT TYPE=SUBMIT>
</FORM>

<SCRIPT>
function fnSubmit() {
var objPwd=document.forms[0].elements['myPWD'];
}
</SCRIPT>
```

Beware that passwords entered in this way are not secure, and are appended to the URL as a query.

Two events are supported by the Password object:

- onBlur
- onFocus

Properties

Property	Introduced	Description
defaultValue	JavaScript 1.1	Indicates the default value for the password.
form	JavaScript 1.0	References the form to which the Password object belongs.
name	JavaScript 1.0	Indicates the name of the Password object. Corresponds to the NAME attribute.
type	JavaScript 1.1	Indicates the type of element, corresponding to the TYPE attribute. This will return "password".
value	JavaScript 1.0	Indicates the value of the element, corresponding to the VALUE attribute.

Methods

Method	Introduced	Description
blur	JavaScript 1.0	Causes the element to lose focus.
focus	JavaScript 1.0	Causes the element to receive focus.
select	JavaScript 1.0	Selects the input area of the Password object.

Radio

Represents a radio button in a form. Introduced in JavaScript 1.0, JScript 1.0. A number of radio buttons can be created with an array of HTML <INPUT> elements with a TYPE attribute set to "RADIO" and with the same name; assigning different names will cause the radio buttons to belong to different groups, so the user will be able to select any number. The array of radio buttons can be accessed through the elements array of a Form object; an individual button can then be accessed through an index of this array:

```
<FORM ONSUBMIT=fnSubmit()>
<INPUT TYPE="RADIO" NAME=radBtn>Yes
<INPUT TYPE="RADIO" NAME=radBtn>No
<INPUT TYPE="RADIO" NAME=radBtn>Don't care
<INPUT TYPE=SUBMIT>
</FORM>

<SCRIPT>
function fnSubmit() {
   var arrRad=document.forms[0].elements['radBtn'];
   var objRad=arrRad[2];
   if (objRad.checked==true) {
     alert("'Don't care was made to care'");
   }
}
</SCRIPT>
```

The Radio object supports the events:

❑ onBlur

❑ onClick

❑ onFocus

Properties

Property	Introduced	Description
checked	JavaScript 1.0	Indicates whether a specific radio button is currently checked.
defaultChecked	JavaScript 1.0	Indicates whether a specific radio button is checked by default.
form	JavaScript 1.0	References the form to which the Radio object belongs.
name	JavaScript 1.0	Indicates the name of the Radio object. Corresponds to the NAME attribute.
type	JavaScript 1.1	Indicates the type of element, corresponding to the TYPE attribute. This will return "radio".
value	JavaScript 1.0	Indicates the value of the element, corresponding to the VALUE attribute.

Methods

Method	Introduced	Description
blur	JavaScript 1.0	Causes the element to lose focus.
click	JavaScript 1.0	Simulates a mouse-click on the element and fires the onClick event.
focus	JavaScript 1.0	Causes the element to receive focus.

Reset

The Reset object represents a reset button in a form. Introduced in JavaScript 1.0, JScript 1.0. A Reset object is created with an HTML <INPUT> element with the TYPE attribute set to "RESET" and referenced through the elements array of a Form object:

```
<FORM>
<INPUT TYPE="RESET" NAME="myReset">
</FORM>

<SCRIPT>
var objReset=document.forms[0].elements['myReset'];
</SCRIPT>
```

The Reset object supports the events:

- ❑ onBlur
- ❑ onClick
- ❑ onFocus

Properties

Property	Introduced	Description
form	JavaScript 1.0	References the form to which the Reset object belongs.
name	JavaScript 1.0	Indicates the name of the reset button. Corresponds to the NAME attribute.
type	JavaScript 1.1	Indicates the type of element, corresponding to the TYPE attribute. This will return "reset".
value	JavaScript 1.0	Indicates the value of the element, corresponding to the VALUE attribute.

Methods

Method	Introduced	Description
blur	JavaScript 1.0	Causes the element to lose focus.
click	JavaScript 1.0	Simulates a mouse-click on the element and fires the onClick event.
focus	JavaScript 1.0	Causes the element to receive focus.

screen

Represents the client's screen and contains information about the display capabilities of the client. Introduced in JavaScript 1.2, JScript 3.0. The screen object is automatically and can be referenced through the screen keyword:

```
alert("Available area: "+screen.availHeight+" x "+screen.availWidth+
      "\nTotal area: "+screen.height+" x "+screen.width);
```

Properties

Method	Introduced	Description
availHeight	JavaScript 1.2	Indicates the vertical range of the screen potentially available to the browser (in pixels).
availWidth	JavaScript 1.0	Indicates the horizontal range of the screen potentially available to the browser (in pixels).
colorDepth	JavaScript 1.0	Indicates the number of bits used for colors on the client's screen.
height	JavaScript 1.0	Indicates the vertical range of the screen (in pixels).
width	JavaScript 1.0	Indicates the horizontal range of the screen (in pixels).

Select

Represents a selection list in a form. Introduced in JavaScript 1.0, JScript 1.0. Created with an HTML <SELECT> element and referenced through the elements array of a Form object:

```
<FORM ONSUBMIT=fnSubmit()>
Please select your favorite food:
<SELECT NAME="mySelect">
<OPTION>Black pudding
<OPTION>Broccoli
<OPTION>Caviar
</SELECT>
<BR><INPUT TYPE=SUBMIT>
</FORM>

<SCRIPT>
function fnSubmit() {
    var objSelect=document.forms[0].elements['mySelect'];
    if (objSelect.selectedIndex==0) {
        alert("Mine too!");
    }
}
</SCRIPT>
```

The Select object supports the events:

❑   onBlur
❑   onChange
❑   onFocus

Properties

Property	Introduced	Description
form	JavaScript 1.0	References the form to which the Select object belongs.
length	JavaScript 1.0	Returns the number of options in the selection list.

Property	Introduced	Description
name	JavaScript **1.0**	Indicates the name of the Select object. Corresponds to the NAME attribute.
options	JavaScript **1.0**	Returns an array of the Option objects in the selection list.
selectedIndex	JavaScript **1.0**	Returns the index of the first selected option.
type	JavaScript **1.1**	Indicates the type of element, corresponding to the TYPE attribute. This will return "select-multiple" for a multiple selection list or "select-one" if only one item in the list may be selected.

Methods

Method	Introduced	Description
blur	JavaScript **1.0**	Causes the element to lose focus.
focus	JavaScript **1.0**	Causes the element to receive focus.

Submit

The Submit object represents a submit button in a form. Introduced in JavaScript 1.0, JScript 1.0. Created with an HTML <INPUT> element with the TYPE attribute set to "SUBMIT" and referenced through the elements array of the Form object:

```
<FORM ONSUBMIT=fnSubmit()>
<INPUT NAME="sbmtBtn" TYPE=SUBMIT>
</FORM>

<SCRIPT>
function fnSubmit() {
var objSubmit=document.forms[0].elements['sbmtBtn'];
objSubmit.value="Don't touch me again!";
}
</SCRIPT>
```

The Submit object supports the events:

❑ onBlur
❑ onClick
❑ onFocus

845

Properties

Property	Introduced	Description
form	JavaScript **1.0**	References the form to which the Submit object belongs.
name	JavaScript **1.0**	Indicates the name of the submit button. Corresponds to the NAME attribute.
type	JavaScript **1.1**	Indicates the type of element, corresponding to the TYPE attribute. This will return "submit".
value	JavaScript **1.0**	Indicates the value of the element, corresponding to the VALUE attribute.

Methods

Method	Introduced	Description
blur	JavaScript **1.0**	Causes the element to lose focus.
click	JavaScript **1.0**	Simulates a mouse-click on the element and fires the onClick event.
focus	JavaScript **1.0**	Causes the element to receive focus.

Text

Represents a textbox. Introduced in JavaScript 1.0, JScript 1.0. Created with an HTML <INPUT> element with the TYPE attribute set to "TEXT" and referenced through the elements array of the Form object:

```
<FORM ONSUBMIT=fnSubmit()>
<INPUT TYPE="TEXT" NAME="myText">
<INPUT TYPE="SUBMIT">
</FORM>

<SCRIPT>
function fnSubmit() {
    objText=document.forms[0].elements['myText'];
    if (objText.value=="") {
      alert("You must enter a value.");
    }
}
</SCRIPT>
```

Text objects support the following events:

- ❑ onBlur
- ❑ onChange
- ❑ onFocus
- ❑ onSelect

Properties

Property	Introduced	Description
defaultValue	JavaScript 1.0	Indicates the default value for the textbox.
form	JavaScript 1.0	References the form to which the Text object belongs.
name	JavaScript 1.0	Indicates the name of the textbox. Corresponds to the NAME attribute.
type	JavaScript 1.1	Indicates the type of element, corresponding to the TYPE attribute. This will return "text".
value	JavaScript 1.0	Indicates the value of the element, corresponding to the VALUE attribute.

Methods

Method	Introduced	Description
blur	JavaScript 1.0	Causes the element to lose focus.
focus	JavaScript 1.0	Causes the element to receive focus.
select	JavaScript 1.0	Selects the input area of the Text object.

Textarea

Represents a textarea in a form. Introduced in JavaScript 1.0, JScript 1.0. Created with an HTML <TEXTAREA> element and referenced with the elements array of the Form object:

```
<FORM ONSUBMIT=fnSubmit()>
<TEXTAREA ROWS=5 COLS=30 NAME="myText">
Enter your text here.
</TEXTAREA>
<INPUT TYPE="SUBMIT">
</FORM>

<SCRIPT>
function fnSubmit() {
    objText=document.forms[0].elements['myText'];
    if (objText.value=="") {
        alert("You've got to enter something");
    }
}
</SCRIPT>
```

The Textarea object supports seven events:

- ❑ onBlur
- ❑ onChange
- ❑ onFocus
- ❑ onKeyDown
- ❑ onKeyPress
- ❑ onKeyUp
- ❑ onSelect

Properties

Property	Introduced	Description
defaultValue	JavaScript **1.0**	Indicates the default value for the textarea.
form	JavaScript **1.0**	References the form to which the `Textarea` object belongs.
name	JavaScript **1.0**	Indicates the name of the textarea. Corresponds to the NAME attribute.
type	JavaScript **1.1**	Indicates the type of element, corresponding to the TYPE attribute. This will return `"textarea"`.
value	JavaScript **1.0**	Indicates the value of the element, corresponding to the VALUE attribute.

Methods

Method	Introduced	Description
blur	JavaScript **1.0**	Causes the element to lose focus.
focus	JavaScript **1.0**	Causes the element to receive focus.
select	JavaScript **1.0**	Selects the input area of the `Textarea` object.

window

Represents a window or frame in the browser. Introduced in JavaScript 1.0, JScript 1.0. A `window` object is automatically created for every browser window open, and can be referenced with the `window` keyword. However, we can call the methods and properties of the `window` object without explicitly naming the object, so, to see whether the current window is closed, we can write:

```
alert(closed);
```

instead of:

```
window.alert(window.closed);
```

The window object supports six events:

- ❑ onBlur
- ❑ onError
- ❑ onFocus
- ❑ onLoad
- ❑ onResize
- ❑ onUnload

Properties

Property	Introduced	Description
closed	JavaScript **1.1**	Indicates whether a window is closed.
defaultStatus	JavaScript **1.0**	Indicates the default text displayed in the window's status bar.
document	JavaScript **1.0**	Returns a reference to the document object in the current window.
frames	JavaScript **1.0**	Returns an array of the frames in the window.
history	JavaScript **1.1**	Returns a reference to the history object for the window.
length	JavaScript **1.0**	Returns the number of frames in the window.
location	JavaScript **1.0**	Returns the location object for the current window.
name	JavaScript **1.0**	Indicates the name of the window. Corresponds to the NAME attribute.
offscreenBuffering	JavaScript **1.2**	Specifies whether offscreen buffering is to be used to update objects in the window before they are made visible.
opener	JavaScript **1.1**	Returns a reference to the window which called the current window.
parent	JavaScript **1.0**	Returns a reference to the window or frame to which the current frame belongs.
self	JavaScript **1.0**	Returns a reference to the current window.
status	JavaScript **1.0**	Indicates the current message in the status bar.
top	JavaScript **1.0**	Returns a reference to the topmost window.

Methods

Method	Introduced	Description
alert	JavaScript **1.0**	Displays a dialog box containing a message and an OK button.
blur	JavaScript **1.0**	Causes the element to lose focus.
clearInterval	JavaScript **1.2**	Cancels an interval set with the setInterval method.

Table Continued on Following Page

Method	Introduced	Description
clearTimeout	JavaScript **1.0**	Cancels a timeout set with the setTimeout method.
close	JavaScript **1.0**	Closes the window.
confirm	JavaScript **1.0**	Displays a dialog box containing a message and OK and Cancel buttons.
focus	JavaScript **1.1**	Causes the element to receive focus.
moveBy	JavaScript **1.2**	Moves the window by the specified number of pixels in the x- and y-axes.
moveTo	JavaScript **1.2**	Moves the top-left corner of the window to the specified position in the x- and y-axes.
open	JavaScript **1.0**	Opens a new window.
print	JavaScript **1.2**	Prints the contents of the window or frame.
prompt	JavaScript **1.0**	Displays a dialog box with a message, an input area and OK and Cancel buttons.
resizeBy	JavaScript **1.2**	Resizes the window by the specified x- and y-offsets by adjusting the position of the bottom-right corner.
resizeTo	JavaScript **1.2**	Resizes the window to the specified dimensions by adjusting the position of the bottom-right corner.
scroll	JavaScript **1.1**	Scrolls the window to the specified co-ordinates.
scrollBy	JavaScript **1.2**	Scrolls the window by the specified x- and y-offsets.
scrollTo	JavaScript **1.2**	Scrolls the window to the specified co-ordinates, such that the specified point becomes the top-left corner.
setInterval	JavaScript **1.2**	Evaluates the given expression every time the specified number of milliseconds elapses.
setTimeout	JavaScript **1.0**	Evaluates the given expression (once only) after the specified number of milliseconds has elapsed.

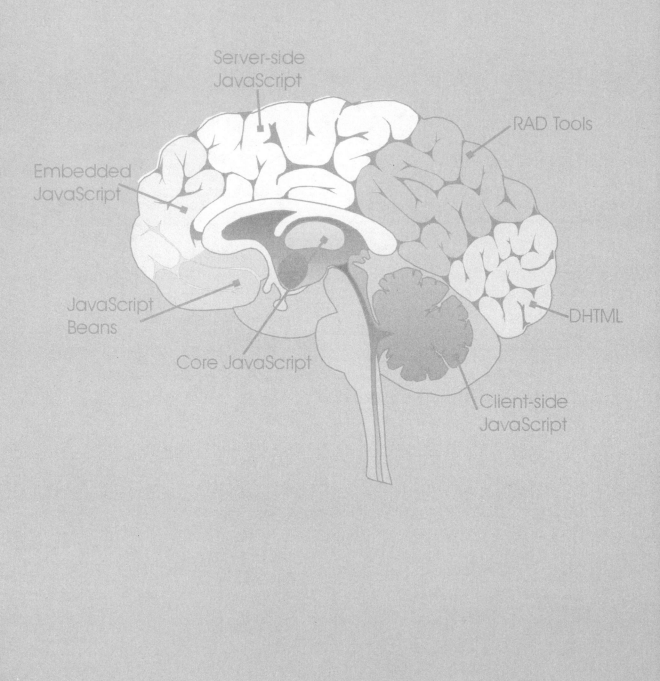

JavaScript Server Reference

This appendix covers those features of JavaScript which relate only to its use on the server-side. We cover here only Netscape JavaScript, as it is used in Enterprise Server 3.x, since the peculiarities of JScript on the server are covered in the appendix on ASP (Appendix G). Also, because ECMAScript is confined to the core language, none of the features in this appendix are supported by ECMA-262. Enterprise Server 3.x supports JavaScript to version 1.2, so any features introduced in JavaScript 1.3 and 1.4 are not available in server-side JavaScript.

Version Reference

The following table illustrates the correspondence between versions of Netscape Enterprise Server and the supported versions of the JavaScript language.

Language Version	Enterprise Server Version
JavaScript 1.1	2.0
JavaScript 1.2	3.0

Operators

As for the core language, except that the strictly equal (===) and not strictly equal (!==) comparison operators (introduced in JavaScript 1.3), and the in and instanceOf object operators (introduced in JavaScript 1.4) are not supported.

Statements

Identical to those of the core language, except that the exception statements `throw` and `try...catch` (introduced in JavaScript 1.4) are not supported.

Top-Level Functions

Top-Level Properties

These are not supported.

Top-Level Methods

All of the top-level methods of the core language are supported, except for `isFinite`. The following top-level functions are also supported:

Function	Introduced	Description
addClient	JavaScript **1.1**	Adds information about the client to a URL.
addResponseHeader	JavaScript **1.2**	Adds the specified name/value pair to the response header.
blob	JavaScript **1.1**	Returns a `blob` object from the specified file.
callC	JavaScript **1.1**	Calls a native function.
debug	JavaScript **1.1**	Prints the specified value in the Trace window of Enterprise Server's Application Manager.
deleteResponseHeader	JavaScript **1.2**	Removes the specified field from the response header.
flush	JavaScript **1.1**	Sends all data from the output buffer to the client.
getOptionValue	JavaScript **1.1**	Returns the value of a specific selected option in an HTML `<SELECT>` element.
getOptionValueCount	JavaScript **1.1**	Returns the number of selected options in an HTML `<SELECT>` element.
redirect	JavaScript **1.1**	Redirects the client to the specified URL.
registerCFunction	JavaScript **1.1**	Registers a native function so that it can be called from within JavaScript.

Function	Introduced	Description
ssjs_generateClientID	JavaScript **1.2**	Generates an identifier for a specific client object.
ssjs_getCGIVariable	JavaScript **1.2**	Returns the value of the specified environment variable.
ssjs_getClientID	JavaScript **1.2**	Returns an identifier for a specific client object.
write	JavaScript **1.1**	Writes the specified string to the HTML page sent to the client.

Objects

In addition to the objects of the core language (except for those specific to JScript: the ActiveXObject, Enumerator and VBArray objects), server-side JavaScript.

blob

Represents a Binary Large Object, or BLOB. This is a large block of data stored in binary format, and typically consists of an image. Introduced in JavaScript 1.1. A blob object cannot be created directly, but may be refernced through a field of the cursor object which contains a BLOB. For example, the following code connects to the Northwind database through an ODBC DSN, sets the cursor to the Employees table and for each entry sets a blob object to equal the photo field and writes this to the client:

```
<SERVER>
database.connect("ODBC","NWind","","","");
objCursor=database.cursor("SELECT * FROM Employees");
while (objCursor.next()) {
    objBlob=objCursor.photo;
    write(objBlob.blobImage("bmp"));
}
objCursor.close();
</SERVER>
```

Methods

Method	Introduced	Description
blobImage	JavaScript **1.1**	Creates an HTML < IMG> element of the specified MIME type for the blob object.
blobLink	JavaScript **1.1**	Creates an HTML <A> element which links to the BLOB data.

This object also inherits the methods watch and unwatch from the Object object.

client

Represents a client currently connected to the server. Introduced in JavaScript 1.1. A client object is automatically created for each client as it connects to the server. This object can be accessed through the client keyword:

```
var objClient=client;
```

Methods

Method	Introduced	Description
destroy	JavaScript **1.1**	Destroys the client object.
expiration	JavaScript **1.1**	Specifies the number of seconds a client may be inactive before the client object will be destroyed.

This object also inherits the methods watch and unwatch from the Object object.

Connection

Represents a connection to a database. Introduced in JavaScript 1.2. Connection objects are created with the connection method of the DBPool object. For example, the following code connects to the Jet Northwind database through an ODBC DSN, creates a Connection object with the name "myConnection" and a timeout value of 30 seconds and calls its SQLTable method to return an HTML table containing the results of a SQL query to the browser:

```
<SERVER>
objDBPool=new DbPool("ODBC","NWind","","","");
objConn=objDBPool.connection("myConnection,30);
objConn.SQLTable("SELECT * FROM Employees");
</SERVER>
```

Properties

Property	Introduced	Description
prototype	JavaScript **1.2**	Returns the prototype for the object, which can be used to extend the object's interface.

Methods

Method	Introduced	Description
beginTransaction	JavaScript **1.2**	Marks the beginning of a new transaction.
commitTransaction	JavaScript **1.2**	Commits the transaction.
connected	JavaScript **1.2**	Indicates whether the Connection object is connected to a database.

Method	Introduced	Description
cursor	JavaScript 1.2	Creates a cursor object on the connection with the supplied SQL statement.
execute	JavaScript 1.2	Executes the SQL statement supplied as an argument.
majorErrorCode	JavaScript 1.2	Returns the code for an error raised by the database server or ODBC.
majorErrorMessage	JavaScript 1.2	Returns the descriptive message for an error raised by the database server or ODBC.
minorErrorCode	JavaScript 1.2	Returns an additional code for an error raised by the database server or ODBC.
minorErrorMessage	JavaScript 1.2	Returns an additional message for an error raised by the database server or ODBC.
release	JavaScript 1.2	Releases the Connection object back into the database pool for reuse.
rollbackTransaction	JavaScript 1.2	Aborts the transaction.
SQLTable	JavaScript 1.2	Creates an HTML table displaying the results of the given SQL query.
storedProc	JavaScript 1.2	Creates a Stproc object and runs the specified stored procedure on the database server.
toString	JavaScript 1.2	Converts the Connection object into a string.

This object also inherits the methods watch and unwatch from the Object object.

Cursor

Represents a cursor returned from the database due to a SQL query. Introduced in JavaScript 1.1. Created through the cursor method of the Connection or database object:

```
<SERVER>
database.connect("ODBC","NWind","","","");
objCursor=database.cursor("SELECT * FROM Products");
</SERVER>
```

Properties

Property	Introduced	Description
column_name	JavaScript **1.1**	Returns the named column in the cursor.
prototype	JavaScript **1.1**	Returns the prototype for the object, which can be used to extend the object's interface.

Methods

Method	Introduced	Description
close	JavaScript **1.1**	Closes the cursor.
columnName	JavaScript **1.1**	Returns the name of the column in the cursor with the specified index value.
columns	JavaScript **1.1**	Returns the number of columns in the cursor.
deleteRow	JavaScript **1.1**	Deletes the current row in the specified table.
insertRow	JavaScript **1.1**	Inserts a new row into the specified table.
next	JavaScript **1.1**	Moves to the next row in the cursor.
updateRow	JavaScript **1.1**	Saves changes to the current row of the specified table to the database.

This object also inherits the methods watch and unwatch from the Object object.

database

Used to represent a database. Introduced in JavaScript 1.1. The database object is always available, but to use any other methods, we must first call its connect method to connect to a database. We must specify the type of database ("ORACLE", "SYBASE", "INFORMIX", "DB2", or "ODBC"), the name of the server (or for an ODBC connection, the Data Source Name), the user name and password with which the connection is to be made, and the name of the database to connect to (or " " if multiple databases are not supported):

```
database.connect("ODBC","my_server","user_name","password","");
```

We can additionally supply a value for the maximum number of connections and a flag to indicate whether transactions are to be committed or rolled back when the connection is released.

Properties

Property	Introduced	Description
prototype	JavaScript **1.1**	Returns the prototype for the object, which can be used to extend the object's interface.

Methods

Method	Introduced	Description
beginTransaction	JavaScript **1.1**	Marks the beginning of a transaction.
commitTransaction	JavaScript **1.1**	Commits the transaction.
connect	JavaScript **1.1**	Connects to a database (see above).
connected	JavaScript **1.1**	Indicates whether the `database` object is connected to a database.
cursor	JavaScript **1.1**	Creates a `cursor` object from the database with the supplied SQL statement.
disconnect	JavaScript **1.1**	Severs all connections from the database.
execute	JavaScript **1.1**	Executes the SQL statement supplied as a parameter.
majorErrorCode	JavaScript **1.1**	Returns the code for an error raised by the database server or ODBC.
majorErrorMessage	JavaScript **1.1**	Returns the descriptive message for an error raised by the database server or ODBC.
minorErrorCode	JavaScript **1.1**	Returns an additional code for an error raised by the database server or ODBC.
minorErrorMessage	JavaScript **1.1**	Returns an additional message for an error raised by the database server or ODBC.
rollbackTransaction	JavaScript **1.1**	Aborts the transaction.
SQLTable	JavaScript **1.1**	Creates an HTML table displaying the results of a SQL query against the database.
storedProc	JavaScript **1.2**	Creates a `Stproc` object and runs the specified stored procedure on the database server.
storedProcArgs	JavaScript **1.2**	Creates a prototype for a stored procedure which supports input and output parameters. Used to indicate the direction of the parameters.
toString	JavaScript **1.1**	Converts the `database` object into a string.

This object also inherits the methods `watch` and `unwatch` from the `Object` object.

DbPool

Represents a pool of connections to a database. Introduced in JavaScript 1.2. Created with the `DbPool` constructor, which takes the same arguments as the `database` object's `connect` method. For example:

```
objDbPool=new DbPool("ODBC","NWind","user_name","password","");
```

Properties

Property	Introduced	Description
`prototype`	JavaScript **1.2**	Returns the prototype for the object, which can be used to extend the object's interface.

Methods

Method	Introduced	Description
`connect`	JavaScript **1.2**	Connects to a database.
`connected`	JavaScript **1.2**	Indicates whether the `DbPool` object is connected to a database.
`connection`	JavaScript **1.2**	Retrieves a `Connection` object from the pool.
`disconnect`	JavaScript **1.2**	Severs all connections in the pool from the database.
`majorErrorCode`	JavaScript **1.2**	Returns the code for an error raised by the database server or ODBC.
`majorErrorMessage`	JavaScript **1.2**	Returns the descriptive message for an error raised by the database server or ODBC.
`minorErrorCode`	JavaScript **1.2**	Returns an additional code for an error raised by the database server or ODBC.
`minorErrorMessage`	JavaScript **1.2**	Returns an additional message for an error raised by the database server or ODBC.
`storedProcArgs`	JavaScript **1.2**	Creates a prototype for a stored procedure which supports input and output parameters. Used to indicate the direction of the parameters.
`toString`	JavaScript **1.2**	Converts the `DbPool` object into a string.

This object also inherits the methods `watch` and `unwatch` from the `Object` object.

File

Represents a file on the server. Introduced in JavaScript 1.1. Created with the `File` constructor, which takes as an argument the name of the file to be opened; if the file doesn't already exist, it will be created. The following code opens a file for appending, writes a line of text to it and closes it:

```
<SERVER>
objFile=new File("Test.txt");
objFile.open("a");
objFile.writeln("Line successfully added to file.");
objFile.close();
</SERVER>
```

The following flags are available for use with the `open` method:

- a. Open the file for appending.
- a+. Open the file for appending and reading.
- r. Open the file for reading.
- r+. Open the file for reading and writing.
- w. Open the file for writing.
- w+. Open the file for writing and reading.

Properties

Property	Introduced	Description
constructor	JavaScript 1.1	Used to reference the constructor function for the object.
prototype	JavaScript 1.1	Returns the prototype for the object, which can be used to extend the object's interface.

Methods

Method	Introduced	Description
byteToString	JavaScript 1.1	Converts a byte value into a string.
clearError	JavaScript 1.1	Resets the `error` property.
close	JavaScript 1.1	Closes the file.
eof	JavaScript 1.1	Indicates whether the pointer is at a point beyond the end of the file.
error	JavaScript 1.1	Returns an integer indicating whether any errors have occurred.
exists	JavaScript 1.1	Indicates whether the specified file exists.

Method	Introduced	Description
flush	JavaScript **1.1**	Writes the contents of the buffer to the file.
getLength	JavaScript **1.1**	Returns the length of the file in bytes or characters.
getPosition	JavaScript **1.1**	Returns the position of the pointer in the file.
open	JavaScript **1.1**	Opens the specified file for specific functions (see above).
read	JavaScript **1.1**	Returns a string containing the specified number of characters from the file.
readByte	JavaScript **1.1**	Returns the value of the current byte from the file and moves the pointer to the next byte.
readln	JavaScript **1.1**	Returns a string containing the current line in the file and moves the pointer to the next line.
setPosition	JavaScript **1.1**	Moves the pointer to the specified position in the file.
stringToByte	JavaScript **1.1**	Converts the first character of the specified string into a byte value.
write	JavaScript **1.1**	Writes a string to the file.
writeByte	JavaScript **1.1**	Writes a byte value to the file.
writeln	JavaScript **1.1**	Writes the specified string as a line of text to the file.

This object also inherits the methods watch and unwatch from the Object object.

Lock

Represents a lock on an object which can be used to prevent multiple clients simultaneously accessing that object. Introduced in JavaScript 1.2. Created with the Lock constructor:

```
objLock=new Lock();
```

Properties

Property	Introduced	Description
constructor	JavaScript **1.2**	Used to reference the constructor function for the object.
prototype	JavaScript **1.2**	Returns the prototype for the object, which can be used to extend the object's interface.

Methods

Method	Introduced	Description
isValid	JavaScript **1.2**	Indicates whether the Lock object is valid.
lock	JavaScript **1.2**	Returns a reference to the lock. If the object is currently locked, this method will wait for the lock to be released until the specified timeout value has elapsed.
unlock	JavaScript **1.2**	Releases the lock.

This object also inherits the methods watch and unwatch from the Object object.

project

Represents an application running on the server. Introduced in JavaScript 1.1. Created automatically and referenced with the keyword project.

Methods

Method	Introduced	Description
lock	JavaScript **1.1**	Locks the project.
unlock	JavaScript **1.1**	Unlocks the project.

This object also inherits the methods watch and unwatch from the Object object.

request

Represents the request received from the client. Introduced in JavaScript 1.1. The request object is generated automatically and can be referenced with the request keyword. The following code uses the request object to read the value submitted in a textbox:

```
<FORM>
<INPUT NAME="myText" TYPE=TEXT>
<INPUT TYPE=SUBMIT>
</FORM>

<SERVER>
write("You wrote:<BR>"+request.myText);
</SERVER>
```

Properties

Property	Introduced	Description
agent	JavaScript **1.1**	Returns a string containing information about the browser in use by the client.
imageX	JavaScript **1.1**	Returns the x-coordinate of the mouse pointer when the user clicks on an image map.
imageY	JavaScript **1.1**	Returns the y-coordinate of the mouse pointer when the user clicks on an image map.
input_name	JavaScript **1.1**	Represents the named < INPUT > element in an HTML form (as used in the example above).
ip	JavaScript **1.1**	Returns the client's IP address.
method	JavaScript **1.1**	Returns the HTTP method used to submit the form ("get" or "post").
protocol	JavaScript **1.1**	Returns the level of HTTP protocol supported by the client.

Methods

This object inherits the methods watch and unwatch from the Object object.

Resultset

Represents a recordset returned from the database server when a stored procedure is executed. Introduced in JavaScript 1.2. Created with the resultSet method of the Stproc object. The following code creates a resultSet object by executing the byroyalty stored procedure in the SQL Server pubs database:

```
<SERVER>
database.connect("ODBC","pubs","user_name","password","");
objStProc=database.storedProc("byroyalty",40);
objRS=objStProc.resultSet();
</SERVER>
```

Properties

Property	Introduced	Description
prototype	JavaScript **1.2**	Returns the prototype for the object, which can be used to extend the object's interface.

Methods

Method	Introduced	Description
close	JavaScript **1.2**	Closes the `resultSet` object.
columnName	JavaScript **1.2**	Returns the name of the column with the specified index number.
columns	JavaScript **1.2**	Returns the number of columns in the `resultSet` object.
next	JavaScript **1.2**	Moves the pointer to the next row in the `resultSet`.

This object also inherits the methods `watch` and `unwatch` from the `Object` object.

SendMail

Represents an e-mail message. Introduced in JavaScript 1.2. Created with the `SendMail` constructor:

```
objMail=new SendMail();
```

Properties

Property	Introduced	Description
Bcc	JavaScript **1.2**	A comma-delimited string containing the names of blind-CC recipients for the mail message.
Body	JavaScript **1.2**	Contains the body of the e-mail.
Cc	JavaScript **1.2**	A comma-delimited string containing the names of CC recipients for the mail message.
constructor	JavaScript **1.2**	Used to reference the constructor function for the object.
Errorsto	JavaScript **1.2**	The e-mail address to which error reports are to be sent. The default is the address of the sender.
From	JavaScript **1.2**	The name of the sender of the e-mail.
Organization	JavaScript **1.2**	Contains information about the organization.
prototype	JavaScript **1.2**	Returns the prototype for the object, which can be used to extend the object's interface.
Replyto	JavaScript **1.2**	The address of the user to whom any replies to the message should be sent. By default, this will be the address of the sender.
Smtpserver	JavaScript **1.2**	The name of the SMTP server.
Subject	JavaScript **1.2**	Contains the subject of the e-mail.
To	JavaScript **1.2**	A comma-delimited string containing the names of the primary recipients for the mail message.

Methods

Method	Introduced	Description
errorCode	JavaScript **1.2**	Returns an error code indicating whether the e-mail was successfully sent or whether errors occurred.
errorMessage	JavaScript **1.2**	Returns a description of any error that occurred when the attempt was made to send the e-mail.
send	JavaScript **1.2**	Sends the e-mail.

This object also inherits the methods watch and unwatch from the Object object.

server

An object representing the server. Introduced in JavaScript 1.1. The server object is automatically created and can be accessed through the server keyword.

Properties

Property	Introduced	Description
host	JavaScript **1.1**	Returns a string containing the name of the server, together with the name of the subdomain and domain in which it resides.
hostname	JavaScript **1.1**	Returns a string containing the full hostname of the server, consisting of the host property and the port number. If the port number is 80 (the default), this is omitted and the host and hostname properties have the same value.
port	JavaScript **1.1**	Returns the number of the TCP port used by the server (usually 80).
protocol	JavaScript **1.1**	Returns a string containing the communication protocol used by the server (for example, "http:" or "https:").

Methods

Method	Introduced	Description
lock	JavaScript **1.1**	Locks the server object.
unlock	JavaScript **1.1**	Releases the lock.

This object also inherits the methods watch and unwatch from the Object object.

Stproc

Represents a stored procedure on the database. Introduced in JavaScript 1.2. Created through the storedProc method of the database or Connection object. Calling this method causes the stored procedure to be executed. The following code executes the byroyalty stored procedure on the SQL Server pubs database (passing in a parameter with a value of 40):

```
<SERVER>
database.connect("ODBC","pubs","user_name","password","");
objStProc=database.storedProc("byroyalty",40);
</SERVER>
```

Properties

Property	Introduced	Description
prototype	JavaScript 1.2	Returns the prototype for the object, which can be used to extend the object's interface.

Methods

Method	Introduced	Description
close	JavaScript 1.2	Closes a Stproc object.
outParamCount	JavaScript 1.2	Indicates the number of output parameters returned by a stored procedure.
outParameters	JavaScript 1.2	Returns the value of the output parameter with the specified index position.
resultSet	JavaScript 1.2	Returns a new resultSet object.
returnValue	JavaScript 1.2	Returns the value of the return value parameter of the stored procedure.

This object also inherits the methods watch and unwatch from the Object object.

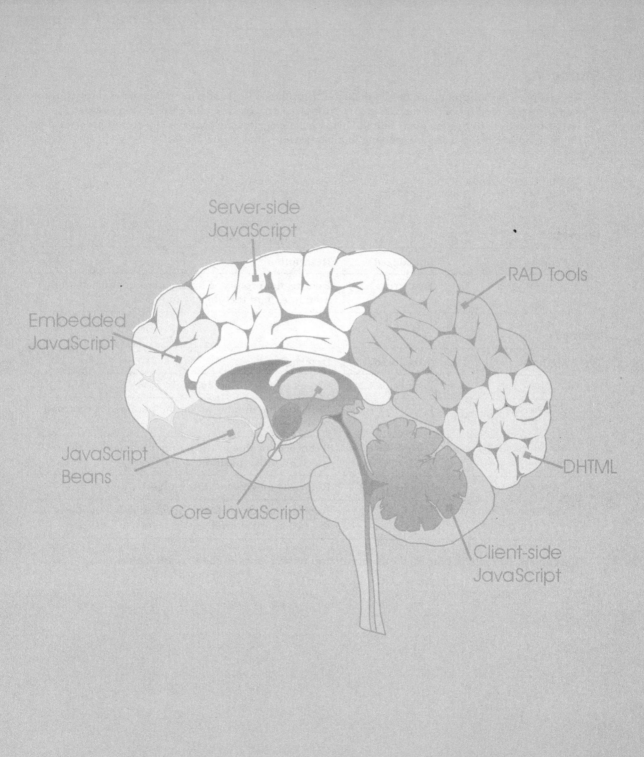

The Wrox Ultimate HTML Database Listing

This section lists all the HTML element tags in alphabetical order, showing which versions of HTML and which browsers support each one. For each element, we also list all the available attributes for use with it. Again, each one shows which versions of HTML and which browsers support each attribute.

!– –

Denotes a comment that is ignored by the HTML parser.

!DOCTYPE

Declares the type and content format of the document.

A

Defines a hypertext link. The HREF or the NAME attribute must be specified. **ALL**.

Attributes	2.0	3.2	4.0	N2	N3	N4	IE2	IE3	IE4/5
<event_name>=script_code	✗	✗	✓	✗	✗	•	✗	•	•
ACCESSKEY=key_character	✗	✗	✓	✗	✗	✗	✗	✗	•
CHARSET=*string*	✗	✗	✓	✗	✗	✗	✗	✗	✗
CLASS=*classname*	✗	✗	✗	✗	✗	✓	✗	✓	✓
COORDS=*string*	✗	✗	✓	✗	✗	✓	✗	✗	✗
DATAFLD=column_name	✗	✗	✗	✗	✗	✗	✗	✗	✓
DATASRC=id	✗	✗	✗	✗	✗	✗	✗	✗	✓
DIR=LTR|RTL	✗	✗	✓	✗	✗	✗	✗	✗	✗
HREF=url	✓	✓	✓	✓	✓	✓	✓	✓	✓
HREFLANG=langcode	✗	✗	✓	✗	✗	✗	✗	✗	✗
ID=*string*	✗	✗	✓	✗	✗	✓	✗	✓	✓
LANG=language_type	✗	✗	✓	✗	✗	✗	✗	✗	✓
LANGUAGE=JAVASCRIPT|JSCRIPT|VBSCRIPT|VBS	✗	✗	✗	✗	✗	✗	✗	✗	✓
METHODS=*string*	✓	✗	✗	✗	✗	✗	✗	✗	✓
NAME=*string*	✓	✓	✓	✓	✓	✓	✓	✓	✓
REL=SAME|NEXT|PARENT|PREVIOUS|*string*	✓	✓	✓	✗	✗	✗	✗	✓	✓
REV=*string*	✓	✓	✓	✗	✗	✗	✗	✓	✓
SHAPE=CIRC|CIRCLE|POLY|POLYGON|RECT|RECTANGLE	✗	✗	✓	✗	✗	✗	✗	✗	✗
STYLE=*string*	✗	✗	✓	✗	✗	✓	✗	✓	✓
TABINDEX=*number*	✗	✗	✓	✗	✗	✗	✗	✗	✓
TARGET=<window_name>|_parent|_blank|_top|_self	✗	✗	✓	✓	✓	✓	✗	✓	✓
TITLE=*string*	✓	✓	✓	✗	✗	✗	✗	✓	✓
TYPE=BUTTON|RESET|SUBMIT	✗	✗	✓	✗	✗	✗	✗	✗	✓
URN=*string*	✓	✗	✗	✗	✗	✗	✗	✗	✓

ABBR

Indicates a sequence of characters that compose an acronym (e.g., "WWW"). **HTML 4.0, IE4, IE5**.

Attributes	2.0	3.2	4.0	N2	N3	N4	IE2	IE3	IE4/5
<event_name>=script_code	✗	✗	✓	✗	✗	✗	✗	✗	✓
CLASS=classname	✗	✗	✓	✗	✗	✗	✗	✗	✓
DIR=LTR|RTL	✗	✗	✓	✗	✗	✗	✗	✗	✗
ID=*string*	✗	✗	✓	✗	✗	✗	✗	✗	✓
LANG=language_type	✗	✗	✓	✗	✗	✗	✗	✗	✓
LANGUAGE=JAVASCRIPT| JSCRIPT|VBSCRIPT|VBS	✗	✗	✗	✗	✗	✗	✗	✗	✓
STYLE=*string*	✗	✗	✓	✗	✗	✗	✗	✗	✓
TITLE=*string*	✗	✗	✓	✗	✗	✗	✗	✗	✓

ADDRESS

Specifies information such as address, signature and authorship. **ALL**.

Attributes	2.0	3.2	4.0	N2	N3	N4	IE2	IE3	IE4/5
<event_name>=script_code	✗	✗	✓	✗	✗	✗	✗	✗	✓
CLASS=classname	✗	✗	✓	✗	✗	✓	✗	✗	✓
DIR=LTR|RTL	✗	✗	✓	✗	✗	✗	✗	✗	✗
ID=*string*	✗	✗	✓	✗	✗	✓	✗	✗	✓
LANG=language_type	✗	✗	✓	✗	✗	✗	✗	✗	✓
LANGUAGE=JAVASCRIPT| JSCRIPT|VBSCRIPT|VBS	✗	✗	✗	✗	✗	✗	✗	✗	✓
STYLE=STRING	✗	✗	✓	✗	✗	✓	✗	✗	✓
TITLE=STRING	✗	✗	✓	✗	✗	✗	✗	✗	✓

APPLET

Places a Java Applet or other executable content in the page. **HTML 3.2, N2, N3, N4, IE3, IE4, IE5, deprecated in HTML 4.0.**

Attributes	2.0	3.2	4.0	N2	N3	N4	IE2	IE3	IE4/5
`<event_name>=script_code`	✗	✗	D	✗	✗	✗	✗	✗	✗
`ALIGN=TOP|MIDDLE|BOTTOM|LEFT|RIGHT|ABSMIDDLE|BASELINE|ABSBOTTOM|TEXTTOP`	✗	✓	D	✓	✓	✓	✗	✓	✓
`ALT=text`	✗	✓	D	✓	✓	✓	✗	✓	✓
`ARCHIVE=url`	✗	✗	D	✗	✓	✓	✗	✗	✗
`BORDER=number`	✗	✗	D	✗	✗	✗	✗	✗	✗
`CLASS=classname`	✗	✗	D	✗	✗	✓	✗	✗	✓
`CODE=filename`	✗	✓	D	✓	✓	✓	✗	✓	✓
`CODEBASE=Path|url`	✗	✓	D	✓	✓	✓	✗	✓	✓
`DATAFLD=column_name`	✗	✗	✗	✗	✗	✗	✗	✗	✓
`DATASRC=id`	✗	✗	✗	✗	✗	✗	✗	✗	✓
`DOWNLOAD=number`	✗	✗	✗	✗	✗	✗	✗	✓	✗
`HEIGHT=number`	✗	✓	D	✓	✓	✓	✗	✓	✗
`HSPACE=number`	✗	✓	D	✗	✗	✓	✗	✓	✓
`ID=string`	✗	✗	D	✗	✗	✓	✗	✗	✓
`MAYSCRIPT=YES|NO`	✗	✗	✗	✗	✗	✓	✗	✗	✗
`NAME=string`	✗	✓	D	✗	✗	✗	✗	✓	✓
`OBJECT=string`	✗	✗	D	✗	✗	✗	✗	✗	✗
`SRC=url`	✗	✗	✗	✗	✗	✗	✗	✗	✓
`STYLE=string`	✗	✗	D	✗	✗	✓	✗	✗	✓
`TITLE=string`	✗	✗	D	✗	✗	✗	✗	✓	✓
`VSPACE=number`	✗	✓	D	✗	✗	✓	✗	✓	✓
`WIDTH=number`	✗	✓	D	✓	✓	✓	✗	✓	✓

AREA

Specifies the shape of a "hot spot" in a client-side image map. **ALL except HTML 2.0.**

Attributes	2.0	3.2	4.0	N2	N3	N4	IE2	IE3	IE4/5
`<event_name>=script_code`	✗	✗	✗	✗	✗	✓	✗	✗	✓
`ALT=text`	✗	✓	✓	✓	✓	✓	✗	✓	✓
`CLASS=classname`	✗	✗	D	✗	✗	✓	✗	✓	✓
`COORDS=`*string*	✗	✓	✓	✓	✓	✓	✓	✓	✓
`DIR=LTR`|`RTL`	✗	✗	✓	✗	✗	✗	✗	✗	✗
`HREF=url`	✗	✓	✓	✓	✓	✓	✓	✓	✓
`ID=`*string*	✗	✗	D	✗	✗	✓	✗	✓	✓
`LANG=language_type`	✗	✗	D	✗	✗	✗	✗	✗	✓
`LANGUAGE=JAVASCRIPT`|`JSCRIPT`|`VBSCRIPT`|`VBS`	✗	✗	✗	✗	✗	✗	✗	✗	✓
`NAME=`*string*	✗	✗	✗	✗	✗	✓	✗	✗	✗
`NOHREF`	✗	✓	✓	✓	✓	✓	✓	✓	✓
`NOTAB`	✗	✗	✗	✗	✗	✗	✗	✓	✗
`SHAPE=CIRC`|`CIRCLE`|`POLY`|`POLYGON`|`RECT`|`RECTANGLE`	✗	✓	✓	✓	✓	✓	✓	✓	✓
`STYLE=`*string*	✗	✗	D	✗	✗	✓	✗	✗	✓
`TABINDEX=number`	✗	✗	✓	✗	✗	✗	✗	✓	✓
`TARGET=<window_name>`|`_parent`|`_blank`|`_top`|`_self`	✗	✗	✓	✓	✓	✓	✗	✓	✓
`TITLE=`*string*	✗	✗	D	✗	✗	✗	✗	✓	✓

B

Renders text in boldface where available. **ALL**.

Attributes	2.0	3.2	4.0	N2	N3	N4	IE2	IE3	IE4/5
`<event_name>=script_code`	✗	✗	✓	✗	✗	✗	✗	✗	✓
`CLASS=classname`	✗	✗	✓	✗	✗	✓	✗	✗	✓
`DIR=LTR|RTL`	✗	✗	✓	✗	✗	✗	✗	✗	✗
`ID=string`	✗	✗	✓	✗	✗	✓	✗	✗	✓
`LANG=language_type`	✗	✗	✓	✗	✗	✗	✗	✗	✓
`LANGUAGE=JAVASCRIPT|JSCRIPT|VBSCRIPT|VBS`	✗	✗	✗	✗	✗	✗	✗	✗	✓
`STYLE=string`	✗	✗	✓	✗	✗	✓	✗	✗	✓
`TITLE=string`	✗	✗	✓	✗	✗	✗	✗	✗	✓

BASE

Specifies the document's base URL. **ALL**.

Attributes	2.0	3.2	4.0	N2	N3	N4	IE2	IE3	IE4/5
`HREF=url`	✓	✓	✓	✓	✓	✓	✓	✓	✓
`TARGET=<window_name>|_parent|_blank|_top|_self`	✗	✗	✓	✓	✓	✓	✗	✓	✓

BASEFONT

Sets the base font values to be used as the default font when rendering text. **HTML 3.2, N2, N3, N4, IE2, IE3, IE4, IE5 deprecated in HTML 4.0.**

Attributes	2.0	3.2	4.0	N2	N3	N4	IE2	IE3	IE4/5
`CLASS=classname`	✗	✗	✗	✗	✗	✓	✗	✗	✓
`COLOR=color`	✗	✗	D	✗	✗	✗	✗	✓	✓
`FACE=font_family_name`	✗	✗	D	✗	✗	✗	✗	✓	✓
`ID=string`	✗	✗	D	✗	✗	✓	✗	✗	✓
`LANG=language_type`	✗	✗	✗	✗	✗	✗	✗	✗	✓
`LANGUAGE=JAVASCRIPT|JSCRIPT|VBSCRIPT|VBS`	✗	✗	✗	✗	✗	✗	✗	✗	✓
`SIZE=1|2|3|4|5|6|7`	✗	✓	D	✓	✓	✓	✓	✓	✓

BDO

Turns off the bidirectional rendering algorithm for selected fragments of text. **HTML 4.0**.

Attributes	2.0	3.2	4.0	N2	N3	N4	IE2	IE3	IE4/5
CLASS=classname	✘	✘	✓	✘	✘	✘	✘	✘	✘
DIR=LTR|RTL	✘	✘	✓	✘	✘	✘	✘	✘	✘
ID=*string*	✘	✘	✓	✘	✘	✘	✘	✘	✘
LANG=language_type	✘	✘	✓	✘	✘	✘	✘	✘	✘
STYLE=*string*	✘	✘	✓	✘	✘	✘	✘	✘	✘
TITLE=*string*	✘	✘	✓	✘	✘	✘	✘	✘	✘

BGSOUND

Specifies a background sound to be played while the page is loaded. **IE2, IE3, IE4, IE5**.

Attributes	2.0	3.0	4.0	N2	N3	N4	IE2	IE3	IE4/5
BALANCE=number	✘	✘	✘	✘	✘	✘	✘	✘	✓
CLASS=classname	✘	✘	✘	✘	✘	✘	✘	✘	✓
ID=*string*	✘	✘	✘	✘	✘	✘	✘	✘	✓
LANG=language_type	✘	✘	✘	✘	✘	✘	✘	✘	✓
LOOP=number	✘	✘	✘	✘	✘	✘	✓	✓	✓
SRC=url	✘	✘	✘	✘	✘	✘	✓	✓	✓
TITLE=*string*	✘	✘	✘	✘	✘	✘	✘	✘	✓
VOLUME=number	✘	✘	✘	✘	✘	✘	✘	✘	✓

BIG

Renders text in a relatively larger font than the current font. **HTML 3.2, 4.0, N2, N3, N4, IE3, IE4, IE5**.

Attributes	2.0	3.2	4.0	N2	N3	N4	IE2	IE3	IE4/5
`<event_name>=script_code`	✗	✗	✓	✗	✗	✗	✗	✗	✓
`CLASS=classname`	✗	✗	✓	✗	✗	✓	✗	✗	✓
`DIR=LTR|RTL`	✗	✗	✓	✗	✗	✗	✗	✗	✗
`ID=string`	✗	✗	✓	✗	✗	✓	✗	✗	✓
`LANG=language_type`	✗	✗	✓	✗	✗	✗	✗	✗	✓
`LANGUAGE=JAVASCRIPT|JSCRIPT|` `VBSCRIPT|VBS`	✗	✗	✗	✗	✗	✗	✗	✗	✓
`STYLE=string`	✗	✗	✓	✗	✗	✓	✗	✗	✓
`TITLE=string`	✗	✗	✓	✗	✗	✗	✗	✗	✓

BLINK

Causes the text to flash on and off within the page. **N2, N3, N4**.

Attributes	2.0	3.2	4.0	N2	N3	N4	IE2	IE3	IE4/5
`CLASS=classname`	✗	✗	✗	✗	✗	✓	✗	✗	✗
`ID=string`	✗	✗	✗	✗	✗	✓	✗	✗	✗
`STYLE=string`	✗	✗	✗	✗	✗	✓	✗	✗	✗

BLOCKQUOTE

Denotes a quotation in text, usually a paragraph or more. **ALL**.

Attributes	2.0	3.2	4.0	N2	N3	N4	IE2	IE3	IE4/5
`<event_name>=script_code`	✗	✗	✓	✗	✗	✗	✗	✗	✓
`CITE=url`	✗	✗	✓	✗	✗	✗	✗	✗	✗
`CLASS=classname`	✗	✗	✓	✗	✗	✓	✗	✗	✓
`DIR=LTR|RTL`	✗	✗	✓	✗	✗	✗	✗	✗	✗
`ID=string`	✗	✗	✓	✗	✗	✓	✗	✗	✓
`LANG=language_type`	✗	✗	✓	✗	✗	✗	✗	✗	✓
`LANGUAGE=JAVASCRIPT|JSCRIPT|` `VBSCRIPT|VBS`	✗	✗	✗	✗	✗	✗	✗	✗	✓
`STYLE=string`	✗	✗	✓	✗	✗	✓	✗	✗	✓
`TITLE=string`	✗	✗	✓	✗	✗	✗	✗	✗	✓

BODY

Defines the beginning and end of the body section of the page. **ALL.**

Attributes	2.0	3.2	4.0	N2	N3	N4	IE2	IE3	IE4/5
<event_name>=script_code	✗	✗	✓	✗	✗	✓	✗	✗	✓
ALINK=color	✗	✓	D	✓	✓	✓	✗	✓	✓
BACKGROUND=*string*	✗	✓	D	✓	✓	✓	✓	✓	✓
BGCOLOR=color	✗	✓	D	✓	✓	✓	✓	✓	✓
BGPROPERTIES=FIXED	✗	✗	✗	✗	✗	✗	✓	✓	✓
BOTTOMMARGIN=number	✗	✗	✗	✗	✗	✗	✗	✗	✓
CLASS=classname	✗	✗	✓	✗	✗	✓	✗	✓	✓
DIR=LTR|RTL	✗	✗	✓	✗	✗	✗	✗	✗	✗
ID=*string*	✗	✗	✓	✗	✗	✓	✗	✓	✓
LANG=language_type	✗	✗	✓	✗	✗	✗	✗	✗	✓
LANGUAGE=JAVASCRIPT|JSCRIPT|VBSCRIPT|VBS	✗	✗	✗	✗	✗	✗	✗	✗	✓
LEFTMARGIN=number	✗	✗	✗	✗	✗	✗	✓	✓	✓
LINK=color	✗	✓	D	✓	✓	✓	✓	✓	✓
RIGHTMARGIN=number	✗	✗	✗	✗	✗	✗	✗	✗	✓
SCROLL=YES|NO	✗	✗	✗	✗	✗	✗	✗	✗	✓
STYLE=*string*	✗	✗	✓	✗	✗	✓	✗	✓	✓
TEXT=color	✗	✓	D	✓	✓	✓	✓	✓	✓
TITLE=*string*	✗	✗	✓	✗	✗	✗	✗	✗	✓
TOPMARGIN=number	✗	✗	✗	✗	✗	✗	✓	✓	✓
VLINK=color	✗	✓	D	✓	✓	✓	✓	✓	✓

BR

Inserts a line break. **ALL**.

Attributes	2.0	3.2	4.0	N2	N3	N4	IE2	IE3	IE4/5
CLASS=classname	✗	✗	✓	✗	✗	✓	✗	✓	✓
CLEAR=ALL|LEFT|RIGHT|NONE	✗	✓	D	✓	✓	✓	✓	✓	✓
ID=string	✗	✗	✓	✗	✗	✓	✗	✗	✓
LANGUAGE=JAVSCRIPT|JSCRIPT|VBSCRIPT|VBS	✗	✗	✗	✗	✗	✗	✗	✗	✓
STYLE=string	✗	✗	✗	✗	✗	✓	✗	✗	✓
TITLE=string	✗	✗	✓	✗	✗	✗	✗	✗	✓

BUTTON

Renders an HTML button, the enclosed text used as the button's caption. **HTML 4.0, IE4, IE5**.

Attributes	2.0	3.2	4.0	N2	N3	N4	IE2	IE3	IE4/5
<event_name>=script_code	✗	✗	✓	✗	✗	✗	✗	✗	✓
ACCESSKEY=ley_character	✗	✗	✓	✗	✗	✗	✗	✗	✓
CLASS=classname	✗	✗	✓	✗	✗	✗	✗	✗	✓
DATAFLD=column_name	✗	✗	✗	✗	✗	✗	✗	✗	✓
DATAFORMATAS=HTML|TEXT	✗	✗	✗	✗	✗	✗	✗	✗	✓
DATASRC=id	✗	✗	✗	✗	✗	✗	✗	✗	✓
DIR=LTR|RTL	✗	✗	✓	✗	✗	✗	✗	✗	✗
DISABLED	✗	✗	✓	✗	✗	✗	✗	✗	✓
ID=string	✗	✗	✓	✗	✗	✗	✗	✗	✓
LANG=language_type	✗	✗	✓	✗	✗	✗	✗	✗	✓
LANGUAGE=JAVSCRIPT|JSCRIPT|VBSCRIPT|VBS	✗	✗	✗	✗	✗	✗	✗	✗	✓
NAME=string	✗	✗	✓	✗	✗	✗	✗	✗	✗
STYLE=string	✗	✗	✓	✗	✗	✗	✗	✗	✓
TABINDEX=number	✗	✗	✓	✗	✗	✗	✗	✗	✗
TITLE=string	✗	✗	✓	✗	✗	✗	✗	✗	✓
TYPE=BUTTON|RESET|SUBMIT	✗	✗	✓	✗	✗	✗	✗	✗	✓
VALUE=string	✗	✗	✓	✗	✗	✗	✗	✗	✗

CAPTION

Specifies a caption to be placed next to a table. **ALL except HTML 2.0**.

Attributes	2.0	3.2	4.0	N2	N3	N4	IE2	IE3	IE4/5
<event_name>=script_code	✗	✗	✓	✗	✗	✗	✗	✗	✓
ALIGN=TOP|BOTTOM|LEFT|RIGHT	✗	✓	D	✓	✓	✓	✓	✓	✓
CLASS=classname	✗	✗	✓	✗	✗	✓	✗	✗	✓
DIR=LTR|RTL	✗	✗	✓	✗	✗	✗	✗	✗	✗
ID=*string*	✗	✗	✓	✗	✗	✓	✗	✗	✓
LANG=language_type	✗	✗	✓	✗	✗	✗	✗	✗	✓
LANGUAGE=JAVASCRIPT|JSCRIPT|VBSCRIPT|VBS	✗	✗	✗	✗	✗	✗	✗	✗	✓
STYLE=*string*	✗	✗	✓	✗	✗	✓	✗	✗	✓
TITLE=*string*	✗	✗	✓	✗	✗	✗	✗	✗	✓
VALIGN=BOTTOM|TOP	✗	✗	✗	✗	✗	✓	✓	✓	✓

CENTER

Causes enclosed text and other elements to be centered on the page. **HTML 3.2, N2, N3, N4, IE2, IE3, IE4, IE5, deprecated in HTML 4.0**.

Attributes	2.0	3.2	4.0	N2	N3	N4	IE2	IE3	IE4/5
<event_name>=script_code	✗	✗	✗	✗	✗	✗	✗	✗	✓
CLASS=classname	✗	✗	✗	✗	✗	✓	✗	✗	✓
ID=*string*	✗	✗	✗	✗	✗	✓	✗	✗	✓
LANG=language_type	✗	✗	✗	✗	✗	✗	✗	✗	✓
LANGUAGE=JAVASCRIPT|JSCRIPT|VBSCRIPT|VBS	✗	✗	✗	✗	✗	✗	✗	✗	✓
STYLE=*string*	✗	✗	✗	✗	✗	✓	✗	✗	✓
TITLE=*string*	✗	✗	✗	✗	✗	✗	✗	✗	✓

CITE

Renders text in italics. **ALL**.

Attributes	2.0	3.2	4.0	N2	N3	N4	IE2	IE3	IE4/5
<event_name>=script_code	✗	✗	✓	✗	✗	✗	✗	✗	✓
CLASS=classname	✗	✗	✓	✗	✗	✓	✗	✗	✓
DIR=LTR|RTL	✗	✗	✓	✗	✗	✗	✗	✗	✗
ID=*string*	✗	✗	✓	✗	✗	✓	✗	✗	✓
LANG=language_type	✗	✗	✓	✗	✗	✗	✗	✗	✓
LANGUAGE=JAVASCRIPT|JSCRIPT|VBSCRIPT|VBS	✗	✗	✗	✗	✗	✗	✗	✗	✓
STYLE=*string*	✗	✗	✓	✗	✗	✓	✗	✗	✓
TITLE=*string*	✗	✗	✓	✗	✗	✗	✗	✗	✓

CODE

Renders text as a code sample in a fixed width font. **ALL**.

Attributes	2.0	3.2	4.0	N2	N3	N4	IE2	IE3	IE4/5
<event_name>=script_code	✗	✗	✓	✗	✗	✗	✗	✗	✓
CLASS=classname	✗	✗	✓	✗	✗	✓	✗	✗	✓
DIR=LTR|RTL	✗	✗	✓	✗	✗	✗	✗	✗	✗
ID=*string*	✗	✗	✓	✗	✗	✓	✗	✗	✓
LANG=language_type	✗	✗	✓	✗	✗	✗	✗	✗	✓
LANGUAGE=JAVASCRIPT|JSCRIPT|VBSCRIPT|VBS	✗	✗	✗	✗	✗	✗	✗	✗	✓
STYLE=*string*	✗	✗	✓	✗	✗	✓	✗	✗	✓
TITLE=*string*	✗	✗	✓	✗	✗	✗	✗	✗	✓

COL

Used to specify column based defaults for a table. **HTML 4.0, IE3, IE4, IE5**.

Attributes	2.0	3.2	4.0	N2	N3	N4	IE2	IE3	IE4/5
<event_name>=script_code	✗	✗	✓	✗	✗	✗	✗	✓	✗
ALIGN=CENTER|LEFT|RIGHT|JUSTIFY|CHAR	✗	✗	✓	✗	✗	✗	✗	✓	✓
CHAR=string	✗	✗	✓	✗	✗	✗	✗	✗	✗
CHAROFF=string	✗	✗	✓	✗	✗	✗	✗	✗	✗
CLASS=classname	✗	✗	✓	✗	✗	✗	✗	✗	✓
DIR=LTR|RTL	✗	✗	✓	✗	✗	✗	✗	✗	✗
ID=string	✗	✗	✓	✗	✗	✗	✗	✗	✓
SPAN=number	✗	✗	✓	✗	✗	✗	✗	✓	✓
STYLE=string	✗	✗	✓	✗	✗	✗	✗	✗	✓
TITLE=string	✗	✗	✓	✗	✗	✗	✗	✗	✓
VALIGN=BOTTOM|MIDDLE|TOP|BASELINE	✗	✗	✓	✗	✗	✗	✗	✗	✓
WIDTH=number	✗	✗	✓	✗	✗	✗	✗	✗	✓

COLGROUP

Used as a container for a group of columns. **HTML 4.0, IE3, IE4, IE5**.

Attributes	2.0	3.2	4.0	N2	N3	N4	IE2	IE3	IE4/5
<event_name>=script_code	✗	✗	✓	✗	✗	✗	✗	✗	✗
ALIGN=CENTER|LEFT|RIGHT|JUSTIFY|CHAR	✗	✗	✓	✗	✗	✗	✗	✓	✓
CHAR=string	✗	✗	✓	✗	✗	✗	✗	✗	✗
CHAROFF=string	✗	✗	✓	✗	✗	✗	✗	✗	✗
CLASS=classname	✗	✗	✓	✗	✗	✗	✗	✗	✓
DIR=LTR|RTL	✗	✗	✓	✗	✗	✗	✗	✗	✗
ID=string	✗	✗	✓	✗	✗	✗	✗	✗	✓
SPAN=number	✗	✗	✓	✗	✗	✗	✗	✓	✓
STYLE=string	✗	✗	✓	✗	✗	✗	✗	✗	✓
TITLE=string	✗	✗	✓	✗	✗	✗	✗	✗	✓
VALIGN=BOTTOM|MIDDLE|TOP|BASELINE	✗	✗	✓	✗	✗	✗	✗	✓	✓
WIDTH=number	✗	✗	✓	✗	✗	✗	✗	✓	✓

COMMENT

Denotes a comment that will not be displayed. **HTML 4.0, IE2, IE3, deprecated in IE4/5**.

Attributes	2.0	3.2	4.0	N2	N3	N4	IE2	IE3	IE4/5
ID=*string*	✗	✗	✗	✗	✗	✗	✗	✗	✓
LANG=language_type	✗	✗	✗	✗	✗	✗	✗	✗	✓
TITLE=*string*	✗	✗	✗	✗	✗	✗	✗	✗	✓

DD

The definition of an item in a definition list, usually indented from other text. **ALL**.

Attributes	2.0	3.2	4.0	N2	N3	N4	IE2	IE3	IE4/5
<event_name>=script_code	✗	✗	✓	✗	✗	✗	✗	✗	✓
CLASS=classname	✗	✗	✓	✗	✗	✓	✗	✓	✓
DIR=LTR|RTLR	✗	✗	✓	✗	✗	✗	✗	✗	✗
ID=*string*	✗	✗	✓	✗	✗	✓	✗	✓	✓
LANG=language_type	✗	✗	✓	✗	✗	✗	✗	✗	✓
LANGUAGE=JAVASCRIPT|JSCRIPT| VBSCRIPT|VBS	✗	✗	✗	✗	✗	✗	✗	✗	✓
STYLE=*string*	✗	✗	✓	✗	✗	✓	✗	✓	✓
TITLE=*string*	✗	✗	✓	✗	✗	✗	✗	✗	✓

DEL

Indicates a section of the document that has been deleted since a previous version. **HTML 4.0, IE4, IE5**.

Attributes	2.0	3.2	4.0	N2	N3	N4	IE2	IE3	IE4/5
<event_name>=script_code	✗	✗	✓	✗	✗	✗	✗	✗	✓
CITE=url	✗	✗	✓	✗	✗	✗	✗	✗	✗
CLASS=classname	✗	✗	✓	✗	✗	✗	✗	✗	✓
DATETIME=date	✗	✗	✓	✗	✗	✗	✗	✗	✗
DIR=LTR|RTL	✗	✗	✓	✗	✗	✗	✗	✗	✗
ID=*string*	✗	✗	✓	✗	✗	✗	✗	✗	✓
LANG=language_type	✗	✗	✓	✗	✗	✗	✗	✗	✓
LANGUAGE=JAVASCRIPT|JSCRIPT| VBSCRIPT|VBS	✗	✗	✗	✗	✗	✗	✗	✗	✓
STYLE=*string*	✗	✗	✓	✗	✗	✗	✗	✗	✓
TITLE=*string*	✗	✗	✓	✗	✗	✗	✗	✗	✓

DFN

The defining instance of a term. **ALL except HTML 2.0**.

Attributes	2.0	3.2	4.0	N2	N3	N4	IE2	IE3	IE4/5
`<event_name>=script_code`	✗	✗	✓	✗	✗	✗	✗	✗	✓
`CLASS=classname`	✗	✗	✓	✗	✗	✓	✗	✗	✓
`DIR=LTR|RTL`	✗	✗	✓	✗	✗	✗	✗	✗	✗
`ID=string`	✗	✗	✓	✗	✗	✓	✗	✗	✓
`LANG=language_type`	✗	✗	✓	✗	✗	✗	✗	✗	✓
`LANGUAGE=JAVASCRIPT|JSCRIPT|` `VBSCRIPT|VBS`	✗	✗	✗	✗	✗	✗	✗	✗	✓
`STYLE=string`	✗	✗	✓	✗	✗	✓	✗	✗	✓
`TITLE=string`	✗	✗	✓	✗	✗	✗	✗	✗	✓

DIR

Renders text so that it appears like a directory-style file listing. **ALL, except deprecated in HTML 4.0**.

Attributes	2.0	3.2	4.0	N2	N3	N4	IE2	IE3	IE4/5
`<event_name>=script_code`	✗	✗	D	✗	✗	✗	✗	✗	✓
`CLASS=classname`	✗	✗	D	✗	✗	✓	✗	✗	✓
`COMPACT`	✓	✓	D	✗	✗	✓	✗	✓	✗
`DIR=LTR|RTL`	✗	✗	D	✗	✗	✗	✗	✗	✗
`ID=string`	✗	✗	D	✗	✗	✓	✗	✗	✓
`LANG=language_type`	✗	✗	D	✗	✗	✗	✗	✗	✓
`LANGUAGE=JAVASCRIPT|JSCRIPT|` `VBSCRIPT|VBS`	✗	✗	✗	✗	✗	✗	✗	✗	✓
`STYLE=string`	✗	✗	D	✗	✗	✓	✗	✗	✓
`TITLE=string`	✗	✗	✗	✗	✗	✓	✗	✗	✗
`TYPE=CIRCLE|DISC|SQUARE`	✗	✗	✗	✗	✗	✓	✗	✗	✗

DIV

Defines a container section within the page, and can hold other elements. **ALL except HTML 2.0.**

Attributes	2.0	3.2	4.0	N2	N3	N4	IE2	IE3	IE4/5
<event_name>=script_code	✗	✗	✓	✗	✗	✗	✗	✗	✓
ALIGN=CENTER|LEFT|RIGHT	✗	✓	D	✓	✓	✓	✗	✓	✓
CHARSET=*string*	✗	✗	✓	✗	✗	✗	✗	✗	✗
CLASS=classname	✗	✗	✓	✗	✗	✓	✗	✓	✓
DATAFLD=column_name	✗	✗	✗	✗	✗	✗	✗	✗	✓
DATAFORMATAS=HTML|TEXT	✗	✗	✗	✗	✗	✗	✗	✗	✓
DATASRC=id	✗	✗	✗	✗	✗	✗	✗	✗	✓
DIR=LTR|RTL	✗	✗	✓	✗	✗	✗	✗	✗	✗
HREF=url	✗	✗	✓	✗	✗	✗	✗	✗	✗
HREFLANG=langcode	✗	✗	✓	✗	✗	✗	✗	✗	✗
ID=*string*	✗	✗	✓	✗	✗	✓	✗	✓	✓
LANG=language_type	✗	✗	✓	✗	✗	✗	✗	✗	✓
LANGUAGE=JAVASCRIPT|JSCRIPT| VBSCRIPT|VBS	✗	✗	✗	✗	✗	✗	✗	✗	✓
MEDIA	✗	✗	✓	✗	✗	✗	✗	✗	✗
NOWRAP	✗	✗	✗	✗	✗	✓	✗	✓	✗
REL=relationship	✗	✗	✓	✗	✗	✗	✗	✗	✗
REV=relationship	✗	✗	✓	✗	✗	✗	✗	✗	✗
STYLE=*string*	✗	✗	✓	✗	✗	✓	✗	✗	✓
TARGET	✗	✗	✓	✗	✗	✗	✗	✗	✗
TITLE=*string*	✗	✗	✓	✗	✗	✗	✗	✗	✓
TYPE	✗	✗	✓	✗	✗	✗	✗	✗	✗

DL

Denotes a definition list. **ALL**.

Attributes	2.0	3.2	4.0	N2	N3	N4	IE2	IE3	IE4/5
`<event_name>=script_code`	✗	✗	✓	✗	✗	✗	✗	✗	✓
`CLASS=classname`	✗	✗	✓	✗	✗	✓	✗	✓	✓
`COMPACT`	✓	✓	D	✗	✗	✓	✗	✓	✗
`DIR=LTR|RTL`	✗	✗	✓	✗	✗	✗	✗	✗	✗
`ID=string`	✗	✗	✓	✗	✗	✓	✗	✓	✓
`LANG=language_type`	✗	✗	✓	✗	✗	✗	✗	✗	✓
`LANGUAGE=JAVASCRIPT|JSCRIPT|` `VBSCRIPT|VBS`	✗	✗	✗	✗	✗	✗	✗	✗	✓
`STYLE=string`	✗	✗	✓	✗	✗	✓	✗	✓	✓
`TITLE=string`	✗	✗	✓	✗	✗	✗	✗	✗	✓

DT

Denotes a definition term within a definition list. **ALL**.

Attributes	2.0	3.2	4.0	N2	N3	N4	IE2	IE3	IE4/5
`<event_name>=script_code`	✗	✗	✓	✗	✗	✗	✗	✗	✓
`CLASS=classname`	✗	✗	✓	✗	✗	✓	✗	✗	✓
`DIR=LTR|RTL`	✗	✗	✓	✗	✗	✗	✗	✗	✗
`ID=string`	✗	✗	✓	✗	✗	✓	✗	✗	✓
`LANG=language_type`	✗	✗	✓	✗	✗	✗	✗	✗	✓
`LANGUAGE=JAVASCRIPT|JSCRIPT|` `VBSCRIPT|VBS`	✗	✗	✗	✗	✗	✗	✗	✗	✓
`STYLE=string`	✗	✗	✓	✗	✗	✓	✗	✗	✓
`TITLE=string`	✗	✗	✓	✗	✗	✗	✗	✗	✓

EM

Renders text as emphasized, usually in italics. **ALL**.

Attributes	2.0	3.2	4.0	N2	N3	N4	IE2	IE3	IE4/5
<event_name>=script_code	✗	✗	✓	✗	✗	✗	✗	✗	✓
CLASS=classname	✗	✗	✓	✗	✗	✓	✗	✗	✓
DIR=LTR|RTL	✗	✗	✓	✗	✗	✗	✗	✗	✗
ID=*string*	✗	✗	✓	✗	✗	✓	✗	✗	✓
LANG=language_type	✗	✗	✓	✗	✗	✗	✗	✗	✓
LANGUAGE=JAVASCRIPT|JSCRIPT|VBSCRIPT|VBS	✗	✗	✗	✗	✗	✗	✗	✗	✓
STYLE=*string*	✗	✗	✓	✗	✗	✓	✗	✗	✓
TITLE=*string*	✗	✗	✓	✗	✗	✗	✗	✗	✓

EMBED

Embeds documents of any type in the page, to be viewed in another suitable application. **N2, N3, N4, IE3, IE4, IE5**.

Attributes	2.0	3.2	4.0	N2	N3	N4	IE2	IE3	IE4/5
ALIGN=ABSBOTTOM|ABSMIDDLE|BASELINE|BOTTOM|LEFT|MIDDLE|RIGHT|TEXTTOP|TOP	✗	✗	✗	✗	✗	✓	✗	✗	✓
ALT=text	✗	✗	✗	✗	✗	✗	✗	✗	✓
BORDER=number	✗	✗	D	✗	✗	✓	✗	✗	✗
CLASS=classname	✗	✗	✗	✗	✗	✓	✗	✗	✓
CODE=filename	✗	✗	✗	✗	✗	✗	✗	✗	✓
CODEBASE=url	✗	✗	✗	✗	✗	✗	✗	✗	✓
HEIGHT=number	✗	✗	✗	✓	✓	✓	✗	✓	✓
HIDDEN=*string*	✗	✗	✗	✗	✗	✓	✗	✗	✗
HSPACE=number	✗	✗	✗	✗	✗	✓	✗	✗	✓
ID=*string*	✗	✗	✗	✗	✗	✓	✗	✗	✓
NAME=*string*	✗	✗	✗	✓	✓	✓	✗	✓	✓
PALETTE=FOREGROUND|BACKGROUND	✗	✗	✗	✗	✗	✓	✗	✓	✗
PLUGINSPAGE=*string*	✗	✗	✗	✗	✗	✓	✗	✗	✗

Attributes	2.0	3.2	4.0	N2	N3	N4	IE2	IE3	IE4/5
SRC=url	✗	✗	✗	✓	✓	✓	✗	✓	✓
STYLE=*string*	✗	✗	✗	✗	✗	✓	✗	✗	✓
TITLE=*string*	✗	✗	✗	✗	✗	✗	✗	✗	✓
TYPE=*mime-type*	✗	✗	✗	✗	✗	✓	✗	✗	✗
UNITS=EN|EMS|PIXELS	✗	✗	✗	✗	✗	✓	✗	✓	✓
VSPACE=number	✗	✗	✗	✗	✗	✓	✗	✗	✓
WIDTH=number	✗	✗	✗	✓	✓	✓	✗	✓	✓

FIELDSET

Draws a box around the contained elements to indicate related items. **HTML 4.0, IE4, IE5**.

Attributes	2.0	3.2	4.0	N2	N3	N4	IE2	IE3	IE4/5
<event_name>=script_code	✗	✗	✓	✗	✗	✗	✗	✗	✓
ALIGN=CENTER|LEFT|RIGHT	✗	✗	✗	✗	✗	✗	✗	✗	✓
CLASS=classname	✗	✗	✓	✗	✗	✗	✗	✗	✓
DIR=LTR|RTL	✗	✗	✓	✗	✗	✗	✗	✗	✗
ID=*string*	✗	✗	✓	✗	✗	✗	✗	✗	✓
LANG=language_type	✗	✗	✓	✗	✗	✗	✗	✗	✓
LANGUAGE=JAVASCRIPT|JSCRIPT|VBSCRIPT|VBS	✗	✗	✗	✗	✗	✗	✗	✗	✓
STYLE=*string*	✗	✗	✓	✗	✗	✗	✗	✗	✓
TITLE=*string*	✗	✗	✓	✗	✗	✗	✗	✗	✓

FONT

Specifies the font face, size, and color for rendering the text. **HTML 3.2, N2, N3, N4, IE2, IE3, IE4, IE5, deprecated in HTML 4.0.**

Attributes	2.0	3.2	4.0	N2	N3	N4	IE2	IE3	IE4/5
<event_name>=script_code	✗	✗	✗	✗	✗	✗	✗	✗	✓
CLASS=classname	✗	✗	D	✗	✗	✓	✗	✗	✓
COLOR=color	✗	✓	D	✓	✓	✓	✓	✓	✓
DIR=LTR|RTL	✗	✗	D	✗	✗	✗	✗	✗	✗
FACE=font_family_name	✗	✗	D	✗	✓	✓	✓	✓	✓
ID=*string*	✗	✗	D	✗	✗	✓	✗	✗	✓
LANG=language_type	✗	✗	D	✗	✗	✗	✗	✗	✓
LANGUAGE=JAVASCRIPT|JSCRIPT|VBSCRIPT|VBS	✗	✗	✗	✗	✗	✗	✗	✗	✓
POINT-SIZE=*string*|number	✗	✗	✗	✗	✗	✓	✗	✗	✗
SIZE=number	✗	✓	D	✓	✓	✓	✓	✓	✓
STYLE=*string*	✗	✗	D	✗	✗	✓	✗	✗	✓
TITLE=*string*	✗	✗	D	✗	✗	✗	✗	✗	✓
WEIGHT=*string*|number	✗	✗	✗	✗	✗	✓	✗	✗	✗

FORM

Denotes a form containing controls and elements, whose values are sent to a server. **ALL**.

Attributes	2.0	3.2	4.0	N2	N3	N4	IE2	IE3	IE4/5
<event_name>=script_code	✗	✗	✓	✗	✗	✓	✗	✓	✓
ACCEPT-CHARSET=*string*	✗	✗	✓	✗	✗	✗	✗	✗	✗
ACTION=*string*	✓	✓	✓	✓	✓	✓	✓	✓	✓
CLASS=classname	✗	✗	✓	✗	✗	✓	✗	✗	✓
DIR=LTR|RTL	✗	✗	✓	✗	✗	✗	✗	✗	✗
ENCTYPE=*string*	✓	✓	✓	✓	✓	✓	✗	✗	✓
ID=*string*	✗	✗	✓	✗	✗	✓	✗	✗	✓
LANG=language_type	✗	✗	✓	✗	✗	✗	✗	✗	✓

Attributes	2.0	3.2	4.0	N2	N3	N4	IE2	IE3	IE4/5
LANGUAGE=JAVASCRIPT|JSCRIPT| VBSCRIPT|VBS	✗	✗	✗	✗	✗	✗	✗	✗	✓
METHOD=GET|POST	✓	✓	✓	✓	✓	✓	✓	✓	✓
NAME=*string*	✗	✗	✗	✗	✗	✓	✗	✗	✓
STYLE=*string*	✗	✗	✓	✗	✗	✓	✗	✗	✓
TARGET=<window_name>|_parent| _blank|_top|_self	✗	✗	✓	✓	✓	✓	✗	✓	✓
TITLE=*string*	✗	✗	✓	✗	✗	✗	✗	✗	✓

FRAME

Specifies an individual frame within a frameset. **HTML 4.0, N2, N3, N4, IE3, IE4, IE5**.

Attributes	2.0	3.2	4.0	N2	N3	N4	IE2	IE3	IE4/5
<event_name>=script_code	✗	✗	✗	✗	✗	✓	✗	✗	✓
ALIGN=CENTER|LEFT|RIGHT	✗	✗	✗	✗	✗	✓	✗	✓	✗
BORDERCOLOR=color	✗	✗	✗	✗	✓	✓	✗	✗	✓
CLASS=classname	✗	✗	✓	✗	✗	✓	✗	✗	✓
DATAFLD=column_name	✗	✗	✗	✗	✗	✗	✗	✗	✓
DATASRC=id	✗	✗	✗	✗	✗	✗	✗	✗	✓
FRAMEBORDER=NO|YES|0|1	✗	✗	✓	✗	✓	✓	✗	✓	✓
ID=*string*	✗	✗	✓	✗	✗	✓	✗	✗	✓
LANG=language_type	✗	✗	✗	✗	✗	✗	✗	✗	✓
LANGUAGE=JAVASCRIPT|JSCRIPT| VBSCRIPT|VBS	✗	✗	✗	✗	✗	✗	✗	✗	✓
LONGDESC=url	✗	✗	✓	✗	✗	✗	✗	✗	✗
MARGINHEIGHT=number	✗	✗	✓	✓	✓	✓	✗	✓	✓
MARGINWIDTH=number	✗	✗	✓	✓	✓	✓	✗	✓	✓
NAME=*string*	✗	✗	✓	✓	✓	✓	✗	✓	✓
NORESIZE=NORESIZE|RESIZE	✗	✗	✓	✓	✓	✓	✗	✓	✓
SCROLLING=AUTO|YES|NO	✗	✗	✓	✓	✓	✓	✗	✓	✓
SRC=url	✗	✗	✓	✓	✓	✓	✗	✓	✓
STYLE=*string*	✗	✗	✓	✗	✗	✗	✗	✗	✓
TITLE=*string*	✗	✗	✓	✗	✗	✓	✗	✗	✓

FRAMESET

Specifies a frameset containing multiple frames and other nested framesets. **HTML 4.0, N2, N3, N4, IE3, IE4, IE5.**

Attributes	2.0	3.2	4.0	N2	N3	N4	IE2	IE3	IE4/5
`<event_name>=script_code`	✗	✗	✓	✗	✗	✗	✗	✗	✗
`BORDER=number`	✗	✗	D	✗	✓	✓	✗	✗	✓
`BORDERCOLOR=color`	✗	✗	✗	✗	✓	✓	✗	✗	✓
`CLASS=classname`	✗	✗	✓	✗	✗	✓	✗	✗	✓
`COLS=number`	✗	✗	✓	✓	✓	✓	✗	✓	✓
`FRAMEBORDER=NO|YES|0|1`	✗	✗	✗	✗	✓	✓	✗	✓	✓
`FRAMESPACING=number`	✗	✗	✗	✗	✗	✗	✗	✓	✓
`ID=string`	✗	✗	✓	✗	✗	✓	✗	✗	✓
`LANG=language_type`	✗	✗	✗	✗	✗	✗	✗	✗	✓
`LANGUAGE=JAVASCRIPT|JSCRIPT| VBSCRIPT|VBS`	✗	✗	✗	✗	✗	✗	✗	✗	✓
`ROWS=number`	✗	✗	✓	✓	✓	✓	✗	✓	✓
`STYLE=string`	✗	✗	✓	✗	✗	✗	✗	✗	✓
`TITLE=string`	✗	✗	✓	✗	✗	✗	✗	✗	✓

HEAD

Contains tags holding uNiewed information about the document. **ALL.**

Attributes	2.0	3.2	4.0	N2	N3	N4	IE2	IE3	IE4/5
`CLASS=classname`	✗	✗	✗	✗	✗	✓	✗	✗	✓
`DIR=LTR|RTL`	✗	✗	✓	✗	✗	✗	✗	✗	✗
`ID=string`	✗	✗	✗	✗	✗	✓	✗	✗	✓
`LANG=language_type`	✗	✗	✓	✗	✗	✗	✗	✗	✗
`PROFILE=url`	✗	✗	✓	✗	✗	✗	✗	✗	✗
`TITLE=string`	✗	✗	✗	✗	✗	✗	✗	✗	✓

Hn

The six elements (H1 to H6) render text as a range of heading styles. **ALL**.

Attributes	2.0	3.2	4.0	N2	N3	N4	IE2	IE3	IE4/5
`<event_name>=script_code`	✗	✗	✓	✗	✗	✗	✗	✗	✓
`ALIGN=CENTER|LEFT|RIGHT`	✗	✓	D	✓	✓	✗	✓	✓	✓
`CLASS=classname`	✗	✗	✓	✗	✗	✓	✗	✗	✓
`DIR=LTR|RTL`	✗	✗	✓	✗	✗	✗	✗	✗	✗
`ID=string`	✗	✗	✓	✗	✗	✓	✗	✗	✓
`LANG=language_type`	✗	✗	✓	✗	✗	✗	✗	✗	✓
`LANGUAGE=JAVASCRIPT|JSCRIPT|VBSCRIPT|VBS`	✗	✗	✗	✗	✗	✗	✗	✗	✓
`STYLE=string`	✗	✗	✓	✗	✗	✓	✗	✗	✓
`TITLE=string`	✗	✗	✓	✗	✗	✗	✗	✗	✓

HR

Places a horizontal rule in the page. **ALL**.

Attributes	2.0	3.2	4.0	N2	N3	N4	IE2	IE3	IE4/5
`<event_name>=script_code`	✗	✗	✓	✗	✗	✗	✗	✗	✓
`ALIGN=CENTER|LEFT|RIGHT`	✗	✓	D	✓	✓	✓	✓	✓	✓
`CLASS=classname`	✗	✗	✓	✗	✗	✓	✗	✓	✓
`COLOR=color`	✗	✗	✗	✗	✗	✗	✓	✓	✓
`DIR=LTR|RTL`	✗	✗	✓	✗	✗	✗	✗	✗	✗
`ID=string`	✗	✗	✓	✗	✗	✓	✗	✓	✓
`LANG=language_type`	✗	✗	✓	✗	✗	✗	✗	✗	✓
`LANGUAGE=JAVASCRIPT|JSCRIPT|VBSCRIPT|VBS`	✗	✗	✗	✗	✗	✗	✗	✗	✓
`NOSHADE`	✗	✓	D	✓	✓	✓	✓	✓	✓
`SIZE=number`	✗	✓	D	✓	✓	✓	✓	✓	✓
`SRC=url`	✗	✗	✗	✗	✗	✗	✗	✗	✓
`STYLE=string`	✗	✗	✓	✗	✗	✓	✗	✓	✓
`TITLE=string`	✗	✗	✓	✗	✗	✗	✗	✗	✓
`WIDTH=number`	✗	✓	D	✓	✓	✓	✓	✓	✓

HTML

The outer tag for the page, which identifies the document as containing HTML elements. **ALL**.

Attributes	2.0	3.2	4.0	N2	N3	N4	IE2	IE3	IE4/5
DIR=LTR|RTL	✗	✗	✓	✗	✗	✗	✗	✗	✗
LANG=language_type	✗	✗	✓	✗	✗	✗	✗	✗	✗
TITLE=*string*	✗	✗	✗	✗	✗	✗	✗	✗	✓
VERSION=url	✗	✗	✓	✗	✗	✗	✗	✗	✗

I

Renders text in an italic font where available. **ALL**.

Attributes	2.0	3.2	4.0	N2	N3	N4	IE2	IE3	IE4/5
<event_name>=script_code	✗	✗	✓	✗	✗	✗	✗	✗	✓
CLASS=classname	✗	✗	✓	✗	✗	✓	✗	✗	✓
DIR=LTR|RTL	✗	✗	✓	✗	✗	✗	✗	✗	✗
ID=*string*	✗	✗	✓	✗	✗	✓	✗	✗	✓
LANG=language_type	✗	✗	✓	✗	✗	✗	✗	✗	✓
LANGUAGE=JAVASCRIPT|JSCRIPT| VBSCRIPT|VBS	✗	✗	✗	✗	✗	✗	✗	✗	✓
STYLE=*string*	✗	✗	✓	✗	✗	✓	✗	✗	✓
TITLE=*string*	✗	✗	✓	✗	✗	✗	✗	✗	✓

IFRAME

Used to create in-line floating frames within the page. **HTML 4.0, IE3, IE4, IE5.**

Attributes	2.0	3.2	4.0	N2	N3	N4	IE2	IE3	IE4/5
ALIGN=ABSBOTTOM|ABSMIDDLE| BASELINE|BOTTOM|LEFT|MIDDLE| RIGHT|TEXTTOP|TOP	✗	✗	D	✗	✗	✗	✗	✗	✓
BORDER=number	✗	✗	D	✗	✗	✗	✗	✗	✓
BORDERCOLOR=color	✗	✗	✗	✗	✗	✗	✗	✗	✓
CLASS=classname	✗	✗	✓	✗	✗	✗	✗	✗	✓
DATAFLD=column_name	✗	✗	✗	✗	✗	✗	✗	✗	✓
DATASRC=id	✗	✗	✗	✗	✗	✗	✗	✗	✓
FRAMEBORDER=NO|YES|0|1	✗	✗	✓	✗	✗	✗	✗	✗	✓
FRAMESPACING=number	✗	✗	✗	✗	✗	✗	✗	✗	✓
HEIGHT=number	✗	✗	✓	✗	✗	✗	✗	✗	✓
HSPACE=number	✗	✗	✗	✗	✗	✗	✗	✗	✓
ID=*string*	✗	✗	✓	✗	✗	✗	✗	✗	✓
LANG=language_type	✗	✗	✗	✗	✗	✗	✗	✗	✓
LANGUAGE=JAVASCRIPT|JSCRIPT| VBSCRIPT|VBS	✗	✗	✗	✗	✗	✗	✗	✗	✓
LONGDESC=url	✗	✗	✓	✗	✗	✗	✗	✗	✗
MARGINHEIGHT=number	✗	✗	✓	✗	✗	✗	✗	✗	✓
MARGINWIDTH=number	✗	✗	✓	✗	✗	✗	✗	✗	✓
NAME=*string*	✗	✗	✓	✗	✗	✗	✗	✗	✓
NORESIZE=NORESIZE|RESIZE	✗	✗	✗	✗	✗	✗	✗	✗	✓
SCROLLING=AUTO|YES|NO	✗	✗	✓	✗	✗	✗	✗	✗	✓
SRC=url	✗	✗	✓	✗	✗	✗	✗	✗	✓
STYLE=*string*	✗	✗	✓	✗	✗	✗	✗	✗	✓
TITLE=*string*	✗	✗	✓	✗	✗	✗	✗	✗	✓
VSPACE=number	✗	✗	✗	✗	✗	✗	✗	✗	✓
WIDTH=number	✗	✗	✓	✗	✗	✗	✗	✗	✓

ILAYER

Defines a separate area of the page as an inline layer that can hold a different page. **N4 only**.

Attributes	2.0	3.2	4.0	N2	N3	N4	IE2	IE3	IE4/5
<event_name>=script_code	✗	✗	✗	✗	✗	✓	✗	✗	✗
ABOVE=object_id	✗	✗	✗	✗	✗	✓	✗	✗	✗
BACKGROUND=*string*	✗	✗	✗	✗	✗	✓	✗	✗	✗
BELOW=object_id	✗	✗	✗	✗	✗	✓	✗	✗	✗
BGCOLOR=color	✗	✗	D	✗	✗	✓	✗	✗	✗
CLASS=classname	✗	✗	✗	✗	✗	✓	✗	✗	✗
CLIP=number[,number,number,number]	✗	✗	✗	✗	✗	✓	✗	✗	✗
ID=*string*	✗	✗	✗	✗	✗	✓	✗	✗	✗
LEFT=number	✗	✗	✗	✗	✗	✓	✗	✗	✗
NAME=*string*	✗	✗	✗	✗	✗	✓	✗	✗	✗
PAGEX=number	✗	✗	✗	✗	✗	✓	✗	✗	✗
PAGEY=number	✗	✗	✗	✗	✗	✓	✗	✗	✗
SRC=url	✗	✗	✗	✗	✗	✓	✗	✗	✗
STYLE=*string*	✗	✗	✗	✗	✗	✓	✗	✗	✗
TOP=number	✗	✗	✗	✗	✗	✓	✗	✗	✗
VISIBILITY=SHOW|HIDE|INHERIT	✗	✗	✗	✗	✗	✓	✗	✗	✗
WIDTH=number	✗	✗	✗	✗	✗	✓	✗	✗	✗
Z-INDEX=number	✗	✗	✗	✗	✗	✓	✗	✗	✗

IMG

Embeds an image or a video clip in the document. **ALL**.

Attributes	2.0	3.2	4.0	N2	N3	N4	IE2	IE3	IE4/5
`<event_name>=script_code`	✗	✗	✓	✗	✗	✓	✗	✗	✓
`ALIGN=BASBOTTOM|ABSMIDDLE|BASELINE|` `BOTTOM|LEFT|MIDDLE|RIGHT|TEXTTOP|TOP`	✓	✓	D	✓	✓	✓	✓	✓	✓
`ALT=text`	✓	✓	✓	✓	✓	✓	✓	✓	✓
`BORDER=number`	✗	✓	D	✓	✓	✓	✓	✓	✓
`CLASS=classname`	✗	✗	✓	✗	✗	✓	✗	✓	✓
`CONTROLS`	✗	✗	✗	✗	✗	✗	✓	✓	✗
`DATAFLD=column_name`	✗	✗	✗	✗	✗	✗	✗	✗	✓
`DATASRC=id`	✗	✗	✗	✗	✗	✗	✗	✗	✓
`DIR=LTR|RTL`	✗	✗	✓	✗	✗	✗	✗	✗	✗
`DYNSRC=string`	✗	✗	✗	✗	✗	✗	✓	✓	✓
`HEIGHT=number`	✗	✓	✓	✓	✓	✓	✓	✓	✓
`HSPACE=number`	✗	✓	✓	✓	✓	✓	✓	✓	✓
`ID=string`	✗	✗	✓	✗	✗	✓	✗	✓	✓
`ISMAP`	✓	✓	✓	✓	✓	✓	✓	✓	✓
`LANG=language_type`	✗	✗	✓	✗	✗	✗	✗	✗	✓
`LANGUAGE=JAVASCRIPT|JSCRIPT|VBSCRIPT` `|VBS`	✗	✗	✗	✗	✗	✗	✗	✗	✓
`LONGDESC=url`	✗	✗	✓	✗	✗	✗	✗	✗	✗
`LOOP=number`	✗	✗	✗	✗	✗	✗	✓	✓	✓
`LOWSRC=url`	✗	✗	✗	✓	✓	✓	✗	✗	✓
`NAME=string`	✗	✗	✗	✗	✗	✓	✗	✗	✓
`SRC=url`	✓	✓	✓	✓	✓	✓	✓	✓	✓
`START=number|string`	✗	✗	✗	✗	✗	✗	✓	✓	✗
`STYLE=string`	✗	✗	✓	✗	✗	✓	✗	✓	✓
`TITLE=string`	✗	✗	✓	✗	✗	✗	✗	✓	✓
`USEMAP=url`	✗	✓	✓	✓	✓	✓	✓	✓	✓
`VSPACE=number`	✗	✓	✓	✓	✓	✓	✓	✓	✓
`WIDTH=number`	✗	✓	✓	✓	✓	✓	✓	✓	✓

INPUT

Specifies a form input control, such as a button, text or check box. **ALL**.

Attributes	2.0	3.2	4.0	N2	N3	N4	IE2	IE3	IE4/5
`<event_name>=script_code`	✗	✗	✓	✗	✗	✓	✗	✓	✓
`ACCEPT=string`	✗	✗	✓	✗	✗	✗	✗	✗	✗
`ACCESSKEY=key_character`	✗	✗	✓	✗	✗	✗	✗	✗	✓
`ALIGN=CENTER|LEFT|RIGHT`	✓	✓	D	✓	✓	✓	✓	✓	✓
`ALT=text`	✗	✗	✓	✗	✗	✗	✗	✗	✗
`CHECKED=FALSE|TRUE`	✓	✓	✓	✓	✓	✓	✓	✓	✓
`CLASS=classname`	✗	✗	✓	✗	✗	✓	✗	✓	✓
`DATAFLD=column_name`	✗	✗	✗	✗	✗	✗	✗	✗	✓
`DATAFORMATAS=HTML|TEXT`	✗	✗	✗	✗	✗	✗	✗	✗	✓
`DATASRC=id`	✗	✗	✗	✗	✗	✗	✗	✗	✓
`DIR=LTR|RTL`	✗	✗	✓	✗	✗	✗	✗	✗	✗
`DISABLED`	✗	✗	✓	✗	✗	✗	✗	✗	✓
`ID=string`	✗	✗	✓	✗	✗	✓	✗	✓	✓
`LANG=language_type`	✗	✗	✓	✗	✗	✗	✗	✗	✓
`LANGUAGE=JAVASCRIPT|JSCRIPT|` `VBSCRIPT|VBS`	✗	✗	✗	✗	✗	✗	✗	✗	✓
`MAXLENGTH=number`	✓	✓	✓	✓	✓	✓	✓	✓	✓
`NAME=string`	✓	✓	✓	✓	✓	✓	✓	✓	✓
`NOTAB`	✗	✗	✗	✗	✗	✗	✗	✓	✗
`READONLY`	✗	✗	✓	✗	✗	✗	✗	✗	✓
`SIZE=number`	✓	✓	✓	✓	✓	✓	✓	✓	✓
`SRC=url`	✓	✓	✓	✓	✓	✗	✓	✓	✓
`STYLE=string`	✗	✗	✓	✗	✗	✓	✗	✓	✓
`TABINDEX=number`	✗	✗	✓	✗	✗	✗	✗	✓	✓
`TITLE=string`	✗	✗	✓	✗	✗	✗	✗	✓	✓

`TYPE=BUTTON|CHECKBOX|FILE|HIDDEN|`
`IMAGE|PASSWORD|RADIO|RESET|SUBMIT|`
`TEXT`
	✓	✓	✓	✓	✓	✓	✓	✓	✓

`USEMAP=url`	✗	✗	✓	✗	✗	✗	✗	✗	✗
`VALUE=string`	✓	✓	✓	✓	✓	✓	✓	✓	✓

INS

Indicates a section of the document that has been inserted since a previous version.**HTML 4.0, IE4, IE5**.

Attributes	2.0	3.2	4.0	N2	N3	N4	IE2	IE3	IE4/5
`<event_name>=script_code`	✗	✗	✓	✗	✗	✗	✗	✗	✓
`CITE=url`	✗	✗	✓	✗	✗	✗	✗	✗	✗
`CLASS=classname`	✗	✗	✓	✗	✗	✗	✗	✗	✓
`DATETIME=date`	✗	✗	✓	✗	✗	✗	✗	✗	✗
`DIR=LTR|RTL`	✗	✗	✓	✗	✗	✗	✗	✗	✗
`ID=string`	✗	✗	✓	✗	✗	✗	✗	✗	✓
`LANG=language_type`	✗	✗	✓	✗	✗	✗	✗	✗	✓
`LANGUAGE=JAVASCRIPT|JSCRIPT|` `VBSCRIPT|VBS`	✗	✗	✗	✗	✗	✗	✗	✗	✓
`STYLE=string`	✗	✗	✓	✗	✗	✗	✗	✗	✓
`TITLE=string`	✗	✗	✓	✗	✗	✗	✗	✗	✓

ISINDEX

Indicates the presence of a searchable index. **ALL. Deprecated in HTML 4.0**.

Attributes	2.0	3.2	4.0	N2	N3	N4	IE2	IE3	IE4/5
`ACTION=string`	✗	✗	✗	✓	✓	✓	✓	✓	✗
`CLASS=classname`	✗	✗	D	✗	✗	✓	✗	✗	✓
`DIR=LTR|RTL`	✗	✗	D	✗	✗	✗	✗	✗	✗
`ID=string`	✗	✗	D	✗	✗	✓	✗	✗	✓
`LANG=language_type`	✗	✗	D	✗	✗	✗	✗	✗	✓
`LANGUAGE=JAVASCRIPT|JSCRIPT|` `VBSCRIPT|VBS`	✗	✗	✗	✗	✗	✗	✗	✗	✓
`PROMPT=string`	✗	✓	D	✓	✓	✓	✓	✓	✓
`STYLE=string`	✗	✗	D	✗	✗	✓	✗	✗	✓
`TITLE=string`	✗	✗	D	✗	✗	✗	✗	✗	✗

KBD

Renders text in fixed-width font, as though entered on a keyboard. **ALL**.

Attributes	2.0	3.2	4.0	N2	N3	N4	IE2	IE3	IE4/5
`<event_name>=script_code`	✗	✗	✓	✗	✗	✗	✗	✗	✓
`CLASS=classname`	✗	✗	✓	✗	✗	✓	✗	✗	✓
`DIR=LTR|RTL`	✗	✗	✓	✗	✗	✗	✗	✗	✗
`ID=`*string*	✗	✗	✓	✗	✗	✓	✗	✗	✓
`LANG=language_type`	✗	✗	✓	✗	✗	✗	✗	✗	✓
`LANGUAGE=JAVASCRIPT|JSCRIPT|` `VBSCRIPT|VBS`	✗	✗	✗	✗	✗	✗	✗	✗	✓
`STYLE=`*string*	✗	✗	✓	✗	✗	✓	✗	✗	✓
`TITLE=`*string*	✗	✗	✓	✗	✗	✗	✗	✗	✓

KEYGEN

Used to generate key material in the page. **N2, N3, N4**.

Attributes	2.0	3.2	4.0	N2	N3	N4	IE2	IE3	IE4/5
`CHALLENGE=`*string*	✗	✗	✗	✗	✗	✓	✗	✗	✗
`CLASS=classname`	✗	✗	✗	✗	✗	✓	✗	✗	✗
`ID=`*string*	✗	✗	✗	✗	✗	✓	✗	✗	✗
`NAME=`*string*	✗	✗	✗	✗	✗	✓	✗	✗	✗

LABEL

Defines the text of a label for a control-like element. **HTML 4.0, IE4, IE5**.

Attributes	2.0	3.2	4.0	N2	N3	N4	IE2	IE3	IE4/5
<event_name>=script_code	✗	✗	✓	✗	✗	✗	✗	✗	✓
ACCESSKEY=key_character	✗	✗	✓	✗	✗	✗	✗	✗	✓
CLASS=classname	✗	✗	✓	✗	✗	✗	✗	✗	✓
DATAFLD=column_name	✗	✗	✗	✗	✗	✗	✗	✗	✓
DATAFORMATAS=HTML|TEXT	✗	✗	✗	✗	✗	✗	✗	✗	✓
DATASRC=id	✗	✗	✗	✗	✗	✗	✗	✗	✓
DIR=LTR|RTL	✗	✗	✓	✗	✗	✗	✗	✗	✗
FOR=element_name	✗	✗	✓	✗	✗	✗	✗	✗	✓
ID=string	✗	✗	✓	✗	✗	✗	✗	✗	✓
LANG=language_type	✗	✗	✓	✗	✗	✗	✗	✗	✓
LANGUAGE=JAVASCRIPT|JSCRIPT|VBSCRIPT|VBS	✗	✗	✗	✗	✗	✗	✗	✗	✓
STYLE=*string*	✗	✗	✓	✗	✗	✗	✗	✗	✓
TITLE=*string*	✗	✗	✓	✗	✗	✗	✗	✗	✓

LAYER

Defines a separate area of the page as a layer that can hold a different page. **N4 only**.

Attributes	2.0	3.2	4.0	N2	N3	N4	IE2	IE3	IE4/5
`<event_name>=script_code`	✗	✗	✗	✗	✗	✓	✗	✗	✗
`ABOVE=object_id`	✗	✗	✗	✗	✗	✓	✗	✗	✗
`BACKGROUND=string`	✗	✗	✗	✗	✗	✓	✗	✗	✗
`BELOW=object_id`	✗	✗	✗	✗	✗	✓	✗	✗	✗
`BGCOLOR=color`	✗	✗	D	✗	✗	✓	✗	✗	✗
`CLASS=classname`	✗	✗	✗	✗	✗	✓	✗	✗	✗
`CLIP=number[,number,number,number]`	✗	✗	✗	✗	✗	✓	✗	✗	✗
`ID=string`	✗	✗	✗	✗	✗	✓	✗	✗	✗
`LEFT=number`	✗	✗	✗	✗	✗	✓	✗	✗	✗
`NAME=string`	✗	✗	✗	✗	✗	✓	✗	✗	✗
`PAGEX=number`	✗	✗	✗	✗	✗	✓	✗	✗	✗
`PAGEY=number`	✗	✗	✗	✗	✗	✓	✗	✗	✗
`SRC=url`	✗	✗	✗	✗	✗	✓	✗	✗	✗
`STYLE=string`	✗	✗	✗	✗	✗	✓	✗	✗	✗
`TOP=number`	✗	✗	✗	✗	✗	✓	✗	✗	✗
`VISIBILITY=SHOW|HIDE|INHERIT`	✗	✗	✗	✗	✗	✓	✗	✗	✗
`WIDTH=number`	✗	✗	✗	✗	✗	✓	✗	✗	✗
`Z-INDEX=number`	✗	✗	✗	✗	✗	✓	✗	✗	✗

LEGEND

Defines the title text to place in the 'box' created by a FIELDSET tag. **HTML 4.0, IE4, IE5**.

Attributes	2.0	3.2	4.0	N2	N3	N4	IE2	IE3	IE4/5
<event_name>=script_code	✗	✗	✓	✗	✗	✗	✗	✗	✓
ACCESSKEY=key_character	✗	✗	✓	✗	✗	✗	✗	✗	✗
ALIGN=BOTTOM|CENTER|LEFT|RIGHT|TOP	✗	✗	D	✗	✗	✗	✗	✗	✓
CLASS=classname	✗	✗	✓	✗	✗	✗	✗	✗	✓
DIR=LTR|RTL	✗	✗	✓	✗	✗	✗	✗	✗	✗
ID=*string*	✗	✗	✓	✗	✗	✗	✗	✗	✓
LANG=language_type	✗	✗	✓	✗	✗	✗	✗	✗	✓
LANGUAGE=JAVASCRIPT|JSCRIPT|VBSCRIPT|VBS	✗	✗	✗	✗	✗	✗	✗	✗	✓
STYLE=*string*	✗	✗	✓	✗	✗	✗	✗	✗	✓
TITLE=*string*	✗	✗	✓	✗	✗	✗	✗	✗	✓
VALIGN=BOTTOM|TOP	✗	✗	✗	✗	✗	✗	✗	✗	✓

LI

Denotes one item within an ordered or unordered list. **ALL**.

Attributes	2.0	3.2	4.0	N2	N3	N4	IE2	IE3	IE4/5
<event_name>=script_code	✗	✗	✓	✗	✗	✗	✗	✗	✓
CLASS=classname	✗	✗	✓	✗	✗	✓	✗	✓	✓
DIR=LTR|RTL	✗	✗	✓	✗	✗	✗	✗	✗	✗
ID=string	✗	✗	✓	✗	✗	✓	✗	✓	✓
LANG=language_type	✗	✗	✓	✗	✗	✗	✗	✗	✓
LANGUAGE=JAVASCRIPT|JSCRIPT|VBSCRIPT|VBS	✗	✗	✗	✗	✗	✗	✗	✗	✓
STYLE=*string*	✗	✗	✓	✗	✗	✓	✗	✓	✓
TITLE=*string*	✗	✗	✓	✗	✗	✗	✗	✗	✓
TYPE=1|a|A|I|I|DISC|CIRCLE|SQUARE	✗	✓	D	✓	✓	✓	✓	✓	✓
VALUE=*string*	✗	✓	D	✓	✓	✓	✓	✓	✓

LINK

Defines a hyperlink between the document and some other resource. **HTML 2.0, 3.2 & 4.0, IE3, IE4, IE5**.

Attributes	2.0	3.2	4.0	N2	N3	N4	IE2	IE3	IE4/5
`<event_name>=script_code`	✗	✗	✓	✗	✗	✗	✗	✗	✗
`CHARSET=charset`	✗	✗	✓	✗	✗	✗	✗	✗	✗
`CLASS=classname`	✗	✗	✓	✗	✗	✗	✗	✗	✗
`DIR=LTR|RTL`	✗	✗	✓	✗	✗	✗	✗	✗	✗
`DISABLED`	✗	✗	✗	✗	✗	✗	✗	✗	✓
`HREF=url`	✓	✓	✓	✓	✓	✓	✗	✓	✓
`HREFLANG=langcode`	✗	✗	✓	✗	✗	✗	✗	✗	✗
`ID=`*string*	✗	✗	✓	✗	✗	✓	✗	✗	✓
`LANG=language_type`	✗	✗	✓	✗	✗	✗	✗	✗	✓
`MEDIA=SCREEN|PRINT|PROJECTION|` `BRAILLE|SPEECH|ALL`	✗	✗	✓	✗	✗	✗	✗	✗	✓
`METHODS=`*string*	✓	✗	✗	✗	✗	✗	✗	✗	✗
`REL=relationship`	✓	✓	✓	✓	✓	✓	✗	✓	✓
`REV=relationship`	✓	✓	✓	✓	✓	✓	✗	✓	✗
`STYLE=`*string*	✗	✗	✓	✗	✗	✓	✗	✗	✗
`TARGET=<window_name>|_parent|` `_blank|_top|_self`	✗	✗	✓	✗	✗	✗	✗	✗	✗
`TITLE=`*string*	✓	✓	✓	✓	✓	✓	✗	✓	✓
`TYPE=MIME-type`	✗	✗	✓	✗	✗	✓	✗	✓	✓
`URN=`*string*	✓	✗	✗	✗	✗	✗	✗	✗	✗

LISTING

Renders text in fixed-width type. Use PRE instead. **HTML 2.0, deprecated 3.2, supported IE2, IE3, IE4, IE5**.

Attributes	2.0	3.2	4.0	N2	N3	N4	IE2	IE3	IE4/5
`<event_name>=script_code`	✗	✗	✗	✗	✗	✗	✗	✗	✓
`CLASS=classname`	✗	✗	✗	✗	✗	✗	✗	✗	✓
`ID=string`	✗	✗	✗	✗	✗	✗	✗	✗	✓
`LANG=language_type`	✗	✗	✗	✗	✗	✗	✗	✗	✓
`LANGUAGE=JAVASCRIPT|` `JSCRIPT|VBSCRIPT|VBS`	✗	✗	✗	✗	✗	✗	✗	✗	✓
`STYLE=string`	✗	✗	✗	✗	✗	✗	✗	✗	✓
`TITLE=string`	✗	✗	✗	✗	✗	✗	✗	✗	✓

MAP

Specifies a collection of hot spots for a client-side image map. **ALL except HTML 2.0**.

Attributes	2.0	3.2	4.0	N2	N3	N4	IE2	IE3	IE4/5
`<event_name>=script_code`	✗	✗	✗	✗	✗	✗	✗	✗	✓
`CLASS=classname`	✗	✗	✓	✗	✗	✓	✗	✗	✓
`ID=`*string*	✗	✗	✓	✗	✗	✓	✗	✗	✓
`LANG=language_type`	✗	✗	✗	✗	✗	✗	✗	✗	✓
`NAME=`*string*	✗	✓	✓	✓	✓	✓	✓	✓	✓
`STYLE=`*string*	✗	✗	✓	✗	✗	✓	✗	✗	✓
`TITLE=`*string*	✗	✗	✓	✗	✗	✗	✗	✗	✓

MARQUEE

Creates a scrolling text marquee in the page. **IE2, IE3, IE4, IE5**.

Attributes	2.0	3.2	4.0	N2	N3	N4	IE2	IE3	IE4/5
<event_name>=script_code	✗	✗	✗	✗	✗	✗	✗	✗	✓
ALIGN=TOP|MIDDLE|BOTTOM	✗	✗	✗	✗	✗	✗	✓	✓	✗
BEHAVIOR=ALTERNATE|SCROLL|SLIDE	✗	✗	✗	✗	✗	✗	✓	✓	✓
BGCOLOR=color	✗	✗	D	✗	✗	✗	✓	✓	✓
CLASS=classname	✗	✗	✗	✗	✗	✗	✗	✗	✓
DATAFLD=column_name	✗	✗	✗	✗	✗	✗	✗	✗	✓
DATAFORMATAS=HTML|TEXT	✗	✗	✗	✗	✗	✗	✗	✗	✓
DATASRC=id	✗	✗	✗	✗	✗	✗	✗	✗	✓
DIRECTION=DOWN|LEFT|RIGHT|UP	✗	✗	✗	✗	✗	✗	✓	✓	✓
HEIGHT=number	✗	✗	✗	✗	✗	✗	✓	✓	✓
HSPACE=number	✗	✗	✗	✗	✗	✗	✓	✓	✓
ID=*string*	✗	✗	✗	✗	✗	✗	✗	✗	✓
LANG=language_type	✗	✗	✗	✗	✗	✗	✗	✗	✓
LANGUAGE=JAVASCRIPT|JSCRIPT| VBSCRIPT|VBS	✗	✗	✗	✗	✗	✗	✗	✗	✓
LOOP=number	✗	✗	✗	✗	✗	✗	✓	✓	✓
SCROLLAMOUNT=number	✗	✗	✗	✗	✗	✗	✓	✓	✓
SCROLLDELAY=number	✗	✗	✗	✗	✗	✗	✓	✓	✓
STYLE=*string*	✗	✗	✗	✗	✗	✗	✗	✗	✓
TITLE=*string*	✗	✗	✗	✗	✗	✗	✗	✗	✓
TRUESPEED	✗	✗	✗	✗	✗	✗	✗	✗	✓
VSPACE=number	✗	✗	✗	✗	✗	✗	✓	✓	✓
WIDTH=number	✗	✗	✗	✗	✗	✗	✓	✓	✓

MENU

Renders the following block of text as individual items. Use lists instead. **ALL, deprecated in HTML 4.0**.

Attributes	2.0	3.2	4.0	N2	N3	N4	IE2	IE3	IE4/5
`<event_name>=script_code`	✗	✗	D	✗	✗	✗	✗	✗	✓
`CLASS=classname`	✗	✗	D	✗	✗	✓	✗	✗	✓
`COMPACT`	✓	✓	D	✗	✗	✓	✗	✓	✗
`ID=string`	✗	✗	D	✗	✗	✓	✗	✗	✓
`LANG=language_type`	✗	✗	D	✗	✗	✗	✗	✗	✓
`LANGUAGE=JAVASCRIPT|JSCRIPT|VBSCRIPT|VBS`	✗	✗	✗	✗	✗	✗	✗	✗	✓
`STYLE=string`	✗	✗	D	✗	✗	✓	✗	✗	✓
`TITLE=string`	✗	✗	D	✗	✗	✗	✗	✗	✓
`TYPE=CIRCLE|DISC|SQUARE`	✗	✗	✗	✗	✗	✓	✗	✗	✗

META

Provides various types of unviewed information or instructions to the browser. **ALL**.

Attributes	2.0	3.2	4.0	N2	N3	N4	IE2	IE3	IE4/5
`CHARSET=string`	✗	✗	✗	✗	✗	✗	✗	✓	✗
`CONTENT=metacontent`	✓	✓	✓	✓	✓	✓	✓	✓	✓
`DIR=LTR|RTL`	✗	✗	✓	✗	✗	✗	✗	✗	✗
`HTTP-EQUIV=string`	✓	✓	✓	✓	✓	✓	✓	✓	✓
`LANG=language_type`	✗	✗	✓	✗	✗	✗	✗	✗	✗
`NAME=metaname`	✓	✓	✓	✓	✓	✓	✗	✓	✓
`SCHEME=string`	✗	✗	✓	✗	✗	✗	✗	✗	✗
`TITLE=string`	✗	✗	✗	✗	✗	✗	✗	✗	✓
`URL=url`	✗	✗	✗	✗	✗	✗	✗	✓	✓

MULTICOL

Used to define multiple column formatting. **N2, N3, N4**.

Attributes	2.0	3.2	4.0	N2	N3	N4	IE2	IE3	IE4/5
CLASS=classname	✗	✗	✗	✗	✗	✓	✗	✗	✗
COLS=number	✗	✗	✗	✗	✓	✓	✗	✗	✗
GUTTER=number	✗	✗	✗	✗	✓	✓	✗	✗	✗
ID=*string*	✗	✗	✗	✗	✗	✓	✗	✗	✗
STYLE=*string*	✗	✗	✗	✗	✗	✓	✗	✗	✗
WIDTH=number	✗	✗	✗	✗	✓	✓	✗	✗	✗

NEXTID

Defines values used by text editing software when parsing or creating the document. **HTML 2.0 only**.

Attributes	2.0	3.2	4.0	N2	N3	N4	IE2	IE3	IE4/5
N=*string*	✓	✗	✗	✗	✗	✗	✗	✗	✗

NOBR

Renders text without any text wrapping in the page. **N2, N3, N4, IE2, IE3, IE4, IE5**.

Attributes	2.0	3.2	4.0	N2	N3	N4	IE2	IE3	IE4/5
ID=*string*	✗	✗	✗	✗	✗	✗	✗	✗	✓
STYLE=*string*	✗	✗	✗	✗	✗	✗	✗	✗	✓
TITLE=*string*	✗	✗	✗	✗	✗	✗	✗	✗	✓

NOEMBED

Defines the HTML to be displayed by browsers that do not support embeds. **N2, N3, N4**.

NOFRAMES

Defines the HTML to be displayed in browsers that do not support frames.**HTML 4.0, N2, N3, N3, IE3, IE4, IE5.**

Attributes	2.0	3.2	4.0	N2	N3	N4	IE2	IE3	IE4/5
ID=*string*	✘	✘	✘	✘	✘	✘	✘	✘	✓
STYLE=*string*	✘	✘	✘	✘	✘	✘	✘	✘	✓
TITLE=*string*	✘	✘	✘	✘	✘	✘	✘	✘	✓

NOLAYER

Defines the part of a document that will be displayed in browsers that don't support layers. **N4.**

NOSCRIPT

Defines the HTML to be displayed in browsers that do not support scripting. **HTML 4.0, N3, N4, IE3, IE4, IE5.**

OBJECT

Inserts an object or other non-intrinsic HTML control into the page. **HTML 4.0, IE3, IE4, IE5.**

Attributes	2.0	3.2	4.0	N2	N3	N4	IE2	IE3	IE4/5
<event_name>=script_code	✘	✘	✓	✘	✘	✘	✘	✘	✓
ACCESSKEY=key_character	✘	✘	✘	✘	✘	✘	✘	✘	✓
ALIGN=ABSBOTTOM | ABSMIDDLE | BASELINE | BOTTOM | LEFT | MIDDLE | RIGHT | TEXTTOP | TOP	✓	✓	D	✘	✘	✘	✘	✓	✓
ARCHIVE=urllist	✘	✘	✓	✘	✘	✘	✘	✘	✘
BORDER=number	✘	✘	D	✘	✘	✘	✘	✓	✘
CLASS=classname	✘	✘	✓	✘	✘	✘	✘	✘	✓
CLASSID=*string*	✘	✘	✓	✘	✘	✘	✘	✓	✓
CODE=filename	✘	✘	✘	✘	✘	✘	✘	✘	✓
CODEBASE=url	✘	✘	✓	✘	✘	✘	✘	✓	✓
CODETYPE=url	✘	✘	✓	✘	✘	✘	✘	✓	✓
DATA=*string*	✘	✘	✓	✘	✘	✘	✘	✓	✓
DATAFLD=column_name	✘	✘	✘	✘	✘	✘	✘	✘	✓

Table Continued on Following Page

Attributes	2.0	3.2	4.0	N2	N3	N4	IE2	IE3	IE4/5
DATASRC=id	✘	✘	✘	✘	✘	✘	✘	✘	✔
DECLARE	✘	✘	✔	✘	✘	✘	✘	✔	✘
DIR=LTR|RTL	✘	✘	✔	✘	✘	✘	✘	✘	✘
EXPORT	✘	✘	✔	✘	✘	✘	✘	✘	✘
HEIGHT=number	✘	✘	✔	✘	✘	✘	✘	✔	✔
HSPACE=number	✘	✘	✔	✘	✘	✘	✘	✔	✘
ID=string	✘	✘	✔	✘	✘	✘	✘	✘	✔
LANG=language_type	✘	✘	✔	✘	✘	✘	✘	✘	✔
LANGUAGE=JAVASCRIPT|JSCRIPT| VBSCRIPT|VBS	✘	✘	✘	✘	✘	✘	✘	✘	✔
NAME=string	✘	✘	✔	✘	✘	✘	✘	✔	✔
NOTAB	✘	✘	✘	✘	✘	✘	✘	✔	✘
SHAPES	✘	✘	✔	✘	✘	✘	✘	✔	✘
STANDBY=string	✘	✘	✔	✘	✘	✘	✘	✔	✘
STYLE=string	✘	✘	✔	✘	✘	✘	✘	✘	✔
TABINDEX=number	✘	✘	✔	✘	✘	✘	✘	✔	✔
TITLE=string	✘	✘	✔	✘	✘	✘	✘	✔	✔
TYPE=MIME-type	✘	✘	✔	✘	✘	✘	✘	✘	✘
USEMAP=url	✘	✘	✔	✘	✘	✘	✘	✔	✘
VSPACE=number	✘	✘	✔	✘	✘	✘	✘	✔	✘
WIDTH=number	✘	✘	✔	✘	✘	✘	✘	✔	✔

OL

Renders lines of text that have <LI> tags as an ordered list. **ALL**.

Attributes	2.0	3.2	4.0	N2	N3	N4	IE2	IE3	IE4/5
<event_name>=script_code	✖	✖	✓	✖	✖	✖	✖	✖	✓
CLASS=classname	✖	✖	✓	✖	✖	✓	✖	✖	✓
COMPACT	✓	✓	D	✓	✓	✓	✖	✓	✖
DIR=LTR|RTL	✖	✖	✓	✖	✖	✖	✖	✖	✖
ID=string	✖	✖	✓	✖	✖	✓	✖	✓	✓
LANG=language_type	✖	✖	✓	✖	✖	✖	✖	✖	✓
LANGUAGE=JAVASCRIPT|JSCRIPT| VBSCRIPT|VBS	✖	✖	✖	✖	✖	✖	✖	✖	✓
START=number	✖	✓	D	✓	✓	✓	✓	✓	✓
STYLE=string	✖	✖	✓	✖	✖	✓	✖	✓	✓
TITLE=string	✖	✖	✓	✖	✖	✖	✖	✖	✓
TYPE=1|a|A|I|I	✖	✓	D	✓	✓	✓	✓	✓	✓

OPTGROUP

Creates a collapsible and hierarchical list of options.

Attributes	2.0	3.2	4.0	N2	N3	N4	IE2	IE3	IE4/5
<event_name>=script_code	✖	✖	✓	✖	✖	✖	✖	✖	✖
CLASS=classname	✖	✖	✓	✖	✖	✖	✖	✖	✖
DISABLED	✖	✖	✓	✖	✖	✖	✖	✖	✖
DIR=LTR|RTL	✖	✖	✓	✖	✖	✖	✖	✖	✖
ID=string	✖	✖	✓	✖	✖	✖	✖	✖	✖
LABEL=string	✖	✖	✓	✖	✖	✖	✖	✖	✖
LANG=language_type	✖	✖	✓	✖	✖	✖	✖	✖	✖
STYLE=string	✖	✖	✓	✖	✖	✖	✖	✖	✖
TITLE=string	✖	✖	✓	✖	✖	✖	✖	✖	✖

OPTION

Denotes one choice in a SELECT drop-down or list element. **ALL**.

Attributes	2.0	3.2	4.0	N2	N3	N4	IE2	IE3	IE4/5
`<event_name>=script_code`	✗	✗	✓	✗	✗	✗	✗	✗	✓
`CLASS=classname`	✗	✗	✓	✗	✗	✓	✗	✗	✓
`DIR=LTR|RTL`	✗	✗	✓	✗	✗	✗	✗	✗	✗
`DISABLED`	✗	✗	✓	✓	✓	✗	✗	✗	✗
`ID=string`	✗	✗	✓	✗	✗	✓	✗	✗	✓
`LABEL=string`	✗	✗	✓	✗	✗	✗	✗	✗	✗
`LANG=language_type`	✗	✗	✓	✗	✗	✗	✗	✗	✗
`LANGUAGE=JAVASCRIPT|JSCRIPT|` `VBSCRIPT|VBS`	✗	✗	✗	✗	✗	✗	✗	✗	✓
`PLAIN`	✗	✗	✗	✓	✓	✓	✗	✗	✗
`SELECTED`	✓	✓	✓	✓	✓	✓	✓	✓	✓
`STYLE=string`	✗	✗	✓	✗	✗	✓	✗	✗	✗
`TITLE=string`	✗	✗	✓	✗	✗	✗	✗	✗	✗
`VALUE=string`	✓	✓	✓	✓	✓	✓	✓	✓	✓

P

Denotes a paragraph. The end tag is optional. **ALL**.

Attributes	2.0	3.2	4.0	N2	N3	N4	IE2	IE3	IE4/5
`<event_name>=script_code`	✗	✗	✓	✗	✗	✗	✗	✗	✓
`ALIGN=CENTER|LEFT|RIGHT`	✗	✓	D	✓	✓	✓	✓	✓	✓
`CLASS=classname`	✗	✗	✓	✗	✗	✓	✗	✓	✓
`DIR=LTR|RTL`	✗	✗	✓	✗	✗	✗	✗	✗	✗
`ID=string`	✗	✗	✓	✗	✗	✓	✗	✓	✓
`LANG=language_type`	✗	✗	✓	✗	✗	✗	✗	✗	✓
`LANGUAGE=JAVASCRIPT|JSCRIPT|` `VBSCRIPT|VBS`	✗	✗	✗	✗	✗	✗	✗	✗	✓
`STYLE=string`	✗	✗	✓	✗	✗	✓	✗	✓	✓
`TITLE=string`	✗	✗	✓	✗	✗	✗	✗	✗	✓

PARAM

Used in an OBJECT or APPLET tag to set the object's properties. **ALL except HTML 2.0.**

Attributes	2.0	3.2	4.0	N2	N3	N4	IE2	IE3	IE4/5
DATAFLD=column_name	✗	✗	✗	✗	✗	✗	✗	✗	✓
DATAFORMATAS=HTML|TEXT	✗	✗	✗	✗	✗	✗	✗	✗	✓
DATASRC=id	✗	✗	✗	✗	✗	✗	✗	✗	✓
ID	✗	✗	✓	✗	✗	✗	✗	✗	✗
NAME=*string*	✗	✓	✓	✓	✓	✓	✗	✓	✓
TYPE=*string*	✗	✗	✓	✗	✗	✗	✗	✓	✗
VALUE=*string*	✗	✓	✓	✓	✓	✓	✗	✓	✓
VALUETYPE=DATA|REF|OBJECT	✗	✗	✓	✗	✗	✗	✗	✓	✗

PLAINTEXT

Renders text in fixed-width type without processing any tags it may contain. **Deprecated in HTML 2.0, 3.0, N2, N3 and N4, supported in IE2, IE3, IE4, IE5.**

Attributes	2.0	3.2	4.0	N2	N3	N4	IE2	IE3	IE4/5
<event_name>=script_code	✗	✗	✗	✗	✗	✗	✗	✗	✓
CLASS=classname	✗	✗	✗	✗	✗	✗	✗	✗	✓
ID=*string*	✗	✗	✗	✗	✗	✗	✗	✗	✓
LANG=language_type	✗	✗	✗	✗	✗	✗	✗	✗	✓
LANGUAGE=JAVASCRIPT|JSCRIPT|VBSCRIPT|VBS	✗	✗	✗	✗	✗	✗	✗	✗	✓
STYLE=*string*	✗	✗	✗	✗	✗	✗	✗	✗	✓
TITLE=*string*	✗	✗	✗	✗	✗	✗	✗	✗	✓

PRE

Renders text in fixed-width type. **ALL**.

Attributes	2.0	3.2	4.0	N2	N3	N4	IE2	IE3	IE4/5
`<event_name>=script_code`	✗	✗	✓	✗	✗	✗	✗	✗	✓
`CLASS=classname`	✗	✗	✓	✗	✗	✓	✗	✗	✓
`DIR=LTR|RTL`	✗	✗	✓	✗	✗	✗	✗	✗	✗
`ID=string`	✗	✗	✓	✗	✗	✓	✗	✗	✓
`LANG=language_type`	✗	✗	✓	✗	✗	✗	✗	✗	✓
`LANGUAGE=JAVASCRIPT|JSCRIPT|VBSCRIPT|VBS`	✗	✗	✗	✗	✗	✗	✗	✗	✓
`STYLE=string`	✗	✗	✓	✗	✗	✓	✗	✗	✓
`TITLE=string`	✗	✗	✓	✗	✗	✗	✗	✗	✓
`WIDTH=number`	✓	✓	✓	✓	✓	✓	✗	✗	✗

Q

A short quotation, such as the URL of the source document or a message. **HTML 4.0, IE4, IE5**.

Attributes	2.0	3.2	4.0	N2	N3	N4	IE2	IE3	IE4/5
`<event_name>=script_code`	✗	✗	✓	✗	✗	✗	✗	✗	✓
`CITE=url`	✗	✗	✓	✗	✗	✗	✗	✗	✗
`CLASS=classname`	✗	✗	✓	✗	✗	✗	✗	✗	✓
`DIR=LTR|RTL`	✗	✗	✓	✗	✗	✗	✗	✗	✗
`ID=string`	✗	✗	✓	✗	✗	✗	✗	✗	✓
`LANG=language_type`	✗	✗	✓	✗	✗	✗	✗	✗	✓
`STYLE=string`	✗	✗	✓	✗	✗	✗	✗	✗	✓
`TITLE=string`	✗	✗	✓	✗	✗	✗	✗	✗	✓

S

Renders text in strikethrough type. **Supported in HTML 3.2, N3, N4, IE2, IE3, IE4, IE5 deprecated in HTML 4.0**.

Attributes	2.0	3.2	4.0	N2	N3	N4	IE2	IE3	IE4/5
<event_name>=script_code	✗	✗	D	✗	✗	✗	✗	✗	✓
CLASS=classname	✗	✗	D	✗	✗	✓	✗	✗	✓
DIR=LTR|RTL	✗	✗	D	✗	✗	✗	✗	✗	✗
ID=*string*	✗	✗	D	✗	✗	✓	✗	✗	✓
LANG=language_type	✗	✗	D	✗	✗	✗	✗	✗	✓
LANGUAGE=JAVASCRIPT|JSCRIPT|VBSCRIPT|VBS	✗	✗	✗	✗	✗	✗	✗	✗	✓
STYLE=*string*	✗	✗	D	✗	✗	✓	✗	✗	✓
TITLE=*string*	✗	✗	D	✗	✗	✗	✗	✗	✓

SAMP

Renders text as a code sample listing, usually in a smaller font. **ALL**.

Attributes	2.0	3.2	4.0	N2	N3	N4	IE2	IE3	IE4/5
<event_name>=script_code	✗	✗	✓	✗	✗	✗	✗	✗	✓
CLASS=classname	✗	✗	✓	✗	✗	✓	✗	✗	✓
DIR=LTR|RTL	✗	✗	✓	✗	✗	✗	✗	✗	✗
ID=*string*	✗	✗	✓	✗	✗	✓	✗	✗	✓
LANG=language_type	✗	✗	✓	✗	✗	✗	✗	✗	✓
LANGUAGE=JAVASCRIPT|JSCRIPT|VBSCRIPT|VBS	✗	✗	✗	✗	✗	✗	✗	✗	✓
STYLE=*string*	✗	✗	✓	✗	✗	✓	✗	✗	✓
TITLE=*string*	✗	✗	✓	✗	✗	✗	✗	✗	✓

SCRIPT

Specifies a script for the page that will be interpreted by a script engine. **HTML 3.2, 4.0, N2, N3, N4, IE3, IE4**.

Attributes	2.0	3.2	4.0	N2	N3	N4	IE2	IE3	IE4/5
ARCHIVE=url	✗	✗	✗	✗	✗	✓	✗	✗	✗
CHARSET=charset	✗	✗	✓	✗	✗	✗	✗	✗	✗
CLASS=classname	✗	✗	✗	✗	✗	✓	✗	✗	✓
DEFER	✗	✗	✓	✗	✗	✗	✗	✗	✗
EVENT=<event_name>	✗	✗	✗	✗	✗	✗	✗	✗	✓
FOR=element_name	✗	✗	✗	✗	✗	✗	✗	✗	✓
ID=*string*	✗	✗	✗	✗	✗	✓	✗	✗	✓
LANGUAGE=JAVASCRIPT|JSCRIPT|VBSCRIPT|VBS	✗	✗	D	✓	✓	✓	✗	✓	✓
SRC=url	✗	✗	✓	✗	✓	✓	✗	✓	✓
STYLE=*string*	✗	✗	✗	✗	✗	✓	✗	✗	✓
TITLE=*string*	✗	✗	✗	✗	✗	✗	✗	✗	✓
TYPE=*string*	✗	✗	✓	✗	✗	✗	✗	✓	✓

SELECT

Defines a list box or drop-down list. **ALL**.

Attributes	2.0	3.2	4.0	N2	N3	N4	IE2	IE3	IE4/5
`<event_name>=script_code`	✗	✗	✓	✗	✗	✓	✗	✗	✓
`ACCESSKEY=key_character`	✗	✗	✗	✗	✗	✗	✗	✗	✓

`ALIGN=ABSBOTTOM|ABSMIDDLE|`
`BASELINE|BOTTOM|LEFT|MIDDLE|`
`RIGHT|TEXTTOP|TOP`
	✗	✗	✗	✗	✗	✗	✗	✗	✓

`CLASS=classname`	✗	✗	✓	✗	✗	✓	✗	✗	✓
`DATAFLD-column_name`	✗	✗	✗	✗	✗	✗	✗	✗	✓
`DATASRC=id`	✗	✗	✗	✗	✗	✗	✗	✗	✓
`DIR=LTR|RTL`	✗	✗	✓	✗	✗	✗	✗	✗	✗
`DISABLED`	✗	✗	✓	✗	✗	✗	✗	✗	✓
`ID=string`	✗	✗	✓	✗	✗	✓	✗	✗	✓
`LANG=language_type`	✗	✗	✓	✗	✗	✗	✗	✗	✓
`LANGUAGE=JAVASCRIPT|JSCRIPT|` `VBSCRIPT|VBS`	✗	✗	✗	✗	✗	✗	✗	✗	✓
`MULTIPLE`	✓	✓	✓	✓	✓	✓	✓	✓	✓
`NAME=string`	✓	✓	✓	✓	✓	✓	✓	✓	✓
`SIZE=number`	✓	✓	✓	✓	✓	✓	✓	✓	✓
`STYLE=string`	✗	✗	✓	✗	✗	✓	✗	✗	✓
`TABINDEX=number`	✗	✗	✓	✗	✗	✗	✗	✗	✓
`TITLE=string`	✗	✗	✓	✗	✗	✗	✗	✗	✓

SERVER

Used to run a Netscape LiveWire script. **N2, N3, N4**.

Attributes	2.0	3.2	4.0	N2	N3	N4	IE2	IE3	IE4/5
`CLASS=classname`	✗	✗	✗	✗	✗	✓	✗	✗	✗
`ID=string`	✗	✗	✗	✗	✗	✓	✗	✗	✗

SMALL

Specifies that text should be displayed with a smaller font than the current font. **HTML 3.2, 4.0, N2, N3, N4, IE3, IE4, IE5**.

Attributes	2.0	3.2	4.0	N2	N3	N4	IE2	IE3	IE4/5
`<event_name>=script_code`	✗	✗	✓	✗	✗	✗	✗	✗	✓
`CLASS=classname`	✗	✗	✓	✗	✗	✓	✗	✗	✓
`DIR=LTR|RTL`	✗	✗	✓	✗	✗	✗	✗	✗	✗
`ID=string`	✗	✗	✓	✗	✗	✓	✗	✗	✓
`LANG=language_type`	✗	✗	✓	✗	✗	✗	✗	✗	✓
`LANGUAGE=JAVASCRIPT|JSCRIPT| VBSCRIPT|VBS`	✗	✗	✗	✗	✗	✗	✗	✗	✓
`STYLE=string`	✗	✗	✓	✗	✗	✓	✗	✗	✓
`TITLE=string`	✗	✗	✓	✗	✗	✗	✗	✗	✓

SPACER

Used to specify vertical and horizontal spacing of elements. **HTML 3.2, 4.0, N2, N3, N4, IE3, IE4, IE5**.

Attributes	2.0	3.2	4.0	N2	N3	N4	IE2	IE3	IE4/5
`ALIGN=ABSBOTTOM|ABSMIDDLE| BASELINE|BOTTOM|LEFT|MIDDLE| RIGHT|TEXTTOP|TOP`	✗	✗	✗	✗	✓	✓	✗	✗	✗
`CLASS=classname`	✗	✗	✗	✗	✗	✓	✗	✗	✗
`HEIGHT=number`	✗	✗	✗	✗	✓	✓	✗	✗	✗
`ID=string`	✗	✗	✗	✗	✗	✓	✗	✗	✗
`SIZE=number`	✗	✗	✗	✗	✓	✓	✗	✗	✗
`STYLE=string`	✗	✗	✗	✗	✗	✓	✗	✗	✗
`TYPE=BLOCK|HORIZONTAL|VERTICAL`	✗	✗	✗	✗	✓	✓	✗	✗	✗
`WIDTH=number`	✗	✗	✗	✗	✓	✓	✗	✗	✗

SPAN

Used (with a style sheet) to define non-standard attributes for text on the page. **HTML 4.0, IE4, IE5**.

Attributes	2.0	3.2	4.0	N2	N3	N4	IE2	IE3	IE4/5
<event_name>=script_code	✗	✗	✓	✗	✗	✗	✗	✗	✓
CLASS=classname	✗	✗	✓	✗	✗	✓	✗	✗	✓
CHARSET=*string*	✗	✗	✓	✗	✗	✗	✗	✗	✗
DATAFLD=column_name	✗	✗	✗	✗	✗	✗	✗	✗	✓
DATAFORMATAS=HTML|TEXT	✗	✗	✗	✗	✗	✗	✗	✗	✓
DATASRC=id	✗	✗	✗	✗	✗	✗	✗	✗	✓
DIR=LTR|RTL	✗	✗	✓	✗	✗	✗	✗	✗	✗
HREF=url	✗	✗	✓	✗	✗	✗	✗	✗	✗
HREFLANG=langcode	✗	✗	✓	✗	✗	✗	✗	✗	✗
ID=*string*	✗	✗	✓	✗	✗	✓	✗	✗	✓
LANG=language_type	✗	✗	✓	✗	✗	✗	✗	✗	✓
LANGUAGE=JAVASCRIPT|JSCRIPT|VBSCRIPT|VBS	✗	✗	✗	✗	✗	✗	✗	✗	✓
MEDIA	✗	✗	✓	✗	✗	✗	✗	✗	✗
REL=relationship	✗	✗	✓	✗	✗	✗	✗	✗	✗
REV=relationship	✗	✗	✓	✗	✗	✗	✗	✗	✗
STYLE=*string*	✗	✗	✓	✗	✗	✓	✗	✓	✓
TARGET	✗	✗	✓	✗	✗	✗	✗	✗	✗
TITLE=*string*	✗	✗	✓	✗	✗	✗	✗	✗	✓
TYPE	✗	✗	✓	✗	✗	✗	✗	✗	✗

STRIKE

Renders text in strikethrough type. **HTML 3.2, N3, N4, IE3, IE4, IE5, deprecated in HTML 4.0.**

Attributes	2.0	3.2	4.0	N2	N3	N4	IE2	IE3	IE4/5
`<event_name>=script_code`	✗	✗	D	✗	✗	✗	✗	✗	✓
`CLASS=classname`	✗	✗	D	✗	✗	✓	✗	✗	✓
`DIR=LTR|RTL`	✗	✗	D	✗	✗	✗	✗	✗	✗
`ID=string`	✗	✗	D	✗	✗	✓	✗	✗	✓
`LANG=language_type`	✗	✗	D	✗	✗	✗	✗	✗	✓
`LANGUAGE=JAVASCRIPT|JSCRIPT|` `VBSCRIPT|VBS`	✗	✗	✗	✗	✗	✗	✗	✗	✓
`STYLE=string`	✗	✗	D	✗	✗	✓	✗	✗	✓
`TITLE=string`	✗	✗	D	✗	✗	✗	✗	✗	✓

STRONG

Renders text in bold face. **ALL**.

Attributes	2.0	3.2	4.0	N2	N3	N4	IE2	IE3	IE4/5
`<event_name>=script_code`	✗	✗	✓	✗	✗	✗	✗	✗	✓
`CLASS=classname`	✗	✗	✓	✗	✗	✓	✗	✗	✓
`DIR=LTR|RTL`	✗	✗	✓	✗	✗	✗	✗	✗	✗
`ID=string`	✗	✗	✓	✗	✗	✓	✗	✗	✓
`LANG=language_type`	✗	✗	✓	✗	✗	✗	✗	✗	✓
`LANGUAGE=JAVASCRIPT|JSCRIPT|` `VBSCRIPT|VBS`	✗	✗	✗	✗	✗	✗	✗	✗	✓
`STYLE=string`	✗	✗	✓	✗	✗	✓	✗	✗	✓
`TITLE=string`	✗	✗	✓	✗	✗	✗	✗	✗	✓

STYLE

Specifies the style properties (i.e. the style sheet) for the page. **HTML 3.2, 4.0, N4, IE3, IE4, IE5**.

Attributes	2.0	3.2	4.0	N2	N3	N4	IE2	IE3	IE4/5
DIR=LTR|RTL	✗	✗	✓	✗	✗	✗	✗	✗	✗
DISABLED	✗	✗	✗	✗	✗	✗	✗	✗	✓
ID=*string*	✗	✗	✗	✗	✗	✓	✗	✗	✗
LANG=language_type	✗	✗	✓	✗	✗	✗	✗	✗	✗
MEDIA=SCREEN|PRINT|PROJECTION|BRAILLE|SPEECH|ALL	✗	✗	✓	✗	✗	✗	✗	✗	✓
SRC=url	✗	✗	✗	✗	✗	✓	✗	✗	✗
TITLE=*string*	✗	✗	✓	✗	✗	✗	✗	✓	✓
TYPE=*string*	✗	✗	✓	✗	✗	✓	✗	✓	✓

SUB

Renders text as a subscript using a smaller font than the current font. **HTML 3.2, 4.0, N2, N3, N4, IE3, IE4**.

Attributes	2.0	3.2	4.0	N2	N3	N4	IE2	IE3	IE4/5
<event_name>=script_code	✗	✗	✓	✗	✗	✗	✗	✗	✓
CLASS=classname	✗	✗	✓	✗	✗	✓	✗	✗	✓
DIR=LTR|RTL	✗	✗	✓	✗	✗	✗	✗	✗	✗
ID=*string*	✗	✗	✓	✗	✗	✓	✗	✗	✓
LANG=language_type	✗	✗	✓	✗	✗	✗	✗	✗	✓
LANGUAGE=JAVASCRIPT|JSCRIPT|VBSCRIPT|VBS	✗	✗	✗	✗	✗	✗	✗	✗	✓
STYLE=*string*	✗	✗	✓	✗	✗	✓	✗	✗	✓
TITLE=*string*	✗	✗	✓	✗	✗	✗	✗	✗	✓

SUP

Renders text as a superscript using a smaller font than the current font. **HTML 3.2, 4.0, N2, N3, N4, IE3, IE4, IE5.**

Attributes	2.0	3.2	4.0	N2	N3	N4	IE2	IE3	IE4/5
`<event_name>=script_code`	✗	✗	✓	✗	✗	✗	✗	✗	✓
`CLASS=classname`	✗	✗	✓	✗	✗	✓	✗	✗	✓
`DIR=LTR|RTL`	✗	✗	✓	✗	✗	✗	✗	✗	✗
`ID=string`	✗	✗	✓	✗	✗	✓	✗	✗	✓
`LANG=language_type`	✗	✗	✓	✗	✗	✗	✗	✗	✓
`LANGUAGE=JAVASCRIPT|JSCRIPT|` `VBSCRIPT|VBS`	✗	✗	✗	✗	✗	✗	✗	✗	✓
`STYLE=string`	✗	✗	✓	✗	✗	✓	✗	✗	✓
`TITLE=string`	✗	✗	✓	✗	✗	✗	✗	✗	✓

TABLE

Denotes a section of `<TR>` `<TD>` and `<TH>` tags organized into rows and columns. **ALL except HTML 2.0.**

Attributes	2.0	3.2	4.0	N2	N3	N4	IE2	IE3	IE4/5
`<event_name>=script_code`	✗	✗	✓	✗	✗	✗	✗	✗	✓
`ALIGN=CENTER|LEFT|RIGHT`	✗	✓	D	✗	✗	✓	✓	✓	✓
`BACKGROUND=string`	✗	✗	✗	✗	✗	✗	✓	✓	✓
`BGCOLOR=color`	✗	✗	D	✗	✓	✓	✓	✓	✓
`BORDER=number`	✗	✓	D	✓	✓	✓	✗	✓	✓
`BORDERCOLOR=color`	✗	✗	✗	✗	✗	✗	✓	✓	✓
`BORDERCOLORDARK=color`	✗	✗	✗	✗	✗	✗	✓	✓	✓
`BORDERCOLORLIGHT=color`	✗	✗	✗	✗	✗	✗	✓	✓	✓
`CELLPADDING=number`	✗	✓	✓	✓	✓	✓	✗	✓	✓
`CELLSPACING=number`	✗	✓	✓	✓	✓	✓	✗	✓	✓
`CLASS=classname`	✗	✗	✓	✗	✗	✓	✗	✓	✓
`CLEAR=ALL|LEFT|RIGHT|NONE`	✗	✗	✗	✗	✗	✗	✗	✓	✗
`DATAPAGESIZE=number`	✗	✗	✗	✗	✗	✗	✗	✗	✓

Attributes	2.0	3.2	4.0	N2	N3	N4	IE2	IE3	IE4/5
DATASRC=id	✗	✗	✗	✗	✗	✗	✗	✗	✓
DIR=LTR|RTL	✗	✗	✓	✗	✗	✗	✗	✗	✗
FRAME=ABOVE|BELOW|BORDER|BOX| HSIDES|LHS|RHS|VOID|VSIDES	✗	✗	✓	✗	✗	✗	✗	✓	✓
HEIGHT=number	✗	✗	✗	✓	✓	✓	✗	✗	✓
HSPACE=number	✗	✗	✗	✗	✗	✓	✗	✗	✗
ID=string	✗	✗	✓	✗	✗	✓	✗	✓	✓
LANG=language_type	✗	✗	✓	✗	✗	✗	✗	✗	✓
LANGUAGE=JAVASCRIPT|JSCRIPT| VBSCRIPT|VBS	✗	✗	✗	✗	✗	✗	✗	✗	✓
NOWRAP	✗	✗	✗	✗	✗	✗	✗	✓	✗
RULES=ALL|COLS|GROUPS|NONE|ROWS	✗	✗	✓	✗	✗	✗	✗	✓	✓
SUMMARY	✗	✗	✓	✗	✗	✗	✗	✗	✗
STYLE=string	✗	✗	✓	✗	✗	✓	✗	✓	✓
TITLE=string	✗	✗	✓	✗	✗	✗	✗	✗	✓
VALIGN=BOTTOM|TOP	✗	✗	✗	✗	✗	✗	✓	✓	✗
VSPACE=number	✗	✗	✗	✗	✗	✓	✗	✗	✗
WIDTH=number	✗	✓	✓	✓	✓	✓	✗	✓	✓

TBODY

Denotes a section of **\<TR>** and **\<TD>** tags forming the body of the table. **HTML 4.0, IE3, IE4, IE5**.

Attributes	2.0	3.2	4.0	N2	N3	N4	IE 2	IE3	IE4/5
\<event_name>=script_code	✗	✗	✓	✗	✗	✗	✗	✗	✓
ALIGN=CENTER|LEFT|RIGHT|JUSTIFY|CHAR	✗	✗	✓	✗	✗	✗	✗	✗	✓
BGCOLOR=color	✗	✗	D	✗	✗	✗	✗	✗	✓
CHAR=*string*	✗	✗	✓	✗	✗	✗	✗	✗	✗
CHAROFF=*string*	✗	✗	✓	✗	✗	✗	✗	✗	✗
CLASS=classname	✗	✗	✓	✗	✗	✗	✗	✓	✓
DIR=LTR|RTL	✗	✗	✓	✗	✗	✗	✗	✗	✗
ID=*string*	✗	✗	✓	✗	✗	✗	✗	✓	✓
LANG=language_type	✗	✗	✓	✗	✗	✗	✗	✗	✓
LANGUAGE=JAVASCRIPT|JSCRIPT|VBSCRIPT|VBS	✗	✗	✗	✗	✗	✗	✗	✗	✓
STYLE=*string*	✗	✗	✓	✗	✗	✗	✗	✓	✓
TITLE=*string*	✗	✗	✓	✗	✗	✗	✗	✗	✓
VALIGN=BASELINE|BOTTOM|CENTER|TOP	✗	✗	✓	✗	✗	✗	✗	✗	✓

TD

Specifies a cell in a table. **HTML 3.2, 4.0, N2, N3, N4, IE3, IE4, IE5.**

Attributes	2.0	3.2	4.0	N2	N3	N4	IE2	IE3	IE4/5
`<event_name>=script_code`	✗	✗	✓	✗	✗	✗	✗	✗	✓
`ABBR=`*string*	✗	✗	✓	✗	✗	✗	✗	✗	✗
`ALIGN=CENTER│LEFT│RIGHT│JUSTIFY│CHAR`	✗	✓	✓	✓	✓	✓	✓	✓	✓
`AXIS=cellname`	✗	✗	✓	✗	✗	✗	✗	✗	✗
`BACKGROUND=`*string*	✗	✗	✗	✗	✗	✗	✓	✓	✓
`BGCOLOR=color`	✗	✗	D	✗	✓	✓	✓	✓	✓
`BORDERCOLOR=color`	✗	✗	✗	✗	✗	✗	✓	✓	✓
`BORDERCOLORDARK=color`	✗	✗	✗	✗	✗	✗	✓	✓	✓
`BORDERCOLORLIGHT=color`	✗	✗	✗	✗	✗	✗	✓	✓	✓
`CHAR=`*string*	✗	✗	✓	✗	✗	✗	✗	✗	✗
`CHAROFF=`*string*	✗	✗	✓	✗	✗	✗	✗	✗	✗
`CLASS=classname`	✗	✗	✓	✗	✗	✓	✗	✓	✓
`COLSPAN=number`	✗	✓	✓	✓	✓	✓	✗	✓	✓
`DIR=LTR│RTL`	✗	✗	✓	✗	✗	✗	✗	✗	✗
`HEADERS=` *string*	✗	✗	✓	✗	✗	✗	✗	✗	✗
`HEIGHT=number`	✗	✓	D	✗	✗	✓	✗	✓	✗
`ID=`*string*	✗	✗	✓	✗	✗	✓	✗	✓	✓
`LANG=language_type`	✗	✗	✓	✗	✗	✗	✗	✗	✓
`LANGUAGE=JAVASCRIPT│JSCRIPT│VBSCRIPT│VBS`	✗	✗	✗	✗	✗	✗	✗	✗	✓
`NOWRAP`	✗	✓	D	✓	✓	✓	✗	✓	✓
`ROWSPAN=number`	✗	✓	✓	✓	✓	✓	✗	✓	✓
`SCOPE=ROW│COL│ROWGROUP│COLGROUP`	✗	✗	✓	✗	✗	✗	✗	✗	✗
`STYLE=`*string*	✗	✗	✓	✗	✗	✓	✗	✓	✓
`TITLE=`*string*	✗	✗	✓	✗	✗	✗	✗	✗	✓
`VALIGN=BASELINE│BOTTOM│CENTER│TOP`	✗	✓	✓	✓	✓	✓	✗	✓	✓
`WIDTH=number`	✗	✓	D	✓	✓	✓	✗	✓	✗

TEXTAREA

Specifies a multi-line text input control. **ALL**.

Attributes	2.0	3.2	4.0	N2	N3	N4	IE2	IE3	IE4/5
<event_name>=script_code	✗	✗	✓	✗	✗	✓	✗	✗	✓
ACCESSKEY=key_character	✗	✗	✗	✗	✗	✗	✗	✗	✓
ALIGN=BASBOTTOM|ABSMIDDLE|BASELINE|BOTTOM|LEFT|MIDDLE|RIGHT|TEXTTOP|TOP	✗	✗	✗	✗	✗	✗	✗	✗	✓
CLASS=classname	✗	✗	✓	✗	✗	✓	✗	✗	✓
COLS=number	✓	✓	✓	✓	✓	✓	✓	✓	✓
DATAFLD=column_name	✗	✗	✗	✗	✗	✗	✗	✗	✓
DATASRC=id	✗	✗	✗	✗	✗	✗	✗	✗	✓
DIR=LTR|RTL	✗	✗	✓	✗	✗	✗	✗	✗	✗
DISABLED	✗	✗	✓	✗	✗	✗	✗	✗	✓
ID=*string*	✗	✗	✓	✗	✗	✓	✗	✗	✓
LANG=language_type	✗	✗	✓	✗	✗	✗	✗	✗	✓
LANGUAGE=JAVASCRIPT|JSCRIPT|VBSCRIPT|VBS	✗	✗	✗	✗	✗	✗	✗	✗	✓
NAME=*string*	✓	✓	✓	✓	✓	✓	✗	✓	✓
READONLY	✗	✗	✓	✗	✗	✗	✗	✗	✓
ROWS=number	✓	✓	✓	✓	✓	✓	✓	✓	✓
STYLE=*string*	✗	✗	✓	✗	✗	✓	✗	✗	✓
TABINDEX=number	✗	✗	✓	✗	✗	✗	✗	✗	✓
TITLE=*string*	✗	✗	✓	✗	✗	✗	✗	✗	✓
WRAP=PHYSICAL|VERTICAL|OFF	✗	✗	✗	✓	✓	✓	✗	✗	✓

TFOOT

Denotes a set of rows to be used as the footer of a table. **HTML 4.0, IE3, IE4, IE5**.

Attributes	2.0	3.2	4.0	N2	N3	N4	IE2	IE3	IE4/5
<event_name>=script_code	✗	✗	✓	✗	✗	✗	✗	✗	✓
ALIGN=CENTER|LEFT|RIGHT|JUSTIFY|CHAR	✗	✗	✓	✗	✗	✗	✗	✗	✓
BGCOLOR=color	✗	✗	D	✗	✗	✗	✗	✗	✓
CHAR=*string*	✗	✗	✓	✗	✗	✗	✗	✗	✗
CHAROFF=*string*	✗	✗	✓	✗	✗	✗	✗	✗	✗
CLASS=classname	✗	✗	✓	✗	✗	✗	✗	✓	✓
DIR=LTR|RTL	✗	✗	✓	✗	✗	✗	✗	✗	✗
ID=*string*	✗	✗	✓	✗	✗	✗	✗	✓	✓
LANG=language_type	✗	✗	✓	✗	✗	✗	✗	✗	✓
LANGUAGE=JAVASCRIPT|JSCRIPT|VBSCRIPT|VBS	✗	✗	✗	✗	✗	✗	✗	✗	✓
STYLE=*string*	✗	✗	✓	✗	✗	✗	✗	✓	✓
TITLE=*string*	✗	✗	✓	✗	✗	✗	✗	✗	✓
VALIGN=BASELINE|BOTTOM|CENTER|TOP	✗	✗	✓	✗	✗	✗	✗	✗	✓

TH

Denotes a header row in a table. Contents are usually bold and centered within each cell. **HTML 3.2, 4.0, N2, N3, N4, IE2, IE3, IE4, IE5.**

Attributes	2.0	3.2	4.0	N2	N3	N4	IE2	IE3	IE4/5
<event_name>=script_code	✗	✗	✓	✗	✗	✗	✗	✗	✓
ABBR=*string*	✗	✗	✓	✗	✗	✗	✗	✗	✗
ALIGN=CENTER|LEFT|RIGHT|JUSTIFY| CHAR	✗	✓	✓	✓	✓	✓	✓	✓	✓
AXIS=cellname	✗	✗	✓	✗	✗	✗	✗	✗	✗
BACKGROUND=*string*	✗	✗	✗	✗	✗	✗	✓	✓	✓
BGCOLOR=color	✗	✗	D	✗	✓	✓	✓	✓	✓
BORDERCOLOR=color	✗	✗	✗	✗	✗	✗	✓	✓	✓
BORDERCOLORDARK=color	✗	✗	✗	✗	✗	✗	✓	✓	✓
BORDERCOLORLIGHT=color	✗	✗	✗	✗	✗	✗	✓	✓	✓
CHAR=*string*	✗	✗	✓	✗	✗	✗	✗	✗	✗
CHAROFF=*string*	✗	✗	✓	✗	✗	✗	✗	✗	✗
CLASS=classname	✗	✗	✓	✗	✗	✓	✗	✓	✓
COLSPAN=number	✗	✓	✓	✓	✓	✓	✗	✓	✓
DIR=LTR|RTL	✗	✗	✓	✗	✗	✗	✗	✗	✗
HEADERS= *string*	✗	✗	✓	✗	✗	✗	✗	✗	✗
HEIGHT=number	✗	✓	D	✗	✗	✓	✗	✗	✗
ID=*string*	✗	✗	✓	✗	✗	✓	✗	✓	✓
LANG=language_type	✗	✗	✓	✗	✗	✗	✗	✗	✓
LANGUAGE=JAVASCRIPT|JSCRIPT| VBSCRIPT|VBS	✗	✗	✗	✗	✗	✗	✗	✗	✓
NOWRAP	✗	✓	D	✓	✓	✓	✗	✓	✓
ROWSPAN=number	✗	✓	✓	✓	✓	✓	✗	✓	✓
SCOPE=ROW|COL|ROWGROUP|COLGROUP	✗	✗	✓	✗	✗	✗	✗	✗	✗
STYLE=*string*	✗	✗	✓	✗	✗	✓	✗	✓	✓
TITLE=*string*	✗	✗	✓	✗	✗	✗	✗	✗	✓
VALIGN=BASELINE|BOTTOM|CENTER|TOP	✗	✓	✓	✓	✓	✓	✓	✓	✓
WIDTH=number	✗	✓	D	✓	✓	✓	✗	✓	✗

THEAD

Denotes a set of rows to be used as the header of a table. **HTML 4.0, IE3, IE4, IE5**.

Attributes	2.0	3.2	4.0	N2	N3	N4	IE2	IE3	IE4/5
`<event_name>=script_code`	✗	✗	✓	✗	✗	✗	✗	✗	✓
`ALIGN=CENTER|LEFT|RIGHT|JUSTIFY|` `CHAR`	✗	✗	✓	✗	✗	✗	✗	✓	✓
`BGCOLOR=color`	✗	✗	D	✗	✗	✗	✗	✗	✓
`CHAR=string`	✗	✗	✓	✗	✗	✗	✗	✗	✗
`CHAROFF=string`	✗	✗	✓	✗	✗	✗	✗	✗	✗
`CLASS=classname`	✗	✗	✓	✗	✗	✗	✗	✓	✓
`DIR=LTR|RTL`	✗	✗	✓	✗	✗	✗	✗	✗	✗
`ID=string`	✗	✗	✓	✗	✗	✗	✗	✓	✓
`LANG=language_type`	✗	✗	✓	✗	✗	✗	✗	✗	✓
`LANGUAGE=JAVASCRIPT|JSCRIPT|` `VBSCRIPT|VBS`	✗	✗	✗	✗	✗	✗	✗	✗	✓
`STYLE=string`	✗	✗	✓	✗	✗	✗	✗	✓	✓
`TITLE=string`	✗	✗	✓	✗	✗	✗	✗	✗	✓
`VALIGN=BASELINE|BOTTOM|CENTER|` `TOP`	✗	✗	✓	✗	✗	✗	✗	✓	✓

TITLE

Denotes the title of the document and used in the browser's window title bar. **ALL**.

Attributes	2.0	3.2	4.0	N2	N3	N4	IE2	IE3	IE4/5
`DIR=LTR|RTL`	✗	✗	✓	✗	✗	✗	✗	✗	✗
`ID=string`	✗	✗	✗	✗	✗	✓	✗	✗	✓
`LANG=language.type`	✗	✗	✓	✗	✗	✗	✗	✗	✗
`TITLE=string`	✗	✗	✗	✗	✗	✗	✗	✗	✓

TR

Specifies a row in a table. **HTML 3.2, 4.0, N2, N3, N4, IE3, IE4, IE5.**

Attributes	2.0	3.2	4.0	N2	N3	N4	IE2	IE3	IE4/5
<event_name>=script_code	✗	✗	✓	✗	✗	✗	✗	✗	✓
ALIGN=CENTER|LEFT|RIGHT|JUSTIFY|CHAR	✗	✓	✓	✓	✓	✓	✓	✓	✓
BACKGROUND=string	✗	✗	✗	✗	✗	✗	✓	✗	✗
BGCOLOR=color	✗	✗	D	✗	✓	✓	✓	✓	✓
BORDERCOLOR=color	✗	✗	✗	✗	✗	✗	✓	✓	✓
BORDERCOLORDARK	✗	✗	✗	✗	✗	✗	✓	✓	✓
BORDERCOLORLIGHT=color	✗	✗	✗	✗	✗	✗	✓	✓	✓
CHAR=string	✗	✗	✓	✗	✗	✗	✗	✗	✗
CHAROFF=string	✗	✗	✓	✗	✗	✗	✗	✗	✗
CLASS=classname	✗	✗	✓	✗	✗	✓	✗	✓	✓
DIR=LTR|RTL	✗	✗	✓	✗	✗	✗	✗	✗	✗
ID=string	✗	✗	✓	✗	✗	✓	✗	✓	✓
LANG=language_type	✗	✗	✓	✗	✗	✗	✗	✗	✓
LANGUAGE=JAVASCRIPT|JSCRIPT|VBSCRIPT|VBS	✗	✗	✗	✗	✗	✗	✗	✗	✓
NOWRAP	✗	✗	✗	✗	✗	✗	✗	✓	✗
STYLE=string	✗	✗	✓	✗	✗	✓	✗	✓	✓
TITLE=string	✗	✗	✓	✗	✗	✗	✗	✗	✓
VALIGN=BASELINE|BOTTOM|CENTER|TOP	✗	✓	✓	✓	✓	✓	✓	✓	✓

TT

Renders text in fixed-width type. **ALL**.

Attributes	2.0	3.2	4.0	N2	N3	N4	IE2	IE3	IE4/5
`<event_name>=script_code`	✗	✗	✓	✗	✗	✗	✗	✗	✓
`CLASS=classname`	✗	✗	✓	✗	✗	✓	✗	✗	✓
`DIR=LTR|RTL`	✗	✗	✓	✗	✗	✗	✗	✗	✗
`ID=string`	✗	✗	✓	✗	✗	✓	✗	✗	✓
`LANG=language_type`	✗	✗	✓	✗	✗	✗	✗	✗	✓
`LANGUAGE=JAVASCRIPT|JSCRIPT| VBSCRIPT|VBS`	✗	✗	✗	✗	✗	✗	✗	✗	✓
`STYLE=string`	✗	✗	✓	✗	✗	✓	✗	✗	✓
`TITLE=string`	✗	✗	✓	✗	✗	✗	✗	✗	✓

U

Renders text underlined. **HTML 3.2, N3, N4, IE2, IE3, IE4, IE5, deprecated in HTML 4.0.**

Attributes	2.0	3.2	4.0	N2	N3	N4	IE2	IE3	IE4/5
`<event_name>=script_code`	✗	✗	D	✗	✗	✗	✗	✗	✓
`CLASS=classname`	✗	✗	D	✗	✗	✓	✗	✗	✓
`DIR=LTR|RTL`	✗	✗	D	✗	✗	✗	✗	✗	✗
`ID=string`	✗	✗	D	✗	✗	✓	✗	✗	✓
`LANG=language_type`	✗	✗	D	✗	✗	✗	✗	✗	✓
`LANGUAGE=JAVASCRIPT|JSCRIPT| VBSCRIPT|VBS`	✗	✗	✗	✗	✗	✗	✗	✗	✓
`STYLE=string`	✗	✗	D	✗	✗	✓	✗	✗	✓
`TITLE=string`	✗	✗	D	✗	✗	✗	✗	✗	✓

UL

Renders lines of text which have `<LI>` tags as a bulleted list. **ALL**.

Attributes	2.0	3.2	4.0	N2	N3	N4	IE2	IE3	IE4/5
`<event_name>=script_code`	✗	✗	✓	✗	✗	✗	✗	✗	✓
`CLASS=classname`	✗	✗	✓	✗	✗	✓	✗	✓	✓
`COMPACT`	✓	✓	D	✓	✓	✓	✗	✓	✗
`DIR=LTR|RTL`	✗	✗	✓	✗	✗	✗	✗	✗	✗
`ID=`*string*	✗	✗	✓	✗	✗	✓	✗	✓	✓
`LANG=language_type`	✗	✗	✓	✗	✗	✗	✗	✗	✓
`LANGUAGE=JAVASCRIPT|JSCRIPT|` `VBSCRIPT|VBS`	✗	✗	✗	✗	✗	✗	✗	✗	✓
`STYLE=`*string*	✗	✗	✓	✗	✗	✓	✗	✓	✓
`TITLE=`*string*	✗	✗	✓	✗	✗	✗	✗	✗	✓
`TYPE=CIRCLE|DISC|SQUARE`	✗	✓	✓	✓	✓	✓	✗	✗	✓

VAR

Renders text as a small fixed-width font. **HTML 2.0, 3.2, 4.0, IE2, IE3, IE4, IE5**.

Attributes	2.0	3.2	4.0	N2	N3	N4	IE2	IE3	IE4/5
`<event_name>=script_code`	✗	✗	✓	✗	✗	✗	✗	✗	✓
`CLASS=classname`	✗	✗	✓	✗	✗	✗	✗	✗	✓
`DIR=LTR|RTL`	✗	✗	✓	✗	✗	✗	✗	✗	✗
`ID=`*string*	✗	✗	✓	✗	✗	✗	✗	✗	✓
`LANG=language_type`	✗	✗	✓	✗	✗	✗	✗	✗	✓
`LANGUAGE=JAVASCRIPT|JSCRIPT|` `VBSCRIPT|VBS`	✗	✗	✗	✗	✗	✗	✗	✗	✓
`STYLE=`*string*	✗	✗	✓	✗	✗	✗	✗	✗	✓
`TITLE=`*string*	✗	✗	✓	✗	✗	✗	✗	✗	✓

WBR

Inserts a soft line break in a block of NOBR text. **N2, N3, N4, IE3, IE4, IE5**.

Attributes	2.0	3.2	4.0	N2	N3	N4	IE2	IE3	IE4/5
CLASS=classname	✗	✗	✗	✗	✗	✓	✗	✗	✓
ID=string	✗	✗	✗	✗	✗	✓	✗	✗	✓
LANGUAGE=JAVASCRIPT|JSCRIPT|VBSCRIPT|VBS	✗	✗	✗	✗	✗	✗	✗	✗	✓
STYLE=string	✗	✗	✗	✗	✗	✓	✗	✗	✓
TITLE=string	✗	✗	✗	✗	✗	✗	✗	✗	✓

XMP

Renders text in fixed-width typeface, as used for example code. Use PRE or SAMP instead. **HTML 2.0, N2, N3, N4, IE3, IE4, IE5, deprecated in HTML 3.2.**

Attributes	2.0	3.2	4.0	N2	N3	N4	IE2	IE3	IE4/5
<event_name>=script_code	✗	✗	✗	✗	✗	✗	✗	✗	✓
CLASS=classname	✗	✗	✗	✗	✗	✓	✗	✗	✓
ID=string	✗	✗	✗	✗	✗	✓	✗	✗	✓
LANG=language_type	✗	✗	✗	✗	✗	✗	✗	✗	✓
LANGUAGE=JAVASCRIPT|JSCRIPT|VBSCRIPT|VBS	✗	✗	✗	✗	✗	✗	✗	✗	✓
STYLE=string	✗	✗	✗	✗	✗	✓	✗	✗	✓
TITLE=string	✗	✗	✗	✗	✗	✗	✗	✗	✓

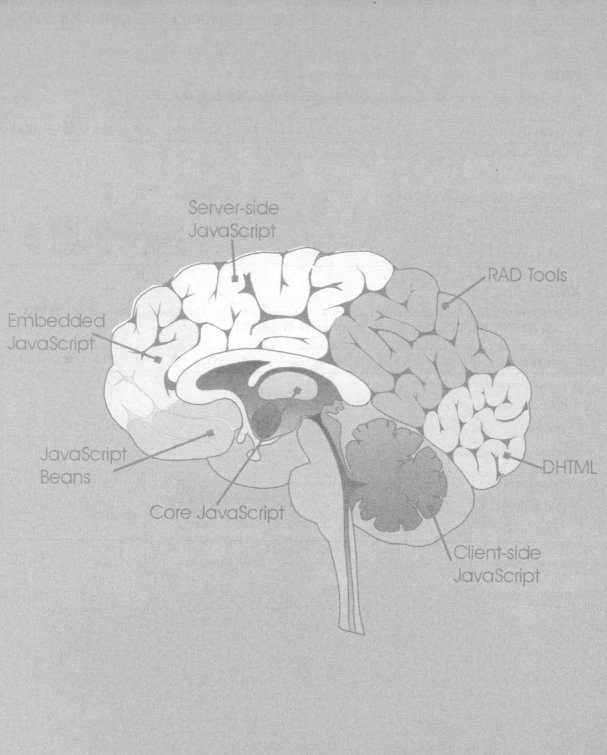

The IE Browser Object Model

The IE5 Dynamic HTML object model contains 23 **objects** and 29 **collections**. Most of these are organized into a strict hierarchy that allows HTML authors to access all the parts of the browser, and the pages that are loaded, from a scripting language like JavaScript or VBScript.

The Object Model In Outline

The diagram (overleaf) shows the object hierarchy in graphical form. It is followed by a list of the objects and collection, with a brief description. Then, each object is documented in detail, showing the properties, methods, and events it supports.

Note that we haven't included all of the objects and collections in the diagram. Some are not part of the overall object model, but are used to access other items – such as dialogs and HTML elements.

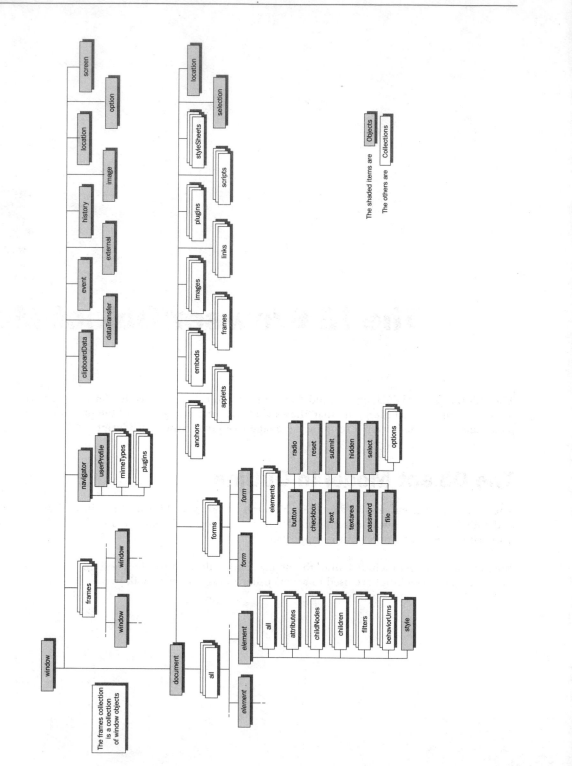

The frames collection is a collection of window objects

The shaded items are Objects

The others are Collections

Object Name	Description
Attribute	An object-representation of an attribute or property.
clipboardData	Used with editing operations to provide access to data contained on the clipboard.
currentStyle	Represents the cascaded format and style of its parent object.
custom	A user-defined element.
dataTransfer	Used with drag-and-drop operations to provide access to data contained on the clipboard.
document	An object that exposes the contents of the HTML document through a number of collections and properties.
event	A global object that exposes properties that represent the parameters of all events as they occur.
external	Allows access to the object model of any application hosting Internet Explorer components.
history	Exposes information about the URLs that the client has previously visited.
location	Exposes information about the currently displayed document's URL.
mimeType	An object that provides information about a MIME type.
navigator	Exposes properties that provide information about the browser, or user agent.
rule	A style (i.e. a selector and one or more declarations) within a cascading style sheet (CSS).
runtimeStyle	Represents the cascaded format and style of its parent object, overriding global stylesheets, inline styles and HTML attributes. Overwrites the values of the currentStyle object but not the style object.
screen	Exposes information about the client's monitor screen and system rendering abilities.
selection	Represents the currently active selection on the screen in the document.
style	Represents an individual style element within a style sheet.

Table Continued on Following Page

Object Name	Description
styleSheet	Exposes all the styles within a single style sheet in the styleSheets collection.
textNode	A string of text, represented as a node on the document hierarchy.
textRange	Represents sections of the text stream making up the HTML document.
textRectangle	A set of the four coordinates that represent the rectangle containing a line of text of TextRange object.
userProfile	Allows a script to request read access to and perform read actions on a user's profile.
window	Exposes properties, methods and events connected to the browser window or a frame.

Collection Name	Description
all	Collection of all the tags and elements in the body of the document.
anchors	Collection of all the anchors in the document.
applets	Collection of all the objects in the document, including intrinsic controls, images, applets, embeds, and other objects.
areas	Collection of all the areas that make up the image map.
attributes	Collection of all the attributes of the object.
behaviorUrns	Collection of all the behaviors attached to the element (as a set of URN strings).
bookmarks	Collection of all the ADO bookmarks tied to the rows affected by the current event.
boundElements	Collection of all the elements on the page that are bound to a dataset.
cells	Collection of all the <TH> and <TD> cells in the row of a table.
childNodes	Collection of all the object's children.
children	Collection of all the object's direct descendents.
controlRange	Collection of the BODY's elements.
elements	Collection of all controls and elements in the form.

Collection Name	Description
embeds	Collection of all the embed tags in the document.
filters	Collection of all the filter objects for an element.
forms	Collection of all the forms in the page.
frames	Collection of all the frames defined within a `<FRAMESET>` tag.
images	Collection of all the images in the page.
imports	Collection of all the imported style sheets defined for a stylesheet object.
links	Collection of all the links and `<AREA>` blocks in the page.
mimeTypes	Collection of all the document and file types supported by the browser.
options	Collection of all the items in a `<SELECT>` element.
plugins	An alias for collection of all the embeds in the page.
rows	Collection of all the rows in the table, including `<THEAD>`, `<TBODY>`, and `<TFOOT>`.
rules	Collection of all the `rule` objects defined in a `styleSheet`.
scripts	Collection of all the `<SCRIPT>` sections in the page.
stylesheets	Collection of all the individual style `property` objects defined for a document.
tBodies	Collection of all `TBODY` objects in the table.
TextRectangle	Collection of all the `TextRectangle` objects in the object.

The Objects in Detail

This section lists all the properties, methods and events available for each object in the browser hierarchy. Brief descriptions of these properties, methods and events can be found in Appendix B, and the collections are briefly described above.

It's worth noting that there's a set of attributes that are common to almost all of the DHTML elements. These attributes provide properties, methods, and events for manipulating the specific object. This commonality makes it simpler to use the exact same scripting style and techniques to deal with nearly every element in the document object model. Thus, you'll see a certain amount of repetition in these lists.

The Attribute Object

An object-representation of an attribute or property.

Properties nodeName nodeType nodeValue specified	
Methods None	
Events None	
Collections None	

The clipboardData Object

Used with editing operations to provide access to data contained on the clipboard.

Properties None
Methods None
Events None
Collections None

The currentStyle Object

Represents the cascaded format and style of its parent object.

Properties backgroundAttachment backgroundColor backgroundImage backgroundPositionX backgroundPositionY backgroundRepeat borderBottomColor borderBottomStyle borderBottomWidth borderColor borderLeftColor borderLeftStyle borderLeftWidth borderRightColor borderRightStyle borderRightWidth borderStyle borderTopColor borderTopStyle borderTopWidth borderWidth bottom clear clipBottom clipLeft clipRight clipTop color cursor direction display fontFamily fontSize fontStyle fontVariant fontWeight height layoutGrid layoutGridChar layoutGridCharSpacing layoutGridLine layoutGridMode layoutGridType left letterSpacing lineHeight listStyleImage listStylePosition listStyleType margin marginBottom marginLeft marginRight marginTop overflow overflowX overflowY padding paddingBottom paddingLeft paddingRight paddingTop pageBreakAfter pageBreakBefore position right styleFloat tableLayout textAlign textDecoration textIndent textTransform top unicodeBidi verticalAlign visibility width zIndex	
Methods None	
Events None	**Collections** None

The custom Object

A user-defined element.

Properties accessKey canHaveChildren className clientHeight
clientLeft clientTop clientWidth currentStyle dir document id
innerHTML innerText isTextEdit lang language offsetHeight
offsetLeft offsetParent offsetTop offsetWidth outerHTML
outerText parentElement parentTextEdit readyState recordNumber
runtimeStyle scopeName scrollHeight scrollLeft scrollTop
scrollWidth sourceIndex style tabIndex tagName tagUrn title

Methods addBehavior applyElement attachEvent blur clearAttributes
click componentFromPoint contains createControlRange
detachEvent doScroll focus getAdjacentText getAttribute
getBoundingClientRect getClientRects getElementsByTagName
getExpression insertAdjacentHTML insertAdjacentText
mergeAttributes releaseCapture removeAttribute removeBehavior
removeExpression replaceAdjacentText scrollIntoView setAttribute
setCapture setExpression

Events onafterupdate onbeforecopy onbeforecut onbeforeeditfocus
onbeforepaste onbeforeupdate onblur onclick oncontextmenu
oncopy oncut ondblclick ondrag ondragend ondragenter
ondragleave ondragover ondragstart ondrop onerrorupdate
onfilterchange onfocus onhelp onkeydown onkeypress onkeyup
onlosecapture onmousedown onmousemove onmouseout onmouseover
onmouseup onpaste onpropertychange onreadystatechange onresize
onscroll onselectstart

Collections all behaviorUrns children filters

The dataTransfer Object

Used with drag-and-drop operations to provide access to data contained on the clipboard.

Properties dropEffect effectAllowed

Methods clearData getData setData

Events None

Collections None

The document Object

An object that exposes the contents of the HTML document through a number of collections and properties.

Properties activeElement aLinkColor bgColor cookie defaultCharset designMode documentElement domain expando fgColor fileCreatedDate fileModifiedDate fileSize lastModified linkColor location parentWindow protocol readyState referrer selection uniqueID URL vlinkColor

---

Methods attachEvent clear clearAttributes close createElement createStyleSheet createTextNode detachEvent elementFromPoint execCommand getElementById getElementsByName getElementsByTagName mergeAttributes open queryCommandEnabled queryCommandIndeterm queryCommandState queryCommandSupported queryCommandValue recalc releaseCapture write writeln

---

Events onbeforecut onbeforeeditfocus onbeforepaste onclick oncontextmenu oncut ondblclick ondrag ondragend ondragenter ondragleave ondragover ondragstart ondrop onhelp onkeydown onkeypress onkeyup onmousedown onmousemove onmouseout onmouseover onmouseup onpaste onpropertychange onreadystatechange onstop

---

Collections all anchors applets childNodes children embeds forms frames images links scripts styleSheets

---

The event Object

A global object that exposes properties that represent the parameters of all events as they occur.

Properties altKey button cancelBubble clientX clientY ctrlKey dataFld dataTransfer fromElement keyCode offsetX offsetY propertyName qualifier reason recordset repeat returnValue screenX screenY shiftKey srcElement srcFilter srcUrn toElement type x y

---

Methods None	**Events** None

Collections bookmarks boundElements

The external Object

Allows access to the object model of any application hosting Internet Explorer components.

Properties menuArguments

Methods AddChannel AddDesktopComponent AddFavorite AutoCompleteSaveForm AutoScan ImportExportFavorites IsSubscribed NavigateAndFind ShowBrowserUI

Events None	**Collections** None

The history Object

Exposes information about the URLs that the client has previously visited.

Properties length	
Methods back forward go	
Events None	**Collections** None

The location Object

Exposes information about the currently displayed document's URL.

Properties hash host hostname href pathname port protocol search	
Methods assign reload replace	
Events None	**Collections** None

The mimeType

An object that provides information about a MIME type.

Properties description enabledPlugin name	
Methods None	
Events None	**Collections** suffixes

The navigator Object

Exposes properties that provide information about the browser, or user agent.

Properties appCodeName   appMinorVersion   appName   appVersion   browserLanguage   cookieEnabled   cpuClass   onLine   platform   systemLanguage   userAgent   userLanguage   userProfile
Methods javaEnabled   taintEnabled
Events None
Collections plugins

The rule Object

A style (i.e. a selector and one or more declarations) within a cascading style sheet (CSS).

Properties readOnly runtimeStyle selectorText style	
Methods None	
Events None	**Collections** None

The runtimeStyle Object

Represents the cascaded format and style of its parent object, overriding global stylesheets, inline styles and HTML attributes. Overwrites the values of the currentStyle object but not the style object.

Properties background backgroundAttachment backgroundColor backgroundImage backgroundPosition backgroundPositionX backgroundPositionY backgroundRepeat border borderBottom borderBottomColor borderBottomStyle borderBottomWidth borderColor borderLeft borderLeftColor borderLeftStyle borderLeftWidth borderRight borderRightColor borderRightStyle borderRightWidth borderStyle borderTop borderTopColor borderTopStyle borderTopWidth borderWidth bottom clear clip color cssText cursor direction display filter font fontFamily fontSize fontStyle fontVariant fontWeight height layoutGrid layoutGridChar layoutGridCharSpacing layoutGridLine layoutGridMode layoutGridType left letterSpacing lineHeight listStyle listStyleImage listStylePosition listStyleType margin marginBottom marginLeft marginRight marginTop overflow overflowX overflowY padding paddingBottom paddingLeft paddingRight paddingTop pageBreakAfter pageBreakBefore pixelBottom pixelHeight pixelLeft pixelRight pixelTop pixelWidth posBottom posHeight position posLeft posRight posTop posWidth right styleFloat tableLayout textAlign textDecoration textDecorationBlink textDecorationLineThrough textDecorationNone textDecorationOverline textDecorationUnderline textIndent textTransform top unicodeBidi verticalAlign visibility width zIndex	
Methods None	
Events None	**Collections** None

The screen Object

Exposes information about the client's monitor screen and system rendering abilities.

Properties availHeight availWidth bufferDepth colorDepth fontSmoothingEnabled height updateInterval width	
Methods None	
Events None	**Collections** None

942

The selection Object

Represents the currently active selection on the screen in the document.

Properties `type`	
Methods `clear` `createRange` `empty`	
Events None	**Collections** None

The style Object

Represents an individual style element within a style sheet.

Properties `background` `backgroundAttachment` `backgroundColor` `backgroundImage` `backgroundPosition` `backgroundPositionX` `backgroundPositionY` `backgroundRepeat` `border` `borderBottom` `borderBottomColor` `borderBottomStyle` `borderBottomWidth` `borderColor` `borderLeft` `borderLeftColor` `borderLeftStyle` `borderLeftWidth` `borderRight` `borderRightColor` `borderRightStyle` `borderRightWidth` `borderStyle` `borderTop` `borderTopColor` `borderTopStyle` `borderTopWidth` `borderWidth` `bottom` `clear` `clip` `color` `cssText` `cursor` `direction` `display` `filter` `font` `fontFamily` `fontSize` `fontStyle` `fontVariant` `fontWeight` `height` `layoutGrid` `layoutGridChar` `layoutGridCharSpacing` `layoutGridLine` `layoutGridMode` `layoutGridType` `left` `letterSpacing` `lineHeight` `listStyle` `listStyleImage` `listStylePosition` `listStyleType` `margin` `marginBottom` `marginLeft` `marginRight` `marginTop` `overflow` `overflowX` `overflowY` `padding` `paddingBottom` `paddingLeft` `paddingRight` `paddingTop` `pageBreakAfter` `pageBreakBefore` `pixelBottom` `pixelHeight` `pixelLeft` `pixelRight` `pixelTop` `pixelWidth` `posBottom` `posHeight` `position` `posLeft` `posRight` `posTop` `posWidth` `right` `styleFloat` `tableLayout` `textAlign` `textDecoration` `textDecorationBlink` `textDecorationLineThrough` `textDecorationNone` `textDecorationOverline` `textDecorationUnderline` `textIndent` `textTransform` `top` `unicodeBidi` `verticalAlign` `visibility` `width` `zIndex`	
Methods `getExpression` `removeExpression` `setExpression`	
Events None	**Collections** None

The styleSheet Object

Exposes all the styles within a single style sheet in the styleSheets collection.

Properties disabled id owningElement parentStyleSheet readOnly type	
Methods addImport addRule removeRule	
Events None	
Collections imports rules	

The textNode Object

A string of text, represented as a node on the document hierarchy.

Properties data length nextSibling nodeName nodeType nodeValue previousSibling	
Methods splitText	
Events None	**Collections** None

The textRange Object

Represents sections of the text stream making up the HTML document.

Properties boundingHeight boundingLeft boundingTop boundingWidth htmlText offsetLeft offsetTop text	
Methods collapse compareEndPoints duplicate execCommand expand findText getBookmark getBoundingClientRect getClientRects inRange isEqual move moveEnd moveStart moveToBookmark moveToElementText moveToPoint parentElement pasteHTML queryCommandEnabled queryCommandIndeterm queryCommandState queryCommandSupported queryCommandValue scrollIntoView select setEndPoint	
Events None	**Collections** None

The textRectangle Object

A set of the four coordinates that represent the rectangle containing a line of text of TextRange object.

Properties bottom left right top	
Methods None	
Events None	
Collections None	

The userProfile Object

Allows a script to request read access to and perform read actions on a user's profile.

Properties None		
Methods `addReadRequest` `clearRequest` `doReadRequest` `getAttribute`		
Events None		
Collections None		

The window Object

Exposes properties, methods and events connected to the browser window or a frame.

Properties `clientInformation` `clipboardData` `closed` `defaultStatus` `dialogArguments` `dialogHeight` `dialogLeft` `dialogTop` `dialogWidth` `document` `event` `external` `history` `length` `location` `name` `navigator` `offscreenBuffering` `opener` `parent` `returnValue` `screen` `screenLeft` `screenTop` `self` `status` `top`
Methods `alert` `attachEvent` `blur` `clearInterval` `clearTimeout` `close` `confirm` `detachEvent` `execScript` `focus` `moveBy` `moveTo` `navigate` `open` `print` `prompt` `resizeBy` `resizeTo` `scroll` `scrollBy` `scrollTo` `setInterval` `setTimeout` `showHelp` `showModalDialog` `showModelessDialog`
Events `onafterprint` `onbeforeprint` `onbeforeunload` `onblur` `onerror` `onfocus` `onhelp` `onload` `onresize` `onunload`
Collections `Frames`

HTML and Form Controls Cross Reference

Dynamic HTML provides the same integral control types as HTML 3.2. However, there are many more different properties, methods and events available now for all the controls.

The following tables show the properties, methods and events that are most relevant to HTML form elements. For a full list of the tags available in HTML 4.0 and the attributes they support, check out Appendix D.

Control Properties	checked	dataFld	dataFormatAs	dataSrc	defaultChecked	defaultValue	maxLength	readOnly	recordNumber	selectedIndex	size	status	type	value
HTML button	✗	✓	✓	✓	✗	✓	✗	✗	✓	✗	✓	✗	✓	✓
HTML checkbox	✓	✓	✗	✓	✓	✓	✗	✗	✓	✗	✓	✓	✓	✓
HTML file	✗	✓	✗	✓	✗	✓	✗	✗	✓	✗	✓	✗	✓	✓
HTML hidden	✗	✓	✗	✓	✗	✓	✗	✗	✓	✗	✗	✗	✓	✓
HTML image	✗	✓	✗	✓	✗	✓	✗	✗	✓	✗	✓	✗	✓	✓
HTML password	✗	✓	✗	✓	✗	✓	✓	✓	✓	✗	✓	✗	✓	✓
HTML radio	✓	✓	✗	✓	✓	✓	✗	✗	✓	✗	✓	✓	✓	✓
HTML reset	✗	✓	✗	✓	✗	✓	✗	✗	✓	✗	✓	✗	✓	✓
HTML submit	✗	✓	✗	✓	✗	✓	✗	✗	✓	✗	✓	✗	✓	✓
HTML text	✗	✓	✗	✓	✗	✓	✓	✓	✓	✗	✓	✗	✓	✓
APPLET tag	✗	✓	✗	✓	✗	✗	✗	✗	✗	✗	✗	✗	✗	✗
BUTTON tag	✗	✓	✓	✓	✗	✗	✗	✗	✗	✗	✗	✗	✓	✓
FIELD SET tag	✗	✗	✗	✗	✗	✗	✗	✗	✓	✗	✗	✗	✗	✗
LABEL tag	✗	✓	✓	✓	✗	✗	✗	✗	✓	✗	✗	✗	✗	✗
LEGEND tag	✗	✗	✗	✗	✗	✗	✗	✗	✗	✗	✗	✗	✗	✗
SELECT tag	✗	✓	✗	✓	✗	✗	✗	✗	✓	✓	✓	✗	✓	✗
TEXTAREA tag	✗	✓	✗	✓	✗	✓	✗	✓	✗	✗	✗	✗	✓	✓
XML tag	✗	✗	✗	✗	✗	✗	✗	✗	✗	✗	✗	✗	✗	✗

Control Methods	add	blur	click	createTextRange	focus	item	remove	select
HTML button	✘	✔	✔	✔	✔	✘	✘	✔
HTML checkbox	✘	✔	✔	✘	✔	✘	✘	✔
HTML file	✘	✔	✔	✘	✔	✘	✘	✔
HTML hidden	✘	✘	✘	✔	✘	✘	✘	✘
HTML image	✘	✔	✔	✘	✔	✘	✘	✔
HTML password	✘	✔	✔	✔	✔	✘	✘	✔
HTML radio	✘	✔	✔	✘	✔	✘	✘	✔
HTML reset	✘	✔	✔	✔	✔	✘	✘	✔
HTML submit	✘	✔	✔	✔	✔	✘	✘	✔
HTML text	✘	✔	✔	✔	✔	✘	✘	✔
APPLET tag	✘	✔	✔	✘	✔	✘	✘	✘
BUTTON tag	✘	✔	✔	✔	✔	✘	✘	✘
FIELDSET tag	✘	✔	✔	✘	✔	✘	✘	✘
LABEL tag	✘	✔	✔	✘	✔	✘	✘	✘
LEGEND tag	✘	✔	✔	✘	✔	✘	✘	✘
SELECT tag	✘	✔	✔	✘	✔	✘	✘	✘
TEXTAREA tag	✘	✔	✔	✔	✔	✘	✘	✔
XML tag	✘	✘	✘	✘	✘	✘	✘	✘

Control Events	onafterupdate	onbeforeupdate	onblur	onchange	onclick	ondblclick	onfocus	onrowenter	onrowexit	onselect
HTML button	✗	✗	✓	✗	✓	✓	✓	✗	✗	✗
HTML checkbox	✓	✓	✓	✗	✓	✓	✓	✗	✗	✗
HTML file	✗	✗	✓	✗	✓	✓	✓	✗	✗	✗
HTML hidden	✗	✗	✗	✗	✗	✗	✓	✗	✗	✗
HTML image	✗	✗	✓	✗	✓	✓	✓	✗	✗	✗
HTML password	✗	✗	✓	✗	✓	✓	✓	✗	✗	✗
HTML radio	✗	✗	✓	✗	✓	✓	✓	✗	✗	✗
HTML reset	✗	✗	✓	✗	✓	✓	✓	✗	✗	✗
HTML submit	✗	✗	✓	✗	✓	✓	✓	✗	✗	✗
HTML text	✗	✗	✓	✓	✓	✓	✓	✗	✗	✓
APPLET tag	✗	✗	✓	✗	✓	✓	✓	✓	✓	✗
BUTTON tag	✗	✗	✓	✗	✓	✓	✓	✗	✗	✗
FIELDSET tag	✗	✗	✓	✗	✓	✓	✓	✗	✗	✗
LABEL tag	✗	✗	✓	✗	✓	✓	✓	✗	✗	✗
LEGEND tag	✗	✗	✓	✗	✓	✓	✓	✗	✗	✗
SELECT tag	✗	✗	✓	✓	✓	✓	✓	✗	✗	✗
TEXTAREA tag	✓	✓	✓	✓	✓	✓	✓	✗	✗	✓
XML tag	✗	✗	✗	✗	✗	✗	✗	✓	✓	✗

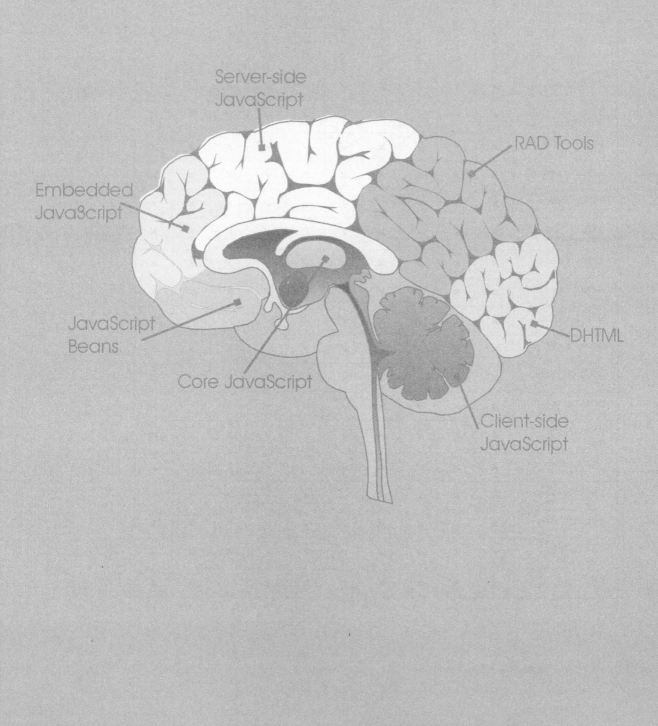

The Netscape Browser Object Model

The Dynamic HTML Object Model for Netscape Navigator contains 38 **objects** and 17 **arrays**. Most of these are organized into a strict hierarchy that allows HTML authors to access all the parts of the browser, and the pages that are loaded, from a scripting language like JavaScript.

The Object Model In Outline

The diagram shows the object hierarchy in graphical form. It is followed by a list of the objects and arrays, with a brief description. Then, each object is documented in detail, showing the properties, methods, and events it supports.

Note that not all the objects and arrays are included in the diagram. Some are not part of the overall object model, but are used to access other items such as dialogs or HTML elements.

The Browser Objects

Objects	Description
`anchor`	An object that represents an anchor created with `<A NAME="..">` in the document.
`area`	An area created within a `<MAP>` element by an `<AREA>` tag.
`button`	An object that represents a control created with an `<INPUT>` tag where `TYPE=BUTTON`.
`checkbox`	An object that represents a control created with an `<INPUT>` tag where `TYPE=CHECKBOX`.

Objects	Description
document	Exposes the contents of the HTML document through a number of arrays and properties.
element	An object that represents a control in the array of all the controls on a `<FORM>`.
event	The global event object exposed for accessing an event's parameters.
fileUpload	An object that represents a control created with an `<INPUT>` tag where `TYPE=FILE`.
form	An object that represents the section of a page contained within a `<FORM>` tag.
frame	An object that represents a `<FRAME>` within a `<FRAMESET>`.
hidden	An object that represents a control created with an `<INPUT>` tag where `TYPE=HIDDEN`.
history	Contains information on the URLs that the client has visited.
image	An object that represents an element created with an `<IMG>` tag.
layer	An object that represents a `<LAYER>` or `<ILAYER>` in a document.
link	An object that represents a link created in the page with an `<A HREF="..">` tag.
location	Contains information about the current URL being displayed.
mimeType	Contains information about the MIME types supported by the browser.
navigator	An object representing the browser itself, and its properties.
option	An individual `<OPTION>` item in a list created by a `<SELECT>` tag.
password	An object that represents a control created with an `<INPUT>` tag where `TYPE=PASSWORD`.
plugin	An object that represents the features of an installed plugin component.
radio	An object that represents a control created with an `<INPUT>` tag where `TYPE=RADIO`.
reset	An object that represents a control created with an `<INPUT>` tag where `TYPE=RESET`.
screen	Contains information about the client's screen and rendering abilities.
select	An object that represents a list control created with a `<SELECT>` tag.
submit	An object that represents a control created with an `<INPUT>` tag where `TYPE=SUBMIT`.
text	An object that represents a control created with an `<INPUT>` tag where `TYPE=TEXT`.
textarea	An object that represents a text area control created with a `<TEXTAREA>` tag.
window	An object that provides information about the current browser window.

The Browser Object Arrays

Arrays	Description
anchors	Array of all the anchors in the document.
applets	Array of all the objects in the document, including intrinsic controls, images, applets, embeds and other objects.
areas	Array of all the areas that make up an image map.
arguments	Array of all the arguments supplied to a function.
classes	Array of all the style classes defined in the document.
elements	Array of all controls and elements in the form.
embeds	Array of all the embed tags in the document.
forms	Array of all the forms in the page.
frames	Array of all the frames defined within a <FRAMESET> tag.
ids	Array of all the individual element styles defined in the document.
images	Array of all the images in the page.
layers	Array of all the layers in a document or another layer.
links	Array of all the links and <AREA> blocks in the page.
mimeTypes	Array of all the supported MIME types.
options	Array of all the items in a <SELECT> list.
plugins	Array of all the plugins available.
tags	Array of all the elements in the document.

The Browser Objects in Detail

This section documents all the properties, arrays, methods and events available for each object in the browser hierarchy. The JavaScript objects are covered at the end of this reference section.

The Anchor Object

An object that represents an anchor created with <A NAME="..."> in the document.

Property	Attribute	Description
name	NAME	Specifies the name to use to refer to the anchor.

Methods	Description
eval	Evaluates the object and returns a representation of its value
toString	Returns a string containing a textual representation of the object's value.
valueOf	Returns the primitive value of an object, or the name of the object itself.

The Area Object

An area created within a `<MAP>` element by an `<AREA>` tag.

Properties	Attribute	Description
hash		The string following the # symbol, the anchor name, in the HREF value.
host		The hostname:port part of the location or URL.
hostname		The hostname part of the location or URL.
href	HREF	The destination URL or anchor point.
pathname		The file or object path name following the third slash in a URL.
port		The port number in a URL.
protocol		The initial sub-string indicating the URL's access method.
search		Any query string or form data following the ? in the complete URL.
target	TARGET	Specifies the window or frame where the new page will be loaded.

Methods	Description
eval	Evaluates the object and returns a representation of its value
handleEvent	Invokes the appropriate event handling code of the object for this event.
toString	Returns a string containing a textual representation of the object's value.
valueOf	Returns the primitive value of an object, or the name of the object itself.

Events	Description
onDblClick	Occurs when the user double-clicks on the area.
onMouseOut	Occurs when the mouse pointer leaves the area.
onMouseOver	Occurs when the mouse pointer first enters the area.

The Button Object

An object that represents a control created with an **<INPUT>** tag where **TYPE=BUTTON**.

Properties	Attribute	Description
form		Reference to the form object that contains the element.
name	NAME	Specifies the name to use to refer to the button.
type	TYPE	Must be **"BUTTON"** for a Button element.
value	VALUE	The caption of the button.

Methods	Description
blur	Causes the element to lose the focus, and fire its **onBlur** event.
click	Simulates a click on the element, and fires its **onClick** event.
eval	Evaluates the object and returns a representation of its value
focus	Causes the element to receive the focus, and fire its **onFocus** event.
handleEvent	Invokes the appropriate event handling code of object for this event.
toString	Returns a string containing a textual representation of the object's value.
valueOf	Returns the primitive value of an object, or the name of the object itself.

Events	Description
onBlur	Occurs when the button control loses the focus.
onClick	Occurs when the button control is clicked or 'pressed'.
onFocus	Occurs when the button control receives the focus.
onMouseDown	Occurs when the user presses a mouse button.
onMouseUp	Occurs when the user releases a mouse button.

The CheckBox Object

An object that represents a control created with an `<INPUT>` tag where `TYPE=CHECKBOX`.

Properties	Attribute	Description
checked	CHECKED	Indicates that the checkbox is selected (i.e. 'on' or ticked).
defaultChecked		Denotes if the checkbox is checked by default.
form		Reference to the form object that contains the element.
name	NAME	Specifies the name to use to refer to the checkbox.
type	TYPE	Must be `"CHECKBOX"` for a Checkbox element.
value	VALUE	The value of the control when checked.

Methods	Description
blur	Causes the control to lose the focus, and fire its `onBlur` event.
click	Simulates a click on the control, and fires its `onClick` event.
eval	Evaluates the object and returns a representation of its value.
focus	Causes the control to receive the focus, and fire its `onFocus` event.
handleEvent	Invokes the appropriate event handling code of the object for this event.
toString	Returns a string containing a textual representation of the object's value.
valueOf	Returns the primitive value of an object, or the name of the object itself.

Events	Description
onBlur	Occurs when the checkbox loses the focus.
onClick	Occurs when the mouse button is clicked on the checkbox.
onFocus	Occurs when the checkbox receives the focus.

The Document Object

Exposes the entire HTML content through its own arrays and properties, and provides a range of events and methods to work with documents.

Properties	Attribute	JSS Equivalent	Description
alinkColor	ALINK	color	Color of the active links on the page, i.e. those where the mouse button is held down.
bgColor	BGCOLOR	background -color	Background color of the page.
cookie			String value of a cookie stored by the browser.
domain			Security domain of the document.
fgColor	TEXT	color	Color of the document foreground text.
lastModified			Date the document was last modified.
linkColor	LINK	color	The color of the unvisited links in the page.
referrer			URL of the page containing the link that loaded this page, if available.
title	TITLE		The title of the document as defined in the <TITLE> tag
URL	URL		Uniform Resource Locator of the page.
vlinkColor	VLINK	color	Color of the visited links in the page.

Arrays	Description
anchors	Array of all the anchors defined in the document.
applets	Array of all the objects in the document, including intrinsic controls, images, applets, embeds and other objects.
classes	Array of all the style classes defined in the document.
embeds	Array of all the <EMBED> tags in the document.
forms	Array of all the forms defined in the document.

Arrays	Description
`ids`	Array of all the individual element styles defined in the document.
`images`	Array of all the images defined on the document.
`layers`	Array of all the layers defined in the document.
`links`	Array of all the links and `<AREA>` blocks defined in the document.
`plugins`	An alias for array of all the embeds defined in the document.
`tags`	Array of all the elements defined in the document.

Methods	Description
`captureEvents`	Instructs the document to capture events of a particular type.
`close`	Closes an output stream to a document and updates the display.
`eval`	Evaluates the object and returns a representation of its value
`getSelection`	Returns a string containing the text currently selected in the document.
`handleEvent`	Invokes the appropriate event handling code of the object for this event.
`open`	Opens a new browser window.
`releaseEvents`	Instructs the document to stop capturing events of a particular type.
`routeEvent`	Passes an event that has been captured back up through the normal event hierarchy.
`toString`	Returns a string containing a textual representation of the object's value.
`valueOf`	Returns the primitive value of an object, or the name of the object itself.
`write`	Writes text and HTML to a document in the specified window.
`writeln`	Writes text and HTML followed by a carriage return,

Events	Description
`onClick`	Occurs when the mouse button is clicked on the document.
`onDblClick`	Occurs when the user double-clicks on the document.
`onKeyDown`	Occurs when the user presses a key.

Table Continued on Following Page

Events	Description
onKeyPress	Occurs when the user presses and releases a key.
onKeyUp	Occurs when the user releases a key.
onMouseDown	Occurs when the user presses a mouse button.
onMouseMove	Occurs when the user moves the mouse pointer.
onMouseUp	Occurs when the user releases a mouse button.

The Element Object

An object that represents a control in the array of all the controls on a `<FORM>`.

Properties	Attribute	Description
checked	CHECKED	Indicates that a checkbox or radio element is selected (i.e. 'on' or ticked).
defaultChecked		Denotes if a checkbox or radio element is checked by default.
defaultValue		The text displayed as the initial contents of a text-based control.
form		Reference to the form object that contains the element.
length		Returns the number of elements in an element sub-array.
name	NAME	Specifies the name to use to refer to the element.
selectedIndex		An integer specifying the index of the selected option in a `<SELECT>` element.
type	TYPE	The type of the element, such as TEXT, BUTTON or RADIO.
value	VALUE	The default value of text/numeric controls, or the value when the control is 'on' for Boolean controls.

Methods	Description
blur	Causes the element to lose the focus, and fire its onBlur event.
click	Simulates a click on the element, and fires its onClick event.
eval	Evaluates the object and returns a representation of its value.

Methods	Description
focus	Causes the element to receive the focus, and fire its **onFocus** event.
handleEvent	Invokes the appropriate event handling code of object for this event.
select	Highlights the input area of a text-based element.
toString	Returns a string containing a textual representation of the object's value.
valueOf	Returns the primitive value of an object, or the name of the object itself.

Events	Description
onBlur	Occurs when the control loses the focus.
onChange	Occurs when the contents of the control are changed.
onClick	Occurs when the mouse button is clicked on the control.
onFocus	Occurs when the control receives the focus.
onKeyDown	Occurs when the user presses a key.
onKeyPress	Occurs when the user presses and releases a key.
onKeyUp	Occurs when the user releases a key.
onMouseDown	Occurs when the user presses a mouse button.
onMouseUp	Occurs when the user releases a mouse button.
onSelect	Occurs when the current selection in the control is changed.

The Event Object

The global object provided to allow the scripting language to access an event's parameters. It provides the following properties, and the three standard methods:

Properties	Description
data	The URLs of the objects dropped onto the Navigator window, as an array of strings.
layerX	Horizontal position of the mouse pointer in pixels in relation to the containing layer.
layerY	Vertical position of the mouse pointer in pixels in relation to the containing layer.
modifiers	String containing the names of the keys held down for a key-press event.

Table Continued on Following Page

Properties	Description
pageX	Horizontal position in pixels of the mouse pointer or a layer in relation to the document's window.
pageY	Vertical position in pixels of the mouse pointer or a layer in relation to the document's window.
screenX	Horizontal position in pixels of the mouse pointer on the screen for an event.
screenY	Vertical position in pixels of the mouse pointer on the screen for an event.
target	The name of the object where the event was originally sent.
type	The type of event, as a string.
which	ASCII value of a key that was pressed, or indicates which mouse button was clicked.

Methods	Description
eval	Evaluates the object and returns a representation of its value.
toString	Returns a string containing a textual representation of the object's value.
valueOf	Returns the primitive value of an object, or the name of the object itself.

The FileUpload Object

An object that represents a control created with an **< INPUT >** tag where **TYPE=FILE**.

Properties	Attribute	Description
form		Reference to the form object that contains the element.
name	NAME	Specifies the name to use to refer to the element.
type	TYPE	Must be **"FILE"** for a FileUpload element.
value	VALUE	The text value of the control.

Methods	Description
blur	Causes the element to lose the focus, and fire its **onBlur** event.
eval	Evaluates the object and returns a representation of its value.
focus	Causes the element to receive the focus, and fire its **onFocus** event.
handleEvent	Invokes the appropriate event handling code of object for this event.
toString	Returns a string containing a textual representation of the object's value.
valueOf	Returns the primitive value of an object, or the name of the object itself.

Events	Description
onBlur	Occurs when the control loses the focus.
onChange	Occurs when the contents of the control are changed.
onFocus	Occurs when the control receives the focus.

The Form Object

An object that represents the section of a page contained within a `<FORM>` tag.

Properties	Attribute	Description
action	ACTION	The URL where the form is to be sent.
encoding	ENC_TYPE	Defines the type of encoding to be used when submitting the form.
length		Returns the number of elements in the form.
method	METHOD	How the form data should be sent to the server; either GET or POST.
name	NAME	Specifies the name to use to refer to the form.
target	TARGET	Specifies the window or frame where the return page will be loaded.

Array	Description
elements	Array of all controls and elements in the form.

Methods	Description
eval	Evaluates the object and returns a representation of its value
handleEvent	Invokes the appropriate event handling code of object for this event.
reset	Simulates a mouse click on a RESET button in the form.
submit	Submits the form, as when the SUBMIT button is clicked.
toString	Returns a string containing a textual representation of the object's value.
valueOf	Returns the primitive value of an object, or the name of the object itself.

Events	Description
onReset	Occurs when the RESET button on the form is clicked, or the form is reset.
onSubmit	Occurs when the SUBMIT button on the form is clicked, or the form is submitted.

The Frame Object

An object that represents a `<FRAME>` within a `<FRAMESET>`.

Properties	Attribute	Description
length		Returns the number of frames in a frames sub-array for the frame.
name	NAME	Specifies the name to use to refer to the frame.
parent		Returns the parent frame or window in the hierarchy.
self		A reference to the current frame.
window		Reference to the window object that contains the frame.

Array	Description
frames	Array of all the frames defined within a `<FRAMESET>` tag.

Methods	Description
blur	Causes the frame to lose the focus, and fire its onBlur event.
clearInterval	Cancels a timeout that was set with the setInterval method.
clearTimeout	Cancels a timeout that was set with the setTimeout method.
eval	Evaluates the object and returns a representation of its value.
focus	Causes the frame to receive the focus, and fire its onFocus event.
handleEvent	Invokes the appropriate event handling code of object for this event.
print	Prints the contents of the frame, equivalent to pressing the Print button.
setInterval	Denotes a code routine to execute every specified number of milliseconds.

Methods	Description
setTimeout	Denotes a code routine to execute once only, a specified number of milliseconds after loading a page.
toString	Returns a string containing a textual representation of the object's value.
valueOf	Returns the primitive value of an object, or the name of the object itself.

Events	Description
onBlur	Occurs when the frame loses the focus.
onFocus	Occurs when the frame receives the focus.
onMove	Occurs when the frame is moved.
onResize	Occurs when the frame is resized.

The Hidden Object

An object that represents a control created with an **<INPUT>** tag where **TYPE=HIDDEN**.

Properties	Attribute	Description
name	NAME	Specifies the name to use to refer to the element.
type	TYPE	Must be **"HIDDEN"** for a Hidden element.
value	VALUE	The text value of the control.

Methods	Description
eval	Evaluates the object and returns a representation of its value.
toString	Returns a string containing a textual representation of the object's value.
valueOf	Returns the primitive value of an object, or the name of the object itself.

The History Object

Contains information about the URLs that the client has visited, as stored in the browser's History list, and allows the script to move through the list.

Properties	Description
current	The current item in the browser's history list.
length	Returns the number of items in the browser's history list.
next	Refers to the next item in the browser's history list.
previous	Refers to the previous item in the browser's history list.

Methods	Description
back	Loads the previous URL in the browser's history list.
eval	Evaluates the object and returns a representation of its value.
forward	Loads the next URL in the browser's history list.
go	Loads a specified URL from the browser's history list.
toString	Returns a string containing a textual representation of the object's value.
valueOf	Returns the primitive value of an object, or the name of the object itself.

The Image Object

An object that represents an element created with an `<IMG>` tag.

Properties	Attribute	JSS Equivalents	Description
border	BORDER	borderWidths()	Specifies the border to be drawn around the image.
complete			Indicates if the image has completed loading.
height	HEIGHT	height	Sets the height for the image in pixels.
hspace	HSPACE		The horizontal spacing between the image and its neighbors.
lowsrc	LOWSRC		Specifies the URL of a lower resolution image to display.
name	NAME		Specifies the name to use to refer to the image.
prototype			A reference to the base object used to construct the object.
src	SRC		An external file that contains the source data for the image.
vspace	VSPACE		The vertical spacing between the image and its neighbors.
width	WIDTH	width	Sets the width for the image in pixels.

Array	Description
areas	Array of all the **<AREA>** tags defined within an image map's **<MAP>** tag.

Methods	Description
eval	Evaluates the object and returns a representation of its value.
handleEvent	Invokes the appropriate event handling code of object for this event.
toString	Returns a string containing a textual representation of the object's value.
valueOf	Returns the primitive value of an object, or the name of the object itself.

Events	Description
onAbort	Occurs if the downloading of the image is aborted by the user.
onError	Occurs when an error arises while the image is loading.
onKeyDown	Occurs when the user presses a key.
onKeyPress	Occurs when the user presses and releases a key.
onKeyUp	Occurs when the user releases a key.
onLoad	Occurs immediately after the image has been loaded.

The Layer Object

An object that represents a **<LAYER>** or **<ILAYER>** element in a document.

Properties	Attribute	JSS Equivalents	Description
above	ABOVE		Indicates that the layer should be above another element in the z-order of the page, or returns the element above it.
background	BACKGROUND	backgroundImage	URL of an image to display behind the elements in the layer.

Table Continued on Following Page

Properties	Attribute	JSS Equivalents	Description
below	BELOW		Indicates that the layer should be below another element in the z-order of the page, or returns the element below it.
bgColor	BGCOLOR	backgroundColor	Specifies the background color to be used for the layer.
clip.bottom	CLIP		Y co-ordinate of the bottom of the clipping rectangle for the layer.
clip.height			Height of the clipping rectangle for the layer.
clip.left	CLIP		X co-ordinate of the left of the clipping rectangle for the layer.
clip.right	CLIP		X co-ordinate of the right of the clipping rectangle for the layer.
clip.top	CLIP		Y co-ordinate of the top of the clipping rectangle for the layer.
clip.width			Width of the clipping for the layer.
left	LEFT		Position in pixels of the left-hand side of the layer in relation to its containing layer or the document.
name	NAME		Specifies the name to use to refer to the layer.
pageX	PAGEX		Horizontal position of the mouse pointer in pixels with respect to the layer.
pageY	PAGEY		Vertical position of the mouse pointer in pixels with respect to the layer.
parentLayer			Reference to the layer that contains the current layer.

Properties	Attribute	JSS Equivalents	Description
siblingAbove			Reference to the layer above the current layer if they share the same parent layer.
siblingBelow			Reference to the layer below the current layer if they share the same parent layer.
src	SRC		An external file that contains the source data for the layer.
top	TOP		Position of the top of the layer.
visibility	VISIBILITY		Defines whether the layer should be displayed on the page.
zIndex	Z-INDEX		Position in the z-order or stacking order of the page, i.e. the z co-ordinate.

Methods	Description
captureEvents	Instructs the layer to capture events of a particular type.
eval	Evaluates the element and returns a representation of its value
handleEvent	Invokes the appropriate event handling code of the object for this event.
load	Loads a file into the layer, and can change the width of the layer.
moveAbove	Changes the z-order so that the layer is rendered above (overlaps) another element.
moveBelow	Changes the z-order so that the layer is rendered below (overlapped by) another element.
moveBy	Moves the layer horizontally and vertically by a specified number of pixels.
moveTo	Moves the layer so that the top left is at a position x, y (in pixels) within its container.
moveToAbsolute	Moves the layer to a position specified in x and y with respect to the page and not the container.
releaseEvents	Instructs the layer to stop capturing events of a particular type.
resizeBy	Resizes the layer horizontally and vertically by a specified number of pixels.

Table Continued on Following Page

Methods	Description
resizeTo	Resizes the layer to a size specified in x and y (in pixels).
routeEvent	Passes an event that has been captured back up through the normal event hierarchy.
toString	Returns a string containing a textual representation of the object's value.
valueOf	Returns the primitive value of an object, or the name of the object itself.

Events	Description
onBlur	Occurs when the layer loses the focus.
onFocus	Occurs when the layer receives the focus.
onLoad	Occurs immediately after the layer's contents have been loaded.
onMouseOut	Occurs when the mouse pointer leaves the layer.
onMouseOver	Occurs when the mouse pointer first enters the layer.

The Link Object

An object that represents a hyperlink created in the page with an `<A HREF=".."> ` tag.

Properties	Attribute	Description
hash		The string following the # symbol, the anchor name, in the HREF value.
host		The hostname:port part of the location or URL.
hostname		The hostname part of the location or URL.
href	HREF	The destination URL or anchor point.
pathname		The file or object path name following the third slash in a URL.
port		The port number in a URL.
protocol		The initial sub-string indicating the URL's access method.
search		Any query string or form data following the ? in the complete URL.
target	TARGET	Specifies the window or frame where the new page will be loaded.

Methods	Description
eval	Evaluates the object and returns a representation of its value
handleEvent	Invokes the appropriate event handling code of object for this event.
toString	Returns a string containing a textual representation of the object's value.
valueOf	Returns the primitive value of an object, or the name of the object itself.

Events	Description
onClick	Occurs when the mouse button is clicked on the link.
onDblClick	Occurs when the user double-clicks on the link.
onKeyDown	Occurs when the user presses a key.
onKeyPress	Occurs when the user presses and releases a key.
onKeyUp	Occurs when the user releases a key.
onMouseDown	Occurs when the user presses a mouse button.
onMouseOut	Occurs when the mouse pointer leaves the link.
onMouseOver	Occurs when the mouse pointer first enters the link.
onMouseUp	Occurs when the user releases a mouse button.

The Location Object

Contains information on the current URL. It also provides methods that will reload a page.

Properties	Attribute	Description
hash		The string following the # symbol, the anchor name, in the HREF value.
host		The hostname:port part of the location or URL.
hostname		The hostname part of the location or URL.
href	HREF	The destination URL or anchor point.
pathname		The file or object path name following the third slash in a URL.
port		The port number in a URL.
protocol		The initial sub-string indicating the URL's access method.
search		Any query string or form data following the ? in the complete URL.

Methods	Description
eval	Evaluates the object and returns a representation of its value.
reload	Reloads the current page.
replace	Loads a page replacing the current page's session history entry with its URL.
toString	Returns a string containing a textual representation of the object's value.
valueOf	Returns the primitive value of an object, or the name of the object itself.

The MimeType Object

Provides information about the page's **MIME** data type.

Properties	Description
description	Returns a description of the MimeType.
enabledPlugin	Returns the plug-in that can handle the specified MimeType.
name	Specifies the name of the MimeType.
suffixes	A list of filename suffixes used with the specified MimeType.

Methods	Description
eval	Evaluates the object and returns a representation of its value.
toString	Returns a string containing a textual representation of the object's value.
valueOf	Returns the primitive value of an object, or the name of the object itself.

The Navigator Object

This object represents the browser application itself, providing information about its manufacturer, version, and capabilities.

Properties	Description
appCodeName	The code name of the browser.
appName	The product name of the browser.
appVersion	The version of the browser.
language	Returns the language the browser was compiled for.
platform	Returns the name of the OS the browser was compiled for.
userAgent	The user-agent (browser name) header sent as part of the HTTP protocol.

Array	Description
mimeTypes	Array of all the MIME types supported by the browser.
plugins	Array of all the plugins that are installed.

Methods	Description
eval	Evaluates the object and returns a representation of its value.
javaEnabled	Indicates if execution of Java code is enabled by the browser.
toString	Returns a string containing a textual representation of the object's value.
valueOf	Returns the primitive value of an object, or the name of the object itself.

The Option Object

An individual <OPTION> item in a list created by a <SELECT> tag.

Properties	Attribute	Description
defaultSelected		Denotes if a list item is selected by default.
index		Returns the ordinal position of the option in a list.
length		Returns the number of elements in an element sub-array.
selected	SELECTED	Indicates that this item in a list is the default.
selectedIndex		An integer specifying the index of the selected option in a list.
text	TEXT	The text displayed in the list.
value	VALUE	The text value of the option when selected.

Methods	Description
eval	Evaluates the object and returns a representation of its value.
toString	Returns a string containing a textual representation of the object's value.
valueOf	Returns the primitive value of an object, or the name of the object itself.

The Password Object

An object that represents a control created with an `<INPUT>` tag where `TYPE=PASSWORD`.

Properties	Attribute	Description
defaultValue		The text displayed as the initial contents of the control.
form		Reference to the form object that contains the control.
name	NAME	Specifies the name to use to refer to the control.
type	TYPE	Must be `"PASSWORD"` for a Password control.
value	VALUE	The text value of the control.

Methods	Description
blur	Causes the control to lose the focus, and fire its `onBlur` event.
eval	Evaluates the object and returns a representation of its value.
focus	Causes the control to receive the focus, and fire its `onFocus` event.
handleEvent	Invokes the appropriate event handling code of object for this event.
select	Highlights the input area of the control.
toString	Returns a string containing a textual representation of the object's value.
valueOf	Returns the primitive value of an object, or the name of the object itself.

Events	Description
onBlur	Occurs when the control loses the focus.
onFocus	Occurs when the control receives the focus.

The Plugin Object

An object that represents the features of an installed plugin component.

Properties	Attribute	Description
description		Returns a description of the MIME type.
filename		The name of the file that implements the plugin.
length		Returns the number of plugins.
name	NAME	Specifies the name to use to refer to the plugin.

Methods	Description
eval	Evaluates the object and returns a representation of its value.
refresh	Updates the information to reflect changes to installed plugins.
toString	Returns a string containing a textual representation of the object's value.
valueOf	Returns the primitive value of an object, or the name of the object itself.

The Radio Object

An object that represents a control created with an `<INPUT>` tag where `TYPE=RADIO`.

Properties	Attribute	Description
checked	CHECKED	Indicates that the radio button is selected (i.e. 'on').
defaultChecked		Denotes if the radio button is checked by default.
form		Reference to the form object that contains the element.
length		Returns the number controls in a sub-array.
name	NAME	Specifies the name to use to refer to the radio button.
type	TYPE	Must be `"RADIO"` for a Radio element.
value	VALUE	The value of the control when checked.

Methods	Description
blur	Causes the control to lose the focus, and fire its **onBlur** event.
click	Simulates a click on the control, and fires its **onClick** event.
eval	Evaluates the object and returns a representation of its value.
focus	Causes the control to receive the focus, and fire its **onFocus** event.
handleEvent	Invokes the appropriate event handling code of the object for this event.
toString	Returns a string containing a textual representation of the object's value.
valueOf	Returns the primitive value of an object, or the name of the object itself.

Events	Description
onBlur	Occurs when the radio button loses the focus.
onClick	Occurs when the mouse button is clicked on the radio button.
onFocus	Occurs when the radio button receives the focus.

The Reset Object

An object that represents a control created with an **<INPUT>** tag where **TYPE=RESET**.

Properties	Attribute	Description
form		Reference to the form object that contains the element.
name	NAME	Specifies the name to use to refer to the element.
type	TYPE	Must be **"RESET"** for a Reset element.
value	VALUE	The text used for the reset button's caption.

Methods	Description
blur	Causes the control to lose the focus, and fire its **onBlur** event.
click	Simulates a click on the control, and fires its **onClick** event.
eval	Evaluates the object and returns a representation of its value.
focus	Causes the control to receive the focus, and fire its **onFocus** event.
handleEvent	Invokes the appropriate event handling code of the object for this event.
toString	Returns a string containing a textual representation of the object's value.
valueOf	Returns the primitive value of an object, or the name of the object itself.

Events	Description
onBlur	Occurs when the control loses the focus.
onClick	Occurs when the mouse button is clicked on the control.
onFocus	Occurs when the control receives the focus.

The Screen Object

The **Screen** object provides the scripting language with information about the client's screen resolution and rendering abilities.

Properties	Description
availHeight	Height of the available screen space in pixels (excluding screen furniture).
availWidth	Width of the available screen space in pixels (excluding screen furniture).
colorDepth	Maximum number of colors that are supported by the user's display system.
height	Overall height of the user's screen in pixels.
pixelDepth	Returns the number of bits used per pixel by the system display hardware.
width	Overall width of the user's screen in pixels.

Methods	Description
eval	Evaluates the object and returns a representation of its value.
toString	Returns a string containing a textual representation of the object's value.
valueOf	Returns the primitive value of an object, or the name of the object itself.

The Select Object

An object that represents a list control created with a **<SELECT>** tag.

Properties	Attribute	Description
form		Reference to the form object that contains the list element.
length		Number of items in the list.
name	**NAME**	Specifies the name to use to refer to the list element.
selectedIndex		The numeric position within the list of the selected item.
type		Indicates the type of list, i.e. **SELECT-ONE**, **SELECT-MULTI**, etc.
text		The text of the currently selected item.

Methods	Description
blur	Causes the control to lose the focus, and fire its **onBlur** event.
eval	Evaluates the object and returns a representation of its value.
focus	Causes the control to receive the focus, and fire its **onFocus** event.
handleEvent	Invokes the appropriate event handling code of the object for this event.
toString	Returns a string containing a textual representation of the object's value.
valueOf	Returns the primitive value of an object, or the name of the object itself.

Events	Description
onBlur	Occurs when the control loses the focus.
onChange	Occurs when an item in the list is selected so that the selection is changed.
onFocus	Occurs when the control receives the focus.

The Submit Object

An object that represents a control created with an **<INPUT>** tag where **TYPE=SUBMIT**.

Properties	Attribute	Description
form		Reference to the form object that contains the element.
name	NAME	Specifies the name to use to refer to the element.
type	TYPE	Must be **"SUBMIT"** for a Submit element.
value	VALUE	The text for the submit button's caption.

Methods	Description
blur	Causes the control to lose the focus, and fire its **onBlur** event.
click	Simulates a click on the control, and fires its **onClick** event.
eval	Evaluates the object and returns a representation of its value.
focus	Causes the control to receive the focus, and fire its **onFocus** event.
handleEvent	Invokes the appropriate event handling code of the object for this event.
toString	Returns a string containing a textual representation of the object's value.
valueOf	Returns the primitive value of an object, or the name of the object itself.

Events	Description
onBlur	Occurs when the control loses the focus.
onClick	Occurs when the mouse button is clicked on the control.
onFocus	Occurs when the control receives the focus.

The Text Object

An object that represents a control created with an `<INPUT>` tag where `TYPE=TEXT`.

Properties	Attribute	Description
defaultValue		The text displayed as the initial contents of the control.
form		Reference to the form object that contains the element.
name	NAME	Specifies the name to use to refer to the element.
type	TYPE	Must be **"TEXT"** (or omitted) for a text element.
value	VALUE	The text currently within the text box.

Methods	Description
blur	Causes the control to lose the focus, and fire its **onBlur** event.
click	Simulates a click on the control, and fires its **onClick** event.
eval	Evaluates the object and returns a representation of its value.
focus	Causes the control to receive the focus, and fire its **onFocus** event.
handleEvent	Invokes the appropriate event handling code of the object for this event.
select	Highlights the input area of the control.
toString	Returns a string containing a textual representation of the object's value.
valueOf	Returns the primitive value of an object, or the name of the object itself.

Events	Description
onBlur	Occurs when the control loses the focus.
onChange	Occurs when the contents of the element are changed.
onFocus	Occurs when the control receives the focus.
onSelect	Occurs when the current selection in the control is changed.

The TextArea Object

An object that represents a text area control created with a **<TEXTAREA>** tag.

Properties	Attribute	Description
defaultValue		The text displayed as the initial contents of the control.
form		Reference to the form object that contains the element.
name	**NAME**	Specifies the name to use to refer to the element.
type		Information about the type of the control.
value	**VALUE**	The text currently within the text box.

Methods	Description
blur	Causes the control to lose the focus, and fire its **onBlur** event.
eval	Evaluates the object and returns a representation of its value.
focus	Causes the control to receive the focus, and fire its **onFocus** event.
handleEvent	Invokes the appropriate event handling code of the object for this event.
select	Highlights the input area of a form element.
toString	Returns a string containing a textual representation of the object's value.
valueOf	Returns the primitive value of an object, or the name of the object itself.

Events	Description
onBlur	Occurs when the control loses the focus.
onClick	Occurs when the mouse button is clicked on the control.
onFocus	Occurs when the control receives the focus.
onKeyDown	Occurs when the user presses a key.
onKeyPress	Occurs when the user presses and releases a key.
onKeyUp	Occurs when the user releases a key.

The Window Object

The **window** object refers to the current window. This can be a top-level window, or a window that is within a frame created by a **<FRAMESET>** in another document.

Properties	Attribute	Description
closed		Indicates if a window is closed.
defaultStatus		The default message displayed in the status bar at the bottom of the window.
document		A reference to the document object from a contained element or object.
innerHeight		Height of the window excluding the window borders.
innerWidth		Width of the window excluding the window borders.
length		Returns the number of frames in a window.
location		The full URL of the document being displayed.
locationbar		Defines whether the address bar will be displayed in the browser window.
menubar		Defines whether the menu bar will be displayed in the browser window.
name	NAME	Specifies the name to use to refer to the window.
opener		Returns a reference to the window that created the current window.
outerHeight		Height of the window including the window borders.
outerWidth		Width of the window including the window borders.
pageXOffset		Horizontal offset of the top left of the visible part of the page within the window in pixels.
pageYOffset		Vertical offset of the top left of the visible part of the page within the window in pixels.
parent		Returns a reference to the parent window.
personalbar		Defines whether the user's personal button bar will be displayed in the browser window.
scrollbars	SCROLLING	Defines whether the window will provide scrollbars if all the content cannot be displayed.
self		A reference to the current window.

Table Continued on Following Page

Properties	Attribute	Description
status		The text displayed in the current window's status bar.
statusbar		Defines whether the status bar will be displayed in the browser window.
toolbar		Defines whether the toolbar will be displayed in the browser window.
top		Returns a reference to the topmost window object.
window		Reference to the window object that contains the window.

Array	Description
frames	Array of all the frames defined within a `<FRAMESET>` tag.

MethodName	Description
alert	Displays an Alert dialog box with a message and an OK button.
back	Loads the previous URL in the browser's history list.
blur	Causes the window to lose the focus, and fire its **onBlur** event.
captureEvents	Instructs the window to capture events of a particular type.
clearInterval	Cancels a timeout that was set with the **setInterval** method.
clearTimeout	Cancels a timeout that was set with the **setTimeout** method.
close	Closes the current browser window.
confirm	Displays a Confirm dialog box with a message and OK and Cancel buttons.
disableExternalCapture	Prevents a window that includes frames from capturing events in documents loaded from different locations.
enableExternalCapture	Allows a window that includes frames to capture events in documents loaded from different locations.
eval	Evaluates the code and returns a representation of its value.
find	Returns **true** if a specified string is found in the text in the current window.

MethodName	Description
focus	Causes the window to receive the focus, and fire its onFocus event.
forward	Loads the next URL in the browser's history list.
handleEvent	Invokes the appropriate event handling code of the object for this event.
home	Loads the user's Home page into the window.
moveBy	Moves the window horizontally and vertically.
moveTo	Moves the window so that the top left is at a position x, y (in pixels).
open	Opens a new browser window.
print	Prints the contents of the window, equivalent to pressing the Print button.
prompt	Displays a Prompt dialog box with a message and an input field.
releaseEvents	Instructs the window to stop capturing events of a particular type.
resizeBy	Resizes the window horizontally and vertically.
resizeTo	Resizes the window to a size x, y specified in pixels.
routeEvent	Passes an event that has been captured up through the normal event hierarchy.
scrollBy	Scrolls the document horizontally and vertically within the window by a number of pixels.
scrollTo	Scrolls the document within the window so that the point x, y is at the top left corner.
setInterval	Denotes a code routine to execute every specified number of milliseconds.
setTimeout	Denotes a code routine to execute once only, a specified number of milliseconds after loading the page.
stop	Stops the current download, equivalent to pressing the Stop button.
toString	Returns a string containing a textual representation of the object's value.
valueOf	Returns the primitive value of an object, or the name of the object itself.

EventName	Description
onBlur	Occurs when the window loses the focus.
onDragDrop	Occurs when the user drops a file or object onto the Navigator window.
onError	Occurs when an error loading a document arises.
onFocus	Occurs when the window receives the focus.
onLoad	Occurs when a document has completed loading.
onMouseMove	Occurs only when event capturing is on and the user moves the mouse pointer.
onMove	Occurs when the window is moved.
onResize	Occurs when the window is resized.
onUnload	Occurs immediately prior to the current document being unloaded.

HTML Controls Cross Reference

Dynamic HTML provides the same integral control types as HTML 3.2. However, there are more properties, methods and events available now for all the controls.

The following tables show those that are relevant to controls. For a full description of the properties, methods and events for each element, check out Sections **A** and **B**.

Control Properties	checked	defaultChecked	defaultSelected	defaultValue	form	index	length	name	seleced	selectedIndex	text	type	value
Button	✗	✗	✗	✗	✓	✗	✗	✓	✗	✗	✗	✓	✓
Checkbox	✓	✓	✗	✗	✓	✗	✗	✓	✗	✗	✗	✓	✓
FileUpload	✗	✗	✗	✗	✓	✗	✗	✓	✗	✗	✗	✓	✓
Hidden	✗	✗	✗	✗	✗	✗	✗	✓	✗	✗	✗	✓	✓
Option	✗	✗	✓	✗	✗	✓	✓	✗	✓	✓	✓	✗	✓
Password	✗	✗	✗	✓	✓	✗	✗	✓	✗	✗	✗	✓	✓
Radio	✓	✓	✗	✗	✓	✗	✓	✓	✗	✗	✗	✓	✓

Control Properties

	checked	defaultChecked	defaultSelected	defaultValue	form	index	length	name	seleced	selectedIndex	text	type	value
Reset	✗	✗	✗	✗	✓	✗	✗	✓	✗	✗	✗	✓	✓
Select	✗	✗	✗	✗	✓	✗	✓	✓	✗	✓	✓	✓	✗
Submit	✗	✗	✗	✗	✓	✗	✗	✓	✗	✗	✗	✓	✓
Text	✗	✗	✗	✓	✓	✗	✗	✓	✗	✗	✗	✓	✓
Textarea	✗	✗	✗	✓	✓	✗	✗	✓	✗	✗	✗	✓	✓

Control Methods

	blur	click	eval	focus	handleEvent	select	toString	valueOf
Button	✓	✓	✓	✓	✓	✗	✓	✓
Checkbox	✓	✓	✓	✓	✓	✗	✓	✓
FileUpload	✓	✗	✓	✓	✓	✗	✓	✓
Hidden	✗	✗	✓	✗	✗	✗	✓	✓
Option	✗	✗	✓	✗	✗	✗	✓	✓
Password	✓	✗	✓	✓	✓	✓	✓	✓
Radio	✓	✓	✓	✓	✓	✗	✓	✓
Reset	✓	✓	✓	✓	✓	✗	✓	✓
Select	✓	✗	✓	✓	✓	✗	✓	✓
Submit	✓	✓	✓	✓	✓	✗	✓	✓
Text	✓	✓	✓	✓	✓	✓	✓	✓
Textarea	✓	✗	✓	✓	✓	✓	✓	✓

Control Events	onBlur	onChange	onClick	onFocus	onKeyDown	onKeyPress	onKeyUp	onMouseDown	onMouseUp	onSelect
Button	✓	✗	✓	✓	✗	✗	✗	✓	✓	✗
Checkbox	✓	✗	✓	✓	✗	✗	✗	✗	✗	✗
FileUpload	✓	✗	✓	✓	✗	✗	✗	✗	✗	✗
Hidden	✗	✗	✗	✗	✗	✗	✗	✗	✗	✗
Option	✗	✗	✗	✗	✗	✗	✗	✗	✗	✗
Password	✓	✗	✗	✓	✗	✗	✗	✗	✗	✗
Radio	✓	✗	✓	✓	✗	✗	✗	✗	✗	✗
Reset	✓	✗	✓	✓	✗	✗	✗	✗	✗	✗
Select	✓	✓	✗	✓	✗	✗	✗	✗	✗	✗
Submit	✓	✗	✓	✓	✗	✗	✗	✗	✗	✗
Text	✓	✓	✗	✓	✗	✗	✗	✗	✗	✓
Textarea	✓	✗	✓	✓	✓	✓	✓	✗	✗	✗

JavaScript Style Properties

These properties provide access to the individual styles of an element. They could have been previously set by a style sheet, or by an inline style tag within the page. The equivalent HTML attributes are shown where appropriate.

JavaScript Style Property	Attribute	CSS Equiv.
align	ALIGN	float
Specifies the alignment of the element on the page		
backgroundColor	BGCOLOR	background-color
Specifies the background color of the page.		
backgroundImage	BACKGROUND	background-image
Specifies a URL for the background image for the page.		

JavaScript Style Property	Attribute	CSS Equiv.
borderColor	BORDERCOLOR	

The color of the bottom border for an element.

| borderBottomWidth | MARGINHEIGHT | border-bottom-width |

The width of the bottom border for an element.

| borderLeftWidth | MARGINWIDTH | border-left-width |

The width of the left border for an element.

| borderRightWidth | MARGINWIDTH | border-right-width |

The width of the right border for an element.

| borderStyle | | border-style |

Used to specify the style of one or more borders of an element.

| borderTopWidth | MARGINHEIGHT | border-top-width |

The width of the top border for an element.

| borderWidths() | BORDER | border |

Allows all four of the borders for an element to be specified with one attribute.

| clear | CLEAR | clear |

Causes the next element or text to be displayed below left-aligned or right-aligned images.

| color | COLOR | color |

Defines the color to be used for the element, by name or as a number.

| display | | display |

Specifies if the element will be visible (displayed) in the page.

| fontFamily | FACE | font-family |

Specifies the name of the typeface, or 'font family'.

| fontSize | SIZE | font-size |

Specifies the font size.

| fontStyle | | font-style |

Specifies the style of the font, i.e. normal or italic.

| fontWeight | WEIGHT | font-weight |

Sets the weight (boldness) of the text.

Table Continued on Following Page

JavaScript Style Property	Attribute	CSS Equiv.
`height`	`HEIGHT`	`height`

Specifies the height at which the element is to be rendered on the page.

`lineHeight`		`line-height`

The distance between the baselines of two adjacent lines of text.

`listStyleType`	`TYPE`	`list-style-type`

The type of bullets to be used for a list.

`marginBottom`		`margin-bottom`

Specifies the bottom margin for the page or text block.

`marginLeft`		`margin-left`

Specifies the left margin for the page or text block.

`marginRight`		`margin-right`

Specifies the right margin for the page or text block.

`marginTop`		`margin-top`

Specifies the top margin for the page or text block.

`margins()`		`margin`

Allows all four margins to be specified with a single attribute.

`paddingBottom`		`padding-bottom`

Specifies the spacing between an element's contents and the bottom border of the element.

`paddingLeft`		`padding-left`

Specifies the spacing between an element's contents and the left border of the element.

`paddingRight`		`padding-right`

Specifies the spacing between an element's contents and the right border of the element.

`paddingTop`		`padding-top`

Specifies the spacing between an element's contents and the top border of the element.

`paddings()`		`padding`

Allows all four paddings to be specified with a single attribute.

`textAlign`	`ALIGN`	`text-align`

Indicates how text should be aligned within the element.

JavaScript Style Property	Attribute	CSS Equiv.
textDecoration		text-decoration

Font decorations (underline, overline, strikethrough) added to the text of an element.

| textIndent | | text-indent |

The indent for the first line of text in an element, may be negative.

| textTransform | | text-transform |

Transforms the text for the element.

| verticalAlign | VALIGN | vertical-align |

Sets or returns the vertical alignment of the element on the page.

| whiteSpace | | white-space |

Indicates whether white space in an element should be collapsed or retained, as in text formatting.

| width | WIDTH | width |

Specifies the width at which the element is to be rendered on the page.

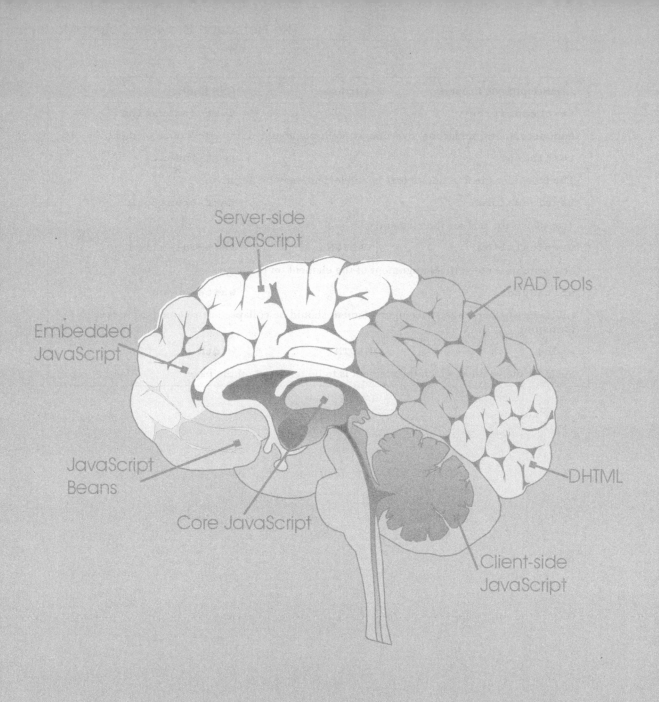

ASP 2.0 Object Model

Microsoft Active Server Pages Object Library Reference

Objects

Name	Description
Application	The main ASP application – defined as 'all the .asp files in a virtual directory and its sub-directories'.
Request	Retrieves the values passed from the client browser to the server during an HTTP request.
Response	Used for sending output to the client.
ScriptingContext	The Active Server Pages scripting context.
Server	Provides access to methods and properties on the server.
Session	Allows storage of information needed for an individual user session.

The Application Object

Methods

Name	Returns	Description
Lock		Prevents other Active Server Pages from modifying the Application
UnLock		Enables other Active Server Pages to modify the Application object

Properties

Name	Returns	Description
Contents	Dictionary	Collection of contents associated with application. Read only
StaticObjects	Dictionary	Collection of static objects associated with application. Read only

Events

Name	Returns	Description
OnStart		Occurs when a page in the application is first referenced
OnEnd		Occurs when the application ends

The Request Object

Methods

Name	Returns	Description
BinaryRead	Variant	Reads data returned by the client in a POST request

Properties

Name	Returns	Description
ClientCertificate	Dictionary	Collection of client certificate fields (specified in the X.509 standard). Read only
Cookies	Dictionary	Collection of cookies sent as part of the Request. Read only
Form	Dictionary	Collection of form elements. Read only
QueryString	Dictionary	Collection of query string values. Read only
ServerVariables	Dictionary	Collection of predetermined environment variables. Read only
TotalBytes	Integer	Total number of bytes that the client will return in the request body. Read only

The Response Object

Methods

Name	Returns	Description
AddHeader		Adds an HTTP header
AppendToLog		Adds a string to the end of the Web server log entry for this Request
BinaryWrite		Writes content without any character (Unicode to ANSI) conversion
Clear		Erases any buffered content
End		Causes Active Server Pages to stop processing and return any buffered output
Flush		Sends buffered output immediately
PICS		Adds an HTTP pics header. Read/Write
Redirect		Sends a '302 Redirect' status line
Write		Writes content with character (Unicode to ANSI) conversion

Properties

Name	Returns	Description
Buffer	Boolean	Indicates whether page output is buffered. Read/Write
CacheControl	String	The HTTP Cache-control header. Read/Write
CharSet	String	The HTTP Character set header. Read/Write
ContentType	String	The HTTP content type. Read/Write
Cookies	Dictionary	Collection of cookies sent as part of the Response. Write only
Expires	Integer	The length of time in minutes until the Response expires. Read/Write
ExpiresAbsolute	Date	The absolute date and time that the Response expires. Read/Write
IsClientConnected	Boolean	Indicates whether the client connection is still valid. Read only
Status	String	Value of the HTTP status line. Read only

The Server Object

Methods

Name	Returns	Description
CreateObject	Object	Creates an instance of a server component
HTMLEncode	String	Applies HTML encoding to a specified string
MapPath	String	Maps the specified relative or virtual path to the corresponding physical directory on the server
URLEncode	String	Applies URL query string encoding rules, including escape characters, to a specified string
URLPathEncode	String	Applies URL path encoding rules, including escape characters, to a specified string

Properties

Name	Returns	Description
ScriptTimeout	Integer	The maximum length of time in seconds before a script is terminated. Read/Write

The Session Object

Methods

Name	Returns	Description
Abandon		Destroys a Session object and releases its resources

Properties

Name	Returns	Description
Contents	Dictionary	Collection of all the items added to the Session through script commands. Read only
CodePage	Integer	The code page used when writing text to, or reading text from, the browser. Read/Write
LCID	Integer	The LCID used when writing text to, or reading text from, the browser. Read/Write
SessionID	String	Returns a Session ID for this user. Read only
StaticObjects	Dictionary	Collection of static objects associated with session. Read only
Timeout	Integer	The length of time in minutes before session state is destroyed after non-use by an individual user. Read/Write

Events

Name	Returns	Description
OnStart		Occurs when a page in the session is first referenced
OnEnd		Occurs when the session ends, is abandoned, or times out

The ObjectContext Object

Methods

Name	Returns	Description
SetAbort		Indicates that as far as the ASP page is concerned the transaction should not be completed
SetComplete		Indicates that as far as the ASP page is concerned the transaction can be completed

Events

Name	Returns	Description
onTransactionAbort		Raised when a transaction has been aborted
onTransactionComplete		Raised when a transaction has been completed

Method Calls Quick Reference

Application

*Application.*Lock
*Application.*UnLock

Request

*Variant = Request.*BinaryRead(*pvarCountToRead As Variant*)

Response

*Response.*AddHeader(*bstrHeaderName As String, bstrHeaderValue As String*)
*Response.*AppendToLog(*bstrLogEntry As String*)
*Response.*BinaryWrite(*varInput As Variant*)
*Response.*Clear
*Response.*End
*Response.*Flush
*Response.*Pics(*bstrHeaderValue As String*)
*Response.*Redirect(*bstrURL As String*)
*Response.*Write(*varText As Variant*)

Server

Set *Object* = *Server*.CreateObject(*bstrProgID As String*)
String = *Server*.HTMLEncode(*bstrIn As String*)
String = *Server*.MapPath(*bstrLogicalPath As String*)
String = *Server*.URLEncode(*bstrIn As String*)
String = *Server*.URLPathEncode(*bstrIn As String*)

Session

Session.Abandon

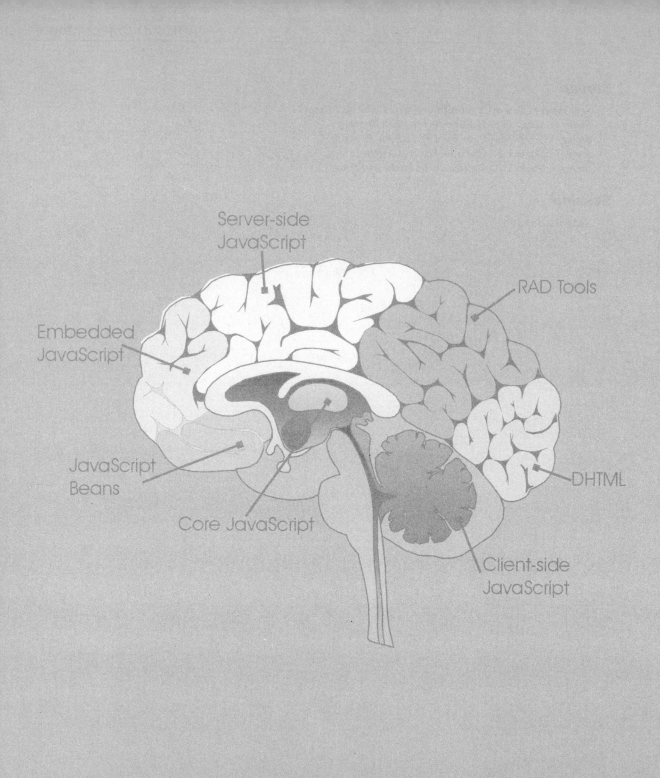

The ScriptEase Interpreters

This appendix describes the main features of the ScriptEase JavaScript interpreters available from Nombas Inc. The interpreters are all based around a common core interpreter but are available in several forms. This allows you to deploy them into situations where JavaScript has previously not been available as a design choice. Each of these interpreters is discussed in a separate chapter:

❑ Chapter 22 – ScriptEase:ISDK

❑ Chapter 21 – ScriptEase:Desktop (SE:DT)

❑ Chapter 12 – ScriptEase:Web Server Edition (SE:WSE)

You would use the ISDK version to embed a JavaScript interpreter into your own application software. The Desktop version provides a way to develop JavaScript control of a desktop or workstation computer. The Web Server Edition is a means of writing server side JavaScript to generate web pages. However, it need not be used just to generate web pages and the scripts can also be executed stand alone just like any other shell script in the UNIX environment.

ScriptEase Extensions to the JavaScript Language

The ScriptEase interpreters extend the base JavaScript language in a number of important ways. The JavaScript interpreter runs in a server context rather than a client. This has important implications for the kind of things you would design the scripts to do.

For example, you wouldn't expect to display a window and receive a mouse click. In a server context, however, you would expect to process some input, make some decisions based on the values you have been passed, and generate some output. Generally that would result in a stream of outgoing HTML, but note that other data formats are supported.

Accessing files in the client machine's file system is not possible with client-side JavaScript – there's too much of a security risk for the client. However, this is one of the main things you need the ability to do on a server, so it is a very useful thing to have the file I/O extensions which ScriptEase gives you.

ScriptEase provides a very powerful and advanced form of JavaScript. The ScriptEase interpreter allows you to run scripts locally, so you can use ScriptEase to write fully fledged programs. In addition, ScriptEase has added commands and directives that increase and extend its power without interfering with the operation of standard JavaScript. These enhancements include preprocessor directives such as #link, #include and #define, the C library access, and the built-in Buffer object.

In the next few sections, we'll discuss various specific extensions to the JavaScript language that you will find available in the ScriptEase interpreter.

ScriptEase File Types

Normally you store JavaScript include files for inclusion into HTML pages in js files. These would contain JavaScript that will end up being executed on the client. ScriptEase uses the following file extensions:

File Type	Description
JSE	A ScriptEase JavaScript file normally available for execution at the users request. Some extensions libraries for inclusion use this file type.
JSH	An includable header with ScriptEase extension functions. Not normally callable from the user's browser directly. Normally used in the #include directives of a JSE script.
JSB	A pre-compiled ScriptEase script.
HMM	A function wrapper file type used with the #include directive.
CMM	An old style function wrapper.
SO	Shared library for use with the #link directive on some platforms.
DLL	Shared library for use with the #link directive on some platforms.

ScriptEase Data Types

In a few operations, it is important to specify data types so that the values being passed can be accessed in the correct way. ScriptEase standardizes on the following data type values which are automatically created by the interpreter as pre-processor manifest constant values.

Data Type	Description
\<array\>	The size of the array is used to indicate how large a buffer to create or read from.
\<positive-integer\>	The value in bytes is indicated.
\<string\>	The length of the string is taken as a size value and if appropriate, its UNICODE setting is also inherited by default.
\<structure-definition\>	The structure size is used to size the read or write.
FLOAT32	Four byte floating point value.
FLOAT64	Eight byte floating point value.
FLOAT80	Ten byte floating point value. (this is not supported on Win32 platforms).
SWORD16	Signed two byte word.
SWORD24	Signed three byte word.
SWORD32	Signed four byte word.
SWORD8	Signed byte value.
UWORD16	Unsigned two byte word.
UWORD24	Unsigned three byte word.
UWORD32	Unsigned four byte word.
UWORD8	Unsigned byte value.

Initialization and Termination

When scripts run, the ScriptEase interpreters go through several phases:

❑ **Import parameters**
The SE:WSE interpreter assimilates CGI parameters from HTTP request headers as well as the command line and the query values in the URL. The desktop version would take them from a command line or the environment.

❑ **Pre-process**
The pre-processor carries out all the header includes, processes the defines and assembles the conditional code blocks. Some of the pre-processor operations may invoke a function call.

❑ **Run the initialization**
Any piece of code in a script that is not contained in any function is part of the global initialization function. This code is executed first, before calling any function (unless a function is called from this initialization code). Any variables referenced in the initialization section must be global. You don't have to call this explicitly. It gets executed automatically by the interpreter. It is part of the pre-processing of the script, you could imagine that what happens is that after including all the necessary external files and executing the #defines, #ifdef and other conditionals, all of the function blocks are extracted leaving a sequence of code that exists outside the scope of any function. This remaining global code is executed as if it were enclosed inside a function called INIT() which gets called at the outset and before calling main().

❑ **Run the main() function**
After the initialization has been performed, the main() function is called and is given the arguments that the operating system passed to the ScriptEase interpreter. If there is no main() function, the program will end after running through all of the steps in the initialization. Again, you don't need to explicitly do anything. The interpreter will load the script and look for the main() function to execute it. If there is one, it gets processed; if not, only the globally accessible initialization code gets called. That may invoke other functions but that would not be good style. It is best to have a main() function and execute it conventionally.

❑ **Run the exit handler**
If you used the Clib.atexit() function to define any functions to call as the script terminates, these will be executed last of all.

The main() function

ScriptEase is far less picky about the main() function than C is. While a C program must have a main() function, in ScriptEase this is not the case. The following two programs do exactly the same thing:

```
var b = 20;
var a = b*b;
cgi.out ("Content-Type: text/html\r\n\r\n");
cgi.out ("<HTML>");
cgi.out ("<BODY>");
cgi.out (a);
cgi.out ("</BODY>");
cgi.out ("</HTML>");
```

and:

```
function main(argc, argv)
{
  var b = 20;
  var a = b*b;
  cgi.out("Content-Type: text/html\r\n\r\n");
  cgi.out("<HTML>");
  cgi.out("<BODY>");
  cgi.out(a);
  cgi.out("</BODY>");
  cgi.out("</HTML>");
}
```

These two programs both set the value of a to 400 and then output an HTML page. There are some differences in the way the variables will be handled, however. In the first example, a and b are global variables, and are available to any function in the program. In the second, a and b are local variables, and are only available to the main() function.

One advantage to the main() function is that it receives any parameters included on the command line when the script was first called. The call to the main() function looks exactly like the main() function in a C program. Strictly it is really main(argc, argv). It is passed the number of command line arguments in argc and an array of them in argv. In the example above they are omitted because no command line values are assumed to have been passed in. You can leave them out if you are not going to access them. On the other hand, it won't hurt to put them in and ignore them.

The argc variable tells you how many command line arguments were passed, while the variable argv is an array of all of the arguments. The first value in the argv array (argv[0]) is the name of the script being called, so if argc = 1 then no actual command line arguments were passed. These variables behave like any other local variable. If you don't need to pass parameters to main(), it is recommended that your program have a main() function anyway, but with no parameters; in this case the parenthesis following the main() function declaration should be left empty.

The argc variable in the main() function is a copy of the global _argc variable. The argv array is a copy of the global _argv array. It is convenient that argc and argv content is also available in _argc and _argv. To be consistent with C language usage, the names without leading underscores are available inside the main() function. To be consistent with the scope rules that apply when you define arguments to functions, these have to be local to the main() function and therefore cannot be global variables with the same name. Therefore, to be available globally (which is very convenient sometimes) the underscore is placed in front of the global copy. Now, since it would make no sense to modify the content of these variables, whether they are actually a duplicated copy or are actually the same variable accessible under two names and scopes is something we could spent all day arguing about.

To execute code automatically when the script terminates, see the Clib.atexit() function.

Pre-processor Directives

If you have used the C language before, you should be familiar with what the C pre-processor does for you. Because ScriptEase extends the functionality of JavaScript in many ways that are similar to the functionality of a C language compiler, you should be very comfortable with using these extended features.

Documentation and installation kits can be downloaded and viewed online at http://www.nombas.com/

Be careful not to confuse linkable libraries with includable source files. They are two different kinds of files. Linkable libraries contain compiled code that supports low-level access to the operating system and its resources. They present an API to the scripting environment that is consistent and convenient to use from JavaScript. Includable files, on the other hand, contain JavaScript source code which may be needed to be reused over and over again without having to type the same function definitions into each script. Often there is an #include-able wrapper library that encapsulates the #link-able binary module.

#define

The pre-processor #define directive allows manifest constants to be created in the same way as you would for the C language.

This is useful for setting the value of debug flags or constants that are used in many files. It means you only end up setting the value once. You might imagine that it is easier to assign a value to a variable but if that value is used in a lot of places, even if you define it as a global variable, it is not quite as convenient as a #define that sets a constant. Here are some examples:

```
#define SCREEN_HEIGHT 25
#define LANGUAGE_FLAG "en"
#define START_EMPHASIS "<FONT COLOR=RED>"
#define END_EMPHASIS "</FONT>"
```

#option

The #option directive provides configuration switches for the ScriptEase interpreter. They are most likely going to be helpful when you are debugging new scripts as you develop them. These are the various options:

Option	Description
#option DefaultLocalVars	All variables declared inside functions are local to that function regardless of whether the var keyword is used. Only variables declared outside functions are globally available.
#option !DefaultLocalVars	Variables declared in functions with the var keyword are local but if the var keyword is omitted they will be globally scoped even though they are declared within a function body.

Option	Description
`#option MathErrorWarnings`	Warnings are generated on mathematical exceptions such as divide by zero, operation on NaN values and invalid type conversions.
`#option !MathErrorWarnings`	Warnings on math exceptions are suppressed.
`#option RequireFunctionKeyword`	Functions cannot be declared without the `function` or `cFunction` keyword.
`#option !RequireFunctionKeyword`	Functions may be declared without the `function` or `cFunction` keyword.
`#option RequireVarKeyword`	Variables cannot be declared without the `var` keyword. This helps avoid type and scope errors and problems with undefined variables.
`#option !RequireVarKeyword`	The `var` keyword is not mandatory.

#include <source-library>

The #include directive provides a way to reuse code blocks in multiple projects from a single source. Basically they are a means of creating libraries of functions that you can bind as needed. You can select regions of the file to be included. You can designate parts of the file with labels and elect to include only those sections. Alternatively, you can mark a beginning and end of an includable section and incorporate just that part. Here is an example that selects one heading style or another based on the label selected. These lines are contained in a file called style.jsh:

```
:style1 function heading()
:style1 {
:style1 cgi.out("<h2>");
:style1 }

:style2 function heading()
:style2 {
:style2 cgi.out("<h3>");
:style2 }
```

This line in the top of your CGI script chooses style set 1:

```
#include <styles.jsh, null, :style1>
```

This line selects style set 2 instead:

```
#include <styles.jsh, null, :style2>
```

Now let's mark the beginning and end sections. Our include file is called `defaults.jsh` and contains several sections of alternative data. Here is the relevant part of it:

```
//BEGIN UNIX
#define PLATFORM_NAME "The UNIX system"
//END UNIX

//BEGIN OTHER
#define PLATFORM_NAME "A non UNIX Server"
//END OTHER
```

On a UNIX system we might use this form:

```
#include <defaults.jsh, 0, 0, //BEGIN UNIX, //END UNIX>
```

On a non-UNIX system, this line would be used:

```
#include <defaults.jsh, 0, 0, //BEGIN OTHER, //END OTHER >
```

The ScriptEase documentation provides more examples of how to use this functionality.

#if, #ifdef, #elif, #else, #endif

There are times when you want to make particular things happen in the pre-processor only if certain conditions are true. You might have some platform dependant code for instance. The conditional pre-processing works very similarly to the C language pre-processor. You can use this to make sure your ScriptEase JavaScript files are portable across a variety of platforms. Conditional sections of code are usually made dependant on pre-defined constants. You will need to consult the Nombas manuals for more detail and for a list of the available pre-defined values.

The `#if` and `#ifdef` are not quite the same. `#if <expression>` can be used to test the result of evaluating a JavaScript function. The `#ifdef` is equivalent to `#if defined(<var>)`.

Let's take the example with the `#include` blocks a little further. Instead of manually including one or another section of the `defaults.jsh` file, let's allow the pre-processor to make the decision:

```
#ifdef (_UNIX_)
#include <defaults.jsh, 0, 0, //BEGIN UNIX, //END UNIX>
#else
#include <defaults.jsh, 0, 0, //BEGIN OTHER, //END OTHER >
#endif
```

#link <binary-library>

The #link directive provides a way to incorporate additional libraries of compiled code into the ScriptEase interpreter. These libraries are modules of executable code that have been compiled and linked to form DLL or shared library binaries. They will be platform specific and you may need to consult additional Nombas documentation to make the best use of them. Only access binary library modules with the #link directive. You should not #link plain text source JavaScript files (.jsh files). They should always be used with the #include directive.

Includable Headers

ScriptEase interpreters ship with a collection of includable source text files. These are called JavaScript Header files or jsh files for short. You must use the #include directive to access these as they won't work with the #link directive.

Since these libraries of code are external to ScriptEase and are in an editable source form, you can modify them if you need to. A slightly different set is shipped with the Desktop and Web Server Edition versions of ScriptEase. The ISDK does not include the libraries of source script.

There are some useful functions available in the Desktop set which are not in the Web Server Edition and so if you are deploying a web server, you may want to download one of the Desktop kits and get a copy of the files in the #include library.

Both interpreters come with a variety of sample files as well and these are good starting point. We won't list the sample files here but the includable jsh header files are worth enumerating. The table indicates which set the files are in. Where the files are available in the WSE and DT versions, they may not be identical. If there is a duplication, use the one that was supplied with the interpreter you are using, just in case there are differences that are necessary to support that interpreter variant.

You can build your own includable files but they must contain text source form JavaScript.

Here is a list of the includable files shipped with SE:DT and SE:WSE:

Include File	Desktop	WSE	Description
array.jsh	✓		A collection of tools for manipulating arrays. There are functions in here to convert arrays, copy elements, edit arrays, extract sections of arrays, fix index ranges and insert arrays into each other. Although this is shipped with SE:DT, it might have some useful functionality for SE:WSE use as well.
cmdline.jsh	✓		This provides some help with processing command lines. It is probably only useful in the SE:DT environment.
copyfile.jsh	✓		Facilities for copying one file to another. Could be useful in SE:WSE although it is shipped only in SE:DT at present.

Include File	Desktop	WSE	Description
dspfile.jsh	✓		Support for distributed scripting protocol.
error.jsh		✓	Handle an error message by generating an HTML response. This clears the current buffer contents and replaces it with a hardwired error page. You could roll your own if you prefer a different error page.
file.jsh	✓		A collection of useful functions for handling files. Some platform limitations exist although you may be able to create edited versions of the functions to work round that. The functions are generally to do with managing file attributes. This might be useful on SE:WSE.
filename.jsh	✓		Filename tools useful for breaking paths into arrays and such like. This could be useful in SE:WSE as well as SE:DT scripts.
fileobj.jsh	✓		A set of functions to support access to files within an object representation of the file. Since the file is now an object, it can have properties and methods associated with it. Useful for all kinds of things.
filepack.jsh	✓		A mechanism for packing multiple files into an archive.
formease.jsh		✓	A collection of useful functions for accessing form data. These functions create fragments of HTML for you rather than whole pages. There are also field conversion routines that help you get values out of submitted forms.
ftp.jsh	✓		Wrapper functions for performing FTP access to a remote server. This could be useful in a SE:WSE environment where an FTP server is not available on the internet and can be 'front-ended' by a web page. The http access to a CGI script could request the file which is then accessed in the web server via ftp and returned in the request body. The web server then behaves as a proxy for a hidden ftp server.
general.jsh	✓		Generally useful functions and constants. This might be helpful for SE:WSE developers as well.
getopt.jsh	✓		Support for a UNIX like getopt facility. This is probably useful in the SE:DT environment but probably not in SE:WSE.

Include File	Desktop	WSE	Description
grflib.jsh		✓	A collection of routines to help build graphs and such like. It relies on the GD library having been #link-ed in and provides wrapper functions for its capabilities. This used to be shipped as grflib.hmm and there may be an old copy of that file on your system. Use the jsh file out of preference.
html.jsh		✓	Useful page output routines. Using these functions simplifies the creation of pages and builds tag pairs as nested function calls. Heavy nesting of tables within tables may become more complex with this technique.
htmlcopy.jsh		✓	HTML template handler. With this, you can load a template and replace particular strings in it.
idsp.jsh	✓		The distributed scripting protocol support.
idspodbc.jsh	✓	✓	This include file contains some wrapper functions that help when accessing remote ODBC data sources. Use this instead of odbc.jsh when the ODBC database client access is on another machine. odbc.jsh is for a locally supported ODBC client connection.
imglib.jsh		✓	Image library helper functions for creating GIF data on the fly. These are additional wrappers for the GD image library that is accessed though the #link directive. There may be an older imglib.hmm file on your system. Use the jsh version if there is.
item.jsh	✓		An item list manager. Provides a way of splitting strings of items into an array and back again. This could be really useful in the SE:WSE environment.
key.jsh	✓		Support for keyboard access. Not useful in a web server but dead handy for the SE:DT environment.
lock.jsh	✓	✓	File locking functions. This implements a cooperative locking scheme.
mail.jsh	✓	✓	TCP/IP mail access routines. This provides mail send and receive capabilities.
memsrch.jsh	✓		This is a fast memory search. However, because some of it is implemented in machine code, it is not portable and only works on Windows platforms.

Include File	Desktop	WSE	Description
nntp.jsh	✓		Support for access to Usenet newsgroups. A web based news group front end could be built with this support if you add this to your SE:WSE system.
objtools.jsh	✓		A collection of functions for copying, storing and comparing objects. This includes arrays and primitives. This could also be useful in an SE:WSE environment.
odbc.jsh	✓	✓	A library of more useful functions to help with ODBC access. The ODBC binary library will be required (it gets #link-ed by this header). These functions are built on top of that as convenience wrappers. Here you can access data sources and tables to make queries on the database. You can do some quite complicated things here but beware because you could also completely wreck the database as well.
odbcease.jsh	✓	✓	Some more ODBC help. This is a layer that is built on top of the odbc.jsh wrapper functions. Some additional convenience code is provided to access tables more easily.
optparms.jsh	✓		More optional command line parameter handling. This is related to the functions in getopt.jsh.
sqlconst.jsh	✓	✓	Some SQL constants that might be helpful when accessing SQL databases through the odbc.jsh and odbcease.jsh functions.
string.jsh	✓	✓	Useful string handling functions. These are implemented by extending the String and Clib object prototypes with additional functions. This is a large function collection of editing, conversion and insertion tools that will save a lot of time and effort.
struct.jsh	✓	✓	Structure initialization support for bulk loading data into arrays of structure members.
table.jsh		✓	Useful functions when building HTML tables from data structures retrieved from the database.
tinyhtml.jsh		✓	A way to output HTML with function based tag pairs. This is somewhat experimental.

Include File	Desktop	WSE	Description
`url.jsh`	✓	✓	Grab the text of a page given the URL.. This is an excellent example of how to open and read from a remote socket on another web server.
`winini.jsh`	✓	✓	Interface for accessing windows ini file structures (profiles). These crop up in a variety of systems these days as Windows applications are ported to other platforms. This is provided to gain access on non windows based systems.

Linkable Libraries

Nombas publish a description of the run-time linkable libraries on their website. The online documentation describes the functionality for each one. There is a developer kit for building these libraries if you feel particularly ambitious. These libraries are updated and made available on new platforms from time to time and the latest information on status and availability should be obtained directly from Nombas. Here is a summary of the modules commonly available with ScriptEase:

Library	Description
SESOCK	Routines for working with sockets. You can create socket listeners and clients with these extensions. Send and receive mechanisms are also available. This means you can extend the back end of your server to remotely query other systems, connect to mail servers and all manner of remote services accessible via IP and port address.
ODBC	Routines for providing ODBC database connectivity. Please note that the ODBC version for 16 bit windows is a `.jsh` file, and not a `#link` file as with the other operating systems.
GD	This library lets you create `.gif` files on the fly. See the EST clock and Piechart demos on the Nombas web site for examples that use this library. Two libraries of wrapper functions go with this library: `grflib.jsh`, for creating graphs, and `imglib.jsh`, for creating images.
REGEXPSN	Routines for regular expression searches. The normal JavaScript regular expression object is available. This provides an alternative with some subtle differences in functionality. This is designed for in memory searches. File system searches can be done through the C Lib extensions (via a `system()` call).
OLEAUTOC	Routines for OLE Automation. These are only really useful on Windows systems. The support basically allows for methods to be invoked in OLE objects. You can set or get properties and test objects to see if they are accessible.

Utility Scripts Provided With ScriptEase

The following utility scripts are in the utility folder and are available to all ScriptEase platforms. These utilities are useful applications when administering a computer:

Script Name	Description
alldirs.jse	Perform a command in the current folder and all subfolders under it.
attrib.jse	View or set the attributes of files.
autoexec.jse	Automatically loaded by a ScriptEase interpreter when the command line shell is being used. Among other things the script defines command line aliases. Good source of examples for technical applications. Within the shell environment, typing the name of a script and pressing the return key causes the script to run in the shell.
autoload.jse	Automatically loaded by a ScriptEase interpreter when being run as a shell. Its main purpose is to implement a ScriptEase shell. Good source of examples for technical applications.
batch.jse	Interprets a DOS batch file, allowing many such batch files to be run on non-DOS platforms.
compdate.jse	Compares the date and timestamp of two files and returns the result as an error level indicating whether one file is newer, older, or the same age as another file.
compile.jse	Compiles scripts to binary files that are similar to the executable files that ScriptEase Desktop Pro can create but which are not self-executable.
copy.jse	Copies files in a way similar to the DOS copy command.
cron.jse	A scheduler program with a Unix like interface.
cstrargs.jse	A utility that converts C strings to strings that are acceptable on a command line.
date.jse	View the system date and, on some platforms, set it.
datediff.jse	Display the difference between two dates.
del.jse	Deletes files in a way similar to the DOS del command.
delold.jse	Delete files older than a specified period.
deltree.jse	Delete or kill an entire subtree.
dir.jse	Shows a directory of a folder in a way similar to the DOS dir command.
dirdiff.jse	Compare two directories, looking for differences in file name, file date, or file size.
filecomp.jse	Do a binary comparison of two files.

Script Name	Description
findenv.jse	Aids in converting variable names in older scripts to the JavaScript requirements in current ScriptEase.
geturl.jse	Process, open, and print the page to which a specified URL points.
inclist.jse	List the files included using the #include preprocessor directive in scripts. Will work with any source texts that use C like include directives.
keycode.jse	Display numeric values for keys when they are pressed.
makedir.jse	Make a directory or folder in a way similar to the DOS md command.
more.jse	Display a text file by pausing with each screenful of text.
move.jse	Move files by combining the functionality of the DOS move and rename commands.
print.jse	Print a text file.
rmdir.jse	Remove a directory or folder in a way similar to the DOS rd command.
shellchr.jse	Automatically loaded by a ScriptEase interpreter when being run as a shell. Adds special key character handling to the ScriptEase shell. Good source of examples for technical applications.
time.jse	Same as date.jse.
treplace.jse	Find and replace strings in text files.
ver.jse	A version command for a ScriptEase shell.
which.jse	Find which file in the path matches a specified file specification. Useful to determine which file will be run first if there are more than one files with the same name in your path.
wrldfrct.jse	Implements a fractal routine in an interesting way.
xcopy.jse	Copies files with extended capabilities in a way similar to the DOS xcopy command.
zipview.jse	View the contents of ".zip" files.

Sample Scripts

The following sample scripts are in the sample folder and are available to all ScriptEase platforms. These samples illustrate ScriptEase usage in a variety of ways, some useful and some just for show:

Script Name	Description
99btls.jse	Display the words to "99 Bottles of Beer," as if it were being sung.
args.jse	Displays the parameters argc and argv that are received by the main function. Useful in debugging.
ascii.jse	Displays the ASCII character set and numeric codes.
border.jse	Draw a border of asterisks on a ScriptEase screen or window.
cast.jse	A general chat program, server and client.
dos2unix.jse	Convert a DOS style text file to Unix.
duplines.jse	Displays the line numbers of duplicate lines in a text file.
fibonacc.jse	Displays fibonacci numbers until a key is pressed.
fileobj.jse	Demo script to illustrate some of the features of the File object in fileobj.jsh.
frantick.jse	Watch an asterisk as it is frantically bounced around inside of a ScriptEase screen or window.
getnews.jse	Gets news articles from news servers.
hello.jse	The seemingly ubiquitous and required "Hello" program.
hellocnt.jse	A "Hello" program with a counter.
history.dat	Data for the history questions in history.jse.
history.jse	Tests your knowledge of history with random questions about history.
htmlxlat.jse	Convert a standard HTML file to a specialized file for ScriptEase Web Server Edition.
httpd.jse	A simple web server you can modify to your heart's content! This server is powerful enough to handle the entire Nombas web site. It shows how easy it is to do web and TCP/IP related programming with the ScriptEase language and tools.
inn.jse	One of the files of the INN chat demo.
innbard.jse	One of the files of the INN chat demo.
inncli.jse	One of the files of the INN chat demo.
iso9660.jse	Check filenames for compliance with the ISO9660 standard.
jseedit.jse	A simple text file editor.

Script Name	Description
julian.jse	Show a Julian month and day when the number of a day in a year is entered.
lgrade.jse	Displays a letter grade based on a number grade.
loan.jse	Calculates monthly payments for a loan.
mailsamp.jse	Demo for the mail.jsh library for working with e-mail.
quote.jse	Displays random quotes.
sortrand.jse	Reads lines of text from standard input and scrambles their order to standard output.
startup.jse	Dynamically control startup programs.
string.jse	Demo for the routines in string.jsh. See the many ways that strings can be manipulated.
Struct.jse	Demo program for struct.jsh.
ttt.jse	A simple game of Tic-Tac-Toe.
Write.jse	Demo for the enhanced output routines in write.jsh.

Win32 platform special includes

The following script libraries are in the win32\include folder and are written for Windows 95/98/NT/2000. Like all platform specific scripts, there are also utility and sample scripts. Only the library scripts will be described here and only for Win32.

Script Name	Description
clipbrd.jsh	Routines for working with the clipboard.
colors.jsh	Definitions and routines for working with colors in ScriptEase screens and windows.
com.jsh	Routines to interface with the Component Object Model.
dlgdemo.jsh	Demonstrates dialog box functions and routines
dropsrc.jsh	Routines to facilitate drag and drop operations.
gdi.jsh	Routines to interface with graphics functions in the API.
globlmem.jsh	Routines to work with global memory allocation.
hotkey.jsh	Routines for the creation of hotkeys.
icon.jsh	Routines to work with icons.

Script Name	Description
keypush.jsh	Routines to control or mimic the pushing of keys on the keyboard. The functions in this library work by sending virtual keystrokes to an active window. Allows a user to control other windows and applications, especially when used in conjunction with menuctrl.jsh.
menuctrl.jsh	Routines to control or create menus. Allows a user to control other windows and applications, especially when used in conjunction with keypush.jsh.
message.jsh	Routines to send and post message to windows.
msgbox.jsh	Routines to work with the standard message box. The most common message boxes are predefined.
pickfile.jsh	Pick a file using a common dialog.
profile.jsh	Routines to work with profile or INI files. Largely superceded by the Profile object in profobj.jsh.
profobj.jsh	Creates a Profile object to work with profile or INI files.
progman.jsh	Work with the program manager through DDE.
registry.jsh	Routines to work with the registry. Largely superceded by the Registry object in regobj.jsh.
regobj.jsh	Creates a Registry object to work with the registry.
screen.jsh	Adds methods to the Screen object that enhance working with ScriptEase screens and windows.
shortcut.jsh	Routines to work with shortcut, link, files.
useful.jsh	Miscellaneous routines that are useful in the Windows environment.
window.jsh	Creates a Window object for working with windows. When used in conjunction with winutils.jsh, encompasses all windows routines.
winexec.jsh	Multiple ways to execute applications. Allows for eccentricities encountered when working in the windows environment.
winsock.jsh	Routines for working with winsock.
wintools.jsh	Routines for working with windows. Largely superceded by window.jsh and winutils.jsh.
winutil.jsh	Routines for working with windows. Largely superceded by window.jsh and winutils.jsh.
winutils.jsh	Utility routines for working with windows. When used in conjunction with window.jsh, encompasses all windows routines.
winvers.jsh	Get version information.

String Extensions

There are a few areas where strings behave slightly differently in ScriptEase. These are all extensions to the underlying JavaScript functionality.

Escape Sequences for Characters

The most common way to indicate that data is a string is to put it in double or single quotes. All the usual Unicode support is available. Special characters will need to be escaped and ScriptEase supports several minor extensions to the normal JavaScript string literal set. The table below lists the ScriptEase extension escape sequences:

Escape	Description
\a	Audible bell
\v	Vertical tab
\0	Null character

Single-quote Strings

Because single quoted strings have special meaning in C language, it is recommended not to use them for string literals in preference to double-quoted strings. In any case, they behave differently inside cFunction modules and this can cause some headaches when debugging code that you may have pasted into a cFunction from a JavaScript function.

Back-quote Strings

ScriptEase provides the back-quote (`), also known as the back-tick or grave accent, as an alternative quote character to indicate that escape sequences are not to be translated. This may be useful but will render your scripts less portable.

String Concatenation

In JavaScript you can use the '+' symbol to concatenate strings together. If you try to concatenate a string containing non numeric characters with a number, the result will be a string. ScriptEase adds a small refinement that means the '+' symbol is optional. All of these lines will result in the variable containing an identical string:

```
string = "aaa123";
string = "aaa" + 123;
string = "aaa" 123;
```

Array Additions

ScriptEase supports two kinds of arrays. The first is the normal JavaScript array. These are objects that belong to the class `Array`. ScriptEase also creates arrays automatically when they are needed. These arrays are of class `Object`. You can get the `length` property of an Array object but not an Object object. To measure the length of automatically created arrays, use the `getArrayLength()` global function. The best description of these arrays is located in the comment section of the `array.jsh` file supplied with SE:DT.

Goto and Labels

You may jump to any location within a function block (see functions) by using the `goto` statement. The keywords is reserved in JavaScript but is un-implemented in other interpreters. ScriptEase provides the `goto` functionality in the same way as it works in C Language. The syntax is:

```
goto LABEL;
```

where `LABEL` is an identifier followed by a colon (`:`). Like this:

```
beginning:
a = Clib.getche(); //get a value for a
if (a<2)
{
 goto beginning;
}
Clib.printf("%d", a);
```

Some programmers consider this to be bad practice and many heated debates have been aired about it. Whether that is true or not, this should be used sparingly to avoid making the program flow difficult to follow.

Functions

ScriptEase extends the behavior of functions over and above the normal facilities of JavaScript. Here are some particular points to take into account when using any of the ScriptEase interpreters.

Duplicate Function Names

ScriptEase allows you to have two functions with the same name. The interpreter will use the function nearest the end of the script; that is, the last function to load is the one that will be executed. This is unexpected, as you would normally anticipate the first one that is encountered to be used. Because of this though, you can write overriding functions that supersede the ones included in the pre-processor from the `.jsh` files. Beware of this capability though. Some interpreters may execute the first named instance of a duplicated function. Having duplicate named functions might make your scripts non portable and is more dangerous than it is useful.

Error Checking for Functions

Some functions will return a special value if they failed to do what they are supposed to do. The function Clib.fopen() opens or creates a file for a script to read or write to but returns null if it cannot. If you try to read or write to the file the script will not operate correctly. Normal practice in C language programming is to test for the null by checking the result of an assignment. You can use the same technique in ScriptEase and it looks almost identical to the C code it emulates. Like this:

```
if (!(fp = Clib.fopen("myfile.txt", "r")))
{
  ErrorMsg("Clib.fopen returned null");
}
```

You will still have to abort the script or manage the problem another way.

cfunction keyword

The ScriptEase cfunction keyword defines a function that behaves somewhat differently than standard JavaScript functions. This is for the benefit C programmers who are used to the way the C language handles functions and variables. Avoid using the cfunction if you intend to run your scripts with other interpreters because it is non standard JavaScript.

In a function declared with the cfunction keyword, there is no data conversion between numbers and strings. Instead of being treated as a special data type, strings are presented as an array of bytes. The first character of the string is assigned to string[0], the second to string[1], and so on until the end of the string.

The last character of a string is always '\0', which defines the end of the string. If you assign a variable to a string, defining the string in double quotes, this character will automatically be appended to the end of the string. To assign a string to a variable without appending the '\0' character, put the string in single quotes. This is most often done with single characters. For example, if

```
aaa = "m";
bbb = 'm';
```

then the variable aaa is an array: aaa[0] = 'm' and aaa[1] = '\0'. The variable bbb is a character, containing the letter 'm'. Internally, characters are converted to numbers according to the ASCII code set standard.

You can change the contents of strings by assigning individual array entries with new character values.

String concatenation syntax becomes pointer arithmetic inside a cFunction. Beware that if you try and concatenate a value to the end of a string, you may relocate its starting point inadvertently. You can still access the original data because negative offsets work as well. This can be quite confusing.

Logical operators may be affected as well. You might compare two strings for equality. Equality and identity are not the same and here inside a cFunction the equals operator is testing for identity and not value. Two strings are only equal in a cFunction if they point at an identical location in memory. They can have the same contents copied to them but they will still not satisfy the test for equality because the contents are stored in different memory locations.

In functions declared with the function keyword, variables are compared by value, so the actual values of two strings are compared. In this case the result of the comparison is true if they both contain the same data regardless of where they store it. This is a subtle and sometimes confusing difference.

Automatic Variable Type Conversion

When a ScriptEase variable is used in a context where it makes sense to convert it to a different type, ScriptEase will automatically coerce the variable to the appropriate type. This most commonly happens with numbers and strings.

Converting numbers to strings is usually quite easy. However, when converting strings to numbers there are a number of coercions that are tricky and its mostly to do with promoting the value to higher type. While subtracting a string from a number (or vice versa) converts the string to a number and subtracts the two, adding the two converts the number to a string and concatenates them. The string will always convert to a base 10 number, and must not contain any string that cannot legally scan as a numeric value. The string "110e" will not convert to a number, because the ScriptEase interpreter doesn't know what to make of the 'e' character.

You can override this to make a more strict conversion by using the ParseInt() and ParseFloat() methods.

Extensions to the Global Object

These are extension functions to the global object supported by ScriptEase:

Function	Description
Defined(<var>)	This function returns true if the variable is defined. If the variable is of type undefined, it returns false. This gets round a problem in JavaScript where undefined variables are hard to detect. Because there is no keyword for the undefined value, and it is different to a null value, detecting an undefined variable in standard JavaScript depends on seeing if they contain a null value. If you had assigned a value of null to them, they would be defined but would still fail the test. Using the defined() function in an if statement can distinguish the difference.
Undefine(<var>)	This function changes the type of a variable to undefined. Any data contained in the variable will be lost. This function is identical to the delete keyword and the variable is thereafter genuinely undefined which is a different state to being nulled.

Function	Description
getArrayLength (<array> [, <minIdx>])	Use this with dynamically created arrays (those other than the ones created using the Array() constructor. This useful for arrays created automatically by ScriptEase which may not respond to the .length property requestor.
setArrayLength (<array> [,<minIdx>], <length>)	Used to set the new length for dynamic arrays.

There are also conversion functions such as ToBoolean() which converts a value to a Boolean. These are available for all the data types that ScriptEase supports and are named consistently. Here is a list:

- ❑ ToBoolean
- ❑ ToBuffer
- ❑ ToBytes
- ❑ ToInt32
- ❑ ToInteger
- ❑ ToNumber
- ❑ ToObject
- ❑ ToPrimitive
- ❑ ToString
- ❑ ToUint16
- ❑ ToUint32

The Clib Object

ScriptEase allows you to include the standard C library as an object in your code. Each method in the Clib object corresponds to one of the standard C library functions. A significant part of the JavaScript Math object is duplicated in the Clib object.

Clib - String Manipulation Functions

Generating HTML is likely to require much string manipulation and I/O functionality. These are the C library functions available in ScriptEase for that task. In fact, there are extensions here for caseless comparisons that are not generally available in C language libraries:

Method/Property	Description
Clib.rsprintf (<format-string> [, ...])	Return a formatted string. It behaves like printf(), fprintf(), and sprintf() except that in this case the string is returned to the caller. This has no counterpart in the C language. The same method is also available as a method in the SElib object.
Clib.sprintf(<string>, <format-string> [, ...])	Performs a formatting operation like printf() but store the output into a string variable.
Clib.sscanf(<string>, <format-string> [, ...])	Read and interpret text from a string.
Clib.strcat(<target>, <source>)	Append <source> to <target>.
Clib.strchr(<target>, <char>)	Search <string> for the location of <char>.
Clib.strcmp(<string1>, <string2>)	Compare two strings for equality.
Clib.strcmpi(<string1>, <string2>)	Compare two strings for similarity. Differences in case are ignored, so the string ABCD is equal to abcd.
Clib.strcpy(<target>, <source>)	Copy <source> onto <target>. The contents of <target> are destroyed in the process.
Clib.strcspn(<string>, <character-set>))	Return the offset to the first character in <string> that is present in <character-set>
Clib.stricmp(<string1>, <string2>)	An alternative to Clib.strcmpi().
Clib.strlen(<string>)	Return the length of the <string>.
Clib.strlwr(<string>)	Convert the string to lower case.
Clib.strncat(<target>, <source>, <max-length>)	Append <source> to <target> up to the end of <source> or <max-length> whichever happens soonest.
Clib.strncmp(<string1>, <string2>, <max-length>)	Compare <max-length> characters of <string1> with <string2>. This test is case sensitive.
Clib.strncmpi(<string1>, <string2>, <max-length>)	Compare <max-length> characters of <string1> with <string2>. This test is case insensitive.

Method/Property	Description
`Clib.strncpy(<target>, <source>, <max-length>)`	Copy `<max-length>` characters of `<source>` onto `<target>`. The contents of `<target>` are destroyed in the process. If `<source>` is longer than `<max-length>`, then only `<max-length>` characters are copied.
`Clib.strnicmp(<string1>, <string2>, <max-length>)`	Case insensitive comparison between two strings for a specified length.
`Clib.strpbrk(<string>, <character-set>)`	Search `<string>` for any characters in `<character-set>`. When the first one is found, return the remainder of `<string>` from that point to the end of the string.
`Clib.strrchr(<target>, <char>)`	Search `<string>` for the location of `<char>` in reverse, starting at the end of the string.
`Clib.strspn(<string>, <character-set>)`	Return the offset to the location of the first character in `<string>` that is not in `<character-set>`.
`Clib.strstr(<string>, <sub-string>)`	Searches for `<sub-string>` inside `<string>`. Returns the string starting at the location where the match is found.
`Clib.strstri(<string>, <sub-string>)`	Searches for `<sub-string>` inside `<string>`. Returns the string starting at the location where the match is found. The comparison ignores character case.
`Clib.strtod(<string> [, <end>])`	Converts the string to a decimal value (if it can). The `<end>` variable is set to a string commencing where the conversion ceased.
`Clib.strtok(<source>, <delimiter>)`	Tokenize a string with a delimiter. The first time this is called, the source string is buffered internally within the `strtok` handler. Subsequent calls should replace the `<source>` with a null. Each call returns the next token delimited by the same string.
`Clib.strtol(<string> [, <end> [, <radix>]])`	Converts the string to a long decimal value (if it can). The `<end>` variable is set to a string commencing where the conversion ceased. The `<radix>` indicates the number base for conversion.
`Clib.strupr(<string>)`	Convert the string to upper case.
`Clib.toascii(<char>)`	Convert the character to ASCII.
`Clib.tolower(<char>)`	Convert the character to lower case.
`Clib.toupper(<char>)`	Convert the character to upper case.

Clib - String Classification Functions

The C language support includes some useful character classification functions. These are helpful when scanning and parsing data that you import for processing. In the C language these tests only apply to a single character. In ScriptEase, they apply to a whole string at once.

Method/Property	Description
Clib.isalnum(<string>)	Returns TRUE only if all the characters are letters or numbers.
Clib.isalpha(<string>)	Returns TRUE only if the string is composed entirely of letters.
Clib.isascii(<string>)	Returns TRUE if the string can be encoded non destructively in ASCII. A UNICODE string with special currency symbols would fail this test. This has no C language counterpart and is available only in ScriptEase.
Clib.iscntrl(<string>)	Returns TRUE if the string contains any control characters.
Clib.isdigit(<string>)	Returns TRUE if the string is composed entirely of numbers.
Clib.isgraph(<string>)	Returns TRUE if the whole string consists of printable characters other than spaces.
Clib.islower(<string>)	Returns TRUE only if the whole string is lower case.
Clib.isprint(<string>)	Returns TRUE if the string contains only printable characters including spaces.
Clib.ispunct(<string>)	Returns TRUE if there are any punctuation characters in the string.
Clib.isspace(<string>)	Returns TRUE if the string contains any space characters.
Clib.isupper(<string>)	Returns TRUE if the string contains only upper case characters.
Clib.isxdigit(<string>)	Returns TRUE if the string could be successfully converted to a numerical value through a hexadecimal scanner.

Clib - File I/O

If you want to operate on files stored in the server's local file system, then these functions will be useful:

Method/Property	Description
Clib.fclose(<file-pointer>)	Close the file pointed at by the file pointer.
Clib.feof(<file-pointer>)	Check to see if we have read to the end of the file.
Clib.fflush(<file-pointer>)	Flush any pending output writes to the file.
Clib.fgetc(<file-pointer>)	Collect a single character from the input file.
Clib.fgetpos(<file-pointer>, <position>)	Get the current position within the file. This value can be used to rewind back to the same position if necessary.
Clib.fgets(<file-pointer>)	Get a string from the file. The string ends when enough characters have been read or we encounter a newline character.
Clib.flock(<file-pointer, <lockFlag>)	Lock or unlock a file to prevent simultaneous access to a file.
Clib.fopen(<file-name>, <mode>)	Open a file for reading, writing or appending to. The full range of text and binary flags are supported as you would expect to have available in a C language standard library.
Clib.fprintf(<file-pointer>, <format-string> [, ...])	Print a formatted string to a file.
Clib.fputc(<character>, <file-pointer>)	Put a character into the output stream of a file.
Clib.fputs(<string>, <file-pointer>)	Put a string into the output stream of a file.
Clib.fread(<destination>, <length>, <file-pointer>)	Read <length> bytes from file into the destination.
Clib.fread(<destination>, <type>, <file-pointer>)	Read a value of <type> into the destination from the file. The type values are the usual ScriptEase UWORD32 etc values.
Clib.fread(<destination>, <structure-definition>, <file-pointer>)	Read the contents of a structure from a file.
Clib.freopen(<file-name>, <mode>, <old-file-pointer>)	Close and reopen a file in a different mode or to a different device.

Method/Property	Description
`Clib.fscanf(<file-pointer>, <format-string> [, ...])`	Read and interpret incoming text from a stream.
`Clib.fseek(<file-pointer>, <offset> [, <mode>])`	Relocate the file position indicator to a new position. This will affect where the next read or write operation takes place.
`Clib.fsetpos(<file-pointer>, <position>)`	An alternative file position relocate function which can use the result obtained from an earlier `Clib.fgetpos()` call. In this case, you may be accessing a large file. Small files may be better managed with `Clib.fseek()` calls.
`Clib.ftell(<file-pointer>)`	The `Clib.ftell()` function complements `Clib.fseek()`. Be wary of using this with text mode files.
`Clib.fwrite(<source>, <buffer-length>, <file-pointer>)`	Write the source data to the file.
`Clib.fwrite(<source>, <data-type>, <file-pointer>)`	Write data to a file stream according to the data type value.
`Clib.getc(<file-pointer>)`	This is an alternative way to read characters from a file. It is identical to `Clib.fgetc()` so it is probably best to use `Clib.fgetc()` and ignore this one.
`Clib.getch()`	Read characters from the keyboard in a desktop environment without echoing the keystrokes.
`Clib.getchar()`	Read the next character from the standard input stream.
`Clib.getche()`	Read characters from the keyboard in a desktop environment, echoing the keystrokes to the screen as they are typed.
`Clib.gets()`	Read a string of characters from the keyboard, only returning the whole string when the return key is pressed.
`Clib.kbhit()`	Returns true if there are keystrokes waiting to be collected. Only appropriate in Desktop environments.
`Clib.printf(<format-string> [, ...])`	Print a formatted string to the standard output stream.

Method/Property	Description
`Clib.putchar(<character>)`	Put a character into the standard output stream.
`Clib.puts(<string>)`	Put a string into the standard output stream. A newline character is added automatically.
`Clib.putc(<char>, <stream>)`	An alternative to `fputc()` which is functionally identical.
`Clib.remove(<file-name>)`	Delete a file whose name is `<file-name>`.
`Clib.rename(<old-file-name>, <new-file-name>)`	Rename a file.
`Clib.rewind(<file-pointer>)`	Reset the file position indicator to the start of a file. This will affect any subsequent reads or writes.
`Clib.scanf(<format-string> [, ...])`	Read and interpret incoming text from the standard input stream.
`Clib.tmpfile()`	Create a temporary file that is destroyed automatically when the script exits. You cannot access the file by name.
`Clib.tmpnam([<string>])`	Generate a unique name for use when opening a temporary file. Use this to create temporary files which need to persist after the script has completed execution. However, unless you note the name somewhere, it is unlikely you will ever be able to find it again.
`Clib.ungetc(<char>, <stream>)`	Push a character back onto a stream ready to be collected again later. This is not good style and only one character is guaranteed to be retrievable again.

Clib - Math functions

Many of these methods may already be supported by the Math object in standard JavaScript. They are provided here as alternatives:

Method/Property	Description
`atof(<str>)`	Convert the string to a floating point value.
`atoi(<str>)`	Convert the string to an integer value.
`atol(<str>)`	Convert the string to a long integer value.

`Clib.div(<numerator>, <denominator>)`	This divides the numerator by the denominator and returns an object with two properties. The properties are the quotient and the remainder. Here is how to access them:
	`aa = Clib.div(bb, cc);`
	`qq = aa.quot;`
	`rr = aa.rem;`

`fabs(<x>)`	Return the absolute, non-negative value of a floating point number.
`fmod(<x>, <y>)`	Returns the remainder of `<x>` divided by `<y>`.
`Clib.frexp(<float>)`	Fracture a floating point number into a mantissa and exponent.
`labs(<x>)`	Returns the absolute, non-negative value of a long integer
`Clib.ldexp(<number>, <n>)`	This is the complement of `Clib.frexp()` and returns the number multiplied by 2 to the power `<n>`.
`ldiv(<num>, <denom>)`	Performs a `div()` operation on long integer values. Functionally identical to the `div()` function.
`Clib.log10(<x>)`	Returns the base 10 logarithm of `<x>`.
`Clib.modf(<x>, <i>)`	Splits a value into integer and fractional parts, returning the integer part in the variable `<i>` and the fractional part as the result.
`srand(<seed>)`	Seeds the random number generator.
`rand()`	Return a random number between 0 and `RAND_MAX` and may be affected by the `srand()` call.
`Clib.cosh(<x>)`	Returns the hyperbolic cosine of `<x>`.
`Clib.sinh(<x>)`	Returns the hyperbolic sine of `<x>`.
`Clib.tanh(<x>)`	Returns the hyperbolic tangent of `<x>`.

Clib - Environment Variable Access

If you construct any environment within which the ScriptEase interpreter runs, you can pass in values from that environment with these functions:

Method/Property	Description
Clib.getenv([<env-var-name>])	If you specify an environment variable name, the value that it contains will be returned. If you omit the names, an array of all environment variables is returned. This is an extension to the normal C language functionality.
Clib.putenv(<env-var-name>, <value>)	This function allows you to set an environment variable. There is an issue of non-portability in that some shells will allow you to modify the parent environment. DOS shells allow this for example. UNIX shells emphatically will not. However, setting an environment variable makes that variable available to the current execution later and to any child processes that it may spawn. In that sense, it can be used as a variable having a global scope that extends outside the current process.

Clib - Time Functions

Here is a list of the time functions supported. C library time values work with time values in several formats. The values returned by time() is a binary representation of the time now. It is machine specific. Convert it through localtime() to get it stored in a time object which has the time values broken down into component values. You can operate in these values individually and then print them out through one of the time formatters. These are distinctly different time functions to the JavaScript Date object methods. It is arguable as to which has more functionality but your choice as to which to use is likely to depend on what you want to do with a time value. It is likely that the object oriented approach is better for presenting time values to user while the Clib time functions may be better for internal time value computations. If you want to know more about them, then you should consult the manual supplied with ScriptEase or an ANSI C language reference manual:

Method/Property	Description
Clib.asctime(<time>)	Convert time to text from component time structure.
Clib.clock()	Get processor time used since starting ScriptEase.
Clib.ctime(<time>)	Convert machine specific time to text.
Clib.difftime(<time0>, <time1>)	Return the difference in seconds between two machine specific times.

Method/Property	Description
`Clib.gmtime(<time>)`	Convert calendar time to universal coordinated time.
`Clib.localtime(<time>)`	Convert a machine specific time to a component time object.
`Clib.mktime(<time>)`	Reconstruct a machine specific time value from a component time object.
`Clib.strftime(<string>, <format-string>, <time>)`	String formatted time presentation. Converts time objects to strings with a variety of formatting options on the individual time components.
`Clib.time(<time>)`	Get a time value in machine specific form. You will need to use some of the other functions to operate on this value as it is not usefully formatted.

Clib - Error Handling Functions

These functions provide support for error handling situations:

Method/Property	Description
`Clib.clearerr(<file-pointer>)`	Clear the error status for a file buffer.
`Clib.ferror(<file-pointer>)`	Examine a file streams error indicator.
`Clib.errno`	A globally available error property. Normally this is zero but internal functions can set this when an exception occurs. You can test this for non zero after calling a function. There are many possible values for this and you should consult the Nombas documentation for details.
`Clib.perror([<string>])`	Prints and returns an error message appropriate to the value in the `Clib.errno` property.
`Clib.strerror(<error-number>)`	Returns a string appropriate to the value in the `Clib.errno` property.

Clib - Sorting Functions

Access to and management of data structures will be facilitated by these functions:

Method/Property	Description

`Clib.bsearch(<key>, <sorted-array>,`
`        [<element-count>,]`
`        <compare-function>)`
	Perform a binary search on an array.

`Clib.qsort(<array>,`
`        [<element-count>,]`
`        <compare-function>)`
	Sort an array according to the result of the compare function.

Clib - Script Execution Functions

These functions facilitate script execution in various ways. They provide ways to exit and call external system level commands.

Method/Property	Description
`Clib.abort([<abortAll>])`	Kill the current execution thread. If the `<abortAll>` flag is true then all nested interpretations are aborted.
`Clib.assert(<logical-expression>)`	Evaluate an expression that returns a boolean result. If it is not `true`, print a message and abort the script.
`Clib.atexit(<string>)`	Register a stack of functions to call at exit via this function.
`Clib.exit(<exit-status>)`	Exit normally out of the script.
`Clib.system(<command-line>)`	Execute a command line and return the result. The DOS version of this has a slightly different syntax making the scripts non-portable. You can use a conditional pre-processor block to include the one you want.
`Clib.chdir(<dirPath>)`	Change to a different current working directory.
`Clib.getcwd()`	Return the current working directory.
`Clib.mkdir(<dirPath>)`	Make a new directory.
`Clib.rmdir(<dirPath>)`	Remove a directory.

Clib - Variable Argument List Support

Some C language functions such as `printf` have a variable number of arguments. You can implement your own functions that take a variable number of arguments by using a C-like mechanism provided by ScriptEase. These facilities are omitted here because JavaScript already supports this activity by enumerating through the arguments array in a `for` loop like this:

```
for (ii=0; ii<arguments.length; ii++)
{
 printf("Argument - %d is |%s|", ii, arguments[ii]);
}
```

You might conceivably need the variable argument support when operating on blobs and buffers. Here is a list of the variable argument handling functions:

- ❏ va_arg
- ❏ va_end
- ❏ va_start
- ❏ vprintf
- ❏ rvsprintf
- ❏ vfprintf
- ❏ vfscanf
- ❏ vscanf
- ❏ vsprintf
- ❏ vsscanf

Clib - Memory manipulation

These functions are rather like the string functions but operate on arbitrary byte ranges rather than string variables. Since we are operating on raw data, we need to tell ScriptEase the start and end points of the data to operate on. The corresponding string functions don't need this because ScriptEase knows how long the strings are already.

Method	Description
memchr(<array>, <char> [, <size>])	Search a byte array (perhaps a blob object) for a character.
memcmp(<array1>, <array2> [, <len>])	Compare <len> bytes of <array1> and <array2>.
memcpy(<dest>, <source> [, <len>])	Copy <len> bytes from the source to the destination.
memmove(<dest>, <source> [, <len>])	Move <len> bytes from the source to the destination. However, in ScriptEase, this is functionally identical to memcpy().
memset(<buf>, <char> [, <len>])	Set <len> bytes of <buf> to <char>.

The UNIX Object

In the example HTTPD web server implemented entirely in JavaScript, there is evidence of a Unix object. This provides some additional mechanisms that are useful on a server and may be helpful in the CGI handler. These are based on evidence found in the SE:DT install kit for Solaris. Although it is there, the functionality appears to be undocumented and may not be available on all platforms. There may be other undocumented functions belonging to the Unix object.

Method/Property	Description
Unix.setsid()	This creates a new session ID so that sub-processes in the UNIX environment can be collected together into a process group. This is a helpful precursor to forking child processes.
Unix.fork()	Fork the current process into a child and parent. This duplicates the current process at the point of calling the fork. A different value is returned by the fork call depending on whether it is in the child or parent process. A parent would use this to return to the top of a spawn loop while a child would drop into the child process code.
Unix.setuid (<user-id>)	This sets the user ID for the current process. In the web server example, this prevents the web server from running under the root account even though that is where it may have been started. Specifying the user ID of a process internally may sometimes be necessary for security purposes.
Unix.setgid (<group-id>)	This sets the group ID for the current process. In UNIX systems, users belong to groups and this is part of the UNIX security model. You would set the group ID for much the same reasons as setting the user ID.
Unix.waitpid(<pid>, <status>, <options>)	This is used to wait for a process to complete. However it is a special non-blocking wait that allows multiple child processes to be created if the options are set correctly. The <pid> value indicates which process to wait on. Positive numbers indicate a specific process to wait for. Zero indicates a wait for any child in the same process group as the calling process. The -1 value signifies that any child process regardless of process group ID. Any other negative values indicate the process group to monitor. The process group is indicated by the absolute value of the negative number that is passed. The options are WNOHANG or WUNTRACED and the resulting status is returned in the variable indicated by the status parameter.

The Buffer Object

The buffer object provides a way to manipulate data at a very basic level. This is a special feature of ScriptEase. It is useful when the relative location of data in memory is important. Any type of data may be stored in a buffer object. Buffer objects have two important properties that determine how data is read from them: `cursor` and `window`. The `cursor` property indicates the place in the buffer that data will be read from. The `window` property indicates how much data is to be considered. Creating a new buffer object is done like this:

```
new Buffer(<source> [[,<isUnicode>] ,<bigEndian>]);
```

The `isUnicode` and `bigEndian` flags are optional and indicate settings for the `unicode` data flag and memory architecture. The buffer can simply be created with defaults like this:

```
newBuffer = new Buffer(<source>);
```

The `<source>` value can be one of the following:

Source	Description
integer	Creates a buffer of integer bytes size.
string	Creates a buffer big enough to hold the string and derives the unicode settings from it. A sub-string can be specified.
array	Creates a buffer big enough to hold the array. A section of the array can be specified to make a smaller buffer.
buffer	An existing buffer can be copied to make a new one.

Buffer objects have the following properties and functions available for enquiry: They can also be accessed in an array-like manner.

Method/Property	Description
Buffer.size	Returns the size of the buffer content in bytes.
Buffer.bigEndian	Returns a flag indicating the byte ordering within the buffer.
Buffer.unicode	Returns a boolean flag indicating whether the buffer is UNICODE or ASCII.
Buffer.cursor	Returns the current cursor position in the buffer.
Buffer.data	Refers to the internal data within a buffer object.

Method/Property	Description
`Buffer.comparableTo(<buffer>)`	This method tests to see whether <buffer> refers to the same internal data as the Buffer object.
`Buffer.compareEnds(<buffer>)`	Checks to see whether <buffer> and the current Buffer object refer to the same data; if so, this method returns the relative values of the ends of their respective windows.
`Buffer.compareStarts()`	This method returns the relative values of the starts of their respective windows. An error is generated if they do not refer to the same data.
`Buffer.getCursor()`	This returns the position of the cursor relative to the absolute beginning of data in the buffer.
`Buffer.getSize()`	This object gets the current window size, i.e. how much data can be read at once.
`Buffer.isValidIndex(<index>)`	This function determines whether <index> is a valid index for the buffer.
`Buffer.setCursor(<offset>)`	This sets the value of the cursor to be equal to <offset>. Offset must be a number between 0 and `Buffer.getMaximumSize()`.
`Buffer.setSize()`	This method sets the size of the window, i.e. how much data it can read at once.
`Buffer.shift()`	This method shifts the cursor value by the amount specified by offset; this may be a positive or a negative amount. An attempt to shift the cursor past either end of the data will trigger an error.
`Buffer.shiftWindow()`	This method shifts the cursor but the size of the window remains constant. If the cursor is so close to the end of the data that there is not enough to fill the window, the size of window will shrink.
`Buffer.getUint32([<offset>] [, <endian-flag>])`	Retrieve an unsigned 32 bit word from the buffer.
`Buffer.getUint16([<offset>] [, <endian-flag>])`	Retrieve an unsigned 16 bit word from the buffer.

Method/Property	Description
`Buffer.getFloat([<offset>]` `        [, <endian-flag>])`	Retrieve a floating point value from the buffer.
`Buffer.getUNICODEValue([<offset>]` `        [, <endian-flag>])`	Retrieve a unicode character from the buffer.
`Buffer.getByte([<offset>]` `        [, <endian-flag>])`	Retrieve an 8 bit signed byte from the buffer.
`Buffer.getChar([<offset>]` `        [, <endian-flag>])`	Retrieve an arbitrary unsigned character from the buffer.

`Buffer.getASCIIString([<offset>`
`        [, <length>]]`
`        [, <endian-flag>])`
	Retrieve an ASCII string from the buffer.

`Buffer.getUNICODEString([<offset>`
`        [, <length>]]`
`        [, <endian-flag>])`
	Retrieve a UNICODE string from the buffer.

`Buffer.getString([<offset>`
`        [, <length>]]`
`        [, <endian-flag>])`
	Retrieve a string of arbitrary characters from the buffer.

`Buffer.getString([<length>])`	Retrieve a string of arbitrary characters from the buffer using the current cursor position.
`Buffer.getValue([<valSize>,` `        <valType>])`	Retrieve a value from the buffer using the current cursor position.

`Buffer.setUint32(<value>`
`        [,<offset>]`
`        [, <endian-flag>])`
	Store a 32 bit unsigned word in the buffer.

`Buffer.setUint16(<value>`
`        [, <offset>]`
`        [, <endian-flag>])`
	Store a 16 bit unsigned word in the buffer.

`Buffer.setFloat(<value>`
`        [, <offset>]`
`        [, <endian-flag>])`
	Store a floating point value in the buffer.

`Buffer.setUNICODEValue(<value>`
`        [, <offset>]`
`        [, <endian-flag>])`
	Store a UNICODE character in the buffer.

`Buffer.setByte(<value>`
`        [, <offset>]`
`        [, <endian-flag>])`
	Store a signed byte value in the buffer.

`Buffer.setChar(<value>`
`        [, <offset>]`
`        [, <endian-flag>])`
	Store an unsigned character value in the buffer.

`Buffer.setUNICODEString(<val>`
`        [, <offset> [, <len>]]`
`        [, <endian-flag>])`
	Store a UNICODE string in the buffer.

Method/Property	Description
`Buffer.setASCIIString(<val>` `[, <offset>` `[, <length>]]` `[, <endian-flag>])`	Store an ASCII string in the buffer.
`Buffer.setString(<value>` `[, <offset>` `[, <length>]]` `[, <endian-flag>])`	Store an arbitrary character string in the buffer.
`Buffer.putString(<string>)`	Store a string in the buffer at the cursor position.
`Buffer.putValue(<value>` `[,<valueSize>` `[,<valueType>]])`	Store a value in the buffer at the cursor position.
`Buffer.subBuffer(<beginning>,` `<end>)`	Returns another buffer object consisting of part of the source buffer.
`Buffer.toString()`	Converts the buffer to a string.

The Blob Object

Blobs are a way of representing large collections of arbitrary binary data. This may just be a collection of bytes or words or perhaps something with structural properties. These are especially useful when building dynamic link calls to the API's of some systems.

Method/Property	Description
`Blob.get(<blob>, <offset>,` `<data-format>)`	Get some data out of a blob object. Various formatting rules determine how the data is parsed out to the receiving variable.
`Blob.put(<blob>, <offset>,` `<data-format>)`	Store some data into a blob object. Rules about how the bytes are to be parsed in are indicated in the data format value.
`Blob.size(<definitions>)`	Get or set the size of a blob object in memory.

The SELib Object

The methods in this object extend the functionality of JavaScript. Like the Clib object, the SELib object is a collection of convenient functions that let you work with files and how they are stored on your system, memory, script execution, etc.

The SELib object also contains operating system specific functions. For example, it contains functions that let you create windows and process window messages which may only be used on systems running Windows. Functions that are only valid in certain operating systems will have the pertinent system indicated to the right of the function name.

SElib - Miscellaneous Functions

Here is a list of the miscellaneous functions:

Method/Property	Description
SElib.rsprintf(<format-string> [, ...])	Return a formatted string. It behaves like printf(), fprintf(), and sprintf() except that in this case the string is returned to the caller. This has no counterpart in the C language.
SElib.getArrayLength(<array>, <min-index>)	Measure an array and return its length. This is also implemented as a function belonging to the global object. It is used to measure the length of automatically created arrays in the ScriptEase interpreter. These do not have a length property since they are a member of the Object class and not the Array class.

SElib - Memory Access functions

The following properties deal with memory, how it is accessed and managed. These are likely to be operating system specific in some cases:

Method/Property	Description
SElib._BigEndianMode	Some platforms order the bits and bytes in memory so that 2, 4 and 8 byte values (and others) are constructed in a different way. Referring to the variables by name hides this but if you need to access the memory byte by bye, this can make a difference. Big-endian and Small-endian systems refer to whether the multi-byte words are formed right to left or left to right in ascending order of memory locations.
SElib.address(, <offset>)	DOS and 16 bit windows segment address conversion help.

Method/Property	Description
SElib.interrupt(<interrupt>, <reg-in> [, <reg-out>])	DOS and 16 bit windows interrupt configuration settings.
SElib.segment(<buffer>)	DOS and 16 bit windows pointer management for segment addressing.
SElib.offset	DOS and 16 bit windows pointer management for segment offset calculations.
SElib.pointer(<var>)	Return the address in memory where the data contained by the variable <var> is stored.
SElib.peek(<address> [, <dataType>])	Access the memory directly to retrieve data according to the <dataType> from the <address> specified.
SElib.poke(<address>, <data> [, <descriptor>])	Write the <data> at <address> according to the <descriptor> for data type formatting.

SElib - Operating system functions

The following functions deal with your operating system, its directories and sub-directories, and the way that scripts are executed:

Method/Property	Description
SElib.directory([, <file-spec> [, <sub-dirs> [, <inc-attr> [, <req-attr>]]]])	List the contents of a directory.
SElib.fullpath(<path-spec>)	Work out an absolute path within the file-system.
SElib.interpret(<code> [, <interpret-flags> [, <error-string>]])	Interpret the string as if it were JavaScript code. This is more powerful and flexible than the JavaScript eval function however. Refer to the Nombas manual for full details.
SElib.compile(<script> [, <isFile>])	Compile a script and store it into a file as a pre-compiled script object. The <script> parameter may be source script or a file name where the script is already saved. Set the <isFile> value true if it is a file. The result is a buffer object.
SElib.spawn(<mode>, <exec-spec> [, <arg1> [, <arg2> [,...]]])	Create a child process to run some other activity in the machine. There are various options that allow the child process to run on its own or overlay the parent. These are somewhat operating system dependant in their availability and operation.

Method/Property	Description
SElib.splitFileName (<file-spec>)	This breaks a file specification into component parts so you can access the directory, name and extension type.
SElib.suspend(<delay>)	This holds up execution for a short while. The accuracy of the delay may depend on the accuracy of timing functions in the underlying operating system. The delay value is measured in milliseconds.
SElib.multiTask (<logical-expression>)	Provided to allow multitasking to be turned on and off. Use this facility with great care. Refer to the Nombas manual for details. Only available in 16 bit Windows.
SElib.instance()	Return the instance of this ScriptEase session for when multiple instances are running. Only available in 32 bit Windows.
SElib.Eset(<file-spec>)	Write the environment variables to a file. Only available in 32 bit Windows and OS/2.
SElib.interpretInNewThread (<file-name>, <source-text>)	Run scripts within a multiple threaded environment. Thread safe programming techniques need to take account of the fact that processes share many resources with one another and you can compromise the activity of another thread inadvertently. For example, the number of file buffers available to a process are shared amongst all threads in that process. ScriptEase provides some protection but you will need to synchronize the threads yourself. Only available in 32 bit Windows and OS/2.

SElib - Hardware Port Access Functions

The following functions are only applicable in OS/2, DOS and Windows 3.x systems; they allow you to read and write data to hardware ports:

Method/Property	Description
SElib.inport(<port>)	Read a byte from an input port.
SElib.inportw(<port>)	Read a word from an input port.
SElib.outport(<port>, <value>)	Write a byte to an output port.
SElib.outportw(<port>, <value>)	Write a word to an output port.

SElib - Windows UI Access Functions

There are a collection of very platform specific window access routines that are different for every system. This applies by and large to the Windows and OS/2 environments only. Syntactically, the API calls are different on each platform and in some cases the function names themselves are also different. You will need to consult the documentation that covers your platform for more details. These functions provide a way to create and destroy windows, attach ScriptEase functions to the message manager and access DLL code. Although these won't be relevant to using the SE:WSE interpreter, they will be helpful in SE:DT.

The Screen object

Access to a character cell terminal screen is effected through the Screen object. This object supports the following methods and properties:

Method/Property	Description
clear()	Clears the display.
cursor([<col> [,<row>]])	Returns the current cursor position.
handle()	Returns the window handle of a ScriptEase screen.
setBackground(<color> | <r>, <g>, <b>)	Set the color for the text background.
setForeground(<color> | <r>, <g>, <b>)	Set the color for the text foreground.
size([<col> [,<row>]])	Returns the screen size.
write(<data>)	Write some data to the screen.
writeln(<data>)	Write some data to the screen and automatically add a new line at the end.

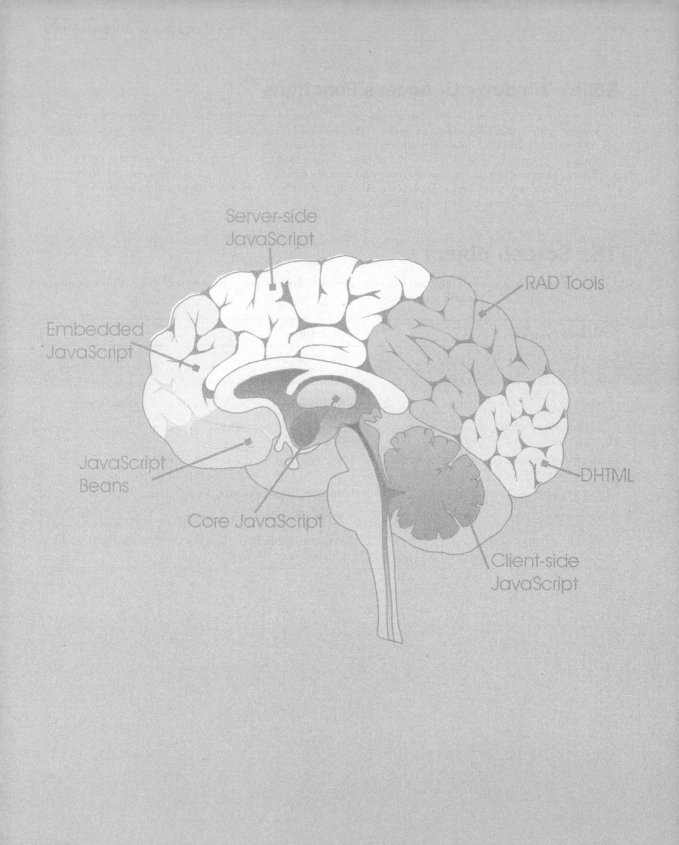

JavaScript Bean Tag Reference

A JavaScript Bean (JSB) file defines a single component. This file contains plain text that can be parsed according to SGML rules. Because a JSB file is in plain text format, you can create it with any editor capable of producing unformatted text. JavaScript components must also contain a constructor function to initialize the component and define the actual code for the components methods and events.

As with HTML tags, the tags used to define the JSB are enclosed in angled brackets and may contain attributes. Most JSB tags have attributes that provide unique tag information. The names you assign to attributes must be unique throughout a JSB file and should not duplicate JavaScript or JSB reserved words.

The <JSB> and </JSB> tags identify the beginning and ending of a component. Typically, the skeleton of a JSB file looks like the following:

```
<JSB>
    <JSB_DESCRIPTOR ...>
    <JSB_ICON...>
    <JSB_PROPERTY ...>

    <JSB_EVENT ...>

    <JSB_METHOD ...>
        <JSB_PARAMETER ...>
    </JSB_METHOD>

    <JSB_CONSTRUCTOR ...>
    </JSB_CONSTRUCTOR>
</JSB>
```

<JSB_DESCRIPTOR>

The first tag embedded in a component definition is the <JSB_DESCRIPTOR>. This tag is used to identify the component, its environment type, display name, and descriptions used for the component.

CUSTOMIZER attribute

Usage: Optional
Default Value: (none)
Description: Specifies a Java class used to customize the component.
For example:

```
CUSTOMIZER="packagename.packageclass"
```

Notes:

❑ `packagename` is the name of the Java package to use.

❑ `packageclass` is the name of the class to use for customizing the JavaScript component.

DISPLAYNAME attribute

Usage: Required
Default Value: (none)
Description: Specifies a name for the component that can be used for display purposes.
For example:

```
DISPLAYNAME="componentclassname"
```

Notes: If this attribute is not provided, it is assigned the value of the NAME attribute.

ENV attribute

Usage: Optional
Default Value: `either`
Description: Specifies the environment where the component runs.
For example:

```
ENV="value"
```

Notes: `value` can be one of the values in the following:

❑ **`client`**: The component instance will execute on the client. If you set the ENV to `client` then when the JSB file is processed, its code is automatically placed within `<SCRIPT>` tags in the HTML document.

❑ **`server`**: The component instance will execute on the server. If you set the ENV to `server` then when the JSB file is processed, its code is automatically placed within `<SERVER>` tags in the HTML document. For any component that can run on the server, you must create a separate `.js` file on the server that defines the components constructor function, and point to that file in the SRC attribute of the `<JSB_CONSTRUCTOR>` tag.

❑ **`either`**: (default) The application developer will decide where execution should occur.

❑ **`both`**: Two instances of the component will be created, one on the client and one on the server. If this setting is specified, then each property and method defined for the component must specify individual ENV attributes to specify where they are instantiated at run time.

EVENTMODEL attribute

Usage: Optional
Default Value: JS
Description: Specifies which event model is used by this component.
For example:

```
EVENTMODEL="model"
```

Notes: model can take the following values:

- ❑ **JS**: A method body is created by VJS and assigned to the Java Script object.
- ❑ **AWT11**: Add and remove listener methods are used at run time to connect components.
- ❑ **HTML**: Permits connection to HTML built-in objects (e.g., form elements).

If EVENTMODEL is omitted in <JSB_DESCRIPTOR>, you must supply a separate EVENTMODEL attribute for each event and property that uses an event.

HELP_URL attribute

Usage: Optional
Default Value: (none)
Description: Specifies a string containing a valid URL for a page containing the help info for a component. Visual JavaScript developers can view this page by choosing **More Info** from the VJS menu.
For example:

```
HELP_URL="uniformresourcelocator"
HELP_URL="$INSTALLDIRuniformresourcelocator"
```

Notes:

- ❑ uniformresourcelocator is a valid URL for the help page,
- ❑ $INSTALLDIR is a string literal, that, if present, requires that the help page be located in a directory relative to the installation directory.
- ❑ A URL that is not stored relative to the install directory can start with http:// or file:///. Use http:// when a user is connected to the Internet and the help file resides remotely on an Internet server. Use file:/// for a local help file that resides on the user's machine.

ISHIDDEN attribute

Usage: Optional
Default Value: (none)
Description: Specifies to a component development tool, such as VJS, that a component should not be visible in a WYSIWYG view of the application page where the component resides.
For example:

```
ISHIDDEN
```

Notes:

- ❑ This attribute is not assigned a value. It is the existence of this attribute that causes it to be in effect.
- ❑ If omitted, the component is displayed. If present, the component is not displayed in a WYSIWYG view.

NAME attribute

Usage: Required
Default Value: (none)
Description: Specifies the unique identifier for the component.
For example:

```
NAME="packagename.componentname"
```

Notes:

- ❑ `packagename` is the name of the package containing the component.

- ❑ `componentname` is the unique name of a component in the specified package.

- ❑ The `NAME` attribute of the `<JSB_DESCRIPTOR>` tag is used to generate the default ID of each instance of the component.

NEEDSFORM attribute

Usage: Optional
Default Value: (none)
Description: Indicates that a component must be placed in a form on an HTML page, and instructs Visual JavaScript to create a form for the component if necessary.
For example:

```
NEEDSFORM
```

Notes: This attribute is not assigned a value. It is the existence of this attribute that causes it to be in effect.

SHORTDESCRIPTION attribute

Usage: Optional
Default Value: (none)
Description: Provides a brief description of the component class that is displayed in the development tool's Tool Tips.
For example:

```
SHORTDESCRIPTION="tiptext"
```

VISUAL attribute

Usage: Optional
Default Value: (none)
Description: Specifies the name of a class used to provide the design time visual appearance of a component.
For example:

```
VISUAL="packagename.packageclass"
```

Notes:

- ❑ `packagename` is the name of the Java package to use.

- ❑ `packageclass` is the name of the class to use for providing the components design time appearance. Instances of this class are passed to the engine for Layout view. In Visual JavaScript, `packageclass` must be one of `HTMLFlowable`, `HTMLContextMenu`, `ActionListener`, or `RemovablePropertyChangeListener`.

Icon Descriptor <JSB_ICON>

A component definition can include an optional <JSB_ICON> tag that defines icon information for the component, including the name of the file that contains the GIF for the component.

ICONNAME attribute

Usage: Optional
Default Value: (none)
Description: Specifies the name of a class used to provide the design time visual appearance of a component.
For example:

```
ICONNAME= "filename"
```

Notes:

❑   filename is a standard file name that can include an optional extension.

❑   The GIF file specified is expected to be 16 x 16 pixel color GIF.

❑   Since some development tools require a 16 x 16 pixel image while others, such as Visual JavaScript, require both a 16 x 16 and a 32 x 32 pixel image. The ICONNAME attribute is used to determine the 32x32 pixel image, if needed. . The 32 x 32 pixel files name is assumed to be the same as the filename provided, except it will have 32 appended. For example, if ICONNAME is assigned the string value jsbicon.gif, then the 32 x 32 pixel file will be assumed to have the name jsbicon32.gif.

❑   Only one icon file can be specified per JavaScript Bean component.

Property Descriptors <JSB_PROPERTY>

The <JSB_PROPERTY> property descriptor tag is used to define a property in the JSB file. This descriptor tag defines the property's name and data type. It can optionally specify a property editor class, and the Get and Set methods that enable an application to retrieve and set the property's value. If the Get and Set methods are specified for a property, the JSB file must also contain the corresponding method descriptors for those methods.

DEFAULTVALUE attribute

Usage: Optional
Default Value: (none)
Description: Provides a default value for a property if no other value is assigned
For example:

```
DEFAULTVALUE="value"
```

Notes: value represents any valid JavaScript data type or fully qualified Java class.

DESIGNTIMEREADONLY attribute

Usage: Optional
Default Value: (none)
Description: Indicates that at design time the value of this property can be examined, but cannot be at runtime.
For example:

```
DESIGNTIMEREADONLY
```

Notes: This attribute is not assigned a value. It is the existence of this attribute that causes it to be in effect.

DISPLAYNAME attribute

Usage: Required
Default Value: (none)
Description: Specifies a name for the property that can be used for display purposes.
For example:

```
DISPLAYNAME="propertyname"
```

Notes: If this attribute is not provided, it is assigned the value of the NAME attribute.

ENV attribute

Usage: Optional
Default Value: either
Description: Specifies the environment where the application can set or retrieve a property's value.
For example:

```
ENV="value"
```

Notes: Specifying ENV is only meaningful if the component descriptors ENV attribute was set to both. value can be one of the following values:

❑ **client**: the property value is set and retrieved on an instance of the component found on the client.

❑ **server**: the property value is set and retrieved on an instance of the component found on the server.

❑ **both**: (default) the property value is set and retrieved on an instances of the component found on both the client and the server.

EVENTMODEL attribute

Usage: Required if a global EVENTMODEL is not specified in the <JSB_DESCRIPTOR> tag, or if the event model used by this property overrides the globally assigned event model.
Default Value: JS
Description: Specifies which event model is used by this property.
For example:

```
EVENTMODEL="model"
```

Notes: If EVENTMODEL is omitted in <JSB_DESCRIPTOR>, you must supply a separate EVENTMODEL attribute for each event and property that uses an event. It can take the following values:

❑ **JS**: A method body is created by VJS and assigned to the Java Script object.

❑ **AWT11**: Add and remove listener methods are used at run time to connect components.

❑ **HTML**: Permits connection to HTML built-in objects (e.g., form elements).

ISBOUND attribute

Usage: Optional
Default Value: (none)
Description: Specifies that an onChange event is thrown when a property's value is changed.
For example:
    ISBOUND

Notes: This attribute is not assigned a value. It is the existence of this attribute that causes it to be in effect.

ISDEFAULT attribute

Usage: Optional
Default Value (none)
Description: Indicates that this property is the default property of the component.
For example:
    ISDEFAULT

Notes:

❑ This attribute is not assigned a value. It is the existence of this attribute that causes it to be in effect.

❑ If ISDEFAULT is omitted for all component properties, the first property listed in the JSB file automatically becomes the default property. If more than one property is assigned the ISDEFAULT attribute, the first property with this attribute becomes the default, and all other ISDEFAULT attributes for properties are ignored.

ISEXPERT attribute

Usage: Optional
Default Value: (none)
Description: Indicates that this property should not be displayed by the component inspector.
For example:
    ISEXPERT

Notes: This attribute is not assigned a value. It is the existence of this attribute that causes it to be in effect.

NAME attribute

Usage: Required
Default Value: (none)
Description: Specifies the unique identifier for the property.
For example:
    NAME="propname"

Notes: propname is a unique property name within the component.

PROPERTYEDITOR attribute

Usage: Optional
Default Value: (none)
Description: Specifies the Java class the development tools inspector uses to edit the property's value.
For example:

```
PROPERTYEDITOR="packagename.classname"
```

Notes:

❑　packagename is the name of the package containing the property editor

❑　componentname is the unique name of the editor within the specified package.

PROPTYPE attribute

Usage: Optional
Default Value: (none)
Description: Determines how a property is stored in the HTML document, and how the property is treated if it is a bound property.
For example:

```
PROPTYPE="value"
```

where value is one of:

Notes: PROPTYPE takes one of the following values:

❑　JS: Stores a property using JavaScript inside a <SCRIPT> tag to form a parameter object that is passed to the constructor.

❑　TagAttribute: Stores a property in the HTML document as an attribute of the property tag.

❑　HTML: Indicates that a property is accessed exclusively through Get and Set methods, like a JavaBeans component.

READMETHOD attribute

Usage: Optional
Default Value: (none)
Description: Specifies the name of the Get method used to retrieve the value of the property at run time.
For example:

```
READMETHOD="methodname"
```

Notes:

❑　The return value of the specified Get method must correspond to the property's TYPE attribute.

❑　methodname must correspond to the name of a <JSB_METHOD> tag defined elsewhere in the JSB file.

RUNTIMEACCESS attribute

Usage: Optional
Default Value: (none)
Description: Specifies the runtime access for a property.
For example:
```
RUNTIMEACCESS="accesstype"
```

Notes: accesstype takes one of the following values:

- ❑ FULL: Property is read and write accessible. This is the default for a property if RUNTIMEACCESS is not specified.

- ❑ READONLY: Property is read only at run time, and is not available for property connections at design time.

- ❑ NONE: Property is not accessible at run time, and is not available for property connections at design time.

SHORTDESCRIPTION attribute

Usage: Optional
Default Value: (none)
Description: Provides a brief description of the property when displayed in the development tool's Tool Tips.
For example:
```
SHORTDESCRIPTION="tiptext"
```

TYPE attribute

Usage: Required
Default Value: (none)
Description: Defines the data type of the value stored in the property.
For example:
```
TYPE="datatype"
```

Notes: datatype may be a JavaScript data type, a primitive Java data type, or the fully qualified package name of a Java class that describes a data type.

WRITEMETHOD attribute

Usage: Optional
Default Value: (none)
Description: Specifies the name of the Set method used to set the value of the property at runtime.
For example:
```
WRITEMETHOD="methodname"
```

Notes: methodname should contain the name of a <JSB_METHOD> tag defined elsewhere in the JSB file. This tag should define a set method with a single parameter that corresponds to the property's data type.

VALUESET attribute

Usage: Optional
Default Value: (none)
Description: Specifies a range of allowed values for the property.
For example:

```
VALUESET="range"
```

Notes:

❏   `range` should hold a string containing a list of possible values.

❏   Because `VALUESET` is a string, the property editor must be able to parse values in the string. The interpretation of the string depends upon the data type of the property:

❏   For string properties, the `VALUESET` should be a comma-delimited list of strings. For numeric properties, `VALUESET` can be a comma delimited list of values or ranges, where a range follows a `min:max` pattern.

<JSB_METHOD>

Methods are functions that execute within a component. Unlike properties, which can be set at either design time or at runtime, a method can only be executed at runtime. Any data that a method acts upon is supplied by either the calling routine as a parameter or from a property previously set in the object. To create a method, use the `<JSB_METHOD>` and `</JSB_METHOD>` descriptor tags. This tag pair will define what function will execute when that method is called, its the type of data it will return, if any, and any arguments it might take. The method should have some function defined with the same name, typically contained within the JSB constructor. When the method is called, it is this function which is executed.

DISPLAYNAME attribute

Usage: Required
Default Value: (none)
Description: Specifies a name for the method that can be used for display purposes.
For example:

```
DISPLAYNAME="methodname"
```

Notes: If this attribute is not provided, it is assigned the value of the `NAME` attribute.

ENV attribute

Usage: Optional
Default Value: `either`
Description: Specifies the environment where the where the method resides.
For example:

```
ENV="value"
```

Notes: Specifying ENV is only meaningful if the component descriptors ENV attribute was set to both. value can be one of the following values:

❑ **client**: the property value is set and retrieved on an instance of the component found on the client.

❑ **server**: the property value is set and retrieved on an instance of the component found on the server.

❑ **both**: (default) the property value is set and retrieved on an instances of the component found on both the client and the server.

ISEXPERT attribute

Usage: Optional
Default Value: (none)
Description: Indicates that this method should not be displayed by the component inspector.
For example:
    ISEXPERT

Notes: This attribute is not assigned a value. It is the existence of this attribute that causes it to be in effect.

NAME attribute

Usage: Required
Default Value: (none)
Description: Specifies the unique identifier for the method.
For example:
    NAME="methodname"

Notes: methodname is a unique property name within the component.

SHORTDESCRIPTION attribute

Usage: Optional
Default Value: (none)
Description: Provides a brief description of the method when displayed in the development tool's Tool Tips.
For example:
    SHORTDESCRIPTION="tiptext"

TYPE attribute

Usage: Required
Default Value: (none)
Description: Defines the data type of the return value of the method.
For example:
    TYPE="datatype"

Notes: datatype may be a JavaScript data type, a primitive Java data type, or the fully qualified package name of a Java class that describes a data type.

<JSB_EVENT>

Events are triggered when a certain condition occurs within a component. When an event is thrown, an event handler method may be executed. The <JSB_EVENT> event set descriptor tag specifies the name of the event, the event model to which the event conforms, and, depending on the specified event model, a listener type parameter that specifies the name of the interface used by the component.

ADDLISTENERMETHOD attribute

Usage: Required for the AWT11 event model if the listener methods belong to another object, optional otherwise.
Default Value: (none)
Description: Specifies the name of the method used to add a listener method for the event.
For example:

    ADDLISTENERMETHOD= "addMethod"

Notes: addMethod should contain the name of the method that adds a listener method for the event.

DISPLAYNAME attribute

Usage: Required
Default Value: (none)
Description: Specifies a name for the event that can be used for display purposes.
For example:

    DISPLAYNAME="eventname"

Notes: If this attribute is not provided, it is assigned the value of the NAME attribute.

EVENTMODEL attribute

Usage: Required if a global EVENTMODEL is not specified in the <JSB_DESCRIPTOR> tag, or if the event model used by this property overrides the globally assigned event model.
Default Value: JS
Description: Specifies which event model is used by this property.
For example:

    EVENTMODEL="model"

Notes: If EVENTMODEL is omitted in <JSB_DESCRIPTOR>, you must supply a separate EVENTMODEL attribute for each event and property that uses an event. It can take the following values:

- ❑ **JS**: A method body is created by VJS and assigned to the Java Script object.
- ❑ **AWT11**: Add and remove listener methods are used at run time to connect components.
- ❑ **HTML**: Permits connection to HTML built-in objects (e.g., form elements).

ISDEFAULT attribute

Usage: Optional
Default Value (none)
Description: Indicates that this event is the default event of the component.
For example:

    ISDEFAULT

Notes:

❑ This attribute is not assigned a value. It is the existence of this attribute that causes it to be in effect.

❑ If ISDEFAULT is omitted for all component events, the first event listed in the JSB file automatically becomes the default event. If more than one event is assigned the ISDEFAULT attribute, the first event with this attribute becomes the default, and all other ISDEFAULT attributes for events are ignored.

ISEXPERT attribute

Usage: Optional
Default Value: (none)
Description: Indicates that this event should not be displayed by the component inspector.
For example:
```
ISEXPERT
```

Notes: This attribute is not assigned a value. It is the existence of this attribute that causes it to be in effect.

LISTENERTYPE attribute

Usage: Required for the AWT11 event model, optional otherwise
Default Value: (none)
Description: Specifies the name of the Java package and class that implements the listener interface that must be supported by the receiving object.
For example:
```
LISTENERTYPE="eventListener"
```

Notes: eventListener should contain the name of a <JSB_INTERFACE> tag which in turn specifies the event listener interface.

NAME attribute

Usage: Required
Default Value: (none)
Description: Specifies the unique identifier for the method.
For example:
```
NAME="eventname"
```

Notes: eventname is a unique property name within the component.

REMOVELISTENERMETHOD attribute

Usage: Required for the AWT11 event model, optional otherwise
Default Value: (none)
Description: Specifies the name of a method used to remove a listener method for the event.
For example:
```
REMOVELISTENERMETHOD="deleteMethod"
```

Notes: deleteMethod contains the name of the method that deletes a listener method from the event.

SHORTDESCRIPTION attribute

Usage: Optional
Default Value: (none)
Description: Provides a brief description of the event when displayed in the development tool's Tool Tips.
For example:

```
SHORTDESCRIPTION="tiptext"
```

<JSB_PARAMETER>

Defines a parameter for a method belonging to the component. Parameter tags are always embedded within `<JSB_METHOD>` tags in a JSB file. `<JSB_PARAMETER>` is primarily modeled on the JavaBeans `ParameterDescriptor` object.

DISPLAYNAME attribute

Usage: Required
Default Value: (none)
Description: Specifies a name for the parameter that can be used for display purposes.
For example:

```
DISPLAYNAME="paramname"
```

Notes: `paramname` contains the unique parameter name for the method. If this attribute is not provided, it is assigned the value of the `NAME` attribute.

SHORTDESCRIPTION attribute

Usage: Optional
Default Value: (none)
Description: Provides a brief description of the parameter when displayed in the development tool's Tool Tips.
For example:

```
SHORTDESCRIPTION="tiptext"
```

TYPE attribute

Usage: Required
Default Value: (none)
Description: Defines the data type of the return value of the method.
For example:

```
TYPE="datatype"
```

Notes: `datatype` may contain a JavaScript data type, a primitive Java data type, or the fully qualified package name of a Java class that describes a data type.

<JSB_CONSTRUCTOR>

The constructor tag is used to define the component's functions used for its methods and is used to create an instance of the component at runtime. All JavaScript components must have a constructor definition, or must point to an external .js file on a server that provides the definition. A script must, at a minimum, define a function that matches the NAME attribute of the <JSB_DESCRIPTOR> tag, except that embedded dots in NAME must be replaced by underscores in the function definition. The constructor is identified by the <JSB_CONSTRUCTOR> and </JSB_CONSTRUCTOR> tag pair enclose the JavaScript code.

SRC attribute

Usage: Required for a component that can be created on the server or the client – that is, when JSB_DESCRIPTOR ENV="either"; optional otherwise
Default Value: (none)
Description: Specifies the .js file containing the script used to construct a component.
For example:

    SRC="filename"

Notes:

❑   filename should contain the name of the .js file containing the constructor script for the component.

❑   The script in the .js file must compile in the server environment. It must reside in the root of the package hierarchy.

❑   If you specify the SRC attribute, then the body of the constructor in the JSB file must be empty.

<JSB_INTERFACE>

The <JSB_INTERFACE> tag describes the interface information a component returns to an external object that implements the actual interface. Using an external object to handle events enables sharing of event handlers across JavaScript components

NAME attribute

Usage: Required
Default Value: (none)
Description: Specifies the unique identifier for the interface class.
For example:

    NAME="eventname""packagename.class"

Notes:

❑   packagename is the fully qualified package name containing the interface class.

❑   class is the name of the interface in the package.

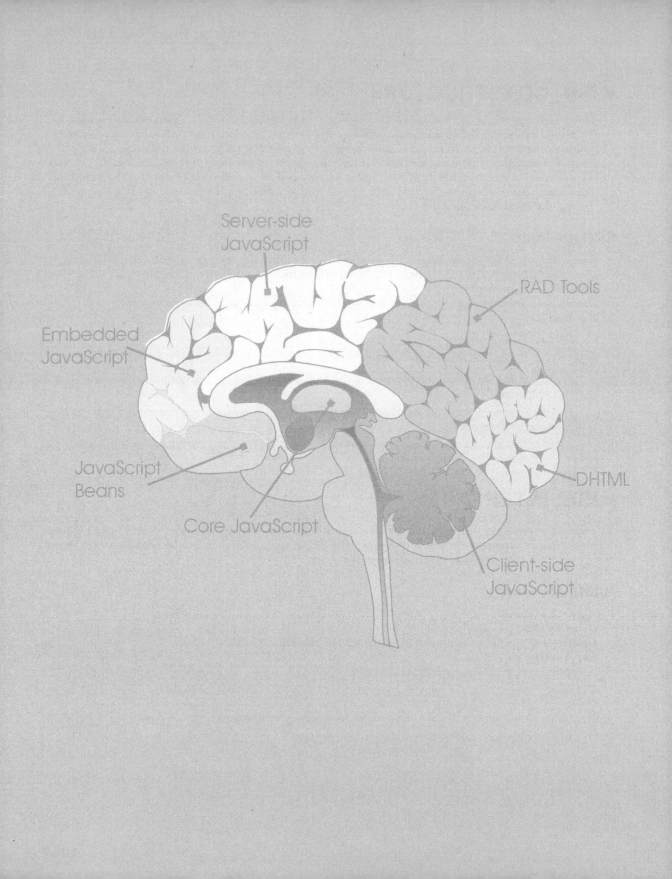

HTTP Request and Response

The Hypertext Transfer Protocol (HTTP) is an application-level protocol for distributed hypermedia information systems. It is a generic, stateless protocol, which can be used for many tasks beyond its use for hypertext. A feature of HTTP is the typing and negotiation of data representation, allowing systems to be built independently of the data being transferred.

The first version of HTTP, referred to as HTTP/0.9, was a simple protocol for raw data transfer across the Internet. HTTP/1.0, as defined by RFC 1945 improved the protocol by allowing messages to be in a MIME-like format, containing meta-information about the data transferred and modifiers on the request/response semantics. The current version HTTP/1.1, first defined in RFC 2068 and more recently in RFC 2616, made performance improvements by making all connections persistent and supporting absolute URLs in requests.

URL Request Protocols

A URL is a pointer to a particular resource on the Internet at a particular location and has a standard format as follows:

```
Protocol Servername Filepath
```

In order, the three elements are the protocol used to access the server, the name of the server and the location of the resource on the server. For example:

```
http://www.mydomain.com/
https://www.mydomain.com:8080/
ftp://ftp.mydomain.com/example.txt
mailto:me@world.com
file:///c:|Windows/win.exe
```

The `servername` and `filepath` pieces of the URL are totally dependent on where files are stored on your server and what you have called it, but there are a standard collection of protocols, most of which you should be familiar with:

- ❑ `http`: Normal HTTP requests for documents.
- ❑ `https`: Secure HTTP requests. The specific behavior of these depends on the security certificates and encryption keys you have set up.
- ❑ `JavaScript`: Executes JavaScript code within the current document.
- ❑ `ftp`: Retrieves documents from an FTP (File Transfer Protocol) server.
- ❑ `file`: Loads a file stored on the local (Client) machine. It can refer to remote servers but specifies no particular access protocol to remote file systems.
- ❑ `news`: Used to access Usenet newsgroups for articles.
- ❑ `nntp`: More sophisticated access to news servers.
- ❑ `mailto`: Allows mail to be sent from the browser. It may call in assistance from a helper app.
- ❑ `telnet`: Opens an interactive session with the server.
- ❑ `gopher`: A precursor to the World Wide Web.

This book exclusively deals with the first five of these.

HTTP Basics

Each HTTP client (web browser) request and server response has three parts: the request or response line, a header section and the entity body.

Client Request

The client initiates a web page transaction – client page request and server page response – as follows.

The client connects to an HTTP-based server at a designated port (by default, 80) and sends a request by specifying an HTTP command called a method, followed by a document address, and an HTTP version number. The format of the request line is:

```
Method          Request-URI     Protocol
```

For example,

```
GET    /index.html    HTTP/1.0
```

uses the `GET` method to request the document `/index.html` using version 1.0 of the protocol. We'll come to a full list of HTTP Request Methods later.

Next, the client sends optional header information to the server about its configuration and the document formats it will accept. All header information is sent line by line, each with a header name and value in the form:

```
Keyword: Value
```

For example:

```
User-Agent:     Lynx/2.4 libwww/5.1k
Accept:         image/gif, image/x-xbitmap, image/jpeg, */*
```

The request line and the subsequent header lines are all terminated by a carriage return/linefeed (\r\n) sequence. The client sends a blank line to end the headers. We'll return with a full description of each HTTP Header value later on in the Appendix.

Finally, after sending the request and headers the client may send additional data. This data is mostly used by CGI programs using the POST method. This additional information is called a request entity. Finally a blank line (\r\n\r\n) terminates the request. A complete request might look like the following:

```
GET /index.html HTTP/1.0
Accept: */*
Connection: Keep-Alive
Host: www.w3.org
User-Agent: Generic
```

HTTP Request Methods

HTTP request methods should not be confused with URL protocols. The former are used to instruct a web server how to handle the incoming request while the latter defines how client and server talk to each other. In version 1.1 of the HTTP protocol, there are seven basic HTTP request methods:

Method	Description
OPTIONS	Used to query a server about the capabilities it provides. Queries can be general or specific to a particular resource.
GET	Asks that the server return the body of the document identified in the Request-URI.
HEAD	Responds similarly to a GET, except that no content body is ever returned. It is a way of checking whether a document has been updated since the last request.
POST	This is used to transfer a block of data to the server in the content body of the request.
PUT	This is the complement of a GET request and stores the content body at the location specified by the Request-URI. It is similar to uploading a file with FTP.
DELETE	Provides a way to delete a document from the server. The document to be deleted is indicated in the Request-URI.
TRACE	This is used to track the path of a request through firewalls and multiple proxy servers. It is useful for debugging complex network problems and is similar to the traceroute tool.

Server Response

The HTTP response also contains 3 parts.

Firstly, the server replies with the status line containing three fields: the HTTP version, status code and description of status code, in the following format.

```
Protocol    Status-code    Description
```

For example, the status line:

```
HTTP/1.0    200    OK
```

indicates that the server uses version 1.0 of the HTTP in its response. A status code of 200 means that the client request was successful.

After the response line, the server sends header information to the client about itself and the requested document. All header information is sent line by line, each with a header name and value in the form:

```
Keyword: Value
```

For example:

```
HTTP/1.1 200 OK
Date: Wed, 19 May 1999 18:20:56 GMT
Server: Apache/1.3.6 (Unix) PHP/3.0.7
Last-Modified: Mon, 17 May 1999 15:46:21 GMT
ETag: "2da0dc-2870-374039cd"
Accept-Ranges: bytes
Content-Length: 10352
Connection: close
Content-Type: text/html; charset=iso-8859-1
```

The response line and the subsequent header lines are all terminated by a carriage return/linefeed (\r\n) sequence. The server sends a blank line to end the headers. Again, we'll return to the exact meaning of these HTTP headers in a minute.

If the client's request if successful, the requested data is sent. This data may be a copy of a file, or the response from a CGI program. This result is called a **response entity**. If the client's request could not be fulfilled, additional data sent might be a human-readable explanation of why the server could not fulfill the request. The properties (type and length) of this data are sent in the headers. Finally a blank line (\r\n\r\n) terminates the response. A complete response might look like the following:

```
HTTP/1.1 200 OK
Date: Wed, 19 May 1999 18:20:56 GMT
Server: Apache/1.3.6 (Unix) PHP/3.0.7
Last-Modified: Mon, 17 May 1999 15:46:21 GMT
ETag: "2da0dc-2870-374039cd"
Accept-Ranges: bytes
Content-Length: 10352
Connection: close
Content-Type: text/html; charset=iso-8859-1
```

```
<!DOCTYPE HTML PUBLIC "-//W3C//DTD HTML 4.0 Transitional//EN"
"http://www.w3.org/TR/REC-html40/loose.dtd">
<html>

   ...

</html>
```

In HTTP/1.0, after the server has finished sending the response, it disconnects from the client and the transaction is over unless the client sends a `Connection: KeepAlive` header. In HTTP/1.1, however, the connection is maintained so that the client can make additional requests, unless the client sends an explicit `Connection: Close` header. Since many HTML documents embed other documents as inline images, applets and frames, for example, this persistent connection feature of HTTP/1.1 protocol will save the overhead of the client having to repeatedly connect to the same server just to retrieve a single page.

HTTP Headers

These headers can appear in requests or responses. Some control how the web server behaves, others are meant for proxy servers and some will affect what your browser does with a response when it is received. You should refer to the HTTP 1.1 specification for a full description. You can download it from:

```
ftp://ftp.isi.edu/in-notes/rfc2616.txt
```

The authentication is covered in a little more detail in:

```
ftp://ftp.isi.edu/in-notes/rfc2617.txt
```

Other RFC documents from the same source may be useful and provide additional insights.

This table summarizes the headers you'll find most helpful. There are others in the specification but they control how the web server manages the requests and won't arrive in the CGI environment for you to access:

Header	Request	Response	Description
Accept:	✓		Lists the types that the client can cope with.
Accept-Charset:	✓		Lists the character sets that the browser can cope with.
Accept-Encoding:	✓		List of acceptable encodings or none. Omitting this header signifies that all current encodings are acceptable.
Accept-Language:	✓		List of acceptable languages.

Table Continued on Following Page

1063

Header	Request	Response	Description
Age		✓	A cache control header used to indicate the age of a response body.
Allow:		✓	Determines the available methods that the resource identified by the URI can respond to.
Authorization:	✓		Authorization credentials. Refer to RFC2617 for more information on Digest authentication.
Cache-Control:	✓	✓	A sophisticated proxy-controlling header. Can be used to describe how proxies should handle requests and responses.
Code:	✓		Defines an encoding for the body data. This would normally be Base64.
Content-Base:		✓	Used to resolve relative URLs within the body of the document being returned. It overrides the value in the Content-Location header.
Content-Encoding:		✓	Specifies encodings that have been applied to the body prior to transmission.
Content-Language:		✓	This specifies the natural language of the response content.
Content-Length:		✓	The length of the body measured in bytes should be put here. CGI responses may defer to the web server and allow it to put this header in.
Content-Location:		✓	The actual location of the entity being returned in the response. This may be useful when deploying resources that can be resolved in several ways. The specifically selected version can be identified and requested directly.
Content-MD5:		✓	This is a way of computing a checksum for the entity body. The receiving browser can compare its computed value to be sure that the body has not been modified during transmission.

Header	Request	Response	Description
Content-Type:		✓	The type of data being returned in the response is specified with this header. These types are listed later in this appendix.
Expires:		✓	The date after which the response should be considered to be stale.
From:	✓		The client e-mail address is sent in this header.
Host:	✓		The target virtual host is defined in this header. The value is taken from the originating URL when the request is made.
Last-Modified:		✓	This indicates when the content being returned was last modified. For static files, the web server would use the file's timestamp. For a dynamically generated page, you might prefer to insert a value based on when a database entry was last changed. Other more sophisticated cache control headers are provided in the HTTP specification. Refer to RFC2616 for details.
Location:		✓	Used to redirect to a new location. This could be used as part of a smart error handling CGI.
Referrer:	✓		The source of the current request is indicated here. This would be the page that the request was linked from. You can determine whether the link was from outside your site and also pick up search engine parameters from this too, if your URI was requested via Yahoo, for example.
User-Agent:	✓		This is the signature field of the browser. You can code round limitations in browsers if you know this. Be aware of some of the weird values that can show up in this header now that developers are building their own web browsers and spiders.
Warning:		✓	This is used to carry additional information about the response and whether there are risks associated with it.

Server Environment Variables

By and large, the headers in the request correspond with environment variables that are present when a CGI handler executes. Not all headers make it as far as the CGI environment. Some may be 'eaten up' by a proxy server, others by the target web server. Some environment variables are created as needed by the web server itself, without there having been a header value to convert.

Here is a summary of the environment variables you are likely to find available. There may be others if the web server administrator has configured them into the server or if the CGI adapter has been modified to pass them in. You can access them with the Clib.getenv() function. These are considered to be standard values and they should be present:

(Editor's Note: This list is written with respect to ScriptEase CGI scriptwriters. The server variables are also accessible from ASP as members of the Request.ServerVariables collection. The notes made here also apply to ASP scripts).

AUTH_TYPE

The value in this environment variable depends on the kind of authentication used in the server and whether the script is even security protected by the server. This involves server configuration and is server specific and also protocol specific. The value may not be defined if the page is insecure. If it is secure, the value indicating the type of authentication may only be set after the user is authenticated. An example value for AUTH_TYPE is BASIC.

CONTENT_LENGTH

If the request used the POST method, then it may have supplied additional information in the body. This is passed to the CGI handler on its standard input. However, ScriptEase will assimilate this for you, extract any query strings in the body and decode them into variables that you can access more conveniently.

CONTENT_TYPE

The data type of any content delivered in the body of the request. With this, you could process the standard input for content bodies that are some type other than form data. This is relatively unexplored territory and likely to be very much server and platform dependent. If it works at all, you might choose a reading mechanism based on content type and then use other headers to process the binary data in the body. If you are using this just to upload files, then the HTTP/1.1 protocol now supports a PUT method which is a better technique and is handled inside the server.

DOCUMENT_ROOT

This is the full path to the document root for the web server. If virtual hosts are being used and if they share the same CGI scripts, this document root may be different for each virtual host. It is a good idea to have separately owned cgi-bin directories unless the sites are closely related. For example, a movie site and a games site might have separate cgi-bin directories. Three differently branded versions of the movie site may have different document roots but could share the same cgi-bin functionality. In some servers, this may be a way to identify which one of several virtual hosts is being used.

FROM

If the user has configured their browser appropriately, this environment variable will contain their e-mail address. If it is present, then this is a good way to identify the user, given the assumption that they are the owner of the computer they are using.

GATEWAY_INTERFACE

You can determine the version number of the CGI interface being used. This would be useful if you depend on features available in a later version of the CGI interface but you only want to maintain a single script to be used on several machines.

HTTP_ACCEPT

This is a list of acceptable MIME types that the browser will accept. The values are dependent on the browser being used and how it is configured and are simply passed on by the web server. If you want to be particularly smart and do the right thing, check this value when you try to return any oddball data other than plain text or HTML. The browser doesn't say it can cope, it might just crash on the user when you try and give them some unexpected data.

HTTP_ACCEPT_LANGUAGE

There may not be a value specified in this environment variable. If there is, the list will be as defined by the browser.

HTTP_CONNECTION

This will indicate the disposition of the HTTP connection. It might contain the value "Keep-Alive" or "Close" but you don't really have many options from the ScriptEase:WSE-driven CGI point of view. You might need to know whether the connection to the browser will remain open but since SE:WSE won't currently support streaming tricks it won't matter much either way.

HTTP_COOKIE

The cookie values sent back by the browser are collected together and made available in this environment variable. You will need to make a cookie cutter to separate them out and extract their values. Which particular cookies you receive depend on whereabouts in the site's document root you are and the scope of the cookie when it was created.

HTTP_HOST

On a multiple virtual host web server, this will tell you the host name that was used for the request. You can then adjust the output according to different variations of the sites. For example, you can present different logos and backgrounds for www.mydomain.com and test.mydomain.com. This can help solve a lot of issues when you set up a co-operative branding deal to present your content via several portal sites. They do like to have their logo and corporate image on the page sometimes.

HTTP_PRAGMA

This is somewhat deprecated these days but will likely contain the value "no-cache". Cache control is handled more flexibly with the new response headers available in HTTP/1.1. Caching and proxy server activity can get extremely complex and you may want to study the HTTP specification for more info - ftp://ftp.isi.edu/in-notes/rfc2616.txt

1067

HTTP_REFERER

This is the complete URL for the page that was being displayed in the browser and which contained the link being requested. If the page was a search engine, this may also contain some interesting query information that you could extract to see how people found your web site. There are some situations where there will be no referrer listed. When a user types a URL into a location box, there is no referrer. This may also be true when the link was on a page held in a file on the user's machine. There are some browser dependent issues as well. Some versions of Microsoft Internet Explorer do not report a referrer for HTML documents in framesets. If you have the referrer information it can be useful, but there are enough times when the referrer may be blank that you should have a fall back mechanism in place as well.

HTTP_USER_AGENT

The User Agent is a cute name for the browser. It is necessary because the page may not always be requested by a browser. It could be requested by a robot or so called web spider. It may be requested by offline readers or monitoring services and it's not uncommon for static page generators to be used on a site that was originally designed to be dynamic. Rather than try to cope with all variants of the browsers, you should focus on determining whether you have a browser or robot requesting your documents. That way, you can serve up a page that is more appropriate to a robot when necessary. There is no point in delivering a page that contains an advert, for example. You can make your site attractive to the sight-impaired user community by detecting the use of a text-only browser such as Lynx. You could then serve a graphically sparse but text rich page instead. When examining this value, be aware that there is much weirdness in the values being returned by some browsers. This may be intentional or accidental, but since the Netscape sources were released, developers have been busy writing customized browsers. Some of these will send User-Agent headers containing control characters and binary data. Whether this is an attempt to exploit bugs in web servers, CGI handlers or log analysis software is arguable. You will encounter e-mail addresses, URLs, command line instructions and even entire web pages in this header.

PATH

This is the list of directories that will be searched for commands that you may try and execute from within your CGI handler. It is inherited from the parent environment that spawned the handler. It is platform dependent and certainly applies to UNIX systems. It may not be present on all of the others.

PATH_INFO

This is a way of extracting additional path information from the request. Here is a URL as an example: http://www.domain.com/cgi-bin/path.jsh/folder1/file. This will run the SE:WSE script called path.jsh and store the value /folder1/file in the PATH_INFO environment variable. This can be an additional way of passing parameters from the HTML page into the server-side script.

PATH_TRANSLATED

This is only implemented on some servers and may be implemented under another environment variable name on others. It returns the full physical path to the script being executed. This might be useful if you have shared code that you include into several scripts.

QUERY_STRING

The query string is that text in the URL following a question mark. This environment variable will contain that text. SE:WSE will unwrap it and present the individual items as variables you can access directly.

REMOTE_ADDR

This is the remote IP address of the client machine that initiated the request. You might use this to control what is displayed or to deny access to users outside of your domain.

REMOTE_HOST

It is very likely this value will be empty. It requires the web server to resolve the IP address to a name via the DNS. Whether that would even work depends on the remote user's machine even being listed in a DNS database. It is most often disabled because it imposes significant performance degradation if the web server needs to perform a DNS lookup on every request. You could engineer a local DNS and run that separately, only looking up IP addresses when you need to. Even so, that would still impose a turnaround delay on handling the request and time is definitely of the essence here.

REMOTE_IDENT

This is a deprecated feature. It relies on both the client and server supporting RFC 931 but, since the end user can define the value to be anything they like, the chances of it being useful are quite small. This is probably best avoided altogether and you will be very fortunate if you ever see a meaningful value in it. Of course, in a captive intranet situation where you have more control, you might make use of it.

REMOTE_USER

If the user has been authenticated and has passed the test, the authenticated username will be placed in this variable. Other than that, this variable and AUTH_TYPE are likely to be empty. Even after authentication, this value may be empty when the request is made for a document in a non-secured area.

REQUEST_METHOD

This is the HTTP request method. It is likely you will only ever see GET or POST in here. You usually don't need to deliver different versions of a document based on this value but it might be important to verify that the access was made correctly from your page via the correct method. Apart from the size of the data being larger with a POST, there is another more subtle difference between GET and POST. Using a GET more than once should always result in the same data being returned. Using POST more than once may result in multiple transactions to the back-end. For example, placing an order more than once due to reposting a form. This is one area where the back button on the browser works against you and you may want to interlock this somehow within your session-handling code to prevent duplicate financial transactions happening. You should be aware that this is happening when the browser displays an alert asking whether you want to repost the same form data.

SCRIPT_FILENAME

This is effectively the same as the PATH_TRANSLATED environment variable. It is the full path to the script being executed. Once you have established which of these your server provides (if any), you should be able to stick with it.

SCRIPT_NAME

This is the logical name of the script. It is basically the Request-URI portion of the URL that was originally sent. It is the full path of the script without the document root or script alias mapping. This would be portable across several virtual hosts where the SCRIPT_FILENAME/PATH_TRANSLATED values might not be. This is also useful for making scripts relocatable. You can use this value to rebuild a form so that it will call the same script again. The result is that the script does not then contain a hard coded path that will need to be edited if it is renamed or moved.

SERVER_ADMIN

If it is configured, the e-mail address of the server administrator is held in this environment variable. You could build this into the security mechanisms to alert the administrator when a potential break-in is detected. Be careful not to mailbomb the server administrator with thousands of messages though.

SERVER_NAME

This is the name of the server and may, on some systems, be equivalent to the HTTP_HOST value. This can be useful for manufacturing links elsewhere in a site or detecting the site name so you can build site-specific versions of a page.

SERVER_PORT

The port number that the request arrived on is stored here. Most web sites operate on port 80. Those that don't may be test sites or might operate inside a firewall. It is possible that ancillary servers for adverts and media may use other port numbers if they run on the same machine as the main web server. Most web servers allow you to configure any port number. In the case of the Apache web server you can set up individual virtual hosts on different ports. This means that you could develop a test site and use this value to activate additional debugging help knowing that it would be turned off if the script were run on the production site.

SERVER_PROTOCOL

This is the protocol level of the request being processed. This area is quite ambiguous in the specifications and previously published books. The browser can indicate a preferred protocol level that it can accommodate. This is the value it puts in the request line. However, the server may choose to override that and serve the request with a sub-set of that functionality that conforms to an earlier protocol level. The server configuration may determine a browser match and override it internally or the request may be simple enough that it can be served by HTTP/1.0 protocol even though the browser indicates that it could cope with HTTP/1.1 protocol. From a CGI scripting point of view, it is unlikely you would need to build alternate versions of a page according to this value. It might determine whether you could provide streaming media but that technique is not currently supported by SE:WSE anyway.

SERVER_SOFTWARE

For example, Apache/1.3.6, but dependent on your server.

UNIQUE_ID

This is available in CGI environments running under an Apache web server that has been built with the `unique_id` module included. You could select the first one of these that arrives in a session, and use it as the session key thereafter, as another alternative way of generating unique session keys. It also might provide some useful user-tracking possibilities.

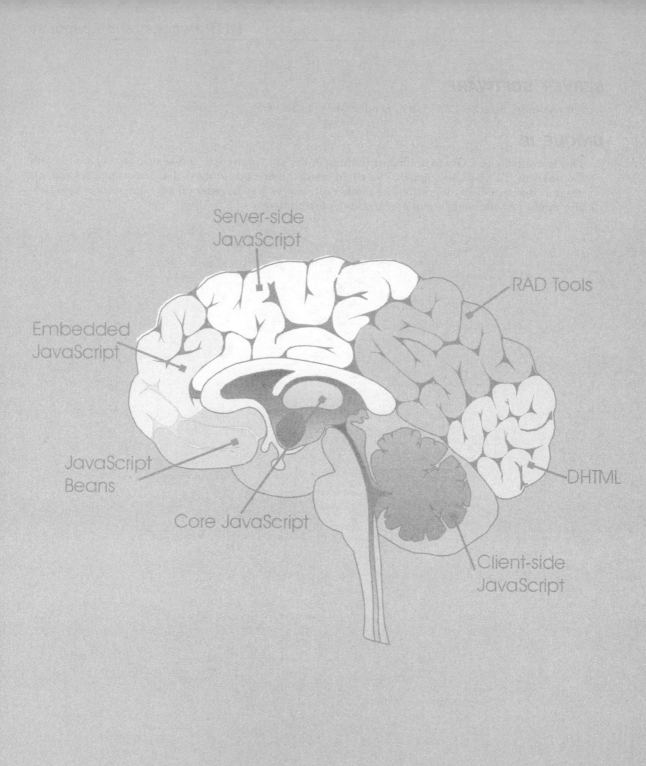

Server-side
JavaScript

RAD Tools

Embedded
JavaScript

JavaScript
Beans

DHTML

Core JavaScript

Client-side
JavaScript

Bibliography

In this appendix, you'll find a complete list of the books and websites mentioned during the book, along with a number of other references you may like to explore in order (even) more on JavaScript.

Wrox Links and Books

Wrox Home Page : http://www.wrox.com
Professional JavaScript homepage:
http://www.wrox.com/Consumer/Store/Details.asp?ISBN=186100270X
Code Download : http://www.wrox.com/Consumer/Store/Download.asp
Errata Page : http://www.wrox.com/Consumer/Forums/Default.asp

JavaScript Objects by Nakhimovsky and Myers (ISBN 1-861001-84-9)
Instant UML by Pierre-Alain Muller (ISBN 1-86100-xx-x)
XML in IE5 Programmer's Reference by Alex Homer (ISBN 1-861001-57-6)
Instant Netscape DHTML Programmer's Reference by Homer et al. (ISBN 1-861001-19-3)
IE5 DHTML Programmer's Reference by Homer et al., ISBN 1-861001-74-6
Professional IE4 Programming by Enfield et al. (ISBN 1-861000-70-7)
Beginning Java 2 by Ivor Horton (ISBN 1-861002-23-8)
Professional Java Server Programming by Patzer et al (ISBN 1-861002-77-7)
Professional Web Site Optimization by Ware et al (ISBN: 1-861000-74-X)
Windows Script Host Programmer's Reference by Dino Esposito (ISBN: 1-861002-65-3)

Product Download Links

Internet Explorer : http://www.microsoft.com/downloads/search.asp?
Netscape Navigator : http://www.netscape.com/computing/download/
Netscape Enterprise Server : http://www.iplanet.com/downloads/testdrive/
Netscape Directory Server : http://www.iplanet.com/downloads/testdrive/
ScriptEase : WebServer Edition : http://www.nombas.com/us/download/
ScriptEase : Desktop : http://www.nombas.com/us/download/
Mozilla : http://www.mozilla.org
Opera : http://www.opera.com
NeoPlanet : http://www.neoplanet.com
The Be Browser: http://www.be.com.
The Ant Browser: http://www.ant.co.uk
Macromedia (ShockWave/Flash): http://www.macromedia.com
SSJSLDAP library download site: http://courses.unt.edu/mewilcox/ldap/
LDAP Java SDK Download: http://devedge.netscape.com/directory
Browscap.ini: http://www.asptracker.com
Microsoft JScript: http://msdn.microsoft.com/scripting/jscript/default.htm
Sun JDK 1.2.2: http://java.sun.com
FESI Homepage: http://home.worldcom.ch/jmlugrin/fesi/.
SATAN: http://www.fish.com/satan/
SAINT: http://wwdsilx.wwdsi.com/saint/
OLEView download page: http://www.microsoft.com/com/resource/oleview.asp
MS Windows Script Host: http://msdn.microsoft.com/scripting/

Web Standards

ECMA Standard : http://www.ecma.ch/stand/ECMA-262.htm
ECMA Components Standard: http://www.ecma.ch/stand/ECMA-290.htm
The Document Object Model Level 1 : http://w3.org/TR/REC-DOM-Level-1.htm
The Unicode Standard : http://www.unicode.org
The HTML 4.0 Standard : http://www.w3.org/TR/REC-html40
Wireless Application Protocol : http://www.wapforum.org/what/technical.htm
The CGI standard: http://hoohoo.ncsa.uiuc.edu/cgi/
The XML Specification v1.0: http://www.w3.org/TR/1998/REC-xml-19980210
HTTP 1.1: ftp://ftp.isi.edu/in-notes/rfc2616.txt
HTTP 1.1 Authentication: ftp://ftp.isi.edu/in-notes/rfc2617.txt
HTTP Media types: ftp://ftp.isi.edu/in-notes/iana/assignments/media-types

Introduction

ECMAScript 262 Standard : http://www.ecma.ch/stand/ECMA-262.htm
The Document Object Model : http://w3.org/TR/REC-DOM-Level-1.htm
ScriptEase : http://www.nombas.com/

Chapter 1

The Unicode Standard : http://www.unicode.org
The Mozilla Group : http://www.mozilla.org
The IEEE : http://www.ieee.org

Chapter 3

More on prototype inheritance
http://www.sunlabs.com/research/self/papers/papers.html
http://developer1.netscape.com:80/docs/manuals/communicator/jsobj/

More on regular expressions
JavaScript Objects by Nakhimovsky and Myers (ISBN 1-861001-84-9)
JavaScript : Definitive Guide by David Flanagan (ISBN 1-56592-392-8)
JavaScript Bible by Danny Goodman (ISBN 0-7645-3188-3)
http://www.asptoday.com/articles/19990330.htm
http://www.microsoft.com/mind/1098/jscript/jscript.htm
http://www.asptoday.com/articles/19990629.htm

Chapter 4

The .HTC file :
http://msdn.microsoft.com/workshop/essentials/versions/IE5behave.asp
The HTML 4.0 Standard : http://www.w3.org/TR/REC-html40
The VBArray Object :
http://msdn.microsoft.com/scripting/jscript/doc/jsobjVBArray.htm
Opera : http://www.opera.com
NeoPlanet : http://www.neoplanet.com
The Be Browser: http://www.be.com.
The Ant Browser: http://www.ant.co.uk
Mozilla : http://www.mozilla.org
The Cryptozilla Organization/Project : http://www.cryptozilla.org
WebTV : http://www.webtv.com
EnReach Technologies : http://www.enreach.com/
Acorn Computers : http://www.acorn.com
Adobe Acrobat : http://www.adobe.com/
Wireless Application Protocol Consortium: http://www.wapforum.org
Yahoo (for browser stats) : http://www.yahoo.com
Browser Statistics : http://www.statmarket.com
The World Wide Web Commission (W3C) : http://www.w3c.org
The Document Object Model : http://w3.org/TR/REC-DOM-Level-1.htm
USENET JavaScript newsgroup: comp.lang.javascript

Chapter 5

Netscape's NetHelp : http://developer.netscape.com/
Microsoft's HTML Help:
http://msdn.microsoft.com/workshop/author/htmlhelp/default.asp
Tooltips using Dynamic HTML :
http://members.aol.com/MHall75819/dhtml/tooltips.html

Chapter 6

More on DHTML Behaviors:
XML in IE5 Programmers Reference by Alex Homer (ISBN 1-861001-57-6)
http://msdn.microsoft.com/workshop/author/behaviors/overview.asp
mouseOver Event Applet: http://www.omegagrafix.com/mouseover/mousover.html
Netscape LiveCache:
http://www.home.it.netscape.com/navigator/v3.0/using/cachesetup.html

Using Java with JavaScript :
`http://developer.java.sun.com/developer/onlineTraining/Programming/JDCBook/perf.html`
pnglets : `http://www.elf.org/pnglets/`
JavaScript scrolling effects: `http://javascript.internet.com/scrolls/`
Netscape's how-to page (JavaScript functions for building graphs) :
`http://developer.netscape.com:80/docs/technote/javascript/graph/`
LiveAudio plug-in documentation:
`http://developer.netscape.com:80/docs/manuals/js/client/jsguide/liveaud.htm`
Macromedia (ShockWave/Flash): `http://www.macromedia.com`
HTML Document Tree Viewer :
`http://www.microsoft.com/windows/ie/webaccess/webdevaccess.exe`
IE5 DHTML Programmers Reference support web site :
`http://webdev.wrox.co.uk/books/1746/`
DHTML sample pages and web resources :
`http://www.webreview.com/wr/pub/guides/style/style.html`
`http://www.dynamicdrive.com/`
`http://www.htmlguru.com/`

Chapter 7

Storing data in objects, tree menu controllers, JavaScript calculators:
JavaScript Objects by Nakhimovsky and Myers (ISBN 1-861001-84-9)
Windows Explorer-style controller:
`http://www.geocities.com/Paris/LeftBank/2178/foldertree.html`
Date and Time script resources: `http://www.irt.org/articles/js043/index.htm`
General script resources: www.irt.org
Validation routine scripts:
`http://developer.netscape.com/docs/examples/javascript/formval/overview.html`
Regular expressions: `http://www.perl.com/CPAN/doc/manual/html/pod/perlre.html`
Dynamic HTML controller: `http://home.sol.no/~warnckew/tree_menu/`
A simple calculator: `http://www.people.cornell.edu/pages/avr1/calculator.html`
A collection of calculators: `http://www.yahoo.com/Computers_and_Internet/Hardware/Calculators/Online_Calculators/JavaScript/`
Various calculating devices: `http://sun1.bham.ac.uk/s.m.williams.bcm/apps/apps.html`
Fire and forget forms: `http://www.yahoo.com,  http://www.hotbot.com`

Chapter 8

Instant Netscape DHTML Programmer's Reference by Homer et al, ISBN 1-861001-19-3
IE5 DHTML Programmer's Reference by Homer et al., ISBN 1-861001-74-6

CSS-1 Specification: `http://www.w3.org/TR/REC-CSS1-961217.html`
CSS-2 Specification: `http://www.w3.org/TR/REC-CSS2/`
DOM ECMAScript binding: `http://www.w3.org/TR/WD-DOM-Level-2/ecma-script-language-binding.html`.
Netscape mimicry of IE transitions:
`http://developer.netscape.com/viewsource/wyner_transition/wyner_transition.html`
The Document Object Model Level 1 Specification: `http://w3.org/TR/REC-DOM-Level-1.htm`

NC4 DHTML example:
`http://developer.netscape.com/devcon/jun97/key_1/directs.html`
IE4+ DHTML example:
`http://msdn.microsoft.com/workshop/author/dhtml/site/Scale1.htm`
DHTML Animation example:
`http://developer.netscape.com/devcon/jun97/contest/freefall/index.html`
Menu expansion example: `http://msdn.microsoft.com/`

Chapter 9

Communicator Preferences:
`http://developer.netscape.com/docs/manuals/deploymt/jsprefs.htm`
Technical notes on Communicator preferences:
`http://home.netscape.com/browsers/index.html`
Browser extensions:
`http://msdn.microsoft.com/workshop/browser/configuration/clientreg/`
`clientregistrylayout.asp`
`http://msdn.microsoft.com/workshop/browser/ext/overview/overview.asp`
Communicator's command line options:
`http://developer.netscape.com:80/docs/manuals/deploymt/options.htm`
The InternetExplorer object:
`http://msdn.microsoft.com/workshop/browser/webbrowser/reference/objects/In`
`ternetExplorer.asp`
WSH 'event sink' techniques (DOM programmatic control):
`http://msdn.microsoft.com/scripting`
Netscape Netcaster manual:
`http://developer.netscape.com/library/documentation/netcast/devguide/index`
`.html`
LiveConnect documentation: `http://developer.netscape.com`

Chapter 10

Netscape's list.js code library:
`http://developer.netscape.com/docs/technote/dynhtml/collapse/list.js`
list.js documentation:
`http://developer.netscape.com/docs/technote/dynhtml/collapse/index.html`
Netscape's resize.js fix:
`http://developer.netscape.com/docs/technote/dynhtml/collapse/resize.js`
Outline Java applet:
`http://www.demon.co.uk/davidg/outline.htm`

Chapter 11

Mozilla JavaScript Engine: `http://www.mozilla.org/rhino/`
NES and NDS download page:
`http://www.iplanet.com/downloads/testdrive/index.html`
NDS installation instructions: `http://home.netscape.com/eng/server/directory/`
NES installation instructions: `http://home.netscape.com/eng/server/webserver/3.0/`
SSJSLDAP library download site: `http://courses.unt.edu/mewilcox/ldap/`
LDAP Java SDK Download: `http://devedge.netscape.com/directory`
Java Server Pages: `http://java.sun.com/jsp`

Chapter 12

ScriptEase homepage: http://www.nombas.com/
SEWSE download page: http://www.nombas.com/us/download/index.htm#sewse
StoryServer: www.vignette.com
WebObjects: www.webobjects.com
Cold Fusion: www.allaire.com
The CGI standard: http://hoohoo.ncsa.uiuc.edu/cgi/
W3C CGI: http://www.w3.org/CGI/
URL Primer: http://www.ncsa.uiuc.edu/demoweb/url-primer.html
W3C URL Definition: http://www.w3.org/hypertext/WWW/Addressing/Addressing.html

Chapter 13

Browscap Component: http://www.asptracker.com
Setting metabase to allow out-of-process components:
http://msdn.microsoft.com/workshop/server/components/outproc.asp

Chapter 14

Microsoft JScript: http://msdn.microsoft.com/scripting/jscript/default.htm

Chapter 15

Beginning Java 2 by Ivor Horton (ISBN 1-861002-23-8)
Professional Java Server Programming by Patzer et al (ISBN 1-861002-77-7)

Java Browser Plug-in: http://java.sun.com/products/plugin/index.html
Sun Java Tutorials: http://java.sun.com/docs/books/tutorial/
JDK 1.2.2: http://java.sun.com
Netscape Developer Support Site: http://developer.netscape.com

Chapter 16

CORBA: http://www.omg.org
SUN Java Download Page: http://java.sun.com/products/OV_jdkProduct.html
FESI Homepage: http://home.worldcom.ch/jmlugrin/fesi/.
Java API Reference: http://java.sun.com/products/jdk/1.2/docs/api/index.html
Swing/JFC: http://java.sun.com/jfc

Chapter 18

JavaScript security bug information: http://www-genome.wi.mit.edu/WWW/faqs/wwwsf?/html
Netscape Capabilities classes reference:
http://developer.netscape.com/library/documentation/signedobj/javadoc/Package-netscape_security.html
Introduction to the Capabilities Classes (documentation):
http://developer.netscape.com/docs/manuals/signedobj/capabilities/index.html

Netscape object-signing tools:
`http://developer.netscape.com/software/signedobj/jarpack.html`
Netscape Object Signing: Establishing Trust for Downloaded Software:
`http://developer.netscape.com/library/documentation/signedobj/trust/index.htm`
Java Capabilities API and the use of targets:
`http://developer.netscape.com/library/documentation/signedobj/capabilities/index.html.`
Netscape System Targets (documentation):
`http://developer.netscape.com/docs/manuals/signedobj/targets/index.htm`
Testing site security:
    SATAN: `http://www.fish.com/satan/`
    SAINT: `http://wwdsilx.wwdsi.com/saint/`
    JMyth code encryption:
    `http://www.geocities.com/SiliconValley/Vista/5233/jmyth.htm`
SSL certificate vendors:
    VeriSign: `www.verisign.com`
    Thawte: `www.thawte.com`
    Belsign: `www.belsign.com`
    SSL for Apache server: `www.cryptsoft.com`
Simple JavaScript password checking:
    GateKeeper: `http://junior.apk.net/~jbarta/tutor/keeper/index.html`
    ebGate: `http://www.ebutterfly.com/eb/ebgate.html`
Signed and unsigned scripts:
`http://developer.netscape.com/library/documentation/communicator/jssec/index.htm`
The JAR format:
`http://developer.netscape.com/library/documentation/signedobj/jarfile/index.html`
Netscape Signing Tool:
    Zigbert:
    `http://developer.netscape.com/docs/manuals/signedobj/zigbert/index.htm`
    Version 1.0,1.1:
    `http://developer.netscape.com/software/signedobj/jarpack.html`
HTTP Authentication: `http://www.webthing.com/tutorials/login.html`
Netscape's proposal for cookie standards:
`http://www.netscape.com/newsref/std/cookie_spec.html`
Official standard for cookies:
    `http://www.cis.ohio-state.edu/htbin/rfc/rfc2109.html`
    `http://www.w3.org/Protocols/rfc2109/rfc2109`
Managing cookie strings: `http://www.hidaho.com/cookies/cookie.txt`
Web Security: `http://www.doubleclick.com`
Configuring Web servers: *Professional Web Site Optimization* by Ware et al (ISBN: 1-861000-74-X)

Chapter 20

Windows Script Host Programmer's Reference by Dino Esposito (ISBN: 1-861002-65-3)
Professional IE4 Programming by Enfield et al. (ISBN 1-861000-70-7)

The XML Specification v1.0: `http://www.w3.org/TR/1998/REC-xml-19980210`
MS WSH documentation: `http://msdn.microsoft.com/scripting/windowshost/`
OLEView download page: `http://www.microsoft.com/com/resource/oleview.asp`
Windows Script Host newsgroup: `microsoft.public.scripting.wsh`

WSH FAQ: http://wsh.glazier.co.nz/
Win32 Scripting: http://cwashington.netreach.net/
Born's WSHost Bazaar:
http://ourworld.compuserve.com/homepages/Guenter_Born/index0.htm/
Microsoft Scripting Homepage: http://msdn.microsoft.com/scripting/
JScript Run-Time Library Reference:
http://msdn.microsoft.com/scripting/jscript/doc/JSFSOTOC.htm
FileSystemObject Tutorial:
http://msdn.microsoft.com/scripting/JScript/doc/jsfsotutor.htm
OLE/COM Object Viewer: http://www.microsoft.com/com/resource/oleview.asp
Internet Explorer Browser Object Model: http://msdn.microsoft.com/workshop/browser/
Internet Explorer Document Object Model: http://msdn.microsoft.com/workshop/author/

Chapter 22

JavaScript interpreters:
    Mozilla JSRef library: http://lxr.mozilla.org/mozilla/source/js/src/
    Mozilla license agreement: http://www.mozilla.org/NPL/
    FESI: http://home.worldcom.ch/~jmlugrin/fesi/index.html
    Rhino: http://www.mozilla.org/rhino/
    NGS: http://www.debian.org/Packages/stable/interpreters/ngs-js.html
    NGS (Alternate site): http://www.ngs.fi/js/
    WSH: http://msdn.microsoft.com/scripting
JScript library: http://msdn.microsoft.com/scripting
Microsoft Scriptlets:
http://msdn.microsoft.com/workshop/languages/clinic/xmlscript.asp
ScriptEase pre-4.10b errata:
http://www.nombas.com/us/devspace/errata/core/index.htm
    Objects & functions:
    http://www.nombas.com/us/devspace/errata/objfunc/index.htm
    4.03c errata: http://www.nombas.com/us/devspace/errata/link/index.htm
    4.10c errata: http://www.nombas.com/us/devspace/errata/isdk/index.htm
Rhino
    Integration of LiveConnect:
    http://www.mozilla.org/js/liveconnect/lc3_proposal.html
    Changes to the method ScriptableObject.defineClass:
    http://www.mozilla.org/js/rhino/org/mozilla/JavaScript/ScriptableObject.html
    SecuritySupport interface:
    http://www.mozilla.org/js/rhino/org/mozilla/javascript/SecuritySupport.html
    Changes to Context.exit():
    http://www.mozilla.org/js/rhino/org/mozilla/javascript/Context.html
    Source Code (bypassing CVS) http://www.mozilla.org/download.html
    Source Code (in CVS) http://www.mozilla.org/cvs.html
Cygnus (Windows toolkit): http://sourceware.cygnus.com/cygwin/download.html
ActivePerl Perl interpreter: http://www.activestate.com/ActivePerl/download.htm

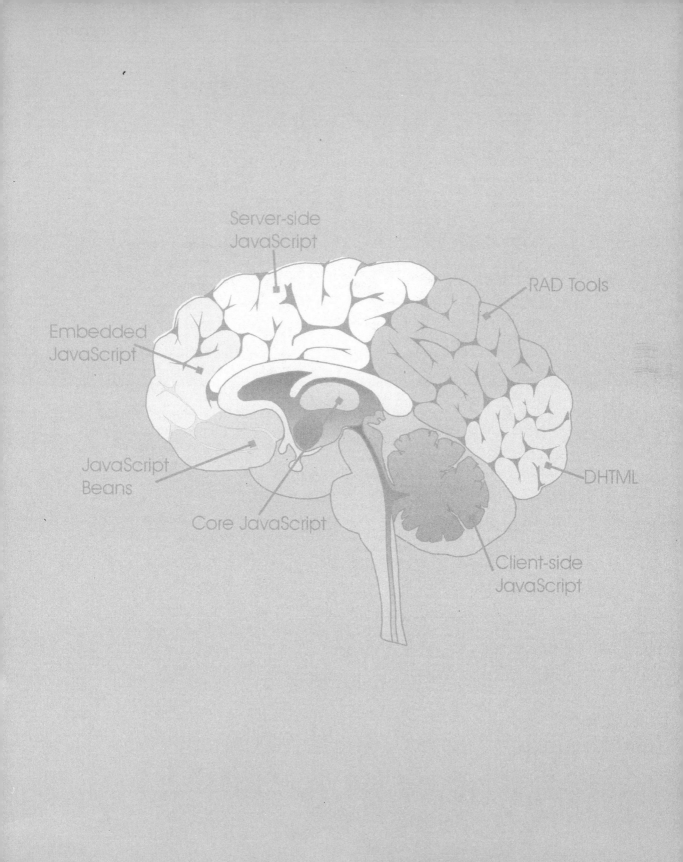

Support and Errata

One of the most irritating things about any programming book is when you find that bit of code you've just spent an hour typing simply doesn't work. You check it a hundred times to see if you've set it up correctly and then you notice the spelling mistake in the variable name on the book page. Of course, you can blame the authors for not taking enough care and testing the code, the editors for not doing their job properly, or the proofreaders for not being eagle-eyed enough, but this doesn't get around the fact that mistakes do happen.

We try hard to ensure no mistakes sneak out into the real world, but we can't promise that this book is 100% error free. What we can do is offer the next best thing by providing you with immediate support and feedback from experts who have worked on the book and try to ensure that future editions eliminate these gremlins. The following section will take you step by step through the process of posting errata to our web site to get that help. The sections that follow, therefore, are:

- ❏ Wrox Developers Membership
- ❏ Finding a list of existing errata on the web site
- ❏ Adding your own errata to the existing list
- ❏ What happens to your errata once you've posted it (why doesn't it appear immediately)?

There is also a section covering how to e-mail a question for technical support. This comprises:

- ❏ What your e-mail should include
- ❏ What happens to your e-mail once it has been received by us

So that you only need view information relevant to yourself, we ask that you register as a Wrox Developer Member. This is a quick and easy process, that will save you time in the long-run. If you are already a member, just update membership to include this book.

Wrox Developer's Membership

To get your FREE Wrox Developer's Membership click on **Membership** in the top navigation bar of our home site – http://www.wrox.com. This is shown in the following screenshot:

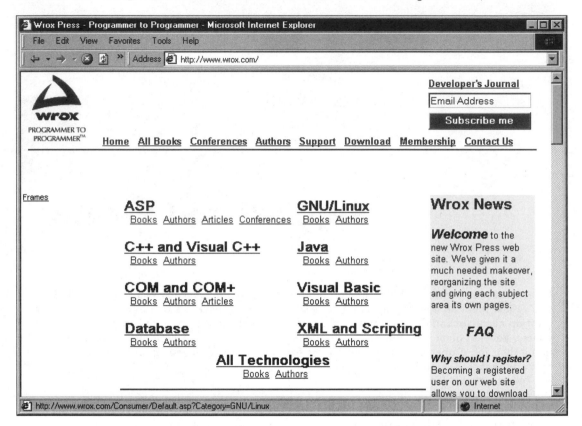

Then, on the next screen (not shown), click on New User. This will display a form. Fill in the details on the form and submit the details using the Register button at the bottom. Before you can say 'The best read books come in Wrox Red' you will get the following screen:

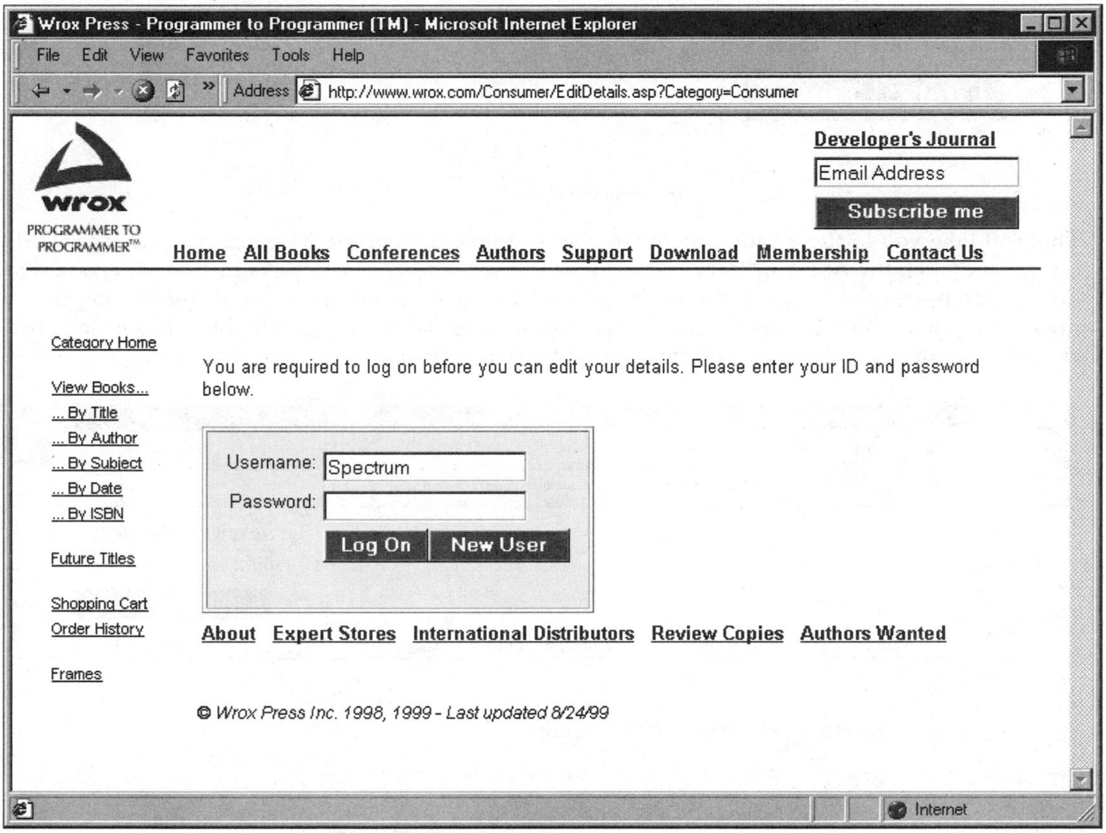

Type in your password once again and click Log On. The following page allows you to change your details if you need to, but now you're logged on, you have access to all the source code downloads and errata for the entire Wrox range of books.

Finding an Errata on the Web Site

Before you send in a query, you might be able to save time by finding the answer to your problem on our web site – http:\\www.wrox.com.

Each book we publish has its own page and its own errata sheet. You can get to any book's page by clicking on Support from the top navigation bar.

Halfway down the main support page is a drop down box called Title Support. Simply scroll down the list until you see Professional JavaScript. select it and then hit Errata.

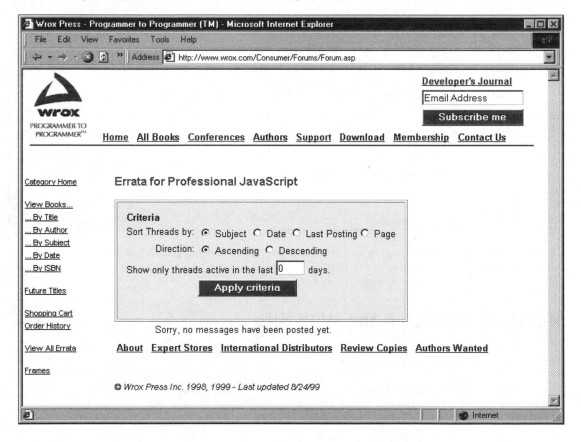

This will take you to the errata page for the book. Select the criteria by which you want to view the errata, and click the Apply criteria button. This will provide you with links to specific errata. For an initial search, you are advised to view the errata by page numbers. If you have looked for an error previously, then you may wish to limit your search using dates. We update these pages daily to ensure that you have the latest information on bugs and errors.

Add an Errata : E-mail Support

If you wish to point out an errata to put up on the website or directly query a problem in the book page with an expert who knows the book in detail then e-mail support@wrox.com, with the title of the book and the last four numbers of the ISBN in the subject field of the e-mail. A typical email should include the following things:

- ❑ The **name**, **last four digits of the ISBN** and **page number** of the problem in the Subject field.
- ❑ Your **name**, **contact info** and the **problem** in the body of the message.

We won't send you junk mail. We need the details to save your time and ours. If we need to replace a disk or CD we'll be able to get it to you straight away. When you send an e-mail it will go through the following chain of support:

Customer Support

Your message is delivered to one of our customer support staff who are the first people to read it. They have files on most frequently asked questions and will answer anything general immediately. They answer general questions about the book and the web site.

Editorial

Deeper queries are forwarded to the technical editor responsible for that book. They have experience with the programming language or particular product and are able to answer detailed technical questions on the subject. Once an issue has been resolved, the editor can post the errata to the web site.

The Authors

Finally, in the unlikely event that the editor can't answer your problem, s/he will forward the request to the author. We try to protect the author from any distractions from writing. However, we are quite happy to forward specific requests to them. All Wrox authors help with the support on their books. They'll mail the customer and the editor with their response, and again all readers should benefit.

What We Can't Answer

Obviously with an ever-growing range of books and an ever-changing technology base, there is an increasing volume of data requiring support. While we endeavor to answer all questions about the book, we can't answer bugs in your own programs that you've adapted from our code. So, while you might have loved the online music store in Chapter 14, don't expect too much sympathy if you cripple your company with a live adaptation you customized from Chapter 14. But do tell us if you're especially pleased with the routine you developed with our help.

How to Tell Us Exactly What You Think

We understand that errors can destroy the enjoyment of a book and can cause many wasted and frustrated hours, so we seek to minimize the distress that they can cause.

You might just wish to tell us how much you liked or loathed the book in question. Or you might have ideas about how this whole process could be improved. In which case you should e-mail feedback@wrox.com. You'll always find a sympathetic ear, no matter what the problem is. Above all you should remember that we do care about what you have to say and we will do our utmost to act upon it.

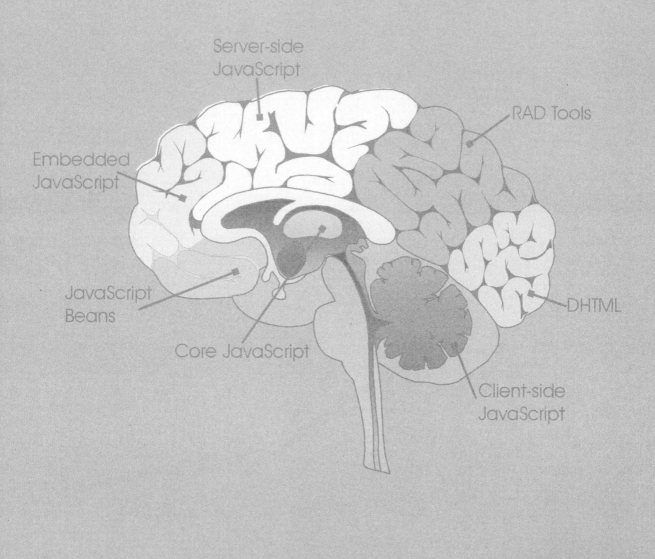

Index

A

Abandon method
Session object, 435
About page
browser windows, 155
Access Database
Web-based voting, 369
voter table, 369
votes table, 369
Acorn set-top browser
JavaScript, browsers, 142
ActionListener interface
JComboBox class, 576
message reminder system, 576
activate() method
netcaster object, 311
Active Desktop
channels, 312
Internet Explorer, 308
Active Directory Service Interfaces
see ADSI
active property
netcaster object, 311
Active Server Pages
see ASP
ActiveX events
event handlers, 120
JavaScript, 120
ActiveX objects
Windows Script Host, 707
ActiveX Scripting component
see Scripting component
ActiveXObject() method
JScript Library, 773
Ad Rotator component
ASP, 441
adClicked() function
Banner Rotator applet, 545
addChannel() method
netcaster object, 311
addElem() function
tree controller, 336
addEntry() function
message reminder system, 576
AddFavorite() method
Internet Explorer, 156
AddHeader method
Response object, 434

addList() method
tree controller, 342
AddOrderItem
stored procedures, 509, 513
AddPrinterConnection() method
Windows Script Host, 685
WshNetwork object, 699
Address book window
browser windows, 156
Netscape Communicator, 156
AddWindowsPrinterConnection() method
Windows Script Host, 685
WshNetwork object, 699
ADO component
ASP, 441
Adobe Acrobat
JavaScript, browsers, 142
ADSI
Windows Script Host, 685
aggregation
JavaScript, 68, 70
without information hiding, 70
OOP, 68
Alarm.esw
message reminder system, 575
album.html
Family Tree Photo Album, 351
alert popup
browser windows, 157
help, providing, 171
alert() method
FESI IDE, 559, 563
Window object, 157
JavaScript, debugging, 596
AlertMessage property
design time changes, 667
JavaScript Beans, 667
all property
collections, 267
Document object, 266
Array object, 266
tag objects, 267
Window object, 267
alwaysRaised option
open() method, 550
signed scripts, 622
ancient browsers, supporting
compatibility techniques
JavaScript, browsers, 146

J

W

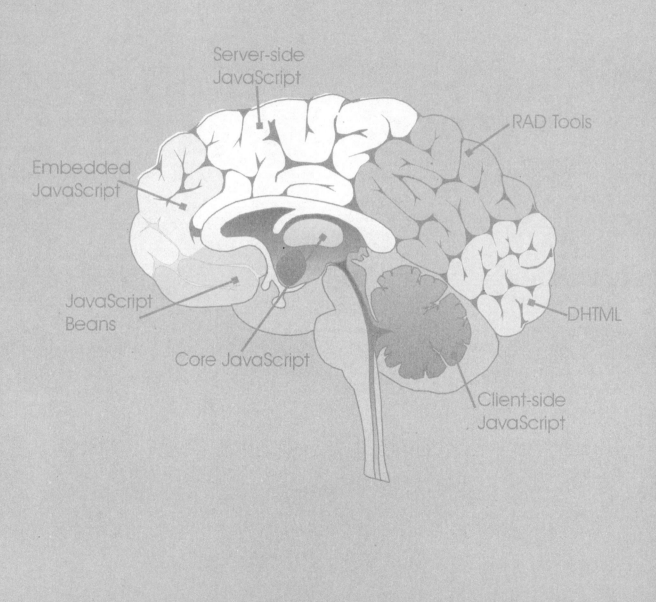